Economics

A Student's Guide

Pearson Education

We work with leading authors to develop the strongest educational materials in business and economics, bringing cutting-edge thinking and best learning practice to a global market.

Under a range of well-known imprints, including Financial Times Prentice Hall, we craft high quality print and electronic publications which help readers to understand and apply their content, whether studying or at work.

To find out more about the complete range of our publishing, please visit us on the World Wide Web at:
www.pearsoneduc.com

Fifth
Edition

Economics

A Student's Guide

JOHN BEARDSHAW

DAVID BREWSTER

PAUL CORMACK

ANDREW ROSS

FINANCIAL TIMES
Prentice Hall

An imprint of **Pearson Education**

Harlow, England · London · New York · Reading, Massachusetts · San Francisco
Toronto · Don Mills, Ontario · Sydney · Tokyo · Singapore · Hong Kong · Seoul
Taipei · Cape Town · Madrid · Mexico City · Amsterdam · Munich · Paris · Milan

Dedicated to John Beardshaw 1943–1995

Pearson Education Limited
Edinburgh Gate
Harlow
Essex CM20 2JE
England
and Associated Companies throughout the world

Visit us on the World Wide Web at:
www.pearsoneduc.com

First published in Great Britain under the Pitman Publishing imprint in 1984
Second edition published 1989
Third edition published under the Longman imprint in 1992
Fourth edition published 1998
Fifth edition published 2001

© John Beardshaw 1984, 1989 and 1992
© Denise Beardshaw and Pearson Education Limited 1998, 2001

ISBN 0 273 65140 4

British Library Cataloguing-in-Publication Data
A catalogue record for this book is available from the British Library

Library of Congress Cataloging-in-Publication Data
Economics : a student's guide / John Beardshaw ... [et al.].-- 5th ed.
     p. cm.
   Includes bibliographical references and index.
   ISBN 0-273-65140-4 (alk. paper)
     1. Economics. I. Beardshaw, John.

  HB171.5 .E3346 2001
  330--dc21   2001023882

10 9 8 7 6 5 4 3 2
06 05 04 03 02

Typeset in 10/12pt Sabon by 30.
Printed and bound in Italy by G. Canale & C. S.p.A.

Contents

Full contents

A Companion Web Site accompanies
ECONOMICS: A Student's Guide

Visit the Companion Web Site at *http://www.booksites.net/beardshaw* to find valuable teaching and learning material.

- Up-to-date web-links
- Questions for further discussion
- Updates for the textbook
- Glossary
- A syllabus manager that will build and host your very own course website

Preface

A fifth edition is an achievement for any textbook but particularly so in a field where there is such a wide range of excellent books to choose from. We believe this success is due to marrying long-established strengths with advances in learning methods, together with an up-to-date and comprehensive presentation of economic theory and practice. You may ask – is this the best economics book to buy? Well, although this book has won number one slot in a review of such texts, John Beardshaw himself stressed that economics tells us that league tables are not necessarily a useful approach to individual choice. Put simply, John saw that product differentiation in the market for economics texts had benefited the student and hence students should make use of this diversity and use the texts which best suit their own needs and preferences. We hope that we have again provided a textbook for those looking for a combination of the best of new and 'traditional' approaches and a thorough but not too technical approach to economics.

While seeking to preserve the strengths of *Economics: A Student's Guide* that have served so well, there is much that is new in this edition. Most noticeable is the extensive restructuring that will allow the AS-level student to master the basics of economics in the first part of the book while retaining the higher level of analysis needed at A-level and for first-year university or professional courses later in the text.

On the macroeconomic side: to reflect changes in syllabuses this book no longer requires the reader to understand the 'Keynesian-cross' 45-degree diagram, but it is still there in self-contained chapters for those syllabuses and readers that require it. The chapter on the fundamental insights of Keynes, introduced to praise in the last edition, is retained. This is because the insights of Keynes are still as relevant as ever to syllabuses and economics, even if the mechanics of representing his ideas have moved on. Accordingly, aggregate demand and supply is used more extensively, but not uncritically, together with a more in-depth treatment of the micro-foundations for more advanced readers. The important topic of national income accounting has also been simplified to reflect the reduced emphasis in importance in many syllabuses. A new applied chapter traces the course of UK macroeconomic policymaking since the Second World War, highlighting the necessary theoretical underpinnings along the way. There is also much that is new on international aspects and a whole new chapter on Europe by a specialist in the field.

On the microeconomic side: there is a new section on the housing market and a new chapter on the leisure industry to meet the needs of A-level syllabuses. New sections on regulation and deregulation of industry plus a comprehensive review of changes to competition policy have been introduced. Changes in the introduction of important microeconomic concepts have been made to reflect new syllabuses but the need for logical development of theory has been retained.

Given recent changes in some syllabuses, no textbook can provide a 'one size fits all' solution and hence there will be parts of the book that you can return to another day as they may not be directly relevant to your course. Where examination boards have provided materials to help students prepare for the board's assessments, students would be foolish not to use these. Equally it would be too narrow an approach not to have access to a main textbook such as *Economics: A Student's Guide* or another of the excellent textbooks that now exist (it would also herald a very unhealthy reduction in competition in the textbook market!). The mapping below shows you how to use this book if you are following the main UK syllabuses at AS/A-level but your tutor will give guidance for other syllabuses such as professional or undergraduate courses. If you are fortunate enough to be able to read the book in its entirety then you will have gained a very substantial introduction to the subject.

Syllabus map for AS/A-level students

Course		Where to find this in the book
AQA		
Module 1	Markets and market failure	Sections I and II (Chapters 1–10)
Module 2	The national economy	Section IV (Chapters 15–18)
Module 3	Markets at work	Section III (Chapters 11–14)
Module 4	Working as an economist	Section IX (Chapters 44–45)
Module 5	Business economics and the distribution of income	Section V (Chapters 19–24) and Section VI (Chapters 25–28)
Module 6	Government policy, the national and international economy	Section VII (Chapters 29–30 and 33), Section VIII (Chapters 34–36, 38–39, 41–43) and Section IX (Chapter 46). (Chapter 40 of Section VIII and Chapter 47 of Section IX can also be read for a more advanced analysis of certain issues)
Edexcel		
Unit 1	Markets – how they work	Section I (Chapters 1–8) and Section III (Chapter 11)
Unit 2	Markets – why they fail	Section II (Chapters 9–10) and Section III (Chapters 13–14)
Unit 3	Managing the economy	Section IV (Chapters 15–18)
Unit 4	Industrial economics	Section V (Chapters 19–24)
Unit 5A	Labour markets	Section VI (Chapters 25–28)
Unit 5B	Economic development	Section VIII (Chapter 34), Section IX (Chapter 46) and Section III (Chapter 12)
Unit 6	The UK in the global economy	Section VII (Chapters 29–30 and 33), Section VIII (Chapters 34–36, 38–39, 41–43) and Section IX (Chapters 44–45). (Chapter 40 of Section VIII and Chapter 47 of Section IX can also be read for a more advanced analysis of certain issues)
OCR		
Module 2881	The market system	Section I (Chapters 1–8), Section III (Chapter 11) and Section V (Chapters 19–24)
Module 2882	Market failure and government intervention	Section II (Chapters 9–10) and Section III (Chapter 13)
Module 2883	The national and international economy	Section IV (Chapters 15 and 17–18) and Section VIII (Chapters 38–39 and 41–42)
Module 2884	Economics of work and leisure	Section III (Chapter 12) and Section VI (Chapters 25–26 and 28)
Module 2885	Transport economics	Section III (Chapter 14) and Section VI (Chapter 27)
Module 2886	Economics of development	Section VIII (Chapter 34) and Section IX (Chapter 46)
Module 2887	The UK economy	Section IV (Chapter 16), Section VII (Chapter 29–30 and 33) and Section VIII (Chapters 35–36 and 43) (Chapter 40 of Section VIII and Chapter 47 of Section IX can also be read for a more advanced analysis of certain issues)
Module 2888	Economics in a European context	Section IX (Chapters 44–45)

The new syllabuses have allowed the introduction of an even greater number of applied chapters dealing with recent economic events and also more case studies. This has enhanced the 'real-life' feel of the book, but we have also been careful to trace through the logical development of the theory that underlies such applied analysis. Without proper attention to this it would be impossible for you to achieve the deep learning necessary for an understanding of the subject matter. thus this edition further embraces and develops an 'active learning' approach but avoids the mistake of confusing active learning with simply providing a set of resources for activities. In short, modern learning methods are employed to make learning more enjoyable and effective but have not replaced the painstaking work required to present the student with a clear exposition of complex subject matter.

This book is packed with **student activities**, **questions** and **data response** exercises, but it is also unashamedly a textbook that seeks to provide the student with a structured and graduated ladder to understanding. Admittedly, written text is a limited medium for interactivity, but we have sought to steer the reader away from those misconceptions and confusions which so frequently block understanding by pointing out common **student misunderstandings** at the point at which these are most likely to occur. This draws on the extensive classroom experience of the authors in teaching economics, but we would be delighted to continue to receive further suggestions for where this powerful technique for avoiding the common misunderstandings taking hold that might block learning could be deployed.

Although exercises, questions, activities and guidance break-up the text, we have deliberately avoided the 'magazine' format favoured by some modern authors. This is not a criticism of their approach but merely a preference that we know accords with many teachers and students. There is room for different approaches and this can only benefit students overall. Such an attitude reflects another difference of approach; within the necessary confines of the syllabus, this book continues to be deliberately more pluralistic than most comparable texts. This is not in anyway an attack on mainstream economics, but simply recognition that other approaches are worthy of at least a mention and indeed provide a contextualisation for mainstream economics. Also, from a learning methodology angle, because considering problems from new perspectives is an important technique for deep learning.

We realise that teachers have a difficult job in recommending the most appropriate learning resources for their students and their own teaching style. For our part we have again attempted to present an informed, readable, uncluttered and well-structured text that more than covers the syllabuses it will be used for. To the extent that it retains its well-established traditional strengths, it is more 'scholarly' than some recent approaches. To the extent that it has utilised findings from recent research in teaching and learning, it is more worldly, digestible and interactive than more technical and didactic approaches. But we have also been mindful that the book should continue to do justice to the discipline of economics itself. Economics profoundly affects all our lives and its principles can be applied in everyday life as well as business. For these and many other reasons you should find it an interesting subject. This book does require effort by the reader for no-one claims that economics is an easy subject. We hope this new edition continues to make studying economics interesting and successful for many more students.

David Brewster
Paul Cormack
Andrew Ross

About the authors

John Beardshaw

John Beardshaw graduated from the London School of Economics and taught at colleges in and around London before becoming Senior Tutor in Banking Studies and Lecturer in charge of Economics at Southgate College. John maintained his regular teaching throughout a career which included authorship, examining and awards moderation, consultancy for a major merchant bank and a highly successful series of intensive revision courses for A-level students.

He began writing on economics with the intention of producing a book for students which was both comprehensive and comprehensible. Since his first and very successful publication in the late 1970s, he went on to write other well received textbooks, workbooks and articles on economics. This work brought him international recognition as a leading author in his field.

David Brewster

David Brewster teaches economics at the Westminster Business School, part of the University of Westminster. He studied at Reading University and at Brunel University. He taught economics at Thames Valley University for over twenty years and then briefly at the University of North London before moving to Westminster. He has also been a Visiting Professor at California State University, Fullerton. He has written a number of articles in the fields of business economics and industrial economics, and is the author of *Business Economics: decision-making and the firm* (Thomson Learning Business Press).

Paul Cormack

Paul Cormack is a Senior Lecturer in the School of Environment and Development at Sheffield Hallam University. He is a graduate of Hull University and holds an MA from Leicester University and an MBA from Thames Valley University. He taught A-level economics in London schools for three years before moving into higher education, where he has taught since 1978. He has a special interest in transport and environmental economics, but his current research is into costs in higher education.

Andy Ross

Andy Ross began working life as a telephone engineer. After A-levels as a mature student, he studied full-time at the LSE and then as a postgraduate at Birkbeck College London. He gained a distinction for the teaching certificate at Garnett College and taught A-level economics for five years before lecturing in higher education. Since then he has held the post of Head of Department of Economics, Head of the School of European and International Studies, and Director of the College of Undergraduate Studies at Thames Valley University. Currently Head of Branch at the Office for National Statistics, Andy has recently become an Economic Advisor in the Government Economic Service.

Acknowledgements

Thanks goes to Brian Ardy of South Bank University for updating the chapters on Europe and international institutions, adding much interesting new material. Acknowledgement must also go to Malcolm Cummings, Chris Faux, Andreas Kyriacou and David Palfreman for their contributions to previous editions. A particular thank you is given to Denise Beardshaw for her advice and comments on previous editions.

Permission has been sought from the many newspapers and statistical sources used and these are noted as appropriate, but if any have been inadvertently overlooked, the publishers will be pleased to make the necessary arrangement at the first opportunity.

Appreciation also for the support, guidance and patience of the team at Pearson Education, especially Paula Harris, Laura Prime and Liz Tarrant.

As usual, the authors accept responsibility for any mistakes or shortcomings.

Publishers' acknowledgements

We are grateful to the following for permission to reprint copyright material:

Ashgate Publishing Limited for Table 45.3 from *The Economics of European Integration*, 3rd edition, by W. Molle (1997); Atlantic Syndication Partners for 'The French put tax on hard work' by Peter Shard in *Daily Mail*, 28 August 1997; BEQB for Figure 38.11; Figure 29.3 (a) and (b) used with permission of the Confederation of British Industry; The Economist Newspaper Limited, London, for extracts from the articles 'Bashing the Unions' in *The Economist*, 14 September 1996, 'A Good Start' in *The Economist*, 10 May 1997, 'Labour stats aren't working' in *The Economist*, 7 February 1998, 'The Air War' in *The Economist*, 11 September 1999, 'Snarl-up' in *The Economist*, 15 April 2000, 'Loosening the Belt' in *The Economist*, 15 July 2000, and 'Motoring down-hill – Tourism in Scotland' in *The Economist*, 5 August 2000; Tables 1.2 and 45.4 from *Eurostat*; Table 11.1 adapted from *General report on the activities of the EU*, 1998, and Tables 20.2 and 45.9 from Pratten (1989) *The Cost of Non-Europe*, Vol. 2, Office for the Official Publications of the European Communities, Luxembourg; Table 40.4 adapted from EMEP data; Figure 45.5 and Tables 45.11 and 45.12 from European Commission (1999a and b), Tables 45.5 and 45.6 from the European Commission website: http//www.europarl.eu reproduced by permission of the European Commission; Guardian Newspapers Ltd for extracts from 'Analysis' by Larry Elliott in *The Guardian*, 11 September 1977, 'Rouble devalued by Soviet Union' in *The Guardian*, 26 October 1989, 'Putting trade in its place' in *The Guardian*, 27 May 1996, 'Dedicated followers of fashion' in *The Guardian*, 18 August 1997, 'Whisper it . . . takeovers don't pay' by Lisa Buckingham and Dan Atkinson in *The Guardian*, 30 November 1999; the International Monetary Fund for Figures 19.1 and Tables 44.1, 44.2, 45.1 and 45.2; Figure 19.1 reproduced by permission of KPMG, London; 'Money, a telling law' by Dorothy Rowe in *The Observer*, 31 August 1997, and 'Inwardly troubled' by Simon Caulkin in *The Observer*, 16 April 2000; the Office for National Statistics for permission to reprint the many tables and figures which are shown credited to them in the text; the Office for the Official Publications of the European Communities for Figures 1.2 and 45.5 and Tables 12.1, 20.3, 45.3, 45.8, 45.11 and 45.12; the OECD for Tables 30.3 and 34.1; Palgrave Publishers Ltd for extracts from 'The General Theory Of Employment, Interest And Money' in *The Collected Writings of John Maynard Keynes* by John Maynard Keynes (CUP, 1936); Syndication International for the article 'Feelgood factor boost for firms' by Kevin Relly in the *Daily Mirror*, 30 June 1997; The World Bank for an extract from *World Development Report 1990*, IBRD; the *Financial Times* for permission to reprint 'Cuba's revolution in a class of its own', © *Financial Times*, 20 March 2000; 'Avoiding the trap of transition' plus figure, © *Financial Times*, 11 October 2000; Figure 7.6 from 'UK corporate profitability', © *Financial Times*, 28 September 2000; 'Big oil, big bucks', © *Financial Times*, 18 August 1998; 'Service staff shortages prompt inflation warning' plus figure, © *Financial Times*, 6 June 2000; from 'UK glories in seventh heaven' plus figure, © *Financial Times*, 22 September 2000; 'In defence of domination', © *Financial Times*, 8 November 1999; 'A once-toothless watchdog gets set to bite back', © *Financial Times*, 1 March 2000; 'Central bankers upbeat despite euro slide', © *Financial Times*, 12 September 2000; and 'A hole of its own making', © *Financial Times*, 7 August 1997; and the United Nations for Table 1.1.

While every effort has been made to trace the owners of copyright material, in a few cases this has proved impossible and we take this opportunity to offer our apologies to any copyright holders whose rights we may have unwittingly infringed.

SECTION I

The market system

'It is not from the benevolence of the butcher, the brewer or the baker that we expect our dinner, but from their regard to their own self-interest.'

Adam Smith

1 Introduction: what is economics all about?

Learning outcomes

At the end of this chapter you will be able to:

▶ State what economists mean by **the economic problem** and use this idea to give a definition of economics.

▶ Explain the importance of **economics** for human welfare.

▶ Describe and criticise the **scientific method** in relation to economics.

▶ Define the **price mechanism**.

▶ Contrast **market** and **planned economies**.

▶ Comment on the experience of Eastern European **transition economies**.

The subject matter of economics

Students who can relate economics to the world around them will find it a fascinating subject. This should be easy for you to do, for examples of economic forces at work are all around you and are constantly in the media. This book will help you to recognise and analyse these powerful forces that affect us all.

There is something of interest in economics for almost everyone. This is because it is a very wide-ranging subject. Economics looks at people and production; markets and institutions; enterprise and exploitation; individual behaviour and social relations; scarcity and choice; prosperity and poverty; power and free trade; national economies and globalisation; efficiency and waste; crisis and growth; inequality and welfare; rent and reward; the creation and destruction of resources; the environment and the prospects for the economic future of humankind. It is a dynamic subject that studies changes in the economy and which itself changes as new ideas, and old ones, battle for influence.

Although there is much that economists agree on there are also vast differences between different groups, or *schools*, of economists. They disagree as to what are the important areas of study, the scope and nature of the subject itself, as well as over more technical matters such as the accuracy and interpretation of economic data. This is also true of the natural sciences such as physics at their frontiers of knowledge, but economics is made more involving for the student as its debates are so often the subject of intense media and political interest. Astrophysics, like economics, is a fascinating subject but we are not often called to make judgments on astrophysics when electing governments!

Defining economics

As you may have suspected by now, a single definition of economics is unlikely to cover all its aspects. And yet, economics is as old as the human race. When some cave-dweller went out to hunt while others remained to defend the fire, or when skins were traded for flint axes, we had economics. But economics as an academic discipline is relatively new: the first major book on economics, **Adam Smith**'s *The Wealth of Nations*, was published in 1776. Since that time the subject has developed rapidly and there are now many branches of economics as well as competing schools of thought.

Economics can help explain many of the changes we see around us. Some are dramatic world events such as the collapse of the Soviet bloc, the problems experienced in transition from planned to market economies or recent instability in South East Asian economies. Other changes are more gradual but still profoundly affect the social and economic environments we live in such as economic globalisation, the increase in paid female and part-time employment, increased inequality, rising participation in education, increased road congestion, urban decay and homelessness. Although most people are aware that economic forces affect their lives few could define economics.

Most definitions of economics focus on *scarcity* and *choice*. To the economist virtually everything is scarce, not just diamonds or oil but also bread and water. How can we say this? The answer is that one only has to look around the world to see that there are not enough resources to give people all they want. This is not the same thing as saying there are not enough resources to cloth and feed the world's population, it is rather to point out that it is not only the very poor who feel deprived; even the relatively well-off seem to want more. Whether or not it is immoral to want more affluence while others starve; when economists use the word scarcity they mean that:

All resources are scarce in the sense that there are not enough to satisfy fully everyone's wants. For the individual and for humankind it seems that wants exceed means.

● *Common misunderstanding*

Scarce should not be confused with 'rare'.

It is in this sense that resources are limited both in rich countries and poor countries. The focus for much of economics is to evaluate the choices that exist for the use of these resources. You make such choices everyday, you cannot buy everything you want and so you must choose between the things you want or need. Thus we have another characteristic of economics: it is concerned with choice. Therefore we could define economics as:

The human science which studies the relationship between scarce resources and the various uses which compete for these resources.

The central economic problem

There are many specific economic problems – poverty, inflation, unemployment, etc. However, if we use the term *the economic problem* we are referring to the overall problem of the scarcity of resources. Hence, because they cannot have everything, individuals and societies have to choose carefully when trying to make the best use of scarce resources.

The American Nobel Prize winner **Paul Samuelson** noted that every economic society has to answer three fundamental questions arising from the economic problem: '**What?**', '**How?**' and '**For whom?**'

- *What?* What goods are to be produced with the scarce resources – clothes, food, cars, submarines, television sets, and so on?
- *How?* Given that we have basic resources of labour, land, etc., how should we combine them to produce the goods and services that we want?
- *For whom?* Once we have produced goods and services we then have to decide how to distribute them among the people in the economy.

These are economic questions that exist for all societies, regardless of geography or politics.

STUDENT ACTIVITY 1.1

Look through a newspaper to find an example of any economic concern of the day. Explain why it is part of *the* economic problem of scarcity and choice and how it affects the questions of what, how and for whom.

Economic goods and services

All the things that people want, goods and services, are lumped together by economists and called *economic goods*.

Economic goods are those which are scarce in relation to the demand for them.

As scarce in this sense just means that more of it would be wanted if it were free; clearly there are only a few things that are not economic goods. About the only thing which fits happily into this category is air. But even then clean air is not always available and even things in natural abundance could be made scarce if someone were able to establish property rights over it and hence restrict its supply.

STUDENT ACTIVITY 1.2

Make a list of things which are currently free. Describe ways in which someone who owned all of the free good might restrict its supply and so set a charge. Could a price be set for all the things you have listed? In the light of this explain why a price can be set for most things.

Wealth and welfare

An early definition of economics was that it is the study of wealth. By wealth the economist means all the real physical assets which make up our standard of living – clothes, houses, food, roads, schools, hospitals, cars, oil tankers, etc. One of the primary concerns of economics is to increase the wealth of a society, i.e. to increase the stock of economic goods. However, in addition to wealth we must also consider welfare. The concept of welfare is concerned with the whole state of well-being. Thus it is concerned not only with more economic goods but also with public health, hours of work, law and order, and so on. It would be possible to increase the level of wealth in a society while decreasing its level of welfare. For example, if everyone were to work 50 per cent longer per day the country's wealth would be increased, but it is doubtful if its welfare would, because people would be overtired, have less time for leisure, their health could suffer, and so on.

Hence modern economics has tried to take account not only of the output of economic goods but also of economic 'bads' such as pollution and loss of pleasure from the natural environment.

Wealth and money

Economics is not just about money as many people think. Indeed we could have an economy without money. Also, if we consider economics to be the study of wealth, it should be obvious that

we could print twice as much money without altering the real wealth of the economy.

● *Common misunderstanding*

People often think money is wealth and has value itself. In fact, it is merely paper or metal, or even bank deposits with no physical form at all! Money is just a claim to wealth. Nevertheless, changes in the quantity of money circulating in the economy could affect behaviour and hence change the outcomes of the central questions of the economic problem. Thus, although economics is not directly concerned with money as wealth, economists do study its effects on the outcomes of the central economic questions.

Positive and normative statements

Consider the following two statements:

(a) The death penalty reduces the number of murders.
(b) Murderers deserve to die.

Which statement attempts to state a fact and which is a value judgement? You may agree or not agree with the first statement, but it asserts a relationship that could be investigated through statistical evidence. For example, the murder rate may be compared under regimes that do and do not have capital punishment. If such evidence points clearly one way or the other, investigators may come to agree on whether the relationship exists or not even though they disagree over the second statement. By contrast, the second statement expresses a personal belief, or value judgement, about what ought to happen to murderers – it could not be disproved by any amount of statistical evidence.

Statement (a) is called a *positive statement* and statement (b) is called a *normative statement*:

Positive statements concern what is, was, or will be and hence depend on facts. Normative statements concern what ought to be and hence depend on value judgements as to what is good or bad.

Unfortunately, it turns out that even positive statements are usually difficult to prove or disprove as evidence is often incomplete, conflicting, or capable of being interpreted in different ways.

For example, consider the statement: 'Trade unions are the cause of inflation because in pushing up wage costs they also push up the price of goods.'

This assertion has in fact been extensively investigated, but there is still no consensus of opinion. Even when an apparent relation between trade union power and rising prices seems to have been statistically established, this has not settled the debate. One problem is that union power cannot be measured directly. Does a high percentage membership or changes in that percentage indicate current strength? Is the number of strikes a good measure or is it that powerful unions seldom need to strike? How do we know which of these measures is 'correct'? Another problem is that of the direction of causation: are unions pushing up prices or merely attempting to keep pace with prices that are already rising? Even if unions succeed in pushing up wages and prices in one market will this cause prices to fall in other markets thus off-setting any inflationary effects? Trade unions are just one part of an economic system that itself might be the cause of industrial conflict and wage/price spiraling – so is it a value judgement to single out unions for the blame?

You will not have to study economics for long before realising:

Debates over the truth of positive statements in economics are seldom settled by looking at the facts because the facts are rarely simple and rather than 'speaking for themselves' have to be interpreted.

Does this mean that the investigation of issues by economists is pointless? No! The issues involved are just too important to be left to politicians and the 'lay-person'. Even if disagreement cannot be eliminated, it can be reduced and the areas of disagreement clarified.

Scientific method

Some economists say they attempt to test economic ideas scientifically, but how is this done? Scientific method begins with trying to think of possible explanations for something we observe. For example, we may put forward the idea that the demand for a good is determined by its price. On the basis of this we may reason that as the price is increased, demand goes down, while if the price is decreased the demand will go up. This then is a *hypothesis* that can be tested on observed behaviour. This testing of ideas on the evidence is known as *empiricism*. Having made our observations we may then:

(a) accept the hypothesis as our best attempt so far to explain the facts;
(b) reject it;
(c) amend it in the light of the evidence.

This process is shown in diagrammatic form in Figure 1.1.

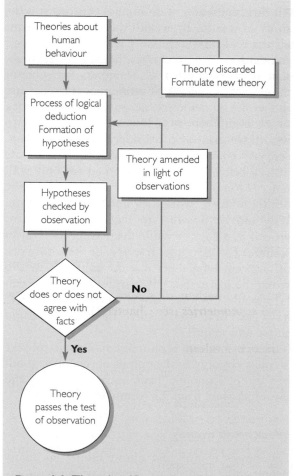

Figure 1.1 The scientific testing of theories

Think of the things you bought this week. What factors do you think affected your decisions to buy those particular things? The price of the items may be one of the variables that affected your decision but list two other things that can be measured. Obviously there may be exceptions to the rule and things that you have left out, but think about how your own behaviour matches up to this theory. Does your behaviour or that of others ever contradict your theory? Later in this book you will read about how economists measure consumer demand. Make a note to compare your theory with the theory of demand in economics.

Ceteris paribus

This is Latin for 'all other things remaining constant'. In physics if we wished to test the effects of heat on something we would not simultaneously change the pressure, altitude, etc. It is the same in economics; if, for example, we wish to examine the effect of price on demand we want to separate out simultaneous changes in incomes, tastes, etc. Therefore, when formulating economic principles, we are usually careful to state that such and such will happen, *ceteris paribus*. This principle presents particular problems in the social sciences because, whereas in the natural sciences we can undertake laboratory experiments to control the variables, this is not possible where human society is concerned – in a real economy we cannot command all things except one to stand still! This is an important problem for economics that is addressed by a specialised branch of mathematics and statistical theory called *econometrics* (see Chapter 2).

Human behaviour

It can be argued that since economics is concerned with human behaviour, it is impossible to reach any firm conclusions. However, while individuals are often unpredictable, people in large numbers are less so. If, for example, we increase everyone's income it is possible that any particular individual may or may not spend more. However, if we examine what happens to a million people as their income increases it is possible to conclude

that overall their expenditure will increase. Thus, examining a large number of people's behaviour allows us to take advantage of the law of large numbers. This law predicts that the random behaviour of one person in a large group will be offset by the random behaviour of another, so that we are able to make predictions about the behaviour of the group as a whole.

Dissenting schools of thought

So far this chapter has tended to outline the *mainstream* or orthodox view of economics which gained almost total dominance after the Second World War and which still dominates economic syllabuses. This approach has emphasised a model of 'scientific economics' with its emphasis on the testing of positive statements by reference to, supposedly, value-free empirical data. But many of the century's most influential economists, such as **Keynes** and **Hayek**, have rejected this methodology. There are deep philosophical considerations here, but the student of economics soon comes to realise that the subject is inherently controversial. Many economists have come to accept that it is misleading to present economics as merely a debate between experts over purely technical matters. Increasingly there is recognition that economics is a value-laden subject (see Chapter 47).

Such is the level of controversy in economics that there is a case for introducing the subject as competing schools of thought rather than a single discipline. Indeed, a more rounded view of a problem can often be gained by considering arguments from various schools of thought, and examiners do give credit to some extent for this. Those who reject the notion that mainstream economics is scientific and value free often prefer the original term of '*political economy*' to 'economics'. Political economists take the view that an economist *necessarily* interprets theories and empirical data through a political perspective. It must be realised here that there is a distinction between bias and dishonesty. In an honest and tolerant world bias should be confessed without shame or loss of argument; dishonesty will be hidden as it would destroy all credibility if discovered.

The syllabuses to which this book is directed do not demand a detailed knowledge of alternatives to the mainstream approach and this book does not pretend to give a proper airing to them. Nevertheless, wider arguments are included where appropriate. The major alternatives to the mainstream approach mentioned in this book are the *New-classical*, *Austrian*, *post-Keynesian* and *Marxian* schools of thought. After completing this book you should return to this chapter, and the exercises at its end, when these terms will mean something to you. In the meantime you will find that there is much to learn from the mainstream approach. All economists study mainstream economics, not just because it is the dominant school of thought but also because it provides many insights into the economic forces at work in the world. Also, it is a route to understanding the writings of modern political economists from the 'right' and the 'left' of the political spectrum.

Different answers to the same questions

We stated earlier in this chapter that each society has to answer three fundamental economic questions: 'What?', 'How?' and 'For whom?' While there are a million variations on answers to these questions, when we look around the world we find that there are only a limited number of ways in which societies have set about answering them. We will now examine these briefly.

Tradition and hierarchy

For most of human history the 'What?', 'How?' and 'For whom?' have been solved by tradition and rulers. The decisions that were not fixed by tradition were taken by command. For example, in feudal society the king or the lord of the manor simply ordered people what to do. We should note that this system lasted for hundreds of years whilst our own has existed for only a relatively short period.

Free enterprise and the price mechanism

The feudal society we have described was largely a non-monetary society; people did not work for wages but merely to produce their food. They did not pay rent for their land but worked for so many days in the lord's fields. Money was used only for the relatively small percentage of things which the local economy could not produce. However, over a period of several hundred years this changed and there was a monetisation of the economy: people grew food not to eat but to sell; labourers worked for wages; rent was paid for land; taxes were paid to the king. Thus was developed the *price mechanism*.

Thus, everything – houses, labour, food, land, etc. – came to have its market price, and it was through the workings of market prices that the 'What?', 'How?' and 'For whom?' decisions were taken. Despite there being no central committees organising shoe production or regulating wages, this resulted not in chaos but order. People, by being willing to spend money, signalled to producers what it was they wished to be produced. The 'How?' question was answered because one producer had to compete with others to supply the market; if that producer could not produce as cheaply as possible then custom would be lost to competitors. The 'For whom?' question was answered by the fact that anyone who had the money and was willing to spend it could receive the goods produced.

A price mechanism is a system where the economic decisions in the economy are reached through the workings of the market: changes in the relative scarcity of goods and services are reflected in changes in prices and these price changes produce incentives for producers to reallocate available resources towards reducing market shortages and surpluses.

The study of the price system forms much of the subject matter of economics and, hence, of this book. It should be said, however, that the *free market*, or *free enterprise* system composed of many competing firms, as envisaged by earlier economists such as **Adam Smith** and **Alfred Marshall**, has been much modified by the growth of large monopolistic businesses and unions. Today huge multinational companies with turnovers bigger than the national income of many countries and *globalisation* (explained in more detail at the end of this chapter) have created economic forces and power beyond that described by earlier economists. Hence many observers prefer the term *capitalism* rather than free market.

Capitalism refers to the private ownership of the means of production.

Collectivism, command and planning

In the twentieth century in many countries there grew up, or was imposed, an alternative to capitalism known as *collectivism*.

Collectivism is the system whereby economic decisions are taken collectively by planning committees and implemented through the direction of collectively owned resources, either centrally or at local level.

Under this system planning committees are appointed and they provide the answers to our three central questions. Thus committees take the decision on whether, for example, more cars or more tractors should be produced. They solve the 'How?' problem by directing labour and other resources into certain areas of production and they decide the 'For whom?' problem not by pricing but by allotting goods and services on the grounds of social and political priorities.

For example, in 1917 a bloody revolution in Russia led to an attempt to set up a state run system of collectivisation run according to communist principles. But the first effects of abolishing the market economy were disastrous, so to boost the economy elements of the free market for smaller businesses and farms were re-introduced. However, in 1924 Stalin came to power determined to make the Soviet Union of communist countries a major world power. He succeeded but his regime was brutal.

Under Stalin a central planing committee called 'Gosplan' had the responsibility for preparing five-year plans and then laying down annual production targets to achieve these plans. Managers who met the targets could expect bonuses and productive workers were honoured, but there was no price mechanism or provision for making profits. Despite this the Soviet system, particularly in its early years, achieved some very high rates of economic growth and the system lasted until the end of the 1980s.

From 1989 the former Soviet bloc countries made dramatic shifts from centrally planned systems towards a market-based price mechanism. By the early 1990s the central planning system had gone. This shift involved rapid large-scale *privatisation*, i.e. the transfer of state-owned industries to private ownership (see also Chapter 24). A large part of the reason for the collapse of the Soviet system was the failure of the planned system to cope effectively with the problems of 'What?', 'How?' and 'For whom?'

- *What?* Unlike the workings of a smoothly operating price mechanism that we will examine in Chapter 6, in a planned economy resources do not automatically move to eliminate shortages and surpluses. The amount of information that planners would need to collect as to wants and resources is immense – it often took months or even years to respond to shortages and surpluses because of bureaucracy and lack of information. Thus there were many farcical examples of tractors being produced even though there were no tyres for them, shortages of toilet paper, surpluses of black and white TVs, while, sometimes tragically, harvests rotted for want of transport and storage facilities. International media crossed borders and the falling behind the West in terms of consumer goods was thus all the more obvious.
- *How?* Factory managers were concerned solely with meeting the output targets that had been set by the central planners. The waste of resources in production and the quality of the finished products were of secondary importance to them. The result was wasted resources, severe pollution and poor quality products.
- *For whom?* The distribution of products and of incomes was largely set centrally. In the Soviet Union basic foodstuffs and housing were available to all, but the cost of this high basic security was a lack of consumer goods and luxuries. The material standard of living was below that of the richer market economies. The control of incomes and overproduction of basics led to bread being so cheap it was fed to cattle even though consumers had no meat. Workers had little incentive to move to new jobs or attempt to improve their income; the result was often a lack of incentive and a drab way of life. Corruption was rife among the bureaucrats who were paid relatively small salaries in comparison to the large amounts of resources they controlled and hence found it easy to collect bribes.

Has transition worked?

As more market elements were introduced some people were bound to suffer at first as the protection of basic living standards under communism was removed. But the people of the former Soviet bloc countries hoped that capitalism would end years of inefficiency and rapidly boost the economy leading to a general increase in economic well-being. In the West there was also excited expectation and even textbooks based on 'scientific' economics were jubilant:

> At the end of a century of experimentation, the much critised, free-market, capitalist system has proved itself superior to centrally planned, or highly government-regulated, systems.
>
> (*Positive Economics* by Lipsey and Chrystal, 8th edition, OUP, 1995)

However, Table 1.1 shows that the transition has not been as successful as expected and that the new *transition economies* have had mixed fortunes. In fact, all the former communist countries initially saw huge declines in output, by as much as 30 per cent. Thus there were massive increases in unemployment, poverty and inflation. Nevertheless, for some such countries, particularly in Central Europe such as Poland and Hungary, transition seems clearly to have led to improved economic performance. For other countries, such as Moldova, Russia and Ukraine there have been disastrous falls in output and it is not possible to say yet that capitalism has proved 'superior' in economic terms. We are ignoring here the benefits of a reformed political system, but this has to be balanced against a truly massive rise in poverty, hardship and crime. The consequences for the rest of the world of the slide of tens of millions of Eastern Europeans into third world poverty may yet be felt.

It may be significant to note that, in sharp contrast to the Soviet transition, China stimulated consumer spending to allow a consumer-led free market capitalism to grow up around, rather than replace, the massive state owned enterprises (SOEs). As private enterprise began to flourish the SOEs were gradually reduced. The combined effect of this took SOE production from 75 per cent of the Chinese economy in the 1970s to 28 per cent by 2000. Again, ignoring important political aspects and noting that China is still not a rich country in terms of income per head, we see that in the 1990s when so many former communist countries suffered massive falls in output, recessions hit Western economies and the 'Asian Crisis' had severe consequences for many other far eastern countries, China maintained an enviable record of growth (see Table 1.1). Ironically perhaps, this growth was propelled by the rapid spread of the price mechanism and private ownership.

Perhaps the mistake in the Soviet transition was to so rapidly privatise the state owned industries and to expect free markets to grow quickly even though consumer demand was weak.

Table 1.1 **World output growth and income per head**

	Average growth of output (annual percentage change)		Income per head (1993 US dollars)	
	1981–1990	1991–1998	1980	1998
World	3.1	3.0	4078	4789
Developed economies	2.8	2.1	18184	25649
Of which				
United States	2.9	2.6	20551	28313
European Union	2.3	1.7	15041	20838
Japan	4.0	1.3	23483	35873
Economies in transition	1.9	−3.4	2261	1206
Developing economies				
By region				
Latin America	1.3	3.2	3262	3395
Africa	2.0	2.3	786	663
Western Asia	−0.6	2.8	6224	3502
East Asia	6.5	5.1	1150	2506
South Asia	5.2	4.8	213	358
China	9.1	10.8	181	777

Source: World Economic and Social Survey, United Nations

Moreover, the rapid privatisation turned the huge centralised industries into privately owned monopolies. Monopolists are often more likely to raise prices and reduce investment rather than the opposite (see Chapter 8). This is because they do have to worry about competition and it can be more profitable to simply raise prices rather than increase costs through investing in more capacity.

The mixed economy

By a mixed economy we mean one in which some economic decisions are taken by the market mechanism and some collectively. In fact all real economies have a mixture of such collective or state ownership and private ownership. (Although, more recently, many nations have increasingly used the state to direct rather than own resources; see Chapter 10.)

All economies are mixed to some extent; even in Stalinist Russia some free markets remained while, at the same time, predominantly capitalist nations such as the United States took some economic decisions collectively, e.g. the provision of national defence.

When we use the term mixed economy it is usually applied to economies where there is a significant component of both collectivism and free enterprise.

Despite the wave of privatisation in the United Kingdom and elsewhere, significant economic decisions are still taken collectively. Education, health care, defence and social security remain in the collectivist section of the economy. In the UK approximately 40 per cent of all expenditure is undertaken by the state. Indeed, Table 1.2 shows that as we enter the new millennium no country in the European Union has state expenditure of less than one-third of the value of national output. Thirteen have state expenditure above 40 per cent, and five above 50 per cent of the country's national output.

Conclusions

The end of history?

Friedrich von Hayek (1899–1992), perhaps the century's greatest champion of capitalism, died with the satisfaction of believing he had lived just long enough to see his prophecy of the collapse of

Table 1.2 **General government expenditure as a percentage of total output in EU countries in year 2000**

Belgium	50.0
Denmark	54.2
Germany	47.2
Greece	42.8
Spain	40.7
France	51.1
Ireland	35.4
Italy	47.8
Luxembourg	43.6
The Netherlands	45.0
Austria	50.3
Portugal	48.3
Finland	47.7
Sweden	56.0
United Kingdom	39.1

Source: Eurostat

communist collectivism come true. Some philosophers have even called it the 'end of history' with the final victory going to capitalism.

As we noted above, facts are seldom so straightforward. We should note, for example, that the Soviet Union was an oppressive and corrupt regime. There was little freedom to express discontent with the performance of the planners or the economy, bribery was rife and there was little scope for reform from within the system. Its leaders also used a high percentage of resources to build up arms and the military during the arms race; this added to the effects of inefficiency and corruption in leaving less resources to provide consumer goods.

We also saw that the transition from communism to capitalism was immediately followed by enormous falls in output from which many of the former Soviet countries have not yet recovered. This has caused some disillusionment, particularly among the older people who remember the comparative stability and basic security of the former system. In contrast, China, despite only limited political changes and a more gradual transition, has been one of the world's fastest growing economies for more than a decade, albeit from a very low base. Perhaps it was the rapid transition of Soviet economies that was a mistake and, had the political situation allowed it, a more gradual transition would have been better for those Eastern European countries without the prerequisites for competitive markets.

The question that the vast majority of economists today are concerned with, however, is less about the extremes and far more to do with how to get the best from a mixed economy:

Accepting the efficiency of market systems and the obvious long-term wealth creation of capitalism, the collapse of the Soviet Union does not prove the superiority of completely free market capitalism over the mixed economy.

Why study economics?

In closing this first chapter we make a plea to avoid the OBE, the One Big Explanation for the economy. You just have to glance through the pages of this book to see that economics is a vast and often complex subject and many of the problems are, as yet, imperfectly understood. This should only encourage our wish to study and so to understand.

We study economics in the belief that through understanding we will be able to increase the welfare of society, and with the conviction that knowledge is better than opinion, analysis better than supposition. What we understand about economics is very important; it influences us all. Perhaps it is as **John Maynard Keynes** wrote in 1936 in one of the most influential economics books of the century, *The General Theory of Employment, Interest and Money*:

The ideas of economists and political philosophers, both when they are right and when they are wrong, are more powerful than is commonly understood. Indeed the world is ruled by little else. Practical men, who believe themselves to be quite exempt from any intellectual influences, are usually the slaves of some defunct economist.

Summary

1 Economics is the human science which studies the relationship between scarce resources and the various uses which compete for these resources.
2 All economic societies have to answer three fundamental questions: 'What shall be produced?', 'How shall it be produced?' and 'For whom shall it be produced?'
3 Wealth is the stock of physical assets while welfare is the general state of well-being.
4 It is difficult to arrive at 'pure' economic decisions since the economic problems are closely bound up with political, moral, sociological and other problems.
5 Mainstream economics lays great emphasis on separating positive from normative problems.
6 There are four main categories of economic society: those run by:
   (a) tradition and hierarchy;
   (b) the market mechanism;
   (c) collectivism and planning; and
   (d) a mixture of the other methods, i.e. the mixed economy.
7 The collapse of the Soviet Union highlights the strengths of the price mechanism but does not prove the superiority of pure capitalism over a mixed economy.

QUESTIONS

1 Comment upon the economic aspects of sport, leisure, religion, transport, television and education.
2 List five economic goods whose production also involves economic 'bads'.
3 Why do economists disagree?
4 Make positive and normative statements about:
   (a) the distribution of income;
   (b) inflation;
   (c) industrial relations;
   (d) health care.
5 Give two examples of goods or services provided by the state owned public sector.
6 What criteria would you use for assessing the effectiveness of an economic society? Are they all positive or are some normative?
7 List the possible strengths and weaknesses of the market economy when compared to the criteria you have produced for question 7.
8 Has economic transition in former Soviet countries been worthwhile?
9 Read the following statements.

The great object of the political economy of every country, is to increase the riches and power of that country.

Adam Smith *The Wealth of Nations*

The history of all hitherto existing society is the history of class struggles. Freeman and slave, patrician and plebian, lord and serf, guild master and journeyman, in a word, oppressor and oppressed, stood in constant opposition to each other, carried on an uninterrupted, now hidden, now open fight, a fight that each time ended, either in a revolutionary reconstitution of society at large, or in the common ruin of the contending classes.

Karl Marx and **Friedrich Engels**
The Communist Manifesto

Economics is a study of mankind in the ordinary business of life.

Alfred Marshall *Principles of Economics*

Economics is a science which studies human behaviour as a relationship between ends and scarce means which have alternative uses.

Lionel Robbins *An Essay on the Nature and Significance of Economic Science*

The economist's value judgements doubtless influence the subjects he works on and perhaps also at times the conclusions he reaches. . . . Yet this does not alter the fundamental point that, in principle there are no value judgements in economics.

Milton Friedman *Value Judgements in Economics*

Debates between economists are not just technical arguments among practitioners but often reflect philosophical and ideological positions which are not always made explicit.

Sam Aaronovitch *Radical Economics*

'Do you have anything on economics?' asked a colleague in his local bookshop. 'Over there', replied the assistant, 'beyond fiction.'

Anonymous. Quoted in *Financial Times*

Having studied these statements, say which of the statements you consider is the best description of economic society and the study of economics?

Data response A
CUBA AND THE ECONOMIC PROBLEM

Read the following abridged extract from the *Financial Times* of 20 March 2000 and then answer the questions that follow.

1 What three questions have to be answered by any economic system and why is it impossible to avoid these questions?

2 Contrast the ways in which a centralised state planning system and a free market system address these questions?

3 Why have even the most committed communist countries allowed elements of the free market?

4 Why should an economist not be surprised to find that good business management is valued in all societies?

5 Evaluate the claim that a state run company can be more efficient than the best capitalist one. (Chapter 24 looks at this in detail).

6 Would it be impossible to have a price mechanism if all industries are state owned and what problems might arise in attempting to combine state ownership and the price mechanism?

7 Why is there a booming illegal private sector in Cuba?

Data response B
TRANSITION FROM PLANNED TO MARKET ECONOMY

Read the following abridged extract from the *Financial Times* of 11 October 2000 and then answer the questions which follow:

1 By 'insider privatisation' the author means that the huge previously state owned industries were sold off to individuals whose sole interest was to make profits for themselves. As these industries were highly localised and had been run as a single entity they were monopolies. Why is it unlikely that such a monopoly would begin by investing to raise output and may simply raise prices instead? Would this behaviour be any different from a capitalist monopolist?

2 Why might it not be as easy for some countries to move very quickly from a centrally planned economy to a competitive free market as the author suggests?

3 The author points out that the transition countries that are closest to the output levels of a decade ago are the ones that have either reformed least or most. Why do you think this is the case and does it prove that all such countries could or would benefit from a faster transition?

Cuba's revolution in a class of its own

Die hard socialist it may be, but the island is nevertheless hosting a business management course, says **Pascal Fletcher**

Trying to teach capitalist management techniques in one of the world's few remaining diehard Communist states, whose president regularly reviles neo-liberal economics and demonises institutions such as the International Monetary Fund, may appear at first sight as useful as trying to plough the sea.

But the challenge has not discouraged a group of European business school professors who are teaching a business management course in Cuba. Far from experiencing suspicion and resistance, the teachers have encountered enthusiastic pupils and apparently willing cooperation from the Cuban authorities.

'The hunger for knowledge is incredible, it is amazing,' says Francisco Lamolla, the European director of the programme and a professor from Esade in Barcelona, which is among several leading European business schools taking part in the Cuba programme. Prof. Lamolla makes no secret of the fact that Europe's intention in backing the programme is to support and encourage economic reform in Cuba, whose Communist leadership has pledged to remain faithful to socialist economics, including the concept of central planning and pre-dominant state ownership. For this reason, the courses, which include economics, accounting, business strategies and marketing are aimed at career professionals. The course represents an intriguing opening to western-style capitalist management concepts and techniques in a country where neo-liberal economic policies and capitalist financial institutions are regularly pilloried by government leaders from Mr Castro downwards.

The veteran 73-year-old Cuban president, who has completed four decades in power since his 1959 Revolution, opened up the island's state-run economy to foreign businesses and tourism only in the last decade, to counter the effects of economic recession triggered by the collapse of the Soviet bloc. He has made it clear several times since then that he introduced these and other cautious, liberalising reforms out of necessity, not conviction.

It may seem surprising that the programme, which Prof. Lamolla says is unashamedly capitalist in its criteria, has not been construed as 'counter-revolutionary' by the Cuban authorities. But he notes that some of the modern management objectives being taught in the course appear to dovetail with a current government campaign for business improvement, to modernise and reform Cuban state companies to make them more efficient. Government officials say this reform programme is a priority.

'For socialism to be successful, it is essential for socialist state companies to be efficient,' Cuban vice-president Carlos Lage wrote in a letter to Cuban company directors in January. 'Today more than ever, I am convinced that a socialist state company can be more efficient than the best capitalist one,' he added.

Prof. Lamolla says he has noticed that his students have appeared particularly interested in applying what they have learnt to the government's efficiency drive in the state economic sector. However, Mr Castro, Mr Lage and other government leaders take every opportunity to stress that Cuba's limited economic liberalisation and cautious reforms are not intended to return the island to capitalism. Privatisation remains a dirty word and Cubans are not allowed to own or run full-blown businesses, apart from limited private economic activities such as running a home restaurant or renting one's house. These, and tightly regulated self-employed trades and services, constitute Cuba's tiny legal private sector at present, although there is a booming illegal private sector.

Source: Financial Times, 20 March 2000. Reprinted with permission.

Avoiding the trap of transition

by **Martin Wolf**

A successful transition is more than worthwhile. It can be achieved. In its assessment of the experience, published in the latest *World Economic Outlook*, the International Monetary Fund argues that 'where reasonable fiscal discipline was maintained and meaningful structural reforms were pursued, inflation typically remained well contained and output recovered more rapidly than in countries where stabilisation and reform efforts were less consistent and vigorous'. Equally, 'the recorded increases in poverty were sharpest in those countries where the reform process had stalled, stultifying entrepreneurship and new growth opportunities, and where privatisation favouring insiders and poor targeting of social safety nets have permitted a lopsided accumulation of wealth'.

Reform works. But countries with the longest experience of communism and economies most distorted by its mania for large-scale heavy industry, have also found it hardest either to manage reform or achieve a healthy recovery. Communism has left a deep footprint – so deep that many countries are finding it almost impossible to climb out of it.

... Intriguingly, the transition countries that are closest to the output levels of a decade ago are the ones that have either reformed least – Belarus and Uzbekistan – or have reformed most – Hungary, Poland, the Czech republic, the Slovak Republic, Slovenia and Estonia. The former have compelled unreformed enterprises to continue producing, however useless their output. The latter have started to show the dynamism and flexibility of a market economy. In between, neither communist fish nor capitalist fowl, lie the semi-reformed.

These unhappy countries are stuck in a transition trap. It is no accident that they were also among those most marked by the communist experience. But it is possible to describe the trap more precisely.

Much attention has been paid to the supposed failure of many of those advocating reform to recognise its institutional preconditions. But the error is more subtle than that. It concerns the origins of personal behaviour as much as formal institutions.

A sophisticated market rests on an understanding of the distinction between what can be bought and what cannot be: goods, yes; judges, no. The more deeply was communism embedded in people's brains, the more difficult have they found it to make this distinction.

In Russia, for example, the failure to complete price liberalisation for many valuable commodities opened opportunities for huge private gain. So did insider privatisation. What economists call 'rent seeking behaviour' then flourished, to the enrichment of the ruthless few, and impoverishment of the hapless many.

The lesson of experience is the importance of moving as swiftly as possible through the trap. The need is to establish the institutional norms of a proper market economy before entrenched private interests corrode the effectiveness of the state altogether. To have the right sort of market-orientated democratic society, one needs the right kind of state.'

Source: Financial Times, 11 October 2000. Reprinted with permission.

From communism to the market

Transition country	Year transition began	Real output ratio 1999/1989	1999 EBRD* average transition indicator
EU accession (excl Baltics)	**1991**	0.95	3.3
Bulgaria	1991	0.67	2.9
Czech Republic	1991	0.94	3.4
Hungary	1990	0.99	3.7
Poland	1990	1.28	3.5
Slovenia	1990	1.05	3.3
Baltic countries	**1992**	0.68	3.2
Estonia	1992	0.78	3.5
Other south-eastern European	**1990**	0.77	2.5
Bosnia & Herzegovina	n.a.	0.93	1.8
Croatia	1990	0.80	3.0
Macedonia, FYR	1990	0.59	2.8
Commonwealth of Independent States	**1992**	0.53	2.3
Russia	1992	0.55	2.5

* Between 1 and 4
Sources: IMF; *Transition Report 1999*

Mathematical techniques in economics

How to use this chapter

This chapter has been placed near the beginning of the book for ease of reference. You do not need to study all of it before learning economics. You may not need to cover all the learning outcomes (above), depending on what level you are studying at. Treat it as a reference chapter that you can always go back to if you need some help with mathematical techniques.

A number of basic arithmetical and mathematical techniques are used in economics: interpreting graphs and statistics; averages and distribution; using percentages and indices; basic algebra; visual interpretation of correlation. You do not need all these skills immediately. For some syllabuses, some of the skills are not necessary at all. The book is written in such a way that most of the algebra can be avoided if you are seriously allergic to it. However, maths is a useful avenue of understanding in economics, alongside words, statistics and graphs. Use it as an extra language and consider it to be an opportunity rather than a threat!

The use and abuse of statistics

Numbers often appear to have a magical authority about them. Politicians and economists produce statistics to 'prove' their case. However, we must treat figures with caution for three reasons. Firstly, there may be inaccuracies in the compilation of data. Secondly, figures can be 'presented' in such a way as to distort them. This does not mean that we abandon statistics. It means that we need to study them more carefully in order to appreciate what they really do mean. Thirdly, the compilation of statistics usually reflects a particular way of looking at a problem and thus they seldom speak for themselves.

We will first consider the visual presentation of data.

Interpreting graphs

Data presented in tables can also be presented in graph format. This format allows you to see all the information at once in a pictorial form. Analysis and discussion of the data is often easier when the data is presented in this way. It is important that you understand how to interpret graphs, as we shall be using them a great deal. Most graphs have a vertical and a horizontal axis, with different information being measured on each axis. If you look at Figure 2.1(a) (taken from Chapter 6, p. 89) you will see a dashed line going across from 100 on the vertical (price) axis to the curve marked D at the point marked X

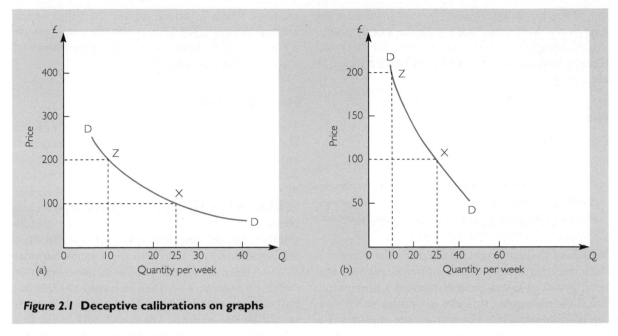

Figure 2.1 Deceptive calibrations on graphs

(you will later recognise it as a demand curve). A vertical line then drops down from X to the horizontal (quantity) axis to the point marked 25. What does this mean? In this case it means that at a price of £100, 25 units of the product will be purchased every week. More generally you should see that a point like X brings together two pieces of information: price (from the vertical axis) and quantity (from the horizontal axis). Each point on the graph has a different pair of price and quantity values that are associated. For instance, at point Z a price of £200 would reduce purchases to only 10 a week. The important point is to find your way around graphs like this. Start at a chosen point on the vertical axis, go across to the curve and drop down vertically to the horizontal axis to find the quantity associated with that price.

STUDENT ACTIVITY 2.1

Using Figure 2.1(b) work out roughly what quantity would be purchased if the price was £150.

Visual deception

The choice of scale in graphs can be deceptive. Figure 2.1(a) has been redrawn using a different scale in Figure 2.1(b). Both graphs show the same information (check points X and Z) but because of the different scales used, a very different impression is gained from (a) than from (b).

Figure 2.2 shows a graph as it might appear in a newspaper. This gives an extremely misleading impression but is typical of the way statistics are presented in the media. The vertical axis, as you

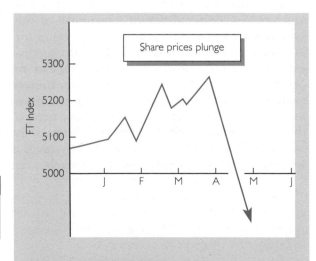

Figure 2.2 Visual deception
The graph of share prices gives a misleading impression of the magnitude of changes in the index of share prices in the first six months of the year.

see, does not start at zero but at 5000 and the gap in the horizontal axis with the graph plunging through it gives the impression that the figures have broken some sort of barrier when, in fact, none exists.

Numerical deception

Consider the following two statements:

> In the last four years annual government borrowing has grown by no less than £25 billion.

> In the last four years annual government borrowing has shrunk from 6 per cent of the national income to 5 per cent of the national income.

Which of the statements is correct? The answer is that they both may be, if national income has been growing faster than government borrowing. The first statement suggests government borrowing is in crisis, while the second one suggests it is being brought under control. Each statement emphasises the viewpoint of the writer.

Averages and distribution

Most people are familiar with the idea of an *average*, or to use the correct name, an *arithmetic mean*. Table 2.1 shows figures for the GDP (national income) of various countries. You can see that the average figure (GDP divided by population) gives a very different impression of the economies involved than the aggregate figure for GDP. However, the average figure can also be misleading. Does the fact that GDP per head in Kuwait was higher than that of the United Kingdom mean that the typical Kuwaiti citizen

Table 2.1 **Population and income (1998)**

Country	Population (millions)	GDP ($m)	GDP/head ($)
Kenya	29.3	9 669	330
India	979.7	421 271	430
China	1238.6	928 950	750
Brazil	165.9	758 163	4 570
Malaysia	22.2	79 920	3 600
UK	59.1	1 264 740	21 400
Singapore	3.2	96 192	30 060
USA	270.0	7 921 800	29 340
Kuwait	1.4	30 373	21 695

Source: World Development Report, IBRD

enjoys a living standard higher than that of the average Briton? No! This is not the case because we also need to know about the *distribution* of income in the two countries.

Means and medians

Means can be very misleading. For example, in many countries the bulk of the national income is enjoyed by very few of the people. The mean income would therefore give us a very poor idea of the income of the average family. We therefore have another measure of the 'average', which is termed the *median*. The median is the middle number, i.e. the one which is half-way between the highest and the lowest in the sample. Suppose that we lined up all the people in the country in order of income and then selected the person half-way down the line. This person's income would be the median. Thus, one-half of the line of people would have a larger income and the other half a smaller income.

The median is nearly always smaller than the mean. This is because the people earning less than median income mainly earn only a little less than the median income. A reasonably large number of those earning above the median earn substantially more than the median income. This pulls the mean above the median. With an understanding of these two measures of average you should now be able to make sense of statements like 'the majority of people earn less than average'!

The mode

A third concept of the 'average' is the *mode*. The mode is the most commonly occurring figure in the sample. We can further explain these concepts by taking a numerical example. Table 2.2 shows the distribution of annual incomes in a community of 51 households. The total income for the community is £650 000 so that this gives an arithmetic mean of £12 745 per household. The most commonly occurring level of income, however, is £7001–£10 000 and this therefore is the mode. As there are 51 households in the community the median income is that of the 26th household, which is £9307. These figures are presented graphically in Figure 2.3(b). You can see that the mode is the highest point of the distribution

Table 2.2 Distribution of household incomes

Number of households	Annual income (£)
1	less than 3 000
3	3 001–4 000
5	4 001–5 000
7	5 001–7 000
13	7 001–10 000
12	10 001–15 000
7	15 001–25 000
2	25 001–50 000
1	more than 50 000
Total 51	650 000

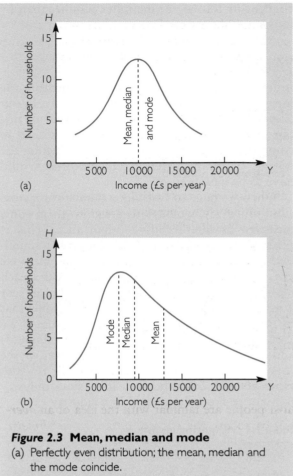

(a)

(b)

Figure 2.3 Mean, median and mode
(a) Perfectly even distribution; the mean, median and the mode coincide.
(b) A 'skewed' distribution.

curve, while the median and mean are displaced to the right. This is referred to as *skewedness*. By comparison, Figure 2.3(a) shows how the curve would look if the distribution were **normal**, i.e. evenly distributed on each side of the mean.

STUDENT ACTIVITY 2.2

Given the following incomes, work out the mean, the mode and the median:

   120; 150; 150; 200; 300; 400; 500.

Is the distribution skewed?

The existence of these various measures of the average should warn us to treat statistics with care. The mode or the median may give a much better idea of the typical unit in a sample than does the arithmetic mean.

Indices

What is an index number?

Index numbers or indices are another commonly used statistical technique in economics. An index is a method of expressing the change of a number of variables through the movement of one number. The technique consists of selecting a base, which is given the value of 100, and then expressing all subsequent changes as a movement of this number. This is most easily explained by taking the change in just one variable. Say, for example, that we consider the output of cars in

the economy (see Table 2.3). If year 1 is adopted as the base, then this is given the value of 100. In year 2, production is 15 per cent higher and therefore the index becomes 115, and so on. The table records a fall in production in year 4 below the level of year 1, and so the index number is less than 100. As you can see in Table 2.3, it is rather easier to judge the magnitude of the

Table 2.3 Index of car production

Year	Output of cars	Index number
1	1 502 304	100
2	1 727 609	115
3	1 906 003	127
4	1 400 005	93
5	1 679 294	112
6	1 699 024	113

changes by looking at the index number than by looking at the output figures.

Weighting

Index numbers are usually used to measure the movement of many things simultaneously. In our example so far we have used the output of just one commodity, cars. However, if we wished to compile an index of all industrial production the output of many different commodities would have to be measured.

When we have to consider a number of factors simultaneously, we have to assign to them some measure of their relative importance. This is referred to as *weighting*. Table 2.4 gives a simplified example of how this may be done. Here we are concerned with five industries. In year 1 each industry's output has an index of 100, but in year 2 industry A's output has risen to 115, while that of industry B has fallen to 90, and so on. If we then add up the five index numbers in column (3) and average them out by dividing by five, we see that the index number for year 2 is 106. However, this could be misleading since industry B might be more important than industry C.

Table 2.4 **Weighting an index**

Industry	Index of output, year 1	Index of output, year 2	Weight (no. of people) employed)	Year 2 index multiplied by weight ((3) × (4))
(1)	(2)	(3)	(4)	(5)
A	100	115	2	230
B	100	90	7	630
C	100	95	9	855
D	100	120	2	240
E	100	110	3	330
Total	500	530	23	2 285
Index	100	106	–	99

How, therefore, do we decide whether the 15 per cent rise in industry A is more significant than the 10 per cent fall in industry B? As a measure of their relative importance we have taken the number of people they employ, and this is shown in column (4). To weight the index we now multiply the index number by the weight. This gives a value of 230 for industry A and 630 for industry B, and so on. When this has been done we total

the figures in column (5) and divide by the sum of the weights. Thus we arrive at an overall index number of 99 for year 2.

Thus the unweighted index made it appear that industrial output overall had risen, while the weighted index shows that it has fallen. This is because the rises in output were in the industries that employed few people, while the industries that employed more people experienced falls in output.

Price indices

The most frequently used index is that which measures prices, the retail price index (RPI). In this we have to combine the movements in prices of thousands of different commodities. This is described in detail in Chapter 35. The weighting technique, however, is exactly as described above.

● *Common misunderstanding*

*It is assumed that you understand what a percentage is, but one feature of percentages often causes problems in economics and that is the **base** on which the percentage is calculated. If a person earns £100 a week and gets an increase of 10 per cent then their income rises to £110. Many people assume that if their income falls by 10 per cent the following year, then their income will return to £100. This is not the case because 10 per cent of £110 is £11. Their income would fall to £99. This is because we have changed the base on which the percentage is calculated from £100 to £110.*

Rebasing an index

It may be the case that you are presented with index numbers but the base year chosen is not appropriate to your needs. For example, the index is based on 1989 but you wish to show it with reference to the current year (or another one).

In Table 2.5 we show an index that is based on 1989, but we would prefer it to be based on 1993. The method is to take the index for each year shown and to divide it by the index number of the year chosen for the rebasing. Thus we obtain:

$$\frac{\text{Old base year}}{\text{Required base year}} \times \frac{100}{1} =$$

New index with required year = 100

Can you complete the calculations for the remaining years in Table 2.5?

Table 2.5 **Rebasing an index**

Year	Index	Calculation	New index 1993 = 100
1989	100.0		
1990	138.2		
1991	147.3		
1992	182.7		
1993	186.2		
1994	170.6	170.6/186.2 × 100 =	91.6
1995	186.2	186.2/186.2 × 100 =	100.0
1996	200.7	200.7/186.2 × 100 =	107.8
1997	210.6		
1998	233.3		

Algebra

Some people develop an allergy to algebra when studying maths. A few simple techniques are a great help in understanding economic theory. Some of the more difficult algebra discussed below is simply an alternative route to understanding graphs which you may prefer to understand at a verbal, visual or numerical level. If you really find algebra a problem, use these alternative routes to understanding.

Symbols

We make use of *symbols* in economics. In so doing we are adopting a kind of shorthand. The symbols are common to most economics books so that once they are learnt they should help us to speed up our writing on the subject. Typical examples of such symbols are:

Y = income
Q = output or quantity
S = savings

Unfortunately, arrays of symbols in texts can look forbidding, but the student should remember that they are not in themselves mathematical, just *abbreviations*.

Functions

We will often find that the magnitude of one factor is affected by another. For example, the demand for a good is affected by its price. In mathematical terms we could say that demand is a *function* of price. This can be written as:

$$Q = f(P)$$

where Q is the quantity demanded and P the price.

Often the value of the factor we are considering will be affected by several variables. These we can add to the function. Thus, for example:

$$Q = f(P, Y, P_n ... P_{n-1})$$

This tells us that demand is a function of the price of the commodity (P), consumers' income (Y) and the price of other commodities (P_n, P_{n-1}).

Writing things in this fashion is, again, just a form of shorthand because no values have been ascribed to P, Y, etc. Once we put in values, we obtain one of two kinds of function.

(a) *Linear functions*. This is where, if we plotted the figures as a graph, we would obtain a straight line. For example, consider the function:

$$C = 0.8Y$$

where C is total consumer spending and Y is income. This expression tells us that consumption is always 0.8 (80 per cent) of income. This would produce a straight line graph.

● *Common misunderstanding*

Many students are unable to relate decimals to percentages and believe they are talking about completely different things. As the example above shows, you can turn a decimal into a percentage by moving the decimal point two places to the right. If there aren't two places put some extra zeros in: 0.8 is the same as 0.80. Adding a zero after the 8 is adding nothing!

(b) *Non-linear functions*. Any function which does not give a straight line when plotted as a graph is a non-linear function. (Students up to GCE A level economics will not be required to handle non-linear functions in examinations.)

The economist makes extensive use of graphs. These are both an illustration and a means of analysis. Once again the practised economist will tell you that they are also a form of shorthand and a method by which often complex relationships can be reduced to a few lines on a page.

Graphs are a method of showing the relationship of one variable to another. On the horizontal (or x) axis of the graph we place the *independent variable*, and on the vertical (or y) axis we place the *dependent variable*.

Consider the following figures:

Year	Sales of product Z (thousands/year)
1993	5
1994	10
1995	12
1996	7
1997	14

Which is the independent variable? Obviously, in this case, it is time (the year) since that depends upon no other factor, whereas the quantity of sales depends upon the year we are considering. Thus if we plot these figures on a graph we obtain Figure 2.4.

The graph in Figure 2.4 shows only positive values on the *x* and *y* axes. However, it is possible to have graphs with negative values, in which case the axes (or coordinates) would be as shown in Figure 2.5. We will come across negative values for *y* when we plot the marginal revenue of a business in Chapter 23, and Figure 4.8 (Chapter 4) shows negative values for *x*.

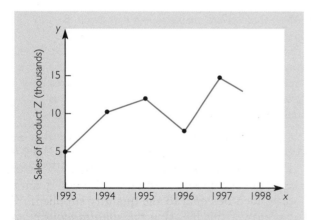

Figure 2.4 The independent variable
The independent variable (time) is plotted on the *x* axis and the dependent variable (sales of Z) on the *y* axis.

Equations and graphs

If we have the equation for two related variables, such as the quantity of a good supplied and its price, then we can plot a graph to show them.

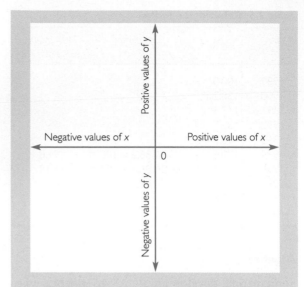

Figure 2.5 Plotting positive and negative values of *x* and *y*

Suppose we have the equation:

$$P = 2Q$$

Then in order to plot the graph we have to ask ourselves what if the value of Q were 1, what if it were 2, and so on? Knowing that Q is always half the value of P, we would obtain the figures in Table 2.6.

What type of unit must we assign to P and Q? That need not concern us at the moment. We can simply have them as one unit of P or two units of P and so on. We can decide later whether we are talking about pounds or kilograms or tonnes.

If we plot the figures in Table 2.6, we obtain the graph in Figure 2.6. The graph slopes upwards from left to right. This is said to be a *positive slope* since as the value of P increases so does the value of Q.

Table 2.6 Values of P and Q(1)

Values of Q (x)	Values of P (y)
1	2
2	4
3	6
4	8
5	10

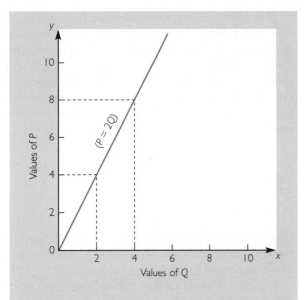

Figure 2.6 The slope of line given by the equation: *P* = 2*Q*

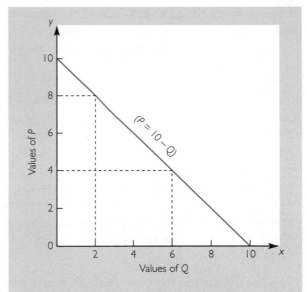

Figure 2.7 The slope of a line given by the equation *P* = 10 – *Q*

The graph we have drawn is an example of a *supply curve*. In plotting it we have departed from mathematical convention because Q has been placed on the x axis. However, it is, strictly speaking, the dependent variable because the quantity supplied depends upon the price and so should go on the y axis. The reason for plotting it as we have is that when economists such as **Alfred Marshall** first began to plot supply and demand curves, they plotted them in this way. If they were plotted as they should be they would appear very unfamiliar to economists. We will therefore adhere to this convention for demand and supply curves. However, elsewhere we keep to the correct mathematical convention.

Suppose that we have a function which is:

$$P = 10 - Q$$

Now what happens if we ask ourselves the question, what is the value of P if Q is 1? We obtain the result that P must be 9. If we continue for other values of Q then we obtain the figures in Table 2.7. If these figures are plotted as a graph, as in Figure 2.7, we see that this produces a downward-sloping line. This is referred to as a *negative slope* since as the value of Q increases, the value of P decreases.

Table 2.7 **Values of P and Q(2)**

Values of Q (x)	Values of P (y)
2	8
4	6
6	4
8	2
10	0

Problem solving

The graph we have constructed above is a *demand curve*, showing the quantity of a product which is demanded at various prices. Suppose that we ask ourselves the question, at what price will quantity demanded be equal to the quantity supplied? We can answer this by using the *simultaneous equation* technique.

We have the values:

$$P = 2Q \text{(supply)} \tag{1}$$

and:

$$P = 10 - Q \text{(demand)} \tag{2}$$

We can find where the price (P) for demand and supply will be the same by substituting the value for P in equation (1) into equation (2):

$$2Q = 10 - Q \tag{3}$$

If we move all the Q to one side of the equation and the numbers to the other, we obtain:

$$3Q = 10 \qquad (4)$$

Thus:

$$Q = 3\tfrac{1}{3} \qquad (5)$$

To obtain the value for P we now need only insert the value of Q into expression (1) and we obtain:

$$P = 2 \times 3\tfrac{1}{3}$$
$$P = 6\tfrac{2}{3}$$

We can check that this result is correct by doing a similar exercise with expression (2):

$$P = 10 - 3\tfrac{1}{3}$$
$$P = 6\tfrac{2}{3}$$

Thus the quantity is the same for both supply and demand when price equals $6\tfrac{2}{3}$. You can check that this is so by superimposing Figure 2.6 on Figure 2.7. You will see that this is the point where the two curves intersect. The student who is unsure about this analysis should now attempt the relevant questions at the end of the chapter. It is important to master this, because questions are set on it.

The approach we have adopted here might be criticised as being too specific to one set of problems (demand and supply). Many books prefer to conduct this analysis in purely abstract terms of x and y. We have adopted the price and quantity approach because this is the most usual area for problems. However, the student should remember that the algebra can be applied to any linear functions.

Statistics

Correlation

Correlation exists when there is a connection between two variables. We establish the existence of a correlation by collecting information.

Figure 2.8 shows two scatter diagrams. Both diagrams show information about the same group of 20 male adults. Figure 2.8(a) depicts the relationship between income and expenditure while Figure 2.8(b) shows the relationship between income and height. It is clear that there is a possible correlation between income and expenditure, but none between income and height.

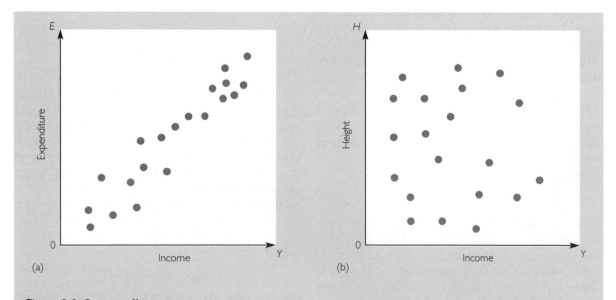

Figure 2.8 Scatter diagram
(a) This shows a possible correlation between the income of the 20 persons in the sample of their expenditure.
(b) There is no correlation between income and height.

Regression

To measure the relationship between two variables when correlation appears to exist, we need to indulge in a regression analysis. How this is done is illustrated in Figure 2.9. Here we have drawn two regression lines. This has been done visually to obtain a line of best fit. Visually they both may appear sound, but if we wish to find the best regression line then we must obtain the so-called line of least squares. This is done by drawing a line from each of the dots to the regression lines A and B. We then measure the length of each line and square it. Then the total of these squares is found for the two regression lines. The regression line with the smaller total is the better fit. In this case it is line B. You will not be required to undertake regression analysis yourself, but it is useful to know what it is.

The slope of the regression line now tells us the regression coefficient of the two variables.

In our example we have shown the regression of expenditure on income. This could be, for example:

$$E = 0.6Y$$

telling us that expenditure (E) is 0.6 of income (Y).

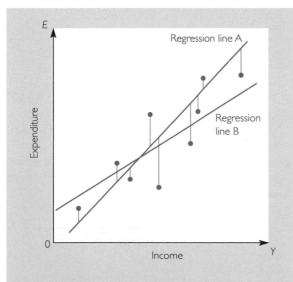

***Figure 2.9* Least squares**
The line of best fit is the one which has the smallest total of the squares of the distances of the dots from it.

Correlation and causation

The fact that there appears to be a correlation between two variables does not prove that one causes the other. Two major problems exist.

(a) *Wrong-way causation.* It is a proven fact that in the cities of northern Germany there is a correlation between the number of babies born and the number of storks' nests. Should this then be taken as proof that storks do indeed deliver babies? The causation is, of course, the wrong way round. Cities that have more children have more houses and, therefore, more chimneys for storks to build their nests in.

(b) *Spurious causation.* It is a statistical fact that during the 1970s there was a positive correlation between the rise in the cost of living in London and the number of foreign tourists visiting the city. Does this therefore prove that rising prices caused more people to visit London? Here the correlation is 'spurious' because increased prices do not cause increased tourism, and increased tourism does not cause rising prices. They are both the result of more fundamental broader-ranging phenomena.

We have used here rather humorous examples to illustrate the problem, but it is a very serious and common error in the subject. Correlation is often taken by politicians (and some economists) as proof positive of their argument.

Consider one of the most serious of our economic problems, inflation. One can demonstrate a close correlation between inflation and the rise in wages. Politicians are therefore often heard to say, 'We all know that rising wages cause inflation'. Is this a true correlation? Is it a wrong-way causation or is it a spurious correlation? At the same time we can show a strong positive correlation between increases in the money stock and rising prices. Some politicians (often the same ones) therefore state with equal confidence, 'Increases in the money supply cause inflation'. A moment's reflection will tell you that if it is increased wages which are the cause of inflation it cannot at the same time be increases in the money stock.

It would be presumptuous of us to suggest a glib answer to the above problem, as it is one of the thorniest in modern economics, but we hope by the end of the book to have shed some light on the issue. Suffice it to say that correlation is not causation. In addition to correlation, we need an explanation of why one factor relates to another.

Summary

1 Numerical and statistical information can be used both to inform and deceive.
2 There are several types of 'average'. These are the mean, the median and the mode.
3 Index numbers are a method of expressing the change in a number of variables through the movement of one number. They are frequently used to measure such things as the price level.
4 Symbols are used in economics as a convenient means of abbreviation.
5 Functions can be used to express the relationship of one variable to another.
6 Equations can be translated to draw graphs.
7 Correlation in a graph does not imply causation.

? QUESTIONS

1 Define the following: mean; median; mode; index numbers; correlation.
2 Suppose that you wanted to describe the 'average' intelligence of the population. What measure(s) would you use and why? If instead you wanted to describe the average ownership of wealth in the economy, how would your choice of measure differ and why?
3 Construct a graph which is calculated to deceive someone, e.g. showing changes in the exchange rate in the last 12 months.
4 Re-read the section on numerical deception and then explain how the same information could lead to the two seemingly contradictory statements.

5 Describe how an index might be compiled to measure prices.
6 Construct a graph and on it draw the line which would illustrate the following functions: $y = 3x$ and $y = 10 - x$. State the value of x and y where the two lines intersect.
7 Construct a graph to illustrate the following function:

$$y = 4 + 5x$$

8 In the following situations, determine the points at which x and y are equal, i.e. where the graphs would intersect.
   (a) $y = 1 + 3x$
       $y = 25 - x$
   (b) $y = 20 + 5x$
       $y = 100 - x$
   (c) $y = 10 + x$
       $y = 2x - 4$

Data response A
INDEX NUMBERS

Study the information in the table below, and then attempt the questions which follow.

	1981	1986	1991	1995
Bus prices	100	139	198	252
Rail prices	100	137	201	246
Petrol and oil prices	100	145	156	203
RPI (all prices)	100	137	185	208

Source: Adapted from *Social Trends* 1996, National Statistics. © Crown Copyright 2001

1 Which form of transport, car, bus or rail, has gone up most in the period? Which has gone up least? How do you expect this to affect demand for each type of transport?
2 Compare the period 1981–6 and 1991–5. In which period has public transport become relatively more competitive than the car?

Data response B
REBASING AN INDEX

The data below on bus prices is not collected for calendar years. Although 1992 = 100, it is difficult to see what is happening. Rebase the index to find out how much more bus prices have been rising than general prices (RPI) between 1993–4 and 1995–6; 1992 = 100.

	Bus prices	RPI
1992–3	101.3	100.4
1993–4	105.9	102.2
1994–5	110.9	105.0
1995–6	116.0	108.4

Adapted from the *Annual Abstract of Statistics* 1997

Data response C
MAPS AND MODELS

Look at the drawings of a house in Figures 2.10(a) and 2.10(b). Each of the drawings can be thought of as a 'model' of the house, giving some information about it.

1 (a) What information is *not* included in each drawing?
  (b) Which would be most useful to someone thinking of buying the house?
  (c) Is there any way of presenting more information on paper about the house?
2 Explain as fully as possible what the use of models is in economics.

FRONT ELEVATION   SIDE ELEVATION

Figure 2.10(a) **Front and side elevations**

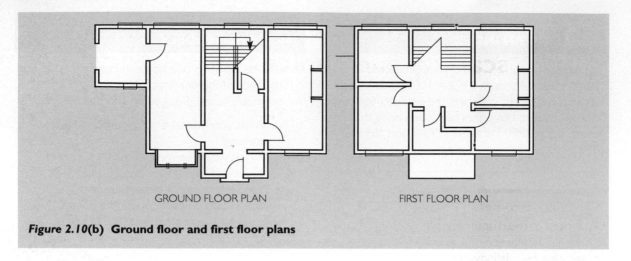

GROUND FLOOR PLAN   FIRST FLOOR PLAN

Figure 2.10(b) **Ground floor and first floor plans**

The economic problem: resources, scarcity and choice

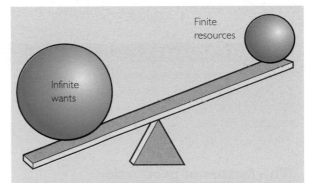

Figure 3.1 The economic problem: finite resources and infinite wants

Wants and needs

We saw in Chapter 1 that the fundamental economic problem is the scarcity of all resources. Therefore all economic decisions involve choice in terms of what to produce, how to produce it and who will receive the output thus produced. We must now turn to another aspect of the economic problem – the *insatiability* of human wants.

Finite resources and insatiable wants

It is literally impossible to satisfy human wants because as one economic want is satisfied another appears to be created. We may liken this to a seesaw with, on the one hand, the finite resources of the world, while on the other hand are infinite wants (see Figure 3.1). It may be possible to satisfy human needs, so that we could say, for example, a person needs three shirts, two pairs of

shoes, good health care, etc., but this is not the same thing as human wants. If we give people enough to eat then they appear to want better or different foods; if we give them enough to wear then they want more fashionable clothes, and so on. Thus, in this sense, the economic problem is insoluble. There have always been a few people who reject this materialistic view, e.g. monks and nuns. In recent decades supporters of 'Green' politics have also questioned whether the view of 'more is better' is a desirable or sustainable goal.

Conspicuous consumption

The problem of the insatiability of human wants has been the subject of much thought in economics. The great American economist **Thorstein Veblen** (1857–1929), in his book, *The Theory of the Leisure Class*, first described what is termed *conspicuous consumption*. This refers to the tendency of those above the subsistence level, i.e. the 'leisure class', to be concerned mainly with impressing others through standards of living, taste and dress.

In more recent times Professor Galbraith has also pointed out that in most advanced industrial economies most people have gone beyond the level of physical necessity. Consumers may be observed to flit from one purchase to another in response to pressures of fashion and advertising. These arguments still do not apply to the poor of the world.

Whether it is a matter of need or want, decisions have to be made in the economy about what to produce, how to produce, and which factors of production to use in each industry.

STUDENT ACTIVITY 3.1

List the goods and services you (or your parents) have consumed in the last week under one of the following headings:
(a) needs; (b) wants; (c) conspicuous consumption.

The factors of production

The economic resources that provide for our economic wants are termed the *factors of production*. Traditionally, economists have classified these under four headings. They are (together with their 'factor rewards'):

(a) labour   (wages)
(b) land   (rent)
(c) capital   (interest)
(d) enterprise   (profit)

The first two are termed primary factors since they are not the result of the economic process; they are, so to speak, what we have to start with. The secondary factors (capital and enterprise) are a consequence of an economic system.

Labour

Labour may be defined as the exercise of human mental and physical effort in the production of goods and services.

Included in this definition is all the labour that people undertake for reward, in the form of either wages and salaries or income from self-employment. There is a problem with labour that is undertaken without payment. Housework,

gardening and decoration are often undertaken by the owners of a house, and this is clearly labour because we would have to pay workers to do this work if we did not do it ourselves. This kind of work is not included in measures of the size of the economy because it cannot be easily valued, having no price. This problem is discussed in more detail in Chapters 15 and 34. In more technical terms the working population constitutes the supply of labour. This is discussed in Chapters 26 and 39.

Land

Land may be defined as all the free gifts of nature.

As such, land constitutes both the space in which to organise economic activity and the resources provided by nature. Thus, included within the definition are all mineral resources, climate, soil fertility, etc. The sea, since it is a resource for both fishing and mineral exploitation, would also fall within the definition of land. The economist, therefore, uses the word *land* in a special way.

In practice it may be very difficult to separate land from other factors of production such as capital but, theoretically, it has two unique features that distinguish it.

First, it is fixed in supply. Since, as we saw above, the sea is included in the definition, we are thus talking about the whole of the planet, and it is obvious that we can never acquire more land in this sense. Indeed, environmentalists emphasise how economic growth is using up the planet's resources.

Second, land has no cost of production. The individual who is trying to rent a piece of land may have to pay a great deal of money, but it has never cost society as a whole anything to produce land. This last point may seem rather abstract but forms an important component of some political ideologies such as Marxism.

Capital

We define capital as the stock of wealth existing at any one time. As such, capital consists of all the real physical assets of society. An alternative formulation would be:

Capital is all those goods that are used in the production of further output.

Capital can be divided into *fixed* capital, which is such things as buildings, roads, machinery, etc., and *working*, or circulating, capital, which consists of stocks of raw materials and semi-manufactured goods. The distinction is that fixed capital continues through many rounds of production while working capital is used up in one round; for example, a machine for canning beans would be fixed capital, while stocks of beans to go into the cans would be circulating capital.

As stated previously, capital is a secondary factor of production, which means that it is a result of the economic system. Capital has been created by individuals forgoing current consumption, i.e. people have refrained from spending all their income immediately on consumer goods and have saved resources which can then be used in the production of further wealth. Suppose we consider a very simple economy in which the individual's wealth consists entirely of potatoes. If the individual is able to refrain from consuming all the potatoes, these may be planted and, thus, produce more potatoes in the future. From this example it can be seen that a capital good is defined, not from what it is, but from what it does, i.e. in our example the potato is a capital good if it is used in the production of more potatoes.

Education as capital

One of the purposes of education is to increase the skills and therefore the productivity of labour. The higher wages paid to workers with higher levels of education are thought to reflect this increased productivity. Improving workers' skills and abilities in this way is sometimes called 'human capital'. You can consider the course you are currently following as an investment that will increase your income in the future.

Enterprise

Some economists have cast doubt on whether enterprise is a separate factor of production while others argue that the entrepreneur is the most important factor without which the other factors will be used inefficiently, if at all. Enterprise fulfils two vital functions:

(a) It hires and combines the other factors of production.

(b) It takes a *risk* by producing goods in anticipation of demand.

It may be fairly easy to identify the role of the entrepreneur in a small business. However, in a large business the entrepreneurial function will be split up between many managers and departments, as well as being shared with the shareholders of the business. Despite the difficulties involved in identifying the entrepreneur, the role of enterprise is clearly vital to the economic process, since it is the decision-making factor. It therefore provides an important tool in our understanding of how businesses work. In recent years there has been great political stress on the importance of 'the enterprise culture' in promoting economic progress. This emphasis has not lessened with the election of the Labour government in 1997, which claims to be 'business friendly'.

Factor incomes

The revenue from selling goods and services is passed to the factors of production. The various incomes which the factors receive can also be termed *factor rewards* or factor returns. Labour receives *wages and salaries*, land earns *rent*, capital earns *interest* and enterprise earns *profit*. The precise meaning of these economic terms often causes some confusion to begin with, because these words are used in a slightly different sense in everyday conversation. Accountants may also use the terms differently. For instance in every day use, the term 'rent' is used to mean the payment for using a building, whether it is a flat, an office or a factory. Not all of the payment will be rent in the economic sense of the word. Some of the payment may cover repairs and maintenance, which is mainly labour. The building itself is clearly capital which attracts the reward of interest. In addition the landlord will not stay in the business unless a reasonable level of profit is earned – otherwise there would be no point in organising the other factors of production to provide this service.

Another example of people using terms differently is when accountants calculate the profit for a business without taking into account the capital that has been put into the business by its owner. Part of the profit is really interest on the owner's capital, but it may not appear like that in the accounts.

● *Common misunderstanding*

When thinking about which factors receive a reward for helping to produce a product, students often become puzzled about raw materials and partly finished products bought in from outside the business. For instance, if a toilet in a building needs a new handle (which the landlord must supply as part of the rental agreement), which factors of production does this expenditure reward? The answer is that the four factors of production will have all been involved in making the toilet handle, in the business that has made it. This business will also have brought in raw materials from other businesses. What about the raw material (metal) needed to make the handle? Ultimately we find something that has come from land (natural resources). If you follow the logic of this process you will find that many different industries have contributed to something as simple as a handle. This exercise will help you to understand how interdependent modern economies are.

STUDENT ACTIVITY 3.2

Using either a train or a bus journey as your example, identify which resources used can be categorised as land, labour, capital and enterprise. Carry out the same exercise for your school/college/university.

The division of labour

Specialisation

The expression *division of labour* refers to the dividing up of economic tasks into specialisations. Thus few workers these days produce the whole commodity but undertake only particular parts of the production process. This process lies at the very heart of the modern exchange economy. The enormous advantages of the division of labour were recognised early by Adam Smith and he illustrated them by the use of what is now, possibly, the most famous example in economics – pin making. In *The Wealth of Nations* he described pin making thus:

> One man draws out the wire, another straights it, a third cuts it, a fourth points it, a fifth grinds it; to make the head requires two or three distinct

operations, to put it on is another peculiar business, to whiten the pin is another, it is even a trade by itself to put them into paper.

The resulting increase in output is phenomenal.

It is important to grasp the significance of this idea of *specialisation*. It is not necessary that any new technique be invented; the specialisation itself will result in increases in production. The ultimate extension of the principle is that of the specialisation of nations, which is the basis of the theory of international trade. This international division of labour is discussed at the end of this chapter.

Advantages of the division of labour

(a) *Increase in skill and dexterity*. 'Practice makes perfect', as the saying goes; the constant repetition of tasks means that they can be done more expertly. The authors can report that their typing speeds have improved as a result of writing this book!

(b) *Time saving*. If a person has to do many different tasks then a considerable period of time is taken between operations. Time can also be saved in the training of people. If, for example, a person has to be trained as an engineer, this takes many years, but a person can be quickly trained to fulfil one operation in the engineering process.

(c) *Individual aptitudes*. The division of labour allows people to do what they are best at. Some people are physically very strong, while others have good mental aptitudes. With the division of labour there is a greater chance that people will be able to concentrate on those things at which they are best.

(d) *Use of machinery*. As tasks become subdivided it becomes worthwhile using machinery, which is a further saving of effort. For example, consider wine production: if production is only a few hundred bottles then specialist bottling equipment is hardly justified; but if production rises to tens of thousands of bottles, then it becomes worthwhile to use a specialist machine to do this.

(e) *Managerial control*. Some economists have argued that the division of labour, in breaking down processes into separate tasks, allows managers to monitor workers more closely.

Moreover, operatives on a production line are more easily coerced than more skilled workers, who can withhold information from managers and may not be so easily replaced.

Disadvantages of the division of labour

A modern economy without the division of labour is inconceivable. Thus when we speak of its disadvantages it should be realised that these are not arguments against specialisation but, rather, problems associated with it.

(a) *Interdependency.* Specialisation inevitably means that people are dependent upon each other. In the UK today we are dependent for our food upon people thousands of miles away and beyond our control.

(b) *Dislocation.* Because of interdependency the possibilities for dislocation are very great. For example the miners' strike in 1984 would have brought the whole country to a halt, had it not been for massive police intervention. A more recent example is the havoc caused by the 'dump the pump' campaign against high fuel prices in 2000, which threatened to curtail essential services after only a few days.

(c) *Unemployment.* Specialisation means that many people have a narrow training and experience. This can mean that if their skill is no longer required, it may be difficult for that person to find alternative work. In the rapidly changing technology of the twenty-first century this can represent a problem unless workers are prepared to retrain for new skills or professions, or engage in 'lifelong' education, updating themselves continuously as technology changes the nature of their jobs.

(d) *Alienation.* This refers to the estrangement many workers feel from their work. If, for example, a person's job is simply to tighten wheel nuts on a car production line, it is understandable that they should feel bored or even hostile towards the work. This may have repercussions on labour relations and productivity. In response, some manufacturers have undertaken job enrichment schemes, putting the division of labour into reverse, as it were, in order that people may have more varied tasks.

The alienation of the workforce is a major part of Marxist sociology. Capitalists might reply that although jobs may be dull, working hours are made shorter and leisure is enriched by greater wealth. However, alienation is not a problem that should be ignored, either at work or in society in general.

Because of these problems with the division of labour, there has been a counter tendency in the last decade towards 'multi-skilling' of workers to increase their flexibility and enrich their jobs. In education, the so-called 'transferable skills' such as communication, literacy, numeracy, teamworking and IT skills have been emphasized. This move away from the division of labour is known as 'post-Fordism'.

Economies of scale

Economies of scale exist when the expansion of a firm or industry allows the product to be produced at a lower unit cost. As such, economies of scale are an aspect of the division of labour. Economies of scale are possible only if there is sufficient demand for the product. For example, we would hardly expect to find scale economies in the production of artificial limbs, because there simply are not enough of them demanded. As Adam Smith put it, 'the extent of the division of labour is limited by the size of the market'. Economies of scale cannot be achieved quickly because large-scale investment in capital (factories, machinery, etc.) is necessary to achieve them. Indeed, the short period is defined in economics as the period in which capital cannot be varied (this period of time will differ according to the industry). The achievement of economies of scale is therefore a long-run objective.

Internal and external economies of scale

Internal economies of scale are those obtained within one organisation, while *external* economies are those that are gained when a number of organisations group together in an area. Industries such as chemicals and cars provide good examples of internal economies, where the industry is dominated by a few large organisations. Historically, the most famous example of external economies of scale was the cotton industry in Lancashire, where many hundreds of businesses concentrated in a small area made up the industry. A more up-to-date example might be the grouping of firms offering specialist financial services in the City of London, or the concentration of the computing industry and the film industry on the west coast of the USA.

Types of internal economy

(a) *Indivisibilities*. This occurs where there is a 'lumpiness' about output which means a minimum size is necessary to use current technology. For example, for most railway routes only one track is needed in each direction. As demand for rail services increases, the total cost of providing the track increases only slowly.

(b) *Increased dimensions*. In some cases it is simply a case of bigger is better. For example, an engine that is twice as powerful does not cost twice as much to build, or use twice as much material. This is partly due to area–volume relationships. As a rule of thumb, engineers use the *law of two-thirds*, which states that as the volume of a container (pipe, ship, plane) is doubled, its surface area is increased by only two-thirds. The surface area determines how much it costs to construct, while the volume determines its output. Doubling the volume of a ship doubles its ability to carry cargo, but only increases its construction costs by about two-thirds. Hence large ships are much more efficient than small ships. This explains the development of massive oil tankers and bulk cargo carriers. Jumbo jets (e.g. Boeing 747s) are also an example of this principle.

(c) *Economies of linked processes*. Technical economies are also sometimes gained by linking processes together, e.g. in the iron and steel industry where iron and steel production is carried out by the same plant, thus saving both transport and fuel costs.

(d) *Commercial*. A large-scale organisation may be able to make fuller use of sales and distribution facilities than a small-scale one. For example, a company with a large transport fleet will probably be able to ensure that it transports mainly full loads, whereas a small business may have to hire transport or despatch part-loads. A large firm may also be able to use its commercial power to obtain preferential rates for raw materials and transport. This is usually known as *bulk buying*.

(e) *Organisational*. As a firm becomes larger, the day-to-day organisation can be delegated to office staff, leaving managers free to concentrate on the important tasks. When a firm is large enough to have a management staff they will be able to specialise in different functions such as accounting, law and market research.

(f) *Financial*. Large organisations often find it cheaper and easier to borrow money than small ones, as banks are less worried that they might go out of business.

(g) *Risk bearing*. All firms run risks, but risks taken in large numbers become more predictable. In addition to this, if an organisation is so large as to be a monopoly, this considerably reduces its commercial risks.

(h) *Overhead processes*. For some products very large overhead costs or processes must be undertaken to develop a product, e.g. an aeroplane. Clearly if more units of the product are made, the development costs attributed to each unit will fall.

(i) *Diversification*. Most economies of scale are concerned with specialisation and concentration. However, as a firm becomes very large it may be able to safeguard its position by diversifying its products, processes, markets and the location of production.

(j) *Economies of common multiples*. For any product we consider, the various processes which are needed to produce it may not have the same optimal scale of production. For example, a large blast furnace may produce 75 tonnes of pig iron but a steel furnace may be able to handle only 30 tonnes; we would thus need more than one steel furnace for every blast furnace. In fact the smallest optimal size for the whole process is the lowest common multiple of the individual processes involved. In our steelmaking example this would give us a plant consisting of two blast furnaces and five steel furnaces:

$$2 \times 75 \text{ tonnes} = 150 \text{ tonnes}$$
$$5 \times 30 \text{ tonnes} = 150 \text{ tonnes}$$

Thus the smallest optimal size is 150 tonnes.

Types of external economy

(a) *Economies of concentration*. When a number of firms in the same industry band together in an area they can derive a great deal of mutual advantage from one another. Advantages might include a pool of skilled workers, a better infrastructure (such as transport, specialised warehousing, banking, etc.) and the stimulation of improvements. The lack of such external economies is a serious handicap to less developed countries.

(b) *Economies of information*. Under this heading we could consider the setting up of specialist research facilities and the publication of specialist journals.

(c) *Economies of disintegration*. This refers to the splitting off or *subcontracting* of specialist processes. A simple example is to be seen in the high street of most towns where there are specialist photocopying firms.

It should be stressed that what are external economies at one time may be internal at another. To use the last example, small firms may not be able to justify the cost of a sophisticated photocopier, but as they expand there may be enough work to allow them to purchase or rent their own machine.

Efficiency and economies of scale

Where an economy of scale leads to a fall in unit costs because less resources are used to produce a unit of a commodity, this is economically beneficial to society. If, for example, a large furnace uses less fuel per tonne of steel produced than a small one, then society benefits through a more efficient use of scarce fuel resources. It is possible, however, for a firm to achieve economies through such things as bulk buying, where its buying power is used to bargain for a lower price. This benefits the firm because its costs will be lower, but it does not benefit society as a whole since no saving of resources is involved.

Diseconomies of scale

Diseconomies of scale occur when the size of a business becomes so large that, rather than decreasing, the unit cost of production actually becomes greater. Diseconomies of scale usually flow from administrative and social, rather than technical problems.

(a) *Bureaucracy*. As an organisation becomes larger there is a tendency for it to become more **bureaucratic**. Decisions can no longer be made quickly at the local level but must follow centrally laid-down procedures or be referred up to higher levels of management. This may lead to a loss of *flexibility*.

(b) *Loss of control*. Large organisations often find it more difficult to monitor effectively the performance of their workers. **Industrial relations** can also deteriorate with a large workforce and a management which seems remote and anonymous.

Optimal plant and company size

Achieving the best size of business is not simply a question of getting bigger, but of attaining the optimal size of business or plant.

The typical size of plant will vary greatly from industry to industry. In capital-intensive industries such as chemicals the typical unit may be very large, but in an industry like catering the optimum size of a restaurant is quickly reached and, beyond this, diseconomies may set in. If a restaurant business wishes to expand, it does so by opening new branches (e.g. McDonald's, Burger King) in other locations.

Economics of scale and returns to scale

Confusion frequently arises between economies of scale and *returns to scale*. Economies of scale reduce the unit cost of production as the scale of production increases; returns to scale are concerned with physical input and output relationships. If, for example, the input of factors of production were to increase by 100 per cent but output were to increase by 150 per cent, we would be said to be experiencing increasing returns to scale. Conversely, if inputs were to be increased by 100 per cent but output were to increase by less than this, then we would be experiencing decreasing returns to scale.

Increasing returns to scale should result in decreasing costs. However, it does not follow that every economy of scale that reduces costs is a result of a return to scale. To take the most obvious example, bulk buying may reduce costs to the business but it does not involve returns to scale since no change in the input–output relationship is involved.

New technology

Improvements in technology are obviously of fundamental importance to the economy. New technology brings improved productivity and is therefore beneficial. However, the impact of a major new technology can also bring major dislocation and uncertainty to the economy and society. We will consider two such technical revolutions to illustrate this point, one of which is now widely accepted but continues to make considerable changes in our lives (information technology); and the other is only just being introduced and is the subject of some misgivings (biotechnology and GM crops).

Information technology

The term 'information technology' (IT) covers a series of inventions: computer hard disks; silicon chips; fibre optic cable for telecommunications; Windows-based software and the world wide web. Together these new technologies have revolutionised the way in which we live and work. The changes have affected almost every aspect of production and many aspects of consumption. Information can now be accessed and sent rapidly using the Internet. The growing power of computers allows them to control many precise and complex engineering tasks, for example robots can assemble electrical components. The music industry has been affected by the free exchange of MP3 files on the Internet. The computer games industry has grown from nothing over the last 20 years to become a major player in the home entertainment market. Major new technologies such as this may result in the closure of firms that fail to keep pace, and unemployment or low paid employment for workers who fail to acquire the new skills. In the case of IT, it has even resulted in a new category of poverty: the 'information poor'. On the other hand, dot.com millionaires, e-tailers, and whole new industries benefit as new areas of the economy expand. The full potential of the information technology revolution has still not been reached and it seems likely that it will have a more significant effect on the way we live than the original industrial revolution. It is always difficult to forecast where a technology is moving next, but there seem to be clear signs that the computing, telecommunications and television technologies are converging, with the development of WAP mobile phones and access to the Internet via telephone and television without the need for an intervening PC. The important point to note in this process is that changing technology will require resources to be allocated differently, and we need a system to re-allocate resources as technology changes. The market is the system that usually achieves this objective, although the state may also have a role to play.

The Industrial Revolution

Economic history tells us that vast leaps in technology have been made before. The industrial revolution began in the UK in the second half of the eighteenth century, and continued to gather pace in the nineteenth century. For example, within ten years of its invention each spinning jenny was able to replace 100 workers in the cotton industry. In the wake of the industrial revolution there was poverty and misery for millions, but in the long run the expansion of the economy was able to provide employment for most (labour is after all our most valuable resource) and a higher standard of living. The nature of the jobs available changes after the technological revolution. Only a small proportion of people work in the agricultural industry nowadays, although this was the most common occupation before the industrial revolution. It is sometimes argued that we are going through a second industrial revolution at the present – an information revolution. This sometimes allows countries to leapfrog more established economies by moving straight into the new technology without passing through all the historical stages needed to get there. For instance, the software industry has established itself in India before that country has shifted most of its workers from agriculture to industry.

Many people view new technology with alarm, seeing it purely as a method of making workers redundant. In the nineteenth century there was a movement of workers called Luddites, who smashed industrial machinery because they saw it as a threat to their livelihood. It is important to see that new technology both destroys old jobs and creates new jobs, bringing opportunity and wealth to those individuals and countries able to exploit its potential. It also may bring poverty and unemployment to those less able to adapt.

Biotechnology

From a new technology which is now widely accepted, and which has had a clear, largely beneficial impact on the economy, we now turn to a technology that is much newer and less certain in its effects. Biotechnology has been with us for some time, particularly the use of enzymes to produce certain chemicals. More recently, the Genome project has successfully outlined the genetic blueprint of the human race. These more advanced biotechnological techniques have also led to the development of genetically modified (GM) crops. This innovation has allowed the development of crops that are resistant to insecticides, allowing the more intensive use of such chemicals to kill off mankind's principal competitors for food. Such technology has raised concerns about the ecological effects of this new form of agriculture. Concerns have also been expressed about the unknown effects on humans of food products changed in this way. These concerns have led to direct action to destroy GM crops by environmentalists opposed to the new technology. Will these environmental protesters be seen as the Luddites of today when people look back on this era, or as the saviours of the environment? It is too early to say whether such fears are justified, but it may also be too late to prevent such crops spreading through natural germination.

Another example of this type of technology is the proposed use of genetically engineered fungus to attack cocaine and heroine poppy crops in Colombia and Afghanistan as part of the war against drugs. While scientists can test to make sure these organisms do not attack other crops, there is always the risk of mutation in the wild.

The use of this technology to grow replacement organs, or create 'designer' babies also raises complex ethical questions. Biotechnology gives us the opportunity to improve output in agriculture and medicine, but brings with it many difficult problems and risks.

Increasing costs and diminishing returns

We have been examining factors that help people to exploit the resources of the world. However, the basic law of economics is that of scarcity. We must now consider the factors that place constraints upon our exploitation of resources.

The law of diminishing returns

Why can we not grow all the world's food in one garden? A silly question perhaps, but it illustrates a very important principle. We can get a greater output from a garden of fixed size by working longer hours or adding more seeds, etc., but the extra output we obtain will rapidly diminish. Indeed, if we just go on dumping more and more seeds in the garden, total output may even go down.

The principle involved here is known as the *law of diminishing returns*. This law is one of the most important and fundamental principles involved in economics. We may state it thus:

If one factor of production is fixed in supply and successive units of a variable factor are added to it, the extra output derived from the employment of each successive unit of the variable factor must, after a time, decline.

We can illustrate this by the use of a simple numerical example. Suppose that the fixed factor of production is a farm (land). If no labour is employed there will be no output. Now let us see what happens if people are employed. Suppose that one person is employed in the first year, two in the second, and so on. Table 3.1 shows the resulting output from the various combinations of the factors. The first person results in 2000 tonnes of produce. When two people are employed output rises to 5000 tonnes, so that the second person has resulted in 3000 extra tonnes being produced. However, after this, diminishing returns set in and the employment of a third person results in only 2000 tonnes more being produced, while a fourth person adds just 1000 tonnes to production. Were a fifth person to be employed there would be no extra output at all.

Table 3.1 The law of diminishing returns

Number of people employed	Total output (tonnes)	Extra output added by each additional unit of labour
0	0	
		2000
1	2000	
		3000
2	5000	
		2000
3	7000	
		1000
4	8000	
		0
5	8000	

The law of diminishing returns comes about because each successive unit of the variable factor has less of the fixed factor to work with.

The law of diminishing returns may be offset by improvements in technology, but it cannot be repealed.

The short run and the long run

At any particular time any business must have at least one of the factors of production in fixed supply. For example, the buildings that a firm uses cannot be expanded overnight, so that if the firm wants to obtain more output it must use more of the variable factors such as labour.

The period of time in which at least one factor is fixed in supply is defined as the *short run*. Given time, all the factors may be varied, i.e. new buildings can be constructed, more land acquired, etc. The period of time in which all factors may be varied and in which firms may enter or leave the industry is defined as the *long run*. The length of time involved will vary from business to business. Obviously it will take much longer for an oil refinery to vary its fixed factors by constructing a new refinery than it would, for example, for a farmer to rent more land.

The law of diminishing returns is thus a short-run phenomenon because, by definition, it is concerned with a situation in which at least one factor is fixed in supply.

The law of increasing costs

The law of diminishing returns concerns what happens to output if one factor remains fixed in the short run; in the long run their may be either economies or diseconomies of scale as discussed above. The *law of increasing costs* examines what happens to production, and therefore to costs, as output is increased in one industry by increasing the use of all factors of production. Output of other industries will have to be reduced.

Let us imagine we are faced with the choice that Hermann Goering gave the German people in 1936: we can produce either guns or butter. Table 3.2 shows a list of alternative possibilities and if we start at possibility C, where we are producing 10 000 guns and 10 million kg of butter, and then try to produce more guns, this involves switching resources from farming to industry. To reach possibility B we have had to give up 5 million kg of butter to gain 4000 guns. If we want still more guns, to reach possibility A we have to give up a further 5 million kg of butter to gain only 1000 guns. Thus the cost of guns in terms of butter has risen sharply.

Table 3.2 Increasing costs: a production possibility schedule

Possibility	Guns (thousands)	Butter (millions of kg)
A	15	0
B	14	5
C	10	10
D	5	14
E	0	15

It would also work the other way. If we started from possibility C and tried to increase our output of butter, the cost in terms of guns not produced would become greater and greater. Figure 3.2 shows this graphically. As we move to either end of the *production possibility frontier* we can see that it is necessary to give up a greater distance on one axis to gain a smaller distance on the other axis. Why should this be? It is because, as we concentrate more and more resources on the output of a particular commodity, the resources we use become less and less suitable. For example, if we tried to produce more and more butter we would, inevitably, be forced to graze cows on land that is better suited to other uses such as forestry.

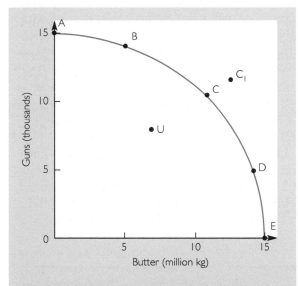

Figure 3.2 Production possibility frontier
Society can attain any combination of guns and butter on line AE or any combination within it such as U, but is unable to attain a position beyond line AE such as C_1.

Opportunity cost

Limited resources have alternative uses; for example, the bricks and labour we use to build a house could have been used to build a factory or a hospital. Thus the cost of any product may be looked at in terms of other opportunities forgone. In the example of guns and butter used above, any movement along the production possibility line tells us the *opportunity cost* of guns in terms of butter or vice versa.

Opportunity cost calculations often come up with different answers according to the viewpoint taken. For instance, if a person is unemployed what is the opportunity cost of them taking a job? From the viewpoint of the individual, leisure time must be given up, so there is a positive opportunity cost. From the point of view of the economy as a whole, the labour was previously unproductive, so the opportunity cost is zero. From the point of view of the government, they no longer have to pay unemployment benefit, and their tax revenues will rise as the individual earns income. In this section it is the opportunity cost to the economy as a whole that is being considered.

STUDENT ACTIVITY 3.4

What is the opportunity cost to (a) society and (b) yourself of undertaking your present course of study? Choose from the following list of items to be included in each case:

(a) Your leisure time.
(b) Your income if you had a job instead.
(c) Your output if you had a job instead.
(d) The cost of producing your education.
(e) Any fees or other expenses which you pay because of your course.
(f) The increase in productivity that will result from your education.
(g) The increase in your income that will result from your education.
(h) The cost to your parents of supporting you financially.
(i) The money you are able to earn in the holidays.
(j) The social advantages of mixing with many people of your own age.

The production possibility frontier

If we plot the figures in Table 3.2 as a graph we obtain Figure 3.2. This is termed a production possibility frontier because it shows the limit of what it is possible to produce with present resources. Society may attain any point on the line, such as point C, or, through the unemployment or inefficient use of resources, any point within the frontier, such as U.

However, point C_1 is unattainable at present. Point C_1 may become attainable as the production possibility shifts rightwards as a result of economic growth and improvements in technology.

You will note that the line is bowed outwards (concave to the origin). This is because of the law of increasing costs. A few moments experimenting with a ruler on the graph will show you that the rate of exchange of guns for butter, or vice versa, worsens continually as we move up or down the line. This is the typical shape for a production possibility.

Of course, in any real economy there will be many more than two products. Presenting the production possibility frontier is not possible in graphical form if we have more than three products (and even then it's difficult). A real PPF would have to be presented using complicated maths, which you would probably not enjoy. This is an early example of how economics simplifies complex reality in order to get at the essential nature of the economy.

Three possibilities for a line

To check that you have understood this idea let us consider the three possibilities for the shape of the production possibility frontier. These are illustrated in Figure 3.3. In Figure 3.3(a), as we move down the vertical axis each 20 units of Y given up gains smaller and smaller amounts of X. Moving from position A to position B we give up 20 units of Y but gain 50 units of X. However, as we move from position B to position C, a further 20 units of Y given up now gains us only 22 units of X. The ratio of exchange continues to deteriorate until the last 20 units of Y given up gains only three units of X. Review your understanding of this principle by considering it in reverse, i.e. as we move from point F to point E it costs only three units of X given up to gain 20 units of Y, but moving from position B to position A involves giving up 50 units of X to gain 20 units of Y. Thus the ratio of exchange of X for Y (or Y for X) deteriorates whichever way we move along a line that is concave to the origin of the graph. Such a line illustrates increasing costs (or diminishing returns).

In Figure 3.3(b) we show a constant cost case, i.e. that product X can be exchanged for product Y at a constant rate. You will find various applications of such a line in this book, starting with a discussion of economic growth and international trade below. It is sometimes easier to assume constant returns to scale as this simplifies an

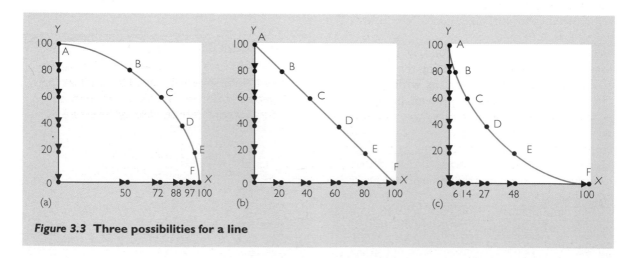

Figure 3.3 Three possibilities for a line

otherwise complicated situation and allows us to concentrate on the important issues.

If we look at a line which is bowed inwards (convex to the origin) this shows increasing returns (or decreasing costs), i.e. the ratio of exchange of X for Y (or Y for X) gets better as we move towards the ends of the line. In Figure 3.3(c) moving from position A to position B involves giving up 20 units of Y to gain six units of X but the next 20 units of Y given up gains eight units of X and so on until the last 20 units of Y given up gains us 52 units of X. This could come about if, for example, specialising in X allowed us to gain more and more economies of scale. Again check your understanding of the principle by moving the other way along the line and seeing that the ratio of exchange of Y for X also improves, i.e. the first 20 units of Y cost us 52 units of X given up but the next 20 only 21 and so on. As we have stated above, a production possibility line is most likely to be concave, but we shall encounter various applications of these properties of lines throughout the book.

Economic growth: outward shifts in the production possibility frontier

Over time, economies are able to achieve economic growth by shifting their production possibility frontiers outwards as in Figure 3.4. More of both products can be produced as a result of economic growth. If the economy was operating at point A, it can now produce at point D; if it was previously at point C it can shift out to point E. Economic growth need not take place evenly over all parts of the economy. It is often the case that a few sectors are driving the change with strong technical innovation, as with the case of information technology at present. In Figure 3.4. economic growth has been stronger in industry Y, with a 30 per cent increase in maximum output compared with only 10 per cent in industry X. However, if consumer demand prefers the output of industry X, the country may still end up with a point like E, with the emphasis on X production.

The main way in which growth can be achieved is by the introduction of new technology as discussed earlier in the chapter, but it can also be achieved if people are willing to work harder, or a larger proportion of the population is willing

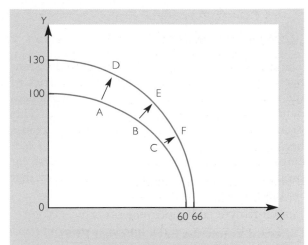

Figure 3.4 Economic growth shifts the production possibility frontier outwards

to work. The debate about how to encourage investment in new technology, and how to persuade people to work harder, forms a large part of the subject matter of economics. We will return to these questions in Chapters 11, 28 and 34. Some economies have managed to grow at substantially faster rates than others. The economies of Germany and Japan grew faster than most other countries in the period after the Second World War. While both these countries have had much slower growth in the 1990s, other countries have been more successful, notably the Republic of Ireland and China, while the USA has also enjoyed sustained growth throughout this decade.

STUDENT ACTIVITY 3.5

1 Which industries have experienced the biggest growth rates in recent years? Do you think that is because of increasing productivity in those industries, consumer demand, or a mixture of the two?

2 How could you study more efficiently to increase your educational output? Classify your answer in terms of
   (a) working harder
   (b) organising your time better
   (c) using more effective techniques
   (d) making better use of class time
   (e) buying equipment

International trade

The discussion so far has been limited to decisions occurring inside one economy. The countries of the world are rapidly becoming more interdependent, a process known as *globalisation*. This process means that much economic growth comes because of trade between nations, with each specialising in the products they are best at producing. It is to this aspect of the economy that we turn next.

Different countries have different PPFs

Not all countries will face the same conditions of production, and as a result, their production possibility frontiers will be different. Whenever there is a difference between countries PPFs, a possibility for trade exists. There are many possible reasons why PPFs could be different:

(a) *Differences of climate.* Agricultural productivity may vary between countries, or certain plants may be more suited to one climate than others. Growing grapes in Scotland is very difficult, but oats are easily produced.

(b) *Differences of skill.* Education or tradition may result in differing levels of skill in different countries. Countries without an industrial tradition may not have the necessary skills among the workforce to compete internationally.

(c) *Differences in the proportions of factors of production.* Europe and much of South East Asia are densely populated. This results in them using intensive methods of farming to get as much out of the limited land as possible. This can lead to problems of diminishing returns. By contrast, Australia and the mid-West of the USA are relatively thinly populated, leading them to use much less intensive methods.

(d) *Differing technology.* This last point also extends to capital, both in terms of its quantity and its quality, which will affect the productive capacity of a country.

(e) *Differences in enterprise.* Cultural differences in countries may also be important. If there is a tradition of innovating new products and new methods of production, as is the case in the more dynamic capitalist countries, then

they will have an advantage in these areas of production, while other countries may concentrate on more traditional manufacture.

(f) *Differences in work effort.* The productivity of different countries may vary simply because of how long, or how hard people are willing to work. Once again this may be a matter of local culture.

(g) *Differences in population.* This will also make a difference to the total output of a country, although output per person may actually be lower than in a smaller country.

Specialisation and the gains from trade

These differences are illustrated in Figure 3.5, where country A is clearly better at producing good Y, while country B is much better at producing good X. If it helps you, choose your own products and name the countries. **David Ricardo,** the nineteenth-century British economist who first thought carefully about these issues, chose England and cloth, to compare with Portugal and wine. To make the example easier we will assume constant returns to scale, so that the PPFs are straight lines.

To make the comparison between the situation before and after specialisation and trade easier still, we have assumed that the two countries start off at the same point M, producing and

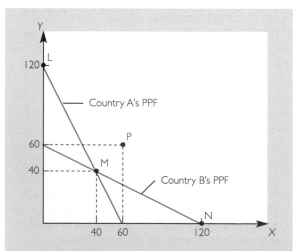

Figure 3.5 **The benefits of international trade**

consuming 40 units of output of both products. This point is on the PPF of both countries, so both of them can produce this combination of X and Y on their own without trade.

If country A decides to specialise in producing good Y (because they are clearly more efficient at it) they will be able to triple production to 120 units at point L on their PPF, but they will have no output of good X. Country B will likewise be able to triple output of good X to 120 units at point N on their PPF, but will have no good Y output. Country A decides to trade 60 units of its good Y production, leaving it 60 units for its own consumption. Country B decides to trade 60 units of its good X production, also leaving it 60 units for its own consumption. After the two countries have traded their surplus production they will each be able to consume 60 units of each product at point P. Simply as a result of specialisation and trade, both countries have experienced a 50 per cent growth in their economies compared with the starting point M.

Incentives for trade

What would make the two countries behave in this way? The answer is the market system, which is the subject of the next few chapters. Each country will specialise in the product they are most efficient at producing, because that is where their businesses can make the most profit. The situation is more complicated than this, because each country will use its own currency. In order that trade (other than barter) can take place, an exchange rate has to be worked out between the two countries. Once again it is the market system that will work out the value of one currency in terms of another according to the laws of supply and demand.

Limits to trade

Trade does not take place in all products or between all countries. Here are some of the barriers to trade:

(a) *Non-tradables*. It is not easy to import or export some products. Exporting a haircut or a meal in a restaurant cannot be easily done. Such products form the non-tradable sector of the economy.

(b) *Transport and transactions costs*. The cost of transporting goods and the costs of dealing in more than one currency also limit the extent of trade. The adoption of the euro as a common currency would reduce transaction costs.

(c) *Protectionism*. Quotas and import duties are two methods countries use to protect themselves against imports which are either cheaper or better quality than domestic products. Despite the overall gains from trade indicated above, there will always be some losers from the less efficient part of the economy. This argument is discussed in more detail in Chapter 41.

(d) *Self-sufficiency*. If countries specialise too much they may become overly dependent on another country's output. In times of war, or other crises, they may wish to be more independent. This argument is often used in relation to the agriculture and defence industries.

Regional specialisation and trade

In the same way that countries specialise and trade, different regions of a country will specialise in different types of production. Trade will be easier, because there are no trade barriers and the same currency and language is used. Transport may also be easier. Some regions may specialise in tourism; others with lower population densities may have more agricultural output; London specialises in financial services, while there is more manufacturing in the midlands and the north of England.

The EU is an interesting case, as the adoption of a common currency by most EU countries (but not the UK at present) has made their trade more like regional than international trade. In theory, the easier trading conditions inside the EU ought to create economic growth.

Absolute versus comparative advantage

The example of trade worked out in Figure 3.5 above is an example of absolute advantage. Each country has an absolute advantage over the other in the production of one good. A more difficult case, where trade is still advantageous, is the case of comparative advantage. What if one country is better than another country at producing both products?

The *principle of comparative advantage* is used to explain why trade is still beneficial. In Figure 3.6, both countries have the same resources but country A is more efficient at producing both good X and good Y. It can produce more of either and has an absolute advantage in both products over country B. Gains from trade can still be made by looking at comparative advantage. Country A is 150 per cent better at producing good Y but only 25 per cent better at producing good X. It follows that country A should specialise in producing good Y and country B in good X because that is where their comparative advantages lies.

Table 3.3 **The principle of comparative advantage**

	Before specialisation		After specialisation		After trade	
	Y	X	Y	X	Y	X
Country A (S)	50	50	(U) 90	10	60	50
Country B (R)	20	40	(T) 0	80	30	40

The starting point in Figure 3.6 is R (20Y and 40X) for country B, and S (50Y and 50X) for country A. Country B specialises in good X, producing 80 units and moving from R to T on its PPF. This not quite enough to meet demand (40X plus 50X) so country A has to produce 10 units of X. Country A's specialisation is not complete, but they can still move from point S to point U where 90 units of Y are produced, leaving a surplus of 40Y.

As long as country A exchanges less than these 40 units of Y for the 40 units of X they need to meet demand, they will have made a gain from trade. As long as country B gets more than 20 units of Y for their surplus of 40X, they will also have made a gain from trade. If they share the gains equally, the result will be as in Table 3.3, and both will have made a gain of 10 units of good Y.

Exchange rates

In the case of absolute advantage it was easy to see how businesses in each country could make a profit by selling their specialist products in the other market, which was less efficient at producing it. It is more difficult to see how this can happen in cases of comparative advantage. How can the less efficient country sell its products in the markets of the more efficient country? The answer is that the exchange rate will move down until this becomes profitable. This will happen as a result of the market mechanism because nobody will want to buy country B's currency until it has become cheap enough for the country to trade profitably.

Where the principle of comparative advantage operates between regions in the same country, the exchange rate cannot be used to oil the wheels of trade. Instead, wages will rise in the more efficient region and be held back in the less efficient region until trade is profitable.

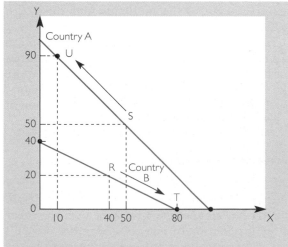

Figure 3.6 **The principle of comparative advantage**

Summary

1 The economic problem is that of infinite human wants but only limited resources with which to fulfil them.
2 Economic resources are traditionally divided into the four factors of production: labour, land, capital and enterprise.
3 Division of labour is the subdivision of the economic process into specialist tasks. The resultant increase in output is the basis of economic prosperity.
4 Economies of scale exist when the production of a product in large numbers allows its unit cost to be decreased. There are both external and internal economies of scale.
5 The law of diminishing returns states that if one factor is fixed in supply, but more and more units of a variable factor are employed, the resultant extra output will decrease.
6 The law of increasing costs is encountered when one type of production is expanded at the cost of others. It comes about because less suitable resources have to be used.
7 The production possibility line shows all the combinations of products which it is possible to produce with a given quantity of resources.
8 Economic growth can result from new technology or from incentives to work hard.
9 Regional or international specialisation and trade can contribute to economic growth.

? QUESTIONS

1 Define increasing costs, returns to scale and the law of diminishing returns.
2 Evaluate the extent to which the disadvantages of division of labour outweigh the advantages.
3 Show the effect upon society's production possibility line in Figure 3.2 if technological improvements increased productivity in the production of guns but not of butter.
4 If in a given situation the quantity of land could be increased but labour could not, would the law of diminishing returns still operate? Explain your answer.
5 Assess the extent to which each of the following products is affected by available economies of scale:

petroleum; milk; electricity; cars; frozen peas; coal; luxury yachts.
6 Evaluate the role which prices play in helping to answer the economic problem.
7 Consider the opportunity cost of:
  (a) Leaving school at 16.
  (b) Spending 5 per cent of GDP on defence.
  (c) Building a fifth terminal at London Heathrow airport.
  (d) The construction of a new motorway.
8 If imports of cheap overseas products result in a local factory being closed down, are there any gains from trade?

Data response A
COSTS AND CHOICE

Table 3.4 presents information for the JSB Audiomax Speaker Company, showing how the cost of producing loudspeakers varies with the output produced per week.

Table 3.4 Costs of the JSB Audiomax Speaker Company

Units of output produced per week	Total costs of production (£)
1 009	85 025
1 998	110 014
3 004	130 010
4 014	160 002
4 997	209 889
6 011	280 015
7 003	370 000
7 990	479 917

1 From this information construct a graph to show how the cost of producing a loudspeaker (unit or average cost) varies with the quantity of loudspeakers produced each week.
2 State the range of output over which the company experiences:
  (a) increasing returns to scale;
  (b) decreasing returns to scale.
3 What is the most productively efficient level of output for JSB?
4 Distinguish between economies of scale and returns to scale.
5 What economies of scale are likely to be available to JSB?

Data response B
GROWTH, WAGES AND POVERTY

Read the following passage which is taken from the
World Development Report of 1990.

Growth, real wages, and poverty: the United Kingdom and the United States, 1770 to 1920

The history of the *industrial revolution* in the United Kingdom
and the United States suggests links among growth, real
wages, and poverty. In both countries development in the
early phase of the revolution was *capital-intensive*. Since at the
same time the labour supply was increasing, the *real wages* of
unskilled workers grew slowly, and economic growth had only
a small effect on poverty. After about 1820 in the United
Kingdom and 1880 in the United States, however, real wages
began to rise, and poverty began to decline.

Britain's industrial revolution began around 1770, but until
1820 real wages barely increased. In the first twenty years of
the nineteenth century the earnings of adult male unskilled
workers grew at just 0.2 per cent a year. The next fifty years
saw a much faster and steadier increase at 1.7 per cent a
year. After about 1840 the GDP of the United States grew
significantly faster than that of the United Kingdom at a
comparable stage, but real wages for urban unskilled labour
increased by less than 0.2 per cent a year between 1845 and
1880. Then, as in the United Kingdom, they accelerated and
grew by 1.3 per cent a year for the next 40 years.

In both countries technological advances initially favoured
capital-intensive and *skill-intensive* industry over *labour-intensive* agriculture. Slow growth in labour demand

coincided with dramatic population growth to restrict the
growth of real wages. Several decades after the start of the
industrial revolution, technological progress in farming led to
a more *balanced pattern of growth*, and the labour-saving bias
of early industrialisation gave way to a neutral or labour-intensive bias. Lower birth-rates and stricter immigration
laws slowed population growth, and real wages increased at
a faster rate.

In the United Kingdom pauperism declined after 1840.
The most reliable data for the United States, from records in
New York State, suggest that poverty increased up to 1865,
when 8 per cent of the population was receiving local relief.
After that, poverty declined until the end of the century. In
both countries growth in the real wages of unskilled labour
reduced the incidence of poverty.

Answer the following questions.

1 Explain the terms in italics.
2 If population increased rapidly what would you
   expect to happen to the level of real wages?
   Explain what principle is at work in this situation.
3 Construct a production possibility curve to
   illustrate what would happen if technology
   increased rapidly in industry but not in agriculture.
4 State the conditions necessary for there to be an
   increase in population accompanied by growth in
   real wages.
5 Poverty is still a worldwide problem. Do the
   developments described in the article have any
   lessons for poor countries today? Explain your answer.

4 The allocation of resources in competitive markets

Learning outcomes

At the end of this chapter you will be able to:
- List factors that will affect consumers' decision to demand.
- List factors that will affect the producer's decision to supply.
- Predict how the market will respond to disequilibrium positions.
- Explain the functions of the market.
- Identify areas in which the market system may not meet social objectives.

The price system

Micro- and macroeconomics

Owing largely to the work of the great British economist **John Maynard Keynes**, it has been customary to divide economic theory into *microeconomics* and *macroeconomics*. As its name implies, microeconomics is concerned with small parts of the economy and the interrelationships between these parts, while macroeconomics is concerned with the behaviour of broad aggregates affecting the whole economy. Explanations of the price of food, or houses (discussed in detail in Chapter 11) are examples of microeconomic topics. Macroeconomic topics, which are discussed in detail in Sections IV, VII and VIII, come under the four headings of *inflation*, *unemployment*, *the balance of payments* and *growth*.

Defining the price system

When we speak of the *price system* we mean situations where the vital economic decisions are taken through the medium of prices. A market price is the result of the interaction between the consumers' demand for a good and the supply of that product by producers. However, in order to produce goods, the producers must have used factors of production. Ultimately all factors in the economy are owned by consumers, so that the producers must buy the use of these factors from consumers. There are therefore, in addition to markets for products, markets for the factors of production. This is illustrated in Figure 4.1. This shows the critical importance of prices as the connecting, or communicating, mechanism between consumers and producers.

Types of markets

In this chapter we will concern ourselves with the essentials of the price mechanism, which forms the nub of microeconomic theory. It is necessary to build up the logical structure of the theory first, before going on to apply it to the real world in Section 3. In this chapter we concentrate on a type of market known as 'perfect competition' which has the following characteristics:

- Many buyers and sellers.
- Freedom of entry into, and exit from the market.
- Homogeneous products.
- Perfect knowledge of the market by buyers and sellers.

As the name 'perfect' competition implies, this is an ideal market structure, which ensures that prices reflect the costs of production, and which eliminates inefficient firms. As will be seen later in this section, this type of competition also ensures that resources follow demand. If demand for one product increases, then there are incentives in the market for firms to increase production. Your

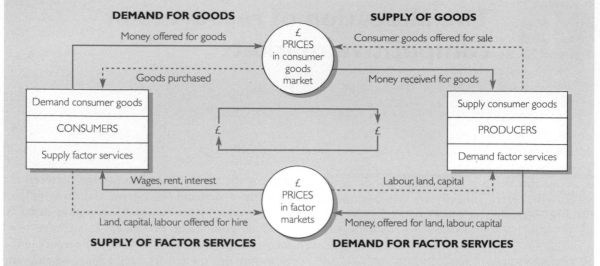

Figure 4.1 The price system
The prices of consumer goods and services are determined by the interaction of consumer demand and supply from producers. Similarly, the price of factors of production is determined by the interaction of producers' demand for factor services and the supply of factors of production from consumers.

experience of the world may lead you to believe that it is not in fact perfect. It is the same in economics. No real world market is without some imperfections, and the consequences of this are discussed for specific markets in Sections II and III. The other main types of market are monopoly (a single seller) and oligopoly (competition among a few firms). We will consider these other types of market later in Chapter 8 and Section V (Chapter 22 and 23).

The discussion of perfectly competitive markets is divided up into demand for the product and supply of the product. We will discuss these separately before looking at interactions between the two.

Demand

Market demand

The demand for a commodity is the quantity of the good that is purchased over a specific of period of time at a certain price. Thus there are three elements to demand: price, quantity and time. This is the effective demand for a good, i.e. the desire to buy the good, backed by the ability to do so – it is no use considering a person's

demand for a product if they do not have the money to make the purchase.

We may distinguish between *ex ante* demand and *ex post* demand. *Ex ante* demand is the quantity consumers will wish to demand at a particular price, while *ex post* demand is the amount they actually succeed in buying. The difference between the two may be brought about, for example, by a deficiency of supply in the market (see the section below on excess demand).

It is usually the case that as the price of the commodity is lowered, a greater quantity will be demanded. The intuitive reason for this is that the product is now **better value for money**. As discussed in the previous chapter, because resources are scarce relative to demand, choices have to be made. For the individual this scarcity is experienced as a limited income, and in order to get the most satisfaction from this limited income, the individual has to consider not just how much satisfaction they get from each product, but also whether it is good value for the money spent. Another way of saying this is that consuming one good rather than another involves an opportunity cost. If the price of a product falls, it becomes better value for money and consumers are more likely to buy it.

● **Common misunderstanding**

The reader may object that when the price of products fall, they do not always buy more of them, or indeed buy them at all. The theory of demand is about what happens in the whole market, so this objection does not hold. As long as at least one extra purchase takes place, then demand will have gone up in response to a fall in price.

There are many factors which influence the demand for a product, of which price is only one. These factors include tastes and preferences, income, and the prices of other goods and are discussed shortly. Initially we will assume that these other factors have not changed and concentrate on the relationship between price and quantity demanded.

You may have observed that the discussion of demand centres around ideas like value and satisfaction. Modern economics originated in the eighteenth century from philosophers' discussions of these ideas. For a more detailed discussion of this aspect of economics, see Chapter 40.

The demand curve

The data in Table 4.1 is a hypothetical demand schedule for commodity X. It illustrates the first law of demand.

All other things remaining constant (ceteris paribus), more of a good will be demanded at a lower price.

Table 4.1 Demand schedule for commodity X

	Price of commodity X (£/kg)	Quantity of X demanded (kg/week)
A	5	110
B	4	120
C	3	150
D	2	200
E	1	250

Such information is usually expressed as a graph called a demand curve. As you can see in Figure 4.2, the graph marked DD slopes downwards from left to right; this is nearly always the case. The relationship between price and the quantity demanded is an **inverse relationship**, since as

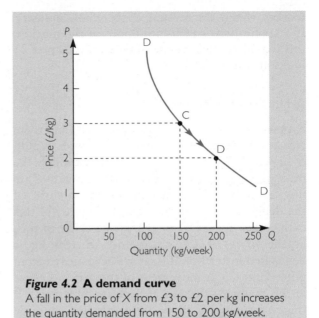

Figure 4.2 A demand curve
A fall in the price of X from £3 to £2 per kg increases the quantity demanded from 150 to 200 kg/week.

price goes down the quantity demanded goes up. If the price is lowered from £3 per kg to £2 per kg, then the quantity demanded grows from 150 kg to 200 kg per week. This can be shown as a movement down the existing demand curve from C to D. This is termed an extension of demand. Conversely, if the price of X were raised then this could be shown as a movement up the curve, which is termed a contraction of demand. An extension or contraction of demand is brought about by a change in the price of the commodity under consideration *and by nothing else*.

Demand and revenue

The *total revenue* is the total sales receipts in a market at a particular price. In Table 4.1 you can see that if the price were £3 per kg the quantity demanded would be 150 kg per week. Consequently the total revenue would be £450. Thus we can say that:

Total revenue (*TR*) = Price (*P*) × Quantity (*Q*)

If the price were lowered to £2 the total revenue (*P* × *Q*) would be £400. You can see in Figure 4.2 that the total revenue can be represented as a rectangle drawn under the demand curve (represented by the dashed lines). In a perfectly competitive market, this is the revenue of the whole industry. If a single firm had a monopoly of the market, this would be the revenue of the firm (Chapter 23 looks at this in detail).

An increase in demand

Suppose that the product X was wheat, and there was a failure of the potato crop. People would then wish to buy more wheat, even though the price of wheat had not fallen, because potatoes are not available. This is shown as a shift of the demand curve to the right. In Figure 4.3 this is the move from DD to D_1D_1: as a result of this, at the price of £3, a quantity of 150 kg is demanded instead of 100, as we have moved from point C to C_1. A movement of the demand curve in this manner is termed an increase in demand. If the curve were to move leftwards, for example from D_1D_1 to DD, this would be termed a decrease. An increase or decrease in demand is brought about by a factor *other than change in the price* of the commodity under consideration. In this case it would be the higher price of potatoes resulting from the shortage that would have shifted the demand for wheat to the right.

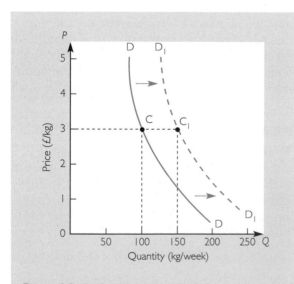

Figure 4.3 An increase in demand
The shift of the curve from DD to D_1D_1 shows that more is demanded at every price, e.g. demand at £3/kg increases from 100 to 150 kg/week.

It is important not to confuse an *increase in demand* with an *extension of demand*. An extension of demand is brought about by a fall in the price of the product, whereas an increase in demand is brought about by a change in any other factor affecting demand except the price of the product.

The determinants of demand

Demand for a product will be affected by price in the way explained above, but other determinants of demand can be identified:

(a) The *price of other products* will affect demand, particularly if they are substitutes or complements. Coffee is a substitute for tea. If the price of coffee increased, then some people might switch into tea, increasing the demand for tea. On the other hand, milk is a complement for tea, and an increase in the price of milk might result in a slight decrease in the demand for tea.

(b) Changes in *population*. Demand is influenced both by the overall size of the population and by the age, sex and geographical distribution. It is fairly easy to see that if the population increased in size, the number of products purchased would increase. The structure of the population might also affect the pattern of demand. If the proportion of children rises in a society, more education will be demanded.

(c) *Tastes, habits and customs*. These are extremely important as most people tend to continue their habits of eating etc. A change in taste in favour of a commodity causes an increase in demand.

(d) *Income* will in general increase the demand for goods as people have more money to spend. However, there may be less expenditure on some products if consumers have moved 'up market'. The *distribution of income* can also affect the pattern of demand. A more even distribution of income, for example, might increase the demand for hi-fi equipment but decrease the demand for luxury yachts.

(e) *Seasonal factors*. In addition to the factors listed above, the demand for many products such as clothing, food and power is influenced by the season. This is a factor which is more important to some products than others and not always included in the list.

STUDENT ACTIVITY 4.1

There is an increase in the demand for cars brought about by increased levels of employment and income as the economy comes out of the recession. Draw a diagram to show what has happened to the demand curve. If price remains the same, what will happen to the total revenue of the car companies?

Supply

The supply curve

We will now turn to the other side of the market, which is *supply*.

By supply we mean the quantity of a commodity that suppliers will wish to supply at a particular price.

This is illustrated by Table 4.2. As you can see, the higher the price is, the greater the quantity the supplier will wish to supply. If the price decreases there will come a price (£1) at which suppliers are not willing to supply because they cannot make a profit at this point.

As with demand, we can plot the supply information as a graph. This is illustrated in Figure 4.4. As you can see the supply curve slopes upwards from left to right. This is a direct relationship, i.e. as price goes up the quantity supplied will go up. If the price increases from £2 per kg to £3 per kg, then the quantity suppliers are willing to supply goes up from 90 kg to 150 kg. As with the demand curve, this movement along the supply curve from D to C in called an *extension of supply*. A movement down the curve would be called a *contraction of supply*. As with

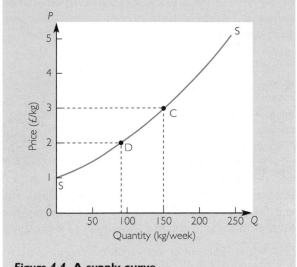

Figure 4.4 A supply curve
An increase in the price of X from £2 to £3 per kg causes the quantity supplied to increase from 90 to 150 kg/week.

demand, an extension or contraction is brought about by a change of the price of the commodity under consideration – *and nothing else*.

The first principle of supply is that, all other things remaining constant (*ceteris paribus*), a greater quantity will be supplied at a higher price.

The reason for this is that at a higher quantity, increased costs can be incurred. We have already dealt in Chapter 3 with two principles – the *law of diminishing returns* and the *principle of increasing costs* – both of which would suggest that costs increase with supply. Suppliers will need a higher price to persuade them to increase their production, if they are to make a profit on this extra production. This argument is examined in more detail in Chapter 21, and below in the section on producer surplus.

The law of diminishing returns applies in the short run, when capital is fixed. The principle of increasing costs applies in the long run when further output of a product runs into problems of diseconomies of scale. It is important to notice that the law of diminishing returns ensures that the supply curve slopes upwards in the short-run, but if there are economies of scale there is the possibility that the supply curve might slope downwards in the long run. In the market

Table 4.2 Supply schedule for commodity X

	Price of commodity X (£/kg)	Quantity of X suppliers will wish to supply (kg/week)
A	5	240
B	4	200
C	3	150
D	2	90
E	1	0

place we are usually concerned with short-run responses, so the supply curve is normally drawn as upward sloping.

● *Common misunderstanding*

When asked why more is supplied at a higher price, students frequently reply 'because increased profits can be made'. You can now see that this is not so. Suppliers need the incentive of higher prices because costs are rising.

The determinants of supply

Progress can be made in understanding the supply side of the economy by simply listing the factors that can influence the supply of a product.

(a) *Price.* The most important determinant of supply is price. As we have just seen, a change in price will cause a movement up or down the supply curve. The remaining determinants of supply can be termed the *conditions of supply*. A change in the conditions of supply causes an increase or decrease in supply, shifting the supply curve leftwards or rightwards. For example, suppose that the product we are considering is tomatoes; then very bad weather would have the effect of decreasing the supply. In Figure 4.5 you can see that this has the effect of shifting the supply curve leftwards. Conversely, unexpectedly good growing weather would shift the curve rightwards.

(b) *Price of factors of production.* Since output is produced by combining the factors of production, their price is an important determinant of supply. An increase in the price of a factor will increase the costs of a firm and this shifts the supply curve leftwards. Labour costs (wages) tend to rise in periods of full employment. Interest rate rises increase the cost of capital purchased by loans.

(c) *The price of other commodities.* If, for example, there is a rise in the price of barley but not of wheat, this will tend to decrease the supply (shift the curve leftwards) of wheat because farmers will switch from wheat to barley production. Economic theory envisages resources switching easily and rapidly from one type of production to another in response to price changes. In practice, though, this may be a slow and often painful process.

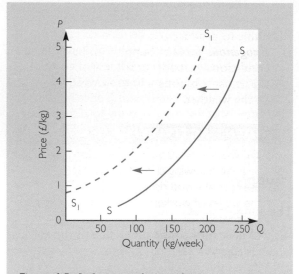

Figure 4.5 A decrease in supply
The shift of the supply curve leftwards from SS to S_1S_1 shows that less is supplied at every price.

(d) *Technology.* Changes in the level of technology also affect supply. An improvement in technology allows us to produce more goods with fewer factors of production. This would therefore have the effect of shifting the supply curve to the right. This has been well illustrated in recent years by the effect of microchip technology upon the supply of such things as pocket calculators, watches and personal computers.

(e) *Tastes of producers.* In theory suppliers are perfectly rational beings interested only in obtaining the highest return for their efforts. However, producers may have preferences and be willing to tolerate lower returns if, for example, they find the business stimulating or worthwhile or socially prestigious. Conversely, producers may avoid unpleasant lines of work.

(f) *Entry and exit from the industry.* In the short run new firms will not be able to enter the industry because it takes time to set up production. In the long run firms may enter or leave the industry in response to the profitability of the industry. A good example of this is provided by North Sea oil. UK oil costs four or five times as much to extract as Saudi Arabian oil. The low prices of the 1950s and early 1960s would certainly not have allowed

the UK to extract the oil profitably, but as the price rocketed in the 1970s it became profitable to produce oil.
(g) *Exogenous factors*. Supply can be affected by conditions outside market forces. Perhaps the most obvious example of this would be the weather.

Regressive supply curves

Supply curves usually slope upwards from left to right. Sometimes, however, they change direction, as in Figure 4.6, and are said to become *regressive*; this might be the case with the supply of labour where there may be a high leisure preference. In coalmining, for example, where the job is extremely unpleasant, it has often been noticed that as wage rates have been increased miners have worked shorter hours. This is because instead of taking the increased wage rate in money the miners are taking it in increased leisure. There has also been a noticeable long-term historical trend for hours of work to be reduced as countries become richer.

A similar effect may be observed in some undeveloped peasant economies where producers have a static view of the income that they require. In these circumstances a rise in the price of the crop they produce causes them to grow less because they can now obtain the same income from a smaller crop.

Equilibrium prices

The formation of an equilibrium price

We shall now combine our analysis of demand and supply to show how a competitive market

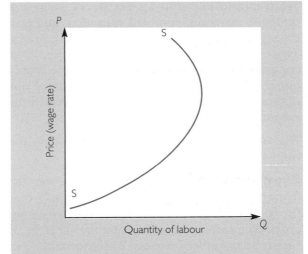

Figure 4.6 A regressive supply curve
As the wage rate continues to rise, people eventually work shorter hours, preferring to take the improvement in wages as increased leisure rather than increased income.

price is determined. Table 4.3 combines the demand and supply schedules. The motives of consumers and producers are different in that the consumer wishes to buy cheaply while the supplier wishes to obtain the highest price possible. Let us examine how these differences are reconciled.

If, for example, we examine row A in Table 4.3, here the price is £5 per kg and 240 kg will be supplied per week. However, at this price consumers are willing to buy only 110 kg. As unsold stocks of goods begin to pile up, suppliers will be forced to reduce their prices to try to get rid of the surplus. There is a downward pressure on prices. Conversely, if we examine row D, where the price is £2 per kg, suppliers are willing to supply only 90 kg per week but consumers

Table 4.3 The determination of the equilibrium price

	Price commodity X (£/kg)	Quantity demanded of X (kg/week)	Quantity supplied of X (kg/week)	Pressure on price
A	5	110	240	Downward
B	4	120	200	Downward
C	3	150	150	Neutral
D	2	200	90	Upward
E	1	250	0	Upward

are trying to buy 200 kg per week. There are therefore many disappointed customers, and producers realise that they can raise their prices. There is thus an upward pressure on price. If we continue the process we can see that there is only one price at which there is neither upward nor downward pressure on price. This is termed the *equilibrium price*.

The equilibrium price is the price at which the wishes of buyers and sellers coincide.

If we superimpose the supply curve on the demand curve we can see (in Figure 4.7) that the equilibrium price occurs where the two curves cross. The surplus of supply and the shortage of supply at any other price can be shown as the gap between the two curves. The arrows in Figure 4.7 show the equilibrium forces that are at work pushing the price towards the equilibrium.

Equilibrium prices ration out the scarce supply of goods and services. There are no great queues of people demanding the best cuts of meat, or the best quality organically grown vegetables; a high price for a product ensures that only the rich or those who derive great satisfaction from them will choose to buy them. Neither are there vast unsold stocks of meat or vegetables in the shops, the equilibrium price having balanced the

demand and supply. It might be argued that the price mechanism is socially unjust, but if we do away with price as the rationing mechanism we only have to put something else, perhaps equally unacceptable, in its place. Examples of such alternative systems for allocating products are considered in Section 3.

Excess demand and supply

If the price is above the equilibrium, more will be supplied than is demanded. This surplus of supply over demand is termed *excess supply*. Conversely, if the price is below the equilibrium, this will result in a situation of *excess demand*. For example, in Table 4.3 on page 53 if the price is £2 per kg, then 200 kg per week is demanded but only 90 kg is supplied and there is therefore an excess demand of 110 kg per week. It is possible to plot a graph that shows the excess demand function at all prices (having just one graph which combines both the demand and supply curves is more convenient for such things as computer modelling). This is done in Figure 4.8. The graph crosses the vertical axis at the equilibrium price; at higher prices the graph shows that there is negative excess demand (usually termed excess supply) and at lower prices there is positive excess demand.

Shifts in demand and supply

If there is an increase in demand this will cause a shift to a new equilibrium price. This is illustrated in Figure 4.9(a). Similarly, in Figure 4.9(b) you can see the effect of a decrease in supply upon the equilibrium price.

The problems associated with changes in equilibrium price are discussed at greater length in Chapter 6.

If there is a change in the equilibrium price and quantity this brings about a reallocation of resources. For example, let us consider the increase in demand shown in Figure 4.9(a). Suppose that this shows an increased preference for tomatoes. The increase in demand raises the price of tomatoes and this encourages more people to produce them so that resources are switched away from other forms of market gardening and into tomato production. No planning

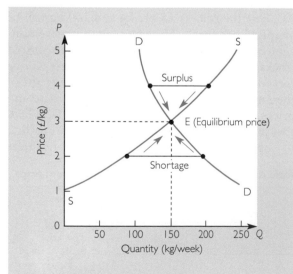

Figure 4.7 The equilibrium price
At the price of £3/kg the quantity that is offered for sale is equal to the quantity people are willing to buy at that price.

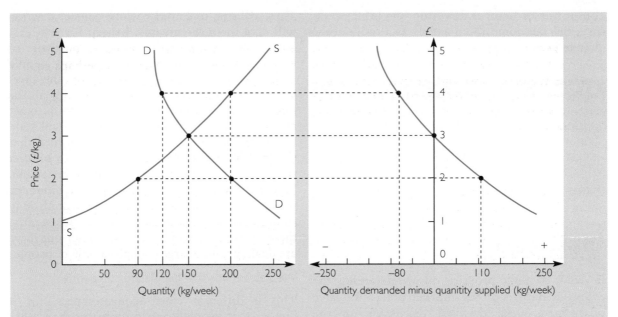

Figure 4.8 The excess demand curve

If the quantity supplied is subtracted from the quantity demanded it gives the excess demand function, e.g. at a price of £4/kg 120 kg are demanded but 200 kg are supplied, giving a negative excess demand (excess supply) of 80 kg.

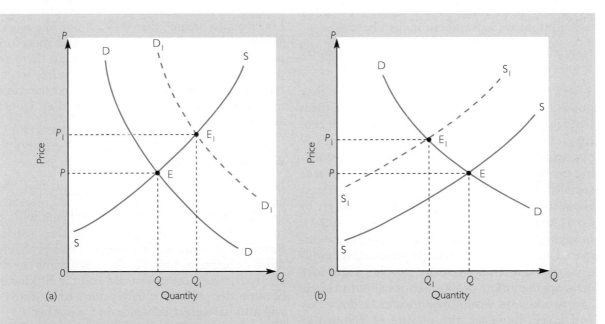

Figure 4.9 Changes in the equilibrium

A shift of either the demand or the supply curve creates a new equilibrium price.

(a) An increase in demand gives a higher price and a greater quantity.

(b) A decrease in supply gives a higher price and lower quantity.

committee or central direction has been necessary; this has come about simply as a result of the change in price.

STUDENT ACTIVITY 4.3

Cup final tickets often change hands at substantially above the official price. What does this tell you about equilibrium in this market? Draw a diagram to show the situation. Why are the official prices of cup final tickets not increased to remedy this situation?

Demand in detail

In order to make progress on understanding the essential nature of the market place, we have postponed some detailed discussion of the demand curve until this point in the chapter.

Assumptions about human behaviour

In examining the functioning of the price system we are not dealing with abstract forces but with people. It is therefore necessary to set out the assumptions we make about human behaviour.

First, we assume that people are maximizers: they try to gain as much wealth or pleasure as possible.

Those things for which people strive, be they goods, services or leisure, are said to give them benefit, or as the eighteenth and nineteenth century economists called it '*utility*' (this idea is discussed in detail in Chapter 40 for those studying the subject at a higher level). Perhaps in a true socialist state people would strive for the greatest good for all (although such a society has yet to exist), but this is not generally true of our society. In saying this we are implying that people are primarily economic creatures. If political, religious or aesthetic motives overcame people's acquisitive instincts then most of our theories about markets and production would begin to break down. By and large, however, the picture of acquisitive society seems to hold true.

In addition to this we also assume that people are rational.

They will stop to consider which course of action will give them the greatest benefit for the least cost. This somewhat unlovely portrait of humankind is not a suggestion of how people should be, but an observation of how they are! Of course, not everyone behaves like this all the time, but it is sufficiently close to the truth to act as a model of human behaviour, which will yield useful predictions. **Milton Friedman** argued that the purpose of economic theory was to *predict* rather than *explain* or *describe* human behaviour. Friedman is helped by the *law of large numbers*, which points out that although individuals may sometimes act irrationally and inconsistently, these aberrations will cancel each other out if we are dealing with a large enough sample of people.

We also assume that people are competitive.

This is different from acquisitiveness, for it implies that people want to do better than other people. We can also see from this that people are *individualistic*. In a competitive society such as ours, not only are people forced to compete but also the good working of the system depends upon them doing so.

In addition to assuming that people generally compete to gain as much personal benefit as they can, we also assume that they do not like work. Work is said to have *disbenefit* and therefore people have to be paid to encourage them to undertake it. There are people who do like work, but, in general, if people were offered the same money for shorter hours of work they would accept it.

Consumer sovereignty

In the price system it is sometimes said that 'the consumer is king', meaning that a consumer decides what is to be produced by being willing to spend money on those particular goods. Rather than *consumer sovereignty*, it is probably more accurate to say that there is a joint sovereignty between the consumer and the producer, because the producer's behaviour and objectives will also have great influence on the market.

The price system is also said, by some people, to be democratic in that every day consumers 'vote' for what they want to be produced by spending their money. Although to some extent this is true, it is considerably modified by the fact that money 'votes' in the economy are unevenly distributed. Thus those with a high income have more 'voting' power than those who are poor.

Exceptions to the law of demand

There are a number of exceptions to the first law of demand, i.e. situations when a fall in the price of a good actually causes people to buy less of it, or a rise in price causes them to buy more.

(a) *Snob goods.* With some expensive items, e.g. a Rolls-Royce, or Chanel perfume, the consumer may buy the commodity *because* it is expensive. The price is part of the attraction of the article and a rise in price may render it more attractive.

(b) *Speculative demand.* This is where purchasers believe that a change in price is the herald of further price changes. On a stock exchange, for example, a rise in the price of a share often tempts people to buy it and vice versa. The housing market also can be seen to work like this, particularly during price booms and slumps.

(c) *Giffen goods.* Sir Robert Giffen, a nineteenth-century statistician and economist, noticed that a fall in the price of bread caused the 'labouring classes' to buy less bread and vice versa. Giffen saw this as a refutation of the first law of demand. It is now recognised as an exception rather than a refutation. When people are very poor and depend on one main food such as rice or bread, an increase in the price of this food makes them poorer. As a result they can no longer afford the small quantity of more luxurious foods that they used to eat and switch more of their expenditure into buying rice (or potatoes). When the price of this food falls, they have more income left to spend on other foods and switch out of buying rice (or potatoes).

The effect of income on demand

Since *effective demand* is the desire to buy a good backed by the ability to do so, it is obvious that there must be a relationship between the demand for a firm's product and the consumer's purchasing power. Purchasing power is usually closely linked to income. The nature of the relationship between income and demand will depend upon the type of product considered and the level of consumers' income. Under normal circumstances a rise in income is hardly likely to send most consumers out to buy more bread, whereas it might cause them to buy a new car.

Other things being equal, if the demand for a commodity increases as income increases it is said to be a normal good.

In Figure 4.10 line (a) represents the income demand curve for **normal goods**. As you can see, demand rises continuously with income. However, the graph tends to flatten out at higher levels of income because people will not want more and more cars and more and more swimming pools, etc. For some normal goods the income demand curve will flatten very quickly as people reach their desired level of consumption of, say, fresh vegetables.

With a small number of products, usually inexpensive foodstuffs such as salt, the demand tends to remain constant at all but the very lowest levels of income. The income demand curve for such products is shown by line (c) in Figure 4.10.

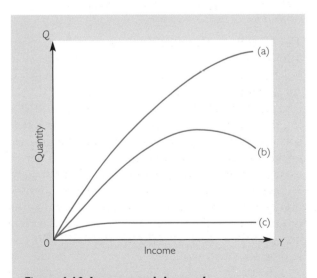

Figure 4.10 **Income and demand**
(a) Normal goods, (b) Inferior goods, (c) Inexpensive foodstuff, e.g. salt.

Inferior goods

The final possibility, line (b) in Figure 4.10, is that demand will decline as income increases. Such products are termed inferior goods and may be defined as follows:

Other things being equal, if, as income rises, the demand for a product goes down it is said to be an inferior good.

The effect may be observed with products such as bread and potatoes. At low levels of income people will tend to consume large amounts of these products but, as their incomes rise, they will buy other foods – more meat, fish, fruit, etc. – and thus require less bread and potatoes.

You should note that the demand for inferior goods behaves like the demand for normal goods at lower levels of income. All *inferior goods* start out as normal goods and become inferior only as income continues to rise. For example, cotton sheets might be considered inferior if, as you become very wealthy, you substitute silk sheets. In other words the goods are not intrinsically inferior, but become inferior as income rises. In different periods of history, different products will be inferior as income rises over time.

Relationships between products

The demand for all goods is interrelated in the sense that they all compete for consumers' limited income. There are two types of interrelationships of demand: goods may be *substitutes* one for another, or they may be *complementary*. Examples of substitute commodities would be tea and coffee, or butter and margarine. Complementary products are demanded jointly, for instance cars and petrol, or strawberries and cream. In all these cases there is a relationship between the price of one commodity and the demand for the other. This is illustrated in Figure 4.11. In Figure 4.11(a) you can see that as the price of cars is lowered so the demand for petrol increases, whereas in Figure 4.11(b) as the price of butter increases so the demand for margarine increases.

Advertising and marketing

A successful advertising campaign obviously increases the demand for a product, but may also be designed to emphasise the characteristics of a product which make it different from its substitutes. There are two main kinds of advertising: informative and persuasive. Informative advertising

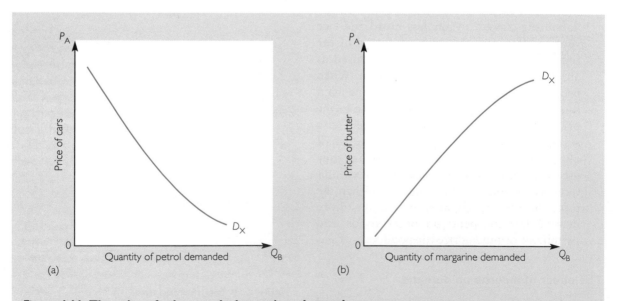

Figure 4.11 **The price of other goods determines demand**
(a) Complements. A fall in the price of cars increases the demand for petrol.
(b) Substitutes. A rise in the price of butter causes an increase in the demand for margarine.

may actually make the market mechanism work better by giving consumers the information they need to make the best purchasing decisions. Persuasive advertising uses people's emotions (envy, greed, sexual attraction, machismo, pride) rather than information to shift their expenditure. In addition to advertising, marketing techniques may be used to influence people's choices, ranging from attractive packaging, and special offers to attract the customer's attention, to careful choice of retail outlets or alternative selling methods to reach the target customers. These techniques are less often found in perfect markets, because one firm's adverts will benefit the whole industry rather than just that firm. It is sometimes the case that the whole industry will advertise, either by getting together to mount an advertising campaign, or with government assistance. Advertising and marketing techniques are more often found when there is market power or differentiated products.

STUDENT ACTIVITY 4.4

Taking current newspaper, magazine or television advertisements as your examples, decide whether particular advertisements are mainly informative or persuasive.

Consumer surplus and willingness to pay (WTP)

A useful way of looking at the demand curve is that it represents the willingness to pay (WTP) of successive consumers. It is therefore a measure of the benefit that consumers receive when they consume a good, if we regard WTP as a measure of benefit. Looking at the demand curve in this way allows us to make the observation that most people buying a product are in fact willing to pay more for the product than the market price. In Figure 4.12, the column represents the purchase of one unit of a good. It can be seen that while the market price is £1, the consumer would have been willing to pay £2 to purchase this unit of the good. The difference between the two yields the value of consumer surplus, in this case £1. If this procedure is repeated for all purchases, the total consumer surplus for the product can be identi-

fied as the shaded triangle ABC. The area of this triangle is all the consumer surplus values added together. This idea will be useful when examining public policy in Chapters 9 and 10.

Producer surplus

Although it is not part of the theory of demand, producer surplus is presented in this section because it is the counterpart of consumer surplus. It is found by looking at the difference between the market price and cost. As has already been argued earlier in this chapter, suppliers will need a price at least equal to the cost of producing an extra unit of production, to persuade them to supply that unit. The supply curve does therefore actually represent the cost of producing each extra unit. In Figure 4.12 it can be seen that the cost of producing the extra unit is in fact only 50p. Since the extra revenue from selling this unit is £1, it follows that there has been an addition if 50p to profits, which is the producer surplus from producing this unit of output. You can see that both producers and consumers have gained from the production and sale of this unit, resulting in a gain for society as a whole. Further consumer and producer surplus will continue to result from increased production until we reach the point

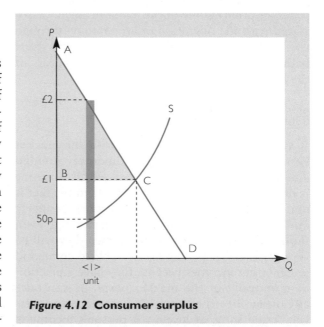

Figure 4.12 Consumer surplus

where the supply and demand curves cross, the point of equilibrium. This is another way of showing the beneficial effects of the market place. Left to its own processes, the market will automatically arrive at the point of maximum social benefit. Reservations about this conclusion are explored in Chapters 9, 10 and 28.

The price system assessed

The price system provides an answer to the fundamental problem of any economic society. Through prices, the economy decides what to produce, i.e. anything people are willing to spend money on that can be produced profitably. We have also seen that techniques of production are also dependent on (factor) prices, since it involves producers buying the services of the factors of production in factor markets. The income generated in these factor markets also determines who will have the money to buy the goods that are produced.

The price system is also automatic in its operation and is self-regulating when changes occur in the economy. Whether or not this produces the best possible use and distribution of resources is one of the most important topics in economics, and much of this book consists of an attempt to answer this question. For the time being we will consider briefly some of the major problems associated with the operation of an economy through the price system. A fuller treatment of this must wait until we have considered all the aspects of the market.

The distribution of income

A serious problem associated with the market system is that income is very unevenly divided among the population. In theory people's income is determined by demand and supply in the factor markets. If the market does not work properly and a person's labour is not demanded even though they are willing to work, then they will be very poor. Other people may be able to command much larger incomes because they have a position of monopoly in the market place, or can take advantage of other people's ignorance to make very large sums of money. A person's income is also influenced by inheritance. Such are the inequalities in income that nearly all governments are forced to intervene in markets to alleviate the worst excesses. For example, the provision of old-age pensions in the UK has been necessary to avoid mass poverty among the old, and benefit for those who are unemployed is also necessary, if poverty is to be limited. People who are in work but on low incomes still receive benefits from the state to buy the essentials of life. You may have noticed that this problem with the market place depends upon your attitude to those in difficulties. To make up your own mind about this you will have to decide on your attitude to those in poverty. You may feel that it is the responsibility of the individual or family or of charities rather than the taxpayer. You may feel that giving people benefit gives them no incentive to provide for themselves. These arguments are taken further in Chapters 11 and 28.

Dangerous products and environmental hazards

A minor interference with the market system that is forced on nearly all governments is the regulation of dangerous products. Thus, for example, governments may forbid the sale of arms or dangerous drugs. These are extreme examples, but many products have harmful side-effects. Pollution results from our production of electricity by burning fossil fuels, or from the exhausts of motor vehicles. Many production processes have adverse effects on the air, the soil, or rivers and oceans. The government has to intervene to limit these environmental hazards. This topic is considered in detail in Chapter 13.

Competition

The picture of the economy we have been developing in this chapter depends upon there being competition between suppliers. This, said Adam Smith, along with the 'invisible hand' of self-interest, leads to an optimum allocation of resources. But the invisible hand will not work if there is not free competition. When we turn to examine the economy we find that there are many monopolies and restrictions upon trade.

A monopoly [said Smith] granted either to an individual or a trading company has the same effect as a secret in trade or manufactures. The monopoly – by keeping the market constantly understocked, never supplying the effectual demand, sell their commodities much above the natural price, and raise emoluments, whether they consist in wages or profit, greatly above their natural rate.

Despite these reservations we continue to study the competitive market because it provides a model by which we can judge the economic success of the real world. Situations where there is market power are considered in Chapters 23 and 24.

Allocation of resources

The market has many functions in the economy, most of which can be thought of as an aspect of the allocation of resources:

(a) *Changing pattern of demand*: If demand for a product is declining, then price in the market place will fall. This will act as a *market signal* to producers, some of whom may decide to exit the industry as their profits fall. This will shift the supply curve to the left, reducing the capacity of the industry in line with falling demand. If on the other hand the demand for another product is rising, then price will rise in that market leading to higher profits, tempting entrepreneurs to enter that industry. This will push the supply curve to the right, increasing capacity in line with changing demand. It is not only entrepreneurs who will switch industries, as the more profitable expanding industry will be in a better financial position and will be able to bid other factors of production (land, labour, capital) away from the declining industry.

(b) If *costs of production* are rising in an industry, then market prices will once again act as a signal, persuading consumers to switch to other products that are now better value for money, and re-allocating resources as a result.

(c) The market brings people together to trade who would not have been able to under a system of barter or in a command and control type of economy. This is of particular importance in the *capital markets*, bringing savers and entrepreneurs together.

The costs of running the market

The discussion of the market so far in this chapter assumes that it costs nothing to run. In fact many people are employed solely to help run the market place rather than producing anything themselves. A ticket inspector on a train is not producing transport, merely making sure the train company gets its revenue. A policeman arresting a thief is merely ensuring that the system of property rights on which the market system depends, is properly enforced. The market can also go spectacularly wrong:

(a) In *speculative* markets, individuals can lose (or gain) very large amounts of money. When stock exchanges crash or currencies collapse, individuals can often bear a large part of the cost.

(b) When market economies go into *recession*, the labour market can function badly for a number of years, leading to severe poverty for those unlucky enough to be unemployed at the time. Once again, individuals often bear a large part of the cost.

STUDENT ACTIVITY 4.5

Classify the following as products, costs of operating the market, or problems of the market (you may find yourself putting them under more than one category).

(a) Prisons
(b) Banks
(c) Lorries
(d) Pollution
(e) Cars
(f) Unemployment benefit

Summary

1 The price system is a method of operating the economy through the medium of market prices.
2 The law of demand tells us that, other things being equal (*ceteris paribus*), more of a product is demanded at a lower price.
3 A change in price, *ceteris paribus*, causes an extension or contraction of demand, while a change in any other determinant causes an increase or decrease of demand.

4 The first principle of supply is that, *ceteris paribus*, a greater quantity is supplied at a higher price because at a higher price increased costs can be incurred.
5 An increase or decrease in supply is caused by a change in one of the conditions of supply.
6 The determinants of supply are price (the price of factors of production and the price of other commodities) the state of technology, the tastes of producers, and other exogenous factors.
7 The equilibrium price is the price at which the wishes of buyers and sellers coincide.
8 At any price other than the equilibrium there is either upward or downward pressure on price caused by either excess demand or excess supply.
9 Consumer and producer surplus are both gained to the left of the equilibrium point.
10 Our view of the price system as a method of achieving the optimum allocation of resources is modified by problems associated with the distribution of income and by the lack of competition in the economy.

QUESTIONS

1 Describe the factors that determine the supply of wheat.
2 Make a list of as many cases as you can of where the government intervenes with the automatic working of the price system, e.g. food and drugs legislation.
3 Describe precisely how excess supply in a market causes the price to fall.
4 What would happen to the market demand for steak as the result of each of the following?
   (a) An increase in the average income per head.
   (b) An increase in the size of population.
   (c) Increased advertising for lamb and pork.
   (d) An increase in the price of lamb.
   (e) A decrease in the price of pork.
5 What would happen to the equilibrium price and quantity of butter if:
   (a) the price of margarine increased?
   (b) the cost of producing butter increased?
6 Discuss the problems associated with using the price mechanism as a way to deal with:
   (a) the allocation of university places;
   (b) traffic problems in cities.

7 Explain the difference between partial equilibrium and general equilibrium analysis.
8 'When some people are very wealthy while others are poor, the whole notion of consumer sovereignty in a market economy is misleading and prejudicial.' Discuss.
9 St Thomas Aquinas in the thirteenth century wrote: 'To sell a thing for more than it's worth, or to buy it for less than it's worth, is in itself unjust and unlawful.' Discuss the problems that might be associated with the application of this view to a modern economy.
10 'If the price mechanism did not exist it would be necessary to invent it.' Discuss.
11 For the mathematically minded: suppose that a demand curve is given by the equation $y = 1000 - x$ and the supply curve by the equation $y = 100 + 2x$.
   (a) What will be the equilibrium price?
   (b) What is the excess demand or supply if the price is: (i) 900; (ii) 400?
   (c) Devise an equation for the excess demand function based on the demand and supply schedules in this example.
   (Remember y = price and x = quantity.)

Data response A
EQUILIBRIUM PRICES

The following figures give the demand and supply schedules for product Z.

Price of Z (£/kg)	Quantity demanded of Z (kg/week)	Quantity supplied of Z (kg/week)
9	100	800
7	300	600
5	500	400
3	700	200
1	900	0

From these figures:

(a) Draw the demand and supply curves.
(b) Determine and state the equilibrium price.
(c) What is the excess demand or supply if the price is: (i) £7 per kg; (ii) £2 per kg?
(d) Suppose that demand were now to increase by 50 per cent at every price. Draw the new demand curve and determine the new equilibrium price.
(e) From the original figures, construct the excess demand function.

(f) From the original demand curve calculate the total revenue to be gained from the sale of product Z at £1, £2, £3, etc. Then plot this information on a graph, putting total revenue on the vertical axis and quantity on the horizontal axis. State the quantity at which total revenue is maximised.

Data response B
ECONOMISTS AND THE MARKET

People of the same trade seldom meet together, even for merriment and diversion, but the conversation ends up in a conspiracy against the public, or in some contrivance to raise prices.

Adam Smith *The Wealth of Nations*

Fundamentally, there are only two ways of coordinating the economic activities of millions. One is central direction involving the use of coercion – the technique of the army and the modern totalitarian state. The other is voluntary cooperation of individuals – the technique of the market place.

Milton Friedman *Capitalism and Freedom*

1 Both Smith and Friedman are great advocates of free market economics. Analyse these seemingly contradictory statements.
2 For what reasons do modern states find it necessary to interfere in the 'voluntary cooperation' of the market place?
3 To what extent do you consider that the collapse of many East European economies is a vindication of Friedman's view

5   Elasticities of demand and supply

Learning outcomes

At the end of this chapter you will be able to:

▶ Understand the concept of elasticity of demand.

▶ Calculate a range of elasticities from data.

▶ Understand the implications for a firm's pricing policy of different price elasticity values.

▶ Use intuitive methods for estimating price elasticity of demand.

▶ Predict which goods will grow in demand terms over time using income elasticity.

▶ Understand the relationship between elasticity and time for both supply and demand.

Introduction

In the previous chapter we have considered how demand and supply determine prices. The first law of demand, for example, tells us that if we lower the price of a commodity, other things being equal, a greater quantity will be demanded. In this chapter we seek to measure and quantify those changes.

Everyone is familiar with the idea that if there is a glut of a commodity its price usually falls. As long ago as the seventeenth century **Gregory King**, the English writer on population, noted that when there was a good harvest not only did prices fall but farmers appeared to earn less. In other words bad harvests seemed to be better for farmers (see Chapter 11). King, without knowing it, was commenting on an application of the principle of elasticity of demand.

Elasticity of demand

Price elasticity of demand defined

There are several different types of elasticity. The most important is price elasticity of demand and is sometimes abbreviated to PED. We may define it thus:

Price elasticity of demand measures the degree of responsiveness of the quantity demanded of a commodity to changes in its price.

It is worthwhile remembering this definition since it can be readily adapted to give the definition for any other type of elasticity. Responsiveness is measured by comparing the percentage change in the price with the resultant percentage change in the quantity demanded. This is best explained by taking a numerical example. Two very different demand curves are shown in Figure 5.1. In both cases the price has been cut by the same amount, from £10 to £5, but this has had very different effects upon the quantity demanded. In (a) the quantity demanded has expanded a great deal, from 100 units to 300 units, but in (b) the demand has grown only from 100 units to 125. Thus the same percentage cut in the price has resulted in different percentage changes in the quantity demanded. Diagram (a) is said to illustrate an *elastic* demand because it is responsive to price changes, whereas diagram (b) illustrates an *inelastic* demand because it is relatively unresponsive to price changes.

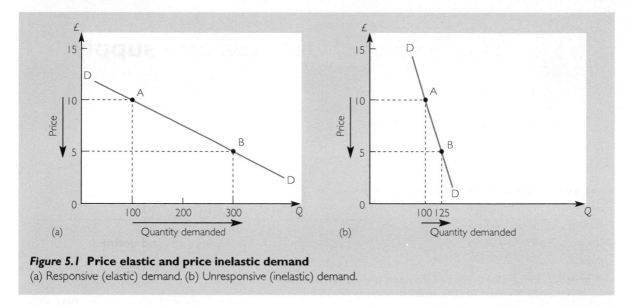

Figure 5.1 Price elastic and price inelastic demand
(a) Responsive (elastic) demand. (b) Unresponsive (inelastic) demand.

● *Common misunderstanding*

Note that it is the demand that is elastic or inelastic, not the product. Which category of elasticity the demand for a product falls into depends upon the product we are considering. A 50 per cent drop in the price of salt, for example, would hardly send everyone dashing out to the shops, but a 50 per cent drop in the price of cars might well have people queueing at the showrooms.

Price elasticity of demand and total revenue

Price elasticity can also be defined and categorised by the effect of a price change on the total revenue of the firm. There are three categories of price elasticity of demand: elastic, inelastic and unitary. Which category any particular demand falls into depends upon the relative percentage changes in price and quantity demanded and the resultant effect upon the total revenue.

Elastic demand

Demand is price elastic when a percentage cut in price brings about a greater percentage expansion in demand so as to increase total revenue.

The relationship between elasticity and total revenue is illustrated in Figure 5.2. Total revenue, as

explained in the previous chapter, is calculated by multiplying the price of the commodity by the quantity demanded. In diagram (a) of Figure 5.2 a reduction in price from £5 to £3 increases total revenue from £500 to £900. The shaded rectangle A shows the revenue that has been given up by lowering the price, but you can see that this is greatly outweighed by the shaded rectangle B, which is the extra revenue gained from increased sales. This, therefore, is an elastic demand because, as the price is lowered, total revenue increases.

It should be noted that this process works in reverse. With an elastic demand, a price increase results in a loss of revenue. You should check this for yourself by raising the price from £3 to £5 in Figure 5.2 (a) and seeing what happens to revenue.

Inelastic demand

Demand is price inelastic when a percentage cut in price brings about a smaller percentage expansion in demand so as to decrease total revenue.

In diagram (b) a reduction in price from £100 to £50 results in total revenue declining from £400 to £250. This is because the demand is inelastic. As with elastic demand, this relationship works in reverse. An increase in price will raise total revenue.

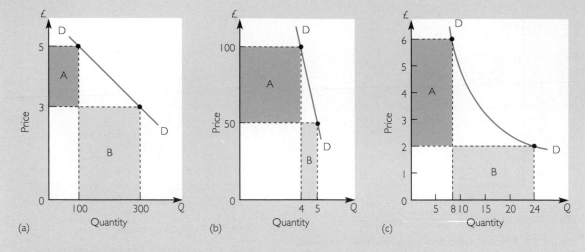

Figure 5.2 Price elasticities of demand and total revenues
(a) Price elastic demand. Total revenue increases as price falls.
(b) Price inelastic demand. Total revenue decreases as price falls.
(c) Unitary demand. Total revenue remains constant whatever happens to price.

Unitary elasticity

Demand has unitary price elasticity when a percentage cut in price brings about an exactly equal expansion of demand so as to leave total revenue unchanged.

In diagram (c) the cut in price is exactly matched by the increase in quantity and therefore, although the price has fallen from £6 to £2, the total revenue remains constant at £48. Area A is exactly equal to area B. We therefore have unitary elasticity of demand. If you check the other points on the demand curve in diagram (c) you will discover that whatever is done to price, the total revenue remains the same. A graph such as this is called a rectangular hyperbola. The curve has the property that any rectangle drawn under it has a constant area (the area represents total revenue).

Price elasticity of demand and the firm's decision making

Pricing with an inelastic demand curve

If a firm faces an inelastic demand curve, then pushing up price will always increase revenue. Raising price will reduce output so costs must be falling at the same time. With revenue rising and costs falling, profits must go up. Checking the logic in reverse, it is always a mistake to lower price if facing an inelastic demand curve, because revenue will fall and costs will rise with output. Profits must, therefore, decline.

Pricing with an elastic demand curve

The firm has a more difficult decision if facing an elastic demand curve. The firm knows it can increase its revenue by lowering price, but this will also increase output and therefore costs. The question is, which has gone up more, revenue or costs? The firm needs to know more about its costs and this decision is discussed in more detail in Chapters 7 and 21.

● *Common misunderstanding*

If you look back over Figures 5.1 and 5.2 you will see that the price elastic demand curves tended to be rather flat whereas the price inelastic curves were steep. The appearance of the curves, however, can be most deceptive. In Figure 2.1 (see page 17) you will see that both demand curves show the same information: one is steep and the other is rather flat simply because the scales have changed. (As a convention, textbooks do use steep-looking curves to depict inelastic demand, and flatter ones for elastic demand.)

The calculation of price elasticity of demand

The effect of price changes upon total revenue has given us only three broad categories of price elasticity: elastic, inelastic and unitary elasticity. The definition can, however, be restated as a mathematical formula to give us an actual value for the price elasticity of demand (E_D), provided we know details of the demand curve:

$$E_D = \frac{\text{Percentage change in quantity demanded}}{\text{Percentage change in price}}$$

Since this method of measuring elasticity is based on a comparison of percentage changes, in this case between demand and price, it is referred to as the *percentage formula*. In Figure 5.3 a small part of a demand curve has been extracted so that we may examine it in detail and use this formula to calculate the value of price elasticity. In moving from point A to point B on the demand curve the price has fallen from £400 to £350. To calculate this as a percentage we divide the change in price (ΔP) of £50 by the original price (P) of £400, and then multiply the result by 100:

$$\text{Percentage change in price} = \frac{\Delta P}{P} \times \frac{100}{1}$$

The same thing must then be done for quantity demanded, which has expanded from 800 to 1000. We can then arrange the formula for price elasticity as follows:

$$E_D = \frac{\Delta Q/Q \times 100/1}{\Delta P/P \times 100/1}$$

Since 100/1 is common to both numerator and denominator we may cancel it out, giving us the formula:

$$E_D = \frac{\Delta Q/Q}{\Delta P/P}$$

Let us now complete the calculation from Figure 5.3:

$$E_D = \frac{\Delta Q/Q}{\Delta P/P} = \frac{200/800}{-50/400} = \frac{200}{800} \times \frac{400}{-50} = -2$$

Note that the formula can be rearranged as:

$$E_D = \frac{\Delta Q}{\Delta P} \times \frac{P}{Q} = \frac{200}{-50} \times \frac{400}{800} = -2$$

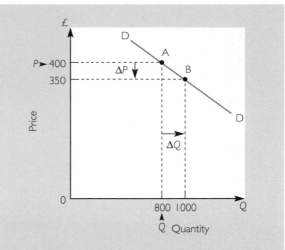

Figure 5.3 The coefficient of price elasticity of demand
As price falls from £400 to £350 the quantity demanded expands from 800 to 1000. Thus the original $P = £400$ and $\Delta P = £50$, while $Q = 800$ and $\Delta Q = 200$:
$$E_D = \frac{200/800}{-50/400} = -2$$

In this example we have a value of two for elasticity. It is simply stated as a number and is independent of the units used to measure price and quantity.

For price elasticity of demand, the value will always be negative because if price goes down then quantity goes up and vice versa.

That is why in the example above ΔP is shown as –£50 and the value for elasticity is given as –2.

Ranges of price elasticity values

● *Common misunderstanding*

When looking at Figure 5.3 it might be thought that the value of price elasticity is the value of the slope of the demand curve. This is not so. What is being measured is not the slope of the curve but the relative movements along the axes. This is yet another warning not to be deceived by the appearance of the curve.

There are two cases, however, when the slope of the curve does tell us the value of price elasticity. These are shown in Figure 5.4. In diagram (a) the demand curve is horizontal, showing that

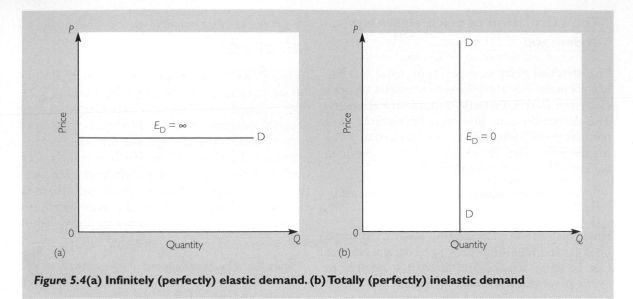

Figure 5.4(a) Infinitely (perfectly) elastic demand. (b) Totally (perfectly) inelastic demand

consumers are willing to buy any amount at this price, but a price of even one penny higher would result in no sales at all. This is termed an infinite (or perfectly) elastic demand and the value of elasticity is infinity. In diagram (b) it would appear that consumers will buy exactly the same amount of the product whatever the price. There is therefore no responsiveness of demand to price changes. This is termed a totally (or perfectly) inelastic demand and the value of elasticity is zero.

For the in-between case of unitary demand, which results in constant revenue whatever the price, the value of elasticity is one.

Having considered these three extreme cases we can state the boundaries of the values of the different categories of elasticity.

Note that it is the value of the coefficient itself that is important in determining the category of elasticity; the negative value or sign can be ignored in this regard:

(a) If elasticity is greater than one but less than infinity then demand is price elastic.
(b) If elasticity is exactly equal to one then demand has unitary price elasticity.
(c) If elasticity is less than one but greater than zero then demand is price inelastic.

The main values of price elasticity of demand (ignoring the minus sign) are summarised in Table 5.1.

Table 5.1 Price elasticities of demand

Category	Value	Characteristics
Perfectly inelastic	$E_D = 0$	Quantity demanded remains constant as price changes
Inelastic	$0 < E_D < 1$	Proportionate change in quantity is less than proportionate change in price
Unitary	$E_D = 1$	Proportionate change in quantity is the same as proportionate change in price
Elastic	$1 < E_D < \infty$	Proportionate change in quantity is greater than proportionate change in price
Perfectly elastic	$E_D = \infty$	Any amount will be bought at a certain price but none at any other price

STUDENT ACTIVITY 5.1

The only real way of making sure you understand elasticity is to do some calculations yourself. Use the information in Table 5.2 to calculate price elasticity. Start at the top price of 10 and work your way down to zero. You need not calculate elasticity at every price on the way, but make sure you calculate elasticities in the elastic and inelastic sections of the demand curve as illustrated in Figure 5.5

Notes on your calculations:
1   Don't worry if some values are infinity or zero. This should happen at the top and bottom of the demand curve.
2   Notice that price elasticity varies continuously along this (or any other) straight line demand curve.
3   An increase (+) in price will cause a fall (−) in quantity and, conversely, a decrease (−) in price will cause a rise (+) in quantity. If we divide the change of quantity by the change in price the value of the answer must always be negative.

Table 5.2 A demand schedule

	Price of commodity (£/kg)	Quantity demanded (kg/week)	Total revenue (£)	Category of price elasticity
A	10	0	0	
B	9	10	90	
C	8	20	160	Elastic
D	7	30	210	
E	6	40	240	
F	5	50	250	Unitary
G	4	60	240	
H	3	70	210	
I	2	80	160	Inelastic
J	1	90	90	
K	0	100	0	

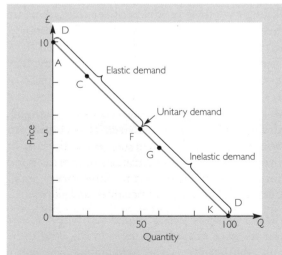

Figure 5.5 One demand curve can have all three price elasticities
The value of elasticity decreases from infinity at point A through unity at point F to zero at point K.

Factors determining price elasticity of demand

Although we know how to measure price elasticity we have not yet discussed the reasons why some demands are elastic and others not so. Why is it, for example, that the demand for wheat is very inelastic while the demand for cakes, which are made from wheat, is much more elastic? Understanding the factors lying behind price elasticity is very useful, because frequently there is insufficient information in the real world to know exactly where a demand curve lies. Intuitive estimates of price elasticity are therefore useful to entrepreneurs.

Ease of substitution

This is by far the most important determinant of price elasticity. If we consider food, for example, we will find that food as a whole has a very inelastic demand, but when we consider any particular food, e.g. cream cakes, we will find that the elasticity of demand is much greater. This is because, while we can find no substitute for food, we can always substitute one type of food for another. In general we can conclude that:

The greater the number of substitutes available for a product, the greater will be its price elasticity of demand. Also the closer the substitutes are the greater the price elasticity of demand.

A great deal of advertising expenditure is devoted to persuading consumers that a particular brand of a product is significantly different from its competitors. If the consumer can be convinced that other brands are not a good substitute for the product, then its demand will have been made more inelastic.

● *Common misunderstanding*

It may be thought that price elasticity may be determined by whether or not a product is a necessity. To some extent this is true. The 'bare necessities' do tend to have low elasticities of demand. However, this can be a misleading idea because what is a luxury to one person may be a necessity to another. Tobacco, for example, can hardly be considered a 'necessity' and yet to many people it is, because there is no substitute available. The idea of necessity determining price elasticity is also further undermined when we discover that demand for many luxury goods, e.g. diamonds, is relatively inelastic. It is not therefore the 'expensiveness' which determines elasticity, but the availability of substitutes. For instance, when the international oil cartel OPEC more than trebled oil prices in 1973–4 and doubled them again in 1979, demand did not fall dramatically. There is no real substitute for petrol, but there is a substitute for oil in generating electricity. Coal or gas can be burnt instead to generate electricity, but it takes time to convert power stations from one fuel to the other.

The proportion of incomes spent on the product

If the price of a box of matches were to rise by 50 per cent, for example from 10p to 15p, it would discourage very few buyers because such an amount is a minute proportion of their income. However, if the price of a car were to rise from £10 000 to £15 000 it would have an enormous effect upon sales, even though it would be the same percentage increase.

We can state this principle as:

The greater the proportion of income which the price of the product represents the greater its price elasticity of demand will tend to be.

If we apply this principle to individual consumers it will be clear that those with high incomes may be less sensitive to changes in the price of products than those with low incomes. Similarly, if we consider the growth in national income over the years it is apparent that products which seemed expensive luxuries some years ago, e.g. colour televisions, are now regarded by many as 'necessities'. This is partly because the product now represents a much smaller proportion of their income.

Time

The period of time we are considering also plays a role in shaping the demand curve. In general the longer the period of time, the more elastic the demand curve. This is due to a number of different factors. First, people make many purchases as a matter of habit and do not change their spend-ing habits immediately. Second, even if they are willing to reconsider their spending patterns, it may take time to find an acceptable alternative. Third, consumers may be locked into a particular technology. If the price of electricity rises sharply, people cannot immediately switch to gas if they have electric cookers. Since buying gas cookers is expensive they will probably wait until it is time to replace their electric cooker before switching fuels. This principle we may state as:

Following a change in price, price elasticity of demand will tend to be greater in the long term than the short term.

Whether or not this is a noticeable effect will depend upon whether or not consumers discover adequate substitutes.

Addiction

Where a product is habit forming, e.g. cigarettes or alcohol, this will tend to reduce its price elasticity of demand. In extreme cases of addiction, such as with heroin or crack, a person's income is no longer a constraint on the price that can be charged. If drug addicts run out of money, then they will steal in order to maintain their habit.

Complementary goods

Although we treat products as separate, they are often used in a complementary way. For instance, car tyres are only demanded for use with cars. When goods are complementary in this way, they are said to be 'jointly demanded'. If the price of tyres goes up by 10 per cent then demand for tyres will not be significantly changed; although tyre prices have risen by a significant amount, they are only a small part of the cost of motoring, so the price of the composite good 'motoring' will have risen by only a very small percentage. This idea can be stated as follows:

Where a good is jointly demanded with another good, its price elasticity of demand will tend to be lower: the smaller is the expenditure on such a product as a proportion of total expenditure on the composite good, the more inelastic is the demand.

Use the intuitive approach for estimating elasticity implicit in the above arguments to give an idea of the price elasticity value for the following products:

1　Carrots
2　Vegetables
3　Petrol
4　Bread
5　Cigarettes
6　Chocolate
7　A brand of chocolate, e.g. Mars bars
8　Replacement windscreen wipers

Arc elasticity

The percentage method of calculating elasticity which we have developed is given by the formula:

$$E_D = \frac{\Delta Q/Q}{\Delta P/P}$$

This can be rearranged as follows:

$$E_D = \frac{\Delta Q}{Q} \times \frac{P}{\Delta P} = \frac{\Delta Q}{\Delta P} \times \frac{P}{Q}$$

This formula gives the right answer for straight line demand curves, as we shall see below. It does not work for curved demand curves, however. If looked at as a way of estimating elasticity of demand *between* two points, it appears to give contradictory answers even with straight line demand curves. To check that this is so, perform the calculations in Student Activity 5.3.

In Student activity 5.1 you were asked to calculate elasticity of demand moving down the demand curve. Recalculate some of the elasticity values from Table 5.1 but move up the demand curve instead of down it. You should get different values from those you calculated in Student activity 5.1. As you move up from a price of 7 to 8, you will get a different value from moving down from a price of 8 to 7, although it is the same stretch of the demand curve.

The reason why different values are found depending on whether the calculation moves up

or down the demand curve is that values for P and Q are determined by the starting point of the calculation. Different values for P and Q will be used according to whether we start at the top or the bottom of a section of the demand curve.

If we have a curved demand curve there is an additional problem. If we look at a small section of the demand curve, a different value for $\Delta Q/\Delta P$ is found than if we look at a longer stretch. This is illustrated in Figure 5.6 which shows the demand curve from the data in Table 5.3.

Table 5.3 **A demand schedule for a demand curve**

P	Q
0	100
1	81
2	64
3	49
4	36
5	25
6	16
7	9
8	4
9	1

If we calculate the elasticity of demand using the percentage method of a decrease in price from 7 to 3 then the result is:

$$E_D = \frac{\Delta Q}{\Delta P} \times \frac{P}{Q} = \frac{40}{-4} \times \frac{7}{9} = \frac{70}{9} = -7\tfrac{7}{9}$$

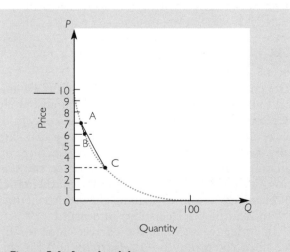

Figure 5.6 **Arc elasticity**

The answer we get from reducing price from 7 to 6, using a shorter section or 'arc' of the demand curve, is closer to the true value of $-4\frac{2}{3}$ (which is calculated in the section on point elasticity below):

$$E_\mathrm{D} = \frac{\Delta Q}{\Delta P} \times \frac{P}{Q} = \frac{7}{-1} \times \frac{7}{9} = \frac{49}{9} = -5\frac{4}{9}$$

The inaccuracy of the answer is minimised by considering as small a change as possible. If we are able to consider the slope of the curve at one spot we will obtain a value known as point elasticity. Before moving on to this, we can make improvements to our estimate by using *arc elasticity*.

Arc elasticity is the average value of price elasticity of demand over a segment of the curve

The formula for arc elasticity is the same as for the percentage method except that an average of the values of P and Q at either end of the arc of the demand curve is used. This means that the same value for elasticity is found whether moving up or down the demand curve. The formula is given below together with a calculation of its value between a price of 7 and 6 on the demand curve in Figure 5.6:

$$E_\mathrm{D} = \frac{\Delta Q}{\Delta P} \times \frac{(P_1 + P_2)/2}{(Q_1 + Q_2)/2} = \frac{7}{-1} \times \frac{6.5}{12.5} = -3\frac{16}{25}$$

This value is between the correct value of $-4\frac{2}{3}$ at a price of 7 and the correct value of -3 at a price of 6. The convention now is to use the arc elasticity method when measuring price elasticity of demand.

Point elasticity

The content of this section is rather more technical than the rest of the chapter and not absolutely necessary for an understanding of the concept of elasticity of demand. If you prefer you can skip this section and move on to the section on income elasticity of demand. However, the section is useful in understanding the mathematics of elasticity and in explaining the precise method for measuring price elasticity of demand.

    In order to calculate the correct value for E_D we need to employ *point elasticity* and for this we need to use some simple calculus. It was noted

in the section on arc elasticity that as the arc of the demand curve being considered was shortened, the result got closer to the true value. In calculus, when the value of ΔQ gets close to zero, $\Delta Q/\Delta P$ becomes dQ/dP, the first derivative of Q with respect to P. This is in fact the inverse of the slope of the demand curve:

$$E_\mathrm{D} = \frac{P}{Q} \times \frac{dQ}{dP}$$

Point elasticity is the value of price elasticity at any one point on the curve.

The ratio dQ/dP is the derivative of quantity with respect to price, while P and Q are price and quantity at the point where we wish to measure elasticity. In geometric terms the chord AC in Figure 5.6 is first shortened to AB and ultimately, when ΔQ equals zero, it becomes the tangent to the demand curve at point A.

    In order to calculate dQ/dP we must have the equation of the demand curve. The data in Table 5.3 (which is also shown in Student activity 5.4) have been calculated from the following formula:

$$Q = 100 - 20P + P^2$$

When differentiated with respect to P this gives a value of:

$$dQ/dP = -20 + 2P$$

If we apply this formula to the example used in Figure 5.6 for the price of £7 and a quantity of 9 then:

$$dQ/dP = -20 + (2 \times 7) = -6$$

Therefore, the precise value of elasticity at this point is:

$$E_\mathrm{D} = \frac{P}{Q} \times \frac{dQ}{dP} = \frac{7}{9} \times (-6) = -4\frac{2}{3}$$

STUDENT ACTIVITY 5.4

Use the data from the information given below (taken from Table 5.3) to calculate the value of point elasticity at other points along the demand curve. Identify the elastic and the inelastic range of the demand curve.

P	Q	P/Q	dQ/dP	E_D
0	100	0	20	0
1	81	1/81	18	
2	64		16	
3	49		14	
4	36		12	
5	25		10	
6	16		8	
7	9		6	$-4\frac{2}{3}$
8	4		4	
9	1		2	

If we are considering straight line demand curves, the percentage method of calculating elasticity will give an absolutely accurate answer. This is because dQ/dP, the inverse of the slope of the demand curve, will be the same at every point along the demand curve and will be equal to ΔQ/ΔP. The percentage method appears to be measuring the elasticity for a move along a stretch of the demand curve, but in fact gives the right answer for point elasticity.

It is important to understand the differences between the percentage method, arc elasticity and point elasticity. However, you will not be required to calculate point elasticity unless you go on to higher-level theoretical economics.

Income elasticity of demand

Income elasticity defined

In the previous chapter we saw how the demand for a product has several determinants. The most important of these is price, and so far in this chapter we have been concerned with how demand alters in response to price changes. Another determinant of demand is income (Y). The response of demand to changes in income may also be measured.

Income elasticity of demand measures the degree of responsiveness of the quantity demanded of a product to changes in income.

The value of income elasticity can be calculated by the following formula:

$$E_Y = \frac{\text{Percentage change in quantity demanded}}{\text{Percentage change in income}}$$

In the same way as price income elasticity of demand, this formula can be reduced to:

$$E_Y = \frac{\Delta Q/Q}{\Delta Y/Y} = \frac{\Delta Q}{\Delta Y} \times \frac{Y}{Q}$$

where Y is income.

Categories of income elasticity

As was explained in the previous chapter, demand might increase or decrease in response to a rise in income, depending upon whether the product we are considering is a normal good or an inferior good. The demand for normal goods increases with income and so these are both positive movements; consequently the value of income elasticity will be positive. With inferior goods, as income rises demand falls and the value is therefore negative. A third possibility exists, which is that demand will remain constant as income rises. In this case there is said to be zero income elasticity. These possibilities are illustrated in Figure 5.7. (You will note in Figure 5.7 that quantity demanded is on the vertical axis and income on the horizontal axis. This is because we have returned to the correct mathematical procedure of placing the dependent variable on the vertical axis (see pages 21–2).)

You will recall that price elasticity of demand is always negative. Income elasticity can be either positive or negative and it is therefore very important to include the sign (+ or –) when stating its value. Positive income elasticity can still fall into the three categories of elastic, inelastic and unitary. The possibilities are summarised in Table 5.4.

Table 5.4 Income elasticities of demand

Category	Value	Characteristics
Negative income elasticity	$E_Y<0$	Demand decreases as income rises
Zero income elasticity	$E_Y = 0$	Demand does not change as income rises or falls
Income inelasticity	$0<E_Y<1$	Demand rises by a smaller proportion than income
Unit income elasticity	$E_Y = 1$	Demand rises by exactly the same proportion as income
Income elasticity	$1<E_Y<\infty$	Demand rises by a greater proportion than income

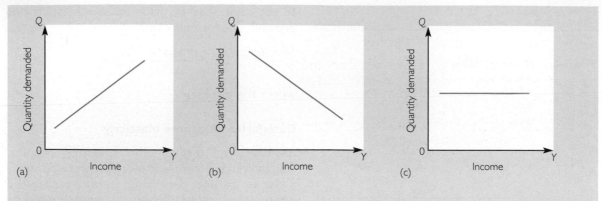

Figure 5.7 Income elasticities: three possibilities
(a) Positive income elasticity as demand increases with income, e.g. colour television sets.
(b) Negative income elasticity as demand falls with income, e.g. potatoes.
(c) Zero income elasticity; demand remains constant as income rises, e.g. salt.

When we examined elasticity of demand we discovered that one demand curve might have all three categories of elasticity. This is also so with income elasticity of demand. Consider a product like potatoes. If an economy is very poor then as income rises people will be pleased to eat more potatoes and therefore potatoes will be a normal good. As income continues to rise and people buy other types of food to supplement their diet, the demand for potatoes remains constant and there is therefore zero income elasticity. As the economy becomes richer people consume such quantities of meat and other vegetables that they need fewer potatoes. There will now be negative income elasticity of demand for potatoes. This is illustrated in Figure 5.8.

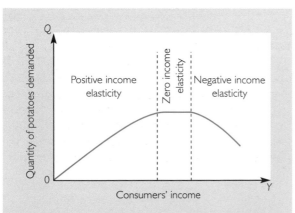

Figure 5.8 The demand for potatoes may have all three types of income elasticity

The importance of income elasticity

Economic growth increases the income of a country and this is generally considered to be a good thing. However, for those engaged in the production of goods with negative income elasticities, this will mean a declining demand for their product. Even when we consider products with positive income elasticities, there is a great variability of response. For example, with commodities such as food and clothing, although demand may rise with income, it might not rise fast enough to offset improvements in productivity, so that the result may still be unemployment for some in the industry. The booming industries tend to be those making products which have highly income elastic demands such as personal computers and foreign holidays. A downturn in national income, however, may well mean a rapid decline in the demand for these types of goods.

Income elasticity therefore has a most important effect upon resource allocation. We should not be surprised to find that the prosperous areas of the economy are often those associated with products which have a high income elasticity. In recession the opposite will be true.

Cross elasticity of demand

The demand for many products is affected by the price of other products. Where this relationship can be measured we may express it as the cross elasticity of demand.

Cross elasticity of demand measures the degree of responsiveness of the quantity demanded of one good (B) to changes in the price of another good (A).

The value of cross elasticity may be calculated in the same way as price and income elasticity. The formula is:

$$E_x = \frac{\text{Percentage change in quantity demanded of B}}{\text{Percentage change in price of A}}$$

This we may write as:

$$E_x = \frac{\Delta Q_b/Q_b}{\Delta P_a/P_a} = \frac{\Delta Q_b}{\Delta P_a} \times \frac{P_a}{Q_b}$$

In the case of complementary goods, such as cars and petrol, a fall in the price of one will bring about an increase in the demand for the other. Thus we are considering a cut in price (−) bringing a rise in demand (+). This therefore means that for complements, E_x is negative. Conversely, substitute goods such as butter and margerine or own brands versus name brands as in many supermarket products like cereals, washing powders and coffee might be expected to have a positive E_x; a rise in price of one (+) will bring about a rise in the demand for the other (+) as was discussed in the previous chapter.

The value of E_x may vary from minus infinity to plus infinity. Goods which are close complements or substitutes will tend to exhibit a high cross elasticity of demand. Conversely, when there is little or no relationship between goods then E_x will be near to zero. These possibilities are summarised in Table 5.5.

Table 5.5 Cross elasticities of demand

Category	Value	Characteristics
Substitute	$0 < E_x < \infty$	Quantity demanded of product B changes in same direction as price change of product A
No relationship	0	Quantity demanded of product B unchanged as price of A changes
Complement	$-\infty < E_x < 0$	Quantity demanded of product B changes in opposite direction to price change of product A

STUDENT ACTIVITY 5.5

Comment on the possible income elasticity values for the following products:

1 Carrots
2 Cheap bottles of wine
3 Salt
4 Foreign holidays

Now comment on the possible cross elasticity values for the following pairs of products:

1 Beef and veal
2 Sugar and sugar substitutes
3 Flights to and hotels in a particular destination
4 Computers and wool

Price elasticity of supply

Price elasticity of supply defined

Much of what we have said about price elasticity of demand will hold true for price elasticity of supply. Indeed the definition is very similar. Price elasticity of supply measures the degree of responsiveness of quantity supplied to changes in price.

The value of price elasticity of supply can be calculated by the formula:

$$E_s = \frac{\text{Percentage change in quantity supplied}}{\text{Percentage change in price}}$$

This may be written as:

$$E_s = \frac{\Delta Q/Q}{\Delta P/P} = \frac{\Delta Q}{\Delta P} \times \frac{P}{Q}$$

This appears to be identical with the formula for price elasticity of demand. However, you will recall (see page 67) that price elasticity of demand is always negative. Price elasticity of supply, however, is positive since the supply curve slopes upwards from left to right. There is a possibility that we may encounter a backward-bending supply curve (see page 53), in which case the backward-sloping position of the supply curve would have negative elasticity.

Supply curves

When we examined demand curves we discovered that it was dangerous to infer the value of elasticity from the slope of the curve. With supply, however, things are much easier. Any straight line supply curve that meets the vertical axis will be price elastic and its value will lie between one and infinity. A straight line supply curve that meets the horizontal axis will be price inelastic and its value will lie between zero and one. Any straight line supply curve through the origin will have unitary elasticity.

Thus in Figure 5.9 both S_1 and S_2 have unitary elasticity. (This is because at any point on the supply curve P, Q and ΔP, ΔQ form similar triangles with the supply curve.) This you may confirm by experimenting with curves of different slopes. Supply curves of more complex shapes pose similar problems to demand curves. The category of price elasticity of supply at any point on a supply curve may be judged by drawing a tangent to the point of the curve we wish to know about. If the tangent hits the vertical axis then supply is elastic at that point. If it hits the horizontal axis, as in Figure 5.10, then it is inelastic.

The importance of elasticity of supply

Business organisations, the government and public corporations all take a keen interest in price elasticity of demand and are interested in its precise measurement. This is not hard to understand for they will be interested in how price changes affect their revenues. However, no conclusions about total revenue can be arrived at

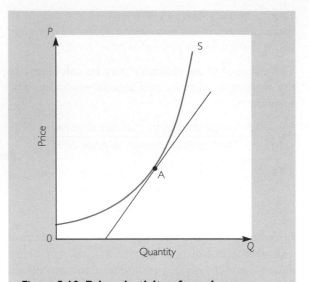

Figure 5.10 **Price elasticity of supply curve**
The elasticity of supply at point A can be judged from a tangent drawn to the curve at that point.

from the supply curve. The precise measurement of E_S is, therefore, of less interest.

Although we have dealt with price elasticity of supply only briefly here, it should not be thought that it is unimportant. Indeed, since the long-run shape of the supply curve is dependent upon the costs of production, it can be readily appreciated that its slope is of the utmost importance. In later chapters, when we come to consider costs and the theory of production, we will be investigating the factors which shape the supply curve.

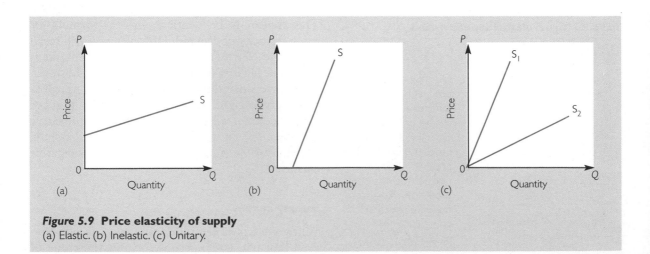

Figure 5.9 **Price elasticity of supply**
(a) Elastic. (b) Inelastic. (c) Unitary.

Periods of supply

Price elasticity of supply increases with time as producers have longer to adjust to changes in demand. **Alfred Marshall** maintained that there were three periods of supply – the momentary, short-run and long-run periods – defined as follows:

(a) *Momentary*. In the momentary period supply is fixed and E_S is zero.
(b) *Short run*. In the short run supply can be varied with the limit of the present fixed assets (buildings, machines, etc.).
(c) *Long run*. In the long run all factors may be varied and firms may enter or leave the industry.

Suppose we consider an increase in the demand for candles as a result of a strike in the electricity supply industry. In the momentary period we have only whatever stocks of candles already exist in shops. In the short run the existing candle factories can work longer hours, take on more labour, etc. If the increase in demand for candles were to be permanent, then in the long run more candle factories could be built. The effect of periods of supply on costs is discussed in Chapters 7 and 20.

Periods of supply and the equilibrium price

If we accept the Marshallian periods of supply then we should be able to observe them in their effect on equilibrium price. Figure 5.11 follows Marshall's analysis. Suppose that the diagram represents the market for fresh fish. In each diagram the effect of the same increase in demand is considered. This increase might have been brought about by, for example, the BSE crisis in the beef industry causing people to switch to fish.

In each diagram E represents the original equilibrium. In diagram (a) the supply of fish is fixed at whatever the present landings are. The only response therefore is for price to rise (E_1) but there is no variation in supply. In diagram (b) the fishing industry responds by working longer hours, using more nets, taking on more labour, etc. The price falls from the momentary high of E_1 to E_2 as there is some expansion of supply. Diagram (c) shows what happens if there is a long-term increase in demand. Now in response to the increase in demand the industry is able to build more boats (vary the fixed assets) and new businesses enter the industry. The result is that the price falls to E_3 and considerably more is supplied. It was Marshall's contention that E_3 would be higher than E, i.e. that the supply curve is upward sloping. Marshall assumed that the industry had already benefited from economies of scale and that any expansion of the industry, in relation to others, would cause it to suffer from increasing costs (see pages 38–9). Since S_L is more price elastic than S_M or S_S we may conclude that:

Price elasticity of supply tends to increase with time.

It should not be thought that the equilibrium price leaps from E_1 to E_2. More usually it is a gradual process as price elasticity of supply

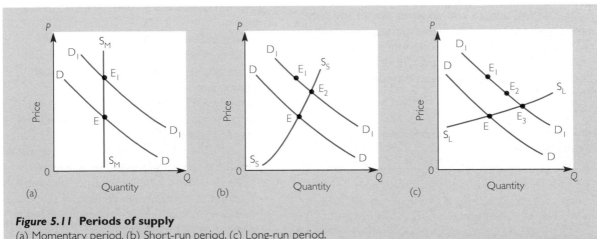

Figure 5.11 **Periods of supply**
(a) Momentary period. (b) Short-run period. (c) Long-run period.

increases with time. In the next chapter we will be considering changes in demand and supply. It is worthwhile remembering that when changes occur the effects may be possible to isolate in three phases, as we have seen here.

Determinants of price elasticity of supply

As with demand, there are a number of factors which affect price elasticity of supply:

(a) *Time*. This is the most significant factor and we have seen how elasticity increases with time.
(b) *Factor mobility*. The ease with which factors of production can be moved from one use to another will affect price elasticity of supply. The higher the factor mobility, the greater will be the elasticity.
(c) *Natural constraints*. The natural world places restrictions upon supply. If, for example, we wish to produce more vintage wine it will take years of maturing before it becomes vintage.
(d) *Risk taking*. The more willing entrepreneurs are to take risks the greater will be the price elasticity of supply. This will be partly influenced by the system of incentives in the economy. If, for example, marginal rates of tax are very high this may reduce the price elasticity of supply.

This chapter has concentrated on the theoretical aspects of the elasticities of demand and supply. You will find, however, that it is a concept which has widespread uses. It can be applied to exports and imports to assess the effects of depreciation in the currency. The Chancellor of the Exchequer will be concerned with it in determining the level of indirect taxes, and of course firms are vitally concerned with it in their price and output policy. You will find references to it throughout the book and especially in the next chapter and Chapter 11; therefore make sure you have understood this chapter thoroughly.

Summary

1 Any value of elasticity is arrived at by dividing the percentage change in the quantity demanded (or supplied) by the percentage change in the determinant which brought it about (price, income, price of other goods).

2 Price elasticity of demand measures the responsiveness of quantity demanded to changes in price. Demand may be elastic, inelastic or unitary depending upon whether a cut in price raises, lowers or leaves total revenue unchanged.
3 Price elasticity of demand is primarily determined by the ease of substitution.
4 Elasticity measured along a segment of a curve is referred to as arc elasticity while elasticity measured at one spot on a curve is called point elasticity.
5 Income elasticity measures the responsiveness of demand to changes in income and may be positive, negative or zero, depending upon whether quantity demanded goes up, goes down or remains constant as income increases.
6 Cross elasticity measures the responsiveness of the quantity demanded of one good to changes in the price of another. It may be either positive or negative depending upon whether the two products considered are substitutes or complements.
7 Price elasticity of supply may be elastic, inelastic or unitary depending upon whether, following a price rise, the quantity supplied rises by a greater, smaller or equal percentage.
8 Price elasticity of supply increases with time. This can be analysed in Marshall's three supply periods: momentary, short run and long run.

? QUESTIONS

1 Explain the factors which determine price elasticity of supply.
2 Compare and contrast the responsiveness of demand of primary products and manufactured products with respect to changes in price and changes in income.
3 Explain how OPEC has exploited its knowledge of the price elasticity of demand for oil. Evaluate the success of its policy.
4 Explain how the value of price elasticity of demand will affect the success of the following actions.
   (a) Cinema owners increase the price of admission in order to increase their receipts.
   (b) London Transport reduces underground train fares to attract more customers and increase its receipts.

5 Consider the following information:

	1971	1981	1986	1991	1994	1997
Disposable income at constant prices (1990 prices)	46.6	58.5	85.5	99.9	104.7	116.3
Cigarette sales (millions)	136	121	101	98	86	82

Are cigarettes inferior goods? Justify your answer. If you were asked to account for the observed variation in cigarette sales, what additional information would help you?

6 Examine the effect that price elasticity of demand would have on government tax revenues if the government were to increase the tax on:
(a) alcohol;
(b) video cassettes.

7 Discuss the effects of (a) a fall in the price of supermarket own brands of cornflakes on the demand for name brands and (b) an increase in the price of video recorders on the demand for video cassettes.

Data response A
BEEBOP TRAINERS

The information in Table 5.6 represents the demand and supply for BEEBOP trainers.

Table 5.6

Price per pair (£)	Quantity of trainers pairs/week Supplied	Demanded
100.00	20 000	1 250
85.00	16 250	3 125
70.00	12 500	5 000
55.00	8 750	6 875
35.00	3 750	9 375
25.00	1 250	10 625
20.00	0	11 250

From this information:

1 Determine the equilibrium price and quantity of BEEBOP trainers.
2 Calculate the price elasticity of demand (E_D) and supply (E_S) at the equilibrium price.
3 What would be the new equilibrium price if demand were to increase by 50 per cent at every price?
4 Why would it be useful to the owners of BEEBOP to know the price elasticity of demand for their product? In what other circumstances is knowledge of the value of elasticity of demand likely to prove useful?
5 What does price elasticity of demand tell us about the relative power of consumers, sellers and producers in given market situations?

Data response B
PRICE AND INCOME ELASTICITIES

The figures in Table 5.7 show the values of price and income elasticity of demand for selected products in the UK.

Table 5.7 Price and income elasticities for selected products

Product	Price elasticities	Income elasticities
Consumer durables	−0.9	1.5
Foreign travel	−1.8	3.3
Bread	−0.1	−0.2
Milk	−0.2	0.0
Fresh meat	−1.4	0.0
Wine	−1.2	2.6
Petrol	−1.0 (short run) −0.5 (long run)	1.3
Beer	−0.4	0.5

Various sources

1 Explain the values of price and income elasticity of demand for as many of the products as you can.
2 With reference to the price elasticity values comment on their implications for pricing policies in the industries concerned.
3 With reference to the income elasticity values comment on the implications of a rapid rate of economic growth for the industries concerned.

Markets in movement

In Chapters 4 and 5 we have examined the factors that shape demand and supply curves, and the formation of equilibrium prices. We will now go on to analyse how changes in demand and supply affect market prices. We will start by recalling some important points.

Some important ideas reviewed

Equilibrium price

This occurs where the demand curve cuts the supply curve and is the point at which the wishes of buyers and sellers coincide. Equilibrium prices also have an important allocative and distributive function in a free enterprise economy, helping us to answer the *What?*, *How?* and *For whom?* questions. An equilibrium price, however, is not permanent; it lasts only so long as the forces that produced it persist. A change in the conditions of demand or supply will bring about a new equilibrium price.

Ceteris paribus

It is possible to make predictions about price and quantity as long as we keep the rule of considering only one change at a time. Most statements in microeconomics should be prefaced with the phrase 'all other things remaining constant' also known by the Latin equivalent, '*ceteris paribus*'. In economics it is not easy to perform experiments of the type used in the physical sciences, because society cannot be brought into the laboratory. It is possible to perform 'thought experiments', however, where we change just one thing and work out the logical consequences.

Changes in demand and supply

In Chapter 4 the difference between shifts in the demand curve, and movements along it were first introduced. The same distinction was made for the supply curve. Figure 6.1(a) illustrates a movement along a demand curve from point A to point B, sometimes termed an extension of demand. This movement has been caused by a reduction in price. If the move had been in the reverse direction from B to A, this would be termed a contraction in demand. However, if there is a rise in income (for example) so that more is demanded at each price than before, this shifts the demand curve to the right. This is termed an increase in demand and is illustrated in diagram (b). These principles hold true for supply as well and are illustrated in diagrams (c) and (d).

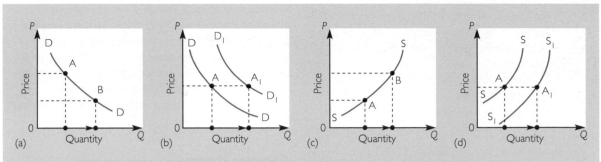

Figure 6.1 Shifts in demand and supply curves versus movements along them
A change in the price of the commodity causes a change in the quantity demanded (a) or supplied (c).
A change in constant factors behind the curves shifts the curve, so that more is demanded (b) or supplied (d) at any given price.

A movement along an existing supply curve is termed an extension or contraction of supply and a shift to a new supply curve is termed an increase or decrease in supply.

Changes in market price

Four possibilities for change

If we consider all the possible changes in demand and supply it will be apparent that only four basic movements in the equilibrium are possible. These are illustrated in Figure 6.2.

Other things being equal, an increase in demand will bring about an extension of supply so that more is supplied at a higher price (Figure 6.2(a)).

A decrease in demand leads to a contraction of supply, with less bought at a lower price (Figure 6.2(b)). Conversely, an increase in supply causes an extension of demand so that more is demanded at a lower price (Figure 6.2(c)); and a decrease in supply causes a contraction of demand so that less is bought at a higher price (Figure 6.2(d)).

> **STUDENT ACTIVITY 6.1**
>
> If you refer back to the determinants of demand and supply in Chapter 4, you will see what factors might have brought about these changes. Can you match the following four examples with the correct diagrams in Figure 6.2?

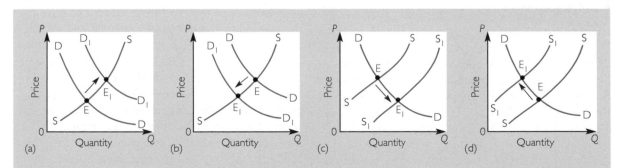

Figure 6.2 Changes in the equilibrium
(a) Increase in demand results in more being bought at a higher price.
(b) Decrease in demand results in a smaller quantity being bought at a lower price.
(c) Increase in supply results in more being supplied at a lower price.
(d) Decrease in supply results in less being supplied at a higher price.

1. In the computer industry there has been a reduction in the cost of silicon chips.
2. An exceptionally poor summer affects tomato production.
3. The impact on the beef market of a rise in consumers' incomes.
4. The impact on the potato market of a rise in consumers' incomes.

You should have got: 1 (c); 2 (d); 3 (a); 4 (b). (Remember that potatoes are usually considered an inferior good.)

● *Common misunderstanding*

A mistaken argument is often advanced which goes something like this. 'If supply increases (Figure 6.2(c)) the price will fall, but if the price falls then more will be demanded. This rise in demand will then put up the price, increased price will cause less to be demanded and so on. Therefore it is impossible to say what the effect of the original increase in supply will be.'

This argument confuses changes in supply and demand with movements along supply and demand curves. The original increase in supply does not cause demand to change. For example, technological advance means that many more pocket calculators can be supplied very cheaply. This does not alter the conditions of demand. It does not, for example, increase people's incomes. Instead it means that the suppliers of pocket calculators have many more to sell and this they do by lowering the price. This causes a greater quantity to be demanded. If there is no further change a new equilibrium will have been reached, with more calculators bought at a lower price.

Complex changes

We were only able to reach any firm conclusions in the analysis above because we stuck to the rule of *ceteris paribus*, i.e. of considering only one change at a time. It is, of course, possible – even likely – that more than one factor may vary at a given point in time. Suppose, for example, that there is a large rise in the demand for apples because of a successful advertising campaign to promote them. This is followed by an unexpected bumper crop of apples. What will be the final effect upon the equilibrium price?

If you study Figure 6.3 you will see that both diagrams could illustrate the example we have just mentioned. However, although the quantity demanded and supplied increases in both cases, in diagram (a) the price falls while in (b) it rises.

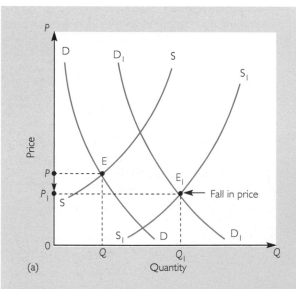
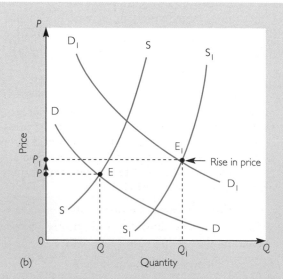

Figure 6.3 **Complex shifts in demand and supply**
In both cases there is an increase in demand and supply, but in (a) this results in a lower equilibrium price and in (b) a higher equilibrium price. This is because of the different magnitudes of shifts in demand and supply.

When multiple shifts in demand and supply curves are considered it may be impossible to reach any firm conclusion about the effect on the equilibrium price unless the precise magnitudes of the changes are known.

This conclusion has important consequences for anyone undertaking an examination in economics. Suppose you are asked to consider the effect of a number of changes in the demand and supply of a particular product. It is obvious from Figure 6.3 that no firm conclusion can be reached unless both changes move in the same direction; for example, an increase in supply coupled with a decrease in demand will definitely lower the equilibrium price. What is the solution? The answer is to explain one change at a time. In the examples used above, for instance, first explain the effect of an increase in demand and draw a diagram to illustrate it. Then explain the effect of the increase in supply and draw another diagram to illustrate this. Always keep to the rule of explaining one thing at a time unless you have precise details of the demand and supply.

Multiple choice examinations

If your examination contains a multiple choice element it is quite likely that you may find yourself faced with a diagram similar to Figure 6.4. In this case we can answer questions about multiple changes in demand and supply because we know the precise magnitude of them (they are shown in the diagram). Suppose the question was:

Figure 6.4 shows the original equilibrium price of margarine. However, many people are discouraged from eating butter because of articles in the press suggesting it is dangerous. This is followed by a large rise in the cost of the oils from which margarine is made. What will be the new equilibrium price for margarine? A? B? C? D? E?

The best way to answer the questions is to locate position O and the demand and supply curves that cross at that point. Ignore the other DD and SS curves for the moment. Then follow the question one step at a time. The articles in the press

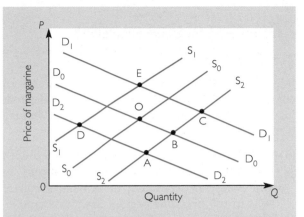

Figure 6.4 **Multiple shifts in demand and supply**

will decrease the demand for butter and thus increase the demand for margarine; we are thus at the intersection of S_0S_0 with D_1D_1. In the second step, consider the increase in the cost of oils, which will decrease the supply of margarine S_0S_0 to S_1S_1. Thus we will move to point E, which is the correct answer.

If there are more questions on the same diagram always remember to return to the original equilibrium O. Then follow the same procedure as outlined above.

STUDENT ACTIVITY 6.2

Using Figure 6.4 and starting again at O, what will be the new equilibrium position in each of the following cases?

(a) There is a massive increase in the price of bread, but the EU decides to subsidise margarine production.
(b) New evidence suggests that butter is healthier for you after all, and crop failures push up the price of margarine's constituents.
(c) The wages council covering agricultural production is abolished resulting in a fall in wages in the agriculture sector. Butter prices remain the same because they are covered by an EU price guarantee scheme. The economy as a whole is going into recession.

The effect of time on prices

Time lags

Supply often takes some time to respond to changes in demand. This *time lag* will vary depending upon the product we are considering. We may distinguish between two types of response:

(a) *One-period time lag.* This is associated with agricultural products, where the supply in one period is dependent upon what the price was in the previous period. Say, for example, that there is an increase in demand for barley. This will cause the price to rise, but there will be no immediate response from supply; it will have to wait until more barley has been planted and grown. Then at the next harvest there will be a sudden response to the previous year's increase in price. The period need not be a year; if the product we were considering was timber it might take a good deal longer to grow more trees.

(b) *Distributed time lag.* This is associated with manufactured goods. For example, if there is an increase in the demand for cars then manufacturers can respond to this by using their factories more intensively. However, if this does not satisfy the demand then supplying more will have to wait upon the building of new factories. The response is thus more complex and distributed over time.

Time lags and prices

It is easiest to consider one-period time lags. A possible effect is shown in Figure 6.5. Suppose that the diagram illustrates the demand and supply of barley. The move from DD to D_1D_1 shows the effect of an increase in the demand for barley. However, at the time of harvest the supply of barley is absolutely fixed and can be represented by the vertical supply curve S_1. The only response of the market, therefore, is for the price to rise to E_1, but there is no change in supply. Seeing the increase in demand, however, farmers plant more

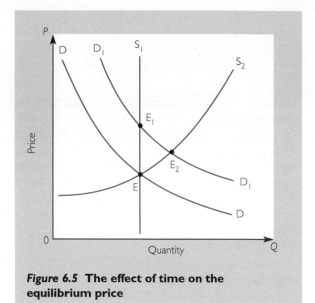

Figure 6.5 The effect of time on the equilibrium price

barley and so next year there is more supplied and we arrive at E_2. The extra supply in year 2 has thus been called forth by the high price in year 1.

This is a development of the idea of elasticity of supply explained in Chapter 5. The further implications of this are discussed at the end of this chapter.

Government interference with equilibrium prices

The problem

We have seen that prices fulfil an *allocating function* in distributing scarce goods between different users or consumers. Income, however, is unevenly distributed, so that although goods may be readily available, people may not be able to buy them. If these goods are the essentials of life it is very hard for a democratic government not to interfere. Suppose, for example, rents are extremely high so that people cannot afford housing. The government could build more houses; this, however, is very expensive. It is very tempting for the government, therefore, to think that it can get round the problem by freezing the rent of houses below the equilibrium price. It is the object of this section to show that such interferences, almost invariably, have some undesirable side effects. Examples from agriculture, housing and minimum wages (among other industries) are introduced here, but are discussed in full in Chapter 11 after market failure concepts have been introduced.

Any price artificially imposed by law may be termed a *flat price*. Where the authorities stipulate a maximum price for a commodity this may be termed a *ceiling price* and where a minimum price is stipulated this is termed a *price floor*.

The objectives

Governments do not just freeze prices at a low level; they sometimes maintain them at artificially high levels. It is possible for a government to be fixing some prices too high and others too low at the same time. This is because of different policy objectives:

(a) *Cheapness*. It may be the objective of the government to keep the price of a product at a level at which it can be afforded by most people, e.g. housing or food.
(b) *The maintenance of incomes*. The government may want to keep the incomes of producers at a higher level than that which would be produced by market prices. This is often true of farm incomes.
(c) *Price stability*. If there is a wide variation in the price of produce from year to year, e.g. agricultural products, the government may wish to iron out these variations in the interests of both producers and consumers.

Interpreting diagrams

As the policies that are being analysed become more complex, so unfortunately do the diagrams! In Chapter 4 you were introduced to the idea of total revenue being represented by a rectangle on the demand curve diagram (see Figure 4.2). When we are comparing different revenues on the same diagram, this can get quite complicated. We simplify this process by labelling the corners of the various rectangles by capital letters, so they can be referred to more easily. The point where price

and quantity are both zero, and the two axes meet, is known in mathematical terms as the origin and will be given the letter O. Labelling points on the diagram also helps to explain shifts in equilibrium, the extent of excess supply or demand, price and quantity levels, and the incidence of taxes. The price level OT in Figure 6.6 is measured by starting at the origin (O) and moving up to point T on the price axis. The associated quantity ON is the distance along the quantity axis from the origin to point N. The excess demand LN referred to in the next section is the distance from L to N, or could be thought of as ON minus OL. It may take you a little while to get used to this way of labelling diagrams, but will make things easier in the long run.

Ceiling prices

Governments in many countries have often interfered in the economy to fix the price of a commodity below the equilibrium. Good examples of this are to be found in wartime. In the UK during the Second World War almost everything was in very short supply. If the price of a basic commodity such as meat or eggs had been left to

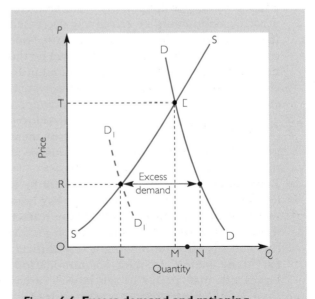

Figure 6.6 Excess demand and rationing
The price set below the equilibrium brings about excess demand of LN. D₁ shows an artificial equilibrium created by the imposition of rationing.

find its own level it would have been very high, and beyond the means of many people. In Figure 6.6 this is shown as price OT. A ceiling price is shown as OR. At this price consumers will wish to buy ON but suppliers who were willing to supply OM when the price was OT are now willing to supply only OL. There is therefore an excess demand of LN. Thus price is failing to fulfil its *rationing function*, and some other method will have to be used. This might lead to long queues outside butchers' shops or to butchers serving only their regular customers. This often happened in Russia and the other former communist states, where prices were kept low despite chronic deficiencies of supply. This meant that other rationing measures had to be put in place such as allowing meat to be sold on only one day of the week, thus limiting demand. Three examples of intervention in the market are considered below:

(a) *Wartime controls.* During the Second World War the UK adopted a system of rationing. This meant that in addition to the price, customers also had to have a coupon issued by the government that entitled them to so many ounces of meat per week. Therefore, in effect, a new money-plus-coupon price had been created. Demand could be effectively decreased to equate with supply by regulating the issue of coupons. In Figure 6.6 this is shown by the new demand curve D_1 and thus an equilibrium, of sorts, was arrived at. This system still had drawbacks; for example, a coupon entitled a person to a number of ounces (or grammes in today's measures) of meat per week but it did not specify the quality of the meat.

(b) *Rent control.* Such interference has not been limited to wartime. In the UK there has been rent control since the First World War. Rather than providing cheap accommodation for all, this had the effect of making it very difficult for many people to rent accommodation. Landlords may prefer to sell houses rather than let them at low rents; sitting tenants with protected tenancies have clung to their accommodation even when it is no longer suitable for their needs. Thus rent control has had the opposite effect from that which was

intended. Similar controls in France discouraged building between 1914 and 1948. Rent controls in the UK led to massive **distortions** in the housing market. They were, for example, one of the reasons for the high level of owner occupation. The Conservative government abolished most of the remaining controls in 1988. Although this return to market economics got rid of distortions in the market, it did not solve the problem of how to house the poorest people in society, many of whom ended up in unsatisfactory bed and breakfast accommodation. This discussion is continued in more detail in Chapter 11.

(c) *Interest.* In the Middle Ages charging interest on money was condemned by the church as the sin of usury, and since the sixteenth century many countries have placed a ceiling on the interest that can be charged. The best example of this in recent years has been regulation in the USA, which was intended to give cheap loans and mortgages to people. The drawback was that it also frequently created a shortage of funds for these purposes. The USA began to phase out restrictions on interest charges in 1981. Once again, it is often the poorest people who suffer when the market is allowed to work without interference because only less reputable lenders, sometimes known as 'loan sharks', are willing to lend to them. Islamic economics also has to get around this problem, since charging interest is forbidden by the Koran. They mostly achieve this by making investors share the risk of the investments they make, thus turning interest into profit.

Price floors

If the government establishes a floor below which prices may not fall, and this price is above the equilibrium, then excess supply will be created. This is illustrated in Figure 6.7. Here the price has been fixed at OT and this has caused demand to contract from OM to OL. However, at the higher price suppliers wish to sell more and supply expands to ON. The excess supply is shown as line AB. We will consider three examples of this:

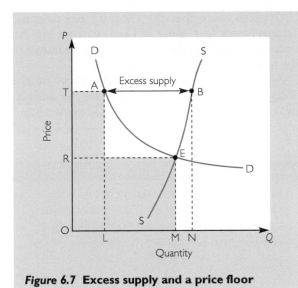

Figure 6.7 **Excess supply and a price floor**

was passed to set minimum wage levels in a variety of industries, such as agriculture and catering, where wages were low. At one time wages councils were laying down the minimum wage levels for three million workers. The Conservative government, however, followed Milton Friedman's argument and set about dismantling many of the wages councils during the 1980s, believing that this would enlarge employment. Since the Labour government introduced the minimum wage, employment has risen, but it may be that other factors are responsible for this.

It is necessary to return to this argument after macroeconomics has been considered in some detail. If poorer people spend a higher proportion of their income then increased expenditure may result in more employment in the economy as the minimum wage is increased. This argument is discussed in more detail in Chapters 11 and 28.

(a) *Agricultural prices.* In the USA and Europe, governments frequently set guaranteed high prices for agricultural products in order to protect the incomes of farmers. The Common Agricultural Policy (CAP) of the EU does this and Europeans are familiar with the excess supply it creates in the form of 'butter mountains' and 'wine lakes' (see Chapter 11). It also results in high prices for the consumer, once again creating problems for the poorest people in society.

(b) *Minimum wages.* Where wages are very low a government may try to improve the lot of workers by insisting on a minimum wage. This may, however, have the effect of encouraging employers to employ fewer people and instead substitute other factors of production. Thus the workers that remain in employment are better off but others may have lost their jobs. This is illustrated in Figure 6.7. Here the diagram shows that not only are fewer people employed but also the possibility that the total amount of money paid in wages has declined. If OT is the minimum wage then the total amount paid in wages is OTAL, whereas at the lower wage rate of OR the amount paid is OREM.

In the USA, **Milton Friedman** has argued that minimum wage regulations have significantly reduced the employment of young black people and have depressed the total paid in wages, as in Figure 6.7. In the UK, on the other hand, the Wages Councils Act 1969

STUDENT ACTIVITY 6.3

What do you think would be the consequence of imposing a standard minimum wage on the following groups of workers?
(a) Machinists in the clothing industry.
(b) Cleaners in the NHS.
(c) School leavers of 16.
(d) Accountants.
(e) Part-time Saturday jobs.

(c) *Exchange rates.* Where the value (exchange rate) of a currency is fixed by a government, it is possible for its price to be set too high (or too low). Suppose that the rurit, the currency of Ruritania, has a real value of:

10 rurits = £1 or 1 rurit = 10p

However, the Ruritanian government insists on an exchange rate of 2 rurits = £1. This now values the rurit at 1 rurit = 50p. At this exchange rate Ruritanians will find UK exports and holidays in the UK extremely attractive. However, they will not find anyone willing to sell them pounds at this rate unless they are sufficiently desperate for Ruritanian goods to pay five times their true value. Thus commerce between the two countries will be all but impossible.

Many of the former communist states of Eastern Europe insisted on rates as unrealistic as the one described above. Thus, their citizens found it very difficult, or impossible, to obtain pounds or dollars to buy imports or to travel abroad. Foreign currency earnings came from tourists who were willing to pay the unrealistic exchange rate in order to visit the country. Exports and imports had to be arranged by special agreements with foreign governments or companies. The difficulties of attempting to move to a realistic exchange rate led to the almost total collapse of the rouble (see Data response B at the end of the chapter).

Informal markets

Whenever a government intervenes to fix a price too high or too low, it means that there is another price at which both buyers and sellers are willing to trade. Such fiat prices thus tend to bring so-called *informal markets* (also known as black markets) into being, as people begin to make illegal arrangements to circumvent the government price.

During rationing in the Second World War there were active informal markets in the USA, the UK and occupied Europe. Rent control had led to potential tenants making payments to land-lords for 'furniture and fittings' or as 'key money' in order to obtain a tenancy. In the USA ceilings on interest payments frequently led banks to offer other inducements to attract accounts. Potential depositors were often offered gifts to open an account, the gifts varying from electric toasters to, on one occasion, a Rolls-Royce. The reader may be more familiar with the informal market in tick-ets for tennis at Wimbledon or the FA Cup Final.

When we turn to prices set too high we find comparable attempts at circumvention. Anyone who has visited a country that does not allow its currency to be determined by market forces will be aware of the efforts of residents to buy foreign currency at informal market rates. Wages set too high can also cause difficulties; for example, people are often employed illegally thus not only receiving a low wage but also defrauding the gov-ernment of income tax. Employers also get round legislation by employing outworkers who work in their own homes rather than in a factory or office. The rates of pay for such work are often incredibly low. The artificially high prices of the

CAP often mean that the EU itself has to make arrangements to dispose of the excess supply. An example of this was the sale of cut-price butter to the former USSR.

Not all these are informal markets in the accepted sense, but they do illustrate the difficul-ties caused by interfering with equilibrium prices.

STUDENT ACTIVITY 6.4

You are working in a government department which has been asked to look at the way in which FA Cup Final tickets are distributed. The options which you have been asked to look at are:

1 Leave the system to the open market with no intervention from the government or the FA.
2 Offer tickets at a rate lower than the market rate only to supporters of the two clubs in the final and sell any that are left on the open market.
3 Offer a limited number of tickets to the supporters of both teams and further tickets to supporters of other football teams. Offer the same controlled price to everyone.

Advise the government which is the best system. Can you think of any alternative systems? What informal market activity is likely to occur in each case?

Price stabilisation

Agricultural products are often subject to unplanned variations in supply, i.e. because of the influence of such things as the weather and dis-eases the actual output in any particular year may be greater or smaller than that which farmers planned. If we consider a product with a rela-tively inelastic demand, such as wheat, then comparatively small variations in supply may cause large variations in the price. This is illus-trated in Figure 6.8. S_0 represents the planned supply, with farmers happy to produce 20 million tonnes of wheat at £260 per tonne. A bad harvest might decrease the supply to S_2 while a good one might increase it to S_1. High prices in bad years might suit farmers but might cause distress or even famine to consumers. Although consumers might be delighted with low prices in good years,

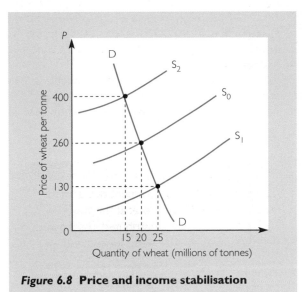

Figure 6.8 Price and income stabilisation

these prices might result in bankruptcy for many farmers. In extreme cases the price may fall so low that it does not even cover harvesting and distribution costs and the crops may be ploughed back into the soil.

It would seem desirable, therefore, to attempt to stabilise prices and incomes. This could be done by a producers' cooperative or by a government agency. Suppose that we have the situation represented by S_1 in Figure 6.8, with supply totalling 25 million tonnes. If an agency were to buy up 5 million tonnes and store them, this would drive up the price to £260 per tonne. Suppose that in the subsequent year the crop was very poor so that now only 15 million tonnes is produced. By releasing 5 million tonnes from store the agency can keep the price down to £260 per tonne, thus bringing stability and order to the situation.

This policy is not easy to implement because it is difficult to determine the correct price for a product and to be certain in any year how much to build up or to release. Nevertheless many such schemes have been tried. (This subject is developed further in Chapter 11.)

Taxes and subsidies

Types of tax

Taxes fall into two main groups, direct and indirect. *Direct taxes* are those which are levied directly on people's incomes, the most important being income tax. *Indirect taxes* are those which are levied on expenditure. We are here concerned only with expenditure or outlay taxes and their effect upon demand and supply. (Taxes are more fully discussed in Chapters 10 and 29.)

The two most important indirect taxes in the UK are *value-added tax* (VAT) and *excise duty*. VAT is an *ad valorem* (by value) tax, i.e. it is levied as a percentage of the selling price of the commodity. Excise duty is a specific (or unit) tax which is levied per unit of the commodity, irrespective of its price; for example, the same excise duty is levied per litre of wine irrespective of whether it is ordinary table wine or the finest vintage.

VAT is levied on most goods, with only a few essentials being exempt from it. Excise duty is levied mainly on alcohol, tobacco and petrol. VAT is levied after excise duty and consequently the purchaser may end up paying a tax on a tax. Thus products such as petrol have both a specific and an *ad valorem* tax on them.

The effect of a tax

If we wish to demonstrate the effect of a tax upon the demand and supply situation, this is done by moving the supply curve vertically upwards by the amount of the tax. The tax may be regarded as a cost of production. The producer has to pay rent and wages and now must also pay the tax to the government. The effect of indirect taxes is shown in Figure 6.9.

In diagram (a) £1 specific tax has raised the supply curve from S to S_1. You can see that the new supply curve is £1 above the old curve at every point. In diagram (b) the effect of a 50 per cent *ad valorem* tax is shown and you can see that the new supply curve diverges from the old one as the tax increases with price.

The incidence of a tax

If we use the phrase 'the *incidence* of taxation' this means who the tax falls upon. The *formal* (or legal) incidence of a tax is upon the person who is legally responsible for paying it. In the case of alcohol, for example, this is the producer or importer. It is possible, however, that some or all of the tax may be passed on to the consumer, in

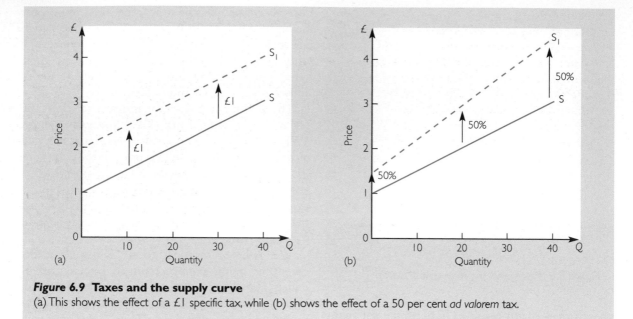

Figure 6.9 Taxes and the supply curve

(a) This shows the effect of a £1 specific tax, while (b) shows the effect of a 50 per cent *ad valorem* tax.

which case the incidence is said to be shifted so that the actual incidence (or **burden**) of the tax is wholly or partly upon the consumer.

It is often thought by the consumer that if the government places a tax upon a commodity the price of that commodity will immediately rise by the amount of the tax. This is usually not so. Consider what might happen if a tax of £1 per bottle were placed on wine. If the price were to be put up by £1 consumers would immediately begin to look for substitutes such as beer, spirits or soft drinks. The wine merchants, being worried about their sales, might well reduce their prices. In other words they have absorbed part of the tax. Thus the incidence has been distributed between the producers and consumers of wine.

This situation is analysed in Figure 6.10. Here you can see that the original price of a bottle of wine was £2.50 and that 25 000 bottles were sold. The imposition of a £1 tax might be expected to raise the price to £3.50. This you can see is not so; the new equilibrium price is £3.10 and the quantity sold is 21 000 bottles. The price to the consumer has thus risen by 60p. The price the producer receives is now £3.10 but £1 of this must be given to the government, so the producer is effectively receiving only £2.10, i.e. 40p less than previously. Thus the incidence of the tax is 60 per cent to the consumer and 40 per cent to

the producer. In Figure 6.10, BC is paid by the consumer and CD by the producer. This conclusion is dependent on there being a competitive market in wine. If the wine merchants have any

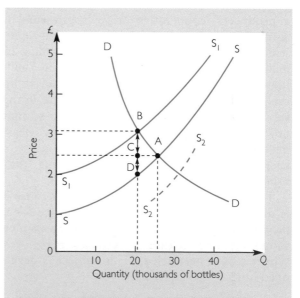

Figure 6.10 The effect of a £1 specific tax

The original equilibrium is at A, with price £2.50 per bottle and 25 000 bottles sold. After the imposition of a £1 tax the new equilibrium price is £3.10 and the quantity sold is 21 000 bottles. S_2 shows the effect of £1 per unit subsidy.

degree of market power, they may be able to pass on more of the tax to the consumer.

The extent to which the tax is passed on to the consumer will be determined by the elasticity of demand and supply – the more inelastic the demand the greater will be the incidence upon the consumer. Consider what would happen in Figure 6.10 if the demand curve were vertical. The price would rise to £3.50 and all the tax would be passed on to the consumer. The more elastic is the demand the less the producer will be able to pass on the tax.

STUDENT ACTIVITY 6.5

(a) Can you determine the amount of revenue the government will receive from wine sales in Figure 6.10?

(b) Would you expect the incidence of a tax on each of the following products to be more on the producer or more on the consumer?
  (i) petrol
  (ii) carrots
  (iii) chocolate

Subsidies

The government sometimes subsidises a product by giving an amount of money to the producers for each unit they sell. This was the case with many agricultural products in the UK before its entry into the EU. The benefit of the subsidy will be split between the producer and the consumer. The division will, once again, depend upon the elasticity of demand. In Figure 6.10 S_2 shows the effect of a £1 per unit subsidy. In this case the price falls to approximately £2.10 so that the consumer is receiving 40p of the subsidy and the producer 60p. Although subsidies may be regarded as supporting an inefficient industry they do not result in disequilibrium (see also Chapter 11).

Government tax revenues

If the government is trying to raise more revenue it will increase taxes on those products that have inelastic demands. If it were to increase the tax on those products with elastic demands the money it collected would actually decline. Figure 6.11 illustrates this in a simplified form by omitting the

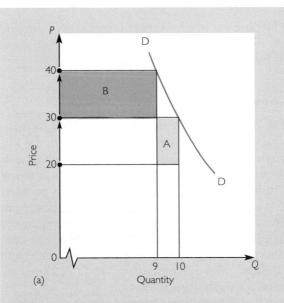
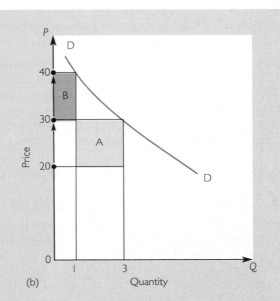

Figure 6.11 Revenue from an indirect tax
(a) Inelastic demand. (b) Elastic demand. B is the revenue gained by raising the tax and A the revenue lost. Only if B is greater than A will increasing the tax be worth while.

supply curves. In diagram (a) you can see that if the tax is increased from £10 a unit to £20 a unit, tax revenue increases from £100 to £180, but in (b) the same increase in the tax causes revenue to fall from £30 to £20.

It would follow, therefore, that if a government wanted to increase its tax revenue from those products with elastic demands it would do best to lower the tax. This point was well illustrated when the nineteenth-century UK prime minister Robert Peel reduced the import duties on many commodities and thereby considerably increased the revenues of the exchequer.

Problems with demand and supply analysis

In the last two sections of the chapter we will examine some of the shortcomings of demand and supply analysis and suggest some ways in which these might be remedied. It is best to think of supply and demand analysis as a model of how the market works. Like all models, it makes certain assumptions about the nature of reality, and when those assumptions do not apply, the model may not predict accurately. The reader should be aware of situations where the analysis is not appropriate in order to avoid making mistakes. The following situations may be identified:

(a) Situations where there is significant *economic power*, either on the part of buyers or sellers, are not best analysed using supply and demand analysis. Alternative models have been developed for these situations. They will be introduced in Chapter 8 and further elaborated in Section V.

(b) Where there is *speculative* demand, the normal laws of demand do not apply, as has already been noted in Chapter 4 (page 57). Ways of analysing this situation are found below, and further explored in Chapter 11 in the section on the housing market.

(c) Where there is a considerable *time lag* there may be instability in the market. We have already pointed out earlier in the chapter how prices may take some time to reach their eventual equilibrium point. Below we discuss situations in which a time lag results in the market moving further away from equilibrium. This is of relevance to the discussion of the agricultural industry in Chapter 11.

(d) Where there are constant changes in the conditions of supply and demand, a market may never be in equilibrium. It may move towards equilibrium but be pushed in another direction by a new change in conditions before it gets there. Such a market can be thought of as being permanently in *disequilibrium*. Some financial markets go through phases like this.

(e) Prices may appear to reflect costs, but if there are substantial *social costs*, which are disregarded by the market place, the market may allocate private resources adequately but leave society with problems like pollution. The problem of social costs is dealt with in Chapters 9–13, and in more detail in Chapter 27.

(f) Much of demand and supply analysis assumes that consumers have a *perfect knowledge* of the market. In practice this is not so and *ignorance* constitutes a major criticism of the effectiveness of the market mechanism. As with the last point, the market will arrive at an equilibrium price, but this need not be interpreted as reflecting consumer preferences.

The problem of time lags and speculative demand are now dealt with in more detail, leaving some of the other problems for later chapters.

Comparative statics

The demand and supply analysis which we have developed so far has been concerned with the formation of an equilibrium price. Any change in the market condition has then moved us to a new equilibrium. For example, the analysis predicts that an increase in supply will lead to a new equilibrium at a lower price with a greater quantity supplied (see Figure 6.2(c). We arrive at this conclusion by comparing one static equilibrium with another. This method of analysis is therefore termed *comparative statics*.

It has already been pointed out in this chapter that a time element may enter into the formation of prices. This being the case, we need a theory that will explain the movement of prices with respect to time. Such a study is termed *dynamic analysis*. We may indeed find when we use dynamic analysis that a market may never be in a state of equilibrium. This does not mean, however, that we shall abandon comparative static analysis. Comparative statics is a useful way to explain changes in a market and is the basis of our understanding of the forces involved, i.e. its predictions are often correct.

Ceteris paribus – again

It has been emphasised throughout this section of the book that we can only reach any firm conclusions if we hold all other things constant and just consider the influence of one factor at a time. A moment's reflection will tell us, however, that in the real world all other things are not constant; in reality the demand for a particular product will be the result of the influence of price, incomes, tastes, the price of other goods and dozens of other factors all acting upon prices simultaneously. If we were to be limited to our comparative static analysis we should perhaps end up with a situation like Figure 6.4, with both demand and supply curves shifting upwards and downwards simultaneously. Thus if we wish to enter the real world of economic measurement and forecasting we must have a method of analysis which allows us to combine all these factors together but nevertheless allows us to identify the separate influence of each factor.

The cobweb theorem

We may develop a simple dynamic theory of market price by considering the *cobweb theorem*. Let us return to the problem depicted in Figure 6.5 where we considered the effect of time lags. We would normally say that quantity supplied is determined by the current price. A mathematical way of expressing this idea (which may not help all readers) is that supply is a *function* of price, which we could write as:

$$S = f(P_t)$$

where t is the time period we are considering. However, it has been pointed out that for some products, especially agricultural ones, it is the price in the previous period that determines the supply. For example, farmers will look at this year's price in determining how much barley to plant for next year. Thus we can write:

$$S_t = f(P_{t-1})$$

Or putting it verbally, the supply in the period we are considering (S_t) is determined by the price in the previous period (P_{t-1}).

Let us consider the effect this might have upon the market situation. Examine Figure 6.12, where P and Q represent the equilibrium situation for the market for barley. Suppose in year 1 that for some reason the crop is less than intended, so that supply is Q_1(A). This will mean that the price is P_1. You can see that at this price farmers would wish to supply Q_2(B) and are therefore encouraged to plant this much for year 2. You can see, however, that an output of Q_2 can be sold only for a price of P_2 and so the price falls to this level (C). The low price discourages farmers from planting barley and so they only produce

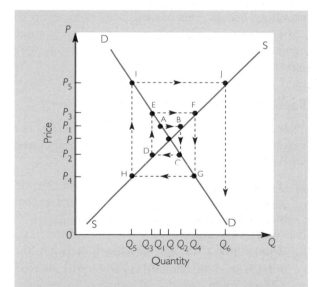

Figure 6.12 An unstable or diverging cobweb
The supply in one time period, e.g. Q_3, is determined by the price in the previous period, i.e. P_2. Thus:
$$S_t = f(P_{t-1})$$
For example:
$$Q_3 = f(P_2)$$

Q_3 in the following year and there is thus a deficiency of supply, which drives the price up to P_3. The high price of P_3 encourages farmers to overproduce, and so on. You can see from the graph how the cobweb theorem gets its name.

Thus when we introduce a time lag into the situation we may introduce *instability* into the system, or even permanent disequilibrium. Figure 6.12 illustrates a diverging or unstable cobweb. This is brought about because the slope of the supply curve is less than (flatter than) the slope of the demand curve. In Figure 6.13 you can see a converging or stable cobweb. In this situation any disequilibrium will reduce and, other things being equal, an equilibrium price will eventually be reached. This is brought about when the slope of the supply curve is greater than (steeper than) the slope of the demand curve.

These predictions may appear fanciful but were in fact developed from Professor Ezekiel's observations of the 'corn–hogs cycle' in the USA. In this, a low price of corn caused farmers to switch to hogs (pigs) so that corn became dear and hogs cheap. This caused farmers to revert to corn and so on. The inherent instability of some agricultural markets is one of the reasons why governments intervene to aid farmers.

Factors modifying the cobweb

There are a number of factors that modify the extent of oscillations in the market associated with the cobweb theorem:

(a) Producers learn from experience and thus do not vary their behaviour to the full extent predicted by the theory.

(b) We have examined only one-period time lags. Distributed time lags (discussed earlier in the chapter), on the other hand, will modify the cobweb.

(c) The cobweb depends upon actual supply equalling planned supply. *Unplanned variations* in supply can occur, particularly in the agricultural industry. These will further modify the cobweb, either diminishing or increasing its effect.

(d) Prices may be inflexible, in which case prices may change too slowly to bring about significant changes in supply.

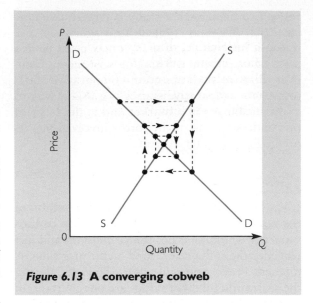

Figure 6.13 A converging cobweb

Having considered all these points, we may still conclude that some markets are inherently unstable.

Speculative demand

The predictions of supply and demand analysis also run into problems in the case of speculative demand. Speculative demand is likely to occur whenever a product is not just a commodity, wanted for its own sake, but also an asset capable of making capital gains or losses for its owner. Good examples can be found in the housing market, foreign currency, and the stock exchange. In times of normal trading, the commodity aspect of these products dominates, with housing providing shelter, foreign exchange providing the means to buy foreign goods, or go on holiday, and shares providing an annual income. If the price of these commodities rises, less will be purchased. If these markets move into a speculative phase however, the normal logic of the market place is overturned. If people believe that the value of a house, a foreign currency or a share is about to rise, then demand will increase as people try to make a capital gain. Likewise, if prices fall there will be a scramble to sell, as people try to avoid making a capital loss. How far will this upward or downward spiral of prices continue until sanity returns to the market place? It is difficult for the economist to tell, as it all depends on the beliefs of the participants in the market. As long as they think that the rise in prices is sustainable, then prices will continue to rise as more capital gains are possible. As long as they think prices are continuing to fall, it will make sense not to buy, as they will be able to buy more cheaply in the future.

The system is automatic

Much is often made of the fact that supply decisions seem to happen automatically and that adjustments to changing demand conditions happen without central coordinating bodies. We should be careful not to equate 'automatic' with 'good'. Some rivers flood automatically every year but few people suggest that we do nothing about this; in a similar way it may sometimes be necessary to regulate the 'automatic' price mechanism. It can be said that interferences with the price mechanism often lead to undesirable side effects, but the social or political reasons for intervening in markets may outweigh the economic disadvantages. These questions are dealt with further in Chapters 9–13

Summary

1 Increases or decreases in demand or supply will move the DD and SS curves rightwards or leftwards respectively. If we keep to the rule of *ceteris paribus* there are then only four basic changes which occur in the equilibrium.
2 Time may affect the ability of supply to respond to changes in demand.
3 Any government interference with equilibrium prices is likely to have undesirable side effects which often lead to the opposite result from that desired by the government.
4 The incidence of an indirect tax will be determined by the elasticity of demand and supply for the product.
5 The shortcomings of demand and supply analysis place limitations upon its usefulness.
6 The cobweb theorem predicts constant disequilibrium for some markets.

? QUESTIONS

1 The following information concerns the demand and supply of oranges.

Price (£/box)	Quantity demanded (boxes/week)	Quantity supplied (boxes/week)
8	500	1700
7	800	1200
6	1100	700
5	1400	200
4	1700	0

(a) Determine the equilibrium price and quantity.
(b) As part of the CAP support system orange growers are guaranteed a price of £7 per box. What are the likely consequences of this?
(c) Suppose that in the original situation demand were to increase by 50 per cent at every price. What would be the equilibrium price now?

2 'A decrease in demand leads to a decrease in price.' 'A decrease in price leads to a rise in the quantity demanded.' Reconcile these statements.

3 In July 1997 the price of commodity X was £700 and 60 units were demanded. In July 1998 the price of commodity X was £800 and 80 units were demanded. Show that these observations are consistent with demand and supply analysis.

4 The following information is known about the elasticities of demand of three products X, Y and Z. For X, $E_D = 2$; for Y, $E_D = 1$; and for Z, $E_D = 0.75$. Each bears a sales tax of 15 per cent. Last year the tax revenues were as follows: product X = £200 million; product Y = £100 million; and product Z = £300 million. This year the government wishes to raise its total revenue from the sales tax on these products to £700 million. What advice would you give the government?

5 Why is the price of some agricultural products inherently unstable?

6 Contrast the incidence of a commodity tax imposed in the market for peaches with that of a similar tax in the market for potatoes.

7 Product K has linear demand and supply curves such that $DD = Y = 10 - X$ and $SS = Y = 1 + 2X$.

Further suppose that $S_t = f(P_{t-1})$. If the quantity produced in period 2 were to be $O_S = 1$, what would be the price and quantity supplied of product K in period 3?

Data response A
FOOTBALL PRICING

Study the following passage and then answer the questions below.

The concern over safety at football matches has resulted in all-seater stadia in the Premier League. The effect of this change has been to substantially reduce the number of fans who can get into the stadium, as people take up more space sitting down than they do standing up.

The more civilised atmosphere that results from all-seater stadia, together with the major efforts of the police and clubs to stamp out football hooliganism, has resulted in a widening of the appeal of the game. More 'middle class' fans are spending Saturday afternoon at the football ground, and the proportion of women fans has risen to 25 per cent at some clubs. This civilisation of the game has reached its ultimate stage with the development of corporate hospitality, with major companies reserving some of the best seats to entertain their clients.

The top clubs have taken advantage of this situation to raise their prices. Increasingly, they are now public limited companies floated on the stock exchange with a responsibility to their shareholders to provide a good return on their investment. Even with the higher prices, the clubs are able to regularly fill their stadiums.

Inevitably these changes have brought some resentment from traditional fans, often from a more working class culture, with incomes to match. One wonders whether the high prices will deter poorer parents from taking their children to see their teams on a regular basis. Who knows what effect this might have on the inspiration of the next generation? We may see the cost of such developments in the quality of our footballers in decades to come.

1 Depict the changes that have taken place in terms of a supply and demand diagram.
2 What intervention in the market place would be necessary to help younger, poorer fans see their teams?
3 Is it in the interest of the clubs themselves to introduce such policies or does the government need to take action?
4 Should football clubs operate as profit-maximising companies responsive to their shareholders, or local institutions responsive to their fans? Is there necessarily any conflict between these two alternatives?

Data response B
ROUBLE DEVALUED BY SOVIET UNION

Read the following article by Jonathan Steele which appeared in *The Guardian* on 26 October 1989. The Russian economy has continued to have difficulties with stabilising its economy since this time, but this is a good example from recent history of observing an economy shifting from a socialist economy with managed prices over to a market economy.

Answer the following questions:

1 With the aid of demand and supply diagrams explain the existence of a black market in foreign currency in the Soviet Union prior to the changes mentioned in the article.
2 Assume that the exchange rate before the devaluation was 60 kopeks to the dollar and also assume that the new rate of 6 roubles 26 kopeks is the correct exchange rate. Demonstrate the proposed changes with the aid of a diagram.
3 What is the effect of the change in the value of the rouble for:
   (a) the standard of living in the former USSR, and
   (b) value for money for tourists visiting the area?

Rouble devalued by Soviet Union

The Soviet Union has dropped the rouble to one-tenth of its previous value against the dollar in some transactions, in a sweeping attempt to defeat the flourishing black market.

The massive devaluation, which comes into effect on 1 November is a blow to Soviet citizens who need hard currency to go abroad.

It is not yet clear how it will benefit tourists coming in or the resident foreign community.

A terse four-paragraph notice from the official news-agency, Tass, said that the USSR State Bank had taken the decision 'to serve Soviet and foreign citizens'. But the notice made no further reference to visiting or resident foreigners.

Soviet citizens going abroad will have to pay 6 roubles 28 kopeks for a dollar, instead of the 60 to 65 kopeks that they pay at the moment.

They used to be allowed to get up to $200 at the favourably high rate of the rouble.

With so many Soviet citizens travelling abroad since President Gorbachev started his reform programme, there has been a serious drain on the country's hard currency reserves.

The new rate makes foreign travel more of a luxury and will soak up more of the population's spare cash.

For foreigners holding hard currency, the official rate was absurd, as a brief commentary in the government newspaper *Izvestia*, accepted last night.

'If a businessman could unofficially get 10 000 roubles for $1000 instead of 600 roubles at the official rate, the temptation to change on the black market was too high,' the newspaper said.

The devaluation was a 'more than decisive measure' against the black market, it added.

Senior officials at the State Bank were unavailable for comment last night, but it was assumed that the new exchange rate would work for cash transactions for foreigners as well as for Soviet citizens.

It was not clear whether it would change the system whereby foreigners have to make certain purchases in roubles, exchanged at the present high rate, such as hotel rooms and rents. Nor is it clear how it affects foreign trade. Tass said that two rates for the rouble would apply in future.

'The rouble's special rate will be published monthly, along with the official rate of the USSR State Bank, in the newspaper *Izvestia*, before the two rates come into force,' Tass said.

The devaluation is a partial step towards the full convertibility of the rouble which President Gorbachev has put forward as his eventual goal.

It is the first official admission that the present exchange rate was unrealistic.

Source: *The Guardian*, 26 October 1989

7 The business organisation, costs and profits

Learning outcomes

At the end of this chapter you will be able to:
- Distinguish between the main types of business organisation.
- Distinguish between the terms the short run and the long run.
- Understand the concepts of total costs, fixed costs and variable costs.
- Explain the shut-down conditions for a firm in the short run and in the long run.
- Understand the concepts of average costs and marginal costs and appreciate the relationship between them.
- Appreciate the distinctions between both normal and abnormal profits and implicit and explicit costs.

Types of business organisation

There are many different types of business organisation, all of which trade goods and services in exchange for money. In this chapter we shall deal with those business organisations that operate in the *private sector* and which, we shall assume, exist mainly with the intention of *maximising profits*. Thus, public corporations, like the Post Office, that operate in the *public sector* and which do not exist primarily to maximise their profits are temporarily excluded from the analysis (see Chapter 24).

Plants, firms and industries

The *plant* (or *establishment*) is the unit of production in industry: it can be a factory, a shop, a farm, a hotel or any economic unit that carries on its business at one geographic location.

The firm is the unit of ownership and control.

A firm may consist of just one plant, in which case it is referred to as *single plant*. However, many large firms are likely to comprise a number of plants: they are *multiplant*. We can make the distinction between plants and firms clearer by taking an example: ICI is a firm but it has over 40 sites in the UK.

An industry is all the firms concerned with a particular line of production.

The government's (1992) Standard Industrial Classification (SIC (92)) divides industries into 17 sections (some of which are split into subsections) and then into 60 industrial divisions (which are further broken down into groups and classes). The main sections are shown below:

A   Agriculture, Hunting and Forestry
B   Fishing
C   Mining and Quarrying
D   Manufacturing
E   Electricity, Gas and Water Supply
F   Construction
G   Wholesale and Retail Trade; Repair of Motor Vehicles, Motorcycles and Personal and Household Goods
H   Hotels and Restaurants
I   Transport, Storage and Communication
J   Financial Intermediation
K   Real Estate, Renting and Business Activity
L   Public Administration and Defence; Compulsory Social Security
M   Education
N   Health and Social Work
O   Other Community, Social and Personal Service Activities

P   Private Households
Q   Extra-Territorial Organisations and Bodies

Thus, section D is manufacturing, subsection DB denotes the manufacture of textiles and textile products and division 17 is the manufacturing of textiles alone.

The SIC groupings are made according to the production processes used rather than the substitutability of their products for consumers. This characteristic can be seen at the broadest level of aggregation, sections. Hotels and rented accommodation can be viewed as substitutes in terms of the demand created by local authority tenancies or by lengthy business trips. However, hotels are listed in section H and rented accommodation in section K of SIC(92). This is a problem when instead of looking at the industry share of a firm the economist wishes to focus on its market share.

An industry is defined in terms of close substitutability in production, whereas a market is defined in terms of close substitutability of consumption.

Substitutability in consumption is measured by cross elasticity of demand (see Chapter 5): the higher the (positive) value of cross price elasticity the greater the degree of substitutability. The problem for the economist is that economic theory does not tell us the value of the elasticity at which we can assume that products are in separate markets. Moreover, data on cross elasticities are not usually available. Industries are also difficult to define rigorously as one firm may operate in more than one industry. However, despite these definitional problems and the differences between the two terms, markets and industries, they are often used interchangeably.

STUDENT ACTIVITY 7.1

Can you think of any other examples of products that are considered substitutes by consumers, yet may be classified as belonging to different industries? Refer to SIC(92) if possible.

Classification of firms

There are many ways in which we might classify firms: for example, we could do it by size. However,

the most important distinction as far as the economist is concerned is the type of competition under which a firm operates; this is discussed in the next chapter and in Section V. Before turning to this aspect, though, we must first look at the *legal forms of business*. As a prelude to this we will look at the development of the modern business organisation.

The development of the business organisation

As society evolved from feudalism to *laissez-faire* and then to capitalism, so the forms of business organisations evolved. The earliest forms were the sole trader and the partnership. The joint stock company did not become common until the nineteenth century, although its origins can be found much earlier in the *commercial revolution* of the sixteenth and seventeenth centuries. During this period the capitalist system of production became well established, i.e. a system where there was a separation of functions between the capital-providing employer on the one hand and the wage-earning worker on the other.

The joint stock form of organisation developed not from industry but from foreign trade. In order to raise the necessary capital and spread the risk of early trading ventures a company form of organisation was adopted. The *joint stock company*, which had a continuous existence and was run by a board of directors and owned by its shareholders, became much more popular. The most important of these early companies was the East India Company. This was founded in 1600 and became a joint stock company in 1660.

Limited liability (see page 102) was first introduced in 1662 but it was granted to only three companies. Dealings in shares took place from the beginning but the first stock exchange was not established until 1778. By this time there was a flourishing capital and insurance market centred on a number of coffee houses in the city of London. The most famous of these was Lloyd's. A great speculative boom known as the South Sea Bubble ruined many people and caused the passing of the Bubble Act 1720. This made it illegal to form a company without a Royal Charter and effectively hindered the development of companies for many years.

The importance of the joint stock company and the need to raise large capital sums received a massive boost during the *industrial revolution* that occupied most of the second half of the eigtheenth and the first half of the ninteenth centuries. The demand for British manufacturing goods in overseas markets and a spate of technical innovations, especially the creation of steam power, produced the necessary conditions for the rapid development of large-scale manufacturing industry. The building of canals (from 1761 onwards) required vast amounts of capital. In the nineteenth century the building of railways involved hundreds of joint stock companies and by 1848 their quoted share capital was over £200 million. The development of joint stock banking in the UK dates from 1826.

Throughout the nineteenth century the family business remained the dominant form of organisation in industry. It is interesting to note that at this time, when industry and commerce were finding it necessary to adopt the joint stock form of organisation, the government was also finding it impossible *not* to interfere in the economy; just as the sophistication of industry and commerce needed regulation through company legislation, so the increasingly complex urban world demanded government intervention to ensure adequate drainage, street lighting, education, etc.

Much of the organisation of institutions which evolved at this time, such as hospitals and schools, was modelled on factories. These forms have survived the *scientific revolution* of the twentieth century. We are now in the midst of what may turn out to be great changes in our economy which is being brought about by the *microprocessor revolution* and now also through the use of the *new technologies* involved in the use of the Internet and the development of e-commerce. If we are tempted to cling to the forms of organisation of the past it should be recalled that they originated in the need to exploit large steam engines as a source of power.

Legal forms of firms

The sole trader

A sole trader is a business organisation where one person is in business on their own, providing the capital, taking the profit and standing the losses themselves.

Typical areas of commercial activity for the sole trader are retailing and building, i.e. activities which are not usually capital intensive. Sole traders are often wrongly termed 'one-man businesses'. Sole traders are indeed *owned* by one person but the business may *employ* many people.

Limits are placed on the growth of a sole trader's activities by two main constraints. First, finance: economic growth depends largely on the availability of capital to invest in the business, and sole traders are limited to what can be provided from their own resources or raised from banks, etc. Second, organisation: one person has only limited ability to exercise effective control over and take responsibility for an organisation. As a business grows, a larger and more complicated business organisation will generally replace the sole trader.

The sole trader is in a potentially vulnerable financial position. The profits may all accrue to one person but so do the losses, and many sole traders are made bankrupt each year.

Limited capital resources often make the sole trader particularly vulnerable, not only to sustained competition from large business units but also to bad capital investments, e.g. a grocer opening a delicatessen in an area which turns out to prefer more mundane food or the introduction of a restaurant in an area where a number of others already exist.

It can be argued, however, that a sole trader is able to weather a short reduction in consumer spending far better than a large business unit. The sole trader can adapt quickly to the level of demand and, if necessary, can make personal economies until business improves.

Sole traders remain the most common business unit in the UK and they are the backbone of the business structure on which the country depends, although, in terms of capital and labour resources employed, sole traders are of limited importance. None the less, in the 1980s and 1990s there was a substantial increase in the number of sole traders partly as a result of government encouragement of the 'enterprise culture'. During this time the UK has had the fastest rate of growth of self-employment (the self-employed usually operate as sole traders) of any major industrial country. However, there was also a record number of bankruptcies. Some of the reasons for the failure of sole traders are listed below:

(a) Lack of capital to invest in new premises, equipment and materials.
(b) Lack of expertise in every aspect of the business resulting in inefficiency, e.g. the sole traders may be good at selling but bad at administration.
(c) Lack of advice and guidance about the operations of the business – consultancy is usually too expensive to be considered.
(d) Competition from chain stores and other larger business units which are able to benefit from various economies of scale.
(e) Increased overheads resulting from bureaucratic functions imposed by law, e.g. VAT collection, which sole traders are often disinclined and ill-equipped to perform (this is less quantifiable as a reason but still important).
(f) Interest rates that were extremely high in the late 1980s and early 1990s. Since many businesses relied heavily on borrowed money this, therefore, put up their costs substantially. This occurred at a time when sales were considerably down because of recession in the economy.

Yet sole traders survive and even flourish. As a business organisation they offer attractive advantages when compared with others. The initial capital investment may be very small and the legal formalities involved are minimal. In sharp contrast to joint stock companies, they offer financial secrecy and the 'personal touch' (a subjective but often important factor). Sole traders are also able to alter their activities to adapt to the market without legal formality or major organisational problems.

Excluding the legal point just mentioned all these factors could apply equally to any *small business* whatever its legal form. The reasons for the continued existence of small business are discussed at the end of Chapter 19.

Partnerships

The Partnership Act 1890 defines a partnership as 'the relation which subsists between persons carrying on a business in common with a view of profit'.

Many partnerships are very formal organisations, such as a large firm of solicitors or accountants,

but two people running a stall in a local Sunday market would almost certainly be in partnership with each other and subject to the same legal rules as a firm of city solicitors with an annual turnover that may run into many millions of pounds.

Two or more persons in partnership can combine their resources and, in theory, form an economically more efficient business unit, producing a better return on the capital invested. In most cases each partner has unlimited liability and is responsible for any debts of the business without limit. A rare form of this type of enterprise is the limited partnership in which sleeping partners, who take no part in the management of the business, have limited liability.

The maximum number of members possible in most partnerships is fixed by law at 20. The professional partnerships that are allowed to exceed this number – solicitors, accountants and members of a recognised stock exchange – are often organisations of some size, with considerable capital resources and offering economies of scale and the benefits of specialisation. It is unusual, however, to find a trading partnership consisting of more than five or six partners, for corporate status as a company with limited liability is usually more attractive.

Quite apart from the rules of professional bodies, which usually prohibit their members from forming a company, a partnership is a business organisation generally more suited to professional people in business together than to manufacturers or traders. In the former, the risk of financial failure is less of a disadvantage. For all but the small trading ventures, or where there are particular reasons for trading as a partnership, registration as a company with limited liability is usually preferred.

The joint stock company

A joint stock company may be described as an organisation consisting of persons who contribute money to a common stock, which is employed in some trade or business, and who share the profit or loss arising. This common stock is the capital of the company and the persons who contribute to it are its members. The proportion of capital to which each member is entitled is their share.

The need for more capital explains both the development of partnerships and, later, the development of joint stock companies. As soon as it became possible to do so, many partnerships chose to become registered joint stock companies with limited liability. Today, in terms of capital and labour resources employed, the joint stock company is the dominant form of business organisation.

The principle of limited liability is extremely important to a company. Limited liability means that an investor's liability to debt is limited to the extent of their shareholding.

Thus, for example, if you own a hundred £1 shares in a company, in the event of it becoming insolvent, then the most you can lose is the £100 originally invested. This encourages investment because it limits the risk investors take to the amount they have actually invested. It is possible for even very large companies to go bankrupt, as we saw with the failure of Polly Peck in 1990. At the time Polly Peck was in the *Financial Times* top one hundred companies; another example was the failure of the airline carrier PanAm in the USA in 1992. Without limited liability, it is likely that none but the safest business venture would ever attract large-scale investment. In particular, the institutional investors, such as life assurance companies and pension funds, would not hazard their vast funds in any speculative venture and would invest only in the gilt-edged market (government securities).

Public and private companies

To the outsider the most obvious distinction between *public and private limited companies* is that a public limited company has the letters PLC after its name as, for example, Marks and Spencer plc, while private limited companies have the abbreviation Ltd after their name. A public limited company may own subsidiaries which are private limited companies. When one company owns and controls others it is often referred to as a *holding company*.

Legally speaking, a public company is a company limited by shares (or guarantee) which has been registered as a public company with the Registrar of Companies. It has two or more members and can invite the general public to subscribe for its shares or debentures. A private company is any company which does not satisfy the requirements for a public company. In common with a public company it has two or more members.

Thus the essential distinction between a public and a private company is that the former may offer its shares or debentures to the public while the latter cannot. It is a criminal offence to invite the general public to subscribe for shares or debentures in a private company.

The private company at present is in some respects a transitional step between the partnership and the public company; typically it is a family business. In common with a public limited company, it possesses the advantage of limited liability, but in common with a partnership it has the disadvantage of only being able to call upon the capital resources of its members (supplemented by possible loans from its bank). Since public companies can offer their shares to the public – the shares of many (but certainly not all) public companies are quoted on the stock exchange – they are able to raise considerable sums of money to finance large-scale operations.

A private company used to be limited to a membership of 50, was unable to invite the public to subscribe for its shares and had by its articles to restrict the right to transfer its shares, e.g. only to existing shareholders. Some of these restrictions on membership and transfer of shares no longer exist. This means that private companies have the prospect of growth and development previously open only to public companies. Non-public share offers, e.g. through business contacts or bankers, are now possible. As a result, some private companies, like Amstrad and Virgin, can become extremely large organisations, although in terms of capital public companies usually dwarf private companies; public companies have also been responsible for the immense growth in investment this century. The typical public company can carry on such diverse activities as manufacture cars, give overdrafts or sell insurance – in other words, there is no such thing as a 'typical' public company.

● *Common misunderstanding*

A public limited company is not part of the public sector, nor is it owned by the public at large. It operates in the private sector and is owned by those people who have purchased its shares, the shareholders.

Consumer and worker cooperatives

A consumer cooperative is a registered retail business that is owned essentially by the people who shop there and who wish to make a minimum deposit on a share in the organisation.

Each shareholder has a vote at the annual meeting, where a committee to run the business is elected. Profits (having allowed for taxes and investments) used to be distributed to members in proportion to the value of their purchases, but this policy has now mainly been superseded by the issue of trading stamps that can then be used in exchange for goods in the retail outlets.

Consumer cooperatives originated in the UK in the mid-nineteenth century, but their numbers have fallen quite dramatically in the last 20 to 30 years as people increasingly prefer to shop in the large stores operated by the main supermarket chains.

A worker cooperative is a registered form of business that is owned and controlled by some or all of its employees, who share any profits.

Worker cooperatives originated over a hundred years ago and then declined in popularity. Recently their numbers have revived as workers have taken over businesses threatened with closure, although these new organisations have met with a mixed degree of success.

STUDENT ACTIVITY 7.2

Give examples of the different legal forms of business enterprise in your area. State which you think is the most common type of organisation and which has the most local impact.

Costs of production

In Chapter 4 we gave considerable attention to the theory of demand. We also need to turn our attention to the other side of the market, that is to say, to supply. This part of economics is sometimes called the *theory of the firm* since the firm is the unit of supply; an important element within the theory of the firm and an important consideration for all forms of business organisation is the subject of their costs of production.

We have noted the significance of demand and revenue for a firm; costs of production represent the other side of the profit equation. We shall examine costs fairly briefly here, before returning to the topic in more detail in Chapter 20.

It will be seen in the next chapter that firms can operate under different types of competition, but no matter what market conditions a firm operates under the basic elements of its cost structures will be similar. Thus the cost structures which we investigate in this chapter can apply to all types of competition, from perfect competition to monopoly.

It is convenient to split up the costs of the business organisation in various ways because it allows us to understand its behaviour more fully. For present purposes we shall concentrate on the division of total costs into its fixed and variable components, before distinguishing between average costs and marginal costs. In Chapter 20 we shall extend the analysis by examining the reasons for the shape of particular cost curves in the short run and the long run. The firm itself will analyse its own cost structures in order to try to improve its performance.

Total costs (TC)

Total costs (TC) are the costs of all the resources necessary to produce any particular level of output.

Total costs *always rise with output*. This is because obtaining more output must always require more input. Thus, no matter what the scale of production, obtaining another unit of output must involve, say, the input of some raw materials or labour, no matter how small the amount, so that a greater output must always involve a greater total cost.

We can obtain a better understanding of total costs by splitting them into their two main components: fixed costs and variable costs.

Fixed costs (FC)

Fixed costs (FC) are those costs which do not alter with output in the short run.

Fixed costs are derived from fixed factors of production. (For the definitions of the short run and the long run see Chapter 3.)

Fixed costs usually comprise such things as hiring plant and equipment, the interest on borrowed capital, insurance costs, property taxes, most managerial and administrative expenses, depreciation costs (that depend on the ageing of any fixed assets) and an advertising campaign that runs for a set period. These costs will exist (and remain constant) whether the business is producing as much as possible or nothing at all. If a business wishes to expand beyond the capacity of its present fixed assets, then it must build or acquire new premises, capital, equipment, etc. The period of time necessary for it to do this is said to be the *long-run* period.

Variable costs (VC)

As a firm produces more output, so it needs more labour, raw materials, power, etc. The cost of these factors which *vary with output* is termed variable costs. Examples include most wage costs, raw material expenses, heating and lighting, depreciation costs (that are associated with the use of the capital equipment) and sales commissions.

Variable costs (VC) are those which vary with output. Variable costs are zero when output is zero and rise directly with output.

Thus, total cost comprises *fixed costs* and *variable costs*. This we can state as:

$$TC = FC + VC$$

This is illustrated in Table 7.1, where you can see that whatever the level of output, fixed costs remain constant at £116 per week. If there is no output there is no variable cost, but as output increases, so do variable costs.

Table 7.1 Total costs, fixed costs and variable costs

Output units per week, Q	Total costs, TC (£)	Fixed costs, FC (£)	Variable costs, VC (£)
0	116	116	0
1	140	116	24
2	160	116	44
3			60
4	200	116	
5	240	116	124
6	296	116	180
7			252
8	456	116	

The figures in Table 7.1 are illustrated in Figure 7.1. Here you can see that fixed costs are constant whatever the level of output in the short run. Variable costs are zero when output is zero and rise with output. The *TC* curve is obtained by aggregating the *FC* and *VC* curves.

Why does the *VC* curve (and thus the *TC* curve) begin to rise more rapidly at higher levels of output? The reason for this is that after a certain output, the business has passed its most efficient use of its fixed assets (buildings etc.) and *diminishing returns* begin to set in.

Figure 7.2 illustrates the effect of a change in fixed cost in the long run. As plant size is expanded, this causes a shift from one level of total cost to another. Thus:

In the long run all costs are variable.

Digression 1: the short run and the long run

We have already defined the short run and long run in Chapter 3, but it is useful here to restate the definitions in terms of the costs of the firm.

The short run may be defined as the period during which output may be varied within the limits of the

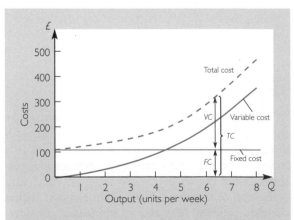

Figure 7.1 Total costs are fixed costs plus variable costs

present fixed assets. It is not possible for new firms to enter the industry or for existing firms to leave it.

The long run may be defined as the period in which all factors of production and hence all costs are variable and new firms may enter the industry or existing firms leave it.

The short run and the long run are *periods of supply* and refer to the ability of the business to vary its behaviour within the market. They are *not* chronological periods of time, e.g. we *cannot* say the short run period is, say, six months. How long the supply period is will depend upon the industry. In the motor vehicle industry, for example, the short run may extend for a very long time, e.g. five to ten years for the business to vary its fixed assets, i.e. build a new plant or re-equip an existing one, while in the retail trade it may be possible for a business to acquire new premises in a relatively short time, e.g. three to six months depending on the length of the lease.

● *Common misunderstanding*

The relationship between the terms the short run and the long run and precise periods of time needs to be made completely clear. While the short run may extend for quite a long period, the long run may actually only be a quite a brief amount of time. At any one time a firm is almost bound to have some fixed factors of production, such as plant and equipment; hence, it is almost permanently in a short-run position. At the time the firm makes the long-run decision to invest in a new plant it is

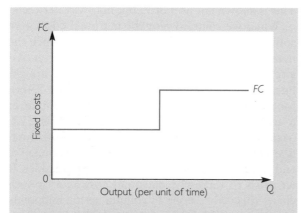

Figure 7.2 Fixed costs in the long run
The increase in fixed costs as the firm expands its capacity in the long run causes a 'kink' in the curve

in a short-run situation; it remains in that position until the new plant is up and running. Then it will be in a new short-run situation.

Digression 2: short-run shut-down conditions

Suppose that a business is running at a loss. Obviously in the long run it will go out of business, but what is the best policy in the short run? Will it make a smaller loss if it stays open so long as there is still some money coming in, or is it best to close down immediately?

The answer to this conundrum lies in the *variable costs*.

So long as the revenue the business is getting in is greater than the variable costs, it is worth its while staying open in the short run because it will make a smaller loss than it would do by closing immediately. However, if the revenue it is earning from selling its product is less than its variable costs, then it will make a smaller loss by closing immediately.

Ultimately, though, in the long run all costs must be covered if the business is to remain in the industry.

Let us consider the case of an apple grower. The cost of planting the trees and of renting the land could be regarded as fixed costs, since the farmer can shed them only by going out of business. Other costs, such as harvesting the crop and transporting it to the market, will vary with output and can therefore be described as variable costs. This being the case, it is apparent that if the price of apples were low the apple grower could not recover all the costs, but would still continue to sell apples in the short run if variable costs could be covered. In other words, if the money from the sale is greater than the costs of picking and selling the apples, it would appear that in the short run the grower will produce and ignore fixed costs.

Conversely, if the cost of harvesting, transport, etc., were greater than sales revenue, the apple grower would be better off closing down immediately and saving the variable costs.

● *Common misunderstanding*

A firm does not need to recover all its costs in the short run in order to stay in production. It is worthwhile remaining open as long as revenue covers its variable costs, since the fixed costs have to be paid anyway. Thus, a firm makes a smaller loss by staying open than by closing down.

...You can check your understanding of this point by trying Data response B at the end of this chapter.

Average costs (AC) and marginal costs (MC)

Average or unit cost (AC) is the total cost divided by the number of units of the commodity produced.

This can be expressed as:

$$AC = \frac{\text{Total cost}}{\text{Output}} = \frac{TC}{Q}$$

Using the same figures for output and total costs as in Table 7.1, average costs can be calculated. These are shown in Table 7.2 and the relevant curve is plotted in Figure 7.3. Since the average costs figures are total cost divided by output in each case, they are also commonly referred to as *average total costs* or *ATC*.

Table 7.2 Average costs and marginal costs

Output units per week, Q	Total costs, TC (£)	Average cost AC (£)	Marginal cost, MC (£)
0	116	∞	
			24
1	140	140.00	
			20
2	160	80.00	
			16
3	176	58.60	
			24
4	200	50.00	
			40
5	240	48.00	
			56
6	296	49.30	
			72
7	368	52.60	
			88
8	456	57.00	

You can see that the *AC* or *ATC* curve is 'U'-shaped. This, in fact, is always the case in the short run. This is due to the law of diminishing returns: the curve starts at infinity and initially it declines until the point of **optimum efficiency** or **optimum capacity** is reached (at an output of 5). Average costs then begin to rise as diminishing returns set in. As will be seen in Chapter 20 the *ATC* curve can also be viewed as the sum of the *AFC* and *AVC* curves; its shape, therefore, is also dictated by the shape of these curves.

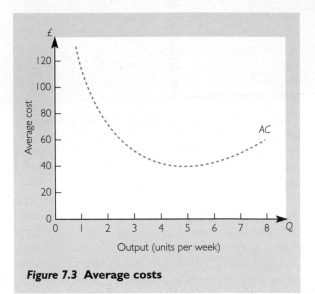

Figure 7.3 Average costs

Marginal cost (MC) may be defined as the cost of producing one more (or less) unit of a commodity.

Like all the other costs we have considered marginal cost may be calculated from the total cost schedule. We arrive at marginal cost by subtracting the total costs of adjacent outputs. We may illustrate this by using the same total cost figures we have used previously. In Table 7.2 you can see that it is the cost involved in moving from one level of output to the next. The figure is therefore plotted half-way between the two outputs. Hence if we produce 6 units the total cost is £296, whereas if we produce 7 units total cost rises to £368. The cost involved in producing 7 units is therefore £72. This is shown not at 6 or 7, but half-way between.

When we come to plot the marginal cost curve some particular problems are involved. Since the marginal cost is the cost of moving *between* two levels of output, it is plotted as a horizontal straight line between these outputs. Thus, in Figure 7.4(a), for example, the cost of moving from an output of 6 units per week to 7 units per week is £72. Marginal cost is therefore plotted as a horizontal line between these outputs. When this is done we end up with a graph looking like a step-ladder. If we wish to represent marginal cost as a smooth curve, this can be done by joining up the midpoints of each step. This is done in Figure 7.4(b).

The step-ladder graph and the smooth curve represent two different concepts of marginal cost. The step-ladder shows that costs move in **finite** steps from one output to the next, whereas the

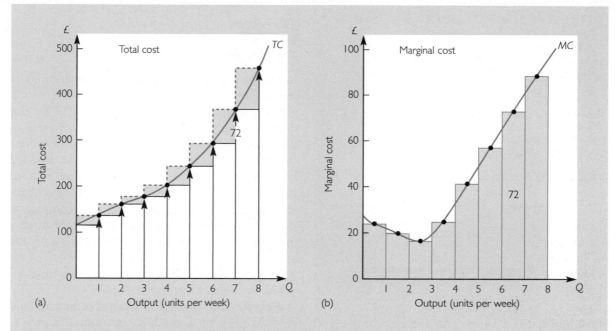

Figure 7.4 **Total cost and marginal cost output of 6 units/week to 7**
Marginal cost is the difference between successive levels of total cost, e.g. the cost of moving from an output of 6 units/week to 7 units/week is £72. You can see that the distance in (a) corresponds to the same distance in (b). Thus the value of the shaded areas in both diagrams is equal.

smooth *MC* curve suggests that costs are infinitely variable between outputs. Thus we would see the marginal cost of producing 1.1 units, 1.2 units, 1.3 units and so on. The step-ladder therefore shows *discrete* data and the smooth curve *continuous* data. These conditions apply to all marginal figures. It is increasingly becoming the practice in economics texts to adopt the discrete data approach at this level of the subject. However, it is usually more convenient to adopt the continuous data approach, and this we shall do for most purposes.

You will see in Figure 7.4(b) that the *MC* curve at first falls and then rises, presenting a similar 'U'-shape to the *AC* curve. This is because the same principles of diminishing returns apply to marginal cost in the short run as they do to all the other cost structures. As we shall see in subsequent chapters, the firm is almost invariably concerned with the levels of output where marginal cost is rising. The student should not be surprised therefore if sometimes economic texts present marginal cost as continuously upward-sloping lines.

The relationship between *MC* and *AC*

In Figure 7.5 we have brought together the figures for *MC* and those for *AC*. A most important point is revealed:

The *MC* curve cuts the *AC* curve at the lowest point of *AC*.

As you can see in Figure 7.5, this occurs at an output of 5 units per week.

Why does this relationship occur? The reasons are mathematical rather than economic and the explanation is this. So long as *MC* is less than *AC*, then it will draw *AC* down towards it, but as soon as *MC* is greater than *AC* then it will pull up the *AC* curve. Thus, the *MC* curve must go through the bottom point of the *AC* curve. This applies to both short-run and long-run situations.

This principle applies to the relationship between any marginal and average figure. Consider the following example.

A batsman in the county cricket championship has an average score of 25 runs after 10 innings. In the next match (*marginal*) he scores 13 runs. What happens to his average? It falls because the

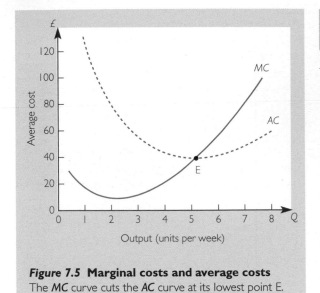

Figure 7.5 Marginal costs and average costs
The *MC* curve cuts the *AC* curve at its lowest point E.

marginal score is below the average. In the next match he scores 18. Although his marginal score has risen, his average is still brought down because the marginal is still less than the average. However, were he to score 30 in the next match, the marginal score, now being greater than the average, would pull up the average.

The student should also note that the same principle applies to the marks or grades awarded on school or college courses!

STUDENT ACTIVITY 7.4

Complete the following table for total, average and marginal costs:

Output units per week Q	Total costs, TC (£)	Average costs, AC (£)	Marginal costs, MC (£)
0	40	∞	
			8
1		48.0	
			7
2	55		
3	60	20.0	
			8
4	68		
5		16.4	
			17
6	99		
			27
7	126		
8	156	19.5	

Profits

The role of profit

In Chapter 3 we noted that profit is traditionally regarded as the earnings of enterprise or of the entrepreneur; it is essentially the reward for the risk of producing goods and services in anticipation of demand. We also noted that in large corporations the entrepreneurial function may be divided between many people and may therefore be hard to identify. In fact, as we shall see in the next chapter, it may be the case that when a large company is run entirely by managers and not by profit earners they may be less interested in maximising profits and more interested in such things as growth of the company and job security. They may therefore act as risk avoiders rather than risk takers.

Nevertheless, profit still has a specific and vital role to play in a modern economy. Someone always has to take the risk of producing ahead of demand. In a mixed economy many production decisions are taken by the government, but there are still many more taken by private persons and for them profit remains the overriding goal. Adam Smith argued that the 'invisible hand' of self-interest guided the economy to the best possible use of its resources. This was because, to produce profitability, the business would not only have to produce the goods which people wanted but also have to produce them at minimum cost in order to compete with its rivals. Profit acts not only as an incentive to encourage businesses to produce but also as an indicator. If, for example, profits are high in one particular line of business, this indicates that people want more of that good and encourages more firms to produce it. Also if one firm in an industry is making more profit than another this could indicate that its methods are more efficient, and the other firms will therefore have to emulate this greater efficiency or go out of business.

Joseph Schumpeter (1883–1950) saw profit and economic development inextricably bound up with each other: 'Without development there is no profit, without profit no development. For the capitalist system it must be added that without profit there would be no accumulation of wealth.'

Thus profit acts as an *incentive* to firms to encourage them to take risks, as a *measure of efficiency* and as a *spur* to the introduction of new products and processes.

The accountant's and the economist's views contrasted

To the accountant profit is essentially a residual figure, i.e. the money which is left over after all the expenses have been paid. Even so, one might talk of profits before tax or after tax, distributed or undistributed. There is also a difference between profit and dividends. To understand these figures fully requires a working knowledge of accounts and is beyond the scope of this book. We may say, however, that there are many judgemental elements at work in accounts. Accountancy is often regarded as an exact study but in arriving at a figure for profit the accountant will have to exercise judgement in *estimating* many figures in the accounts; for example, estimates will have to be made in arriving at figures for the value of stock, debts and assets. These calculations are made all the more difficult when the accountant must also estimate the effects of inflation. It is therefore possible for a company to have a healthy-looking balance sheet but be near to insolvency, or to appear to be making virtually no profit at all but be very sound.

It is possible that a firm owns some of the resources it uses; for example, it may have the freehold on its premises. In these circumstances it is essential to its effective running that these are costed and accounted for as if they were rented. This point is developed below.

It is possible for a business to make an accounting profit but an economic loss. This is perhaps best explained by taking a simple example. Imagine the case of a self-employed solicitor who works in premises he or she owns. At the end of the year the solicitor has made £100 000 above the running costs of the practice and therefore regards this as profit. The economist, however, will always enquire about the *opportunity cost*, i.e. what else could have been done with the resources of capital, labour, etc? We may find on examination that the solicitor could have rented the building out for £20 000 per annum, that the capital involved would have earned

£20 000 interest if invested elsewhere and that £70 000 could have been earned working as a solicitor for the local council. Under these circumstances the solicitor could be £10 000 per annum better off as a result of closing down the practice and placing the resources elsewhere.

Normal and abnormal profits

At its simplest, profits are the difference between total revenue (TR) and total costs (TC). However, economists also have a view of the *normal profit* for a firm.

Normal profit is the minimum amount of profit which is necessary to keep the firm in the industry.

It is obvious that the firm must pay for the labour it uses, pay rent for its site and pay for its raw materials. It must also pay for the capital that it uses: the owners of the business must be rewarded or they will not consider it worthwhile supplying the necessary financial capital. We may thus regard some profit as a legitimate cost of the business. We therefore include this in the costs of the business; this is because if profits fall below a certain level it will no longer be considered worthwhile producing the product and the owners of capital will transfer their money elsewhere. Thus:

Normal profit represents the opportunity cost of supplying capital to a business. Any profit in excess of this is termed abnormal profit (or, sometimes, pure, excess or supernormal profit). As will be noted in the next chapter when there is relative freedom of entry to the industry, like in perfect competition or monopolistic competition, any abnormal profit will attract new firms into the industry. However, with monopoly or oligopoly, barriers to entry are likely to exist and any abnormal profit may persist.

The concept of normal profit is an essential tool in explaining the behaviour of a firm. What the normal level of profit is may vary both from industry to industry and even between firms within an industry. Some investments, or some lines of business, are more risky than others. What sort of investment people undertake depends on their attitude towards risk: the more risky the investment, the higher the expected return or level of normal profit. Shareholders in a company that has a secure position in an established market are likely to be content with a lower, but more certain, return on their investments than are the suppliers of capital to a business that is, say, introducing a new product into a relatively volatile or uncertain market, such as fashion or films.

Implicit and explicit costs

In arriving at a calculation of profit a firm needs to consider both explicit and implicit costs. These are both measured in terms of their opportunity costs. For resources *not owned* by the firm their opportunity costs are simply the prices the firm has to pay for their use. Thus, explicit costs are those which the firm is contracted to pay, such as wages, rates, electricity, etc. In the case of resources *owned* by the firm their costs are implicit; they are what the resources could earn in their next best alternative use. For example, suppose a firm owns the site on which it operates; the economist would argue that in addition to its wages bill, its electricity bill, etc., the firm should pay itself the market rent for the site, otherwise it is making an uneconomic use of its resources because it is conceivable that it could do better by closing down and renting the site to someone else. We are thus once again speaking of the concept of opportunity cost.

An example may make the point clearer. Many years ago a company called Lyons (now part of the Allied Domecq group) had 'Corner House' cafés on many of the most prominent sites in London. These appeared to be making a profit. However, Lyons discovered that if it were to close the cafés, dispose of the sites and invest the money gained it could make more than its present level of profit. Lyons had been ignoring the implicit costs of its business. Having considered these costs Lyons decided to sell off many of these sites and London lost some of its most familiar landmarks.

● *Common misunderstanding*

Normal profit is not part of profit in the accounting sense. It is actually regarded as a cost of production. It is the minimum reward necessary for the owners of the business to continue supplying the necessary capital, given the risks involved. Thus, normal profit represents the implicit costs of ownership.

STUDENT ACTIVITY 7.5

A person decides to set up a travel business and invests £100 000 of their own money, which could have earned 10 per cent in a high-interest bank or building society account. The person could also have earned £40 000 p.a. working for someone else. He/she takes a salary of £30 000 from the travel business in the first year of operation, when the business had revenues of £185 000; its costs of production total £150 000. Calculate:

(a) The level of profit according to an accountant.
(b) The level of profit according to an economist.

Discuss the reasons for any difference.

Conclusion

In this chapter we have examined the development of the business organisation and have compared the main legal forms of business enterprise. We have also noted the distinctions between fixed costs and variable costs, between marginal costs and average costs, between normal profit and abnormal profit and between implicit and explicit costs.

Summary

1 The firm is the unit of ownership and control in industry. It is usually assumed that all businesses in the private sector seek to maximise profits.
2 The main types of business are sole traders, partnerships, joint stock companies and cooperatives.
3 Total costs (TC) comprise fixed costs (FC) and variable costs (VC). Fixed costs are fixed in the short run, while variable costs start at zero and increase with output.
4 A firm will stay in business in the short run so long as it is recovering its variable costs. In the long run all costs must be covered.
5 Average (unit) cost is total cost divided by output; the AC curve is 'U'-shaped in the short run.
6 Marginal cost (MC) is the cost of producing one more unit of a commodity.
7 The MC curve is plotted in a special incremental manner. It intersects with the AC curve at the lowest point of AC.

8 Normal profit is the minimum amount of profit which is necessary to keep a firm in an industry; it varies with the degree of risk in a market.

? QUESTIONS

1 Distinguish between plants and firms. Comment on any problems that may exist in comparing markets and industries.
2 What are the advantages and disadvantages of sole proprietorship as a method of owning and running a business?
3 To what extent is having corporate status an asset for a business?
4 Of the following list – wages, managerial salaries, rent, heating and lighting, sales commisssions, raw materials, interest and depreciation – which are fixed costs and which are variable? How will the answer vary between the short run and the long run?
5 Using your knowledge of short-run shut-down conditions explain the factors that a hotelier would take into account in deciding to stay open in the off-peak season.
6 Define marginal costs and average costs; explain the shape of and relationship between the MC and AC curves.
7 Explain what are meant by implicit and explicit costs. How is it possible for a firm to be making an accounting 'profit' but an economic loss?

Data response A
UK CORPORATE PROFITABILITY

Examine Figure 7.6 on the relative profitability of UK companies in manufacturing and services taken from *Financial Times* of 28 September 2000 and answer the following questions:

1 Why is profit important for firms?
2 Can you think of any reasons why there might be differences between rates of return (i.e. profitability) in services and manufacturing?

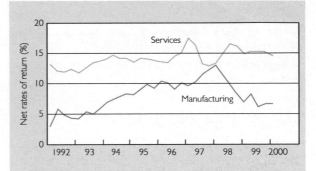

Figure 7.6 UK corporate profitability
Source: Financial Times, 28 September 2000. Reprinted with permission.

3 Why do you think profits have fallen in manufacturing industry since 1997/98? (Hint: think in terms of exports and also in terms of changes in commodity prices.)

Data response B
SHORT-RUN SHUT-DOWN CONDITIONS

Suppose that a farmer is able to rent an orchard at a cost of £5000 per year and other fixed costs amount to a further £500 per week. Itinerant labour to pick the apples can be hired at a wage of £240 per week and each labourer can pick 600 dozen apples per week. Other variable costs such as packaging and transport amount to 10 pence per dozen. Under these conditions:

1 What is the minimum price per dozen that the apple grower would be willing to accept in the short run?
2 Suppose that the apple grower employs five workers for five weeks picking apples to gather the complete harvest. Assuming that all costs and productivities stay the same as stated above, what is the minimum price per dozen the apple grower will look for to remain in the industry in the long run?

In both cases explain your answer as fully as possible.

8 Market structures

In the same way that the market demand curve is a horizontal summation of individual demand curves, so market supply is the horizontal summation of firms' supply curves.

In Figure 8.1 we envisage a market which is supplied by two groups of firms, A and B. At a price of £4 per unit group A supplies 60 units and group B 80 units, whereas at a price of £2 A would supply 20 units and B 30 units. If we total the amount supplied at each price we obtain the market supply, i.e. 140 units at £4 and 50 units at £2.

Supply

We noted in the previous chapter that the firm is the unit of supply; hence, if we are able to explain the behaviour of one firm we may explain the behaviour of market supply by aggregating all firms' supply.

Profit maximisation

One of the basic assumptions on which the whole theory of business behaviour is based is that firms will seek to maximise their profits, i.e. they not only attempt to make a profit but attempt to make the last penny of profit possible. At the end

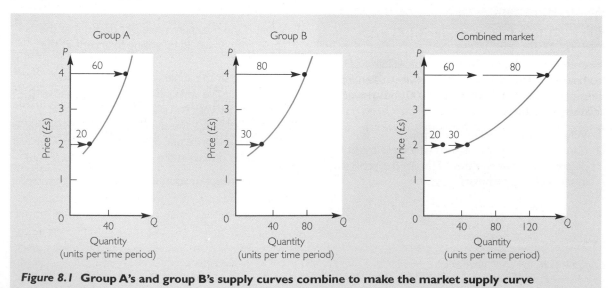

Figure 8.1 Group A's and group B's supply curves combine to make the market supply curve

of the chapter we are going to suggest some modifications to this view, although it is generally accepted that no other comprehensive explanation of the behaviour of firms has been put forward and certainly no other that stands up well to the rigours of empirical testing and benefits from widespread supportive evidence. Thus, we will find that whatever type of competition we consider, profit maximisation can be regarded as a unifying principle.

Types of competition

When the economist classifies types of firms it is usually with respect to the type of competition under which they exist. At one extreme we have perfect competition, which represents the theoretically optimal degree of competition between firms, while at the other extreme we have monopoly, where the firm is synonymous with the industry and there is no competition at all.

Figure 8.2 gives a diagrammatic representation of the possibilities. We have inserted a gap in the line between perfect competition and all other types since perfect competition is only a theoretical possibility. Economists refer to these as different types of *market structure*. The structure of a market is indicated by those characteristics that determine the *conduct* of firms or how they behave (i.e. their pricing policies) and ultimately their levels of *performance* (e.g. their profitability). The key structural 'characteristics' of a market are the number and relative size of firms in a market (i.e. the level of market concentration), the extent of the freedom that firms have to enter and leave a market and the nature of the product (i.e. the degree of similarity between the products of the various firms in a market).

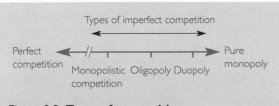

Figure 8.2 **Types of competition**

Perfect competition

In perfect competition firms are price-takers, i.e. they have no power to affect the market price, although they can sell all they want to at this prevailing price.

For a state of perfect competition to exist in an industry the following conditions have to exist:

(a) A large number of buyers and sellers of the commodity.
(b) Freedom of entry and exit to the market for both buyers and sellers.
(c) Homogeneity of product, i.e all goods being sold have to be identical, and are perfect substitutes.
(d) Perfect knowledge of the market on the part of both the buyers and sellers.

STUDENT ACTIVITY 8.1

Explain why each of the above assumptions is necessary for price-taking to exist.

It is obvious that all these conditions cannot exist in one market at once. There are, however, close approximations to perfect competition, e.g. the sale of wheat on the commodity market in Canada. In this situation there are thousands of sellers and ultimately millions of buyers and it is relatively easy for farmers to enter or leave the market by switching crops; as far as homogeneity is concerned, once graded, one tonne of wheat is regarded as identical with another. In addition to this, when wheat is sold on the commodity market both sides have a good knowledge of the market and it appears to the farmers that they can sell all they want at the market price even though, individually, a farmer is unable to influence it. The perfection of the market is, however, flawed by farmers banding together in cooperatives to control the supply, by widespread government intervention in agriculture and by some very large buyers in the market.

It might be argued that developments in information technology and in the use of the internet will, by making information more freely available and by bringing more buyers and sellers into closer contact, increase the prospects of perfect competition. There is no doubt that the use of the internet reduces the search costs of information for both buyers and sellers and can introduce more competition into markets, but there are still costs involved in obtaining and employing the requisite technology to which not all buyers or even sellers are able to subscribe and even then there is little chance of them having access to perfect information. It will be interesting to view future developments, however!

If there were perfect competition the individual firm would *appear* to face a horizontal or infinitely elastic demand curve for its product. If it raised the price of its product it would no longer be on the demand curve and would sell nothing. Conversely, it would have no incentive to lower its prices since it appears to be able to sell any amount it likes at the market price. The organisation is thus a **price-taker** and its only decision, therefore, is how much to produce (see Figure 8.3). The price may of course change from day to day, as it does in the case of wheat, but to the farmer the demand curve always appears horizontal. The industry demand curve, on the other hand, is typically downward-sloping.

● *Common misunderstanding*

There is sometimes confusion about the nature of the demand curve facing the individual firm in perfect competition compared with the demand curve for the industry as a whole. The individual producer is said to face a horizontal or infinitely elastic demand curve for the product. However, the industry demand curve will remain a normal downward-sloping one; indeed the world demand curve for wheat is fairly inelastic, large changes in price bringing only relatively small changes in demand.

Why study perfect competition?

If perfect competition is purely a theoretical state the student may legitimately ask why we study it. To this we could answer on three grounds:

(a) It represents an idealised functioning of the free market system. Thus, although we cannot eliminate all imperfections in the market, we may try to minimise them, as a motor engineer attempts to minimise friction in a car engine. This idealised view is examined in Chapter 27.

(b) For the student attempting a serious study of economics, study of the perfect market is essential since no understanding of the literature of microeconomics over the last century can be achieved without it. We will also see that perfect competition is vital to the neo-classical view of the macroeconomy (see Chapter 32).

(c) On a rather more mundane level, students will find themselves confronted with questions on perfect competition in examinations!

STUDENT ACTIVITY 8.2

Can you think of any other market situations that may approximate to perfect competition?

Imperfect competition

We will now turn to look at imperfect markets. All markets are to a greater or lesser extent imperfect. This is not an ethical judgement on the organisations which make up the markets. There is nothing morally reprehensible about being an imperfect competitor; indeed this is the 'normal' state of affairs. It could be the case, however, that firms contrive imperfections with the object of maximising their profits to the detriment of the consumer.

In imperfectly competitive markets firms are price-makers; they have the power to determine their own prices.

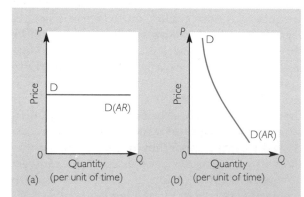

Figure 8.3 The demand curve under perfect competition
(a) The demand curve for the individual firm's product.
(b) The industry demand curve. Note: In the theory of the firm the demand curve is usually labelled *AR* (average revenue).

The main influence on whether firms can set their own prices is the degree of *product differentiation* that exists in a market. This is the extent to which similar products are perceived to be different by consumers; the differences may be due to actual physical differences in, say, quality or they may be the result of advertising and policies to develop a particular brand image. Jeans may vary in quality according to their manufacturer, but some makes also have a particular brand image perpetuated through advertising; Levis, for example, are associated with durability and a certain tough, 'macho' image as well as being regarded as a fashion article.

In other words, the products in imperfect markets are not perfect substitutes for each other.

As a result, all imperfect competitors share the characteristic that the demand curve for their individual firm's product slopes downward, i.e. if the firm raises its prices it will not lose all its customers as it would under perfect competition. Conversely, it can sell more of the product by lowering its prices.

In addition to this the firm can be affected by the action of its competitors. In Figure 8.4, for example, the decrease in demand DD to D_1D_1 could have been brought about by a competitor lowering prices. If, for example, Ford were to drop the prices of its cars by 5 per cent it would probably bring about a fairly substantial decrease in demand for cars produced by other manufacturers. This would not be so in the case of perfect competition. If, for example, Farmer Jones were to cut the price of wheat by 5 per cent it would scarcely affect the sales of the thousands of other farmers who make up the market.

Imperfectly competitive markets are also characterised by imperfect information: firms may be unsure of how their rivals are going to behave in any situation and consumers are unlikely to possess enough information to distinguish adequately between the products of all the firms in a market. Furthermore, firms in imperfectly competitive markets are unlikely to be completely free to enter or leave it.

It is possible to distinguish several types of imperfect competition. These distinctions arise chiefly out of the number and size of firms in a market, the degree of product differentiation and the ease with which

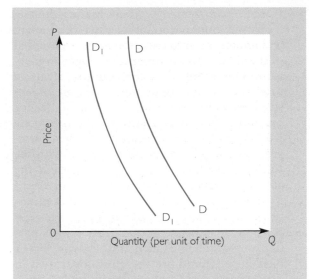

***Figure 8.4* The demand curve for an individual firm's product under imperfect competition**
The firm has some choice over price and output, but can also be affected by competitors. The decrease in demand from DD to D_1D_1 could have been brought about by a fall in the price of a competitor's product.

firms can enter (or leave) a market. The latter depends on the extent of barriers to entry (and exit) to and from a market.

Barriers to entry and exit

Barriers to entry, hardly surprisingly, make it difficult for new firms to enter a market; in such circumstances the established firms, or incumbents, may be able to charge a higher price and make more profit than if entry to the market was relatively easy.

The main barriers to entry are:

(a) *Economies of scale.* When there are significant economies of scale in an industry (see Chapter 3), only a few firms may be able to supply the market efficiently, i.e. at lowest possible cost. A new firm trying to enter on a relatively small scale would face higher unit costs than the incumbents and hence would find it difficult to survive. In the extreme case, where unit costs continue to fall beyond the level of market demand, just one firm can benefit from economies of scale; a *natural monopoly* exists.

(b) *Capital requirements*. Many manufacturing industries employ capital-intensive production techniques; a large capital outlay, a potential obstacle to entry, is required to begin production. The problem is compounded if, as in many consumer goods industries, an expensive advertising campaign is required or, as for example in pharmaceuticals, a large-scale R&D programme is necessary. Evidence suggests that capital requirments, along with the relevant technical knowledge, represent the greatest obstacle to entry in many industries.

(c) *Product differentiation*. Product differentitation can create **brand loyalty**, whereby consumers associate good quality with a particular brand name (such as Rolex watches or Parker pens) and are therefore loyal to it in their purchases. To overcome brand loyalty a new firm may have to spend more on advertising than the incumbents. Established firms may also make it difficult for new firms to enter a market by each supplying several brands; such **brand proliferation** occurs among beers and lagers, breakfast cereals, cigarettes and soaps and detergents.

(d) *Lower unit costs*. Incumbents may have lower unit costs than potential entrants for a variety of reasons: knowledge of operating in the industry may give them favoured access to managerial talent, suppliers and superior locations; *patent rights* give firms the right to supply a product for a specified number of years.

(e) *Pricing policies*. Incumbents may engage in **limit pricing** if their costs are lower than those of the new entrant. Instead of trying to maximise their own short-run profits the incumbents may eliminate the potential for profits on the part of the entrant by charging a price only up to the level of the new firm's costs.

(f) *Legal restrictions*. Patent rights represent one form of legal restriction on firms selling certain products. In addition, in the UK the Post Office has the legal right to be the sole supplier of letter deliveries under 50 pence. Licences are required to sell alcohol (whether on or off the premises). Legal permission is required to supply banking services, although the deregulation of the financial services market in the1980s means that firms in the industry can also sell other financial products (e.g. banks offer mortgages and life insurance policies).

(g) *Sunk costs*. These are costs that cannot be recovered once a firm leaves an industry. Specialist capital equipment often falls into this category, as does most marketing costs, like advertising. Firms are unable to recoup these costs. These act as **barriers to exit** for incumbents given the large capital outlays involved. They also represent barriers to entry for new firms, which may be reluctant to enter an industry if faced with the prospect of substantial sunk costs should they not be successful.

Barriers to entry can be divided into structural barriers, which tend to occur naturally in an industry. They include capital requirements and economies of scale. There are also behavioural or strategic barriers, the result of intentional decisions by the incumbents.

Limit pricing is an example of the latter. Product differentiation, however, may be categorised as either type: most consumer goods are naturally prone to a certain level of advertising in order to inform the public about the products, although established firms in these industries may also advertise with the express intent of raising costs for potential entrants. Incumbents can also use excess capacity, R&D expenditure and predatory pricing as intentional actions to ward off would-be entrants, although this is a controversial area and is hotly disputed by industrial economists.

Traditionally, it has been assumed that barriers to entry are fairly extensive in many industries, especially in manufacturing. The Austrian school views barriers to entry as rather less formidable: most, it is assumed, can be overcome over time. Legal barriers are regarded as the most effective obstacles to entry according to the Austrian view and are also thought to be the most likely to persist.

Monopoly

Monopoly lies at the opposite end of the competitive 'spectrum' to perfect competition. It literally means a situation where there is only one seller of a commodity, although in practice a dominant firm may be able to exert a considerable amount of monopoly power with far less than 100 per cent of the market.

Monopoly power refers to the ability of a firm to determine its own pricing policy and make monopoly profits; these are likely to persist into the long run should barriers to entry exist. Legally speaking, an organisation may be treated as a monopoly under the Competition Act 1998 if it has more than 25 per cent of the market, although if one or more firms acting together 'abuse' their monopoly position in some way then a 40 per cent rule applies. (For more detail on UK policy towards monopolies see Chapter 23.) In principle, for a monopoly to exist there should also be no close substitutes for the firm's product. However, in most cases a certain amount of competition is likely to occur with other similar products. Thus, the railways compete with other forms of transportation, such as road, air and even sea. The Post Office is in competition with firms such as DHL and Federal Express for parcel deliveries.

The monopoly power of a firm is partly determined by the size of its regional market. Thus, if a village has a single hairdressing salon it will have some monopoly power, since customers will not wish to travel far to get their hair done.

The sources of monopoly

The ability of firms with market power to make long-run monopoly profits means that most governments have a policy towards monopolies. To some extent the government's attitude is determined by how the monopoly arose; hence it is important to assess the *sources* or *bases* of monopoly:

(a) *Natural conditions.* This source arises out of the geographical conditions of supply. For example, South Africa has an almost complete monopoly of the Western world's supply of diamonds.

(b) *Historical.* A business may have a monopoly because it was first in the field and no one else has the necessary know-how or customer goodwill. Lloyd's of London has a command of the insurance market that is largely based on historical factors.

(c) *Capital requirements.* The supply of a commodity may involve the use of such a vast amount of capital equipment that new competitors are effectively excluded from entering the market. This is the case with the chemical industry.

(d) *Technological.* Where there are many economies of scale to be gained it may be natural and advantageous for the market to be supplied by one or a few large companies. This is the case of the natural monopoly mentioned earlier in the chapter and would apply to the utilities, like gas, electricity and water distribution and the railway network.

(e) *Legal.* The government may confer a monopoly upon a company. This may be the case when a business is granted a patent or copyright. The right to sole exploitation is given to encourage people to bring forward new ideas.

(f) *Public.* Public corporations such as the Post Office may have a monopoly, as already noted. This can also be cited as an example of a monopoly conferred by statutory or legal right.

(g) *Contrived.* When people discuss the potential evils of monopoly, it is not necessarily the above forms of monopolies they are thinking about as those that are deliberately contrived through firms' conduct or behaviour. Business organisations can contrive to exploit the market either by taking over, or driving out of business, the other firms in the industry (*scale monopoly*) or by entering into an agreement with other business to control prices and output (*complex monopoly*). It is this type of monopoly at which most legislation has traditionally been aimed and it has often aimed at firms that belong to oligopolies (see Chapter 23). It should also be pointed out that there are schools of thought that take a very different view towards monopoly, i.e. that it is not altogether a 'bad' thing and may even be positively beneficial. The Austrian school, for example, emphasises the attainment of monopoly power because of the lower relative costs of production of particular firms, possibly the result of successful R&D strategies.

Oligopoly

The word oligopoly, like monopoly, is derived from the Greek and means a situation where there are only a few sellers of a commodity.

In other words, there is a high degree of seller concentration. 'Few' is never strictly defined, but can mean anything from two to, say, 10 firms. The situation where just two firms dominate a market is known as a *duopoly* and is regarded as a special case. In a few instances, such as cement, steel and aluminium production, oligopolists produce virtually identical products and compete in terms of prices; they are referred to as *perfect oligopolies*. However, in most cases oligopolies are characterised by a high degree of product differentiation and little price competition and are known as *imperfect oligopolies*. Many manufacturing industries in the UK can be classified as oligopolies: motor vehicles, electrical goods, confectionery, glass manufacture, pharmaceuticals and so on. A growing number of service markets, e.g. banking and insurance and food retailing, are also dominated by a few, large sellers. The tobacco industry and the manufacture of soaps and detergents are examples of duopolies.

Monopolistic competition

When there are a large number of sellers producing a similar but differentiated product, then a state of monopolistic competition is said to exist.

Thus, seller concentration is quite low and the products tend to be fairly close substitutes. Such a market is also characterised by the frequent entry and exit of firms. It is called monopolistic competition because, owing to imperfections in the market, each organisation has a small degree of monopoly power.

Examples of monopolistically competitive markets are more likely to be found in the service sector: estate agents, dry cleaners, restaurants and various forms of retailing. However, as noted previously, in a small town one or two individual sellers may possess considerable local market power. The various types of competition are summarised in Table 8.1.

● *Common misunderstanding*

The fact that firms may appear to face little competition does not mean that these firms do not compete. Take the case of advertising. It is paradoxical that under perfect competition very little competition is visible since there is no advertising and promotion of products, whereas under all types of imperfect competition rivalry between firms is only too obvious. Thus, even firms with significant market power advertise. Tate and Lyle, for example, which has a large share of the market for cane sugar production, not only promotes its product but extols the virtues of free competition. It is a case, as Professor Galbraith wrote in The Affluent Society, *of competition being advocated 'by those who have most successfully eliminated it'.*

Table 8.1 **Different market forms**

Type of competition	Number of producers and degree of product differentiation	Barriers to entry	Influence of the firm over prices
Perfect competition	Many producers, homogeneous products	None	None
Imperfect competition:			
Monopoly	Single producer no close substitutes	Very likely	Considerable
Oligopoly	Few dominant producers	Likely	Considerable
Perfect	Homogenous products		
Imperfect	High degree of product differentiation		
Monopolistic competition	Many producers, product differentiation	Very low	Fairly small

Alternative objectives

While we shall assume that profit maximisation remains the key objective of the firm, whatever the level of competition, alternative theories postulating different objectives have been advanced from time to time.

The managerial theories of the firm that originated in the 1950s and 1960s refer particularly to large firms in which, it is assumed, there is a divorce between ownership and control.

Shareholders, the owners of the firm, are interested in maximising profits, while the managers, it is argued, have other objectives from which they obtain prestige, power and increased monetary rewards. Thus, **William Baumol** suggested that the prime objective of management is to maximise sales revenue, while **Robin Marris** postulated that the main managerial aim is to maximise the rate of growth of the firm; managerial salaries and prestige are thought to be more closely associated with sales and the size of the firm than with profit alone. **Oliver Williamson** put forward a more general model in which managerial interests are met by the optimisation of a utility function comprising salaries, the number of subordinates, fringe benefits, such as plush offices and company cars, and control over a firm's resources.

In each model the firm is expected to achieve a certain level of profits in order to provide the shareholders with an acceptable return on their investments. This reduces the risk of them selling their shares and so lessens the threat of takeover. The profit also helps to provide the necessary funds for capital investment purposes.

Another theory of the firm developed in the 1960s was the *behavioural model*, mainly associated with **H.A. Simon**. The firm is seen as a coalition of interest groups, including managers, shareholders, employees, customers and suppliers. Each group has goals and these may conflict. However, since each group has limited knowledge of the firm's operations and of the aims of the other groups, a coalition of interests results. *Satisficing* rather than maximising behaviour ensues: a satisfactory level of sales, profits, wages or quality of product is sought. Each goal takes the form of an *aspiration level*, which changes if targets are not met or if there is a change of emphasis (a larger market share, say, to counteract the growth of a competitor) by coalition members.

Both the managerial and behavioural theories incorporate the concept of 'organisational slack'. Where there is a lack of competition members of the firm may receive payments over and above what is required for the continued existence of the organisation; in other words, a firm is likely to produce at above minimum cost.

Slack can accrue to any member of a firm, but managers are thought to be in the best position to receive such payments, which can take the form of higher salaries and fringe benefits or reduced effort.

Small firms, such as sole traders and many partnerships, may also have non-profit-maximising objectives. One of the prime reasons for the continued existence of the small concern is the desire to be one's own boss; once this desire is met entrepreneurs may be content with a relatively quiet life and the achievement of a satisfactory level of profit.

Consumer cooperatives are supposed to be mainly concerned with satisfying the interests of their customers, while worker cooperatives may have a particular concern for protecting jobs.

Summary

1 The theory of the firm is the basis of the theory of supply, since if we are able to explain the behaviour of the firm we can then explain the operation of industry supply.

2 The traditional theory of the firm is based on the profit maximisation hypothesis.

3 Perfect competition represents the ideal functioning of the market system. The two most important conditions of perfect competition are that:
   (a) no individual buyer or seller can influence market price;
   (b) there is freedom of entry and exit to the industry.

4 The main types of imperfect competition are monopoly, oligopoly and monopolistic competition. All firms operating under these conditions have some control over the market price.

5 The principal types of barrier to entry are economies of scale, capital requirements, product differentiation, lower unit costs, pricing policies, legal restrictions and sunk costs, the last of which is also the main barrier to exit. Barriers to entry are most likely to feature in monopoly and oligopoly markets.

6 The sources of monopoly vary from natural conditions and technological factors to the contrived factors which are the direct result of firms' policies.

7 There are alternative theories of the firm that assume non-profit-maximising objectives. However, profit remains an important feature of any theory.

? QUESTIONS

1 Contrast perfect competition and monopoly as market forms. Discuss whether one is superior to the other from society's point of view.

2 Discuss why profit is important for a firm.

3 If the government imposes a price ceiling on a product (see page 85) does that make the firms that sell the product price-takers, regardless of whether or not they are perfect competitors? Give reasons for your answer.

4 List five products you have bought in the last week. Assuming that they were not bought from perfect competitors how did the supplier compete for your business with other rival suppliers?

5 Outline the main barriers to entry. Discuss whether they are likely to occur naturally in an industry or are more the result of the deliberate actions of the incumbent firms.

6 Explain why managers in large firms may have objectives other than profit. Is profit the sole objective of small concerns?

Data response A
BARRIERS TO ENTRY

Read the following passage and answer the questions.

The traditional view of the degree of profit in economic theory is associated with market structure, that is to say the degree of competition existing in an industry. Monopoly, for example, may experience profits above the normal because other firms are excluded from competition. In theory profits should be lower when there is a great deal of competition. When firms set out to exclude other firms there are said to be barriers to entry; they can also arise naturally in an industry. There seems to be some debate, however, about the extent and persistence of barriers to entry in many industries.

1 What do you understand by the term 'barriers to entry'? How do barriers to entry arise?

2 Assess the importance of barriers to entry for the following industries:
   (a) motor vehicle production;
   (b) the manufacture of video cassette recorders;
   (c) fresh fruit and vegetable supply;
   (d) aircraft construction;
   (e) plumbing services.

3 Explain what is meant by the concept of normal profit.

4 What action might a government take to reduce barriers to entry?

Data response B
BIG OIL, BIG BUCKS

Read the article on page 121 which is taken from the *Financial Times* of 18 August 1998 and answer the following questions.

1 Explain what is meant by oligopoly.

2 What do you think are the chief sources of the monopoly power of the large oil companies?

3 Discuss the different ways by which firms compete in the oil industry.

4 Given the significant market power of the large oil firms why do you think they bother to advertise?

Big oil, big bucks

The proposed BP Amoco merger underlines the themes of modern business: market dominance and the instinct to survive. By **Peter Martin**

You run one of the worlds' biggest companies, selling huge volumes of a commodity that is steadily falling in price in real terms. You have a historically evocative brand name, but your customers buy on price. You have spent most of the past decade downsizing the company, but need to find new ways of reducing costs. So what do you do?

The answer, if you are Sir John Browne of British Petroleum or Larry Fuller of Amoco, is simple: you double your bets. Putting together these two giant oil companies to form BP Amoco offers lots of scope for cost savings. . . .

. . . What has allowed them to survive the new era? Skilful management has certainly played a role. But a broader answer must surely be oligopoly: a collective market dominance which has allowed Big Oil to prosper despite the past quarter-century's roller-coaster prices.

Though convenience and price, not branding, are the decisive factor in most customers' purchasing decisions, the oil companies have several big advantages. Their decades of headlong expansion, fuelled by those upstream profits, have given them a disproportionate share of attractive retail locations.

The scale of their operations has given them economies of scale. And their studious attempts to create micro-monopolies – geographical areas of local market dominance – have given them a degree of protection from the unfettered operation of market pricing.

Modern business relies on these slivers of elbow-room to achieve acceptable levels of profitability. In most industries, it is branding that plays the critical role, allowing a company with a good name and reputation slightly greater scope for pricing freedom.

The oil industry is unusual both because its branding opportunities are limited, and because the downward pressure on its prices has been so marked. In this respect, it offers useful lessons for the rest of business, which is faced with increasing consumer resistance to paying extra for brands.

One response to these conditions is to abandon branding altogether: to compete purely on costs and scale as a commodity business. Some of the retailing independents have taken this approach.

Yet none of the big oil companies has done so. They continue to believe that it makes sense to spend money on persuading customers to buy from green filling-stations rather than yellow or red ones. They persist with loyalty schemes that only a marketing manager could love.

This obstinacy reflects the corporate survival instinct. Companies are more than simply instruments for increasing shareholder value. They are also living entities, carrying the burden of the innate human desire for immortality.

Brands are the outward symbol of that yearning for institutional survival. Preserving the Amoco brand in the US was sensible commercial move, since it has greater resonance there than BP's. But it was also a guarantee to Amoco's employees that the company lives on.

Other industries faced with downward pricing pressures could usefully learn two lessons from the oil industry. The companies that survive the process of consolidation will be those that exploit every little pocket of market power to preserve margins. They will also be the ones that best exploit the instinct for corporate survival to reshape themselves and form alliances for the future.

Source: Financial Times, 18 August 1998. Reprinted with permission.

SECTION II

Market failure and government intervention

'Would you really tax General Motors for selling unsafe cars? Isn't that selling the right to destroy human life?' The economist thought for a moment and replied, 'Surely it is better than giving that right free of charge.'

W. Baumol and W. Oates

9 The mixed economy: market failure vs government failure

Learning outcomes

At the end of this chapter you will be able to:

▶ Identify the various roles of the government in the economy.

▶ Explain the main ideas of economists who have influenced thinking in this question.

▶ Relate the growth of government involvement in the economy to both economic ideas and events in history.

▶ Identify the main causes of market failure and government failure.

▶ Apply the concepts of efficiency and equity to economic problems.

What is a mixed economy?

The twentieth century saw massive increases in the involvement of the government in the economy – until the 1980s. In the last two decades this growth was halted, and been put into reverse in many countries.

In its most dramatic form this reverse can be seen in the collapse of communism in Russia and Eastern Europe in the late 1980s. In China, the communists have retained control, but have enthusiastically embraced the market. Japan and the USA always had a lower involvement of government in the economy, and this has not changed. The new 'tiger' economies of the Far East, such as Malaysia and Singapore, have developed largely using the private sector. In Western Europe, following the lead taken by the UK from 1979 onwards under Mrs Thatcher's Conservative government, the state has withdrawn from many activities, mainly by the process of privatisation (discussed in Chapters 10 and 24). Despite these efforts, levels of government spending have remained obstinately high and these economies can still be referred to as mixed economies.

● *Common misunderstanding*

Many people believe that privatisation reduced public spending considerably, and was a major part of the reduction in the size of the state in the 1980s and 1990s. While it is true that the number of people employed by the state fell as a result of privatisation, there was not much reduction in spending because most of the nationalised industries, as monopolies, were able to make a profit. Some loss making sectors, like the railways and social housing, continue to be subsidised now they are in the private sector. It has proved necessary to regulate many of the privatised industries (see Chapters 10 and 24), so the government remains involved in these industries. It is true that the proceeds from the sale of state-owned assets averaged over £5bn a year in the UK during this period, but this was an increase in revenue rather than a reduction in expenditure. It is also a one-off increase that can no longer be relied on in the government finances once the privatisation process is complete. It is therefore true to say that the period of privatisation changed the role of the government in the economy, rather than the size of government expenditure.

All economies of the world can be said to be 'mixed', to a greater or lesser degree, in that there is no economy where there is no state activity (this would be anarchy), and no economy where the market has no role at all. However, we usually reserve the term 'mixed' for those economies where there is both a large element of a market economy, together with a significant degree of state control. It is thus a term that can still be applied to most of the countries of Western

Europe. It is important to see why the government continues to have a role in the economy. To explore this question we will look at a brief history of the development of the mixed economy in the UK. We will also look at the economists who have influenced ideas on the role of the state in the economy.

STUDENT ACTIVITY 9.1

List the main goods and services provided by the state in your country. Which of them are paid for by the consumer, using prices rather than taxes? Which of them can also be provided by the market?

Socialism and capitalism

Capitalism is the organisation of production through the private sector. Socialists are those who believe that the means of production should be publicly owned. The idea of socialism is often associated with the nineteenth-century German philosopher and economist, **Karl Marx**. He was pessimistic about the ability of capitalism to solve its problems of unemployment and poverty, and believed that capitalism would eventually collapse and be replaced by socialism.

Ironically, in the late twentieth century, it is the socialist economies that have collapsed in Eastern Europe, to be replaced by capitalism.

It is important to realise that the two problems of poverty and periodic unemployment remain a problem for capitalism to this day. Governments are often judged by their ability to deal with these perennial difficulties.

In Western Europe a non-revolutionary, constitutional form of socialism emerged during the twentieth century. The two main strands were the further development of the welfare state, and the nationalisation of industries with monopoly power, such as rail, electricity, gas and telecommunications. Although the state has reduced its role substantially in the last two decades, 'mixed economy' socialism remains a strong tradition. Socialist thinking in the UK probably owes more to **Sidney** and **Beatrice Webb** and other great Fabian socialists, than to **Marx** and

Lenin. The UK Prime Minister, Harold Wilson, once remarked that 'British socialism owed more to Methodism than Marxism'.

Measuring the size of the public sector

The size of the public sector is usually compared to the size of the whole economy. We must first have a measure of how big the economy is before comparing with public sector with the whole economy. There are several different measures that can be used for the size of the economy, but the most commonly used is Gross Domestic Product (GDP). This measures the value of the output of the whole economy. It includes investment goods as well as consumption goods, and goods produced by the public sector, and will be discussed in more detail in Chapter 15. The value of the output of the whole economy is the same as the income of all factors of production receiving factor rewards. The money received from selling the output of the economy will all end up as somebody's income, whether it is wages, interest, rent or profit (as discussed in Chapter 3).

The size of the public sector relative to the whole economy, is found by dividing government spending (G) by the value of output of the whole economy (GDP) and expressing it as a percentage:

$$\frac{G}{GDP} \times \frac{100}{1}$$

The results of this calculation over a number of years can be found in Table 9.1. More recent values will be found in Case study 10.1 in the next chapter.

Table 9.1 Growth of public expenditure as a percentage of GDP at market prices

1965–6	36.5%
1970–1	39.5%
1975–6	46.75%
1979–80	42.5%
1985–6	43.25%
1990–1	39.0%
1995–6	41.5%
1999	37.5%

Source: ONS *National Income and Expenditure Blue Book*, 2000, National Statistics. © Crown Copyright 2001

The origins of the mixed economy

Adam Smith and *laissez-faire*

The economy of the UK in the nineteenth century was one in which people and organisations were in a state of unfettered competition. It was believed that the economy would operate best if the government did not intervene in it.

Such beliefs were based on the writings of the Scottish economist and moral philosopher **Adam Smith** (1723–90), who argued that competition was the best regulator of the economy. The belief that internal and external trade should be left to regulate itself became known by the French expression *laissez-faire* – which roughly translates as 'leave to do'.

Adam Smith saw the economy as made up of millions of individuals and small businesses guided by the invisible hand of the market. He observed at first hand the world's first industrial revolution in the UK of the late eighteenth century and saw the benefits that the market could bring.

> Every individual endeavours to employ his capital so that its produce may be of greatest value. He generally neither intends to promote the public interest, nor knows how he is promoting it. He intends only his own security, only his own gain. And he is led in this by an *invisible hand* to promote an end which was no part of his intention. By pursuing his own interest he frequently promotes that of society more effectively than when he really intends to promote it.

To Smith, therefore, the economy was a self-regulating structure. For this to happen properly he believed that government should interfere in the economy as little as possible, for interference disturbed the mechanism of the market.

● *Common misunderstanding*

It is often thought that free competition is the 'natural' state of the economy. This is not so: it is almost entirely a nineteenth-century phenomenon. Before this time monarchs felt free to regulate the economy as they saw fit. On the other hand, in the twentieth century the economy was dominated by the government and by giant business organisations. Only in a few sectors of the economy could free competition be said to exist today.

In his book *The Wealth of Nations*, Smith argued that the many taxes and regulations that surrounded the commerce of the country hindered its growth. Business organisations should be free to pursue profit, restricted only by the competition of other business organisations. From about 1815 onwards government began to pursue this policy. The UK, already a wealthy country, grew wealthier still. The success of industries such as textiles and iron appeared to prove the wisdom of Adam Smith. Belief in the 'free market' system became the dominant economic ideology. This was confirmed towards the end of the century, when the British economist **Alfred Marshall** formalised Smith's ideas in the laws of supply and demand that you have already studied in Chapters 4, 5 and 6 and will go on to study further in an applied setting in Section III.

As the nineteenth century progressed, however, it became apparent that the free market system had three major defects.

(a) Although efficient at producing some products such as food and clothing, the free market system failed to produce effectively things such as sanitation or universal education.

(b) Competition could easily disappear and give way to monopoly, as occurred with the railways.

(c) Competition has winners but it also has losers. Society has to find some way of helping the losers – the incompetent, the sick and the unemployed.

It was to combat these three problems that the state began to intervene in the economy. In the case of (a) the government did not take a conscious decision to depart from *laissez-faire* philosophy; rather, action was forced upon it by the severity of the problems. This is well illustrated by the 1848 Public Health Act. In this case cholera epidemics forced the government to promote better drainage and sanitation. In the case of (b) there was a more conscious effort to regulate monopolies. This may be illustrated by the measures, which began as early as 1840, to regulate the activities of railway companies (a problem we still have to deal with today – see Chapter 14). Lastly, with 'one man, one vote' being achieved in the 1870s in the UK, and women being given the vote in the 1920s, government came under pressure to help all people in society. In the case of (c) above, real changes in policy had to wait for the twentieth century, although the *welfare state* did have humble beginnings in the late nineteenth century. Its development and subsequent problems are discussed later in this chapter and in Chapters 10, 11 and 28.

Thus the nineteenth century presents a picture of governments believing in a free market economy but gradually being forced to regulate its most serious excesses.

Does the labour market work? Keynes and crisis in the 1930s

Following the stock exchange crash of 1929 in the USA, unemployment spread throughout the world in the 1930s, with as many as 25 per cent of the workforce being unemployed in the UK during the worst years (1932–33). This is an example of markets not working very well. The market for labour is in theory no different from the market for any other commodity. Labour can be bought and sold, has a supply (people willing to work), a demand (employers willing to take on workers) and a price (wages). If there is unemployment it can be thought of as excess supply (see Figure 11.10, page 171).

If there is an excess supply of potatoes, this is dealt with by a reduction in the price of potatoes. Can we solve the problem of unemployment in the same way? Keynes argued that a cut in wages would result in workers cutting their spending, leading to more unemployment, not less. He suggested the only way out of this situation was for the government to step in and give the economy a kick start by increasing its spending. His views on the economy appeared so radical at the time that they were not accepted by governments in the 1930s. However in the period after the Second World War, governments were determined not to go back to the unemployment of the 1930s, and government intervention to correct problems in the labour market became fashionable in many countries. The arguments about how to deal with unemployment are dealt with in detail in Sections IV, VII and VIII. As will be seen later in this chap-

ter, Keynes's ideas were questioned in the last two decades of the twentieth century. The correct policies to deal with this problem are still a matter of debate. The UK Conservative government of the mid-1990s used Keynes' methods to cure unemployment, as did the Japanese government when faced with similar problems in the late 1990s. However, many governments of the last two decades have rejected his ideas in favour of letting the market work.

This argument is introduced in this chapter because it is relevant to the question of government spending and government intervention in the economy. It is usually thought of as a macroeconomic question, however, so we will leave further discussion until later in the book.

The post-war consensus 1939–1979

A period of forty years in the middle of the century was characterised by much greater intervention in the economy, producing the modern idea of a mixed economy. The main components of the mixed economy were:

(a) A free enterprise sector, where economic decisions are taken through the workings of the market.
(b) Government intervention in the economy through spending, taxes and regulations.
(c) Public ownership of some industries especially where there was monopoly.
(d) The welfare state providing free education and health care plus a contributory scheme of state insurance providing sick benefit, unemployment benefit and an old-age pension.

In this list (a) constitutes the private sector of the economy while (b) to (d) are the public sector. (See Data response A at the end of this chapter for recent trends in public spending.)

The first three decades of this period enjoyed steady economic growth, low unemployment and modest inflation. There were of course minor changes to policy in this period, with the Conservatives shifting the economy towards the market, and the Labour party shifting it towards government intervention. The economy remained a very mixed economy throughout this period, with substantial state and market sectors.

During the 1970s many Western economies were faced with the dual pressures of rising inflation and rising unemployment. There were two oil crises during the decade, in 1973–4 when the oil cartel OPEC raised oil prices fourfold and in 1979 when they were doubled again. This pushed most economies into unemployment, inflation and balance of payments deficit simultaneously, and slowed growth rates. Keynes ideas clearly couldn't cope with all these problems, and the policy of intervention in the economy became less popular. The American economist, **Milton Friedman**, was foremost in advocating a return to free market economics to solve these problems. The popular name, at the time, for these economists was *monetarists* but the counter-revolution against Keynes' ideas was much wider than monetarism. It might be better to refer to those advocating a return to market values as the *neo-classicists* or *new classicists*.

Rolling back the frontiers of the state 1979–1997

Milton Friedman was successful in persuading governments to adopt 'monetarist' rather than Keynesian policies. The Austrian economist, **Friedrich Hayek**, was probably more influential with Mrs Thatcher's government, since he persuaded her that she should attempt to 'roll back the frontiers of the state'. There followed a period of privatisation of all the industries nationalised by the Labour party in the late 1940s, shifting the UK substantially towards the capitalist end of the socialist–capitalist spectrum. The welfare state has been retained, but efforts have been made to make it more market-oriented. These reforms are considered in Chapter 10. Efforts to reduce the share of the economy accounted for by public expenditure have proved more difficult. Public expenditure has however been stabilised after a long period of growth (see Table 9.1)

● *Common misunderstanding*

Most people believe that the Conservative government from 1979 onwards reduced public expenditure. This is not the case for many of their years in office and in 1994–5 public expenditure was 42 per cent of gross domestic product (a measure of national income; see next chapter), exactly the same level as in 1979–80.

Which way in the twenty-first century?

The 1980s and 1990s have given time for the return to the market to be evaluated, and while there are clearly many benefits in terms of lower prices and better services from some privatised industries, there have also been problems in terms of two major recessions (in the early 1980s and early 1990s) with unemployment rising to three million in the UK on both occasions. Home ownership has risen spectacularly, but there was a major crisis in confidence in the housing market in the early 1990s. House prices collapsed leaving many people with mortgage debts greater than the value of their houses. The housing market has now recovered with a house price boom in the late 1990s, but income distribution has widened with the better-off doing disproportionately well under the system. These problems have meant that reservations about the market have grown again. **George Soros**, the financier and currency speculator, claimed (1997) that with the demise of communism, the greatest enemy of the open society was the invasion of the market into too many aspects of life. **Will Hutton**, in his influential book, *The State We're In*, wrote:

> The overall judgement on the market experiment must be at best mixed, at worst negative. The economy has been taken on a ferocious switchback ride; a period of deep recession in the early eighties, then an unsustainable boom and then a second chronic recession . . . it has made the business sector understandably cautious about undertaking new investment. In area after area implementation of the market principle . . . has failed to benefit the community.

At the same time the spectacular growth of the 'tiger' economies of South Korea, Taiwan, Singapore and Malaysia has provided a major challenge to the competitiveness of many European economies. With the massive Chinese population ready to follow in their footsteps, there is no doubt that Europe and the USA are in for a period of fierce competition. Increasingly *multinational companies* move jobs around the world, looking for the most competitive workforce. This *globalisation* of the world economy reduces the power of individual governments to control events. Is involvement in the global market place the only way to defend jobs and create growth? Is the welfare state affordable under these circumstances? These are questions with which any future government has to grapple.

The Labour government has opted for what it calls the 'Third Way', combining market economics and 'flexible labour markets' with the government-provided welfare state.

Criteria for government intervention in the market

In the remaining sections of this chapter we will consider the various ways in which the government intervenes in the UK economy. We shall be using the categories invented by the American public finance economist, **Richard Musgrave**. He argued that governments intervened in the economy for three principal reasons: the stabilisation role, the allocative role and the distributive role. We will concentrate on the second of these two roles because the stabilisation role involves macroeconomic policy and is discussed in depth in Sections IV and VII. We will also be introducing ideas invented by the British economist, **Pigou**. He argued that the market does not deal well with certain types of goods that he called 'public goods'. Public goods like defence are best provided by the public sector. He also pointed out that market transactions sometimes have 'external' effects on other people. A good example of this would be the pollution created by industrial activity. He argued that the state is justified in preventing the market from acting in such anti-social ways.

The allocative role: provision of goods and services

Privatisation has substantially reduced the number of goods and services provided by the state, but there are still quite a large number of services that remain in state hands even after the nationalised industries have been sold off. These services have one thing in common: they are for one reason or another difficult or unsuitable for provision through the market. Defence, roads, health, education, law and order are provided by the state in almost every country to some extent.

These services are not, of course, free, since we pay for them indirectly through taxes and national insurance schemes. Some are controlled directly by central government, e.g. defence and motorway construction, while in other cases the service may be decided upon by central government but administered by local government, e.g. local education authority schools. Services such as street lighting and refuse collection may be entirely controlled by local authorities. Some services may be provided by bodies set up by the government, but which are not regarded as either central or local government bodies, an example being health authorities and trusts. Such bodies are termed *quangos* (quasi-autonomous non-governmental organisations). The operation of these organisations is discussed more fully in the next chapter.

Public goods and services

Public goods are those where consumption of the product by one person does not diminish the consumption by others.

The classic example of this is that of a lighthouse, where the fact that the light guides one ship does not detract from its ability to guide others. More significantly in the modern economy, such things as defence, street lighting, law and order, and roads are considered to be public goods. It is difficult to charge people for services that, once provided for one person, are immediately available to everyone! Parts of the road system can be charged for: bridges, tunnels and motorways have limited entry and exit points. It is more difficult to imagine a pricing system for the road system as a whole, although new technology may provide this soon (see Chapter 14). Defence is usually considered to be a pure public good which governments are responsible for. However, a distinction is made between provision and production. Just because the government has to provide defence, does not mean that it has to produce it. Much of the armaments industry, producing the hardware of war, is in private hands. Some governments even hire mercenary (private sector) soldiers rather than running a large army. The case of law and order is more mixed, with some firms and individuals providing their own protection. As with defence, some services are produced in the private sector while being provided by the public sector (e.g. prisons run by firms such as Group 4). The overall level of law and order cannot be left entirely in private hands, or we would be faced with vigilante activity and mob rule.

External benefits and costs

Some services benefit people other than those purchasing them. Communicable diseases are best treated or they will affect others. An unhealthy workforce is not so productive; this may also affect the shareholders of the companies for which they work. Education increases people's potential productivity, which may result in higher economic growth, from which everyone benefits. These arguments are sufficient to suggest that the state should at least subsidise these activities. Further arguments that the state should be more involved are presented below. The state also intervenes to reduce *external costs* such as pollution from industry. These issues are discussed further in applied settings in Chapters 13 and 14. More detail on the theory can be found in Chapter 27. **Pigou** argued that the way to deal with the problem of externality was to impose a tax on products equal in value to the external costs they caused. In the case of external benefits, the solution was to provide a subsidy. In this way, it was argued that the externality was 'internalised' and the social costs treated as if they were private costs. The result of imposing a tax or giving subsidies was discussed in Chapter 6 (page 91).

Merit goods and services

These are products that are allocated to the members of the public, not according to the consumers' preferences but according to the paternalistic judgements of the government.

Thus, for example, state-financed education is given to everyone as a right between the ages of 5 and 16, irrespective of their willingness or ability to pay. It is assumed that everyone has a need for education, however poor. Choice is removed from this market and education is compulsory. Health services may be concerned to change people's behaviour rather than meet their demands. Improved diet, giving up smoking and other drugs are questions of health promotion decided upon by governments or professionals.

Sociologists often speak of a 'cycle of deprivation' where lifestyles leading to poverty, crime and other anti-social behaviour are passed from generation to generation. The idea of paternalistic intervention is to try to break this pattern. The extent to which government should over-rule people's personal choices about their lifestyle is a political argument which cuts across party lines. More *authoritarian* politicians, on both the right and left wing, argue that intervention is necessary for the good of society. More *libertarian* politicians can also be found on the left and the right, who stress the importance of individual choice.

It is usual for merit goods to be provided free, or to be means tested so that poorer people do not have to pay for them. If the government wishes to insist on people consuming a service, it is very difficult to also insist on payment. This can result in problems of over-consumption of the good (see Chapter 10). Paradoxically, it is sometimes found that if people do not pay for a service themselves, they do not value it. If they are required to make a payment, then they expect to get value for money, and start to act more like a consumer than a recipient of charity, or of authoritarian requirements to consume, for instance, education. This is one of the arguments behind the introduction of fees for undergraduate students in the UK. This idea that people behave differently according to the role assigned to them is a sociological rather than an economic idea.

The state and monopoly power

Many major industries in the UK were at one time nationalised. In most cases these industries had a degree of monopoly power (e.g. gas, electricity, telecommunications) and the idea of nationalisation was to protect the consumer from exploitation. These industries, and their subsequent privatisation, are discussed in detail in Chapters 10 and 24. After privatisation the government has continued to influence how these industries operate, but by regulation rather than ownership. Initially the regulation was in the form of price controls to prevent the privatised monopoly taking advantage of their monopoly power, but more recently the emphasis has been on reforming the industries so that more competition can be introduced. It is now possible to choose which company will provide your gas, your electricity and your telephone service. This has not been possible in all privatised industries, and many people have no choice over things like local buses, trains, or water companies. In these areas regulation is still necessary to protect the consumer.

It is not only the former nationalised industries that have market power. Many companies strive to dominate the market they find themselves in by means of merger, takeover, or restrictive practices. In oligopolistic industries, firms sometimes cooperate to raise price for their mutual benefit. The state needs to regulate such industries to prevent them from exploiting the consumer, for reasons of equity. As will be argued in more detail below, the restriction of demand by high prices also results in too few resources being attracted into such industries. This is considered to be inefficient. A more general discussion of the question of regulating monopoly power is found in Chapter 23.

STUDENT ACTIVITY 9.3

Put arguments for and against the following being in the public sector. Try to use the following terms in your arguments: merit good, public good, external benefits and costs, monopoly.

(a) school education
(b) healthcare
(c) higher education
(d) roads
(e) police
(f) defence
(g) electricity

The distributive role: transfer payments

Table 9.2 shows that the largest single item on the list of public expenditure is social security. This heading covers old-age pensions, unemployment benefit, sickness benefit, and working family's tax credit for those on inadequate incomes. These payments are known as transfer payments, since they are not in return for productive work, but simply transfer income from taxpayers to the groups of people receiving benefit. The government now takes responsibility for the poor and disadvantaged in our society, but other groups have taken this responsibility in the past. The family, the church (in the case of Christianity) and charities still continue to take some responsibility, but the twentieth century has seen the state shoulder the largest part of this burden. The number of pensioners is rising, and the number of unemployed has at times been fairly high in recent years, so this is a commitment that the government cannot easily avoid.

Some services which are provided free, like education and health, can be regarded as

Table 9.2 **Functional government expenditure (percentage of total)**

	1991	1995	1999
Defence	10.1	7.3	7.3
Public order	5.1	5.0	5.6
Education	10.9	10.7	11.5
Health	12.3	12.6	14.2
Social protection	35.9	39.2	39.1
Housing/amenities	3.6	2.5	1.5
Other	22.1	22.7	20.8
General government expenditure (£b)	232.5	304.7	336.9
GDP at market prices (£b)	548.5	714.0	891.1

Source: ONS *National Income and Expenditure 'Blue Book'*, 2000, National Statistics. © Crown Copyright 2001

redistribution in kind, providing a higher level of service in these two areas than the individuals would have been able to afford themselves. This raises an additional argument for these two services to be provided through the public sector. Consumers are still at liberty to choose to pay for their education and health through the private sector if they wish.

The welfare state

You do not have to be a socialist to believe that everyone is entitled to education, health services and social security. The origins of the welfare state can be traced back to Lloyd George and the Liberal party at the beginning of the twentieth century, but in its modern form was designed by the Beveridge Report of 1942.

The Beveridge Report recommended a national health scheme for 'every citizen without exception, without remuneration limit and without an economic barrier'. Beveridge also stated that the basis for comprehensive social security must be the certainty of a continuing high level of employment. A White Paper, Employment Policy, which embodied this idea, was published in 1944 and accepted by both the major political parties. Subsequently, full employment was to become a first priority for all governments. The wheel had come full circle from the workhouses of 1834, which were designed to be so unpleasant that they would force people to find work.

However, from 1988 onwards, market-based reforms of the welfare state that stopped short of privatisation were introduced by the Conservative government. The details of these reforms are discussed in the next chapter, but consisted largely of introducing market mechanisms into the welfare state and privatising support services.

Criteria for the allocation of resources

Market failure

Monopoly power, public goods and externality are all kinds of *market failure*. The idea of market failure can only be understood if you

have a measure of market success. The main role of markets is to allocate resources in such a way as to meet peoples' preferences. In Chapter 4 we introduced the idea of using willingness to pay for goods as a measure of benefit. In Chapter 3 we introduced the idea of opportunity cost. Using resources in one industry is the opportunity cost of not using them in another. The marginal cost of production is the total value of the resources used in producing the last unit of production. The price of factors of production in the market place is what other industries are willing to pay for them. It follows that we can use the marginal cost curve to represent the opportunity cost of resources, in the same way that we use the demand curve to represent willingness to pay. We can put these two ideas together to work out a criterion of market success. In Figure 9.1 it can be shown that where willingness to pay for the last unit of output (price) is equal to the opportunity cost of resources (marginal cost) then the best outcome has been found. The optimality of producing where price is equal to marginal cost can be demonstrated by looking at situations where price is not equal to marginal cost and showing how an improvement can be made. If output is below the best point, then each unit produced is adding more to benefit than cost. At an output of q_1, willingness to pay, at R is above the cost of resources at S. There is a net benefit to

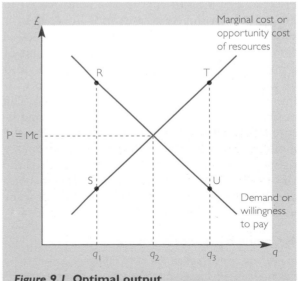

Figure 9.1 **Optimal output**

society of producing this unit. We should therefore carry on increasing output until this is no longer true (i.e. up to the point where P = MC at an output of q_2). If, on the other hand, we are producing at a point beyond the best point, like q_3, then we have added less to benefit than cost in this industry and the resource would be better used in another industry where there is greater willingness to pay. Willingness to pay at q_3 is only at U, while the cost of resources is higher at point T. The cost to society is thus greater than the benefit.

The optimality of perfect competition

The rule for the most efficient output is met by perfect competition. In Figure 9.1 the willingness to pay curve is the demand curve and the marginal cost curve is the supply curve. Where the two curves intersect, we have the most efficient outcome, but also the point of equilibrium in perfect competition. This is one of the strongest arguments for more competition in the economy, as it moves us towards an efficient allocation of resources.

Now that we have a criterion for market success, it is easier to see why monopoly, externality, and public goods are thought of as market failures. In the case of externality, the market does not take into account all the costs. The market reflects private costs but not social costs. Output is higher than it should be. On the other hand, monopolists restrict output in order to push up price, and as a result end up at a point like q_1 in Figure 9.1. In this case, output is lower than it should be. The marginal cost of a public good is zero. It costs nothing to produce an extra unit of a public good, and therefore the price should also be zero. Clearly, no entrepreneur would be willing to supply goods at a price of zero! The position of public goods is a little more complicated than this. They are not produced by the market, because you cannot create property rights for them. Once defence is provided for the UK, everyone in the country is defended. If someone in central London said 'actually I don't want to be defended' they can do nothing about it.

● *Common misunderstanding*

In everyday conversation the word efficiency is used to mean producing things at minimum cost, or getting the most output out of factors of production. While it is

necessary to meet this condition in order for something to be efficient in the economist's meaning of the word, this is not enough. For a market to be efficient, it must produce the right output, so that the correct amount of resources is allocated to that industry. If output is too low, more net benefit could be gained by shifting resources into the industry. If output is too high, greater net benefit could be gained by transferring resources to other industries. The efficient level of output is where P = MC.

Efficiency and equity

The criterion of efficiency is only one half of the story. If a situation is efficient, it tells us that resources are allocated according to willingness to pay. This gives more influence over the economy to those who are rich than to those who are poor. We also need to discuss the question of equity, or fairness. Economists have very different positions on the question of equity, because it is an ethical question and people have different value judgements. It is possible to take the view that rich people get rich by working hard and saving their money, while poor people become poor by avoiding work, and by not providing for their old age, or for periods of unemployment or sickness by saving or insurance schemes. It is possible to take the view that redistributing income to the poor will only remove their incentive to work. This would be a very right-wing view. A more left-wing view might be that rich people get like that by inheritance, or exploiting workers and consumers, while poor people often have no power in the market place and often end up without employment through no fault of their own. It is not the job of this book to tell you what to think about such matters. It is the job of this book to tell you that you can't decide about economic policy unless you do have an opinion of one sort or another about equity. Redistribution and its effects are discussed in Chapters 11 and 28.

Government failure

We have suggested that if there is market failure, the situation can be remedied by the government stepping in to put things right. Advocates of the market complain that the government often does no better than the market place, and that its intervention can often have harmful effects. Some examples of their criticisms are:

(a) Where the state produces something like education or health, they decide on the standards for the whole population, whereas consumers will have different preferences.
(b) Production in the public sector can often have monopoly features, because there is one large producer.
(c) This means there is no competition to drive down costs or innovate new products or techniques of production.
(d) It also means that some public sector workers will be in a position of power, which allows them to earn 'rents' like a private sector monopolist. This might be in the form of conditions of work rather than income.
(e) The growth of regulations puts burdens on the private sector which discourages enterprise.
(f) Bureaucracies have got a tendency to grow in size.

These arguments must be set against the arguments about market failure we discussed earlier. Countries have to find a balance between the public sector and the private sector that takes into account both sides of the argument. As has been discussed earlier, after rapid growth in the government sector through most of the twentieth century, the last two decades have experienced a switch back towards the market.

STUDENT ACTIVITY 9.4

Create a list of areas of the economy that the government intervenes in which you think it should move out of, or be less involved in. Do the same for areas where you think it should be more involved.

The political process as a substitute for the market

Economic policy, however, must function within the political framework. In practice this gives the consumers very little economic choice. However detailed the manifesto is on which a government is elected, it will only roughly approximate to the wishes of even its own supporters. Politics also places another constraint upon the mixed

economy. At least once every five years the government must seek re-election. It is possible to argue that any major economic policy should last for much longer than this and that therefore the real welfare of the country is being subjected to the government of the day's desire to ensure re-election. Thus politicians are led to ask themselves what most people want, while the economist would maintain that the correct question should be 'what do people want most?'

Conclusion

Despite the changes wrought by the Conservative governments of the 1980s and 1990s the UK economy is still a mixed economy with the public sector accounting for over 40 per cent of GDP (see Table 9.1). However, it is a very different economy than it was twenty years ago, with substantial areas of industry privatised and competition in much of what is left of the public sector.

Summary
1 Despite a belief in *laissez-faire*, governments of the nineteenth century were forced to intervene in the economy.
2 Classical economics proved unable to explain or cure the mass unemployment of the 1920s and 1930s.
3 Keynesian interventionist policies proved unable to deal with the inflationary problems of the 1970s, prompting a return to the market.
4 The mixed economy is a compound of *laissez-faire*, government management, public ownership and welfare state.
5 A profound change of direction came about in the 1980s and 1990s through privatisation and measures to make the economy more market orientated.
6 In the early twenty-first century the mixed economy faces new problems, in particular globalisation and the power of multinational business. The role of the state is once more a subject of great political controversy.
7 The state has three roles in the economy: stabilisation, allocative and distributive.

8 Market failure in the form of public goods, externality and monopoly gives rise to government intervention.

9 Government failure in the form of standardised output, high costs of production and bureaucracy may offset the advantages of such intervention.

10 In addition to efficiency, equity is also an important criterion for intervention.

❓ QUESTIONS

I Attempt to categorise each of the following as merit goods, public goods, goods with external benefits or costs, or private goods:

(a) roads
(b) dental care
(c) electricity
(d) rail travel
(e) libraries
(f) toothpaste
(g) lighthouses
(h) chocolate bars.

2 Distinguish between monetarists and Keynesians in relation to intervention in the economy.

3 Why do governments have to take notice of events in the rest of the world economy when formulating their policy?

4 Distinguish between the allocative, distributive and stabilisation roles of state intervention.

5 Explain why all economies are really mixed economies.

Data response A
PUBLIC EXPENDITURE ANALYSIS

Using the figures in Table 9.2 (page 132) answer the following questions:

I Which categories of public expenditure have been growing fastest as a percentage of total public expenditure?

2 What has been happening to public expenditure as a percentage of GDP at market prices?

3 Which of the categories of public expenditure in Table 9.2 are in the public sector for which of the following reasons:

(a) They are public goods.
(b) There are external costs and benefits.
(c) There is a redistribution of income.

10 Government intervention in the market

Learning outcomes

At the end of this chapter you will be able to:
▶ Identify the main problems of public expenditure control.
▶ Explain the main market-oriented reforms of the public sector.
▶ Understand the difficulties of making decisions in the absence of the market.
▶ Recognise policy areas where there are trade-offs between equity and efficiency.
▶ Identify areas where the market appears not to work well, and government regulation needs to be considered.

Introduction

Reasons for the government intervening in the economy were discussed in the last chapter. If part of the economy is in the public sector, its output should be produced in an *efficient* way. We do not necessarily have the market to fall back on as an automatic pressure towards efficiency. This chapter explores the way in which the public sector attempts to deal with the problem of efficiency and with conflicts with other *objectives* that the government may be trying to achieve.

This is a case study chapter. The cases can be treated as data response articles and there will be no further data responses at the end of the chapter. Student activities are to be found at the end of each case study.

Case study 10.1
THE GROWTH OF PUBLIC EXPENDITURE

The growth of public expenditure is a twentieth-century phenomenon. In the nineteenth century, the public sector accounted for 12 per cent, or less, of total national income (see Chapter 9). In the twentieth century we see a continuous increase until figures between 40 and 50 per cent become common in European countries. Figures for the USA and Japan are lower, but have also been growing. This case study explores the reason for this growth and the methods that have been used to control public expenditure growth.

Public expenditure is organised by a bureaucracy, the Civil Service, under the control of the government. This contrasts with the private sector, which operates through the market. Recent reforms have tried to simulate the market in the public sector, particularly in education and health. The case studies in this chapter therefore try to look at the public sector from the point of view of microeconomics.

Components of public expenditure

As can be seen from Table 10.1, the main components of public expenditure are pensions and benefits (social protection), defence, health, education, and law and order (Public Order/Safety). These industries are not exclusively provided by the public sector. There are flourishing private sector schools and health care services. In some countries health care is provided mainly by the private sector (e.g. the USA). Defence and law and order are nearly universally provided by the public sector, although private security firms do exist to protect property. Pensions can also be provided through the private sector.

Table 10.1 Functional composition of general government expenditure in 1999 (percentage of total)

	1999
Defence	7.3
Public order/safety	5.6
Education	11.5
Health	14.2
Social protection	39.1
Housing/amenities	1.5
Other	20.8

Source: ONS *National Income and Expenditure 'Blue Book'*, 2000, National Statistics. © Crown Copyright 2001

Reasons for growth in public expenditure

● *Common misunderstanding*

Since it was the Conservative party's policy to reduce public expenditure from 1979, most people assume this was achieved. In fact all it succeeded in doing was to prevent further growth, and in some years did not even succeed in doing this. Compare the figures for 1979–80 and 1995–6 in Table 10.2

Table 10.2 Public expenditure as a percentage of GDP at market prices

1991	39.7%
1992	42.5%
1993	43.0%
1994	42.4%
1995	42.7%
1996	40.5%
1997	39.3%
1998	38.5%
1999	37.8%

Source: *National Income 'Blue Book'* 2000, National Statistics. © Crown Copyright 2001

Income elasticity of demand

It is argued that the services that are normally provided by the public sector, also have high income elasticities of demand. The process by which this is turned into extra production is the political process rather than the market process. Voters are a bit like consumers because when they vote they are choosing a government that will provide public services. Governments which meet the 'voter–consumer's' demand for more education and health tend to get elected, although cutting taxes is also popular! Of course, choosing a government is much more complicated than this, with issues other than public expenditure, but if a government fails to produce essential services at the right level, people are more likely to vote them out at the next election.

The idea that demand for public sector output tends to grow faster than the rest of the economy is called **Wagner's law** after its German inventor. Although people want more and better public services, they also dislike having to pay higher taxes to pay for them. It is for this reason that governments have been trying to make the consumers of public services pay for some or all of the service. A good example is the shift away from grants to students in higher education and over to loans. Following the Dearing Report on Higher Education (1997) the Labour government introduced tuition fees for students (although this does not cover the full cost of higher education). Increases in prescription charges, introduced by the Conservatives but maintained by the Labour government have also helped to pay for the National Health Service (NHS).

Demographic change

The age structure of the population has changed dramatically over the last century as people live longer. In the UK there was a surge in births immediately after the Second World War, known as the **baby boom**. The baby boom generation will start to reach the age of 60 in the year 2005. Health care for elderly people is estimated to be up to six times as expensive as for young people. The number of people drawing the state pension will continue to rise over the next decade. Since health and social security are a large part of public expenditure (see Table 10.1), these increased demands on public services will place upward pressure on government spending.

Efficiency in the public sector

Rising demand on its own need not lead to increasing expenditure. The massive rise in the demand for computers has been accompanied by a massive reduction in their price and an increase in their power because of rapid technical progress. It is argued that service industries find it more difficult to reduce their costs because it is more difficult to introduce assembly line techniques. In the health service, for instance, it is difficult to introduce technology to reduce the number of nurses per patient. In fact introducing more capital sometimes increases the demand for nurses (e.g. in intensive care wards). It may be difficult to reduce costs in services, but it is not impossible. In some services new technology has significantly reduced labour needs, e.g. banking. By contrast, labour-saving inventions in hairdressing are few and far between and basically there is still one hairdresser per customer. Many of the industries in the public sector fall into the service industry category, so this problem makes reducing costs difficult. If increases in pay were only related to productivity increases then there would be less of a problem. If we wish to continue to persuade talented people to become teachers, doctors and nurses, then to attract them into these professions the state must pay them competitive wages. The difficulty of raising productivity in these public service industries contributes to public expenditure growth.

The business cycle

When the economy is booming, the ratio of public expenditure to GDP goes down. This is for two reasons. First, GDP is going up, and second, because spending on unemployment benefit is falling, public expenditure will be falling. For the opposite reasons, during a recession, the ratio will rise. When trying to judge the success of a government in reducing public expenditure, you should take into account the level of unemployment. The generally higher level of unemployment that has been experienced in Europe and North America in the 1980s and 1990s has contributed to the difficulty in reducing the percentage of GDP going to public expenditure.

● *Common misunderstanding*

It is sometimes thought that the nationalised industries added to the growth of public expenditure until they were privatised in the 1980s and 1990s. This is true for certain industries and certain periods, but is generally not true for most of the industries, most of the time. Telecommunications, gas, and electricity were profitable in most years for the simple reason that they were monopolies. Rail consistently made a loss, but continues

to need large subsidies now that it has been privatised. The coal industry did need subsidy and has largely been closed down after privatisation. There were certain industries which were nationalised in the 1970s because they were 'lame ducks' which could not survive in the private sector. An example is British Leyland (now known as Rover). The idea here was to return them to the private sector once they returned to profitability. There are some good examples of this policy (Cable and Wireless, Amersham International) but the car industry continued to need subsidy. Finally, there was one period when the nationalised industries did make a loss, when the government refused to let them increase their prices as part of its anti-inflation policy between 1974 and 1976. Further discussion of nationalised industries and privatisation can be found in Chapter 24.

Strategies for the control of public expenditure

The range of policies that have been used to control public expenditure is very wide, but policies can be grouped together:

(a) *Privatisation* can only reduce public expenditure if the privatised industry was making a loss when it was in the public sector. Proceeds from the sale of nationalised industries and other state owned assets create a one-off increase in revenue for the government. This allows them to increase public expenditure in that year without unpopular increases in tax. Alternatively, privatisation revenue allows a one-off reduction in tax. For a fuller discussion of privatisation, see Chapter 24.

(b) *Price indexation*. By indexing pensions to prices rather than wages in the 1980s, the government ensured that pensions would grow more slowly than national income. This may keep public expenditure under control, but pensioners do not think it was such a good idea. When inflation falls to low levels then the increase in money terms can seem very low. The 75p a week increase in 2000 was politically unpopular because it appeared to be so mean.

(c) *Charges* can be introduced or increased for public services resulting in a lower net expenditure. The charges for prescriptions and dental treatment were increased under the Conservative administration, although free provision was retained for children, pensioners and low-income groups. In higher education the replacement of much of the student grant by loans has a similar effect, as does the introduction of tuition fees.

(d) *Cost reduction* in services provided have largely been achieved by the introduction of competition by various means. The development of an *internal market* within the public sector in health and education is discussed below in Case studies 10.2 and10.3. *Compulsory competitive tendering* (CCT) has been introduced for many government departments and local government services. This means that the public sector bureaucracies have to compete with alternative bids from the private sector for the production of services.

(e) *Means testing* can be introduced for services previously offered free. Care of the elderly in residential homes is offered free only if a person has less than £16 000 of assets. Home help services are also means tested.

STUDENT ACTIVITY 10.1

Ask your teacher how it is possible to reduce the costs of your education without also reducing its quality. To what extent is it possible to substitute capital for labour by using technology? Should you be becoming more of an 'independent learner' so your teacher can teach more students? Should your teacher receive pay increases only when productivity has risen?

STUDENT ACTIVITY 10.2

How can the following expenditures be reduced by introducing charges?

(a) dentistry
(b) in-patient hospital treatment
(c) school
(d) pensions

Case study 10.2
REFORM OF THE NHS: TECHNICAL EFFICIENCY AND TRANSACTIONS COSTS

Why is health care in the public sector?

In Chapter 9 the rationale for government involvement in the market was discussed in some detail. *Externality* is one of the reasons for government involvement, both because people spread diseases if untreated, and because an unhealthy population is unproductive. There are *equity* reasons for government involvement, so that poor people can achieve a minimum standard of health. There are *paternalistic* reasons because richer people may wish to redistribute income to poorer people in this particular way. The market may not work well because of *ignorance* about health in the population, so the government may concentrate on *preventive medicine* and health education. It can be seen that there is no simple reason for the government to intervene, and different aspects of health care may have different reasons for government intervention. This is a complex area that you must think about carefully before jumping to conclusions.

It is also clear that if people have the money, they may naturally wish to buy the best medical attention as quickly as possible. It is also evident that there are services supplied to the patient in hospital that are clearly private goods and have little to do with health. The so-called *hotel services* of a hospital can be provided at many levels to satisfy the preferences and ability to pay of the consumer–patient. Food, accommodation, furnishing and entertainment are necessary in a hospital but are not part of health care.

The size of the NHS budget

In 1999, the NHS spent £49.9 billion, representing 14.8 per cent of government spending. The NHS was created in 1948 out of a mixture of private and local authority hospitals. The belief of its founders was that by providing free health care, people's health would improve and costs would be reduced. While this may be true when people are younger, the success of the health industry in keeping people alive until they reach old age has meant a considerable increase in expenditure. Elderly people are more costly to the NHS as they need more care for chronic conditions. The advance of medical technology has meant that many illnesses such as heart disease and cancer, which afflict the elderly, can be treated with expensive surgery or drugs and operations.

As the elderly represent an increasing proportion of the population, this means that expenditure on the health service has to keep rising constantly just to provide the same level of service to everyone. The important questions are how to keep costs under control and how to pay for the service.

How to pay for the service?

The private sector

In the private sector the method of payment is usually by insurance, where a person pays annually, whether they need treatment or not. In the USA where health care is mainly private, this is the usual method of payment. It is not necessarily the case that such insurance will pay all costs and there may be a maximum payment for treatment in a particular year. It is of course more expensive to join such schemes as you become older, since the risk of expensive illnesses rises. What happens to poor people who cannot afford medical health insurance? In the USA there is a **safety net** of charity and publicly provided medicine. The quality of service in this sector is obviously lower, otherwise people would not choose to pay for expensive private health insurance. The USA spends more on health care as a percentage of GDP than almost any other country. This could be partly explained in terms of the high income elasticity of demand for health care, and the high US standard of living (Wagner's law). There is also a suspicion that because of ignorance on the part of the patients, and fear of litigation on the part of the doctors, that more is spent on health care than is strictly necessary. If a doctor making decisions about the right treatment for you is also likely to profit from your treatment, it is possible the doctor will take advantage of the situation, although it is hoped that this would not happen often.

Public provision and private production

In Germany, each person pays a proportion of their income tax for health care. If a person has no income they pay nothing. As their income rises they will pay more until a point comes where it would be cheaper for them to opt out of the system and pay for private health care insurance. In this case the government has effectively nationalised the insurance part of the health care system and introduced a pricing system based on **ability to pay** rather than **willingness to pay**. The **production** of health care could be in the private sector under such a system, but its **provision** can remain in the public sector. It is important to make this distinction between production and provision because the role of the state is different in each case. If the state provides a service, it is paying for it, not producing it. The industry is not nationalised.

Public subsidy

In France payment is made for certain types of health care, such as a visit to the doctor, and the patient is reimbursed by the government. In this system patients sometimes have to pay a proportion of the cost themselves. It is argued that if a good is free it will be overused (see Figure 10.1). If a person has to pay something towards a visit to the doctor then they will not make visits that are trivial. Against this argument it is pointed out that people are often ignorant about the importance of symptoms that

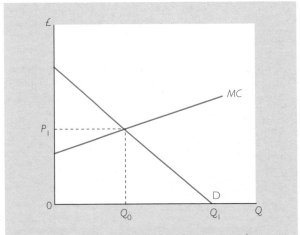

Figure 10.1 **Excessive demand at zero price**

they may suffer from, and may delay going to the doctor. An earlier appointment could have saved money and suffering by successful treatment of the disease in its early stages.

Bureaucratic control

The NHS in the UK before the recent reforms was organised in a bureaucratic way. Funds were channelled down from the government to Regional and Area Health Authorities which were responsible for delivering health care in their part of the country (see Figure 10.2). Since the NHS is 'free at the point of use' there will be a tendency for demand to be very high (see Figure 10.1). If price is not used to allocate resources in health care, then rationing is likely. It is possible to imagine so many resources being put into health care by the government that all demands on it could be met, but this has never been the case since the NHS was set up. The NHS has always prioritised emergencies and serious illness.

As a result **waiting lists** have developed in non-urgent surgery and treatment. This is similar to a situation of excess demand because the price (set at zero) is below the market clearing price as indicated in Figure 10.1. Health care is being **rationed** on the basis of **need** rather than **willingness to pay**. In effect doctors are taking the decision about who should be treated first rather than the market. There is not only a problem of allocating resources between different types of medical expenditure; there is also the problem of how much should be put into the health care system as a whole. Total expenditure on the NHS has often been a major political issue in the UK.

The internal market

The idea of a market in the public sector was put forward in a White Paper in 1989 and was implemented in the early 1990s. It is not a market in the full sense since customers do not use their own money to buy services. It is sometimes referred to as a **quasi-market** because it does not have all the characteristics of a market. It is also described as an **internal market** because the market is inside the NHS, between different parts of the organisation.

The NHS was split up into different parts so they could trade with each other. The main features of the changes are depicted in Figure 10.2. The principle behind all market reforms in the public sector is the **purchaser– provider split**. In the case of the NHS it is the hospitals which are largely the providers, and the family doctors (general practitioners or GPs) who are the purchasers. Initially, under the Conservatives, then GP practices with just a few GPs acted as a business unit and entered into contracts with hospitals. More recently, under the Labour party, larger groups of GPs and other healthcare professionals such as community nurses have been put together in primary care trusts (**PCT**s). These groups are much larger, serving an average of 100 000 patients.

If you go to your doctor with a problem that needs further treatment, then the doctor will purchase this treatment for you from a hospital. The doctors receive money for each patient who registers with them whether they are sick or well. It can be seen that the doctors are undertaking the insurance function of health care in this way. This is one of the reasons for increasing the size of purchaser organisation from the doctor's surgery to the larger PCT – the risks are spread over a wider group. A second reason, is the cost of operating the market. It costs more if there are many contracts between hospitals and all the GP surgeries that may use them,

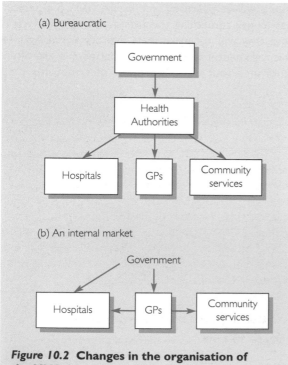

Figure 10.2 Changes in the organisation of the NHS

rather than just a few contracts with the larger PCTs. Finally, there is an argument about the principle of comparative advantage (see Chapter 3): should doctors spend their time on medicine, or on running a small business?

Trusts and fundholding

Eventually all hospitals became independent **trusts**. The status of a trust is very different from a private company. It does not have shareholders and is not trying to maximise profits. It does have revenues and costs, and will normally try to break even or reinvest any surplus. Unlike bureaucratic organisations in the public sector it will try to build up a small **reserve** to cushion it for times when it cannot break even. Like private companies it will face competition from other trusts for its services, and doctors (or PCTs) are able to choose the cheapest, or the best service for different kinds of standard treatment. It is argued that people in a position of power within non-profit-making organisations may pay themselves a **rent** (see Chapter 25) in the form of high wages or advantageous conditions of employment.

The other main organisational reform of the internal market, GP **fundholding**, was organised differently. GPs have always been self-employed, so there was no need to set up trusts. GP practices are partnerships (see Chapter 7) that receive more income as more patients are registered. The main effect of the reforms was to transfer the funds allocated for treating patients in hospital from Health Authorities to GP practices. If GP practices do not spend all this money, they were allowed to spend any surplus on the surgery, but given the insurance function of fundholding, they are well advised to hold money in reserve in case their patients are less healthy the following year. Not all GP practices elected to take fundholding status and patients from non-fundholding practices continue to have their hospital treatment funded by the local Health Authority. The recent shift to the PCT system has removed much of the ambiguity about what to do with surpluses.

Efficiency and transactions costs in the internal market

The central principle that the NHS should be **free at the point of use** has been retained, but competition has replaced bureaucratic control. Competition

should drive down costs or improve service quality. The question that arises is whether this has happened in practice. The problem is that treatments were not costed individually before the reforms, so comparison is difficult. One measure that has been used is the length of waiting lists. Targets to reduce waiting to less than a year were initially met, but the problem returns from time to time as demand increases and resources do not keep pace. However, if the cost of keeping all waiting lists at less than one year is bringing non-urgent cases in earlier, but delaying some more serious cases, then needs are not being prioritised correctly. There have been attempts to place hospitals in league tables but these have also run into some difficulties. An early study of heart treatment in Scotland put the most prestigious hospital at the bottom of the list. Since it had the most seriously ill patients, it had the highest death rate. This underlines the difficulty of making such comparisons.

There has been a reduction in the number of nurses employed in the NHS since the reforms were introduced, but this has been more than offset by increases in the number of administrative and management staff. Competition may well have reduced costs, but the costs of setting up and administering the market must also be taken into account. These transactions costs are the main drawback of the reforms. The PCT proposal is an attempt to reduce **transactions costs**, but it should be noted that it reduces competition too.

Equity and the internal market

A second undesirable by-product of the internal market was the advantage that fundholding GPs had in their dealings with hospitals. The waiting time for the patients of non-fundholding GPs was longer on average than for those of fundholding GPs. This was because the hospitals were keen to keep their new customers happy. The Labour government instructed hospitals to end this inequitable practice. The early Labour moves against bureaucracy and inequity seem reasonable, but defenders of the reforms are concerned that competition will disappear.

Relationships between the public and private sectors

The largest provider of private medicine in the UK is the NHS! This surprising answer takes us back to a much older debate about how the NHS is run. When asked about how he had persuaded the doctors to support the nationalisation of the health service, Beveridge is reputed to have said 'I stuffed their mouths with gold'. It certainly seems to be the case that senior consultants can quite happily combine their contract with the NHS and their private work, even undertaking both activities in one hospital in some cases. If there is a waiting list for an operation on the NHS, a patient can 'jump the queue' by becoming a private patient, and may even be operated on by the same doctor possibly in the same hospital. Waiting lists have never been a problem for those who can afford the treatment or insurance. It is therefore not true to say that, before the introduction of the internal market, the NHS always operated in an entirely equitable way. There is also evidence to suggest that more articulate, educated middle-class patients are better at 'working the system' to obtain second opinions, or to challenge unsatisfactory treatment. However bureaucratic a system may be, market forces have a habit of making themselves felt, particularly if it is a matter of life and death.

STUDENT ACTIVITY 10.3

Which of the following scenarios for the development of the health service do you think is preferable? Use the concepts of equity, efficiency and transactions costs in your answer.

(a) A bureaucratically run health service; free at the point of use; owned by the state; where doctors cannot work for the private sector; with treatment prioritised solely by need.

(b) A private sector backed up by a private insurance system with a lower-quality state safety net system.

(c) An internal market primarily run by the state but with cooperative relationships with the private sector.

Case study 10.3
MARKETS IN EDUCATION: ALLOCATIVE EFFICIENCY

Opting out

The 1988 Education Reform Act (ERA) introduced the market into state education. Before the ERA,

education was largely run by local government; a mixture of local democracy and local bureaucracy. After ERA schools could choose (provided they had the support of their parents) to opt out of local government control and receive funding directly from the Department for Education (later known as the Department for Education and Employment – DfEE). Initially such direct funding was more attractive, to encourage more schools to opt out. Funding was on a per student basis so that the more successful a school was in attracting 'customers', the more money it received. This principle of *formula funding* was later extended to all schools including those remaining under local authority control. All schools have been given much greater control of their own budget under a scheme known as the local management of schools (LMS).

Competition?

Schools now have to compete to attract 'customers' in order to increase revenue. They have to manage their resources in order to keep costs under control. They can make a profit or a loss. Are they like firms in private sector competition? In some important respects they are. They are rewarded for successful operation of their 'businesses'. They can reinvest any surplus that they make. Successful schools are more likely to attract new investment if an expansion of capacity is needed. However, there are some important respects in which they are not like private companies:

(a) They do not have shareholders and do not distribute profits.

(b) They cannot usually take over other schools.

(c) If a school gets into financial difficulty it is difficult for it to 'exit' the market because of its responsibility to its students. A change of management (head teacher) is more likely.

(d) They have no control over pricing, but must accept the price set nationally (for opted out schools) or locally (for those remaining under local government control).

Choice?

For allocative efficiency to exist, the consumer must have *choice*. Is this the case with the market in the state schools system? Certainly there has been a big increase in the apparent choice of schools available to students, but there is a conflict between two government objectives. One objective is to reduce costs, which can be best achieved by getting rid of spare capacity and making sure every class is full. This can conflict with choice because successful schools have reduced the *spare capacity* that would allow them to accept extra students who want to attend them. Less successful schools may have spare capacity because students have not chosen to enrol with them.

Who chooses whom?

Where there is no spare capacity the schools will choose which students to accept. In the market place, the question of which consumer will buy the best products is usually settled by who is willing to pay the highest price. Could the problem of who should attend the best schools be solved in this way? There is a problem here with an equity concept, the idea of *equality of opportunity*. In practice, schools will tend to accept students who they believe will enhance their reputation. Systems designed to discover which students have the greatest potential, such as exams or interview, tend to be manipulated best by middle-class parents. The question of equality of opportunity therefore arises again. Even where there is 'comprehensivisation' of schools, local people tend to know which is the 'best' comprehensive to get into. They may even be willing to move house to get into the catchment area of the school. Temporary religious conversions have not been unknown!

Measuring success: the value-added debate

In order to help consumers choose the right school, the government has published league tables to show which ones are doing best. These league tables have largely been at A level and GCSE level but SAT results have also been published to show relative performance at younger ages. Critics of such league tables argue that they are not measuring the schools, but the students in them. Schools which select their students, or which recruit from an affluent middle-class area, are likely to do better than inner city schools recruiting from poor areas with high unemployment. This might sound like a suggestion that middle-class children are more intelligent than working-class children. Far from it; this view suggests that there is no difference in intelligence at birth, but the affluent middle-class environment will generally provide the motivation, advice and role model for a

student to succeed. There will of course also be intelligent, self-motivated, successful working-class students, and rebellious, lazy, cerebrally challenged middle-class students.

Conclusion

Creating competition in schools does not automatically bring improvement to the school system as a whole. International comparisons of school students' abilities suggest that the UK competes well at the top end of the distribution, but our average students are doing less well than the average students of our competitors. Generating excellent schools at the top end will not necessarily help our competitiveness in world markets, which depends on the abilities of the vast majority of our workforce. The question is whether the opting out system will drive the performance of all schools or just benefit the élite. The Labour government's first response on this question is to continue initially with league tables, but to be more pro-active in changing the culture of 'failing schools'. The replacement of the management and many of the teachers of schools identified by the education regulator (OFSTED) is one approach. This process has gone as far as identifying 'failing' local authorities, which have been replaced by outsiders. The idea of private sector companies running failing schools is also being considered, although such companies are, unsurprisingly, expressing an interest in running successful schools as well. Money has also been made available to reduce the class size of under seven-year-olds to below 30. It remains to be seen whether this approach is more successful than that of their predecessors.

STUDENT ACTIVITY 10.4

(a) What measures could be used to improve exam results in your school or college?
(b) Study the results of the following two schools and put forward possible explanations for the differences. How could School A's results be improved?

Number of pupils achieving five A–C grades

School A *Inner city comprehensive*	School B *Suburban grammar school*
27%	95%

Case study 10.4
MONOPOLY AND PRIVATISED INDUSTRIES

The privatisation of the nationalised industries

The most dramatic change in the role of the state has been the privatisation of the nationalled industries mainly achieved by the Conservative government of 1979 to 1997, led first by Mrs Thatcher, and then by John Major. Most of the industries were nationalised in the 1940s, after the Second World War, mainly because they were thought to be monopolies, and needed to be controlled by the government in order to protect the consumer from exploitation. Not all industries fell into this category however, the steel and coal industries being examples of industries that were potentially competitive, but nationalised for political reasons, or because of their strategic importance. This case study looks at the ways in which the problem of monopoly was overcome after privatisation.

Natural monopoly and networks

The term natural monopoly is used to describe the situation where having more than one competitor would raise costs and cause wasteful competition. Examples can be found from industries that are based on large physical distribution networks. Many of the nationalised industries fell into this category. The gas and water industries use pipelines, which would be expensive to duplicate. The telephone and electricity industry distribute their products through wires. Road and rail both have extensive track for the distribution of their service.

Separating the natural monopoly from the competitive service

Initially when privatisation took place, nationalised industries were privatised as single companies, with some provision for competition. British Telecom had limited competition from a company called Mercury, which had access to BT's network, but only a small network of its own. The electricity industry was considered to be sufficient competition for British Gas. Later privatisations attempted to separate the natural monopoly element from the potentially competitive services. The electricity industry was separated into the National Grid, a national monopoly which distributes bulk electricity around the country; the regional electricity companies, local monopolies which distribute electricity to homes and businesses; the generating companies which produce the electricity; and supply companies who provide a billing and meter reading service, but buy everything else from the other companies. This is perhaps the most complicated example, but the principle is the same with other industries, with a natural monopoly network and competition between suppliers. The natural monopoly still needs regulating of course, or else could exploit other companies or consumers. The privatised industries are regulated by bodies such as Oftel, Ofwat and Ofgen, which limit price increases in the natural monopoly part of the industry, and set rules about competitive practices. In the case of the telecommunication industry, a new technology (fibre optic cable) has reduced the cost of duplicating the network, leading some people to argue that it is no longer a natural monopoly. The privatised industries are considered in detail in Chapter 24.

Controlling other monopolies

Monopolies arise in other circumstance than the privatised industries. The 1998 Competition Act allows the government to take action if a monopoly sets unfair selling or purchase prices. Action may also be taken if monopolies limit production, markets or technical developments; discriminate between customers or suppliers; or enforce other firms to sign contracts with unconnected unfavourable obligations. A firm is considered to have a monopoly if they control 25 per cent of the market, but the Director-General of Fair Trading is only compelled to act if the market share reaches 40 per cent. Similar rules apply to groups of companies acting together to create restrictive practices such as fixing prices, limiting production, or acting in other ways like a monopoly. Firms can be fined up to 10 per cent of UK turnover for up to three years if they break these rules.

The regulators of the privatised industries are now expected to implement these rules and refer companies that break them. Some people are speculating that this new legislation is so strong that it may replace the need for separate regulators in some of the industries altogether.

Identify the natural monopoly element in each of the following industries and discuss which elements are potentially competitive. What kind of regulations would be needed in each case if the product is provided through the private sector?

(a) Parcel and letter delivery.
(b) Secondary school education in the 'National Curriculum' system.
(c) The railways.

Case study 10.5
REGIONAL PROBLEMS

The government intervenes to help those areas of the economy that are doing less well in terms of employment. Before looking at such policy, we will consider some of the factors which affect the location of economic activity.

The location of industry

There are many factors which affect the attractiveness of a location for a business. These are examined below in two groups: those occurring spontaneously in the economy, and those engineered by the government. We might imagine that organisations weigh all the possible advantages and disadvantages carefully and site their business so as to minimise their costs. It is doubtful whether this is ever totally the case; historical accident may well play a big part in location. For example, William Morris started car manufacture in Oxford because that is where his cycle shop was. Equally, business people tend to be gregarious and will often site their organisation where there are lots of others. However, no one will begin a business or site a new factory without considering some of the following factors.

Spontaneous factors

(a) *Raw materials.* Extractive industries must locate where the raw materials are, and this may in turn attract other industries, e.g. the iron and steel industry was attracted to coalfields, and engineering industries were then often attracted to the same location. Thus around Glasgow

there were the Lanark coalfield, an iron and steel industry and shipbuilding. Today, when many raw materials are imported, industries frequently locate at or near ports.

(b) *Power.* The woollen industry moved to the West Riding of Yorkshire to take advantage of the water power from Pennine streams. In the nineteenth century most industries were dependent upon coal as a source of power. Since coal was expensive to transport, they tended to locate on coalfields. Most industries now use electricity or nuclear power, which is readily available anywhere in the country. This means that the availability of power is not an important locational influence today. An exception to this is the aluminium industry, which uses vast quantities of electric power. The industry is therefore centred in countries where there is a lot of cheap hydro-electric power, such as in Canada and Norway.

(c) *Transport.* Historically, transport was a vital locational influence. Water transport was the only cheap and reliable means of transporting heavy loads. Most industries, therefore, tended to locate near rivers or the coast. Canals and, later, railways allowed industry to spread to other locations. Today, access to good transport facilities is still a locational influence. This is illustrated by the town of Warrington in Cheshire, which experienced a renaissance in its industrial fortunes partly as a result of standing at the intersection of three motorways.

Max Weber, a famous economic historian and sociologist, developed a theory of the location of industry. Weber maintained that industrialists would try to minimise their transport costs. This means that if a commodity *lost weight* during manufacture the industry would tend to locate near the raw materials, whereas if it *gained weight* during manufacture it would tend to locate near the market. Steel is an example of a commodity which loses weight during manufacture. To manufacture steel near the market would mean transporting several tonnes of raw materials but selling perhaps only one tonne of finished product. Brewing, however, is an industry in which the product gains weight during manufacture. It is therefore more economical to transport the hops, barley and sugar to the market, where water is added and the brewing takes place. Traditionally, brewing was a widely-dispersed industry, although in recent years it has become more centralised. Weber's theory is modified by the value of the commodity. Whisky, for example, is so expensive that transport costs are only a small percentage of the price and are therefore not a locational influence.

(d) *Markets.* Service industries, such as catering, entertainment and professional services, have nearly always had to locate near their markets. In the twentieth century many industries initially located with respect to markets. Goods which are fragile and expensive to transport, such as furniture and electrical goods, may be better produced near to where they are to be sold; however, the globalisation of production, with many industries now dominated by large multi-national firms, means that this factor is far less significant as a locational force than it once was.

(e) *Labour.* The existence of a pool of highly-skilled labour may be a locational influence but, increasingly, manual skills can be replaced by automated machinery. An exception to this may be 'foot-loose' industries. Since they are not dependent upon other specific locational influences they may therefore be attracted to cheap labour.

(f) *Industrial inertia.* This is the tendency of an industry to continue to locate itself in an area when the factors which originally located the industry there have ceased to operate. An example of this would be the steel industry in Sheffield, although this may be explained, partly, by external economies of scale and the existence of skilled labour.

(g) *Special local circumstances.* Such factors as climate or topography may affect the location of an industry. The oil terminal at Milford Haven is located there because of the deep-water anchorage available. A further example is provided by the market gardening industry in the Isles of Scilly, located there to take advantage of the early spring.

(h) *'Sunrise' industries.* This is the term given to industries such as computer software which are associated with the 'new technology'. They could be regarded as 'footloose' industries since they are relatively free from apparent locational constraints. However, many of them have become concentrated in the so-called 'M4 corridor', which is the area either side of the M4, stretching from Slough towards Bristol. Reasons that have been suggested for this, apart from the natural gregariousness of business people, are the good communications and, more importantly, the fact that, freed from other obvious constraints, business people have opted to live and work in the pleasant environment of Berkshire and Oxfordshire.

Government influences and the location of industry

The old staple industries, such as iron and steel, shipbuilding and coal-mining, were in decline for most of the twentieth century, but have suffered from serious crisis in the last 20 years. Areas such as Glasgow, South Yorkshire, the North East and South Wales have been heavily affected, as have old ports such as Liverpool and Hull, which cannot handle the new container traffic as effectively as Southampton or Felixstowe. The operation of free market economics seemed powerless to alleviate the consequent economic distress of these areas. This meant that from the 1930s, the government brought in an increasing number of measures to try to attract industry to these areas. We used to explain things in terms of the decline of the old staple industries and the rise of the new industries such as motor vehicles, electronics and chemicals. However, since the 1970s some of these 'new' industries have been in decline, or at least have not been experiencing any significant growth in sales, so that previously prosperous areas, such as the West Midlands, themselves became areas of industrial dereliction during the depression of the early 1980s. Subsequently, as the economy moved into a further recession in the early 1990s, yet more such industries and areas experienced difficulties. A good example of this is the recession in the financial services industries in London and the south-east during the early 1990s, although such new industries often bounce back fastest when economic recovery occurs.

Over the years since the Second World War governments of both the major parties built up such an armoury of legislative controls and financial inducements that government came to be one of the most important influences upon the location of industry. However, the 'Thatcher revolution' in the 1980s meant that by the early 1990s many of the controls and incentives had disappeared. Nevertheless, some controls and incentives did remain, provided by both the British government and the EU. We will now consider the most important of these.

(a) *Financial incentives*. Financial incentives to encourage organisations to move to depressed areas started with the Special Areas Act 1934. After the Second World War various Acts increased regional assistance. The Industry Act 1972 designated large areas of the country as Special Development Areas (SDAs), Development Areas (DAs) and Intermediate Areas (IAs), all of which qualified for financial assistance.

Successive Conservative governments in the 1980s and early 1990s drastically reduced both the amount of regional aid and the extent of the areas which could receive aid, although Northern Ireland continued to receive considerable assistance. At present there are two types of Assisted Area that qualify for regional aid, **Development Areas** and **Intermediate Areas**, the distinction between Development Areas and Special Development Areas having been dropped in 1984.

The reasons for the decrease in regional assistance were the government's disinclination to intervene in the economy, stemming from its belief that market forces are the best way to ensure a healthy economy, and its desire to cut public expenditure.

In 1988 Regional Development Grants (RDGs), available to manufacturing and some service projects that created or increased capacity in Assisted Areas, were replaced by discretionary Regional Selective Assistance (RSA). The latter focused more on helping new firms to set up in Assisted Areas rather than on aiding the more traditional industries in those areas. RSA is available to both manufacturing and service firms that create or safeguard jobs and benefit the local economy. Small firms (defined in this instance as those employing less than 25 people) in Assisted Areas can apply for Regional Enterprise Grants (REGs) to aid investment and innovation.

A development in 1980 was the introduction of Enterprise Zones. These are small areas of inner cities, averaging in size approximately 150 hectares. Currently there are 30 such zones in existence in the UK. Firms setting up in Enterprise Zones get a stream of incentives for their first 10 years of operation: no rates; 100 per cent capital allowances on all commercial and industrial property; and generally less bureaucracy and fewer planning regulations. Another development in the 1980s was the creation of a number of Urban Development Corporations (UDCs). These virtually independent bodies have freedom from many planning constraints, together with tax privileges. The most famous of these is the Docklands Development Corporation, which was associated with the 'yuppiefication' of London's docklands.

In 1988 the Action for Cities Programme was launched, which was aimed at coordinating government policy on the inner cities and at encouraging private investment. In 1994 this was largely replaced by the Single Regeneration Budget (SRB) under the control of the Department of the Environment.

The EU makes some funds available from the European Regional Development Fund (ERDF), which is part of the broader EU Structural Funds. In principle, EU financial assistance is supposed to be additional to help given by national governments, but often the DTI has deducted the amount of any ERDF grant from any assistance it may have given. EU guidelines reducing those parts of the population currently included in the regional policy 'net' are being implemented, thus reducing the Assisted Area coverage.

Whether interventionism works or whether free market forces are more effective, there can be no doubt that in the 1990s massive regional disparities still existed in the UK.

(b) *Legislative controls*. The government can influence the location of industry by the negative method of forbidding or discouraging new building where it does not want it. Between 1947 and 1974 successive governments created a whole series of legislative controls designed to encourage firms to move to SDAs and DAs. The controls required all new industrial or office developments first to obtain Industrial Development Certificates (IDCs). However, in December 1981 the government suspended the regulations. This was done partly because of the government's desire to reduce the role of government intervention in the economy and partly because of the need to facilitate development of all kinds in an effort to alleviate unemployment.

Thus, to all intents and purposes, planning regulations are the same throughout the country. The exceptions are Enterprise Zones and the Urban Development Corporations, where regulations are less strict.

(c) *Direct intervention.* The government can place orders for goods and services in development areas. It was also able to encourage the nationalised industries (pre-privatisation) to do so. In addition to this, it could decentralise government departments, as it did when the Inland Revenue administration was moved to Middlesbrough. The Distribution of Industry Acts of 1945 and 1950 allowed the government to build factories in Development Areas and lease or sell them. Today, the government may lease a factory to a firm, rent free, for two years if it creates enough jobs.

The New Towns Act 1946 and the Town Development Act 1952 brought a number of new towns into existence, the first of which was Stevenage in Hertfordshire. In August 1981 the government decided to curtail the activities of new towns and eight of the New Town Corporations had to dispose of £140 million of their assets.

(d) *Persuasion.* By advertising and information, businesses may be persuaded to locate in the regions. This policy is followed through both centrally and locally. The Local Employment Act 1960 set up development councils in depressed regions. In 1965 the whole of the UK was covered by 11 regional economic planning councils, each of which was responsible for devising an economic strategy for its region and for publicising opportunities in the region. Advertisement placed by regional authorities and by New Town Corporations are a familiar sight in UK newspapers. The DTI provides information and advice, both from its headquarters in London and from its regional offices. An assessment of regional policy is included in Chapter 39.

The Labour government of 1997 has placed a new emphasis on regional development, setting up nine English Regional Development Authorities (RDAs), similar to those established in Wales and Scotland. Their boundaries are the same as regional planning councils and their functions are similar, but also include some of the work of the SRB plus the functions of the Rural Development Commisssion. In negotiations with the EU, the UK's poorest regions are to receive £1.5 billion p.a. for seven years from 2000, provided a similar amount is forthcoming from UK public or private sources.

The Rodgers Report (2000) emphasised the need to regenerate British cities on more European lines with greater use of brownfield sites (old industrial land), better public transport and revitalised city centres. This vision of cities as a place which people find attractive, rather than places people try to escape, has been mirrored in the Government's Urban White Paper which attempts to implement the Rodgers Report.

Markets allocate resources between different regions of one country with results that sometimes create political difficulties. The data in Table 10.3 illustrate the way in which unemployment (see Chapters 18 and 39) and the standard of living vary considerably within one country. It is possible to explain this in terms of the principle of comparative advantage (see Chapter 3), with the high incomes going to the more productive region. Exchange rates cannot be adjusted to offset different levels of productivity, so wages are higher in the more productive region instead. Capital is naturally attracted to the more dynamic areas of the country where the skill and education levels are higher, so there is less unemployment in these regions.

The question arises as to whether the government should intervene to help the areas by improving transport links; spending money to raise educational achievement; 'regenerate' declining city centres and inner city areas by pumping in money to finance an improvement in amenities and housing; and provide subsidies to attract foreign multinational firms to set up in the area.

STUDENT ACTIVITY 10.6

Study Table 10.3. Which of the regions has the worst problems? What policies could be used to try and improve the performance of their economy? If you live in one of the regions, use your local knowledge to decide what makes your region successful or unsuccessful.

Table 10.3 **Regional disparity**

	Population (million)	GDP per capita UK = 100	Unemployment %	% of pupils gaining 5 GCSEs A–C	Net migration (1998) (thousands)
North West	6.89	88.2	6.2	46.0	−4
North East	2.59	78.8	10.1	40.8	−12
Yorkshire and the Humber	5.04	87.8	6.5	41.9	−4.4
East Midlands	4.17	94.8	5.1	47.1	−11.4
West Midlands	5.33	91.7	6.8	45.1	−6.6
East	5.38	114.2	4.1	52.2	+19.3
Greater London	7.19	130.4	7.6	46.7	−47.7
South East	8.00	116.7	3.6	53.8	+20
South West	4.90	91.9	4.7	52.8	+27
Wales	2.93	79.4	7.0	47.5	+3.2
Scotland	5.12	95.6	7.4	57.8*	−3.8
Northern Ireland	1.69	75.8	7.2	56.0	−1.6

Source: *Regional Trends* No. 35, National Statistics. © Crown Copyright 2001
*Highers at 17 rather than GCSEs at 16

Summary

1 There has been considerable growth in public expenditure as a percentage of GDP throughout the twentieth century.

2 The efforts of the Conservative government from 1979–97 have resulted in, at best, a stabilisation of public expenditure as a percentage of GDP.

3 Factors which make the control of public expenditure difficult include the increasing proportion of older citizens in the population, and increasing demand for services such as health and education which are traditionally produced in the public sector.

4 The construction of internal markets, compulsory competitive tendering and franchising may have made contributions to increased efficiency.

5 The costs of setting up mechanisms which simulate the market must be set against any benefits which accrue.

6 The quasi-markets in health and education do not perfectly simulate the market and there are areas of concern.

7 In addition to efficiency, equity must be used as a criterion for most publicly-provided services.

8 Although it is possible to make some progress in placing values on costs and benefits that do not pass through the market, in many cases there will be large areas of ignorance.

9 The government has a role in controlling by regulation the behaviour of large firms which dominate their markets.

10 Regional disparities result from the market, which the government tries to remedy by investment in people and infrastructure, and with regional assistance.

Markets in operation

We must look at the price system as a mechanism for communicating information if we want to understand its real function.

Friedrich August von Hayek

Now Maple were Sam's Mon-o-po-ly; That means it were all 'is to cut. And nobody else adn't got none; So'e asked Noah three ha'pence a foot.

Marriott Edgar for Stanley Holloway

The market in practice: agriculture, housing and labour

Introduction

The structure of the chapter

This is another case study chapter, which may be regarded as a series of data response exercises with student activities being placed at the end of each case. The three case studies in the operation of the market cover agriculture, housing and labour.

Case study 11.1
AGRICULTURAL PRICES

Interventionist policies

In this case we look at the application of demand and supply theory to agriculture. Agriculture has been called the UK's most successful industry: output and productivity boomed in the second half of the twen-tieth century. This has been achieved by extremely *interventionist* policies on the part of the government; the average Briton supports farmers through artificially high prices and through taxes.

The UK policy is now effectively decided in Brussels. The role of the Common Agricultural Policy (CAP) is an area of vigorous political debate. The budget for the CAP is larger than all other EU expenditures put together and is a constant cause of argument. On the international scene there have been disputes between the EU and other World Trade Organisation (WTO) members. The USA and many of the poorer members of the WTO have often argued that the EU is unfairly subsidising agriculture and *discriminating* against their exports. Farming practices are also a subject of disagreement; for example, many of the 'Green' lobbies maintain that the use of fertilisers, insecticides, GM crops etc. are damaging the environment.

It is, perhaps, a curious paradox that agriculture is the economist's most used example of the market place. We use it to illustrate shifts in demand and supply and all the workings of the free market system. But no market is more interfered with than agriculture. Governments, not only in the UK, but in most other nations, constantly interfere to regulate and manipulate production and farm incomes. In many nations the quantity of next year's crop is as likely to be affected by government policy as it is by market forces and the weather.

The UK system of subsidy after 1947

Farming's privileged status can be traced back to the Agriculture Act 1947. The experience of two world wars had taught the UK the danger of being over-reliant on imported foodstuffs. Agriculture was therefore supported by government grants for improvements, tax relief, fixed prices for milk and 'deficiency' payments on many products to bring prices up to a guaranteed level and enable farmers to compete with imports. The detail of the schemes need not concern us, but we can say that the main effect was a heavy **subsidisation** of farm prices. The effect of this is shown in Figure 11.1. Here you can see that, although 'inefficient' farmers are being propped up, no disequilibrium is created because the lower price brought about by the subsidy encourages consumers to buy more. The price before subsidy was OG and the quantity demanded was q_1. After the subsidy, the price has fallen to OD, and the quantity demanded has been extended to q_2. This form of support, as well as helping farm incomes, also benefits the consumer because some of the subsidy comes back to the taxpayer by way of lower prices. This particularly benefits **low-income groups**, to whom the price of food is very important. The cost of this kind of policy is quite high, shown by the shaded area ABCD in Figure 11.1. It is clear that not all this cost comes back to the consumer, and in Figure 11.2 the savings from buying the same amount of food as was bought prior to the subsidy is only GEFD. On the other hand consumers also decide to buy more agricultural products to the value of FCq_2q_1. This extra consumption is not necessarily a good thing, as the market is being **distorted** away from the consumers' true preferences by a manipulation of costs.

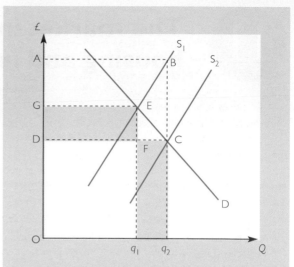

Figure 11.2 The benefit to the consumers of subsidising agriculture

The Common Agricultural Policy (CAP)

When the UK joined the EC the subsidy system just described was replaced by **guaranteed high prices** and a stable **import levy** to keep cheap non-EC food out of Europe. This situation is illustrated in Figure 11.3. Transitional arrangements were made to protect the UK's traditional suppliers, particularly New Zealand. The farmers' incomes are supported by artificially high prices instead of subsidies. The

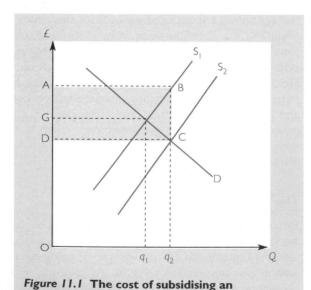

Figure 11.1 The cost of subsidising an agricultural product

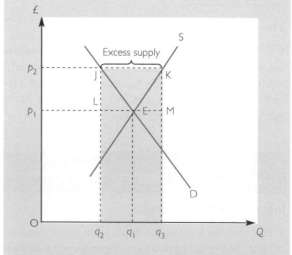

Figure 11.3 The cost of imposing floor prices in agriculture

consumer is worse off because of these higher prices. It is argued that this is offset by lower taxes to support the scheme because there are no expensive subsidies. The main problem with the CAP is its tendency to create a disequilibrium of **excess supply**, this excess supply being familiar to us as the butter mountain, the wine lake, etc. This situation is illustrated in Figure 11.3. Point E is the original equilibrium with a market price of p_1 and an output of q_1. The CAP guaranteed-prices policy raises the price to p_2. This contracts demand to q_2 but expands supply to q_3. CAP intervention agencies are then forced to buy up the excess supply of q_2q_3. The EU is thus committed to additional expenditure of the shaded area q_2 JKq_3. Of course, some surplus of agricultural products in storage is an advantage, acting as a buffer against poor harvests. It is only when these stocks become excessive that there is a problem.

What shall we do with the surplus?

The argument put forward in the previous paragraph (that the CAP is cheaper to the taxpayer than a subsidy-based system) has a weakness. What does the EU do with the excess supply? The hope that the uncertainties of agricultural production would result in surplus years being balanced out by years of shortage was not borne out by experience. Mountains of butter and beef, and a lake of wine, all grew in the 1970s and 1980s. Theoretically the EU could sell the excess output on world markets at a price of p_1, making a loss of p_1p_2 for each unit sold. The cost of the system would then be reduced to area JKML in Figure 11.3. The problem with this solution is that it breaks international agreements about trade. Selling a product abroad below the domestic price is known as **dumping**. Offloading large surpluses on world markets could depress the world price for certain products, reducing the incomes of farmers in poorer countries. It can also be argued that the resources used to produce food that no one eats could be better employed producing goods that are in demand. The costs of storing excessive surpluses must also be included as a waste of resources.

The surpluses have mainly been dealt with in the following ways:

(a) Sale to old-age pensioners at a reduced price. This is a form of price discrimination (see Chapter 23) but clearly benefits poorer sections of society.

(b) Sale to non-market economies. Considerable quantities of butter were sold to the former USSR (Russia). Since these economies were not part of the world market system, selling them the surpluses did not have much effect on world prices. Most of these countries have now become capitalist, so this solution is decreasingly available.

(c) Downgrading the product, e.g. turning wine into vinegar.

Features of the agriculture industry

Problems for the UK

There are some differences between farming in the UK and much of Western Europe. The UK's cool, damp climate favours barley and pasture, but rules out crops such as olives, tobacco, vines and maize – all products which feature largely in the CAP budget. The UK has much of the poor quality hill grazing in the EU and in consequence rears almost 50 per cent of the EU sheep. The UK also has a large average size of farm, three times as large as the average French farm and four times as large as the average German farm. The UK has one of the higher population densities of the EU, approximately twice that of France, although less than Belgium and The Netherlands. Agricultural self-sufficiency is more difficult as a result, particularly as many of the less populated areas in Scotland and Wales are mountainous.

Partly as a result of these differences the UK has less than 2 per cent of its workforce employed in agriculture, the lowest of any European country. Other countries are likely to put a greater emphasis on the maintenance of farming incomes because the farming 'lobby' is a larger percentage of the electorate, although the recent involvement of farmers in the 'dump the pump' campaign has raised their profile (see Chapters 13 and 14).

Productivity growth

There have been spectacular increases in the productivity of the UK's agriculture, in terms of output per hectare and output per worker. These improvements are due to increased mechanisation, which has halved employment from 700 000 to 307 000 in 1990. Increased use of fertilisers and pest control agents is thought to account for about 30 per cent of the increased productivity.

Against these spectacular rises in productivity must be set concerns about the environment particularly arising from **intensive farming**. The environment lobby argues that the destructive effects of new farming methods upon the environment should be taken into account when deciding on farming policy. This is an example of externalities, discussed in Chapter 9. The most recent concern, GM crops, has been discussed in Chapter 3 in the section on new technology, page 36.

Instability in agricultural markets

As we have already seen, prices in markets for agricultural products are inherently unstable because of **unplanned** variations in supply. This is further complicated by long production lags, resulting in Cobweb effects of the kind discussed in Chapter 6. Governments therefore usually intervene in agricultural markets, with the object of **stabilising** both farm incomes and consumer prices. However, complete price stabilisation would lead farmers' incomes to vary directly with output, making them high in bumper years and low in times of bad harvest. This is the complete opposite of the normal state of affairs.

● *Common misunderstanding*

People often believe that a good harvest must be good for farmers and a poor harvest will result in problems for them. This is the complete opposite of the case. Because of the inelasticity of demand for agricultural products, farmers' incomes usually vary inversely with output (as long as all other farmers suffer the same conditions).

A sensible scheme will therefore probably aim not at total stability but rather at limiting fluctuations in prices and incomes. This will be difficult to achieve in practice because of the following:

(a) *Imperfect knowledge.* The government does not possess perfect knowledge about the shape of the consumers' demand curve, or about the absolute state of supply at any particular moment. Much estimation would therefore be involved.
(b) *Political pressure.* In most European countries farmers are a strong **political lobby** and there is therefore great pressure to set the target price and income too high. This results in the government holding greater and greater surpluses of products and the scheme costing a great deal of money, as has occurred with the CAP.

(c) *The vagaries of climate.* In recent years different parts of Europe have suffered from drought and floods. There is concern that the climate is becoming more unstable, possibly as a result of global warming (see Chapter 13).

Recent developments in policy

Pressure for reform of the CAP has come from WTO, the USA and also from the UK whose pattern of agriculture contrasts with that of many of its EU partners. The EU also faced internal pressure to restrain spending on the CAP in order to reduce the size of the CAP budget (see Table 11.1). The existence of persistent surpluses has also been something of an embarrassment to the EU. In addition to the stabilisation of the budget in many areas, the 1998 report announced a 30 per cent cut in intervention prices in beef in the period 2000–2002; a 15 per cent reduction in milk intervention prices (2000) and a 20 per cent reduction in cereal intervention prices.

Table 11.1 **CAP appropriations by sector (items over 1 billion ECU)**

	Billion ECU		
	1993	1997	1999 (budget)
Arable crops (including land withdrawal)	10.6	17.4	17.8
Sugar	2.2	1.6	1.9
Milk/milk products	5.2	3.0	2.6
Beef and veal	4.0	6.6	4.9
Sheep/goats	1.8	1.4	1.8
Other	10.8	9.1	11.4
Total	34.6	39.1	40.4

Source: Adapted from data in the *General Report on the Activities of the EU*, 1996 and 1998

Set-aside

One solution to the problem of excess supply has been the introduction of **set-aside**. This is a policy where farmers are literally paid not to produce on 15 per cent of their land. The cost of this payment is offset because the excess supply problem has been reduced. The warehousing costs and the losses made on sales of old surpluses are therefore avoided. The policy is illustrated in Figure 11.4. It can be seen that production has been reduced by q_2q_3 resulting in the elimination of the surplus, while retaining the high price that guarantees income to the farmer on the land which is farmed. The farmer also receives income from the EU for the land that is not used from the set-aside fund. This policy was successful in reducing surpluses. EU stocks of cereal fell from 27 million tonnes in May 1993 to only 7 million tonnes in May 1995. The butter mountain was reduced to a sixth of its former size and the beef mountain virtually eliminated during this period. Because of the set-aside payments, however, the CAP budget continued to grow.

The environmental impact of this policy has good and bad aspects. The land that lies fallow attracts wildlife that might not have survived on farming land. On the other hand, there are pressures to farm the remaining land even more intensively with the bad side-effects of fertilisers, insecticides, removal of hedgerows, etc. Environmentalists argue that policies to encourage *less intensive* farming using **organic** methods would be better. The set-aside policy illustrated in Figure 11.4 demonstrates that prices remain high for the consumer.

EU expansion

The opening of negotiations with Poland, Hungary, the Czech Republic, Estonia, Slovenia and Cyprus will create problems for the CAP because the income of

these countries and their agricultural efficiency is so far below that of existing members. In July of 1997 the EU launched plans to shift the emphasis away from price support and set-aside and towards **targeted** support for those farmers in greatest need of additional income, as noted in the discussion of reduced intervention prices above. It remains to be seen whether this shift away from price support and towards income support will reduce the overall CAP budget of some 40.4 billion ECU (1999). The accession of new states brings concerns that the budget may actually increase further unless the subsidies are better targeted at those who need them.

It is argued that the main effect of subsidies going to efficient farmers is to increase the value of agricultural land. This process is known as **capitalisation**, where a subsidy or tax on a product is transferred into the capital values. Farmers appear not to be making very excessive profits, but that is because the cost of acquiring the land is set against profits. If the increased value of the land was regarded as a **capital gain** rather than a cost, it can be seen that removal of subsidies would not necessarily result in lower profits, but simply in lower land prices. The farmer is clearly in two markets: the agricultural products market, and the market for land. Holders of land would of course make capital losses when subsidies were removed, but they would make this loss in their role as speculators in the land market, rather than as producers in the agriculture business. Of course some farmers who had taken on large loans to purchase land would suffer serious cash flow problems and might go bankrupt.

A comparison of three policies

The three policies discussed in this chapter are summarised in Figure 11.5. A proper comparison of them requires us to consider what the objectives of EU policy might be in intervening in the agricultural market. Since the EU is not a government, but is composed of many countries, it is also necessary to consider what conflicts of interest there might be between different countries.

Policy objectives

(a) To stabilise agricultural prices. Political pressures to stabilise them at too high a level are a problem for this policy goal.

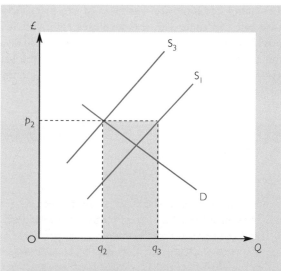

Figure 11.4 The effect of set-aside on agriculture surpluses

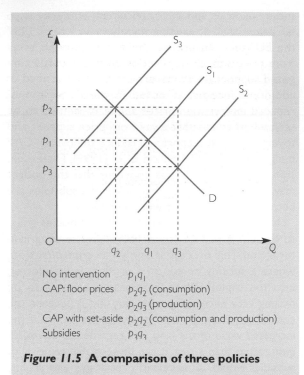

No intervention p_1q_1
CAP: floor prices p_2q_2 (consumption)
                         p_2q_3 (production)
CAP with set-aside p_2q_2 (consumption and production)
Subsidies p_3q_3

Figure 11.5 **A comparison of three policies**

(b) To maintain farmers' incomes which are under pressure from world competition. Obviously this is an objective that will interest countries with large, low income, farming communities.
(c) To maintain rural communities. Many European countries experienced industrialisation and urbanisation later than the UK and are concerned to maintain a viable rural community.
(d) To increase efficiency in farming in order to compete with the rest of the world, and to reduce the size of the CAP budget.
(e) To farm in a way which is friendly towards the environment.
(f) To achieve overall self-sufficiency in agriculture in the EU.
(g) To provide the population with affordable food in sufficient quantity.

Not all of these possible policy objectives are necessarily achievable at the same time. Different countries will put a higher priority on different objectives. EU policy making will therefore have a strong political component as countries fight for their own interest.

Non-intervention

Non-intervention results in a price of p_1q_1. Farmers' incomes in all but the most efficient cases will be pulled down towards those in poorer countries who compete in world agricultural markets. Marginal farmers will leave the industry and the EU will fail to be self-sufficient in agriculture. A large balance of payments deficit may develop in this sector. These consequences make this an unlikely policy option.

Subsidy

This results in p_3q_3, which allows farmers to compete in world markets, and gives consumers low prices and plentiful food. The subsidy is costly to the taxpayer and can be interpreted by other countries as protectionist. In order to prevent the farmer leaving the industry as described in the previous section, it is necessary to set subsidies at a reasonably high level.

Price floor

This results in p_2q_2 (consumption) and p_2q_3 (production), the difference between the two being surplus production which is difficult to dispose of. This is once again protectionist, but this time with high prices and lower consumption than the subsidy case.

Set-aside

The same consumption result as in the price floor case but this time with the surpluses removed. It is possibly more costly than a price floor because of the set-aside payments. It can be argued that the set-aside payments should be targeted at lower-income farmers to limit the cost of such a policy.

STUDENT ACTIVITY 11.1

1 Which of the objectives listed above do you think are in the interests of the UK?
2 How would the priorities of countries like Ireland or France differ from those of the UK?
3 Which of the policies described above would be in the interests of each of these countries?
4 Explain how the expansion of the EU eastwards is likely to affect the size of the CAP budget.

What policies would you advocate to contain this expansion of the budget?

5 If the bulk of the CAP budget is targeted towards low income, small, inefficient farmers, how can we make sure that these farmers have an incentive to become more efficient?

6 Design a policy towards agriculture that has, as its highest priority, a concern for the environment.

7 Indicate on Figure 11.5 the following:
   (a) The cost of a price floor if the excess supply cannot be sold.
   (b) The cost of a price floor if the surplus can be sold at world market prices.
   (c) The benefit to the consumer in lower prices if a subsidy policy is used.
   (d) The cost to the taxpayer in the case of a subsidy.
   (e) The amount of agricultural production reduced by the set-aside policy.

8 Show using diagrams what the effect of introducing price ceilings in agriculture would be at a level below the market clearing price. Would the objective of providing people with cheap, plentiful food be achieved?

9 What are the advantages to a country of being self-sufficient in food?

Case study 11.2
THE HOUSING MARKET

Housing market sectors

The twentieth century saw a large number of experiments in housing policy. A small introduction into the four main sectors of the housing market will help you to understand these policies. The **owner occupied sector** is made up of property which is owned by the households living in the property, or which is being bought by them using a mortgage. The **private rented sector** consists of property owned by individuals or companies and then rented out to households who either cannot afford to buy their own property, or are currently choosing not to. Properties owned by (usually local) government form the **public rented sector**. With the retreat of the state, noted in the previous two chapters, the **voluntary sector** has grown in importance. This sector can be a mixture of rented

and owner occupied property as occupiers are sometimes able to switch between renting and purchasing. While finance for this sector usually comes from the state, the operation of the sector is by independent charitable trusts.

Government policy has had four main objectives, although the relative emphasis on each of these policies has varied over time:

(a) to protect poorer households from exploitation;
(b) to improve the quality and quantity of housing;
(c) to encourage owner occupation;
(d) to minimise homelessness.

The history of housing intervention

The private rented sector dominated in the nineteenth century, although there were interesting examples of voluntary sector provision, particularly by philanthropic industrialists. Homelessness was largely dealt with by the workhouse. Rent controls to protect poorer households were introduced from 1914 onwards. The role of the state as a provider of housing started in a small way in the 1920s and 1930s but really took off in the 1950s and 1960s as the UK attempted to restore and increase its housing stock after the damage of the Second World War and in response to the baby boom which followed it. The consequent decline of the private rented sector and its concentration on poorer households led governments to regard this sector as an appropriate area for interventionist social policy. Rent Acts in the 1960s and 1970s imposed not only rent controls but also protected tenancies. The consequences of this policy for the private rented sector are discussed in the next section. The advent of Thatcherism in the 1980s marked the return to more market-oriented solutions and a retreat from state intervention. The reintroduction of short rents for new tenancies in the 1980s and 1990s effectively removed the right to new protected tenancies. The introduction of a right to buy for council house tenants began to reduce the size of the public sector stock of council houses. Housing benefit replaced rent controls as a policy for helping poorer households. Local authorities were permitted to place homeless families in bed and breakfast accommodation and hostels, rather than provide them with genuine housing. The growth in this type of housing together with the growth in numbers presenting themselves as homeless, is presented in Table 11.2.

Table 11.2 **Local authority homeless acceptances in Great Britain**

	1980	1985	1990	1995	1998
No. of households	76 342	111 323	171 516	151 201	116 720
Bed and breakfast	1 330	5 360	11 130	4 500	6 070
Hostels	3 380	4 730	9 010	9 660	8 820

Source: Housing Finance Review 1999, National Statistics. © Crown Copyright 2001

The reduction in subsidy to the rented sectors was matched by reduced help for households buying their own houses. The tax relief on interest paid on mortgages was phased out over a twenty year period from 1980. Initially the amount of the mortgage debt eligible for tax relief was capped at £25 000. This was raised only once, to £30 000 but was then pegged at that level. Inflation has then steadily eroded the real value of this tax relief. However, in the middle and late 1990s, inflation rates fell substantially, slowing down the erosion of the real value of the tax relief. The government then progressively lowered the rate of tax at which relief could be claimed from the standard rate of income tax, to 15 per cent, and then 10 per cent. The value of the relief was by this time so small that it could be removed altogether in 1999 without much complaint from mortgage holders. A mortgage of £30,000 attracted interest of £1800 at 6 per cent, resulting in £180 tax relief at 10 per cent, which worked out at about 50p a week.

Intervention in the private rented sector

We can use supply and demand analysis to investigate the likely consequences of intervention in the private rented sector. The introduction of rent controls is a kind of price control, as landlords can only raise rents with permission. Unlike the price controls introduced by the CAP, discussed in the last case study, this price will often be below the market-clearing rate. This is referred to as a price ceiling (as opposed to a price floor in agriculture) and is illustrated in Figure 11.6. In the free market this would be described as a situation of excess demand (of Q_1Q_3) and would result in prices rising from P_1 to P_2 with quantity demanded falling from Q_3 to Q_2. A question can be asked at this stage: if the price did rise, would the reduction in demand mean people would become homeless? The answer is not necessarily. Young people may choose to remain living with their parents; old people may decide to live with their children. It can be seen that there are social conse-

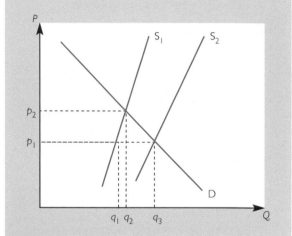

Figure 11.6 Price ceiling vs the free market in rented properties

quences of changes in the housing market. A more complicated answer may be that the average size of dwelling may be reduced, leaving tenants paying the same rent, but landlords receiving more in total. In order to make the analysis simpler, we have assumed that all rented dwellings are the same size, to be consistent with the idea of homogeneous output in perfect competition. In reality this is not true, of course, and landlords can adjust both the size and quality of dwellings in response to market forces.

In the long run the higher rents will increase the landlords profits and attract new entrants into the market, increasing the supply and reducing price, possibly to P_1Q_3. This may be quite a slow process, however, and in the meantime tenants are faced with higher rents, worse living conditions, or possibly are forced to live with relatives when they would rather be more independent.

Price ceilings, capitalisation and locking in

The introduction of rent controls will prevent the market responding in the way described in the previous section. What will be the impact of such government intervention? It can be argued that without protected tenancies, it is likely that some landlords will exit the market, evicting their tenants and selling their properties to owner-occupiers. The argument is that poor returns on their investment make it more profitable to sell their properties. They would then transfer their money into alternative assets such as stocks, shares, or other business ventures where the returns may be better. There would therefore be a shift of the supply curve to the left as dwellings are shifted out of the private rented sector, as illustrated in Figure 11.7.

Governments would not be happy with this outcome, since the situation of excess demand has been worsened. In the 1960s and 1970s the policy of rent controls was supplemented with protected tenancies. Landlords were not able to evict their tenants simply because they wanted to sell their property. If they wished to exit the industry, they now had to sell their property with the tenants in it. A gulf emerged between the value of a property with 'sitting' tenants, and a similar property that was empty. This is because of the phenomenon of **capitalisation**. This idea has already been discussed in the previous case study, where rising agricultural land prices were attributed to artificially high agricultural prices. In the case of private rented housing, the capital value of properties with sitting tenants is reduced because the rents are controlled.

A new landlord entering the market would compare the return on the property with other possible investments (shares, stocks, deposit accounts, other business ventures, etc.). Since the profit on letting properties has been artificially reduced, a new landlord would only agree to buy a property if the price allowed a reasonable rate of return. For instance, if a property is worth £100 000 on the market without tenants, but has an annual profit of £5000 (a return of 5 per cent) then a new landlord would be willing to buy only if 5 per cent was better than the rate of return obtainable elsewhere. If other investments would bring a return of 10 per cent, then the new landlord would only be willing to pay £50 000 for the property.

It is sometimes said that landlords were 'locked in' by the combination of rent controls and protected tenancies, since they can only exit the market by taking a capital loss. This situation resulted in windfall gains for some tenants, who were offered cash sums to give up their tenancy, or prices below the free market rate to purchase them. The system also had the unintended consequence of biasing the market towards students and young professionals who were much more likely to move on, rather than stay and take advantage of their protected tenancy. Poorer people, for whom the legislation was intended were, ironically, discriminated against.

Creating protected tenancies will slow down, rather than prevent the transfer of properties from the private rented to the owner occupied sector. It will also act as a powerful disincentive against entering the private rented sector, since the value of any property transferred into the sector will fall as a result of capitalisation. These adverse consequences of regulation in this sector, led the Conservative government of the 1980s to reform the private rented sector. New short tenancies were introduced by the Housing Act 1988, which meant the tenancy was only protected for the letting period. While some protected tenancies remain, this more flexible type of contract has now become the norm.

The public sector

History

The public sector grew rapidly in the 1950s and 1960s, constituting almost one third of all dwellings by tenure (see Table 11.3). As a method of meeting housing demand in the period after the Second World War, it must be regarded as a success. Housing of this type

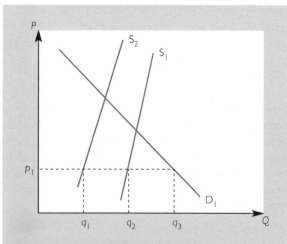

Figure 11.7 **Price ceilings and exit**

Table 11.3 **Dwellings by tenure**

	1971	1981	1991	1997
Owner occupier	50.5	56.4	66.3	67.3
Private rented	18.9	11.0	9.5	10.4
Housing Association	–	2.2	3.0	4.8
Local authority rented	30.6	30.4	21.4	17.4

Source: Housing Finance Review 1999, National Statistics. © Crown Copyright 2001

was largely financed centrally, but built and administered by local authorities (or councils – hence the name 'council housing'). The number of houses built became one of the key statistics used in general election debates of the time. The quality of some of the council houses built at this time was however poor, and some of these properties have already been demolished. The experiment in high-rise council flats in the 1960s is also largely regarded as a failure, with many of these towers being demolished because of their unpopularity and inconvenience, rather than because they had failed structurally. The key question about public sector housing from the 1970s onwards became one of finance and pricing because of the subsidy given to this type of tenure.

Waiting lists

Once again, supply and demand analysis can be used to analyse the consequences of subsidising council housing. By setting price too low, excess demand develops as indicated in Figure 11.8. If it is agreed that a subsidy is appropriate, the policy question is how to deal with such excess demand of q_1q_2. Rather than using the price mechanism, local authorities used a waiting list system to deal with this problem. People on the waiting list were awarded points according to how long they had been waiting, and other measures of social need (numbers of children, age, etc.). When properties became available they were allocated to the household on the waiting list with the most points. This will be recognised as a rationing system, using social criteria rather than willingness to pay in order to allocate resources.

Subsidy

In the 1970s and 1980s, council housing became a major area of dispute in political debate. The Labour party argued for continuing subsidy to the council

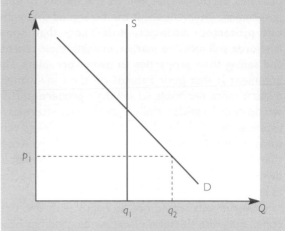

Figure 11.8 **Excess demand for council housing**

housing sector, despite the fact that about a third of all households lived in council housing and some of them were quite well off. The Conservatives privatised much of the council housing sector. They achieved this objective by introducing the 'right to buy', with the price reduced in line with the period of tenancy. This can also be regarded as a kind of subsidy.

It has been alleged that both parties attempted to bribe voters living in council houses, the Labour party by subsidising rents, and the Conservative party by offering council houses for sale at reduced prices. Whatever the politics of housing, the economic issues are based on the best allocation of resources (efficiency) and questions of justice in society (equity). Unless there is market failure, the objective of efficiency is best met by allowing the market to work as competitively as possible. In the case of housing, there are some externalities in terms of noise, visual intrusion, and nuisance, but these are best dealt with by legal means. In practice it is a reasonably competitive market, so the efficiency criterion suggests free market solutions.

This may be in conflict with the equity criterion, however, as housing of an acceptable quality may be placed beyond the means of ordinary people in some areas. The role of inelastic supply and speculative demand in this situation is discussed in the section on owner-occupiers below. If people need help with housing for reasons of equity, a number of questions need to be answered:

- Who should be subsidised?
- How should subsidy to housing be related to other kinds of income support?

- Should housing be subsidised, or the tenants?
- Should the subsidy go in upfront capital subsidy or an annual subsidy?

The problem with a blanket subsidy of all council tenants is that not all of them need to be subsidised. Even if people need subsidy when they first become council tenants, it is likely that many people's circumstances will change and the subsidy may be no longer necessary. It can be argued that it is inequitable to pay subsidies to people who do not need it. It is a wasteful use of scarce public funds that could have been spent on people in greater need, or in a general improvement of public sector services. Alternatively, without such expenditure, taxes could have been reduced.

These arguments suggest that it is people who should be subsidised rather than types of housing tenure. People who are unable to afford acceptable housing because of poverty should be helped. It should be made clear that this is a '*value judgement*'. It is possible to hold the view that people who cannot afford housing of an acceptable standard should be turned out on to the street, or allowed to live in overcrowded unsanitary conditions. Most governments of industrialised countries do not hold these views, but some of their citizens do! Before deciding your own views about housing policy, you should consider what your value judgements might be.

The voluntary sector

The role of providing social housing was progressively shifted from local authorities (councils) to Housing Associations in the 1980s and 1990s. Housing Associations are in the voluntary sector. They attempt to breakeven after the subsidies given to them by the government. They also try to pursue social objectives. The main difference from the era of council housing, is that they are controlled and financed by central government rather than local government. Unlike the local authorities, they cannot cross-subsidise between housing and other local activities. They also allow households to switch between tenures more easily, allowing tenants to become owner occupiers without having to move house. They are more likely to follow social rather than political objectives, since they are not elected.

The owner occupied sector

Housing finance

Most people don't have enough money to buy a house without borrowing. Of course, many products are purchased using credit but usually such credit is repaid within a few years. In the case of housing, the purchase is so large that it often takes as many as 25 years to repay the debt. Until the debt is repaid the house is 'mortgaged' to the lender, which means that it may become the lender's property if the purchaser is unable to keep up their repayments. In practice, lenders will not exercise this right straight away, but will allow the purchaser some time to rectify the situation.

When home ownership was at a lower level, most people borrowed money from building societies, which are cooperative organisations owned by their customers and borrowers. In line with shifts in the economy towards the market in the 1980s and 1990s, many building societies were sold to the private sector, resulting in a windfall profit to their customers and borrowers. This type of sale is known as 'demutualisation' and has some similarities with privatisation (see Chapter 24). Banks have also entered the home loans market because of the increased volume of business.

Repayment mortgages

Mortgages are repaid on a monthly basis. The monthly payments are fixed as long as the rate of interest remains the same. There are two main kinds of mortgages: repayment mortgages and endowment mortgages. Repayment mortgages payments are made up of an interest element and a capital repayment element. Towards the end of a mortgage, the monthly payments are made up mainly of capital repayments with hardly any interest. By contrast, at the beginning of the mortgage, the monthly payments consist almost entirely of interest with only a little capital repayment. This process can be illustrated by a numerical example. If you borrow £30 000 to buy a house and the interest rate is 10 per cent, then you will have to pay £3000 a year in interest. If your mortgage payments are set at £300 per month, at the end of the year you will have paid £3600. This means that, after interest payments, you have reduced the amount you owe by £600 to £29 400.

Your interest payments in the following year will therefore be reduced to £2940, allowing you to reduce your debt by a further £660 to £28 740. Each year, the interest payment element falls and the capital repayment element increases. The lender will calculate the amount of your monthly repayment so that your debt is completely repaid by an agreed date. If interest rates change, the lender has to recalculate your monthly repayment.

Endowment mortgages

In the case of endowment mortgages, no repayment of capital is made until the end of the period. Instead payments are made into an endowment insurance policy, which is calculated to cover repayment of the capital at the end of the period. The monthly payments to the lender are for the interest element only. This was a popular method in the 1980s, but has become less popular recently with the removal of tax advantages, and by the failure of some endowment policies to fully pay off the capital at the end of the period. Since monthly premiums for the endowment policy are invested on the stock exchange, the value of the endowment policy at the end of the period depends on the performance of stocks and shares. Some insurance companies in the 1980s over-estimated the likely value of such shares, leaving endowment policy holders unable to fully repay their mortgages. Using this type of mortgage therefore involves speculating on the stock exchange. All speculation brings with it the possibility of loss as well as gain, and this point has been forcibly brought home to some home-buyers recently who believed, erroneously, that because endowment policies had always paid of in the past, they would continue to do so in the future.

Variations

The two most important types of mortgage have been discussed, but there are variations on these basic types. Some borrowers opt for fixed interest mortgages, which carry the same interest rate for a number of years. Another variation on this theme is the capped interest rate mortgage, where the lender agrees the interest rate will not go above a certain rate, even if market rates do. With the lost tax advantages and reputation of the endowment policy, other financial schemes such as PEPs and ISAs have

been used to accumulate the money to pay off the capital at the end of the mortgage period. These two tax-free methods of saving are discussed further in Chapter 28, but may also have some of the speculative problems of the endowment policy.

The housing market

The housing market will be analysed using supply and demand analysis, but at the outset it should be recognised the housing market has special features, which result in instability and volatility:

- The supply of housing is inelastic because even if the building industry works flat out, it cannot increase the housing stock by much more than 2 per cent a year.
- The housing market is a speculative market. When people buy a house it is partly for somewhere to live, and partly an investment with strong possibilities of large capital gains – or losses.
- The housing market is markedly different in different regions, or even in different areas close by each other. Location is one of the most important characteristics of a house.
- The demand for housing is affected by its complementary service: finance. If interest rates change there will be a change in the demand for housing because of the effect on mortgage payments.
- Since mortgage payments are often a large portion of income, the demand for housing will depend heavily on the level of employment and income.
- The government can affect the demand for housing by changes in the tax system.
- It must be remembered that different sectors of the housing market are substitutes for each other. Changes in other sectors of the market will affect the owner occupied sector.

As with our earlier discussion about rented accommodation, it is necessary to assume a homogeneous product in order to discuss the market in terms of supply and demand. Sometimes the average house price is used to discuss changes in the market, but it must be remembered that the composition of the housing stock changes over time. More detached houses are being built as people become richer (although often they have smaller gardens). The semi-detached house is often taken as the standard house in the UK, but again, it must be remembered that apparently similar houses will vary in price because of location, the quality of kitchen and bathroom fittings, size of garden and a host of other characteristics that may be important to the buyer. Any supply and demand analysis must state which sector of the market is being considered, and even then a certain amount of averaging is necessary. Before moving on to consider the housing market in detail, factors that affect location must be considered.

Housing and the price of land

Housing is only one use of land and is in competition with other uses. Agriculture, offices, warehouses, factories, recreation and transport all use land. Land is at its most expensive in the central business district (CBD) because retailers and headquarters offices have most to gain from this location and are willing to pay very high rents. Moving out from the city centre means higher transport costs into the centre for work, shopping and recreation, so land prices usually fall as you move further away from the centre. People are willing to pay less because of poorer access to the city centre. However, the supply of land near to the city centre is smaller than in the outer suburbs, as you will discover in the student activities below.

This usually results in higher density housing as you get nearer to the city centre. This pattern of land values is presented in Figure 11.9. This diagram will not represent the actual value of land in any real city, because many other factors will come into play.

- The development of '**green belts**' around the edge of cities to prevent them sprawling into attractive recreational space around the city will raise land values at the edge of the city and in the green belt surrounding the city. Development is severely limited in the green belt.
- The '**inner city**' has declined in many industrial towns and cities, partly because the housing stock is older, and partly because factories and warehouses often locate nearer to the motorway system on the edge of the city. Industry originally located near to the railway, but most freight is now carried by road (see Chapter 14).
- The growing middle classes cannot all fit into the suburbs, nor afford the city centre. This leads to '**gentrification**' of former inner city areas, which

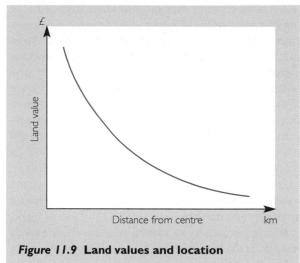

Figure 11.9 **Land values and location**

are renovated and become fashionable, raising their price.

- Local geographical and historical features will alter house prices. Good views, fine architecture or access to transport systems may increase prices. Poor quality housing or high levels of air pollution may have the reverse effect.
- Education has an effect on house prices in the UK. It is usually easier to get a place in a state school if you live near by. If a school gains a reputation for good results, families will want to move into the area, forcing up prices.
- The previous points may force a social separation of the city with pronounced working class and middle class areas. This also happens with other groupings, particularly ethnic minorities who often choose to live in communities.
- Subsidiary business centres will develop in larger towns and cities, resulting in local increases in land values away from the CBD.
- The 1980s and 1990s saw the development of large out of town shopping centres which were easier for people to reach because of the growth of car ownership. Land in or near such developments will rise in value.

The price of houses

When discussing the price of houses, it is best to separate normal trading periods from speculative periods. In times of normal trading, supply and demand analysis can be used to predict the consequences of various changes. Increases in income, in employment, in prices in the rented sector, or reductions in interest rates will all shift the demand curve up to the right. There will be an increase in average house prices and the quantity of houses in the owner occupied sector. This need not be the result of more homes being built – it may be partly due to properties switching out of the various rented sectors. Supply may shift as a result of demolition of old housing, the building of new housing, or the switch of properties into or out of other housing sectors. Supply may also shift between different parts of the owner occupied sector if, for instance, a large house is converted into flats.

It is important to be careful to understand exactly what is meant by the housing market. Do we mean the properties which are currently being bought and sold (**option A**), or do we mean the entire stock of properties, most of which are not being traded, but are nevertheless demanded by the current owner occupiers (**option B**), that is, if you decide not to sell your property, then you are demanding it! The analysis in this case study is based on option B, but you will be asked to think about option A in the student activities.

Within the owner occupied sector, it is also important to recognise that there are different sectors, although they may overlap. The market for a detached house in an affluent suburb is not usually a substitute for a small flat in the inner city. At any given time, prices may move differently in different sectors. If, for instance, there was a shift in fashion towards city living, this would impact differently in different sectors. A shortage of flats, relative to demand for them, may push up prices in this sector, while a surplus of detached houses in the suburbs may drive down their price.

Speculative periods

During normal trading, a rise in the price of a product will result in there being fewer buyers. A speculative market works in exactly the opposite way, as has already been discussed in Chapter 6. If people believe that prices will continue to rise, then there is the chance of making a capital gain by buying now. If this opportunity is not taken now, the property may become too expensive to buy at a later date. The speculative process in other markets (shares, foreign exchange etc.) usually includes a period of 'profit taking' where the asset is sold and the capital gain is 'realised'. Although some buyers may behave in this way in the housing market, the majority of people will not take profit in this way, because the asset they are speculating in is also their home. They may wait until children leave home, or a job move shifts them to another part of the country before 'taking their profit'.

The speculative process in housing works in the following way, once people believe that prices will continue to rise. People who are thinking of becoming owner occupiers will bring their decision to buy forward, because they fear that house prices will rise beyond their reach. The same argument applies to people considering moving up the housing market to a more expensive property. They fear that the difference in price between their current property and the one that they wish to buy may increase. Both these situations lead to an increase in demand. Some people considering selling their house may delay because they hope to obtain a higher price in the future. This will include houses being sold by relatives after the death of the occupant, or properties being sold by landlords who wish to exit the renting industry. This will reduce the number of houses on the market. How can people afford to buy houses when prices double within a few years? The answer is that most people use the sale of their current house to finance most of the new purchase. The people who really suffer during these periods are first time buyers who suddenly have to borrow much more, or accept a more modest property. The fluctuations in the housing market can be seen in Table 11.4 which looks at the period 1986 to 1998, through one housing boom and one slump in house prices followed by the beginning of the next boom at the end of the century.

Table 11.4 Annual house price changes 1986–98

	86	87	88	89	90	91	92	93	94	95	96	97	98
% change in price	14.7	10.6	23.1	15.9	6.8	0.1	−0.2	1.6	9.8	2.8	4.6	5.8	5.0

Source: Housing Finance Review 1999, National Statistics. © Crown Copyright 2001

Negative equity

The spiralling upwards of house prices will eventually reach a turning point. It may be an economic recession, rising interest rates, or the inability of ordinary people to buy the cheapest house, or a mixture of these factors. It will always include a belief that the boom is over and that house prices can only come down. The speculative process then goes into reverse. People will put off buying a house because they believe it will be cheaper to do so in the future; this will reduce demand. Households in financial difficulties because of high interest payments or unemployment will be forced to sell, increasing the number of properties on the market. This will create a downward spiral of prices. For those unfortunate to have bought at the top of the boom, the value of their home may fall below the mortgage they used to buy it. This is known as negative equity.

The equity that a person holds in their home is the proportion that they actually own. For instance, if a person buys a house for £100 000 with a mortgage of £80 000, then they have a 20 per cent equity in their home. If over time the value of their property rose to £160 000, then they would have 50 per cent equity. If the value of the house fell below £80 000 there would be negative equity because mortgage debt exceeds the value of the house.

House prices and demography

Considerable changes in how long people live, and the way in which they live have occurred in the last 50 years. As people get older, they often continue to live in the family home for emotional reasons, even though it is a bigger property than they need. This tendency 'locks up' part of the housing stock that could otherwise be available to younger families. Like any restriction in supply, it creates an upward pressure on prices.

The increased divorce rate, and consequent increase in the number of single parent families, raises the total number of households that need to be housed. The type of housing demanded by these households may be smaller, however, because the same income now has to finance two properties. Changes in the number of households can be seen in Table 11.5.

Table 11.5 Number of households (million)

1961	1971	1981	1991	1998–9
16.3	18.6	20.2	22.4	23.7

Source: *Social Trends 2000*, National Statistics. © Crown Copyright 2001

Regional variations in house prices

Much has been made of the 'North–South' divide, not only in house prices, but also in employment and income. Average house prices are highest in London and the south east of England and lowest in the north of England and Wales. These differences can be explained in terms of factors influencing supply and demand as can be seen in Table 11.6. Areas with large inward migration, high income and employment levels are in general areas of high prices (see previous chapter). Given the inelastic supply of housing, a situation of excess demand will force up prices. The lower priced areas are characterised by low income and employment levels, as well as outward migration. This results in an excess supply of housing forcing prices down.

Table 11.6 Average house prices and rents by region (1998)

Region	(Greater London = 100)	
	Average house price	Average rent (semi-detached house)
North	50.2	43.0
Yorkshire and Humberside	54.1	44.7
North west	57.0	48.6
East Midlands	57.5	39.7
West Midlands	62.5	54.2
East Anglia	65.3	47.5
South west	69.8	56.4
South east	90.5	77.7
Greater London	100.0	100.0

Source: *Housing Finance Review 1999*, National Statistics. © Crown Copyright 2001

Of course, these are gross generalisations, and will not apply equally to all parts of a region. There will be affluent areas that are in demand in the north of England, and areas in the south of England that are in relative decline. Some of the factors which create house price variation within a city or region are discussed above in the section on 'Housing and the price of land'.

Housing and the environment

The age of the housing stock may have a bearing on global warming since older houses are often less well-insulated, more draughty, and sometimes damper than modern housing. It can be very expensive to remedy these problems. Houses built in the first half of the twentieth century mostly do not have cavity walls, which provide insulation and may be filled with further insulating material. Houses from the nineteenth century and before do not normally have damp courses to prevent rising damp, which is expensive to dry out. Double glazed windows only began to be fitted as standard in the 1990s. The implications of this are discussed further in Chapter 13 on environmental economics.

Housing and the labour market

The way in which the UK housing market impacts on the labour market has been the subject of much critical comment in recent years. In today's rapidly changing economies it is important that factors of production (other than land) are mobile. The housing market can act as a barrier to labour movement in a number of ways.

- Large regional variations in house prices can act as a strong disincentive for people moving from the lower priced areas of the country. Unfortunately, it is in the higher priced areas where there are more jobs.
- The existence of council house or housing association waiting lists can make it difficult for people who do not own their own property to move to the higher priced areas. The lack of affordable private rental sector housing in some areas may compound this problem.
- The planning system acts as a brake on high-density development and green belt development in the growing areas of the economy.
- In periods of falling house prices such as the early 1990s, owner occupiers may be effectively 'locked in' because of the problem of negative equity.
- Policies to encourage owner occupation have resulted in a very small private rented sector, which makes moving areas difficult.

Housing and the planning system

The problems that have been discussed in this case study create dilemmas for planning decisions by local authorities. Local councils in the UK have to prepare a structure plan, which takes into account the forecasts of future demand for housing in the area. What should planners do if there is a forecast of inward migration from other regions, as is the case of the south east of England? Allowing planning permission for the extra houses may result in higher density housing or encroachment on the green belt; other parts of the infrastructure may come under pressure, such as transport or schools. Refusing permission, on the other hand, may create a situation of excess demand and soaring property prices. The UK government has encouraged the use of brownfield developments for new housing. Brownfield development is the use of old industrial land that is more expensive to develop than new green belt sites.

STUDENT ACTIVITY 11.2

1. Using option A in the section 'The Price of Houses', use demand and supply curve shifts to show what happens to the price of houses in a speculative period.
2. What is the best way of supplying affordable housing to the poorer people in society? Providing cheap council houses; subsidising council rents; regulating the private sector by controlling rents and assuring tenancies; housing association properties; giving people housing benefit and letting the market system work.
3. Would you take out a repayment or an endowment mortgage? How might ISAs be a better alternative to endowment policies?
4. Given today's market conditions, what kind of property do you think would give you the largest capital gain (think about location and type of property).
5. Using the formula for the area of a circle (πr^2, where $\pi = 3.142$), how much land is there 1 km, 2 km, 3 km, 4 km, and 5 km from the city centre.
6. What are the effects on land values of zoning land for commercial, residential, industrial and rural (green belt) use?

Case study 11.3
MINIMUM WAGE LEGISLATION

Historical background

The shift towards the market at the end of the twentieth century also applied to the labour market. The labour market in the 1960s and 1970s in the UK was characterised by strong trade unions negotiating with industries, often at the national level. The 1980s marked a period of conflict between the trade unions and Mrs Thatcher's Conservative government, which largely resulted in a victory for the government. The right to strike was limited in various ways, and union membership fell. There was a move, supported by both Conservative and later Labour governments, towards *'flexible' labour markets* which made it easier for companies to hire and fire workers, and made employment contracts more flexible.

Workers in low paid employment did not benefit from strong trade unions. In the 1960s and 1970s, such workers were covered by 'wages councils' set up by the government to protect workers with weak bargaining power in the so-called 'sweated trades'. In effect this worked as a kind of minimum wage for these industries. The 1980s saw the abolition of the wages councils as part of the move towards more flexible labour markets.

The Labour government introduced the minimum wage at £3.60 in 1999 in order to help low paid workers. In 2000 they cautiously raised it to £3.70. The Conservative opposition initially argued against this policy, but have more recently agreed to retain it. Most other EU countries have a minimum wage policy of some kind. There are strong arguments both for and against this policy that will be examined below.

The debate

If the labour market is working perfectly, then the wage paid in any occupation will just balance out supply and demand. Everyone who wants to work at the going wage rate will find employment. If this is the case, there is no argument in terms of efficiency for intervening in the market. There may be an argument in terms of equity, if the equilibrium wage rate is too low to provide an acceptable standard of living. If society decides on a minimum standard of living (sometimes referred to as the 'poverty line') below which people should not fall, then it becomes a question of how to achieve this objective. Should the state keep people above the poverty line, or do employers have this responsibility? Are workers being exploited by businesses if they are paid wages that cannot support an acceptable standard of living?

It can be argued that there are some market failures in the labour market because of information, mobility and deficient demand. This can be seen from the regional data already discussed in Chapter 10.

Arguments about excess supply

If the market was in equilibrium before the government intervened to place a floor price on labour, then the minimum wage legislation (MWL) will create a situation of excess supply of L_1L_2 in Figure 11.10. Fewer workers will be demanded by businesses than before, although more people may wish to look for work at these wages than before the introduction of the minimum wage. This is the essential argument against the minimum wage. Unemployment will rise amongst the least well off in society. It is also argued that MWL will force the market for cheap labour out of the regulator's reach particularly by the device of home working. This is a pattern of employment found particularly in the clothing industry, where employers send work out to people who work in their own homes. Since they do not come to a place of employment, such workers can be regarded as self-employed, usually receiving payment for their output rather than their time. Paying someone for what they produce, rather than how long they work, is called piecework.

Arguments about international competition

It is argued that the consequences for unemployment of MWL are particularly severe when the industry faces strong international competition, particularly if this competition comes from less developed countries with low pay rates. If workers are employed in an industry which exports much of its output, or an industry which faces considerable competition from imported goods, then the arguments about minimum wages and unemployment become stronger.

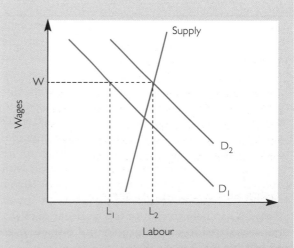

Figure 11.10 **Excess supply in the labour market**

If on the other hand workers are employed in the non-traded part of the economy, the argument is weaker, since such workers do not face competition from abroad. Sectors of the economy which are non-traded include services which require the person giving the service to be present, such as hair dressing.

There is an argument that an advanced economy does not want jobs that are competing with labour from developing countries. Higher wages also force employers to think about investment both in capital and in the workforce in order to increase productivity in line with wages.

Arguments about poverty and social policy

Poorer people spend a higher proportion of their income. Increasing their wages will ensure higher levels of spending in the economy, thus pushing employment back up again. This is illustrated in Figure 11.10 with a shift to D_2. The shift depicted here returns the economy to equilibrium in the labour market but the actual shift may be smaller or larger than this. This is essentially a macroeconomic argument that we have referred to in Sections IV and VII. What will be the net effect of MWL on employment? It depends on whether the excess supply effects (discussed above), or the increased demand effects of MWL are stronger. The evidence that we have at the moment is that unemployment has fallen since the MWL was introduced. This is not conclusive proof that MWL increases employment, however. Other forces pushed employment up as the economy continued to expand in 2000. The business cycle which alternately creates unemployment and then employment is also discussed further in Sections IV and VII.

A second argument about poverty concerns incentives. The UK benefit system overlaps with the tax system to create disincentives. People are paid benefit if they are on low incomes. If they increase their income they will pay tax *and* lose benefit. This creates a serious disincentive to work or indeed to become employed, if people are not much better off if they make the effort to improve their income. Increasing the minimum wage is not enough on its own to solve this problem, but in combination with other policies, such as a starting rate of tax of 10 per cent and no national insurance payments on lower incomes, it can help to reduce this disincentive effect. Further discussion of the problem of disincentives can be found in Chapter 28.

The arguments so far in this case study are about efficiency, that is about how markets work. There are also arguments about equity – what is a fair payment for people in employment? It is possible to make a value judgement about such matters. This does not mean that efficiency is forgotten. There may be some increased unemployment from such a policy, but if so other policies could be introduced to offset this problem, such as improved education and training.

STUDENT ACTIVITY 11.3

1 Why is it difficult to be sure what the effects of MWL will be?
2 If you believe that there is a minimum wage that people should be paid, what other policies might you also need to maintain levels of employment?
3 Think of some other jobs in the non-traded sector of the economy.

Summary

1 UK agriculture has been supported since the Second World War. This support mainly took the form of price subsidies, in contrast with the CAP system of guaranteed high prices.
2 The pattern of agriculture and land ownership in the UK is very different from much of the rest of the EU, which has created friction with other member states.
3 Productivity has increased greatly in terms of output per hectare and output per worker. However, there are environmental concerns about 'industrial' farming techniques.
4 Agricultural markets are inherently unstable so that governments usually intervene to stabilise prices and farm incomes.
5 Agricultural policy is complicated by imperfect knowledge, political pressure and administrative costs.
6 The housing market is divided into owner occupied, private rented, public rented and voluntary sectors.
7 Regulation of the market can result in unintended consequences.
8 Prices are affected by location, type of housing, the state of the economy and speculative factors.
9 It is not possible to be sure about the disincentive effects of minimum wage legislation. If they do exist, other policies may be needed to offset them.

12 The leisure industry

Learning outcomes

At the end of this chapter you will be able to:

▸ Understand what the leisure industry comprises.
▸ Identify the main leisure activities, both at home and away from home, in the UK.
▸ Appreciate the impact of tourism on the UK economy.
▸ Understand the structure of the package holiday market in the UK.
▸ Be aware of key aspects of the economics of the English football Premier League.

As an economy grows and people become wealthier, so they are able to devote more time to leisure activities. The more time that people have at their disposal for leisure, the greater the range and quality of activities on offer. This is true for all societies, at least in theory, although the priority for many people in the poorest countries of the world is simply to be able to earn a sufficient living for survival rather than concern themselves with leisure pursuits and their time is often solely devoted to this end.

We shall begin this chapter by investigating what exactly the leisure industry comprises and what types of leisure activities people in the UK undertake. This is followed by an examination of the impact of tourism on the UK economy and of the package holiday industry in the UK. The chapter concludes with a brief analysis of the economics of the football industry, with specific reference to the English Premier League.

The meaning of leisure

Deciding exactly what leisure constitutes is no easy matter. It is a *highly diversified* set of activities, includ-ing holidays, reading and watching television, eating out, DIY and gardening and sport.

Most, but not all, leisure activities are services. However, it also covers the consumption of complementary manufactured goods such as books, televisions, stereos, sporting goods and so on.

STUDENT ACTIVITY 12.1

Make a list of products (services and goods) that you think might be classified as belonging to the 'leisure' industry. Do you think there are any problems in defining such an industry?

In the last thirty years leisure spending has increased faster than consumer spending as a whole and, as Table 12.1 indicates, it now constitutes about 17 per cent of total household expenditure. However, this may be an underestimate since spending on leisure goods and services excludes items like spending on clothing and footwear (e.g. sportswear), tobacco and alcohol, at least some of which, it might be argued, can be said to comprise leisure activities. It can also be seen from Table 12.1 that the households in the highest income groups spend a higher proportion of their incomes on leisure goods and services than do those in the lower groups; the households in the top fifth of the income distribution spent 20 per cent of their income on leisure goods and services in 1997/98, whereas those in the lowest fifth only spent 13 per cent of their income on these products. This implies that the demand for leisure products tends to be income elastic, i.e. they are classified as *luxuries*, in the sense that demand for them increases proportionately more than increases in income.

Table 12.1 **Percentage household expenditure by income grouping, 1997–98, UK**

| | Quintile groupings of households* | | | | | |
	Bottom fifth	Next fifth	Middle fifth	Next fifth	Top fifth	All households
Food	23	20	19	16	14	17
Leisure goods and services	13	15	16	17	20	17
Motoring and fares	11	15	16	19	18	17
Housing	16	16	15	15	16	16
Household goods and services	13	13	14	13	14	13
Clothing and footwear	6	5	5	6	6	6
Fuel, light and power	6	5	4	3	3	4
Alcohol	4	4	4	5	4	4
Tobacco	3	3	2	2	1	2
Other goods and services	4	4	5	4	4	4
All household expenditure (=100%)(£ per week)	171	218	305	407	556	331

* Equivalised disposable income (i.e. allowing for household size and composition) used for ranking households into quintile groups.
Source: *Social Trends*, Office for National Statistics, Vol. 30, 2000 edition. © Crown Copyright 2001

● *Common misunderstanding*

It should be stressed that leisure activities do not just come under the service sector umbrella. Products such as sportswear, sports goods like tennis rackets and cricket bats and even televisions can all be classified as belonging to the leisure industry, yet they are all manufactured goods and hence are part of the manufacturing sector of the economy (or are imports).

Types of leisure activities

Table 12.2 shows that the most popular home-based leisure activity remains watching television, an activity undertaken by 99 per cent of the population aged over 16. This is followed by visiting or entertaining friends and relatives and listening to the radio. Reading books is more popular among women than men, with DIY being more of a male preserve. Dressmaking and knitting remains a predominantly female activity, although less popular than it was, a reflection of the fact that more women work and have less time for such activities as well as having more money to spend on buying clothes.

The most popular leisure activity outside the home continues to be 'visiting the pub'. In a government survey in 1998–99 about 18 per cent of

people aged 16 or over in Great Britain had made such a visit the day prior to being interviewed, men being more likely than women to visit a public house. Driving for pleasure and spectating at a sporting event are also more popular among men than women.

Participating in sporting and physical activities tends to be more popular for men than for women: about 71 per cent per cent of men and 57 per cent of women participate in at least one such activity on a regular basis. Walking is the most popular physical activity for both men and women, followed by snooker or pool for men and keep fit or yoga for women. The trend towards a more healthy lifestyle has meant that participation in physical activities has become more popular in the last twenty years, especially among the younger age groups, although recently concern has been expressed in a number of quarters that sport may now have lower priority than it once did in the crowded school curriculum.

The proportion of the adult population attending cultural events has remained fairly constant during the last decade or so, as evinced by Table 12.3, the one exception being the growth in popularity of cinema-going. Cinema attendance has seen a resurgence in popularity after 40 years of decline: cinema admissions in Great Britain fell

Table 12.2 Percentage participation* in home-based leisure activities, by gender, Great Britain

	1977	1987	1996–97
Males			
Watching TV	97	99	99
Visiting/entertaining friends or relatives	89	94	95
Listening to radio	87	89	90
Listening to records/tapes/CDs	64	76	79
Reading books	52	54	58
DIY	51	58	58
Gardening	49	49	52
Dressmaking/needlework/knitting	2	3	3
Females			
Watching TV	97	99	99
Visiting/entertaining friends or relatives	93	96	97
Listening to radio	87	86	87
Listening to records/tapes/CDs	60	71	77
Reading books	57	65	71
DIY	22	30	30
Gardening	35	43	45
Dressmaking/needlework/knitting	51	47	37

* Percentage of those aged 16 or over participating in each activity in the four weeks before interview.

Source: *Social Trends*, Office for National Statistics, Volume 30, 2000 edition. © Crown Copyright 2001

from 1.4 billion in 1951 to reach a low point of 53 million in 1984. This was undoubtedly due to the advent of a strong substitute product in television; the use of video recorders simply hastened the downward trend in cinema-going. Its revival (cinema admissions were 123 million in 1998) has been linked with the investment and expansion in multiplex cinemas in recent years.

Table 12.3 Percentage attendance* at cultural events in Great Britain

	1987–88	1991–92	1997–98
Cinema	34	44	54
Theatre	24	23	23
Art galleries/exhibitions	21	21	22
Classical music	12	12	12
Ballet	6	6	6
Opera	5	6	6
Contemporary dance	4	3	4

*Percentage of resident population aged 15 and over attending 'these days'.

Source: *Social Trends*, Office for National Statistics, Volume 30, 2000 edition. © Crown Copyright 2001

Day trips are another increasingly popular leisure activity. They have risen by 15 per cent between 1994 and 1998 as people have more time and a greater amount of disposable income to devote to such activities. The two most popular reasons for taking day visits away from home are to go out for a meal or drink or to visit friends or relatives.

The proportion of adults in the UK taking at least one holiday a year of four nights or more has remained fairly constant at around 60 per cent for the past 25 years. The proportion of adults taking two or more holidays a year, however, increased steadily to 27 per cent by 1995, although since then the proportion has levelled out. In 1998, 56 million holidays of four nights or more were taken by UK residents, 36 per cent more than in 1971, a reflection of rising living standards. The number of holidays taken in the UK has been fairly stable over the last decade, but the number taken abroad has increased steadily; in 1998 for the first time the number of holidays taken abroad outnumbered those taken in the UK. Spain remains the most popular overseas destination for UK holiday-makers, followed by France and the USA. The latter has become an increasingly popular holiday destination for the British in the last decade due to a combination of rising real incomes and the fall in the real price of travel following deregulation in the airline industry. It is also of interest to note that a number of the foreign holiday destinations, especially in Europe, are substitutes for each other: people choose between travelling to Spain or France, for example. Thus, there is likely to be a positive cross price elasticity between them (see Chapter 5).

We shall next take a look at the importance of travel and tourism to the UK economy and then briefly investigate the structure of the package holiday industry in the UK.

Travel and tourism

The impact of tourism on the economy

Tourism spending in the UK as a *share of* GDP was 3.6 per cent in 1999, a proportion which has remained fairly static over the last twenty years. In 1999 earnings from tourism in the UK reached almost £32 billion, which was split more or less equally between earnings from overseas visitors and earnings from domestic tourism. Spending on domestic tourism (excluding day trips) represented 5.7 per cent of total UK consumer spending in 1999, a share which also has been relatively constant during the last two decades. The British Tourist Authority (BTA) spends almost £40 million p.a. promoting the UK as a tourist destination.

Tourism makes a very important contribution to the *balance of payments* (see Chapter 42). It accounts for a quarter of exports of all service industries, or invisible exports, and 4.5 per cent of all exports. It is also a *significant employer*. It is estimated that there are just over 1.75 million people, including the self-employed, employed in tourism and tourism-related industries in the UK (this covers travel agencies and tour operators; hotels and other accommodation; restaurants, cafés and snack bars; pubs, bars and nightclubs; libraries, museums and other cultural events; and sporting and other recreational activities). This figure represents about 6.5 per cent of the employed labour force.

● *Common misunderstanding*

It would be wrong to think that when UK residents travel abroad and spend money there that this represents an invisible export. In this case pounds are exchanged for foreign currencies; this then is an import, in this case an invisible one, in the same way as when a car is imported from, say, France, pounds are exchanged for francs in order to pay for the car. When foreign tourists come to the UK, however, and spend money here they exchange their currencies for pounds; foreign exchange is earned in this way and hence these earnings from overseas visitors represent the invisible export.

The figures given so far represent the direct impact of tourism on the economy. However, there may also be further indirect effects of tourism that can benefit the economy. This is due to the *multiplier effect* that expenditures such as tourism spending can have. Spending by tourists has benefits not just for tourism and tourist-related industries, but in others such as retailing, financial services, transport and so on. The spending adds to incomes and jobs in these industries and this additional income is then spent by the people working in them on consumption goods and services, which in turn creates a further round of income and job creation, and so on. A multipler effect has been initiated. (For a more detailed explanation of the multiplier process see Chapter 32). It is estimated, for example, that for every job created in the tourist industry, half of an indirect job is created elsewhere in the economy. The concept of the multiplier can also be used to study the impact of tourism on a local or regional economy, such as the south west of England. In this case, the multiplier effect is likely to be smaller, since quite a lot of the expenditure will 'leak' out of the region to firms based in other parts of the country.

STUDENT ACTIVITY 12.2

Provide examples of how tourist expenditure will leak out of a particular locality to benefit firms and households in other parts of the country.

There are also possible negative effects of tourism for an economy, or certain parts of it, and these can provide examples of *market failure* (see

Chapter 9). When foreign tourists visit London they may impose *external costs* on those who live and work there, such as increased congestion and pollution. The costs for any additional services, like refuse collection, fall on the local authorities. One possible solution is for the government to intervene and to impose some kind of road pricing scheme, with the aim of having tourists pay the full social costs of their decision to visit the capital. The problem with this is that it may well reduce the number of visitors to London and the amount that they spend. Any road pricing charges do not fall just on foreign visitors, of course!

The package holiday market in the UK

The package holiday industry in the UK is an *imperfect oligopoly* (see Chapter 8). It is dominated by four large firms: Thomson (which was acquired by Preussag, Germany's market leader, in 2000) has 28 per cent of the market for package holidays; Airtours, has a 21 per cent market share; Thomas Cook has 19 per cent of the market; and First Choice, has a 17 per cent share of the package holiday market. This gives a concentration ratio for the four largest firms for UK package holidays of 85.0, i.e. $C_4 = 85.0$ (see Chapter 19). The product that these firms sell is highly differentiated, based on strong corporate branding and advertising strategies.

There is a fringe of smaller firms in the industry that mainly cater to specialist markets. Kuoni, for example, specialises in long haul and adventure holidays, while Saga deals in holidays for the older traveller. Many other smaller tour operators as well as travel agents exist. This suggests that it is relatively easy to enter the industry and it is true that it may not take much to set up as an independent holiday provider. However, there is little doubt that there are significant barriers to entry to becoming a large-scale producer in the industry. Apart from the capital requirements involved, the dominant firms take advantage of economies of scale and there are the product differentiation barriers of advertising and brand loyalty that would have to be overcome by any prospective new entrant. There is also a significant amount of *vertical integration* in the industry, with the largest players owning their own travel agencies and/or charter airlines.

Thomson, for example, has the Lunn Poly travel agency chain plus Britannia Airways, the market leader. In fact, the possibility that the travel agency chains may concentrate on selling the products of their parent companies was investigated in 1997 by the competition authorities (see Chapter 23), although on this occasion the industry was found to be operating efficiently and not against the public interest.

Competition is likely to intensify in the industry in the future. The package holiday market is a mature one, with little likelihood of significant growth. Further consolidation in the industry is probable; in 1999 the Airtours proposed takeover of First Choice was blocked by the EU authorities on competition grounds. Price wars have been a feature of the industry and may well increase if the impact of technology continues to erode market shares and profit margins (currently at 3–4 per cent). People are now able to book foreign travel and accommodation via the internet or their television screens. While 54 per cent of UK holidays abroad in 1999 were inclusive tours, the balance seems to be turning towards people making more independent travel arrangements and booking the individual components of their holidays separately. In order to maintain their shares of what may be a stagnant or even dwindling market the large players are employing more diverse strategies, such as allowing customers to devise their own package holidays from within their product ranges.

> ### STUDENT ACTIVITY 12.3
>
> Discuss what strategies firms might pursue in order to protect their market shares in a market which is intensely competitive and which has limited growth prospects.

Some economic aspects of the English Premier League

The football industry in England was shaken up in the early 1990s by the establishment of the Premier League. For the 1992–93 season the twenty leading clubs that had comprised the Football League division one became part of an entirely separate entity, the Premier League. Divisions two, three and four in the original format became the first three divisions of the new Football League. (The leading Scottish clubs followed suit in 1998–99, the Scottish Premier League teams voting to break away from the Scottish Football League.)

It is no coincidence that the establishment of the Premier League has coincided with a huge influx of television money into football. For the years 1997–2001 BSkyB paid £670 million for the rights to broadcast live matches (compared with £214 million for the rights to the previous five years). In addition, the Premier League receives £73 million from the BBC for recorded highlight rights. (The total television rights for the Premier League for the three years from 2001 amounts to £1.6 billion.) Currently half the television income is divided equally between the Premiership clubs, 25 per cent is divided on merit depending on their League positions and the remaining 25 per cent is allocated to clubs when their matches are broadcast, split between the home and away teams. For the 1998–99 season, Arsenal, second in the table, received £10.95 million television income, more than double the earnings of Nottingham Forest, the bottom club in the League. Despite the fact that the Football League teams negotiate their own separate television deals, the loss of finance in not being part of the Premier League means that there is a significant opportunity cost involved.

In 1999 the deal between the Premier League and BSkyB was referred to the Restrictive Practices Court by the Director General of Fair Trading in that it was thought to be anti-competitive and hence would infringe competition rules (see Chapter 23). There were two issues at stake: first, whether the twenty Premiership clubs in effect illegally acted as a *cartel* by negotiating the television deal collectively; and second, whether the Premier League could legally prevent anyone other than BSkyB from televising or recording matches. However, on both counts the Restrictive Practices Court found that the existing deal was not against the public interest, given that the product demanded by both the viewing public and broadcasters was the Premier League championship as a whole and that, furthermore, any

resulting diminution of income for the clubs would prevent them from improving the quality of their stadia and other facilities. (The competition authorities had previously prevented a takeover bid for Manchester United by BSkyB in 1998, citing the possible conflict of interest with the latter's possession of the overall television rights for Premier League matches.)

Changing technology, like the introduction of Pay-per-View television, is likely to herald even greater increases in television revenues in the future. Middlesbrough was the first British club to launch its own satellite television channel. Manchester United (and Rangers in Scotland) are other teams following a similar path.

Since its inception the Premier League has seen an increase in overall attendances of over 16 per cent. The rise in real ticket prices during the period has meant that total match receipts have more than doubled, suggesting a price inelastic demand overall for Premiership matches.

Each year the top three teams (the third chosen by play off) are promoted from the first division of the Football League and three are relegated from the Premier League. Of course, the key barrier to entering the Premier League is failing to secure one of the three available promotion slots, but being promoted to the Premier League is one thing, staying there is quite another. It is common for at least one of the newly promoted teams to be relegated again the following season. The costs involved in running a successful Premier League club are enormous and represent a significant barrier to entry for many other clubs. The main cost per club is players' wages; since the establishment of the League the average Premiership wage has more than trebled. This has been helped by the 'Bosman ruling' of 1995, a European Court decision to allow players to change clubs freely when their contracts expire. In order to keep their star players, the supply of whom is price inelastic, clubs are prepared to meet their even higher wage demands. The possible end of the transfer system between clubs for players under contract would tip the balance of power even more in favour of the top players in the future.

The most successful clubs, like Manchester United and Chelsea, are increasingly able to exploit their brand names, particularly with regard to customer loyalty, in order to secure greater revenues to help finance these wage demands. Manchester United gets only about one-third of its more than £100 million a year turnover from ticket sales and a further one-sixth from television. The rest comes from sponsorships, conferences and catering and in particular from the merchandising of its products, especially its replica shirts. Chelsea's owner, Chelsea Village, has a hotel, flats and offices on its stadium site, in a prime area of West London, all promoted under the Chelsea name. (In fact, it is not unusual for English teams to own their own stadia, in contrast to the situation in many other European countries, where they are often rented from city councils.) The desire to tap further sources of funding has meant that a number of clubs have sought a stock market listing: ten Premiership clubs, nine Football League teams and two Scottish clubs have so far followed this particular route.

Much of the extra revenues entering football go into players' wages and transfer fees, or alternatively into redeveloping and updating stadia. Therefore, it is no surprise to find that most clubs, even in the Premiership, are not very profitable, even though those listed on the Stock Exchange now have to try to generate a satisfactory return for the external shareholders who have invested in the club. Four Premier League clubs are included in the world top twenty in terms of turnover, with Manchester United heading the list, although few of them are able to combine consistent footballing success with profitability. However, it is unlikely anyway that clubs would regard themselves as profit maximisers. For most of them securing playing success while maximising sources of revenue are more likely options; this means staying in the Premier League and trying to secure qualification for one of the European competitions, especially the extremely lucrative Champions League.

Conclusion

The leisure industry is a diverse one, comprising a range of different activities, both home-based and away from home. Leisure spending represents a higher proportion of spending for those people in the higher income groups than those in the lower income groups.

One of the key leisure activities is travel and tourism. Tourism is one of the most important industries in the UK economy. It is a significant employer and makes an important contribution to the balance of payments. The indirect effects of tourism spending on other industries are incorporated in the multiplier effect. There are, however, external costs of tourism spending to consider.

Summary

1 The leisure industry comprises a highly diversified set of activities, including both services and manufactured goods.
2 Higher income groups spend a higher proportion of their incomes on leisure goods and services.
3 The most popular home-based leisure activity is watching television, followed by visiting or entertaining friends and relatives. The most popular activity away from home is visiting the pub; there has also been a significant increase in cinema-going in the last decade.
4 More adults in the UK now take two or more holidays a year. The numbers taking overseas holidays also continues to increase in significance.
5 The tourism industry is an important employer and makes a significant contribution to the balance of payments; the tourism multiplier also means that there are indirect benefits for other industries. However, there are external costs of tourism spending to consider.
6 The package holiday industry in the UK is an imperfect oligopoly. There is intense competition among the leading firms in the industry.
7 The English Premier League has witnessed a significant increase in attendances and match revenues since its inception. There has also been a dramatic influx of television money into football.
8 The main cost for clubs is players' wages. The leading teams are able to exploit their brand names in order to enhance revenues from a variety of sources.

? QUESTIONS

1 Explain what is meant by the leisure industry and discuss the problems in defining it.
2 Comment on the key changes in leisure spending by the British public in the last twenty years.
3 'Leisure is a luxury good.' Explain and discuss.
4 Comment on the significance of the tourism industry for the UK economy.
5 Discuss what barriers to entry may exist for firms wishing to become one of the leading players in the UK package holiday industry.
6 Price competition is not generally thought to be a significant feature in oligopolistic industries, yet price wars are rife among the leading firms in the package holiday industry in the UK. Explain why you think this may be so.
7 Use the concepts of price elasticty of demand and supply to help explain why both the costs for clubs and attendance prices have increased significantly since the inception of the English Premier League.

Data response A
TOURISM IN SCOTLAND

Study the passage taken from *The Economist* of 5 August 2000 and answer the following questions.

1 Why is tourism important for the Scottish economy?
2 Why do you think the number of foreign tourists to Scotland fell in 1999 compared with the previous year?
3 What steps could the Scottish Tourist Board take to rectify the situation?
4 Given that there are negative as well as positive effects of tourism spending for an economy, should the Scottish Tourist Board do anything to rectify the situation?

Motoring downhill

Save perhaps for the annual migration of the British aristocracy to the grouse-shooting moors, Scotland will never be a destination for the touring masses. Sunshine is not guaranteed, and the best that can be said for swimming in the sea is that it is 'bracing'. Yet tourism is a vital part of the Scottish economy. It is reckoned to employ 177,000 people – 8% of the workforce – more than the oil, gas and whisky industries combined. In some parts of the country, such as the Highlands, looking after visitors keeps 15% of the population in a job.

But hoteliers are worried that heather-clad mountains and ancient castles may no longer be doing the trick. This summer, the Scottish Tourism Board caused a shock when it revealed that the number of foreign visitors to Scotland fell by 11% in 1999, compared with 1998. By contrast the number of foreigners coming to England was down by only 1%. Scotland's receipts from tourism also fell slightly to £2.5 billion ($3.8 billion).

These figures caused the kind of political panic that used to break out in Scotland when a colliery or a steelmill was threatened with closure. Henry McLeish, the tourism minister in Scotland's devolved government, announced four sets of action plans – all different – within as many days. Efforts to discover what foreign visitors thought about Scotland threw up a variety of dislikes, from dreary food to the infuriating habits of the midge, a tiny biting insect which attacks in swarms in the Highlands. One survey suggested that over half of first-time visitors to Scotland would think twice about returning because of the midges.

Actually, the likelist reasons for the decline are simple, and sadly only marginally more susceptible to reason than the midge. One is the strength of the pound against the euro which, according to Tom Buncle, the tourist board's chief executive, has made holidays in Scotland about 20% more expensive than they used to be for Europeans.

The other is the cost of petrol, which astounds Americans in particular. Driving 750 miles in Britain costs around £100, about 12% more than in France and 20–30% more than in most European countries. Mr Buncle fears that as most foreign visitors to Scotland arrive first in the south-east of England, motoring costs may be causing car hirers to turn back before they reach the Scottish border.

Since it is 160 miles from Edinburgh, the Scottish capital, to Inverness, the main town in the Highlands, the remoter parts of the country which depend most heavily on tourist income are suffering worst. Mr Buncle thinks that these costs explain why a survey of foreign visitors last year found that 20% of Germans (and 10% of Americans) thought that Scotland was too expensive.

Scottish hoteliers are hoping that their salvation will lie in special-interest holidays – hill-walking, bird-watching, golf, and so forth. The Scots are also learning from the Irish by devising holidays themed around traditional music, which is highly popular in Germany and Scandinavia. Tourism officials in the Scottish Borders recently asked local folk-music bands to collect addresses from their audiences when they toured the continent. A subsequent mail-shot persuaded about 200 of these people to attend a festival of folk music in the Borders.

Unsurprisingly, the Scottish National Party is making much of the damage being done by the strong pound and dear petrol – more policies designed for south-eastern England damaging Scotland, say the nationalists. But they are less keen to point out that, unlike other Europeans, the English visited Scotland in greater numbers last year – and now make up almost 50% of total visitors.

Source: © The Economist Newspaper Limited, London, 5 August 2000. Reprinted with permission.

The economics of the environment

An introduction to the environment

This chapter begins with a discussion of the range of possible policies to deal with pollution. It continues with a discussion of the different characteristics of pollutants and their relationship to the choice of policy. Finally these ideas are applied in case studies on the economics of the environment, which should be treated as data response articles. As a result there are no data response articles at the end of the chapter. Student activities appear at the end of each case. By coming to the problem of environmental pollution from these three different directions there will be some repetition, but the reader will see how the nature of the pollution affects policy.

Environmental problems

The impact of economic activity on the environment was not widely discussed until a group of academics known as the Club of Rome reported in the early 1970s that the planet faced pressures from the overuse of *resources*, the growth of *pop-* *ulation* and the increase in **pollution**. These three issues are frequently interrelated. The contribution of economists in helping to solve the problems of the environment date back to Pigou and his concept of *externality*. As discussed in Chapter 9:

An externality is a side effect of economic activity that affects people or companies not directly involved in that activity.

The usefulness of this concept is best illustrated by describing some of the most pressing environmental problems that result from economic activity. A minimum amount of understanding of the science behind these (usually chemical) problems allows us to trace the environmental problem back to its economic source.

(a) *Global warming* is a gradual heating of the earth, which has been traced to the increased production of carbon dioxide (CO_2). Every time we burn fossil fuels (petrol, oil, gas, coal) we add to this problem. The economic source of this problem is the transport and gas and electricity industries. Methane and CFCs (see below for a discussion of the ozone layer) are also global warming gases.

(b) *Acid rain* results from burning sulphur or nitrogen to produce oxides, which then turn into acids (sulphuric, nitric, nitrous etc.) when in contact with water in the atmosphere. The acid falls in a dilute form in rainfall, often hundreds of miles from its origin, adversely affecting tree growth rates, agricultural productivity, paint, metal and stonework.

(c) *Depletion of the ozone layer.* This problem is caused by a group of chemicals called CFCs used as propellants for spray cans and refrigerants for fridges and freezers. Oxygen is found in two main molecular forms in the atmosphere: with two atoms of oxygen (O_2), which is the type we breathe; and with three atoms (O_3) which is known as *ozone*. Ozone is an irritant to the lungs at ground level, and is regarded as a pollutant. However when found in the upper atmosphere it performs a very useful function: it reflects harmful radiation away from the planet's surface. When CFCs deplete the ozone layer, they allow in more radiation which reduces agricultural productivity and increases the incidence of skin cancer.

(d) *General air pollution* results from the build up of a number of gases at ground level including ozone as discussed above. Other problems include carbon monoxide (CO), nitrous-oxide (N_2O), volatile organic compounds like benzine (VOCs), particulate matter which are tiny specks of carbon (PM_{10}). They originate mainly from fossil fuel burning, so transport and energy industries are to blame again. Their main impact is on lung irritation, causing major problems for people with lung conditions and asthma sufferers.

There are of course many other environmental problems, some of which are discussed below. The case study on acid rain covers more advanced techniques than are used at this stage of the book and can be found in Chapter 40.

Sustainability and intergenerational equity

The Brundtland Commission report (1987) promoted the idea of *sustainable development* (see also Chapters 33 and 40). The main idea of sustainable development is that current economic growth should not be to the detriment of future generations. While stressing the need for development to get rid of poverty, particularly among less developed countries, the report points out that economic growth uses up the finite resources of the planet (oil, gas, coal) and degrades the environment by pollution. Sustainable development takes account of these problems by passing on the planet to the next generation in good condition. The idea is best summarised in the environmentalist slogan 'we have only borrowed the earth from our grandchildren'. You should recognise that, in economic terms, sustainability is an equity concept – intergenerational equity.

Another new concept that it introduces is the idea that we have two forms of capital – environmental capital and man-made or human capital.

Ideas about sustainability come in two forms: *strong* and *weak sustainability*. In the strong form of sustainability, the earth's environmental capital should be passed on intact to the next generation. This is very difficult to do in practice because the fossil fuels are clearly being used up. Some people argue that there is little point in having the fossil fuels, unless they are used up at some point by someone! The weaker form of sustainability argues that using up environmental capital is acceptable, as long as it is replaced by human capital. Critics of this view argue that human capital is not always a very good substitute for environmental capital. In the case of fossil fuels, the argument from weak sustainability would be that it is acceptable to use up fossil fuels, as long as we are investing in research into alternative methods of generating power, such as nuclear fusion or solar cells. The argument between the two often boils down to a question of optimism or pessimism about the ability of science to provide a 'technical fix' to current environmental problems. Supporters of strong sustainability argue that in many cases human capital is not a good substitute for environmental capital.

Policies to deal with the environment

When looking at the case studies, you should distinguish between *market instruments*, which affect price, such as taxes and subsidies, and *regulations*, which affect technology or output directly. Each policy is discussed separately below. There is a bias among more right wing politicians towards using the market wherever possible to deal with environmental problems. More left wing politicians tend to prefer regulation. As will be seen in the discussion below, the picture is more complicated than this, and regulations are more suited to some environmental problems, while others are more suited to market instruments.

Taxation

Two good examples of using taxation to deal with an environmental problem are cigarettes and petrol. The idea is to make people pay the full cost of their activity, including the external costs as well as the private costs. The main problem faced by such a policy is inelastic demand (see Figure 13.2 on page 189). In our two examples, the government has increased the tax massively over the last decade. In the case of cigarettes this has met with some success (see Table 13.1), but in the case of petrol, car demand continues to rise (see Table 13.2). If such high taxes are not having a big impact on demand, it is reasonable to ask whether they are effective polices. Some people have argued that the government is also addicted – to cigarette and petrol revenues. Raising taxes on these products allows them to keep income tax rates down and retain the support of the electorate.

Taxation is not a single policy, as there is choice over what to tax. The government can tax the private good associated with the externality (cigarettes and petrol above) or they could tax the pollution itself (this usually costs too much to measure). Finally they could tax a proxy input like the carbon content of fossil fuel (see the global warming case study below).

When considering the benefits of taxation, the costs of measurement and of tax collection should be considered. Governments often like the idea of the taxation solution because it allows them to keep other taxes like income tax lower than they otherwise would be. You should be familiar enough with demand curves by now to know that you can control both price and quantity. When using tax as the 'price of polluting', producers and consumers are left to decide what quantity of pol-

lution they want to produce at that price. This may not be a good idea if it is important to keep pollution down below an agreed safe limit. Since tax is effectively the price of pollution, it is also easier to get people to accept it if the costs imposed by the pollution are easy to value. It is then possible to justify the tax in relation to identifiable costs (e.g. treatment of asthma patients suffering from general air pollution).

Subsidy

Taxes attempt to persuade people not to do a 'bad' thing. Subsidies try to persuade people to do a 'good' thing. Two examples are public transport and loft insulation, which both help in cutting down global warming by reducing CO_2 emissions. The use of public transport also improves general air quality and road congestion (see Chapter 14). The main drawback with subsidies is that they increase public spending, which means the government has to raise more in taxation. Subsidies are a good idea to deal with poorer groups in society (loft insulation for pensioners), or where the introduction of more taxation is difficult (e.g. public transport subsidy, instead of petrol tax).

Tradable permits

Tradable permits work by allowing firms to buy the right to pollute from the government. The government can set the global amount of pollution that they will allow in any given year. The firms are then either allocated the permits in line with their current pollution levels (sometimes called grandfather rights) or have to bid for the rights. Once the pollution permits have been distributed, a market is established and firms can buy and sell the permits.

The USA has experimented with the idea of tradable permits to control water and air pollution, and has also proposed them for CO_2 outputs where it hopes to buy rights to pollute from Russia. Under the Kyoto agreement of 1997, the USA will have to reduce its output of CO_2 to 93 per cent of 1990 levels by 2012, but it hopes to buy pollution rights from countries whose allowance for pollution leaves them with 'spare capacity' like Russia. The insistance of the USA

Table 13.1 **Number of smokers (percentage of the population (16+)**

	1972	1998/9
Male	52	28
Female	42	26

Table 13.2 **Passenger kilometres (total distance travelled) by car, van and taxi (billion)**

1980	1998
388	616

on the tradeable permits approach was a major cause of the breakdown of talks in The Hague (2000) to implement the Kyoto agreement.

Tradable permits have the advantage over taxation that the global quantity of pollution is fixed. On the other hand they may not be suitable for pollution that has local effects, as a large firm may decide to buy up permits with disastrous effects on a local neighbourhood. There may also be problems if the industry is oligopolistic (see Chapter 8). There is evidence from some schemes that firms may use the permits as a barrier to entry into the market. If they refuse to sell pollution permits to firms hoping to enter the industry, they may be able to exercise market power.

Eco-labelling

A market works best if there is perfect information. Eco-labelling improves the flow of information to the consumer. The best examples in recent years are the ozone layer and lead. In the late 1980s and early 1990s spray cans were labelled as 'ozone friendly' if they didn't contain the CFCs that were destroying the ozone layer. Customers could choose not to be polluters because they had the necessary information. In the same way, lead-free petrol reduced air pollution, and consumers could choose to drive in a less polluting way. In both these cases, the pollutant has now been phased out completely, but producers needed time to develop alternative technology.

Quantity regulation

It is often argued that the market is the best way to regulate pollution, but there are situations where regulation is still best. If the policy target is zero pollution, then quantity regulation is the best policy (e.g. CFCs). If there is a threshold level that it is important not to exceed, then quantity regulation is the best option, because taxes leave the choice about output to the market (e.g. low level radiation from nuclear power plants). If it is difficult to trace the producer of the nuisance then regulation, and fines if they are caught, may be the best option (e.g. noise from lorries or carbon monoxide from vehicle exhausts). Regulation can often be inefficient, however, because everyone has to reduce their levels of pollution by the same amount. With taxation, the polluters who can reduce the pollution most cheaply will do so. If the tax is more than the cost of pollution reduction then it is profitable to reduce that unit of pollution.

Safety regulation

Health and safety regulations are applied to check that accidents are minimised and workers and consumers are not exposed to unnecessary risk. Where the problem is pollution resulting from an accident, safety regulation is the best answer. The idea here is to create preventative measures to avoid catastrophes such as the Chernobyl nuclear accident in the former USSR. The same kind of logic applies to oil tanker accidents at sea, which can cause major pollution for coastal areas. Where people are exposed to hazards for which they have no obvious source of information (for instance in the workplace), then health and safety regulations are appropriate.

Zoning (regulation)

In the case of pollution that is local, sometimes separating the polluters from their potential victims is the best solution. Separating shoppers from cars by shopping malls or pedestrianised areas is a good way to reduce the impact of noise pollution and reduce accidents at the same time. Further examples of this solution will be considered below shortly.

Pollution characteristics

When looking at any pollution, you should know what the characteristics of the pollution are before deciding what the best policy is. Each pollution has its own 'personality' which will be made up of a combination of the following characteristics.

Operational and accidental pollution

It is helpful from the point of view of policy to make a distinction between pollution that occurs as a normal by-product of industrial activity (*operational pollution*) and *accidental pollution* when something goes wrong, as in the case of the accident at the Chernobyl nuclear power plant in the former Soviet Union. The production of carbon dioxide as a result of burning fossil fuels is clearly operational. Operational pollution can more frequently be dealt with by *market-based incentives*, while accidents nearly always require regulations to prevent frequent occurrence.

Local, international or global

A bad smell from a factory may only affect the immediate locality, while the gases that cause acid rain (sulphur dioxide and NO_x) can affect countries 2000 miles away. Carbon dioxide, the main global warming gas, affects the climate of the whole planet. It is important to know how wide the scope of the damage is, when deciding policy. As noted above, local pollution can often be dealt with simply by separating the polluter from potential victims. Smokers can be restricted to certain areas. Town planners can insist that certain parts of a city can be reserved for industrial use, and separated from residential areas. This type of solution to problems of local pollution is called *zoning*, and is a form of regulation.

Elastic or inelastic demand

As noted above, if a product is being taxed because of its environmental effects, an inelastic demand will result in little change in consumers' behaviour. One possible response to this is to say that consumers have paid for the external cost of their activity and should be allowed to pollute the environment. Welfare economists call this situation efficient (see Chapter 9).

The problem with this approach is that while the consumers have paid for this cost, it is possible that the victims of the pollution have not been compensated. For instance, motorists may continue to add to global warming, but the victims may be future generations who cannot easily be compensated by the current generation and have no say in what is happening. This is a question of *intergenerational equity*. It is also a question of who owns the environment (clearly without intervention from the government, the motorists believe they do). If global warming is increasing desertification and tropical storms (as some climate experts believe) then the argument is similar,

although we are talking about *international equity*. General air pollution is often worst in poorer parts of the city near urban motorways and industrial areas. Motorists and industrialists are claiming ownership over the air and reducing the quality of life of poorer people. This is also a question of equity and ownership of the environment.

Traceable or difficult to trace

If the pollution is easy to trace, then it is much easier to place taxes on it. If it is difficult to trace, then a regulatory approach with fines for those caught infringing the rules is more appropriate. Noise from lorries is a good example that has already been mentioned.

Stock or flow

A *flow* pollutant is one that enters the environment, creates a harmful effect, but does not build up in the environment. A *stock* pollutant, however, is one that does build up in the environment. For instance, noise is a good example of a flow pollutant. On the other hand, the effect of CFCs, CO_2 or radioactive substances is cumulative and these are stock pollutants. As students of economics you should be aware of this distinction already: wealth is a stock, while income is a flow; capital is a stock, while interest is a flow. Carbon dioxide builds up in the atmosphere making global warming gradually worse. Acidity of the soil as a result of acid rain can also build up over time. The ozone layer takes a long time to recover after CFCs have broken it down. On the other hand, some pollutants disappear almost as soon as they arrive. Noise from an aeroplane dies away. Many chemical smells are temporary. Oil pollution of the sea will eventually be dissipated (there are at least 90 organisms which eat oil!).

● *Common misunderstanding*

It is not always easy to distinguish between a stock and a flow in practice because given time, the ozone layer will recover, and radioactive substances will decay to less harmful substances. These processes take a very long time, however, and in practice we are distinguishing between very short-term pollutants (flow) and very long-term pollutants (stock).

Certain or uncertain in its effects

Acid rain is known to cause considerable damage to buildings, plants and lakes. The effect of CFCs in depleting the ozone layer is known to increase the risk of skin cancer. Lead is known to have an adverse effect in the development of young people's brains. These are fairly certain effects. The impact of global warming is still argued over. There are still a minority of scientists who dispute the existence of the effect. There may even be some beneficial effects if the climate warms. Unfortunately models of ocean currents suggest the Gulf Stream, which raises the temperature of the UK by about 5 degrees above what is expected at this latitude, will change direction if global warming continues. This is a pollutant of uncertain effects. Policy to deal with pollution that is certain in its effects will be more urgent and more stringent. Where pollution is less certain in its effects, policy will be more hesitant, and more open to political objection from people losing out from the policy (see the section 'Dump the pump' on page 190).

Easy or difficult to value

Even when we are certain of the effects of an environmental pollutant, we will not always be able to place a value on these effects. It is quite easy to place a value on lost agricultural output, or erosion of buildings by acid rain, because products are involved which have prices. We can go some way to valuing the effects of ill health caused by pollution in terms of its treatment costs, but pain and suffering are more difficult to place a value on. How much is someone's life worth? What value would you place on the natural beauty of a landscape? How do we value environmental costs that will be suffered by future generations? These are more difficult questions to answer and will often affect how seriously the environmental problem is taken. Some approaches to these questions are found in Chapter 40. As has been noted above, the existence of a widely accepted value for environmental damage will legitimise the use of a tax, which is supposed to reflect that value.

Fixed or variable technology

Taxing a product that is produced by a fixed technology will have the effect of reducing the output of that product and the environmental problem will be reduced in proportion. Taxing petrol will reduce demand and CO_2 output will be reduced in proportion by the fixed technology of the internal combustion engine. Taxing electricity will not have the same effect, because electricity can be produced by wind power, hydro, nuclear power, gas, oil or coal burning power stations, all of which have a different output of CO_2 in relation to electricity produced.

Case study 13.1
GLOBAL WARMING

The scientific background

Global warming is a rise in the average temperature of the whole planet. The scientific theory that suggests that global warming will be a significant problem in the twenty-first century is known as the *greenhouse effect*. The sun's rays warm the earth during the day, but when this energy is reflected back into outer space it is trapped, much as energy in a greenhouse is trapped. The increase in the production of certain gases (since the industrial revolution started in the late eighteenth century) is responsible for this effect. Carbon dioxide, nitrous oxides, CFCs (see the Case study 13.2 on ozone depletion on page 192) and methane are the main gases responsible. The expected effects on temperature are shown in Figure 13.1.

Some of the effects of global warming are beneficial. The agricultural productivity of more northerly countries such as the UK should improve and their climates could become more pleasant. However, other countries such as Ethiopia could suffer from increased desertification and problems of famine. Patterns of rainfall are likely to change. The greatest threat comes from the projected rise in sea level. Sea level will rise as warmer water expands, but more seriously, the polar ice-caps may start to melt. As a result, countries such as Bangladesh and Egypt with large populations in low-lying coastal river deltas may suffer. Much of the projected costs of global warming comes from the loss of agricultural production from these fertile areas, or from the cost of providing them with sea defences. It is also believed that the strength and frequency of hurricanes is related to seawater temperature in the tropics. There is uncertainty about many of the projected effects of global warming, but there is a possibility that the climate of the UK could become colder. If the Gulf Stream, which carries warm water to our shores, changes direction, our climate would become more like that of other North European countries.

The link with the economy

The main source of man-made carbon dioxide is from the burning of coal, oil and gas. The main industries responsible for adding carbon dioxide to the atmosphere are electricity, gas and transport. These are industries that are vital to production and distribution in a developed economy. The lifestyle of consumers in industrialised countries is also highly energy intensive. As more countries successfully industrialise, so the problem will worsen.

Transfrontier pollution

Global warming is an example of an externality that crosses frontiers. If individual countries attempt to deal with the problem on their own, much of the benefit will in fact go to other countries, while the cost of reducing the pollution will fall on their own country. Where there is *transfrontier pollution*, progress can only be made if there is international agreement about common policy to be followed by all countries. Such agreements usually take the form of agreed targets for each country, and it is then up to each country to achieve that target in the way it thinks best. The Rio environmental summit in Brazil (1992) formed the basis of many such agreements. In the case of global warming, countries agreed to limit their output of carbon dioxide to 1990 levels by the year 2000. This may not seem like a very dramatic control policy, but it is set against the background of sharply increasing output levels in previous decades. The failure to make progress on the implementation of the Kyoto agreement in The Hague (2000) has further delayed action on global warming for the time being.

Intergenerational externality

The problem with global warming is that the predicted adverse effects are not expected to become serious until later in the twenty-first century. Predictions of how much sea level will rise vary and there are even some scientists who remain sceptical about the whole thing. What we are faced with here is an external effect of uncertain magnitude occurring in the future. Figure 13.1 shows the range of temperature forecasts by the International Panel on Climate Change (IPCC) and compares these forecasts with historical evidence. The costs of reducing the externality are borne by the current generation, while the benefits will accrue to future generations. This situation is known as an *intergenerational externality*. This may explain the fairly conservative management policy being advocated at present. World environmental policy on global warming can best be described as holding carbon dioxide output levels steady while we check what the effects really are.

Sustainable development

The Brundtland Commission (1987) popularised the notion that when faced with intergenerational externalities of this kind, the right approach was to try to follow a path of *sustainable development*. Sustainable development means that we should try to achieve economic growth in such a way as not to affect future generations adversely. This may be easier for developed nations than those undergoing a process of industrialisation. We can hardly complain if China or India attempt to achieve the same standard of living as Europe, increasing their use of energy per capita to our levels. Clearly an extra two billion people consuming energy at that level is likely to have a major impact on

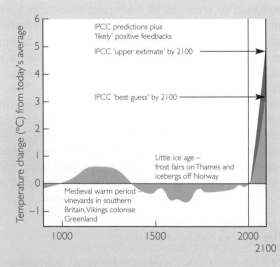

Figure 13.1 Global warming

global warming. The main problem with the idea of sustainable development is that optimists argue that there will be a **technical fix** for the problems as science progresses and that we need not worry too much. Pessimists would argue the opposite, so policy will depend upon attitudes towards the **uncertainty** of future events.

Policies

VAT on fuel

In 1993 the government introduced a VAT rate of 8 per cent on gas and electricity, which had previously been zero rated. Plans to increase VAT to the standard rate (now 17.5 per cent) the following year had to be abandoned owing to strong political opposition. After its election in 1997, the Labour government announced its intention to reduce this tax to 5 per cent as soon as was prudent (this is the lowest rate of VAT that can be charged under EU regulations). In Chapter 9 we discussed Pigou's idea of imposing a tax equal to the value of the externality. The idea of such a tax is that consumers pay the full social costs of their energy consumption. The use of this form of taxation to deal with energy pollution runs into a number of problems that are discussed in the following sections.

● *Common misunderstanding*

Most people believe that there was no tax on energy before the introduction of VAT on gas and electricity. This is not the case because of the way in which VAT works (see Chapter 28 for a fuller discussion). VAT is levied on the value of the output of companies at each stage of production. There is a rebate of the tax already charged on inputs from earlier stages in production. Inputs such as energy that did not themselves attract tax are taxed when they are used to produce other goods and services. The introduction of VAT on energy was therefore only on domestic energy, since industrial and commercial use of energy was already taxed in the way described in this paragraph.

Targeting the externality

Because the tax is on the private good rather than on the externality itself, it is not well **targeted**. The tax does not discriminate well between different sources of energy that have different effects on the environment. For instance, nuclear energy, although it may have other external effects, does not produce any carbon dioxide at all. Electricity production works by burning fossil fuels to create high-pressure steam, which turns turbines, which generate the electricity. Not all fuels produce the same amount of carbon dioxide per unit of energy produced. Gas is more environmentally efficient at producing energy, both when used directly and when used for generating electricity. It also has a lower sulphur content and is therefore also preferable because it produces less acid rain). It is because there are a number of alternative energy technologies available that a tax on energy is badly targeted.

Incidence and equity

The demand for energy is very inelastic, so the reduction in consumption is small compared with the increase in tax (see Figure 13.2). Most of the incidence of the tax will be on the consumer because of the inelasticity of demand. In addition to questions about the effectiveness of the tax in meeting its objectives, there is a problem of **equity**. The poorest people in society also spend the highest proportion of their income on energy. The elderly and families on low income with young children both need warmth in winter to stay well, so this is a matter for social concern. However, it can be argued that the

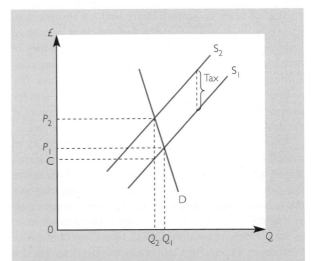

Figure 13.2 The incidence of a tax on domestic energy

government should concentrate on getting relative prices to reflect social costs properly, and then deal with problems of income distribution separately, increasing pensions and social security payments to poorer households so that they can afford to maintain their energy consumption at an adequate level.

On the plus side it must be said that the absence of a tax on domestic energy consumption was encouraging excessive use of this energy by lowering its price relative to the prices of the majority of products which do attract VAT. Paradoxically, greater efficiency following the privatisation of the electricity industry will have the effect of lowering prices and increasing consumption! A further advantage of using VAT is that it is rebateable on exported goods, so it does not adversely affect the country's balance of payments. Finally, as noted below, higher energy prices may persuade people to take energy-saving measures.

The petrol tax escalator

In the 1990s, the Conservative government decided to discourage use of the car by increasing the excise tax on petrol by 5 per cent a year in real terms. This policy was continued by the Labour government, until the protests of the motorists and the freight transport industry persuaded them not to make any further increases after 1999. Once again this is a tax on a price inelastic product, so the reduction in demand is likely to be small as in the case of domestic energy illustrated in Figure 13.2. However, this time the tax is much better targeted because the choice of fuels is limited. There will be an incentive for consumers to use more fuel-efficient means of transport. Unfortunately the high income elasticity of demand for transport will constantly be moving consumers in the opposite direction. This time the poorer people in society are likely to bear a smaller proportion of the costs because public transport is generally more fuel efficient per passenger carried.

One problem for this kind of tax is the volatility of the oil market. At the same time as the tax was introduced, the recession of the early to mid-1990s drove the price of oil down to $12 a barrel, offsetting the tax increases. As the economic recovery progressed in the West and the Far East began to recover from its late 1990s recession, OPEC (the Organisation of Petroleum Exporting Countries) managed to get the price of a barrel above $30, increasing petrol prices sharply just as the government was trying to ease back on the petrol escalator policy.

'Dump the pump'

In the same way that there had been political resistance to the tax on gas and electricity, a campaign was mounted in September 2000 by farmers, truckers and people living in more remote areas, against the rise in petrol prices. It could be argued that these were the groups that had been most affected by the higher prices. The campaign took the form of direct action to prevent the distribution of petrol, and soon had the effect of bringing the country to a standstill. Paradoxically, the government had stopped further rises in petrol duty just before this protest. It was the rise in world oil prices that was pushing up petrol prices.

This campaign demonstrates that making decisions to tax the environment to reflect its external costs may make sense in efficiency terms (allocating resources) but can have a serious impact on the income of a small group of people in the economy (equity). There was no real environmental problem with lowering taxes on petrol in 2000, because world oil prices were doing the job that the taxes were doing before – creating disincentives for using petrol. There is however a problem for the government's finances. If tax revenues from petrol go down, then one of three things must happen to the government's budget:

1 taxes must be increased on income or other products to make up the shortfall in revenue; or
2 government spending must fall to reflect this reduced revenue; or
3 if the government budget is in deficit, this deficit will rise resulting in higher borrowing; if it is in surplus then this surplus will fall, postponing the repayment of the National Debt.

Some supporters of the dump the pump campaign have argued that they would be less concerned about the tax on petrol if the money had been spent on upgrading and/or subsidising the public transport alternative. In the long run, meeting the restrictions of the Kyoto agreement will probably mean some restrictions on car use. The problem is, how to achieve this?

Infrastructure

Decisions about investment in transport *infrastructure* can also affect carbon dioxide output. Public transport consumes less fuel than car transport for each passenger mile travelled. Building more roads reduces congestion and makes travelling on the roads more attractive. Any decision to curb the road building programme must be accompanied by greater investment in **public transport**, possibly with greater **subsidies** if people are to be persuaded by lower prices to use it. Transport is fundamental to the operation of market economies because markets depend on the free movement of labour, goods and services. Other aspects of this problem area are discussed in Chapter 14.

Information technology

To the extent that information technology reduces the need for transport, by video conferencing, faxes, file transfers on the world wide web, e-mail, etc., it reduces the demand for energy and is environmentally beneficial. People are more able to work at home some of the time, using a modem instead of a car. Information transmitted electronically is also less intensive than paper.

Subsidy for loft insulation

Energy-saving measures such as loft insulation and double glazing do pay for themselves eventually, but may cost a great deal of money. A universal subsidy was available in the 1970s when the oil crisis led the government to put a premium on saving energy and reducing expensive oil imports. Currently this subsidy is limited to old age pensioners. A tax on energy may have the result of persuading more people to take energy-saving measures. As part of its initiative to get younger people off unemployment benefit, the Labour government announced the setting up of environmental task groups to help with loft insulation, among other environmental tasks.

The carbon tax

Although not implemented, this has often been advocated as a good method of reducing carbon dioxide output. Instead of placing the tax on the private good, electricity, the tax is levied on the **carbon content** of the fossil fuel. This acts as an effective **proxy** for the real thing we wish to tax: carbon dioxide.

The recession

The recession of the early 1990s made it easier for the UK to meet its targets, since energy use is related to GDP. This is not a policy as such, and indeed it may persuade people that pollution control is going well. The economy recovered strongly from the mid-1990s onwards, leading to increased environmental problems and a need for stronger policy to help meet targets.

Nuclear power and the fossil fuel levy

Nuclear power does not use fossil fuels and creates no global warming effects. It seems, on the face of it, to be an ideal solution to the problem. Unfortunately, nuclear power has externalities of its own, both in terms of the low-level **radioactive waste** that nuclear power plants produce routinely, and the more dramatic **accidents** that sometimes occur. The relatively recent Chernobyl disaster has worried some people about the use of nuclear energy. Nevertheless the UK government initially subsidised the nuclear industry after the rest of the electricity industry had been privatised, by charging a levy on all fossil fuel (coal, oil, gas). This levy has now been phased out.

Renewable energy

The revenue from the fossil fuel levy was also used to subsidise renewable sources of energy, such as wind power, but only a small fraction of the total went on this kind of sustainable energy production. The fossil fuel levy was phased out with the privatisation of the nuclear industry in 1997. **Alternative energy** is the technology of the future, if global warming is to be tackled successfully. Unfortunately these technologies are mostly more expensive to produce at present. Most of them use the energy from the sun, directly or indirectly. Direct solar energy can be used to heat water or generate electricity using **solar cells**. **Wind turbines** in windier (usually mountainous) areas of the country are using indirect solar energy. In Iceland **geothermal** energy is used by pumping water down to hot parts of the earth's crust (which are near the surface), which then returns as steam to drive turbines. The most urgent need in the case of renewable technologies is research and development to drive down the costs of producing energy in this way. If significant progress can be made in reducing these costs, the hottest countries may become the natural location for energy-intensive industry.

Trees and the rainforests

● *Common misunderstanding*

*Many people believe that trees grow out of the soil. In fact they largely grow out of the air! Trees are mainly made of carbon, which they obtain by 'breathing in' carbon dioxide from the air through their leaves, removing the carbon, and then 'breathing' out the oxygen through their leaves. This is very useful as human beings and other animals need this oxygen to live. It is also useful because it reduces the amount of carbon dioxide in the atmosphere, so growing trees reduces the greenhouse effect. The trees act as a **carbon sink** effectively storing the carbon. All plants have this effect, but trees are the bulkiest and therefore the most effective store of carbon.*

There are many reasons for protecting the rainforests. They have a vast variety of animal and plant species that may be of medical value to humankind. Water evaporates from them and falls as much needed rainfall in more arid regions. They are the natural home of indigenous peoples. But most of all they are the world's biggest carbon sink. The argument about sustainable development arises again here (see earlier in the chapter). Europeans cut down their vast forests over a period of thousands of years as their populations grew and their economies developed. Are Europeans in a strong position to argue that tropical countries should not do the same? The tropical areas include some of the world's poorer countries (in Central Africa), but also some of the world's faster-growing developing countries such as Brazil and the 'Asian tiger' economies (Malaysia, Thailand, Indonesia). Cutting down trees in these forests is no problem in itself as long as they are replanted. If the trees are turned into wood products like furniture they will continue to act as a carbon store while new trees are growing. *Sustainably managed* rainforests used for commercial timber add to the carbon sink and are more environmentally desirable.

Consumer information and self-interest

Some reduction in energy use can be achieved by more energy-efficient homes and vehicles. The introduction of official miles per gallon (mpg) figures for cars helped consumers both to save money and help the environment. Energy use figures for washing machines and dishwashers have the same effect. Campaigns to persuade people to insulate their lofts, or install double glazing, will also save people money in the long run. These are examples of **eco-labelling**.

STUDENT ACTIVITY 13.1

Undertake a survey of your school/college/university listing the areas where energy saving might be possible. List the measures you suggest in terms of rising expense. You can undertake a similar activity for your own home as an individual exercise.

STUDENT ACTIVITY 13.2

● Which are the easiest policies to implement from the above list?
● What are the best ways of reducing carbon dioxide output from domestic heating and transport respectively?
● Which policies would have less impact on poorer people?

STUDENT ACTIVITY 13.3

Using Figure 13.2, indicate how much of the incidence of the tax on domestic energy consumption is on the consumer and how much is on the producer.

**Case study 13.2
OZONE DEPLETION**

What does ozone do?

The ozone layer is high in the earth's atmosphere and acts to deflect ultraviolet (UV) radiation away from the surface of the planet. Ozone is in fact a form of oxygen that has three atoms in each molecule (O_3) instead of the normal two (O_2), which we breathe at ground level. Ozone found at ground level is a pollutant, which irritates the lungs. A group of chemicals known as **CFCs** (chlorofluorocarbons) have the effect of breaking down the ozone molecules. As a result, more UV radiation reaches ground level. The main harmful result to humankind is an increased incidence of skin cancer, which can be fatal. Agricultural productivity might also be affected in the long run as radiation can affect growth. The main use of CFCs was as a propellant for aerosol spray cans and as a coolant for refrigerators and freezers.

Characteristics of the externality

This once again is a transfrontier externality. Although most CFC use has been in North America and Europe, the first measurable effect was the 'ozone hole' that has appeared over the Antarctic. Ozone thinning has also been detected in the northern hemisphere. The ozone layer does eventually recover but it is thought that this process might take up to 80 years. It is thus also an intergenerational externality. Since it is associated with the operation of a particular product, it is an operational externality. In addition it is a stock pollutant, since, once CFCs have destroyed the ozone layer, it takes a long time to build up again naturally.

Eco-labelling

Not all manufacturers had the ability to switch to alternative spray propellant technology immediately. Although CFCs have now been banned, there was an interval while the new technology was being introduced when reduction in output was dependent on the consumers' unwillingness to pollute the environment. Spray cans were labelled as 'ozone friendly' if they did not contain CFCs. This approach is known as *eco-labelling* and relies on providing information to consumers to help them make the right decision, rather than telling them what to do by introducing regulations. It works well as a transitional policy while new technology is being introduced. It works best when the issues are straightforward and simple for the consumer to understand. Another example of eco-labelling is lead-free petrol, although this was combined with a tax differential between leaded and unleaded petrol to encourage people to switch. Biodegradable detergents in the washing powder business are an example of eco-labelling which is less clear, because the time taken for the chemicals to degrade safely varies between different brands, and the consumer has no way of knowing what the acceptable period should be. This is perhaps an area where government regulation of environmental standards is needed to bolster simple eco-labelling.

Certainty

Clearly, stock pollutants are more worrying in the long run, but there are sometimes scientific *uncertainties* about the nature of the environmental threat. Forecasting well into the future also brings with it uncertainties. The appearance of the ozone hole over the Antarctic confirmed scientific hypotheses and led to strict action globally, and the development of the Montreal Protocol for phasing out CFCs. Because of the increased certainty that ozone depletion is taking place and is causing harmful effects, policy has been stricter in this area and international agreement has been easier to achieve. Furthermore, since CFCs are also global warming gases, taking firm action on this problem allowed a little more time to think about the more difficult problem of reducing CO_2 levels.

Technology transfer

Although technologies which do not use CFCs exist for both aerosols and fridges, they are not necessarily easily accessible to less developed countries because of patents held by companies based in developed countries. As these countries industrialise they may use cheap polluting technology in their production techniques. The solution to this problem is to *transfer new technology* to developing countries by providing information, waiving patent fees, and giving technical assistance and training. Profit-making countries are unlikely to do this of their own accord, so government involvement would be necessary.

STUDENT ACTIVITY 13.4

Make a list of supermarket products that make environmental claims. Are they easily understood by the average consumer? Are they confirmed by any body other than the producers themselves? Which products would you purchase as a result of the information made available in this way?

Case study 13.3
RUBBISH AND RECYCLING

The costs of rubbish

Industrial economies produce an enormous quantity of waste, which must be disposed of in some way. The majority of waste is disposed of in landfill sites, which are eventually covered in earth and returned to other uses. The costs of this process are:

(a) the loss of land for agricultural and other purposes;

(b) those that arise because of the 'chemical soup' in the tip, the land may be unsuitable for any other purpose for a long period after tipping has ceased and may cost a considerable amount of money to make safe at a later date;

(c) the cost of the materials thrown away instead of being recycled, including the energy needed to replace materials like glass and aluminium;

(d) the energy costs of transporting waste to distant landfill sites.

Policy

Refuse collection

Local authority collection is not a solution to the problem of waste but it prevents it from becoming a local nuisance. The service is frequently produced by private sector companies, given the franchise by local authorities.

Recycling

There are four main products that are recycled: paper, glass, aluminium and plastic. In addition batteries are sometimes recycled because they contain heavy metals, and CFCs from fridges are recycled because of their impact on the ozone layer. The purpose of this recycling varies from material to material.

Biodegradability

A substance is said to be **biodegradable** if it quickly decomposes into environmentally beneficial substances. Paper and cardboard are biodegradable but are still recycled for three reasons. First, recycling reduces the demand on forestry for raw materials. Second, it reduces the bulk of refuse considerably, much of which comes from cardboard packaging and newspapers. Third, biologically useful degraded materials are no use to anyone if mixed with toxic materials. Plastics and glass are not biodegradable, and aluminium is not a useful biological material.

Food waste and some garden waste can be turned into soil by **composting** in compost heaps in people's gardens.

Energy saving

Glass and aluminium production are both energy-intensive processes and considerable energy savings can be achieved by using recycled materials. The benefit of energy saving is not only the money saved; it is a contribution to the reduction of global warming (see Case study 13.1, page 187). This energy saving must be offset against the energy costs of getting the materials to recycling centres.

Rubbish tax

The introduction of a **tax on landfill** makes this way of disposing of rubbish less attractive. It is not a tax on the manufacturers who produce packaging, or directly on the households who throw it out. It falls on the refuse disposal firms who are presumably able to pass it on to the local authorities who pay for their services. Most of the disincentive effects therefore fall on these firms and local authorities rather than on households and manufacturers. It might be argued that making sure that manufacturers meet the cost of disposing of their products and packaging, as in Germany, might change the behaviour of those causing the problems, rather than concentrating on those who have to clear them up. Landfill tax can be avoided mainly by persuading households to recycle rather than throw out by providing separate collection services (paper and card) or local recycling centres. Indirectly, households may benefit from a lower council tax, but individual households may act selfishly if recycling costs them too much time or effort.

Summary

1 Pollution can be dealt with by market instruments or regulation.
2 Transfrontier pollution requires international agreement before progress can be made.
3 Operational pollution is more likely to be dealt with by market instruments, although regulation will be used if zero or closely controlled emissions are required (e.g. CFCs and nuclear waste).
4 Accidental pollution is usually best dealt with by regulatory methods.
5 Eco-labelling works well for easily understood straightforward cases.
6 Intergenerational pollution requires us to develop in a sustainable way.
7 Stock pollutants such as carbon dioxide need monitoring because above a certain level serious consequences may result.
8 The certainty or uncertainty of the harmful effects will influence how seriously governments take any pollutant.

? QUESTIONS

1 Why is global warming a problem? What are the best policies available to deal with it?
2 Why are international agreements needed to deal with transfrontier pollutants?
3 What is meant by optimal pollution? What information would you need to arrive at an estimate of what level of a pollutant is optimal? Why do 'deep green' environmentalists disagree with this idea?
4 In what way is sustainable development different from most industrialisation that has taken place in the twentieth century?
5 Explain why market instruments are often better for operational pollution, while regulation is more likely to succeed with accidental pollution.
6 What are the benefits of recycling materials?

14 Transport and the economy

Learning outcomes

At the end of this chapter you will be able to:
- Apply appropriate cost concepts and market structures to different transport situations.
- Recognise that different solutions are needed to solve the problem of congestion in different situations.
- Relate pricing to cost structure and market environment.

Introduction

This is a case study chapter so the cases may be regarded as examples of data response exercises as well as giving an opportunity to apply economics in a new area.

The transport sector of the economy is important in both production (principally freight transport) and consumption (mainly passenger). It provides us with a rich range of economic problems to discuss. There are problems of *monopoly* (rail), *deregulation* (airlines), *social cost* (most transport), *pricing* (roads, rail, air), *privatisation* (rail). Although each of these *modes* of transport are separate they are often in competition with each other. The Channel tunnel has created strong competition not only for the cross Channel ferries, but also for the airlines on the London–Paris and London–Brussels routes. Car, rail and bus compete in the commuter market. The social costs of transport include congestion, noise, global warming and acid rain, some of which have already been discussed in Chapter 13 on environmental policy. A few technical transport terms will be

introduced as the need arises in this chapter, but the emphasis will be on the application of ideas you should already be familiar with. The chapter is presented as a series of case studies, each focusing on a different problem.

More complex issues are discussed in Chapter 40 on advanced policy issues. Case 40.2 (see page 592) considers the problems encountered in road investment decisions and Case 40.3 (see page 595) investigates the complex cost structure of the railway industry and implications for pricing.

Case study 14.1
ROAD CONGESTION

The transport problem that most people are familiar with is **congestion**: sitting in queues of traffic sometimes for long periods of time. The existence of a queue usually means a situation of excess demand (see Chapter 4). The usual response of the market to a situation of excess demand is to raise price in the short run, and increase capacity if the problem persists in the long run. It is necessary to examine the special features of the road market that make this difficult to achieve.

Do roads have public good characteristics?

It is easy to find bits of the road system that have the characteristics of a **private good**. It is not difficult to set up charging systems for bridges and tunnels. In France and Italy, there are also tolls on the motorways. The reason why these parts of the road system can be easily charged for is that there are limited entry and exit points where toll booths can be placed. This means that people can be **excluded** from using this part of the road network. Exclusion is an important characteristic of a private good. The time savings offered by bridges, tunnels or motorways will mean that many people are willing to pay to use that part of the road system.

This argument cannot be easily applied to the road system as a whole. If tolls are set up at regular intervals in the road network, then people will find routes that miss these tolls. Such a charging system would drive people off the main roads and on to the side roads in a bid to minimise their toll payment. This would create more congestion in the side roads and would be socially undesirable for local residents. The only way to stop people from engaging in this behaviour would be to set up toll points at every road intersection. While this might solve the problem of unemployment, it would be clearly too expensive and would in any case probably add to the problem of congestion that it is trying to solve. It appears that it is difficult to exclude people from the road system as a whole and that therefore the road system has some public good characteristics.

Pricing systems for the roads

Road users do pay for the road network, however, by a system of taxes. In the UK an annual road tax provides an entry price on to the road system (and allows the authorities to keep track of which vehicles are on the road so they can be regulated). Although it is difficult to price the road system, it is easy to put a tax on petrol, which cars need to use the road system. The petrol tax system of charging for roads also has the advantage that car users pay in proportion to their use, and that heavier vehicles which take up more room and create more wear and tear on the road system will pay more. On top of this there is a built-in incentive to use more fuel-efficient vehicles, which has environmental benefits. The system has to be run by the government because taxes rather than prices are being used, but seems on the face of it to be a good pricing system.

Peak and off-peak demand

Two features of the transport market create problems for the tax system of pricing. First, demand is not regular over time. There is a strong *peak demand* in the morning 'rush hour' as people drive to work, and a similar problem in the evening as they

return. On its own variation in demand need not matter. Christmas cards have a strong peak demand in December, but can be produced over a longer period and stored in a warehouse. Unfortunately, transport is not so easy to *store*. Road space that is not used in the afternoon cannot be stored and used in the evening!

In rail passenger transport a higher price is charged in the peak period, and a lower one in the *off-peak* period to encourage off-peak use and remove pressure on the system from the peak period (see Case study 14.2 on page 200). This option is not available for the road system, because the 'pricing' is based on the petrol tax. Petrol bought in the off-peak period can be used in the peak period. The pricing system is not sensitive to the time and place of use of the road system.

The road pricing solution to excess demand

Economists have long been aware of this problem and many have advocated a *road pricing* solution. The analysis of the problem in terms of demand and costs is well established, but the technical solution has been missing. An early suggestion was to bury electronic devices in the road, which would transmit a signal to a meter in each vehicle as it passed overhead, but this idea was rejected as being too expensive. The advent of the smart card may have solved the technical problem, since a smart card bought in advance and placed in the windscreen can be electronically 'zapped' on passing selected points on the road. The price could be raised at certain times of the day, when demand is at a peak. Trials have been conducted to see if the system would work in principle and local authorities have been given the power to implement such schemes. However popular campaigns against rising petrol taxation (see Chapter 13) has made the introduction of such schemes less likely in the near future. The best price to charge in Figure 14.1 is zero for the off-peak and p_1 for the peak, thus eliminating all congestion. It was noted in the last chapter that demand for car transport is inelastic, so the price necessary to eliminate all congestion could be quite high!

Congestion as an externality

It is also possible to think of congestion in terms of the *externality* concept. Motorists will decide

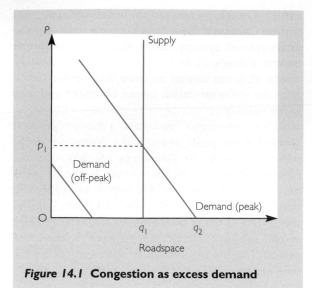

Figure 14.1 Congestion as excess demand

whether or not to make a journey on the basis of their valuation of the benefits from the journey and their valuation of the alternatives forgone in terms of time and money for petrol and other variable costs. They will not consider, however, the additional cost imposed on others owing to increased congestion. This cost can be regarded as an external cost to the motorist, and one therefore which the motorist will not take into account when making decisions. The solution to an externality is to impose a tax (see Chapters 9 and 13). This gives us the same result as in the previous paragraph, a road pricing solution.

Other pricing solutions

Since the road pricing solution above has been technically infeasible until recently, practical pricing solutions have concentrated on reducing the prices of competing modes of transport such as rail and bus, rather than increasing the price of using the roads. This has often resulted in *subsidies*.

One of the main arguments for subsidising public transport has been to reduce congestion on the roads. Such arguments may become weaker if road pricing is successfully introduced, but it must be remembered that public transport is also more fuel efficient. The discussion in Chapter 13 on global warming noted that fuel use in transport is proving more difficult to contain than other fuel use.

Parking charges in central urban areas can also be used as a road pricing measure because, like petrol, parking is jointly consumed with road use. Drivers have to put the vehicle somewhere at the end of their journey. While this will not affect motorists who have access to private parking, on-street parking can be priced in this way. Special arrangements may have to be made to allow local residents parking rights where the housing stock does not have adequate off-street parking facilities. Through traffic is of course unaffected by this type of policy. *Park and ride* schemes encourage motorists to leave their vehicles on the edge of towns and travel in to the centre on subsidised public transport.

Rationing solutions

When rationing was first discussed in Chapter 6, it was suggested that it was most appropriate in situations of acute shortage, such as during famines, or in the immediate aftermath of war. It is also appropriate when the pricing system is not working well, as in the case of roads. Parking restrictions, such as the yellow lines and red routes used in the UK, ration the use of the road as a parking area by preventing parking on busy streets, or limiting it to off-peak periods. This reduces congestion by improving traffic flow. *Pedestrian-only zones* also ration the amount of road space available to the motorist. This solution is often used in medium-sized cities and large towns in association with an inner ring road as indicated in Figure 14.2. Its main benefit is the separation of shoppers from traffic. It is a *zoning solution* to an externality problem (see Chapter 13). Sometimes the cheapest solution to an externality problem can be to separate the polluter from the polluted in this way, particularly if the externality is local. *Bus lanes* are also a good example of rationing. By giving priority to buses during the peak period, bus lanes speed up the buses and make them a more attractive alternative.

Investment solutions

Building additional roads to increase capacity in cities is difficult because roads already occupy about 25 per cent of the land available in the city. Further road building is difficult without displacing existing residents or facilities outwards. Expansion of the city in this way is only likely to increase demand for transport and make matters worse. Table 14.1 demonstrates the sharp rise in demand which suggests that any new roads built would themselves

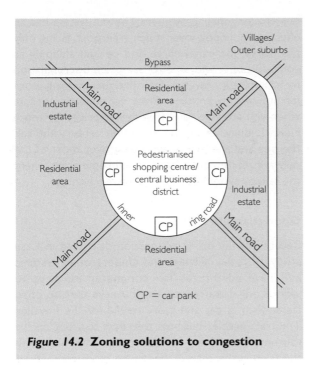

Figure 14.2 **Zoning solutions to congestion**

Table 14.1 **Passenger transport by mode (bn passenger km)**

	1980	1990	1998
Bus and coach	52	46	43
Car, van, taxi	388	588	616
Motor cycles	8	6	4
Pedal cycles	5	5	4
Rail	35	39	42
Air (domestic)	3	5	7
Total	491	689	716

Source: Transport Statistics 1999, National Statistics. © Crown Copyright 2001

soon become congested. Indeed some people have argued that building more roads actually increases demand. The environmental problems of global warming discussed in the last chapter suggest that we should not be encouraging more car use. Investment in city transport systems therefore often takes the form of *public transport infrastructure*. The Victoria and Jubilee Underground lines and the Docklands light railway in London; the Newcastle-upon-Tyne Metro system; and new 'supertram' systems in Manchester and Sheffield are all good examples of major investments of this kind over the last few decades. Investment in computerised

traffic management systems, to speed up traffic and prevent *gridlock*, try to make better use of the existing road system rather than to extend the volume of roads.

The construction of a motorway network, the upgrading of major roads to dual carriageways and the construction of bypasses round towns have been the major areas of road investment in the second half of the twentieth century. This investment programme is in a constant race to keep up with demand. The M25 around London was completed in 1986, but had to be upgraded from three to four lanes along its busiest sections in the early 1990s. This massive investment programme is justified by the demand forecasts of the Ministry of Transport, but its detractors argue that it is the building of the motorways that is inducing demand growth. The environmental arguments against traffic growth have been discussed already in Chapter 13. Policy is also influenced by the freedom that the car brings to individuals. The question of investment is discussed further in Case 40.2 (page 595).

Conclusions

The car brings enormous freedom to consumers and greater flexibility than most forms of transport. Its development and use represents a large portion of economic growth in the second half of the twentieth century. On the other hand it also brings with it considerable social and environmental costs. Any policy has to balance these two considerations.

Given the complexity of the market it is unlikely that any one solution will be sufficient on its own. It is necessary to have a range of solutions to cover different aspects of the problem.

STUDENT ACTIVITY 14.1

Discuss the best solution to congestion caused by each of the following types of traffic:

(a) Commuter traffic going into London (or your nearest major city).
(b) Heavy goods vehicles travelling through cities, towns and villages on their way to ports or the Channel tunnel.
(c) Cars on their way to the coast on a public holiday.
(d) Heavy use by all vehicles of major motorways such as the M25 or M6.

Case study 14.2
PRIVATISING A LOSS-MAKING MONOPOLY

The railways are a monopoly in the sense that they have a monopoly over rail transport. This is true even after privatisation, although the monopolies have in most cases become local monopolies. There is no point in having a monopoly, however, if there is insufficient demand for your product, or if very good substitutes make the demand for your product elastic. In many cases it is better to think of railways as taking part in a very *competitive market in transport*, rather than having a monopoly. In some cases, however, the railways have retained some market power.

In the last decade of the nineteenth century, regulations had to be introduced to prevent the railways overcharging their customers. The rail system had an effective monopoly over much transport, facing only the horse, the canal barge and coastal shipping as competitors. It was able to use price discrimination to maximise its revenue from freight, charging more for higher-value products. Price discrimination occurs when you are able to charge higher prices for more inelastic demands. In the twentieth century the car, the bus and the lorry have taken over most of the railway's market, but there are still some areas where the railway system has a competitive advantage.

Good markets for rail

Because of the urban congestion discussed in Case study 14.1, the railways and Underground systems still have advantages for commuter journeys to work. Long-distance intercity journeys are also often faster than by car and more restful for the traveller. The train enables business travellers to work on the journey. The airlines are the main competitor with the train in this market, becoming more competitive as distance increases. The lorry has almost completely supplanted the train for *short-haul freight* transport and is usually more effective for small and medium consignments, but the railways retain some competitiveness on *long-haul routes*, particularly if one customer can provide a train-load of goods to transport. The opening of the Channel tunnel has increased the amount of long-haul freight routes.

A short history of closure: Beeching and Serpell

The car took off as a popular means of transport in the UK in the 1950s. This coincided with the early period of nationalisation of British Rail in 1947. It became clear that British Rail was unprofitable in the 1950s and the immediate response was a modernisation plan which began to replace steam by electric and diesel power. However, the Beeching Report (1963) argued that the only way to regain profitability was to reduce capacity radically by closing nearly half of the route distance. It was largely small branch lines that were closed, but local resistance to closure meant that the network was only reduced from 16 000 miles to 11 000 miles. The extent of the network at the time of the later Serpell Report is shown in Figure 14.3.

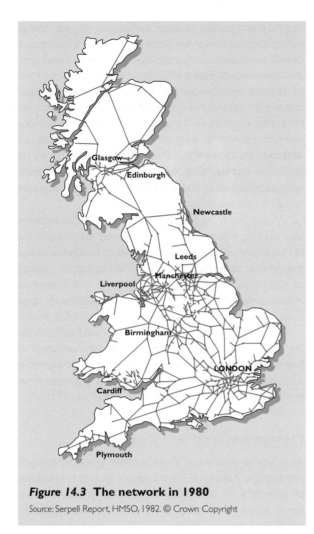

Figure 14.3 The network in 1980

Source: Serpell Report, HMSO, 1982. © Crown Copyright

Figure 14.4 The profitable network

Source: Serpell Report, HMSO, 1982. © Crown Copyright

The railways continued to make losses throughout the 1960s and early 1970s until this state of affairs was recognised in 1974 with an official annual subsidy known as the *public service obligation* (PSO). In 1982 the Serpell Report concluded that only the major intercity routes and a few commuter lines were profitable. The profitable network is shown in Figure 14.4 which should be compared to Figure 14.3. Freight and the remaining commuter lines could be run at a small loss, but the major loss-makers were the *provincial routes* to towns in the regions. The PSO was a payment to British Rail for carrying out this non-commercial part of its services.

Reasons for subsidising commuter routes have been discussed in the case study above about congestion. It may be the cheapest way of relieving congestion in some urban areas. The reasons for sub-

sidising provincial routes has more to do with access to a national transport system for those without use of a car. The young, the elderly and the poor are the main groups who have generally less access to car transport. It can be seen that the PSO was a kind of *social policy* in the transport sector, keeping open routes which might be closed on purely commercial grounds.

As the Serpell Report rightly pointed out, this social policy might be more cheaply achieved by subsidising bus and coach transport instead. An additional argument for subsidising a rail link to a town and more importantly to a region is to generate local economic growth. If a region is not linked to the network, it may make attracting inward investment more difficult. One of the policy options put forward by the Serpell Report was that all towns which had a population over 25 000 should be connected to the rail network. This may seem a little arbitrary, but any size for the route network will be a compromise and involve subjective opinions.

● *Common misunderstanding*

Many people believe British Rail became a loss maker after nationalisation. This is simply not the case; the privately owned railways struggled with lorry and bus competition in the 1920s and 1930s and were largely unprofitable. Some of this may have been due to the depression of the 1930s, and the way in which the railways were forced to publish their prices, while the lorry owners were not. After nationalisation, the railways were faced with further competition from the car and any privately owned rail system would have faced similar problems.

Privatisation

Which parts of the railway system have monopoly power?

As with many of the later privatisations (see Chapter 10 and 24) British Rail has been privatised in a way that separates the natural monopoly from the potentially competitive parts of the industry. The track and signalling are an unavoidable monopoly that has been privatised as a separate company known as Railtrack. This company is regulated to prevent it exploiting its market position. The operation of rail services on the monopoly track can be arranged in a more competitive way. In some cases, other modes will provide sufficient competition. Where rail services do not face strong competition from other modes, price regulation is necessary, particularly as, in the case of commuter routes, low prices may be desirable to reduce congestion.

Franchises

The provision of passenger services has been split into a large number of *franchises*. Each franchise operates a group of services for a fixed period of time after which the franchise must be renegotiated. This introduces an element of competition in two ways. First, the company which puts in the highest bid for the franchise will believe that it can operate the franchise most profitably. Initially, until the companies have experience of operating franchises, they

may make mistakes in their estimation of profitability, but this should improve with experience. Exploitation of the consumer can be avoided by putting price control agreements in the franchise agreement. If the level of service falls below an agreed level, then penalty clauses or early termination of the franchise also protect the consumer. Second, the quality of service offered can form part of the decision making on whether to extend the franchise when it comes up again for competitive bids. This technique is already well established in the case of regional TV franchises which are in many ways similar.

Where rail transport is provided for social reasons, loss making will not attract companies to provide the service without some inducement. In these cases, the ***lowest negative bid*** will be accepted, so subsidy of these parts of the rail network will continue. Presumably, if the negative bids reach a sufficiently large level, a decision might be made to close services down.

The rolling stock has been largely sold off to leasing companies. This enables the smooth handover of franchises from one company to another. It also creates a market in rolling stock which is separate from the franchisees' market in railway services.

Problems with rail privatisation

The way in which the Conservative government privatised the railway system has put as much emphasis as possible on competition. Critics of the process have highlighted the problems of coordination between different companies. The main problems of dividing up the railways into so many franchises are the following:

(a) It becomes more difficult to create a coordinated timetable with connections between trains run by different franchises. Railtrack has been given this coordinating role.

(b) Buying a ticket on a route that uses several different franchise companies requires coordination between them if a single ticket is to be issued. If this fails to happen, the passenger will pay for several short journeys instead of one long journey, probably at a higher price.

(c) In the same way, methods must be found to continue with timetable and ticketing coordination between different modes of transport, such as bus and rail, which may have been easier when they were both in the public sector.

(d) Where two franchises use the same section of track, the question of who should pay for it arises. The prices charged can make a major difference to the apparent profitability of the two franchises. The marginal cost of using the track is low, but the average cost is quite high. Soon after Railtrack was set up this was illustrated in a dramatic way when rolling stock which needed servicing was sent by lorry because it was cheaper than the price asked for by Railtrack! This problem is discussed in more detail in Case 40.3 on page 595.

Accountability

A major problem of accountability has emerged with Railtrack and the Franchise Operators arguing with each other about the reasons for lateness. Since lateness is one of the main quality measures with associated financial penalties, this can be a major problem. Safety is also a major issue, responsibility for which was initially given to Railtrack. The recent Hatfield train accident, brought to light problems with cracking rails, which has resulted in partial closure of the system while the problem is rectified. It has been pointed out that Railtrack has a conflict of interests between the maintenance of safety and the minimisation of costs. A question has been raised as to whether it has got the balance right between these two objectives. Reform of the system may change the balance of power with the new Strategic Rail Authority taking a stronger hold of safety issues. The emphasis is likely to be more on the provision of service levels than the achievement of profit. Longer franchise periods may help Franchise Operators take a longer view of their businesses. The safety issue has raised many concerns about the railway, but in fact the railway remains one of the safer modes of transport per kilometre travelled as can be seen in Table 14.2

Alternative methods of privatisation

Two main alternative methods of privatising the railways were suggested. The railway could have been broken up into the old *regional* companies that existed before 1939. This would have improved coordination within the region but it would have left the regional company as a regulated monopoly. This

Table 14.2 **Passenger deaths per billion passenger kilometres**

	Average 1988–97
Motorcycles	89.9
Walking	68.2
Pedal cycles	46.0
Car	3.6
Rail	0.7
Bus/coach	0.4
Air	0.1

goes against the principle used in most later privatisations (see Chapter 24) of separating the potentially competitive parts of the industry from the natural monopoly – in this case Railtrack. The other alternative would have been to separate British Rail into its constituent businesses: intercity, freight, commuter and provincial. This idea would still run into the problems of accountability and cost allocation discussed above, but would have none of the competitive advantages of the franchise system. As with the first idea, greater coordination would probably be achieved at the cost of reduced competition.

STUDENT ACTIVITY 14.5

You have been asked to bid for a rail franchise for the next five years. The franchise is for a small branch line (in reality franchises are much bigger than this). You are required to provide 10 passenger trains a day in each direction, which can be accomplished by leasing one train. The following information has been provided to help you decide on your bid. Assume zero inflation in your calculations.

Current annual passenger kilometres	1 000 000
Regulated price per passenger kilometre	10p
Cost of leasing a train	£10 000
Variable costs per single train journey (fuel, labour)	£10
Payments to Railtrack per single journey	£5
Administrative costs	£20 000

A private survey you have commissioned suggests that passenger kilometres have been declining by 10 000 a year, but points out that this was during a recession and the economy is now growing strongly.

Submit your bids to your teacher/lecturer. Be prepared to justify your proposed bid.

The Department of Transport has been asked by the Treasury to reduce its subsidy to the rail industry as part of its contribution to reducing public expenditure. As a civil servant in the department you have to prioritise the following proposals to achieve this objective. Assume each of them saves the same amount of money.

(a) Close 1000 miles of provincial rail lines mainly in the north of Scotland, north and central Wales, Devon, Cornwall, Lincolnshire and Norfolk (if you are studying outside the UK choose areas of low population without much industry).
(b) Increase franchise bids due for renewal by:
    (i) allowing higher prices on commuter routes;
    (ii) reducing frequency on off-peak and provincial services.

Case study 14.3
AIR TRANSPORT

The discussion of roads was about creating a market where one does not fully exist at the moment. The discussion on the railways was about replacing a state monopoly with a privatised, competitive system. In the case of air the emphasis is on the removal of *collusive* arrangements between airlines operating in the international market. It is helpful to start with a discussion of costs, pricing and market structure so the reader is familiar with the details of the industry being studied.

Costs

The airlines have a very similar cost structure to the railways. Like the railways, they have indivisible units of output. You cannot fly with half a plane! This means that the marginal costs of a plane which is not full are very close to zero, while the average costs are quite high. As with all forms of transport, the product is not *storable* and so the question of load factor again becomes important. Raising load factor is an important way of reducing average costs.

The major difference in air transport is the way in which the costs of take-off and landing at airports influence costs, as illustrated in Figure 14.5. These costs incurred at the airport can be thought of as *fixed costs* since no matter how long the flight, a plane will have to take off and land. The longer the flight the lower the *average fixed costs* of take-off and landing per passenger kilometre travelled. Since the variable costs of operating the plane at cruising speed are fairly constant, there are *economies of range*. The further the plane is flying, the lower its *average total costs* will be. The unit of output is the seat kilometre (that is the total number of seats times the number of kilometres travelled), but passenger kilometres (the total distance travelled by all the passengers added together) are what bring in the revenue.

Of course, if a European airline is flying to Sydney in Australia, it will usually break the journey in a number of places to take on extra passengers and fuel. It might stop in Dubai, Delhi and Singapore on the way. Each of the parts of the total journey is referred to as a *stage*. Each stage involves one take-off and one landing, so economies of range refer to

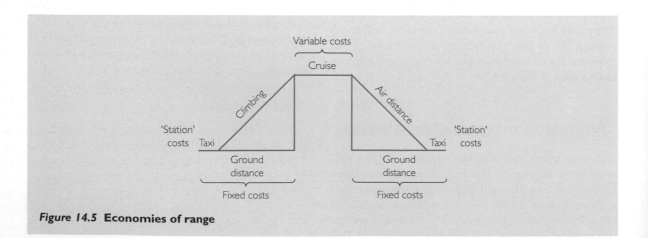

Figure 14.5 Economies of range

the individual stage lengths, not the whole route. Flights are divided into short haul, usually internal flights within a country, or between neighbouring countries; medium haul, across continents; and long haul, between continents.

Pricing

The main basis of pricing in the scheduled market is the separation of leisure and business traffic. At first sight this may be seen as a straightforward case of price discrimination with the higher prices being charged for the relatively inelastic business market and lower prices for the more elastic leisure market. As with rail pricing, the separation of the two markets is achieved by ticket conditions. Business travellers want the ability to book up to the last moment, and also to cancel if their plans change. The leisure market is separated out by the **APEX** (advanced passenger excursion) ticket which cannot be cancelled and must be bought some specified time in advance. Although this ticket is substantially cheaper, business travellers would not want its inflexibility. Last-minute purchase of **IPEX** (instant purchase excursion) tickets is also cheap because it enables airlines to fill empty seats. **Stand-by** tickets are available even more cheaply to travellers who are prepared to wait for a seat to be available.

APEX tickets also allow an airline to reduce its costs. These tickets are not available for all flights, but will be mainly directed towards the off-peak times of travel that are less popular with business travellers. This enables the airlines to increase their load factor (how full their planes are on average), and so reduce their average costs. Different prices for different seasons also try to shift demand into flights where lower load factors are expected. The prices of airline tickets will also reflect the level of service offered. The three main service levels are economy, cabin class and first class with a progressively higher quality of service, comfort and leg room.

As in the discussion of railway pricing, it can be seen that standard textbook models of pricing are useful in understanding what is happening, but real-world pricing will often be a mixture of different pricing strategies; in this case both demand-related and cost-related strategies are being followed. The view that price differences are not merely a question of price discrimination is confirmed by the fact that these pricing strategies have survived the introduction of greater competition in international air

transport. Price discrimination should only occur where there is monopoly or collusive oligopoly.

Market structure: scheduled and charter

There is a major distinction between the **scheduled** market which is timetabled and open to bookings from all members of the public, and the **charter** market which mainly operates to take package tour holiday makers to their destination. In most cases there is 'vertical integration' in the charter market in that the charter airlines are often owned by package holiday companies. This means that competition is really between the holiday companies, not the charter airlines themselves.

The charter airlines have cost advantages over the scheduled airlines for two main reasons. First, they are usually able to plan their activities well in advance so that they achieve very high load factors. Second, they usually offer a lower level of service than the scheduled airlines, since they are not trying to attract business travellers.

Market structure: bilateral agreements and IATA

Scheduled airlines operating on international routes do so only with the permission of the governments of the countries in which they land. The Paris Convention of 1919 decided that the air space over a country belongs to that country and as a result a system of bilateral agreements between each pair of countries is necessary to give permission for airlines to overfly countries other than their own, and to land in their airports. Until the late 1970s, this resulted in most international routes being operated by the two **national flag carriers**. In many countries the flag-carrying airlines were nationalised and private sector airlines were mainly confined to the charter market, or a small secondary role.

Deregulation

The bilateral agreements varied a great deal in how much competition they allowed for. The most restrictive resulted in the airlines from each country operating almost as a single monopoly company, sharing costs and revenues. In all bilaterals, pricing was determined by the International Airlines Trade Association (IATA). The USA led the way in dismantling this restrictive system in the late 1970s and early 1980s. The first route to be partly deregulated was the North Atlantic route between the USA and Europe. After an initial successful period when prices fell and profits rose, a vicious price war ended with the bankruptcy of one operator (Laker) and massive losses for the others (PanAm, TWA and BA). After this experience, and the court case which followed it (settled out of court), airlines became more careful about starting price wars in case they were accused of anti-competitive practices. It should be noted that the term deregulation is a relative one. Even after deregulation, only two airlines from each country were allowed to fly on each route. Not all airports in each country were open to international traffic. This is a long way from an *open skies* policy.

A single European market in air transport?

Curiously, although most international air transport became more deregulated, European air transport remained heavily regulated. There were certain exceptions like the Anglo-Dutch bilateral agreement which was very liberal, but in general progress was slow. The coming of the European Single Market and the Maastricht Treaty meant that this had to be re-examined. Proposals for the development of a single air transport market met strong resistance and the policy was only in place in 1997. The reasons for resistance were as follows:

(a) There was a sharp difference of culture between the largely privatised and profitable airlines of Northern Europe, and the largely subsidised and nationalised airlines of Southern Europe.

(b) Airlines such as Air France and Greece's Olympic Airlines were granted extensions in order to get their finances in order. A competitive market cannot work if some of the competitors are in receipt of massive subsidies from their governments.

(c) Traditional nationalised flag carriers were concerned about being taken over by the stronger privatised airlines. A reserve of nationalism remains associated with national airlines even in a single market!

(d) There was a recognition that most airlines in Europe were not as large as their American and Far Eastern rivals and therefore did not benefit

from the same *economies of scale*. This further fuelled nervousness about takeovers.

Further difficulties are expected when the policy is fully implemented because:

(e) *Slots* at airports are in limited supply. A slot is a take-off or landing time at a given airport. With strong growth in demand there is a shortage of slots at the busiest of European airports. How should this limited supply be allocated? The most common method is *grandfathering*. This means that those who have always had slots continue to have slots. This makes it very difficult for new competition to break into an airport. The building of the fifth terminal at Heathrow and the second runway at Manchester are both attempts to increase capacity.

(f) *Hubs* are airports that act as junctions for airline routes as illustrated in Figure 14.6. They are the aviation equivalent of Crewe or Clapham junction on the railways. It is not economic for regular flights to take place between each pair of airports, so some airports, often because of geographical position, become *interline* centres where people change planes. Heathrow is the busiest hub in Europe, followed by Frankfurt. Airlines based at such airports have a competitive advantage.

(g) *Cabotage*. The provisions of the single market in air transport include the right of airlines to compete on the internal routes of another country. BA could take passengers from Paris to Marseilles, for instance. This invasion of the domestic markets of other countries is likely to meet resistance.

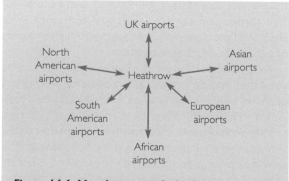

Figure 14.6 **Heathrow as a hub airport**

(a) Which airlines do you think will benefit most from the deregulation of European air transport and which ones will have the most difficulty?

(b) Do you think that it would be better to have lots of small airlines competing in Europe, or a few large ones to compete with other large world airlines?

(c) Is it a good idea to increase airport capacity in Manchester and Heathrow in order to make them more effective as hub airports from the point of view of:
   (i) the balance of payments;
   (ii) UK employment;
   (iii) local residents;
   (iv) global warming?

Which of these criteria is most important?

You are working for a new airline that has started up with one aircraft with 200 seats and a single route. You have commissioned research that suggests the elasticity of demand is −0.4 for business traffic but −1.6 for leisure traffic at the current price of £100. Currently you are achieving 50 per cent load factor split evenly between the business and leisure sectors.

(a) Calculate the effect on revenue and load factor of a 10 per cent increase in business prices and a 10 per cent reduction in leisure prices.

(b) What are the likely effects on cost and profits?

(c) What pricing strategies can you use to separate business and leisure traffic?

Case study 14.4
THE CHANNEL CROSSING: INTERMODAL COMPETITION

The ferries

Before the Channel tunnel was built the Channel crossing was often used as a good example of an oligopolistic market. The crossing was dominated by Sealink (later taken over by Stena) and P&O European Ferries (formed by a merger in 1985) with small competition from the Sally line. The airlines provided effective competition for the business and weekend-break markets, but for the growing car tourism market and freight to the continent, the ferries were in a strong position. Demand growth was strong with the numbers of cars crossing doubling between 1985 and 1995.

The tunnel

The arrival of the Channel tunnel provided a competitor to both the airlines (from Eurostar) and the ferries (from LeShuttle) and has made substantial inroads into both markets. The usual behaviour of oligopolistic markets faced with entry is to engage in price wars either to establish market share in the case of the entrant, or to protect it in the case of the existing firms (see Chapter 22). As with the case of deregulation of air transport on the North Atlantic (see Case study 14.3 on page 204), it was the new entrant who initiated the price war by nearly halving prices in 1995. The ferries had no choice but to respond to protect market share. They also considered merger in 1996 in order to rationalise and reduce costs. The western crossings of the Channel to ports like Cherbourg and Caen are less affected by the tunnel, because cars with destinations in the west of France would have a long way to drive after going through the tunnel.

Is the tunnel profitable?

The price war may have established the tunnel's market share (roughly equal to that of the two main ferry operators put together) but it did nothing for its profitability. As with many large projects, the final cost of building the tunnel was almost twice the original estimate, and together with early operational losses, Eurotunnel ended up with debts of £8.5 billion. It has now started to cover operational costs and make small contributions towards debt interest, but it is clearly not going to be able to repay any of the capital in the near future. If you owe the bank £1000 you have a problem, but if you owe the bank £8.5 billion, the bank has a problem! Eurotunnel's creditors from banks and other financial institutions have taken the only sensible step and converted much of the debt into equity holdings with the hope of making a long-term return.

The impossibility of exit

The problem that the ferries face in this situation is the impossibility of the tunnel *exiting* the market. If Eurotunnel goes bankrupt, the tunnel will still exist and could be sold by the liquidator to a new business. It would then only have to cover its variable costs. The tunnel's costs are nearly all *sunk* costs and the variable costs are quite small by comparison.

The competitive response

The ferries have responded by introducing so-called superferries on to the route achieving economies of vessel size, faster turnarounds and a better quality service on board. The longer crossing time is being marketed as an advantage, allowing drivers to relax and take a break. The ferry is reconstructed as a resort in itself. Profits from duty-free sales have been eroded by competition from Eurotunnel and are due to be phased out in any case as a result of the single market. The *Herald of Free Enterprise* disaster of 1987 made some people concerned about ferry safety. The fire in the Channel tunnel has now worried some people about safety in the tunnel. The effect of these two events probably cancel each other out. There remains excess capacity on the route and the competitive position of the ferries has been much weakened. After the initial price war, both sides accepted the other is there to stay, and we have now returned to a period of more sensible pricing which may return profitability to the ferries and give the bankers some of their money back. For the consumer, who has enjoyed very low prices, the party may be over.

STUDENT ACTIVITY 14.9

(a) Using the ideas developed in the other case studies, suggest ways in which the ferries could increase their load factors by offering special deals.
(b) If prices rise, how could the government tell if the operators were simply using more sensible prices to cover their costs, or whether they were engaging in covert collusion to exploit the consumer?

Summary

1 The combination of non-storable outputs and peak and off-peak demand in transport industries results in considerable price variations.
2 Price differences between the peak and off-peak also allow transport to shift demand away from the peak and economise on capital expenditure.
3 Congestion can be dealt with by pricing, investment or rationing, or a combination of these three methods.
4 Subsidy of the railways has been continued after privatisation. This policy can be explained in terms of environmental objectives, congestion reduction and equity considerations.
5 Deregulation of European airlines is facing difficulty from loss-making nationalised airlines and 'ownership' of slots.
6 When considering competition, exit is as important as entry as in the case of the Channel tunnel.

SECTION IV

The national economy

Let us beware of this dangerous theory of equilibrium which is supposed to be automatically established. A certain kind of equilibrium, it is true, is re-established in the long run, but it is only after a frightful amount of suffering.

Simonde de Sismondi

What is the macroeconomy?

Pre-Keynesian attitudes

With the exception of Marxists, few economists in the latter half of the nineteenth century or at the turn of the twentieth century questioned the *overall* stability of capitalism. Indeed, there was little, if any, distinction made between how individual markets work and how the economy as a whole functions. It was believed that if there were any overall imbalances in the economy supply and demand would simply adjust to remove them, in exactly the same way as markets clear in microeconomics. For example, unemployment was believed to be the result of wages being too high in exactly the same way as a surplus occurs in any other market when the price is above the equilibrium. Such analysis based on demand and supply clearing markets across the economy belongs to the *neo-classical* school. This school of thought is today again the dominant school of economics, although its macroeconomics is now more developed than in its former pre-Keynesian form.

This belief in the self-righting mechanisms of capitalism was deeply held. It was thought that if there were genuinely unemployed people looking for work their efforts would create an excess supply that would cause wages to fall hence erad-

icating unemployment. If the 'so-called' unemployment persisted then it could not really be unemployment at all! Some workers might band together in unions, or trades guilds, and hold wages above the equilibrium in some labour markets, but this would simply tend to divert those seeking work to other markets where there were no such restrictions on opportunity.

The great depression and Keynes

Looking at Figure 15.1 you will see that it is difficult to square the microeconomic explanation for unemployment with the history of unemployment. We see that in Victorian times up until the First World War there were regular trade cycles of strong magnitude, in the interwar years and 1980s and 1990s there were very high levels of chronic unemployment. Although in the interwar years some may have blamed emerging unions or 'welfare' pay-

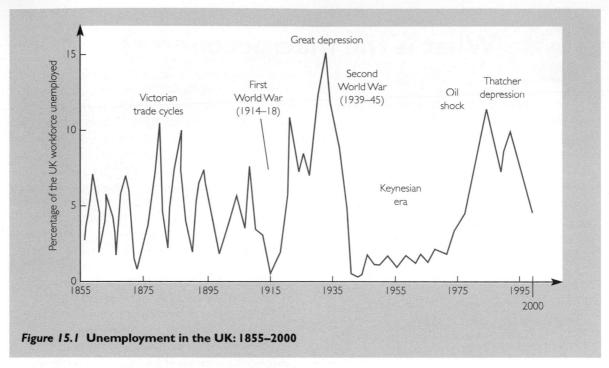

Figure 15.1 **Unemployment in the UK: 1855–2000**

ments for causing unemployment, there was no convincing and 'respectable' alternative theory to explain chronic involuntary unemployment.

The economic depressions of the interwar year, however, raised doubts about whether capitalism was, after all, a stable system. The over-riding problem of the 1920s was mass unemployment and it seemed that rather than market failure being confined to individual markets, the economy as a whole was failing. Millions of people found themselves involuntarily unemployed. Output fell and poverty and misery grew.

The severe economic depressions between the two world wars in Western economies forced economists and politicians to consider a new type of question 'Is capitalism as an economic *system* stable?'

When economists look at how the whole economy responds to changes, they are looking at how *aggregates* behave rather than at how individuals or individual markets behave. This approach owes much to the work of the Cambridge economist John Maynard Keynes (1883–1946). He wrote one of the most influential of all books of the twentieth century – *The General Theory of Employment, Interest and Money* (1936). This book, usually

called simply *The General Theory*, led to what is often described as the Keynesian 'revolution' in economics. Indeed, from the mid–1940s until the early 1970s Keynes's economics was the foundation stone of macroeconomic policy making.

Macroeconomics

In macroeconomics we are concerned with the behaviour of broad aggregates in the economy, e.g. the total level of investment or the volume of employment for the economy as a whole.

In microeconomic theory we are concerned with such things as the determination of employment in particular industries, but in macroeconomics we are concerned with the general level of employment in the economy. Similarly, a microeconomic view can be used to explain the determination of the relative prices of products, i.e. the price of one product in terms of other products, whereas in macroeconomics we are concerned with the general level of all prices in the economy. Keynes's *General Theory* clearly used a macroeconomic approach.

Demand management

Keynes argued that although the forces of supply and demand work well to establish equilibrium in individual markets, the economy as a whole could experience periods of severe instability.

In *The General Theory*, Keynes analysed the workings of the economy and put forward his solution to unemployment. In contrast to microeconomic models of supply and demand he emphasised fluctuations in the levels of aggregate flows around the economy.

Keynes maintained that it was not the demand for individual resources which was important but the level of total (aggregate) demand in the economy.

He argued that a fall in the level of demand would mean that there was over-production; this would lead to the accumulation of stocks (inventories). Employers would not wish to go on producing more than they could sell and so would begin to cut back on production. As this happened, people across the economy would lose their jobs and hence be thrown into unemployment. The unemployed would also lose their purchasing power and therefore the level of demand would sink still further, and so on in a vicious circle. Cutting wages, advocated by the conventional wisdom of the time, would not therefore cure unemployment but it could actually make it worse by further reducing purchasing power.

Keynes seemed to have presented a convincing and comprehensive explanation of how a collapse in demand in the economy as a whole could throw millions of workers out of work and into chronic unemployment, even though they were eager to work. But his theory was in stark contrast to the prevailing economic orthodoxy of the time which emphasised market equilibrium and that therefore seemed to have no convincing explanation for how such steep increases in mass unemployment could occur. It is important, however, to understand the context of Keynes's work as a response to the problems of his day, modern macroeconomics has moved on but the debate between Keynesians and neo-classical economists concerning the overall stability of the economy is still very much alive.

If, as Keynes maintained, the economy is not self-regulating, then there is a clear case for government intervention. Keynes's solution was that, if there was a shortfall in demand in the economy, the government should make it up by public spending. In order to do this the government would have to spend beyond its means, i.e. spend more than it collected in taxes (i.e. a **budget deficit**). In the 1930s this solution was not politically acceptable. There was a firm belief in sound public finances and balancing the books. If anything the conventional wisdom suggested 'tightening belts' in hard times and spending less. As Galbraith has written: 'To spend money to create jobs seemed profligate; to urge a budget deficit as a good thing seemed insane.' It took the Second World War to bring Keynes's ideas into the operation of government policy.

● *Common misunderstanding*

Students sometimes confuse Keynes's ideas with socialism. Keynes was not a socialist. He was a supporter of capitalism and wrote enthusiastically about market forces. He was not a supporter of the common ownership of the means of production and certainly was not advocating a command system to replace market forces.

The social and economic background to *The General Theory*

In order to understand the context and impact of Keynes's *General Theory* it is necessary to know something of the economic and political events of the times. Keynes was responding to the experience of the interwar depression in the Western economies that had seen unemployment reach levels perhaps as high as a quarter of the workforce. This had caused much accompanying misery, poverty and loss of dignity for millions of people. In the UK there was also widespread social unrest such as the general strike of 1926. Perhaps because free market capitalism appeared to be in crisis, working class political movements and the trade unions were growing in strength.

Although things were not as politically dangerous as before the revolution in Russia of 1917, the belief in *laissez-faire* capitalism was shaken by these events. Then in 1929 the USA stock market on Wall Street saw share prices crash. Many had their wealth, held in stocks and shares, wiped out, there followed a spate of bank failures. The Wall

Street crash was followed by prolonged depression and this cast further doubt on the stability of capitalist economies. Back in the UK, it was clear that the soldiers of the First World War had not come home to a land 'fit for heroes' that they had been promised. Events such as the Jarrow hunger march in 1936, when unemployed shipbuilders marched from Jarrow in the north of England to London to lobby the government, troubled consciences across the country.

Post-war politicians of all parties had their political outlook shaped by these events and these memories formed the backdrop for much subsequent policy making. Indeed, until Margaret Thatcher came to power in 1979, all governments after the Second World War explicitly accepted a responsibility for maintaining 'full employment'. Hence, although Keynes's ideas were not immediately adopted, and events were eventually over-shadowed by the Second World War, the Great Depression of the interwar years led to a political climate in which many politicians and economists were looking for new ideas (particularly young ones wishing to upstage their tutors!).

In the period following the Second World War Keynes's ideas triumphed over the former emphasis on *laissez-faire* capitalism. His theories were interpreted and developed and became the mainstream orthodoxy of macroeconomics. Governments of all parties accepted an explicit responsibility for the maintenance of 'full employment'.

Conclusion

The Keynesian school remains an important school today, but since the Keynesian era it has lost its dominance due to the resurgence of the neo-classical macroeconomic schools. The use of Keynesian demand management through fiscal measures has therefore declined as a central tool of economic management and a mixture of schools of thought and experiences today influences macroeconomic policy. Perhaps it is a useful lesson that, often, in time, both sides of a debate are seen to be lacking.

Summary

1 Pre-Keynesian mainstream economics did not seem able to explain or cure the mass unemployment of the 1920s and 1930s.
2 Before Keynes there was little distinction between micro- and macroeconomics.
3 Macroeconomics analyses the movements of broad aggregates such as the overall level of employment, output and inflation.
4 Keynes's most famous book *The General Theory of Employment, Interest and Money* reflected the economic, social and political conditions of the interwar years.
5 Keynes's insights into the workings of the economy revolutionised the subject.
6 Keynes argued that governments could use demand management to stabilise the macroeconomy.
7 All UK Governments from 1945 to 1979 accepted a responsibility for maintaining full-employment
8 In the 1970s there was a resurgence of neo-classical theories offering explanations for macroeconomic changes.
9 The neo-classical schools again dominate economics but the debate with the Keynesians is far from settled.

? QUESTIONS

1 Why did pre-Keynesian theory predict that mass unemployment could only be a temporary phenomenon?
2 Explain why Keynesian theory changed the way many people perceived the unemployed.
3 Read a newspaper and list references to the things that you think relate to macroeconomic aggregates.
4 Explain how, in a Keynesian recession, the government might boost the output of the private sector through its own spending and taxation.
5 Why did many people regard Keynes's proposed solutions as 'reckless'?
6 Distinguish between the aims of Keynes and the aims of socialists.

Data response A
KEYNES AND THE CLASSICS

Read the following extract from Keynes's *The General Theory of Employment, Interest and Money* and then answer the questions that follow.

So long as the classical* postulates hold good, unemployment, which in the above sense is involuntary, cannot occur. Apparent unemployment must, therefore, be the result either of temporary loss of work of the 'between jobs' type or of intermittent demand for highly specialised resources or of the effect of a trade union 'closed shop' on the employment of free labour. Thus writers in the classical tradition,* overlooking the special assumption underlying their theory, have been driven inevitably to the conclusion, perfectly logical on their assumption, that apparent unemployment (apart from the admitted exceptions) must be due at bottom to a refusal by the unemployed factors to accept a reward which corresponds to their marginal productivity. A classical economist may sympathise with labour in refusing to accept a cut in its money wage, and he will admit that it may not be wise to make it to meet conditions which are temporary; but scientific integrity forces him to declare that this refusal is, nevertheless, at the bottom of the trouble.

J.M. Keynes, *The General Theory of Employment, Interest and Money*, 1936, CUP

* Keynes used the term 'classical' to refer to the prevailing economic theory of the time that he was challenging.

1 Keynes makes a distinction between temporary unemployment and involuntary unemployment, why was the concept of involuntary unemployment a break with pre-Keynesian economic theory?
2 A 'closed shop ' refers to a situation where one cannot work for certain employers unless one is a member of the relevant union. Show how the operation of a closed shop could result in an excess supply of labour to an industry. Is this a convincing explanation for mass unemployment throughout the whole economy?
3 Pre-Keynesian economists laid the blame for mass unemployment on the refusal of workers to accept a cut in wages. How did Keynes attempt to break free from this conclusion ?
4 Did the fact that there was mass unemployment prove Keynes right? Refer to the media to list alternatives to Keynesian policies.

16 Measuring the macroeconomy

Learning outcomes

At the end of this chapter you will be able to:
▶ List the four main macroeconomic measures and targets of policy.
▶ Outline how they are measured and why they are important.
▶ Convert changes in nominal national income to changes in real national income.
▶ Understand the limitations of national income statistics for international comparisons.

The four macroeconomic policy targets

The previous chapter explained that macroeconomics is concerned with aggregate economic phenomena and processes. In practice, there are four such aggregates that are the targets of macroeconomic policy.

The four targets of macroeconomic policy are the balance of payments, inflation, growth and unemployment.

These four variables are taken to indicate the overall 'health' of the economy. The importance of each of these targets is now briefly described.

1 The balance of payments is a record of a country's transactions with the rest of the world. It is rather like a person's bank account in that it shows whether that country is 'living within its means'. Ultimately, if a country is spending more abroad than it earns from the rest of the world then corrective action will be necessary, e.g. to maintain the value of the country's currency in relation to other countries' currencies.

2 Inflation refers to a rise in the general level of prices, e.g. if all prices doubled in a year inflation would be 100 per cent for that year. This does not mean everyone is automatically worse off for wages and salaries are simply the price of labour and hence wages may have doubled also. Economists debate the extent to which inflation is harmful, but there is reason to suspect that it could be and all agree that at a high level it is damaging. Inflation also tends to be cumulative, i.e. once begun the inflation rate begins to accelerate. Experience shows that policy to reduce inflation often depresses employment and output and so most economists and governments are inflation-adverse and will seek to avoid allowing it to build-up to unacceptable levels.

3 Growth refers to an increase in the overall output of the economy. If the output each year is increasing then, *ceteris paribus*, there is more of everything to share out. Hence, growth is linked to real income and economic welfare and is particularly important for a country's long term standing in the world community.

4 Unemployment is people wanting to work but not being able to find jobs. Not only is this a waste of available resources, but it can cause personal misery and wider social problems.

Measuring national income

The growth of the economy is measured by changes in national aggregate output. We can measure this by looking at the main components of national output. The official UK statistics for national output can be found in the following UK publications from the Office for National Statistics (and published by the Stationery Office) – the *United Kingdom National Accounts 'The Blue Book'*, *Economic Trends, Annual Abstract of Statistics* or the *Monthly Digest*. They are also available free from the National Statistics website at *www.statistics.gov.uk*. A thorough understanding of those statistics is vital for anyone who wishes to be a serious economist, for the accounts provide a rich source of information on the economy, but there are potential pitfalls too. To reflect changes in syllabuses only a broad understanding is given here, but you are encouraged to look at these publications or on the website. As already mentioned, national income and its growth may have important implications for welfare (see Chapter 34). Here we concentrate only on how it is defined and measured.

The circular flow of national income

The national product

National product is a term we use to describe the total of all the output of goods and services produced by an economy over a specific period of time. As this output is the real income of the economy for the period, national product is also known as national income.

STUDENT ACTIVITY 16.1

Suppose the output of a country in a year consists of 10 000 hairgrips, 2000 toothbrushes, 5 million kilowatts of electricity, 18 luxury motor cars, 500 basic motor cars, 4000 hours of solicitors' advice, 8000 hours of housework, 5000 ball bearings, 400 tonnes of steel, 2590 tyres, 70 tonnes of pollutant gases, 5000 hours of entertainment, 6000 hours of gardening, 16 kilometres of egg noodle, 3000 cardboard boxes and 4000 sausages. The economy also exports 50 cars and imports 40 motorcycles. How might you go about producing a single measure for the output or real income of this economy? What problems will arise in this exercise? Make a list of the problems you have identified and tick them off as you read through this chapter.

There are several different measures of national product, the most commonly used being *gross*

domestic product (GDP) and *gross national product* (GNP). Gross domestic product refers to the value of all goods and services produced within the country's boundaries, gross national product also includes net income from investments abroad. Most countries use similar measurements and quarterly summaries for 24 industrialised nations can be found in the Organisation for Economic and Co-operation and Development's (OECD) *Economic Outlook* or at *www.oecd.org*.

The first problem you will have encountered in Student activity 16.1 is that to aggregate all the various outputs of the economy by counting or weighing them would be nonsensical. Perhaps you realised that the best way to aggregate these disparate outputs would be to use prices, this is indeed how it is done.

● *Common misunderstanding*

The monetary measures of national income can suggest that it is the flow of money that is the focus of measurement. It is important to bear in mind that it is the flow of output of goods and services that the national income accountant is actually trying to measure. It is this flow that is the real income of the economy.

The circular flow

The circular flow method of looking at the flow of economic aggregates was used by Keynes as the foundation of his macroeconomics. Figure 16.1 illustrates a very simple circular flow model in which there is no foreign trade and no government intervention. Here we see two of the main sectors of the macroeconomy, households and firms. These sectors are identified not by who they are but by what they do, i.e. firms produce while households consume. Everyone in the economy must belong to a 'household' since everyone must consume. The households also own the factors of production. In order to produce, firms must buy factor services from households. In return for the factor services, firms pay households wages, rent, interest and profit. The size of these payments will give us the total income from producing and therefore the value of the national product.

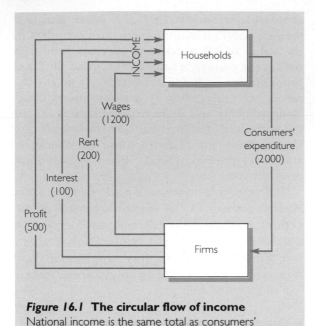

Figure 16.1 The circular flow of income
National income is the same total as consumers' expenditure

This payment for factor services is known as income and is usually abbreviated to the letter Y (the letter I is reserved for investment). It should be clear that income is derived from the expenditure of others, e.g. if you buy something your expenditure becomes the income of the factors of production that produced the item. In other words, for any given period the amount spent must be identically equal to the amount received as income. Hence, if we totalled all consumers' expenditure (C) on the right-hand side of Figure 16.1 it should be equal to all the factor incomes on the left-hand side. We can conclude:

There are (at least) two methods of measuring the national product: by measuring either national income or national expenditure.

If we return to Figure 16.1 you will be able to see why this view of the economy is often referred to as the circular flow of income. Firms receive money from households which they then pay out as wages etc. This income is then spent creating more income for firms and so on. Everyone's income is someone else's expenditure.

Both these measures are used in calculating the total. Not only is the amount spent equal to the amount received but it must also be equal to the value of the goods and services so exchanged. At its simplest imagine that only two goods are sold, say 20 loaves of bread and four kgs of rice. If the price of a loaf of bread is 30p and the price of rice £2 per kg, then the total expenditure is £6 + £8 = £14. Thus we have a third measure of national income known as the 'output' measure which is conceptually the most direct way of measuring national product, i.e. the sum of the monetary values of all *final goods and services* (see Student activity 16.2 to discover why the term 'final' goods and services has been used).

This very simplified example should have made it clear that for the economy as a whole, within a specified time period, total income must equal total expenditure which must equal total product. Hence the basic income accounting identity is:

National income ≡ National Expenditure ≡ National product

The components of national income

So far we have been considering a very simple economy which produces only consumer goods and has no government intervention and no foreign trade. However, all these things must be included in the actual calculation of national income or product. We will consider each of these in turn.

Capital goods

In order to produce consumer goods we need capital goods in the form of buildings, machines and stocks. Therefore an economy must produce not only consumer goods (C) but also investment in capital goods (I). We count both consumer goods and investment goods as part of the gross national product (GNP). Although we may not actually consume factories or machines, if our stock of them increases then the economy has become wealthier because we have a greater ability to produce wealth. We therefore need to count investment goods as part of the national product. From this we can see that national product is going to include the output of consumer goods plus investment goods ($C + I$).

The government and the national product

When we are calculating national expenditure, as well as consumer spending (C) and private investment spending (I), we add all government expenditure on goods and services (G), so that the total demand for goods and services will now be $C + I + G$.

Included within government expenditure are such things as the cost of new schools and the salaries of school teachers, soldiers and the cost of tanks and guns. In short, it is the wages of all government employees plus goods (medicines, paper, roads, buildings, etc.) which the government buys from the private sector. This can also be split into government consumption (e.g wages) and capital formation (i.e. investment).

This does not, however, include *all* government spending. We do not include items such as expenditure on old-age pensions or sickness benefits. These are termed ***transfer payments***. The reason for this is that these are not payments for productive services and therefore are deemed to have nothing to do with the creation of the national product in the current year.

Foreign trade and the national product

So far the economy we have considered has been a ***closed economy***. The UK, however, is an ***open economy***, i.e. one which trades with the rest of the world. The sale of UK goods and services abroad creates income for people in the UK and we therefore include that in our calculation of the national product. On the other hand, much of what is spent in the UK is expenditure on imported goods and services which creates

income for people overseas. This is therefore subtracted from the national product. When we have done this we can arrive at a full statement for all the components of the national product, which is:

$$Y = C + I + G + (X - M)$$

Figure 16 2 extends the circular flow model of Figure 16.1 which can still be seen in the left of the diagram. The government and international sectors have now been added and for completeness the flows of savings and borrowing are also included as dotted lines. It should be realised, however, that C, I, G, X and M are more than just flows of money, for each there is a real flow of goods and services in the opposite direction. It is these expenditures which contribute to aggregate demand.

National income accounts

We have already seen that the value of the national product can be arrived at in three different ways from output, expenditure and income. Table 16.1 shows a simplified representation of the national income accounts (figures have also been rounded for convenience).

STUDENT ACTIVITY 16.3

Consumers' expenditure includes an imputed rent for owner occupied dwellings. Why do you think this is done? (Hint: Think what would happen to national expenditure if all householders suddenly decided to sell their houses and pay rent.)

● *Common misunderstandings*

(a) *The various measures of the national product give us a tally of the nation's income for a year. However, this does not measure the nation's wealth. The nation has a great stock of capital goods. This stock of national capital is the sum total of everything that has been preserved from all that has been produced throughout our economic history. Interestingly, perhaps the greatest asset of modern economies is the skill and education of the workforce. This is called 'human capital' but is not included in measures of net capital stock because of the difficulty of measuring it.*

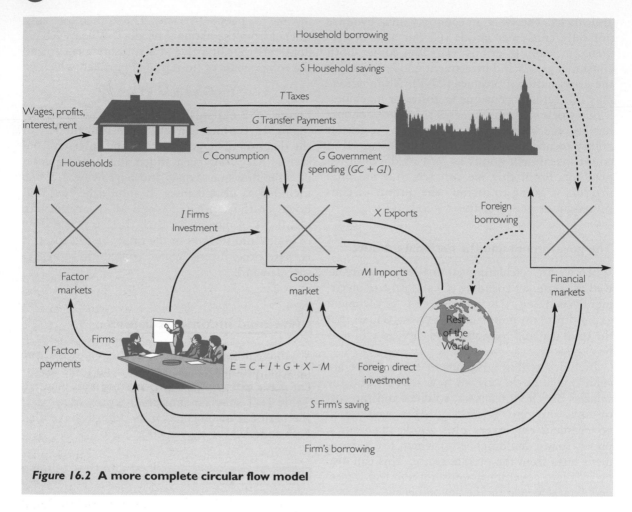

Figure 16.2 **A more complete circular flow model**

Table 16.1 **Simplified National Accounts (figures approximate) UK gross domestic product 1999 (£bn = £1000 million pounds)**

Expenditure method		
(C)	Final consumption	587
(G)	Government final consumption	163
(G)	Government investment	14
(I)	Private sector investment	143
(X)	Exports	229
(M)	Less Imports	245
Gross domestic product		**891**
Income method		
Profit, rent and interest		337
Wages and salaries		491
Self employment		63
Gross domestic product		**891**

Table 16.1 continued

Output method	
Agriculture, hunting, forestry and fishing	11
Mining and quarrying	21
Manufacturing	168
Electricity, gas and water supply	21
Construction	46
Wholesale and retail trade; repairs; hotels and restaurants	133
Transport, storage and communication	78
Financial intermediation, real estate, renting and business activities	250
Public administration, national defence and compulsory social security	46
Education, health and social work	105
Other services	47
Adjustment for financial intermediation services indirectly measured	−35
Gross domestic product	**891**

Source: Adapted from National Statistics, *Blue Book.* © Crown Copyright 2001

(b) *If we were assessing someone's wealth, one of the first things we would look at is how much money they had and also whether they owned stocks and shares. However, these are excluded from the calculation of national wealth. Why? The answer is because we have already counted them in the form of real wealth such as buildings and machines. Money and other financial assets are only claims upon wealth and hence are simply paper certificates of ownership. Similarly, varying the amount of money in the economy does not directly make it any richer or poorer.*

Inflation and national product

The national income accountant is attempting to measure a flow of real output. Thus a problem faced when comparing one year's national product with another is that of inflation. If, for example, the money value of national product at current prices were to grow by 10 per cent but this simply reflected inflation of 10 per cent, then in real terms the national product would not have grown at all.

● Common misunderstanding

'Current prices' does not mean today's prices it means the prices of the year in question. For example, '1996 GDP at current prices' refers to the value of gross domestic product valued at the prices that existed in 1996. Constant prices means that the prices of some base year has been used, so that '1996 GDP at constant (1995) prices' means the value of the output in 1996 measured in 1995 prices.

It is useful to have a measure that shows changes in real national product. Measuring national product in constant prices does this. This can be calculated by *deflating* the figures by the amount of inflation that has taken place. Inflation itself is measured by means of index numbers. The best-known index of inflation is the retail price index (RPI) (see Chapter 34). Although there are other measures, it is the percentage change in the RPI which is usually referred to as *the rate of inflation*. The RPI is not, however, an appropriate measure for the purpose of deflating the national product because it measures only consumers' expenditure and, as we have seen, the national product also includes expenditure on investment and expenditure by the government. Therefore a more complex index is needed and this is termed the *GDP deflator*.

Let us consider an example (using approximate numbers). The GDP in current prices was £713 980 million in 1995 and £891 100 million in 1999. The GDP deflator for these years was 100 in 1995 (base year) and 112 in 1999 respectively. This therefore gives the overall price inflation for the components of GDP between these years as 12 per cent. To express the GDP in constant price terms we divide by the deflator and multiply by 100. Thus we obtain:

1995 in constant (1995) prices = £713 980 million ÷ 100 × 100 = £713 980 million

1999 in constant (1995) prices = £891 100 million ÷ 112 × 100 = £795 625 million

Thus, the 'real value' of the GDP in 1999 was £795 625 million in terms of 1995 prices, rather than its current price value of £891 100 million. Put another way, the real value of the GDP increased by 11.4 per cent between 1995 and 1999 while its monetary value increased by 24.8 per cent. GDP at current prices is sometimes called *nominal* GDP to distinguish it from the real measure in constant prices.

There are tables in the *National Income and Expenditure* 'The Blue Book' which have already applied the deflator in this way and hence show GDP at current and constant prices.

Growth

Economic growth is a prime objective for most countries. Even a small percentage difference in current rates of growth will produce wide differences in the income of countries over a few decades.

Strictly speaking growth refers to an outward shift of the production possibility frontier. Hence, in Figure 16.3 the movement from X to Y might simply be caused by the economy recovering from a previous recession. A movement from Y

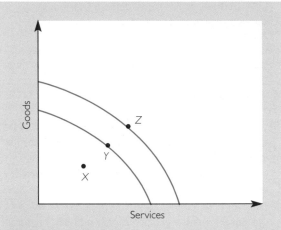

Figure 16.3 **Difficulties in comparisons through time**

to Z would be 'true' economic growth. Such a shift could be caused by an increase in productivity and/or technical progress or an increased supply of resources to the economy. In practice, however, such a distinction is not often made and the increase in real gross domestic product (GDP at constant prices) from one year to another is taken to be the growth rate.

The limitations of GDP or GNP growth as an indicator of improvements in welfare is explored further in Chapter 34 but it should be obvious that human welfare depends on many things not just material well-being, e.g. quality of community life, peace, health and the environment. The main problem of comparing GDP through time is that the mix of goods and services changes. For example, how do we compare the output mix at the beginning of the twentieth century with that at the end? At the beginning of the century there were no TV's, video players, mobile phones, few cars or domestic appliances, the service sector accounted for about half of UK output in 1900, by 2000 about two-thirds. The quality of product and services has also changed substantially making it difficult to compare, say, gas mantles with designer interior lighting.

Such considerations are fairly unimportant over short periods and it is easy to re-base the GDP deflator to adjust for changes in output, but over longer periods we are not really comparing like with like.

International comparisons

Obviously in comparing different countries it is the amount of GDP per person that is important rather than the absolute size of GDP. Dividing GDP by a country's population gives GDP per head for that country, this is also known as GDP per capita. Of course, this is only the average, very different distributions of income could give the same figure for GDP per head. Also when comparing richer and poorer countries we might need to adjust for the level of output that is home produced or traded by direct barter and is therefore not recorded as a market transaction, for example, food production for one's own consumption. It is also the case that some countries spend a far higher percentage of their resources on defence than other countries.

In addition to the problems of comparison caused by very different distributions of income within countries, the differing percentages of economic activity conducted through non-monetary transactions and the differing effects of government expenditure, particular problems for international comparisons are caused by 'distortion' due to exchange rates.

Most countries' exchange rates 'float', i.e. the international value of their currencies change in the market from day to day. So, for example, as exchange rates move against the dollar the estimates for per capita income as measured in dollars also change. For example, in 1988 GNP per capita for Japan was $21 020 and thus more than the $19 840 for the USA at that time. But if the same figures for GNP are measured in dollars at 1990 exchange rates, the figure for Japan becomes $18 658, i.e. less than that for the USA. When we are considering a large number of nations, each of whose exchange rates is varying, the possibilities for inaccuracy are multiplied.

Unemployment

Not all unemployment is considered a problem. For example, workers may be temporarily unemployed as they enter the workforce from school or as they move between jobs. Unemployment of this sort is part of the *frictional unemployment* that will always exist as part of the normal functioning of the economy. We saw, however, in the last chapter that the level of unemployment has shown great changes over time. This is due to changes in the level of *involuntary* unemployment. Involuntary unemployment exists when someone is actively seeking a job but simply cannot find one because there are not enough jobs to go around (see also Chapter 39). This is clearly both distressing and a waste of resources.

There are two main measures of unemployment: (a) the number of people eligible for state welfare unemployment benefit and (b) the International Labour Office definition of unemployment of 'actively seeking work' which is measured by conducting surveys of the unemployed. The number of unemployed is divided by the total workforce, i.e. the total number of working and unemployed persons, to give the percentage unemployed. As unemployment benefit arrangements vary greatly between countries, the ILO definition is the one usually used for international comparisons. Figure 16.4 shows that since 1992 unemployment has fallen steadily and in September 2000 the claimant count figure had reached low levels not seen since the mid-1970s.

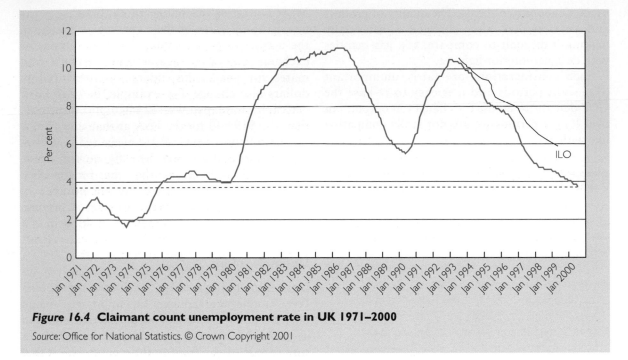

Figure 16.4 Claimant count unemployment rate in UK 1971–2000

Source: Office for National Statistics. © Crown Copyright 2001

The Balance of Payments

We complete this chapter by briefly describing how transactions with the rest of the world are measured. This is explained in more depth in Chapter 42. The detailed Balance of Payments accounts for the UK are compiled by National Statistics in 'The Pink Book' (yes, the blue book is blue and the pink book is pink). Here we are interested only in a broad understanding of what is measured and why it matters for policy rather than a detailed knowledge of the accounts themselves.

The balance of payments is an account of all the transactions of everyone living and working in the UK with the rest of the world. It is measured by two sections of the accounts: (a) the 'current account' and (b) the 'capital and financial account'.

The current account

This account shows how much the UK earns from the rest of the world and how much it spends. The biggest component of this account records the *trade in goods and services*. It records the balance of the receipts earned by selling exports on the one hand and the payments made to purchase imports from other countries on

the other. This is also often referred to as the *balance of trade*. The inward flow of income is recorded as 'credits' and the outflow as 'debits'. If the income earned from selling exports is greater than the UK's expenditure on imports then there is a trade surplus and vice versa for a trade deficit.

● *Common misunderstanding*

It is a common fallacy that it is only the export of goods which earns money for the country. In fact, the sale of services such as banking, insurance and tourism is also a major source of overseas income for the UK. Indeed, for the UK there is typically a deficit in the trade of 'visibles', i.e. goods, and a surplus in the trade of 'invisibles', i.e. services.

Current income can also be earned from UK workers working abroad or from the return to investments made abroad. There will also be debits from foreign workers in the UK taking money out of the country and from the return on investment made in the UK by residents of other countries. These credits and debits are recorded in the *income* component of the current account. The last section of the UK current account is *current transfers* and consists of credits and debits arising from transfer of monies between governments and other bodies such as the European Union. Overseas aid and maintaining a military presence abroad are also included as debits in this account.

The capital and financial account

The capital and financial account shows movements of investment funds between the UK and the rest of the world. This may be *direct investment* where businesses are set up in another country, or *portfolio investment* where financial instruments such as shares or government-backed securities are purchased from another country. Inward investment causes a credit and outward investment a debit.

● Common misunderstanding

Investment funds and investment earnings are often confused. The earnings from investments abroad show up in the current account whereas the movement of funds shows up in the capital and financial account. Hence, a debit caused by investment overseas will tend to cause an inflow in future years as income is earned from that investment.

From Table 16.2, you will see that, when allowance is made for the inevitable errors and omissions, the sum of the current and capital and financial accounts is zero. However, this is for a trivial reason only. The capital and financial account also records changes to the UK stock of *international reserve assets*, e.g. gold and holdings of foreign currencies. Obviously, if more money has flowed out of the country than into it then the reserves are depleted by this amount. But as this outward flow of reserves is matched by an inward flow of pounds it is given a plus sign on the balance of the accounts and therefore, in an accounting sense only, the balance of payments always balances! It should be clear, however, that an inflow of pounds from selling reserve assets is a depletion of wealth rather than income earned.

For the purposes of examining macroeconomic policy in this section we will be looking at the current account. As stated earlier, a country with a chronic current account deficit is rather like an individual living beyond his or her means, eventually that country must take action if it is to avoid running out of international reserves or its currency losing value. A current account surplus is not such a pressing problem, but there is little point in endlessly accumulating money if it is not to be used for consumption or investment.

Conclusion

In order to gain an overview of the macroeconomy this chapter has looked at the definition and measurement of each of the four macroeconomic aggregates. Although the priority given to each

Table 16.2 UK balance of payments: 1999

	Credits	Debits	Balance
1 Current account			
A Goods and services			
Goods	165 667	192 434	−26 767
Services	63 982	52 444	+11 538
B Income	109 099	100 767	+8 332
C Current transfers	18 278	22 362	−4 084
Total current account	357 026	368 007	−10 981
2 Capital and financial accounts			
A Capital account, direct investment, portfolio investment and other investment	187 559	181 569	+5 990
B Reserve assets		−639	+639
C Net errors and omissions	4 352		+4 352
Total			0

Source: Adapted from National Statistics. © Crown Copyright 2001

varies between governments and over time, these aggregates are a concern for any government no matter what its politics. An in-depth look at these aggregates can wait until Section VIII of this book; for now, you should know enough to be able to follow the analysis of UK macroeconomic policy in Chapter 18. But first, in the next chapter, we move from definition and measurement to some simple tools of analysis in order to understand how macroeconomic policy works (and also fails!).

Summary

1 The four macro-economic aggregates targeted by the economic policies of any government are the balance of payments, growth, inflation and unemployment.

2 National income is a measure of the output of goods and services produced over a given period of time.

3 Income, expenditure and output are different methods of measuring the same entity.

4 Government expenditure and the net figure from foreign trade also form part of the national product.

5 The components of GDP may be summarised as:

$$Y = C + I + G + (X - M)$$

6 Changes in the 'real' value of GDP can be arrived at by using an index of inflation to deflate GDP at current prices to GDP at constant prices.

7 Problems arise in the interpretation of national income accounts and their use as a measure of welfare.

8 Growth is measured by increases in GDP at constant prices.

9 The balance of payments records a country's monetary transactions with the rest of the world, the accounts have two main sections: (a) the current account and (b) the capital and financial account.

10 The problems associated with an unsatisfactory level for each of the four economic targets differ, but ultimately a problem with any or all may lead to a serious loss of overall welfare.

? QUESTIONS

1 $Y = C + I + G + (X - M)$. Give the precise names of all the terms in this formula.

2 Distinguish between wealth and income.

3 Many people are turning to 'do-it-yourself' for household improvements. Does the GDP (which includes the cost of DIY components) therefore over- or underestimate the 'true' value of the national product?

4 In 1987 Subtopia had a GDP of $7 750 million which had risen to $21 000 million by 2000. Over the same period the GDP deflator rose from 100 to 250. Meanwhile, population had also increased from 54.2 million to 58.7 million. What was the change in the real GDP per capita in Subtopia over this period?

5 Suppose that Germany has a population of 77 million and a GDP of DM5000 billion, whereas the UK has a GDP of £800 billion and a population of 56 million. The exchange rate is £1 = DM3. Compare their relative prosperity. What other information would be useful in order to assess the standard of living in the two countries?

6 Suppose that in one year there is a large outflow of investment finance that puts the balance of payments into deficit, does this mean that the country is poorer?

7 Why would it not be a sensible policy to try to reduce measured unemployment to zero?

8 Give reasons why attempting to achieve a satisfactory level of one of the four macroeconomic targets might cause unsatisfactory levels of another.

Data response A
MACROECONOMIC MOVEMENTS

Study the charts in Figure 16.5 and answer the following questions.

1 What has happened to the rate of inflation since 1990?

2 Compare the balance on 'visibles' with the balance on 'invisibles'.

3 Identify the years of recession for the UK.

4 Explain the relationship between growth of GDP and level of unemployment.

5 What has been happening to economic growth since 1995 and why might this account for a deterioration in the balance of trade?

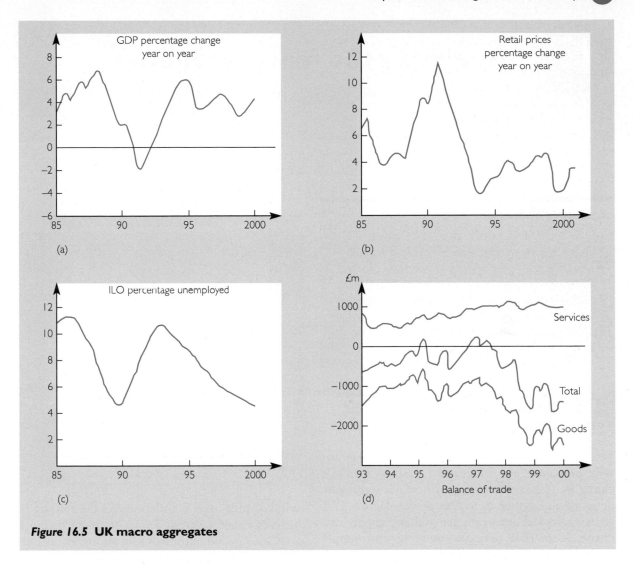

Figure 16.5 **UK macro aggregates**

17 Analysing the macroeconomy

Learning outcomes

At the end of this chapter you will be able to:
▶ Draw aggregate demand and supply diagrams.
▶ Describe the factors affecting the slope of these aggregate curves.
▶ Show the effects of changes in the conditions of demand and supply.
▶ Use aggregate demand and supply to analyse macroeconomic changes.

The aggregate demand and supply curve approach

This chapter provides an introductory analysis that will help you to understand macro-economic changes. The tools developed here are *aggregate demand* and *aggregate supply* curves. Figure 17.1 shows a typical aggregate demand and supply diagram. Note that, like the demand and supply curves of microeconomics, they are plotted with price on the vertical axis. Here, however, the vertical axis shows the aggregate level of prices, it is thus an index of all the prices of goods and services produced by the economy. Therefore an upward movement along the axis means that there has been an increase in the general level of prices. The discussion of the GDP deflator in the last chapter should have made you familiar with such a concept, but a simple way to think about it (often actually used in macroeconomics) is to assume that only one product is produced by the economy, say, 'fudge'. This fudge is of course really a 'composite volume index' of all goods and services produced, but it is simpler to think of the aggregate price as the price of a unit of this fudge. Similarly, the hori-

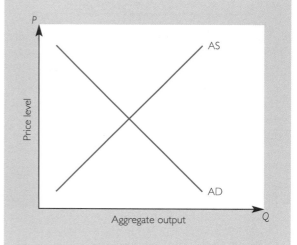

Figure 17.1 Aggregate demand and supply curves

zontal quantity axis simply becomes the amount of this fudge that is demanded or supplied within a given time period, although it is also really a composite volume for all goods and services produced by the economy.

The curves in Figure 17.1 look very much like the demand and supply curves you have encountered already in analysing market equilibrium (and this will make it easier to understand this chapter). But it is important for you to bear in mind that aggregate demand and supply curves are very different from the demand and supply curves for individual markets. Indeed, in Chapter 15 we saw that Keynes was emphasising that the macroeconomy does not necessarily behave in the way predicted by the demand and supply analysis of individual markets. Here we give a simplified account of aggregate demand and supply analysis, but when using it you should always bear in mind that there is more involved than in micro-economic demand and supply analysis. What lies behind these aggregate curves is looked at in greater depth in Section VII of this book.

The derivation of the aggregate demand curve

Aggregate demand is the total quantity of all goods and services demanded in a certain time period.

Aggregate demand can also be thought of as the total volume of real national product demanded within a certain time period. Aggregate demand is therefore the sum of the demands of house-holds, firms, governments and overseas buyers for UK products. Thus the derivation of the aggregate demand curve is fairly straightforward; we simply have to recall the components of expenditure we identified in the previous chapter and see how they are affected by a change in the level of prices. These components are shown again here:

Expenditure =

Consumption + Investment + Government Spending + Exports – Imports

or

Aggregate Demand depends on $C + I + G + X - M$

To derive the aggregate demand curve we have to relate aggregate demand to the price level. We begin this by considering the effect of changes in the price level on the value of the *stock of money* in the economy.

At any one time, there will be a certain amount of money held by households, firms and banks. This is more than just the notes and coins in cir-culation, in fact the biggest element is bank deposits. These coins, notes and deposits are measured in nominal terms, e.g. as having a money value equal to so many pounds sterling, but their real value depends on the price level, i.e. how much could be purchased with them. Thus, although the nominal (or 'face') value stays the same, a change in the general level of prices changes the real value of money. In particular, an increase in all prices would lower the real value of a unit of money and a decrease in all prices would increase the real value of money.

We shall now follow through the effects of a decrease in the level of prices, *ceteris paribus*, on the components of aggregate demand. As explained above, a decrease in the level of prices will increase the real value of a given supply of money, i.e.

$$\text{Prices} \downarrow \Rightarrow \frac{\text{Money supply (fixed)}}{\text{Prices}} \uparrow \Rightarrow \text{Real money supply} \uparrow$$

For example, halving the general level of prices would double the real purchasing power of a constant nominal money supply.

Taking each of the elements of aggregate demand expenditure in turn, an increase in the real money supply will tend to increase the volume of aggregate demand for the following reasons:

(a) As the nominal wealth of households' held in money becomes worth more in real terms members of these households are likely to use this increase in wealth to consume more.

(b) Also, the increase in the real money supply will tend to reduce the cost of borrowing money (i.e. the interest rate) and thus expen-diture on items such as cars and household appliances will tend to rise, particularly if the price of these items has also fallen.

(c) The fall in interest rates is also likely to lead to more investment by firms.

Thus the effect of the fall in the price level has been to increase both consumption and investment.

(d) The effect of a general fall in prices on the real value of government expenditure will depend on how that government reacts. But, *ceteris paribus*, any given level of nominal government spending will be greater in real terms at a lower price level. Therefore we may again assume that the fall in prices, *ceteris paribus*, will tend to lead to a higher level of aggregate demand in real terms.

(e) At lower prices the demand for exports is also likely to increase as the domestic price level falls relative to foreign markets, i.e. the country's exports become relatively cheaper compared to goods and service in other countries. In addition, there might be a decrease in the demand for imports as domestically produced goods become cheaper relative to imports. An increase in exports and a fall in imports clearly adds to the demand for UK goods and services.

Therefore, for all these reasons:

We assume the aggregate demand curve to be downward sloping.

● *Common misunderstanding*

Clearly the overall price level seldom actually falls, but that does not mean we cannot think of an extension of demand. The nominal money supply is usually also rising and hence the rate of increase in prices need only fall below the rate of expansion of the nominal money supply for the real money supply to expand. In short, the model can be represented in dynamic terms in which a slowing of the rate of increase in prices leads to an expansion of the real money supply and hence an extension of aggregate demand. If you want to you can think of a fall in the level of prices as really a slowing of inflation. Its much simpler though to show this as an aggregate demand and supply diagram and as an actual fall in the level of prices leading to an extension of demand.

A decrease in the general price level will tend to cause an extension of aggregate demand and thus a higher level of demand for goods and services in real terms.

The precise *transmission mechanism* may vary (see Chapter 37) but the end result is that at the lower price level there has been an extension of demand for the output of the economy.

The conditions of aggregate demand

This terminology is the same as for the microeconomic demand curves – recall that we reserved the term *extension* to describe a rise in demand caused by a fall in the price level. This is the same for aggregate demand. You will not be surprised to learn that the term *an increase* in aggregate demand is reserved to describe a rightward shift of the AD curve, i.e. more goods and services demanded at any given price than before (see Figure 17.2). As with microeconomic demand an increase in aggregate demand is caused by a change in the conditions of demand, i.e influences other than the price level itself. The conditions of demand in this case are the components of expenditure which go to make up aggregate demand, i.e. $C, I, G, X–M$. Hence, an increase in aggregate demand is caused by an increase in one of these components for any given price level.

For example, if firms are optimistic about the future they are likely to invest more in order to prepare for a higher level of sales. An increase in investment will then cause an increase in aggregate demand. Similarly, if households feel more secure about their future income, or expect it to increase, they are likely to save less and consume more thereby also increasing aggregate demand.

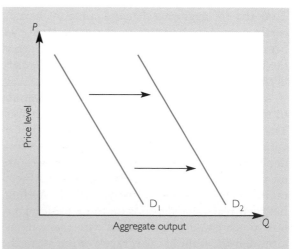

Figure 17.2 **An increase in aggregate demand caused by an increase in one or more of the components of expenditure for any given level of prices**

Changes in expectations have an important effect on consumption and investment spending.

STUDENT ACTIVITY 17.2

It should be fairly easy for you now to explain why an increase in the nominal money supply will cause an increase in the aggregate demand for any level of prices. But what do you think will happen to aggregate demand if the government decreases its budget deficit?

As you will see in the next chapter, the interest rate is a very important determinant of aggregate demand. If the Bank of England judges that inflation is likely to exceed the target set it will act by raising interest rates. The mechanism for this is explained in the next chapter, but it should be understood here that by making money more expensive to borrow this will tend to reduce consumption and investment spending and hence constrain aggregate demand.

The derivation of the aggregate supply curve

In the 1970s there was a debate between Keynesian economists and the monetarists. Textbooks of the time portrayed this as Keynesians arguing that fiscal policy has a more powerful influence on aggregate demand than monetary policy and the monetarists (hence the name) arguing that monetary policy had the more powerful effect on aggregate demand. But today the debate has moved on to a more fundamental debate about the functioning of capitalism. Just about every economist today accepts that if either fiscal or monetary policy is applied strongly enough it will shift aggregate demand (see later in this chapter) the real debate is now over the shape of the aggregate supply curve.

The shape of the aggregate supply curve we draw depends crucially on the assumptions we make. These assumptions vary markedly between schools of thought. The differences in the assumptions made by different schools reflect deep differences in belief as to how the economy works, but the main distinction is between the Keynesian schools and the modern neo-classical macroeconomic schools such as monetarism.

Keynesian schools interpret and develop the writings of Keynes to argue that capitalism is prone to instability but that it can be corrected by the appropriate government intervention to manage aggregate demand. Neo-classical schools use standard demand and supply analysis to arrive at the result that capitalism is quickly self-righting and that hence demand management is not necessary. Indeed, neo-classical macroeconomists tend to think that macroeconomic policy does more harm than good. Clearly then, Keynesians tend to be to politically to the 'left' of neo-classical economists such as monetarists.

Keynesian aggregate supply

Keynesians today continue to argue that the macroeconomy behaves in ways that differ from the predictions of microeconomic analysis. They argue, for example, that in the real world firms are constrained in how much they can sell by the level of aggregate demand in the economy. In particular, firms will not produce more than they can sell but typically would be glad to sell more at the same price. Rather than firms responding to a given price by selling only up to the profit maximising point as in perfect competition, firms set a mark-up on their estimate of average cost (see also Chapter 22) and then sell as much as consumers will buy. Thus, an increase in demand allows firms to sell more and they will happily do so even at the same price as before.

Keynesians argue that the aggregate supply curve has a horizontal section whereby firms are willing to supply more even at the same prices.

STUDENT ACTIVITY 17.3

We are confident that you have never walked into a shop and been told by the shopkeeper 'I'm sorry, but I have already sold up to the point at which my profits are maximised, if you want to buy anything you must pay more than the prices on display'. Does this prove that Keynesians are correct in saying that an increase in demand does not necessarily cause prices to rise? Explain why it would be impossible for the aggregate supply curve to be horizontal no matter how high the level of output.

Obviously, Keynesian economists recognise that as output expands the economic problem will eventually bite. For example, as the pool of unemployed persons gets smaller so wages may be bid up and this increase is passed on to the consumer, or, firms unable to produce more begin to raise prices instead. Equally as firms bid for the other remaining scarce resources the price of these inputs rise and firms faced with rising unit costs may pass this on to consumers as a price rise. Thus as output increases, at some point, the aggregate supply curve begins to slope upwards. When the supply of resources to firms cannot expand further, e.g. when full employment is reached, the aggregate supply curve becomes vertical.

The resulting Keynesian aggregate supply curve is shown in Figure 17.3.

Neo-classical macroeconomic aggregate supply curves

Neo-classical economists emphasise that the market mechanism acts through demand and supply to establish an equilibrium in which all economic agents are doing what they want to do given the prices they face. Hence, not only is this equilibrium reached 'naturally' it is a desirable outcome. For example, if there were people without jobs wanting to work, those unemployed persons would represent an excess supply in the labour market. This would cause wages to fall and firms to employ more until everyone who still wants to work can do so. This is shown in Figure 17.4

● *Common misunderstanding*

It might be thought that equilibrium in the labour market means that there is no unemployment. But there will always be people wishing to change jobs or who remain unemployed while searching for the job they want. Keynesians tend to refer to full employment while modern neo-classical economists speak of the natural rate of unemployment, both accept that overall equilibrium is compatible with the existence of a level of this 'frictional' unemployment

Thus:

In neo-classical macroeconomics the economy will naturally move to a point at which the demand and supply for resources and for goods and services are in equilibrium.

What does this mean for the aggregate supply curve? It means that at any one point of time there will be a level of output, and hence employment, that the economy will naturally move towards. This 'natural' level of employment/

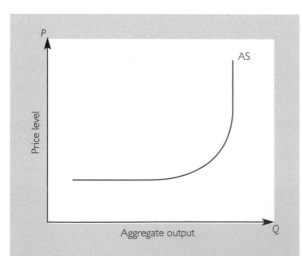

Figure 17.3 The Keynesian aggregate supply curve
Well below the point of full employment increases in aggregate demand increase output and employment without any inflation, as full employment is approached the price level begins to rise as well, at full employment increases in demand will cause only inflation.

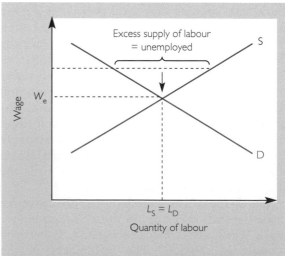

Figure 17.4 Flexible wages acting to eliminate unemployment

unemployment and output will be set by the equilibrium of the labour market and by the overall demand and supply of goods and services. Therefore, in neo-classical macroeconomics, in the long run at least, the aggregate supply curve will be vertical at the natural rate of output. This is shown in Figure 17.5. Note that in this case the only long-term effect of an increase in aggregate demand is to raise the level of prices, i.e. inflation will occur with no change in output or employment/unemployment.

At the two extremes, the Keynesians assume that the aggregate supply curve is horizontal while neo-classical macroeconomists assume it is vertical!

Keynesian and neo-classical macroeconomic equilibrium

We noted above that Keynesians tend to be politically to the 'left' of neo-classical economists. In this sense we mean 'left' to refer to those who believe that free market capitalism has serious flaws and the 'right' to refer to those who have a strong belief that the capitalist economy is self-adjusting and quickly moves to a desirable equilibrium. Those on the right argue that government intervention should be kept to a minimum and as we saw above, an increase in aggregate demand in neo-classical macroeconomics will most likely lead only to inflation. In contrast, if you look at

Figure 17.6 you will see that there is nothing to guarantee that the equilibrium in Keynesian models has desirable properties.

At point Q_X the level of aggregate demand is insufficient for the economy to reach the full-employment level of output. Hence, there is a waste of potential output as well as the individual misery and social problems associated with unemployment. There would thus therefore be very good reason for the government to act to increase aggregate demand so as to lower unemployment and increase real GDP.

Beliefs about how the economy works are often intertwined with political outlook.

Increases in the aggregate supply curve

It is important to remember that the position of the supply curve reflects the real supply of resources to the economy. Hence, in both the neo-classical and Keynesian views, anything that increases this flow of resources, e.g. more capital, greater productivity or more incentive or willingness to work, will shift the aggregate supply curve to the right. Neo-classical economists will think of a vertical aggregate supply curve shifting as the *natural rate* of output increases. Keynesians will show an upward-sloping aggregate supply curve shifting and improving the inflation output/employment trade-off. In both schools such a shift will tend to lower inflation and increase output (see Figure 17.7).

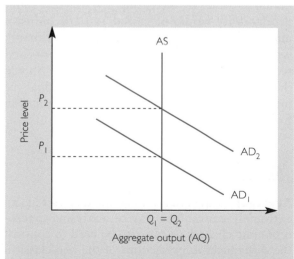

Figure 17.5 Neo-classical long-run aggregate supply

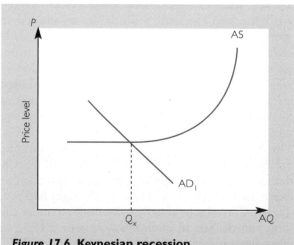

Figure 17.6 Keynesian recession

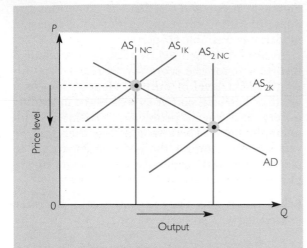

Figure 17.7 Successful supply side policy
For neo-classical economists (NC) inflation is reduced and
the natural level of output/employment increased. For
Keynesian economists (K) the inflation output/employment
trade-off is improved. For both schools equilibrium output
is increased and prices lowered.

● *Common misunderstanding*

*Students sometimes think that because the price level is
almost always rising (i.e. there is always some inflation)
aggregate demand must permanently be exceeding
aggregate supply. More complex models, however, take
account of this persistent tendency for inflation. Thus a
rightward shift of the aggregate supply curve can be
considered to reduce inflation rather than actually cause
the price level to fall.*

Labour market supply side measures associated
with the neo-classical schools are examined in
more detail in Chapter 33. These measures include
reduced welfare payments, reduced taxation,
reduced trade union power and the abolition of
wage floors. Those who believe that government
intervention in the economy should be as little as
possible often advocate these policies, others are
more doubtful that they work as simply as this.
The balance of evidence is unclear, for example,
the introduction of the minimum wage in the UK
did not seem to shift aggregate supply to the left or
cause unemployment as those on the right had predicted. Conversely many economists attribute the
long-run decline in unemployment since 1992 to
more flexible labour markets.

The interventionist policies associated with the
left of the political spectrum in the UK have also
increasingly been couched in terms of supply side
economics. Such analysts point out that the
evidence of the effects of 'free market' supply
measures is inconclusive. They believe that the
major effects of such policies have been an
increase in poverty and the deterioration of
working conditions. Keynesians continue to
maintain that significant increases in employment
and economic forces can be achieved by intervention in the economy and changes to the structure
and regulation of the economy.

Interventionist policies suggested to shift the
aggregate supply have also included increased
provision and subsidisation of education and
training. This has recently been given strong
emphasis in the UK by the Prime Minister, Tony
Blair, who once declared that his Government's
policy was 'Education–Education–Education!'.
This might increase labour productivity but its
effects may take a long time. Another way to
increase productivity might be to increase the
level of investment by deliberately directing
resources towards it, e.g. by tax allowances and
grants. Left-wing analysts also criticise the financial markets of the UK for maintaining very high
levels of overseas investment (see balance of payments in previous chapter). Some would take
measures to redirect this investment towards UK
manufacturing. By increasing investment, labour
productivity would be raised and UK industry
made more competitive. On the other hand,
would it simply discourage investment and
reduce income from wealth held overseas? Should
the investment decisions of private individuals be
interfered with and could it lead to retaliation
from other countries?

Conclusion

Aggregate supply and demand analysis is an
extremely convenient way of analysing macroeconomic changes. It can also be used to contrast
the differences in predictions of the neo-classical
macro-schools such as monetarism and those of
the Keynesians. The questions at the end of this

chapter will give you practice in manipulating AS and AD to predict the effects of changes in policy and circumstances. You should never forget, however, that economics often involves far more than moving lines across a page. Having said that, you will find in the next chapter that with only a little more theory, AS and AD analysis can give an understanding of a great deal of UK macroeconomic policy from the mid-twentieth century through to today.

Summary

1 Aggregate demand and supply analysis provides a simple tool for analysing many macroeconomic changes and policies.
2 Aggregate demand and supply curves are plotted with a measure of the overall price level on the vertical axis and a measure of aggregate output on the horizontal axis.
3 The terms contraction, extension, increase and decrease are used in the same way as for microeconomic demand and supply.
4 A fall in the price level, *ceteris paribus*, will tend to cause an extension of demand as the real value of money increases encouraging consumption and investment, the real value of government expenditure is increased and exports increase while imports decrease.
5 The shape of the aggregate supply curve is more controversial than the shape of the aggregate demand curve.
6 Keynesians believe that the aggregate supply curve has a flat or sloping section at levels of output below full employment. This means there is a role for demand management to control the levels of employment/unemployment and inflation.
7 Neo-classical macroeconomists, such as monetarists, emphasise that aggregate supply is fixed by the real supply of resources to the economy and that markets clear. Hence, equilibrium in the labour market eradicates unemployment and determines the level of employment and hence output. The long-run aggregate supply curve is thus vertical at this 'natural' level of output and employment.
8 Aggregate demand will shift when the conditions of demand change. For example, a rightward shift (an increase) may be caused by an increase in the money supply, the Bank of England lowering interest rates, rising consumer and business confidence, an increase in government expenditure or a decrease in taxation, an increase in exports or a decrease in imports for any level of prices.
9 An aggregate supply shift may be caused for example by a change in: technology, the capital stock, the workforce, incentives and willingness to work, productivity, the encouragement of enterprise, training and education. These tend to be longer term effects compared to shifts in aggregate demand. Changes in the costs of inputs can have a quicker effect on aggregate supply, e.g. a rise in wages or the cost of a major input such as oil.
10 In practice, changes in aggregate demand and supply tend to affect the rate of inflation rather than actually change the direction of prices.

? QUESTIONS

1 Refer to Figure 17.3 to show the effects of increasing demand over the various sections of the Keynesian aggregate supply curve.
2 Assuming an upward sloping aggregate supply curve, show the likely change in the aggregate equilibrium of:
   (a) a decrease in the interest rate;
   (b) a strike by petrol tanker drivers;
   (c) an increase in the incomes of Germans;
   (d) an increase in the incomes of public sector workers;
   (e) increasing economic optimism;
   (f) a shares crash.
3 What will be the effect of an increase in demand on the level of imports? Explain why this change will only reduce and not reverse the increase in AD.
4 Explain how a reduction in the rate of income tax could affect both aggregate supply and demand. Which is the more certain to change?

5 Draw the effects on aggregate supply of an increase in wage pressure or a loss of industrial capacity. What will be the effect on employment and inflation in a neo-classical macroeconomic model?

6 A former Chancellor of the Exchequer once likened the level of unemployment to the level of crime by saying that it is a social rather than a government problem. Was he a Keynesian or a monetarist?

7 Using the Keynesian aggregate supply curve sketch out the implied relationship between unemployment and inflation.

8 Could an increase in wages be associated with an increase in aggregate demand *and* aggregate supply? Explain your answer.

Data response A
KEEPING AN EYE ON PRICES

Read the following article from the *Financial Times* of 6 June 2000 and then answer the questions that follow:

1 Use aggregate demand and supply analysis to show and explain how shortages of skilled labour may be associated with increasing inflation.

2 Draw a diagram to show the short-run effects of the Bank of England raising interest rates. How might the longer term effects be different?

3 List the things in the article that will tend to (a) increase inflation, (b) lower inflation. Illustrate each of these influences using aggregate demand and supply diagrams.

Service staff shortages prompt inflation warning

By **Christopher Adams,** Economics Correspondent

Service sector labour costs are rising at their fastest rate for at least four years, driven higher by severe staff shortages, according to fresh survey evidence.

The Chartered Institute of Purchasing and Supply warned in its latest report yesterday that the tight labour market was fuelling inflationary pressure.

Many companies are successfully passing on the higher costs to consumers, in part because of strong demand.

With unemployment falling fast, shortages of skilled staff had worsened, it said. Service industry companies reported that biggest monthly rise in costs in May since the survey began in mid-1996. Higher fuel and energy costs were also blamed for upward price pressure. The biggest increases were in transport and communications.

The report comes as the Bank of England's monetary policy committee begins a two-day meeting to set interest rates. Signs of looming inflation may worry those members of the committee who believe that interest rates may have to rise again in coming months.

Separate figures today from the British Retail Consortium show spending on the high street remains healthy.

Annual growth in retail sales eased in May to 3.2 per cent on a like-for-like basis, from 7.4 per cent in the previous month, when the figures were distorted by the timing of Easter.

The BRC said that underlying growth was steady. The buoyant housing market supported sales of furniture and electrical goods. Demand for widescreen televisions, mobile phones and digital video discs was especially strong.

Clothing and footwear benefited from sunny weather at the beginning of the month, but sales suffered later.

'Retailers have been relieved by continued steady growth through spring,' said Bridget Rosewell, the BRC's chief economic adviser. 'The figures show a return to a more comfortable trading environment. However, it should be remembered that pricing is still tight.'

On their own, the data were unlikely to influence the monetary policy committee, said economists.

The Bank is widely expected to keep its base interest rate at 6 per cent tomorrow following recent evidence of a slowdown in economic growth.

There are extra uncertainties this month. Christopher Allsopp an Oxford academic, and Professor Stephen Nickell, a labour market

The rate debate

Case for a rate rise

- Pay growth remains robust. Although headline annual growth in average earnings growth slipped in March from 6 to 5.8 per cent, it is well above the level regarded by the Bank as consistent with meeting the inflation target in the long run.

Average earnings
Headline annual rate %

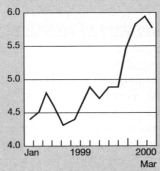

- Service sector output remains robust. And, worryingly, price pressures are rising. Staff shortages will push up the cost of labour and feed through to higher inflation.

Source: Primark Datastream

Case for a no change

- The record-breaking surge in house prices may be running out of steam. Figures from the Nationwide building society show the average price of a house fell last month, for the first time in almost two years. The drop suggests that the boost to consumer spending from housing and market buoyancy will be short-lived.

House prices
Annual % change in Nationwide House Price Index

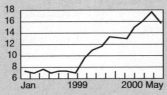

- A surprise fall in retail sales in April, blamed in part on wet weather, suggests consumers may be more cautious. This, combined with a sharp slowdown in final domestic demand growth in the first quarter GDP data, point to slower economic activity.

Domestic demand
% change (quarter on quarter).

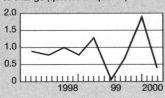

expert from the London School of Economics, vote for the first time after joining the committee last week.

The overall pace of expansion in services slowed slightly, said the survey of purchasing managers. The institute's composite index of activity dipped from April's 59.5 to 59.2. One in three companies reported increased activity.

'Strong corporate and consumer demand are driving growth,' said the institute's Roy Ayliffe.

However, there were signs that recent interest rate rises could damp the pace of expansion. Business confidence eased, for the second month in succession, and is at its lowest level since February last year

Source: Financial Times, 6 June 2000. Reprinted with permission.

Managing the macroeconomy: problems and policies

Learning outcomes

At the end of this chapter you will be able to:
▶ Give a brief overview of the history of UK macroeconomic policy.
▶ Explain the application of fiscal and monetary policy.
▶ Understand most of the coverage of the economy in the media.

Having learned some tools of macroeconomic analysis in the last chapter we will now apply aggregate demand and supply curves to a brief analysis of UK macroeconomic policy in the second half of the twentieth century through to October 2000. To understand events and policy, we will also introduce in passing aspects of *monetary policy* and the effects of changes in international *exchange rates*, the *balance of trade* and the *balance of payments*. All of these areas of economics, including aggregate demand and supply itself, are developed in more depth later in the book.

The good news for you as you begin this important chapter is that even an introductory treatment of macroeconomic analysis can explain a very great deal of the economic events and topics that are daily discussed in the media. Table 18.1 shows the movements of the four macroeconomic objectives discussed in the last chapter over the period, it will be useful to refer occasionally to this table when reading through this chapter.

Although the analysis is kept as simple as possible it covers a great deal of ground and may require several readings, but you will be able to understand and follow most of the macroeconomic coverage in the media.

The major objectives of government policy

Even within political parties, opinions differ as to the most important objectives of policy, but in general terms all governments have pursued similar objectives. Nevertheless, the priority given to the four macroeconomic targets changes with the times as well as with the political persuasion of governments. But the first economic priority after the Second World War was to prevent unemployment returning to the levels of the interwar years of economic depression and we will begin by looking at the unemployment record to illustrate the changing macroeconomy.

The control of unemployment

From 1945 until the 1970s, UK governments appeared to be remarkably successful in achieving near full employment. However, in the mid-1970s and early 1980s unemployment rose to very high levels, peaking at 3.4 million or 12.3 per cent in the early part of 1986. In the late 1980s unemployment fell to under 2 million. However, with the recession in the early 1990s it rose above 3 million once again. Recovery in the mid-1990s meant that unemployment had fallen below 1.5 million by mid-1997. Although this was still high by post-war standards many economists and politicians from the right came to believe that the experience of the 1980s and 1990s simply showed that the natural rate of unemployment was higher than before. But from 1992 to 2000 the unemployment rate has fallen back to the levels of the mid-1970s (refer again to Figure 16.4, page 224).

Table 18.1 **The four macroeconomic objectives**

	Percentage unemployed	Annual change in real GDP	Inflation: percentage change in RPI	Balance of payments: current account (£m)
1950	1.3	3.1	3.1	386
1952	2.2	0.6	9.2	263
1954	1.5	4.4	1.8	194
1956	1.3	1.0	4.9	285
1958	2.2	0.3	3.0	426
1960	1.7	5.3	1.0	−171
1962	2.1	1.3	4.3	241
1964	1.7	5.5	3.3	−260
1966	1.6	1.9	3.9	218
1968	2.5	4.1	4.7	−147
1970	2.6	2.5	6.4	911
1972	2.8	3.5	7.1	344
1974	2.0	−1.7	16.0	−3 179
1976	4.1	2.8	16.6	−727
1978	4.3	3.4	8.3	1 433
1980	5.0	−2.2	18.0	3 166
1982	9.4	1.9	8.6	4 107
1984	10.5	2.3	5.0	1 209
1986	11.0	4.2	3.4	−2 285
1988	7.9	5.1	4.9	−17 537
1990	5.7	0.7	9.5	−19 513
1992	9.6	0.1	3.7	−10 082
1994	9.2	4.4	2.4	−1 458
1996	7.2	2.6	2.4	−600
1998	4.7	2.2	3.4	−80
1999	4.3	2.1	1.5	−10 981

Source: National Statistics. © Crown Copyright 2001

1945 to the early 1970s

Unemployment

All UK governments in this period accepted a responsibility to maintain 'full employment'. This followed the acceptance (finally) of Keynesian theories that predicted that the government could control the level of unemployment through demand management. This 'tuning' of the economy was done mainly through fiscal policy, i.e. adjusting the level of taxation and government expenditure to regulate aggregate demand and thus the volume of output and employment. Monetary policy was geared mainly to keeping interest rates low so as not to discourage investment and to reduce the burden of the government's debt.

Figure 18.1 shows an increase in aggregate demand from AD_1 to AD_2 achieved through increasing government expenditure and/or reducing taxation. We can assume that, *ceteris paribus*, as the output of the economy increases so firms will need more labour and hence employment falls. Thus as Q (the quantity or level of aggregate output) increases along the horizontal axis in Figure 18.1 employment is increasing and unemployment falling. Eventually as output continues to increase a level of output is reached at which there is full employment, this is marked Q_f.

It follows that to the left of Q_f the level of output is insufficient to sustain full employment. All governments of this period believed that the economy could get 'stuck' in an undesirable equilibrium such as Q_{e1} due to insufficient aggregate

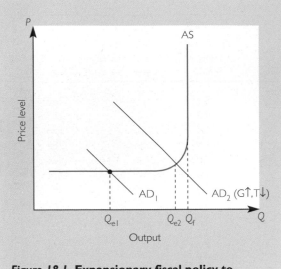

Figure 18.1 Expansionary fiscal policy to increase output and reduce unemployment

demand. The accepted Keynesian prescription was to use fiscal policy to increase aggregate demand to AD_2 thereby moving to a new equilibrium at Q_{e2} nearer full employment.

This may seem too easy to be true, and there were indeed problems which we will turn to in a moment, but Figure 15.1 shows that this policy at least appeared to be very successful in keeping unemployment low. In fact, the overwhelming majority of economists of the time believed that Keynes had provided the policies to maintain a stable equilibrium at, or near, full employment.

What then were the macroeconomic problems of the times? These problems were mainly in the form of a trade-off between high employment and the other macroeconomic targets, in particular the balance of trade and as, the period went on, inflation.

Balance of payments

Problems with the balance of trade tended to set in as aggregate demand was raised to increase employment and deal with unemployment. This is because higher output and more employment meant that incomes rose. As incomes rose so consumers bought more imports and UK firms found it easier to sell in the home market thereby reducing the incentive to export. This often caused the value of imports to exceed the value of exports

and caused a deficit on the *balance of trade* in turn resulting in a deficit on the current account of the balance of payments. Governments committed to free trade resisted putting up barriers to imports (which might have caused other countries to retaliate in any case) and so as a balance of payments crisis developed the only course of action available was to reduce aggregate demand again!

As aggregate demand began to fall again it would relieve the balance of payments problem by reducing incomes and thus imports. However, this falling demand also decreased the consumers' demand for UK goods and this again led to firms laying off workers and hence to rising unemployment. The level of unemployment would then become an embarrassment for the government and so they took action to increase aggregate demand again. This led to what was called the *stop–go cycle* (see Figure 18.2).

Growth

The series of fluctuations described in Figure 18.2 was obviously damaging to economic growth. For example, firms held back investing in the upturns for fear of being caught over extended in the downturn. It must also be the case that if the economy is fluctuating between full and less than full employment, on average the economy is running at below its potential output.

Inflation

Although this was very moderate by what was to follow in the late 1970s and early 1980s, inflation was nevertheless still a macroeconomic target to be kept low. It seemed, however, that as full employment was neared inflation began to set in. There was thus the ever present danger that reducing the rate of unemployment would result in increases in the rate of inflation. Indeed, in 1958 the engineer and economist **Alban Phillips** derived a curve that was interpreted as mapping the trade-off between inflation and unemployment. Such a *Phillips curve* is represented in Figure 18.3.

For politicians, concerned with practical aids to policy making, the Phillips curve seemed to offer a stable 'menu for policy choice'. It seemed that the government could choose a position on

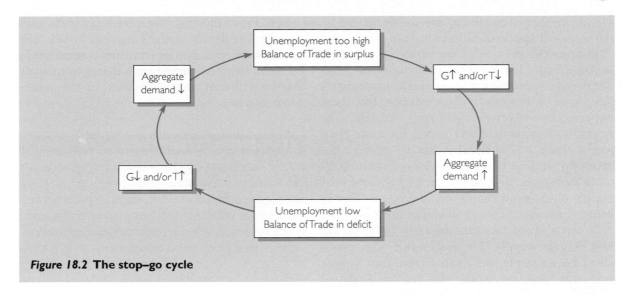

Figure 18.2 **The stop–go cycle**

the curve for a trade-off between the two bads of inflation and unemployment. Note in Figure 18.3 that at high levels of unemployment inflation may be slightly negative (i.e. the price level would be falling) but as full employment is approached the rate of inflation increases sharply. There were several attempts to improve this trade-off by governments directly intervening in the economy to set limits to increases in prices and wages. Such prices and incomes policy prohibited firms from granting wage increases or making price rises above the limits laid down by the government of the day.

These *prices and incomes* policies had varying success but were heavily criticised for over-riding

the freedom of the market and for distorting the price mechanism. They also caused periods of severe industrial and political unrest as unions fought to end such government-imposed limits on wage rises. In any case, by the end of the period the former apparent trade-off appeared to have worsened as both inflation and unemployment began to rise together. Some economists and politicians began to look for an alternative to Keynesian economics.

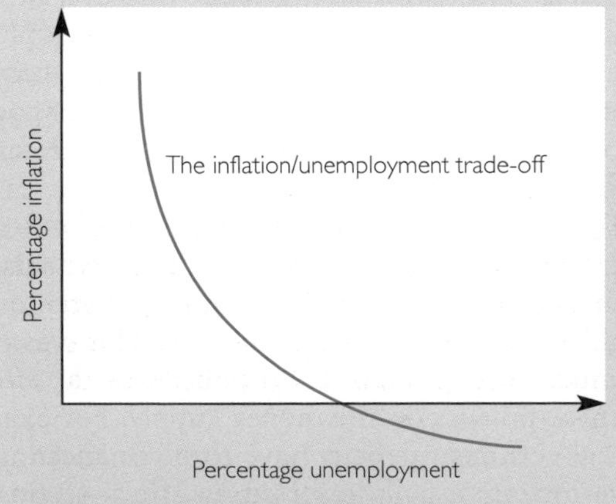

STUDENT ACTIVITY 18.1

Experiment with the shape of the aggregate supply curve to see what shape is most consistent with the Phillips curve shown in Figure 18.3.

1974–1982

The beginning of this period saw rising unemployment and steeply increased inflation. Looking at Table 18.1 you will see that high inflation came to be associated with higher unemployment and a slowing of growth or even a contraction of the economy. The word *stagflation* was coined to describe this combination of stagnant output and high inflation. The 'new' phenomenon of a simultaneous increase in both inflation and unemployment seemed to contradict the trade-off suggested by the Phillips curve. The

Figure 18.3 **The Phillips curve**

old 'menu for policy choice' previously offered by the trade-off appeared to have broken down.

Despite the previous long period of apparent success, this led to the growing view that Keynesian economics was, after all, inadequate. Keynesian economists, however, dispute that these experiences 'disproved' Keynes's theories. For example, Keynes had advocated far more than just a crude use of fiscal policy to manage the economy and he had acknowledged the importance of demand *and* supply. He had concentrated mainly on demand simply because he saw this as being at the root of the problems of his times.

It was also the fact that the early 1970s period saw massive supply side shocks and other problems. For example, the Arab–Israeli Yom Kippur war was won by Israel and led to Arab oil producers using the OPEC cartel (Organisation of Petroleum Exporting Countries) to restrict the output of crude oil. This caused huge increases in the price of oil and its derivatives such as petrol. In 1973–4 oil prices rose fourfold and, after falling back, doubled again in 1979. This was at a time when the economies of Western countries had become very dependent on the use of cheap oil from the Gulf states. The price increases added very substantial costs to producers for the energy and transport they used and as a direct input into many production processes such as plastics.

There was also much industrial unrest in the UK during this period aimed at thwarting the Conservative government's prices and incomes policy. Things came to a head as a miner's strike led to power stations running out of coal and the shortage of electricity putting industry on a three-day week. The Conservative's leader, Prime Minister Edward Heath, called an election to give him the mandate to deal with the powerful National Union of Miners. He lost the election in 1974 and unions emerged strengthened. In 1978–9 there was the 'winter of discontent' when several strikes combined to cause widespread chaos in an attempt to defy the Labour Government's incomes policy. The Labour party then lost the election of 1979 to the Conservatives, led by Mrs Thatcher, who had by then become an ardent supporter of *monetarism.*

On the demand side of the economy, there were changes to the regulation of the banking sector. The Competition and Credit Control (CCC) regulations of 1971 were an important change in

policy. From this date interest rates were supposed to be determined by market forces. The result of the reduction of constraints upon banks led to an unprecedented rise in the money supply that contributed to the inflation of the subsequent years.

STUDENT ACTIVITY 18.2

Show how the supply side changes of high oil prices and poor industrial relations would shift the aggregate supply curve. What would be the effect of this shift on inflation, output and employment? Is this necessarily inconsistent with demand management being a useful tool of economic policy?

Whatever the rights and wrongs concerning the strengths or shortcomings of Keynesian economics, the attention of many economists turned to reviving the pre-Keynesian theories of neo-classical economics. This led to the emergence of modern neo-classical schools of macroeconomics. The first of these schools to make an impact on the previous Keynesian dominance was the *monetarist school* led by **Milton Friedman** from Chicago University (sometimes known as *The Chicago School*). Friedman, in keeping with neo-classical theory, asserted that the free market economy is essentially stable. That is, he argued that the long-run aggregate supply curve is vertical (see previous chapter for an explanation of this).

If the long-run supply curve is vertical, it follows that demand management to reduce unemployment would only cause inflation in the longer term with no long reduction in unemployment. Further, if higher inflation damaged economic performance then the aggregate supply curve may even be backward bending at some higher price levels.

Friedman argued that, although the *long-run* aggregate supply curve is vertical, governments in their futile attempts to fine tune the economy could cause short-term fluctuations. This was not so much through their fiscal policies as the effect of these policies on the money supply. For example, government deficits have to be financed and governments usually resorted, in effect, to financing deficits by 'printing money' (in Chapter 35 you will see that it's not necessary to actually print money in order to create more of it, but its easier to think of it in this way for the present). For monetarists it was this expansion of the money supply that was the root cause of inflation.

The monetarists see changes in the money supply as the main determinant of aggregate demand. Hence the name 'monetarist' was given to contrast with Keynesian economists who were often called **Fiscalists**, especially in the US. The monetarists argued that a government budget deficit only increased aggregate demand through increasing the money supply.

Although they argued that the long-run aggregate supply curve is vertical, monetarists did accept that an increase in aggregate demand could temporarily raise output and lower unemployment. But they put forward the following arguments against doing this:

(a) Any benefits from reduced unemployment from demand side boosts are short-lived and at the expense of longer term damage to the economy from higher inflation.

(b) Governments cannot accurately predict the course of the economy and it takes time to implement government policies. Thus there is no guarantee that when demand management takes effect the economy is in the same condition as when the policy was formulated. Thus demand management could exacerbate fluctuations in the economy rather than smooth them.

(c) Boosting aggregate demand may appear to improve the functioning of the economy but this is before the longer term undesirable effects show up. Thus political parties in government may unscrupulously increase aggregate demand before elections in order to fool the electorate into thinking that there had been real long-term improvements. Such a temptation for political parties in power could cause *electoral business cycle* fluctuations for the economy.

(d) Neo-classical economists place much less emphasis on the existence of involuntary unemployment than do Keynesian economists. For neo-classical economists, apart from the effects of unions in particular markets, unemployment is largely voluntary (see Chapter 39). For example, people may be unemployed because they are looking for a

better wage than the jobs that they have so far found on offer. If inflation acts upon both wages and prices these workers are likely to think that the higher wages now on offer match the levels they were looking for. They therefore accept a job only to realise later that prices have also increased. When they realise that the real wage is not that which they sought, they drop back to being unemployed to resume their search. Thus the reduction in unemployment was the result of *money illusion* fooling people into taking jobs they would not have otherwise accepted.

In neo-classical macroeconomic schools, such as monetarism, demand management to reduce unemployment is neither necessary nor desirable.

Freidman's short-run Phillips curve

Money illusion was used by **Friedman** to explain why an unexpected boost to aggregate demand might temporarily raise output and raise employment/lower unemployment. This is shown in Figure 18.4. But as the money illusion caused by an unexpected increase in inflation wears off, i.e. people's expectations adapt to the higher level of prices, the economy returns to its natural equilibrium.

STUDENT ACTIVITY 18.3

Use this process of expectations adapting to inflation to show what would happen if governments persistently tried to lower unemployment below its natural level. What would happen if after several years of doing this the government suddenly reduced aggregate demand and brought inflation back more or less to its starting point?

Neo-classical macroeconomics and the *laissez-faire* tradition

Monetarists revived many of the old traditions of *laissez-faire*. Instead of governments actively manipulating aggregate demand to maintain full employment, monetarists argued that governments should leave the economy to reach its

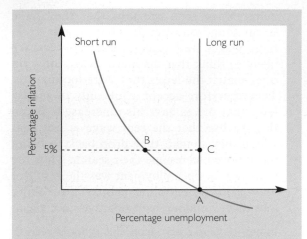

Figure 18.4 Friedman's short-run Phillips curve
The government increases aggregate demand and inflation rises from −0 to 5 per cent. Workers are fooled by rising wages and accept job offers previously rejected. When the money illusion wears off, the inflation is anticipated and workers resume their search for higher real wages from B to C.

natural equilibrium. Equally, they argued, the demand and supply of exports and imports would cause exchange rates to adjust to maintain an equilibrium on the balance of trade. Indeed, for monetarists, demand and supply would work efficiently through the whole economy taking the macroeconomy to a point on the production possibility frontier corresponding to the natural rates of output and unemployment.

For neo-classical economists, the 'natural' levels of output and employment/unemployment are reached through the voluntary choices of millions of economic agents responding to the real constraints of economic scarcity.

Instead of active demand management, monetarists emphasised that governments should maintain a stable economic environment and not interfere with the natural workings of the economy. **Milton Friedman** from the Chicago School and **Freidrich von Hayek** of the Austrian School were the intellectual champions of this resurrection of the pre-Keynesian *laissez-faire* beliefs. They both emphasised free markets as the best method of coordinating the allocation and utilisation of resources. Friedman and Hayek differed

greatly in their approaches to economics, but both combined a strong belief in the superiority of free markets with a liberal philosophy that political freedoms and *laissez-faire* economics go hand in hand. Both scorned the governments of the Keynesian era as having meddled with free choice to the detriment of economic performance.

As monetarists blamed fluctuations in the money supply for fluctuations and instability, they also advocated that policy makers should follow pre-set rules that did not allow for such discretion to alter the amount of money in the economy. Instead of governments using their discretion to alter economic policy in response to the trends of the economy, monetarists argued for non-discretionary policy rules that would not be deviated from because of short-term concerns. A pre-set target rate of expansion of the money supply would then determine the rate of inflation, and then employment and growth could find their own 'natural' levels.

Margaret Thatcher and the monetarists

The Labour government of the late 1970s was in fact influenced by monetarism, but it was the election of the Conservative government under Mrs Thatcher in 1979 that led to the explicit adoption of monetarism as the mainstay of UK macroeconomic policy. Despite strong objections at the time from the majority of UK economists, who feared massive increases in unemployment, Mrs Thatcher's government made the substantial reduction of inflation the immediate and prime target of government policy. Acting on the demand side of the economy, in the medium term, she intended to establish a non-inflationary economic environment in which businesses and the market economy could thrive. Her government adhered to the advice of monetarists and specified a pre-set series of diminishing targets for the rate of growth of money in the economy. This strict policy to reduce inflation was laid out in what was called the Government's *Medium Term Financial Strategy* (MTFS).

It was announced that the primary purpose of the MTFS was to reduce inflation and that this would be done by progressively constraining the growth of the money supply. In contrast to the previous era of active demand management where the government used its discretion in the light of changes in the four macroeconomic objectives, the diminishing targets for the rate of growth of the money supply specified in the MTFS were not to be deviated from. Indeed, to assist the adjustment of expectations to a lower rate of inflation, Mrs Thatcher boasted that her government would not be moved from these targets come what may. She was often called the 'Iron Lady' by her critics as well as by her admirers.

Accepting Friedman's assertion that the main cause of excessive money supply growth was the government's own budget deficit, Mrs Thatcher's government attempted to reduce the *Public Sector Borrowing Requirement* (PBSR) (now known as the *Public Sector Net Cash Requirement* or PSNCR). Roughly speaking, the PSBR is the difference between the expenditure of the public sector and the revenues it collects by way of taxation, for our purposes here we can regard it as G minus T in our model. As a right-wing politician, Mrs Thatcher rejected raising taxation as a means of reducing the need for government borrowing, and so her government set out significantly to reduce public expenditure (i.e. the spending of the state/public sector).

Mrs Thatcher also turned her attention to, in effect, shifting the aggregate supply curve to the right. The following measures were expected to improve the supply side of the economy:

(a) The reduced borrowing of the public sector would free more investment funds for the private sector; it was argued that less private sector investment would be *crowded-out* by the government's own demand for funds and resources. This increase in productive investment would in turn increase the productive capacity of the economy thereby increasing aggregate supply.

(b) It was believed that lower taxation and restrictions on unemployment benefits would increase the incentive to work and thereby increase the supply of labour and so shift the aggregate supply curve to the right.

(c) It was argued that inflation made it harder to read the signals provided by the price mechanism that are essential to its efficient functioning. By reducing the distortion of market signals, it was believed that lower inflation would increase economic growth. Thus again shifting the aggregate supply curve to the right over the longer term.

(d) In addition to all this, Mrs Thatcher's government acted to reduce union power through legislation and adopted a very unyielding stance towards striking public sector workers. This was intended to reduce inflation and unemployment and provide more freedom for entrepreneurial decision making.

STUDENT ACTIVITY 18.4

Use aggregate demand and supply analysis to show how Mrs Thatcher's government's policy was meant to work in reducing inflation and increasing growth over the medium term. (To make this easier, assume that a reduction in the price level represents a reduction in the rate of inflation.)

Monetary policy

Monetary policy is the direction of the economy through the supply and price of money.

What does the term 'the supply of money' mean? First, it is important to realise that money is not just notes and coins, in fact money is mainly in the form of bank and building society deposits which are used to finance transactions.

Money can be defined as anything which is readily acceptable as a means of payment or in settlement of debt.

You will not be surprised to know that by far the largest percentage of spending is actually transacted through the transfer of deposits held in financial institutions such as banks and building societies. When cheques are drawn or credit cards used, these deposits are transferred as debts between financial institutions and do not necessarily involve the transport of actual notes and coin.

The slippery supply of money

To non-economists, it usually seems obvious what money is. But as is explained in detail in Chapter 35, money is not a straightforward commodity at all and hence controlling its supply proved to be far more difficult than expected.

Why was it so difficult to control the money supply? In a developed financial sector, there are very many different types of accounts, deposits and other financial instruments and hence very many different ways of measuring money. Also, there are very many ways for financial institutions to lend. When a financial institution extends new credit to its customers, it is creating new money as the borrower can use this newly created deposit to purchase goods and services. Indeed, if financial institutions wish to lend and their customers wish to borrow then it is in fact very difficult for a government to control this. There are, however, several methods by which a government can attempt to control the supply of new credit from financial institutions. Controlling credit restricts the growth of new deposits and hence the money supply.

For example, we saw that the MTFS involved attempts to reduce the PSBR and hence prevent the injection of money into the economy that occurs when the government is forced to create new money. This happens when the government 'borrows' new money from the *Bank of England* to finance its deficit. Now, the Bank of England is the UK's *central bank* and the role of a central bank in an economy is crucial in relation to the functioning of its financial sector. Hence, the most direct method of constraining the growth of money is for the central bank to raise the prevailing rate of interest in order to discourage the growth of borrowing. Indeed this was the main instrument used in the shorter term to control monetary growth.

Why does a rise in the interest rate constrain the growth of the aggregate amount of money in the economy? The interest rate is the price of money; it is what must be paid to borrow someone else's money for a period. For example, if the interest rate is 10 per cent per year and you borrowed £100, at the end of the year you would owe £110 to the lender. Less obviously, it is also the opportunity cost of holding money in ways that do not earn interest. Thus if the interest rate is raised by the central bank less borrowing is demanded by consumers and less for investment in capital by firms, the ability of financial institutions to supply new money is thereby reduced

and this constrains the growth of the amount of money in the economy.

The precise mechanism whereby a rise in the rate of interest set by the Bank of England works through to a general rise in interest rates is more complicated than we need to understand for this chapter, but an outline may be helpful: although financial institutions can in fact create new money in the form of deposits they cannot do this without limit. For example, if a commercial bank creates too many new deposits it would be in danger of more people wishing to take money out of its deposits than is being put in. If a major bank could not meet its debts and went bankrupt this would be a disaster for the financial system and would have severe knock-on effects for the rest of the economy. The Bank of England therefore stands by to provide money to the banking sector, in particular to those financial institutions that specialise in volatile short-term lending and are thus most exposed. To cover for this eventuality these specialist finance institutions will raise the interest rate at which they lend and this then works through to all interest rates.

Did the monetarist experiment work?

Looking at Table 18.1 we can see that after rising sharply at first, inflation fell from 19 per cent in 1979 to 3.4 by 1986. For many, this achievement and the greater reliance on market forces together with reducing the role of the state and unions set the foundation for subsequent improved growth. But did the experiment work as anticipated by the monetarists?

As with the earlier apparent success of the Keynesian era, alternative explanations can be offered. For example, as was predicted by Keynesian economists (notably **Nicholas Kaldor** of Cambridge University), in most years of the monetarist experiment the actual rate of growth of the money supply exceeded the targets laid down by the MTFS. Also, as predicted by the Keynesians, rather than a short term peak in unemployment as expectations adjusted to decreased inflation, unemployment rose massively to numbers not seen since the great depression of the interwar years. In worst hit areas the economies of whole communities were destroyed. One fifth of the UK's manufacturing output disappeared within two years. By January 1981 the economy had plummeted to the worst post-war slump in Britain. For the next twenty years the percentage of the workforce unemployed was to stay very high by previous standards.

The importance of the exchange rate

The *exchange rate*, i.e. the rate of exchange between international currencies affects the prices of exports and imports and hence the current account on the balance of payments (this is explained below). Throughout the 1950s and 1960s the pound was 'pegged' to the dollar, i.e. its price was fixed against the dollar. This lack of price flexibility meant that the pound could not freely adjust to restore a balance between exports and imports. Thus, as we have seen, in the long Keynesian era increases in aggregate demand would suck in imports and cause a current account deficit that could only be corrected by reducing aggregate demand again.

In 1972 the fixed exchange rate was abandoned and this allowed the exchange rate to adjust thereby making it easier to expand the economy without running into a current account deficit on the balance of payments. But *floating exchange rates* brought a different set of problems. In fact, to fully understand why unemployment doubled between 1979 and 1982 it is necessary to trace the following chain of causation involving the exchange rate.

(a) In an attempt to restrain the growth of money in the economy the Conservative government raised interest rates.
(b) The high interest rate caused the pound sterling to 'strengthen' against other currencies, i.e. the exchange rate went up as the pound became worth more in terms of other currencies.
(c) The increase in the exchange rate made UK exports uncompetitive on the world market.

The first step in this train of events has already been explained: despite the determination to stay within the announced monetary targets, Mrs Thatcher's government was failing to achieve this. To curtail the growth in the amount of money interest rates were increased to record levels. But why does this cause the second step whereby an increase in interest rates leads to an increase in the pound sterling's exchange rate?

To understand the effect of the interest rate on the exchange rate we can again turn to demand and supply analysis. The exchange rate can be thought of as the price of a nation's currency. If the pound strengthens against other currencies the UK exchange rate is said to have increased. This is because it now takes more of a foreign currency to buy a pound on the world's currency markets. As the exchange rate is the price of a pound the demand and supply of pounds on the world's international currency markets determines this price.

In the previous chapter, we saw that the balance of payments included not only flows of exports and imports on the current account but also flows of investment and finance. All of these flows cause changes in the supply of and demand for pounds.

For example, in order to buy imports from the US, pounds must be sold to buy the US dollars necessary to pay the US exporters. Equally, pounds will be sold in order to pay for investment in the US or to buy US financial assets. Thus pounds are being supplied on the world's currency markets in order to buy dollars.

A supply of pounds to the world's currency markets is caused by imports to the UK and UK investment and finance flows to other countries.

Conversely when exports of goods and services or financial assets are sold by the UK to other countries, or other countries invest in the UK, foreigners must obtain pounds to pay for this.

Exports from the UK and investment and finance flows into the UK cause a demand for pounds on the world's currency markets.

Figure 18.5 shows a supply and demand curve for pounds. As usual the horizontal axis shows the quantity, in this case the number of pounds supplied and demanded. The vertical axis is the price of pounds in terms of other currencies, you can think of it as dollars or some other currency if you wish. A 'strengthening' of the pound against other currencies thus describes an increase or appreciation in the exchange rate.

We can now return to our question, why did the increase in UK interest rates cause an increase

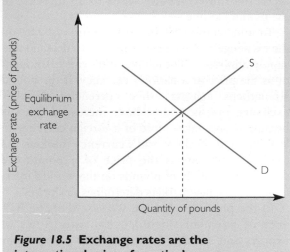

Figure 18.5 Exchange rates are the international price of a nation's currency

in the pound's exchange rate? The reason lies chiefly in the vast flows of money around the world seeking the highest interest rate. If UK interest rates become higher than elsewhere, financial investors will take their money out of financial investments in other countries in order to buy UK financial assets and deposits so as to take advantage of the higher UK interest rate. This inward flow of financial capital thus increases the demand for pounds. As is shown in Figure 18.6 this caused a sharp appreciation of the exchange rate.

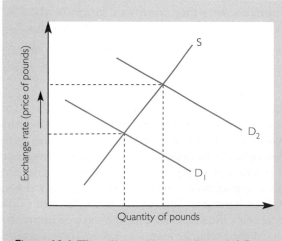

Figure 18.6 The effect of inward financial flows on the exchange rate

It is now quite simple to explain the last step in the chain of causation from high UK interest rates to a decrease in UK exports. Suppose a UK car costs £100 in the UK and the exchange rate is one pound to the dollar, i.e. £1 buys $1. Ignoring shipping costs etc., we can also say that the car costs $100. Now if the pound strengthens against the dollar, in other words the exchange rate appreciates to, say, £1 = $2, the cost of the UK car in the US doubles to $200. Similarly, as the exchange rate appreciates against other currencies the price of UK exports in those countries becomes uncompetitive and hence the demand for UK exports contracts.

● *Common misunderstanding*

Although an increase in the exchange rate means that pounds will buy more in other countries, a 'strengthening' of the pound is not necessarily a good thing for the UK.

Hence, in the early 1980s aggregate demand was constrained by the effect on consumption and investment of record high interest rates, the decreased demand for UK exports due to the high pound and the tight fiscal stance being maintained to control the PSBR. There was thus a fall in real GDP for the first time since the oil shock of the early 1970s.

Dutch disease, North Sea oil and the collapse of UK manufacturing

Obviously the macroeconomic objective of growth was badly affected in the early 1980s, but from Table 18.1 it can be seen that another objective, that of the current account of the balance of payments, was in substantial surplus despite the uncompetitiveness of UK exports. What were the reasons for this? The first reason was that the fall in domestic demand reduced in turn the demand for imports. The second reason was the coming on stream of UK-produced oil from the North Sea.

Although the export of North Sea oil compensated for the weakness of other UK exports and brought a surplus on the current account, it actually added to the problems of other UK exporters. It should be clear by now why the export of oil from the UK caused an increase in the demand for pounds from foreign importers. This increased demand for pounds added to the appreciation of the exchange rate shown in Figure 18.6. But again this appreciation of the exchange rate damaged other industries that were previously large exporters, one might say that they were 'crowded-out' by the flow of North Sea oil's effect on the exchange rate. This was named the *Dutch disease* (as the discovery of natural gas had once had a similar impact on Holland's economy in the 1950s.)

As services may involve personal contact and are therefore often more difficult to export or import, it is manufactured goods that are particularly exposed to changes in the exchange rate. There was already a long-term decline in manufacturing as a percentage of UK economic activity, but the combination of falling domestic demand from the monetarist experiment, high interest rates and Dutch disease led to a 'collapse' of UK manufacturing. In just the two years from 1979 to 1981 UK manufacturing output fell by one-fifth with a loss of almost one-quarter of manufacturing employment.

Postscript to the monetarist experiment

Monetary targets had been found to be impractical and were subsequently abandoned but the monetarist experiment seemed to have considerable success in reducing inflation. It could be argued, however, that this reduction was simply due to throwing the economy into recession rather than any success for monetarist economics.

Another objective, the current account on the balance of payments, was held in surplus by North Sea oil. But the revenues from North Sea oil disguised the massive import penetration of many of the UK's markets. Growth was also badly affected by the contraction of the economy and a fall in industrial investment. Of most direct effect for the welfare of those affected, unemployment rose to levels unprecedented since the great depression and brought much misery.

The experiment had not seemed to have worked as had been predicted by monetarist economic theory. The monetarists defended themselves by claiming that it had not been a proper monetarist experiment as the money supply had not been

controlled. Many on the right of politics nevertheless claimed it had been the unpleasant tasting 'medicine' that laid the foundation for subsequent improved economic growth. For example, the struggle to reduce the power of the trade unions was to culminate in a bitter year-long struggle with the powerful National Union of Miners. The strike ended in March 1985 this time with the defeat of the NUM. The number of strikes subsequently fell to a record low. There was also high growth by previous standards in the second half of the 1980s and it was claimed that this justified the earlier tough policies to reduce inflation, but, as shall see now, this growth was short lived.

1982–1996

The failure to meet monetary targets led to less reliance being placed on the monetarist prescription that governments should concentrate economic policy almost entirely on controlling the growth of the money supply. Concern at the continuing high unemployment had also shifted the emphasis away from regarding inflation as the single most important objective of policy. Hence a reduction in interest rates and a less contractionary fiscal stance led to some economic recovery at the beginning of this period.

With the recovery unemployment at last began to fall, but it also brought increased inflation. Previous attempts to control inflation through monetary measures had clearly brought severe problems. Instead, policy turned away from monetary targets to targeting the exchange rate as a means of controlling inflation. A high exchange rate acted to lower inflation by keeping import costs low and this both lowered the costs of inputs to UK industry and increased price competition for UK goods. Reduced costs and price competition from imports encouraged producers to avoid increasing the price of their products.

Whereas the government, through the Bank of England, had previously manipulated interest rates in an attempt to restrict monetary growth and inflation, it was now using interest policy to control the exchange rate as a means of keeping inflation down and avoiding damaging fluctuations in the value of the pound. But as the recovery continued into the mid-1980s consumer confidence rose and increasing house prices gave households collateral to secure new loans. The Conservative Chancellor of the Exchequer, Nigel Lawson, further added to the ability of households to spend by reducing income tax. Then in 1987 share prices around the world crashed, and, fearing that a loss of confidence could lead to a recession, monetary policy was further relaxed. The anticipated recession did not materialise and the combination of factors stoking aggregate demand led to severe 'overheating' of the economy – now known as the 'Lawson Boom'.

These increases in spending and expansionary policies had led to increased domestic demand that turned recovery into a dangerous economic boom. As inflation began to rise sharply and the balance of payments on current account reached record deficits the government was forced to act, it again used interest policy to squeeze out excess demand through raising interest rates. This worked by discouraging consumption and bringing down house price rises from over 30 per cent per year to minus figures within a year. Inevitably, unemployment began to rise again and the government needed to find a credible macroeconomic policy.

In October 1990 the UK joined the *European Exchange Rate Mechanism* (ERM). In this arrangement certain European Community countries were meant to act together to keep their exchange rates within agreed bands of permitted fluctuations. The UK Government's hope was that membership of the ERM would assist in maintaining confidence in the pound. This would mean that holders of pounds would be less worried about sudden changes in the pound's exchange rate and therefore more willing to hold pounds. This in turn should allow interest rates to be set lower without causing a fall in the exchange rate which could set off inflation. Nevertheless, the main day to day instrument to maintain the agreed UK exchange rate was again the use of interest rate policy.

Partly because of her opposition to closer UK ties with the European Union, Mrs Thatcher's euroscepticism was becoming incompatible with the new policy. The Conservative Party voted Mrs Thatcher out as their leader and John Major was voted in as the new leader and hence Prime Minister, but again economic policy did not work out quite as planned. Many observers had felt that the UK had entered the ERM at too high an exchange rate against the other ERM currencies, certainly towards the end of 1992 there was a widespread belief that the pound was going to fall below its agreed exchange rate.

Currency speculators therefore began to sell their holdings of pounds in massive amounts. They could not lose; if the pound did not fall then they were no worse off, if it did fall they would have avoided losses and could buy more pounds than before, once the price had fallen. Faced with the massive financial flows out of pounds the government was reduced to relying on its single policy instrument of manipulating the interest rate to maintain the exchange rate. This proved insufficient, as Mrs Thatcher reminded her party 'You can't buck the market'. Despite very large increases in short-term interest rates, and massive selling of UK gold and foreign currency reserves to buy pounds by the Bank of England, the downward market pressure on the pound forced the UK to leave the ERM. The pound was thus allowed to fall to a more realistic exchange rate.

With the UK out of the ERM the government had suddenly lost its macroeconomic policy. Moreover, it feared that the very steep fall in the exchange rate as the pound left the ERM would set off new inflationary price rises through increased import costs. This fear was added to by the PSBR rising to record levels as unemployment rose – thereby simultaneously reducing the revenue from the income tax take and increasing welfare payments. The lesson seemed to be that single instrument approaches to macroeconomic policy such as manipulating the interest rate, and inflexible monetary or exchange rate targets, were insufficient for effective macroeconomic management.

During the ERM period there was an unresolved conflict caused by using the interest rate as the sole instrument of policy: a high interest rate was needed to hold up the exchange rate but a low interest rate was needed to stimulate consumption and investment to deal with the recession. Hence, attention turned again to a wider set of policy instruments. Also, for the first time, inflation itself was given an explicit target.

The final years of the seventeen years of Conservative government since 1979, were dominated by a concern for 'sound public finances'. This was driven by the alarming increase in the PSBR that had continued to climb from minus borrowing (i.e. the government was repaying public debt – PSDR) in the late 1980s to peak at some £50bn in 1993. The new Chancellor, Kenneth Clarke, emphasised long-term goals and that the job of government was simply to pursue stability through controlling inflation, this would create a 'benign' economic environment where the usual risks of business were not added to by sharp macroeconomic changes.

1997 onwards

In May 1997 Tony Blair's New Labour Party won the election. Strong commitments had been given in the build-up to the election not to increase taxation and this prevented increasing income tax to reduce the PSBR, which had been falling but was still high. The Labour government therefore confirmed that it would stick to the previous government's expenditure targets in order to continue to bring down the PSBR/PSNCR. In the event, stronger than expected growth from 1997 to 1998 and a rapid fall in unemployment quickly turned the PSBR back into a PSDR (Public Sector Debt Repayment).

In the same month that Labour won power, the new Chancellor of the Exchequer, Gordon Brown, announced that the government was giving up its right to set interest rates by giving operational independence to the Bank of England. Decisions on interest rates were to be taken by a *Monetary Policy Committee* (MPC) chaired by Eddie George, the Governor of the Bank of England. The Chancellor of the Exchequer laid down a target for inflation of $2\frac{1}{2}$ per cent and the job of the MPC is to set interest rates so as to achieve this.

The New Labour government has not returned to the use of fiscal policy for discretionary Keynesian type demand management. Instead it has committed itself to following a 'golden rule' for public finances. This is a rule whereby public sector receipts cover all public sector 'current expenditure' (i.e. administration, welfare benefits and public sector wages) over the economic cycle. Public sector investment (e.g. roads and schools) is exempted from this zero borrowing rule as it may contribute towards economic growth.

Keynesian policy in the first period we looked at relied on the government using its discretion to respond appropriately to economic change by altering economic policy. It is thus clear that the New Labour government has not returned to discretionary policy; with monetary policy given over to an independent MPC charged with meeting a pre-set inflation target, and with fiscal policy tied to a golden rule, there now seems little scope for discretionary demand management. Gordon Brown has emphasised that 'This Government will not return to short-termism and the damaging cycles of boom and bust'.

Keynesians today largely accept that fine-tuning the economy is impractical, but they point out that the danger with set rules is that they may become inappropriate when economic circumstances change unexpectedly. This was the criticism of the monetarist experiment, i.e. an inflexibility of policy allowed an unacceptably deep recession. So far the Labour government's policy rules appear to have had considerable success, but perhaps they have just built on the foundations laid by Kenneth Clarke? Alternatively, the current period may reflect external factors such as the long period of growth in the US (see below). Nevertheless, growth and inflation have been on target and unemployment has fallen to levels not seen since before Mrs Thatcher's government. The real test of this government's policy rules will come if the course of the economy begins to give cause for concern.

At the time of writing, October 2000, the balance of trade is being pulled into deficit as the export of goods fails to keep up with imports, and there are other danger signs. For example, OPEC is again presiding over substantial increases in the price of oil which is in turn pushing up firms' costs – and there is renewed Arab–Israeli conflict. Company indebtedness has been increasing and business confidence falling a little, and investment growth is weakening. The

Chancellor has announced he will now use the surplus built up on the public finances to fund substantial new amounts of public spending. Some observers are saying this could spark off inflation. It is hoped that the UK economy will continue its recent pattern of low unemployment, low inflation and steady growth, by the time that you read this you will know whether the self-righting forces of the economy have avoided the need to depart from set policy rules.

International interdependence and 'globalisation'

The danger of the analysis so far is that it may give the impression that all changes in the economy reflect changes in UK government policy or purely domestic trends, i.e. forces internal to the national economy. Indeed, the electorate in democracies do often associate economic success or failures with the incumbent government. Perhaps increasingly, however, it is clear that in economic terms countries are not wholly their own masters but are also affected by powerful international economic forces and events.

Figure 18.7 tracks the recent paths of GDP growth for the 'G7' countries; if you study this chart you will see that even the world's largest economies often tend to move together. This, of course, is not the whole story and countries are also subject to forces, internal and/or external, which affect them in particular and so they change position in the growth league or even move in an opposite direction to the overall trend. Japan, for example, has often topped the G7 growth rates but in the late 1990s was suffering from a severe recession while other G7 countries were enjoying steady growth.

Nevertheless, despite the differences between these economies at any one time, Figure 18.7 clearly shows that there is also much interdependence and suggests that there are common causes for these mutual trends.

National economic trends often reflect international trends

The main international 'transmission mechanisms' that cause economies to be so interdependent are (a) international trade, (b) international financial movements and (c) the foreign direct investment practices of multinational companies

The volume of trade and financial movements between nations grew in magnitude in the latter half of the twentieth century to the extent that some

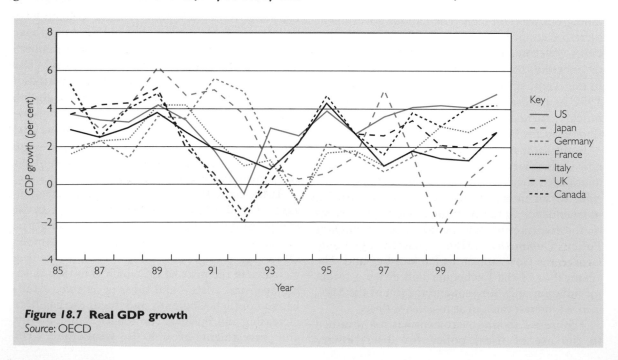

Figure 18.7 Real GDP growth
Source: OECD

economists and many politicians now call this process 'globalisation'.

In its extreme version globalisation is portrayed as a world capitalism that has grown beyond the control of nation states. Governments across the world are seen as powerless to counter the global economic forces, which may at times favour their economies and at other times be disadvantageous. Many economists reject this extreme and point out that international interdependence is not new and that the formation of major trading blocs, cooperation between the larger economies and the formation of national policies that take account of global interdependence could control these powerful global economic forces. We will now look at these international forces in more detail.

Trade

International trade has grown faster than the real GDP of OECD countries and hence these economies have become more 'open', i.e. international trade has grown as a proportion of these countries' national income and hence changes in the level of trade have a bigger influence on domestic economies. In fact, as you will see in Chapter 42, the UK has been a particularly open economy for longer than most, but the extent to which growing international interdependence exacerbates fluctuations in trade means the UK is also more subject to changes than before.

Looking at the categories for expenditure in GDP again:

$$Y = C + I + G + X - M$$

we can see that if exports fall this will tend to reduce aggregate demand. Also this is likely to cause a trade deficit unless domestic demand is also reduced. Falling exports and attempts to control the balance of trade are likely to reduce GDP. But of course, as one nation's GDP falls so will its consumption, and part of this consumption consists of imports from other countries. It is easy to see how this could result in a vicious cycle of falling trade reducing GDPs across the world leading to further reductions in trade and so on. Indeed, some writers (such as **Micklethwait** and

Wooldridge in their book *A Future Perfect*) argue that the world was more globalised 100 years ago but that trade and capital flows were then greatly reduced from 1918 by protectionist trade policies and nationalistic capital controls.

Financial flows and foreign direct investment

OECD export volume has grown at 6 per cent per year for the last 20 years and output by 3 per cent, but financial flows have grown much faster than either and today well over a trillion dollars of assets are traded each day in foreign exchange markets. As explained above, much of this huge financial flow is of 'footloose' or 'hot' monies seeking the highest available interest rate and having no allegiance to any particular country. Its owners move this hot money in an instant from one country to another through modern foreign exchange markets and by switching between holding deposits in foreign banks.

Thus if one country raises its interest rates, relative to that of other countries, there will be a large inflow of funds to that country. This will cause its exchange rate to appreciate and those of other countries experiencing an outflow of funds to depreciate. As funds become scarcer in other countries this may drive up their interest rates also, but in any case it is unlikely that other countries will be prepared to accept the effects of the outflow of funds and so are likely to retaliate by raising their own interest rates. As with falls in trade there is a danger that the uncoordinated policies of countries result in a vicious cycle of beggar my neighbour policies causing worldwide depression.

The growth of multinational or transnational companies has also been seen as a challenge to the sovereignty of nation states. Quite simply, if a globalised company does not like the domestic policies of any particular country it may stop investing in it. For example, it may dislike the domestic union laws, levels of corporate taxation or whether that country should or should not be part of trading blocs such as the European Union. As such Foreign Direct Investment (FDI) can account for jobs in an area and boost the domestic economy governments may take this into account when setting domestic policy.

Conclusion

This chapter has given an overview of the development of macroeconomic management policies since the Second World War. Policies have changed according to developments in the actual economy and as economists produce new explanations of these developments. It has always been difficult to simultaneously achieve satisfactory levels for all four of the macroeconomic targets but this is now made even harder by high levels of international interdependence. The Labour Chancellor of the Exchequer, Gordon Brown, has placed the same emphasis on stability and the control of inflation as did his predecessor, the Conservative Chancellor, Kenneth Clarke. Since 1992 the performance of the UK economy has been remarkably solid and Gordon Brown has underlined the pursuit of long-term stability by giving independence to the Bank of England to achieve the inflation target. There are some danger signs, however, and the extent to which global economic forces create disadvantageous trends may depend very much on how willing and able the major economies of the world are to coordinate their economic policies.

Summary

1 After the Second World War there followed a long period in which Keynesian policy dominated economics and government macroeconomic policy.

2 Increasingly it became difficult simultaneously to achieve full employment, satisfactory balance of payments and level of inflation. Prices and incomes policies led to industrial unrest and did not seem to control inflation in the long run.

3 In the early 1970s economic trends and events made Keynesian economics seem less relevant. Monetarists were arguing that the sole cause of inflation was excessive growth of the money supply and that demand management to control unemployment is unnecessary.

4 The monetarist experiment of Mrs Thatcher's Government failed to meet the monetary targets of the Medium Term Financial Strategy but eventually saw inflation fall. This may have had more to do with economic recession than monetarist theory.

5 Monetary policy has shifted from attempts to control the money supply to using the Bank of England's influence on interest rates to act on the demand for money.

6 A rise in the exchange rate will, *ceteris paribus*, reduce inflation by lowering import prices and increasing price competition for exports.

7 The UK was forced to leave the ERM but the emphasis on controlling inflation as the long-term guarantor of growth and lower unemployment has remained. This is easier now that the interest rate does not have to control both inflation and maintain a fixed exchange rate.

8 Both the current Chancellor and his predecessor have emphasised long-term economic stability over active short-term economic management.

9 The handing over, to the Bank of England's Monetary Policy Committee, of operational independence to take decisions on interest rates is a marked reduction in the government's discretionary economic power.

10 The future for the UK economy depends not just on domestic policy but also on international economic trends and events.

? QUESTIONS

1 Describe how fiscal policy might be used to reduce unemployment.

2 Why is it often difficult to achieve simultaneously satisfactory levels for the four main economic policy targets?

3 What events and economic trends in the 1970s led to a revival for neo-classical macroeconomics?

4 Monetarists accepted that governments could temporarily reduce unemployment. How does this occur in monetarist models and why is it not desirable to do so in such models?

5 Evaluate the success or otherwise of the monetarist experiment.

6 Describe the link between interest rates and the exchange rate. What are the problems in trying to use interest rates alone to control inflation, the exchange rate and unemployment?

7 Why does stability and economic growth in the rest of the world benefit the UK and what are the dangers of uncoordinated policies across the nations of the world?

8 Refer to the National Statistics web site (*www.statistics.gov.uk*) to see what has been happening since this chapter was written. Describe and explain the recent course of the economy.

Data response A
MACRO HEAVEN?

Read the following article by Christopher Adams from the *Financial Times* of 22 September 2000, then answer the questions that follow.

1 Explain why increases in share prices and house prices can lead to consumer expenditure 'bubbling' over.
2 Describe how the Bank of England can reduce inflation through raising interest rates. Why does

the author write that 'If the inflationary support of a highly-valued currency is removed, the Bank of England will face possibly its toughest test since independence in 1997?'
3 List and explain the dangers mentioned in the article that could end the current long period of UK uninterrupted growth and rising employment.
4 Why is economic convergence so important for countries wishing to share a common currency?

UK glories in seventh heaven

Several more years of robust expansion are predicted but the recent decline in sterling could pose new inflationary threats. By **Christopher Adams,** Economics Correspondent

Since emerging from one of the worst recessions in living memory in 1992, the British economy has enjoyed seven years of uninterrupted growth and rising employment.

In a glowing report published in June, the Organisation for Economic Co-operation and Development (OECD) said that UK's performance over the past two years had been 'enviable'. Not only had Britain avoided recession, but the danger of a consumer boom had been recognised, it said.

Twelve months ago, the economy was at risk of a consumer boom. Fuelled by rising share prices and house prices, personal wealth was rising fast. Unemployment continued to decline and wages grew strongly.

The result was a surge in borrowing and a collapse in saving to levels not seen since the end of the last big spending boom in the 1980s. Consumer expenditure was about to bubble over.

The Bank of England, however, reacted swiftly. Since September

last year, interest rate rises have dampened demand and house prices have come off the boil.

Output growth, which had accelerated sharply, is slowing again. Pay growth, a significant source of inflationary concern for most of last year, has fallen back, despite falls in unemployment that have taken the number of people out of work down to the lowest level in 20 years.

The Bank last raised interest rates in February, by a quarter-point to 6 per cent. Moderating

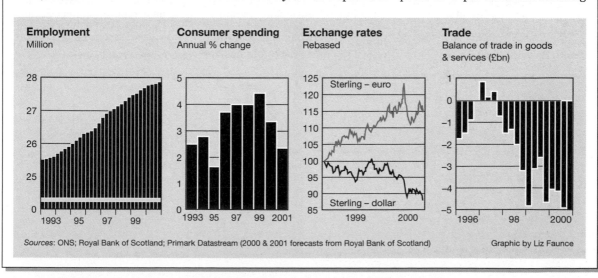

Sources: ONS; Royal Bank of Scotland; Primark Datastream (2000 & 2001 forecasts from Royal Bank of Scotland)   Graphic by Liz Faunce

demand has stayed its hand, but most economists expect another rate rise before the end of the year.

The UK is likely to enjoy continued expansion over the next few years. The Bank predicts that GDP growth will slow from an annual 3.1 per cent to 2.5 per cent, close to the economy's long-run rate, before picking up slightly again.

Inflationary risks remain. Sterling, which had previously stubbornly defied expectations of a fall, has weakened spectacularly, threatening to stoke price pressures. The pound has tumbled more than 10 per cent against the dollar since January, to $1.40 by mid September, its lowest level since March 1993, alleviating some of the pain inflicted by its past strength on manufacturers. It remains strong against the euro.

If the anti-inflationary support of a highly-valued currency is removed, the Bank will face possibly its toughest test since independence in 1997.

A deep split between members of the Bank's monetary policy committee over the likely future path of sterling has already made the pound into a policy dilemma. The impact of a sharp slide in its value would add to uncertainty surrounding inflation. 'If sterling does fall further, this will allow more of the strength of domestic costs to feed through to inflation, adding to pressure for higher base rates,' says Michael Saunders at Schroder Salomon Smith Barney in London.

Manufacturers, who have struggled to compete with overseas rivals, say sterling remains too strong. Britain's trade deficit with the rest of the world has continued to widen, reaching £4.1bn in the second quarter.

Further interest rate rises are therefore likely to exacerbate the divide between weak manufacturing and robust services, and will be unpopular with industry.

Demand, though, is still robust and will probably have to slow further to prevent inflation overshooting the targeted annual rate of 2.5 per cent. Higher oil prices, if sustained, will fuel price pressure.

Government spending is also set to rise sharply, by 6.7 per cent in real terms this year, the biggest annual increase since 1974, as more resources are pumped into public services.

The biggest danger to growth could come from out-side. A collapse in the US stock market, for instance, would be felt across the globe. Britain's Labour government, though, is riding high on the strength of the economy. Though its credibility has suffered some damage from the chaos caused by recent oil price protests, it will use promises of higher spending on health and education to woo voters in the general election, expected next year.

A thornier issue will be the question of euro-zone membership. Labour says it is in favour of joining the single currency, but only if the economic conditions are right. A decision to join would be subject to a public referendum.

In recent months, several independent reports have suggested economic convergence may be taking place. According to the OECD, the 'output gap' – the difference between current output and the economy's long-term potential – is likely to converge with that of the euro-zone over the next two years. And, while interest rates are projected to remain divergent, that could change quickly if the prospect of joining the single currency becomes reality.

The Treasury gave the OECD report a cautious endorsement. It will publish an assessment of its own five economic tests for joining early in the next parliament.

Analysts say the government's tests, which include an assessment of convergence, are vague and likely to be decided by political expedience.

Gordon Brown the chancellor, remains publicly mute on the prospects for convergence. His stance has angered pro-euro industrialists who argue that the government should be pushing membership more aggresively.

The biggest stumbling block to membership may be the pound. As long as sterling continues to fluctuate, and stays well above a rate against the euro regarded by business as competitive, negotiations over an entry level will be fraught.

Source: *Financial Times*, 22 September 2000. Reprinted with permission.

SECTION **V**

Business economics

It seems improbable that a firm would emerge without the existence of uncertainty.

Ronald H. Coase

19   The size and growth of firms

Learning outcomes

At the end of this chapter you will be able to:
- Understand the concepts of market and aggregate concentration ratios.
- Distinguish between internal and external methods of growth of firms.
- Identify the main reasons why firms merge.
- Appreciate the reasons for strategic alliances.
- Appreciate the significance of multinational firms.
- Identify the reasons for the survival of small firms.

The size of firms

Of the estimated three million business units in the UK, the vast majority (probably over 90 per cent of all business units) are classified as *very small firms*, each having less than 10 employees. Most of these businesses are sole traders, although they may also comprise some partnerships. These firms tend to be more labour intensive than firms in general, evidence of which is shown by the fact that they account for approximately 26 per cent of total employment in the economy but only 13 per cent of total sales revenue. Such very small concerns occur in all industrial sectors, especially services; they are particularly prevalent in the construction, hotel and catering and distributive industries.

Manufacturing firms tend, on average, to be larger than businesses in other sectors of the economy because they have a higher degree of capital intensity. *Small firms*, each employing less than 100 people, predominate numerically, comprising over 96 per cent of all manufacturing firms, yet they are only responsible for a quarter of manufacturing employment and a fifth of manufacturing output.

There is a high concentration of production in the sense that large firms in manufacturing, each of which has more than 5000 employees, number less than 100 individual enterprises but account for almost 30 per cent of manufacturing employment and over 34 per cent of output in the sector.

Concentration of production

The degree of concentration of production can be measured in two ways, or to be more precise, at two levels: (a) the market or seller concentration ratio and (b) the aggregate concentration ratio.

The market or seller concentration ratio

This measures the share of employment or output of the largest few firms in a market or industry.

In the UK the five-firm concentration ratio (C_5) is usually employed; this measures the share of a market taken by the five largest firms. In other countries three-firm (C_3) and four-firm (C_4) concentration ratios are commonly adopted. Manufacturing industries are usually the most highly concentrated: the five largest firms in the tobacco industry are responsible for over 99 per cent of total output (C_5 = 99.5), in iron and steel production the equivalent figure is over 95 per cent (C_5 = 95.3), for motor vehicles it is almost 83 per cent (C_5 = 82.9), for the supply of domestic electrical goods the figure is 57 per cent (C_5 = 57.0), for pharmaceuticals it is above 51 per cent (C_5 = 51.5) and for footwear a little over 48 per cent (C_5 = 48.2). On the other hand, the figures for the production of leather goods and the processing of plastics are 15 per cent (C_5 = 15.0) and 8.8 per cent (C_5 = 8.8) respectively. There is also evidence of increasing concentration of production in service industries like food retailing and in financial services, such as banking and insurance.

High concentration is associated with a high degree of market or monopoly power on the part of the largest firms in an industry.

The degree of market concentration grew rapidly in many manufacturing industries in the 1950s and 1960s, mainly as a result of the high level of merger activity. Since then, on average, market concentration has remained fairly stable, although there is some evidence that concentration increased again in a number of industries in the second half of the 1990s. The level of concentration in many industries in the UK is reckoned to be somewhat higher than in similar industries in most other industrial economies.

Concentration varies between industries because in some cases economies of scale may become exhausted at fairly low levels of industry output, allowing several firms to benefit fully from them, whereas in others economies of scale may account for almost all the total industry output, thus allowing only one or two firms to survive and prosper in the industry. Other barriers to entry, the level of merger activity and simple chance factors (like, for example, a successful advertising campaign which allows one firm to grow faster than others in an industry) may also account for differences in levels of seller concentration.

Concentration ratios are fairly simple to employ and evidence about them is widely available. One problem with them, however, is that the level of concentration for each industry varies depending on the number of firms included in the ratio. They also take no account of the distribution of output within the leading few firms in an industry. Five firms may each produce 15 per cent of output in one industry, whereas in another one firm may produce 35 per cent and the largest four others 10 per cent each; in both cases $C_5 = 75.0$, but in the first industry all the firms are of equal size whereas in the second industry one firm dominates. Furthermore, concentration ratios refer only to domestic output; therefore, they overestimate the extent of concentration in a market where there is a significant amount of competition from imports. On the other hand, in industries like motor vehicles and consumer electronics the domestic suppliers may import finished products from their overseas branches and resell them in the home market; in these circumstances concentration ratios underestimate the degree of concentration in a market. Concentration ratios also understate the true level of concentration where local or regional monopolies exist, as in food retailing. Since people usually only shop for food locally, the market comprises a fairly narrow area which tends to be dominated by two or three of the large supermarket chains.

The aggregate concentration ratio

This measures the share of total employment or output contributed by the largest firms in the whole economy, or in large sectors of it.

The 100 largest manufacturing firms in the UK account for about 38 per cent of total manufacturing output ($C_{100} = 38.0$). As is the case with market concentration, aggregate concentration in the UK increased quite rapidly until the late 1960s, since when the level has stabilised.

● Common misunderstanding

When using concentration ratios care should be taken to avoid confusing the absolute and relative sizes of firms. It is not the actual or absolute size of firms that is important, it is their size relative to the market as a whole. The absolute size of the firm is indicated by the actual value of sales revenue or the total number of employees; the relative size is measured by size relative to the market or to the sector in general. Thus, it may be possible for firms which are quite small in terms of their actual numbers of employees to hold a significant amount of market power (and hence for there to be a high degree of seller or market concentration). This can be the case in services like catering and dry cleaning where the market is considered very localised, such as a small town; two or three small firms may dominate such a market. However, in most manufacturing industries large relative size is also equated with large absolute size.

In the UK any increase in absolute firm size that is implicit in rises in concentration has occurred more by firms taking over or merging with other firms and thus acquiring more plants than through increases in the average size of plant.

The growth of firms

Firms can grow in size, for example by increasing sales, in one of two ways: (a) through *internal*

STUDENT ACTIVITY 19.1

The respective market shares of the leading five firms in two industries, A and B, are as follows:

	A	B
Firm 1	32%	12%
Firm 2	12%	12%
Firm 3	8%	12%
Firm 4	5%	12%
Firm 5	3%	12%

Calculate the C_3 and C_5 ratio for each industry. What do your answers tell you about the benefits of using concentration ratios as a measure of market power?

growth, by investing in new plant and equipment; and (b) *externally*, through mergers and takeovers. These are the two main *methods* of growth, although a third, growth through *strategic alliances*, has become increasingly popular in recent years.

Internal growth

Internal growth can take the form either of increased penetration into one's existing market or via some kind of diversification strategy involving new products and/or new markets (perhaps in other countries). Whichever direction of expansion a firm may take, internal growth is likely to have some kind of relationship with its existing product base, either through operating in similar markets or by adopting similar production techniques. The main source of finance for such expansion for firms in the UK is *internal funds* derived from ploughed-back profit, although an increased proportion of funds has come from bank borrowing and new share issues in recent years.

The main motive for internal growth for a firm is to dominate its market and so obtain the benefits of greater monopoly power; the increase in size that accompanies growth may well also yield greater economies of scale.

Of course, whatever method of growth a firm chooses, there are *limits* to how fast it can grow. There may be limits to how much finance a firm can obtain: more borrowing raises the firm's 'gearing' (its ratio of borrowed to share capital) and increases the level of risk of not being able to repay the loans; a new share issue may cause the price of all shares to fall unless profits are projected to increase; more retained profit means less available to pay out in dividends. Should shareholders feel that profits are not likely to rise in the future, they may sell their shares leading to a fall in the share price and possibly making the firm ripe for takeover. In addition to the financial constraints on a firm's growth, it also faces a demand constraint: expansion in its own market means price reductions in order to attract ever more marginal customers and this may lead to a fall in profits; there is a limit to diversification into other markets because this places an increased burden on management in having to cope with the additional requirements of producing different products and possibly selling them in different parts of the world; in other words, there is also a managerial constraint to growth.

Mergers and takeovers

A *merger* refers to the combination of two (or more) firms to form a new legal entity. A *takeover* occurs when one company buys out another; if this happens without the consent of the acquired company's management it is known as a *hostile takeover*. The two terms, mergers and takeovers, are often used interchangeably, as they will be here, although there are obvious distinctions between them.

There are three main types of merger:

(a) A *horizontal merger*, or horizontal integration, occurs when two firms in the same industry and that are at a similar stage of production combine. For example, if an oil company which already owned a string of petrol stations were to take over another competitive chain, this would be horizontal integration.

(b) A *vertical merger*, or vertical integration, is a combination of two firms at different stages of production in the same industry. Vertical integration can either involve a firm expanding *backwards* towards its sources of supply or *forwards* towards its markets. For example, an oil company which bought oil wells would be engaging in backward integration, while if it purchased filling stations this would be forward integration.

It is possible for a firm to undertake both horizontal and vertical integration. Figure 19.1 illustrates the case of an oil company which is vertically integrated from its ownership of oil wells to its control of filling stations and is horizontally integrated by controlling several chains of filling stations.

(c) A *conglomerate merger*, or conglomerate integration, refers to the combination of two firms with no obvious common link between them. In the UK, GEC and Trafalgar House are examples of conglomerates that have expanded largely by acquiring companies in non-related industries.

Mergers usually occur in waves, with periodic increases in activity.

In the UK there were several such merger waves in the twentieth century: in the 1920s, during the late 1960s and early 1970s, in the mid- to late 1980s and again in the mid- to late 1990s. There is no satisfactory explanation for these sudden bursts of activity, although each wave has coincided with peaks in share prices. In the two earliest waves and in the latest wave horizontal mergers were by far the most popular form of acquisition. In the wave during the 1980s conglomerate deals predominated, comprising over half of all mergers. Large companies, hitherto immune from takeover, have also become more prone to acquisition in the more recent merger waves.

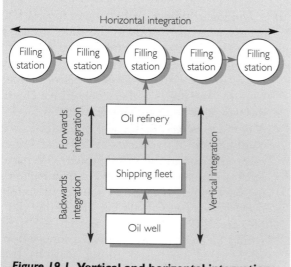

Figure 19.1 Vertical and horizontal integration

British and American firms have traditionally been regarded as the most merger active, both at home and in other countries, and they continue to be so. However, in the last decade there has been a significant increase in merger activity by firms from other West European countries, such as France and Germany, especially abroad. Within these continental European economies the acquired companies have tended to be smaller concerns. This is because there are fewer companies whose shares are freely tradable on the stock markets compared with the UK and the USA. Firms in continental Europe are also much more likely to be able to issue shares to friendly third parties, such as family board members and banks with whom the companies have long-established ties; these groups would be likely to vote against any proposed acquisition by another firm. In Japan the *keiretsu* system of extensive cross-shareholdings between companies restricts takeover activity there. These features also explain the relative rarity of hostile takeovers in the non-Anglo-American economies.

Reasons for mergers and takeovers

(a) *Economies of scale.* It is argued that the growth in size should lead to economies of scale. For this to happen the new business must be reorganised, otherwise the resultant situation may be less efficient than when the firms were separate (see the full discussion of economies of scale on pages 33–5).

(b) *Market domination.* One of the most frequent motives for horizontal mergers is simply to dominate the market and thus be able to reap the advantages of monopoly power.

(c) *Reduced uncertainty.* Mergers can reduce uncertainty in a variety of ways. A horizontal merger can reduce uncertainty through the acquisition of a rival; the fewer the rivals, the less the uncertainty concerning their actions. A vertical merger is often undertaken to establish a more secure source of supply of raw materials and components or to maintain the quality of the finished product in retail outlets.

Diversification into different product areas via conglomerate merger activity spreads a firm's risks. By avoiding the uncertainty of 'having all one's eggs in one basket' a firm may be able to offset periodic declines in sales in one of its products against increases in sales elsewhere. BAT (British American Tobacco) has diversified into hotels, frozen foods and many other lines to protect itself against the risk of a decline in tobacco sales.

(d) *For growth*. Mergers provide a quicker, and sometimes cheaper, form of growth than via internal expansion. This may be a particularly important motive for mergers if the managers of a firm are more interested in growth than in profits as an objective (see Chapter 7). The increased size that results from growth may also make the firm less vulnerable to takeover by other firms.

(e) *Asset stripping*. This occurs when a company is taken over with the object of closing all or part of it down so that its assets may be realised. This can occur when a company's real assets (land, capital equipment, etc.) have a greater value than its stock market valuation. Asset stripping has often been criticised, especially when a going concern has been closed down. In strict economic terms, however, asset stripping amounts to a more productive use of resources.

The success of mergers and takeovers

To determine if mergers are successful it is first necessary to define success. If it is defined in terms of improved profitability (resulting, say, from lower costs due to economies of scale and/or from increased market power), then the evidence suggests that most mergers are not very successful: many merged firms have proved to be no more profitable, and sometimes less profitable, than had the individual firms remained separate. This applies particularly to horizontal mergers. On the other hand, some conglomerates have grown quite rapidly and successfully through merger activity. The shareholders of the acquired firms also often benefit from a fairly substantial rise in the share price just before takeover. In general, however, the evidence on the performance of merged firms is fairly disappointing: there is no evidence that, on balance, the best run and presumably therefore the most profitable companies naturally acquire the least profitable ones, thereby leading to an overall improvement

in efficiency. Since there is also no evidence of a downward trend in merger activity, in fact quite the reverse, then it has to be concluded that many mergers are undertaken with insufficient prior knowledge or appraisal of potential targets by the acquiring firms.

● *Common misunderstanding*

Given the popularity of mergers and the amount of media attention that some of the largest achieve, it would be expected that most of them were successes. However, generally this is not the case: mergers allow firms to grow in size quite quickly, but they do not appear to result in improved profitability for the firms concerned. It may be concluded from this that many mergers are undertaken more to satisfy the interests of managers than those of the shareholders, especially in the firms doing the acquiring.

STUDENT ACTIVITY 19.2

Find examples of recent mergers from the financial press and state which type of merger you think they represent (note: some mergers may belong to more than one category).

Strategic alliances

Strategic alliances (SAs) have become an increasingly popular method of growth in the last twenty or so years. They can be rather informal agreements between firms, sometimes called *networks*, such as in the airline industry whereby a number of firms will employ code-sharing arrangements so that customers can use several airlines on a single ticket. Alternatively, *joint ventures* are much more formal relationships, involving an exchange of ownership and the establishment of a newly-created organisation. Between these two extremes there are a whole host of other types of collaboration, such as licensing agreements, franchising and distribution and supply arrangments. Many SAs occur in relatively 'high-technology' industries, such as microelectronics, aeronautics, defence, pharmaceuticals and vehicle production and involve the development and diffusion of technical knowledge.

SAs are most likely to take place when there are high costs and risks involved in a particular venture, such as research and development (R&D), and a shared arrangement is thought to be preferable to going it alone. Alternatively, they may also occur when other routes to new markets are difficult. Procter and Gamble and IBM have both built up large sales in Japan via a system of alliances, for example.

Many SAs are relatively short-lived and end with the sale of one or more of the partners to another. The incompatibility in combining different methods of doing business, especially if collaborating with a firm in another country, and concern about giving key rivals too much access to vital information are two of the problems most commonly cited for SAs.

One form of collaboration that warrants special mention is *franchising*: one party, the *franchisor*, sells the right to another, the *franchisee*, to supply and market the product, possibly for a specified period of time. The franchisor supplies the brand name, parts and materials and managerial advice, whereas the franchisee, who pays an intial fee and receives a percentage of the sales or profits, supplies capital and local market knowledge.

Franchising is a popular business technique of certain multinational firms in the fast-food and hotel industries, such as McDonald's, Burger King, Kentucky Fried Chicken and Holiday Inn, offering as it does relatively easy and cheap access to foreign markets for the firms concerned. In the UK growing numbers of petrol stations and public houses are now franchised and the system has also been adopted for the railway operators, among many local bus companies and for most local authority cleaning, catering and refuse collection services (see also Chapter 24). Franchising can provide relatively cheap access to, or growth within, an industry, often for an established brand name, although problems may arise in ensuring quality standards are mantained and in agreeing the length of the contract.

Multinational firms

The size of the firm and the economic power that it can wield is taken to its extreme in the case of the multinational corporation (MNC). This is a firm that has production facilities (i.e. plants that it owns and controls) in more than one country.

In setting up these plants or subsidiaries the MNC engages in *foreign direct investment* (FDI). MNCs invest abroad for a variety of reasons: to gain access to raw materials and to markets, to avoid trade barriers, to take advantage of lower labour costs, to exploit their technological and organisational advantages (such as superior managerial skills) over local firms and simply because their main domestic rivals have already undertaken overseas investment or are about to do so. The largest MNCs (e.g. Shell, Ford, General Motors, IBM, Nestlé and Unilever) have subsidiaries worldwide and exercise enormous economic power by being able to transfer resources across virtually any national boundary.

The capital resources, technological knowledge and jobs that MNCs can bring to an economy create intense competition among national governments (as well as among regional authorities within countries) to try to attract these firms to their areas through the offer of various financial inducements. Whether such financial incentives are entirely warranted can depend upon the nature of the inward investment. For example, many of the Japanese car-producing and consumer electronic plants set up in Western Europe prior to the creation of the Single Market in the EU in 1993 are essentially assembly operations with relatively little local content. In this sense they are 'footloose' and are not dependent on particular locational advantages. The initial inflow of funds has a positive impact on the capital account of the balance of payments (see Chapter 42) and new jobs are created. However, there are also future outflows of profits and managerial royalties to consider and any export earnings on sales from the plant may have to be weighed against the import of components from the home country (in this case Japanese) suppliers.

The continuation of the small business

Despite the fact that both national and international business is dominated by the large firm, the small firm remains the most popular form of business enterprise.

There are various reasons for its survival:

(a) *Limited economies of scale.* In some industries, such as agriculture, only limited economies of scale can be gained. However, small firms may still exist in industries where there are considerable economies of scale, as you may see by considering the remaining points in this list.

(b) *'Being one's own boss'.* Entrepreneurs may accept smaller profit for the social prestige of working for themselves or the possibility of making a profit in the future.

(c) *Goodwill.* A small business may survive on a fund of goodwill where its customers might tolerate higher prices for a more personal service.

(d) *Banding together.* Independent businesses may band together to gain the advantages of bulk buying while still retaining their independence. This is so among UK grocery chains such as Spar and others.

(e) *Specialist services or products.* Businesses may gain a market niche by providing specialist products for particular market segments, e.g. a few small car manufacturers exist in the UK making specialist sports cars, such as Morgan and TVR.

(f) *Subcontracting.* Since the 1980s there has been a trend in many countries, notably the UK and the USA, for greater flexibility in production. One method of achieving this, so it is claimed, is by large firms subcontracting what are regarded as peripheral activities, such as design, marketing, accounting services and even basic research, to smaller concerns.

Professor Galbraith in his book *Economics and the Public Purpose* suggests two more reasons for the survival of the small firm. First, he says: 'There are limits to the toil that can be demanded in the large firm, but the small businessman is at liberty to exploit himself and in this role he can be a severe taskmaster.' He goes on to suggest that some industries are particularly suited to this kind of discipline which 'rewards diligence and punishes sloth' and he singles out agriculture, suggesting that this is one reason it adapts badly to socialism. The second reason he gives is that as society fulfils its more fundamental economic needs, people begin to demand aesthetic satisfaction from products, thus creating a role for the artist in the economic process, e.g. interior design.

STUDENT ACTIVITY 19.3

Examine some small firms in your area and suggest reasons for their continued existence.

Conclusion

This chapter has examined the size and growth of firms in the UK. There has been a trend towards a greater concentration of production in many industries, although there are a number of very important reasons why small concerns still predominate numerically.

Firms can grow in size both internally and externally, or via some kind of strategic alliance. The largest firms of all, multinationals, can set up production facilities in most parts of the world and many countries now compete for their investments.

Summary

1 Small concerns are by far the most numerous type of business organisation, but there is a significant concentration of production in the hands of a relatively few large firms in many industries.
2 Firms can grow through internal or external means, or via strategic alliances.
3 Takeovers and mergers are common in the UK and have contributed significantly towards the increased concentration of production, although many mergers do not appear to be particularly successful.
4 Multinational firms dominate international production. Firms invest abroad for a variety of reasons and many countries compete to attract them to their shores.
5 Despite the concentration of production, many small businesses survive.

? QUESTIONS

1 Account for the continued existence of so many small firms.
2 Explain why and how firms grow in size.
3 Distinguish between market and aggregate concentration. Account for the growth in the concentration of production in the UK.

4 Why do mergers and takeovers take place? Discuss whether they are in the public interest.

5 Account for the fact that, despite the concentration of production in UK industry, the average size of plant remains relatively small.

6 Why do firms invest in production facilities abroad? Discuss why countries compete to attract such investments.

7 Explain what is meant by franchising. Discuss the relative merits of this form of business activity.

Data response A
MERGERS AND TAKEOVERS

Read the article below (taken from *The Guardian* of 30 November 1999) which is included to indicate the problems of mergers, and then attempt the following questions.

1 For what reasons do mergers and takeovers take place?

2 Are mergers successful?

3 Discuss the reasons why many mergers may not yield their expected benefits.

4 Discuss the implications of the article for public policy towards mergers.

Data response B
INWARD INVESTMENT

Study the article on pages 268–9 which is taken from *The Observer* of 16 April 2000 and answer the following questions.

1 Explain what is meant by the term 'inward foreign direct investment'.

2 Distinguish between investment through mergers and takeovers and so-called greenfield investment.

3 Is substantial inward investment a good thing for a country such as the UK?

4 What effect might the high value of the pound have on both inward investment by foreign firms and outward investment by British firms?

Whisper it . . . takeovers don't pay

Mergers don't add up, admits new force in mergers. By **Lisa Buckingham** and **Dan Atkinson**

There were red faces all round at accountancy firm KPMG yesterday after a report was published disclosing that fewer than one in five takeovers produces any value for shareholders.

The research is, however, distinctly unsettling for everyone in M&A, particularly as it has surfaced so shortly after the launch of the world's two largest hostile takeover contests – Vodafone's bid for Mannesmann and Pfizer's assault on fellow drugs group Warner Lambert.

The survey shows a remarkable lack of analysis by the companies in the current bout of takeover frenzy. Although their deals are doing little if anything for investors – the people who actually own the companies – they are clearly doing a lot for executive egos. Some 82% of those surveyed by KPMG regarded the major deal in which they had been involved as a success. But KPMG found that, using its own criteria, only 17% of mergers added value, while as many as 53% destroyed shareholder value.

So what is driving the late 90s merger frenzy, and why is it that companies remain so bad at assessing whether a deal is likely to be rewarding for their shareholders?

One of the factors pushing towards top-dollar takeover prices is the buoyancy of shares. The value of targets is rising but so is the ability to pay, as predators are able to issue highly rated shares.

In fields such as telecoms, banking and pharmaceuticals, it is the fashion for gigantism that has produced a rush towards the holy grail of market leadership.

There are technical issues at play, too.

3i made no bones about the fact that its bid for rival Electra was partly motivated by a fear that it would drop out of the FTSE100 index, which usually has a dramatically negative effect on share prices, unless it could keep getting bigger.

Smaller companies too are rushing to 'get married' in order to qualify in terms of size for the FTSE250 list, according to John Kelly of KPMG's M&A department.

Despite the current enthusiasm, however, history shows that re-invention and innovation are clearly more important than simply getting bigger, particularly in a field which is rapidly going out of style.

Few commentators of the industrial scene in the lead-up to the first world war would now recognise Coast Viyella, the textiles group which has just dropped out of the list of the UK's top 350 companies. It had merged with another textiles giant, Paton, and topped off a period of frenetic corporate activity by combining with Carrington Viyella. At its zenith, it towered above Shell and General Electric.

Conversely, examples of successful re-invention include WPP, the global advertising group, which started out as a maker of shopping trolleys, while EMI, the world's third largest music company, has jettisoned more brand names than most of us can think of.

One factor undermining the success of big deals is that the 'M' in 'M&A' is usually a fig leaf: there have been 'only a handful of true mergers ever ... most ... are acquisitions,' according to KPMG's Mr Kelly. This may explain the 'victor mentality' noticeable in post-deal environments, when the stronger partner displays a 'not invented here' attitude towards the working practices, personnel and even equipment of the weaker.

The failure to deal with management and boardroom issues ahead of a merger is one of the principal reasons that mergers do not deliver anywhere near the expected benefits, while a refusal to deal with conflicts of culture can also undermine hopes of success – just look at the disastrous acquisition merger of US banks Wells Fargo and First Interstate.

It is noticeable that UK-US deals – still about 50% of all cross-border deals – are 45% more likely than the average to succeed, whereas US-Europe deals were 11% less likely to succeed than average.

One recent example of this has been the seemingly remarkably smooth acquisition of Asda supermarkets by the American retail giant Wal-Mart. The culture and operating ethos of both were similar; indeed Asda had already modelled itself on Wal-Mart.

As to why investors continue to tolerate the enthusiasm of their costliest employees – the directors – for M&A activity, given its abysmal record on delivering shareholder value, Mr Kelly suggested too many accepted at face value the boardroom view of merger 'success'.

Executives tend to be confident individuals, not prone to probing their own mistakes. Fewer than half the boards of merged companies conduct any proper post-deal evaluation; the balance often seemed virtually to declare the merger a success simply because it had taken place.

And, while KPMG's survey might not highlight the point, many managements are persuaded of the merits of takeovers by their corporate finance advisers. Too few are prepared to stand out from the crowd in rejecting their advice.

Source: *The Guardian*, London, 30 November 1999. Reprinted with permission.

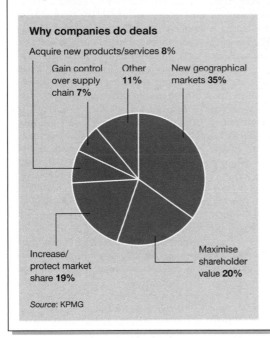

Why companies do deals

Acquire new products/services **8%**

Gain control over supply chain **7%**

Other **11%**

New geographical markets **35%**

Increase/protect market share **19%**

Maximise shareholder value **20%**

Source: KPMG

Inwardly troubled

The UK attracts investment – because the economy is full of holes, says **Simon Caulkin**

Search for 'inward investment' on the Web, and of the pages and pages of hits, apart from a couple for Tahiti, the Dominican Republic and France, almost all extol the unrivalled delights of investing in the UK: Barnsley, York, Wales, Scotland, London, Cumbria and Fermanagh on the first page alone.

A trawl through the newspaper cuttings reinforces the impression that inward investment is almost entirely a UK story, and a glowing success story at that: 'Investors prefer UK despite euro, uncertainty'; 'Investment into Britain jumps by 90 per cent to reach record high'; 'Rising tide of investment flows from overseas'. These are just a few of the recent headlines.

It is true that Britain attracts a proportionately large amount of mobile investment. With just 1 per cent of the world's population, it consumes nearly 8 per cent of all direct cross-border investment, second only to the US. In Europe, the UK is the self-proclaimed inward investment champion, gobbling up half the available total, compared with a meagre 5 per cent for France and 3 per cent for Germany.

The figures are huge. In 1998 foreign companies invested £40 billion in the UK, according to the United Nations Conference on Trade and Development. As many as 25 000 UK companies are estimated to be under foreign ownership, and 25 per cent of 'British' output comes from foreign-owned factories.

So that's all right, then. Well, not quite. Inward investment has gone unchallenged for so long as a plank of economic policy that people have forgotten to ask the more troubling questions. If foreign direct investment (FDI) is such a good thing, why is it only the UK that makes such a big thing of it? What does all the investment consist of? And what does it say about the functioning of the British economy as a whole?

The truth is that like so much of British management under scrutiny this 'triumph' is not nearly as wonderful as it seems. In the first place, much FDI activity represents mergers and acqusitions, which have replaced greenfield investment – building new factories – as the largest component of inward investment in developed countries.

As Bob Bischof, chairman of direct marketer McIntyre & King, points out, that makes it 'instead-of' investment, not 'additional' investment. In effect it is 'outward divestment' by UK companies rather than extra inward investment, the total of which is quite small.

Semantics? Not when you relate it to the way the economy is currently run. The implications of foreign ownership and an unsympathetic economic policy are horribly illustrated by the Rover debacle. Twenty-five per cent of UK manufacturing is in the same position as Rover. Ford is considering shutting Dagenham, Bischof notes, and his own former company, Boss Group, the UK arm of German forklift manufacturer Jungheinrich, is also in peril from the high pound.

In that situation, where would you like the decisions made, Munich or Birmingham? 'It's the "furthest away from headquarters" syndrome,' says Bischof. 'If you're in London, the Newcastle or Welsh plant goes first. Exactly the same applies internationally.'

By the same token, the vaunted 'clusters' of foreign investment in the North East or 'Silicon Glen' are fragile things. 'They are not embedded in the local economy,' says David Johnson, director of Durham Business School's Barclays Centre for Entreprenership. Without the anchorage of special skills or particular know-how in the area – as at homegrown Cambridge, centred on the university – there is little to tie them in when the going gets rough.

None of this is to deny the economic benefits that some inward investment provides. The National Institute of Economic and Social Research (NIESR) estimates that a third of UK industrial productivity growth since the mid-1980s can be attributed to the 'ripple-through' effect of better work practices imported by the incomers, principally the Japanese. Despite the strength of sterling, Japanese implants have also done much to sustain export figures in sectors such as cars and electronics.

But there is no such thing as a free lunch. Why has Johnny Foreigner (with the exception of BMW) been able to make a go of industries which British companies are abandoning in droves – cars, electronics, televisions, utilities? Why has it taken foreign management to restore a measure of credibility to British quality and British labour?

A large part of the answer lies in vastly better management at every level. For foreign firms, the opportunity to buy cheap assets and cheap labour with which to compete in a wildly over-priced UK market is a no-brainer, particularly since ease of entry and investment are matched by ease of exit.

Meanwhile, spurning the opportunities on their doorstep, UK firms have become the world leaders in exporting capital. Last year they invested a towering $212bn overseas, more even than the US. Unlike the US, the UK is a huge net *outward* investor.

Bischof believes that the steady evacuation by British firms of the most competitive commercial arenas is no accident. It is driven, he argues, by fierce short-term pressures from shareholder institutions which won't tolerate the high investments, patience and determination that long-term competition requires.

Thus, in what is supposed to be the financial centre of the world, there is no British representation left in investment banking, the most globally strategic and competitive area. UK banks have retreated to the High Street – where their cartel is now under increasing pressure.

Too often, the ownership transaction isn't just a swap of accents or assets. What happens in the rust belt has a knock-on effect at the posh end of the economy.

For example, a foreign acquirer often appoints a foreign bank to replace overdraft-obsessed British ones. A foreign insurer follows. Foreign managers and continental suppliers complete the picture – initially reluctantly, says Bischof, when domestic suppliers can't make the quality standards, then systematically because of uncompetitive prices as a result of the strength of sterling.

So when the press whips up the next Mexican wave in favour of glowing inward investment figures, ponder instead what is slipping away, and why that investment was needed in the first place.
simon.caulkin@observer.co.uk

Source: *The Observer*, 16 April 2000. Reprinted with permission.

20 Costs in the short run and the long run

Learning outcomes

At the end of this chapter you will be able to:
▶ Understand the concepts of average total costs (ATC), average fixed costs (AFC) and average variable costs (AVC).
▶ Account for the nature of long-run average costs in theory and practice.
▶ Appreciate the significance of the minimum efficient scale (MES) level of output.
▶ Explain the effects of changes in fixed costs and variable costs.

In Chapter 7 we saw that total costs can be divided into fixed costs and variable costs. We also distinguished between average costs and marginal costs and examined the relationship between them.

In this chapter we shall take the analysis further by examining the nature of average costs in the short run and the long run and by investigating the effects of changes in costs. Before we do this it is important to point out that, although there are different kinds of competition ranging from perfect competition to monopoly, no matter what market conditions a firm operates under its cost structures will be similar.

Average costs in the short run

Since total costs can be divided into fixed costs and variable costs, it would follow that average cost can be divided in the same way:

$$\text{Thus, average costs } (AC) = \frac{\text{Total cost}}{\text{Output}} = \frac{TC}{Q}$$

Therefore:

$$\text{Average fixed costs} = \frac{\text{Fixed costs}}{\text{Output}}$$

or

$$AFC = \frac{FC}{Q}$$

and

$$\text{Average variable costs} = \frac{\text{Variable costs}}{\text{Output}}$$

or

$$AVC = \frac{VC}{Q}$$

It would therefore follow that:

$$AFC + AVC = ATC \text{ (average total costs)}$$

Using the same figures as in Chapter 7, we may illustrate these various concepts. It should be apparent to the student that we can calculate all these various figures once we have the total cost schedule (see Table 20.1).

AFC declines continuously with output in the short run as fixed costs are spread over a greater and greater number of units of output.

● **Common misunderstanding**

While total fixed costs are by definition fixed in quantity and do not vary with output, when these fixed costs are divided by units of output the resulting average fixed costs inevitably declines as the output increases. Hence, the AFC curve declines continuously with output; it is not a horizontal straight line as with the FC curve.

Table 20.1 **The costs of the firm**

Output units per week, Q	Total costs, TC (£)	Fixed costs, FC (£)	Variable costs, VC (£)	Average fixed costs, FC + Q = AFC (£)	Average variable costs, VC + Q = AVC (£)	Average total costs, AFC + AVC = ATC (£)
0	116	116	0	∞	–	∞
1	140	116	24	116.00	24.00	140.00
2	160	116	44	58.00	22.00	80.00
3	176	116	60	38.60	20.00	58.60
4	200	116	84	29.00	21.00	50.00
5	240	116	124	23.20	24.80	48.00
6	296	116	180	19.30	30.00	49.30
7	368	116	252	16.60	36.00	52.60
8	456	116	340	14.50	42.50	57.00

Whether *AVC* increases or decreases depends upon the rate at which total cost is increasing. We can arrive at *ATC* either by adding *AFC* and *AVC* or by dividing total cost by output. We can also verify the fact that:

$$AFC + AVC = ATC$$

For example, if the output is 5 units per week, then *AVC* is £24.80 while *AFC* is £23.20, thus giving *ATC* as £48.00.

Figure 20.1 shows *AFC*, *AVC* and *ATC* plotted graphically. You can see that *AFC* slopes downwards continuously and is **asymptotic**

to the axis, i.e. it gets nearer and nearer to the horizontal axis but never touches it. The *AVC* curve at first falls and later rises owing to the effects of diminishing returns.

The most important curve, as far as we are concerned, is the *ATC* curve. This, you will see, is an elongated 'U'-shape. This is always so in the short run. *ATC* always starts at infinity and then falls rapidly as the fixed costs are spread over more and more units. It continues to fall until the point of **optimum efficiency** or **optimum capacity** is reached (output of 5). Average costs then begin to rise as diminishing returns set in and the increase in *AVC* outweighs the fall in *AFC*. Economically speaking, therefore, the best output is 5 (in our example) because here the article is being produced at the **lowest unit costs**. If output were to be any greater or any less then unit costs would rise. It should also be noted that, as average fixed costs gets progressively smaller, the distance between the *AVC* and *ATC* curves narrows. This can be confirmed from Table 20.1 and Figure 20.1. Note also that, for the same reasons that were spelled out in Chapter 7 where it was explained that the *MC* curve always cuts the *AC* curve at its lowest point, the *MC* curve cuts the lowest point of the *AVC* curve. This can be seen in Figure 20.2.

The efficiency of a business can be judged by the extent to which it is managing to minimise its unit costs. This is an important point which we will return to later.

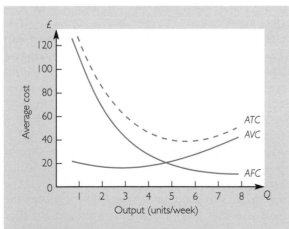

Figure 20.1 Average costs

Average total cost is average variable cost plus average fixed cost.

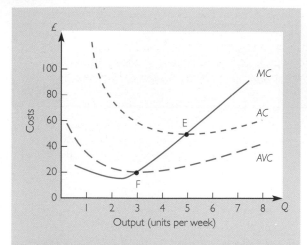

Figure 20.2 Marginal cost, average cost and average variable cost
The *MC* curve cuts the *AC* curve at point E, the lowest point of average cost, and the *AVC* curve at point F, the lowest point of average variable cost.

Output units per week, Q	Total costs, TC (£)	Average fixed costs, AFC (£)	Average variable costs, AVC (£)
0	40		
1	48		
2	55		
3	60		
4	68		
5	82		
6	99		
7	126		
8	156		

Shut-down conditions – again

In the section in Chapter 7 on short-run shut-down conditions, we stated the principle that the firm should continue to operate in the short run so long as it covers its variable costs. Now we can re-examine the principles involved in terms of average cost. If, for example, the variable costs of the business were £68 per week and output was 400 units, then the business would have to recover at least 17 pence per unit to stay in business, i.e. £68/400. This we can now recognise as the average variable costs (*AVC*) of production. Thus we can restate the short-run condition as:

The firm will continue to produce in the short run so long as the price of the product is above *AVC*.

If you are in doubt about this, then re-read this section carefully and attempt Data response A at the end of the chapter. It is important to understand this principle because it is a necessary component of the theory of the firm.

STUDENT ACTIVITY 20.1

You are given the following information regarding units of output and total costs. Calculate the schedules for average fixed cost (*AFC*) and average variable cost (*AVC*).

Average costs in the long run

It has already been stated that the average cost curve is 'U'-shaped in the short run because of the law of diminishing returns. In the long run, however, the fixed factors of production can be increased to get round this problem.

What effect does this have on costs?

If the business has already exploited all the possible technical economies of scale, then all it can do is build an additional factory which will reproduce the cost structures of the first. However if, as the market grows, the business is able to build bigger plants which exploit more economies of scale then this will have a beneficial effect upon costs.

In Figure 20.3 SAC_A is the original short-run average cost curve of the business. As demand expands the business finds it possible to build larger plants which are able to benefit from more economies of scale. Thus it arrives at SAC_D. SAC_M represents a repeat of the process with a larger scale of production.

Exactly what size of plant a firm should choose to produce a certain output is an extremely important decision. For example, if the firm decides to produce output OQ it chooses the plant size that gives the lowest unit cost for that particular level of output. This is SAC_D, yielding unit costs of OC. SAC_D represents the plant size that can produce OQ most efficiently. Note that OQ could be produced by operating a smaller plant, SAC_A, at optimum capacity (i.e. at its

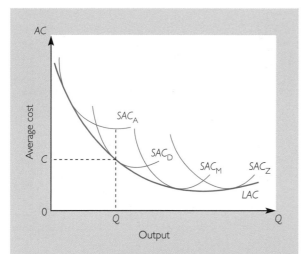

Figure 20.3 Smooth envelope curve
SAC_A to SAC_Z represent an indefinite number of short-run average cost curves created as plant size is increased. LAC is the long-run average cost curve (smooth envelope) which is tangential to the SAC curves. Both SAC and LAC are 'U'-shaped.

lowest point). However, it is better that the firm **underutilises** the larger plant, SAC_D, than operates the smaller plant at its lowest point. Such a process continues until all available economies of scale have been exhausted. Beyond this level of output successive SAC curves, such as SAC_Z, lie higher and to the right owing to the existence of diseconomies of scale. Increased size adds to bureaucracy and leads to control loss. In addition, highly specialised labour can create repetitive work. Both can have the effect of reducing productivity and raising unit costs. In these circumstances (i.e. where diseconomies of scale exist) it is preferable for a firm to **overutilise** a smaller plant than to operate a larger plant at its most efficient level.

Every plant size, or level of fixed input, is represented by an SAC curve; each SAC curve is tangent to the long-run average cost curve. The LAC curve is often referred to as the envelope curve of all the SAC curves. It shows the minimum attainable unit cost for each and every level of output.

The curve we have produced is known as a smooth envelope curve. It is drawn on the assumption that there are an infinite number of choices of plant size between SAC_A and SAC_D, and

so on, so that we obtain a smooth transition in long-run average costs (LAC). If on the other hand there were only a limited number of choices of size of plant, this would tend to make the LAC curve more irregular. This is shown in Figure 20.4.

● **Common misunderstanding**

In the long run the firm is not likely to operate at the minimum point of a short-run average cost curve, even though this is the point of optimum efficiency in the short run. The reason for this apparent anomaly is that, in the long run, the firm can vary the size of its plant. Hence, it will choose the size of plant that minimises unit costs for whatever level of output it chooses to produce. This is why a firm underutilises a plant whenever economies of scale exist and long-run average costs fall and overutilises a plant whenever diseconomies of scale exist and long-run average costs rise. It is only when long-run average costs neither fall nor rise, i.e. at their lowest point, that the relevant short-run average cost curve is tangent to the long-run average cost curve at its lowest point.

We saw above that diminishing returns to scale mean that short-run average costs will eventually increase as output expands. **Alfred Marshall** also assumed that the long-run average cost curve is 'U'-shaped. This implies that expanding firms will always eventually hit diseconomies of scale.

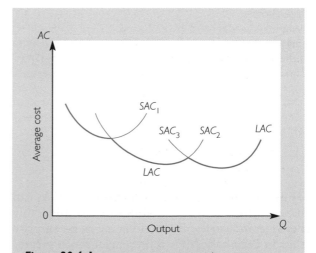

Figure 20.4 Long-run average cost
SAC_1 to SAC_3 represent three possible sizes of plant. The LAC curve is still an envelope of these curves but is no longer smooth.

In practice, evidence suggests that, in those industries investigated, economies of scale exist but diseconomies of scale either do not or are outweighed by economies of scale. In other words, the *LAC* curve is more 'L'-shaped than 'U'-shaped.

A summary of the main evidence for the UK and the EU is given in Table 20.2. The table shows the minimum efficient scale (MES) as a percentage of output in various industries in the UK and the EU.

MES is defined as that level of output where the **LAC** curve first reaches its minimum point, or where all economies of scale have been fully utilised.

Table 20.2 **Evidence of economies of scale in selected manufacturing industries in the UK and the EU**

Industry	MES (% UK output)	MES (% EU output)	Rise in costs (%) at one-third MES
Beer	12	3	5
Cigarettes	24	6	2.2
Oil refining	14	2.6	4
Integrated steel	72	9.8	10
Cement	10	1	26
Petrochemicals	23	2.8	19
Paint	7	2	4.4
Ball bearings	20	2	8–10
Televisions	40	9	15
Refrigerators	85	11	6.5
Glass bottles	5	0.5	11
Washing machines	57	10	7.5
Bricks	1	0.2	25*
Nylon and acrylic	4	1	9.5–12*
Cylinder blocks	3	0.3	10*
Tyres	17	3	5*

*The percentage increase in costs for bricks, nylon, cylinder blocks and tyres is at one-half MES.
Source: Pratten (1989) *The Cost of Non-Europe*, Vol. 2 (Luxembourg: Office for Official Publications of the European Communities)

Thus, in Figure 20.5 MES is given by O*Q*. As can be seen from Table 20.2 MES varies considerably between industries. It should come as no surprise that in each case MES represents a much greater share of UK output than for the EU as a whole, given the latter's much larger market size. In most of the investigations MES is less than 5 per cent of EU output, suggesting that the market can sup-

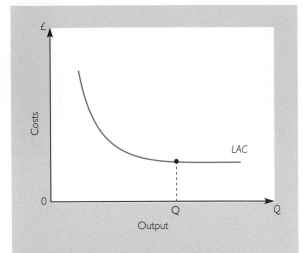

Figure 20.5 **The MES level of output**
This is where the *LAC* curve first reaches its minimum point.

port at least 20 plants. For the UK alone, however, MES is above 10 per cent in most cases, and often substantially so, implying that only a relatively small number of plants can survive in each industry.

The other method of assessing the extent of economies of scale in an industry, as indicated in the last column of Table 20.2, is to observe by how much unit costs increase at a certain percentage of MES output. In the majority of instances the cost disadvantage for plants at a third (or a half) MES is only around 10 per cent; smaller plants do not incur a large cost penalty.

The evidence gives rather contradictory signals about the extent of economies of scale. The data in the table suggests that they are quite extensive in most industries, especially when the UK alone is considered, while the information in the last column implies that they may be rather less so. The general conclusion is that, while economies of scale occur in most industries, they do not preclude smaller units from surviving.

STUDENT ACTIVITY 20.2

Study the data in Table 20.2 and state in which industries you think economies of scale are most or least significant and why.

The mathematics of marginal cost

In Chapter 7 we defined marginal cost (MC) as the cost of producing one more (or less) unit of a commodity. We also derived the typical 'U'-shaped MC curve. It may be useful to remind yourself of these points by re-reading the relevant section in Chapter 7 at this juncture. However, this section may be omitted without impairing your understanding of subsequent chapters.

The method of calculating marginal costs which we have used is quite adequate for the purpose of explaining the behaviour of the firm. However, it is possible to envisage further complications. Suppose that we have figures for total costs as presented in Table 20.3. Here we have output increasing not in single units but in 50 units.

Table 20.3 Total cost schedule

Output, units per week, Q	Total costs (£)
350	12 500
400	13 500
450	15 000

How then do we determine the cost of one more unit? One method would be to take the change in total costs (TC) and divide it by the change in output (Q). Thus, using the figures in Table 20.3, if output increases from 350 to 400 per week, we would obtain the calculation:

$$MC = \frac{TC}{Q}$$

$$= \frac{£1000}{50}$$

$$= £20$$

This, however, is only an approximation because it gives the average increase per unit between 350 and 400 units per week. It would therefore be better to refer to it as the *average incremental cost* (*AIC*) rather than marginal cost (*MC*). The figures in Table 20.3 if plotted as a graph, would give a curved line for MC so that its value would vary all the way from 350 units to 400 units, i.e. MC would be different at each level of output – 300, 301, 302, etc.

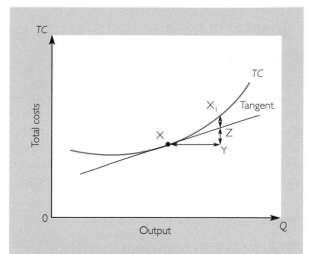

Figure 20.6 Marginal cost
The value of MC at X can be determined by constructing a tangent to the curve at X. Thus $MC = XY/YZ$.

This can be better understood by considering Figure 20.6. In measuring MC we have so far taken a method which depends upon comparing distance XY with distance YX_1. That is to say, if XY represents an increase in output of 1 unit then YX_1 is the resulting increase in total cost, i.e. the MC. It would be mathematically more precise to define MC as the slope of the TC curve at any particular point; that is:

$$MC = \frac{d\,(TC)}{dQ}$$

which the mathematically minded will recognise as the way of saying that:

Marginal cost is the first derivative of cost with respect to output.

That is to say, it is the change in cost associated with an infinitesimally small movement along the TC curve. In Figure 20.6 we can demonstrate this by the construction of a tangent to the TC curve at the point we wish to measure. Then the value MC at point X is:

$$MC = \frac{XY}{YZ}$$

By turning our stepped MC curve into a smoothed-out one we are in fact making an approximation to the correct mathematical way of calculating MC.

Changes in costs

A change in fixed costs

Suppose that a firm's fixed costs were to increase – for example, its rent might be doubled – but its variable costs were to remain unchanged. What effect would this have upon the cost structures? The answer to this question is found in Figure 20.7. The marginal cost is not affected because it shows the change in cost associated with increasing output. Therefore:

Marginal cost is unaffected by fixed cost.

The average cost, however, is increased at every level of output so that it shifts upwards from AC_1 to AC_2. You will note that the MC curve cuts both AC curves at their lowest points.

A change in variable costs

In Table 20.4 we have doubled the level of variable costs at each level of output. As you can see this affects both the average cost and the marginal cost. In Figure 20.8 you can see that both the AC and MC curves have shifted upwards as a result of the change. The intersection of MC and AC is now *at a lower level of output*. Once again you can see that MC cuts AC at its lowest point.

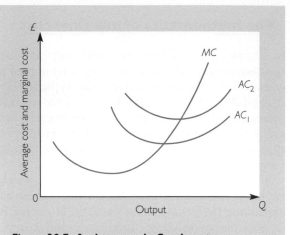

Figure 20.7 An increase in fixed costs
If fixed costs are increased but variable costs are not, then the MC curve is unaffected by the AC curve moving upwards from AC_1 to AC_2.

As we shall see in subsequent chapters, there will be consequences for the output policy of firms as a result of these changes in cost structures.

Conclusion

We have now all but completed our examination of the costs of the firm; it only remains in the next section of the book to demonstrate the

Table 20.4 **The effect of an increase in variable costs**

Output units per week, Q	Original total cost, TC_1 (£)	New total cost, TC_2 (£)	Original average cost, AC_1 (£)	New average cost, AC_2 (£)	Original marginal cost, MC_1 (£)	New marginal cost, MC_2 (£)
0	116	116	∞	∞		
					24	48
1	140	164	140	164		
					20	40
2	160	204	80	102		
					16	32
3	176	236	58.6	78.6		
					24	48
4	200	284	50.0	71.0		
					40	80
5	240	364	48.0	72.8		
					56	112
6	296	476	49.3	79.3		
					72	144
7	368	620	52.6	88.6		
					88	176
8	456	796	57.0	99.5		

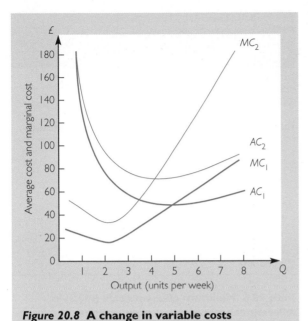

Figure 20.8 A change in variable costs
Both the MC and the AC curves shift upwards as a result of the increase in variable costs.

relationship between cost and diminishing returns. As has already been stated, we may treat the cost structures of the firm as being governed by the same principles no matter what type of competition the firm operates under. It will therefore be

obvious to the astute reader that the differences must lie on the demand side. We will therefore conclude this chapter by restating the essential difference between perfect competition and imperfect competition. This is that under perfect competition the firm's demand curve is horizontal, while under all types of imperfect competition the firm's demand curve is downward sloping. This is illustrated in Figure 20.9. The difference in behaviour thus stems from the relationship of these demand curves with the cost curves. Marginal revenue (MR) is explained in Chapter 22.

Summary

1 Average (unit) cost (AC) is total cost divided by output. It may be divided into average fixed cost (AFC) and average variable cost (AVC). Thus:

$$ATC = AFC + AVC$$

2 In the short run the firm will continue to produce as long as price is above AVC.
3 The AC curve is 'U'-shaped in the short run because of diminishing returns. In the long run the AC curve will also be 'U'-shaped because of economies and diseconomies of scale.

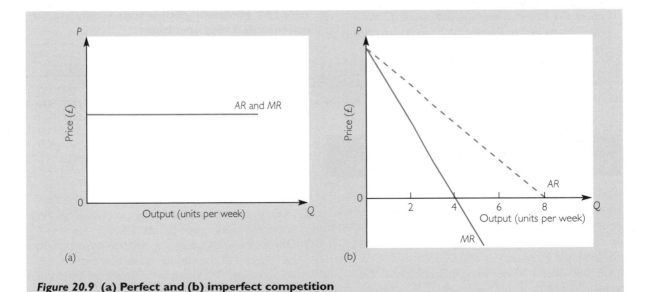

Figure 20.9 (a) Perfect and (b) imperfect competition
The difference is that under perfect competition the firm's demand curve is horizontal while under imperfect competition it is downward sloping.

4 In practice it has been discovered that economies of scale occur in most industries that have been investigated, whereas diseconomies are less likely to exist; hence the long-run average cost curve is actually more 'L'-shaped.
5 A change in fixed costs will affect AC but not MC, whereas a change in variable costs will affect both AC and MC.
6 The cost structures of the firm are the same irrespective of the type of competition. The differences in firm's behaviour originate from the differences in the demand curves, which are a result of the market conditions.

? QUESTIONS

1 Define AFC, AVC and ATC. Explain the shape and relationship of their respective curves.
2 Consider how AC will vary in the long run in theory and in practice.
3 In an industry the MES level of output forms a significant share of total output, yet the cost disadvantage for smaller plants is fairly small. What does this say about the extent of economies of scale in the industry?
4 If an industry experienced neither economies of scale nor diseconomies of scale, how would this affect the long-run average cost curve? Draw a diagram based on Figures 20.2 and 20.3 to illustrate your answer.
5 Distinguish between the effects of a change in fixed costs and in variable costs on the AC and MC curves.

Data response A
OFF-PEAK DECISION FOR A HOTELIER

The manager of a small 20-room hotel in a seaside resort reckons he can charge an average of £15 per room per night during the off-peak season and achieve an occupancy rate of 80 per cent. Total fixed costs off-peak are estimated as £60 000. Variable costs sum to £7000 over a 30-day period. Should the hotel remain open?

Data response B
ECONOMIES OF SCALE IN CAR PRODUCTION

Study the following tables and then answer the questions.

Table 20.5 Index of unit costs in car manufacture

Output units per year	Index of unit costs
100 000	100
250 000	83
500 000	74
1 000 000	70
2 000 000	66
3 000 000	65

Table 20.6 Minimum efficient scale (MES) in different car manufacturing operations

Manufacturing operation	Units per plant per year
Casting of engine blocks	1 000 000
Casting of various other parts	100 000 – 750 000
Power train (engine, transmission) machining and assembly	600 000
Pressing of various panels	1–2 000 000
Paint shop	250 000
Final assembly	250 000

Table 20.7 Minimum efficient scale in different car non-manufacturing operations

Non-manufacturing operation	Optimum units per year
Advertising	1 000 000
Sales	2 000 000
Risks	1 800 000
Finance	2 500 000
R&D	5 000 000

Source: G. Rhys, 'Economics of the Motor Industry', Economics, Winter 1988

1 Discuss the main sources of economies of scale.
2 Discuss the implications for car production of the cost information given in Table 20.5.
3 Discuss the implications for decision-making in the car industry of the various levels of minimum efficient scale (MES) for the different activities given in Tables 20.6 and 20.7.

21 Competitive supply

Learning outcomes

At the end of this chapter you will be able to:
▶ Distinguish between the short-run and the long-run equilibrium positions of the competitive firm.
▶ Understand the derivation of the supply curve in perfect competition.
▶ Appreciate why a perfectly competitive environment will yield an optimum allocation of resources.

Having examined the cost structures of the business, we can now turn to look at how a firm's price and output policy is determined. In this chapter we consider market behaviour under conditions of perfect competition. It should be remembered that the guiding principle of the business is *profit maximisation*. We can therefore say that the firm will be in equilibrium if it is maximising its profits.

The best profit output

Output and profit in the short run

Under perfect competition the firm is a price-taker, i.e. it has no control over the market price. It can only sell or not sell at that price (see page 113). Therefore, in trying to maximise its profits, the firm has no pricing decision to make; it can only choose the output which it thinks most advantageous. For example, in a freely competitive market a farmer could choose how much wheat to plant but could not control the price at which it would be sold when harvested.

The best profit position for any business in perfect competition would be where it equated the price of the product with its marginal cost (MC).

If the cost of producing one more unit (MC) is less than the revenue the producer obtains for selling it, i.e. the price, then profit can be increased by producing and selling that unit. Even when MC is rising, so long as it is less than the price, the firm will go on producing because it is gaining *extra profit*.

It does not matter if the extra profit is only small, it is nevertheless an *addition to profit* and, if the firm is out to maximise profits, it will wish to receive this. This is illustrated in Figure 21.1, where the most profitable output is OM. If the business produced a smaller output (OL), then the cost of producing a unit (MC) is less than the revenue received from selling it (P). The business could therefore increase its profits by expanding output. The shaded area represents the extra profit available to the producer as output expands. At

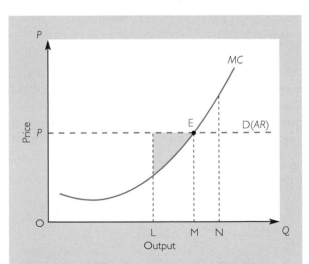

Figure 21.1 Perfect competition in the short run
The firm produces the output at which MC = P.

point E (output OM) there is no more extra profit to be gained. If the firm were to produce a large output (ON), then the cost of producing that unit (MC) would be greater than the revenue from selling it (P) and the producer could increase profits by contracting output back towards OM. Thus the output at which MC = P is an **equilibrium position**, i.e. the one at which the firm will be happy to remain if it is allowed to.

Let us look again at our example from Chapter 7 where we considered the apple grower. Suppose that the orchard owner has produced a crop of apples. The grower now has to harvest them and send them to market. Since apples are highly perishable they will continue to be sent to market while the extra cost (MC) incurred in doing so (labour, transport, etc.) is less than the money received for selling them (P). As soon as the cost of getting them to market is greater than the money received for them the grower will cease to do so, even if it means leaving the apples to rot.

You will notice in Figure 21.1 that we have not included the AC curve. This is because it is not necessary in the short run to demonstrate how much or how little profit the firm is making to be able to conclude that it is the best profit possible. We have already seen that a firm may produce in the short run, even if it is making a loss, so long as it is covering its variable costs.

Therefore we can conclude that so long as price is above AVC a perfectly competitive business will maximise its profits or (which is the same thing) minimise its losses by producing the output at which MC = P.

We shall see in the next chapter that under perfect competition price can be equated with marginal revenue (MR). Thus we could restate the proposition as MC = MR. This then becomes the profit maximisation position for all types of competition.

● *Common misunderstanding*

Profit is not maximised where MR (or the competitive price) exceeds MC; a firm could gain more profit by expanding its output. Profits are maximised at the level of output where MC = MR. (In the case of perfect competition, since P = MR, then profits are maximised where MC = P). At this point all available profit has been obtained; no extra can be gained. Should MR be less than MC it would pay the firm to reduce its level of output.

The long-run equilibrium

Although a business might produce at a loss in the short run, in the long run all costs must be covered. In order to consider the long-run situation we must bring average cost into the picture.

Before doing this it will be useful if we list some of the main points established so far. Check that you fully understand them before proceeding any further.

(a) Under perfect competition there is a freedom of entry and exit to the market.
(b) MC = MR is the profit maximisation output.
(c) MC cuts AC at the lowest point of AC.
(d) At below normal profit, firms will leave the industry; if profit is above normal new firms will be attracted into the industry.

Since the MC curve cuts the AC curve at the lowest point on AC it follows that this intersection must occur at a level which is higher, lower or equal to price. These three possibilities are shown on Figure 21.2. In situation (a) the ATC curve dips down below the AR curve and the business is making **abnormal profit**. Remember that normal profit is included in the costs of the firm. Thus any positive gap between ATC and AR must be abnormal profit. In the long run the abnormal profit attracts new firms into the industry and the profit is competed away. Therefore (a) cannot be a long-run position.

In situation (b) the ATC is at all points above AR and therefore there is no output at which the business can make a profit. It may remain in business in the short run so long as price (AR) is above AVC, but in the long run it will close down. Therefore (b) cannot be a long-run position either.

In situation (c) the ATC is tangential to the AR curve. Thus the firm exists making just normal profit but no abnormal profit. The firm may therefore continue in this position since it is not making enough profit to attract other firms to compete that profit away. Hence (c) is the long-run equilibrium position of the business operating under conditions of perfect competition. We may conclude, therefore, that under perfect competition the long-run equilibrium for the business is where:

$$MC = P = AC = AR$$

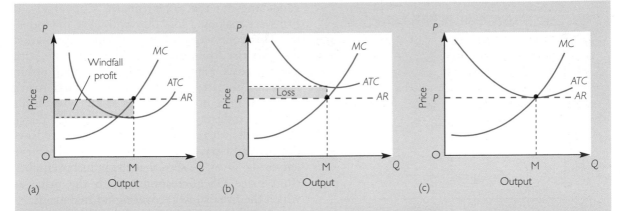

Figure 21.2 **The long-run equilibrium of the firm under perfect competition**
(a) Windfall profits attract new firms to the industry. This lowers price and eliminates the abnormal profits. (b) The firm is making a loss and in the long run will leave the industry. (c) The firm is just recovering normal profit. This is the long-run equilibrium where: $MC = P = AR = AC$.

The average business is hardly likely to look at the process in this way. Profit maximisation is arrived at by practical knowledge of the business and by trial and error. The concepts of marginal cost, average revenue, etc., allow us to generalise the principles that are common to all businesses. Although business people may not be familiar with words like 'marginal revenue', they are nevertheless used to the practice of making small variations in output and price to achieve the best results. Thus, they are using a marginal technique to maximise their profits.

The supply curve

The firm's supply curve

Having demonstrated the equilibrium of the firm we will now go on to consider the derivation of the supply curve.

It will be recalled that the supply curve shows how supply varies in response to changes in price. No matter how the market price changes, the demand curve always appears to be a horizontal line to the individual firm under perfect competition. Therefore as price goes up or down the firm always tries to equate price with marginal cost in order to maximise its profits. In Figure 21.3 as price increases from OP_1 to OP_2 to OP_3 the firm expands output from OM_1 to OM_2 to OM_3. This, therefore, shows how the firm varies output in response to changes in price; in other words it is a supply curve. Thus we may conclude that:

Under perfect competition the firm's *MC* curve, above *AVC*, is its supply curve.

Industry supply

If we can explain the firm's supply curve then we can explain the industry supply curve since, as we saw at the beginning of Chapter 8, the industry supply curve is the horizontal summation of individual firms' supply curves.

A change in supply

Figure 21.4 illustrates a shift in the supply curve; this would be brought about by a change in the ***conditions of supply***. Thus, for example, the leftward shift in the supply curve could have been brought about by an increase in the costs of production.

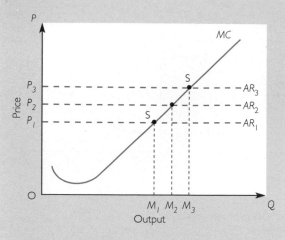

Figure 21.3 Under perfect competition the firm's MC curve is its supply curve
As price rises from OP_1 to OP_2 to OP_3, so the firm expands output from OM_1 to OM_2 to OM_3, in each case equating MC with P. Thus SS is the supply curve.

The equilibrium of the industry

The industry equilibrium occurs when the number of firms in the industry is stable and industry output is stable. As we have seen, above-normal profits will attract new firms into the industry, but the extra output produced by the firms will then depress the market price, thus

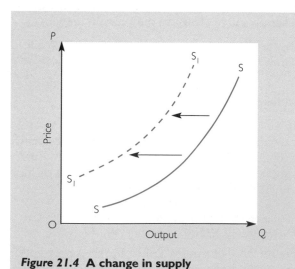

Figure 21.4 A change in supply
The leftwards shift of the SS curve is the result of change in one of the conditions of supply, e.g. a rise in costs.

squeezing out the excess profit. Conversely, if firms are making a loss they will leave the industry. This contraction of output will cause market price to rise, thus bringing price into line with average costs. Figure 21.5 shows the relationship between industry supply and individual firm's supply. If price is OT then this attracts new firms into the industry and shifts the supply curve rightwards, whereas if price is OR firms are leaving the industry, thus shifting the supply curve leftwards. It can be seen that the industry equilibrium price OS corresponds with the price at which the firm is just recovering normal profit.

It should not be thought that the equilibrium for the industry represents a static situation. The equilibrium may be the long-run result of a situation where different firms are constantly entering and leaving the industry, but overall the situation is stable.

The optimality of perfect competition

The optimum allocation of resources

The importance of the idea of perfect competition is that it represents, to many economists, the ideal working of the free market system. The fundamental problem of any economy, it will be remembered, is to make the best use of scarce resources. If we look at the model of perfect competition we will see how it relates to this.

An individual will purchase a product until the marginal utility, or the additional satisfaction gained, from the last unit purchased is equal to its price; at that point no further consumer surplus can be gained from buying the good. The marginal utility curve is, in fact, the basis of the demand curve when expressed in monetary terms.

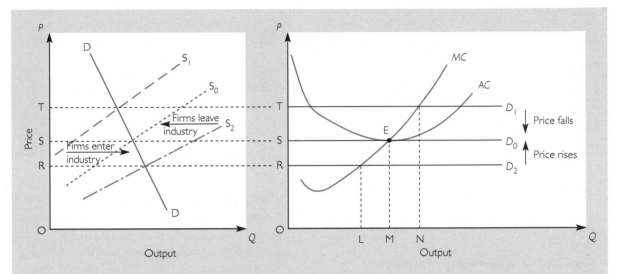

Figure 21.5 Industry equilibrium and firm's equilibrium
If industry price is OT then abnormal profits attract new firms and supply increases from S_1 to S_0 and price falls to S. If industry price is OR firms leave the industry and the supply curve shifts from S_2 to S_0. Industry equilibrium is where S_0 intersects with industry demand curve DD, corresponding to long-run equilibrium for the firm at OM. Note: Industry demand curve is downward sloping but it always appears horizontal to the firm; thus at price OT the firm's demand curve is D_1, at price OS it is D_0, and so on.

In perfect competition $MC = P$ for any level of output. Since $MC = P$, then:

Marginal utility equals marginal cost. This is a welfare-maximising equilibrium position for the individual.

At lower output levels the consumer values any additional unit purchased more than its marginal cost, i.e. $MC < P$, and output should be increased. At higher output levels the individual places a lower value on an additional unit purchased relative to its marginal cost, i.e. $MC > P$; less should be produced. By the aggregation of individual marginal utility (MU) and MC curves it would be possible to demonstrate the welfare-maximising equilibrium for the whole industry.

In addition, in its long-run equilibrium the firm is producing where $MC = AC$, i.e. at the bottom of the AC curve. At this point output costs, i.e. the quantity of resources needed to produce a unit of the commodity, are minimised. Looking at Figure 21.6 you can see that if the firm produced a greater or smaller output the cost of producing a unit would rise. In the long-run equilibrium, therefore, the firm is making an optimum use of its resources. If every firm in the economy operated

under these conditions it would follow that there would be an optimum allocation of resources (since $MC = P$) and every commodity would be produced at a minimum unit cost. Indeed all firms would be producing to consumers' demand curves and therefore not only would the goods be produced at a minimum cost but they would also be the goods which people wanted.

It has already been seen that this view of the economy is subject to two major criticisms. First, that the commodities which people are willing to pay for may not be the goods which are most useful to society, and, second, that income in the economy may be unevenly distributed, meaning that an efficient system may not be socially just (see Chapter 4).

Competition is, however, also important as a political idea. When right-wing parties advocate increasing the amount of free competition in the economy it is in the belief that this will lead to a more efficient use of resources. Even trade unions have advocated 'free competition' in wage bargaining. Free competition in our economy is something of a myth, in that markets often tend to be dominated by large organisations with a great deal of

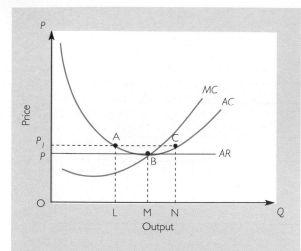

Figure 21.6 The optimality of perfect competition

The long-run equilibrium is at output OM, which corresponds to the lowest unit cost at point B on the AC curve. At any other output, greater or smaller, the unit cost is higher, as at points A and C on the AC curve.

monopoly power. In the same way, in some industries 'free collective bargaining' is dominated by large unions, although the power of the unions generally has declined in recent years. Imperfections in the market are the rule rather than 'free and unfettered competition'. The importance of the model of perfect competition is not that it is attainable but that it gives us a measure with which to assess the imperfections of competition.

Summary

1 The firm under perfect competition maximises its profits by producing the output at which $MC = P$.
2 In the long run the firm's equilibrium is where $MC = P = AR = AC$.
3 Under perfect competition the firm's supply curve is its MC curve and the industry supply curve is the aggregation of individual firms' MC curves.

---

4 The equilibrium for the industry is where output is stable, the number of firms is stable and overall the industry is making normal profit.
5 There is an optimum allocation of resources in the sense that the marginal utilities of consumers are equated with the marginal costs of production.
6 In addition, in the long run firms operate at the bottom of their AC curves; output costs are minimised.

? QUESTIONS

1 'Perfect competition is an ideal state that is unattainable; it has no practical relevance.' Discuss this statement.
2 Explain the 'welfare connotations' of perfect competition.
3 Explain the profit-maximising rule for a perfectly competitive firm.
4 How will a firm's long-run equilibrium differ from its short-run equilibrium under conditions of competitive supply?
5 Contrast the effects on the equilibrium of a competitive firm of a change in its fixed costs with those of a change in its variable costs.
6 The figures in Table 21.1 give the revenue, output and costs of a firm. From this information construct the firm's short-run supply curve. Explain how you establish your answer.

Data response A
THE PUCKBOAT COMPANY

Table 21.2 gives the total cost schedule for Puckboat, a small business making fibreglass dinghies.

1 Calculate Puckboat's average and marginal cost schedules.
2 Assuming that Puckboat is able to sell any quantity of dinghies at a price of £480, construct a graph to show the firm's average cost, marginal cost and marginal revenue.

Table 21.1 Revenue and costs of a firm

Output	0	1	2	3	4	5	6	7	8
Total revenue (£)	0	300	600	900	1200	1500	1800	2100	2400
Total costs (£)	580	700	800	880	1000	1200	1480	1840	2280

Table 21.2 Costs of the Puckboat Company

Output of dinghies per week	Total costs (£)
0	1160
1	1400
2	1600
3	1760
4	2000
5	2400
6	2960
7	3680
8	4560

3 Determine the profit maximisation output for this firm.

4 Consider the long-run effects upon Puckboat of the following price changes, assuming that its cost structure remains unaltered:
   (a) Price falls to £320.
   (b) Price increases to £640.
   In both cases explain your answer as fully as possible.

5 What alternative policy strategies might Puckboat have to that of profit maximisation?

6 What extra information would Puckboat need in order to pursue each of these 'alternative policies'?

Data response B
THE LIBERAL POINT OF VIEW

Read the following passage which extols the merits of the free market.

In a society where the sheer quantity of information necessary for the coordination of the immense number of projects and individual actions is dispersed amongst a large number of individual personalities and surpasses the ability of any individual brain to comprehend, it is the mechanism of the market which allows each of us, and society as a whole, to benefit from the sum total of information, understanding and knowledge in a way which is beyond the capability of any other system of economic organisation.

To put it another way, the superiority of the market mechanism is that it allows us to bring about an optimal distribution of resources, without a full comprehension of all the information and understanding which is scattered throughout society, and without the procedures which must be prescribed under any other economic system. This characteristic, according to Hayek, allows us to bring about the best coordination and thus the best coherence and effectiveness of all decisions and actions of each individual.

It is fundamental to the nature of the market that the knowledge of the things necessary for the well running of a complex society is atomistic and dispersed, because it is founded on the principle that 'each person is free to utilise all the knowledge available, even if it is incomplete, to interact with his environment according to his own designs'. The mechanism of the free market is that which experience has shown to be the most effective at resolving the problems of the mobilisation, communication and accumulation of knowledge.

Henri Lepage *Les Cahiers Français*
(Translated by John Beardshaw)

Answer the following questions:

1 Explain as fully as possible the assumptions on which this liberal view of the market economy is based.

2 With the aid of a diagram(s) explain how perfect competition brings about an optimal distribution of resources.

3 What are the shortcomings of the market system?

(With all these questions you may find it useful to refresh your knowledge of the views of Adam Smith.)

22 Price and output under imperfect competition

Learning outcomes

At the end of this chapter you will be able to:

▶ Explain the techniques for profit maximisation.
▶ Understand the concept of marginal revenue and account for its relationship with price elasticity of demand.
▶ Identify the equilibrium positions of the monopolist and the monopolistic competitor.
▶ Appreciate the notion of oligopolistic interdependence.
▶ Discuss the kinked demand curve model as an explanation of oligopolistic behaviour and be aware of its limitations as a general model.
▶ Account for oligopolistic price collusion.
▶ Appreciate the significance of non-price competition in oligopolies and understand the reasons for price wars.
▶ Recognise the prevalence of mark-up pricing.
▶ Outline the limitations of alternative theories of the firm.
▶ Explain the concept of a contestable market.
▶ Understand the theory of limit pricing.

Perfect and imperfect competition

Perfect and imperfect markets compared

Having considered perfect markets we will now turn to imperfect ones.

An imperfect market is simply one in which one or more of the assumptions of perfect competition does not hold true.

You will recall that the assumptions of perfect competition appeared very unrealistic and, indeed, very few real-life industries even approximate to perfect competition.

In practice virtually all markets deviate from the conditions of perfect competition and hence are imperfectly competitive.

Rejecting perfect competition as a description of how actual markets operate does not mean it is of no importance as a theoretical model. As we have seen, perfect competition provides the conditions under which we can construct a supply curve; it is important to realise that:

A supply curve assumes that firms are responding to a price which is given to them, i.e. beyond their control.

In imperfect competition firms typically decide and set the price themselves. Hence, although demand and supply analysis often provides useful predictions about market behaviour it can be a misleading analysis if applied to imperfectly competitive markets.

We also see in Sections II and VI of this book that perfect competition is also an important assumption in welfare economics. The problem for the economist is that, when looking for a model of the way firms behave in an imperfect competitive world, there are many models to choose from. We will state at the outset that there is no consensus as to which of these alternative approaches is the most useful. Nevertheless, the range of models provides an array of analytical tools from which the economist may choose as seems appropriate to understanding a particular industry.

You will recall that under perfect competition a firm which raises its price will immediately lose all its customers to its competitors. Hence, the demand curve facing the individual firm in perfect competition is horizontal. In imperfect competition such price competition is less fierce because there are fewer competitors for customers to turn to and/or the products of firms are not identical and hence consumers may have a preference for a particular firm's product. This means that a firm which raises its price will lose some but not all of its customers, and hence the demand curve facing the firm is downward sloping. The ability to recognise that a firm facing a downward-sloping demand curve signifies imperfect competition is often called for in economics examinations.

The 'traditional' theory of monopoly

This model is often said to apply to the situation where there is just one firm in an industry, i.e. the monopolist is the sole seller of the product. We shall see that this definition of monopoly is too simplistic (see Chapter 8 and below). But for now it should be appreciated that even complete freedom from competition does not mean the firm can sell any amount at any price it wishes.

● *Common misunderstanding*

It is incorrect to say that a monopolist will always charge the highest price it can. Even within a market a higher price will mean that some consumers can afford to buy less or are induced to switch their purchasing power to other markets. In short, a monopolist faces a downward-sloping demand curve and it is this that dictates the price it can charge for any level of output.

We will now reconsider profit maximisation in the case of such a firm and compare this with profit maximisation under perfect competition.

Profit-maximising techniques

Analysis using total revenue and total cost

We can demonstrate profit maximisation most easily by simply subtracting total cost from total revenue at all levels of output. This is done in Table 22.1. Here we have used the same total cost schedule as in Chapters 7 and 20. The total revenue schedule is derived from the downward-sloping demand curve for the firm's product. As you can see, in this example, the business maximises its profits at an output of 4 units per week where it makes a profit of £184 per week. You will notice that this is *not* the output at which revenue is maximised; this occurs at the output of 5 units per week. We will see the reason for this as we work through the chapter.

Figure 22.1 presents the information from Table 22.1 in graphical form. Total profit (*TP*) is the gap between the total cost curve and the total revenue curve. From the graphs you can see that the firm can make abnormal profits anywhere between the output of 1 unit per week up to an output of about 7 units per week.

Table 22.1 Profit maximisation using total cost and total revenue schedules

Output, units per week, Q	Total revenue, TR (£)	Total cost, TC (£)	Total profit, TP (£)
0	0	116	−116
1	144	140	+4
2	256	160	+96
3	336	176	+160
4	384	200	+184
5	400	240	+160
6	384	296	+88
7	336	368	−32
8	256	456	−200

While profit is increasing the *TC* and *TR* curves must be diverging; while as profit is decreasing *TC* and *TR* must be converging.

Therefore, when profit is maximised the two curves will be neither diverging nor converging, i.e. they will be parallel to each other. At the same output the *TP* curve will be at its maximum and its slope will be zero, since at that point profit will be neither rising nor falling.

We will return to total cost and total revenue curves later when we consider *mark-up pricing*, but now we will turn to the more usual way of presenting profit maximisation, which involves the use of marginal cost, which we met in Chapter 7, and marginal revenue.

Marginal revenue

In order to explain the behaviour of the firm we must introduce the concept of marginal revenue (*MR*):

Marginal revenue is the change to total revenue from the sale of one more unit of a commodity.

Suppose for example that a firm was selling 4 units a week at £10 each. Then the total revenue would be £40, but, since this is imperfect compe-

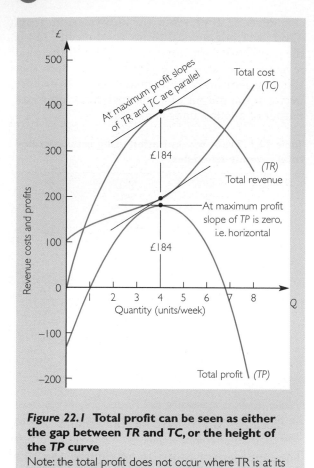

Figure 22.1 Total profit can be seen as either the gap between *TR* and *TC*, or the height of the *TP* curve
Note: the total profit does not occur where TR is at its greatest.

not marginal revenue is positive or negative depends upon whether the gain in revenue from extra sales is greater or smaller than the loss on preceding units. This depends upon which part of a firm's demand curve schedule we are considering.

Table 22.2 gives a demand schedule, a total revenue schedule and, in the last column, the marginal revenue schedule. The marginal revenue can now be seen as the difference between adjacent total revenues. You can see that as price is lowered, total revenue increases until point F in the table and then begins to decrease because the increase in sales is now no longer great enough to offset the fall in price. Thus after point F marginal revenue becomes negative.

Table 22.2 Marginal revenue

	Output, Q (units/week)	Average revenue, P (£/unit)	Total revenue, P x Q (TR)	Marginal revenue, $TR_n - TR_{n-1}$ (MR)
A	0	160	0	
				144
B	1	144	144	
				112
C	2	128	256	
				80
D	3	112	336	
				48
E	4	96	384	
				16
F	5	80	400	
				−16
G	6	64	384	
				−48
H	7	48	336	
				−80
I	8	32	256	
				−112
J	9	16	144	
				−144
K	10	0	0	

tition, if it wishes to sell more it must lower its prices. Therefore, for example, selling 5 units a week may involve dropping the price to £9, in which case the total revenue will now be £45. Thus the change to the firm's total revenue as a result of selling one more unit is £5. This is termed the marginal revenue.

In order to sell more the imperfect competitor must, as we have seen, lower the price. If, for example, sales are 50 units per week at a price of £10 and sales are increased to 51 units by lowering the price to £9, then not only does the firm lose money on the 51st unit but also all the preceding units now all have to be priced at £9. Thus total revenue decreases from £500 to £459, giving a marginal revenue of minus £41. (For the extra £9 sales revenue gained from the 51st unit the firm has sacrificed £1 on the preceding 50 units; thus MR = (£9 − £50) = −£41.) Whether or

Figure 22.2 presents the information for demand and marginal revenue in graphical form. Note that once again the *MR* curve is plotted in a special manner, as was marginal cost.

The mathematical relationship between *AR* and *MR* means that the *MR* curve descends at twice the rate of the *AR* curve.

Thus you can see that the *AR* curve meets the quantity axis at 10 units per week while the *MR* cuts the quantity axis at 5 units per week. This can also be seen in Table 22.2, where you can see that average revenue descends in amounts of £16,

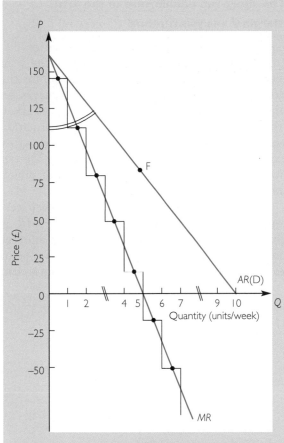

Figure 22.2 Marginal revenue
The *MR* curve descends at twice the rate of the *AR* curve, bisecting the quantity axis.

i.e. £160, £144, £128, etc., while the marginal revenue descends in amounts of £32, i.e. £144, £112, £80, etc. This relationship holds good so long as we have a linear function for *AR*, i.e. the demand curve is a straight line. If the *AR* curve is non-linear (curved) then the relationship becomes more complex. When drawing sketch graphs to illustrate examination answers the student should remember this relationship between *AR* and *MR*; a carelessly drawn graph will show the examiner that you do not appreciate the concepts involved.

Marginal revenue and elasticity

If we examine point F on the *AR* curve in Figure 22.2 we will find that it is when demand is unitary. How can we say this with such certainty? It

---

STUDENT ACTIVITY 22.1

Complete the figures for average revenue (*AR*), total revenue (*TR*) and marginal revenue (*MR*) from the information below:

Output, Q (units/week)	Average revenue, AR (£)	Total revenue, TR (£)	Marginal revenue, MR (£)
0	0	0	
			40
1	40		
2		72	
			24
3	32		
4	28		
5		120	
6		120	
			−8
7	16	112	
8	12		
9	8	72	
			−32
10	4		

is because *MR* is zero at that point. As we descend the demand curve towards point F then the total revenue is increasing; therefore demand must be elastic. Below point F, as price is lowered total revenue decreases and therefore demand must be inelastic. Therefore at point F total revenue must be neither rising nor falling, i.e. it must be constant and thus elasticity must be unitary. You can check this by calculating E_D at F:

$$E_D = \frac{1}{-16} \times \frac{80}{5} = -1$$

Thus we can conclude that:

Demand is elastic when *MR* is positive, inelastic when *MR* is negative and unitary when *MR* is zero.

Marginal revenue and perfect competition

Why did we not consider *MR* when discussing perfect competition? The answer is that, under perfect competition, price and marginal revenue are the same thing. This is because the price is constant so that the firm can sell more without lowering its price. There is thus no loss on

Table 22.3 **Marginal revenue under perfect competition**

Output, Q (units/week)	Average revenue, AR (£/unit)	Total revenue, TR (P × Q)	Marginal revenue, MR ($TR_n - TR_{n-1}$)
0	5	0	
1	5	5	5
2	5	10	5
3	5	15	5
4	5	20	5
5	5	25	5

preceding units as sales expand; each extra unit sold results in the same addition to total revenue. This is illustrated in Table 22.3, where you can see that *MR* and *AR*(P) are both £5. Thus, when we come to draw the *MR* curve for perfect competition it coincides with the *AR* curve as shown in Figure 22.3(a). The short-run equilibrium condition for the firm under perfect competition, which you will recall is:

$$MC = P$$

can now be restated as:

$$MC = MR$$

and the long-run equilibrium as:

$$MC = MR = AC = AR$$

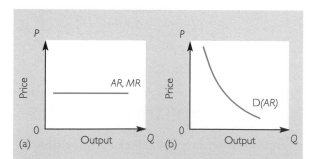

Figure 22.3 The marginal revenue curve
(a) Perfect competition. *MR* and *AR* curves coincide because price is constant.
(b) The industry demand curve remains downward sloping, thus the *MR* curve would look like that in Figure 22.2.

The short-run equilibrium of the firm: marginal analysis method

Let us now revert to the monopoly situation discussed in the previous section (where the firm faces a downward-sloping demand curve for the product) and draw the *MR* and *MC* curves on one graph. We can see from Figure 22.4 (taken from Table 22.4 which shows all the information we have developed in this chapter) that they cross exactly at an output of 4 units per week. We can now state that this will be the output at which the firm will maximise its profits.

How are we able to say this with such certainty? The explanation is this. While *MR* is greater than *MC* the cost of producing another unit of the commodity is less than the revenue to be gained from selling it, so that the business can

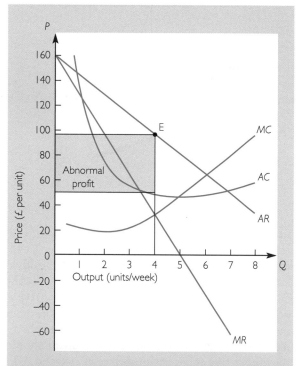

Figure 22.4 The equilibrium price and output of the firm under imperfect competition in the short run
Profit is maximised at an output of 4 units and a price of £96, i.e. where:

$$MR = MC$$

and

$$Profit = (AR - AC) \times Q = £184$$

add to its profits by producing and selling that unit. This remains true so long as *MC* is **less** than *MR*. Thus the business will increase its profits by expanding its output. However, once *MC* is **greater** than *MR* then the cost of producing another unit is greater than the revenue to be derived from selling it and the business could, therefore, increase its profit by contracting output.

We can conclude, therefore, that:

The business will maximise its profits by producing the output at which *MR* = *MC*.

You will see that this is essentially the same analysis as for perfect competition because although we have stated the condition for perfect competition as *MC* = *P*, we now realise that *MR* is the same as *P* under perfect competition (see Chapter 21). Thus:

MC = *MR* is the profit maximisation condition for all types of competition.

In Figure 22.4 the shaded rectangle represents abnormal profit. At an output of 4 units per week *AR* (price) is £96 and average cost (*AC*) is £50. The difference between the two (£46) is profit and the firm has made this profit on 4 units. We could express this as:

$$TP = (AR - AC) \times Q$$
$$= (£96 - £50) \times 4$$
$$= £184$$

Alternatively it could be expressed as:

$$TP = TR - TC$$
$$= (AR \times Q) - (AC \times Q)$$
$$= (£96 \times 4) - (£50 \times 4)$$
$$= £184$$

The mathematically minded will realise that the 'contribution' to total profit can also be calculated by summing all *MR*s at the output of four and subtracting the summation of all the *MC*s at that output. To calculate actual profit, fixed costs must also be subtracted from this contribution, that is:

Total profit = Sum of all *MR*s − Sum of the *MC*s − Fixed cost

or

$$TP = \Sigma MR - \Sigma MC - FC$$

You will recall from Chapter 7 that normal profit is included in the cost of the business. Therefore, the profit discussed above is all **abnormal profit** (also called **excess profit** or **monopoly profit**), i.e. all this profit could be eliminated without forcing the business to leave the industry. How has this abnormal profit been made? The answer is by selling a restricted output at a higher price, i.e. in comparison with perfect competition the monopolist (or any imperfectly competitive firm) has raised the price by **contriving scarcity**.

Table 22.4 **Costs, revenues and profits under imperfect competition**

Output, Q (units/week)		Average revenue, P (£/unit)	Total revenue, TR (P × Q)	Total cost, TC (£)	Total profit, TP (TR − TC)	Marginal cost, MC ($TC_n - TC_{n-1}$)	Marginal revenue, MR ($TR_n - TR_{n-1}$)	Average cost, AC (TC/Q)
A	0	160	0	116	−116			∞
						24	144	
B	1	144	144	140	+4			140
						20	112	
C	2	128	256	160	+96			80
						16	80	
D	3	112	336	176	+160			58.6
						24	48	
E	4	96	384	200	+184	MC = MR		50
						40	16	
F	5	80	400	240	+160			48
						56	−16	
G	6	64	384	296	+88			49.3
						72	−48	
H	7	48	336	368	−32			52.6
						88	−80	
I	8	32	256	456	−200			57

From the information below calculate the total profit, marginal revenue and marginal cost schedules and indicate the profit-maximising level of output:

Output, Q (units/week)	Total revenue, TR (£)	Total cost, TC (£)	Total profit, TP (£)	Marginal revenue, MR (£)	Marginal cost, MC (£)
0	0	87			
1	108	105			
2	192	120			
3	250	130			
4	286	150			
5	302	178			
6	286	220			
7	250	276			
8	192	342			

The equilibrium of the monopolist

This contrived scarcity can be seen in Table 22.4 and Figure 22.4. For the monopolist MR is less than price and hence profits are maximised where $MR = MC$ at an output of 4 units and a price of £96. For firms in perfect competition MR = price and hence output will be increased until $MC = P$ at 6 units of output and a price of £64. Thus, a standard criticism of monopoly is that it tends to restrict output and raise prices to consumers. In fact such 'welfare' aspects of monopoly turn out to be more complicated than this and are considered in the next chapter.

Can you think of any circumstances under which a monopolist may actually charge a lower price than, say, that which operates in a perfectly competitive industry?

The traditional textbook model of monopoly assumes that there is a sole seller of a particular product, which is usually protected by high barriers to entry. In this case there is no one, therefore, able to compete for the monopolist's abnormal profit and, if there were, they would find it difficult to enter such a market. Thus in the traditional theory of monopoly the long-run equilibrium is like the short-run one, i.e. unlike perfect competition abnormal profits are not competed away in the long run. For many examination questions the assumptions of a sole seller and long-run abnormal profits are the distinguishing features of monopoly; in practice it is more accurate to consider degrees of monopoly.

The degree of monopoly

As previously noted in Chapter 8 the traditional view of monopoly as described above is rather simplistic.

In practice, a firm can exert considerable market power with far less than 100 per cent of the market.

In most instances a monopolist is likely to be in competition with firms selling similar products. Furthermore, the breadth of definition of a market must be arbitrary. Thus, the market share of a firm depends on how broadly we choose to define the market. The broader the range of products included as part of the market (or the wider its geographic limitations), the smaller will any firm's market share appear to be, i.e. the market concentration ratio (see Chapter 19) is inversely related to the level of product (or geographic) aggregation.

Industrial economists often use the definitions of industries employed in Standard Industrial Classifications to assess the extent of market domination and the degree of monopoly power. However, as noted in Chapter 7, industries are not necessarily the same as markets and both concepts can be difficult to define and measure with any accuracy.

There is also the question of how long we can assume a relative absence of competition to persist. High profitability may result eventually in new entry or the introduction of more products which are partial substitutes. Indeed, if high profits have hastened the development of a product or new competition (or, if the development of a new product or process led to the establishment of the monopoly in the first place), then the monopoly may be judged to have been beneficial.

The Austrian school of economics emphasises precisely these dynamic benefits of monopoly profit. In fact, while some evidence points towards a positive relationship between the degree of seller concentration and profitability, not all studies support the notion that the average level of profits in an industry rises with seller concentration. It is also not entirely clear whether the higher profits, should they exist, stem from increased monopoly power or from the greater efficiency (i.e. lower costs) of the largest firms in a market compared with their smaller rivals. Such considerations blur the concept of monopoly and its welfare implications. What we can say is this:

Rather than monopoly being an 'either or' situation, we can say that the extent of market domination or degree of monopoly increases the higher a firm's industry and market share; the lower the price elasticity of demand for its product; the lower the cross elasticity with other products; and the higher the barriers to new entry.

These determinants are not independent of one another and, in addition, firms may collude to increase the effective degree of monopoly (see below). **Michael Kalecki**, the great Polish economist, and some modern economists such as **K. Cowling** have suggested that we can expect the mark-up of a firm's price above its unit variable cost to reflect the degree of monopoly (see Figure 22.5). However, there are also other considerations when assessing the relative merits of a particular monopoly situation.

● Common misunderstanding

Monopoly power should not always and automatically be regarded as a 'bad thing' in itself. Most firms with monopoly power are likely to face competition from rival products, although the extent of competition may be quite limited. Monopolists are able to restrict output and raise prices, but, by the same token, monopolists may benefit from lower costs of production compared with those in perfectly competitive conditions. Evidence cannot say with complete accuracy whether lower costs or greater market power are more of a determinant of profitability in highly concentrated industries. These points are pursued in the next chapter when discussing the basis of government policy towards monopoly enshrined in competition policy.

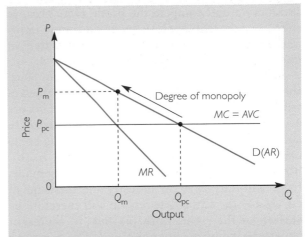

Figure 22.5 Price and the degree of monopoly
In a perfect market, price and output are P_{pc} and Q_{pc}. The greater the degree of monopoly the nearer the firm moves towards situation P_m, Q_m.

The equilibrium of the monopolistically competitive firm

You may, if you prefer, skip this section and move straight on to oligopoly. This model was developed independently by **E.H. Chamberlin** and **J. Robinson** in the 1930s as a response to the inadequacies of perfect competition and traditional monopoly theory.

These economists had noted that in most industries firms tend to differentiate their products either by actual differences or by perceived differences such as brand names.

Monopolistic competition differs from the assumptions of perfect competition in that, although a large number of firms are assumed, firms differentiate their products from competitors.

Thus, as there are no perfect substitutes, firms again face a downward-sloping demand curve. But the model is like perfect competition and different from monopoly in that there is relative freedom of entry to the industry; hence no abnormal profits can persist in the long run.

If one business is seen to be making high profits in a situation where there are lots of competitors in an imperfect market, other businesses will be encouraged to enter that line of production and compete the profit away because there is something close to freedom of entry and exit to the market. This is illustrated in Figure 22.6.

In (a) abnormal profits are being made. Since there is free entry to the market other businesses enter and compete this profit away. This occurs as the demand curves for the existing firms are shifted to the left by new firms attracting some customers by offering similar products. In (b), however, less than normal profits are being made; firms will thus leave the industry and the demand curves for the firms that remain will therefore be shifted to the right. Both (a) and (b) represent short-run equilibrium positions. The long-run equilibrium is (c), where firms are maximising profits by setting *MC* = *MR* but the *AC* curve is tangential to the *AR* curve; thus firms are receiving only normal profits.

An example of this might be found in, say, the fashion industry. A manufacturer who accurately predicts a new fashion trend may enjoy monopoly profit until other firms copy the designs and the excess profit is competed away. Independent traders such as local newsagents may face similar market characteristics.

You will note in Figure 22.6(c) that, unlike perfect competition, the business does not produce at the lowest point of average cost. This is often regarded as a loss of welfare to the economy in that unit cost would be lower in perfect competition. Against this, however, should be put the greater variety to the consumer under monopolistic competition.

As with monopoly *MR* is less than price; hence, as profit maximising is assumed, *MC* is again below price in equilibrium. This would seem to imply a loss of welfare to society, but, as is always the case when the assumptions of perfect competition are relaxed, the welfare implications are muddied. This is because although *MC* is less than price (implying a less than Pareto-optimal output; see Chapter 27) and firms exhibit excess capacity there is also the benefit from greater product variety.

As with all other theories, the theory of monopolistic competition has weaknesses. For example, the assumptions of similar but differentiated products and independent profit maximisation by firms are inconsistent; in practice firms are acutely aware of the reactions from rival firms and this would lead to a far more complex competitive process. It might be countered that as many firms are in the industry changes by one firm go unnoticed by others, but then the model is silent as to the number of firms or the level of differentiation at which behaviour switches from allowing for interdependence to acting entirely independently.

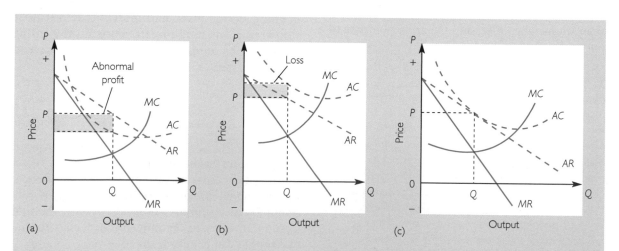

Figure 22.6 The price and output of the firm under monopolistic competition in the long run
(a) The existence of abnormal profits attracts new firms to the industry, which lowers the price and eliminates the profit.
(b) The firm makes a loss at any level of output and in the long run will leave the industry.
(c) The long-run equilibrium, where the firm just recovers normal profit. AC is tangential to AR.

The assumption of product differentiation is also at odds with freedom of entry. A new firm would have to promote its product in order to make its product known and attract customers from established firms. Such 'market penetration' costs could, as research strongly suggests, act as a barrier to entry. As with monopoly we also have the problem of determining the breadth of the industry. Even if it were possible to compile a complete list of cross price elasticities (which it is not), the model would still not tell us the numerical value of such elasticities that would allow inclusion of a firm's product as part of an industry's output – what exactly constitutes 'the same but different' assumption of product differentiation.

Since the degree of product substitutability, barriers to entry and long-run entry are ill-defined, many economists do not feel that the model contributes anything above that offered by a broader treatment of monopoly, e.g. the notion of degrees of monopoly. It is significant, however, that Robinson later rejected the relevance of her model because of its reliance on marginal analysis and certain knowledge of demand and costs.

● *Common misunderstanding*

*While there is debate about the extent of any differences between the different models, nevertheless monopolistic competition is **not** the same thing as monopoly. By differentiating their products firms in monopolistic competition achieve a certain level of monopoly power, but it is assumed that such power is very temporary and can be competed away as new firms enter the industry, unlike in monopoly situations. This is a contentious issue, however, and, as noted above, it may be that we are simply talking about differences in degrees of monopoly power that firms may possess at any one time.*

Oligopolistic competition

Oligopoly – the situation where the market is dominated by a few large firms – is hard to analyse. (Remember from Chapter 8 that the special case of just two firms dominating a market is called duopoly). In perfect competition all firms are so small in relation to the total market that they can ignore changes in the behaviour of individual rivals. This simplifies the analysis as each

firm can be assumed independently to maximise profit. But where there are a smaller number of firms in an industry, they will be affected by changes in one another's behaviour and hence retaliation is likely. This is referred to as *oligopolistic interdependence*.

Oligopolistic interdependence may mean that the competitive process in imperfectly competitive markets is closer to the everyday meaning of the term. In perfect competition firms simply adjust output until marginal cost is equal to a market price which is beyond their control. They do not need to worry about any reactions from other firms. In imperfect competition firms may actively form strategies to gain a competitive advantage over their rivals, and hence competition may be more intense in the sense of trying to beat one's rivals. Such reaction and counter-reaction make for great complexity, all the more so since firms are very **uncertain** about rivals' reactions to changes in their competitive strategies. Thus, predicting the behaviour of the market becomes difficult.

The kinked demand model of oligopoly

This model was developed in 1939 by the economist **P.M. Sweezy**. The model assumes that an oligopolist will expect rival firms to follow any price decrease it makes but not follow any increase. Thus the elasticity of demand for the firm's product is much greater above the ruling price than below it, and hence there is a kink in the demand curve faced by the firm.

For straight line demand curves the marginal revenue line lies half-way between the demand curve and the vertical axis. It is thus easy to show that the kink in the demand curve implies a discontinuity, i.e. a sudden drop, in the marginal revenue curve of the firm (see Figure 22.7).

Marginal cost could thus vary greatly but still pass through this discontinuity in marginal revenue. Equally, changes in market demand could shift demand curves in and out without affecting the height of the kink. In short, profit maximising at $MC = MR$ could leave price unaffected despite considerable fluctuations in costs and demand.

The model has been used to explain why prices appear to fluctuate less in oligopolistic markets

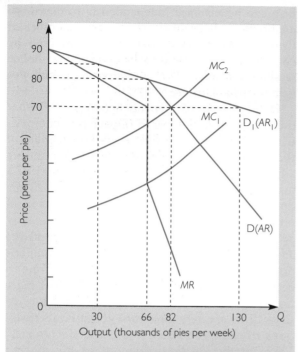

Figure 22.7 A 'kinked' oligopoly demand curve
Assume Meaty is a firm selling meat pies in an oligopolistic market. Meaty's original price is 80p per pie. Meaty raises the price to 85p per pie and sales fall to 30 000. Meaty calculates that if it cuts its prices to 70p per pie sales will expand to 130 000 ($D_1(AR_1)$). However, the cut in price causes competitors to cut prices too and therefore, Meaty's sales are only 82 000. This causes a 'kink' in the demand curve and discontinuity in the MR curve.

than in competitive markets (oligopolistic prices are often said to be 'sticky'). The model has serious flaws, however: again it implies a knowledge of marginal costs and revenue not possessed by real firms; it is not clear that entrepreneurs hold such pessimistic expectations of the reactions of their competitors. But the greatest flaw is that the model does not explain price determination, i.e. it does not explain how the prevailing price was established in the first place or what happens when the price is eventually changed.

Collusion and price leadership

Rivalry usually results in lower profits than could be achieved through firms cooperating with one another.

Such cooperation to limit competition is known as *collusion*, and many economists believe that this is

often a more realistic assumption than rivalry. A more *formal* type of collusion would be a price- or output-fixing ring, known as a *cartel*, in which all firms coordinate their activities so as to maximise joint profits by behaving, in effect, as a monopolist. Such an arrangement is illegal in most countries, but a student should be aware of the term.

Probably the most famous cartel is OPEC, the Organisation for Petroleum Exporting Countries. Its power has somewhat reduced as world non-OPEC oil supplies have increased, but it has survived because as an international organisation it transcends national laws. IATA, the International Air Transport Association, which fixes scheduled air fares, is another international cartel arrangement, although its power has also diminished as the growing deregulation of the world's airline markets has led to excess capacity in the industry. Despite their illegality cartels also persist within countries owing to their profit-raising potential for member firms. Recent examples in the UK have been found among betting shops and cross-Channel ferries and in the glass, insurance, milk, roofing and sugar refining industries. In the EU cartels have been discovered in the steel, PVC and cement industries.

The problem with cartels is that they are inherently unstable and many do not last very long. The members often have difficulty on agreeing how the market should be divided, especially if they are of different sizes or have different costs. The greater the number of firms that belong to the cartel the more difficult that agreement becomes. Such problems are compounded by the possibility of entry of new firms into the industry if entry barriers are low or where the industry is subject to stable or falling demand. Even when agreement has been reached, individual members have a strong incentive to cheat on the arrangement by undercutting the agreed price.

Collusion may instead be more *informal* or *tacit* and take the form of *price leadership* where, instead of competing through price, firms accept one of their number in the industry as a price leader and simply keep their own prices in line with that firm's. Often the dominant firm takes the lead in setting prices. Thus, Ford usually acts as the price leader in the UK car industry and Thomson in the holiday market.

Although these assumptions appear to sidestep the need to analyse oligopolistic interdependence,

interdependence still arises if firms are closely related or if new entry is likely. Moreover, where collusion arises firms can improve their individual position still further by cheating on their 'partners'; hence, collusion has an inherent tendency to break up. Where joint profits are maximised arguments between firms can still arise as to how these profits should be shared. These considerations, together with the illegality of cartels and restrictive practices, suggest that collusion cannot always be assumed.

Price leadership is notoriously difficult to prove as firms will argue that simultaneous price changes are not the result of collusion but reflect the need to respond quickly to changes in the market and the competitive threat of rivals.

Non-price competition and price wars

A common feature of oligopoly is the tendency to avoid competing through price and to use instead other forms of competition such as branding, advertising, competitions and free offers, after-sales services, etc. For example, a car manufacturer will realise that if it cuts the price of a particular model, rival manufacturers can respond almost immediately. If market demand is inelastic, such a price war might do little to expand the market and simply reduce the revenue earned by all the oligopolists. Instead, the firm might introduce a sun roof into the design of the car, or offer a CD player as standard equipment, knowing it may take some time for other firms to respond. In the same way, oligopolistic firms might attempt to use ingenious advertising to steal an advantage over competitors.

There is evidence that the advertising to sales ratio tends to be higher in oligopolistic industries than in industries with either a very low or very high seller concentration ratio.

The advantage of launching an advertising campaign is that it takes a long time (and a lot of expense) for rivals to react by launching a campaign of their own. It is estimated that it takes between £5 million and £7 million, for example, to advertise successfully a new brand of instant coffee.

Nevertheless, price wars do occur in oligopolies, especially where one firm has a much larger market share than its rivals and wishes to drive them out, as has been the case in the daily newspaper market in the UK where News International has used its dominant position to try to increase its market share by significantly reducing prices. A price war is also more likely to occur when market demand is declining and all firms try desperately to hang on to their existing market shares; the cigarette market in the US is a case in point. Finally, a price war is likely to be more prevalent when a new firm enters a market and tries to establish a presence by undercutting its rivals; this happened when the Channel Tunnel was opened in 1994 and Eurotunnel's fares were competitively set to undercut those of the cross-Channel ferries.

STUDENT ACTIVITY 22.4

Think of some industries that you would classify as oligopolies and try to give some practical examples of how the firms in these industries might compete with each other.

Game theory

Game theory attempts to analyse the decision-making behaviour of rivals (players).

It is necessary to assume that players have a finite number of possible courses of action and that they know what the outcome of each possible strategy will be for any given retaliatory strategy played by rivals. The players then assume the worst for themselves in terms of the retaliatory action of rivals. Players thus choose the best of these pessimistically expected outcomes. Usually this anticipation of others' actions results in none of the firms achieving an optimum and hence there are welfare losses for the economy.

The realism of this approach has been questioned and game theory has been described as the 'Argentina' of economics in terms of the gap between potential and achievement. However, given the interdependence and uncertainty that characterises oligopoly, it has been suggested that game theory can provide some insights into oligopolistic behaviour.

Mark-up pricing

It was suggested previously that firms may price, not by using marginal rules (i.e. equating marginal cost and marginal revenue), but via some kind of mark-up procedure above unit variable costs (a technique also known as *cost-plus pricing*). There is plenty of evidence from the UK and the USA that both small and large firms price in this way. The evidence dates back to a survey of oligopolistic firms undertaken in the 1930s by two British economists, **R. Hall** and **C. Hitch**: it was discovered that firms make an estimate of what unit (average) cost will be at the level of output at which they expect to operate (known as the *normal level* of capacity utilisation). A mark-up is then added to this to arrive at a price which covers costs and allows for profit.

According to this approach firms are more likely to adjust their outputs rather than their prices (as implied by the marginal rules) should a change in costs or demand occur.

In principle, therefore, prices would be expected to remain fairly stable or sticky. Since price stickiness is regarded as an important feature of oligopolies, the notion of mark-up pricing has often been closely associated with oligopolistic behaviour. Confirmation of price stickiness is revealed by the fact that, on average, firms change their prices only once or twice a year. They do not like to change prices too often because of the expense involved: current prices have to be checked and, if changes are thought necessary, price lists have to be altered. In addition, firms simply do not like starting price wars.

However, while mark-up pricing may be descriptively accurate of the pricing practices of many firms, this approach is not an analysis of price determination unless the magnitude of, and changes in, the mark-up are explained. In practice, despite the prevalence of cost-based pricing techniques, the main factor that determines price would seem to be market conditions (i.e. the level of demand). Evidence suggests that many oligopolistic firms set their prices at the highest level the market can bear; they are also likely to charge similar prices to their competitors.

● *Common misunderstanding*

Just because most firms seem to price their products according to some kind of mark-up procedure, this does not mean that marginal rules and market conditions are irrelevant. In fact, firms adopt the procedures of traditional theory for pricing even if they do not actually have all the necessary information to equate marginal cost and marginal revenue. Costs are an important factor in setting prices and an increase in costs will often result in an increase in price, just as traditional theory might suggest. However, costs are by no means the only factor that is important in price determination. An increase in demand often leads to a price rise and a fall in demand to a price cut. Rivalry beween firms is another factor that is significant for price determination: one of the key reasons for cutting prices is the price reduction of a rival.

Managerial and behavioural theories revisited

In Chapter 8 it was pointed out that firms may pursue objectives other than profit maximisation. However, the pursuit of profit remains an integral part of both managerial and behavioural theories of the firm. Managerial models deviate from the neo-classical assumption of profit maximisation but are similar in that the firm is regarded as attempting to maximise something, usually with the constraint that there is a minimum of profit which is necessary to prevent takeover and/or keep shareholders happy.

To an extent, the pursuit of growth, employees or sales revenue will coincide with profit making. The point of these models is that managers would be willing to trade off some of the firm's profit in order to get more of what they themselves want. Thus, a general representation of these models might be as shown in Figure 22.8.

However, these models can be criticised. In particular, they do not address the important considerations of oligopolistic interdependence – each firm appears to pursue its managerially chosen ends oblivious of the reaction from rival firms. The evidence as to what is the most general goal of managers and firms is also inconclusive.

It is often claimed that these models predict that price will be raised in the face of an increase in fixed costs in order to preserve the minimum profit constraint. As firms do appear to increase price with increases in fixed costs this is claimed as evidence in support of managerial theories. It has been shown, however, that the predictions of

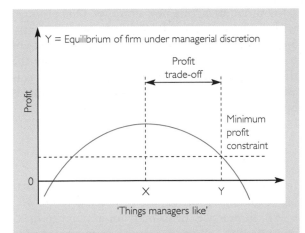

Figure 22.8 Managerial discretion
In this graph profits are plotted against 'things managers like'. Profit maximisation is at X, but left to themselves, managers might go for position Y where the things they like are maximised.

managerial theories vary substantially with minor alterations in their assumptions.

Another line of criticism has been to argue that in most cases the pursuit of managerial goals is ultimately furthered by increasing a firm's profit. For example, growth and sales revenue maximisation in the long run requires substantial investment and the funds for this, whether internally generated or borrowed, depend on the level of profits. Hence, a great deal of intricate analysis can be avoided, with little loss of accuracy, by simply assuming long-run profit maximisation in the first place!

According to behavioural analysis limited knowledge and uncertainty combine to create satisficing rather than maximising behaviour; thus, only a 'satisfactory' market share or level of profit or sales revenue may be sought. To anyone familiar with a large organisation the model is appealing as a description of the way decisions are reached. Again, however, the problem of oligopolistic interdependence is ignored. But by far the biggest problem is that, although in the short term predictable rules of thumb may be adhered to, the model cannot offer any predictions as to how price and quantity will change in response to events which require a new satisficing search.

Contestable markets

Contestability theory argues that the main factor that determines the structure of markets and how firms behave and perform has nothing to do with what is happening in the market itself; instead it has everything to do with the *threat* of entry from outside, i.e. it is *potential* competition that is the key to the nature of the market environment rather than actual competition.

A contestable market is one in which if price is raised sufficiently new entrants will be attracted to the market.

Thus, it is a market in which entry is relatively easy and in which any supernormal or monopoly profits can quite quickly be competed away.

The theoretical extreme is a perfectly contestable market in which any profit at all immediately attracts new entry; it is a market where both entry and exit is free and costless.

In this case, entry will be extremely rapid should profits warrant it. As incumbents can retaliate by lowering price to average cost, entrants will dash into the market (referred to as 'hit and run' tactics) only if they will incur no sunk costs. Thus, in principle, there are no barriers to entry or exit, even in oligopolistic or monopolistic markets. Monopoly profits cannot exist because if they did new firms would be attracted into the market and prices would be driven down to the level of average costs. In the long run the performance of a perfectly contestable market is equivalent to that of a perfectly competitive market. However, a perfectly contestable market is thought to have wider applicability.

The model of perfectly contestable markets was used to justify airline deregulation in the USA in the early 1980s where 'capital on wings' could potentially be quickly rerouted to undercut incumbent airlines or to avoid loss-making routes. Research suggests, however, that actual competition has a far greater influence on price than potential competition and that very few industries have insignificant sunk costs, e.g. airport facilities and advertising constitute fixed costs in civil aviation. Thus, incumbent airlines in the USA were able to overcome the threat of entry by controlling gates at congested airports, investing in computerised reservation systems and undertaking large-scale marketing campaigns.

Limit pricing

In situations where supernormal or monopoly profits exist but are protected by some barriers to entry, then, in order to avoid unwelcome competition, the incumbent firms may hold price below the level at which short-run profits are maximised, i.e. at the **limit price**. In Figure 22.9 it is assumed that the potential entrant has a higher cost curve than the monopolist (or oligopolist) incumbent, the latter having become well established in the market. The incumbent can charge up to price P_L, the limit price, without attracting entry, since the entrant cannot make any supernormal profit at this or at any lower price. It may well be that P_L is below the short-run profit-maximising price, but it is assumed that the incumbent firms are more interested in taking a longer term view in order to maximise long-run profits.

Obviously, the extent to which price must be limited depends on the extent of barriers to entry; the greater these are the higher the price can be

set without attracting new entrants. One problem with limit price models is that barriers to entry are not easily measured. In particular, the extent to which advertising, excess capacity and the threat of predatory pricing by incumbent firms is and can be used to ward off would-be entrants is hotly disputed by industrial economists.

Conclusion

In this and the previous chapter we have seen that profit maximisation implies producing where $MC = MR$. In practice, firms may not attempt to maximise profits and there may be many reasons for the $MC = MR$ rule being of little guidance, e.g. uncertainty and the retaliation of competitors. Nevertheless, we have seen that there is a rich variety of theories which offer insights into actual firm behaviour even though no single model is entirely satisfactory. Having considered the theory of the firm we will continue in the next chapter to examine various ways in which imperfect competition manifests itself in the economy.

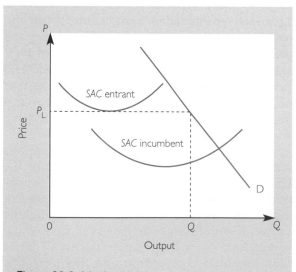

Figure 22.9 Limit pricing
$SAC_{entrant}$ is higher than $SAC_{incumbent}$, giving a limit price of P_L.

Summary
1 Profit maximisation occurs where there is the greatest possible positive difference between total revenue and total cost.
2 Marginal revenue is the change to total revenue as a result of the sale of one more unit of commodity.
3 Profit maximisation always occurs where marginal revenue is equal to marginal cost.
4 For the monopolist abnormal profits may persist in the long run.
5 The long-run equilibrium for the monopolistic competitor occurs where AC is tangential to AR and the firm is just receiving normal profit.
6 In the absence of collusion, oligopoly behaviour is complex and unpredictable.
7 Not only is formal collusion (i.e. a cartel) illegal, but it has a tendency to break up as firms have an incentive to cheat on one another.
8 Mark-up techniques are commonly used to calculate prices, although market conditions remain an important determinant of the actual prices charged.

9 There are many theories of the firm to choose from. Profit maximisation is not always assumed. Each theory, however, has its particular strengths and weaknesses.

10 A perfectly contestable market is one in which there no barriers to entry or exit; it represents a theoretical extreme, but is thought to have wider applicability than perfect competition.

11 Limit pricing represents a model of long-run firm behaviour.

? QUESTIONS

1 Discuss the alternatives that exist to the profit maximisation hypothesis.

2 Explain the relationship between *MR* and elasticity of demand. Examine the significance of a knowledge of this relationship for a firm.

3 Demonstrate that profit maximisation requires *MC* = *MR*. Can firms profit maximise?

4 'Profit maximisation occurs where the difference between *AC* and *AR* is at a maximum.' Discuss.

5 Compare and contrast the long-run equilibrium of the monopolistic competitor with that of the perfect competitor.

6 What explanations exist for oligopolistic behaviour? Discuss the prevalence of price and non-price competition in oligopolistic markets.

7 What are the strengths and weaknesses of the kinked demand theory of oligopoly?

8 Explain how the threat of new entry to the industry may affect the behaviour of a firm.

9 What factors might be taken into consideration in assessing the degree of monopoly in an industry? Explain how these factors are likely to affect prices set within the industry.

10 What is meant by mark-up pricing? To what extent do firms follow such a procedure in setting prices?

Data response A
IN DEFENCE OF DOMINATION

Examine the article from the *Financial Times* of 8 November 1999 on page 302 and answer the questions which follow.

1 Is Microsoft a monopolist?

2 Has the behaviour of Microsoft been beneficial? If so, to whom?

3 On 7 June 2000 Judge Jackson ordered that Microsoft be split into two separate companies, one for operating systems (Windows) and the other for applications (Office and Internet Explorer). Who do you think that this will benefit, if anybody?

Data response B
THE AIR WAR

Study the following extract from *The Economist* of 11 September 1999 on page 303 and answer the questions which follow.

1 Explain what is meant by oligopolistic price collusion.

2 Comment on the pricing policies of the incumbent airlines operating the transatlantic routes from London Heathrow.

3 How do these firms compete?

4 Discuss the possible impact of the entry of new airline carriers, such as British Midland and Singapore Airlines, for these routes.

In defence of domination

FT

Microsoft's response to the court finding that it operates with monopoly power will include a legal appeal strategy and may involve political lobbying, write **Richard Wolffe** and **Louise Kehoe**

It took a year of legal debate, thousands of pages of company e-mails, and millions of dollars in lawyers' fees to state the obvious. In a world where more than 90 per cent of personal computers run on Windows software, the US courts ruled that: 'Microsoft enjoys monopoly power'.

Those four words written by Judge Thomas Jackson begin what amounts to comprehensive demolition of the legal strategy and corporate conduct of the world's largest software company. The 207-page written decision is the first ruling in the most significant US antitrust case since the break-up of AT&T in 1984 and poses a profound threat to Microsoft's way of doing business.

For Microsoft – as well as the US justice department and 19 states which filed their lawsuit in May last year – the severity of the findings was shocking. Few expected such a wide ranging attack as part of a judgment that was intended to set out findings of fact. In theory, the court only now starts to consider whether Microsoft has broken the law.

In practice, it seems highly unlikely that Judge Jackson will find otherwise. That means Microsoft may eventually face remedies ranging in the extreme to being broken up like AT&T. Although Microsoft would almost certainly appeal against any substantial remedy, it finds itself in so weak a legal position, that it may have to seek a settlement.

In a detailed narrative and technical analysis issued late on Friday, Judge Jackson found that the company has wielded monopoly power against a range of rivals and partners across, the industry. Companies developing new technologies – from internet browsing to multimedia software – were bullied into submission or shut out of the market.

'The ultimate result is that some innovations that would truly benefit consumers never occur for the sole reason that they do not coincide with Microsoft's self-interest,' he concluded.

Microsoft continues to deny that it possesses monopoly power. It maintains that its high market share could collapse if technology shifts against it with new products which no longer rely on Windows. But with such a hostile judgment facing it, where can, the world's most highly-valued, company go from here? ...

... Microsoft insists that it must retain the ability to add new features and functions to its products, unfettered by regulatory controls. It is an issue that lies at the heart of the case: can Microsoft add any software technology to Windows regardless of its function or market? After all, that is the basis for Windows 98 – a merging of the company's internet browser with its Windows operating software.

To Mr Gates, Microsoft's ability to improve its products is dependent upon its freedom to build in new capabilities. For example, Microsoft aims to add voice recognition software to Windows, so that PCs can respond to spoken commands.

Competitors would argue that voice recognition software might be sold separately, enabling competition in that emerging market. Yet Mr Gates is adamant. Unless new features are incorporated in Windows, rather than sold separately, the computer operating standard will be bifurcated. This might force all software developers to offer multiple versions of their programs, depending upon which functions are installed on different computers.

On this point, the company and the justice department are as far apart as ever. According to the government and now the judge, Microsoft's strategy against its internet software rival Netscape Communications was to abuse its power over Windows to stop its competitor's products from reaching consumers. First it sought to carve up the market in a meeting between executives in 1995. When that failed, it tied its own internet software to Windows, distributed it for free and restricted its rivals' distribution channels.

For antitrust officials, the concept of tying products together – or integration – represents the bottom line of any settlement. Unless Microsoft's ability to tie products is limited, the government says, the company could stifle any new rival just as it attacked Netscape.

'I am the first to say that Microsoft should innovate. But what I am concerned about is everybody else's opportunity to innovate. That is what this is all about,' said Joel Klein, head of the justice department's antitrust division. ...

Source: Financial Times, 8 November 1999. Reprinted with permission.

The air war

Fed up with waiting for British and American officials to agree, two airlines, British Midland and Singapore Airlines, are campaigning for liberalisation of the transatlantic market to and from London Heathrow. British Midland is spending heavily on an advertising and poster campaign highlighting how business travellers from Heathrow pay through the nose for flights to America. And it is hitching transatlantic flights to the bandwagon of "rip-off Britain". This is a campaign being pushed by Tony Blair's government, which wants to know why the prices of cars, computers and groceries are much higher in Britain than in other European countries or America.

Singapore Airlines also wants to fly to America from London, just as British airlines can fly through Singapore, picking up passengers for onward destinations in Asia. Singapore already has approval from America to do this; only protectionist Britain keeps what is often called "the world's best airline" out of a market in which it could cause untold damage to British Airways and Virgin Atlantic.

British Midland's campaign is, of course, self-serving, but its consumer friendly credentials are good. Its chairman, Sir Michael Bishop, was the darling of Margaret Thatcher when she was prime minister, for his efforts to compete with British Airways on domestic routes and to produce Europe's first liberalised domestic air-market. In similar fashion he went on to make the early stages of European liberalisation a success in the mid-1990s.

With some 200 Heathrow slots (14% of the total, second only to BA with 38%) British Midland is an attractive partner. It is now deciding whether to join Scandinavian Airlines System, which owns a 40% share in it, and SAS's partners (led by Lufthansa and United Airlines) in the Star alliance. It is also being pursued by Air France to join its nascent alliance based on a partnership with America's Delta Air Lines. Air France may be ready to pay a high price to buy out SAS and recruit British Midland, both as a feeder into its hub at Paris Charles de Gaulle and to gain access to Heathrow.

Like Singapore Airlines, British Midland also wants to enter the transatlantic market itself. It could drop some British and European services, where it now faces competition from such low-cost carriers as EasyJet and instead use the slots for transatlantic flights. At the moment the four licensed carriers, BA, Virgin Atlantic, United Airlines and American Airlines, charge virtually identical and anomalously high fares for business-class travel from Heathrow (see chart).

Neither Singapore nor British Midland can do anything without the renegotiation of the Anglo-American air-services agreement. After the glacial progress of liberalisation in the past five years, the British transport department now seems to welcome their campaign. The bureaucrats are preparing a policy review for their minister, John Prescott. This Bishop may soon be preaching to the converted.

Source: The Economist Newspaper Limited, London, 11 September 1999. Reprinted with permission.

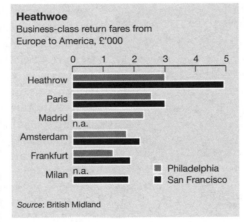

Heathwoe
Business-class return fares from Europe to America, £'000

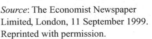

Source: British Midland

23 Aspects of monopoly

Learning outcomes

At the end of this chapter you will be able to:

▶ Understand the rationale underlying competition policy.

▶ Describe the key features of the policies of the UK and the EU authorities towards monopolies, restrictive practices and mergers.

▶ Appreciate the problems involved in establishing a suitable pricing policy towards monopolies.

▶ Recognise the conditions for, and bases of, price discrimination.

▶ Discuss the techniques involved in establishing prices in different market segments.

▶ Understand the concept of predatory pricing.

▶ Describe the relative merits of monopoly for society.

Governments and monopoly

Most governments have a policy towards monopolies, which is usually referred to as **competition policy** (see also Chapter 10). There are two reasons for this.

First, governments recognise the misallocation of resources brought about by monopoly. Second, on the grounds of equity most governments feel obliged to have a policy to limit monopoly profits.

To some extent the government's attitude is determined by how the monopoly arose. As pointed out in Chapter 8, legislation has traditionally been aimed at the contrived basis for monopoly, involving an examination of the anti-competitive behaviour of one or more firms, than at the other sources. It would be useful to remind yourself of the main sources or bases of monopoly power at this stage.

Possibilities for policy

There are three basic policies the government can adopt towards monopolies.

(a) *Prohibition.* The formation of monopolies can be banned and existing monopolies broken up; in other words, it is the structure of the industry which is to be rectified. This has been more the attitude in the USA. 'Antitrust' legislation, as it is called, in the USA, dates back to the Sherman Act of 1890. Very few monopolies are actually broken up nowadays. One exception was the telephone company, AT&T, which was divested of its local services in 1984. Another notable example concerns the recent long-running case against Microsoft and the abuse of its dominant position in the computer software market. In June 2000 it was recommended that it be split into two separate companies, one for operating systems, the other for applications (and see Data response A, Chapter 22). However, there are still a considerable number of monopolies in the USA. Legislation against actions 'in restraint of trade' has tended to be more vigorously prosecuted against unions than against big business.

(b) *Takeover.* The government can take over a monopoly and run it in the public interest. Although many industries and companies have been taken over by the government, it has not usually been done with the object of controlling a monopoly. As the next chapter on the privatisation debate reveals the recent trend has been for firms and industries to be returned to the private sector rather than for them to be taken over by the government.

(c) *Regulation.* The government can allow a monopoly to continue but pass legislation to make sure that it does not act 'against the public interest'. This has traditionally been the attitude of the UK government as part of its *competition policy*, although recently the stance of the competition authorities has become much tougher towards activities that are thought to 'abuse' monopoly power.

The most recent legislation concerning monopolies in the UK is embodied in the Competition Act 1998, the actual policy taking effect from 1 March 2000. This superseded the Fair Trading Act 1973 in various respects, although the main agency for implementing government policy on competition remains the Office of Fair Trading (OFT), originally established as part of the 1973 law. The main aim of the 1998 legislation has been to bring UK policy much more in line with EU competition policy. The Act is divided into two sections or 'chapters', the first dealing with restrictive agreements *between* firms and the second with anti-competitive practices *by* one or more firms and the corresponding abuse of dominant positions. As in the pre-1998 legislation, the Director-General of Fair Trading (DGFT) must keep commercial practices in the UK under review and collect information about them in order to discover monopoly situations and anti-competitive practices. However, the DGFT now has substantially increased powers to investigate and to penalise firms that abuse their monopoly positions. The DGFT also has significantly enhanced powers under the 1998 Act regarding restrictive practices. In addition, the Act gave the DGFT concurrent powers with the director generals of the various regulatory agencies of the privatised utilities to enforce the new anti-competitive legislation in those industries (see also Chapter 24).

Now officers of the OFT have the power to enter and search the premises of firms suspected of acting illegally and seize documents; if found guilty firms can be fined.

Policy on monopolies

At its simplest a monopoly arises when one trading organisation supplies an entire market. This, however, is very rare. The Competition Act 1998 retained the traditional 25 per cent rule for defin-

ing monopoly situations that has long been used in UK competition policy. In other words, a firm or firms acting together with less than a 25 per cent market share, whether it is a national or local market, will not normally be considered dominant. It introduced another threshold, which is that a firm or firms with more than a 40 per cent market share, again for the appropriate market, national or local, would normally be considered dominant. What the situation is for firms with market shares between these two figures is unclear; moreover these are guideline figures and exceptions may be permitted.

The 1998 legislation also introduced much tougher rules regarding the abuse of any dominance that has been established through the above procedures. Chapter 2 of the Competition Act, the 'Chapter 2 prohibition', prohibits any exercise of market power that reduces competition in the UK. If found guilty firms can be fined up to 10 per cent of UK turnover for up to three years. Previously the approach was much more permissive: the OFT could refer a particular case to the Monopolies and Mergers Commission (MMC) for investigation and the Secretary of State for Trade and Industry would decide what action, if any, should be taken. Now abuses of market power come under the four main headings adopted by EU law that are enshrined in Article 82 (originally Article 86) of the Treaty of Rome:

(a) imposing unfair selling or purchase prices;
(b) limiting production, markets or technical developments to the detriment of consumers;
(c) applying dissimilar conditions to equivalent transactions with other trading parties (i.e. discriminatory practices);
(d) enforcing other firms to sign contracts with unfavourable obligations that have no connection with the subject of the contracts.

Examples of policies regarded by the OFT as likely to have significant anti-competitive implications include charging excessively high prices, price discrimination, predatory pricing and various non-price vertical agreements such as exclusive-dealing contracts between a dominant firm and suppliers or customers, refusal to supply a rival with parts and tying the purchase of a product to the purchase of (complementary) products (or 'full-line forcing').

It should be noted that it is the *effects* of any of these practices on competition that is important, not the practice itself. The Competition Commission (CC), the body that has taken over the functions of the MMC, can investigate particular instances of abuse. It also acts as an appeals body, a new function for the competition authorities.

It was felt that the previous legislation was slow and cumbersome; investigations could take an inordinate amount of time and, without financial penalties in cases of wrong doing, it was felt that the legislation lacked teeth. The 1998 Act should rectify these problems and make UK competition law much more compatible with EU legislation, on which it is based. Thus, the basis of EU monopoly policy is similarly the outlawing of the abuse of market dominance and firms can be fined 10 per cent of EU-wide turnover if found guilty. Note that both EU and UK policy do not condemn market dominance *per se*; hence, the possible benefits of monopoly, such as economies of scale and enhanced R&D spending, are recognised within the legislation. There are no market share guidelines for EU monopoly policy, however, although previous decisions suggest that anything under a 40 per cent market share would not be considered worthy of investigation. In addition, UK policy retains much of the 1973 law on complex monopoly situations, whereby the anti-competitive conduct of unrelated firms can be investigated without proof of dominance or of even collusion between them. This, it is felt, gives the authorities in Britain a wider remit to cover certain aspects of oligopolistic behaviour, like excessive advertising in an industry for example, than does the equivalent EU legislation.

● *Common misunderstanding*

*It is not monopoly itself that is condemned by the competition authorities. Furthermore, the fact that a firm or firms may charge very high prices or pursue predatory pricing need not constitute an abuse of monopoly power. It is the job of the DGFT to decide whether the **effects** of such practices in any way hinder or restrict competition. If they do, then the practices are declared illegal and the firm(s) can be fined.*

Restrictive practices

Chapter 1 of the Competition Act 1998 concerns restrictive practices between firms. It replaced the Restrictive Trade Practices Act 1976 and the Resale Prices Act 1976 that had previously dealt with these practices. Pre-1998 firms had to register any formal agreement between firms that restricted competition, such as agreeing to fix prices, restrict output or divide up the market, with the DGFT who could then refer the practice to the Restrictive Practices Court (RPC) to consider whether or not it operated against the public interest. The regime seemed quite tough but only a small minority of cases actually came before the RPC and it only dealt with cases of formal collusion, tacit collusion being outside its remit. With no financial penalties available for cases of illegality, again the legislation lacked any real teeth.

Under Chapter 1 of the 1998 Act, the 'Chapter 1 prohibition', the need for registration has been replaced by a general prohibition. Any agreement that prevents, restricts or distorts competition in the UK is illegal. As with Chapter 2 above, it is the *effects* of any agreement that is all-important in determining whether it should be prohibited. Only those agreements that are deemed to have an *appreciable* effect on competition come within the auspices of the legislation. An agreement will be deemed not to have an appreciable effect if the relevant parties have a combined market share of less than 25 per cent, unless the agreement involves the fixing of prices in some way, in which case any such agreement comes within the legislation's remit. Thus, all price-fixing arrangements are caught!

The practices that are included in the legislation are identical to those specified in Article 81 (originally Article 85) of the Treaty of Rome regarding collusive policies:

(a) fixing prices;
(b) limiting or controlling production, markets, technical development or investment;
(c) sharing markets or sources of supply;
(d) applying dissimilar conditions to equivalent transactions with other trading parties (i.e. discriminatory practices);

(e) enforcing other firms to sign contracts with unfavourable obligations that have no connection with the subject of the contract.

Examples of such restrictive practices include horizontal price-fixing arrangements with rival firms, resale price maintenance policies whereby manufacturers or distributors impose a fixed selling price on the retailers they supply, agreements concerning the restriction of output and the sharing of markets and non-price vertical agreements but only if there is also price-fixing or market dominance. Exemptions apply if agreements improve production or distribution or promote innovation.

As with monopoly policy the aim of the Competition Act 1998 is to make UK restrictive practice legislation compatible with EU law and this it essentially does. Firms can be fined up to 10 per cent of UK turnover for up to three years by the OFT if found guilty of engaging in illegal practices. The new law also encompasses both formal price and output-fixing cartel arrangements as well as more informal practices.

Policy on mergers

The 1998 legislation did not apply to mergers, which are still covered under The Fair Trading Act 1973. This applies to mergers involving the acquisition of gross assets of more than £70 million or where a 'monopoly', defined as 25 per cent or more of the relevant market in the UK or a substantial part of it, would be created or enhanced. Also included are situations where one company acquires the ability to control or materially influence another company without actually acquiring a controlling interest.

The DGFT is responsible for keeping a watchful eye on possible mergers within the Act, but the DGFT's role is only to advise the Secretary of State for Trade and Industry as to whether a reference should be made to the CC; the DGFT may not make a reference directly. This contrasts with the DGFT's powers relating to monopolies above. The Secretary of State has power under the 1973 Act to order that the merger shall not proceed or to regulate any identified adverse effects of a merger or proposed merger.

The approach is broadly neutral, at least in principle, in the sense that each reference is considered on its own merits and on the public interest criteria adopted. The latter encompasses the maintenance and promotion of competition, plus consumer interests, effects on employment and the regional balance of resources and international competitiveness. However, as with monopolies, very few cases are actually investigated. Since 1965, less than 3 per cent of eligible mergers have been referred to the MMC and less than 1 per cent have been declared against the public interest. The fact that most mergers in the UK are consequently regarded as being within the public interest may seem surprising given their relative lack of success (see Chapter 19).

EU legislation on mergers came into force in 1990. The regulations only apply to very large mergers that affect more than one member state. There are two qualifying rules:

(a) the merging companies have a combined global turnover of over €5 billion;
(b) at least two of the companies involved in the merger each have an EU-wide turnover of over €250 million (as long as less than two-thirds of the business is in a single member state, otherwise national laws apply).

The numbers of qualifying mergers in the EU have increased significantly in the last year or so. In the first eight years of the legislation 700 mergers were notified to the European Commission, whereas nearly 300 were notified in 1999 alone. Only nine mergers in total have been banned, however.

UK and EU competition policies compared

The effect of the Competition Act 1998 has been to align UK competition policy much more closely with that of the EU. The effects-based policy has been largely applauded given that it is the abuse of monopoly power that is generally considered harmful rather than monopoly power *per se*. The fact that certain activities and practices are now banned and firms can be fined heavily if caught acting illegally makes for a much more effective policy, at least in principle. In addition, the UK's policy on complex monopolies allows it to investigate aspects of oligopolistic behaviour not covered in EU law. The UK also has wider public interest criteria for investigating mergers than does the EU in general.

Pricing problems

Government policy on monopoly pricing

If a monopoly does exist and the government decides not to break it up but to regulate prices in the public interest or to prohibit certain pricing practices, on what principles should its pricing policy be based? In other words, for what sort of pricing policy should the government, in the form of the competition authorities, be aiming? In the 'normal' monopoly situation, illustrated in Figure 23.1, monopoly legislation could be aimed at making the monopolist produce at point F where $AC = AR$. At this point the price is OR and the output ON. All monopoly profits have been eliminated and the public is obtaining the largest output for the lowest price that is compatible with the monopolist remaining in the industry. Pure economic theory would suggest setting a price where $MC = P$ (called *marginal cost pricing*), but as you can see in Figure 23.1 this would result in the firm actually making a loss. There are also difficulties in determining MC accurately.

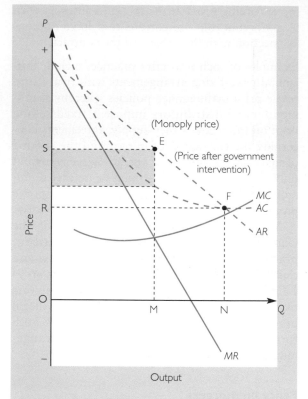

Figure 23.1 Government intervention in monopoly pricing
The monopolist would choose to produce at point E, making maximum profit. Government policy might aim to compel the monopolist to produce at point F where $AC = AR$, thus eliminating abnormal profit.

STUDENT ACTIVITY 23.1

In Figure 23.1 explain (a) why pricing at marginal costs would yield the 'best' solution from society's point of view and (b) why pricing at this level would lead to a loss for the firm in question.

Mark-up pricing and break-even charts

Although an organisation's behaviour may be governed by concepts such as marginal revenue and marginal cost, in practice they may be very difficult to determine, especially when a large organisation is marketing a variety of products. In these circumstances they often try to base their prices on average or unit cost. To do this they must make assumptions about the future volume of sales and likely average cost (which is usually assumed to be constant) at that output. This having been done, a *mark up* of, say, 10 per cent is then added for profit. This fascinatingly simple theory seems realistic, but stops tantalisingly short of telling us why the average mark up should be 40 per cent in one industry and 5 per cent in another (see also Chapter 22).

The reader should take careful note that this is the way the organisation may try to determine the right price for itself, but the customers may or may not be willing to pay the right price or buy the right quantity. Prices in the market are still determined by the forces of supply and demand. The monopolist organisation has great power, of course, to impose its wishes on the market. If an organisation sets its price in this manner then it is relatively easy to draw up a *break-even chart* to demonstrate its profits and losses. In Figure 23.2 the *TR* curve is a straight line because price is assumed to be constant; *TC* is a straight line given the assumption of constant marginal costs and hence constant average variable costs. This way of looking at profits is much closer to the accountants' view than most of the economists' ways of looking at the market.

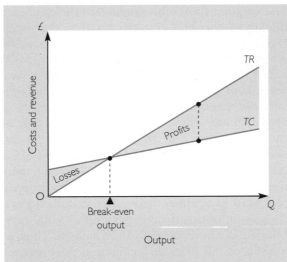

Figure 23.2 A break-even chart
If the price is fixed then *TR* is a straight line. Profits or losses are the vertical distance between the two curves.

Discriminating monopoly

Discriminating monopoly (or price discrimination) is said to exist when different buyers or groups of buyers, in separate market segments, are charged two or more prices for the same product, for reasons not associated with differences in costs.

Thus, price discrimination exists when price differences do not reflect cost differences or when consumers are charged the same price despite cost differences.

The conditions for discriminating monopoly

Every producer knows that there are some consumers who are willing to pay more than the market price for the good. The consumers are therefore in receipt of utility they are not paying for and this is known as a ***consumers' surplus*** (see page 59). A monopolist may be able to eat into this surplus by charging some consumers higher prices than others. For price discrimination to be worthwhile two conditions must be fulfilled:

(a) The monopolist must be able to separate the two markets or market segments in order to avoid the resale of the product from one group of consumers to another. This may be

done geographically, by time or by income. The suppliers of personal services such as doctors and lawyers also often charge different prices for the same service.

(b) The two or more market segments thus separated must have different elasticities of demand, otherwise the exercise would not be worthwhile.

Price discrimination enables a firm to achieve a higher revenue from a given level of sales (and thereby to obtain higher profits).

● *Common misunderstanding*

It should not always be presumed that price discrimination, despite enabling the monopolist to achieve greater profits from a given level of sales, automatically operates against the interests of the consumer. By opening up previously untapped markets, it may also lead to increased output. Price discrimination is regarded as an abuse of monopoly power through either the charging of excessive prices or via the lower prices leading to the exclusion of competitors.

Bases for price discrimination

It perhaps seems unlikely that consumers would willingly pay two different prices for the same product. However, this can happen if consumers are prevented from buying the cheaper product in some way, or if they are unaware that the difference exists. The main ways in which this is achieved are as follows:

(a) *Geographical.* Goods are sold at different prices in different countries. In 1995 the European Commission found that Volkswagen facilitated price discrimination by preventing customers from other countries purchasing cars in Italy; the company was fined €102 million or about £68 million. (See also the example of car prices in general in the EU discussed below.)

(b) *Time.* Some firms with monopoly power sell the same product at different prices at different times. Examples of this are off-peak electricity, weekend returns on the railways and cheaper deals on flights by booking early.

(c) *Income.* Firms may be able to sell their products at different prices to different groups of consumers depending on their levels of income. Thus, doctors and lawyers can charge higher rates to those with higher incomes, children may be charged lower rates than adults in cinemas and on aeroplanes, buses and trains, business passengers may pay more than other travellers and students can often obtain lower prices in restaurants or hairdressers.

(d) *Dumping.* This is a variation on geographical discrimination, but in this case the manufacturer 'dumps' surplus output on foreign markets at below cost price. This often has the object of damaging foreign competition. The EU has often resorted to dumping to get rid of excess agricultural products.

STUDENT ACTIVITY 23.2

Demonstrate that dumping increases a firm's profits so long as the dumped goods are sold at more than *AVC*.

Car prices in the EU: a case study

Despite the protestations put forward by the motor trade, such as differences in tax rates, transport costs and exchange rates (although the effects of the latter should be dimished by the introduction of the euro) it is clear that there is extensive geographical price discrimination in the industry. The reason for this is that the car market in the EU is not truly competitive and for long the car manufacturers have been exempted from some of the effects of competition policy legislation. (See also Data response B at the end of the chapter.)

A survey carried out in 1998 by the European Commission on car prices revealed that the UK was the most expensive market for 61 of the 72 best-selling models. The cheapest country was The Netherlands, which had the lowest prices for 35 of the models, followed by Portugal with the lowest prices for 14 models. The price differential was over 40 per cent for 16 of the 72 models.

We will now proceed to demonstrate by the use of a hypothetical example why price discrimination benefits the manufacturer and how the marketing strategy is determined. Let us assume that the price for a particular make of car is higher in market A than in market B. Figure 23.3 shows the situation for a car manufacturer. The

first diagram shows the situation in the combined market (A plus B). Given this situation the manufacturer would maximise profits by producing where *MR* = *MC*. This gives an output of 25 000 cars a month at a price of £10 000 giving a total revenue of £250 million. However, from experience the manufacturer knows that consumers in market B are willing to pay more for this type of car and therefore sets the price at £11 750 per car, and sells 10 000 per month, thus earning £117.5 million in home sales. In market A, however, there is more price competition and the price is dropped to £9250 to compete with other manufacturers. As a result of this the company sells 15 000 cars, bringing in a revenue of £138.75 million. Thus, as a result of this price discrimination total revenue has increased by £6.25 million per month (£256.25 million – £250 million). This must all be extra profit because output, and therefore costs, are the same as in the combined market.

Figure 23.3 also shows the way in which the market strategy is determined. This is to take the level of *MC* at the *MC* = *MR* intersection in the combined market and then equate this level of *MC* with the *MR* in the separate markets. By then tracing this output to the demand (*AR*) curve the manufacturer is able to determine the best price to charge.

In practice the situation is more complicated. There are indirect taxes to consider, exchange rates and often many different markets. However, our analysis shows the principles underlying the practice. This applies to all types of price discrimination. Thus, when one is offered cheap-day returns on the railways, off-peak electricity or lower prices for children for certain products, it should be remembered that this is all part of a strategy by the producer to increase profits.

Predatory pricing

Sometimes a firm may practice price discrimination with the express intent of removing competition from a market.

Predatory pricing refers to the situation where a large and financially powerful firm prices one or more of its products below costs and, by covering any losses from the funds generated from within other parts of the organisation, intends to secure the demise or the takeover of a smaller rival or rivals.

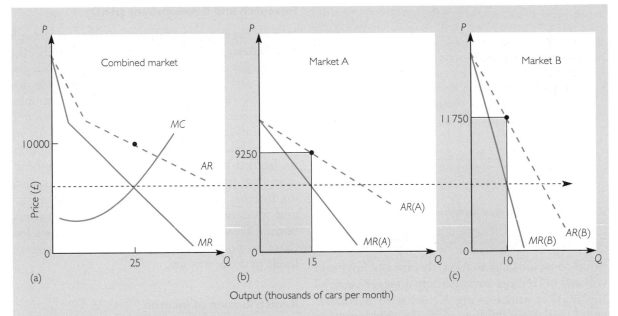

Figure 23.3 Discriminating monopoly
(a) Combined market. (b) Market A (exports). (c) Market B (domestic). The discriminating monopolist divides output between two markets. In the combined market it equates combined *MR* with *MC*; this would give an output of 25 000 cars at a price of £10 000 per car. However, by equating *MR* with *MC* in the separate markets it increases total revenue while keeping the same costs. In market A 15 000 cars are sold at £9250 (*TR* = £138.75m) and in market B the remaining 10 000 cars are sold at £11 750 each (*TR* = £117.5m). This is an increase of £6.25m per month on the combined market price.

Thus, a dominant firm will deliberately make a loss in some aspect of its operations in order to drive competitors out of a market. There is some debate about which costs should be used as evidence of predatory pricing. It is generally accepted that, if price is below average variable cost, this is evidence of predation. In 1993 Wal-Mart, reputed to be the world's largest retailer, was found guilty of predation by deliberately aiming to oust three small pharmacy businesses in Arkansas, USA, by selling prescription drugs at below costs. As soon as the competition vanished, Wal-Mart raised its prices. In the UK, the bus company Stagecoach was found guilty in 1995 of predatory behaviour towards a rival firm, Hylton, by the then Monopolies and Mergers Commisssion.

Monopoly assessed

In this section of the chapter we will consider the advantages and disadvantages of monopoly to the economy. We will first consider two advantages, those of economies of scale and of research and development, and then proceed to the disadvantages.

Economies of scale

In some industries, especially those involving a great deal of capital equipment such as chemicals and motor vehicles, it could be that the larger and more monopolistic a business organisation is the more it is able to take advantage of economies of scale.

In Figure 23.4 the national market for cars is 2 million per year. In our example, the production is divided between two companies, Kruks and Toymota. Toymota has a bigger share of the market (1.1 million) and, because of the economies of scale to be gained, the long-run average cost (*LAC*) curve of the industry is downward sloping. This means that Toymota's average costs (£5000) are lower than Kruks' (£6000). In the

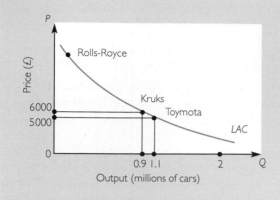

Figure 23.4 **The flat-bottomed average cost curve**

price-conscious car market this means Toymota will sell even more cars, gaining a bigger share of the market and leaving Kruks with a smaller share and even higher costs. In this situation Kruks will eventually go out of business and Toymota will have a complete monopoly. This could be to the public's benefit if continuing economies of scale mean even cheaper cars.

The end result of such a situation, then, is monopoly or some form of oligopoly. This is very much the case in the motor industry, which is dominated by a small number of very large firms. Most medium-sized firms have tended to disappear, but a few companies producing a very small output of specialist cars still exist, e.g. Morgan and TVR in the UK, because they are not so concerned about unit costs. As noted in Chapter 20, while economies of scale occur in most manufacturing industries, they do not preclude the survival of smaller firms.

In the case of natural monopolies, where unit costs continue to fall up to and beyond the level of market demand, it would not be economic sense to break up the monopoly. Indeed, it has been observed that in the UK the government has sometimes promoted the formation of monopolies in these sorts of industry. In these circumstances the government's options are limited either to taking over the industry or to regulating its prices and output, as now occurs in the utilities. Although the choices are very clear in theory, in practice it is often very difficult to acquire enough information to judge what is happening in an industry.

Research and development (R&D)

It has been argued, most notably by **Joseph Schumpeter, 1883–1950**, that it is only the monopolist or the oligopolist that can provide the large sums of money necessary to provide for expensive research and development programmes. Keen price competition can cut profit margins and leave nothing for product development. As we shall see below, it can also be argued that monopoly leads to complacency and lack of development.

In fact, the evidence suggests that R&D spending increases up to a certain medium size of firm and moderate level of industry concentration; beyond these points R&D spending increases less than proportionately with increases in size or levels of concentration.

Redistribution of income

Monopoly brings about a redistribution of income from the consumer to the monopolist. If the consumers are selling their own goods or services in a competitive market then they will be receiving the marginal cost of doing so. The monopolist, however, receives a price above marginal cost and the monopoly rent so earned represents a transfer of income above what is economically necessary. The continued existence of monopolies, therefore, further worsens the unequal distribution of income in the economy.

Allocative inefficiency

The fact that the monopolist produces at a price greater than *MC* represents a misallocation of resources. This point was examined in Section II of the book and is also explained in Section VI. For the moment we can simply note that monopoly power has resulted in *contrived scarcity*. This refers to the fact that, as price exceeds *MC*, extra units of output *could* be produced at a cost below that which the consumers would be prepared to pay. Thus, there seems to be the potential for increasing consumer surplus and the monopolist's profit. This potential gain in welfare, however, does not take place. This is because, unless the monopolist can price discriminate, producing the extra units would cause *MR* to fall below *MC* and hence reduce the monopolist's actual profit. In short, there seems to be an underproduction of the product concerned in that not enough of the nation's resources are being allocated to its production.

Lack of X-efficiency

X-efficiency is the term used to describe the minimisation of cost which occurs under conditions of competition.

It is argued that it is a necessary corollary of profit maximisation that a firm achieves X-efficiency. However, under conditions of monopoly or oligopoly the firm is protected from competition and may therefore not be under pressure to be X-efficient. Adopting the terms of the economist **H. Leibenstein**, the firm will be *X-inefficient*. If this is so it will lead to an upward shift in the cost curves. Figure 23.5 shows an upward shift in the *MC* curve as a result of X-inefficiency, thus further worsening any negative effects of monopoly. Measurement problems mean that evidence of the extent of X-inefficiency is fairly limited, but estimates suggest that it can be quite significant.

◗ Conclusion

Economists since the time of Adam Smith have usually opposed monopoly. As we saw in Chapter 4, Adam Smith wrote:

A monopoly by keeping the market constantly understocked, never supplying the effectual demand, sells their commodities much above the natural price, and raise emoluments, whether they consist in wages or profit, greatly above their natural rate.

It should not be thought, therefore, that the modern capitalist state is the legatee of Smith; free enterprise, indeed, is the very antithesis of much that he argued for.

We have seen, however, that under certain circumstances monopoly can be both efficient and even desirable. It would therefore seem sensible to say that we should not necessarily ban monopoly itself, but rather investigate monopoly practices. Against this it can be argued that full investigation of all such practices would be very expensive. It must also be said that, despite the existence of much legislation on monopoly, there appears to have been a general lack of effectiveness. The most cynical viewpoint on this has been put forward by **J.K. Galbraith**, who argues that the purpose of competition policy is so that the government can be 'seen to be doing something' about monopoly. The state, however, is too wedded to the capitalist structure to want actually to do anything about it. Thus, it is argued, monopoly legislation is a propaganda exercise. It is too early to say whether the new policy in the UK, based largely along pre-existing EU lines, will be much more effective, although the system of banning certain anti-competitive practices and fining firms should improve corporate behaviour.

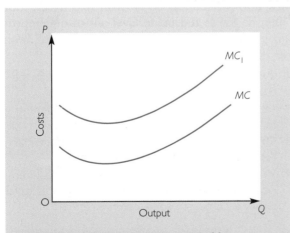

Figure 23.5 Increase in costs caused by X-inefficiency

Summary

1 Government policy on monopoly is now based on the prohibition of certain abuses of monoploy power and restrictive practices; it is an effects-based policy.
2 The chief UK government agencies for competition policy are the Office of Fair Trading (OFT) and the Competition Commission (CC).
3 The EU Treaty of Rome prohibits most restrictive practices; the establishment and abuse of monopoly positions can also both be investigated.
4 Both the UK and the EU have policies towards mergers, although very few cases are actually investigated in either instance.

5 Government policy on monopoly prices could be aimed at getting the monopolist to produce where $P = MC$, but this is impossible if the firm is taking advantage of economies of scale.

6 Discriminating monopoly is a situation where a firm sells the same product at two (or more) different prices.

7 Predatory pricing is where a firm prices below cost in order to oust a competitor or competitors from an industry.

8 Arguments in favour of monopoly include economies of scale and support for research and development.

9 Arguments against monopoly include worsening the distribution of income, allocative inefficiency and the possibility of X-inefficiency.

? QUESTIONS

1 What is the scope for price discrimination for the following:
   (a) British Telecom (BT);
   (b) a wheat farmer;
   (c) the CAP;
   (d) a doctor?

2 Examine the main bases for price discrimination. Discuss the relative merits of price discrimination from the points of view of both the producer and the consumer.

3 Discuss the problems involved in implementing a policy of marginal cost pricing for monopolies.

4 Explain how the Competition Act 1998 has changed monopoly policy in the UK. Discuss the reasons for these changes.

5 'The tragedy of monopoly is not excessive profits. There may indeed be no profits at all, the high price being frittered away in small volume and inefficient production.' Discuss.

6 Discuss the view that breaking up monopolies would increase prices by increasing costs.

7 'While the law [of competition] may be sometimes hard for the individual, it is best for the race, because it ensures the survival of the fittest in every department. We accept and welcome, therefore, as conditions to which we must

accommodate ourselves, great inequality of environment, the concentration of business, industrial and commercial, in the hands of a few, and the law of competition between these as being not only beneficial, but essential for the future progress of the race.'

Critically evaluate this statement by **Andrew Carnegie**, made in 1889.

8 Discuss the view, with reference to official policy, that company mergers are against the public interest.

Data response A
THE OFT's NEW POWERS

Read the following article on pages 315–16 taken from the *Financial Times* of 1 March 2000 on the powers of the Office of Fair Trading (OFT) under the Competition Act 1998 and answer the following questions.

1 Outline the new powers of the OFT under the 1998 legislation.

2 The article refers to 'abuses of dominant market position'. Such as?

3 Discuss the problems that might be encountered in adequately defining the relevant market for a product. How does the Act counter such problems?

4 The government wants a more 'consumerist' competition policy. What do you think this means?

Data response B
UK CAR PRICES

Read the following article on pages 316–17 taken from *The Economist* of 15 April 2000 and answer the following questions.

1 Why has the car industry been investigated by the Competition Commission?

2 How can firms charge different prices in different markets for the same products?

3 On what bases are exemptions allowed for certain restrictive practices?

4 Why might the government and car manufacturers have a common interest in allowing car prices to fall slowly according to some commentators?

A once-toothless watchdog gets set to bite back

Many companies are unaware of the OFT's new powers under the Competition Act write
Kevin Brown and **Jean Eaglesham**

More than half of British businesses are unaware they risk fines of up to 30 per cent of turnover for breaching tough new competition rules that take effect today, according to an unpublished survey by the Office of Fair Trading.

The OFT has carried out a massive education campaign over the past year in a bid to make companies focus on the 1998 Competition Act, which makes it an offence to discuss anything that reduces competition.

But the survey found that the number of companies that were 'spontaneously aware' of the new law was only 11 per cent, compared with 2 per cent a year ago. Only 15 per cent recognised the name of the act, compared with 6 per cent a year ago.

Even after being given a short description, only 44 per cent of companies said they had heard of the legislation, compared with 23 per cent last year. Of those, 68 per cent said their company would be able to comply.

It is hardly the most auspicious star to today's implementation of the 1998 Competition Act, which was intended to transform the OFT from a somewhat toothless competition watchdog to a cartel-busting power to be reckoned with.

John Bridgeman, its director-general, boasted of imposing fines on miscreant companies that would 'make business people's eyes water'

But ministerial frustration at the OFT's perceived unwillingnes to toe the government line on 'rip off' Britain has taken its toll. Five days ago, the OFT announced that Mr Bridgeman would step

down when his five-year term ends in October.

That does not mean companies can be complacent. Lawyers believe Mr Bridgeman's impending exit will not weaken the OFT's resolve to use its new powers.

'The OFT will be keen to show it's still in business,' said Peter Freeman of Simmons & Simmons. 'There will be a big attack on cartels, whoever is the director-general – I don't think it's going to make any difference to that,' says Dorothy Livingstone of Herbert Smith.

The OFT has made no secret of its desire to shift its focus from the red tape of clearing and recording innocuous business agreements to investigations of price fixing and other cartel-type behaviour.

Margaret Bloom, its redoubtable head of competition, has toured the

In the firing line? Sectors that could be in the regulators' sights

- **Buses**
  Highly localised markets make this sector a natural for close inspection by the Office of Fair Trading

- **Cars**
  If the Competition Commission inquiry is not conclusive, the OFT may want to look again at manufacturers' links with dealers

- **Cement/other construction**
  Localised markets with a history of OFT and Brussels investigations

- **Local authority suppliers**
  Already covered by procurement rules, but new powers could trigger inquiries into similarities between tenders

- **PCs, CDs and white goods**
  High cost relative to US makes these perennial favourites, but are there genuine competition concerns?

- **Petrol**
  Will the small number of suppliers tempt the OFT to look for joint market dominance?

- **Rail**
  The rail regulator has advertised for two competition lawyers. It may look at access agreements and competition between long-distance and short-haul operators

- **Television companies**
  The Independent Television Commission has hired the OFT's former head of cartels; it may question whether independent producers get enough airtime

- **Telecoms**
  Oftel is another regulator that may flex its new competition muscles; it's 'probably rubbing its hands', one lawyer said

These sectors are ones where lawyers believe the authorities may investigate competition issues – there is no suggestion that companies in these sectors are involved in cartels.

country promoting the new mantra of 'don't notify – complain'. Cartel members will be offered immunity to promote whistleblowing, and the regulator is expected to use its tough new investigatory powers with relish.

Most competition experts believe the OFT will be looking for a few quick headline successes.

'I think there will be a few high-profile dawn raids rather than them knocking on everybody's doors,' said Elaine Gibson-Bolton of SJ Bervin & Co. Another lawyer thought the watchdog was already trawling in search of 'something spectacular'.

Cartels may make the biggest splash under the new act, but its impact will range much wider. Companies that have never tried to rig the market could still be affected.

The new provisions on 'abuse of dominant market position' replace the formula-driven approach of current legislation with rules focused on the practical effects on competition. As with cartels, offending companies face fines

of up to 30 per cent of their UK turnover – and the number of businesses potentially caught could be much higher.

Many complaints to the OFT will in fact be about abuses of dominance, where there are potentially much more complex issues of market definition, dominance and abuse for businesses to think about,' said Peter Willis, a competition lawyer at Taylor Joynson Garrett.

The act allows the competition authorities to investigate narrowly defined and localised markets. Companies may come under pressure for perceived dominance in very specialised sectors – the classic example cited by lawyers is Boosey & Hawkes, which the European Commission investigated for dominating the market for 'British style brass band instruments'.

There could also be a spate of cases in the courts, since the act makes it much easier for companies to sue rivals for losses suffered as a result of anti-competitive behaviour. Some cases could start very soon. 'There may well be

people around with enough material from previous rulings to start an action,' said Mr Freeman.

The act also extends similar powers to other watchdogs, including the utility regulators. Lawyers believe a number of these, including Oftel and the rail regulator may move swiftly to use their new competition powers. All of which might seem enough to be going on with. But some experts question whether the government, having forced Mr Bridgeman out, will be tempted to interfere further.

The new act is not directly consumer-focused. But Stephen Byers, the trade and industry secretary, has indicated he wants to see a more overtly consumerist competition policy.

Unless the act is changed to give legal expression to this political wish, then however consumer-friendly the credentials of the next director-general of fair trading, the experience of Mr Bridgeman is likely to be repeated.

Source: *Financial Times*, 1 March 2000. Reprinted with permission.

Snarl-up

Newspapers predicted this week that car prices will soon fall dramatically. Don't count on it.

The publication of the Competition Commission's report on the high price of new cars was greeted with headlines predicting that the government would force manufacturers to cut average prices by more than £1000. Some front pages even trumpeted that prices would fill by up to a third.

Buyers should check the fine print before they march down to their local showrooms. Significant price cuts are far from assured, despite the fact that the government has accepted virtually all the commission's recommendations. Stephen Byers, the trade and industry secretary, has said that he is determined to open up the market to more competition. Orders under the Fair Trading Act (1973) will

require manufacturers to give dealers and contract-hire companies the same discounts as fleet operators. Dealers will also be free to advertise new cars for sale at discount prices without fear of retaliation. And manufacturers will be required to publish the number of cars they pre-register, a practice which obscures the prices at which unpopular models are sold.

All this will make the market for cars more transparent. And it should help make new car sales more competitive. But the Competition Commission's report may still have only a limited impact. Mr Byers, advised by his lawyers, has shied away from forcing fundamental change on the industry

before the European block exemption expires in 2002. The block exemption allows manufacturers to insist that their cars are sold only through tightly-controlled exclusive dealerships. So long as manufacturers retain their stranglehold on sales of new cars, dealers will be reluctant to break ranks.

For all the brave words of Mr Byers, there must be doubts about how effective the stop-gap legislation he proposes will be. The central reform – that manufacturers should give ordinary dealers the same preferential discounts they offer fleet operators – appears to be full of holes. Take, for example, a car rental company, such as Hertz. It secures exceptionally favourable discounts of up to 40% because it buys several thousand cars at a time with identical specifications. Not even the largest dealership network, such as Pendragon, buys in such quantities.

Rental companies also pay on delivery. Dealers operate on sale or return. Even when cars are bought outright, dealers get at least two months' credit, allowing them to sell their cars on without having to finance them. Even if the legislation prohibiting preferential discounts is drafted skilfully, it will not be difficult for manufacturers to claim that each deal is different. Alan Pulham of the Retail Motor Industry Federation, which represents three-quarters of Britains 6,000 dealers, has publicly welcomed the report and believes it will exert a downward pressure on prices. But he acknowledges: 'There will always be special terms for special people.'

A degree of scepticism, is also in order about the industry's willingness to change its ways. Its defences are well prepared, long-standing relationships are at stake and it has no intention of surrendering billions of pounds of profit without a fight.

A decade ago, car manufacturers saw off a previous Monopolies and Mergers Commission report, which recommended opening up exclusive franchises, by simply refusing to co-operate. In the end, the government caved in, bleating that it was all far too difficult and that action would have to await a decision in Brussels. Though the ministerial line is tougher this time, the same cry of waiting for Brussels is being heard again. And with car factories at Longbridge and possibly Dagenham under threat, the government is wary of putting too much pressure on the profit margins of British-based manufacturers, for fear of being held responsible for job losses.

Waiting for Brussels to remove the block exemption could take a long time. Though the exemption formally expires in 2002, France, Italy and Germany, who are all anxious to protect their domestic car industries, show no sign of wanting to ban selective and exclusive dealerships.

Professor Garel Rhys of Cardiff Business School points out that both ministers and manufacturers have a common interest in allowing prices to fall slowly. Nick Gaffney of Velo, a leasing and management company, believes that prices are unlikely to fall much in the short term.

Probably the best hope for price cuts is the pressure that will be exerted by the new breed of car importers, which say they can undercut British showroom prices by up to 30% by importing cars from cheaper European markets. If personal imports start to grow fast, the market will have to respond. But there is a sobering table at the back of the Competition Commission's report, which analyses why so few British buyers have chosen the import option. Nearly half said that it had not occurred to them to do so, nearly a third said that it was too difficult and the rest cited a variety of problems, from delays to the inability to trade in their old car. Consumers who are this dozy almost deserve to be overcharged.

Source: The Economist Newspaper Limited, London, 15 April 2000. Reprinted with permission.

24 Public ownership, privatisation, regulation and deregulation

Learning outcomes

At the end of this chapter you will be able to:

▶ Describe the ways in which the former nationalised industries were structured and regulated after privatisation.

▶ Identify the problem of residual natural monopoly and methods used to deal with it.

▶ Understand the arguments for and against privatisation.

▶ Relate differences in regulation to differences in the nature of the industry being regulated.

How to use this chapter

This chapter is divided into case studies on the following issues:

Case study 24.1: The development of nation-alised industries

Case study 24.2: Problems of nationalised indus-try control

Case study 24.3: The privatisation process

Case study 24.4: Privatisation and the introduc-tion of competition

Case study 24.5: The regulation of privatised industries

Case study 24.6: Is privatisation a success?

These cases can be taken in any order but are better in the sequence you find them in. Case studies 24.1 and 24.2 on nationalisation may be omitted by those readers who are less interested in the historical perspective. However, under-standing why the industries were originally nationalised is relevant to the problems they face

as privatised industries, so study of these cases will bring benefits to the student of the privatised industries. Student activities are found at the end of each case as well as at the end of the chapter.

Introduction

What is privatisation?

Undoubtedly privatisation has been one of the most significant trends in economic and social policy in recent years. This has been the case not only in the UK but also in many other industrial nations. Perhaps the most dramatic and difficult privatisation process is taking place in former communist countries in Eastern Europe. At its simplest, privatisation means the denationalisa-tion of state-controlled industries. Everyone understands that the sale of British Gas and British Telecom are examples of privatisation, but privatisation is much wider than this. It also includes the sale of council houses, the sale of the assets of the New Town Corporations and the contracting out of local-authority-controlled ser-vices such as refuse collection.

At a more fundamental level we can see privati-sation as a piece of social economic engineering. It is aimed at reintroducing competition and free market economics to the centre of the economy. It is aimed at changing people's attitudes and bring-ing in what the Conservatives have termed the 'enterprise culture'. It is also aimed at widening the ownership of private property, in both the housing market and the Stock Exchange, developing a greater involvement in *popular capitalism*.

What is a nationalised industry?

The term public 'corporation' is used to describe an industry owned by the state, but set up as a separate organisation and run much like a company. Like companies, the public corporations are run by boards of directors who run the corporation on a day-to-day basis. The difference between a public corporation and a company quoted on the Stock Exchange is that the government is the only shareholder. The public corporation usually has a sponsoring department, whose minister is responsible for the long-term success of the industry, and who can, like the shareholders of a company, change the membership of the board if performance is unsatisfactory.

Occasionally, a nationalised industry will be run, not as a public corporation, but directly by a government department. This was the case with the GPO, which was not set up as a separate public corporation, as the Post Office, until 1969.

By 1979 the state also owned some of the shares in a large number of businesses, such as BP and Amersham International. Such joint ownership may be termed mixed enterprise. Such businesses are only partly nationalised and are not usually referred to as nationalised industries.

It is useful to distinguish between the welfare state (see Chapters 10 and 28) and nationalised industries. The main difference is that the nationalised industries sell their products in the market place like any other company, while the welfare state for the most part offers its services for free. There are a few grey areas in this distinction. Some services of the welfare state have charges, such as prescriptions for medicine, while some nationalised industries were deliberately subsidised, e.g. provincial branch lines of British Rail. Despite these examples, the distinction between the two is fairly clear and widely accepted.

When Margaret Thatcher came to power in 1979 the combined turnover of all public corporations amounted to £44 billion or 22.9 per cent of the gross domestic product. At the same time they employed 1 710 000 people and were responsible for 20 per cent of all investment in the economy. The great majority of these nationalised industries have now been privatised.

Case study 24.1
THE DEVELOPMENT OF THE NATIONALISED INDUSTRIES

It is often thought that nationalised industries are recent developments and the creation of socialist governments. This is not entirely the case. Indeed the Post Office, which has a claim to be the oldest nationalised industry, was largely set up in the seventeenth century.

The early nationalised industries

Nationalisation can be truly said to have started in the UK with the establishment of the Port of London Authority in 1908. The interwar period saw the creation of the Central Electricity Board (1926), the British Broadcasting Corporation (1926), the five London Passenger Transport Boards (1933) and the British Overseas Airways Corporation (1939).

The Labour nationalisations of 1945–51

The major nationalisations of this period included coal, transport (road freight, railways and canals) and electricity generation in 1947, gas in 1948 and iron and steel in 1951. Road freight transport (with the exception of the company BRS) and iron and steel were subsequently privatised again by the Conservative government in 1953. The nationalisations of this period created the bulk of nationalised industries.

The later nationalisations

The scope of nationalisation widened in the 1960s and 1970s. Iron and steel was renationalised in 1967, and aircraft construction and shipbuilding were nationalised in 1977. The GPO ceased to be a government department in 1969 and became, as the Post Office, a public corporation. This was subsequently divided into the Post Office and British Telecommunications in 1981.

Reasons for nationalisation

A socialist would consider the main reason for nationalisation to be control of the means of production, but someone who believes in capitalism may also argue for state ownership in some cases.

Economies of scale and natural monopoly

There are many industries which are best organised on a very large scale. In the extreme case, these economies of scale will result in monopoly creating a strong argument for state ownership, since the advantages of competition are not available and the consumer can easily be exploited. Some industries were thought to be *natural monopolies* because creating competition would result in the wasteful duplication of expensive infrastructure such as rail track, gas pipelines and electricity cables. In most such cases a network exists which transports the service to the customer. Rail, telecommunications, gas, electricity and water were all nationalised partly for this reason.

Lame ducks

A number of private sector companies were taken into public ownership in the 1970s which were clearly not monopolies, but which instead were major employers that faced bankruptcy. Rolls-Royce, the aircraft engine manufacturer, was rescued in this way by a Conservative government, and British Leyland, the car producer, by a Labour government. Such lame ducks can be nursed back to health by the state but are eventually returned to competition.

Capital expenditure

Some industries demand such major investment expenditure that it is argued that only the government is capable of providing the funds. This is particularly the case where large expenditure is associated with considerable risk. Some people argued that the Channel tunnel was too large and risky a project for the private sector to undertake. Its early financial performance with considerable annual losses may be seen as confirmation of this view. Such an argument was advanced to support the nationalisation of the iron and steel industry in 1967. It was also used to support the nationalisation of coal and the railways. In addition to capital expenditure, some industries demand large spending on research and development (e.g. atomic energy and aircraft).

Control of the economy

The nationalisation of industries may enable a government to pursue its economic policies on investment, employment and prices through the operation of the industries concerned. For example, it might hold down prices in the nationalised industries as a counter-inflationary measure as occurred in 1976 or, alternatively, invest to create employment in depressed areas of the economy.

Strategic reasons

The government might find it necessary to nationalise an industry considered vital for the defence of the country. Thus, for example, the aerospace industry in the UK was nationalised to keep it in existence. The defence implications of nuclear power were also a reason for ensuring that this was a nationalised industry. Key industries of less obvious strategic significance, such as iron and steel, coal and transport, might be seen as vital to the defence of the country in times of war.

Political reasons

The coal industry was neither a natural monopoly nor a lame duck when nationalised (although it later faced losses in the 1960s and 1980s when undercut by cheap oil and gas). Issues of safety and the preference of the workforce, together with its influence in the Labour party, may explain this nationalisation. The steel industry is a similar case. The Russian revolutionary leader, Lenin, once described such industries as the 'commanding heights of the economy', which might explain why socialists were keen to nationalise them.

Externalities

Many industries create negative externalities such as pollution, e.g. global warming from the output of carbon dioxide from electricity generation. Another example is commuter rail fares; these are effectively subsidised because if these customers switched to the roads, the resulting congestion would be unacceptable. It should be much easier to control these externalities in nationalised industries than in those under private ownership. However, the experience in many East European states might seem to contradict this. After the collapse of communism in Eastern Europe it became apparent that many governments had put industrialisation before the environment and health of the population, in a way that would not have been acceptable in the West. Market solutions to the problem of externalities are discussed in Chapter 13.

Social costs and equity

Nationalised industries often produced essential goods and services such as heating, lighting and transport, which it was argued should be available to everyone in a civilised society, irrespective of income. Socially needy customers may benefit from preferential treatment. A nationalised industry may offer special low rates to customers such as old age pensioners; free bus passes for old age pensioners might be seen as an example of this. A product or service may be supplied to the public below cost price where this is considered beneficial. An example of this might be postal services supplied to the remoter parts of the country. These factors probably were not the most important when considering whether to nationalise an industry. However, the issues of equity and social costs were important in policy formation in the nationalised industries. They created problems when setting objectives for these industries (see the discussion on political interference below). These problems have not entirely disappeared after privatisation.

STUDENT ACTIVITY 24.1

In each of the following industries, indicate what part is a natural monopoly which must be either nationalised or regulated, and which parts are potentially competitive.

Rail, gas, electricity, telecommunications, coal, steel, car production, roads, the post office.

STUDENT ACTIVITY 24.2

Should the following products be considered as necessary for all citizens in a civilised society: housing, health, heating, food, local transport, education?

If you agree that any of these products should be available for everyone at a reasonable price, what policy (other than nationalisation) would make sure they are available for the poorest people in society?

STUDENT ACTIVITY 24.3

If a major industry is close to bankruptcy, what alternative does the government have to nationalisation as a solution to the 'lame duck' problem? Does it matter if the industry is taken over by a foreign multinational company? If there is no buyer for the industry and the output is replaced by imported goods, what is the effect on the balance of payments and the value of the pound?

Case study 24.2
PROBLEMS OF NATIONALISED INDUSTRY CONTROL

Efficiency

Although it would not be desirable for nationalised industries to maximise their profits, it could be argued that the lack of the profit motive removes the spur to efficiency that private enterprises have. It is argued that nationalisation creates overlarge and over-bureaucratic organisations, which, therefore, suffer from diseconomies of scale.

The abuse of monopoly power

As argued above, many of the nationalised industries were nationalised because they were monopolies. This argument can also be used against nationalisation, however. It could be argued that a state monopoly is more disadvantageous to the consumer than a private one. This is because there is no higher authority to protect the consumer's interests. The consumer therefore has to tolerate the lack of choice and high prices associated with monopoly, with little hope of redress, although there were normally consumer consultative bodies. It is argued by some that the monopoly power of the nationalised industry may be used by trade unions to raise pay and protect jobs by creating restrictive practices. This can be the case even if, as with British Coal, the industry was not a natural monopoly.

● *Common misunderstanding*

Many of the nationalised industries were profitable most of the time, and where this was not the case there was often good reason for the losses. For instance, British Rail *made losses because it was not allowed to close down many of its loss-making provincial branch lines, as identified in the Beeching Report (1963) and the Serpell Report (1982). Instead, from 1974, the government paid British Rail an amount known as the **public service obligation** (PSO) for keeping these services open. Some freight services, intercity and commuter lines into London broke even or better. Other services were kept open for reasons of social cost (congestion on the roads) and equity (access to a national transport network) as discussed above (see also Chapter 14).*

In general it was the natural monopolies in industries like electricity, telecommunications and gas that were profitable. Of course it is not difficult for monopolies to make a profit, as was discussed in Chapter 22. Large losses were made by lame ducks, such as British Leyland, the car manufacturer. Coal, when faced with cheap oil, and steel, when there was world excess capacity and competing subsidies from other national governments, were also frequently loss making.

Political interference

The sound administration of nationalised industries is often undermined by politicians interfering in the industries' policies for short-term political gains. An example of this would be a ministerial order not to raise prices, in an attempt to combat inflation. The National Economic Development Office (NEDO) Report of 1976 (into the performance of nationalised industries) argued that managers should be left with the day-to-day running of the industry, and that the ministers should only be allowed to interfere by setting the long-run strategy of the industry. This suggestion was never taken up, as the Conservative party soon came to power and concentrated on privatisation as their main policy.

Conflicting objectives

Even if nationalised industries are left to meet the objectives set for them by politicians, there is a possibility that these objectives might conflict, or may be vaguely stated. White Papers (statements of government policy) were produced in 1961, 1967 and 1978 to clarify evolving policy towards the nationalised industries. The NEDO Report (1976) made useful comments about the problems of running these

industries. The concerns of these documents can be discussed under the following headings:

(a) break-even and cross-subsidisation;
(b) profit;
(c) pricing;
(d) decreasing cost industries;
(e) the 1978 White Paper.

Break-even and cross-subsidisation

In 1948 the government required industries to meet the demand for their product at a reasonable price, which would allow them to break even over a number of years. The idea of the break-even level of output is illustrated in Figure 24.1. This overall equality of total revenue and total cost allowed for a large disparity between the cost of supplying any one individual and the price charged to this individual. For example, the cost of supplying a telephone line to a farmer in the Welsh mountains would obviously be higher than the cost of providing a telephone line to a business in London. However, the excess of cost over revenue in providing the telephone to the farmer could be met by the excess of revenue over cost in supplying the business in the cities. This cross-subsidisation among consumers was felt, by many observers, to be undesirable, in that the cost to consumers did not always represent the full opportunity cost of the resources they enjoyed.

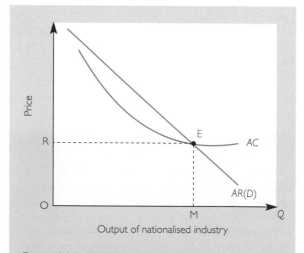

Figure 24.1 The break-even output
This occurs where the AC curve cuts the AR curve at point E. Here: TR = TC.

Profit

Studies of the nationalised industries in the 1950s discovered that the rate of return on capital was higher in the private sector than in the nationalised industries. As a result, the government's 1961 White Paper introduced financial targets for the nationalised industries, and as a consequence downgraded the social objectives. The financial targets were most often expressed as a rate of return on all assets employed by a particular industry. The prevailing market conditions were taken into account in setting these financial targets; hence the required rate of return laid down by the government varied from industry to industry, as well as from year to year. There is no reason why the financial target must always be positive. For example, in 1979–80 the financial target for British Shipbuilders was a maximum trading loss of £100 million.

Apart from asking the nationalised industries not to cross-subsidise, the 1961 White Paper gave no advice on how the financial return was to be achieved. Since many of the industries were monopolies, they could achieve the targets easily by raising their prices without having to consider reducing their costs. The 1967 White Paper retained the idea of financial targets, but introduced a pricing method (marginal cost pricing), which was sometimes inconsistent with making profit, as will be discussed in the next section.

The 1978 White Paper tried to resolve the conflict between profits and social costs. It set a financial target in the form of a required rate of return on capital. It argued that any non-commercial objectives set by the government, such as providing services to remote regions of the country, should be paid for by the government.

Pricing

The 1967 White Paper introduced more explicit guidelines on pricing in nationalised industries. As an attempt to ensure an efficient allocation of resources, a policy of long-run marginal cost pricing was introduced. The prescriptions of modern welfare economics point to the adoption of marginal cost pricing, i.e. prices should be set at the level of marginal cost, as they are in perfect competition. The optimality of marginal cost pricing was described in Chapter 9, while its welfare implications will be discussed more fully in Chapter 27. Attractive as this idea is, it is beset with difficulties.

There are practical difficulties in estimating marginal cost in practice. For example, in transport, vehicles are indivisible; thus the marginal cost of transporting an extra passenger is very close to zero. However, once the vehicle is full and a new vehicle must be laid on, the marginal cost is suddenly very high. There is obviously a problem in attributing increases in costs to individual passengers. Again, in integrated systems such as telecommunications the problem of identifying marginal cost arises. Cables are expensive to lay but relatively inexpensive to use. Also, each phone has access to equipment it may or may not use. It is thus difficult to attribute cost to users who enjoy a potential facility. The NEDO Report (1976) found that with the exception of the electricity industry, nationalised industries were not basing prices on marginal cost, and for the most part did not know what their marginal costs were.

Decreasing cost industries

There are further difficulties when the idea of marginal cost pricing is applied to decreasing cost industries. It is the case that many nationalised industries have large economies of scale which are thought to result in continuously decreasing average costs over the relevant range of output. This should result in a permanent financial deficit for such industries if marginal cost pricing were to be applied.

This is illustrated in Figure 24.2. Here the marginal cost output would be OM at the price OP. This, however, is beyond the break-even output of OL and price of OP_1. This therefore results in a loss, which is shown by the shaded area in the diagram. It has been argued that OM still represents the best situation and that the resultant trading deficit should be financed by taxes. However, the taxes required may have disincentive effects (see Chapters 11 and 28) and might be a cause of allocative inefficiency in the economy as a whole.

There are also some theoretical problems. The first of these is that the MC pricing rule is based on the assumption that costs have been minimised. Thus the policy of MC pricing must be accompanied by pressure to minimise costs in public enterprises. In the private sector this pressure might come from competition and the threat of insolvency or takeover. Although most nationalised industries did face competition in one form or another, it is generally agreed that the threat of closure was less strong

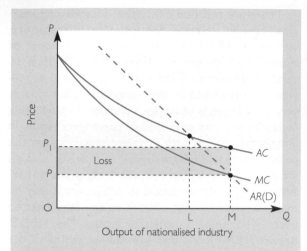

Figure 24.2 **Marginal cost pricing and decreasing costs**
At MC = P the output would be OM and the price OP, but since P is below AC this involves the loss indicated by the shaded areas.

in the public sector. One reason for this is that public enterprises often provide essential services. Another, often related, reason is that where the government itself is seen as the employer, closure would arouse much political opposition. Financial targets might be seen as a substitute for the discipline of the market, but it is difficult to devise acceptable sanctions in the event of these targets not being met. However, if costs are not minimised, *MC* pricing will not ensure a socially efficient allocation of resources.

The second theoretical problem is rather technical and comes under the heading of the theory of second best. Basically this theory demonstrates that setting price equal to marginal cost may not in fact improve efficiency if the conditions assumed in the first optimality theorem do not hold for the rest of the economy.

The 1978 White Paper

This White Paper reintroduced financial targets as a key indicator. The target took the form of a required rate of return on capital. The principle of long-run *MC* pricing was relaxed and the requirement became one of prices being reasonably related to costs. The problem of social costs was dealt with by a proposal that the government should compensate the nationalised industry for any social objective that moved it

away from its financial target objective. This was based on the PSO payment introduced in 1974 for British Rail to pay for provincial and other loss-making services. Just as it appeared that conflicts between the three objectives had been finally resolved, the election of Mrs Thatcher moved the agenda on from the control of nationalised industries to their sale.

STUDENT ACTIVITY 24.4

What are the problems of setting price equal to marginal cost in a natural monopoly? Which formerly nationalised industries would have suffered from this problem? How would a private sector company overcome the problem of loss making by adjusting their price? Would its solution to the problem be in the interests of the customer?

STUDENT ACTIVITY 24.5

Loss-making routes on the railways can sometimes be justified on the grounds of reduced congestion on the roads, or in terms of regional aid to depressed areas of the economy. Who should pay for this social benefit?

(a) Taxpayers at a national level.
(b) Taxpayers at the local level.
(c) Other customers on profit-making parts of the railway.
(d) Road users (via petrol tax).

STUDENT ACTIVITY 24.6

Which of the following regulations should be applied to a nationalised electricity industry? Which of the criteria are consistent with each other?

(a) Make a profit that produces a rate of return on capital equal to the average obtaining in the private sector.
(b) Set price equal to marginal private cost.
(c) Set price equal to marginal social cost.
(d) Set price equal to average cost.
(e) Charge the same price to all areas of the country even if it costs more to supply more remote or sparsely inhabited areas.

Case study 24.3
THE PRIVATISATION PROCESS

The process of privatisation has been a continuous one since 1979. Not only have more and more industries been privatised, but also the approach to privatisation and the regulation, where necessary, of privatised industries have continuously evolved. Table 24.1 shows the dates and proceeds of the principal privatisations.

Table 24.1 **The proceeds of privatisation**

Organisation	Date(s) of sale	Percentage sold	Amount raised (£bn)
British Petroleum	1977,1979, 1983,1987	All	7.40
British Steel	1988	100	2.50
British Telecom	1984	50.2	3.90
	1991,1993	49.8	9.65
Rolls-Royce	1987	100	1.08
British Gas	1986	100	5.40
National Freight	1982	100	0.05
Water	1989	100	5.30
British Aerospace	1981	51	0.15
	1985	49	0.36
British Airways	1987	100	0.90
British Airports Authority	1987	100	1.30
Electricity (distribution)	1990	100	5.18
Electricity (generation)	1991	100	2.10
Electricity (Scottish)	1991	100	2.90
Railtrack	1996	100	1.95

Methods of privatisation

The objective of privatisation is to return state-run industries to private ownership, but this objective can be reached by many different methods. The three principal methods are management buy-out, share flotation and sale to another private company, but parts of an industry can be franchised or contracted out.

Management/employee buy-out

In this form of privatisation shares are offered to managers, workers or both. It differs from a workers' cooperative in that the shares may not be held equally by all employees, and may be sold. The best example of this is the case of National Freight, a road freight business that was privatised in 1982. This form of privatisation is suitable for smaller companies in competitive markets.

Sale to private companies

British Leyland, the nationalised car producer, was sold to British Aerospace (itself a privatised company) in 1986. It was renamed The Rover Group and after a period of collaboration with the Japanese company Honda, it was sold on to the German car producer BMW. Prior to the sale of the company, the lorry section was sold to DAF trucks (a Dutch company) and Jaguar was sold to Ford. BMW failed to make a success of the company, and has now sold it to new UK owners: the Phoenix Consortium.

Share flotation

The large public utilities have been sold by share flotation to the general public. These flotations differ from normal flotations in that the objective is not necessarily to obtain as much money as possible, but also to widen share ownership and thereby to promote the development of popular capitalism. This has been achieved by prioritising small applications for shares and limiting overseas applications. Care has been taken to encourage small share owners to apply by setting the offer price of the share in advance, rather than putting the shares out to tender. Critics of the privatisation process have argued that the shares were often underpriced with the shareholders gaining at the taxpayers' expense.

Franchising

Where part of an industry is run by a franchise, it is possible to simulate some of the characteristics of competition even in situations that appear to be monopolistic. Much of the franchising that has taken place has been in the welfare state or local authority services (e.g. the contracting out of laundry and catering services in the NHS; refuse collection and disposal). These aspects of franchising are discussed in Chapters 10 and 14. However, this form of privatisation has also been used in the transport industry. Although the track and rolling stock have passed into private ownership, the operation of the services is sold as a franchise. The franchise system is particularly useful in attracting firms to run loss-making parts of an industry, such as rural bus routes and provincial rail branch lines, where a negative bid would be expected.

Clearly the terms of the contract are very important so that the subcontracting company can be checked up on, and penalised if it is not fulfilling the terms of the contract. At the end of the agreed period of time, the contract is offered anew, and it is open to other companies to bid for it.

In the early 1990s the principle of competitive tendering was adopted for many government departments and local authority services. Under this arrangement, the existing department of the council could bid against outside companies to decide who should provide the service. This type of tendering was made compulsory for certain services. The idea was that even if the council retained the contract, the process would force its costs down.

STUDENT ACTIVITY 24.7

Imagine you have been asked to set up the franchise agreement for a privatised industry. What conditions would you require of the franchisee before granting the franchise in the case of each of the following?

(a) A rail branch line in a provincial area.
(b) A commuter rail route into London (or another major city).
(c) Catering services for a NHS trust hospital.
(d) Refuse collection for a local authority.
(e) Cleaning services for your school/ college/university.

STUDENT ACTIVITY 24.8

Which of the following considerations are most important when deciding on the right price for a privatisation share issue?

(a) A price that will attract large numbers of ordinary citizens to apply for shares in the knowledge of a certain capital gain.
(b) The maximum price that will give the tax-payer the largest return (even at the risk that a few shares might not initially be sold).

(c) The maximum price that will ensure the sale of all the shares on offer.
(d) A high price in return for the promise of lax regulation after privatisation.

STUDENT ACTIVITY 24.9

The government has a choice of privatising a nationalised industry by the following methods:
(a) share flotation; (b) management buy-out; (c) sale to a private company; (d) franchising. Which do you think would have been most suitable in the case of:

(i)   British Telecom;   (ii)   Jaguar Cars;
(iii) Rover Group;   (iv) Electricity;
(v)   Gas;   (vi) Local water company;
(vii) British Rail;   (viii) Channel 4 TV?

Case study 24.4
PRIVATISATION AND THE INTRODUCTION OF COMPETITION

Although many nationalised industries were monopolies, as the privatisation process continued new methods for introducing competition were invented. Some of these were more successful than others. Where the introduction of competition has been less successful, the government may need to regulate. This section discusses some of the competitive innovations by looking at a number of individual privatisations. The innovations are discussed under three headings:

(a) Vertical disintegration.
(b) Local monopolies competing in the capital markets.
(c) Competition and new technology.

Vertical disintegration

The large public utilities were mainly in a monopoly position before privatisation. The response of the government to this problem has evolved with successive privatisations. Earlier privatisations such as British Telecom and British Gas left the structure of the industry largely unchanged, and have relied on a mixture of regulation and protected competition to overcome the natural monopoly problem. With later privatisations the industries have been restructured extensively prior to privatisation. The objective has been to separate the natural monopoly from the potentially competitive parts of the industry.

Electricity

In the case of electricity, the industry in England and Wales was initially broken into three sectors based on different stages of production (see Figure 24.3). First, electricity generation at power stations is essentially competitive. Second, transmission of electricity from the power stations to different parts of the country takes place via the national grid. This system of pylons and high-voltage cable is a natural monopoly network. The distribution of electricity to homes and businesses is usually effected by underground cable in the UK. This is also a natural monopoly network. However, this is a local network, and had been organised on a local basis before privatisation. The local electricity boards were converted into Regional Electricity Companies (RECs) for different areas of the country (see Figure 24.4). The RECs were also allowed to enter the generation market, initially by producing up to 15 per cent of their own electricity.

The Scottish industry was vertically integrated, by contrast, with Scottish Power providing for the Lowlands, and Hydro for the Highlands. This created two additional competitors in the generation industry. With National Power, PowerGen and Nuclear Electric this makes five major competitors. Imports of electricity from French generators, and competition from the RECs, meant that generation was slowly evolving from an oligopolistic to a more competitive market. The direct sale of electricity from generators to consumers took place initially to large companies. In the late 1990s the supply of electricity (and gas) became a competitive industry with all consumers being able to choose from a range of suppliers. Transmission and distribution companies are paid a regulated fee for transporting the electricity to the consumer.

Gas

Initially the gas industry was privatised as a single company, which was thought of as being in competition with electricity and other fuels. Criticism of the gas industry grew after privatisation, culminating in the loss of the charter mark in the early 1990s

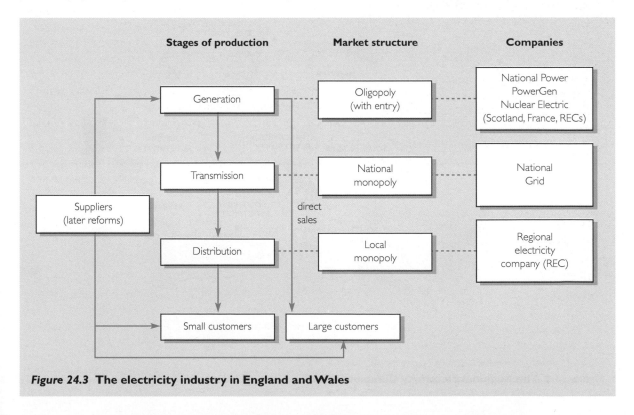

Figure 24.3 **The electricity industry in England and Wales**

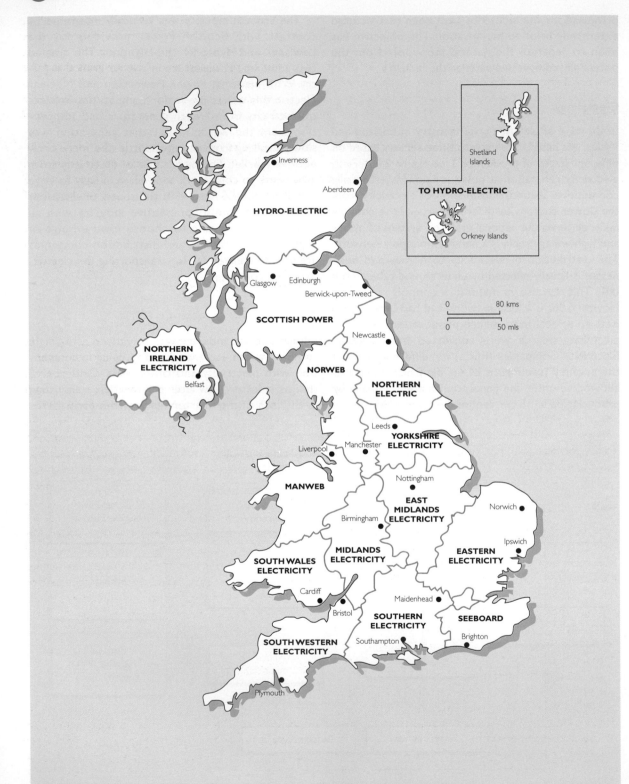

Figure 24.4 **The Regional Electricity Companies (RECs) after privatisation**

originally awarded to the company for good customer service. Monopolies and Mergers Commission reports in 1988 and 1993 suggested that more competition needed to be injected into the industry. Reconsideration of the nature of the gas industry has resulted in more regulation to prevent the abuse of monopoly power. The success of vertical disintegration in the electricity industry led to its introduction in the gas industry. The natural monopoly pipe network, Transco, was separated from the competitive supply of gas. Competing gas suppliers, including British Gas Energy, lease the use of Transco's network to get gas supplies to the consumer. From time to time there are allegations that electricity or gas suppliers get together to fix the price for their industry. Since this is an oligopolistic industry, this is a real possibility, and the regulators have to be careful that this is not easy to do.

In the late 1990s, gas companies started offering electricity supplies and electricity companies began to offer gas, with incentives for customers to buy both products from one company. There is an economy of meter reading and billing in the energy industry, which has led energy supply companies offering both fuels at a reduced rate. Already in the early years of the new century a wide range of companies have moved into these markets, offering to supply (but not necessarily produce or distribute) gas and electricity.

Rail

The natural monopoly in this case is the system of railway tracks and the stations. A separate company, Railtrack, was set up to manage this side of the industry, and was privatised in 1996. The stock of trains was sold off to three companies (known as rolling stock companies or 'Roscos') which lease them back to operators of train services. The train services are operated by companies that have won a time-limited franchise for a part of the rail network. In the case of the rail network, there was a deliberate policy of increasing competition as much as possible by vertical disintegration of the industry. This may create problems of coordination between different companies in the design of an integrated timetable and through-ticketing system. A passenger may use a number of different companies in the course of a long journey. The revenue from a single ticket for the journey must be distributed to the various companies. This distribution process will in itself cost money. This type of cost is referred to as the **transactions cost of setting up the market**, and must be set against any efficiency gains that arise from competition.

There have also been problems of accountability for safety and lateness of trains, which has been discussed in Chapter 14, and has led to the introduction of a stronger regulator in the form of the Strategic Rail Authority. In contrast to electricity and gas, rail is an example of a privatised industry where the problems of social costs have created problems in a competitive setting.

Local monopolies competing in the capital markets

Water and electricity distribution

Where vertical disintegration of industries is difficult to achieve, some degree of competition can occur if the industry can be split up into local natural monopolies. This is the strategy that has been adopted for electricity distribution and for the water industry. This is, of course, not competition from the consumer's point of view since the consumer has no choice but to accept the local supplier. It does, however, create competition in the capital markets, with less efficient companies vulnerable to takeover. Nobody suggests that this type of competition protects the consumer from poor service or overpricing, so considerable regulation is still required in these cases. If there were a national network of water pipes, the water could be separated from the network as in the case of gas. However, the cost of transporting water long distances, sometimes against gravity, would be much greater than for gas.

Competition and new technology

British Telecom

In some cases, after privatisation, competition can be developed to the point where regulation is no longer necessary. New technology can sometimes change a market from being a natural monopoly to being naturally competitive. The introduction of relatively cheap fibre optic cable to replace the old wire system of transmitting telephone calls, and the simultaneous development of mobile phones using radio technology, make a good case study of such a change.

Since its privatisation in 1984, British Telecom has been tightly regulated by price controls, which are discussed in more detail in the section on regulation below. This was necessary initially because of the strong monopoly position of the company. However, the more important action of the regulator (Oftel) was to protect the major new entrant, Mercury. Mercury was wholly owned by Cable and Wireless, itself a recently privatised company specialising in international telecommunications. The problem for a new company in telecommunications is that it does not have a countrywide network of cables. In order to connect customers, it needs to use the network of the dominant firm in the business, British Telecom. This put British Telecom in a very strong bargaining position with Mercury. Oftel protected Mercury by requiring British Telecom to carry Mercury's calls, and by regulating the price. The telecommunications market was opened up to greater competition in the late 1990s as the spread of cable television allowed those companies to offer a competing network, and as the duopoly between BT and Mercury ended, allowing other companies to enter the market. The development of the internet has brought a fresh round of entry into the industry, with ISPs (internet service providers) offering a package service. The convergence of television, computing and telecommunication technologies means that new forms of competition and new products, and combinations of products, are constantly emerging in this industry, particularly with the sudden growth of the internet.

British Airways

The international air passenger market was highly regulated from 1919 to the late 1970s. It was decided by the Paris Convention in 1919 that the air space above a country belonged to that country. Since then, if an airline from one country wishes to carry passengers to another country, the two governments must first sign a *bilateral agreement*. These agreements decide the terms under which airlines can carry passengers between the two countries. Most agreements signed between 1945 and 1975 were very restrictive in nature. In most cases each country could nominate only one airline

to fly on each route, often known as the *flag carrier*. In addition only a limited number of airports were designated as *gate of entry* airports which could be used by airlines from other countries. The prices were largely determined by the International Airlines Trade Association (IATA). In some cases the two airlines on a route would operate a revenue pool, sharing the revenue irrespective of which airline the passengers chose to fly on.

This very uncompetitive state of affairs was challenged by President Carter of the USA in the late 1970s. Since then the bilateral agreements have become progressively more liberal, allowing for two airlines from each country for instance, and designating more airports in each country as international gate of entry airports. Prices are no longer determined by the trade association, IATA. This process of introducing more competition into the airline industry is known as deregulation. It occurred first on the North Atlantic route, particularly between the USA and the UK, and in the USA domestic airline market. It soon spread to other areas of the world where passenger air transport was a large-scale industry. By 1986 when BA was privatised, deregulation was widespread. Curiously enough, despite the Single European Market, deregulation was late to come to the EU. A number of nationalised airlines such as Air France and Iberian Airlines were still being heavily subsidised by their national governments in the late1990s, although these governments had agreed to reduce the subsidy.

The year after BA was privatised it swallowed up its major British rival, British Caledonian, leading to concerns that BA would have too much monopoly power. The growth of international competition because of deregulation has ensured that BA faces international competition. Indeed the development of such competition provides an argument for the expansion of BA so that it can achieve the economies of scale necessary to compete effectively with the giant American airlines in the world market.

There remain some elements of monopoly power in the airline industry. The ownership of *time slots* for take-off and landing at the major British airports based on past practice gives BA an advantage over new British rivals. The ownership of a computer reservation system (CRS) also gives any airline the potential for greater knowledge about customers' and rivals' behaviour.

Television

New technology in the form of satellite broadcasting, cable transmission, and digitisation of the original technology (terrestrial transmission), has led to an enormous increase in the number of competing channels on television. The BBC has had its licence extended and remains in the public sector but has to contend with a more competitive environment.

> ## STUDENT ACTIVITY 24.10
>
> If the government decides to privatise the Post Office consider whether:
>
> (a) it is possible to introduce competition;
> (b) there are any benefits from vertical disintegration of the service;
> (c) the telephone system and the internet are effective substitutes for the postal industry.

Case study 24.5
THE REGULATION OF PRIVATISED INDUSTRIES

It can be seen from the above discussion that although competition can be injected into many of the privatised industries, in many industries natural monopoly and market power remain a problem. For these areas it is necessary for the government to intervene by regulating the industry in order to protect the consumer from excessive price increases.

In most cases the problem of regulating privatised industries is monopoly. The main issues faced by the regulators are:

(a) abnormal profit;
(b) protecting new competition;
(c) efficiency and costs.

Rate of return regulation

In the USA, where regulation was always preferred to nationalisation, the rate of return on capital was the most common form of control on electricity and gas utilities to prevent them from earning excessive profits. A maximum rate of return on capital meant that the firms could not raise their prices too much. This long experience also led the Americans to notice the main drawback of this type of regulation.

If the regulated firm is allowed to make a reasonably good return on capital, it has an incentive to over-invest. Each additional pound spent on capital increases their allowed profit. This unwanted consequence of rate of return regulation is called the **Averch–Johnson effect** after its discoverers.

RPI ± X

The method of regulation adopted in the UK, starting with British Telecom, is to control prices rather than profits. The retail price index (RPI) gives the rate of inflation for the previous year. The privatised industry is allowed to increase its prices, on average, by the rate of inflation minus X. For instance, the initial figure for X in the case of British Telecom was 3 per cent. If the rate of inflation was 5 per cent this would mean that the company could only raise its prices by 2 per cent on average. However, a 2 per cent rate of inflation would mean that a reduction in price by, on average, 1 per cent would be required.

The permitted rate of increase is usually below the rate of inflation, but in one case, water, an RPI ± X formula was used to enable water companies to raise the large sums of money needed to finance investment and meet EU water quality standards. Another variation on the theme occurs where there is a significant input price that is subject to market variations. Coal, oil and gas, prices can significantly affect costs in the electricity industry. The solution in this case is to adopt an RPI − X + Y formula. The Y is to allow for changes in input prices and can itself be negative or positive, depending on whether input prices have fallen or risen.

The big question here is what determines X? Unfortunately, there is no easy answer to this question. Governments are trying to achieve a number of objectives with this single percentage figure and some of them are hard to quantify:

(a) *Reduce abnormal profit* made by the firm. It might seem easy to calculate what the normal rate of profit is that firms should earn, but industries facing more risky environments expect a higher rate of return to compensate them for taking this risk. Unfortunately the assessment of the risk facing a firm is an uncertain and subjective business, unless you have a crystal ball that foretells the future.
(b) *Reduce costs of production* by forcing out any inefficiency. Privatised industries usually have some

inefficiency which can be 'squeezed out' by regulators. The difficulty is knowing how much fat an organisation has. In the case of British Telecom continual increases of the value of X failed to make much impression on its recorded profit (after allowing for redundancy payments) which remained obstinately around the £3 billion level in the early years.

(c) Encourage the adoption of *new technology*. The cost-reducing effects of new technology are always hard to predict in advance.

(d) *Reduce price* for the consumer. This objective will usually be achieved. However, since the formula is normally applied to a basket of prices representing the industry's product range, not all prices will come down by the same amount, and indeed some may actually rise as happened to domestic telephone customers in the early days of privatisation.

Is there a difference?

Some economists argue that there is no real difference between these two forms of regulation, because X gets adjusted upwards if the company continues to make a high profit (or rate of return). This certainly seems to be the case with British Telecom. When a value of 3 per cent for X failed to reduce profits, the regulator, Oftel, kept increasing its value until it reached 7.5 per cent. Competition is the best regulator and the opening of the telecommunications market as we move into the twenty-first century has had the biggest impact on prices, with even British Gas entering the market.

Information problems

The problem faced by regulators is that they do not know enough about the industry they are regulating. This is because the best source of information is the industry itself. It is not in the interest of the industry being regulated to give useful information about itself, if the effect of that information would be tougher regulation and therefore lower profits. This situation is sometimes termed **regulatory capture**, where the industry being regulated is really in charge of the situation. Regulators sometimes have to impose tough price controls despite loud protests from the industry. This can be somewhat of a gamble

by the regulator. If the industry did in fact have lots of potential for reducing costs by shaking out labour, or introducing new technology, then the tough price controls would have been justified. If on the other hand most of the potential for further cost reductions had been exhausted, then tough price controls would substantially reduce profits, and possibly investment as a result.

Regulatory failure

The experience of regulating privatised industries over the last two decades has led to a concept of regulatory failure. In addition to the problems of information identified above, regulators may:

(a) fail to allow a company to be profitable enough to maintain its capital;

(b) fail to adapt quickly enough to the arrival of new technology;

(c) fail to carry political support;

(d) be given inadequate powers to impose needed regulations.

These regulatory failures can be partly avoided if the regulator is:

(a) made as independent as possible;

(b) given a wide range of companies to regulate to avoid capture by any one of them (for instance the Ofgen regulator now covers electricity and gas industries);

(c) given the consumer's interests as the main purpose of regulation.

The windfall tax

The idea that some companies had been sold at below market price led the Labour government to introduce a **windfall tax** on certain privatised companies. This one-off tax was related to the capital gain that an investor would have made by buying at the privatisation price and then selling at the market price. Of course, the new shareholders who actually sold their shares and made this capital gain did not bear this tax. It is the existing shareholders who will lose. Nevertheless the increase in share prices can be taken as a measure of the high profitability of the company and therefore can be taken as a **proxy** for excessive profits made by such companies. Concern expressed by the Labour party while in opposition about the so-called 'fat cat' directors of privatised firms who made enormous sums on share options and other deals, has faded away in government as there is no legal way in which this money can be recovered. The allegations, however, did contribute to the 'sleaze' factor used against the Conservatives in the 1997 election.

Competition: the best regulator

The best regulator is, of course, competition. Sometimes regulation is needed to create and protect this competition. The dominant position of British Telecom in the telecommunications market means that the most important long-term policy of the regulator is to protect new competition. Regulators were at first a little timid in the introduction of competition, allowing only Mercury to challenge British Telecom, and considering electricity to be sufficient competition for gas. This can perhaps be understood in retrospect because of the experimental nature of these reforms. The process of introducing competition into these very large former state monopolies has been an extremely slow process, but considerable progress has been made in telecommunications, and electricity and gas supply.

The 1998 Competition Act, as discussed in Chapter 23 has created a firmer basis for regulators to intervene in their markets with clear penalties for anti-competitive behaviour.

STUDENT ACTIVITY 24.11

A privatised industry is regulated by the formula $RPI - X + Y$, where X is the figure for efficiency gains and Y is a figure allowing for changes in input costs over which the industry has no control.

(a) If the rate of inflation last year was 3 per cent and X is set at 5 per cent, while Y is set at 2 per cent, what will be the average increase in price allowed for the industry in the coming year?
(b) If the industry has already decided to increase its price by 3 per cent on 40 per cent of its output, how must it change the prices on the remaining 60 per cent of its output?

STUDENT ACTIVITY 24.12

An industry is being controlled by rate of return regulation fixed at 10 per cent on the company's assets. Which of the following policies would increase the total profit which the company can earn?

(a) Increased expenditure on capital.
(b) Increases in prices.
(c) Increased expenditure on perks for the management.

Which of the following policies would allow the company to raise its prices?

(a) Increased expenditure on capital.
(b) Increased expenditure on perks for the management.
(c) Increased costs of raw materials.

STUDENT ACTIVITY 24.13

Which of the following parts of privatised industries still need price regulation?

(a) Transco; (b) Gas supply companies; (c) Rover Group; (d) British Telecom; (e) Regional Electricity Companies; (f) National Grid; (g) A rail franchisee (passenger services).

Case study 24.6
IS PRIVATISATION A SUCCESS?

Raising money and transferring wealth

At one level privatisation can be seen as a way for the government to raise money and thus reduce the need for taxation. But more important than this are the ideological motives which underlie the trend. At a superficial level we may view privatisation as a response to the alleged inefficiencies of nationalised industries.

Selling off publicly owned assets was likened by the ex-Conservative Prime Minister, Harold Macmillan, to selling off the family silver. This is a mistaken understanding of the situation. The government does indeed receive wealth from the public, which can be used to lower taxes. However, what happens to the wealth of the nation? Nothing! The ownership of assets has just passed from the public sector to the private. Of course, ownership may go abroad, but that is hardly unusual in today's globalised world.

The political economy of the market

More fundamental than this is the belief that the price system is the most efficient way to run the economy and that the price system brings about an optimum allocation of resources. The classical economists, such as Adam Smith, argued that this optimality was brought about by the invisible hand of self-interest (i.e. everyone striving to maximise their own individual benefit) and was regulated by the forces of competition. Many twentieth-century economists have disagreed with this view. However, in recent years **Milton Friedman** and the Chicago school have argued for a return to classical values. According to this school of thought the market economy is essentially self-regulating and efficient. Thus, in order to have a well-run economy it is essential to reduce the role of the state to a minimum so that the maximum percentage of the economy will be self-regulating. The idea that private enterprise results in more efficient use of resources is also part of the supply side view of economics.

The most influential school of thought in the UK privatisation process has been the Austrian school, particularly the writings of **Hayek**. This school of thought stresses the value of the market, not just as a way of meeting consumer preferences and driving down costs, but also as a source of innovation and investment funds. Abnormal profits may form the basis for investment in new technologies, research and development, and may be regarded as a good thing. It is the view of the Austrian economists (not all of whom are Austrian) that such monopoly power will be challenged in the long run.

Whatever view of privatisation is adopted, the fact remains that reversing the process is very difficult. The cost of renationalising these industries would be prohibitive and could only be achieved at the cost of raising tax rates. This has not been a popular policy proposal in recent elections. The alternative approach of political parties on the left is to concentrate on tighter regulation.

An extension of this argument is that the state sector of the economy has crowded out private investment. During the years of high government intervention there was a high demand upon the investment funds available, of which the state took a large proportion. It is argued by the free market school that the state will take investment decisions on non-economic grounds, for example, it may build coal-fired power stations to keep the miners happy, which will therefore lead to low-yielding investments. It is thus necessary to reduce the role of the state as investor and leave markets to allocate capital in the most efficient manner possible.

We should therefore see the events of recent decades not simply as the selling off of state-controlled industries but as a fundamental shift in the way in which the economy is organised. Initially the sale of assets could be seen as merely a change of emphasis, but as the government extended the role of the market into the operation of the welfare state (see Chapter 10), it became clear that some of the basic principles, which had ordered our society from 1945 to 1979, had been called into question. The election of the Labour government in 1997 has not brought renationalisation with it; indeed further privatisation has not been ruled out.

Performance

One way of deciding whether the policy of privatisation has been a success is to examine the performance of the privatised industries. The results of studies into efficiency have been mixed. Studies of the nationalised industries suggest that they performed moderately well in terms of productivity growth in the 1950s and 1960s, but that they performed rather less well in the 1970s. Curiously enough, their profitability rose in the decade of privatisation, the 1980s! They seem to have done particularly well just before being privatised! Whether this is because the government was deliberately allowing profits to rise in order to get a good share price, or whether the prospect of private sector competition forced it to lower costs, is a matter of dispute.

Increased profitability can be achieved by a number of methods:

(a) *Wages can be reduced.* This does not constitute an increase in productivity, but a redistribution of income. There is evidence that this occurred in some cases of bus and refuse collection privatisations.

(b) *New technology can reduce costs.* A good example here is British Telecom where fibre optic cables and computerised exchanges have revolutionised the technology of the industry. Prices have been driven down continuously in real terms since privatisation. A question that can be legitimately asked here is whether such changes would have occurred as extensively or as rapidly if the industry had remained nationalised. Is the increased productivity due to the privatisation, increased competition, or the new technology? It is difficult to separate out these effects.

(c) *Market power can increase profits.* Where industries have been privatised with relatively little competition, profits have been satisfactory but consumer relationships have not. British Gas lost its charter mark for consumer relations in the early 1990s. The performance of some of the water companies in maintaining supplies has been criticised (although to be fair to them UK rainfall did fall in the mid-1990s). There was at one stage considerable criticism of the reliability of British Telecom public telephone call boxes, but the reliability improved dramatically when Oftel suggested that Mercury could take over provision.

(d) Restrictive practices achieved under nationalisation can be removed. This can result in a substantial reduction in employment in these industries. Closure of loss-making parts of the business can also have a similar effect. Major changes of this kind can create local unemployment, which can take time to eradicate.

Ownership or competition?

A strong view emerging from studies of the privatised industries is that competition is more important than ownership in determining efficiency. Where it has not been possible to introduce competition, privatised industries have needed considerable regulation, and because of the information problems discussed above, this has not always been completely satisfactory. Where it has been possible to introduce competition, results have been better, although where the process of introducing competition has been slow there have been transitional problems. Because it is not always possible to introduce competition, there will always be an argument that nationalisation is still appropriate for some industries which are unavoidably monopolistic.

STUDENT ACTIVITY 24.14

At the time of writing the Post Office had not been privatised. Competition exists in the parcels business for items above a 50p delivery price, but not for letters. If privatised, which sector would you advise a new company to enter?

(a) An urban area with high population density.
(b) A rural area in a remote part of the country.
(c) Mass delivery for companies' 'junk mail'.

What effect will your entry into the market have on:

(a) The revenues and costs of the Post Office?
(b) Wages in the industry?
(c) Numbers of deliveries in the day?
(d) Prices of delivery in rural areas?

STUDENT ACTIVITY 24.15

Transco and the National Grid are natural monopolies where competition is not a sensible option. What are the advantages of privatising and regulating as opposed to nationalisation in such cases?

Summary

1 Industries were nationalised for reasons of monopoly power, social costs, strategic reasons and ideology.
2 There are problems in regulating the nationalised industries because of conflicting objectives: profit, allocative efficiency, social objectives and macroeconomic objectives.
3 Privatisation works best where there is competition. Sources of competition include vertical disintegration, new technologies, deregulation and capital market competition.
4 Regulation is still necessary where there is monopoly power, or in order to protect new entrants into the market.
5 Regulation of privatised industries suffers from shortage of information. Rate of return regulation may lead to over-investment. RPI − X is initially good but difficult to set accurately.
6 There remains a debate about whether competition is more important than ownership.

SECTION VI

Labour markets and the distribution of income

'The first man who, having fenced in a piece of land, said "This is mine," and found people naïve enough to believe him, that man was the founder of civil society.'

Jean-Jacques Rousseau

25 The pricing of productive factors

Learning outcomes

At the end of this chapter you will be able to:

▶ Evaluate the theory of the distribution of income.
▶ Explain the term 'derived demand'.
▶ Account for the significance of the law of diminishing returns in distribution theory.
▶ Define marginal physical product, the average physical product and the marginal revenue product of a factor.
▶ Recognise the importance of measures of productivity.
▶ Explain the derivation of the firm and industry demand curves for a factor.
▶ Account for the fact that the principles underlying resource utilisation are consistent with those supporting cost structures of the firm.
▶ Identify isoquants and isocosts.
▶ State conditions for the least cost combination of factors.

Introduction

In this section of the book we wish to examine the use of the factors of production. In this chapter we will look at the general principles covering the use of resources and the factors which determine their price. In the subsequent chapters we will see how these general principles apply to each factor.

The theory of distribution

Let us return for a moment to the fundamentals of the subject. Economics must answer the *What?*, *How?* and *For whom?* questions in society. In this section we will be completing our explanation of the 'How?' and 'For whom?' questions in a market economy. As we examine the theory of production, this will explain how and why firms use the factors of production, but in doing so it will also explain how the factor incomes – wages, rent, interest and profit – are determined. We will thus be explaining the 'For whom?' question, because it is income that determines people's ability to buy goods. This is termed the *theory of distribution* since it attempts to explain how income is distributed between the factors of production.

The derived demand for the factors of production

When a firm demands a factor of production it is said to be a derived demand, i.e. the factor is not demanded for itself but for the use to which it can be put.

If we examine the demand for such things as bread, these are wanted for *direct* consumption. If, however, a company demands labour it is because it wants to produce something which it can eventually sell. The demand for labour is thus said to be *derived* from the demand for the final product.

Marginal distribution theory

The law of diminishing returns

In order to explain the factors which determine the firm's demand for a factor of production we must turn once again to the law of diminishing returns. The *production function* describes the relationship between output and the factors of production used to produce that output. In the short run the production decision is constrained by the fact that at least one factor is fixed in supply, while the other factors can be varied. For example, a firm will have a factory of a certain size or a farm of a certain area and to this fixed factor the business adds variable factors such as labour and power. Under these circumstances the firm will be affected by the law of diminishing returns, i.e. as the firm adds more and more of the variable factor, e.g. labour, to a constant amount of fixed factor, e.g. land, the extra output per person that this creates must, after a time, be successively reduced.

The marginal physical product (MPP)

As factors of production are combined, in the short run various principles will emerge which will apply to any firm. These are best illustrated by taking a simple example. In Table 25.1 a farmer, whose land is fixed at 10 hectares in the short run, adds more and more units of the variable factor – labour – in order to produce a greater output of wheat. Obviously if no labour is used there will be no output. When 1 unit of labour is used the output of the farm works out at 12 tonnes of wheat per year. If two persons are used the output rises to 36 tonnes.

Table 25.1 **Marginal physical product and average physical product**

Number of people employed	Output of wheat, Q (tonnes/year)	Marginal physical product, MPP (tonnes/year)	Average physical product, APP (tonnes/year)
0	0		0
		12	
1	12		12
		24	
2	36		18
		34	
3	70		23.3
		30	
4	100		25
		20	
5	120		24
		10	
6	130		21.6
		0	
7	130		

The average physical product (APP) per person has risen from 12 tonnes to 18 tonnes. This does not mean that the second person was more indus-

trious than the first but rather that a 10 hectare farm was too big for one person to work and it runs more efficiently with two. The higher average product therefore applies to both workers. It may have been achieved through *specialisation* and *division of labour*, impossible when there was only one worker.

As the employer continues to employ more workers so the total output continues to rise, but eventually the rate at which it increases starts to diminish. The third worker adds 34 tonnes per year to the output, the fourth worker only 30 tonnes, the fifth adds only 20 tonnes per year, and so on. Eventually the seventh worker adds nothing more to total output. The amount added to the total output by each successive unit of labour is the *marginal physical product* (MPP). If we generalise this principle we could define it as:

The MPP is the change to the total output resulting from the employment of one more unit of a variable factor.

STUDENT ACTIVITY 25.1

The number of people employed in a factory and the total output produced are as follows:

Number of people employed	Total output Q (units)	Marginal physical product, MPP	Average physical product, APP
0	0		
1	20		
2	44		
3	69		
4	87		
5	100		
6	106		
7	107		
8	107		

Complete the figures for the MPP and APP of labour.

These figures are illustrated graphically in Figure 25.1. The MPP curve rises as the benefits of division of labour make the utilisation of land more efficient. Between 2 and 3 units labour the curve reaches its highest point and then begins to decline as *diminishing marginal returns* set in.

The APP curve also rises initially. *Diminishing average returns* occur between 4 and 5 units of labour; beyond this point the *APP* curve declines.

Diminishing returns come about because, as more labour is employed, each successive unit of labour has less of the fixed factor – land – to work with. If it were not for the law of diminishing returns we could supply the world's food from one farm simply by adding more and more labour to it. Obviously this is not possible.

You will also see that the *MPP* curve goes through the top of the *APP* curve, the familiar relationship between marginal and average curves. The intersection of the *APP* with the *MPP* tells us when the firm is at its optimum efficiency in terms of its average output or output per unit.

● *Common misunderstanding*

The point of optimum efficiency of the variable factor in terms of either its marginal or average return is not necessarily the output the firm will choose. If, for example, the product we were considering was gold then it might be worthwhile running a very inefficient mine. Eventually, however, because of diminishing returns, MPP may even become negative when total output falls. No business would be willing to employ more resources to get less output.

Once again, because *MPP* is a marginal figure it must be plotted in a particular way. It is the amount added in going from one level of input to one more unit of that input. Hence, in Figure 25.1 *MPP* is plotted half way between 1 and 2 persons, half way between 2 and 3 persons and so on. This is shown by the solid points in Figure 25.1. These can then be joined up to give the *MPP* curve.

Output goes on increasing while *MPP* is positive. Thus in our example total output is maximised when the sixth person is employed. If a seventh person is employed *MPP* becomes negative and total output therefore falls. The relationship between *MPP* and total output is shown in Figure 25.2.

Production and productivity

Production denotes the total amount of a commodity produced by turning factors of production into output, whereas *productivity* is the amount of a commodity produced per unit of resources used. When a firm is improving its efficiency, productivity will be rising; that is, if, by better management, more efficient equipment/technology or better use of labour, the firm manages to produce the same

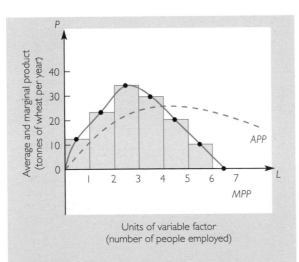

Figure 25.1 The marginal physical curve
The *MPP* shows the amount of extra output produced by each additional unit of the variable factor. Note that the *MPP* curve goes through the highest point of the *APP* curve.

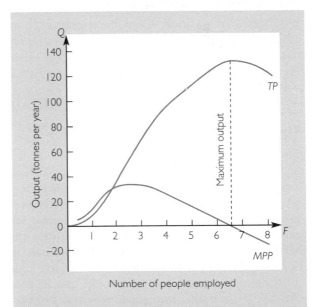

Figure 25.2 Marginal physical product and total product
MPP is zero at the point where total product is maximised.

or a greater amount of product with a smaller amount of resources then it has increased its productivity. However, an increase in output does not necessarily imply an improvement in a firm's efficiency. For example, if the firm produces an increase in output but only at the expense of an even greater increase in resources then, despite the increase in output, its productivity has fallen.

● *Common misunderstanding*

A rise in total output need not involve an increase in productivity. It may be the result of an even greater increase in the firm's resources, in which case productivity will have fallen. Only when an increase in output is the result of a rise in output per person will a firm be more efficient.

Productivity taking account of all inputs is difficult to measure and so one of the most common methods is to simply take the total output and divide it by the number of workers to give *labour productivity*. Measures which take account of all factors are known as *total factor productivity measures*. In the example we have been using, productivity is rising while the *APP* is rising and falling when the *APP* is falling. Productivity is vital to the economic welfare of both individual firms and the nation. It is only by becoming more efficient that we can hope to compete with other businesses or nations. Considerations, such as education and training to improve labour productivity and the level of technology that raises the productivity of capital equipment, are vital issues in productivity.

The marginal revenue product (MRP)

The marginal physical product is so called because it is measured in *physical units* such as tonnes of wheat or barrels of oil, depending upon what is being produced. It is often more convenient, however, to express it in money terms. We can do this by examining how much money the *MPP* could have been sold for. For instance, in our example, if the fourth person employed adds 30 tonnes to output and each tonne can be sold for £750 then the *marginal revenue product* (*MRP*) is £22 500. Thus the *MRP* can be calculated as:

$$MRP = MPP \times P$$

where *P* is the price of the commodity being produced. However, this formula works only if the firm is producing under conditions of perfect competition, i.e. the firm can sell as much of the product as it likes without lowering the price and hence *P = MR*. (The *MRP* under perfectly competitive conditions is often referred to as the *value of the marginal product*, or *VMP*). If, on the other hand, the firm was operating under conditions of imperfect competition then, in order to sell more, it would have to lower the price of the product; the change in a firm's revenue as the result of the sale of one more unit of a commodity, i.e. *MR*, is less than the price. Thus, under conditions of imperfect competition, the *MRP* would be calculated as:

$$MRP = MPP \times MR$$

For the sake of simplicity we will assume conditions of perfect competition for most of this chapter.

The *MRP* may be defined as the change to a firm's revenues as a result of the sale of the product of one more unit of a variable factor.

Table 25.2 gives the *MRP* based upon our example and assuming that wheat can be sold at a price of £750 per tonne.

Table 25.2 The marginal revenue product

Number of people employed	Marginal physical product, MPP (tonnes of wheat)	Price of wheat per tonne, P (£)	Marginal revenue product, MRP = MRP × P (£)
0		750	
	12		9 000
1		750	
	24		18 000
2		750	
	34		25 500
3		750	
	30		22 500
4		750	
	20		15 000
5		750	
	10		7 500
6		750	
	0		0
7		750	
	−10		−7 500
8		750	

If we plot the *MRP* schedule as a graph we will find that its shape is exactly that of the *MPP* but the units which are used on the vertical axis have now become pounds (see Figure 25.3).

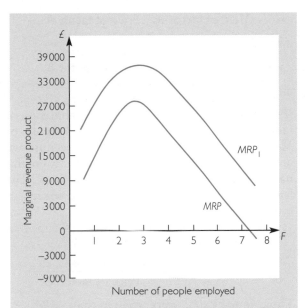

Figure 25.3 The marginal revenue product curve
The shift from *MRP* to *MRP*₁ could be the result of an improvement in technology or an increase in the price of the product.

STUDENT ACTIVITY 25.2

Given a constant price per unit for the product of £800, calculate the *MRP* figures based on the information from Student activity 25.1.

The firm's demand for a factor

We calculate the *MRP* in order that we may explain the quantity of a factor of production which a firm will demand. This we will find is the quantity of the factor at which its *MRP* is equal to the price of the factor. If, for example, the *MRP* of a unit of labour was £25 500 per year and the cost of that unit of labour was £9000 per year, the business would obviously be £16 500 better off as a result of employing that unit of labour. If the *MRP* of the next unit of labour fell to £22 500, but the cost of it remained £9000, the firm would still employ that unit of the factor since it would be a further £13 500 better off. In other words the business will go on demanding a factor of production while the *MRP* of that factor is greater than the cost of employing it.

This is best understood graphically. In Figure 25.4 if the wage rate was £11 250 per person, the best number of people for the firm to employ would be five. The cost of labour would be the area under the wage line, i.e. 5 × £11 250. The shaded area above the wage line and below the *MRP* curve would be the money the business would get back over and above the cost of employing the factor. The firm will always be best off by trying to obtain as much of this shaded area as possible. If, for example, the wage fell to as low as £3750 then the firm would employ six people, but if the wage rose to £18 750 it would be best off employing only four people. Thus:

The firm's *MRP* curve for a factor is its demand curve for that factor provided that the price of the commodity being produced remains fixed.

The industry's demand for a factor

If we consider a fall in the price of the factor, this will have the effect of causing the firm to hire more of the variable factor. However, if all other firms in the industry do the same thing this will cause a rise in output and, therefore, a fall in the price of the product. As a result the *MRP* curve

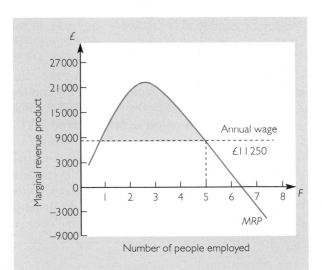

Figure 25.4 The marginal revenue product and wages
The best number of workers for the firm to employ is five. This is where the marginal revenue product is equal to the wage rate.

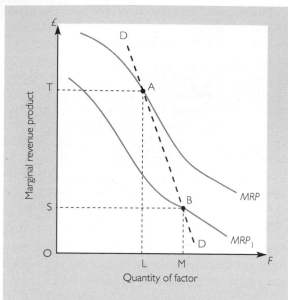

Figure 25.5 Derivation of the demand curve
A fall in the price of the factor from OT to OS causes a fall in the price of the product, which shifts the *MRP* curve to *MRP*₁. The equlilibrium shifts from A to B; thus AB is the demand curve for the firm. The industry demand curve is the horizontal sum of the demand curves of the individual firms.

will shift leftwards. In Figure 25.5 OT represents the original price of the factor and the quantity of the factor employed is OL where the price of the factor coincides with the original *MRP* curve. The leftward movement of the *MRP* curve to *MRP*₁ shows the effect of a fall in the price of the commodity. The price of the factor is now OS and the firm employs OM units of the factor. We have thus moved from point A on curve *MRP* to B on *MRP*₁. If we join up these points this gives the firm's demand curve for the factor, given the effect of a fall in the price of a factor on the price of the product. In these circumstances, the *industry demand curve for a factor* is the horizontal sum of the demand curves of the individual firms; this demand curve is therefore less elastic than the firm's demand curve.

The best factor combination

The profit maximisation equilibrium for a firm would be when the conditions of *MRP* = price of the factor have been fulfilled for each factor. Thus, it will be where:

MRP of factor A = Price of factor A

and

MRP of factor B = Price of factor B

and so on.

If we wish to obtain the least cost combination of factors at any output we must abandon the use of *MRP*s and return to *MPP*s. This is because we are trying to explain simply the least cost combination without reference to revenues (sales). The least cost combination will be achieved when:

$$\frac{MPP \text{ of factor A}}{\text{Price of fatctor A}} = \frac{MPP \text{ of factor B}}{\text{Price of factor B}}$$

$$= \frac{MPP \text{ of factor C, etc.}}{\text{Price of factor C}}$$

Thus, if MPP_B/P_B were greater than MPP_A/P_A then the firm could produce the same output at a lower cost by hiring more of A and less of B until equality was achieved.

The above conditions assume that all factors are variable and are thus long-run conditions. We will return to this at the end of the chapter.

The demand and supply curves for a factor

The *MRP* curve gives us a normal downward-sloping demand curve for factors of production, showing that more of a factor is demanded at a lower price. This is true both for the firm and for the industry. We have so far assumed that the supply curve is horizontal, i.e. that the firm could employ more of a factor without affecting its price. However, if an industry wished to employ more of a factor it is likely that it would have to pay more to attract the factor from other uses. We would thus have a normal upward-sloping supply curve. Therefore, we are often able to analyse factor markets with the same tools of microeconomic analysis that we used for consumer goods markets.

STUDENT ACTIVITY 25.3

Identify those conditions that may cause the industry demand or supply curve for a factor to shift, either to the left or to the right.

Problems with the theory of distribution

The theory explains how the prices of factors of production are determined in competitive markets and thus how incomes are determined. However, there are a number of complications in real life:

(a) *Non-homogeneity*. The theory assumes that all units of a factor are identical. This is not true, either of the quality of a factor or of the size of the units in which it is supplied.

(b) *Immobility*. The theory assumes that factors of production can move about freely, both from industry to industry and area to area. In practice serious difficulties are attached to the free movement of factors.

(c) *Inheritance*. Marginal distribution theory is also supposed to explain how the national income is distributed between the owners of the factors of production. However, in addition to income there is wealth, which may also be a source of income. In the UK, as in most other countries, the majority of wealth is obtained by inheritance and this is outside the operation of market forces.

(d) *Political–legal*. The value of factors such as land is often determined by planning regulations, etc.

(e) *Historical*. The value of factors such as land and labour can also be affected by historical factors such as industrial inertia.

These criticisms notwithstanding, marginal revenue theory is one of the best aids we have to understanding the cost structures of an organisation.

Resources and costs

In this section of the chapter we will demonstrate that the principles associated with the utilisation of resources, which we have just examined, are consistent with the cost structures of the firm which we examined in Section V of this book.

The cost structures of the firm

So far the one cost we have been concerned with has been labour, and in our example we have assumed a wage rate of £11 250 per year. Let us assume that labour costs are the only variable costs of the firm and that fixed costs (land, capital, etc.) amount to £30 000 per year. This having been done, we are able to project the cost schedules shown in Table 25.3.

Table 25.3 **The cost structures of the firm**

Number of people employed	Total output of wheat, Q (tonnes/ year)	Marginal physical product, MPP (tonnes/ year)	Average product, APP (tonnes/ year)	Fixed costs, FC (£)	Variable costs, VC (£)	Total costs, TC (FC+VC)	Average fixed costs, AFC* (FC/Q)	Average variable costs, AVC* (VC/Q)	Marginal costs, MC* (ΔTC/ΔQ)	Average costs, AC* (TC/Q)
0	0		0	30 000	0	30 000	∞	—		∞
		12							938	
1	12		12	30 000	11 250	41 250	2500	938		3438
		14							469	
2	36		18	30 000	22 500	52 500	833	625		1458
		34							331	
3	70		23.3	30 000	33 750	63 750	429	482		911
		30							375	
4	100		25	30 000	45 000	75 000	300	450		750
		20							563	
5	120		24	30 000	56 250	86 250	250	469		719
		10							1125	
6	130		21.6	30 000	67 500	97 500	231	519		750
		0							∞	
7	130		18.5	30 000	78 750	108 750	231	606		837
		−10							—	
8	120		15	30 000	90 000	120 000	—	—		—

* To nearest whole number.

(a) *Variable costs*. In Table 25.3 you can see that variable costs increase as the number of people employed increases. If one person is employed then variable costs are £11 250; if two people are employed this becomes £22 500, and so on.

(b) *Average costs*. We calculate average costs as before by dividing total costs by output. Because the example we have been using in this chapter is based upon the number of people employed, the output increases in rather uneven amounts. Thus if two people are employed, then average costs (*ATC*) are calculated by dividing total costs by the output of 36; if three people are employed then the total costs are arrived at by dividing total costs by the output of 70, and so on. Similar calculations will produce the figures for average fixed costs (*AFC*) and average variable costs (*AVC*) shown in Table 25.3.

(c) *Marginal costs*. It will be recalled that marginal cost is the cost of producing just one more unit of a commodity. However, in our example here we are faced with the problem that output increases in uneven amounts as each additional unit of the variable factor is employed. We can get round this problem, though, by taking the increase in costs as each extra unit of variable factor is employed and dividing it by the number of extra units produced. For example, if the firm employs four people rather than three, then total cost rises from £63 750 to £75 000 and the output rises from 70 to 100 tonnes. Thus, we can obtain marginal cost (*MC*) by dividing the increase in total costs (Δ*TC*) by the increase in output (Δ*Q*); this gives us £11 250/30, which in turn gives the figure of £375 for marginal cost. (This method of calculating *MC* is known in business studies as average *incremental* cost (*AIC*). We have thus obtained an approximation for *MC* which is:

$$MC = \frac{\Delta TC}{\Delta Q}$$

When it comes to plotting these figures graphically we must again plot *MC* half way between the outputs we are considering. Thus, in the figures used above, the marginal cost of £375 would be plotted half way between the output of 70 and 100 tonnes, i.e. at 85 tonnes.

Cost curves

If we use the figures in Table 25.3 to construct average and marginal cost curves, we see that they all accord with the principles discussed in Chapter 20. Once again you can see that in Figure 25.6 the marginal cost curve passes through the bottom of the average cost curves.

Marginal cost and price

So far we have said the firm will try to equate the *MRP* of a factor with the cost of that factor. The *MRP*, however, depends upon the price at which the product can be sold. In Figure 25.3 we assumed that the price of wheat was £750 per tonne and therefore we obtained an *MRP* curve by multiplying *MPP* by the price. We can then proceed to develop the cost structures of the firm based on these assumptions. In Table 25.4 we

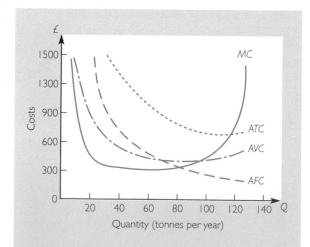

Figure 25.6 Cost curves of the firm
Here:

$$ATC = AFC + AVC$$

and the marginal cost curve cuts through the lowest point of *ATC, AVC*.

demonstrate the best profit output based on these same assumptions about costs and price. We also include in Table 25.4 the *MC* schedule.

Having obtained *MC* from the example we are able to use this to confirm the proposition that, assuming perfectly competitive conditions, the best profit output for the firm is the one at which *MC = P*. In Figure 25.7 you can see that this occurs at the output of 120 tonnes, this being the same output at which *MRP* is equal to the price of the variable factor. Thus the analysis we have developed in this chapter is consistent with the analysis of costs.

As we have assumed so far in this chapter that there is perfect competition, then the price of £750 per tonne is also the marginal revenue (*MR*). This result therefore confirms the proposition that profit maximisation occurs where *MR = MC*.

At the output of 120 tonnes per year the firm makes a profit of £3750 per year. At this output average costs are £718.75 and, since price is £750, this gives a profit per unit of £31.25. Thus, total profit is $TP = (AR - AC) \times Q = (750 - 718.75) \times 120 = £3750$, as confirmed in Table 25.4. However, it should be recalled that this is *abnormal profit* and, therefore, in the long run would attract new firms into the industry. This emphasises the fact that this is a short-run situation.

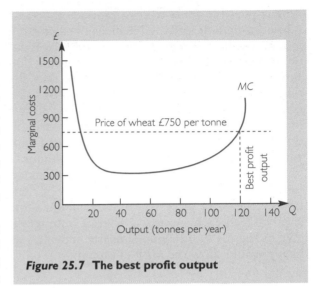

Figure 25.7 The best profit output

Production in the long run

The production function

Our example so far has mainly concerned the short run where at least one factor of production is fixed in supply. In the long run all costs may be varied. To illustrate the principles involved we will use just two factors of production, capital and labour.

Table 25.4 The best profit output of the firm

Number of people employed	Output of wheat, Q (tonnes/ year)	Price of wheat, P (£/tonne)	Marginal revenue product, MRP ($MRP \times P$)	Total revenue, TR ($P \times Q$)	Total costs, TC ($FC \times VC$)	Total profit, TP ($TR - TC$)	Marginal cost, MC^* ($\Delta TC/\Delta Q$)
0	0	750		0	30 000	−30 000	
			9 000				938
1	12	750		9 000	41 250	−32 250	
			18 000				469
2	36	750		27 000	52 500	−28 250	
			25 500				331
3	70	750		52 500	63 750	−11 250	
			21 500				375
4	100	750		75 000	75 000	0	
			15 000				563
5	120	750		90 000	86 250	3 750	
			7 500				1125
6	130	750		97 500	97 500	0	
			0				∞
7	130	750		97 500	108 750	−11 250	
			7 500				−
8	120	750		90 000	120 000	−30 000	

* To nearest whole number.

It is possible for a firm to produce the same output using different combinations of capital and labour, i.e. labour may be substituted for capital or vice versa. Figure 25.8 shows a production function for product X. You can see that the output of 69 units of X can be produced by using 6 units of capital and 1 unit of labour, or 3 units of capital and 2 of labour, and so on. Similarly, an output of 98 units of X could be produced with various, greater, quantities of capital and labour.

If we move horizontally across the production function – for example, if we use 3 units of capital and then add successive units of labour – the gap between each successive level of output will give us the *MPP* of labour. Similarly, moving vertically would show the *MPP* of capital.

Isoquants

If the various combinations of factors of production which produce the same amount of output are plotted as a graph this produces an *isoquant* or *equal product curve*. In Figure 25.9, IQ_1 plots the various combinations of capital–labour which would produce an output of 69 units of product X. Similarly, IQ_2 is the isoquant for the output of

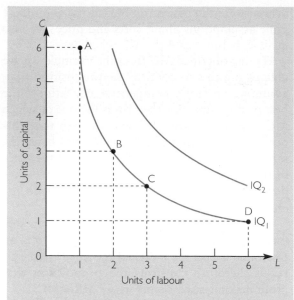

Figure 25.9 Isoquants
Isoquants join the combinations of factors which would produce the same quantity of a product. IQ_1 gives the combinations which would produce 69 units of X and IQ_2 gives the combinations which would produce 98 units of X. A series of IQ curves is termed an isoquant map.

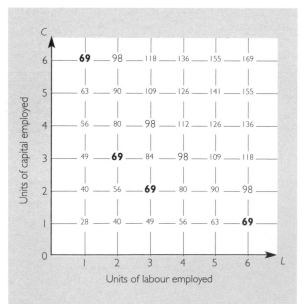

Figure 25.8 Production function
This shows quantities of product X which can be produced by various combinations of labour and capital.

98 units of X. A rightward movement of the isoquant shows a move to a higher level of production and the use of greater quantities of factors of production.

Theoretically we can construct any number of isoquants on the graph to produce an *isoquant map*. (You may notice here the similarity with indifference curves.) What reason is to be found for the shape of isoquants? The reason is that although capital can be substituted for labour or vice versa they are not perfect substitutes. Therefore as we substitute capital for labour, for example, it takes more and more units of capital to replace labour as capital becomes a less and less perfect substitute. In Figure 25.9 if we move from point C to point B, 1 unit of labour can be replaced by 1 unit of capital, but if we move to point A then the next unit of labour given up requires 3 units of capital to replace it. In fact, the substitution ratio of one factor for another at any point on the curve is equivalent to the ratio of their respective marginal physical products.

You can check that you understand this point by starting from point B in Figure 25.9 and examining how the same thing happens in reverse as labour is substituted for capital.

The slope of the isoquant shows the substitution ratios of the factors of production.

Isocost lines

In Figure 25.10, using the same axes, we can construct a graph to show the relative prices of the two factors of production. If, for example, capital costs £100 per unit per time period while labour costs £150 per unit, then a line drawn from 3 units of capital to 2 units of labour would show us all the combinations of capital and labour which could be bought for a cost of £300. Similarly, a line from 6 units of capital to 4 of labour would show combinations costing £600 and so on. The *isocost lines* stay parallel to one another so long as the relative prices of the two factors remain unchanged.

The slope of the isocost shows the ratio of the relative prices of the factors of production.

The least cost combination

If we combine the isocosts and the isoquants on one diagram we can demonstrate how a firm could achieve the least cost combination. This occurs when an isoquant is just tangential to an isocost. For example, if we wish to produce an output of 69 units of X then the cheapest cost at which this can be achieved is £600. This is illustrated in Figure 25.11.

The least cost factor combination occurs where the rate of substitution is equal to the ratio of the relative prices of the factors of production.

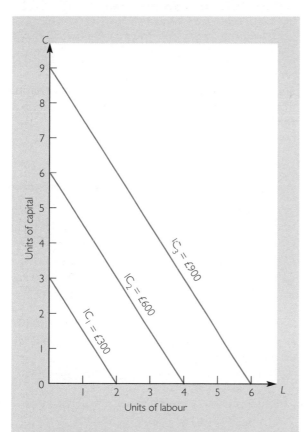

Figure 25.10 Isocosts
Each isocost joins all the combinations of factors which can be bought with the same amount of money. The isocosts here are drawn on the assumption that capital costs £100 per unit and labour costs £150 per unit.

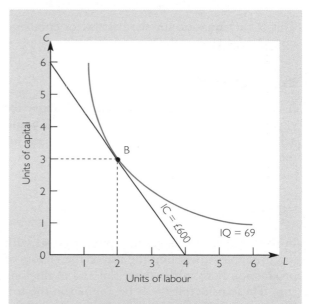

Figure 25.11 The least cost output
The least cost output for the firm is at point B where the isoquant is tangential to the isocost line.

We could explain this by saying either that it is the isocost nearest to the origin which can produce an output of 69 units or, alternatively, that it is the isoquant furthest to the right which can be reached with a budget of £600.

Given the fact that the slope of an isoquant is represented by the ratio of the marginal physical products of the two factors and that the slope of an isocost is given by the ratio of the relative factor prices, then the least cost factor combination occurs at the tangency point of an isoquant with an isocost, where:

$$\frac{MPP \text{ of factor A}}{\text{Price of factor A}} = \frac{MPP \text{ of factor B}}{\text{Price of factor B}}$$

Rearranging gives:

$$\frac{MPP \text{ of factor A}}{\text{Price of factor A}} = \frac{MPP \text{ of factor B}}{\text{Price of factor B}}$$

This is the equation for the best factor combination given earlier in the chapter.

Expansion path

If we undertook the same operation as above for various levels of expenditure, then we could achieve the cost minimisation expansion path for the firm. In Figure 25.12 this is line ABC.

Conclusion

In this chapter we have attempted to deal with the principles governing the use of the factors of production both in the short run and in the long run. These principles will be applied in the following chapters to each of the factors of production. There are, however, important tie-ups with earlier parts of the book, such as the theory of the firm. To check that you have under-

Figure 25.12 An expansion path
As total expenditure increases from IC_1 to IC_2 to IC_3 the least cost combination shifts from A to B to C. Thus this is the expansion path for the firm.

stood the implications of the ideas in this chapter you are advised to work through the questions at the end.

Summary

1 The theory of distribution is concerned with the distribution of income between the factors of production.

2 The marginal physical product is the amount added to production from the employment of one more unit of a variable factor.

3 The marginal revenue product is the change to the firm's revenue from the sale of the marginal physical product.

4 The *MRP* curve of a factor is a firm's demand curve for that factor.

5 The industry demand curve is less elastic than the firm's demand curve for a factor.

6 The demand and supply of a factor can be analysed in a similar way to consumer demand and supply.

7 Marginal productivity theory can also be used to explain the cost structures of a firm.

8 An isoquant shows the various quantities of factors of production which are needed to produce the same quantity of a product.

9 An isocost shows all the combinations of a factor which can be used at a given level of cost.

10 The least cost combination for the firm is where the isoquant is tangential to the isocost, i.e. where the substitution ratio is equal to the relative prices of the factors of production.

? QUESTIONS

1 The following data show the variation in output of product X as inputs of labour are increased.

Labour	1	2	3	4	5	6
Total product	5	15	24	28	30	30

(a) Calculate the marginal and average physical products.

(b) Plot these on a graph.

(c) Indicate on the graph over what output there are increasing returns and over what output there are diminishing returns.

2 Redraft Table 25.4 assuming that fixed costs rise to £60 000, the wage rate increases to £18 000 and the price of wheat increases to £1200 per tonne. Determine the best profit output for the business.

3 What shortcomings are there to marginal distribution theory as an explanation for the distribution of income?

4 Examine Figure 25.4. If Marxists were to look at this diagram they would argue that all the shaded area is the product of labour of which it is being deprived. Do you agree? Give reasons for your answer.

5 Computer technology should increase the MRP curve, thus increasing wages and employment. Reconcile this with the fact that the same technology replaces labour and creates unemployment.

6 Redraw Figure 25.11 assuming that capital increases in cost to £200 per unit. If the firm still wishes to produce 69 units of X what would now be the least cost combination and why?

7 Use the production function in Figure 25.8 to confirm the proposition that the least cost combination is where:

$$\frac{MPP \text{ of labour}}{\text{Price of labour}} = \frac{MPP \text{ of capital}}{\text{Price of capital}}$$

(Note: the answers may be slightly inaccurate owing to rounding the figures to whole numbers.)

8 Under what circumstances will a rise in wages lead to unemployment?

Data response A
THE EVERSHARP PENCIL COMPANY

The data in the table refers to the Eversharp Pencil Company, which manufactures ballpoint pens. The company has premises and machinery which cost it £250 per week.

Table 25.5 Productivity of Eversharp

Number of people employed	Average product (pens/week)
0	0
1	2500
2	2750
3	3500
4	4375
5	4500
6	4250
7	3785.8
8	3187.5

1 From this data calculate the marginal physical product (MPP) schedule of labour at Eversharp and plot it as a graph.

2 Suppose that Eversharp is able to sell any number of ballpoints it wishes to a distributor at a price of 10 pence each. Further suppose that Eversharp is able to employ workers at £200 per person per week. Calculate the marginal revenue product (MRP) schedule and, with the aid of a graph, determine how many workers Eversharp would wish to employ.

3 Assuming that Eversharp's only variable cost is labour determine the profit maximisation output.

4 Calculate the effects of doubling the wage rate to £400. Determine the number of people that

Eversharp will now wish to employ and its profit maximisation output.

5 In question 4 it should be apparent that an increase in the wage rate would cause the business to contract both output and employment. Since the Second World War real wages have risen and, for most of the period, so have output and employment. Explain how this is possible. Your answer should also consider whether marginal revenue product theory has any relevance to the very high levels of unemployment since the late 1970s.

Data response B
HOW TO BRING TECHNOLOGY TO BOOK

Read the following article on the shortcomings of accountancy procedures and then attempt the questions which follow.

Conventional accounting is ill-equipped to deal with modern manufacturing. Technology has left accounting behind and as a result managers are making important decisions about product mix and pricing on the basis of unreliable information.

This is the central thesis behind the work of Robert Kaplan at Harvard Business School. In a series of articles and books published in the latter half of the 1980s, Kaplan and other business academics popularised the idea of 'activity-based costing' – ABC – as a solution to the problem of old-fashioned accounting in a modern factory environment.

The UK's Chartered Institute of Management Accountants (CIMA) is poised to publish the results of a research project into three British companies which have adopted ABC. Two of the case studies by John Innes and Falconer Mitchell of the University of Edinburgh are manufacturers, but one is a large, long-established retail group with several hundred stores and a listing on the London Stock Exchange.

The idea behind ABC is that managers should take a rigorous look at the activities – such as materials-handling, number of orders, size of orders and so forth – which determine overhead costs. By becoming alert to the true 'cost-drivers' of a business, the manager is able to make better decisions about what products to make and how much to charge for them.

Vigorously marketed by squadrons of management consultants from the big accountancy firms, these ideas have been taken up by manufacturing businesses in the US and Europe. The third CIMA case study is unusual because it shows that an activity-based approach can work in an environment very different from that of an automated factory.

The identity of the company is not disclosed; the researchers call it Gamma. It has had a patchy profits record and the regular lurches into losses prompted a review of the company's cost structure.

Over 25 000 separate product lines are bought, distributed and sold by Gamma. Sale volumes are very high, and profitability is highly sensitive to the profit margin achieved on each product. A small change in the volume/margin mix could significantly affect its earnings per share and ultimately its share price.

The essential problem identified by the review was that there was no meaningful data on the cost of the individual product lines. The only information available to the managers was the buy-in cost of each product plus a fixed percentage add-on to cover overheads. Overhead allocation was thus determined solely by the product value, and not by other factors (such as size, weight and fragility) which might influence selling and distribution costs.

'It was obvious our product line costs weren't accurate,' Gamma's commercial manager told the researchers. 'Anyone with basic sense could see that. We needed our costs to reflect the work a product line caused us and the company facilities it used.'

Gamma has four types of cost: the buy-in price of the merchandise; distribution; storage; central overheads and finance charges. The project concentrated on distribution and storage. The aim was to identify the 'cost-drivers' – i.e. the factors which determined storage and distribution costs.

These were identified as: the recording of freight movements; unloading deliveries from suppliers at a central depot; storing suppliers' deliveries; selecting items to comply with store orders; checking orders and loading deliveries to the stores. 'It was clear that the cost associated with these activities varied considerably among Gamma's product lines,' the report says.

The two most important drivers were found to be the size or bulk of the package in which the individual products were contained and the extent to which it was necessary to break open the package when delivered. All the company's product lines were categorised into six classifications around the two drivers.

These classifications were then used as a basis for allocating labour costs from product to product. Occupational costs – such as rates, rent, light and depreciation – were allocated on the basis of the bulk (by cubic feet) of the package.

As a result of this exercise, managers for the first time had net margin figures available for each product line. 'The differences in product line profitability compared with gross margin ... were considerable and extensive. Many popular lines with highly satisfactory gross margins proved to be making net losses due to their high use of distribution and retail resources within Gamma.'

The information helped with management decisions. Those products with a high net margin and a high volume of sales could be considered for extra promotion and display; those with a high margin but low volume would get more advertising those selling in high volume but low net margin could be selected for internal cost reduction, price increases and reductions in promotion. Those products which sold in low quantities and at a low margin could be dropped.

The ABC exercise provided a number of other benefits for management. It increased the visibility of distribution costs and their links to individual products and, as a result, it was easier to identify cost-cutting measures. Management took steps to have suppliers reduce the size of packages, improve the accessibility of the merchandise, and to pack in sizes which removed the need for break-up.

'The danger in using ABC lies too readily in assuming that it provides a panacea which will solve all the problems associated with the provision of costing information to mangement,' the researchers conclude. 'It should be recognised that ABC is not a general purpose system ... suitable, without thought or modification, for use in all areas of control, performance, assessment and managerial decision-making.'

All three companies in this study were optimistic about the future of ABC. They were aware of its limitations but on balance felt that it was a valuable innovation. The Gamma case-study provides a rare example of how ABC can prove valuable in a non-manufacturing environment.

1 Briefly explain what is meant by activity-based costing (ABC).
2 What is the difference between 'the gross profit margin' and the 'net profit margin'?
3 Assess the extent to which the economist's ideas of marginal productivity are relevant to a firm such as Gamma.
4 The report identified several product problems, characters and solutions:

Characteristics	Solutions
High net margin and high sales volume	Extra promotion and display
High margin but low sales volume	More advertising
High sales volume but low net margin	Cost reductions, price increases and reduction in promotion
Low sales volume and low margin	Discontinue sales

Explain what is meant by the terms used to describe the characteristics of products and the rationale behind the proposed policies (solutions).
5 Economists put great emphasis on the importance of marginal costs. Do the points raised in the article support this view? Explain your answer.

Labour and wages

The determination of the wage rate and level of employment

Assuming competitive conditions

The wage rate will be determined by the interaction of the organisation's demand for labour and the supply of labour forthcoming.

In the previous chapter we saw that an organisation's demand for a factor of production is the marginal revenue product (MRP) curve of that factor. The total supply of labour in the economy is represented by the number of workers and the hours worked per unit of labour. The supply of labour to a perfectly competitive firm is horizontal or perfectly elastic because individual firms lack the power to influence wages; they pay the 'going rate'. Without interference from the government or trade unions and assuming perfectly competitive conditions the wage rate and level of employment will be determined by the forces of demand and supply. This is illustrated in Figure 26.1, in which the demand for and supply of labour curves for a particular industry have been

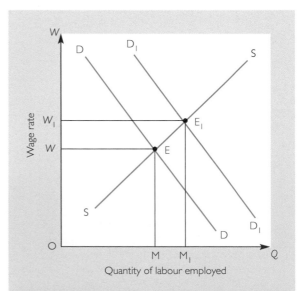

Figure 26.1 The determination of wage rate
The original wage rate is OW at equilibrium E. The movement to E$_1$ and to a higher wage of OW$_1$ shows the effect of an increase in demand for labour.

summed from the demand curves of single firms on the one hand and from the supply curves of individuals on the other. Initially the *equilibrium* level of wages and employment settle at OW and OM respectively. The movement of the demand curve from DD to D_1D_1 leads to a rise in the equilibrium wage rate at OW_1 and an increase in the level of employment to OM_1.

STUDENT ACTIVITY 26.1

What factor(s) may cause a rightward shift in the demand for labour curve, as in Figure 26.1?

Employment and the monopolist

If a firm is the monopoly supplier of a product, then, as the monopolist sells more of the product, it will have to lower the price of the product. Thus the *MRP* for labour is determined by the formula:

$$MRP = MPP \times MR$$

rather than

$$MRP = MPP \times P$$

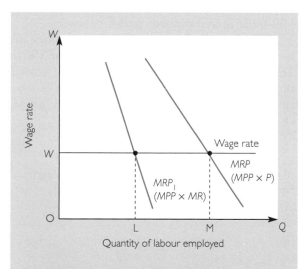

Figure 26.2 Employment and the monopolist
Under perfect competition the business would employ OM units of labour, but under monopoly:

$MRP = MPP \times MR$

and therefore the monopolist restricts employment to OL.

This is illustrated in Figure 26.2. Thus curve *MRP* represents the firm's demand curve for labour as it would be under perfect competition and MRP_1 as it is under monopoly. We have here assumed that the wage rate remains constant. Thus we can see that the monopolist will choose to employ OL units of labour rather than OM as it would under conditions of competitive supply.

Under conditions of monopoly the employer will tend to restrict the employment of a factor.

This restriction of employment in the labour market is associated with the monopolist's restriction of supply of consumer goods. Both situations therefore distort the optimum allocation of resources (see Chapter 23).

The supply of labour

We examined the factors underlying the demand curve for a factor in some depth in the previous chapter, but we did not say much about the supply curve other than that it can be assumed that it is upward sloping. In this section we shall explore those factors determining the supply of labour in a little more detail.

The total supply of labour

The total supply of labour (the *working population* or *workforce*) is determined primarily by non-economic factors such as the size of the population and its age and sex distribution. It may also be influenced by institutional factors such as the school leaving age and social attitudes to such things as women working (although this fact can now be safely taken for granted). In general, therefore, the total supply of labour is highly inelastic, although that is not to say that it may not be varied by exceptional circumstances, as was seen in the Second World War when many women went out to work.

At the beginning of 2000 the workforce in the UK comprised about 29.4 million people out of a total population of 59.5 million. It consists of those people of working age (currently 16–64 for men and 16–59 for women, although a common state retirement age of 65 regardless of gender is being slowly phased in) who are available for work. They are said to be *economically active*. It excludes students, housewives, the sick, those in prison and those taking early retirement; these groups are referred to as the *economically inactive*. The workforce comprises both the employed (employees plus the self-employed) and the unemployed. The *activity* or *participation rate* is the ratio of the working (employed and unemployed) to the total population, or to any section of it whether by age, sex or race.

● *Common misunderstanding*

The workforce does not simply consist of those in full-time jobs. It also consists of part-time workers as well as those registered as unemployed. The workforce comprises those of working age who are available for work; they are the economically active, whether employed or unemployed, in full-time occupations or in part-time positions.

Table 26.1 shows that the workforce has increased in the last decade or so, from 26.7 million in 1984 to 29.5 million in 1999. The total number in employment has varied depending on the state of economic activity. Thus, in the early 1990s there was a fall in employment due to the recession at the time, but since then there has been a fairly significant increase (and a corresponding fall in unemployment) as economic prospects have improved. The increase in the numbers of self-employed in the 1980s was probably more due to the success of policies at the time to encourage the unemployed to become

self-employed rather than to any growth of the entrepreneurial spirit.

What Table 26.1 also indicates is that there has been a steady increase in the number of women working, from 9.1 million in 1984 to nearly 11.5 million in 1999; at the same time, at least until recently when there has been an improvement in employment prospects generally, full-time male employees have been in decline. In fact, while the male participation rate has fallen from about 93 per cent in the early 1970s to 83 per cent in 1994 before increasing slightly to just over 84 per cent in 1999, the female participation rate has risen steadily from 53 per cent in the early 1970s to almost 73 per cent in 1999.

In the last 20 years or so the main change in the pattern of employment has been the fairly dramatic increase in the female participation rate.

The reasons for the growth in female employment include changes in social attitudes and legislation, the fall in the opportunity cost of working due to technological developments in the home such as washing machines, dishwashers and microwaves giving more time to be able to work, an increase in the availability of nursery and pre-school education facilities and the growth of service-sector jobs more geared towards part-time work.

Well over 40 per cent of working women are now employed part-time (defined in the UK as anything up to 16 hours per week). The growth in part-time employment generally is part of what is thought to be a trend in most industrial

Table 26.1 Composition of the workforce, UK (000s)

Year	Employees in employment				Self-employed	Total* employed	Unemployed	Workforce
	Male		Female					
	Full-time	Part-time	Full-time	Part-time				
1984	10829	790	5234	3889	2618	23854	2910	26764
1987	10544	887	5481	4169	2996	24699	2778	27477
1991	10204	1049	5738	4703	3316	25640	2168	27808
1994	9501	1134	5532	4826	3206	24731	2545	27276
1999	11793	1038	6498	4939	3186	27783	1715[†]	29498

* Includes HM forces and training schemes.
† ILO definition used from 1998 (see Chapter 39).

Sources: Economic Review Data Supplement September 1995; Labour Force Survey May 2000

economies, especially the UK and USA, towards more *flexible* patterns of work. It is claimed that, in an increasingly competitive industrial environment and with a more rapid pace of technological change, greater emphasis is now placed on the need to adjust labour inputs to changes in demand as rapidly and as cheaply as possible; improved labour flexibility can achieve this (see Chapter 39).

The rise in the number of service-sector jobs is also a general feature of employment patterns within industrial societies. As manufacturing industry has declined in importance, a process known as *deindustrialisation*, so there has been a corresponding shift in emphasis towards the service sector. This change in the *industrial structure* has been accompanied by a significant alteration in the pattern of sectoral employment. In the early 1970s manufacturing employment accounted for about 33 per cent of total employment, whereas in 1999 this figure had fallen to 16.5 per cent; the equivalent figures for services were 53 per cent and 77 per cent respectively.

Industry supply

If we consider an industry or single firm there is a great deal more elasticity of supply relative to the total labour supply, since offering higher wages will attract workers from other industries. The elasticity of supply will be greater the longer the period of time considered, as people have more opportunity to respond to differentials by retraining etc.

The leisure preference

The supply of labour is also influenced by the length of the working week. Here we are referring to the supply of labour by an individual person (although individual's decisions can also be affected by the labour supply decisions of other members of a household). We encounter the factor known as the *leisure preference*. As real wages have risen over this century people have taken the opportunity not only to consume increased quantities of goods and services, but also to reduce the length of the working week. They have, therefore, consumed part of the income as increased leisure. The possibilities for

the individual confronted with a rise in the wage rate are illustrated in Figure 26.3. In the original situation the wage rate is £5 per hour. The various possibilities for the worker are, therefore, represented by the budget line *TA*. At *T* the worker enjoys 24 hours' leisure but no income, while at A the worker has an income of £120 per day but has to work 24 hours to earn it. Suppose that the worker chooses point E working 10 hours a day, i.e. 14 hours of leisure, and an income of £50. Now suppose that the wage rate doubles to £10 per hour, so that the worker's budget line is now *TB*. As a result of this, three possibilities confront the worker.

First, the worker may continue to work the same number of hours and therefore moves to point Y, so that income now increases to £100 per day. Second, the worker could choose to take some of the increase in more leisure and some as more income; for example, at point X income would rise to £80 per day and the working day decreases to 8 hours. The third possibility is that, in response to the higher wage rate, longer hours are worked; for example, at point Z the working

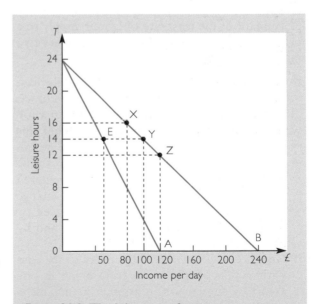

Figure 26.3 The leisure preference
The increase in wages from £5.00 per hour to £10.00 per hour moves the budget line outwards from *TA* to *TB*. Originally the worker supplied 10 hours of work per day (point E). As a result of the increase in pay the worker may move to position X, Y or Z.

day has increased to 12 hours and therefore the wage to £120.

Historically, what seems to have happened is that workers have moved towards the position represented by X, i.e. a shorter working week. The possibility therefore exists for a *perverse* or *backward-sloping supply curve for labour*, where increasing the wage rate (at least, beyond a certain level of real wage) causes less labour to be supplied. Some industries, such as coalmining, where the work is extremely unpleasant, exhibit a very high leisure preference and, thus, effort has sometimes gone down as wages have gone up.

STUDENT ACTIVITY 26.2

Given the possibility of a perverse supply of labour curve, comment on the feasibility of cutting income taxes as an incentive to make people work harder.

Labour mobility

The supply of labour is also affected by labour mobility because the lack of mobility may restrict the supply of labour. Labour mobility is a key determinant of the elasticity of labour supply to a particular industry or type of job. There are two main types of mobility.

(a) *Occupational mobility*. This refers to the ease with which people move from one type of job to another. If a person were to give up a job as a steel worker and become a teacher this would be an example of occupational mobility. This type of mobility is likely to be influenced by the amount of training required for a job, the reluctance of workers to change jobs, the restrictions on job entry placed by unions and professional associations and by the age of the person concerned.

(b) *Geographical mobility*. This refers to the ease with which people move from a job in one area to a similar job in another area. This is restricted by the unwillingness of people to leave the social ties they may have in an area, by the difficulty of finding housing, the reluctance to disturb their children's education, the cost of moving and the lack of information about opportunities elsewhere in the economy.

Surprisingly, in the past geographical mobility has tended to decrease as unemployment has risen because people have become unwilling to risk a new job in an unknown area.

Both types of mobility have tended to be low in the UK compared with a country like the USA. A higher level of mobility would reduce both the level of unemployment and also the differentials between wages. However, moves to make the UK labour market more flexible are designed to raise labour mobility, especially occupational mobility, and reduce demarcation disputes (see below).

Trade unions and wages

Most labour markets are subject to imperfections. These may be both on the demand side (employers) or the supply side (employees). Improving productivity is one of the most certain ways of increasing wages, although there is little that trade unions can do about it *per se*. Trade unions may, of course, be involved in agreements with employers to increase productivity.

Trade unions therefore tend to work by affecting the supply of labour.

In so doing a trade union may act as a *monopoly supplier* of labour.

Restrictive labour practices

A most effective way for trade unions to increase their members' wages is to restrict the supply of labour to a particular occupation. This can be done by *closed shop* practices, whereby all workers in an industry or occupation have to belong to a particular union. These are not always aimed at increasing wages but have certainly been used in the past for this purpose in some industries, e.g. printing and film making. The supply of labour to an occupation could also be limited by the enforcement of long apprenticeships or training periods. Another method is *demarcation*, where particular tasks in a job may be done only by members of a particular union, e.g. plumbers not being allowed to do joiners' jobs in a particular factory. In the past demarcation or 'who does what' disputes have been a frequent cause of unrest in UK industrial relations and have affected a wide variety of industries such as ship-building and printing. In the late 1980s there was a demarcation dispute about the roles of ambulance personnel and paramedics.

Figure 26.4 shows that the effect of restricting the supply of labour is to increase the wage rate from OW to OW$_1$. It also means that the quantity of labour employed declines from OM to OL. It is estimated that unionised workers receive *wage premiums* (i.e. union/non-union wage differentials between groups of similar workers) over their non-union counterparts of about 8–10 per cent in the UK (the estimate for the USA is higher, at between 10–25 per cent).

However, while some workers are receiving higher wages, other people may be unable to obtain jobs. This kind of practice is not restricted to trade unions; the Inns of Court still run a most effective closed shop which restricts the supply of labour to the Bar, thereby keeping out many young lawyers who might like to become practising barristers. This not only has the effect of driving up barristers' fees but also contributes to the delays which bedevil the administration of justice.

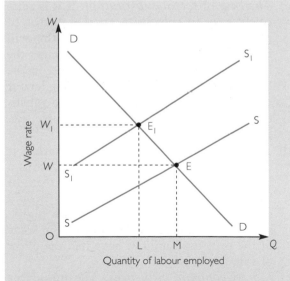

Figure 26.4 The effect of restrictive practices upon the wage rate
By restricting the supply of labour from SS to S$_1$S$_1$ the union is able to raise the wage rate from OW to OW$_1$, but the quantity of labour employed decreases from OM to OL.

Collective bargaining

Working people learned long ago that to ask the employer individually for a wage rise was a good way to lose a job. Trade unions therefore negotiate on behalf of all their members and if agreement is not reached they may take action collectively to enforce their demands. The collective bargaining strength of a trade union varies enormously from industry to industry. Until the unsuccessful strike of 1985 the bargaining strength of coalminers was regarded as great because there was almost 100 per cent membership of the National Union of Mineworkers, a strong community spirit and the possibility of bringing the country to a standstill. On the other hand, the bargaining strength of some workers in the UK has been so poor that the government set up wages councils to determine minimum wage rates. However, the rising tide of unemployment in the 1980s weakened the bargaining power of most workers. Those protected by wages councils saw a further weakening of their position when the government set about restricting the activities of some wages councils and dismantling others. Most were abolished in 1993. Until the establishment of the national minimum wage in 1999, agriculture was the only industry covered by any form of minimum wage legislation, the Agricultural Wages Boards setting minimum wages for various grades of workers. The impact of the national minimum wage is dealt with in the next section.

Figure 26.5 illustrates three possibilities for collective bargaining. Which one occurs will depend upon the strength of the union. Here successful collective bargaining has raised the wage rate from OW to OW$_1$. As a result of this the employer would like to employ less labour (OL instead of OM); this is position A. However, the strength of the union may be such that it is able to insist that the organisation retains the same number of workers as before. This is position B, where the wage rate is higher but the quantity of labour remains OM. As a result of increasing the wage rate more people would like to work for this organisation. In an extreme case the union may be able to insist that the organisation moves to position C where the wage rate is OW$_1$ and the quantity of labour employed is ON. If the organisation is pushed into this position it may

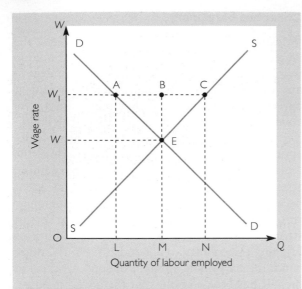

Figure 26.5 Collective bargaining and wages
Collective bargaining raises the wage from the equilibrium level at OW to OW₁, thus creating a disequilibrium. The quantity of labour employed – OL, OM or ON – depends upon the bargaining power of the union.

be forced to close down since AC represents a surplus of labour which it would not choose to employ if it were not forced to do so.

Such *feather-bedding* and *overmanning* have occurred in a number of UK industries, such as newspaper printing, in the past, although the changed industrial relations climate and the effects of the recessions of the early 1980s and 1990s mean that such a scenario is now far less likely to occur.

● *Common misunderstanding*

The establishment of a higher wage through collective bargaining, while quite possibly reducing employment, may not actually create as much unemployment as is first thought. If, in Figure 26.5, the union negotiates a higher wage of OW₁, fewer people may be employed (i.e. position A). In these circumstances LN workers (i.e. the distance AC) comprise the excess supply of labour. Of these, LM workers were previously employed and therefore can be regarded as unemployed as a result of the higher wage rate. However, the remainder, MN workers, have been encouraged to enter the labour market because of the higher wage; it is not quite so obvious that they have become unemployed in consequence. Exactly the same arguments would apply following the imposition of a national minimum wage.

Economic factors affecting bargaining strength

The ability of a trade union to raise wages will be influenced not only by its collective bargaining strength but also by several economic factors, which are listed below.

(a) *The elasticity of demand for the final product.* If the demand for the product for which labour is being used is highly inelastic, it will be relatively easy for the firm to pass increased wage costs on to the consumer. Conversely, an elastic demand will make it difficult to pass on increased costs and, thus, make it difficult for unions to obtain wage rises.

(b) *The proportion of total costs which labour represents.* If labour costs make up a large proportion of total costs this will tend to make it more difficult for workers to obtain wage rises. On the other hand, if the labour costs are a small proportion of the organisation's costs and, more especially, if the worker's task is vital this will tend to make it easier to secure a wage rise. This is referred to by **Professor Samuelson** as 'the importance of being unimportant'.

(c) *The ease of factor substitution.* If it is relatively easy to substitute another factor of production for labour, e.g. capital, this will mean that as unions demand more wages the business will employ fewer workers. In the UK since the Second World War, rising labour costs have encouraged employers to substitute capital for labour wherever possible, e.g. the microprocessor revolution.

(d) *The level of profits.* If an organisation is making little or no profit then the effect of a rise in wages could well be to put it out of business. Conversely, high profits would make it easier for unions to obtain higher wages and job security. High profits in some of the privatised utilities have had the effect of stimulating wage claims.

(e) *Macroeconomic influences.* The influences discussed so far are all microeconomic. However, wage bargaining can be influenced by the macroeconomy. First, the general state of the economy affects wage bargaining. If there is economic growth it is easier for unions to obtain wage rises and wage earners tend to capture a larger share of national income, although the reverse is true in times of economic recession and unemployment. Second, inflation influences wage claims. Inflation decreases the real value of wages and, therefore, stimulates demands for higher money wages. Whether wage earners are able to keep pace with inflation depends upon their relative bargaining power. Inflation may also make it easier to obtain higher money wages if the increased costs can easily be passed on as higher prices because of the inflationary climate.

If trade union activity were successful in the national sense it would increase the proportion of the national income going to wages. Nevertheless, despite all the struggles of trade unions, this is not so. The portion of national income going to wages and salaries now is not significantly different from 45 years ago, being 65 per cent of GNP in 1946, 67 per cent in 1961 and 64 per cent in 1999.

Industrial relations in the UK

The UK's record of industrial relations in the past has not been good compared with other industrialised economies. In particular, the economy has been bedevilled with strikes. However, this situation has changed dramatically since the mid- to late 1980s.

The withdrawal of labour is the ultimate weapon unions possess. The word 'strike' is very emotive and many people believe that previously strikes have been the cause of the UK's economic difficulties. It is more likely, however, that rather than being a cause, strikes have been more a symptom of the UK's industrial malaise. Rather than expressing opinions it is better to examine the facts. Statistics on strikes vary greatly from year to year, but until the mid-1980s you would need to look carefully to find a country with a significantly worse record than the UK.

During 1979 29.5 million man-days were lost to strikes; in 1998 the total was under 400 000. The dramatic fall in strikes meant that the number of days lost from the late 1980s onwards has been among the lowest in the industrialised world. However, the Germans and Japanese have been able to look back on 40 years of good industrial relations.

When the Conservative government was elected in 1979 one of its chief aims was to counter the power of the unions. Legally this was done through the Employment Acts of 1980, 1982, 1988 and 1990, the Trade Union Act of 1984, the Trade Union and Labour Relations Act of 1992 and the Trade Union and Employment Rights Act of 1993. The government saw these as redressing the balance after the privileges given to the unions by the Labour governments of the 1970s.

The 1980 Act made available public funds for secret ballots for such things as electing officers, calling or ending a strike or amending union rules. The Act also gave the Secretary of State wide-ranging power to issue codes of practice 'for the purpose of improving industrial relations'. The 1982 Act, among other things, provided for regular reviews of closed-shop agreements by secret ballot, brought legal immunities for trade unions into line with those of individuals and restricted the meaning of lawful disputes to those between workers and their employers, i.e. it made sympathetic strikes illegal.

The 1984 Trade Union Act made strike action lawful only if sanctioned by a secret ballot of members and it also placed strict limitations on actions such as secondary picketing. This Act also required that every voting member of a union's principal executive committee be (re-)elected by ballot at least every five years.

The 1988 Employment Act made it illegal to dismiss an employee for not wishing to join a union. It also made it unlawful for a union to take action to create or maintain a closed shop. The 1990 Act made all secondary picketing illegal. It also gave any worker the right of complaint to an industrial tribunal if denied employment when not a member of a union.

The 1992 Act consolidated the earlier Acts into a single piece of legislation. The 1993 Act specified that all ballots in support of union action should be postal and gave individuals much greater freedom to join the union of their choice (thereby virtually ending the notion of the closed shop).

Opinions differ as to whether this bout of legislation was an outright attack on trade unions or a much needed attempt to introduce sanity into industrial relations.

Certainly membership of unions has fallen sharply since the early 1980s: in the late 1970s 58 per cent of employees belonged to unions, but by 1999 this figure had fallen to less than 30 per cent of workers. However, this decline in membership has had as much, if not more, to do with the shift in employment from the traditionally more unionised manufacturing sector into services and in the growth of part-time work than with the legislation.

There has been a similar fall in union membership in most other industrialised countries. At the same time there has been a corresponding fall in the proportion of workers covered by some form of collective agreement; the pay and conditions of 35 per cent of UK workers were so determined in 1998, compared with 70 per cent of workers in 1980.

The Conservative government argued that the intention of the legislation was to sweep away restrictive practices and in so doing allow free determination of wages and greater flexibility in the labour market generally. In this way it was hoped that industry would be able to compete successfully with countries such as Japan and Germany. Either coincidentally or as a result of government policy the economy had passed through a huge economic recession in the late 1970s and early 1980s; it did so again in the early 1990s. It was the general economic conditions as much as legislation which broke the grip of the unions. The very low level of strikes in the last decade has lent credence to the view that it was the effects of unemployment rather than legislation which resulted in the reduction in union membership and in the lack of disputes. However, the absence of strikes by itself does not mean that there are good industrial relations. More must be done to create a positive attitude of cooperation and trust between management and workforce if there is to be lasting improvement in economic performance.

In 1999 the Labour government, as part of a pre-election pledge, introduced the Employment Relations Act which allows for statutory union recognition in the workplace as long as at least 50 per cent of the labour force vote in favour of it in a ballot, although the procedure does not apply to firms with less than 21 employees.

The decline in the economic power of the unions has led to a fall in their impact on wage premiums in the UK since the mid-1980s, although some recent evidence has suggested that unionised workers have become more productive than their non-unionised counterparts. Thus, the *efficiency-enhancing* effects of unions may have become at least as significant as their monopolistic influences.

National minimum wage

A *national minimum wage* was introduced by the Labour government in April 1999 at £3.60 per hour for those aged 22 or over (increased to £3.70 per hour in October 2000 and £4.10 per hour in October 2001) and £3.00 per hour for 18–21 year-olds (increased to £3.20 per hour in June 2000) (see also Chapter 11). Whether or not such legislation would bring about an increase in wages for the lower paid or whether it would result in increased unemployment has been a subject of much debate. In Figure 26.5 the imposition of a minimum wage at OW_1 above the equilibrium level OW would lead to a fall in the demand for labour from OM to OL. In fact, the imposition of the minimum wage at a relatively low rate has meant that any job losses have been small, although it is difficult to separate the effect of the minimum wage on employment from the much greater effect of economic growth.

Since its introduction the healthy state of the economy has pushed up employment, thus masking any negative impact that the minimum wage may have had.

STUDENT ACTIVITY 26.3

Given perfectly competitive conditions, if a minimum wage was imposed above the equilibrium level, what factors are likely to influence any resulting job losses in an industry? (Figure 26.5 may help you to decide.)

Monopsony in labour markets

Most labour markets are subject to imperfections. As noted earlier, these may be both on the demand side (employers) and the supply side (employees). We have considered the supply side situation above, i.e. that a trade union may act as a monopoly supplier of labour. If the trade union restricts the supply of labour, it is behaving in a classic monopolist fashion. However, as we have seen, unions may also act to protect jobs, thus departing from typical monopoly behaviour.

Wages and the monopsonist

A monopsony exists when there is only one buyer of a commodity.

This situation exists in labour markets, but much less so than before given the privatisation of many of the previously nationalised industries. Thus, British Rail used to be the sole employer of train drivers, but now more than 20 companies own the rail franchises and compete to employ railway workers; however, the Post Office remains the sole 'purchaser' of postal workers (at least for letter delivery). Under these conditions the employer may influence the wage rate. In Figure 26.6 SS shows the supply curve for labour. Under normal competitive conditions the equilibrium would, therefore, occur where the *MRP* (demand) curve for labour intersects with the supply curve (point E_1), i.e. at a wage rate of OB and a quantity of OM. However, if the monopsonist is a profit maximiser it will wish to equate the *MC* of the factor with the *MRP*. This gives an equilibrium point D. (Note that the *MC* of labour curve lies above the supply curve for labour; this is because when labour is expanded a higher wage is not just paid to the last person employed but to all existing workers). To attract this quantity of labour (OL) the monopsonist must pay a wage of only OA. Thus, the wage is less than that in the competitive market by the amount of AB and the quantity of labour employed is reduced by the amount LM. These conditions could apply to the monopsonistic purchase of any factor, not just labour. Thus we can conclude that:

The monopsonist will tend to employ less of a factor and pay a lower price than in competitive markets.

This imperfection therefore also creates a distortion in the allocation of resources (see the discussion of Pareto optimality in Chapter 27).

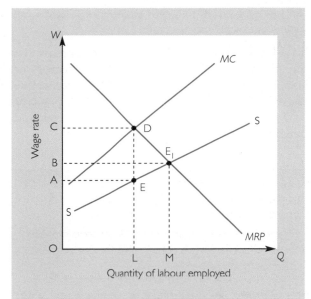

Figure 26.6 Wages and the monopsonist
The profit maximisation equilibrium is where *MC* = *MRP*, i.e. employment of OL, but the business is obliged to pay a wage of only OA. This compares with the competitive wage of OB and employment of OM. Thus both wages and employment are lower under monopsony.

The situation may be further complicated if the monopsonist employer is bargaining with a monopolist union (a situation called **bilateral monopoly**) because under these circumstances the union may be able to prevent the employer moving to position E on the graph. Under these circumstances the income represented by area ACDE becomes a zone of bargaining between employer and union.

STUDENT ACTIVITY 26.4

List the factors that you think are likely to influence the bargaining outcome between a monopolist seller of labour (i.e. a trade union) and a monopsonist buyer of labour (i.e. the employer).

Differentials and disequilibriums

Wage differentials

In 1999 the highest paid 20 per cent of the population received 51 per cent of pre-tax incomes whilst the lowest paid 20 per cent received only just over 2 per cent of pre-tax incomes.

Taxes and social security payments narrow the gap between the richest and poorest sectors of society, but only slightly: in 1999 the respective shares of income of the highest paid 20 per cent and the lowest paid 20 per cent after taxes and benefits were 44 per cent and 7.0 per cent.

STUDENT ACTIVITY 26.5

In fact, incomes are now much less equal than in 1979; then, the richest fifth of the population received 43 per cent of all pre-tax income, while the poorest fifth were responsible for 2.4 per cent. Suggest reasons for this.

Some of the reasons for these widespread differences in income are listed below.

(a) *Non-homogeneity*. Differences may exist in the workforce by way of natural abilities such as strength, intelligence and skill and also because of the **investment in human capital** from training and education.

(b) *Non-monetary rewards*. Workers may receive benefits and payments in kind in addition to their wages, e.g. company cars, cheap loans and mortgages. People may also be willing to work for the non-monetary rewards of a job such as social prestige or pleasant working conditions. Certain jobs such as nursing or teaching are thought to give non-pecuniary advantages to the worker by way of job satisfaction and therefore workers may tolerate lower wages (although this is probably less true now than in the past!). On the other hand, people may have to be rewarded for working in unpleasant or hazardous conditions, like coalminers or steeplejacks.

(c) *Ignorance*. People may simply be unaware of the opportunities which exist elsewhere.

(d) *Barriers to mobility*. As discussed above, barriers may exist to the geographical and occupational mobility of labour, either from the unwillingness of people to move from area to area or because of the restrictions placed on entry to certain jobs.

(e) *Geographical considerations*. Certain areas are considered more desirable to live in than others. The so-called 'sunrise industries' such as computer software have tended to concentrate in areas which are considered geographically desirable. This, however, increases house prices and the general cost of living and therefore higher wages may be necessary. Many employees working in London and the south-east receive an additional 'living allowance' to compensate them for this fact.

Having considered all these problems many economists would maintain that jobs and incomes are still determined by the **principle of net advantage**, i.e. people will still choose their job and move job so as to achieve the greatest net advantage having considered both the pecuniary and non-pecuniary advantages of jobs.

Disequilibriums in the labour markets

It may be surprising that excess demand can exist in a labour market when there is general unemployment or that excess supply can exist when there is generally full employment. However, this is so and a number of factors which may account for this are listed below.

(a) *Non-competing groups*. Since labour is a heterogeneous factor, excess supply in one sector may not influence another; for example, it is quite possible to have an excess supply of history teachers while experiencing a shortage of mathematics teachers.

(b) *Rigidity of wages*. Although it may be possible to increase wages it is very hard to decrease them. Thus successful union pressure may raise wages, creating excess supply, but union bargaining strength may prevent employers from shedding labour (see Figure 26.4).

(c) *Internal promotions*. In many occupations people are recruited relatively young and untrained and then gain specialist training. As a result, **internal labour markets** are established for certain occupations and jobs. These usually require specific knowledge and training, are governed by established rules and procedures and are characterised by internal promotions and 'job ladders'. It thus becomes very difficult for someone outside to compete for the higher grades in such jobs; for example, it would be very unlikely that a person might switch into a senior post in education or local government if their experience is outside the industry, whatever their qualifications may be.

(d) *Information costs.* Seeking a new job or new employee imposes costs on both the employee and the employer. The more senior the post, the more important these costs will tend to become. This point is developed below in search theory.

Search theory

This modern theory of labour markets maintains that both employers and employees will 'search' for the best bargain in the labour market. According to this theory the traditional marginal productivity approach ignores the cost of pay bargaining, information collection and labour mobility.

To the employer the cost of the search may include advertisements for suitable employees, interviewing costs and the costs of doing without the required labour in the interim period. The costs are likely to rise with seniority of the post. For the potential employee there is the opportunity cost of the search, i.e. doing without income until the right job has been found. High levels of unemployment may discourage the worker in the search.

Thus, differentials in incomes may be partly explained by the problems of job search.

Discrimination in labour markets

Another important factor accounting for differences in wages is discrimination in labour markets.

Labour market discrimination occurs when factors such as gender, race or age mean that otherwise identical workers receive different rates of pay for the same job or have different chances of recruitment or promotion

Discrimination can also occur due to differences in appearance and class. While the latter is not quite the issue it used to be, the 'old school tie' syndrome still probably applies in some professions.

Deciding if a particular situation constitutes discrimination is not very easy. Women have traditionally earned less than men. Equal pay legislation has led to a narrowing of the gap between male and female pay in the last twenty odd years, but in 1999 the average gross weekly pay of full-time working women was still only 74 per cent that of equivalent male workers. There is no doubt that the pattern of employment betwen the sexes differs, a higher proportion of men than women being classified as industrial manual workers, while the reverse is the case in administrative and marketing jobs. This fact on its own is not likely to explain the pay discrepancies shown above however, although it is worth noting that the occupations in which women predominate tend to be those which are less heavily unionised.

A key factor in explaining differences in earnings by gender is that it is women who have babies and who are much more likely to take a break from work in order to bring up their young children. Since employers bear at least some of the costs of training workers, they respond by offering more training to male employees, who then benefit from more rapid promotion. Employers expect to get a higher return on their investment in male human capital simply because, on average, men will work a longer number of years. Women also tend to work a shorter working week than men and this can account for some of the gender pay gap; in 1999 the average working week for full-time working women was 34 hours compared with 40 hours per week for men. Such factors, however, are more explanations of the earnings' differences between the sexes than evidence of actual discrimination. This is not to say that sexual discrimination in the workplace does not exist. There are circumstances where women continue to be paid lower rates of pay for performing exactly the same jobs as men even when differences in leaving rates are taken into account.

There are also differences in earnings between racial groups: in 1999 the average hourly rate of pay for workers from minority ethnic backgrounds was 93 per cent that of white workers. Pay differentials even exist within the ethnic minority group as a whole; the hourly pay of workers with a Pakistani/Bangladeshi background is much lower than that of any other group, being only about 75 per cent of the equivalent figure for white workers. Interestingly, these pay differentials between racial groups are due almost entirely to differences among male workers; non-white female workers have similar hourly rates of pay as white women in employment.

On average, workers from the ethnic minorities are less well qualified than white workers and so are less likely to benefit from more highly-skilled jobs that pay better. This is not evidence of labour market racial discrimination in itself, more a reflection of varying qualities and opportunities within the educational system. However, discrimination against ethnic minority workers in the labour market persists both in terms of being offered lower rates of pay for performing similar jobs and via lower rates of recruitment and promotion. Ethnic minority groups also suffer from higher levels of unemployment than white workers: in 1999 the unemployment rate for white workers in the UK was 5.4 per cent, while for those from ethnic minority groups it was 12.2 per cent.

Finally, it is to be expected that earnings would vary by age. As workers get older their earnings are a reflection of accumulated education, training and and work experience. However, beyond a certain point physical frailties set in and attitudes to work change resulting, perhaps, in less intensive efforts being made. It is no surprise to find, therefore, that hourly rates of pay peak for the 35–49 age group. Activity rates decline quite markedly beyond the age of 49 for both men and women. Again this is to be expected as more people take, or are asked to take, early retirement. This makes it doubly difficult for those people trying to re-enter the labour market in their late 40s and early 50s, since employers know that their past experience may make them expensive to take on, while at the same time people of an equivalent age are in the proccess of leaving employment. It is quite likely that 'age discrimination' against such workers exists, although proving that it does is another matter entirely.

Summary

1 The equilibrium wage rate is determined by the interaction of the firm's demand for labour and the supply of labour forthcoming.
2 A monopolist supplier of a product is likely to restrict employment of a factor.

3 The supply of labour as a whole is determined by non-economic factors. The supply of labour is also influenced by leisure preferences and labour mobility.
4 Trade unions attempt to affect wage rates both by restricting supply and by collective bargaining.
5 Factors which affect the bargaining strength of unions are elasticity of demand for the final product, the ease of factor substitution and the proportion of total cost which labour represents.
6 The establishment of the minimum wage has had a fairly insignificant impact on employment so far.
7 A monopsonist is likely to restrict both employment and payment.
8 The differentials which exist between wages are much greater than can be explained by marginal productivity theory.
9 Disequilibriums frequently occur in labour markets irrespective of the overall employment situation.
10 Labour market discrimination by sex, race or age occurs when otherwise identical workers receive different rates of pay for the same job or are given different job market opportunities.

? QUESTIONS

1 Examine the impact of a trade union's ability to raise wages above the equilibrium level in a perfectly competitive labour market. Outline the factors which influence a trade union's ability to raise wages.
2 Explain how wages are determined assuming perfectly competitive conditions. Discuss the factors which account for the differentials in wage rates.
3 'If unions succeed in raising real wages this will lead to less employment and ultimately a smaller total of wages.' Evaluate this statement. (Hint: remember elasticity of demand.)

4 Discuss the factors that determine the total supply of labour. Explain why the supply of labour to a firm or an industry is much more elastic than the supply of labour as a whole.

5 Discuss the extent to which the industrial relations legislation of the 1980s and 1990s has been responsible for the decline in both trade union membership and industrial activity.

6 Explain what is meant by a minimum wage. Discuss the impact of the national minimum wage established in the UK in 1999.

7 Identify and explain an example of:
(a) excess supply;
(b) excess demand in labour markets.
Account for the existence of excess demand in conditions of high unemployment and excess supply when there is full employment.

8 To what extent do you consider unemployment to be an inevitable consequence of the introduction of new technology?

9 Why do accountants earn more than 'dustmen' (household refuse collectors) and yet many teachers earn less than some unskilled labourers on North Sea oil rigs?

Data response A
MALE/FEMALE EARNINGS AND ACTIVITY AND EMPLOYMENT RATES OF ETHNIC GROUPS

Study Figures 26.7 and 26.8. Answer the following questions:

1 Explain what is meant by labour market discrimination

2 To what extent does the data given in Figures 26.7 and 26.8 provide evidence of discrimination?

3 Given the continued existence of various forms discrimination in the UK labour market, what action, if any, can be taken by the government to improve matters?

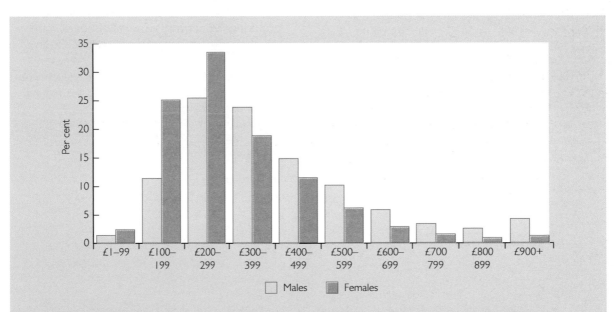

Figure 26.7 **Distribution of gross weekly earnings of full-time employees in the UK for 1999 (not seasonally adjusted)**
Source: Labour Force Survey, May 2000, National Statistics. © Crown Copyright 2001

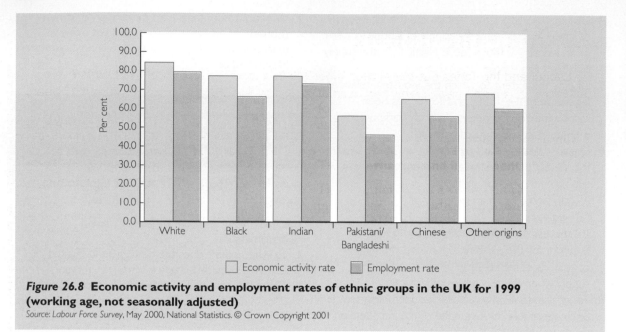

Figure 26.8 **Economic activity and employment rates of ethnic groups in the UK for 1999 (working age, not seasonally adjusted)**
Source: *Labour Force Survey*, May 2000, National Statistics. © Crown Copyright 2001

Data response B
THE DECLINE OF THE UNIONS

Read the following article from *The Economist* of 14 September 1996 and answer the questions which follow.

1 Outline those factors that may have been responsible for the decline in union power since the early 1980s, irrespective of any legislative changes.

2 Discuss the importance of strikes in broad macroeconomic terms (i.e. relative to GDP).

3 'Given the productivity-enhancing effects of unions, they are probably more likely to improve efficiency than act as monopolist suppliers of labour in the UK labour market since the early 1990s.' Explain and discuss.

4 To what extent can it be said that the reduction in the power of the unions has reduced the 'natural' rate of unemployment?

Bashing the unions

As Labour and the Tories out-tough each other with plans to further restrict trade-union 'militancy', it is worth asking what has been achieved by the union reforms of the past 17 years

As an illustration of how much Britain has changed over the past couple of decades, look no further than the dramatic decline of the trade unions, which gathered this week in Blackpool for their annual conference. In the late 1970s, the unions lorded it over the Labour government, eventually bringing it down by engaging in a wave of strikes dubbed the 'winter of discontent'. Now, two high-profile strikes this summer in the public sector notwithstanding, the unions are feared by no one. Even Labour feels able to attack them, competing with the Tories in proposing new limits on union activity that would extend Tory changes to the law (all originally opposed by Labour) which have helped curb the unions since 1979. So what has the unions' decline meant for the economy? Are further legal changes really needed?

The Tories won power in 1979 believing that reducing trade-union power held the key to reviving Britain's economic fortunes. In a series of labour laws since 1980, unions were made liable for the actions of their members and easier to sue for damages when they called strikes illegally. Secondary picketing (the picketing of firms not directly involved in a dispute) and the closed shop (forcing employees in a firm or plant to join a union) were outlawed. Firms were allowed to withdraw recognition of a union. The power of union officials has been cut by giving more influence to individual union members, notably by requiring secret ballots to be held before striking.

These legal reforms went hand in hand with a collapse in union membership, from 13m in 1979 to 8m, and in militancy (see chart [opposite]). During 1979, 29.5m man-days were lost to strikes. Last year, the total was 415 000. This may seem proof enough that the reforms

have paid off handsomely. However, there is much debate among economists both about the impact of the decline of unions on the economy, and how far the Tory legal changes were responsible.

Even if the law had been left unchanged, other factors would have reduced unions' clout. Unemployment soared, making workers less willing to put their jobs at risk. It rose furthest in manufacturing which, outside the public sector, had a far greater union presence than other parts of the economy. Competition between firms increased. Job growth since 1979 has largely been in parts of the labour market where unions have been weakest: in part-time work, especially by women; in the service sector; in smaller firms; and in the South rather than in the North.

Even so, says David Metcalf, of the London School of Economics, the legal changes clearly had a significant impact. He calculates that they resulted in perhaps one-quarter of the decline in membership, and at least one-third of the reduction in union militancy.

Turning to the economic impact of the decline of the trade unions, the most obvious – fewer strikes – is arguably least important. As Mr Metcalf points

out, in terms of their direct impact on GDP, strikes were never that significant: one day lost per worker per year in 1979, five minutes per worker now. What mattered was the inefficient balance of power they symbolised.

Bigger gains came from higher productivity and profits. Unionised firms raised productivity by more than non-unionised ones in the 1980s, as union power declined. Studies have found that between a quarter and a half of the rise in British labour productivity in the 1980s was due to the falling costs of unionisation. Firms that derecognised unions enjoyed the biggest gains. In the early 1980s unionised firms were almost 10 per cent less likely to report above-average profits than non-unionised ones. By 1994 firms with closed shops were still less likely to outperform. But other unionised firms were no longer less likely to report above-average profits than non-unionised ones.

The reason for these gains was that, as union power ebbed, managers found it easier to restructure working practices and to hire and fire. This, rather than the reductions in job protection also pushed through by the Tories, was responsible for the creation of Britain's more flexible labour market. According to John Philpott of the Employment Policy Institute, an independent think-tank, job protection in Britain never amounted to much, unlike the ability of its unions to stop change.

Does the decline in union strength mean that Britain could now enjoy lower unemployment without inflation? In principle, a better match between the supply of labour and demand for it (made possible by greater flexibility) ought to mean that unemployment can now fall further without stirring up inflation than was the

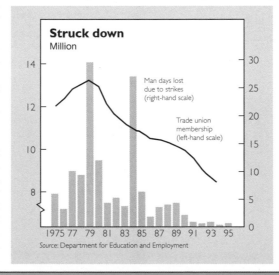

Struck down
Million

Man days lost due to strikes (right-hand scale)

Trade union membership (left-hand scale)

1975 77 79 81 83 85 87 89 91 93 95

Source: Department for Education and Employment

case in, say, the 1970s when the unions were stronger. Most economists think this 'natural' rate of unemployment is now lower, but opinions differ on how much lower.

Patrick Minford, an economist at Liverpool University, thinks that union reforms are one of the main reasons why unemployment could now fall to 3 per cent of the workforce (from its current 7.5 per cent) before inflation started to rise. But Julian Morgan, an economist at the National Institute of Economic and Social Research, reckons that weaker unions have had only a modest effect on unemployment. If the 'natural' jobless rate has fallen, that owes more to social-security reforms and efforts to help the long-term unemployed. So far, lower unemployment has failed to ignite wage inflation, which is good news. Only time will tell how good.

So what need is there for further reform? The current proposals are aimed most at the public sector. There, unions are increasingly holding one-day strikes, so the Tories want to do away with the legal immunities of such strikes. Labour wants more use of conciliation and binding arbitration, and to extend the use of independent pay-review bodies. These ideas are worth considering, but are unlikely to achieve much while the state tries to achieve its broader public-spending goals by squeezing the pay of its own employees without any regard to merit.

Private-sector employers no longer fear the unions, however, and most have little interest in seeing them bashed by politicians. Instead, many firms might be happy to give unions a bigger role if unions became cooperative rather than hostile. This opens up intriguing possibilities. One, proposed by Demos, a think-tank, is for unions to evolve into 'employee mutuals' – organisations which, to overcome job insecurity, become the long-term employer of members, hiring them out, often on short-term contracts, in the flexible labour market.

Source: The Economist Newspaper Limited, London, 14 September 1996. Reprinted with permission.

27 An introduction to welfare economics

Learning outcomes

At the end of this chapter you will be able to:
▶ Apply a precise criterion of efficiency to problems of production and allocation.
▶ Describe the conditions necessary for a market economy to be efficient.
▶ Identify aspects of the real world which do not meet efficincy criteria.
▶ Apply the tax/subsidy solutions to problems of externality.
▶ Identify products for which the market fails to exist.

Introduction

What is welfare economics about?

In Chapter 1 we saw that some economists believe it is possible to have a value-free economics. But whatever the philosophical considerations of such a stance, economists are *inevitably* led to examine the questions of what ought to be done by the very nature of the problems they study. Economics is concerned with the problems of choice in the face of scarcity; it is vital to ask the question 'What would be the best use of existing resources?' (Making the best use of existing resources is of course what is meant by economising!)

The notion of 'best' can only be defined by making normative judgements, i.e. subjectively. I might take it to mean that I should have everything and you have nothing; you, of course, might define it differently. Nevertheless, it would seem absurd for the economist to reply 'I can offer no suggestions as to what might be considered the best allocation of resources'.

It is important, however, that the economist makes clear exactly what value judgements have been made and how economic decisions would be altered if different value judgements were made. In this way the economist can clarify the thinking of the final decision maker without claiming a monopoly of knowledge of what is morally right or wrong.

Welfare economists study both positive and normative questions. The notion of 'best' in economics involves considerations of both efficiency and equity.

Different schools of economists approach the welfare question from different perspectives. Mainstream economists use neo-classical economics to construct welfare criteria and analyse the welfare attributes of market economies. Inevitably, this imparts a bias towards seeing welfare in terms of maximising individual satisfaction in the face of scarcity rather than, say, achieving a contented or 'good' society. This is not to say one bias is better than the other, but in the following account of welfare economics you should be aware of the 'hidden' neo-classical perspective of emphasising the individual rather than the collective welfare.

Partial and general equilibrium

Partial equilibrium

An introduction was made to the subject of welfare economics at the end of Chapter 10. The analysis in that chapter is termed *partial equilibrium* analysis. It is termed partial because it only deals with one small part of the economy, e.g. one market considered on its own. It is important to realise that this type of analysis is possible only when the sector we are studying is *not* sufficiently large as to influence the whole economy. Figure 27.1 attempts a diagrammatic explanation of this point. In Figure 27.1(a), sector A is not big enough to affect the rest of the economy, so that, for example, a rise in price in sector A does not affect the general level of prices in the rest of the economy and therefore there is no appreciable 'feedback' to sector A from the rest of the economy as a result of this change. We are thus able to keep our *ceteris paribus* assumption of all other things remaining constant.

However, in Figure 27.1(b), sector B is sufficiently large that changes in it influence the rest of the economy and that induced changes in the economy then 'feed back' to sector B and so on. Under these circumstances partial equilibrium analysis is no longer possible. We have moved from partial microeconomics to macroeconomics and a new type of analysis is needed.

General equilibrium

You have already been introduced to macroeconomic analysis as the functioning of the whole economy. However, we may note here that a microeconomic explanation of the functioning of the whole of the economy exists. This is termed *general equilibrium* and is illustrated in Figure 27.2. Here we imagine that rather than just looking at the determination of one price we have the thousands upon thousands of prices that go to make up the economy. Prices are thus *interdependent*.

An example of the general equilibrium analysis might be the interrelationship of fuel markets This would involve looking at coalmining, oil

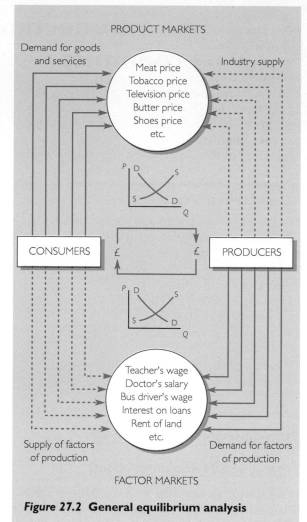

Figure 27.2 **General equilibrium analysis**

tankers, electricity prices, gas exploration and so on, and tracing the ramifications of a change in

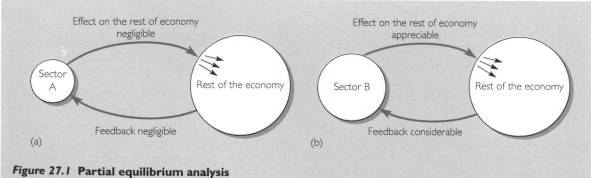

Figure 27.1 **Partial equilibrium analysis**
Partial equilibrium is possible in (a) where we may assume *ceteris paribus*, but feedback effects make it impossible in (b).

any one factor (or group of factors) throughout the economy. General equilibrium analysis is much more complicated than partial equilibrium analysis because the possibility of feedback between sectors now exists.

This effect was illustrated by the rise in oil prices in 1978. OPEC attempted to double prices. The price of a barrel of oil might be considered a microeconomic phenomenon; however, oil was such an important product to most countries that the price rise was sufficient to push their economies into depression. Thus a microeconomic phenomenon became a macroeconomic one. Oil prices are rising sharply again as we move into the twenty-first century, so we must beware of similar effects.

The credit for the invention of general equilibrium analysis is usually given to the French economist, **Leon Walras**. However, the development of it had to wait for the use of matrix algebra, which was the work of **Wassily Leontief**. We will now investigate welfare economics in a general equilibrium setting.

The Pareto criterion

Production or technical efficiency

In neo-classical welfare economics, the term efficiency has a precise meaning. This was first formulated by **Vilfredo Pareto** (1848–1923), an Italian economist and philosopher. He gave a definition of efficiency that sought to separate questions of efficiency from those of equity. Accordingly, he argued that a change is only unambiguously better if no one loses from it. Such an improvement in which no one loses is called a *Pareto improvement*. According to this criterion, if a situation exists, in which it is possible to improve the welfare of someone without making anyone else worse off, then it cannot be efficient to leave the situation as it is. Therefore, inefficiency can be said to exist whenever there is an unexploited potential for a Pareto improvement. This reasoning led to Pareto's definition of efficiency that now underpins neo-classical welfare economics:

'Pareto efficiency' requires that it must not be possible to change the existing allocation of resources in such a way that someone is made better off and no one is made worse off.

This criterion is intended to guard against wasting opportunities for gaining more utility for some people out of existing resources at no expense in terms of lost utility to others.

We can illustrate this idea of efficiency by referring back to the concept of an economy's production possibility frontier (see Chapter 3). In Figure 27.3 we assume that, because of a misallocation of resources, e.g. land best suited to growing wheat is being used for barley production and vice versa, the economy is producing at point A in the diagram. Let us also accept that consumers always desire more of both wheat and

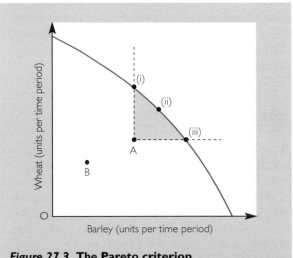

Figure 27.3 **The Pareto criterion**

barley, i.e. 'goods are good'. Now what can be said about point A in terms of the Pareto criterion? Clearly point A is not Pareto optimal, for, by changing the allocation of resources, it would be possible to have:

(i)   more wheat and no less barley;
(ii) more of both wheat and barley;
(iii) more barley and no less wheat.

These three possibilities are shown in Figure 27.3.

If, then, it is possible to have either more of one good and no less of another, or more of all goods, then it follows that it must be possible to distribute this extra output in such a way that all consumers are made better off, or some consumers are made better off without other consumers being made worse off. This is simply because there is more to share out! If this is done a 'Pareto improvement' has been made. You should now be able to explain why a movement from B to A in the diagram also represents a Pareto improvement even though A itself is also an inefficient point.

Points on the production possibility frontier are said to be production, or technically, efficient in that it is not possible to increase the output of one good without decreasing the output of another.

● *Common misunderstanding*

Sometimes students write that a situation is efficient if it is possible to increase the welfare of someone without decreasing the welfare of another. This is clearly not the most efficient or 'optimal' point, because further Pareto improvements can be made. This situation is only described as efficient when no further Pareto improvements are possible.

Allocative efficiency

It is tempting for the student to think that points on the production possibility frontier must represent Pareto-efficient resource allocations. But this is not necessarily the case, as another aspect of efficiency has also to be considered. Although such points *do* demonstrate that production is efficient, this does not ensure that the ***product mix*** is Pareto efficient, i.e. that resources are allo-

cated in the right proportions to producing the various goods. As was the case with productive efficiency, ***allocative efficiency*** again requires that it must not be possible to change the existing product mix in such a way that someone is made better off and no one is made worse off (or, of course, everybody is made better off!). In fact at most points on the production possibility frontier this possibility will arise.

Take for example the point in our wheat/barley example where the production possibility frontier crosses the horizontal axis, i.e. where the economy is producing nothing but barley. It seems most unlikely that consumers as a whole would not be prepared to sacrifice any of this barley in order to obtain some wheat (you might like to think of this as sacrificing some beer, which is made from barley, in order to obtain some bread to eat). If consumers are prepared to make this sacrifice then overall welfare, in the Pareto sense, could be increased by moving along the production possibility frontier, sacrificing barley output in order to increase the output of wheat.

Suppose that consumers as a group are prepared to sacrifice 1 unit of barley in order to obtain 3 units of wheat, but that the economy's production possibility frontier is such that decreasing the output of barley by 1 unit would allow the output of wheat to increase by 4 units. It would thus be possible to use 3 of the 4 extra units of wheat to compensate consumers for their loss of barley and use the remaining unit of wheat to raise overall welfare, i.e. to bring about a Pareto improvement. Only when changes in the product mix can just compensate consumers, and no more, is it no longer worthwhile making further movements along the production possibility frontier. This could also be expressed by saying that it is no longer worthwhile moving further along the production possibility frontier. We will then have reached the Pareto-efficient product mix.

Allocative efficiency exists when it is not possible to bring about a Pareto improvement by changing the product mix.

When the slope of the production possibility boundary is equal to the rate at which consumers as a whole are just prepared to substitute one good for another then at this point there will be both technical (production) efficiency and allocative (product-mix) efficiency – both are needed for Pareto efficiency.

Draw a curved production possibility frontier as in Figure 27.3. Use a ruler to approximate the slope of the line at a point near the vertical axis. Now do the same for a point near the horizontal axis and for a point half-way along the curve. For each of the points, write out in words the rate at which wheat would have to be given up in order to gain one more unit of barley. Now assuming that consumers are prepared to substitute barley for wheat at the rate given by the slope of the line at its centre, explain why a movement along the production possibility frontier towards the centre from the other two points would constitute a Pareto improvement. For Pareto efficiency, what must the relationship be between the rate at which consumers are prepared to substitute barley for wheat and the rate at which it is possible to substitute barley for wheat in production?

Welfare and utility

In Chapter 9, welfare economics was discussed in terms of demand or willingness to pay, which was regarded as the benefit of producing any unit of a product. In this chapter we will take an introductory look at the philosophical arguments behind this. The origin of modern economics lies with the utilitarian philosophers of the nineteenth century, who argued that the objective in running the economy is to achieve the greatest happiness of the greatest number. They argued that happiness, or 'utility' as it was termed was in principle measurable. They also argued that in general, as more of a product is sold to a consumer, the extra (marginal) utility will decline. It is this logic that lies behind both the demand curve. The idea that people will have a rate at which they substitute one good for another as in the argument above, is also based on the idea that people value products by the satisfaction, or utility, that they gain from them. These arguments are considered in detail in Chapter 40.

Efficiency and the free market

The price mechanism and Pareto optimality

We now turn to the important question of whether the allocation of resources as determined by a free market is Pareto efficient. Not surprisingly the answer is no. But it is possible to construct a set of highly unrealistic assumptions under which a free market economy would be Pareto efficient in equilibrium. Economic theory has demonstrated that under these assumptions (the first of which is that perfect competition exists in all markets!) the price mechanism would act automatically to bring about a Pareto-efficient allocation of resources, i.e.:

Under certain conditions, which do not exist in the real world, a price mechanism would automatically bring about production/technical efficiency and allocative/product-mix efficiency.

You may now be asking: 'If Pareto optimality does not exist in the real world, nor will it ever be likely to exist, what is the point of studying it?' The answer is quite simply that unless we are aware of the conditions necessary for Pareto efficiency we will not be able to identify deviations from these conditions. Hence this unrealistic model can, perhaps, provide a useful point of departure for discussing reality.

The conditions for Pareto efficiency

The conditions under which a free market economy, functioning via the price mechanism, would produce a Pareto optimal allocation of resources are summarised in the *first optimality theorem* of modern welfare economics:

If, in all markets, there is perfect competition, no externalities, public goods or market failure connected with uncertainty, then the resulting allocation of resources will be Pareto efficient.

Needless to say, the situation described by this theorem is not even an approximate description of reality. Nevertheless it is often used as a benchmark by economists, with which real-world situations are compared. Movements towards this ideal are often considered to be improvements, hence the tendency of economists to always welcome increases in competition.

Pareto efficiency and perfect competition

If you have understood the chapter so far you will be able to grasp in an intuitive way why the conditions stated in the first optimality theorem will produce Pareto efficiency. Turning first to the question of production or technical efficiency, you should be able to use what you have learned from Chapter 21 to see that the assumption of perfect competition in all markets is sufficient to ensure this result. We can explain this by remembering that the model of perfect competition assumes that firms are profit maximisers and have perfect knowledge of production techniques and factor prices, and that all factors of production are perfectly mobile. Therefore firms will choose the least cost methods of production. In short, firms will hire those factors that are relatively most productive and will use the smallest possible quantity of these factors to produce any given output. This efficient use of factors of production and cost minimisation would ensure that, for any given level of resources, overall output is maximised. That is:

If there is perfect competition in all markets the economy will be operating on its production possibility frontier and will therefore be production (or 'technically') efficient.

Pareto efficiency and market equilibrium

You may recall from Chapter 6 that the theory of demand and supply in competitive markets depended on the assumptions of perfect competition. We saw above that the assumption of perfect competition will bring about production efficiency but you now know enough to understand why an economy composed of competitive markets could also automatically bring about allocative efficiency (ignoring problems of externalities and uncertainty). If there is both productive and allocative efficiency then the economy is Pareto efficient as a whole.

To explain how competitive markets bring about allocative/product-mix efficiency we need to give new interpretations to our familiar demand and supply curves.

Social marginal benefit (SMB)

Under the conditions of perfect competition all consumers are faced with the same price for a product. We also know that consumers will continue to purchase extra units of this product so long as they place a higher monetary value on these units than the price they actually have to pay (this is the concept of consumer surplus, see Chapter 4). They will thus consume extra units of the product up to the point at which the monetary valuation they place on the marginal unit of consumption is equal to its price (see Figure 27.4).

Thus when consumers are in equilibrium, the price of a product will reflect its marginal valuation by consumers (in monetary units). As this price is common to all consumers, it follows that *all* consumers will be attaching the same monetary valuation to their marginal unit of consumption. We will call this monetary valuation the *social marginal benefit* (SMB) of the marginal unit of output of the product concerned. The demand curve for a product, of course, shows how much of the product will be demanded at any market price. Hence by reading off the market price at a specific output, the demand curve automatically shows the social marginal valuation of the product at any level of output (see Figure 27.5).

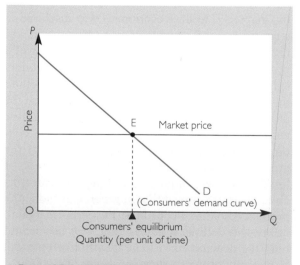

Figure 27.4 Marginal valuation of a product
Point E is where the consumer's marginal valuation of the product is equal to the price of the product.

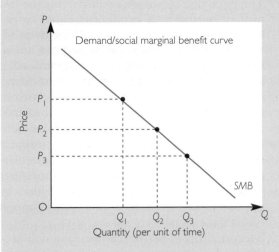

Figure 27.5 The social marginal benefit curve

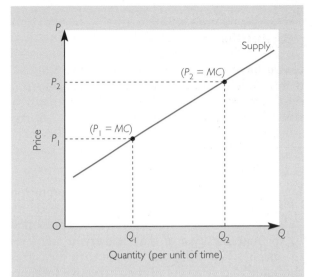

Figure 27.6 The supply curve is the marginal cost curve

We can see that at an output of Q_1 the *SMB*, i.e. consumer valuation of the last unit sold, is equal to P_1. At Q_2 the *SMB* is equal to P_2, and so on. As might be expected, the demand curve for the product shows that the *SMB* of an extra unit falls as output increases.

If all markets in the economy are perfectly competitive (and there are no externalities or uncertainty) the demand curve is also the social marginal benefit curve.

The significance of marginal cost pricing

We now turn to the interpretation of the supply curve under the conditions of perfect competition. Recall that firms in perfect competition will produce up to the level of output at which marginal cost is equal to price. Hence, reading up from the quantity axis, the supply curve tells us what the marginal cost of production is at any level of output (see Figure 27.6).

We can see that at Q_1 the marginal cost of production must be equal to P_1. What, however, is the significance of marginal cost for analysis under these conditions? It turns out that, under the assumptions we have made, marginal cost will measure the valuation by consumers of the alternative products forgone by increasing the output of the product concerned by 1 unit. We can explain this somewhat surprising result as follows. Recall that in perfect competition the

factors of production are free to transfer from one industry to another. Now as marginal cost measures the payment to the factor services needed to produce the last unit of output: the cost of these extra factors, at the margin, must be just sufficient to induce these factors of production away from their best alternative employment. In short, the payment to these extra factors will equal the opportunity cost to these factors of forgoing their best alternative employment in another industry (another way of saying this is that these factors must be paid their transfer earnings; see Chapter 26). Hence if factors are perfectly mobile they must be paid, at the margin, the amount they could earn in their best alternative employment. However, the amount these extra factors could earn in an alternative industry will be equal to the amount that consumers would pay for the alternative products that could be produced by these factors, i.e. the valuation by consumers of the alternative products forgone. Hence we have the result that, under perfectly competitive conditions:

The marginal cost in one industry measures the valuation by consumers (in monetary terms) of the alternative products that are forgone by increasing the output of that industry by 1 unit. This valuation of alternatives forgone is the 'social marginal cost' (*SMC*).

STUDENT ACTIVITY 27.3

You should now work through the following
sequence until you are satisfied that you
understand why MC is also equal to SMC:

MC = Payment to extra factors required
= What these factors could have earned in an
alternative industry = Consumers' valuation of
alternative products forgone = SMC

Let us now run through this new interpretation
of the supply curve. The supply curve of an
industry under perfect competition is represented
by the marginal cost of that industry at any level
of output. This marginal cost in turn measures
the value to consumers of the alternative forgone,
i.e. the SMC. We thus have the result:

If all markets in the economy are perfectly competitive (and there are no externalities or uncertainty)
the supply curve is also the social marginal cost
curve (Figure 27.7).

The welfare significance of equilibrium in a perfect market

The equilibrium price

From the previous section of this chapter we have
derived the following results:

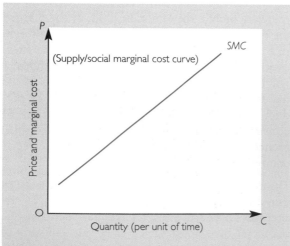

Figure 27.7 The social marginal cost curve

(a) The price that consumers will pay for the last
unit of output of a product is equal to the
marginal valuation by consumers of the product concerned. This is known as the social
marginal benefit of this unit of output and is
shown by the demand curve for the product.

(b) Marginal cost reflects what the factors used to
produce the last unit of output could earn in
their best alternative employment. These earnings in turn reflect the valuation by consumers
of these alternative uses of factors. Hence marginal cost measures the valuation by consumers
of the best alternative products forgone by
increasing production by 1 unit. This valuation
is called the social marginal cost (SMC).

(c) Because firms in perfect competition will produce where price equals marginal cost the
supply curve automatically shows the SMC.

We can now draw the following important conclusion for perfectly competitive markets:

When the market for a product is in equilibrium the
last unit of a product bought is valued equally by
consumers to the best alternative forgone by its production. There is thus an optimum balance between
scarcity and want.

This is illustrated in Figure 27.8.

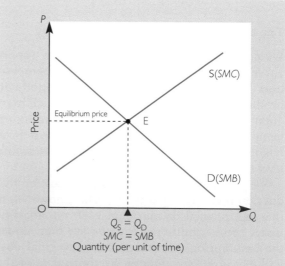

Figure 27.8 The socially efficient price
This occurs where consumers' valuation of the best
alternatives forgone by producing an extra unit (SMC) is
equal to consumers' valuation of an extra unit of the
commodity (SMB).

The Pareto- or socially-efficient level of output

It is now fairly easy to see why an equilibrium of output at which $SMC = SMB$ corresponds to a Pareto-efficient allocation of resources. We need only consider the points either side of the equilibrium level of output.

In Figure 27.9 we can see that at Q_1 consumers value an extra unit of output more than the alternative that would be forgone by its production. The actual gain in welfare available to consumers and hence 'society' from the production of an extra unit at Q_1 is given, in monetary units, by $SMB - SMC$, i.e. the vertical distance between the demand and supply curve is the excess of consumer valuation of the extra unit over its marginal cost of production. The overall welfare loss associated with the output Q_1 can therefore be calculated, in monetary units, by summing the vertical distance between the supply and demand curve for all extra units up to the point at which the level of output is Pareto efficient. Thus the loss of welfare to society associated with the output being at Q_1 rather than the socially efficient output of Q_2 can be represented by a welfare loss triangle (see Figure 27.10).

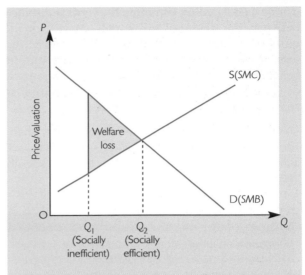

Figure 27.10 **Welfare loss at outputs below the equilibrium**

Welfare loss triangles

It can be seen that under the assumptions of the first optimality theorem, whenever actual output is below the market equilibrium the overall welfare of consumers could be increased by increasing the output of the product, i.e. there exists the potential for a Pareto improvement.

Under the assumptions of the first optimality theorem outputs below the market equilibrium are associated with a 'welfare loss' and hence a socially inefficient allocation of resources.

Conversely, at Q_3 (see Figure 27.11), consumers value the alternative forgone by producing an extra unit more than they value that extra unit of output. There is therefore a welfare loss, as consumers would have preferred the alternative now forgone. The welfare loss associated with the production of this marginal unit can be measured in monetary units by the vertical distance between the demand and supply curve, i.e. $SMC - SMB$. As the overall welfare of consumers could be increased by decreasing the output of the product and diverting resources towards alternatives, it is clear that at outputs above the market equilibrium a potential Pareto improvement exists. The overall welfare loss associated with the output Q_3

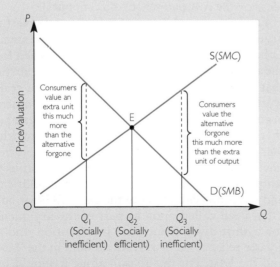

Figure 27.9 **The social efficiency of the equilibrium price**

can be calculated by summing the vertical distance between the demand and supply curves for all units of output from Q_3 down to Q_2. Hence the loss of welfare to society associated with output being at Q_3 rather than the socially efficient output of Q_2 can again be represented by a welfare loss triangle. This is illustrated in Figure 27.11.

Under the assumptions of the first optimality theorem, outputs above the market equilibrium are associated with a 'welfare loss' and hence a socially inefficient allocation of resources.

STUDENT ACTIVITY 27.4

Suppose a politician attempts to bribe the electorate by saying he will print enough money to buy everyone a new washing machine. Explain why the effect of this would tend to decrease the welfare of consumers rather than increase it.

● *Common misunderstanding*

SMB = SMC is often called the socially 'optimal' point and hence often regarded as unambiguously the 'best' level of output. But we were careful to note the individualistic nature of the Pareto criteria. The Pareto criterion says nothing about fairness. For example, the rich may cause a high demand for Rolls-Royce cars and their valuation exceeds their valuation of the alternatives.

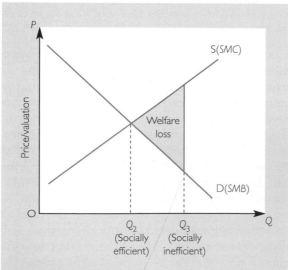

Figure 27.11 **Welfare loss at outputs above the equilibrium**

Conversely the poor may place a high marginal utility on food but lack the money to convert this want into a monetary valuation and hence demand. In short, the rich have more money 'votes' as to how resources should be allocated. Redistributing income would tend to decrease the demand for Rolls-Royces and increase the demand for certain foodstuffs. Thus a new set of Pareto-efficient equilibriums will be established. Thus for every Pareto-efficient equilibrium there is a given income distribution.

The 'invisible hand' theorem

The only point at which it is impossible to change the allocation of resources so as to bring about a Pareto improvement is Q_2. This is the level of output that would be arrived at through the operation of market forces! At this point want and scarcity are brought into balance and the gain, in monetary units, to consumers from the last unit of output is exactly matched by the cost in terms of alternative output forgone. This result that, subject to certain conditions, the equilibrium of an economy in which all markets operate under the conditions of perfect competition will be socially (i.e. Pareto) efficient, is known as the 'invisible hand' theorem. The name of the theorem reflects the belief of some writers that it is a rigorous statement of the ideas of Adam Smith (in Chapter 47 we look at an alternative interpretation of Smith's ideas by the Austrian school of economics).

For some this theorem is taken as a powerful argument in favour of a free market system. Others point out that the assumptions needed for the efficiency of free markets are so unrealistic that the theorem actually demonstrates that real-world markets are socially inefficient. Yet others argue that the theorem is totally abstract and therefore has no implications for real-world market systems. But, whether justified or not, the 'invisible hand' theorem, intuitively or rigorously stated, has had enormous influence in political and economic circles. Since the early 1980s it has often been called upon as part of the argument for a shift away from state intervention and a greater reliance on market forces both in the West and the East. For this reason alone it should be examined carefully, but such welfare economics is now also an important part of economics syllabuses. Its approach is developed and criticised in the rest of this section of the book.

Causes of market failure

In the first part of the chapter we demonstrated that under certain conditions an economy that has perfect competition in all markets has equilibrium positions that are socially (or Pareto) efficient. We can gain insight into why efficiency is not achieved in real-life markets by examining the implications of deviations from the conditions assumed in the first optimality theorem. It will also be necessary to consider the income distribution in society. Efficiency might not be enough on its own without a fair distribution of income. This aspect of the allocation of resources is dealt with in Chapter 28.

We will discuss market failure under the headings of imperfect competition, externality, public goods and merit goods. These ideas have already been introduced to the reader in Chapter 9 and explored in applied situations in Chapters 10–14. We return to them now at a higher theoretical level in the context of welfare economics. Some applied cases are considered in Chapter 4.

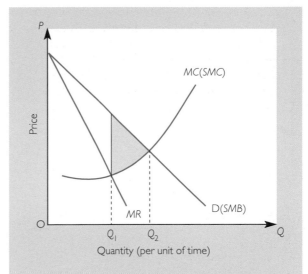

Figure 27.12 Welfare loss under imperfect competition

Q_1 is the profit-maximising output, while Q_2 is the socially efficient output. The shaded area represents welfare loss at the profit maximisation equilibrium.

few resources going to the monopoly industry. Check back to Chapter 23 if you are unsure of this.

Imperfect competition

Welfare loss under imperfect competition

A profit-maximising firm, operating under the conditions of monopoly or monopolistic competition, produces and sells the volume of output at which marginal cost and marginal revenue are equal. Equilibrium will thus occur with marginal cost being less than the market price. From the conditions of the first best optimality theorem, this implies social inefficiency, i.e. a loss of welfare to society. This is illustrated in Figure 27.12, where the shaded area represents the welfare loss to society, with the firm producing output Q_1 rather than Q_2.

● *Common misunderstanding*

It is often thought by students that monopoly pricing is inefficient because it results in high prices for consumers. This is not an efficiency problem in itself, but a separate problem of income distribution. The consumers' loss is the monopolist's gain. The inefficiency results from the misallocation of resources between industries, with too

Cost inefficiencies

So far we have looked only at the loss of social welfare caused by price exceeding marginal cost. However, the lack of competition might also result in cost inefficiency. Firms that are for various reasons insulated from competition, might have the potential to make very large profits and thus are not forced to minimise costs in order to match the prices of their competitors. In such situations firms may have discretion as to the objectives they pursue; for example, they may pursue managerial objectives (see Chapter 7). To the extent that costs are not minimised, this will result in a second kind of efficiency loss caused by unnecessarily high production costs. This welfare loss can again be represented diagrammatically.

In Figure 27.13 the shaded area between the two marginal cost curves, up to Q_1, represents the social loss caused by the cost-inefficient production of Q_1 units of output. If, however, costs are reduced to MC_2 the socially efficient output becomes Q_2. Thus the shaded triangle between Q_1 and Q_2 would also be available as part of the total welfare gain to

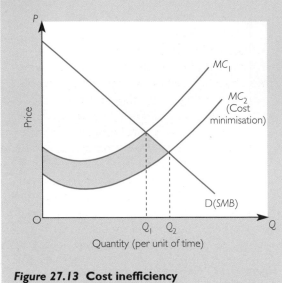

Figure 27.13 Cost inefficiency
If monopoly protects inefficiencies then the cost curve is MC_1 instead of MC_2, which is where it would be under competitive conditions. Thus the shaded area represents the welfare loss to society.

society. The whole of the shaded area therefore represents the welfare loss to society from the wasteful method of production. Some, admittedly inconclusive, empirical evidence has suggested that the welfare loss from cost inefficiency in monopolies is far greater than that caused by underproduction. This has led some observers to state that underproduction due to monopoly pricing policy is of no practical significance. It has been pointed out by other observers, that even a small welfare loss in the present will accumulate into a large long-term welfare loss if left uncorrected. It should also be pointed out that policies designed to decrease monopoly power through increased competition will tend to reduce both types of inefficiency. Government policy towards market power is discussed in Chapters 23 and 24.

Contestable markets, inventions and capital accumulation

The analysis above is in terms of a single period of time. Where there is a longer time frame, some arguments can be put forward to support monopolies. The profits that can be earned by monopolists is often the incentive that leads to innovation. The

American courts have suggested that Microsoft has monopoly power, but it was the prospect of such power that fuelled the search for new software (in this case the DOS interpreter program Windows) and keeping this dominance in the market required continuous innovation. Windows is not completely without competition, but the Apple Mac competitor has a small share of the market, and has to offer Windows compatibility. The Linux system tends to be used only by people with greater computer experience. The Windows system is not without its critics both as a system, and also according to the American courts again, for some restrictive practices. The idea of contestable markets (see Chapter 22) may also be relevant here, as the potential of competition from other systems will keep Microsoft on its toes. In the case of economies with low savings ratios, such as the USA and the UK, monopoly profit may be an alternative method of accumulating the capital necessary for economic growth (see Chapter 34).

Externalities

What are externalities?

Externalities are said to exist when the action of producers or consumers affects not only themselves but also third parties, other than through the normal workings of the price mechanism.

This is likely to result in allocative inefficiency because individuals normally consider only the private costs (the cost incurred by themselves) of their decisions. They largely ignore, or are unaware of, the wider social costs (the full opportunity cost to society) and benefits of their actions. External effects can be either positive or negative. For example, if one person is cured of a contagious disease this obviously gives benefit to others; hence the external effect is said to be positive. On the other hand, airports near residential areas are likely to have negative external effects because of the noise of aircraft taking off and landing.

We can categorise these 'spill-over' effects under four headings:

(a) *Production on consumption.* A negative example of this would be the adverse effects of pollution on recreational areas. A positive externality could result from the warm-water discharge from many industrial cooling processes, making rivers more attractive to bathers.

(b) *Production on production.* A negative externality would result if the release of industrial waste into rivers decreased the catch of commercial fishermen. An important positive externality in this category is that arising from the use of non-patented inventions. As inventors would receive no payment for their efforts this suggests that under *laissez-faire*, too little would be spent on research and development.

(c) *Consumption on production.* Negative externalities might arise from the careless discarding of packaging materials. Alternatively, congestion caused by private motorists will increase the transportation costs of many firms (see Chapter 14). Positive externalities in this category are, in principle, possible, but, in practice, of little significance.

(d) *Consumption on consumption.* Negative externalities include the unwelcome noise from radios and the congestion caused to other private road users of using one's own car. Positive externalities include neighbours enjoying the sight of each other's gardens and the fact that other people's possession of a telephone increases the utility of one's own telephone. A rather controversial negative externality in this category is that of envy (see Chapter 3 on conspicuous consumption, page 29). It is argued that status-orientated consumption by one consumer is likely to reduce the utility of others. However, it might conversely be argued that the copying of others' consumption is due to the information provided by this consumption. This latter argument suggests a positive rather than a negative externality, i.e. people are receiving free information.

It should be noted that the same spill-over effect can simultaneously have both positive and negative effects; for example, the smoke from oil refineries is beneficial to the cultivation of citrus fruits, but it can also be considered as undesirable pollution.

Pecuniary 'external effects'

Pecuniary 'external effects' are the effect of prices in one sector of the economy upon other sectors of the economy.

As we have seen, prices are determined by the interaction of all the economic 'units', i.e. producers and consumers, in the economy. Hence the act of demanding or supplying these units by one group will affect the prices faced by other groups. Although such changes can cause a redistribution of welfare among units, they are not a cause of allocative inefficiency. This is because such effects work *within* the price mechanism; they are not external to it and are therefore not ignored by profit- or utility-maximising decision makers. For example, if firms in one industry increase their demand for a particular factor of production, this is likely to raise the price of this factor of production. It is not a case of market inefficiency because it is the normal working of the price mechanism; the increased price of the factor of production merely reflects the fact that it is scarce in relation to the demand for the products it produces. Such price increases provide an incentive for producers to economise in the use of this factor and conveys to consumers the fact that to have more of one product they must, as a group, have less of another. It is exactly this type of consideration that brought about the efficient balance between wants and scarcity outlined earlier in the chapter.

In view of the confusion between pecuniary externalities and true spill-over effects, it might be better to call the former 'price effects'. However, in a world of imperfect information, pecuniary effects do have an importance as regards efficiency. For example, suppose that one entrepreneur found an ideal but remote location for a hydroelectric dam, but also finds that it would be uneconomical to transmit power to where it is in demand and decides not to go ahead with the project. Further suppose that a separate entrepreneur surveys the same area and finds that it is rich in deposits of bauxite (the ore from which aluminium is extracted). Aluminium smelting requires vast amounts of power, so this entrepreneur also decides not to go ahead with this project. It might thus be the case that if both projects were to go ahead the first entrepreneur would be able to sell electricity at a high enough price to make the dam profitable and the second entrepreneur would be able to buy electricity from the first entrepreneur at a low enough price to make the smelting of aluminium profitable.

The essential point to realise here is that it is not the pecuniary effects themselves that are the cause of market failure; indeed they work in exactly the direction required. It is the lack of information and hence coordination between the entrepreneurs that results in inefficiency. We will return to the problem of market failure caused by incomplete information later in this chapter.

Negative externalities

Consider the soap industry, which, in a free market, would discharge waste products into the air and rivers. This is because owners of soap factories, if they are profit maximisers, will consider only their private costs and ignore the wider social costs of their activities. Indeed, if competition was fierce, they might be unable to incur the cost of purification or non-polluting disposal of their waste products and still match the price of their competitors. Where such negative externalities are present the price mechanism is likely to fail in bringing about a Pareto-efficient allocation of resources. This is because the cost to society in terms of the deterioration of the environment is unpriced by the price mechanism. Private profit makers are given the use of the environment free of charge. It is in this sense that such spill-over effects are external to the price mechanism. The cost to society of the use of this resource is not reflected in the private costs of the individual using it. Individuals are thus 'invited' to destroy these resources at zero price. No incentive is provided by the price mechanism to economise on the use of the environment and hence the price mechanism fails to bring about an efficient balance between the wants of society as a whole and the use of the scarce resources available to it.

Using the analysis we have developed we can again represent the welfare loss resulting from negative externalities in the form of a diagram. This is illustrated in Figure 27.14. It is assumed in the diagram that the soap industry is perfectly competitive. The supply curve of the industry is thus the horizontal summation of the marginal cost curves of all the firms in the industry (see Chapter 21). This curve is represented by the private marginal cost curve (PMC) in the diagram. As firms in perfect competition will equate MC to

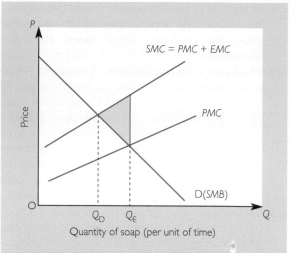

Figure 27.14 Negative externalities
Q_E represents the profit-maximising equilibrium when firms in the industry are able to ignore external marginal costs (EMC). The socially efficient output is Q_D. Thus the shaded area represents the welfare loss to society at the profit-maximising equilibrium.

price, the free market equilibrium output of the industry is thus Q_E. The social marginal cost (SMC) curve represents the full opportunity cost to society of an extra unit of soap production. SMC lies above PMC as SMC includes not only the cost to society in terms of forgone alternative marketed products, i.e. PMC, but also the loss to society in terms of the deterioration of the environment, i.e. the external marginal cost (EMC). EMC represents the loss in value corresponding to what consumers would have been prepared to pay to avoid this loss in utility from the environment associated with extra units of soap production. It can be seen that SMB equals SMC at Q_D units of output.

Thus in terms of social efficiency, as we have defined it above, there is an oversupply of the private good, soap. By summing the excess of SMC over SMB for the units between Q_D and Q_E we again arrive at a monetary measure of the welfare loss to society, i.e. the shaded triangle in the diagram. Because of this overproduction of goods in cases of negative externality, economists have often suggested that the government should intervene in such markets to correct the situation.

The Cambridge economist, **A. Pigou**, suggested that a tax on the private good should be introduced to reflect the cost of the externality. These issues have been discussed in Chapters 9 – 13 and will be considered further in Chapter 4.

STUDENT ACTIVITY 27.5

Suppose that Figure 27.14 represents the costs and benefits associated with flights from a particular airport. The costs are the noise suffered by local residents. The benefits are the willingness of passengers to pay for the flight. The government decides to put a tax on the airlines because of the externality they are producing. Consider the following consequences of this action:

1 What will happen to the number of flights?
2 What will happen to the price of flights?
3 Will the local residents be any better off as a result of this policy?
4 Should the tax revenue be used to compensate the local residents for the remaining level of noise?

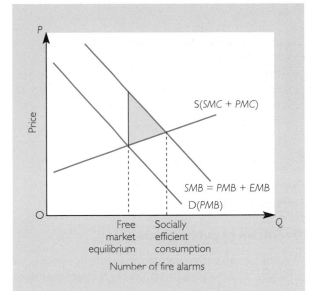

Figure 27.15 Positive externalities
The existence of external marginal benefit (*EMB*) shifts the *SMB* curve to the right. The free market equilibrium is below the socially efficient level of consumption. The shaded area shows the welfare loss brought about by underproduction.

Positive externalities

The same framework as above can be used to analyse the welfare losses associated with positive externalities; for example, those arising from medical care, attractive front gardens, telephone installations and inventions and innovations which can be copied without charge. We could proceed by representing social costs as being less than private costs. It is conceptually easier, however, to represent the positive externality by an upward shift of the marginal benefit curve. This indicates that the benefits of consumption include not only the benefits to the purchaser but also the benefits to those enjoying the positive spill-over effects of this consumption.

We have adopted this procedure in Figure 27.15. Here the upward shift in the *SMB* curve represents the valuation of other residents of having their neighbours' property protected by fire alarms. It can be seen that when positive externalities exist there is a tendency for underproduction of the product in question, i.e. the Pareto-efficient output is greater than the equilibrium output that would occur in an 'uncorrected' free market. Pigou suggested that this situation could be corrected by giving a subsidy to the private good to reflect the external benefit arising from its consumption. Subsidies to public transport and higher education are good examples of this type of policy. Free provision of school education and health care in the UK also reflects the existence of positive externalities. In these cases the policies are also concerned with issues of equity which is discussed later in this chapter. Government policy in this area is discussed in more detail in Chapter 28.

STUDENT ACTIVITY 27.6

Classify the following in terms of positive, negative and pecuniary externalities:

(a) Smoke from a soap factory.
(b) One firm in an industry sets up a training school for its workers.
(c) A mine owner installs a powerful pump which lowers the water table in the area.

(d) A driver makes a right turn on a busy road and causes a traffic jam.
(e) A school leaver decides to go to university.
(f) A home owner plants an attractive front garden.
(g) A crop disease increases the price of bread.
(h) Fred hits Bill.
(i) A reduction in the number of people using buses results in higher prices.

Public goods

Definition of public goods

We have already mentioned public goods in Chapter 9. We will now define them more precisely.

Public goods are defined as products where, for any given output, consumption by additional consumers does not reduce the quantity consumed by existing consumers. Another way of putting this is that the marginal cost of production for an extra person is zero.

There are relatively few pure public goods: defence and lighthouses are the examples usually cited. In cases of pure public goods, it is not possible to think of individual consumption. Provision of public goods is for everyone or no one; either the country is defended against external aggression or it is not. An increase in population would not result in any increase in the cost of defence, but more people would be 'consuming' the good. Public goods are therefore said to be *non-rival in consumption*. This contrasts sharply with purely private goods such as chocolate bars, where consumption by one person rules out the consumption of that chocolate bar by another person. Private goods are said to be *rival in consumption*, which also implies positive marginal cost.

Indivisibility and collective consumption

There is another group of goods which appear to have the characteristics of a public good up to a certain level of consumption, but which then appear to become private goods. Uncongested roads, parks, swimming pools, buses and bridges can all take extra customers at virtually zero costs up to a capacity limit. Once they reach that capacity limit, however, marginal cost rises again, often very substantially. The cost of putting on an extra bus for one extra passenger, because the previous bus has filled up, is very high. When a road reaches its capacity, congestion results in extra costs. These fall on the motorists themselves in terms of wasted time and high car running costs at low speed. These are not cases of public goods, but instances of indivisibility in production. Production is 'lumpy' and can only be increased by large increments. If a congested two-lane motorway needs to be enlarged to meet increased demand, the only way to do it is to increase capacity by 50 per cent by adding a third lane. The term collective consumption, or collective goods is used to describe these situations.

Public goods and property rights

A pure public good has the characteristics of non-rivalry in consumption, as discussed in the previous section. It also is characterised by *non-excludability*. This means that, unlike private goods, it is difficult to create property rights over the product that can be enforced. If you buy a chocolate bar, the property rights over it belong to you. If someone takes the chocolate bar from you by force, they have committed a crime and you could call on the police and the courts to *enforce* your property rights over the chocolate bar. The same arguments do not apply to public goods like defence. The best way to understand this is to imagine door-to-door defence sales people calling at your house, attempting to sell you some of the national or international defence 'product'. After they have interested you in the idea of defending your country, if you are reasonably intelligent you will ask them if they are already producing this product. If they say yes, a selfish person will then say they are not interested in buying the product. This kind of behaviour is called *free riding*. Since the person is already defended they have no interest in paying for the product. The consumers who have already paid for the provision of defence have no means of preventing such 'free rider' consumers from benefiting from their purchase. They have no enforceable property rights over the product because it is a public good.

Of course, if everyone behaves in this selfish way there is a chance that the product will not be produced at all, even though there is considerable demand for it. There is a way around this problem adopted by most governments. Defence is usually provided through the government, not the market, and *citizens* pay compulsory taxes to finance it rather than *consumers* paying voluntary prices. This brings us to a third characteristic of public goods: *non-rejectability*. Some citizens may have a moral or religious objection to violence. This leads them to be opposed to paying for the armed forces. Their objection may be more specific, e.g. opposition to the use of nuclear weapons. They will still have to pay taxes to finance these 'products' which they do not want.

The characteristic of non-rivalness in consumption implies zero marginal cost and therefore, for efficiency, a zero price. This makes public goods unattractive to private enterprise. The characteristic of non-excludability suggests that private enterprise would in any case find it extraordinarily difficult to persuade people to part with their money. Therefore not only is it impossible to charge for the consumption of public goods, it is also undesirable. These considerations obviously make public goods unsuitable for provision through the price mechanism. The characteristic of non-rejectability, however, also provides us with some objections against the provision of public goods by the state!

Collective action

It is possible to object that people are not as selfish as the above discussion of free riders suggests. In practice people act collectively in charities, voluntary social work, religious and political organisations, clubs and societies, trade unions, and youth organisations. The 'voluntary sector' is in fact quite a sizeable chunk of the economy! In the 1960s, Olson argued that small groups were more likely to be effective in setting up such collective action, because the benefits to an individual were quite large compared with the costs of setting up the necessary organisation. He argued that as groups got larger and larger, they became progressively more difficult to mobilise. Social incentives such as status, honours, embarrassment, or even intimidation, might be necessary to make larger organisations work effectively. However, he accepted

that where people are motivated by ideology or faith, their beliefs are sometimes powerful enough to overcome their natural human selfishness.

The voluntary sector is clearly an interesting alternative to government provision for those who wish to reduce the role of the state. Olson's analysis suggests that the government will need to give the voluntary sector encouragement if it is to be a success. A fuller discussion of the role of the state is to be found in Chapters 9 and 10.

STUDENT ACTIVITY 27.7

The difficulty of collective action can be demonstrated by an experiment. Divide your class into groups of about five students (without the help of your teacher/lecturer). Each student should take responsibility for reading up, understanding and explaining one of the following concepts to fellow group members: non-excludability; free riders; non-rejectability; non-rivalness in consumption; indivisibility. Arrange to meet outside normal class time to exchange the information you have gained. At the end of the experiment check how many people refused to cooperate or did not turn up, and how many people listened to other students' explanations but had not done much work themselves (free riders). Remember, this is a small-group situation so you should have some success.

Public goods, efficiency and valuation

The *SMB* curve of public goods

Given all these difficulties, is it possible to decide on the Pareto-efficient level of output of a public good? It was thought too difficult until the American economist, **Paul Samuelson**, put forward a solution in the 1950s. Because all consumers of a public or collective good consume the same output, the social marginal benefit of such products is the vertical summation of all the individual consumers' private marginal benefits. As we shall see in Chapter 40, the estimation of these benefits poses difficult problems. However, we shall ignore these problems for now and assume that we can draw individual demand curves that measure the true willingness to pay of each individual consumer. This is shown in Figure 27.16.

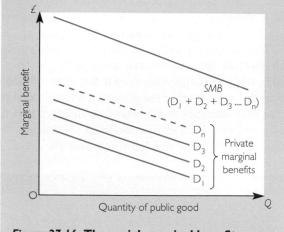

Figure 27.16 The social marginal benefit curve of a public good

The Pareto-efficient output will have been reached when the aggregate valuation of the last unit is equal to the valuation of the best alternative forgone by its production. This is shown in Figure 27.17, where the Pareto-efficient output of a public good is where the *SMC* curve cuts the *SMB* curve. It may appear to the alert reader that the idea of a positive *SMC* for a public good contradicts the idea of non-rivalness in consumption. Earlier in the chapter it was argued that the marginal cost of producing the good to an additional consumer is zero. The *SMC* does not measure the

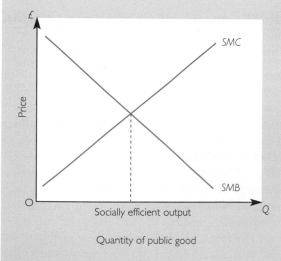

Figure 27.17 The socially efficient output of a public good

cost of providing the same level of defence to an extra person, but the cost of providing more defence to everyone. If the government buys additional fighter aircraft, the level of defence provision has been increased, and clearly the marginal cost of doing so amounts to several million pounds. When thinking about public goods, it is important to understand that there are two concepts of marginal cost. Samuelson appears to have solved the problem of the correct output levels of a public good in theory, but we are left with the problem of estimating people's willingness to pay.

Imperfect knowledge

We now drop the last of the conditions assumed in the first optimality theorem, that of perfect information. Lack of information is probably the most apparent cause of market failure to consumers. We have all no doubt experienced frustration from our less than perfect knowledge of the prices on offer, the qualities and range of commodities on offer and our weakness in resisting persuasive advertising. As workers we also are forced to make decisions based on incomplete information regarding, for example, the wage rates on offer in an area, the jobs available in other areas, even other countries, and career prospects in rival firms. When it comes to the decision to invest in human capital, i.e. in education and training, the problems become even more acute. How are we to know our aptitude for a particular career? What exactly are the best qualifications? How are we to know how future economic changes will affect the prospects from various careers? Producers face similar information problems concerning available supply prices for labour, raw materials and capital. They too face uncertainty when it comes to deciding on investment projects, e.g. will technological change make present processes unprofitable and hence obsolete? What will be the most profitable lines of production in the future? What are the most effective productive methods? Do rival firms have information not possessed by one's own firm?

It is the cost of information which causes many economic decisions to be less than optimal, thus resulting in inefficiency. Information gathering involves inputs of resource and time. In principle it is an easy matter to define the optimum level of 'search'. Search should continue up until the point at which the marginal benefit from search is equal to the marginal cost. However, there is a logical problem here: how can the benefit from extra search be calculated unless the content of the resulting information is known? But if the content of the piece of information is known, there is no need to search for it! As with public goods the application of the $SMC = SMB$ condition raises more problems than it solves.

Conclusion

In this chapter we have outlined the reasons free markets will not, in practice, result in Pareto efficiency. Our conclusion must thus be that it is impossible for a *laissez-faire* market economy to attain a state of Pareto efficiency. In the next chapters we will examine how analysis might be used to design policies intended to help real economies reach a more efficient state. However, we will also note arguments that claim that the first optimality theorem does not provide a fruitful point of departure when it comes to policy formation. We will additionally examine the concept of 'the maximisation of social welfare'; as we can see this is a broader concept than efficiency, in that the former includes considerations of equity as well as efficiency.

Summary

1 Welfare economics is concerned with both positive and normative questions. The notion of best considers both efficiency and equity.

2 Pareto efficiency (often referred to as Pareto optimality) requires that it must not be possible to change the allocation of resources in such a way that someone is made better off and no one worse off.

3 The first optimality theorem states that if in all markets there is perfect competition, no externalities and no market failure connected with uncertainty, then the resulting allocation of resources is Pareto efficient.

4 The social marginal benefit (SMB) is the monetary valuation of the marginal unit of consumption.

5 Social marginal cost (SMC) in one industry measures the valuation by consumers of the alternatives forgone by increasing the output of that industry by 1 unit.

6 Under the conditions stated, where the demand (SMB) curve intersects with the supply (SMC) curve, the resulting equilibrium price is Pareto optimal. Any other level of output involves a welfare loss.

7 When these conditions are met in all markets, there is said to be 'social' efficiency and this is often referred to less accurately as a socially 'optimum' allocation of resources. The conditions necessary for this result are described by the 'invisible hand' theorem.

8 The restriction of output involved in profit maximisation under imperfect competition brings about a welfare loss to society.

9 If monopolistic practices protect inefficient cost structures this also involves a welfare loss.

10 Externalities exist when the actions of producers or consumers affect third parties other than through the price mechanism.

11 Where changes in prices in one market influence other sectors of the economy this is said to be an external pecuniary effect, perhaps better described as 'price effect'.

12 Public goods are those where, at any given output, consumption by additional consumers does not reduce the quantity consumed by existing consumers. An example of this would be defence.

13 The socially efficient output of public goods is where the SMB curve intersects the SMC curve, but this is very difficult to determine.

14 Collective action by the voluntary sector is sometimes a viable alternative to intervention by the state to provide public goods. However, there are difficulties in mobilising collective action.

15 Imperfect knowledge is a major source of inefficiency in markets, both for consumers and producers.

16 Merit goods are normally defined as those distributed on the grounds of merit or need rather than by price. However, the essential reason goods such as health care are thought of as merit goods is the paternalistic consideration that fully informed consumers might not be the best judge of what is best for themselves.

17 Because of the problems caused by such things as externalities, ignorance and merit goods it is impossible for a fully *laissez-faire* economy to be socially efficient.

18 Even with an efficient price mechanism, problems of income distribution are likely to remain.

QUESTIONS

1 Discuss the statement: 'Because of their special training economists are in a better position than politicians to decide which economic policies should be implemented.'

2 'Economists are in agreement on the answers to positive questions; it is over normative issues that they disagree.' True or false?

3 Explain why Pareto efficiency is not necessarily the same thing as the 'best' situation.

4 Examine Figure 27.18 and rank points A, B, C, D and E in terms of Pareto optimality. Is a complete ranking possible? If not why not?

5 Assume that an economy consists of three consumers and two industries. The production function is such that, at present output levels, an increase in the output of barley of 4 units requires a reduction in the output of wheat of 1 unit. The rates at which the consumers are prepared to exchange wheat for barley are given by the following statements:

- Consumer A is prepared to sacrifice 1 unit of wheat for 5 units of barley
- Consumer B is prepared to sacrifice 1 unit of wheat for 3 units of barley
- Consumer C is prepared to sacrifice 1 unit of wheat for 1 unit of barley

  Demonstrate that this does not represent a Pareto-efficient product mix.

6 Assume that an economy has a fixed weekly output of milk and coal. This economy also has two groups of consumers, type A and type B. With the present distribution of output between consumers, group A consumers would be indifferent between a choice of 1 litre of milk and 5 kg of coal. Group B consumers, on the other hand, would be indifferent between a choice of 5 litres of milk and 1 kg of coal. Demonstrate that consumption is not Pareto efficient.

7 Assume that you are given the following information about a two-good, two-consumer economy. An increase in the production of oats of 1 tonne necessarily requires a reduction in the output of rye of 2 tonnes. If both consumers traded 1 tonne of oats for 2 tonnes of rye their levels of satisfaction would be unaltered. What can you say about the efficiency of the existing allocation of resources in this economy?

8 Consider the following two statements:

This so-called perfect market economy constitutes the formal basis for propositions about the advantages of perfect competition.   P. Bohm

Once we have cleansed the impurities in impure value judgement by a rational debate, we are left with factual statements and pure value judgements between which there is indeed an irreconcilable gulf on anyone's interpretation of the concept of 'facts' and the concept of 'values'.   M. Blaug

Attempt to reconcile these two statements.

9 Discuss the view that an unaided price mechanism ensures the best allocation of resources.

10 Demonstrate that if the monopolists were able to practise perfect price discrimination there would be no loss of welfare through inefficiency, i.e. output of the goods would be socially efficient (assume profit maximising behaviour). Explain why this situation might be held to conflict with equity considerations.

11 Assume that a monopolist equates *MR* and *MC* but does not minimise production costs. Draw a diagram indicating the total welfare loss to society resulting from inefficiency.

12 Discuss the view that not enough attention is given to the interest of future generations in taking economic decisions today. Give examples both for and against this argument.

13 Discuss the arguments for and against charging tuition fees for higher education.

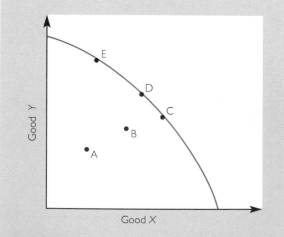

Figure 27.18

14 Explain why collective action is observed to be the preferred solution in the following cases:
   (a) trade unions;
   (b) Oxfam;
   (c) religious groups;
   (d) amateur football clubs.

15 Identify which of the terms on the left below are relevant to the industries on the right below:

   (a) Public good   (1) Water
   (b) Externality   (2) Defence
   (c) Monopoly   (3) Education
   (d) Equity   (4) Electricity
   (e) Collective action   (5) Healthcare
   (f) Merit goods   (6) Roads
   (g) Indivisibility   (7) Rail

Data response A
PRICES, OUTPUT AND WELFARE

Assume that there are two perfectly competitive industries, X and Y, and there is only one factor of production, labour. Labour has no non-monetary preference for working in either industry. The marginal product of labour in industry X, at the present level of output, is one ($MPP = 1$).

Now attempt the following questions:

1 If the wage in industry X is £100, what is the marginal cost (MC) in industry X?

2 The marginal product of labour in industry Y is two ($MPP = 2$) and the price of a unit of Y is £50. Assuming equilibrium, show that the MC of industry X measures the valuation by consumers of the number of units of Y forgone by increasing the output of industry X by 1 unit. (Remember that in perfect competition the wage equals the labour's marginal product multiplied by price.)

3 Using the above information explain why the equilibrium is said to be socially efficient.

4 Demonstrate how the equilibrium would be likely to change if there were an increase in the price of product X.

5 Explain the loss of welfare if the production of product X involved the output of negative externalities.

Inequality and public policy

Learning outcomes

At the end of this chapter you will be able to:
▶ Explain the main forms of taxation.
▶ Understand the arguments about taxes and incentives.
▶ Identify shifts that have taken place in the tax system.
▶ Recognise when criteria other than efficiency may be appropriate, such as paternalism or equity.

Structure of the chapter

This chapter is structured around an introduction to the tax–benefit system and four case studies of current issues in taxation. The introductory section sets out the facts on income and wealth distribution, the ways in which the main taxes work, and some basic concepts. Apart from that, the case studies are self-contained and can be taken in any order. They may be treated as data response articles. Student activities are to be found at the end of each case.

The distribution of income and wealth

In the previous chapter we presented the idea of efficiency as a criterion for economic decision making. In this chapter the often contrasting criterion of equity is considered together with conflicts between the two criteria. This will involve us in a careful consideration of the system of taxes and benefits in the UK together with redistribution in kind, but first we will look at the meaning of the term equity, and arguments for its use as a criterion in economic decision making.

Equity

Even given the attainment of Pareto efficiency, we cannot be sure that the outcome will be socially desirable. The initial distribution of wealth in society may result in a distribution of income with a few wealthy individuals at the top, and a large group of poor people at the bottom. If the labour market does not work well, there may be some people with no income at all without the assistance of charity or the welfare state. Even with a successful labour market, some people may be in this position because of an inability to work, due to sickness, disability, or old age. There is thus an argument for the state to intervene to help those in difficulties, by redistributing the incomes allocated by the market. Feelings of envy or injustice may also persuade politicians that money should be taken away from those who are very rich.

The extent and type of redistribution that you think should take place will depend on your personal value judgements, but economists have put forward a number of reasons why redistribution may be desirable. The *Utilitarians* in the nineteenth century put forward the idea that as income increased, the additional satisfaction gained from it decreased. This is an application of the law of diminishing marginal utility (see Chapter 40) to income. The law of diminishing marginal utility states that as people consume more of good, the utility they gain from each successive unit declines (cream cakes are often used to illustrate this). The utilitarians considered that this principle would apply to income as a whole.

Transferring income from the rich to the poor would therefore increase the some total of human happiness, because the poor would get more satisfaction than the rich for each pound transferred. This argument for redistribution has been criticised for two reasons. First utility is subjective and not measurable directly, and furthermore may differ between individuals. Second, the act of redistribution may change people's behaviour by creating disincentives for work or the accumulation of wealth. The 'cake' of national income may be divided more fairly, but it may be a smaller cake!

A second argument for redistribution, based on market failure, was put forward by **Hochman** and **Rodgers**. They argued that some people were naturally altruistic, and would be willing to transfer some of their income to those worse off than themselves. In utilitarian terms they gained more utility by bringing the income of their fellow human beings up to a certain minimum standard, than they would get from spending the money on themselves. The fact that many charities exist to help people in difficult circumstances supports this view of altruistic redistribution. The problem with this kind of redistribution is the market failure of poor information. It is easy enough to give money when there is a famine in Africa, but how do you know the circumstances of people begging on the streets? Will they spend the money on looking after themselves, or on drugs? How hard have they looked for work? Are they genuinely homeless? These problems of information lead us to the conclusion that the state must step in to establish who is deserving of redistribution. However, alongside market failure, we must also consider government failure (see Chapter 9). How good is the government at establishing who is really in need of assistance? The question of disincentives raised in the previous paragraph also applies here. Austrian economists (see Chapter 47) would argue that these problems mean that we must rely on individual choice and charity rather than state intervention.

A more left wing reason for redistribution, put forward by Marxists and Post-Keynesians (see Chapter 47) is that the market takes money from the poor by market power, and that therefore the poor are justified by taking the money back by political means. This idea of exploitation of the poor by the rich is used to justify democratic intervention in the market, to redress the balance. When the state does step in to redistribute income, there is always some ambiguity about the process. Is the state stepping in to act on behalf of altruistic voters who do not have enough information to act charitably, or is the democratic majority acting to offset market power by taking from the rich to give to the poor? There is a problem with the second of these two ideas. It is not generally the poor who decide elections. The 'floating voter' who holds the balance of power between left and right is usually in the middle income range. Some observers have argued that it is the middle classes who benefit most from redistribution.

A philosophical view put forward by **Rawls** is that when thinking about redistribution you should not consider where you are yourself in the income distribution. Rawls invites us to go 'behind a veil of ignorance' to the point just before we were born. It is in this position that we should make our decision about redistribution policy, without knowing if we are to be born into a rich family or a poor family, whether we have a strong physique or intelligence, whether we are good looking or not. Rawls argues that since most people are 'risk averse' at least when it comes to their whole life, they will choose a policy which does not disadvantage the worst off in society. Rawls' ideas still leave us with the questions about disincentives, since if redistribution leaves us with a 'smaller cake' then the worst off in society may not benefit.

The redistribution of income and wealth in the UK

Redistribution of income and wealth takes place by a number of means. Taxes are used to pay for public expenditure. The tax system can be structured so that richer people pay for a higher proportion of this expenditure. A substantial part of public expenditure consists of benefits to people in need of help from the state. Redistribution can also be 'in kind'. This is where, instead of receiving money income, people receive goods or services either subsidised or completely free. It is argued that this is where the middle classes benefit from redistributive policies, by more intensive use of free services such as libraries, education and health care. This final kind of redistribution is often termed 'merit goods' and is considered in the next section.

The distribution and redistribution of income is shown in Table 28.1 for 1997–8. The population is divided up into five 'quintiles', starting with the lowest 20 per cent of the income distribution and moving up to the highest. The redistribution effect is presented in two stages. First, the effect of the tax-benefit system is calculated for each quintile. Second, the amount of redistribution in kind is estimated, based on the use made of public services (education, health, etc.) by each quintile group (obviously this is an average figure). You will observe that after redistribution, the income for all households has fallen. This is because it is not possible to allocate all public expenditure on an income quintile basis.

The income of the lowest quintile is over three times higher after redistribution. The next highest quintile has grown by 62.7 per cent. The middle group remains approximately the same, while the next group loses income by 22.5 per cent, and the top group by 29.4 per cent. Considering all households lose 10 per cent (the last column) because of unallocated public expenditure, this is not a very considerable cost to the higher income groups. The top quintile still earns approximately four times as much after redistribution as the bottom quintile. Is this enough to maintain incentives in society? We will return to this question in Case study 28.3.

The distribution of wealth is much more unequal than the distribution of income, as can be seen by inspecting Table 28.2. It can also be seen that apart from the very rich, whose share has fallen slightly, the distribution of wealth has been getting wider in recent decades. This widening can be seen to be more extreme if housing is excluded from the calculations. The way in which this wealth is held is shown in Table 28.3. The total of wealth at £3892 bn in 1998 is approximately 4.5 times the size of GDP in that year.

Table 28.2 The distribution of UK wealth

		% owned by (marketable wealth)		% owned by (marketable wealth less value of dwelling)	
		1976	1996	1976	1996
Top	1%	21	19	29	27
	5%	38	39	47	50
	10%	50	52	57	63
	25%	71	74	73	82
	50%	92	93	88	94

Source: *Social Trends 2000*, National Statistics. © Crown Copyright 2001.

Table 28.3 Composition of net wealth (1998) (per cent)

Life assurance/pensions funds	38
Residential buildings net of loans	25
Securities/shares	15
Notes/coins/deposits	15
Other	7

Source: *Social Trends 2000*, National Statistics. © Crown Copyright 2001.

Table 28.1 The distribution and re-distribution of UK household income 1997–8

	Bottom quintile	Next quintile	Middle quintile	Next quintile	Top quintile	All
Original Income	2520	6780	15530	25960	47610	19680
Plus benefits minus tax	4540	7730	12180	17460	31520	14690
Plus benefits in kind*	8430	11030	15330	20120	33590	17700*

* Not all government expenditure is allocatable.
Source: *Social Trends 2000*, National Statistics. © Crown Copyright 2001

Merit goods

Problems of definition

Merit goods can be defined as:

Those products or services that are not distributed through the price system but on the basis of merit or need.

The concept of merit goods is somewhat controversial and is often confused with information and externality problems. Thus health care is often given as an example of a merit good. It is argued that consumers will not know in advance if they are going to need expensive health treatment and thus might underinvest in health insurance; however this is just a market failure due to a lack of information. Alternatively, it is argued that health care benefits people other than just the recipient, and should therefore be subsidised. This analysis is also correct but is an argument based on positive externalities.

The essential reasons why health care and other products might be thought of as merit goods is the idea that fully informed consumers might not be the best judge of what is good for them. This, of course, immediately begs the question, 'Who is the best judge?' It is thus best to state that merit goods arise from a divergence between the values of society (as expressed through government) and the values of individuals. Hence smokers might be fully informed of the health risks to themselves yet society might feel obliged to act in a paternalistic manner by discouraging this activity through taxation. Tobacco, in this case, would be an example of a 'de-merit' good; drugs and pornography might be considered to be other examples. Products considered by governments to be undervalued by many citizens have included opera and art in general, libraries and milk.

Obviously where addiction is involved, e.g. as with a drug addict, consumers themselves might admit that their own immediate preferences are not in their best interests. However, this raises the very deep problems of free will and the determination of tastes. As sociologists point out, the assumption of 'given tastes' is extremely naïve. This again emphasises that modern welfare economics is normative rather than positive; the above analysis implicitly assumes that individuals are the best judges of their own best interest, but individuals' tastes are bound to be influenced by the nature of the society in which the individuals live. How then can they be sure that the present goals, both of themselves and society, are those that will lead to the greatest human happiness? It is considerations such as these that lead some individuals to feel justified in overriding the preferences of others.

Merit goods and future generations

If we accept the definition of merit goods as arising from the fact that consumers might not be the best judges of what is best for themselves, we may see that this is allied to the problems of future generations. If people currently alive cannot take economic decisions in their own best interests, how should we evaluate the welfare of future generations? Investment and consumption decisions taken today often have effects extending far into the future, nuclear waste and indestructible plastics being obvious examples.

Some commentators have argued that advancing technology and economic growth will mean improved living standards. Hence economic decisions should be weighted in favour of existing generations. Other observers argue that pollution, the depletion of non-renewable resources and rapid world population growth will lead to crises. Hence economic decisions should be weighted in favour of the future rather than the present. The essential point for the analysis outlined in the previous chapter is that future generations, and the destitute and animals, have no money votes. Hence their preferences are ignored by the price mechanism. Society then might decide that policies that protect the interests of future generations are desirable, as the wishes of these generations cannot be directly reflected by their own 'money votes' or laws in the present. This issue is explored further in Chapter 40.

Understanding the tax–benefit system

The tax system is a complicated system of laws that are updated and changed annually in the

Chancellor's budget. The law on tax is frequently tested in the courts on questions of interpretation. The objective of this chapter is not to make you an expert on the tax system, but to show how taxation has an impact on the economy. In the course of understanding the impact on the economy, you will have to learn the basics of how the tax system works.

Taxation is studied for its effects on the whole economy (macroeconomics) and its effect on individuals, firms and markets (microeconomics). We have already studied the way in which taxes levied on the retailer may be passed on to the consumer in Chapter 6. We have also discussed its role in fiscal policy.

This chapter concentrates on the details of the taxes, recent changes in the system, and their effects on incentives. A case study approach is taken to focus on different aspects of the tax system, but first a familiarity with the whole tax system is needed.

Why is taxation necessary?

Taxation is needed to finance public expenditure. There are three other methods of financing public expenditure. One is by selling off publicly owned assets (privatisation, discussed in Chapter 24), but this has only financed a tiny proportion of public expenditure. There is a limit to this source of finance because eventually there will be no further assets to sell. Second, borrowing can finance expenditure, but this is just putting off taxation into the future. The National Debt has never been repaid in full, but tax is needed to pay the interest on the National Debt. Third, public expenditure can be financed by direct charges to the users of the service, such as prescription charges for medicines prescribed by doctors in the National Health Service.

The main taxes

The study of taxation is a whole subject in itself, and many people make a living out of keeping up to date with changes in the system and advising individuals and companies. What follows in this section is a very introductory description of the main taxes in use in the UK today. The rates of tax quoted are for 1999–2000. It is possible to

find the up-to-date rates and allowances for the current year by consulting *Tax Which?* or various tax guides published by newspapers and banks. The contribution of each tax to total tax revenue is shown in Table 28.4.

Table 28.4 Central government tax revenues by source, 1999 (£bn)

Income tax	93.7
Corporation tax	32.8
VAT	55.3
Business rates	20.6
Social security contributions	53.0
Fuel duties	22.4
Vehicle excise	4.8
Stamp Duty	6.0
Tobacco	3.7
Alcohol	6.4

Source: *Financial Statistics*, June 2000, National Statistics. © Crown Copyright 2001

Direct taxes

Direct taxes are those levied on the income or earnings of an individual or an organisation. The basic rates can be found in Table 28.5. These are the most important revenue raisers for the government and can be considered under four headings.

Table 28.5 Top and basic tax rates: changes

	1979	1979	1986	1987	1988	1996	1997
Top	83	60	60	60	40	40	40
Basic	33	30	29	27	25	24	23

(a) *Taxes on income.* Before taxing an individual's personal income, personal and other allowances are first deducted. After these tax allowances have been deducted, what is left of a person's income is known as taxable income. For example, if a person had an income of £10 000 p.a. and allowances of £4335, taxable income would be £5665. The marginal rate of tax is the amount of tax a person would pay on each successive unit of taxable income. In 1999/2000 a person paid 10 per cent on the first £1500 of taxable income and 23 per cent on the next £26 500 of taxable income. Taxes on savings income were paid at 20 per cent up to an overall income of £28 000. Only the reasonably well paid would pay the top rate of 40 per cent on taxable income above £28 000. Such a tax is said to be progressive because it takes proportionately more from people with higher incomes. This idea is illustrated in Figure 28.1. The average rate of tax can be calculated by dividing gross income (income before tax) by actual tax paid and converting it into a percentage marginal and average tax rates are perhaps best presented in an algebraic manner:

$$\text{Marginal rate of tax} = \frac{\text{Increase in tax paid}}{\text{Increase in income}} \times \frac{100}{1}$$

or

$$\text{Marginal rate of tax} = \Delta T / \Delta Y$$

The average rate of tax is:

$$\text{Average rate of tax} = \frac{\text{Total tax paid}}{\text{Total income}}$$

or

$$\text{Average rate of tax} = T/Y$$

With progressive taxes it is the case that the marginal rate is higher than the average rate; that is:

$$\Delta T / \Delta Y > T/Y$$

(b) *Corporation tax.* This is the tax levied on the profits of companies. In 1999/2000 the rate of tax started at 20 per cent for small businesses in line with tax on savings income. The

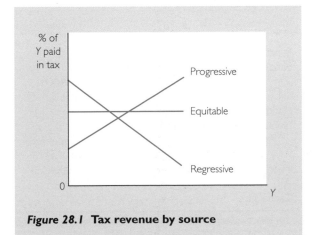

Figure 28.1 **Tax revenue by source**

main rate was 30 per cent. When taxpayers receive dividends from companies that have paid corporation tax, the Inland Revenue treats that income as already taxed at the standard income tax rate of 23 per cent. It can be seen therefore that, in effect, dividends from larger companies are taxed at a rate 10 per cent higher than other types of savings income. This is often justified because of the legal privileges granted to companies. The privilege of limited liability means that shareholders lose a maximum of the capital they put into the company if it should go bankrupt. On the other hand supply side economists argue that this higher rate of tax is a disincentive to investment, enterprise and risk taking.

Corporation tax rates have moved down considerably from the 50 per cent rates that obtained in the 1970s. The new Labour government has shown a willingness to continue with this process. Tax revenues from corporation tax have increased, however, because allowances have been reduced. In the 1970s, industrial companies were allowed to set investment expenditure in the current year against profits before taxes were calculated.

(c) *Taxes on capital.* Capital as such is not taxed, but tax is paid when capital is sold or transferred. The most important taxes are capital gains tax and inheritance tax. After a tax free allowance of £7100 (1999–2000), capital gains are taxed as a part of a person's income. Any increase that is solely due to inflation is also disregarded. The first £231 000 (1999–2000) of a person's estate on death are tax free but after that a marginal tax rate of 40 per cent applies.

(d) *National insurance.* Although not officially classed as a tax, national insurance contributions are in effect a proportional tax, i.e. it takes a constant percentage of income up to a ceiling of £500 (1999/2000) a week, upon employer and employees alike. Originally contributions used to be a fixed rate 'stamp' and could be regarded as a price for an insurance service offered by the state rather than as a tax. While the standard rate of tax has been falling, national insurance contributions have been rising. A lower earnings rate of £66 a week (1999/2000) must be reached before national insurance becomes payable.

Indirect taxes

Indirect taxes are usually taxes on expenditure. They are so called because the tax is not directly on income, but on expenditure. For example, in the case of the duty on whisky it is the distiller who must pay the tax. The *formal* incidence of the tax is said to be on the distiller. The tax is then 'shifted' down the chain of distribution until the burden (or *effective* incidence) of the tax falls also upon the consumer. The determination of the incidence of tax is explained in Chapter 6.

These are the main forms of indirect tax in the UK:

(a) *Customs and excise duty*. Customs duty may be levied on goods coming into the country but this only accounts for 1 per cent of government revenues. Excise duty is levied on a commodity, no matter where it is produced; it is a specific tax, i.e. it is levied per unit of the commodity irrespective of its price. The main duties are on tobacco, alcohol and petrol.

(b) *Value added tax (VAT)*. The most important of indirect taxes, VAT was first introduced in 1973 when it replaced purchase tax. VAT is an *ad valorem* tax, i.e. it is levied on the selling price of the commodity. There are currently three rates of VAT: zero, 5 and 17.5 per cent. Unlike purchase tax, which was only collected from retailers, it is collected from each stage of production. Each company pays VAT on the full selling price of its products, but can claim it back on its purchases from outside the firm. The difference between its sales and its purchases is *value added*.

Taxes on expenditure are generally said to be regressive, i.e. they take a larger percentage of the incomes of the lower paid. The reason for this is that poorer people spend a higher proportion of their income. On the other hand, zero rated or exempt goods like food and children's clothes form a higher proportion of poor people's budget. It can be seen that the actual average rate of tax paid will be different for everyone and will depend on their spending pattern.

Are some taxes really prices?

Other indirect taxes include car purchase tax, road fund and television licences, betting tax and stamp duty. It is sometimes argued that these taxes are really more like prices, paying for goods and services provided by the public sector, such as television and roads. The revenue from these taxes is not necessarily spent on the relevant industry, however. The Treasury rejected a link between tax revenue on a sector of the economy and the amount spent on it (known as *hypothecation*). The last case of hypothecation – between road taxes and expenditure on roads – was abandoned in 1926. Supporters of the 'dump the pump' campaign (see Chapter 14) would argue that a link should be restored as they argue they are currently over-taxed.

STUDENT ACTIVITY 28.1

Using the tax rates and allowances in Table 28.6 calculate the total tax paid and the marginal and average rates of tax for a single person with an income of:

(a) £10 000   (b) £25 000   (c) £40 000

Which income group has the lowest marginal rate of tax? Draw a graph to illustrate how progressive the system is (see Figure 28.1).
(Note: Count national insurance contributions as a tax in your calculations.)

Table 28.6 Current tax rates

Allowances		1999/2000
Personal allowance		4335
Bands	10%	1–1500
	23%	1501–28000
	40%	28000 +
National insurance per week (annual equivalents in brackets)		
	10%	66–500 per week (26000 p.a.)
Inheritance	0%	0–231000
	40%	231000+
Capital gains	0%	0–7100

An engineering company sells 1000 machines a year at £1000 each. Its purchases of raw materials are £300 000 a year and other expenditure (office supplies, telephone, computers, etc.) comes to £50 000. Its labour bill is £500 000 a year and a gross profit of £150 000 is achieved. What will its net value added tax bill be after claiming back VAT on purchases?

Understanding the benefit system

The benefit system is very complex and often subject to change. We will outline the most important features of the system here and some of the main types of benefit that apply.

(a) The old age pension is based on national insurance contributions and is not means tested.
(b) Jobseeker's allowance is payable to people who are looking for work and replaced the old unemployment benefit.
(c) Sickness and disability allowance is payable to people who are unable to work for health reasons.
(d) Child benefit is a non-means tested benefit.
(e) Housing benefit is a means tested benefit paid to people on low incomes who need assistance with their housing costs (usually rent).
(f) Working families tax credit is paid to low income families which have at least one adult in part-time or full-time work, but have not reached a threshold level of income. It is means tested and is gradually withdrawn as the threshold level of income is reached.

Means tested benefits contribute to the poverty trap discussed in Case study 28.3 below.

Case study 28.1
WHAT MAKES A GOOD TAX?

Taxation is a controversial topic. There is disagreement about the purposes of taxes and what constitutes a good tax. More fundamentally there is argument about the effects of taxation upon the economy. The eighteenth-century economist **Adam Smith** was the first to put forward a set of economic principles to guide policy makers.

The canons of taxation

Adam Smith laid down four *canons* (criteria) of taxation. Although taxes have changed a great deal the principles still remain good today. A good tax, said Smith, should have the following characteristics:

(a) *Equitable.* A good tax should be based upon the ability to pay. Today, progressive income tax means that those with higher incomes pay not only a larger amount but also a greater proportion of their income in tax.
(b) *Economical.* A good tax should not be expensive to administer and the greatest possible proportion of it should accrue to the government as revenue. In general, indirect taxes are cheaper to collect than direct taxes, but they are not, however, so equitable.
(c) *Convenient.* This means that the method and frequency of the payment should be convenient to the taxpayer. The introduction of pay as you earn (PAYE) made income tax much easier to pay for most people.
(d) *Certain.* The tax should be formulated so that taxpayers are certain of how much they have to pay and when. This information is widely available today, but is often poorly understood.

Modern economists would add to this list:

(e) *Flexible.* A good taxation system should be readily adaptable to changing circumstances such as changing price levels. VAT goes up automatically as prices rise, but excise taxes do not.
(f) *The benefit principle.* As government expenditure increasingly provides services for 'voter-consumers', it is argued that taxes should be regarded as a kind of price. If people receive the service then they should be paying the 'tax-price'. This principle is often in conflict with the idea of progressivity as will be seen in Case study 28.4 on local taxation.

The redistribution of income

All political parties subscribe to the view that the fiscal system should be used to **redistribute income**. A right-wing view might be that this should be just sufficient to redress the worst inequalities in the economy while left-wingers might wish to see something more drastic done to effect a fundamental shift from the rich to the poor. The redistribution of income is achieved by taking more tax from richer people and giving benefits to poorer people. The provision of free services like health and education also in effect redistributes income.

Progressivity, regressivity and equity

A progressive tax system is one where richer people pay a higher proportion of their income in tax. A good example of a progressive tax is income tax, as the tax rate goes up as income goes up. A regressive tax is one which results in richer people paying a smaller proportion of their income in tax. A good example of a regressive tax is the TV licence, or the poll tax (see Case study 28.4). When all taxpayers pay the same proportion of their income in tax, the system is said to be equitable. Taxes on expenditure come closest to being equitable. Rich people save a higher proportion of their income and avoid paying some expenditure tax in this way making it slightly regressive. On the other hand, poor people spend a higher proportion of their income on goods like food that are exempt from tax, which makes the tax more progressive. These three concepts were illustrated earlier in Figure 28.1.

STUDENT ACTIVITY 28.3

Use Smith's canons of taxation to assess the following taxes:

(a) income tax
(b) VAT
(c) TV licence
(d) Excise duty on beer

Case study 28.2
THE SHIFT TO EXPENDITURE TAXATION

The aspect of the economy that is being taxed is called a tax base. There are four tax bases: income; expenditure; wealth; and existence. The taxation of income is sometimes criticised for taxing what people put into the economy (their labour, capital, land, enterprise), rather than what they take out. A tax on expenditure is based on what people take out of the economy (goods and services). The taxation of income would appear to discourage people from supplying factors of production to the economy. It would also appear to discourage savings that are

needed for investment. Both these disincentives form part of the supply side argument that will be developed in Chapter 39. The arguments about the supply of labour are discussed in Case study 28.3 below. The great advantage of taxing income is that it enables the government to achieve its aims on the redistribution of income.

One of the main changes that have taken place in the last 20 years is the shift away from the taxation of income and towards the taxation of expenditure. Income tax rates have been reduced, especially on higher incomes, and expenditure taxes have been increased, particularly VAT. The main changes that have taken place are discussed below.

Reduction in top income tax rates

● *Common misunderstanding*

In 1979 the top marginal rate of tax on income was 83 per cent. This does not, of course, mean that 83 per cent of a person's income would be taken in tax (that would be an average rate of 83 per cent). The 83 per cent rate was only to be collected on taxable income above the 83p tax threshold. In addition, if more than a certain amount of the person's income was from investment (interest, dividends, etc.) then an investment income surcharge of 15 per cent was collected from this income. This meant that the top marginal rate of tax was effectively 98 per cent. There can be little doubt that such tax rates create disincentives to work or invest. These rates were pointless in a different way, however. Anybody who earned that amount of money could also afford the best tax accountants to advise them on how to avoid paying such high rates of tax by using tax loopholes.

After their return to power in 1979, the Conservative government soon reduced the top rate of tax to 60 per cent and then reduced it further to 40 per cent in 1987. This is one of the lowest top rates of tax in the industrialised world.

Reduction in the standard rate of tax

The standard rate of tax was also gradually reduced from 33 per cent to 23 per cent in 1997, with a new initial 20 per cent band introduced in the 1990s which was then lowered to 10 per cent. This decrease in the standard rate was partly offset by increases in the national insurance contribution. The objective of the Conservatives was to widen the 20 per cent band sufficiently so that it could be regarded as the standard rate. The reductions of the top and standard rates of tax are shown in Table 28.5.

● Common misunderstanding

It is commonly thought that, since the rate of tax on income has gone down considerably in the way described in the two sections above, tax as a whole has gone down. This is not the case because increases in other taxes have more than offset the reductions in income tax, as can be seen in Tables 28.5 and 28.6.

Increases in the rate of VAT

When the Conservatives came to power in 1979 there were two rates of VAT: 8 per cent on standard commodities and 12.5 per cent on luxury items. In 1980 a uniform rate of 15 per cent was introduced which was later raised to 17.5 per cent.

Increases in the scope of VAT

The scope of a tax is the range of items on which it can be raised. Some categories of expenditure are exempt from VAT or are zero-rated. A number of items have recently been included in the VAT net, most notably takeaway foods such as fish and chips and domestic fuels (electricity and gas). VAT on domestic fuel was introduced at the rate of 8 per cent. Although the plan was to impose the higher 17.5 per cent rate on domestic fuel, political pressure resulted in the rate staying at 8 per cent. Since its election the Labour government has reduced this rate to 5 per cent, the lowest that the EU would allow (once a country introduces VAT on a product, EU rules state that it cannot be removed). Food, books, children's clothing and newspapers remain free of VAT but future governments may tap these sources of revenue.

Cross-border shopping

Taxes on alcohol have been reduced recently because of cross-border shopping to France. This is a good example of the bizarre behaviour that a badly designed tax can encourage. British alcoholic products are shipped to Calais where they are sold to British residents who have crossed the Channel to buy them cheaply. The British residents then bring the alcohol back to the UK! Who gains from these extraordinary

transactions? Well clearly the French government gains extra revenue as do the ferry companies, Eurotunnel and the entrepreneurs involved in shipping the products out and selling them in France. The British residents who visit France clearly do better than they would have done if they had bought their alcohol at home, but they have been inconvenienced by having to take such a long trip (unless they were going to France in any case). The clear loser is the UK government with a loss of tax revenue.

The double taxation of savings: TESSAs, PEPs and ISAs

Advocates of expenditure tax argue that saving is taxed more heavily than consumption. This is because saving takes place from taxed income, and then the income from the savings (interest, dividends, etc.) is taxed again. To avoid this, tax-exempt special savings accounts (TESSAs) were introduced. Taxpayers were allowed to put a certain amount into TESSAs each year over a five-year period. Providing they did not touch the money until the end of the period they would not pay any tax on the interest. PEPs worked in a similar way but applied to savings used to buy shares, rather than savings in bank and building society accounts. In the case of PEPs, it was dividends and capital gains that were free from tax. These two systems were combined into ISAs (investment savings accounts) which allowed people a mix of cash savings and investments in securities.

Investment income

Taxation on income from investment was eased in a number of other ways. The basic rate of 20 per cent was applied to all interest from bank and building society accounts in 1996. Indexation was introduced on capital gains. Capital gains tax is charged on any increase in the value of assets when they are sold (the house you live in is exempt). In periods of inflation the price of an asset may rise, but its value may not go up in real terms after allowing for inflation. In periods of inflation capital gains tax may be a tax on inflation, not on real increases in income. Indexation therefore improved the tax situation of people who put their savings in shares. Contributions to pension funds up to a certain percentage of income continue to be allowable against income tax and a tax-free lump sum can be paid in the year of retirement.

Bucking the trend: insurance

Two areas of savings have been treated more harshly since 1979. Premiums paid into an endowment life assurance policy used to be allowable against income tax. An endowment life assurance policy invests the policy-holder's savings over an agreed number of years. At the end of the agreed period (or when the policy holder dies, whichever is the sooner) the policy holder receives a large lump sum or endowment. Since 1984 tax allowances have not been available for new endowment policies, although the old ones have continued to benefit. A rationale for this change is provided by the attitude to risk of the life assurance companies. Since they needed to provide a large lump sum some distance in the future to satisfy their customers, it was argued that they would tend to go for safe, low-risk investments. This may not be the best strategy for an entrepreneurial capitalist economy. The shift away from preferential tax treatment for life assurance can be justified on supply side grounds.

Housing

The tax advantages of owning a home have been reduced in the period since 1979. Home owners who are in the process of buying a house used to be allowed to set the interest on their loans against income for tax purposes. The extent to which they were able to do this was progressively reduced in recent years, until the allowance was finally phased out altogether in 1999. First a ceiling of £25 000 was placed on such tax allowances. Home owners were able to set the interest on the first £25 000 of their mortgage against tax, but any borrowing above that level received no further tax exemption. This ceiling was raised only once, to £30 000, but remained at that level until the interest allowance was phased out in 1999. At the time of its introduction this ceiling seemed quite high and the majority of mortgage holders continued to receive full tax exemption.

Inflation gradually reduced the real value of the ceiling. The success of the Conservative government in curbing inflation in the early 1990s meant that the £30 000 ceiling was no longer being eroded away quickly in real terms. The government acted to cut tax exemption in another way. The rate at which the mortgage holder could claim exemption was progressively reduced to 15 per cent. Someone with a mortgage of £30 000 paying 10 per cent interest with a marginal tax rate of 40 per cent was entitled to a tax exemption of £1200 on the £3000 interest bill before the changes. After the changes the exemption had been reduced in value to £450. The Labour government has continued this trend, first reducing the exemption rate to 10 per cent in their first budget in June 1997, and then abolishing the allowance altogether in 1999.

● *Common misunderstanding*

It may seem odd that a government that claimed it wanted to create a 'property-owning democracy' should remove many of the financial benefits of home ownership. The answer can be found in the same supply side argument used in the previous section. Home ownership is not the kind of risky but potentially successful investment that a dynamic capitalist economy should concentrate on. It must be pointed out, however, that housing continues to receive favourable tax treatment. It is still the case that a person's first house is exempt from capital gains tax (a second house is regarded as a business venture with potential for rent). Some exemption of interest against tax remains. Housing also can be regarded as non-pecuniary income which escapes taxation. If you do not own a home you have to rent from a landlord. The rent you pay is regarded as part of the landlord's taxable income. If you own your own house you can be thought of as your own landlord, but the benefit of the house does not pass through the market, so you pay no tax on it.

The large increase in home ownership in the UK had nothing to do with the tax treatment of housing which became less favourable in the 1980s and 1990s, but had more to do with the subsidised sale of council houses, the house price boom of the mid-1980s and changes in attitudes. The collapse of house prices in the early 1990s left many people with mortgages larger than the value of their homes. This position of so-called 'negative equity' made people more cautious. However, confidence returned to the market by the end of the decade with a fresh round of house price inflation (see Chapter 11).

Conclusion

It can be seen that most tax changes over the last 20 years have been shifting the balance of taxation towards an expenditure base and away from an income base. The two notable exceptions of housing and life insurance can be justified on supply side grounds. The reduction of high marginal tax rates may have had the benefit of reducing disincentive effects for top earners (see Case study 28.3) but also has made the tax system less progressive (see Case study 28.4). The changes have almost certainly made saving more attractive.

STUDENT ACTIVITY 28.4

Work out the value of tax relief in monetary and percentage terms on a mortgage of:

(a) £10 000
(b) £30 000
(c) £60 000

Use current mortgage interest rates.

STUDENT ACTIVITY 28.5

Explain how a rich person can avoid paying tax in ways that are not open to a poorer person.

Case study 28.3
DIRECT TAXES: A DISINCENTIVE TO WORK?

Supply side economists argue that taxes, particularly taxes on income, are a disincentive to work. It is argued that if taxes are cut this will increase incentives because people will be receiving more for their efforts. Thus people will work harder. This will increase productivity and, as the economy expands, create more employment. There will, therefore, be a rise in the level of real national income. If this is the case then it is possible that a greater total amount of tax may be paid. This was the argument put forward by **A. Laffer**.

This argument was accepted by President Reagan in the early 1980s and by the UK Chancellor, Nigel Lawson, in the late 1980s, and was the basis of their tax-cutting budgets.

Income and substitution effects

It seems intuitively correct that high taxes would make working less attractive as there is less take-home pay for each hour's work. On the other hand it can be argued that raising taxes would increase effort as people struggle to maintain their level of disposable income. They might not like higher taxes but, at the end of the month, they have to find the money to pay their mortgage, the electricity bill and so on and are thus forced to work harder.

These two arguments can be restated in terms of the *substitution effect* and the *income effect* explained in Chapter 5. Suppose that we look at the problem in terms of the 'cost' of leisure. If we raise the rate of tax then we reduce the opportunity cost of leisure, because an extra hour's leisure consumed costs less in terms of income forgone. If the substitution effect predominates people may, therefore, work less hard. They are, as it were, 'buying' more leisure because it is cheaper. The substitution effect is associated with the marginal tax rate since this is the tax rate, which applies to the last unit of work effort.

Alternatively, we could argue that increasing taxes reduces people's income and we could, therefore, look at demand for leisure from the point of view of an income effect. As we know, *ceteris paribus*, if income decreases, the demand for a normal good will decrease. If leisure is a normal good, then reducing take-home incomes by raising taxes will decrease the demand for leisure. In other words people will work harder. They are, in effect, 'buying' less leisure because they are poorer and cannot afford it. The income effect is associated with the average tax rate because it measures the percentage by which income has been reduced.

It appears that economic theory on its own cannot settle this question. If taxes are raised, what will happen to the total amount of effort supplied by the labour force will depend upon whether the income effect or the substitution effect is stronger. These alternatives are illustrated in Figure 28.2. Empirical studies to determine which of the two effects are stronger is the only way forward.

Institutional constraints

Apart from the problem of whether people actually regard the situation in this light we have the problem as to whether they can vary their effort at will. For example, if you are a salaried worker then working 10 per cent harder (or less hard) probably has little or no effect upon your immediate wage packet, although it might increase your chances of promotion. If

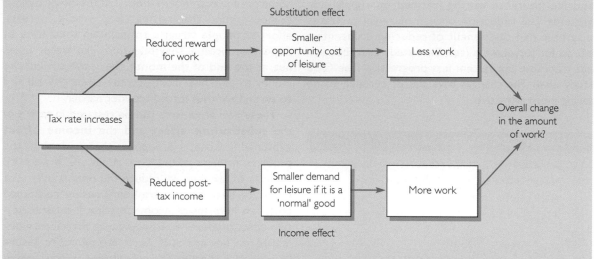

Figure 28.2 Income versus substitution effects – non-determinacy
Raising taxes could cause some people to work harder and others to work less hard. The overall effect depends upon which predominates, the income effect or the substitution effect.

overtime is recognised and paid for, the fact that a person is willing to work overtime is no guarantee that it will be available. If trade unions have negotiated a standard working week (usually somewhere between 35 and 40 hours) then variation of work effort may be quite difficult in practice.

Microeconomic evidence

(a) *Interview evidence.* The balance of evidence from interviews is that there is a slight disincentive effect of higher taxation. The two classic studies quoted are Break (1956) and Fields and Stanbury (1968), but these results have been replicated subsequently. Both interviewed professional people (accountants and lawyers) who could vary their hours of work. It has been noted above that not all workers have this flexibility. Break found that 77 per cent of respondents reported no change in work effort when taxes were increased and only 13 per cent reported disincentive effects as against 10 per cent reporting incentive effects. Fields and Stanbury found slightly higher disincentive effects at 19 per cent with 11 per cent reporting incentive effects, but both studies find the majority of people unaffected.

(b) *Statistical evidence.* Likewise, most microeconomic statistical studies have found inelastic labour supply curves when wages or taxes

change. The only exception to this is the more elastic labour supply of married women. (For those feminists among you, you should note that this is merely a report of how married women do behave, not how they should behave!)

Macroeconomic arguments

Alongside the monetarist revolution of the 1970s came the switch of emphasis to the supply side of the economy. In its earliest phase this consisted mainly of the argument that the problems of the economy could be solved by cutting taxes. Later, other government policies which were thought to constrain supply were included such as planning laws and red tape. The position of the **supply siders** is in some ways similar to the Austrians (see Chapter 47) the further down this line of argument the supply siders go. There is even a concern about the supply side from Keynesians about education and training of the workforce. As you might expect, this Keynesian supply side argument requires an increase in government spending.

The Laffer curve

There is the possibility, pointed out by **Professor Art Laffer** of the USA, that increasing tax rates might, because of the disincentive effect, actually lower tax revenue. Laffer based his argument on the logic that tax revenue would be zero if tax rates were either zero or 100 per cent. If they were zero, obviously no tax would be collected. If they were 100 per cent, all one's income would be taken in tax and then there would be no incentive to work and therefore no income to tax. As real-world tax rates are positioned between zero and 100 per cent, Laffer concluded that there must be a tax rate at which the revenue is maximised. As tax rates rise, initially revenue would also rise as shown in Figure 28.3. At some point, A, tax revenue would reach a maximum and start to fall.

Michael Beenstock made an early estimate of the effects of the Laffer curve for the UK which suggested that a 5 per cent reduction in taxation would result in a 15 per cent increase in GDP. Beenstock's estimates suggest that a peak in the revenue would be reached at an average tax rate of around 60 per cent; only those with an overriding passion for equality would be prepared to squeeze out the last drops of potential revenue. This is because, due to the rounded top of the Laffer curve, these last drops are at the expense of comparatively large increases in the average tax rate.

Tax revenue and GDP

There is a simple mathematical relationship between average tax rates, national income and tax revenue:

$$T = Y \times t$$

where T is tax revenue and t is the average tax rate. Therefore:

$$Y = T/t$$

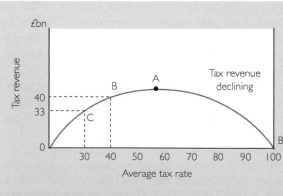

Figure 28.3 **The Laffer curve**

We can use this relationship to explain the effects Laffer was predicting. In Figure 28.3 at point B an average tax rate of 40 per cent (or 0.4) generates tax revenue of £40bn. National income (Y) is therefore equal to £40bn/0.4 or £100bn. A reduction of tax rates to 30 per cent generates a tax revenue of £33bn so national income has risen to £110bn. These numbers are illustrative only and do not reflect any real economy.

Direct taxes: a disincentive to work?

Supply side economists argue that taxes are a disincentive to effort. It is argued that if taxes are cut this will increase incentives because people will be receiving more for their efforts. Thus people will work harder. This will increase productivity and, as the economy expands, create more employment. There will, therefore, be a rise in the level of real national income. If this is the case then it is even possible that a greater total amount of tax may be paid. This was essentially the argument put forward by Laffer.

This argument was accepted by President Ronald Reagan and by Chancellor Nigel Lawson and was the basis of their tax-cutting budgets in the 1980s. (In the USA, at the same time as tax cuts there were massive budget deficits. Logically, therefore, it would be difficult to separate the supply side effects from those of a conventional Keynesian fiscal boost.)

The evidence put forward by Laffer and Beenstock conflicts with much of the microeconomic evidence considered in the previous section, which found only weak evidence that the substitution effect outweighed the income effect. There are criticisms of the Laffer curve approach, mainly from a Keynesian direction. First, there is criticism of the use of the average tax rate when it is remembered that it is the marginal tax rate which is associated with the substitution effect (see above). Second, as noted above, where government spending is not reduced, then cutting taxes will have a fiscal expansionary effect. Keynesians believe that it is this demand side effect which increases output. Supply siders reject this idea, arguing that fiscal policy doesn't work, because increased government borrowing will push up interest rates and reduce demand in the private sector (consumption and investment) as a result. They argue that it must therefore be a supply side effect. As you can see, we are back to the argument between Keynesians and monetarists which will be considered in more detail in Section VII.

Other supply side policies

The supply siders started with tax reduction, but moved on to all kinds of government intervention which prevents entrepreneurial activity, ranging from bureaucratic rules, planning permission, legal support for trade unions. The reform of the welfare state to get rid of the culture of welfare dependency and replace it with one of entrepreneurial activity is also high on their list. The introduction of 'workfare' schemes which tie the receipt of benefit to undertaking some work is the major policy innovation in this area.

STUDENT ACTIVITY 28.6

Explain the effects of a cut in taxes from the viewpoint of:

(a) a supply sider;
(b) a Keynesian.

Tax reform

The poverty trap

One of the worst features of the fiscal system is the **poverty trap**. As Figure 28.4 indicates the poorest people in the economy are the ones facing the highest marginal rates of tax. This is because the tax system and the benefit system overlap. A person who earns a small income may also receive benefit. Until the reforms of the social security system in 1988 marginal tax rates of more than 100 per cent were common. Marginal tax rates are not usually above

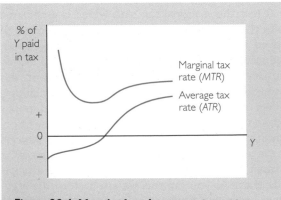

Figure 28.4 Marginal and average tax rates

80 per cent on the poorest group in society now, but this still represents by far the highest marginal rate in the tax system. The working families tax credit system (see above) has improved the situation slightly, as has the introduction of the 10p starting rate of tax.

The reason why the poorest people face such a high marginal rate of tax is because, as their incomes rise, so their benefit is withdrawn (**means tested**). If a person is losing 50 per cent of their benefit as their income rises and is also paying the lower 10 per cent tax rate and national insurance contributions of 10 per cent, then they will face an effective marginal tax rate of 70 per cent. At the same time as facing such a high marginal tax rate, their average rate of tax could well be negative. This will be the case if their total benefit exceeds their total tax paid. It is easier to think about this if you regard a benefit as a negative tax.

Negative income tax

Under this system those above the threshold would pay positive income tax while those below it would receive payments (instead of receiving benefits from the Department of Health and Social Security, etc.). Such payments would thus be a **negative income tax**.

Negative income tax is illustrated in Figure 28.5. In effect, under a negative income tax, everyone in the economy receives a lump sum of Og. Hence someone who had no earned income at all would have a negative tax (i.e. payment from the tax authorities) of Og. Any earned income is then taxed at a constant rate as shown by the constant slope of the line in the diagram. Thus, if Oa is received in earned income the payment of income tax on this earned income will have reduced the net payment from the tax authorities to ae. At a pre-tax income of Ob the income tax paid equals the lump sum so that the net payment of tax is zero. Point b is thus the break-even point or the threshold beyond which the net payment of tax to the authorities becomes positive.

What is important to note is that under such a scheme the marginal tax rate on earned income is constant and thus less than one at all levels of pre-tax income. Thus it always 'pays to work' and the poverty trap has been abolished. Moreover, it is claimed, the system would be cheaper to administer than means-tested flat-rate benefits and thus be more economical in accordance with Adam Smith's canons of taxation.

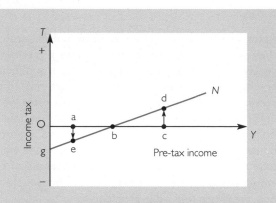

Figure 28.5 Negative income tax
Line *N* represents a constant rate income tax and
negative income tax. At the threshold b no tax is paid.
Above the threshold at Oc the amount of tax paid is
cd. Below the threshold at Oc negative income tax
is received of ae.

The major drawback of the negative income tax
system is that it is, in effect, a universal benefit
system, because everyone implicitly receives Og. This
is, of course, why it works as a solution to the
poverty trap – because there is no means-tested
benefit. The drawback of universal benefit systems is
their expense. If we do not target benefit to those
who really need it, then public expenditure will be
much higher and so will taxes. The other side of the
dilemma is that if we do means test benefits we will
create poverty trap disincentive effects.

This dilemma can be illustrated by asking: what
would be an acceptable minimum income Og that we
could pay someone who has no work and no income?
If we give a conservative estimate of £60 and impose a
tax rate of 25 per cent then the break-even level b
will be £240. Negative income tax is always worked
out relative to the break-even level. The amount of tax
paid can be found in the following way:

$$T = t(Y - b)$$

Verbally, the tax paid (*T*) is the tax rate (*t*) times the
difference between income (*Y*) and the break-even
level of income (*b*).

The consequence of this is that no one earning
less than £240 will pay any income tax! Indeed they
will all be receiving some kind of benefit. People
earning above £240 will have to pay higher rates of
tax to pay for this. Is the result of eliminating the
poverty trap the creation of disincentive effects elsewhere in the income distribution?

The minimum wage

Another way of looking at the problem of the
poverty trap is to ask why people in employment
need the assistance of the state. Employers who do
not give their workers a **living wage** can be thought
of as exploiting them. The Labour government has
promised to introduce a *minimum wage*. The
poverty trap and the benefits bill could be dealt with
at the same time by such a policy. Are there any
drawbacks to this one?

(a) Opponents of the minimum wage argue that it
would destroy jobs. The groups most likely to be
affected in this way are low-paid workers competing with cheap imports from less developed
countries, and young people with few skills and
low productivity. It is likely that a cautiously low
level will be set initially, possibly with a lower
rate for young people.

(b) If a person has a very large family then even a
reasonable level of minimum wage will not provide them with enough. One possible solution to
this is to upgrade child benefit so that family size
is not an issue. The public expenditure consequences of such universal benefits have already
been discussed, however. An alternative approach
is to suggest that having such a large family on a
low income is irresponsible, and refuse to give
benefit to children above a certain number. This
will tend to impact on the children rather
than the parents and would incur the opposition
of the Child Poverty Action Group.

(c) The minimum wage helps those in full-time work,
but those with part-time jobs may still run into
poverty trap problems. Further discussion of the
minimum wage can be found in Chapter 11.

STUDENT ACTIVITY 28.7

Conduct a survey among your parents and working
friends to discover how they are likely to respond
to increases in income tax rates.

STUDENT ACTIVITY 28.8

Explain the difference between the income effect
and the substitution effect. Explain why leisure can
be thought of as a good. Do you think it would be
a normal good in your case?

Case study 28.4
LOCAL TAXATION AND AUTONOMY

Local authority finances have been subject to great changes in recent years. The rating system for domestic property was changed into the community charge but opposition to this was so great that the government was forced to reconsider it. The council tax was introduced as a compromise.

Central government financial support for local authorities comes mainly in the form of the rate support grant. Pressure has been put upon local government to curtail its spending since 1976. This pressure became acute under the Conservative government after 1979. This led to local authorities raising a greater proportion of their revenue as rates. The reluctance, or inability, of local government to make cuts led to more and more draconian measures being taken by the central government. The so-called rate capping Act of 1984 was seen by many people, not just as an attempt to control expenditure, but also as an attack upon local autonomy.

The pattern of local authority expenditure is determined by the services for which it is responsible. The chief form of expenditure for most local authorities is on education, as this is administered at a local level. There is also localised expenditure on roads, social services and housing.

Income and expenditure are the main sources of revenue for governments in modern economies, but wealth taxation is a much older form of taxation. For instance, peasants in the Middle Ages were often taxed on how many cattle they possessed. In capitalist societies, governments are concerned not to discourage the accumulation of capital which drives the economy. Wealth taxation occurs when wealth is handed over from one generation to the next (inheritance tax) and when assets are sold (capital gains tax). Another old form of tax is the poll tax, or head tax, paid equally by all people irrespective of economic position. It is effectively a tax on existence. When introduced by Richard III it resulted in a peasant revolt led by Wat Tyler, and had to be dropped. (When the community charge was introduced by Mrs Thatcher, it was dubbed 'the poll tax' and it too led to widespread protest and riots. Many people believe this was the issue which led to Mrs Thatcher's fall from power.) Poll taxes create no economic disincentives, but have been very unpopular.

Rates

Rates were often criticised as being unfair because they were not related to the services a ratepayer receives from the local authority. This is a difficult argument to maintain since few taxes are related to services received. It was also argued that rates were unfair since they fell only on the head of the household. Thus if, for example, there were two identical houses in a borough but six people lived in one while only one person in the other, the household of six would pay only the same rates as the household of one, creating a free rider problem.

Another criticism of the rating system came from the business community. Rates on business premises in fact raised more money than rates on housing. However, unless the business people happened to live in the same area as their company they got no say in how the money was spent since businesses do not have a vote.

The Conservative government of 1987 was committed to the reform, or abolition, of the rating system. Various proposals were put forward such as local income taxes or complete funding from central government. In the end the government opted for the community charge. Under this system all people over the age of 18 living in a local authority area paid the same amount of tax. It was for this reason that it became known as the poll tax because one would pay tax simply as a result of being on the electoral register. The tax was largely unrelated to income or wealth although some relief was given to various categories of people such as full-time students.

The community charge (poll tax)

The community charge was introduced in Scotland in 1988 and in England and Wales in 1990. The domestic community charge was determined by the local authority. In addition to this there is an industrial rate for business premises which is set nationally. Local authority incomes also continued to be supplemented by transfers from central government and income from other sources continued with central government enforcing council house sales, making local authorities privatise leisure centres and so on.

The community charge was subject to much criticism. It certainly was a highly regressive tax which 'taxes a duke the same as a dustman'. It is hard to see how it accords with the accepted canons of taxation (see Case study 28.1). It proved to be both difficult and expensive to collect. This is because people are more mobile and numerous than houses. In the end the government decided to abolish it and bring in a new council tax. The new tax was to be a mixture of the old rating system, i.e. a tax on property, and a charge on all adults.

Throughout this time the rating system for business properties survived unchanged except for the important fact that it became set by central government. The uniform business rate, as it is known, suffered from problems of its own because property prices were so much higher in the south-east than in other parts of the country. Transitional relief had to be offered to businesses disadvantaged by this change.

The council tax

The council tax is based on the value of a person's house, not the rentable value as had been the case with rates. It is also capped at the top end so that a house of £500 000 pays the same as a house of £1 million. Houses are placed in value bands, but the taxation is regressive for two reasons. First, house prices do not rise as fast as income does, and second, the council tax does not rise directly in proportion to house values.

Conclusion

The government has had to go back to a system of taxing houses at the local level, because houses are not mobile, unlike people. The real problem with the poll tax was that people could avoid paying it by moving around frequently. There are also more people than houses and therefore more bills to send out. Ultimately it was its inequity that led to its demise.

STUDENT ACTIVITY 28.9

Find out your local council tax rates and work out if they are proportional to house prices.

Summary

1 Tax is needed to finance public expenditure.
2 Adam Smith laid down the four canons of taxation: that taxes should be equitable, economical, convenient and certain.
3 There has been a shift away from direct taxation towards indirect taxation over the last 20 years.
4 The progressivity of the income tax system, particularly at the top end, has been reduced over the last 20 years.
5 Evidence about the disincentive effects of income tax is mixed but is more persuasive at the top end of tax rates.
6 The shift from rates to the council tax reflects the increase in home ownership.
7 The poll tax failed because of inequity and collection costs.
8 Discussion of taxation revolves around its effect on efficiency, equity and economic growth.

SECTION VII

Macroeconomic analysis

Who knows when some slight shock, disturbing the delicate balance between social order and thirsty aspiration, shall send the skyscrapers in our cities tumbling.

Richard Wright

Using official statistics to govern the country is like looking up today's trains in last year's timetable.

Harold Macmillan

29 Keynesian macroeconomics

Learning outcomes

At the end of this chapter you will be able to:
- Describe the social and economic events that Keynes was responding to.
- Provide a definition of macroeconomics.
- Explain the elements of the debate between Keynes and the 'classical' economists.
- Describe a sequence of possible events leading up to a Keynesian recession and how Keynesian policy could be used to prevent the recession.

The Keynesian revolution

When economists look at the economy using macroeconomic analysis they are looking at how *aggregates* behave rather than at how individuals or individual markets behave. This approach owes much to the work of the UK Cambridge economist **John Maynard Keynes** (1883–1946). Keynes wrote one of the most influential of all books of the twentieth century – *The General Theory of Employment, Interest and Money* (1936). This book, usually called simply *The General Theory*, led to what is often described as the Keynesian 'revolution' in economics. Indeed, as we saw in Chapter 18, from the mid-1940s until the early 1970s Keynes's economics was the foundation stone of macroeconomic policy making.

Keynes argued that although the forces of supply and demand work well to establish equilibrium in individual markets, the economy as a whole could experience periods of severe instability.

In particular, Keynes presented a convincing explanation of how a collapse in demand in the economy as a whole could throw millions of workers out of work and into chronic unemployment, even though they were eager to work. This was in stark contrast to the prevailing economic orthodoxy of the time which emphasised market equilibrium and which therefore had no convincing explanation for how such steep increases in mass unemployment could occur. Governments of the time thus believed that market forces should be left alone and relied on to eliminate unemployment unaided by government action. Controversially, Keynes argued passionately that governments should take a responsibility for restoring full employment at such times by deliberately regulating the overall, or *aggregate*, level of demand in the economy. Indeed he went further than this and argued for:

> A regime which deliberately aims at controlling and directing economic forces in the interests of social justice and social stability.
>
> Keynes (*Essays in Persuasion*)

The social and economic background to *The General Theory*

In order to understand the context and impact of Keynes's *General Theory* it is necessary to know something of the economic and political events of the times. We have already looked at this in Chapter 15 but recap briefly here. Keynes was responding to the experience of the interwar depression in the Western economies which had seen unemployment reach levels as high as 25 per cent of the workforce. This had caused much accompanying misery, poverty and loss of dignity for millions of people. In the UK there was also widespread social unrest such as the general strike of 1926. Perhaps because free market capitalism appeared to be in crisis, working class political and trade union movements were making great advances.

Although things were not nearly as dangerous as before the revolution in Russia of 1917, the upper and middle classes in Britain were shaken by these events. In the USA the Wall Street crash in 1929 saw the US stock market prices crash; many had their wealth, held in stocks and shares, wiped out. The Wall Street crash was followed by prolonged depression and this cast further doubt on the stability of capitalist economies.

Many post-war politicians of all parties had their political outlook shaped by these events and these memories formed the backdrop for much subsequent policy making. Indeed, until Margaret Thatcher came to power in 1979, all governments after the Second World War explicitly accepted a responsibility for maintaining 'full employment'. Hence, although Keynes's ideas were not immediately adopted, and events were eventually over-shadowed by the Second World War, the Great Depression of the interwar years led to a political climate in which many politicians and economists were looking for new ideas.

In the period following the Second World War, Keynes's ideas triumphed over the former emphasis on *laissez-faire* capitalism. His theories were interpreted and developed and became the mainstream orthodoxy of macroeconomics. Governments of all parties accepted an explicit responsibility for the maintenance of 'full employment'.

● *Common misunderstanding*

Students sometimes confuse Keynes's ideas with socialism. Keynes was not a socialist. He was a wealthy and respected economist and mathematician from a well-established family. He was a well-known patron of the arts and a member of the 'smart' set of the day. He was a supporter of capitalism and wrote enthusiastically about how market forces brought the 'wonderful fruits of the world' to his table. He had a distaste for the 'vulgarity of trade'. Indeed, he dreamed of a time when economic necessity had been overcome and society would be dominated and ordered by a ruling class of cultured intellectuals. He was not a supporter of the common ownership of the means of production and certainly was not advocating a command system to replace market forces in order to achieve social and economic equality.

Macroeconomics

In macroeconomics we are concerned with the behaviour of broad aggregates in the economy, e.g. the total level of investment or the volume of employment for the economy as a whole.

In microeconomic theory we are concerned with such things as the determination of the relative wage rates of particular industries, whereas in macroeconomics we are concerned with the general level of wages in the economy. Similarly, a microeconomic view could be used to explain the determination of the relative prices of products, i.e. the price of one product in terms of other products, whereas in macroeconomics we are concerned with the general level of all prices in the economy. Keynes's *General Theory* clearly used a macroeconomic approach.

Keynes and the 'classics'

Most microeconomic theory revolves around the idea of self-regulating markets. The forces of demand and supply reconcile the disparate aims of producers and consumers through the medium of prices. The equilibrium price clears the market, so that there are no unplanned additions to stocks (excess supply) and also no consumers planning to buy at present prices but unable to find a seller (excess demand). It is possible to view the whole economy as being governed by relative prices. This microeconomic view, in which all markets clear, is called general equilibrium theory. Such ideas of supply and demand equilibrium form the foundations of neo-classical economics in which there is little distinction made between how individual markets function and how the economy as a whole behaves. Keynes argued that the aggregate economy cannot be analysed adequately using microeconomic analysis in which all markets clear. Keynes was thus attacking the dominance of neo-classical economics and introducing a new macroeconomic approach for the analysis of economic aggregates.

In fact, early economists (e.g. **Smith**, **Ricardo**, **Mill** and **Marx**) had used very different approaches to that of neo-classical economics and today these writers would be described as the 'classical' economists. The classical economists used concepts based on social grouping or classes, e.g. workers, capitalists and landlords. They developed theories of instability and of the causes of crisis in capitalist economies. (For example, Smith believed that the spread of more efficient techniques would eventually saturate markets so that economic expansion would eventually slow and then cease altogether.) Ricardo also had a theory that capitalist expansion would reach a 'stationary state' which set an upper limit to the expansion of capitalism. All this is very different to the harmonious equilibrium of neo-classical economics.

Confusingly then, Keynes was *actually* criticising neo-classical economists and the economics which stemmed from the 1870s 'marginalist revolution' (e.g. **Walras**, **Jevons**, **Menger** and, later, **Marshall** and **Pigou**). These neo-classical economists emphasised how market forces act speedily to establish an equilibrium that is efficient and reflects a harmony of interest between freely trading individuals. Class and crisis did not feature in this analysis as in the writings of the classical economists. Keynes, however, (with typical arrogance) lumped together all economists before him under the title of 'classical' economists.

The neo-classical economists put forward the view that the free enterprise economy will automatically reach an equilibrium where there is no involuntary unemployment.

In this analysis, any unemployment which exists can be only a temporary phenomenon. For example, if there were unemployment there would be an excess supply of labour; this would cause wages to fall and therefore employers would be more willing to employ labour; therefore unemployment would be cured (see Figure 29.1) Such analysis was used to support *laissez-faire* economic policy and suggested that unemployment was in fact a voluntary condition and hence not really unemployment at all!

A Keynesian view

As explained above, the idea of a self-regulating economy became increasingly untenable during the 1930s when it was obvious that there was chronic mass unemployment. The (neo-)classical view was thus overturned by Keynes. He argued

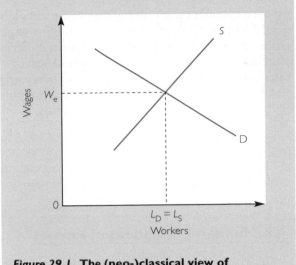

Figure 29.1 The (neo-)classical view of employment determination
In neo-classical analysis the labour market works like any other. Wages adjust until demand equals supply, i.e. anyone who wants to work can.

that equilibrium in the economy was determined by **aggregate demand** and **aggregate supply**. Because these aggregates do not necessarily work in the same way as demand and supply in microeconomics, Keynes argued that it was possible for the economy to be in equilibrium when there was either unemployment or inflation.

According to Keynes the coincidence of the equilibrium level of national income with full employment is a matter of chance.

For example, the neo-classicists argued that lower wages would create more demand for labour. Conversely, Keynes said that, since wages affect the largest component of aggregate demand, lower wages could lead to a lower demand for goods. In the face of this falling demand firms would further reduce their demand for labour. Thus employment and production are pushed into a downward spiral.

Keynes provided reasons for believing that the equilibrium which results from aggregate demand and supply is not necessarily a market clearing equilibrium, i.e. it is possible for there to be unemployed resources, unplanned stocks of goods, or, conversely, excess demand in the form of inflation. If the government were to boost aggregate demand, say by cutting taxes, thereby giving consumers more spending power, retailers would notice a surge of new demand for their products. This would result in new orders being placed with the suppliers of goods and services. Sales and output would rise thereby increasing real national income. In order to produce this extra output more labour would be employed.

Keynes argued that since the economy is not self-regulating it is necessary for the government to intervene to regulate aggregate demand in order to ensure a satisfactory level of national income and employment

The fundamental ideas of Keynes

In *The General Theory* Keynes was concerned with putting across fundamental insights into how free market economies may fall into depression. He suggested ways in which these insights could be worked into a macroeconomic model, but the technical development of such modelling was left for others to develop. In the next few chapters we will outline the theoretical model developed by economists such as **Paul Samuelson** and **Sir John Hicks**. There are, however, many *Keynesian fundamentalists* who argue that these technical models do not adequately capture, or at worst distort, Keynes's original ideas. One such school of economists describes itself as *Post-Keynesian* (see Chapter 47). This school continues to emphasise that:

The fundamental insights of Keynes concern uncertainty, expectations, the nature of money, time and movements in quantities rather than prices.

These ideas will now be explained briefly and then you will see how Keynes used them to explain how an economy could be plunged into a depression.

Uncertainty

Neo-classical economics assumes that economic agents possess a great deal of information. For example, firms in perfect competition have perfect knowledge about production techniques, demand, prices and costs. Likewise, consumers possess much information about their income and the relative prices of products. In stark contrast, Keynes emphasised that the real world is an uncertain place. For example, firms cannot be sure about the levels of future demand. Consumers do not know their future income. The risks of a sudden fall in demand or income are simply not known. Prices, costs, exchange rates and interest rates may change unexpectedly.

Uncertainty is everywhere in the real world and this is not well represented by stable demand and supply curves and diagrams of markets in equilibrium.

Expectations

If many things cannot be known with any certainty, then people are more likely to make decisions based on their expectations.

Expectations are often more important in determining behaviour than what might actually be happening.

This is often apparent in stock exchanges or world currency markets where the price movements of stocks and shares may reflect rumours or waves of optimism or pessimism without there being any real change in the underlying economy itself. Indeed, Keynes likened gambling on a stock exchange to betting on a beauty contest: it is not who you think is the most beautiful that matters but who you think most people will regard as most beautiful. In the same way, individual economic agents are likely to be affected by what they think others are thinking. For example, if entrepreneurs come to believe that consumers are going to cut back on spending they may stop investing in new production plants even though current demand is high. If consumers fear a future rise in unemployment they may reduce their spending even though their current income is high.

Keynes called these changes in expectations which have crowd effects changes in 'animal spirits'.

companies). List the reasons given for the changes in share prices and list those reasons that seem to reflect changes in expectations rather than real changes in the economy.

Equally, if currency speculators believe a currency's value may fall they will sell it and this might actually cause a fall (see Chapter 42).

The nature of money

Keynes emphasised the role of money as a *store of value*. Money does not have to be immediately spent, it can be kept as a store of value to finance future spending. This is because, other than in times of very high inflation, money is a relatively risk-free asset. Money is the most *liquid* of all assets, i.e. it is the most directly 'spendable' asset one can have. It is relatively risk free because it is unique among assets in being the general *medium of exchange*, i.e. it is what one generally uses to buy things. In contrast, houses are *illiquid* as turning them back into money requires an involved and lengthy selling procedure. Whereas the price of any one asset, such as shares, may fall and the owners may lose wealth before they are able to sell, money is unlikely to lose value suddenly against all things. Thus, by holding money rather than other assets the risk of the 'real' world can be avoided.

Other than in times of very high inflation, money is a relatively safe store of value in an otherwise uncertain world.

Time

In much of neo-classical analysis time is virtually ignored. For example, in a supply and demand diagram there is no account of how long it will take to reach an equilibrium. There is also no account of how markets out of equilibrium move through time and what is happening to quantities supplied and demanded during this market 'adjustment'. Keynes emphasised that in the real world adjustments *do* take time. Indeed, sometimes the periods are far too long for the *ceteris paribus* assumption to hold.

Keynesian demand and supply interdependence

In criticising the deceptive nature of *ceterus paribus* assumptions, Keynes stressed that quantities may change long before prices have made a full adjustment. For example, an unexpected fall in demand may see many firms unable to pay back the interest on loans and hence go out of business before an equilibrium is reached on the former supply curve. In the real world debts have to be paid and a recession may cause many firms to go out of business through bankruptcy, this situation is not easily reversed by simply increasing demand again.

Thus in real time supply curves do not sit passively waiting for demand curves to move along them to a new equilibrium; they may themselves start shifting. Unlike the aggregate demand and supply analysis you studied in section four, in Keynesian analysis aggregate supply and demand may not be independent of each other. A fall in demand may result in a fall in supply, also without prices falling! This is particularly likely with a general fall in demand, i.e. a decrease in aggregate demand. If this is the case the distinction between supply and demand as independent forces in the economy becomes less relevant. For example, supply may follow demand quite passively with quantities changing rather than prices. Although it has now become fashionable in textbooks to represent Keynes's ideas in demand and supply diagrams this does, perhaps, rather distort his ideas.

In neo-classical economics prices adjust quickly to restore equilibrium. In Keynesian economics quantities supplied and demanded may change more quickly than prices. Hence the volume of output and employment may change greatly through time.

Keynesian recession and depression

We can now piece together the above ideas to present a Keynesian explanation as to how the level of economic activity may suddenly fall and then stay low in an economy. Suppose, for example, that a dip in company profits across the economy causes investors to expect a fall in the price of company shares. In order to avoid incurring a loss from the falling value of their shares, shareholders may try to sell them before prices fall. But this selling of the shares may actually cause the price of shares to begin to fall. Confirmed in their expectations, investors attempt to increase their selling. If this process continues until there is panic selling the stock market may crash, i.e. share prices in general start to plummet.

As shares lose their value the wealth of shareholders is greatly reduced. Existing shareholders begin to cut back their consumption and companies find it harder to raise finance for investment as former investors either have less wealth or become more reluctant to part with it. Debtors who have lost wealth become unable to repay their debts and hence both creditors and debtors lose wealth. Again consumption and investment is reduced. Instead of money flowing around the economy as before people begin to hold on to their money, either as insurance against loss of income or to avoid the risks associated with investing in the real world.

Money is the refuge from uncertainty; liquidity preference is the desire to hold assets in as liquid a form as possible rather than risk investing in capital investment or spending in the face of an uncertain future income.

As investment and consumption fall so aggregate demand falls. Firms thus face a reduced demand for consumption and investment goods. Some firms may cut back on production. Others, especially those who have borrowed, become unable to cover their debts or operating costs and hence are wound up, either voluntarily or through legal action. Even firms which have strong financial reserves may be reluctant to invest in new capital investment when demand for their output is falling. In all such cases, however, investment is reduced and workers are laid off. Hence investment and consumption falls in a second round of falling aggregate demand which *multiplies* the first falls in aggregate demand.

Faced with falling stock market prices, reduced investment and a rising level of unemployment and business bankruptcies, a wave of pessimism is likely to arise. As gloomy stories about the economy build up it appears riskier than ever to part with money.

A 'retreat into liquidity' may occur, i.e. people and firms hold money in 'idle' money balances rather than spend it or invest it in the real world.

As worsening expectations again multiply the fall in aggregate demand, the recession in the level of economic activity turns a 'collapse' of the economy into depression. The level of output is reduced and millions of previously hardworking people are thrown into unemployment.

STUDENT ACTIVITY 29.2

It is important to note that the initial cause of a reduction in aggregate demand and the sequence of events leading up to economic recession and depression are not important. The point is that real changes and changes in expectations build up into a vicious circle of falling consumption and investment and rising unemployment and business failure. You should now work through a similar scenario for yourself. Think of events that could cause an initial fall in confidence in the economy then work your story through to a full-blown depression. (Hint: if you are stuck as to how to begin the story, search back issues of newspapers, or use a CD-ROM, to locate an article on a change in the level of economic confidence.)

Keynes and Say's Law

At the beginning of the nineteenth century the French economist **Jean-Baptiste Say** (1767–1832) put forward a logical argument that there could not be a shortfall in aggregate demand. He argued that 'supply creates its own demand' and his argument is known as *Say's Law*. Say pointed out that if someone is selling something it is because he wants to use the proceeds to purchase something else. Thus people supplying things create an equal value of demand. Even if the proceeds are saved they will be invested in shares or bonds and hence the money returns to circulation in the economy. A sudden collapse in aggregate demand thus seems ruled out and this became part of the orthodoxy of neo-classical economics.

Keynes challenged Say's law. He pointed out that in a monetary economy the proceeds from supplying may simply be held in the safe form of money, i.e. faced with uncertainty people may be reluctant to part with money and prefer to hold it in '*idle money*' balances. The economist **Alan Coddington** described this as a 'retreat into liquidity'.

Although Say's Law holds for a barter economy it may not hold in a monetary economy.

Government-led recovery

In a Keynesian depression there is no single individual firm or consumer who can break the vicious circle. If workers had jobs then they could spend, and if consumers were spending then firms could sell more and hence take on more workers. If more production were needed firms would begin to invest again and so take on more workers, and so on. But in a Keynesian depression the markets are stuck or 'jammed'. Consumers cannot spend because their income (or expected future income) is low. Firms will not invest because consumers are not even buying up what can be produced within current production capacity. The unemployed cannot get jobs because firms cannot sell and hence they do not need workers. Firms cannot sell because consumers cannot get jobs and hence cannot spend. The economy is thus stuck in depression.

The economist, **Ben Fine** has likened Keynesian recession and depression to people walking round one behind the other in a circle. No one can go faster unless the one in front can also go faster, but that is impossible unless everyone walks faster. What is needed is a ringmaster who can crack a whip to speed everybody up simultaneously. Similarly, in the circular flow model of Keynes, the government is big enough to act as this ringmaster.

If an individual consumer or firm attempted to increase aggregate demand their spending would be a drop in the ocean. The unemployed consumer could spend all his or her precious savings and see no effect in the job market. Equally, firms may make large capital investments and see no increase in consumption; hence they would fail to sell the extra output and get no return on their investment. The government, however, is different. It is in a position to pour massive amounts of spending into the economy through cutting taxes

or increasing its own spending on public sector projects. If all else failed, Keynes argued, the government might simply print money to pay the unemployed to dig holes and fill them in again if there was no other way to get money into the economy (Keynes was demonstrating the power of government here rather than making a serious policy suggestion!).

STUDENT ACTIVITY 29.3

Suppose the government injects some money into the economy through employing previously unemployed workers to mend roads. Why might we expect this to increase income and employment in other activities not directly related to road building?

Government 'pump-priming' of the economy and the multiplier

In fact, Keynes suggested that large injections of spending into the economy by the government is unlikely to be necessary. This is because the initial injection of spending will not stop there, it will go on to create more spending. For example, an initial injection into the economy of £1m may end up increasing spending by £1.5m or perhaps much more. Keynes called this effect the *multiplier*. The multiplier can work through two routes firstly by the direct effect on raising income and therefore spending and secondly by raising expectations.

The direct effect results from increased incomes giving rise to new spending. The government has a wide rage of choices as to how to get extra spending into the economy. For example, the government might give new contracts to firms for public works or defence, it could raise the salaries of public workers, it could directly employ previously unemployed workers, and so forth. Each of these, *ceteris paribus*, will increase incomes. Alternatively, it could lower taxes thereby leaving more spending power in people's pockets. The point is that as incomes and disposable incomes rise, because of such fiscal policy, this will create extra spending as the increased income is spent on additional consumption. This increase in consumption is an increase in aggregate demand and so firms begin to sell more products. To produce more products the firms take on more workers or pay existing workers overtime. There is thus a secondary increase in incomes when these workers are paid and thus a second wave of spending when some of this income is in turn spent. This will continue as each round of spending produces more expenditure.

When does this multiplier process stop? The effect works itself out eventually as each round of income gives rise to a smaller round of expenditure. This is because during each round some of the income 'leaks' out of the process. It may leak through being saved rather than spent, or paid in taxes or spent on imports.

STUDENT ACTIVITY 29.4

Suppose that the government spends £8bn on building new roads and houses. Also assume that half of everyone's income is taxed, saved or spent on imports. Use arithmetic to show that the final increase in GDP would be £16bn.

Depending on the level of consumer and business confidence in the economy, the larger effect of the multiplier may actually be through raising expectations. Once the initial effects of increased government-generated spending were felt expectations may begin to pick up again. As consumers and firms began to 'feel good' about economic prospects consumption and investment would begin to rise in a 'virtuous circle'. Hence, in most cases, Keynes argued, governments would only have to start the process of recovery of, i.e. *pump-prime* the rise in aggregate demand. Indeed, in an extreme case, the simple announcement that the government intended to 'reflate' the economy could spark off such a virtuous circle.

In Keynesian economics mere announcements by the Chancellor of the Exchequer might affect the real economy.

Keynesian trade-off between inflation and unemployment

As noted above, it is quantities rather than prices which adjust during Keynesian recessions.

Output and employment fall while prices may fall only slowly, if at all. Conversely, when a return of confidence injects aggregate demand back into the economy employment and output may rise rapidly and hence aggregate demand could begin to outpace aggregate supply. When this happens full employment or industrial plant capacity may set an upper limit to the expansion of supply even though demand continues to climb. Thus an excess of aggregate demand over aggregate supply will tend to push prices up. You should now satisfy yourself that you understand the next statement (if you do not you should refer to Chapter 17):

Elementary Keynesian theory suggests that there will be an inverse relationship between unemployment and inflation. As unemployment rises inflation will tend to fall or even become negative. When the economy expands output may rise at first but then prices will tend to increase more rapidly as economic capacity is exceeded (see Figure 29.2).

In Keynesian economics there is no automatic 'thermostat' to ensure aggregate demand is kept at the full-employment level. Hence, periods of chronic unemployment or inflation can occur when aggregate demand is below or above the full-employment level.

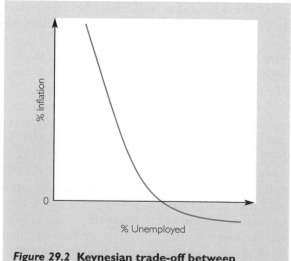

Figure 29.2 **Keynesian trade-off between inflation and unemployment**

The revival of the neo-classical school

A gathering tide of opinion in economics during the 1960s and 1970s questioned the validity of Keynesian economics. In the USA this was associated with **Milton Friedman** of the Chicago Business School. The period from the 1950s to the early 1970s had seen a remarkably stable economy and very low unemployment (see Chapter 18). It began to be thought by many that perhaps this was not the result of Keynesian policies at all but that capitalist economies were, in fact, stable after all. Friedman argued that it was a fundamental misunderstanding to believe that governments had to intervene and regulate aggregate demand. This 'excuse' for government intervention, he argued, had led to a rise in the proportion of government spending as a percentage of the whole economy. Margaret Thatcher later called this 'socialism through the back door'.

In the 1970s inflation and unemployment were rising simultaneously, which appeared to contradict elementary Keynesian theory. The worsening problems of inflation and unemployment and the arguments of Friedman led many politicians to support market-orientated policy prescriptions. These opinions became known as *monetarism* because they advocated that government economic policy should do little more than regulate the growth of the money supply. In the UK and USA these policies became associated with the governments of Margaret Thatcher and Ronald Reagan.

Monetarism is, in fact, just one branch of neo-classical economics. In the later 1980s some of the ideas of the monetarists themselves became discredited as it proved extremely difficult to define, let alone control, the money supply. It was also pointed out that the sudden rises in oil prices created by the Organisation of Petroleum Exporting Countries (OPEC) in the 1970s could explain increases in unemployment and inflation without any contradiction of Keynesian theories.

Conclusion

More recent UK governments have taken a less dogmatic and more pragmatic approach to macro-economic policy. The closer international links between national economies also limit one country's ability to regulate its own domestic demand. Today, a range of *supply side* as well as *demand side* measures are used and far more attention is now given to external effects such as the balance of trade with other countries and the movement of exchange rates.

Summary

1 In his book, *The General Theory*, Keynes was seeking a solution to the major economic problem of the time, i.e. mass unemployment.
2 Macroeconomics looks at how economic aggregates behave rather than individual markets.
3 Keynes was arguing against the economic orthodoxy that free market economies are inherently stable.
4 The fundamental insights of Keynes concern uncertainty, expectations, the nature of money, time and quantity adjustments rather than price movements.
5 Keynesian recessions can occur when pessimistic expectations cause a 'retreat into liquidity'.
6 Keynes argued that unstable economic forces could be corrected by adjusting government taxation and spending. This became the new orthodoxy of economics and government economic policies.
7 Simultaneously rising unemployment and inflation and the arguments of the monetarists led to a move away from crude Keynesian policies.

? QUESTIONS

1 What did Keynes identify as an inherent weakness of free market economies and how did he think this could be corrected?
2 How did Keynes refute that the forces of supply and demand in the labour market would eliminate unemployment?
3 Why was Keynes more concerned with aggregate demand than aggregate supply?
4 Collect evidence on the movements in economic aggregates for the last 20 years. Does this evidence suggest that capitalist economies are inherently stable or unstable?

5 What difficulties may arise for governments in attempting to use taxation and expenditures to offset fluctuations in aggregate demand?

6 How might a Keynesian government go about tackling inflation?

7 To what extent do you think the government of the day is influenced by Keynesian economic policies?

Data response A
THE 'FEELGOOD FACTOR'

Read the following article from the *Daily Mirror* of 30 June 1997 and then answer the questions.

1 Use Keynesian theory to explain the supposed link between the 'feelgood factor' and the rate of business failures.

2 What other explanations might there be for a simultaneous rise in the 'feelgood factor' and a fall in the rate of business failure?

Data response B
EXPECTATIONS AND SPENDING

The first graph (a) in Figure 29.3 below shows the results of surveys of consumers asking them how confident they feel about their economic prospects. The results are converted into an index of consumer confidence. The second graph (b) shows the level of business optimism and the third chart (c) shows yearly changes in the volume of retail sales.

Feelgood factor boost for firms

By Kevin Relly

The number of businesses going bust has fallen to a seven-year low as the feelgood factor continues to boost the economy.

Just 19,962 firms went under in the first six months of the year – the lowest total since 1990. It compares with 20,720 in the first half of 1996 and 32,448 in 1993 at the height of the recession.

But experts Dun and Bradstreet say there's still a long way to go to fall back to the 13,760 that crashed in the first half of 1990.

'These figures show that business failures are set on a downward trend,' says analyst Philip Mellor.

'But the monthly toll of 3,000-plus is still far too high for comfort and companies need to look constantly over their shoulder.'

Drop

The biggest drop came in the East Midlands with the number falling to 980 compared with 1,180 a year ago.

But the neighbouring West Midlands saw an increase in firms collapsing, as did Wales.

Source: *Daily Mirror*, 30 June 1997. Reprinted with permission.

1 Is the relationship between the graphs consistent with Keynesian theory (explain your answer)?

2 Explain how a rise in consumer confidence could result in a drop in unemployment.

3 Why is it not possible to say from this evidence that changes in consumer and business confidence are the cause of fluctuations in the level of economic activity?

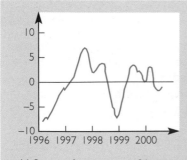

(a) Survey of consumer confidence
Source: CBI

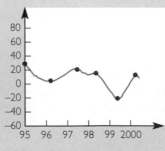

(b) Business optimism
Source: CBI

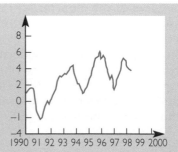

(c) Retail sales volume (% change)
Source: National Statistics. © Crown Copyright 2001

Figure 29.3

30 Changes in aggregate demand: consumption, savings and investment

Learning outcomes

At the end of this chapter you will be able to:

▶ Plot simple relationships between aggregate income and aggregate consumption.
▶ Calculate propensities to consume and save.
▶ List and explain the determinants of consumption, savings and investment.
▶ Identify the causes of changes in, and the interrelationships between, elements of private spending.

Income and consumption

In order to build up a model of the macroeconomy it is first necessary to know more about consumption, savings and investment. Consumers' expenditure (C) in the UK makes up the largest part of national expenditure, being roughly two-thirds of GDP. Consumption is therefore the most important determinant of the level of national income. Conversely, we shall see that the main determinant of consumption is the level of income. There is, therefore, a 'feedback mechanism' between the two which tends to cause consumption and income to rise together in a *multiplier* effect.

Components of consumption

As the country has become wealthier over the years, people have been able to afford a wider range of goods and services. The amount spent on non-durables such as food remains much more constant than that of durables such as cars. It is possible to see changes of demand of up to 25 per cent in a month for cars, whereas this is virtually inconceivable for food. These differing income elasticities for goods cause difficult aggregation problems for economic modelling. Keynes, however, abstracted from such problems by using a very simple relationship whereby aggregate consumption increases in a straightforward way with income.

The consumption function

As income increases, *ceteris paribus*, so does consumption.

Figure 30.1 shows the amount of personal disposable income which has actually been consumed from 1938 to 1999. The 45° line on the diagram shows what would happen if all income were consumed. The line of best fit shows that the proportion of income consumed remains reasonably stable from year to year. The relationship between consumption and income is referred to as the consumption function.

To explain the Keynesian theory of national income we will use a simplified version of the consumption function based on hypothetical data. We will, for the present, ignore foreign trade and government intervention. The figures in Table 30.1 show consumption increasing with income. What is not consumed must be saved and therefore we can calculate savings as:

$$S = Y - C$$

You can see that, at very low levels of income, consumption is actually greater than income so that savings are a negative figure. This is termed *dissaving*. This is caused by consumers who have experienced recent falls in income running down their savings or borrowing. We can plot these figures graphically to obtain a picture similar to Figure 30.1.

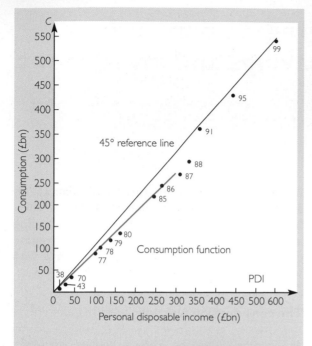

Figure 30.1 The consumption function
This shows the amount of personal disposal income spent (consumed) in the UK in various years from 1938 to 1999. Most years are on or near the line of best fit. The relationship between consumption and income is termed the consumption function.

Figure 30.2 is constructed from the figures used in Table 30.1. The 45° line simply shows all the points of equality between the two axes; hence mathematically its value may be said to be Expenditure (E) = Income (Y).

Table 30.1 A consumption function

	National income, Y ($£bn$)	Planned consumption, C ($£bn$)	Planned savings, S ($£bn$)
A	0	30	−30
B	30	50	−20
C	60	70	−10
D	90	90	0
E	120	110	10
F	150	130	20
G	180	150	30
H	210	170	40
I	240	190	50
J	270	210	60
K	300	230	70

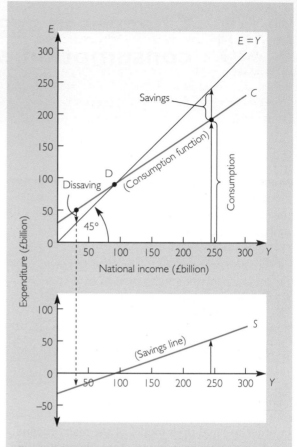

Figure 30.2 The consumption function and savings line

The consumption function (C) passes through the 45° line at the level of income (£90bn) at which savings are zero. To the right of this point savings are positive while they are negative at lower levels of income.

We can use the same figures to construct a graph to show savings. Now where dissaving occurs the graph is below the horizontal axis. It cuts the axis at £90bn where savings are zero and rises above the axis as savings become positive. In the upper graph savings (or dissaving) can be seen as the vertical distance between the consumption function and the 45° line, while in the lower graph it is the distance above or below the horizontal axis.

Autonomous consumption

In Figure 30.2 you can see that when income was zero consumption was still £30bn. This indicates that people plan to consume some quantity of goods and services regardless of their level of income. This corresponds to the dissaving behaviour we have already noted. It is termed *autonomous consumption*. In Figure 30.3 you can see that it is equal to the height at which the consumption function intersects the vertical axis.

Propensities to consume and to save

If we take the amounts saved and consumed and express them as proportions of income, we arrive at the *propensities* to consume and save.

In Figure 30.4 you can see that, of 100 units of income, 10 are saved and 90 are consumed. Thus 9/10 of income is consumed. This is termed the *average propensity to consume* (APC).

The average propensity to consume (APC) is the proportion of income devoted to consumption.

The *APC* is calculated as:

$$APC = C/Y$$

The average propensity to save (APS) is the proportion of income devoted to savings.

The *APS* is calculated as:

$$APS = S/Y$$

In the example used in Figure 30.4 the *APS* is therefore 1/10. It therefore follows that:

$$APC + APS = 1$$

This is always so since 1, here, represents the whole of income, and the whole of income is either consumed or saved.

If national income were to increase, then a proportion of this increase would, similarly, be saved and the rest consumed. In Figure 30.5 you can see that *Y* has been increased by 10 units and, of these 10 units, 4 have been saved and 6 consumed. You will note that in this particular case a smaller proportion of the additional income is consumed.

The marginal propensity to consume (MPC) is the proportion of any addition to income that is devoted to consumption.

The *MPC* may be calculated as the increase in consumption divided by the increase in income:

$$MPC = \Delta C/\Delta Y$$

In the example used in Figure 30.5 it would be:

$$MPC = 6/10$$

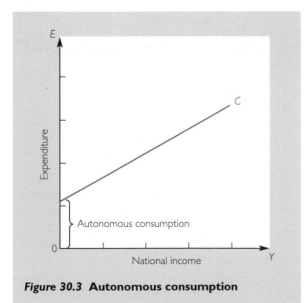

Figure 30.3 Autonomous consumption

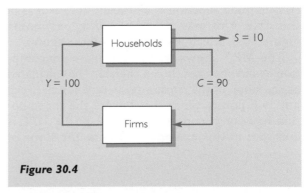

Figure 30.4

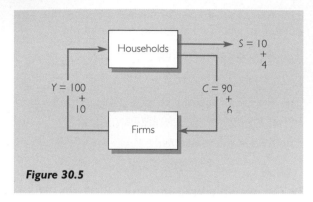

Figure 30.5

Table 30.2 The APC and the MPC

	National income, Y (£bn)	Planned consumption, C (£bn)	Average propensity to consume, APC	Marginal propensity to consume, MPC
A	0	30	∞	0.66
B	30	50	1.67	0.66
C	60	70	1.16	0.66
D	90	90	1.0	0.66
E	120	110	0.92	0.66
F	150	130	0.87	0.66
G	180	150	0.84	0.66
H	210	170	0.81	0.66
I	240	190	0.79	0.66
J	270	210	0.78	0.66
K	300	230	0.77	0.66

The marginal propensity to save (MPS) is the proportion of any addition to income that is devoted to savings.

This could therefore be calculated as:

$$MPS = \Delta S/\Delta Y$$

In our example it would be:

$$MPS = 4/10$$

It also follows that:

$$MPC + MPS = 1$$

because, here, 1 represents the whole of the addition to income. In this theoretical model we assume that APC is greater than MPC. This is because a greater proportion of income is consumed at lower levels of income.

The APC, the MPC and the consumption function

Table 30.2 shows the value of the APC and MPC for various points on a consumption function. As you can see, the MPC remains constant as Y rises while the APC declines. This occurs wherever a consumption function is a straight line, as it is in this case. This may be confirmed by examining Figure 30.6, which is drawn from these figures.

The MPC shows what happens to consumption as income rises. It can therefore be calculated as the slope of the consumption function between any two points. Since the slope of the consumption function is constant, the value of the MPC is constant in this example. Examine the slope of

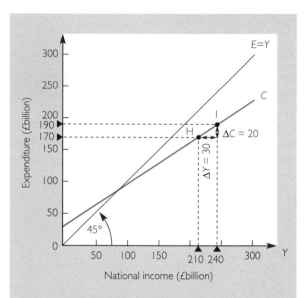

Figure 30.6 The APC and the MPC
The APC can be calculated from any point on the C line, e.g. at point H:

$$APC = \frac{170}{210}$$

whereas the MPC is the slope of the line between two points, e.g. between points H and I:

$$MPC = \frac{20}{30}$$

the C line between points H and I and you will find that income increases by £30bn while consumption increases by £20bn. Therefore we have:

$$MPC = \Delta C/\Delta Y$$
$$MPC = 20/30$$
$$MPC = 0.66$$

The value of the APC can be taken from any point on the line. For example, at point H:

$$APC = C/Y$$
$$= 170/210$$
$$= 0.81$$

We can therefore conclude that the coordinates at any point on a consumption function give us the value of the APC, while the slope between any two points will give us the value of the MPC.

STUDENT ACTIVITY 30.2

A little work with the figures in Table 30.2 should enable you to calculate the APS. For example, satisfy yourself that at point H, APS = 0.19.

Since we know the value of the APC to be 0.81 at this point we are able to confirm that:

$$APS + APC = 1$$

This remains true even when the APC is greater than one because under these circumstances the value of the APS becomes negative.

STUDENT ACTIVITY 30.3

Confirm from Table 30.2 that MPC + MPS = 1.

Determinants of consumption

We have already seen that in our model the most important determinant of consumption is the level of income. However, there are other theories and factors which modify this view. Two of the most important are the *permanent income hypothesis* and *the life-cycle hypothesis*.

The permanent income and life-cycle hypotheses

The hypothesis is that people, in the short run, consume according to an estimation of their permanent income level. If their income were suddenly to increase (or decrease) they would, in the short run, go on spending roughly the same amount because they regard the change as only temporary. Thus a cross-sectional analysis of household incomes would reveal much greater variations in short-term than in long-term propensities to consume.

The permanent income hypothesis is primarily associated with **Milton Friedman**. An alternative formulation is that of the life-cycle hypothesis formulated by **Professors Modigliani, Ando** and **Brumberg**. In the life-cycle hypothesis households are supposed to formulate their expenditure plans in relationship to their expected lifetimes' earnings.

Both formulations attempt to explain the observed variation of actual expenditure patterns from the predicted pattern if expenditure was entirely determined by disposable income levels. Modern econometric models of the economy usually divide consumption (C) into two components: one element is set to vary with the level of disposable income while the other element is not, i.e. it is regarded as autonomous income.

When we consider these theories it brings into question our original proposition that APC declines as income rises. We can now see, and observation confirms this, that consumption and savings may be subject to considerable fluctuation, at least in the short run. However, regarded in the long run, there is greater stability.

Other determinants

(a) *The distribution of income.* Income remains very unequally distributed and different income groups have different MPCs. Understandably the MPC of lower-income groups tends to be much higher than that of the very rich. A movement to a more even distribution of income should therefore lead to a higher MPC for the economy as a whole.

(b) *Consumers' expectations.* Consumers' spending now is influenced by their expectations of the future. Three main factors we might mention are their expectations of inflation, unemployment and income.

(c) *Cost and availability of credit.* Since many goods, especially consumer durables, are bought with the aid of hire purchase or other forms of credit, the terms on which these are available and their cost must have an effect upon the level of consumer demand. A rise in general interest rates will thus tend to decrease consumption.

(d) *Wealth and savings.* Since purchases can be made not only out of current income but also from consumers' assets and savings, the quantity of these can influence consumption. For example, those with savings may be more willing to maintain their level of consumption in the face of falling income. It is also argued that those with a cushion of savings are more willing to spend a greater proportion of their income.

Shifts and movements

If the level of national income increases then we would expect to see a movement along the consumption function to a higher level of consumption. Thus, a change in the level of income need have no effect upon the *MPC*. However, if one of the determinants of consumption changes, such as the availability of credit, this might be expected to lead to a change to a new level of consumption at the same level of income, so that we will have shifted to a new consumption function above or below the old one. We will also have moved to a different average propensity to consume. Figure 30.9 at the end of this chapter shows changes in household final consumption.

Savings

Savings are income not spent; they are thus a withdrawal or leakage from the circular flow of income. The most usual formulation of savings is that they are the proportion of personal disposable income that is not consumed. Savings may be undertaken by households, firms and even by the government. For most of this section of the chapter we will concentrate on household savings.

Savings, income and consumption

We have examined the determinants of consumption and discovered that the most significant factor is the level of income. Since savings are defined as income not spent we have, therefore, also considered the most significant influence upon savings! It would follow, therefore, that as income increases savings will tend to increase both as a total figure and as a proportion of income. There are, however, many other influences which can disturb this relationship.

Motives for saving

Given the income to do so, there are many reasons people save. The motives are often not closely related to current economic circumstances although high rates of inflation or unemployment will alter people's saving habits.

Some of the most important motives are listed below.

(a) *Deferred purchase.* This is saving up to buy something in the future such as a car, a house or a holiday.

(b) *Contractual obligations.* The most significant form of contractual saving is life and pension assurance premiums. Contractual savings form a very significant share of all personal savings.

(c) *Precautionary motives.* Most people will, if they can, put some money by for a 'rainy day'.

(d) *Habits and customs.* Some people and societies save more than others out of habit. This is, internationally, an important determinant of savings.

(e) *Age.* People tend to save and dissave at different times of their life. For example, many young people will be borrowing for house purchase while older people will be saving for their retirement.

(f) *Taxation.* Saving may also be significantly affected by taxation policy towards savings. If, for example, people are able to gain tax relief on assurance premiums this will encourage them to save.

(g) *Expectations.* Expectations of the future economic situation can also be a significant factor.

Savings and the rate of interest

The view of the pre-Keynesian economists was that the amount of savings was determined by the rate of interest, i.e. a rise in the rate of interest would call forth more savings. However, as we have just seen, there are other reasons for saving. This was well demonstrated during the 1970s when, in many years, the real interest rate was negative but people saved significantly more!

The real interest rate is arrived at by subtracting the rate of inflation from the rate of interest.

Thus, if, for example, the interest rate was 10 per cent and inflation was running at 15 per cent, the real rate of interest would be −5 per cent; anyone who saved £100 would, at the end of the year, have purchasing power equal to only £95 in real terms.

This is not to say that interest rates have no effect. High rates of interest may encourage savings while low rates will discourage them. It would appear, however, that other motives, such as deferred purchase, precautionary and expectations, are more important. Differences in rates of interest between financial institutions, however, have a significant effect upon the type of savings that take place.

The savings ratio

A common measure of the amount of savings taking place is the *savings ratio*. This is the amount of savings expressed as a percentage of personal disposable income (PDI). It is thus very similar to *APS* except that it is expressed as a percentage.

Personal savings may be divided into contractual savings and discretionary savings.

Contractual savings are those where a person contracts to save a certain amount per month. The most significant forms of contractual savings are life assurance and superannuation and pension schemes. Discretionary savings are all other forms of savings where people are not obliged to save a specific amount. The most significant forms of discretionary savings are building society deposits, bank deposits and lending to the government.

During the depression of the 1930s the savings ratio was very low as people had to draw on their savings to get by. In the USA in the same period the savings ratio was actually negative. During the Second World War the savings ratio shot up as people were encouraged to lend to the government to help the war effort. After the war the ratio returned to a more normal level but rose again during the 1960s to 9.3 per cent in 1970. From 1973 onwards the ratio began a rapid rise to 14.2 per cent in 1980. However, by 1990 it had fallen back to 8 per cent before rising steeply again, since 1997 it has again been falling and is currently at around 6 per cent. Factors accounting for this volatility include uncertainty and expectations, and demographic change, e.g. young people tend to save less. It might be thought that inflation would discourage saving, but if inflation increases uncertainty and erodes the real value of savings the opposite can be true as in the 1970s when high inflation seemed to lead to a rise in the savings ratio. Table 30.3 shows the volatility of the savings ratio, that the UK has a comparatively low savings ratio for a

Table 30.3 **Savings ratio in OECD countries**

	1985	1987	1989	1991	1993	1995	1997	1999
US	9.2	7.3	7.5	8.3	7.1	5.6	4.5	2.4
Japan	15.6	13.8	12.9	13.2	13.4	13.7	12.6	13.1
Germany	9.5	13.6	14.1	12.2	11.8	10.3	9.5	8.6
France	12.3	10.0	11.6	13.5	15.2	15.9	16.0	15.7
Italy	21.0	19.7	17.0	18.7	17.2	16.6	14.6	12.7
Canada	14.2	10.3	11.5	11.7	10.3	7.5	2.8	1.4
UK	9.6	5.8	5.9	9.7	11.2	10.5	9.6	6.2

Source: Copyright © OECD 2001

European country, and that savings ratios differ markedly between countries and that it has fallen dramatically in North America.

Investment

Investment is both an important component and determinant of the level of national income. When we use the term investment in this context it refers exclusively to the acquisition of new physical capital such as buildings and machines. It is in this sense that we can describe investment as an addition, or an injection, to the circular flow of income.

'Investment' on the Stock Exchange, or in government bonds, is not investment as the term is used in macroeconomics because it only involves the transfer of ownership of pieces of paper.

Types of investment

Investment is not a homogeneous mass; it consists of many different types of things. The different types of investment have differing effects upon the economy; for example, the building of a new oil terminal and the building of an old people's home will have very different consequences, though both are investment.

(a) *Stocks (or inventories)*. Net additions to the physical stocks of materials and goods held by businesses are counted as investment. They are the most volatile component of investment, being subject to change in response to actual changes or expected changes in the level of national income and in response to the financial health of firms. It is possible for the change in stocks to be either positive or negative. Negative stock-building can occur for example when an unexpected surge in demand causes demand to outstrip production.

It is important to recognise that building-up stock to provide for future demand requires resources today. Also, running down stocks by cutting back production can provide important respite from financial pressure. This is the reason why, although it may seem surprising, stocks are usually reduced in recessions; recessions are often associated with financial problems as businesses struggle to pay off their creditors and avoid cash flow problems. One way of doing this is to cut back on production for a while and meet demand instead by running down stock levels.

Changes in stocks are thus not only a consequence of changes in aggregate demand but also a cause of changes in economic activity. Fluctuations in stock levels are hence another important source of fluctuations in private sector aggregate expenditure The volatility of stocks can be seen in Figure 30.9

(b) *Fixed capital*. All investment other than stocks is termed fixed capital formation. Fixed capital is typically divided into three categories, construction, vehicles and plant and machinery. The construction of housing is often included in investment even though it might be more accurate to describe houses as consumer durables. Much investment is to replace worn-out capital. We would have to subtract capital consumption from gross fixed capital formation to give us the net addition to fixed capital stock of the country. Figure 30.9 shows fluctuations in fixed capital investment.

Determinants of investment

Autonomous and induced investment

When we turn to look at the factors which determine investment it is useful to make a distinction between autonomous and induced investment. When we were looking at the determinants of savings we saw that an increase in the level of income was quite likely to induce an increase in saving. Thus the saving had been brought about by a variable (Y) within the model of the economy we are developing. Similarly, investment which is brought about by changes in the level of income may be termed *induced investment*, i.e. investment which is brought about by a factor which is endogenous to (within) the theory. However, much investment is not brought about in this manner. Consider what might happen to a new invention, e.g. 3D television. It is quite likely that firms would go ahead and invest in such a development but there need have been no prior change in income or any other variable within our theory of the economy. Thus the investment would be brought about by something outside or exogenous to the system. Such investment may be termed autonomous.

We normally reserve the term induced investment for that investment associated with the *accelerator principle*, i.e. the relationship between investment and the rate of change of aggregate demand (see the appendix to this chapter, page 435). All other types of investment may be termed autonomous. In practice one may be very hard to disentangle from the other.

Investment and the rate of interest

Here we are concerned with the relationship between the rate of interest and the aggregate level of investment within the economy.

It seems reasonable to assume that firms make the decision to invest on the expectation of making a gain. We may contrast this with the decision to save where, as we saw earlier in the chapter, households will save even if it involves economic loss. Most decisions to invest involve borrowing money we should expect therefore a relationship between the cost of borrowing and the amount of investment taking place.

There is also a relationship between the rate of interest and the capital stock which people will wish to hold. This is illustrated in Figure 30.7 which shows an *MEC* (marginal efficiency of capital) curve. The *MEC* relates the desired stock of capital to the rate of return (yield) an additional unit of capital will produce. The yield is related to the rate of interest. Suppose, for example, that a capital project were to yield 10 per cent; if the rate of interest were 12 per cent investors would not be interested in it. However, were interest to fall to 8 per cent, investors might wish to invest. The capital stock they desire would have increased.

Marginal efficiency of investment

While the *MEC* shows the relationship between the rate of interest and the *desired* stock of capital, the marginal efficiency of investment (*MEI*) shows the relationship between the rate of interest and the *actual* rate of investment per year.

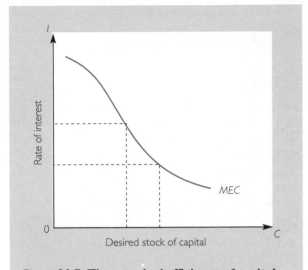

Figure 30.7 The marginal efficiency of capital
A fall in the rate of interest increases the size of the desired stock of capital.

MEC is concerned with a stock while MEI is concerned with a flow.

There will be important differences between the capital stock people desire and the capital investment that takes place. This is because there are physical constraints upon the construction of capital.

Figure 30.8 shows two possibilities for *MEI*. With both we show the effect of dropping the interest rate from 14 per cent to 7.5 per cent. If the curve is relatively flat (*MEI*$_2$) then the rate of investment increases substantially from £18bn to £30bn, but if the curve is steep (*MEI*$_1$) then there is only a small response and the rate of investment increases from £18bn to £21bn.

The MEI reflects the elasticity of investment with respect to the rate of interrest.

Although most economists today believe that there is a relationship between the interest rate and investment, the elasticity of this relationship is often far less important as a determinant of aggregate demand than changes in the other factors that influence the level of investment.

Business expectations

In principle, if a scheme yields 11 per cent and interest is 10 per cent, investment would take

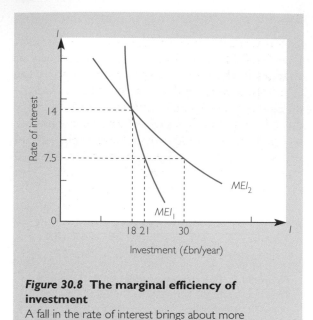

Figure 30.8 **The marginal efficiency of investment**
A fall in the rate of interest brings about more investment; how much more depends on the slope of the *MEI* line.

place. However, we cannot see into the future to be able to judge the profitability of a scheme with such accuracy, nor can we tell whether or not circumstances will change. Because investment decisions take time to accomplish, there may be a great deal of uncertainty about them. Thus what businesses expect to happen in the future is very important. If they are pessimistic about the future, low rates of interest will not encourage them to borrow, whereas if they are optimistic, high rates will not necessarily discourage them.

The level of income

A high level of national income appears to stimulate investment. One reason for this is that it has an effect upon business expectations, i.e. high levels of income tend to make businesses optimistic about the future. Second, a high level of income could mean high profits and therefore businesses have more funds with which to invest. This latter argument is presuming that ploughed-back profits are more significant than borrowed funds. While this has often been so, in recent years borrowed funds have assumed increasing importance.

There is much disagreement about whether or not the level of income determines the level of investment.

Many economists would reverse the causality of the relationship and say that high levels of investment cause high levels of income. It is probably for both reasons that high levels of income are associated with high levels of investment.

The government and investment

The government has a very significant effect upon investment, both indirectly through its policies and directly as the largest investor in the economy. Investment decisions by businesses are influenced by government taxation policies, which may give incentives to investments, and by monetary policy, which plays a significant role in determining interest rates.

There is evidence that public and private investment tend to counterbalance each other, public investment being high when private investment is low and vice versa. It can be argued that this is the government deliberately trying to stabilise the level of total investment, or, conversely, that public investment 'crowds out' private investment from time to time and thus depresses it.

Induced investment: the accelerator

The accelerator hypothesis assumes that it is the size of the capital stock in relation to national income that is the object of decision making. In its simplest form the accelerator hypothesis assumes that firms seek to maintain a constant capital to output ratio. Investment is thus reduced to behaviour which seeks to change the capital–output ratio if it is not at the desired level (see the appendix to this chapter on page 435 for a full explanation).

The capital stock of the nation is several times greater than national income. We may say, therefore, that it takes several pounds of capital to produce £1 of output. For example, say that it takes £3 of capital to produce £1 of output (i.e. the capital–output ratio is 3:1). If total demand in the economy were to rise then, in order to meet the new demand, £3 of capital equipment would have to be built to meet each £1 of new demand. Conversely, if national income were to fall investment could possibly fall to zero if the capital stock is greater than that desired for that particular level of income.

The accelerator hypothesis predicts that it is the rate of change of income rather than its level which determines investment.

In the appendix to this chapter several possible offsetting factors are discussed which make the accelerator effect a matter of some dispute among economists. Nevertheless, although not invented by Keynes himself, the hypothesis accords with his view that the aggregate demand of the private sector is subject to fluctuations which can have a destabilising effect on the economy.

Postscript on investment

There are important theoretical differences between Keynes, the pre-Keynesian economists, and the monetarists about interest, investment and income. We cannot go into these fully until we have had a closer look at income determination and monetary theory. We may simply note here that the pre-Keynesian neo-classicists placed a much greater importance on the rate of interest as a determinant of investment than we do today. As you have seen in this section of the chapter, we have argued that investment might also be determined by factors as diverse as government policy and expectations in general.

● *Common misunderstanding*

Before leaving this chapter we need to note that expenditure and demand are some times taken to mean the same thing. But expenditure is what is actually spent whereas demand is a more theoretical concept. An easy way to see that there is a distinction is to think about what has happened if you placed an order for a product which has in fact already sold out and your money is returned. You will not have actually spent money but you will have added to demand for the product. Equally at the aggregate level, demand may be met by raising prices rather than producing more goods, aggregate demand may result in increased nominal expenditure but the demand for goods and service will have been greater than the amount actually sold.

Exports and imports

As aggregate expenditure can be written $C+I+G+X-M$, we end this section by noting that changes in the level of exports and imports are also both a cause and a consequence of changes in aggregate demand. Imports tend to vary directly with the level of income as consumers buy more goods some of which are imported and firms use a greater volume of materials some of which are also imported. Exports may also decrease or increase somewhat according to how easy it is to sell in the domestic market. As we saw in Chapter 18 and explained in more detail in Chapter 42, exchange rates will also affect the relative prices of imports domestically and exports on the world market. For example, a fall in the UK exchange rate, i.e. a pound buying less in terms of foreign currencies, will make imports more expensive to consumers in the UK and make UK exports relatively cheaper on the world market. Hence, a fall in the exchange rate will tend to 'improve' the balance of trade and hence the current account of the balance of payments. Changes in the balance between exports and imports are shown in Figure 30.9.

Conclusion

Figure 30.9 clearly shows that the components of expenditure are subject to much fluctuation. The ways in which changes in demand affect the economy depend also on the response of aggregate supply, this is examined in depth in the next chapter. One of the difficulties in analysing the causes of economic fluctuations is that the components of demand not only influence levels of income and activity but are also influenced by them, e.g. if consumption has risen this may be the effect rather than the cause of increased income. Nevertheless, changes in the components of aggregate demand are often the causes of changes in expenditure. These changes reflecting autonomous changes in aggregate demand that have an important effect on the economy. For this reason economists closely watch the components of expenditure examined in this chapter in order to monitor and predict changes in the economy.

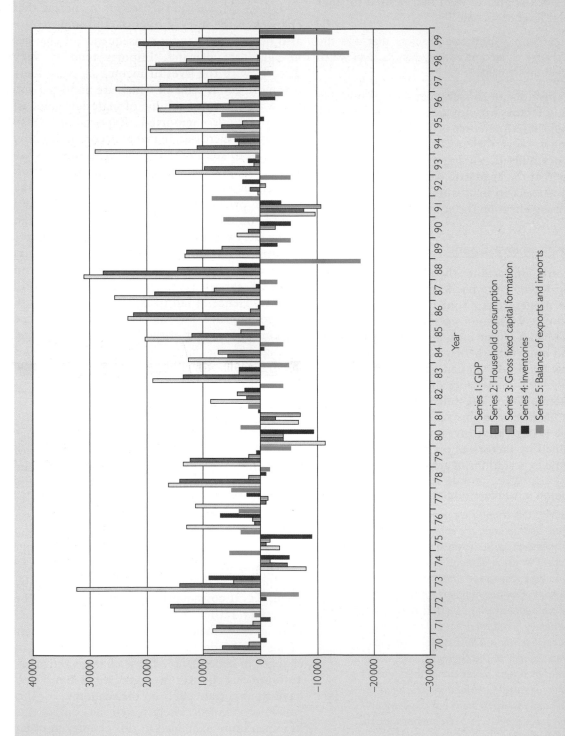

Figure 30.9 Yearly changes in the components of expenditure 1970 to 1999 (constant prices = 1995)

Source: Adapted from National Statistics website (Time zone, www.statistics.gov.uk). © Crown Copyright 2001

Summary

1 The consumption function is the relationship between consumption and income.
2 The APS and APC show the proportions of income which are devoted to savings and consumption respectively. The MPS and MPC show the proportions of any increase in income which are devoted to savings and consumption.
3 A rise in income will bring about a movement along the C line while a change in the other determinants of consumption will cause a shift to a new C line.
4 Saving is a withdrawal from the circular flow of income. It is related to the level of Y and is also motivated by a number of non-economic factors such as habit and age. There is no clearly defined relationship between S and the rate of interest; people will save even when real interest is negative. Savings may be divided into contractual and discretionary. Contractual savings are the more stable.
5 Savings may be undertaken by any sector of the economy.
6 Investment is an injection to the circular flow of income and consists of additions to the real physical stock of capital. There is an equality between realised savings and realised investment.
7 Autonomous investment is determined by exogenous factors such as business expectations. Induced investment is brought about by the rate of change of Y.
8 Changes in the level of stocks are an important source of short-term fluctuations.
9 The balance of exports and imports is also a cause of changes in domestic aggregate demand.

? QUESTIONS

1 What reasons can be advanced to explain the observed variations in the propensity to consume in Figure 30.1? How do you think this diagram would differ if there were no inflation?
2 Explain why a change in autonomous consumption will also lead to a change in induced consumption.
3 Distinguish between induced and autonomous investment.
4 Consider Figure 30.8. What would be the significance of a vertical MEI curve?
5 Prepare a table to compare the percentage of GDP devoted to gross fixed capital formation of four different countries with which you are familiar, e.g. the UK, the USA, Nigeria and Malaysia. Suggest reasons for the observed differences.
6 Examine the role of interest in determining savings and investment.
7 What factors determine investment in a modern economy?
8 What are the determinants of aggregate private investment and why is it likely to fluctuate?
9 In a closed economy with no government intervention:

$$C = 50 + 0.85Y$$

Autonomous investment is constant at 60 units. Induced investment is $I = 0.05Y$ for all levels of Y. At what level of Y will $S = I$? Suppose that autonomous investment were to increase to 80 units. At what level of Y would $S = I$?

Appendix: the accelerator (this section can be skipped without loss of continuity)

A model of the accelerator

To explain the working of the accelerator we will use the model of a very simplified economy. In this economy the initial capital stock is valued at £200m. When fully employed, this stock is just adequate to produce the £100m of goods which constitute the aggregate demand (Y) in the economy for a year, i.e. there is a capital–output ratio of 2:1, which means that a capital stock of £2 is necessary to produce a flow of output of £1. The capital in this economy has a life of five years and is replaced evenly so that a replacement investment of £40m per year is needed to maintain the capital stock.

Aggregate demand (Y)	Capital stock required
£100m	£200m
Replacement	Investment required net
£40m	0

Suppose now that aggregate demand were to rise by 20 per cent to £120m. This would mean that to meet this demand a capital stock of £240m is required. If demand were to be met the following year it would mean that the economy's demand for capital will now be £80m, i.e. £40m for replacement and £40m to meet the new demand. We can summarise it thus:

Aggregate demand (Y)	Capital required
£120m	£240
Replacement	Investment required net
£40m	£40m

Thus, between the first and second years a rise of 20 per cent in aggregate demand has brought about a 100 per cent rise in investment demand. This is an illustration of the accelerator principle.

The accelerator (*a*) is concerned with new (or net) investment demand. In our example £40m of the new investment is necessary to meet a rise in Y of £20m. This is because it takes £2 of capital equipment to produce £1 of output per year. From this we can derive a formula for the accelerator effect which is:

$$I_N = a\Delta Y$$

I_N is the new investment, *a* is the accelerator coefficient (the capital–output ratio, in this case 2) and ΔY is the change in income. Thus in our example we have:

$$I_N = 2 \times £20m$$
$$= £40m$$

To explain the accelerator more fully we need to follow our example through several time periods. This is done in Table 30.4.

Years 1 and 2 in Table 30.4 recapitulate our example. Now assume that in year 3 demand rises to £130m. The capital stock required is now £260m. Therefore there will be a demand for £20m of extra capital but the total demand for capital will have fallen. The capital demand is now £40m for replacement and £20m for new capital. The £40m of extra capital last year will not need

Table 30.4 A model of the economy (capital–output ratio = 2, capital is replaced over a five-year period)

Year	Aggregate demand, Y (£m)	Capital stock required (£m)	Replacement (£m)	Investment Net	Total
(1)	(2)	(3)	(4)	(5)	(6)
1	100	200	40	–	40
2	120	240	40	40	80
3	130	260	40	20	60
4	140	280	40	20	60
5	120	240	–	–	–
6	120	240	40	–	40

replacing for a further five years. Therefore, although aggregate demand is still rising, capital demand has fallen. This is because when the rate of increase of aggregate demand falls, the absolute level of induced investment will decline. You can confirm this by applying the formula.

Further implications of the principle can be observed between years 3 and 4, where the demand for capital is constant because the rate of increase is the same as between years 2 and 3 (remember the increase is ΔY not $\Delta Y/Y$). Between years 4 and 5 aggregate demand drops from £140m to £120m and the capital stock required, therefore, decreases from £280m to £240m. What new investment is required?

If we apply the formula we get:

$$I_N = 2 \times (-£20m)$$
$$= -£40m$$

There is therefore no need to replace the £40m of capital stock which has worn out. In this case it has therefore completely eliminated the need for replacement investment.

Finally, in year 6 demand has stabilised at £120m. The formula predicts that there will be no demand for new capital. However, it is necessary to replace the £40m of capital stock which will have worn out.

The accelerator (*a*) links the rate of change of aggregate demand to the level of new investment demand.

Factors modifying the accelerator

When we look for evidence of the accelerator in the economy we do indeed find that fluctuations in the level of investment demand are significantly greater than those in aggregate demand. But:

(a) they are much smaller fluctuations than those predicted by the theory;
(b) it is very difficult to demonstrate any mathematical relationship between the two.

This does not necessarily mean that the theory is therefore wrong. It could be that a number of factors modify the accelerator and, therefore, mask the effect. Some of these are listed below:

(a) *Businesses learn from experience*. This means that they are unlikely to double their capacity on the strength of one year's orders. Conversely, if demand is dropping, they might be willing to increase their inventories against a rise in demand in subsequent years.
(b) *Capital–output ratios*. These are not as constant as suggested by our example. If demand rose it might be possible to obtain more output from the existing capital stock by varying other factors of production. For example, the workforce might undertake shift work or overtime to meet the extra demand.
(c) *Depreciation*. The replacement of the capital stock may be a function of factors other than time. In our example it was assumed that capital wore out after five years. If there was an increase in demand it might be possible to continue using old capital equipment after was it planned to scrap it. Often the period over which capital is depreciated is an accounting convenience and does not correspond to the physical life of the capital. Conversely, capital may be obsolete before it has physically depreciated.

(d) *Other investment*. It should be recalled that the accelerator applies only to net or new investment resulting from changes in Y. There are other forms of investment such as replacement investment and investment in new techniques.
(e) *Time lag*. New capacity cannot be created immediately after a rise in demand, since plant and machinery take time to build. Also, the time lags will vary depending on the nature of the capital we are considering. We are thus concerned with a distributed time lag. Thus, much more sophisticated mathematics will be needed to measure the effects.
(f) *Capacity*. The operation of the accelerator depends upon the economy being at or near full capacity, otherwise the new demand would be coped with by existing plants expanding their output. However, in apparent contradiction to this, there must be surplus resources (labour, land, etc.) with which to construct the capital equipment.

All these factors make it very difficult for us to observe the accelerator effect in any simple manner.

Data response A
GDP AND COMPONENTS OF SPENDING

Study Figure 30.9 (changes in the components of expenditure) on page 434 and then answer the following questions:

1 Explain why there is such a close relationship between changes in GDP and changes in consumption.
2 Describe and account for the relationship between changes in GDP and changes in the balance of trade.
3 How would the chart be different if it were measured in current prices?
4 What evidence is there for an accelerator effect?

Data response B
WHAT DETERMINES CONSUMPTION?

Study the figures in Table 30.5 relating to income, savings and inflation in the UK. The income figures refer to personal disposable income, i.e. the income of individuals after allowing for deduction of income tax and national insurance contributions. The savings referred to are those of the personal sector.

1 Using graph paper, construct a consumption function for the UK economy based on this data.
2 Determine the marginal propensity to consume (MPC) and the average propensity to save (APS) for the years 1980, 1985, 1989, 1993 and 1998. Explain how you arrived at your answers.
3 How would you account for the observed variations in the size of the APC over this period?
4 What theories have been advanced to explain the determination of the level of consumption in an economy?

Table 30.5 Income, savings and inflation in the UK

Year	Personal disposable income (£m)	Savings (£m)	Consumer price percentage change from previous year (%)
1979	136 152	17 257	13.4
1980	160 735	22 405	18.0
1981	177 594	23 360	11.9
1982	192 614	23 609	8.6
1983	207 457	22 774	4.6
1984	223 092	26 264	5.0
1985	241 362	25 627	6.1
1986	263 448	23 516	3.4
1987	284 483	20 914	4.1
1988	315 787	19 304	4.9
1989	352 097	26 174	7.8
1990	378 325	30 798	7.0
1991	391 316	38 031	7.5
1992	424 838	50 150	4.2
1993	452 810	50 463	2.5
1994	468 883	44 911	2.0
1995	495 337	52 093	2.6
1996	522 089	50 687	2.5
1997	555 518	53 301	1.8
1998	569 496	34 042	1.6
1999	600 259	31 074	1.3

Source: National Statistics; *Monthly Digest of Statistics*, HMSO, and *Economics Trends Annual Supplement.* © Crown Copyright 2001

31 The Keynesian aggregate model

Note: Although this chapter and the next are useful for understanding the mechanics of circular flow models, national accounting and the development of Keynesian economics, the topics covered are no longer required by some UK syllabuses. This book has therefore been written so that this chapter and the next may be skipped without loss of continuity. Alternatively you may wish to skim these chapters to deepen your understanding of aggregate demand and Keynesian economics.

Learning outcomes

At the end of this chapter you will be able to:
▶ Classify the various flows of expenditure and income around, into and out of the circular flow of income.
▶ Use a simple Keynesian circular flow model to identify equilibrium national income.

To explain the determination of economic aggregates, Keynes developed the 'circular flow of income' model as an alternative to the supply and demand model of microeconomics. You have already seen this model in Chapter 15 where Keynes's classification of aggregate expenditures (i.e. *C*, *I*, *G* and *X*) are utilised as a means of national income accounting. In this chapter the model of the circular flow of income will be used, not as a model for accounting for past income and expenditures, but as a simple model for *determining* expenditure and hence income. The model is far too basic and incomplete to be used for actual forecasting, but it is a simple model of income determination that was actually used for some 30 years to teach introductory macroeconomics to students and politicians alike.

It is important when reading this chapter not to lose sight of Keynes's fundamental insights of why aggregate demand might be unstable (see Chapter 29). Indeed, the rather mechanical and deterministic model of this chapter has been criticised as distorting Keynes's fundamental ideas.

These mechanical representations have sometimes been called 'hydraulic models' as they appear to represent the behaviour of water flowing through pipes rather than the subtleties of human behaviour that Keynes appeared to be describing. The derogatory name 'bastardised' Keynesian has also been used to cast doubt on the model's representation of Keynes's fundamental insights.

Many economists who regard themselves as Keynesians, however, are quite happy to use the model as a stepping stone to more complex economic modelling. Indeed, the economist and engineer, **A.W. Phillips**, famous for the Phillips curve which showed a Keynesian-type trade-off between unemployment and inflation (see Chapter 17), actually built a real hydraulic Keynesian 'model' of the economy. It used coloured water and valves, and the water flowing around the various pipes was used to represent income flowing around the economy. The model has recently been reconstructed at the London School of Economics.

Goods and money

In Chapter 16 we saw that there were two sides to the national product: national income and national expenditure. We thus established that:

$$Y = C + I + G + (X - M)$$

We now wish to examine these components of national income more closely.

Figure 31.1 shows again the basic elements of the circular flow of income. Firms produce goods and services and households buy them. The components in the diagram are thus identified not by who they are but by what they do, i.e. firms produce while households consume.

In our simple view of the economy the households own all the factors of production and hence all expenditure flows to firms are paid back out to households as payments for the use of the factors of production. In order to produce, the firms must hire factor services from households. On the other hand, households buy goods from firms in return for which they pay money. The money received by households is termed income (Y) and the money spent by households is termed consumption (C).

You can see in Figure 31.1 that goods and factor services flow one way round the diagram while money flows the other way. Since there is always a flow in the opposite direction, it is convenient to simplify our future diagrams by leaving out the flow of goods and to show only money flows. We shall also use abbreviations wherever possible.

Withdrawals and injections

In Figure 31.1 the value of consumption (C) equals the value of income (Y), i.e. all of income received in one period is directly spent in the next. It appears that there would be no tendency for the level of Y to change, in which case our economy could be said to be in equilibrium. Thus income in the first period is equal to the consumption of the next period. If consumption is the only form of expenditure then it follows that expenditure in this next period must be the same as this consumption. This expenditure, however, is all received by firms and all paid out again as income to factor payments. The model in Figure 31.1 is simply a closed loop with nothing leaking out and nothing being put in from outside. The flow of expenditure and income continues to flow around the circular flow at a constant level. This can be written in simple notation (where t denotes the first time period and $t + 1$ the next time period and so on):

$$C_t = E_t \equiv Y_{t+1} = C_{t+1} = E_{t+1} \equiv Y_{t+2}$$

where $\equiv$ indicates the national accounting identity described in Chapter 16.

However, there are various factors which cause money to be **withdrawn**, or to 'leak', from the system and, conversely, there are also **injections** into it.

Withdrawals

A withdrawal (W) is any part of income that is not passed on within the circular flow.

Savings (S) are an example of a withdrawal. Savings may be undertaken either by households who do not spend all their income or by firms not distributing all their profits but retaining some to finance future development. Equally income taken by the government in taxes (T) may or may not be present, and hence taxes are also a withdrawal. Lastly, income 'escapes' from a country's domestic circular flow through expenditure on imports (M). Hence the total withdrawals from a country's circular flow can be written:

$$W = S + T + M$$

Injections

An injection (J) is an expenditure which is not the consumption of domestic households, i.e. it comes from 'outside' of the circular flow of income.

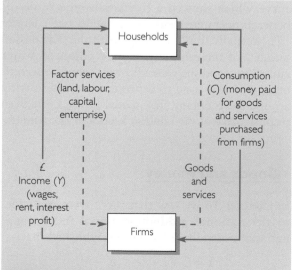

Figure 31.1 **The flow of goods and money between households and firms**

The most obvious example of an injection is exports (X) because the income of the firm selling them comes not from domestic households but from overseas. Less obviously, if a firm produces investment (or capital) goods (I) and sells them to another firm, this is an injection because the flow of income and expenditure has been increased, even though this increase is not a result of extra spending by households. Lastly, government expenditure in the economy (G) may or may not have been financed by current taxation (e.g. it could be financed by past taxation, borrowing or even simply by printing new money). Government expenditure will therefore also be regarded as an injection.

The 'hydraulic' Keynesian model – an overview

In order to understand the dynamics of the simple Keynesian circular flow model it is useful to draw on the analogy with the volume of water flowing through pipes. This is illustrated in the 'cartoon' of Figure 31.2.

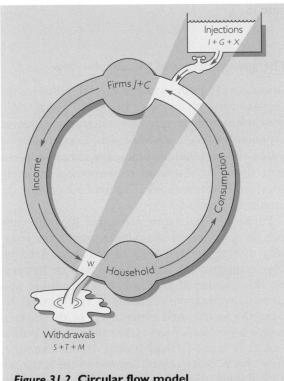

Figure 31.2 Circular flow model

It should be obvious from the cartoon that the flow of water in the circular pipe would be at a constant level when the flow into it (J) is exactly matched by the flow out of it (W). Equally, the flow of water (think 'income') in the pipe will increase whenever the flow of water into it is greater than the flow coming out of it, i.e. J is greater than W. This simple analogy thus makes it clear from the outset that:

The effect of an increase in withdrawals, other things being constant, is to reduce the circular flow of income, whereas an increase of injections will increase it. The circular flow of income is therefore in equilibrium when:

$$I + G + X = J = W = S + T + M$$

If the total of withdrawals is greater than that of injections, national income will contract. This is because the planned expenditure of the economy is insufficient to take up all the goods and services which the firms had planned to produce. Firms will therefore be faced with mounting stocks of unsold goods (inventories) and will cut back on their output, thereby reducing the income of households. (Remember: the costs of the firm are the income of the households.)

Conversely, if injections are greater than withdrawals the planned expenditure will be greater than the planned output of firms. Firms will therefore expand output and thereby raise the level of households' income.

If the total of all withdrawals (W) is equal to the total of injections (J) there will be no tendency for the level of national income to change and it is said to be in equilibrium. Thus the equilibrium condition for the economy is:

STUDENT ACTIVITY 31.1

You will also have noticed an emphasis in this section on the word planned. Another way of stating the equilibrium condition would be to say that it occurs when the planned expenditure is equal to the planned output. Within any one time period it is obvious that all expenditure is received as income and hence the two are identically equal. This is simply the national income accounting identity you saw in Chapter 16. Now use the t, t + 1, t + 2 notation used above to complete the sequence below and to satisfy yourself that, if there are withdrawals and injections, the income in one period is not necessarily equal to the expenditure of the next time period. By doing this you should also be able to demonstrate that when withdrawals equal injections the expenditure in the next time period will be equal to the income of the current period, i.e. the level of aggregate demand is in equilibrium when $W = J$ and this is the same thing as saying planned expenditure equals income.

$$Y_t \to C_{t+1} \overset{\nearrow W_{t+1}}{\underset{\nearrow J_{t+1}}{\to}} E_{t+1} \equiv Y_{t+1}$$

● *Common misunderstanding*

Students sometimes regard $W = J$ and planned $E = Y$ as two separate equilibrium conditions. In the student activity above you will have identified that they are simply alternative ways of stating the same equilibrium condition.

Components of national income

In this section we briefly recap on the various components of the circular flow and describe and define the various injections and withdrawals which constitute the components of national income to construct a simple model of the economy.

Savings (S) are defined as income not spent.

Savings might be undertaken by either households or firms. With households, savings are simply the part of their income which they have not consumed. For firms, savings would consist of profits not distributed to shareholders. For the sake of simplicity in drawing the diagram we shall represent all savings as being undertaken by households.

Investment (I) is any addition to the real capital stock of the nation.

Investment therefore consists of the purchase of new capital equipment, the construction of new buildings and any additions to stocks. It is important to understand that investment is concerned with real capital goods and not with paper claims upon them. For example, purchase of shares on the Stock Exchange is not investment, as used in

this sense, because all that has happened is that the ownership of pieces of paper has changed but there has been no real effect upon the economy.

The open economy

An economy which takes part in international trade, as all do, is described as an open economy. The sale and purchase of goods and services overseas introduce two more components into our model. Imports (M) are a withdrawal because the money paid for them 'leaks' out of the economy and, conversely, exports (X) are an injection because people overseas are now creating income for domestic households and firms.

STUDENT ACTIVITY 31.2

If imports are greater than exports the economy is said to have a trade deficit. Demonstrate that, other things being equal, this will cause the level of national income to fall. Conversely, if exports are greater than imports there is a trade surplus and again, other things being equal, you should be able to show that this will cause the level of national income to rise.

The government and the circular flow

Governments, both local and central, influence the circular flow of income. Taxes (T) are a withdrawal from the circular flow whereas government expenditure (G) is an injection. Taxes might be levied on personal incomes, on expenditure or upon firms, but it is easier to show them as simply being paid by households. This will not destroy the validity of the model.

Earlier in this chapter we stated Keynes's view that the government should intervene in the economy to regulate the level of economic activity. Keynes suggested that this should be done by varying the amount of government expenditure and taxes. Directing the economy in this manner by using the income and expenditure of the government's own budget (or rather that of the public sector) is termed *fiscal policy*. If, for example, there was a deficiency of demand in the economy so that there was unemployment, the government could increase the level of aggregate demand by running a budget deficit, i.e. it could spend more than it collected in as taxes. Conversely, if the government wanted to reduce the level of national income it could withdraw more from the economy in taxes than it put in by way of government expenditure. This would be termed a budget surplus.

The equilibrium of national income

We have now completed our simple model of the macroeconomy. You can see in Figure 31.3 that there are three withdrawals (W) consisting of:

$$W = S + M + T$$

and three injections (J) consisting of:

$$J = I + X + G$$

The figures used in Figure 31.3 indicate that the model is in equilibrium because withdrawals are equal to injections. As you can see, it is not necessary for each withdrawal to be equal to the corresponding injection for an equilibrium to exist, only that the total of all withdrawals is equal to the total of all injections. Thus the equilibrium occurs when:

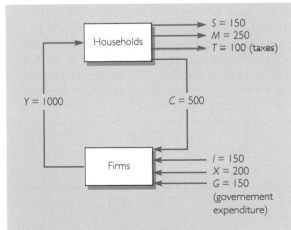

Figure 31.3 The complete model of the economy

Taxes (T) are a withdrawal and government expenditure (G) an injection. This model of the economy is in equilibrium because the total of all withdrawal (S + M + T) is equal to the total of all injections (I + X + G).

$$S + M + T = I + X + G$$

or:

$$W = J$$

or (equivalently):

$$\text{Planned } E = Y$$

It is worth restating that in Keynesian economics there is nothing necessarily desirable about an equilibrium level of national income. The significance of this is that our living standards, employment and well-being depend upon the level of national income and in Keynesian economics governments should not leave these things to chance. In contrast to neo-classical economics where there is less distinction between micro- and macroeconomics and a *laissez-faire* approach particularly at the macro level; Keynesian theory prescribes an **interventionist** role for governments at the macro level. Neo-classical economists believe that governments should pursue 'sound' financial policies which avoid inflations and should not try to influence unemployment and the level of output through macroeconomic policies. Such intervention, they believe, is unnecessary and could do as much harm as good and would present a temptation towards reckless policies based on short-term political objectives rather than long-term economic good. This different attitude towards the role of government is at the heart of the ideological differences between neo-classical and Keynesian economists.

A model of the economy

Assumptions

The economy is an extremely complex entity. Therefore, in order to advance our understanding and to make the construction of our model more straightforward, we will make general simplifying assumptions. Having developed a better understanding of the economy we will then drop these assumptions.

(a) *Potential national income*. Although there is actually a gradual upward trend in UK national income of 2 to 2.5 per cent per annum, assume that at any time there is a fixed level of national income which corresponds to the full employment of all resources; this is given the symbol Y_F. Thus the level of actual national income Y may be less than but no greater than Y_F. If everyone in the economy were to start working overtime it would be possible to exceed the level of Y_F.

(b) *Unemployment.* We assume that there is some unemployment of all factors of production. Thus it is possible to increase the level of Y by bringing these into employment.

(c) *Constant prices.* For most of the time it is convenient to assume that there is no inflation (or deflation). In this way the changes in income which we are looking at are changes in real income.

(d) *Technology.* We also assume that there are no significant changes in the level of technology such as would significantly alter the relationship between inputs and outputs.

Exogenous injections

Here we will make the assumption that injections are constant. Therefore in Figure 31.4 injections (J) are represented as a horizontal straight line at £50bn, determined by exogenous factors (i.e. by influences outside of our model).

Withdrawals

It is to be expected that savings, imports and taxation all increase as income increases. Thus we shall assume, reasonably, that withdrawals increase with income.

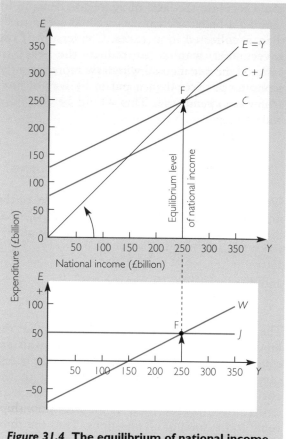

Figure 31.4 The equilibrium of national income

Table 31.1 presents the data for a hypothetical economy. An equilibrium will be reached in this economy when planned withdrawals are equal to injections. As can be seen from Table 31.1, this will occur at row F when national income is

Table 31.1 The equilibrium of national income

	Level of national income, Y (£bn)	Planned consumption, C (£bn)	Planned withdrawals, W (£bn)	Autonomous injections, J (£bn)	Total expenditure, C + J = E (£bn)	Tendency of income to:
A	0	75	−75	50	125	
B	50	100	−50	50	150	
C	100	125	−25	50	175	
D	150	150	0	50	200	Expand
E	200	175	25	50	225	
F	250	200	50	50	250	Equilibrium
G	300	225	75	50	275	
H	350	250	100	50	300	Contract

£250bn. Another way of looking at the equilibrium would be to say that it will occur when total expenditure (*E*) in the economy is equal to total income (*Y*). Total expenditure in this economy has two components: spending on consumer goods (*C*); and expenditure from injections (*J*). Thus total expenditure is *C* + *J*. In Table 33.1 it can be seen that total expenditure is equal to income at the level of £250bn, therefore confirming this as the equilibrium level of income.

Figure 31.4 gives a graphical representation of these figures. In the top graph the *C* + *J* line shows the total of all expenditure in this economy. Since *J* is constant, the *C* + *J* line will be parallel to the *C* line. This line shows the aggregate demand for this economy; this is termed aggregate monetary demand (*AMD*), total final expenditure (*TFE*) or simply aggregate demand (*AD*). The equilibrium level of national income will occur where the aggregate demand line crosses the 45° line, since the 45° line shows all the points at which expenditure is equal to income. This diagram showing the determination of the equilibrium is often called the **Keynesian cross diagram**.

The lower graph demonstrates the relationship of withdrawals and injections. It can be seen that the equilibrium level of national income corresponds to the point at which *W* = *J*. Thus the graph demonstrates, once again, that *W* = *J* is the equilibrium condition for the economy.

The nature of the equilibrium is illustrated in Figure 31.5. Here, if the level of *Y* were below the equilibrium, e.g. OL, then *J* would exceed *W* by AR. Thus injections would be greater than withdrawals and *Y* would rise. Conversely, if *Y* were to be ON then *W* would exceed *J* by TG, so that withdrawals would now be greater than injections and *Y* would fall.

▶ Conclusion

This chapter has explained the simple circular flow model used to explain Keynesian ideas. This model of equilibrium determination can also be represented as a Keynesian cross or 45° line diagram. The mechanics of the model are crude and have a close analogy to the flow of water in pipes

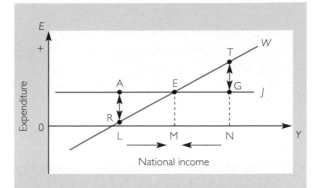

Figure 31.5 The reasons for equilibrium
At income level OL, *J* > *W* and therefore *Y* tends to rise. At income level ON, *W* > *J* and therefore *Y* tends to fall. Therefore OM is the equilibrium level of *Y*, where *W* = *J*.

whereby the level of flow is in equilibrium when the withdrawals (leakages) equal the flow of injections into the pipe. Doubts have therefore been expressed that the model adequately represents Keynes's ideas. Nevertheless, the majority of economists are happy to regard it as a stepping stone to more complex models (e.g. the Treasury model shown in Figure 31.7).

Summary

1 The circular flow of income was used by Keynes as a simple model of national income determination.

2 Micro- and macroeconomics give us contrasting views of the economy.

3 A withdrawal is any part of income that is not passed on within the circular flow, whereas an injection is an addition to the circular flow which does not come from the expenditure of domestic households.

4 The level of the flow of expenditures and income within the circular flow is affected and determined by changes in the balance between injections and withdrawals.

5 An equilibrium level of income is reached where withdrawals are equal to injections or, equivalently, when planned expenditure equals income.

6 Savings (S), imports (M) and taxes (T) are all withdrawals, whereas investment (I), exports (X) and government expenditure (G) are all injections.

7 An equilibrium level of income is reached where:

$$S + M + T = I + X + G$$

? QUESTIONS

1 What is meant by the circular flow of income?

2 Distinguish between microeconomics and macroeconomics.

3 'The economy is in equilibrium when expenditure equals income. In the National Accounts expenditure is always equal to income. Hence the economy is always in equilibrium!' Discuss.

4 In an economy with $C = 2 + 0.8\ Y$ and injections constant at 50 units at all levels of income. What would be the equilibrium level of national income?

5 Study Figure 31.6 which presents a more complex picture of the circular flow. Try to match the following items with the numbered flow which best illustrates it.
(a) Government payment of civil servants' salaries.
(b) A UK householder's purchase of a Volkswagen.
(c) Old-age pensioners' deposits in a building society.

(d) A UK firm's sale of goods to a West African firm.
(e) Income tax.
(f) The government's purchase of arms from a munitions firm.
(g) Disposable income.
(h) A firm ploughing back profit by purchasing new equipment.
(i) VAT.
(j) Corporation tax.

Data response A
THE TREASURY MODEL OF THE CIRCULAR FLOW

Figure 31.7 is a diagrammatic representation of the links between the variables which make up the model used by the UK Treasury. You should be able to see that although this is a far more complex model than the model of this chapter, it still has the Keynesian elements of income and expenditure flows that have been described. Study this diagram for a few minutes and then use it to answer the following questions.

1 Follow the arrows flowing *into* 'Total Final Expenditure' near the centre of the diagram and list the items of expenditure they represent. Classify these items according to the categories C, I, G and X.

2 List the elements which go to make up 'Total personal income' and explain the relationships shown between this and 'Real personal disposable income' and 'Consumers' expenditure'. Briefly, describe how these elements and relationships would complicate the consumption function of our simple model.

3 Check that the expenditure on the import of goods and services does not feed into the box showing 'Total Final Expenditure'. Why is this so? Trace through how an increase in expenditure on imports would lead to a reduction in 'Total Final Expenditure'. What exogenous influences might affect the 'Current Balance' and how would this in turn affect the level of domestic expenditure?

4 Make a list of all those boxes shown in the model which show items which do not appear in our simple model. Attempt to account for why they are included in the Treasury model of the 'real' economy and briefly explain how the simple model of this chapter could be extended to incorporate them.

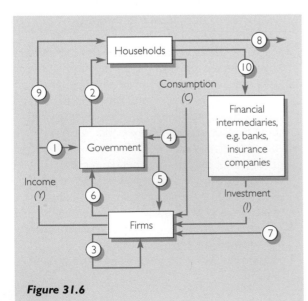

Figure 31.6

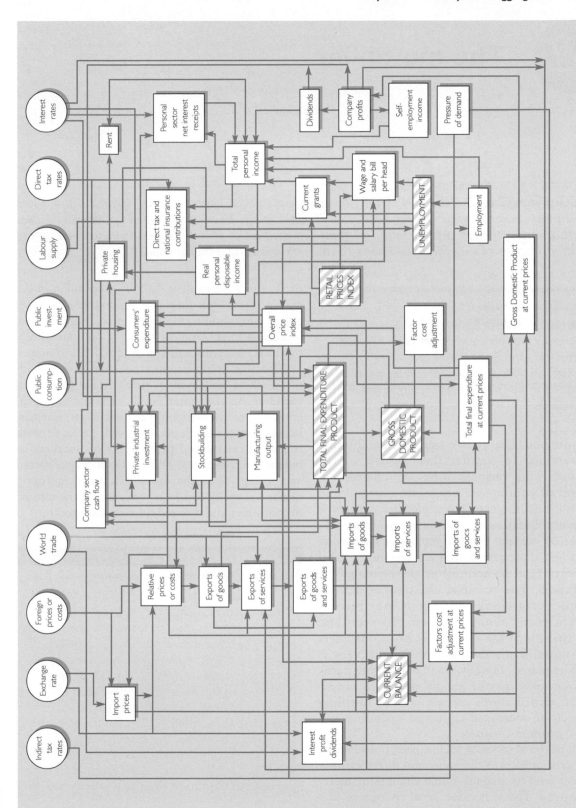

Figure 31.7 The Treasury model of the economy

32 The multiplier

Note: As was explained at the start of the previous chapter, this chapter may be skipped without loss of continuity according to the syllabus you are following. Even if excluded by your syllabus, the authors nevertheless suggest that you skim this chapter as it will deepen your understanding of the multiplier and be useful if you intend to study economics at a higher level.

Learning outcomes

At the end of this chapter you will be able to:
▶ Define the multiplier and demonstrate its effect algebraically and diagrammatically.
▶ Explain and list reasons why the multiplier is modified and thus difficult to identify in real economies.

In the previous chapter we saw how equilibrium is determined in circular flow models of the economy. This chapter looks at changes in the level of equilibrium aggregate demand and hence national income. The *multiplier concept* is an important feature of such Keynesian modes. In Chapter 29 we saw that the multiplier has strong psychological aspects in that changes in the level of activity tend to be reinforced by changes in expectations. For example, as economic activity starts to increase economic agents may become more optimistic about economic prospects and hence firms increase investment and consumers spend more. Thus the pace of the recovery is greatly increased. Equally, small initial downturns in the economy may be greatly magnified as pessimistic expectations create a self-fulfilling prophecy of decreased aggregate spending and reduced economic activity.

Even in the absence of such expectations effects, the process of income determination in the circular flow will tend to magnify initial changes in aggregate demand. This is because initial changes in C, J or W affect subsequent rounds of spending in the circular flow. Thus there is a build-up of *secondary effects* which add to the initial effect. For example, a decrease in government spending on domestically produced weapons will see an initial fall in output and incomes from weapon production. But the laid-off workers will then in turn reduce their own spending on consumer goods. Thus in the local areas around the weapons factories shops, cinemas, licensed drinking places, etc., will be faced with reduced demand and perhaps lay off workers or reduce their payments. This further reduces demand and so on. Thus the initial effect on aggregate demand is multiplied by a reduction in the income of consumers and demand for consumer goods.

STUDENT ACTIVITY 32.1

Take a blank sheet of paper and write '8bn' on it in the currency of your choice, e.g. $8bn. Now 'spend' this 8bn note on an imaginary item also of your choice. Income has thus increased in the item's industry by 8bn. Now suppose that all recipients of this money in the industry concerned spend half of what they receive (i.e. $MPC = 0.5$). You can 'model' this by tearing the sheet of paper in half and 'spending' one half, i.e. 4bn. Income has now increased by 8bn + 4bn = 12bn. But the process will not stop there; tear the sheet in half again and spend 2bn. Income has now risen overall by 8bn + 4bn + 2bn = 14bn. Continue this process to satisfy yourself that the stream of income will increase to a limit of 16bn, i.e. twice the initial 8bn injection. Thus an *MPC* of 0.5 has produced a multiplier coefficient of 2.

The multiplier defined

In Figure 32.1, we show the effect of an increase in the level of injections. Injections have increased by £50bn from J to J_1 and this has the effect of raising the level of national income by £100bn. Thus £50bn of extra injections has brought about £100bn of extra income. This is a diagrammatic example of the multiplier principle. The numerical value of the change is known as the multiplier. The strength of the multiplier, or its coefficient, is given the symbol K. In our example the multiplier would be:

$$K = \Delta Y/\Delta J$$
$$= 100/50$$
$$= 2$$

In this case the multiplier is 2. This means that for every, say, extra £1 of investment that is injected into the economy national income will rise by £2. This effect can also work downwards, so that a decrease in investment would cause a multiple decrease in national income.

The multiplier principle is that a change in the level of injections (or withdrawals) brings about a relatively greater change in the level of national income.

The operation of the multiplier

The operation of the multiplier can be explained by taking a simple example. Assume that investment and savings are the only injection and withdrawal respectively. If a firm decides to construct a new building costing £1000, then the income of builders and the suppliers of the raw materials will rise by £1000.

However, the process does not stop there. If we assume that the recipients of the £1000 have a marginal propensity to consume of 2/3, they will spend £666.67 and save the rest. This spending creates extra income for another group of people. If we assume that they also have an *MPC* of 2/3,

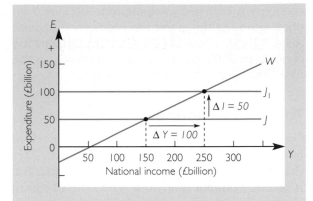

Figure 32.1 The multiplier
An increase in investment of £50bn has increased the equilibrium level of national income by £100bn.

they will spend £444.44 of the £666.67 and save the rest. This process will continue, with each new round of spending being two-thirds of the previous round. Thus a long chain of extra income, extra consumption and extra saving is set up (see Table 32.1).

Table 32.1 A simple example of the multiplier at work

	Increase in income, ΔY (£)	Increase in consumption, ΔC (£)	Increase in savings, ΔS (£)
1st recipients	1000 +	666.67 +	333.33 +
2nd recipients	666.67 +	444.44 +	222.23 +
3rd recipients	444.44 +	296.30 +	148.14 +
4th recipients	296.30 +	197.53 +	98.77 +
5th recipients	197.53 +	131.69 +	65.84 +
	. . .	. . .	. . .
Total	$\Delta Y=£3000$	$\Delta C=£2000$	$\Delta S=£1000$

The process will come to a halt when the additions to savings total £1000. This is because the change in savings (ΔS) is now equal to the original change in investment (ΔI) and, therefore, the economy is returned to equilibrium because $S = I$ once again. At this point the additions to income total £3000. Thus £1000 extra investment has created a £3000 rise in income; therefore, in this case, the value of the multiplier is 3.

Temporary and permanent changes

For the change in the equilibrium level of national income to be permanent it is necessary that the increase in investment is also permanent. If in our example (see Table 32.1) the £1000 of investment were an isolated example, it would create a 'bulge' in national income of £3000 and then the equilibrium would return to its previous level. On the other hand, if £1000 of investment were undertaken in each time period, it would cause a permanent increase in the equilibrium level of national income of £3000. This is illustrated in Figure 32.2.

The multiplier formula

As we have seen, the size of the multiplier is governed by the *MPC*. In our example we saw that additions to income were generated in the following series:

$$Y = £1000 + £666.67 + £444.44 + £296.30 \ldots$$

because the *MPC* was 2/3 and therefore two-thirds of all income received was passed on to create income for someone else. However, if the *MPC* were larger, say 9/10, then the same increase in investment would yield:

$$Y = £1000 + £900 + £810 + £729 \ldots$$

If we followed each series we would find that each successive round of extra income would get smaller and smaller but never quite reach zero. Fortunately such a series is well known in mathematics and is termed a ***geometric progression***. Its value is given by the formula:

$$\frac{1}{1 - r}$$

where r is the value of the common ratio. In the case of the multiplier the common ratio is the *MPC* so that we obtain:

$$K = \frac{1}{1 - MPC}$$

If, therefore, the *MPC* were 2/3 we would obtain:

$$K = \frac{1}{1 - \frac{2}{3}}$$
$$= 3$$

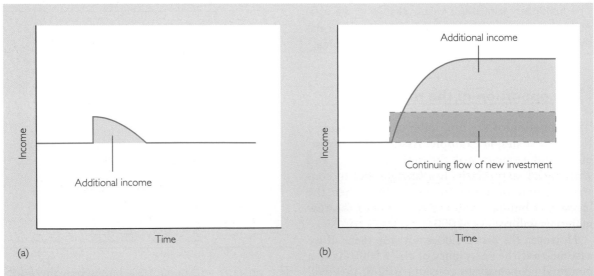

(a)

(b)

Figure 32.2 Effects of investment
(a) The effect of a single act of investment of £1000. (b) The shift to a higher equilibrium level of income caused by a continuous flow of new investment of £1000. Here the value of the multiplier is 3.

whereas if the value of the *MPC* were 9/10 we would obtain:

$$K = \frac{1}{1 - \frac{9}{10}}$$
$$= 10$$

The larger the MPC the larger the multiplier will be.

If in fact the *MPC* were to be one the value of the multiplier would be infinity. However, if everything were consumed there could be no investment anyway, so this is only a theoretical possibility.

STUDENT ACTIVITY 32.2

If you enjoy simple algebra, you should be able to derive the formula for the multiplier for yourself from the following equations of our simple model.

$Y = E$	The equilibrium condition
$E = C + J$	The components of aggregate expenditure
$C = a + bY$	A Keynesian consumption function, where a is autonomous consumption and b is the MPC

Substitute to get:

$Y = a + bY + J$

Thus:

$$Y = \frac{1}{1 - MPC}(a + J)$$

and therefore:

$$\Delta Y = \frac{1}{1 - MPC}\Delta J$$

or:

$$\Delta Y = K\Delta J$$

Equilibrium and the multiplier

In our simple representation, as all extra income is either consumed or withdrawn, we can write:

$$MPC + MPW = 1$$

where *MPW* is the **marginal propensity to withdraw**. In more complex models the derivation of

MPC is complicated by the distinction between *MPC* from gross income and *MPC* from personal disposable income. Here we abstract from such complications by simply assuming that *MPC* refers to the proportion of *gross* income passed on in the circular flow by way of consumption.

It follows in our model that $1 - MPC = MPW$, and thus we could also write the formula for the multiplier as:

$$K = \frac{1}{MPW}$$

Thus, if we know the value of *MPW* we can predict the effect of a change in injections upon national income. The effect will be the change in injections multiplied by K, which we can write as:

$$\Delta Y = K \times \Delta J$$

or as:

$$\Delta Y = \frac{1}{MPW} \times \Delta J$$

To determine the overall *MPW* we must total all the other propensities to withdraw. That is:

$$K = \frac{1}{MPW + MPT + MPM}$$

where $MPW = MPS + MPT + MPM$ and *MPS* is the marginal propensity to save, *MPT* is the marginal propensity of taxation and *MPM* is the marginal propensity to import.

If, for example, $MPS = 0.1$, $MPT = 0.15$ and $MPM = 0.25$ then:

$$K = \frac{1}{0.1 + 0.15 + 0.25}$$
$$= \frac{1}{0.5}$$
$$= 2$$

Thus any permanent increase in investment (I), government spending (G) or exports (X) would lead to a permanent increase in the level of equilibrium national income of twice this amount. For example, an increase in government spending of £1 million would lead to an eventual increase in equilibrium national income of £2 million.

Modifying factors

The multiplier of the simple Keynesian model is far more difficult to identify for a real economy. Partly this is because of the following factors:

(a) *Different MPCs.* Different sections of the population will have different propensities to consume. For example, the poor may have higher *MPCs* than the rich. The great Polish economist, **Michael Kalecki** (who had in fact already developed similar models to Keynes but who did not get the acknowledgement he deserved), distinguished between the *MPC* of those who earned wages/salaries and those who live off unearned income. He showed that these differences in *MPC* mean that income distribution can greatly affect the value of the multipliers and hence equilibrium national income.

(b) *Progressive taxes.* Because of the progressive nature of taxation, any rise in income will tend to increase the proportion paid in tax and hence tend to reduce the multiplier.

(c) *Inflation.* Increases in expenditure may be absorbed by price increases rather than increases in output. Thus output will not increase by as much as aggregate demand. Price increases may also affect people's real wealth and thus change their level of consumption.

(d) *Type of investment.* Different types of investment will have different multiplier effects. For example, extra spending on defence will have a different effect from spending on house building because of the different *MPCs* of the recipients and the different ratio of imported to domestically produced parts and materials. Because of the bulky nature of building materials most will come from domestic producers and hence the multiplier will tend to be larger than for expenditure on manufactured products where many of the components may be imported.

(e) *Endogenous investment.* What would happen if we dropped the assumption that investment is exogenous/autonomous? Suppose that investment were to increase with income. This is shown by the upward-sloping injections function in Figure 32.3(b). This would therefore magnify the multiplier effect as injections could now increase with income. This is also illustrated in Figure 32.3(b).

(f) *Time lags.* The various rounds of spending which cause the multiplier take time to build up. Thus the strength of the multiplier may not be seen for some time. This can cause difficulties for the timing of government macroeconomic policies.

(g) *Expectations.* We have already noted that in Keynesian economics expectations may greatly add to or reduce other effects.

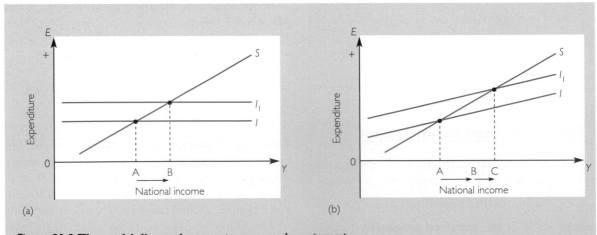

Figure 32.3 **The multiplier and non-autonomous investment**
If investment is constant (a) then the increase in *I* increases *Y* from OA to OB. However, if investment increases with income (b) then the same increase in *I* increases *Y* from OA to OC.

STUDENT ACTIVITY 32.3

Keynes asserted that it could be possible for an increase in the level of planned savings to lead to a fall in the level of actual savings. This he called 'the paradox of thrift'. To explore this possibility, assume that the only injection and withdrawal are investment and savings respectively. It should be clear that an increase in the level of planned savings can be represented by a vertical shift upwards of the withdrawals function, i.e. more saving is planned than before for each level of potential income. Now refer to Figure 32.3 to draw diagrams demonstrating that when injections are constant savings will fall back to their former level and that they could actually decrease if investment is non-autonomous!

Conclusion

In this and the previous chapter we have explained the usual textbook Keynesian model which was the mainstay of macroeconomics teaching for some 30 years. Basically, it is a theory of aggregate demand determination. We have hardly mentioned aggregate supply other than to suggest that it adjusts passively to increases in aggregate demand up until the point of full employment. Indeed, this was essentially the assumption made by Keynes. It is incorrect, however, to say he ignored aggregate supply. Unless there were significant changes in costs or physical supplies of materials, he simply did not think that in a depressed economy aggregate supply mattered very much as a force until full employment is neared. Thus supply followed demand more or less passively and was not an independent force which had to be reconciled with demand through price adjustments. As he was explaining economic depressions rather than inflationary booms he thus tended to suppress the effects of aggregate supply in his analysis.

In the next chapter you will see how aggregate supply can be incorporated into the analysis. But we should also note that as this textbook model is being built up the fundamentals of Keynes's ideas seem harder to discern. For example, the multiplier effects of Chapter 29 were based more on changes in expectations and unjamming of 'jammed' markets than on the size of the mathematical coefficient *MPC*. Post-Keynesians point out that equilibriums and stable functions seem at odds with Keynes's emphasis on instability and uncertainty. Nevertheless, the majority of economists use such simple models of aggregate demand determination as part of more complex models incorporating many additional influences on demand and supply.

Summary

1 An increase in planned consumption or injections will, *ceteris paribus*, tend to increase aggregate demand. An increase in planned savings or other withdrawals will, *ceteris paribus*, decrease aggregate demand.
2 Any initial change in spending results in a larger change in the level of Y as a result of the multiplier effect.
3 The size of the multiplier is determined by the *MPC* and can be calculated from the formula:

$$K = \frac{1}{1 - MPC} \text{ or } \frac{1}{MPW}$$

4 MPW consists of MPS, MPT and MPM.
5 In more complete models the calculation of MPC and MPW becomes more complex, as does the determination of injections when the influences on them are incorporated into the model.
6 In the real world the multiplier is difficult to identify and may change as income levels change.
7 There is a periodicity in the determination of national income such that the output in one period creates the income in the next period. The periodicity may be complicated by the existence of time lags in the economy.

? QUESTIONS

1 List the components of injections to, and withdrawals from, the circular flow of income.
2 Give a brief explanation of the multiplier in the following terms:

(a) common sense
(b) arithmetical
(c) graphical

3 How might the multiplier and the accelerator combine to cause fluctuations in national income and what might set the limits to these fluctuations?

4 What policies might a Keynesian government take to eliminate:
(a) Inflation?
(b) Regional unemployment?

5 List the factors which complicate the identification of the multiplier for 'real' economies.

6 What might happen to the aggregate demand function when it exceeds income at the point of full employment?

7 Assume:

$$C = 40 + \tfrac{2}{3} XY$$

and injections are constant at 50.
    Confirm that $Y = 270$ when the economy is in equilibrium. Increase J by 1 and confirm that Y increases by 3. What is the value of the multiplier and why?

Data response A
PLOTTING THE EQUILIBRIUM

Complete the following table for a hypothetical economy (all figures £bn). Assume that the consumption function is a straight line and that investment is constant at all levels of income.

Y	C	S	I	APC	MPC
0	25		25		
100	100				
200					
300					
400					
500					

1 From this data, draw a graph of the consumption function and of aggregate demand. Underneath this graph draw another to show savings and investment. Demonstrate the relationship between the two graphs.

2 What is the equilibrium level of national income? Show it clearly on the graph.

3 Now assume that I increases by £25bn. What will be the new equilibrium level of national income?

4 Explain the principle that is at work in moving from the first to the second equilibrium.

5 This is a model of a closed economy with no government intervention. What would be the situation if these assumptions were dropped?

Data response B
THE MULTIPLIER

The following table shows the allocation of gross national income in a country:

Gross national income	£276 000m
Direct taxes	£ 24 000m
Retained profits	£ 18 000m
Personal disposable income	£234 000m
Personal savings	£ 20 000m
Indirect taxes	£ 40 000m
Imports	£ 8 100m
Domestic consumption at factor cost	£165 000m

Assuming that additional income would be allocated in the same proportions as above:

1 Calculate the marginal propensity to consume.

2 Using your figure for MPC, calculate the value of the multiplier.

3 (a) What factors determine the value of the multiplier in such a way that its value is decreased as these factors increase?
(b) Show the values of these factors and show how they can be used to calculate the value of the multiplier.

4 (a) If output adjusted instaneously to changes in demand, what would be the change in real GNP following an increase in government expenditure of £100m?
(b) Is it likely that the increase in government expenditure would cause this increase in the volume of output in the real world?

Aggregate demand and supply analysis

Learning outcomes

At the end of this chapter you will be able to:
▶ Give an account of the derivation of aggregate demand and supply curves.
▶ Conduct analysis of macroeconomic changes using aggregate demand and supply diagrams.
▶ Criticise the model as a complete explanation of economic fluctuations.

The aggregate demand and supply curve approach

As we saw in Chapters 16 and 29, Keynes put forward the circular flow model as an alternative to the supply and demand model of microeconomics. Comparatively recently, it has become fashionable to represent macroeconomic interactions in terms of aggregate supply and demand diagrams. Not so long ago textbooks dealt only with demand-determined macro models in which national income and output would expand passively with increases in aggregate demand until full employment is reached (this model was explained in Chapter 31).

Although this allowed a very simple representation of Keynes's ideas it did lead to the supply side of the economy being virtually ignored in introductory textbooks. Keynes himself would have agreed that it is important that supply conditions are also considered.

Indeed, aggregate supply is vital to understanding the various modern neo-classical macro theories such as *monetarism* and *new classical* and for explaining their policy prescriptions which were so influential in the 1980s and 1990s. These modern neo-classical models were part of a revival of the non-interventionist *laissez-faire* political movement. They reversed the emphasis on Keynes and built on pre-Keynesian models.

In contrast to supply behaving passively, in pre-Keynesian models it is aggregate demand which adjusts more or less passively to supply-determined levels of output and employment.

These supply-side-determined models are examined further in Chapter 37 but between these two extremes there can be various balances between the strength of aggregate demand and aggregate supply in the macroeconomy. We shall also note the limitations of, and issues raised by, the practice of representing macroeconomic adjustment in terms of supply and demand diagrams.

● Common misunderstanding

To the student who has read through the micro sections of a textbook the aggregate demand and supply curve diagrams will look deceptively familiar. It is all too easy to engage in the geometrical moving of lines in order to find new 'equilibrium' points of intersection. But unless you are aware of the theoretical underpinning of such curves you are doing little more than moving a ruler across a page.

It is important that you always think about what lies behind these curves and to realise that different schools of thought may offer alternative interpretations and approaches. For now we note that:

Aggregate demand and supply analysis tends to impart a neo-classical bias.

For example, strictly speaking, supply curves imply that firms and consumers are price takers as in perfect competition (see Chapter 21). This is not an assumption that all economists are happy with. Nevertheless, so useful and convenient is this approach that economists of virtually all persuasions will employ it from time to time. Moreover, the concept of a supply curve can be 'stretched' in order to represent different theories, but it must be said that such an approach can sometimes distort rather than elucidate the perspective of some schools of thought, e.g. *monopoly capitalism theorists* (see pages 292 and 710).

We saw in Chaper 17 that, today, the aggregate supply curve is more controversial than the aggregate demand curve. If you were to study economics further you would find that in fact there are some 'lesser; controversies over demand, but for now we are happy to settle for the assumption we made in Chapter 17:

We assume the aggregate demand curve to be downward sloping.

This means that, bearing in mind any multiplier effects, the lower the price level the greater will be the volume of goods and services demanded in the economy. The end result is shown again in Figure 33.1. Remember that it looks like a normal demand curve, but is drawn using an index of the overall price level and plots the aggregate demand for goods and services in the economy as a whole.

The derivation of the aggregate supply curve

The shape of the aggregate supply curve depends crucially on the assumptions we make. In neo-

classical schools perfect competition is assumed. Thus the labour market clears at the level of employment which corresponds to profit maximisation (see Chapter 25). That is:

$$W = MPP \times P$$

or in real terms:

$$\text{Real wage} = W/P = MPP$$

i.e. for the economy as a whole, labour will be employed up until the point at which the real wage (W/P) of the marginal worker is equal to the worker's marginal physical product (MPP).

To understand the idea that the level of employment is determined by the real wage, assume that there is only one output of the economy. Thus workers produce and are paid in the same commodity. We could assume it to be any such commodity, say 'fudge' or any other item that you may prefer. If the price of a unit of fudge were £5 and the money wage were £20 per week, then the real wage would be 4 units of fudge. Thus, assuming diminishing marginal physical product, it would be profitable for employers to employ workers whose MPP exceeded 4 units of fudge but not those extra workers for which MPP falls below 4. If the price of fudge were to rise to, say, £10, then the real wage will have fallen to 2 units of fudge. Thus at the previous level of employment the marginal worker will be producing 4 units of fudge but be receiving only 2 units in wages. It therefore becomes profitable for employers to take on more workers up until the point at which the MPP of labour falls to 2. This relationship between the real wage and the level of aggregate employment is shown in the top half of Figure 33.2.

In the short run the stock of capital (and land) is fixed; hence Figure 33.2 shows that each level of employment will also correspond to a definite level of output. We shall now trace out such a relation.

A Keynesian view of the aggregate supply curve

Keynesians assume that money wages are downwardly sticky, perhaps because of institutional rigidities such as past contracts or union resistance. In the absence of inflation in the prices of goods and services the real wage might thus be

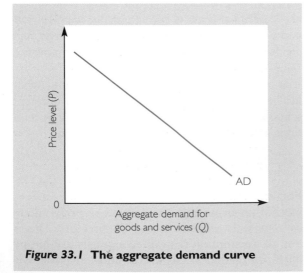

Figure 33.1 **The aggregate demand curve**

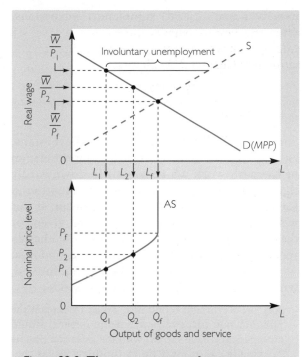

Figure 33.2 The aggregate supply curve
At price level P_1, lower the real wage and more labour is employed (L_2). At price level P_f full employment is reached and the supply curve becomes vertical.

real wage is thus lowered it becomes profitable for firms to employ more workers. As the level of employment increases so will the output of goods and services. Thus:

For any given value of the money wage, we can derive an upward-sloping aggregate supply curve.

Notice, however, that once full employment is reached by raising the price level to P_f the model reverts to the neo-classical case where aggregate supply is fixed. This is because there is nothing to prevent an *increase* in the money wage. Hence any further increase in the price level tending to produce excess demand in the labour market would simply cause money wages to increase so as to hold the real wage and the level of employment and output constant.

STUDENT ACTIVITY 33.1

In neo-classical economics the labour market is regarded as working in the same way as any other market. Hence, wages are fully flexible and will adjust with market forces until the real wage is in equilibrium. Refer to Figure 33.2 to demonstrate that the neo-classical (in macroeconomics this is often called the 'new classical' school) aggregate supply curve will be vertical.

'stuck' at too high a level for the labour market to clear. This is illustrated in the top half of Figure 33.2. The assumption that money wages will not decrease is indicated by the bar over the symbol for money wage, i.e. $\overline{W}$.

It can be seen that at a price level of P_1, the real wage is above the equilibrium. Thus employers are prepared to employ only L_1 of labour and there is an excess supply of labour, i.e. involuntary unemployment. In neo-classical models this excess supply would simply force down money wages until the equilibrium real wage is reached. In this Keynesian case this cannot happen because of the downward stickiness of money wages and hence the involuntary employment can persist.

Figure 33.2 also shows the solution to the unemployment problem. Although money wages will not fall the real wage can be lowered by an increase in the price level of goods and services. Hence, if the government increases the aggregate demand for goods and services through fiscal or monetary means this will tend to increase their prices and thereby lower the real wage. As the

In Figure 33.3 we show aggregate demand and supply based on Keynesian sticky money wage assumptions.

Neo-Keynesians use the same sort of demand and supply approach as neo-classical economists but emphasise that markets do not move smoothly towards market clearing.

Neo-Keynesians emphasise sticky prices and restricted elasticities which prevent rapid market clearing.

The post-Keynesian view is often shown by a completely flat aggregate supply curve as post-Keynesians regard aggregate supply as adjusting passively to demand and set at a level determined by historical and institutional processes. In fact though, post-Keynesians emphasise uncertainty, expectations and dynamic movements through time in their analysis and hence make little use of equilibrium aggregate demand and supply analysis.

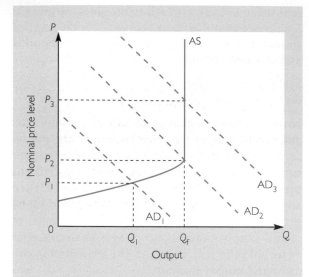

Figure 33.3 **Neo-Keynesian aggregate demand and supply analysis**
Increase in aggregate demand (AD$_1$ to AD$_2$) causes some inflation but a large increase in employment. At full employment (Q$_f$) any further increase in aggregate demand (e.g. to AD$_3$) is turned entirely into inflation with no rise in output or employment.

A neo-Keynesian recession

Let us return to the upward-sloping 'sticky money wage' aggregate supply associated with neo-Keynesians as shown in Figure 33.3. As can be seen, increasing aggregate demand from AD$_1$ to AD$_2$ results in a mild inflation of the price level and a substantial increase in output (and employment). But once full employment has been reached a further increase in aggregate demand to AD$_3$ will be absorbed wholly by an increase in the price level as there is no increase in output.

A common fear among Keynesians is that money wages will begin to rise before full employment is reached, e.g. as union strength increases with the developing shortages of labour, or as bottlenecks in labour markets begin to develop causing employers to bid against each other for the remaining supply of labour. You should now work out the result that this wage inflation will cause the AS curve to shift upwards with increases in AD. Thus government attempts to lower the real wage by reflating the economy might be thwarted. For this reason

neo-Keynesians, and some post-Keynesians, often advocate incomes policies.

Incomes policies attempt to prevent wages rising in the face of increasing aggregate demand and are thus intended to increase the expansionary effects on output of increases in aggregate demand by reducing the effects on inflation.

Some writers, including the post-Keynesians, have challenged the neo-Keynesian interpretation of Keynes's work which identifies downwardly rigid money wages as the critical assumption in Keynes's theory of macro unemployment. If this were the sole reason that Keynes had given for the persistence of unemployment we could hardly speak of a Keynesian 'revolution' in economics. As the Swedish economist, **Axel Leijonhufvud**, wrote in his paper 'Keynes and the Classics':

> Any pre-Keynesian economist, asked to explain the phenomenon of persistent unemployment, would automatically have started with the assertion that its proximate cause must lie in too high wages that refuse to come down.

Some Keynesian economists have thus focused on Keynes's distinction between *nominal* and *effective demand* as holding the key to his analysis. Thus it may be the case that even if the real wage is at the level at which the labour market could nominally clear, the effective demand for labour is constrained by lack of demand in the markets for goods and services. This is illustrated in Figure 33.4. In this diagram the real wage *is* at the level which would cause the labour market to clear in neo-classical analysis. In Keynesian analysis, however, a distinction is drawn between this nominal demand for labour and the *effective demand* for labour as constrained by conditions in the goods market.

In Figure 33.4 we can see that the level of aggregate demand (AD$_1$), as determined in the product market, is insufficient to purchase the level of output associated with full employment (L$_f$) in the labour market. Thus the effective demand for labour is *actually* set by the level of aggregate demand for goods at Q$_1$. Employers will not employ workers past this level, for whatever the potential profit suggested by wages and prices there can be no profit in producing goods and services that no one will actually buy.

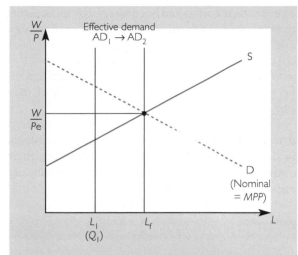

Figure 33.4 Curing a Keynesian recession
Lack of effective demand keeps employment below the full employment equilibrium. This is cured by an increase in government expenditure (ΔG) increasing the level of aggregate demand without changing wages.

This interpretation clearly breaks with the assertion that unemployment is caused by too high a level of the real wage. In this interpretation the 'prices are right' for full employment as it would nominally be profitable for firms to employ all the labour wishing to work. This does not happen, however, as it is profitable to employ the labour only if the products so produced can be sold.

If the produce of labour cannot be sold because of lack of aggregate demand it is not profitable to employ labour whatever the level of the real wage.

STUDENT ACTIVITY 33.2

Adapt Figure 33.4 to show that if a lack of aggregate demand for goods and services is the problem, a fall in wages could actually worsen unemployment, i.e. a reduction in the spending power of workers might further reduce aggregate demand thereby further constraining effective demand in the labour market.

Curing the recession

As is so often the case, the analysis of the problem suggests the cure. In Figure 33.4 we can see how an increase in government expenditure could lift the constraint of effective demand in the labour market by increasing the demand for goods and services. This allows the profitable employment of more workers even if the real wage remains at the same level. Once full employment is reached the model again reverts to the neo-classical vertical AS case, i.e. further increases in aggregate demand will simply cause prices and wages to increase in equal proportion.

The above interpretation of increases in aggregate demand, acting to lift constraints on the quantity of goods that can be sold and consequently the amount of labour employed, implies an AS curve as shown in Figure 33.5.

As can be seen, in this interpretation, increases in AD can increase output until full employment is reached without the need for any price changes or reduction in the real wage.

A neo-classical view

The transmission mechanism

We have seen that in macroeconomic representations of neo-classical economics (e.g. the new classical school) the aggregate supply curve is vertical. If we stick to the assumption of perfectly

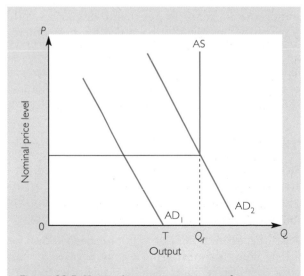

Figure 33.5 Keynesian aggregate supply
An extreme view would allow increases in aggregate demand to increase output, without inflation until full employment is reached.

competitive markets for goods and services and flexible wages there is a monetarist rebuttal to the Keynesian assertion that a lack of AD can forever prevent full employment being reached. If markets are perfectly competitive the lack of effective demand as compared with the level of aggregate supply would cause a persistent downward pressure on prices. Thus, given a constant nominal money supply, the real supply of money will be constantly increasing. The neo-classical monetarist school argues that eventually this increase in the real money supply must 'spill over' into extra spending. This supposed transmission mechanism is explained in more detail on page 538. This will cause AD to increase until eventually full employment is again reached.

The Pigou effect

The increase in consumption due to increased real money balances described above is known as the *real money balances effect* or the 'Pigou effect' after the economist who used it to challenge Keynes's assertion in *The General Theory* that the economy could remain permanently at less than full employment. Many Keynesian economists have responded by accepting its validity as a theoretical solution but insisted that the process would take far too long for policy purposes and hence the increase in aggregate demand would have to be 'artificially' hastened by government-induced reflation.

The debate between Keynesians and neo-classical economists over the Pigou effect relates to the time the effect would take to cure unemployment.

The effect of pricing policies

If we drop the assumption of perfectly competitive markets the Pigou effect loses much of its persuasiveness to the effect that a free market capitalist economy is ultimately self-correcting.

Post-Keynesians point out that it has been known for a long time that most firms are not engaged in marginal cost pricing but in fact set their price according to a pre-determined mark-up on average cost.

Such pricing practices were examined in Chapter 22. Now, much empirical evidence also suggests

that average cost is fairly constant for most firms over a wide range of output. Thus reality may not consist of firms moving up their marginal cost curves in response to increased prices, but instead firms may use some 'rule of thumb' mark-up pricing formula and then sell as much as they can at this price.

Figure 33.6 shows the effect of such mark-up pricing practice. The figure shows that increases in demand may be met by firms increasing their output in response to increased sales without any upward pressure on prices.

STUDENT ACTIVITY 33.3

Taken literally, neo-classical theory suggests that firms will refuse to sell more output at the same price when the point at which $MC = MR$ is reached. Think about your experiences as a consumer and consider which theory of the firm, neo-classical or (neo-)Keynesian, best describes your experiences. But is descriptive accuracy necessarily the most important feature for comparison?

Similarly, firms may respond to decreases in aggregate demand by cutting back output without any change in price. Thus, unlike in perfect

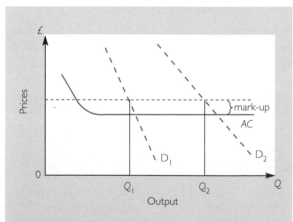

Figure 33.6 The effect of mark-up pricing
The existence of a flat-bottomed *AC* curve and mark-up pricing policies means large changes in demand have no effect upon price. This means that excess capacity can exist without affecting prices. Thus the market might not be self-correcting.

competition, there is not necessarily a tendency for prices to fall as aggregate demand falls. If, following depressed sales, firms competed with one another for increased sales, then the real money supply might again be increased, leading ultimately to a real balance effect. But, particularly in highly concentrated markets, firms may resist the temptation to cut prices for fear of precipitating a self-defeating price war (see discussion of oligopoly behaviour in Chapter 22, page 295).

Mark-up pricing can also be used to explain why the aggregate supply curve might begin to slope, and increase in slope, as full employment is approached. For example, as firms near their maximum potential output production might become less efficient causing average costs to rise. Alternatively, as resources become more fully utilised input costs might rise, again causing unit costs to increase. In either case the increase in unit cost will be passed on as a price rise if a constant mark-up is maintained.

Objections to aggregate supply and demand analysis

We have seen that the slope of the aggregate supply can be used to represent neo-classical and neo-Keynesian views. But economists from both the *laissez-faire* Austrian school and the interventionist post-Keynesian school would challenge the usefulness of aggregate demand and supply analysis. Although at near opposite ends of the political spectrum both of these schools feel that it is misleading to represent the economy in terms of equilibriums. In particular they point out that equilibrium ignores uncertainty and the dynamics of the economy with the passage of time.

For example, an economist looking at aggregate demand and supply diagrams might attempt to reduce inflation by decreasing aggregate demand so as to intersect the aggregate supply curve at a lower level of prices. But this might instead result in a collapse of investment as expectations are adjusted to a downturn in the economy. This collapse of investment in turn means demand is sharply reduced still further. As industrial capacity, job skills and investment in new technology are lost the economy becomes trapped in a downward cycle. If an attempt is made to reflate the economy by restoring aggregate demand the economy is unable to respond quickly by restoring industrial output; hence inflation and imports surge upwards. Instead of a mere adjustment of demand the attempt to reduce inflation has permanently damaged the performance of the economy and made it even more difficult to control inflation! The tendency for equilibrium levels of a variable to gravitate towards actual values is called '*hysteresis*'. Hysteresis suggests that a fall in output and employment may not be easily reversible.

STUDENT ACTIVITY 33.4

Attempt to draw the effects of the analysis of the preceding paragraph using aggregate demand and supply curve diagrams.

Conclusion

Enough has now been said for the reader to appreciate that there is more than one interpretation of aggregate demand and supply diagrams and hence they should not be used unthinkingly. Nevertheless they can provide a convenient way of demonstrating likely macroeconomic interactions. For example, a reduction in the cost of an important raw material can be expected to increase aggregate supply, thereby causing an increase in output and a reduction in the price level.

Summary

1 For many years macroeconomic analysis focused on aggregate demand, following the work of Keynes. The neo-classical school has moved the emphasis to aggregate supply.
2 Deceptively simple aggregate demand and supply curves should be treated with caution. Many assumptions may be used when constructing them, such as that of perfect competition.
3 A fall in the level of prices causes the real money supply to increase, which results in an extension of demand for the output of the economy. Thus the aggregate demand curve is downward sloping. This relationship may be reinforced by changes in imports and exports.

4 The neo-classical view is that the aggregate supply curve is vertical as the real wage adjusts to maintain equilibrium in the labour market.

5 The neo-Keynesian view is that the aggregate supply curve slopes upwards until full employment is reached, when it becomes vertical.

6 Post-Keynesians follow Keynes in emphasising the constraint on employment set by the level of demand in the goods and service market. For such economists the aggregate 'supply' curve may be flat over a wide range.

7 Neo-Keynesians argue for the need for governments to increase the level of aggregate demand to cure unemployment. The neo-classical view is that this causes inflation, not employment.

8 Neo-classicists argue that any lack of effective demand causes prices to fall and thus an increase in real money balances. This causes an increase in demand and eliminates the unemployment. This is sometimes termed the Pigou effect. Keynesians believe the effect would take too long to restore full employment for practical relevance.

9 Uncertainty, imperfections of competition and oligopolistic pricing policies may interfere with the attainment of full employment equilibriums.

10 Supply side improvements can be represented by a rightward shift of the aggregate supply curve.

? QUESTIONS

1 Demonstrate how the aggregate supply curve may be derived from the demand curve for labour.

2 Contrast the different views of the shape of the aggregate supply curve.

3 Discuss the view that the macroeconomy is essentially self-regulating.

4 How may persistent unemployment arise in the macroeconomy according to the neo-Keynesian school of thought?

5 What is the real money balances (or Pigou) effect?

6 Contrast neo-classical and neo-Keynesian views on policies to reduce unemployment.

7 Use aggregate demand and supply curves to demonstrate how inflation occurs.

8 'If the Treasury were to fill old bottles with banknotes, bury them at suitable depths in disused coalmines which were then filled up to the surface with town rubbish, and leave it to private enterprise on well-tried principles of *laissez-faire* to dig the notes up again ... there need be no more unemployment and with the help of the repercussions, the real income of the community, and its capital also, would probably become a good deal greater than it actually is.'

Do you agree with this statement taken from Keynes's *General Theory*? Give reasons for your answer.

9 'Supply siders argue that if the poor have more they work less but if the rich have more they work harder.' To what extent is this statement a fair representation of the arguments of supply side economists?

Data response A
THE EFFECTS OF A MAXIMUM WORKING WEEK

Read the following extract from the *Daily Mail* of 28 August 1997 and then answer the questions that follow:

1 To what extent could there ever be said to be full employment in an economy where the working week is artificially constrained?

2 Accepting the definition of a full-time job as a 35 hour week, what would be the effect on the full employment level of output?

3 Show the effect on an upward-sloping aggregate supply curve of a tax surcharge on workers' extra hours and an obligatory reduction of hours without a proportionate reduction in salary. Explain your answer.

4 What might be the effect on the aggregate demand curve of increased marginal taxation and a shorter working week with a less than proportionate reduction in salary? Explain your answer.

5 What would be the overall effect of the changes in questions 2, 3 and 4 above on (where the overall change is indeterminate explain why this is so):
(a) output;
(b) employment;
(c) the price level?

The French put a tax on hard work

From **Peter Shard** in Paris

French workers face paying extra tax if they work too hard.

Under extraordinary proposals being drafted by Lionel Jospin's Socialist government, anyone labouring more than 39 hours a week will automatically pay an income tax surcharge and more on national insurance.

The plan has been formulated because M Jospin wants to cut the working week to 35 hours to create more jobs. From next year, workers doing official overtime beyond the current working week of 39 hours will have to pay a tax surcharge on their extra hours.

From 2000, all salaried employees will be liable to pay the extra tax for every hour a week they work above 39,

even if it is part of their normal work and not overtime.

The plans are contained in a leaked document prepared for employment minister Martine Aubry.

By law, all French companies have to register employees' hours. Most workers are said to be in favour of the shorter week even if it means earning less. They believe it is a way of helping to persuade companies to take on more employees on shorter working weeks, although the trade unions and bosses are sceptical.

Confederation of industry spokesperson Jean Gandois denounced what he called this 'massive obligatory reduction of hours without a cut in salary

which will seriously harm the competitiveness of our businesses'.

Small firms would be particularly hard hit, Small Businesses Confederation president Lucien Rebuffel warned.

'The reduction in the working week is impracticable because of the way specialised jobs and functions are divided up,' he said.

Louis Viannet, leader of the Communist-backed CGT union, insisted that workers must not be made to suffer. 'This measure must take effect comprehensively and quickly without any reduction in salary' he said. And he warned: 'If the bosses maintain their opposition, there is going to be conflict.'

Source: *Daily Mail*, 28 August 1997. Reprinted with permission.

Data response B
MONEY, EXPECTATIONS AND MARKETS

Read the following extract from *The Observer* of 31 August 1997 and then answer the questions that follow.

1 To what extent might past experience of changes in the economy affect and modify current behaviour?
2 Explain the importance of the distinction between 'private' and 'external' logic, as described in the article, to Keynesian economics.
3 Link fluctuations in money markets to changes in aggregate demand.
4 Use the article and aggregate demand and supply analysis to suggest how a deliberate attempt to reduce inflation could lead to an unintended recession.
5 'The volatility of markets is as much an argument against government macroeconomic intervention as it is for it.' Explain and discuss.

Money: a telling lore

Are buyers and sellers rational people, creating a nice balance between supply and demand?
Theorists think they are, but real life is different, says **Dorothy Rowe**

Money isn't real. It may be a very important means whereby we maintain our sense of identity, but it isn't real. It's simply a set of ideas, some of which we share with other people and some which are our own. We might both agree that this piece of metal is a £1 coin, but is it a lot or a little to pay for a pint of milk? Value is in the eye of the beholder.

If you want to understand why the market does what it does we need to understand ourselves; that is, our own private logic. Nothing pleases me more than when I find some scientific research that supports my theories, especially my theory that to understand why people behave as they do we need to discover each person's private logic.

Research reported by *The Guardian* recently did just that. Here, researchers used artificial-life methods to create computer software working as 'robotraders' to examine classic market theory.

Classic market theory, or the competitive equilibrium model, assumes buyers and sellers behave rationally and thus, in a free market, produce an equilibrium between supply and demand. In real life, markets might produce something like an equilibrium but they also produce much volatility, bubbles and crashes – events that classic theory finds difficult to explain.

Economists, like psychologists, have always been strong on theory. Again like psychologists, they have steadfastly ignored what real people actually do, because real people ruin theories. Some people might do what the theory predicts, but many won't. Instead of asking why this happens, economists and psychologists, since the beginning of their disciplines in the nineteenth century, have seen their task as being that of scientists, of uncovering the orthodox truths that are immanent in nature. In the search for such universal laws, what individuals think is irrelevant.

For psychologists, no word implied such complete rejection and scorn as

'subjective'. The ideal of science towards which they strove was physics, but in such striving they managed to overlook Heisenberg who, in describing his Uncertainty Principle in 1927, said the experimenter was always part of the experiment.

What this means in terms of theory is that the particular theory a person creates or espouses may or may not reflect the real world but will always reflect the individual personal meanings created by those who hold it.

In psychology and economics, theories are never proved or disproved. They simply come into and fall out of fashion.

Freud's theories used to be all the rage while Jung's were seen as the product of an unworldly nutter. Now Freud is deplored or ignored while Jung is extremely popular. In economics, Maynard Keynes went out of fashion and Milton Friedman came in, but now he is on the wane and Keynes is becoming increasingly fashionable.

By ignoring the essence of how we live our lives – the personal meanings we each create – economists and psychologists have developed theories about the world and the people in it from which all sense of personal experience has been removed.

Psychologists have developed models that represent us as being nothing but puppets manipulated by the strings of behaviourist stimulus-response, or of genes, or of unconscious drives. Economists, wrote Paul Ormerod (an economist who is extremely critical of classical economics), 'see the world as a machine – a very complicated one, but nevertheless a machine, whose workings can be understood by putting together carefully and meticulously its component parts'.

'The behaviour of the system as a whole,' he continued 'can be deduced from a simple aggregation of these components. A lever pulled in a certain part of a machine with a certain strength will

have regular and predictable outcomes elsewhere in the machine.'

The Science Museum now houses a model of such a machine made by Bill Phillips, an engineer turned economist. This wonderful contraption has levers to pull, buttons to press, sluice gates and liquids of different colours which, representing economic forces, would rush around the system's tubes.

Such economic machines were not assumed to be thinking. Computers might not think for themselves but they can contain software that simulates thought. This is what the robotrader computers did or, at least, these were models of how their makers, the computer programmers, thought people thought.

They gave their robotraders the ability to adapt to market conditions by using learning algorithms that allow them to try out different buying and selling strategies to optimise their portfolios.

They each reacted individually to events, using the trading rules with which they had been programmed. These rules corresponded to what we can call shared, public logic. However, these robotraders also had a kind of private logic.

We all share a public logic, but each of us has his or her own private logic, which is the set of conclusions we have drawn from our individual experience. No two people ever have the same experience, so no two people ever see any thing in exactly the same way.

The robotraders' programmers created a kind of private logic for their robotraders by running a genetic algorithm, a technique that created a kind of Darwinian evolution in the software, cross-breeding sections of the code to create new strings, some of which then made changes in the external logic rules.

We human beings do this all the time. Your mother might have laid down the rule: 'On your way to school, cross the road only at pedestrian crossings.' You then change that rule to: 'Use a pedestrian crossing only when mother can see you.' Your changed rule is part of your private logic. We use private logic continuously. These robotraders could do so only when the researchers used the genetic algorithm. The researchers ran their experiment 25 times, involving each time some 250 000 trades.

The results were clear. Under certain conditions the efficient market of classic theory emerged. Under other conditions the market that emerged was just like real life – lots of activity, prices bubbling up and then crashing down, the kind of market that pension-fund managers and market-watchers find so hard to predict.

And what were these different conditions? The classic market emerged when the robotraders were using only their external logic, but when the genetic algorithms were used frequently this private logic produced a market very close to real life.

This is a simple scientific replication of what goes on all the time in real life.

In dealing with money, as in dealing with every aspect of our lives, we use both the shared, external logic, which is contained Aristotelian logic, scientific method and laws, mathematics and agreed rules and laws; and our own private, individual logic of the structure of meaning, which gives our sense of identity.

Source: The Observer, 31 August 1997. Reprinted with permission.

SECTION  VIII

Managing the economy: issues and policies

Money is a good servant but a bad master.
Oxford Dictionary of English Proverbs

Our interest will be to throw open the doors of commerce,
and to knock off its shackles, giving freedom to all persons for
the rent of whatever they may choose to bring into our ports,
and asking the same in theirs.

Thomas Jefferson

34 Growth and stability

Economic growth

What is economic growth?

When we speak of *economic growth* we mean an increase in the real GDP of a nation, that is, the money GDP adjusted for inflation. The idea of GDP as a measure of the output of a nation was introduced in Chapter 16, and broadly consists of all the final outputs of the domestic economy. The technical details of adjustment for inflation will be dealt with in Chapter 35, but for the moment you should understand an increase in GDP which is solely the result of increased prices will not make us better off. For economic growth we need an increase in output. We must also consider the effect of *population growth*. Consider the case of a nation whose GDP is growing at 5 per cent per year but whose population is growing at 10 per cent. In this case, in real terms the average GDP per capita is declining. Thus the usual definition of economic growth is:

An increase in the real GDP per capita of a nation.

As we will see later in this chapter, there are some criticisms of this rather narrow economic definition of economic growth, and there is increasing emphasis on other measures of welfare, such as environmental quality, and the amount of leisure time available to enjoy income. Initially, however, we shall concentrate on this narrow version of economic progress, and discuss how some nations are able to achieve higher levels of growth than others. Much economic analysis focuses on the present: how to allocate resources between competing demands; how to solve some immediate problem of unemployment or inflation. The real measure of a successful economy is the growth of its output.

● *Common misunderstanding*

When calculating economic growth, it is important to distinguish between real and nominal increases in GDP. For example, between 1965 and 1995 the GDP of the UK increased from £31.7 billion to £603.2 billion, an increase of 1802 per cent. However, when the effect of inflation is taken into account this amounts to an increase of only 88 per cent. It is the real increase that is important here.

STUDENT ACTIVITY 34.1

A country has a GDP of £100 billion and a population of 10 million. At the end of the year GDP has risen by 10 per cent, but inflation was 5 per cent over the year. Population has risen by 1 per cent. What is the change in real GDP per capita to the nearest pound? Express this as a percentage change. How fast would this economy have to grow in real terms, in order to keep per capita real income at the same level?

The distribution of income

Our simple GDP per capita definition of economic growth is modified by the *distribution of income* within a country. If the increase in GDP is concentrated mainly among the rich, this will obviously have very little effect upon the average living standard. Income tends to be more unevenly distributed in poor countries and this therefore further exacerbates the problems of development. This issue is discussed in detail in Chapter 46.

Environmental considerations

We too often assume in economics that more is better. As we saw in Chapter 13 and 16, economists are becoming increasingly concerned with the fact that the production of *economic goods* also involves the production of *economic bads* such as pollution. If we turn to the very poor nations of the world it is understandable that they tend to downgrade environmental considerations in their fight against the extreme poverty that exists in their countries.

Even in these countries, however, it is being recognised that the environment cannot be ignored. In 1997 uncontrolled forest fires used to clear land for development in Indonesia caused pollution across the whole region, especially when mixed with traffic fumes and other pollutants among Indonesia's more affluent neighbours. The resulting 'haze' made people in South-East Asia think more carefully about the environment as asthmatic and other respiratory conditions spread. A similar event in London in the 1950s resulted in the banning of domestic coal burning in the capital (unless special smokeless fuels were used) after 'smog' killed thousands of elderly people suffering with respiratory complaints.

Such human calamities are the reason why the idea of *sustainable development* (see Chapter 40) is increasingly being put forward by economists as an alternative objective to economic growth. This refers to the aim of meeting the needs of the present generation without harming the needs of future generations by reducing the stock of ecological and socio-cultural assets.

The importance of economic growth

Why worry about economic growth? The answer is that it is this very economic growth that enables us to enjoy a better *standard of living*. As we saw in the early chapters of the book, we assume that people are acquisitive, wishing to acquire more goods, more leisure, more entertainment, etc. All of these acquisitions are made possible by economic growth, as are better education, health care, and so on. Thus, while there are many who condemn the materialistic society, there are few who would deny that they would like a better standard of life.

Growth, power and influence

Economic growth has important political and military dimensions. It is often the wealthy nations of the world that dictate policies. When a country is wealthy it often develops substantial economic interests around the world. It will naturally be interested in the *stability* of countries supplying key raw materials or where multinational businesses have set up production. It may even become concerned about political events in countries neighbouring these countries!

For the European powers in the nineteenth and early twentieth centuries this interest led to *colonisation* of many of the poorer countries of the world. The USA, having itself begun as a group of colonies, was opposed to colonisation, but has intervened politically and militarily in many countries it considers to be in its sphere of influence, particularly in South and Central America and South-East Asia. The USSR intervened with military force in Hungary and Czechoslovakia when these East European states attempted to reject communism and leave the Eastern bloc in 1956 and 1968 respectively. Economic power often leads to political power, but it should be remembered that this political power involves money and resources, which could be used for other activities.

The globalisation of the world economy that has been remarked on in many other chapters means that events far away from a country can have a major impact on its economic growth. It was hoped that the end of the Cold War between communist and capitalist states would increase stability in the world. While this is largely true in Europe and the Americas, political instability in Africa, the Middle East, and parts of the former USSR continue to cause concern.

STUDENT ACTIVITY 34.2

What is the opportunity cost of resources used in military intervention? Should military expenditure count as a benefit or a cost when measuring economic growth?

Growth and the UK

Between 1967 and 1979 the UK economy grew by 32.7 per cent in real terms. Historically, this compares well with growth in the nineteenth century. However, when we compare it with the growth of our main trading partners it is very poor indeed. This is illustrated in Table 34.1. As you can see, the UK's performance overall is disappointing – although marginally better more recently. (In fact, since 1994 the UK's annual average growth rate has been above most of its major competitors.)

Table 34.1 Percentage growth of real GDP for selected countries

	1967–79	1988–98
Japan	83.1%	22.5%
Canada	63.1%	21.9%
Italy	55.8%	15.9%
Australia	54.7%	39.2%
France	52.8%	19.6%
USA	37.8%	27.6%
UK	32.7%	20.6%

Source: OECD and *World Development Report*, various years

● *Common misunderstanding*

It is important to realise that relatively small differences in rates of growth can have very significant differences upon GDP when considered over the medium or long term. This point is often forgotten or ignored, especially by politicians. Over the period 1967–79 the average annual growth in real GDP per capita of the UK was 2.5 per cent while that of Japan was 6.4 per cent. Now consider the information in Table 34.2. Let us assume that the UK is represented by the 2 per cent column, and Japan by the 7 per cent column. If 1990 is the last year we can see how quickly the GDPs begin to diverge. In 10 years' time the UK's GDP increases by 22 per cent but Japan's

doubles. After 30 years the UK's GDP is 82 per cent higher but Japan has increased by a factor of eight. After a century the differences are staggering, with all the implications this has for standards of living and political and military power.

Table 34.2 is also useful in explaining the vast differences that exist between the rich and the poor nations. While the UK, the USA and many European countries have experienced more than two centuries of almost continuous economic growth, many of the poor nations have experienced very little. It is not surprising that if, for example, we examine the GDP per capita of the USA in 1995 we find that it is 79 times greater than that of India. International comparisons are difficult to make because of problems with exchange rates as will be discussed below, but it is clear that Americans are massively more wealthy than citizens of India. Mathematicians refer to the way in which cumulative growth at a steady rate starts off slowly, but then really takes off as in Table 34.2, as *exponential* growth

Table 34.2 How growth rates affect incomes

Year	Index of national income based upon growth rate (%) per year of (1980 = 100)			
	2%	3%	5%	7%
1990	100	100	100	100
2000	122	135	165	201
2020	182	246	448	817
2040	272	448	1218	3312
2050	406	817	3312	13429
2080	739	2009	14841	109660

Factors influencing growth

Stages and theories of economic growth

Many attempts have been made to classify the pattern of economic growth as a passage through a number of definable *stages*. The most famous of these is **Marx's** classification. He saw societies as passing through the following stages: primitive communism; slavery; feudalism; capitalism; and, finally, socialism and communism. Recent historical experience suggests this sequence does not apply and countries may go from feudalism to socialism and then on to capitalism, as in the USSR and China.

Another famous classification is that which appears in **W.W. Rostow's** *Stages of Economic Growth*, which envisages a development of an economy up to the time when there is a 'take off into self-sustaining growth'. In Rostow's view the development of markets and the accumulation of capital are necessary precursors to the 'take off into sustained growth'.

● *Common misunderstanding*

In fact, it is now regarded as fallacious by all but hard-line Marxists to view economies as passing through definite stages. It could even be argued that the idea that economies must pass through certain stages has been harmful, when such a philosophy has been rigorously applied by governments.

There have also been a number of different *theories* of economic growth, which attempt to explain the causes and rates of economic growth. **Adam Smith** pointed out the importance of resources and pointed to the quantity and quality of the factors of production – land, labour and capital – in generating economic growth. In the twentieth century, the *Harrod–Domar model* extended Smith's approach by emphasising the importance of savings and efficiency. The model argued that growth depended on three things:

(a) *The savings rate*. Without savings, capital accumulation was not possible, so the higher the savings the higher the potential growth rate.

(b) *The capital output ratio*. The lower this is, the higher the growth rate as the available capital is being used efficiently.

(c) *The depreciation rate*. The higher this is, the lower the growth rate. If savings are being used up to replace old worn out capital, they not available to increase the total stock of capital goods necessary for growth.

This model suggested growth could best be achieved by policies (such as tax incentives) to encourage savings, and by measures to ensure efficient use of the available resources (such as competition). There was a reaction to this theory by **Solow**, who proposed an alternative theory, suggesting that *technical progress* was the main source of economic growth, and that the market would see to it that the capital–output ratio, and the savings rate, adjusted to the changing needs of the latest technology. This became the accepted model and was well suited to the non-interventionist monetarist period of economic history in the 1970s, 1980s and 1990s. Allowing the market to work was the main policy of the period, with privatisation, deregulation, and reduced international trade barriers and capital controls.

However, it was noticed that growth rates continued to vary enormously between different economies, so critics of Solow's theory began to argue that intervention might be useful after all. Solow's theory is sometimes referred as an '*exogeneous*' theory. This means that the source of the economic growth lies outside economic factors, and comes purely from technical progress. **Chenery** argued that it was easier to explain different growth rates if growth was *endogeneous*, that is determined by things going on inside the economy. In particular, he argued that if workers had more capital they became more efficient at using it. This approach also argues in favour of improving human capital by increased education and training, so that the existing capital stock is more effectively utilised. These ideas are returning us to a more interventionist approach, increasing, as Adam Smith put it, the quality and quantity of the factors of production.

These arguments are very technical, but they point to a number of possble causes of economic growth which will now be examined.

Investment

It is undoubtedly true that investment has an influence on the rate of growth. Increasing the rate of investment reduces consumption of goods and services initially as resources are diverted to the investment industries, but the increased growth rate results in a higher consumption of goods and services in the future which should increase the rate of growth. However, there appears to be no simple relationship between the rate of investment and the rate of growth. In Table 34.3, the share of GDP going to investment is calculated for two separate years. Comparison with the growth rates in Table 34.1 shows that while high investment rates seem to be largely linked to high growth rates, that there are exceptions. The relatively low investment in the UK and the USA don't seem to have handicapped their growth rates in the 1990s, while Japan's high investment rates don't seem to be producing the results in the 1990s that were achieved in the 1970s. The lower figures for the 1988–98 period reflect the worldwide recessions in the 1990s.

It is clear from the figures in Table 34.1 and 34.3 that, as far as the UK is concerned, the low rate of investment over much of the period has been matched by poor performance in the growth league. However, investment on its own cannot explain economic growth.

Table 34.3 **Gross investment as a percentage of GDP: selected countries, selected years**

	1980	1999
Japan	32	29
Canada	24	20
Italy	27	18
Australia	25	22
France	24	17
US	20	19
UK	17	16

Source: World Development Report, 1998/99 and 2000/01, IBRD

Difficulties of comparison

The relationship between investment and growth will also be affected by our old friend *the law of diminishing returns*. Other things being equal, the principle of *marginal productivity* tells us that as we apply more and more investment to an already large stock of capital, the extra output achieved should diminish. This might partly explain why Japan saw a good return on its investment when 'catching up' other countries in 1967–1979, but a poorer rate of return in the 1990s.

We can also point out that a low rate of growth may appear less burdensome to a rich country than to a poor country. Let us consider an analogy with individual incomes. Suppose we consider two individuals, one with an income of £10 000 per year and the other with £100 000. If both their incomes increase by 10 per cent the first individual has an extra £1000 to spend while the second's will increase by £10 000. Thus rich countries with low growth rates may be able to sustain much higher increases in their real living standards than those of poor nations with high growth rates.

It is also possible to consider that geographical conditions may have an effect upon investment. Countries with inhospitable climates or terrains may find that the physical problems of development are disproportionately high. Among the advanced countries, this may affect nations such as Austria, Switzerland and Finland.

Gross and net investment

A major factor influencing the relationship between investment and growth is that of the difference between *gross* and *net investment*. Much investment may simply be to replace obsolete equipment and, thus, will therefore have no effect upon the rate of growth; it is only net investment that increases the wealth of a nation. This is a problem that particularly affects a mature industrial nation such as the UK, since much investment must be to replace out-of-date equipment. This, therefore, has compounded the problem associated with the UK's low rate of investment in the earlier period.

The quality of investment

Units of investment are not homogeneous and it does not follow that there is a constant capital–output ratio even within one industry. We must therefore consider the *quality of investment*. An often repeated argument is that at the end of the Second World War the UK was left with much obsolete and worn-out equipment and investment consisted of patching and infilling. On the other hand, in the then West Germany and in Japan, where the destruction of capital had been almost total, investment was in all-new integrated plant. There is no point in blaming more recent poor performance on such distant historical events. The point is that investment has to be of the right kind to contribute strongly to economic growth.

Inward investment and multinationals

With the increasing globalisation of the world economy, it is increasingly the case that countries are in competition with each other to attract inward investment from multinational companies. Among the features of an economy that a multnational might find attractive are an advantageous tax regime; a well educated workforce; a stable political environment; stable prices and exchange rates; good industrial relations; a good transport infrastructure and flexible labour markets. There is a political question as to how free governments are to create expensive welfare systems under these competitive conditions.

Defence expenditure

All economics is a question of allocating scarce resources in the optimal manner. A significant factor when we come to compare growth rates is defence expenditure. If a nation is devoting a proportion of its precious GDP to defence this must consist of resources which could be used for investment to increase the living standard directly. Table 34.4 shows the proportion of government expenditure devoted to defence expenditure in various countries.

Table 34.4 **Defence expenditure of selected countries**

	% of GDP spent on Defence 1985	1995
Australia	2.7	2.5
Italy	2.2	1.8
Japan	1.0	1.0
Canada	2.2	1.7
France	4.4	3.1
UK	5.1	3.0
USA	6.1	3.8

Source: World Development Report, 1998/9, IBRD

Again it is impossible to draw any simple relationships between defence expenditure and growth. As regards the UK it may have been one more factor restricting economic growth, especially when comparing its position with its European neighbours. Of course it is impossible to estimate the value of defence expenditure to the community in terms of the security it offers. There are also spin-offs in terms of arms sales etc. On the other hand, the burden of defence expenditure can be disproportionately high because it

ties up highly trained personnel as well as some of the most young and vigorous of the workforce.

Two of the most successful economies of the second half of the twentieth century, Japan and West Germany (as was), were prevented from being involved in military activity because of fears they might repeat their aggressive behaviour of the Second World War. It has been suggested that these countries have been able to concentrate their best brains on commercial rather than military activities. Some of the world's poorest countries have spent large amounts on defence, particularly in war-torn areas like the Middle East.

The performance of many developing countries is obstructed by high defence expenditure. Much of their precious foreign exchange goes on importing military hardware.

People and growth

Population growth

As far as advanced economies are concerned it may be debated whether population growth is a spur to economic development or whether increased standards of living have increased population. We could argue, for example, that at the moment the stagnation in population growth in Western Europe has some connection with the lack of economic growth, while faster growing populations such as Australia and the USA have maintained higher economic growth.

If on the other hand we turn to developing countries, there can be little doubt that population growth is one of the main inhibiting factors in increasing GDP per capita. It would appear that any major advance in living standards will, for many countries, depend upon limiting the size of families. In recent years the country to take this most seriously has been China, the most populous nation on earth, where draconian measures have been taken to limit population growth.

Population structure

It is not just the size of the population which is important but also its age, sex and geographic distribution. These factors all have important considerations for economic growth. If, as is the case in most advanced countries, there is an increasing proportion of dependent population (the old, the young, etc.), resources will have to be devoted to caring for them. Thus, valuable investment resources will be channelled into projects of very low productivity such as old people's homes. It could be argued that extra investment put into education will pay dividends in the long run, but such projects will not be conducive to high rates of growth in the short and medium term.

In considering the effect of population upon growth, we must also consider *participation rates*, i.e. the proportion of the population which is economically active. In this respect the UK has one of the highest participation rates of any advanced country, but also a high proportion of part-time workers. Participation rates are governed by such things as school-leaving age, the attitude towards working women, the facilities which exist for child care, the age of retirement, and so on.

The average age of the population may also affect economic growth. By and large, an ageing population tends to inhibit economic growth since older people tend to be more conservative and less inclined to take risks. Again it is possible to argue that the ageing of the UK's population over this century has inhibited growth, although other developed countries have faced a similar situation.

Migration

Migration also has an effect upon economic growth. The growth in population in the USA and Australia has been largely as a result of immigration and has been associated with high growth rates in the 1990s, but it must be noted that these two countries have the space to accomodate a larger population, whereas population densities are quite high in Western Europe and Japan. Immigrants tend to be of working age and therefore beneficial to the economy. Recently, emigrants from the UK have tended to be highly trained personnel such as doctors and scientists. In the early and middle parts of the twentieth century the UK had lower internal migration than its immediate neighbours such as France, Germany and Italy, each of these countries having a large reservoir of labour to draw on, i.e. a drift of the agricultural population to the towns, and

in the case of the then West Germany there was for a time the defection of people from East Germany. Thus, each of these countries had a pool of relatively cheap, easily assimilable labour which could be drawn upon. The immigration which the UK has experienced from overseas has been small by comparison but has posed problems of cultural and social differences. These problems have also been experienced by France and, to a lesser extent, by Germany. Reduced job opportunities during the 1980s and 1990s may have exacerbated these problems.

Education and training

It is often said that the wealth of a country lies in the skill of its population. This being the case, the education, training and attitude of a country's population must be a significant factor in determining its rate of growth. While it may appear unpleasant to speak of investment in people as if they were machines, none the less it is important that a nation makes sure that it has the adequate skills it needs to advance its economy. That is why an investment in people, or more precisely an investment in *human capital*, is considered a priority for the economic well-being of a country. Such investment, whether it takes the form of both formal education or on-the-job training, enhances the skills of the population, raises levels of productivity and ensures a faster rate of economic growth, or so it is often claimed.

Despite the large increase in the numbers receiving higher (or university) education in the UK in the last 10 years, the participation rate (i.e. the percentage of people in the age group receiving such education) is still only just over 30 per cent. This is a lower rate than in most other major OECD economies, such as the USA, Canada, Japan, France and Germany. This discrepancy may have had an adverse effect upon growth when compared with these other countries. We might also regard education, as opposed to training, as a component in the quality of life (i.e. it can be regarded as a consumption good rather than as an investment good). Thus those receiving higher education are consuming an economic product which will improve their standard of living by improving their quality of life.

● *Common misunderstanding*

While it is often claimed that increased investment by a country in its human capital will automatically lead to improved levels of productivity and economic growth, in fact there is not a great deal of supportive evidence. Countries with a greater percentage of the relevant age group in further and higher education tend to have higher levels of per capita GDP, but this does not necessarily prove that the one causes the other. In fact, there may be a two-way relationship between per capita GDP and educational standards: higher GDP may require higher levels of education, but higher standards of living may make it easier to afford better education and a better quality of life.

If you are just embarking upon higher education it will doubtless come as a great comfort to know that there is also a marked correlation between higher education and higher earnings later in life!

Table 34.5 Liberalisation and trade

| | Exports as a percentage of GDP | | Tax as a percentage of GDP |
	1980	1999	1998
Australia	16	21	22.9
Italy	22	27	38.6
US	10	12	20.4
UK	27	29	36.3
Japan	14	11	11.0*
Canada	28	41	18.5*
France	22	27	39.2

* 1996

Source: *World Development Report*, 1998/99 and 2000/01, IBRD

STUDENT ACTIVITY 34.3

If a population has a rising proportion of pensioners and a falling proportion of children of school age what is the implication for growth? Would increased immigration resolve this problem?

Liberalisation and trade

With the demise of socialism, a greater emphasis has been placed on the advantages of the free market and measures that increase trade. The benefits of competition in allowing specialisation and creating efficiency have been noted in several chapters. Table 34.5 shows two possible measures of the liberalisation of an economy; the proportion of exports to GDP, and the proportion of money taken by government in tax. It can be seen that the UK lies between the heavily taxed European economies and the lightly taxed American, Japanese and Australian economies. It also appears as one of the most open economies in the world with a high proportion of GDP being exported. However it is important to be careful about the trade figures, because the larger an economy, the more likely it is to be able to meet its trade requirements internally. The Japanese and USA figures appear low for this reason. Another way of looking at this is to regard the EU

as a single economy when comparing it with the USA or Japan. Since 60 per cent of the UK's exports are to the EU, exports to other countries would only be 11 per cent of GDP in 1996, in line with the USA and not far ahead of Japan.

The UK spearheaded the privatisation process in the 1980s under Mrs Thatcher, bringing greater competition to the utility industries. When making comparisons with other countries, it must be remembered that many non-European countries did not nationalise these industries in the first place.

Problems of international comparisons

The difficulties of making international comparisons of GDP have already been noted in Chapter 16, but are highlighted in Table 34.6, which ranks countries by their GDP expressed in US dollars. These figures are grossly distorted by (sometimes temporary) exchange rate variations, but there is a method for correcting for this called purchasing power parity (PPP). PPP compares prices in different countries and adjusts the exchange rates until prices are on average the same in different countries. There are difficulties with this process because not all countries consume the same types of products. The process is becoming easier now that globalisation is standardising world production. The result of making this adjustment, as seen in Table 34.6, is a much narrower distribution of income than shown from the unadjusted figures. Certain countries move their ranking quite noticeably, such as Japan, the USA, and Canada, while others are

Table 34.6 **Selected developed countries ranked by GDP and PPP**

	GDP $ per capita $	World rank	GDP per capita adjusted for PPP ($)	World rank
Japan	37 850	2	23 400	6
Canada	19 290	18	21 800	10
Italy	20 120	17	20 060	16
France	26 050	11	21 860	11
UK	20 710	15	20 520	14
US	28 740	6	28 740	2
Australia	20 540	16	20 170	15

Source: *World Development Report*, 1998/9, IBRD

relatively unaffected. Incidentally, the top ranked country is Switzerland, which drops to third place after the PPP adjustment, while Singapore is first after the PPP adjustment. Both these countries are special cases with the Swiss Franc grossly inflated in value by the large inflows of foreign capital into their banking system, while Singapore is a city-state.

Sustainable development

A major problem for future growth is the environmental degradation, population expansion, and depletion of resources which has accompanied economic growth. These environmental problems are discussed in Chapters 13 and 40. Sustainable development means economic growth that is not at the expense of future generations. It has been argued that being more careful with our environment will limit the rate at which the world economy can grow. Optimists argue that there will be a 'technical fix' which will enable us to overcome these difficulties.

The problems of the UK economy

Is there a British disease?

There can be little doubt that in the years since the Second World War the UK has possessed many of the advantages which were desirable for economic growth and yet, although it has done well compared with many developing countries, it has not done particularly well compared with

its peers such as France and Germany. The reasons for this are not to be found in complex mathematical models of growth, but rather in a combination of socio-economic factors which together have probably inhibited the growth of the economy.

These factors include government *'stop–go' policies* and the variation in the objectives of government policies, which have had adverse effects upon growth. Government preoccupation with control of the money supply and, more recently, inflation targets, is just the latest in a long line of different policy objectives. This problem is discussed in more detail in Chapter 43.

It has often been the case, especially in the past, that all the problems of UK industry have been blamed on *trade unions*. While this is an exaggeration, restrictive practices and excessive wage demands, when they occurred, may well have had adverse effects upon growth.

It is probably also the case that UK *management* has been too uninventive and unadventurous. In particular, there has been an unwillingness to invest in the future and a spending level on research and development (R&D) which is lower than most of its main competitors.

In addition, while there is no definitive proof of this, it has often been suggested that there has been a tendency for *scientific and technical skills* to be underplayed, while those with qualifications in the arts have often tended to be promoted. It is certainly true that there has been a lack of coordination of research and development programmes by successive governments.

The UK has tended to be a *net exporter of capital*. It can be argued that this flow of funds abroad starves the domestic economy of investment. There is little evidence to demonstrate that this is so. Rather, it may be the case that the other factors discussed combine to limit investment opportunities.

There is some evidence to show that the performance of the economy is damaged by the fact that investment managers go for quick returns on their funds and that, as a result, firms become more concerned with their short-term share values than with more long-term research and development plans. The Bank of England has expressed concern about this. The shares of the majority of large UK companies are traded on the Stock Exchange and it is argued that this situation results in 'casino capitalism'. Contrasts are often made with Germany which has a larger number of private companies which are more likely to be financed through long-term relationships with regional banks rather than by the flotation of shares on the Stock Exchange.

Recent experience

In the middle years of the 1980s growth in the UK economy exceeded that of most of its trading partners and there was some evidence of a *catch-up* process occurring. As you can see from Table 34.7, the UK maintained its improved relative position in the slow growth environment of the early to mid-1990s. At the end of the century UK and US growth rates continued to be strong, while the Japanese are slowly recovering from the recession that hit the Far East in 1998.

The success of the mid-1980s was, at least in part, due to government supply side measures although we should not forget our enormous good fortune in North Sea oil. The government would doubtless claim credit for reducing the power of trade unions and for reintroducing a spirit of competition into the economy.

In the 1980s the economy was recovering from the worst recession for 50 years when we ought to have expected rapid growth. Another large recession in the early 1990s accounted for the lower growth rates at this time and for the higher growth rates subsequently, especially since the UK emerged from the recession earlier than its main European competitors, having also entered it earlier. Unemployment levels improved to levels not seen since the 1970s although many jobs created were part time.

There still remain problems for the economy, such as greater participation in higher education, a lack of coordination in research and development, and poor management, that remain to be tackled. As the UK economy enters the twenty-first century the prospects look better than they have for some time, but slow growth in the USA and Japan may be a problem.

Summary

1 Economic growth is an increase in the real per capita GDP of a nation.
2 The standard of living is not just the income per head but also all the other things which are important to the quality of life, such as health care and literacy.
3 An increase in economic growth may not be the same thing as an increase in economic welfare. We must also consider such factors as the distribution of income and the exploitation of the environment.
4 Whatever its relative merits, economic growth is vital to the improvement of the real standard of living of a nation, in terms of either material wealth or other considerations such as leisure and the general state of well-being.
5 Since the Second World War the UK's economic growth has been rapid but it has nevertheless been much slower than that of its main trading partners, at least until quite recently.
6 Investment is crucial to economic growth but there is no simple relationship between the rate of investment and the rate of economic growth.
7 The efficacy of investment is affected not only by its quantity but also by its quality and type.
8 Economic growth is affected by the size and structure of a population.
9 Although the roots of economic growth are difficult to define, when we examine the UK experience we find that, despite some recent improvements, the economy still seems to be lacking in a number of key areas fundamental to the growth process.

Table 34.7 **Average annual growth in real GDP**

	1980–90	1990–99
Australia	3.4	3.8
Italy	2.4	1.2
USA	3.0	3.4
UK	3.2	2.2
Japan	4.0	1.4
Canada	3.3	2.3
France	2.3	1.7

Source: World Development Report 2000/01, IBRD

QUESTIONS

1 What factors are significant in influencing the growth rate of a nation?
2 Discuss the view that economic growth is the sole indicator of a country's standard of living.
3 What is the relationship between investment in a country and the rate of growth?
4 Explain what is meant by the term 'sustainable development' and account for its significance.
5 How would you account for the UK's relatively poor growth performance since the Second World War?

Data response A
ECONOMIC GROWTH

The sources of social welfare are not to be found in economic growth *per se*, but in a far more selective form of development which must include a radical reshaping of our physical environment with the needs of pleasant living and not the needs of traffic or industry foremost in mind.

E. J. Mishan, *The Costs of Economic Growth*

The anti-growth movement and its accompanying excessive concern with the environment not merely leads to a regressive change in the distribution of resources in the community, it also distracts attention from the real issues of choice which society has to face.

Wilfred Beckerman, *In Defence of Economic Growth*

Compare and contrast these views of economic growth, stating what role the economist should play in attempting to answer the opposing views of the problems they pose.

Data response B
COMPARING COUNTRIES' PERFORMANCE

Taking all the tables in this chapter together as a case study for the selected countries, write an account of each economy describing its growth performance and attempting to explain why its has performed as indicated by the statistics.

35 Money and prices

Learning outcomes

At the end of this chapter you will be able to:

▶ Distinguish between different measures of the money supply.
▶ Use the characteristics and functions of money to determine how well various assets can perform as money.
▶ Compare different measures of inflation.
▶ Understand the link between money and inflation.
▶ Describe the main functions and operations of commercial banks.
▶ Discuss the functions and significance of the money and capital markets.
▶ Outline the functions of central banks.

Introduction

Monetary economics

In this section of the book we will concern ourselves with money. We will look at monetary theory, at institutions which are concerned with the creation and transmission of money and at the monetary policy of the government. Together these subjects constitute the branch of the subject known as monetary economics. Not only is monetary economics an important branch of the subject, it is one of the most controversial areas of modern economics.

In this chapter we shall explain the nature and functions of money in a modern society, as well as the concept of the price level.

The importance of money

'Money', said **Geoffrey Crowther**, 'is a veil thrown over the working of the economic system'. Money may indeed obscure some of the workings of the *real economy* but it also helps it to work effectively. It would be impossible for a complex society to function without money. However, money does more than facilitate the working of the economy; it may also be a powerful influence upon the real economic variables such as consumption, investment, foreign trade and employment. Monetary economics has much to tell us about how changes in the demand, supply and price of money influence the economy.

The development of money

The origins of money

The word money derives from the Latin *moneta* – the first Roman coinage was minted at the temple of Juno Moneta in 344 BC. Before coinage, various objects such as cattle, pigs' teeth and cowrie shells had been used as money. Such forms of money are termed *commodity money* and they are not confined to ancient societies; for example, when the currency collapsed in Germany in 1945, commodity money in the form of cigarettes and coffee took its place.

For most of its history money has taken the form of coins made of precious metal. This kind of money had *intrinsic* value. Many of the units of modern money recall their origin in amounts of precious metal; for example, the pound sterling was originally the Roman pound (12 ounces) of silver. Hence the symbol £ derives from the letter L standing for *libra*, the Latin for a pound. Similarly, dollars were originally one-ounce pieces of silver (the origin of the $ symbol is obscure; it probably derives from the figure 8 on old Spanish 'pieces of eight', which had the same value as a dollar).

From coins to banknotes

Both paper money and modern banking practice originated from the activities of goldsmiths. Goldsmiths used to accept deposits of gold coins and precious objects for safe keeping, in return for which a receipt would be issued which was, in effect, a *promissory note* (a promise to pay the bearer). As time went by these notes began to be passed around in settlement of debts, acting as banknotes do today. Goldsmiths also discovered that they did not need to keep all the gold they had on deposit in their vaults because, at any particular time, only a small percentage of their customers would want their gold back. Thus they discovered that they could lend out, say, 90 per cent of their deposits, keeping only 10 per cent to meet the demands of their depositors. This relationship of cash (assets) retained to total deposits (liabilities) is known as the *cash ratio*.

Let us now consider what happened to the gold which the goldsmith re-lent. This was used by borrowers to pay bills and the recipient would then redeposit it with the same or another goldsmith. This goldsmith issued a promissory note for the deposit and then re-lent 90 per cent of the new deposit of gold. The process would then be repeated with the redeposit of more gold and the writing of more promissory notes. The limit to this process was that the goldsmiths always had to keep, say, 10 per cent of their assets in gold. This would mean that if the goldsmiths kept to a 10 per cent ratio, each £1 of gold could secure a further £9 in promissory notes. Thus, the banker, for this is what the goldsmith had become by this time, could be said to have created money.

The completion of this process came in the 1680s when **Francis Childs** became the first banker to print banknotes. Today the process of credit creation lies at the heart of our money supply. Originally the gold had intrinsic value and the paper money was issued on the faith in the bank. Any currency issued that was not fully backed by gold was called a *fiduciary issue*. Today banks create credit in the form of deposits against the security of Bank of England notes in the same manner that the old banks created bank notes on the security of gold.

● *Common misunderstanding*

*Most people do not question whether money is valuable. They know from their experience that the system works. Today, however, it can be seen that the whole edifice of money rests on **confidence** in the banking system, since all notes are now fiduciary issue. The creation of credit is kept under control by the Bank of England since it issues the banknotes and is responsible for supervising the banks. If you examine a banknote you will see it has written on the side with the Queen's head on it: 'I promise to pay the bearer on demand the sum of five (ten or twenty) pounds.' What would happen if you took a banknote to the Bank of England and asked them to keep their promise? They would exchange it for another banknote of the same value!*

Credit creation

A single-bank system

Let us imagine there is only one bank with which everyone in the country does business. This bank has initial deposits of £10 000 in cash so that its balance sheet would be:

Liabilities (£)	Assets (£)
Deposits 10 000	Cash 10 000

The bank knows from experience, however, that only a tenth of its deposits will be demanded in cash at any particular time and so it is able to lend out £9000 at interest. The people who borrow this money spend it. The shopkeepers and others who receive this money then put it into the bank and the bank finds that the £9000 it has lent out has been re-deposited. This could be described as a created deposit. It is then able to repeat this process, lending out nine-tenths of this £9000 and retaining £900. The £8100 it has lent out will find its way back to the bank again, whereupon it can once more lend out nine-tenths, and so on. This is illustrated in Table 35.1.

Thus at the end of the process, with total cash of £10 000 in the system and a cash ratio of 10 per cent, the bank is able to make loans amounting to £90 000. Although many more deposits have been created, you will see that everything balances out because the bank still has

Table 35.1 **Deposit creation in a single-bank system with a 10 per cent cash ratio**

Liabilities (£) (Deposits)		Loans and advances		Assets (£) Cash retained	
Initial deposit	10 000	1st loan	9 000	$\frac{1}{10}$ of deposit retained	1 000
1st redeposit	9 000	2nd loan	8 100	$\frac{1}{10}$ of redeposit retained	900
2nd deposit	8 100	3rd loan	7 290	$\frac{1}{10}$ of redeposit retained	810
3rd redeposit	7 290	4th loan	6 561	$\frac{1}{10}$ of redeposit retained	729

The maximum possible creation of deposits occurs when

| Liabilities = | £100 000 | Assets = | £90 000 | | + £10 000 |

the necessary one-tenth of its assets in cash to meet its liabilities. You can also see that each horizontal line in Table 35.1 balances assets against liabilities and, therefore, at no stage are accounting principles infringed. The bank's balance sheet at the end of the process would appear as:

Liabilities (£)		Assets (£)	
Initial deposits	10 000	Cash	10 000
Created deposits	90 000	Loans and advances	90 000
	£100 000		£100 000

Note that the bank itself cannot distinguish between its initial deposits and created deposits.

The bank multiplier

The limit to credit creation in this manner is given by the formula:

$$D = \frac{1}{r} \times C$$

where D is the amount of bank deposits, r is the cash ratio and C is the cash held by banks. Thus, in our example we would get:

$$D = \frac{1}{0.1} \times £10 000 = £100 000$$

The value of the expression $1/r$ is known as the bank or *credit creation multiplier*. It shows the relationship between the cash (or reserve assets) retained against total liabilities. In this example the cash ratio is 10 per cent, so the bank multiplier would be 10. However, if the cash ratio were dropped to 5 per cent the multiplier would be 20, whereas if it were raised to 20 per cent it would be only 5.

The effect of any additional deposit of cash into the system upon the level of deposits can be given by the formula:

$$\Delta D = \frac{1}{r} \times \Delta C$$

where ΔD is the effect upon total deposits as the result of a change in cash deposits, ΔC. Note also that there would be a comparable multiple contraction in deposits if cash were lost from the system.

STUDENT ACTIVITY 35.1

In a very small economy with only one bank, what will be the maximum value of deposits the bank can create if the bank holds £100 in cash, and the cash ratio is 10 per cent? What would happen to the maximum value of deposits if:

(a) the cash ratio were changed to 20 per cent;
(b) the bank's holdings of cash rise by £10?

A multibank system

If we consider a system in which there are many banks, credit creation will go on in the same manner, except that money which is loaned out may find its way into a bank other than the one which made it. This is illustrated below, where we assume that there are two banks in the system. Here we have raised the cash ratio to 12.5 per cent, partly to guard against the possibility of deposits being lost to the other bank(s) or leaking out of the banking system altogether. The initial £10 000 of deposits is divided equally between the two banks, and with a cash ratio of 12.5 per cent they are able to create additional deposits of seven times this amount:

Bank X

Liabilities (£)		Assets (£)	
Initial deposits	5 000	Cash	5 000
Created		Loans and	
deposits	35 000	advances	35 000
	£40 000		£40 000

Bank Y

Liabilities (£)		Assets (£)	
Initial deposits	5 000	Cash	5 000
Created		Loans and	
deposits	35 000	advances	35 000
	£40 000		£40 000

Thus, the initial £10 000 is used to support £80 000 of liabilities.

STUDENT ACTIVITY 35.2

What would happen in this situation if account holders in bank X made payments to account holders in bank Y of £2000? Bank X's liabilities would be reduced by £2000 and bank Y's would be increased by £2000. To balance this out bank X would be obliged to make a payment of £2000 to bank Y in cash (in the real world they would make this adjustment through the bank's accounts at the Bank of England). Draw up the banks' balance sheets at the end of these transactions. What has happened to the two banks' cash ratios? What will each bank now try to do to maximise credit creation within the cash ratio constraint? Could bank X be patient and expect some payments in the opposite direction in the next period of time? Will these uncertainties about shifting account balances make banks a little more cautious about credit creation?

Cash ratios and the control of the money supply

The cash ratio was abolished in the UK in 1971 and was replaced by a 12.5 per cent reserve assets ratio, although the clearing banks were expected to keep 1.5 per cent of their assets in cash at the Bank of England. In August 1981 this reserve assets ratio was itself abolished. From this date all banks were required to keep the equivalent of 0.5 per cent (reduced to 0.35 per cent in 1992) of their eligible liabilities in cash at the Bank of England. This is held in non-operational accounts, i.e. the banks may not use this cash. The object of these non-operational, non-interest-bearing accounts is to supply the Bank with funds. In addition to this money, banks have to keep cash at the Bank for the purpose of settling interbank indebtedness (clearing of cheques). Although there is now no cash or reserve assets ratio, banks still need to keep a minimum level of cash and liquid assets, i.e. assets that can quickly be turned into cash in order to meet their obligations on a day-to-day basis. The Bank has laid down guidelines for banks to assess the *prudent* proportion of liquid assets which they need. The asset cover varies according to the kind of deposits (liabilities) the bank has accepted. Thus it is not possible, at present, to state this as a simple ratio.

The functions and attributes of money

We have not as yet defined money. So far we have suggested that coins, banknotes and bank deposits are money. Whether an asset is regarded as money or not depends not so much on what it is but upon what it does.

Money can be defined as anything that is readily acceptable in settlement of a debt.

Thus we have a functional definition of money. For any asset to be considered as money it must fulfil the four functions discussed below. The different forms of money do not all fulfil the functions equally well.

The functions of money

(a) *Medium of exchange*. Money facilitates the exchange of goods and services in the economy. Workers accept money for their wages because they know that money can be exchanged for all the different things they will need.

If there were not money, then exchange would have to take place by barter. For barter to be possible there must be a **double coincidence of wants**. For example, if you have chickens but wish to acquire shoes, you must find someone who has shoes that they wish to exchange for chickens. The difficulties of barter will limit the possibilities of exchange and thus inhibit the growth of an economy. This situation was summed up by the classical economists when they said that, rather than a coincidence of wants, there was likely to be a want of coincidence.

(b) *Unit of account*. Money is a means by which we can measure the disparate components which make up the economy. Thus, barrels of oil, suits of clothes, visits to the cinema, houses and furniture can all be given a common measure which allows us to compare them and to aggregate their value.

It could be argued that there are many things that cannot be given a price. For example, you might possess mementoes of your family or friends which you value highly but which the economist would say were economically worthless. At this stage you might be tempted to agree with Oscar Wilde and say, 'What is a cynic? A man who knows the price of everything and the value of nothing.' The economist, however, is commenting on the exchange value of things within the economy, not the sentimental value which a person may put upon their possessions.

(c) *Store of value*. For a variety of reasons, people may wish to put aside some of their current income and save it for the future. Money presents the most useful way of doing this. If, for example, a person were saving for their old age, it would be impossible to put to one side all the physical things – food, clothing, fuel, etc. – which they would require, apart from the fact that their needs may change. Money, however, allows them to buy anything they require.

In times of high inflation the value of money is eroded and people may turn to real assets such as property. The value of physical assets is, however, also uncertain, in addition to which they may deteriorate physically, which money will not.

(d) *Standard of deferred payment*. Many contracts involve future payment, e.g. hire purchase, mortgages and long-term construction works. Any contract with a time element in it would be very difficult if there were not a commonly agreed means of payment. The future being uncertain, creditors know that all their economic needs can be satisfied with money.

Inflation and the functions of money

Inflation adversely affects the functions of money but it does not affect them all equally. Inflation would have to become very rapid before money became unacceptable as a medium of exchange; for example, when the rate of inflation in the UK was above 20 per cent in the 1970s, shopkeepers showed no disinclination to accept money. Even in the hyperinflation in Germany in 1923, money was still used.

The 'unit of account' function is affected by inflation since it becomes more difficult to compare values over time. For example, we may know that the GDP increased from £44.1 billion in 1970 to £438 billion in 1989, but how much of this was real increase and how much due to inflation? It requires statistical manipulation to deflate the figures and separate the *real* change from the *nominal*. In fact, in the figures used above, the nominal increase of almost ninefold in GDP is reduced to only 37 per cent in real terms when the effects of inflation have been discounted.

The effect of inflation on the store of value function is to reduce the value of people's savings.

This is especially so when *real rates of interest* are negative, as they were in several years in the 1970s. The real rate of interest is the *nominal rate of interest* minus the rate of inflation (this is an approximation but works well for low values). If the nominal rate of interest is 5 per cent and the rate of inflation is 8 per cent then the real rate of interest is minus 3 per cent. If the rate of interest is not even making up for the rate of inflation then, even after interest has been added in, the value of a saver's capital will have fallen in real terms. When real interest rates are negative, the effect of inflation can be, paradoxically, to increase savings as people attempt to maintain the real value of their wealth. This effect was observed in the 1970s. Inflation did, however, encourage people to search for substitute methods of preserving the value of their assets, such as purchasing gold, property or even works of art. In order to encourage people to save in times of inflation, the government introduced *index-linked* financial assets such as 'granny bonds'.

Inflation also affects the 'standard of deferred payment' function. Businesses, for example, may be unwilling to become creditors over long periods of time when they fear a decline in the value of money. Alternatively, special clauses may have to be written into contracts to take account of inflation. On the other side of the coin, people will become more willing to borrow money when they believe that the real burden of the debt will be reduced by inflation.

Inflation may also have an international effect upon the currency. High rates of inflation in a country will make its currency less acceptable internationally and therefore cause adverse effects upon the exchange rate.

The characteristics of money

We have seen that money fulfils four functions and also that many different things have functioned as money. Here we will consider what characteristics an asset should have to function as money.

(a) *Acceptability*. The most important attribute of money is that it is readily acceptable.

(b) *Durability*. Money should not wear out quickly. This is a problem which may affect paper money and to a lesser extent coins. The chief form of money in a modern society, which is bank deposits, suffers no physical depreciation whatsoever as it exists only as numbers on a page, or digits in a computer.

(c) *Homogeneity*. It is desirable that money should be uniform. Imagine, for example, that a country's money stock consisted of £1 gold coins, but that some coins contained 1 gram of gold and others 2 grams. What would happen? People would hoard the 2 gram coins but trade with the 1 gram coins. Thus, part of the money supply would disappear. This is an illustration of *Gresham's law*, that 'bad money drives out good'. Most forms of commodity money will suffer from Gresham's law.

(d) *Divisibility*. Another of the disadvantages of commodity money, such as camels' or pigs' teeth, is that they cannot be divided into smaller units. Modern notes and coins allow us to arrive at almost any permutation of divisibility.

(e) *Portability*. Commodity money and even coins suffer from the disadvantage that they may be difficult to transport. A modern bank deposit, however, may be transmitted electronically from one place to another.

(f) *Stability of value*. It is highly desirable that money should retain its value. In the past this was achieved by tying monetary value to something which was in relatively stable supply, such as gold. It is one of the most serious defects of modern money that it may be affected by inflation. The hyperinflation in Germany in 1923, for example, made the mark worthless.

(g) *Difficult to counterfeit*. Once a society uses money which has only exchange value and not intrinsic value, it is essential that the possibilities for fraud and counterfeit be kept to a minimum.

(h) *Scarcity*. If a commodity used as money is readily available in the environment, there are likely to be distortions in economic activity. For instance, if leaves from trees were the main form of currency, the most lucrative economic activity would be the defoliation of trees (or for those with a longer view, planting trees). This may seem a bizarre example, but the gold rushes in North America in the nineteenth century are an essentially similar phenomenon.

A cashless society?

In today's society we are seeing ever more sophisticated ways of paying for goods and services. Following cheques we have seen the arrival of direct debits, standing orders and credit cards. The late 1980s brought the introduction of EFTPOS (Electronic Funds Transfer at Point Of Sale). Under this system a customer presents the shop with a card that is fed into a machine that automatically debits the amount of the sale from the customer's bank account. It is possible to envisage a future in which there is no need for cash. Cash transactions today account for only a small percentage of the total value of sales, but cash is still used for a large number of small transactions. It is unlikely that cash will be replaced for minor day-to-day transactions such as for slot machines, bus fares and small purchases. The cost of making a payment by card is usually borne by the retailer and is therefore not noticed by the consumer. It is this cost which makes small transactions unviable by card at present.

It seems unlikely that we shall see the end of cash, but the cheque system has declined in relative importance as people switch to credit and debit cards, as can be seen in Table 35.2.

Table 35.2 **Card transactions**

	1991	1998
Number (millions)	2011	4847
Value (£bn)	85	228

Source: Financial Statistics, August 2000, National Statistics. © Crown Copyright

STUDENT ACTIVITY 35.3

1 Assess each of the following possible assets usable as money in terms of the functions and characteristics described above.
   (a) premium bonds; (b) national lottery tickets; (c) daffodil bulbs; (d) Smarties; (e) unshelled nuts; (f) snooker balls.
2 If the rate of inflation is 10 per cent, what will the real rate of interest be for each of the following nominal rates of interest?
   (a) 5 per cent; (b) 10 per cent; (c) 15 per cent.

Measuring the money supply

As we have seen, the vast majority of the number of transactions take place in cash, but in terms of the amount of money spent the most significant form of money is bank deposits. People have deposits of money in a bank that are only fractionally backed by cash, but they are quite happy to write and accept cheques which transfer the ownership of these deposits from one person to another.

● *Common misunderstanding*

Because people use cheques to transfer money in this way, there is a common belief that the cheques themselves are money. However, this is not the case. We could print more or less cheques without making any difference to the money supply. The money supply consists mainly of bank deposits and cash.

Changes in definitions

There was much interest in the money supply during the 1980s by the Conservative government, which originally placed great faith in monetarism. (Monetarists place a great deal of emphasis on control of the money supply – see Chapter 37.) Changes in the financial world and the effort to try to find a 'true' measure of the money supply led to several different measures of the money stock being introduced. In 1987 the Bank of England introduced new definitions of the broader definitions of the money stock. In 1990 definitions were changed again and the Bank of England ceased publication of some of the measures of money stock. There are several measures of the money stock because there are different types of bank account.

Narrow money

Most countries of the world have two measures of the money stock: broad money supply and narrow money supply. Narrow money consists of all the purchasing power that is immediately available for spending. In the UK two narrow measures are currently published. The first, M_0 (or monetary base), consists of notes and coins in circulation and the commercial banks' deposits of cash at the Bank of England. This is shown in Table 35.3.

Table 35.3 M_0 seasonally unadjusted, June 2000

Money stock	£m
Notes and coin in circulation outside the Bank of England	30 642
Bankers' operational deposits with the Bank of England	225
M_0 (wide monetary base)	30 867

Source: Financial Statistics, August 2000, National Statistics. © Crown Copyright 2001

The other measure M_2 consists of notes and coins in circulation and the NIB (Non-Interest Bearing) bank deposits – principally current accounts. Also in the M_2 definition are the other interest-bearing retail deposits of banks and the retail deposits of building societies, although in recent years many of the larger building societies have become banks. Retail deposits are the deposits of the private sector which can be withdrawn easily. Since all this money is readily available for spending it is sometimes referred to as the 'transactions balance'.

Any bank deposit which can be withdrawn on demand without incurring a (loss of) interest penalty is referred to as a *sight deposit*.

Despite some differences in definitions from country to country, similar concepts apply to measures of the money stock(s). These may be seen as relating to the functions of money. This idea is illustrated in Figure 35.1.

The old M_1, NIB M_1 and M_3 measures are no longer published by the Bank of England. M_1 is no longer published because it did not contain building society retail deposits. As building societies came to operate much like banks in the 1980s with cheque books and debit cards, the Bank argued that M_1 was misleading. The Bank ceased publication of M_3 in 1989 following the Abbey National Building Society becoming a bank. Since M_3 did not contain building society deposits, it appeared that there had been a enormous increase in the M_3 supply. The M_2 measure is shown in Table 35.4.

The broad measure of the money supply includes most bank deposits (both sight and

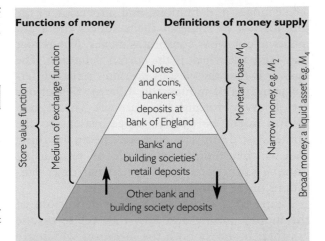

Figure 35.1 Concepts of the money supply
Cash, i.e. notes and coins, are at the apex of the money supply. Similar relationships exist for all countries. Certain deposits may be moved in definitions of the money supply from time to time.

Table 35.4 M_2 seasonally unadjusted, June 2000

Money stock	£m
Notes and coin	25 623
NIB bank deposits	41 725
IB bank deposits in M_2	389 108
Building society deposits in M_2	114 419
M_2	570 879

Source: Financial Statistics, August 2000, National Statistics. © Crown Copyright 2001

time), most building society deposits and some money market deposits such as CDs (Certificates of Deposit). The M_4 definition of the broad money supply is shown in Table 35.5.

Table 35.5 M_4 seasonally unadjusted, June 2000

Money stock	£m
M_2 (see Table 35.4)	570 879
Bank wholesale deposits (incl. CDs)	269 783
Building society wholesale deposits in (incl. CDs)	12 125
	852 787

Source: Financial Statistics, August 2000, National Statistics. © Crown Copyright 2001

The changes in definitions, and suspension of the publication of some of them, reflect the arguments about what constitutes money. The reader may well ask which is the correct definition. The answer is that the various measures reflect different concepts of money and different definitions may be useful for different purposes. The M_4 definition might be said to be equivalent to the monetarist definition of money being anything that is the 'temporary abode of purchasing power'. Keynesians tend to prefer narrower definitions of the money supply.

Figure 35.2 shows the various definitions of the money supply and how they relate to one another. It shows both the measures which are published, and those which are not. The factors determining the size of money stocks are discussed in Chapter 36.

Legal tender

Legal tender is anything that must be accepted in settlement of a debt. In the UK, Bank of England notes have been legal tender since 1833. The notes issued by Scottish and Northern Ireland banks are also legal tender. Royal Mint coins are legal tender too, but the law places limits on the quantities of coin that a creditor is forced to accept. Thus, for example, a creditor can refuse to accept payment of a £1000 debt entirely in 1p coins.

The form of money that the state has decreed to be legal tender may also be termed *fiat* money because it is based solely on the faith of the public in its value. In the UK this means notes and coins. Notes and coins may also be termed *representative* money; this is because their nominal value exceeds the value of the metal or paper of which they are made. Bank deposits are not legal tender but, because of their greater security and convenience, they are often more acceptable than cash in settlement of a debt.

Quasi-money and near money

There are some assets that have some of the attributes of money and fulfil some of its functions, but not well enough to be considered money. Such assets may be termed quasi-money. For example, a postal order may be used as a

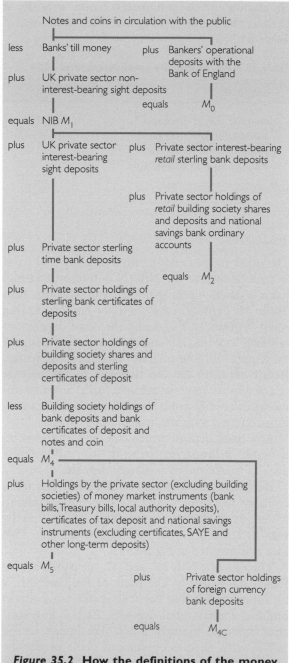

Figure 35.2 How the definitions of the money supply relate to one another

medium of exchange and perhaps also as a store of value, but its usefulness as such is limited and we would say that it is a form of *quasi-money*. Other examples would be book tokens and luncheon vouchers.

Near money is any asset that can quickly be turned into money. This consists of things such as Treasury bills, certificates of deposit and local authority bills. Near money assets provide *liquidity* for banks. They also comprise the main instruments that are dealt with in the money markets.

The quantity equation of money

The equation of exchange

Whatever measure of the money stock we take, it is immediately apparent that none of them equates with the measure of the GDP. All are significantly smaller. This is hardly surprising since each unit of the money supply may be used several times during a year. The number of times that a unit of currency changes hands in a given time period (usually a year) is referred to as the *velocity of circulation* (V).

Consider Figure 35.3. Here we see a simple economy made up of four individuals, A, B, C and D. As in a real economy, each makes their living by selling goods and services to others. Thus, B is producing the goods which A wants, A is producing the goods which D wants, and so on. In each case the value of the goods concerned is £1. Therefore the total value of all the goods exchanged is £4. However, it would be necessary to have a money stock (M) of only £1 because A could pay this to B who in turn uses it to pay C and so on. Thus the value of the total income generated is £4.

This is because income is a flow of money with respect to time, while the amount of money is a stock. An analogy might be a central heating system: the amount of water in the system is the stock, which is constantly being circulated around; the quantity of water passing through any particular part of the system is the flow. The stock may remain constant while the flow becomes greater, or smaller, as the system is speeded up, or slowed down. Similarly, the amount of money in an economy does not depend solely upon the stock of money but also upon how quickly it is used. The total value of money changing hands to finance transactions can be calculated as the *stock* of money (M) multiplied by the velocity of circulation (V). Algebraically this can be represented as:

$$M \times V$$

In the above example this would be £1 × 4 = £4. It is possible to arrive at the same figure by taking the general or *average price level* (P), in our example £1, and multiplying it by the *number of transactions* (T), in our example 4. This would give the same figure of £4. Thus we can derive the formula:

$$M \times V = P \times T$$

This is sometimes known as the quantity equation or, more properly, the equation of exchange. It was first developed by the American economist, **Irving Fisher**.

On the left-hand side we have the total value of money changing hands in a given time period, and on the right-hand side, the total value of the transactions in the same time period. The two sides have to be equal to each other as a matter of logic. Every time there is a sale or transaction, it will be equal in value to the money changing hands. What is true of each transaction will also be true in aggregate.

The velocity of circulation

Let us consider another simplified economy. Suppose that the following is a summary of all the transactions in one time period:

2 shirts sold @ £10	£20
6 pairs of shoes sold @ £5	£30
10 loaves sold @ £1	£10
2 coats sold @ £20	£40
Total value of all transactions	£100

If the money stock is £25, we can then determine the values of the other components in the quantity equation. Since there are 20 transactions in

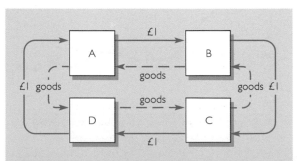

Figure 35.3 **Velocity of circulation**

the time period and the total value of these trans-actions is £100, it follows that the average price of each transaction is £5:

$$£25 \times 4 = £5 \times 20$$
$$(M) \quad (V) \quad (P) \quad (T)$$

The value of V is difficult to measure directly, and must be calculated from the other three values.

The equation of exchange and GDP

In order to relate the equation of exchange to GDP, it is necessary to consider only *final* trans-actions. The distinction between intermediate *transactions* and final transactions was first made in Chapter 7. Intermediate transactions are excluded from GDP because they would result in double counting. In order to relate the exchange equation to GDP, it must be amended so as to cover only final transactions. The letter Y is used to refer to the *number* of final transactions. The equation is rewritten as:

$$M \times V = P \times Y$$

It is important to note that we are using the letter Y in a slightly different way than in the rest of the book, where it is used to denote national income. It should also be noted that the average price level (P)

now also relates only to final products and not intermediate products. This is the version of the price level as used in standard measures of inflation.

Since GDP is equal to the number of final transactions times their average price ($P \times Y$), it is now possible to restate the equation:

$$M \times V = GDP$$

and therefore:

$$V = GDP/M$$

The values for the velocity of circulation are given for recent years in Figure 35.4. The values for M_0 velocity have been rising while those for M_4 have been falling. This implies that M_4 has been rising faster than M_0 and that there is a shift out of cash and into cheque or card methods of payment.

STUDENT ACTIVITY 35.4

(a) If national income is £900bn per annum, M_4 is £600bn, and M_0 is £30bn, calculate the velocity of circulation for each definiton of the money supply.

(b) If $M = 100$; $P = 1$ and $T = 200$, what is the velocity of circulation? What will happen to P if M is doubled and V and T remain the same?

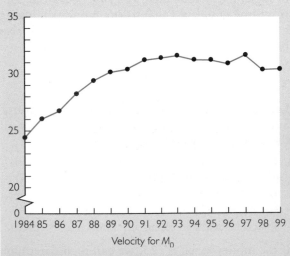

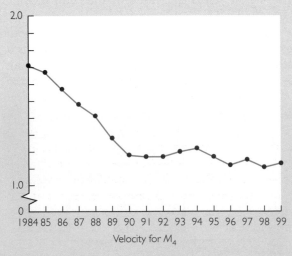

Figure 35.4 The velocity of circulation for M_0 annd M_4

The concept of the general price level

Purchasing power

As we have seen, money is a unit of account and as such we can use it to measure the value of goods and services in the economy. We must now consider how we measure the value of money.

The value of money is determined by its purchasing power. The relative prices of goods and services are always changing but this may not imply any change in the value of money. However, if there is a rise in the general level of prices, so that the value of money declines, we have inflation. Conversely, if the general level of prices were to fall, so that the value of money increased, we would be experiencing deflation. Although an accurate measure of changes in purchasing power over long periods is virtually impossible, Figure 35.5 gives a general idea of what has happened to the value of the pound this century. As you can see, in 1998 it would take £1 to purchase what would have cost only 1.34 pence in 1900 or, put another way, prices rose more than sixtyfold over this period. However, Figure 35.5 also shows the deflation of the interwar period when the value of money increased by some 70 per cent between 1920 and 1935.

Measures of the price level

A measure of the general price level is arrived at by monitoring the price of many individual commodities and combining them together in one index number. By then looking at the rise or fall in the index we are able to see how prices change and consequently how the value of money alters. In the UK, the main indicator of annual changes in the level of consumer prices is the general index of retail prices (RPI), but there are numerous other price indices. These include the wholesale prices index, export prices index, agricultural prices index, pensioner prices index, the consumer expenditure deflator and the taxes and prices index (TPI).

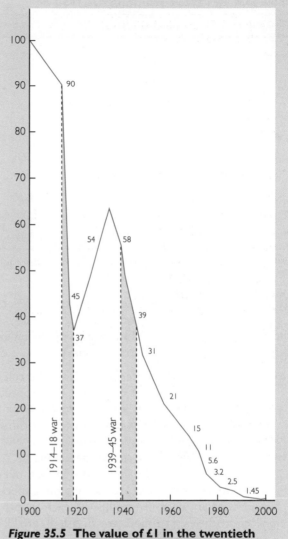

Figure 35.5 The value of £1 in the twentieth century

The index of retail prices (RPI)

The construction of an index number was discussed in Chapter 2. Table 35.6 shows the RPI at five yearly intervals from 1950. The index has been adjusted so that 1985 is equal to 100. It can be seen that after relatively low rates in the 1950s and 1960s, inflation took off in the 1970s with prices almost doubling every five years. Inflation settled down in the 1980s, but did not fall back to the levels found in the 1950s and 1960s. Recent performance in the 1990s shows some improvement.

Table 35.6 RPI at five-year intervals, 1950–90

Year	% increase over five years	RPI
1950		8.8
	31.8	
1955		11.6
	13.8	
1960		13.2
	18.9	
1965		15.7
	24.8	
1970		19.6
	84.2	
1975		36.1
	95.8	
1980		70.7
	41.4	
1985		100.0
	33.3	
1990		133.3
	15.3	
1995		158.6

Source: ONS *Economic Trends Annual Supplement* 1996, National Statistics. © Crown Copyright 2001

To compile an index which gives an accurate reflection of the change in all retail prices is obviously a difficult and complex task. In constructing the index three questions must necessarily be answered.

(a) *Who?* Who is the index thought to be relevant to? In the case of the RPI it is supposed to reflect price changes for the vast mass of the population but it is not relevant for those on very high or very low incomes.

(b) *What?* We must also make decisions as to which goods are to be included – in fact, over 130 000 separate price quotations on a specified Tuesday near the middle of each month. Commodities sampled are divided into 14 main groups and 85 subgroups.

(c) *Weight?* The many different commodities must be allotted an importance, or weight, in the index. A 10 per cent rise in the price of bread would have a very different effect upon the average household from the effect of the same percentage rise in the price of cars.

Calculating the index

The process of calculating an index was discussed in Chapter 2, but is revised below using the simple economy used to illustrate the velocity of circulation earlier in the chapter. The first three columns in Table 35.7 showing price, quantity and expenditure represent the starting point in the economy. The fourth column shows the weight given to each category of expenditure, which is proportional to expenditure. After a period of time a new set of prices develops which are given in the fifth column and calculated as a percentage change in the sixth column. The effect of each price change on the index can be found by multiplying the percentage rise in price by its weight in the index. To find the overall level of inflation, add these effects up. You will notice from the table that some of the price changes may be negative. To simplify this example, we have assumed that changes in relative price have no effect on quantity consumed, and that the economy has not grown. Of course, in the real world neither of these assumptions will apply, but it does enable us to cross-check that in the final column expenditure on the same quantity of products has indeed gone up by 3 per cent as calculated by the method described above. If the index was set at 100 at the beginning of the period, then it will have risen to 103 after the price changes.

Table 35.7 Calculating the RPI

	P_1	Q	E	Weight	New price	Percentage change	Effect on index	New exp.
Shirts	£10	2	£20	0.2	£11	10	+2%	£22
Shoes	£5	6	£30	0.3	£6	20	+6%	£36
Loaves	£1	10	£10	0.1	£1.50	50	+5%	£15
Coats	£20	2	£40	0.4	£15	−25	−10%	£30
Total value			£100	1.0			+3%	£103

Problems associated with the RPI

Having compiled the index, there are problems associated with the interpretation of the figures.

(a) *Time*. Because the compilation of the series has been varied from time to time, and because the weighting has changed significantly, comparisons of prices over many years are difficult. This is well illustrated by the change in the value of weights in Table 35.9 (see page 495). The weights themselves give a picture of the social history of the twentieth century with major shifts away from the necessities of life towards leisure products.

(b) *Quality changes*. As time goes by the quality of products will change, either improving or worsening, but this will not be reflected in the index. For example, television sets are now generally much better than they were some years ago, but only the change in their price will appear in the index. On the other hand some products have built-in obsolescence and don't last as well as in previous years.

(c) *Taxes and benefits*. Changes in indirect taxes such as VAT will be shown in the RPI since they affect prices; changes in direct taxes, however, will not affect the index. Similarly, government price subsidies will influence the index whereas changes in social security benefits will not. Indeed it was partly these limitations which led to the introduction of the TPI (Taxes and Prices Index). The RPIY index takes out the effects of indirect taxes (Table 35.8). It has grown less than the RPI because of the continuous shift of taxation from income to expenditure (noted in Chapter 28).

(d) *Minorities*. While giving a generally good impression of how prices have changed for the mass of the population, the RPI will not be a good guide to how the cost of living has changed for groups whose spending patterns differ greatly from the norm. Examples of such groups are the very rich, the very poor and those with large families. A close look at Table 35.7 will reveal that inflation was 50 per cent on bread but −25 per cent on coats. Poor people are likely to be facing a higher inflation rate than rich people in situations like this. However, the index for a two-person pensioner household (Table 35.8) shows prices rising more slowly for this group recently.

(e) *Mortgage interest* payments are included in the RPI, but this results in perverse behaviour of the index. Governments raise interest rates to discourage spending and curb inflation, but this policy increases inflation because the rate of interest is also a price. Some economists argue that interest rates should be excluded from the index. The RPI without the mortgage element is often referred to as the **underlying** rate of inflation. A comparison of the two measures is found in Table 35.8 which shows considerable variation, which becomes more extreme in periods of sharp interest rate changes.

Interpreting the index

If the RPI increases from 100 to 103, it is obvious that prices have risen 3 per cent. However, high rates of inflation quickly make it difficult to see annual rates of inflation. For example, from 1979 to 1980 the RPI increased from 223.5 to 263.7 (1974 = 100). Some minor mathematics is necessary to see that this is an annual rate of inflation of 18 per cent. This has meant that in recent

Table 35.8 **A comparison of different measures of inflation (1987 = 100)**

Year	RPI		RPIX		RPIY		Two-person household (pensioners)
	Index	% annual change	Index	% annual change	Index	% annual change	
1996	152.7	2.4	152.3	3.0	148.2	2.6	146.9
1997	157.5	3.1	156.5	2.8	151.5	2.2	149.9
1998	162.9	3.4	160.6	2.6	154.5	2.0	151.7
1999	165.4	1.5	164.3	2.3	157.1	1.7	154.2

Source: Economic Trends, August 2000, National Statistics. © Crown Copyright 2001

years it has become common practice to express prices as *X* per cent higher than 12 months previously rather than giving the index number.

● *Common misunderstanding*

*It is commonly assumed that to arrive at an equivalent annual rate from a monthly rate it is necessary to multiply the monthly rate by 12. High rates of inflation have also encouraged the projection of monthly rates into such **annualised rates**. If inflation were to be 1.5 per cent for the last month many people would argue that if this rate of inflation continued all year then the annual rate would be 18 per cent. In fact the correct answer is 19.6 per cent because we have to use the **compound interest** formula. Similarly, if prices rose by 5 per cent a month this would give an annual rate of inflation of 79.6 per cent, not 60 per cent.*

The problem of interpreting inflation data is further complicated by the fact that some sources use the average index value for the year while others use the year end. The situation is further complicated by the use of different base years in different tables.

STUDENT ACTIVITY 35.5

From the following data work out the annual rates of inflation:

	Year 1	Year 2	Year 3	Year 4
RPI	100	110	115.5	127.05

The development of the RPI

The first index of prices compiled by the UK government was the cost of living index. This was introduced in 1914 and continued until 1947. It was designed to measure the costs of maintaining living standards of working-class households. From 1947 to 1956 the interim index of retail prices was similarly angled towards lower-income households. In 1956 the index of retail prices was introduced, and was supposed to reflect changes in prices for the average household.

In 1962 the general index of retail prices (RPI) was introduced. The next major revision of this was in 1974. There is a need to change the index from time to time, partly because with inflation the index number becomes so large, and partly because the composition of the 'basket' of goods in the index changes so greatly. For example, goods such as video cassette recorders were not even in existence when the index of 1974 was compiled.

Although it is difficult to make meaningful comparisons of prices over long periods of time because the weighting changes so much, we have attempted to do so in Figure 35.5, which shows the decrease in the purchasing power of the pound during this century (see page 491).

The weighting of the RPI

The weights for the indexes mentioned above are given in Table 35.9. A profound change has come over the measurement since the first cost of living index in 1914. This was very much a measure of the cost of staying alive and therefore concentrated on the essentials. It was thus of relevance only to those on low incomes. The present RPI is specifically not a cost of living index but a method of measuring changes in all retail prices.

Each set of weights totals 1000. The size of the weight given to each group reflects its relative importance. In the case of the present RPI, the weighting is based on the family expenditure survey (FES) and is revised each January. Thus in 1987 the food groups had a weight of 167; we could therefore consider it as being of 16.7 per cent importance in the index.

As incomes have increased one might have expected to see a decline in the importance of essentials. This is indeed reflected in the decline of the food weight from 350 in 1956 to 143 in 1996. However, when we look at some of the other categories such as housing, we see that they have increased. This is because of the disproportionate rise in the price of these commodities. You will see that the weight for motoring costs has also increased. In this case it is due to the vastly increased car ownership over the period.

Despite the increase in the weights in some categories, the general tendency has been for

Table 35.9 Weights used in calculating the UK retail prices index during the twentieth century

	1914	1947	1956	1974	1987	1996
Food	600	348	350	253	167	143
Catering	–	} 217	–	51	46	48
Alcoholic drink	–		71	70	76	78
Tobacco	–		80	43	38	35
Housing [a]	160	88	87	124	157	190
Fuel and light	80	65	55	52	61	43
Household goods [b]	40	71	66	64	73	72
Household services	–	79	58	54	44	48
Clothing and footwear	120	97	106	91	74	54
Personal goods and services	–	35	59	63	38	38
Motoring expenditure	–	–	} 68	} 135	127	124
Fares and other travel costs	–	–			22	17
Leisure goods	–	–			47	45
Leisure services	–	–			30	65
Total of weights	1000	1000	1000	1000	1000	1000

[a] 1914 and 1947 figures refer only to rent and rates.
[b] 1914 figure refers to all other categories of goods.
Sources: *British Labour Statistics: Historical Abstract/Employment Gazette, Labour Market Trends,* National Statistics. © Crown Copyright 2001

the range of products included in the index to increase. It was this expanding pattern of household expenditure which prompted the 1996 revision. Several new categories of expenditure have been added such as leisure goods and leisure services.

Alternative measures of inflation

The criticisms that have been levelled at the RPI mean that a range of alternative measures have been developed over the years. While they may have their advantages, they have not succeeded in supplanting the RPI for most uses.

The tax and prices index (TPI)

In 1979 the government introduced the TPI. It did this because it believed that changes in the RPI would not give an accurate view of changes in purchasing power because of the government reduction of direct taxes. The TPI is designed to show the increase in gross income (before tax) needed in order to maintain the same level of real net income after taking account of changes in both prices and tax rates and allowances. Alternatively we might describe it as the index formed by averaging changes in taxes including

social security contributions and changes in the prices of goods and services.

Table 35.10 compares RPI and TPI increases over recent years. It can be seen that the gradual reduction in taxation has opened a gap between these two indices (except for the recessionary period from 1992–5).

Table 35.10 A comparison of TPI and RPI (taken at December of each year; January 1987 = 100)

	TPI	[RPI]	Difference
1987	101.4	103.3	1.9
1988	106.3	110.3	4.0
1989	113.1	118.8	5.7
1990	123.3	129.9	6.6
1991	128.2	135.7	7.5
1992	130.1	139.2	9.1
1993	132.7	141.9	9.2
1994	137.2	146.0	8.8
1995	142.1	150.7	8.6
1996	143.6	154.4	10.8
1997	147.6	160.0	12.4
1998	151.5	164.4	12.9
1999	153.4	167.3	13.9

Source: ONS *Economic Trends,* National Statistics. © Crown Copyright 2001

While it is true that the RPI treats changes in direct and indirect taxes differently, the TPI has problems of its own. Are taxes really prices? There are problems in thinking of them as prices of public sector production. Taxes can go up because the price or cost of public sector production has risen, but they can also rise to fund an increased quantity of public sector production (more hospitals, schools, etc.). Alternatively public sector costs can rise, but taxes remain the same if the government chooses to fund its expenditure by borrowing. It is partly for these reasons that the TPI has never replaced the RPI as the principal measure of inflation. An additional reason may be that in the years immediately after its introduction in 1979 it consistently rose faster than the RPI. It also has a tendency to dip just before elections.

International comparisons

The previous section of this chapter has shown that inflation in the UK has sometimes been high, although Table 35.8 shows that inflation has been fairly modest recently. Inflation, however, is an international phenomenon. Figure 35.6 traces

STUDENT ACTIVITY 35.6

Assess how well the RPI would perform in the following situations:

(a) Calculating the wage increase needed to allow workers earning average income to buy the same products as they did last year.
(b) Working out the increase needed for pensions in order to maintain their real standard of living.
(c) Making a similar calculation for a consultant in the NHS.
(d) Calculating how much of the increase in nominal GDP is due to inflation and how much is due to increased output.

the purchasing power of the UK, German and US currencies over this century. In each case it can be seen that the decline in value is comparable. The German mark, however, has had a remarkable history. The hyperinflation of 1923 ended with an exchange rate of 534 910 marks to $1. At this time the price of a loaf of bread in Berlin was 201 000 000 000 marks. The currency was

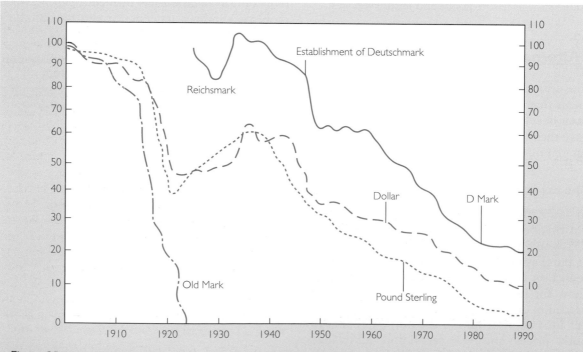

Figure 35.6 The purchasing power of various currencies in the twentieth century compared

re-established in November 1923 but collapsed again after the Second World War. Although there was not the hyperinflation of 1923, marks became almost totally unacceptable and cigarettes and coffee became the money of the country. In 1947 the currency was re-established as the Deutschmark, and has been one of the world's soundest currencies (until replaced by the euro).

Table 35.11 shows the average rates of inflation for selected countries from the 1960s to the 1990s. The general pattern during the 1970s was of a rising trend of inflation worldwide. During the 1980s many nations strove to reduce their rates of inflation. In this the UK was moderately successful, as you can see from the table. Some countries such as Brazil continued to experience runaway rates of inflation.

Table 35.11 **Rates of inflation for selected countries**

	Average annual rate	
	1980–90	1990–99
UK	5.7	2.9
USA	4.2	1.8
Japan	1.7	0.1
France	6.0	1.5
Italy	10.0	4.1
Canada	4.4	1.3
Australia	7.2	1.6
Argentina	389.0	6.2
Brazil	284.0	264.3
Malaysia	1.7	5.0
Russian Federation	2.4	189.6

Source: World Development Report 2000/01, IBRD

Financial institutions

We now move on to consider the operation of those institutions which make up the monetary sector of the economy. We will also examine the money markets and the capital market.

All the institutions involved may be termed financial intermediaries: these are the institutions which channel funds from lenders to borrowers.

Among such institutions are banks, building societies, finance houses (hire purchase companies), insurance companies, pension funds and investment trusts.

Types of financial institution

When we look around the UK and the world we discover many different types of financial institution. In the UK commercial banking is still dominated by the 'big four', although this situation may change as other institutions such as building societies are now able to offer services which have traditionally been the preserve of the banks. Banks themselves can be divided by the type of business they undertake. *Primary banks* are those which are mainly concerned with the transmission of money, i.e. clearing cheques, paying standing orders and so on. This obviously includes the high street banks such as Barclays and Lloyds; less obviously it also includes the discount houses (see below). *Secondary banks* are those which are mainly involved in dealing with other financial intermediaries and providing services other than the transmission of money. A good example is the merchant banks.

(a) *Central banks.* These are usually owned and operated by governments and their most significant functions are in controlling the currency and in implementing monetary policy. They do not generally trade with individuals. Their operations are considered later in the chapter.

(b) *Commercial banks.* These are the profit-motivated banks involved in high street banking activities. In the UK this means the London clearing banks and the Scottish and Northern Irish banks. Many foreign commercial banks now have offices in the UK but they are usually concerned with major commercial types of lending. UK banks also operate extensively overseas; the Barclays Group, for example, operates in over a hundred countries.

(c) *Savings banks.* Originally designed to encourage the small saver, and often non-profit making, these banks have become very significant in some countries. In Germany, for example, these 'Sparkassen' now account for 35 per cent of all deposits and have their own clearing system. In the UK savings banks are represented by the National Savings Bank (NSB), which is fairly insignificant in terms of its total deposits although, via the Post Office network, it has more branches than the rest of the banks put together.

(d) *Cooperative banks and credit unions.* These institutions are much more important in the USA and Europe than in the UK. They are generally small and usually have been established by a group of individuals with a common interest, such as farmers. In France, however, a union of these cooperatives, Crédit Agricole, is now one of the largest banks in the world. The Cooperative Bank in the UK, although established by the cooperative movement, operates more like an ordinary commercial bank.

(e) *Foreign banks.* All industrialised countries have foreign banks operating within them. London, being an important international centre, has many. Some of the foreign banks now compete for the business of domestic commercial banks. The Bank of England issues information on foreign banks which are part of the monetary sector. It issues separate information on American and Japanese banks.

(f) *Building societies.* Many countries possess specialist institutions to assist home buyers and they often enjoy special privileges from the state. Building societies in the UK and savings and loan associations (S&Ls) in the USA have developed to such an extent as to rival the commercial banks. In the UK the Building Societies Act 1986 lifted some of the restrictions on their activities and allowed them to operate more like banks. In fact, a number of the largest societies, such as Abbey National, Halifax and Leeds, have recently legally converted into banks. We have spoken of financial intermediaries as transforming short-term deposits into long-term loans. In the case of building societies we have reached the extreme of this situation as they may grant mortgages for up to 30 years while accepting deposits for as little as seven days or less.

● *Common misunderstanding*

Commercial banks and building societies nowadays offer a very similar range of services, such as current accounts, credit cards, mortgages and pensions. However, there is an important distinction between them: banks are public limited companies, whereas building societies are not; they accept 'shares' in the form of deposits made by their investors.

(g) *Merchant banks.* With merchant banks we have reached the wholesalers in banking. It is often said that commercial banks live on their deposits while merchant banks live on their wits. They act more like banking brokers putting those with large sums of money to lend in touch with borrowers and by offering a wide range of financial advice to companies and even to governments.

(h) *Discount houses.* Peculiar to UK banking, the discount houses make their living by discounting bills of exchange with funds mainly borrowed from the commercial banks.

We will now consider the operation of these various institutions in more detail.

STUDENT ACTIVITY 35.7

List the financial intermediaries that may be found in a typical high street. What types of service do they offer?

Commercial banks

The functions of commercial banks

The most significant function which the commercial bank fulfils is that of **credit creation**, as described earlier in the chapter. The bank itself, however, would not see it in this light as it is not able to distinguish £1 within its deposits from another. It would see its role as accepting money on deposit and then loaning the money out at interest. The commercial banks must compete with other financial intermediaries such as building societies, both in attracting deposits and in making loans.

The **transmission of money** is also a vital function of banks. Customers with current accounts may write **cheques** to pay their creditors. Banks also offer other methods of transmitting money such as **standing orders** and **direct debits**. **Credit cards** are both a method of making a payment and of obtaining credit. Banks also issue **debit cards**, which directly debit the user's account with the amount of the transaction. We can also include **travellers' cheques** as a method of transmitting money.

In addition banks offer *advisory services* to their customers, usually charging for these services. The sort of advisory services which are offered are trusteeship, foreign exchange, broking, investment management and taxation. Since the so-called 'Big Bang' (the deregulation of the financial markets in the late 1980s), the banks are also now able to offer their customers stockbroking services.

Commercial banks may also offer other *financial products* to customers such as mortgages and insurance. In this they will be competing with the more usual suppliers of these services.

Clearing

For payments to be made by cheque it is necessary to have some system of *clearing* the cheques. If a person draws a cheque on their bank and pays it to someone who has an account at the same bank then the clearing can be accomplished without going through the clearing house. If, on the other hand, a payment by cheque involves two different banks then the clearing house becomes involved. This is perhaps best explained by following a cheque through the system. Suppose that Ms Smith draws a cheque on her account with Barclays at its Sheffield branch and gives it to Mr Jones who has an account with HSBC at its Nottingham branch. When Mr Jones has paid in the cheque at the Nottingham branch of HSBC, it is sent with all their similar cheques to the HSBC's clearing department at head office. HSBC then total all the cheques drawn on Barclays and the other banks. The cheques are then taken to the clearing house where they are handed to representatives of the other clearing banks, who in turn hand bundles of cheques to the HSBC. It is then possible to arrive at a figure for the net indebtedness of one clearing bank with the other. This means that instead of hundreds of thousands of separate payments being made by Barclays to HSBC, and vice versa, one payment will settle their accounts. The banks settle their indebtedness to one another by transferring money which they keep in their accounts with the Banking Department of the Bank of England. Thus, at the end of each day their debts have been settled by changes in the book-keeping entries at the Bank of England.

Meanwhile Ms Smith's cheque has been returned to Barclays' head office along with all the others that have been exchanged. Details are then fed into the bank's computer so that the accounts may be debited the next day. Provided that Ms Smith's account is in order her account at the Sheffield branch will then be debited. This process will normally take about three working days. Once the cheque has cleared in this way, Mr Jones's bank will be happy for him to take out the money.

The liabilities of banks

The principal liabilities of the banks are the accounts that people hold with them. The important distinction between different types of account these days is between *sight deposits* and *time deposits*. A sight deposit is any deposit which can be withdrawn on demand without interest penalty. With time deposits notice of withdrawal (e.g. 7 days) is necessary if depositors wish to receive all the interest they are entitled to. The greater the period of notice that is needed the greater the interest a depositor is likely to receive. Large depositors, such as companies, may place money on deposit for periods of three months or more. When this happens it is likely to be by way of special arrangements such as certificates of deposit (CDs – see below). Deposits of foreign currency are very important to UK banks.

● *Common misunderstanding*

Banks used to distinguish between current (cheque) accounts and deposit accounts, current accounts offering instant access to funds but not earning interest, deposit accounts having the opposite characteristics. Nowadays things are a little more complicated. In recent years there has been a decline in the importance of traditional current accounts. In order to attract business away from building societies the banks have introduced such things as instant-access, yet interest-earning, cheque accounts. Other accounts, now mainly referred to as savings accounts, usually earn higher rates of interest although some of these may also be instant access.

Since the banks' liabilities (deposits) form a major portion of the money supply it is understandable that the monetary authorities will wish to supervise them. Since 1981 the Bank of

England's supervision has applied not only to banks but to the whole of the **monetary sector**. The portions of the banks' liabilities which form the basis of control are termed **eligible liabilities** and are those which are of most relevance to the size of the money stock. They comprise, in broad terms, sterling deposit liabilities, excluding deposits having an original maturity over two years, plus any sterling resources obtained by switching foreign currencies into sterling. The banks are then allowed to offset certain of their interbank and money market transactions against their eligible liabilities. Having been defined, these liabilities then form the basis of the various ratios of assets which the banks may be required to maintain.

The clearing banks' assets

Earlier in the chapter we spoke of a cash ratio which banks maintain. In fact the situation is more complex, with banks possessing a whole spectrum of assets from cash, which is the most liquid, to highly illiquid assets such as mortgages that they have made. A bank's assets can be divided into those which are primarily designed to protect liquidity, i.e. those in the balance sheet down to **bills**, and those which are primarily earning assets, or **investments**. Banking business is a conflict between **profitability** and **liquidity**. To earn profits, banks would like to lend as much money as possible at as high a rate of interest as possible. On the other hand they must always be able to meet a depositor's demand for money. Although most business these days is carried out by cheque and credit card, the bank must always be prepared to meet depositors' demands for notes and coins.

When we examine the banks' assets we find that they have different maturity dates; for example, a bank may have loaned money to another bank overnight, while, at the other extreme, it may have granted mortgages which are repayable over 25 years. These days, therefore, the Bank of England, rather than laying down a simple ratio, insists (by a combination of information and persuasion) that the banks hold ratios of assets which are appropriate to the type of liabilities they have accepted. Thus, for example, if a bank has accepted overnight deposits of cash from the money market which are likely to be entirely withdrawn the next day, it is appropriate that these should be 100 per cent covered by highly liquid assets. If, on the other hand, banks have accepted deposits which they will not have to repay for one year, a 5 per cent cover might be appropriate.

The assets cover which a bank requires will therefore depend upon the type of deposits it has accepted. It is no longer possible to state it as a simple ratio; it will differ from bank to bank and from time to time. The clearing banks whose activities are relatively stable might well have a predictable ratio but this will differ from other members of the monetary sector.

The main assets held by the banking sector include:

(a) *Coins and notes*. These are reserves of cash kept by the banks, sometimes referred to as 'till money'. Since 1971 there has been no requirement to keep a specific percentage. In the case of the clearing banks the amount of cash they require is predictable and is a very small portion of their assets. All banks will wish to keep their holdings of cash to a minimum since they earn no interest.

(b) *Cash ratio deposits*. All members of the monetary sector are required to keep 0.35 per cent of their eligible liabilities in cash at the Bank of England. These deposits are kept in non-operational, non-interest-bearing accounts, i.e. the banks and other members of the monetary sector may not use this money, its purpose being to supply the Bank of England with funds rather than for control purposes or for liquidity.

(c) *Other balances*. In addition to the cash ratio deposits the banks keep operational deposits at the Bank of England for the purpose of clearing their debts to one another, as described above. No ratio is laid down by the Bank of England for these deposits.

(d) *Market loans*. The market referred to is the **London money market**, which is discussed in detail later in this chapter. The loans consist of money lent for periods from one day up to three months.

(e) *Discount market*. This is money lent to members of the London Discount Market Association (LDMA) at **call or short notice**. Money lent at call is lent for a day at a time while money lent at short notice is lent for periods up to 14 days. Money lent overnight usually commands a lower rate of interest than that lent for a week, but overnight rates can be very high if the whole market is short of money. After cash these loans are the banks' most liquid assets and will be called in if the banks are short of cash. These loans also form a vital part of the system of money control.

(f) *Other UK banks.* Banks will make and receive short-term loans from other banks and members of the monetary sector to even out their cash flows.

(g) *Certificates of deposit CDs.* If a customer is prepared to make a deposit of cash for a fixed period of time, say three months, the customer will receive a higher rate of interest than in a normal savings account. However, the holder may want the money back before then. The best of both worlds can be enjoyed if the customer accepts a *certificate of deposit.* This is a written promise by the bank to repay the loan at a stated date. The certificate is negotiable, i.e. it can be sold on the money market should the customer require the cash before that date. CDs issued by a bank will, of course, form part of its liabilities, but banks also hold CDs issued by other banks as investments and it is these we see on the assets side of the balance sheet. They are available only for very large deposits.

(h) *Repos.* A similar kind of solution for other assets is found in the repo market where financial institutions which are temporarily short of liquidity sell their assets with an agreement to buy them at an agreed time and price in the near future.

(i) *Local authority loans.* These are loans made through the money market to local authorities, who are now major borrowers. In addition to local authorities, banks may also make short-term loans to companies.

(j) *UK Treasury bills.* The Bank of England sells Treasury bills weekly. These are bought in the first instance by the discount houses. The bills usually have a life of 91 days and they are often acquired by banks from the discount houses when they have five or six weeks left to maturity.

(k) *Other bills.* These are commercial *bills of exchange* issued by companies to finance trade and acquired by the banks on the money market. In the early 1960s commercial bills were almost extinct but they have staged a comeback in the rapid expansion of the money markets over the last two decades.

The primary function of the assets so far discussed is to give liquidity; the remaining items fulfil different functions.

(l) *UK government stocks.* When the term investment is used in banks' balance sheets it refers to their ownership of government stock. The government borrows money by issuing interest-bearing bonds such as Exchequer stock or Treasury stock. These are mainly fixed-interest-bearing, although there are now some which are index linked. Government stocks are termed 'gilts' (gilt edged). The banks will always ensure that they maintain a *maturing portfolio* of bills, stocks, loans, etc., i.e. that a quantity of these mature each week so that the bank has the option of liquidating its asset or reinvesting.

(m) *Advances.* The chief earning assets of the banks are the advances they make to customers. These take the form of overdrafts and loans. In recent years the clearing banks have also made big inroads in the mortgage market.

Liquidity ratios

In the previous chapter we saw that it was necessary for banks to maintain a cash ratio. Today, instead of a cash ratio, the Bank of England requires that banks and other institutions in the monetary sector keep a certain proportion of their assets in a prescribed form. There are two main reasons for this:

(a) In order to ensure the stability of the system. The failure of the Bank of Credit and Commerce International (BCCI) in 1991 and the merchant bank Barings in 1995 emphasised the point that it is still possible for banks to go 'bust'.

(b) It allows the Bank of England to control the credit creation of banks and thus the money supply. Until 1971 the clearing banks were required to keep a *cash ratio* of 8 per cent and a 28 per cent *liquid assets ratio*. In 1971, as part of the Competition and Credit Control regulations, these were replaced by the 12.5 per cent *reserve assets ratio*. Since 1981 there has been no stated ratio and the liquidity ratio which is required of a bank will depend upon the type of business it undertakes. The Bank of England nevertheless still expects banks to maintain appropriate ratios and its control now extends to all institutions in the monetary sector.

The cash which banks require is now a very small and predictable proportion of their assets and it is therefore today of little significance. However, banks must always have an adequate proportion of their assets in highly liquid form. Under the old reserve assets ratio, the items above had to be at least 12.5 per cent of the banks' eligible liabilities, but for prudential reasons banks may require more liquidity than this. At present typical ratios for clearing banks are in the range of 9–12 per cent.

Limits to credit creation by banks

The limits to banks' ability to create credit may be summarised as follows:

(a) *Liquidity ratios*. As we have seen above, the Bank of England lays down liquidity requirements, in addition to which banks will have their own prudential reasons for maintaining ratios.

(b) *Other banks*. If one clearing bank pursued a significantly more expansionist policy of credit creation than all the others, it follows that it would quickly come to grief. This is because a majority of the extra deposits it created would be redeposited with other clearers. The expansionist bank would therefore find itself continually in debt to the other clearers, thus rapidly exhausting its balances at the Bank of England. It would then be forced to reduce its lending to replenish its reserves. Conversely, an overcautious policy of credit creation would decrease the profitability of the bank.

(c) *The supply of collateral security*. A majority of bank lending is in the form of *secured loans*, i.e. the bank has to take something in return, such as a mortgage on a property, an

assurance policy or a bill of exchange, as security in case the loan is not repaid. The supply of such assets will therefore influence a bank's ability to make loans. In particular the supply of money market instruments such as Treasury bills and CDs will greatly influence banks' liquidity. The Bank of England is able to manipulate the supply of such instruments as Treasury bills and government stocks to control banks' credit creation. During the 1980s there was a rapid rise in house prices. Many home owners found themselves in charge of an asset with a rapidly escalating value. A significant number of these used their houses as collateral security to borrow from banks. This money was spent on, for example, buying a holiday home or a new car. This borrowing of money and its use added significantly to inflation.

(d) *The monetary authorities*. Central banks and governments have a variety of weapons at their disposal for influencing bank lending. These are discussed in the next chapter.

> **STUDENT ACTIVITY 35.8**
>
> Suppose a person borrows £1000 from Lloyds bank and thereafter draws a cheque for this sum to buy goods from Cosmic Discount who bank with Barclays. Describe how the money will be paid to Cosmic. If Barclays maintains a liquidity ratio of 20 per cent, how much new lending or investment will it be able to finance as a result of this transaction?

Money markets

The classical and parallel markets

The expression 'money markets' is used to refer to those institutions and arrangements that are engaged in the borrowing and lending of large sums of money for short periods of time.

Most money market transactions are concerned with the sale and purchase of *near money* assets such as bills of exchange and certificates of deposit. Most advanced countries have a money market, but they are most developed in the major banking capitals of the world such as London, New York, Tokyo and Zurich.

In London the money market is geographically very concentrated, all the participants being within a short distance of Lombard Street, although the scope of the market is worldwide through telecommunication computer links.

The *classical money market* is the expression used to describe dealings between the Bank of England, the clearing banks and the discount houses. Traditionally the banks have lent money at call or short notice to the discount houses which they, in turn, have lent out by buying Treasury bills from the Bank of England or by purchasing other first-class bills of exchange. In recent years many new activities have been undertaken on the money market and these are referred to as the *parallel markets*. These include the following:

(a) *The local authorities market.* Local authorities borrow money by issuing bills and bonds which are traded on the money market. They may also place funds when they have a surplus.

(b) *Finance houses.* These institutions, which are involved in hire purchase, obtain some of the funds from the money market.

(c) *Companies.* Large industrial and commercial companies both borrow and place money on the market. If a company lends money to another through the market this is known as an *intercompany deposit*. Companies will also make large deposits with banks in return for a *certificate of deposit*, and these are also traded on the market.

(d) *Interbank market.* This is the borrowing and lending which goes on between banks. It is of great significance in allowing banks to manage their liquidity. It is also important in the determination of interest rates.

(e) *The certificates of deposit market.* As its name implies, this deals with the sale and purchase of CDs in both pounds and other currencies. The repo market operates in a similar way.

(f) *Eurocurrencies.* The market began as the eurodollar market, which referred to the holding of US dollars in European banks. Today a eurocurrency is any holding of currency in a financial institution which is not denominated in the national currency; for example, if a UK bank has holdings of Deutschmarks, this becomes a eurocurrency. The market extends beyond Europe to take in other financial centres such as Tokyo. The main centre of the eurocurrency market is London. Today this market is huge and extremely important. The very large sums held on short-term deposit are a potential source of disequilibrium to a nation, because this so-called 'hot money' may move quickly from nation to nation in search of better interest rates or in anticipation of the change in value of a currency.

Significance of the money markets

The money markets are the place where money is 'wholesaled'. As such the supply of money and the interest rate are of significance to the whole economy. They are also used by the central bank to make its monetary policy effective. Since the abandonment of MLR in 1981, money market indicators have acquired a new significance; for example, the three-month interbank interest rate (the rate at which banks are willing to lend to each other) is now carefully monitored.

Discount houses and discounting

A group of institutions make up the London Discount Market Association (LDMA). They are termed discount houses because their original business was concerned with the discounting of bills of exchange and Treasury bills. Discounting a bill is a method of lending money. We can illustrate the process by considering Treasury bills.

Each week the Bank of England, on behalf of the government, offers Treasury bills for sale. They are a method of borrowing and constitute part of the National Debt. A Treasury bill is a promise by the government to pay a specific sum, e.g. £100 000, 91 days (three months) after the date it is issued.

A discount house might offer to buy the £100 000 bill for, say, £97 500, in which case it will cost the government £2500 to borrow £97 500 for 91 days. This is equivalent to an annual rate of interest of just over 10 per cent. However, the rate on bills of exchange is expressed not as an interest rate but as a *discount rate*. Using the figures above the calculation of a *discount rate* can be illustrated as:

$$\frac{£2500}{£100\,000} \times \frac{100}{1} \times \frac{365}{91} = 10 \text{ per cent}$$

Thus we have arrived at a discount rate of 10 per cent, whereas the true interest rate, or yield, will be higher, in this case 10.28 per cent. If interest rates are falling this will cause discount houses to tender at a higher price. Conversely, if interest rates rise the price the government can expect will obviously fall since the price of the bill and the rate of interest are inversely proportional to each other.

Commercial bills of exchange are discounted in a similar manner. Commercial bills are a method by which a business can borrow money for a short period at advantageous rates. Often they will be to finance a particular transaction. Once a bill has been *accepted*, i.e. guaranteed by a *recognised* bank, it is therefore eligible for discount at the Bank of England. Such *first-class bills of exchange* command the *finest* rates of interest on the money market.

STUDENT ACTIVITY 35.9

Assume that a Treasury bill has a redemption value of £250 000. Suppose that on 8 May, when it still had the full 91 days to run, £222 500 was offered for it. What is the discount rate?

The discount houses and the banks

The discount houses obtain their funds by borrowing money from banks at call or short notice. The rate of interest which they pay is a slightly lower rate than they charge for discounting bills, and in this manner they make their profits. Traditionally the banks have been pleased with this arrangement and have ensured the continued existence of discount houses by not tendering for Treasury bills themselves. The advantage to the banks is that they are lending money for only 24 hours at a time instead of 91 days, thereby giving them an asset almost as liquid as cash but earning some interest. If a bank calls in money from a discount house it is usually to settle an interbank debt. The discount house is then usually able to reborrow the money from the creditor bank.

If the Bank of England is restricting the supply of money it is possible that all the banks will be calling in money from the discount houses. In this situation, if the discount houses cannot find the money anywhere else, they can in the *last resort* borrow from the Bank of England. The Bank does this by *rediscounting* the eligible bills of exchange which the discount houses have. The rate at which the Bank is willing to rediscount is very important, because all other rates move in sympathy with it. The rate is always higher than the Treasury bill rate; the discount houses will, therefore, lose money if they are forced to rediscount with the Bank. Thus, in the event of the Bank restricting the money supply, it is the discount houses which get into difficulties first, therefore providing the banks with a shield, or cushion, against government monetary policy. This is another reason why the banks support the discount houses.

Merchant banks

Merchant banks are so called because they were originally merchants. However, over the course of time they found it more profitable to become involved in the financial aspects of trade rather than the trade itself. Many institutions claim the title of merchant bank; indeed some of the clearing banks have set up merchant banking subsidiaries. Traditionally the term 'merchant bank' was linked to the 16 members of the *Accepting Houses Committee*. This includes such institutions as Hambros, Schroders, Lazards and Morgan Grenfell.

Accepting is a process whereby the accepting house guarantees the redemption of a commercial bill of exchange in the case of default by the company which issued the bill. For this it charges a commission. A bill which has been accepted by a London accepting house becomes a *fine* bill or *first-class bill of exchange*. This makes it much easier to sell on the money market, where it will also command the lowest, or 'finest', discount rate. The bill will also be eligible for rediscount at the Bank of England. In order to be able to guarantee bills in this way, accepting houses have to make it their business to know everyone else's business. A merchant banker will therefore specialise in certain areas of business or in particular areas of the world (companies from all over the world raise money on the London money market); Hambros, for example, specialises in Scandinavian and Canadian business. The regional specialisations often reflect the merchant origins of the bank.

In addition to accepting, merchant banks undertake many other functions. They might undertake to raise capital for their clients or invest in the company themselves. They act as agents in takeover bids and in the issue of new shares. In recent years many merchant banks have become involved in unit trusts and investment trusts. However, merchant banks do not involve themselves in high street banking activities.

The capital market

The capital market is concerned with the provision of longer-term finance – anything from bank loans to investment in permanent capital in the form of the purchase of shares. Unlike the money market, the capital market is very widespread. Some of the participants in this market are as follows:

(a) *Commercial banks*. These are important in providing short- and medium-term loans to industry. In the UK, however, it is unusual for commercial banks to invest in industry by taking shares or debentures, unlike the USA and Germany where this is common practice.

(b) *Merchant banks*. These banks participate in the capital market by assisting companies in the issue of new shares and also by direct investment in industry.

(c) *Insurance companies and pension funds*. Over recent years the institutional investors have become more and more important, so that today the insurance companies and pension funds own well over half the shares in public companies.

(d) *Investment trusts*. There are joint stock companies whose business is investment in other companies. Shares are bought in the normal way and the funds thus raised are used to buy shares in other companies.

(e) *Unit trusts*. Although unit trusts also invest in other companies they are not normal companies. Unit trusts are supervised by the Department of Trade and Industry and are controlled by boards of trustees. They attract small investors who buy units in the trust which can be redeemed if the investor so wishes.

(h) *Private individuals*. The trend for many years has been the decline in the importance of the private individual as an investor. The privatisations of the 1980s did not significantly alter this trend. There are, of course, a few, very wealthy private individuals who are important investors.

(i) *Self-finance*. One of the most important sources of finance to industry is ploughed-back profits. (See also the discussion in Chapter 25.)

Central banking

Every country in the world has a central bank, and there is now also an 'international' central bank for the EU. The oldest central bank is that of Sweden (1668). The Bank of England was founded in 1694, while in the USA the Federal Reserve did not come into existence until 1913. The Bank of England was founded by a group of businessmen headed by a Scotsman, **William Paterson**. In return for a loan to the Crown of £1.2 million the Bank of England acquired several privileges. This began its close association with the UK government which culminated in its nationalisation in 1946.

However, in May 1997 the new Labour government, in a historic step, granted the Bank of England 'operational independence' in the determination of interest rates and hence, in large part, for the operation of monetary policy.

This placed the Bank of England more on a par with the Federal Reserve of the USA and the German Bundesbank, two of the more independent central banks.

An important step in the development of the Bank of England was the Bank Charter Act of 1844. This divided the Bank into two departments, the Issue Department, responsible for the issue of notes, and the Banking Department, which is responsible for all the Bank's other activities. The Act also set in motion the process by which the Bank was to become the sole issuer of notes in England and Wales.

Functions of central banks

Central banks are important to the working of the monetary system. Among their most important functions are the following:

(a) *Government's banker*. Governments pay their revenues into the central bank and pay their bills with cheques drawn on it. The fees which the bank charges for this are an important source of revenue to the bank.

(b) *Banker's bank*. As explained earlier in the chapter, commercial banks keep balances with the central bank. This is both a method of controlling banks and also the way by which interbank indebtedness can be settled.

(c) *Lender of last resort*. The central bank stands ready to support commercial banks should they get into difficulties.

(d) *Banking supervision*. Central banks usually have a major role to play in the policing of the banking system. In some countries this responsibility is shared with other authorities; for example, in the USA the Federal Reserve is supported by the Comptroller of Currency and by the Federal Deposit Insurance Corporation (FDIC).

(e) *Note issue*. In most countries of the world the central bank is responsible for the issue of banknotes. This is not so everywhere. In the USA, for example, the currency is issued by the government.

(f) *Operating monetary policy*. It is usually the central bank which operates government monetary policy.

● *Common misunderstanding*

Besides acting as the government's banker and as the operator of monetary policy, the Bank of England also functions as an ordinary bank. Most central banks do not operate as commercial banks; some, however, such as the Banque de France, compete for ordinary business in the high street with commercial banks.

Other functions of the Bank of England

First, since 1946 it has had the responsibility for 'disposing of the means of foreign payment in the national interest', i.e. all *foreign exchange transactions* are monitored by the Bank. This function is not so important since the abolition of exchange controls in 1979. However, the Bank operates the *Exchange Equalisation Account*. This is a fund, established in 1932, the purpose of which is to buy and sell currency on the foreign exchange market with the object of stabilising the exchange rate. This function is equally important whether there is a fixed or floating exchange rate. The Bank also *sells stock* on behalf of the government. It advises the

government on the issue of new securities, it converts and funds existing government debt, it publishes prospectuses for any new government issues and it deals with the applications for them and apportions the issue. It also *manages the servicing of the National Debt*, i.e. the payment of interest on behalf of the government. The Bank is also responsible for giving the government general *advice on the monetary system*; it publishes large quantities of statistical information on the monetary system, along with studies of various sectors of the economy. (Conscientious students should acquaint themselves with the *Bank of England Quarterly Bulletin* and the accompanying *Monetary and Financial Statistics*, in which much of this information is contained.) Finally, an important function of the Bank is to *represent the government* in relations with foreign central banks and also in various international institutions such as the Bank for International Settlement (BIS) and the International Monetary Fund (IMF).

Summary

1 Modern money can be traced back to the goldsmiths of the late Middle Ages.

2 The majority of the money supply is made up of bank deposits. Banks are able to create credit. The limit on their ability to do so is the prudent cash (or reserve assets) ratio.

3 Money has four main functions: medium of exchange; unit of account; store of value; standard of deferred payment. In order to function as money an asset must have a number of characteristics, or attributes, such as acceptability, divisibility, homogeneity and portability.

4 There are several different measures of the money stock such as M_0 and M_4.

5 The equation of exchange $M \times V = P \times T$ demonstrates that the size of the money stock and the velocity of circulation must be considered when thinking about money.

6 The price level is measured with index numbers, the most well known of which is the RPI. There are many problems associated with the compilation of the RPI. Other measures exist such as the RPIX and the TPI but these also have their problems.

7 Inflation is worldwide. Over the last two decades the UK's rate of inflation has been among the highest of developed nations, but much higher

rates of inflation have been experienced in some other economies, e.g. Argentina.

8 Financial intermediaries are institutions which channel funds between different sectors of the economy.

9 The many different types of bank can be grouped under the two headings, primary and secondary banks. Primary banks operate in the high street and deal with the general public, while secondary banks deal in very large amounts of money with other banking institutions.

10 The main functions of commercial banks are the creation of credit, the transmission of money and the provision of advisory services to customers.

11 Money markets are those institutions and arrangements which are concerned with the borrowing and lending of money on a very large scale for very short periods of time (overnight to three months).

12 The capital market is concerned with the provision of capital for industry, commerce and the government. The market is very widespread and provides capital for periods over three months to permanent.

13 Most central banks act as the government's banker, the banks' bank, lender of last resort and issuer of notes as well as supervising the banking system and operating monetary policy.

14 The Bank of England has other functions such as managing the National Debt and running the Exchange Equalisation Account.

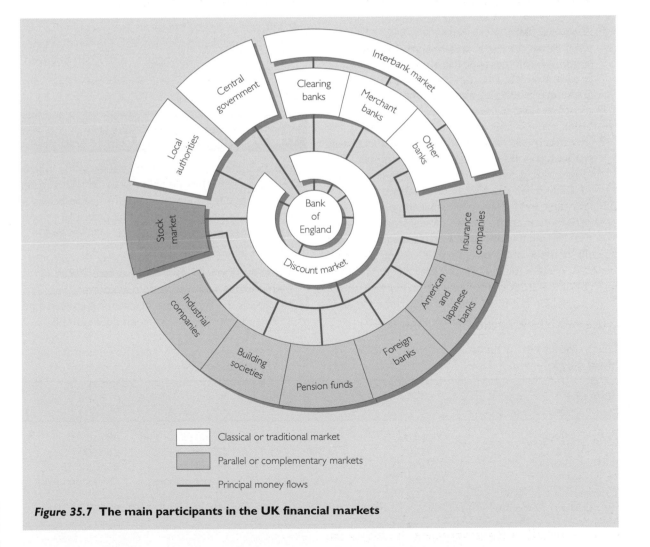

Figure 35.7 **The main participants in the UK financial markets**

? QUESTIONS

1 Discuss the suitability of the following to function as money:
(a) gold; (b) caviar; (c) diamonds; (d) copper; (e) cattle.

2 Examine the extent to which bank deposits possess the attributes of money.

3 Explain how inflation will affect the functions of money.

4 A monopoly bank has deposits of £1000, cash of £250 and loans to customers of £750. It is obliged not to let its cash ratio fall below 10 per cent.
(a) How much credit can it create?
(b) How would the answer to (a) differ if the cash ratio were 12.5 per cent?

5 Distinguish between a change in relative prices and an inflationary change in prices.

6 Assuming that there is to be continuing inflation, what measures might people take to protect themselves from its effects?

7 Explain the difficulties which are associated with the interpretation of changes in the RPI.

8 Describe what is meant by the weighting of an index.

9 The information shown in Table 35.12 about four married couples was obtained in December 1997. Give possible reasons why the change in the cost of living varied so much between those families.

10 Consider the following information about a hypothetical economy: the money stock (M) = £30 million; the velocity of circulation (V) = 4; and the number of transactions is 20 million per year.
(a) What is the general price level (P)?
(b) If the stock of money were to increase to £40 million but the velocity of circulation (V) and the number of transactions (T) were to

remain constant, what would be the new price level (P)?
(c) If in the original situation the velocity of circulation were to rise to $V = 6$ and the number of transactions were to rise to $T = 25$ million, what would be the new general level of prices?

11 A banker might say: 'My bank's books always balance. We simply lend a proportion of my depositors' savings to investors. We do not create money.' To what extent is this true?

12 'Since banks themselves can now determine their own liquidity ratios, there is no effective constraint on their ability to create credit.' Explain and discuss.

13 Assess the advantages and disadvantages of the capital market being dominated by large institutions.

14 What is meant by the terms 'the discount market' and 'the parallel money markets'? To what extent is it possible or meaningful to distinguish between the two?

Data response A
THE UK INFLATION RATE

Figure 35.8 gives the information relating to the index of retail prices (RPI) in the UK in June 1991. The figures in brackets give the weights. The figures in the boxes are the annual change in price in that particular category. Given that the RPI stood at 126.7 in June 1990, attempt the questions which follow.

1 What was the value of the RPI in June 1991? Demonstrate how you arrived at your answer. What was the annual rate of inflation between June 1990 and June 1991? Distinguish between the

Table 35.12

| | Family | | | |
	A	B	C	D
Ages of parents	35 and 32	36 and 28	60 and 58	45 and 43
Total income	£10 000	£22 000	£25 000	£60 000
Ages of children	2, 5 and 10	–	32 and 28	8, 12 and 15
Residence	Rented	Owner occupiers	Owner occupiers	Owner occupiers
Change in cost of living over previous 12 months	9%	2%	5%	0%

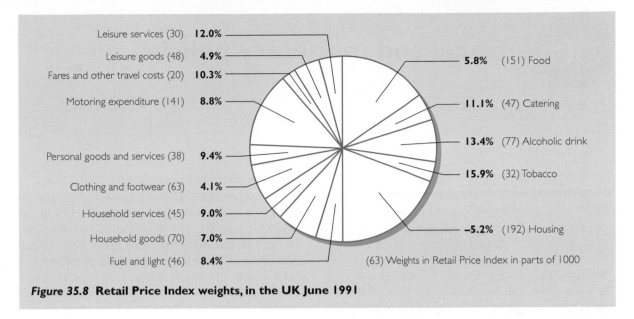

Leisure services (30) **12.0%**
Leisure goods (48) **4.9%**
Fares and other travel costs (20) **10.3%**
Motoring expenditure (141) **8.8%**
Personal goods and services (38) **9.4%**
Clothing and footwear (63) **4.1%**
Household services (45) **9.0%**
Household goods (70) **7.0%**
Fuel and light (46) **8.4%**

5.8% (151) Food
11.1% (47) Catering
13.4% (77) Alcoholic drink
15.9% (32) Tobacco
–5.2% (192) Housing

(63) Weights in Retail Price Index in parts of 1000

Figure 35.8 **Retail Price Index weights, in the UK June 1991**

annual rate of inflation and an annualised rate of inflation.

2 What difficulties are encountered in interpreting RPI figures?

3 It was argued by the Chancellor of the Exchequer that it would be better to take mortgage payments out of the index. Why did he say this? Do you agree with him? Explain your answer.

Fiscal and monetary policies

Learning outcomes

At the end of this chapter you will be able to:

▶ Appreciate the nature, impact and effectiveness of fiscal policy.

▶ Explain the development of monetary policy.

▶ Identify the main weapons of monetary policy.

▶ Appreciate the problems involved in effecting monetary policy.

▶ Identify the relative merits of an independent central bank.

Introduction

In the first part of this chapter we shall deal with *fiscal policy*, or the regulation of the economy through government spending and taxes, which we first encountered in Chapter 15. Here we shall examine the nature of fiscal policy, its potential impact on the economy and its effectiveness.

In the second half of the chapter we will examine the operation of *monetary policy* or the direction of the economy through the supply of and price of money. In this section we shall outline the development of monetary ideas, detail the main weapons of monetary policy and assess the efficiency of the policy operated as it now is by the newly independent Bank of England.

Fiscal policy

Fiscal policy is the regulation of the economy through government spending and taxes.

Government spending in the UK accounts for around 40 per cent of GDP, as Table 36.1 indicates. The main items of expenditure are social security, health, education, defence and law and

order. In fact, although the relative significance of public spending declined a little in the 1980s and 1990s, it has actually increased in importance during the last 40 years. The table also reveals that UK government spending as a proportion of GDP is actually below the average for industrialised economies: some countries, such as Sweden, France and Italy spend far more in proportionate terms, while others like the USA and Japan spend less.

Table 36.1 **Government spending and tax revenue as a percentage of GDP, 1960, 1980, 1998, various countries**

	Government spending			Tax revenue		
	1960	1980	1998	1960	1980	1998
Australia	21.2	31.4	32.9	22.4	28.4	30.3
UK	32.2	43.0	40.2	28.5	35.1	35.3
Canada	28.6	38.8	42.1	23.8	32.0	36.8
France	34.6	46.1	54.3	na	41.7	46.1
Germany	32.4[a]	47.9[a]	46.9	31.3[a]	38.2[a]	37.5
Italy	30.1	42.1	49.1	34.4	30.4	44.9
Japan	17.5	32.0	36.9	18.2	25.4	28.4
Spain	na	32.2	41.8	14.0	23.9	35.3
Sweden	31.0	60.1	60.8	27.2	48.8	53.3
USA	26.8	31.4	32.8	26.5	26.9	28.5
Average	28.3	40.5	43.8	25.1	33.1	37.6

[a] West Germany
Source: The Economist Newspaper Limited, London, 31 July 1999

Most of the expenditure is financed by taxes, but as can be seen from Table 36.1, tax revenue usually forms a lower percentage of GDP than expenditure. Any shortfall between expenditure and revenue is made up by government borrowing.

In the UK the government's spending and taxation plans for the coming financial year (6 April until the following 5 April) are given in the annual **Budget**, which takes place in March. Usually the government plans to spend more than it collects in taxes and so runs a **budget deficit**. It then has to borrow from the Bank of England, issue National Savings certificates or sell government securities. The borrowing details of the public sector are indicated by the **Public Sector Net Cash Requirement (PSNCR)**, which used to be referred to as the Public Sector Borrowing Requirment (PSBR). In fact, while it is normal to run a budget deficit, in 1998 and 1999 the government actually had a **budget surplus**, and collected more taxes than it spent. It can use this surplus to pay off past debts. In this way, the so-called **public sector debt repayment (PSDR)** enables the government to repay some of the **National Debt**, or the accumulated debt from previous years. In 1998 the PSNCR was –£6.4 billion, or, alternatively, the PSDR was + £6.4 billion; in 1999 the PSNCR was –£1.75 billion, giving a PSDR of + £1.75 billion. In both years the surplus funds were able to help pay off some of the National Debt, although as this has accumulated since the establishment of the Bank of England in 1694 and stood at over £421 billion in 1999 it may take some time and some rather large budget surpluses to repay all of it.

The impact of fiscal policy

Fiscal policy can either be expansionary or contractionary depending on its potential impact on the level of economic activity, i.e. spending, output and jobs. If the government raises its expenditure and/or lowers taxes this will either increase the budget deficit or reduce the budget surplus and can have an expansionary (or 'reflationary') effect on the economy by shifting the aggregate demand curve to the right. Such a **loosening** of fiscal policy may also lead to a rise in inflation and a worsening of the current account of the balance of payments. Alternatively, a reduction in the budget deficit or an increase in the budget surplus can have a contractionary (or 'deflationary') impact on demand; this **tightening** of fiscal policy may be accompanied by a fall in inflation and an improvement in the current account of the balance of payments.

The **fiscal stance** of the government, or just how expansionary or contractionary its fiscal policy, depends also on the scale of the current deficit or surplus compared with that in the previous year. An increase in the deficit compared with last year may boost aggregate demand and vice versa, a fall in the deficit relative to the previous year may well reduce aggregate demand. Furthermore, changes in government spending and taxation have to be compared with changes in the other injections and withdrawals in the economy in order to assess their overall impact on aggregate demand (see Chapter 29).

● *Common misunderstanding*

The fact that the government runs a budget deficit over a number of years does not necessarily mean that its fiscal policy is expansionary. First, it is necessary to compare the size of the current budget deficit with that of the previous year; a lower deficit compared with last year may actually reduce aggregate demand. Second, it is important to take into account the scale of changes in the other injections and withdrawals in the economy before the impact of fiscal policy can be properly assessed; the government may increase its level of spending but find that a rise in import spending and/or savings leads to an overall reduction in aggregate demand.

Discretionary and automatic changes

Discretionary fiscal changes are those policies which come about as a result of some conscious decision taken by the government, e.g. changes in tax rates or a change in the pattern of expenditure. Besides trying to influence the level of aggregate demand, discretionary fiscal policies can be used to affect aggregate supply by, for example, lowering tax rates. This, it is argued, provides improved incentives for work and investment. Discretionary policies can also be employed to change expenditure priorities in accord with election manifestos, say, by reducing defence spending and giving more to education and health.

Automatic changes, on the other hand, come about as a result of some change in the economy, e.g. an increase in unemployment automatically increases government expenditure on unemployment benefits. In fact, it is the case that deficits tend to increase automatically in times of recession and decrease in times of recovery. These fiscal weapons which automatically boost the economy during recession and dampen it in times of recovery are referred to as *automatic stabilisers*. It is possible for a government to compound the effects of a recession by raising taxes in order to recover lost revenues. This, according to Keynesians, would cause a contractionary multiplier effect reducing the level of economic activity.

Fiscal drag

Where progressive taxes are concerned, inflation will mean that the Chancellor of the Exchequer takes a bigger and bigger portion of a person's income as increased money wages raise them from a lower to a higher tax bracket. This tendency is known as *fiscal drag* and it is to offset this that the Chancellor frequently raises the tax threshold. There is also a principle known as fiscal boost. This refers to the fact that inflation will reduce the real burden of specific taxes such as excise duty.

STUDENT ACTIVITY 36.1

Explain how the concept of fiscal drag may be instrumental in stalling the recovery from a recession in an economy.

Limitations of fiscal policy

There has been much debate among both economists and politicans about the ability of the government to use fiscal policy to *fine tune* the economy by manipulating aggrgegate demand, or *demand management* policy as it is known. The effect of any shift of the aggregate demand curve on output and employment depends crucially on the assumptions made about the shape of the aggregate supply curve and this was discussed in Chapter 33. Neo-Keynesians (and those on the political left) argue that an expansionary fiscal policy that shifts the aggregate demand curve to the right can have a positive impact on both output and jobs, but there will be mounting inflationary effects as full employment approaches. Neo-classical and monetarist economists (and those on the political right), however, assume the

existence of a vertical aggregate supply curve and this means that an expansion of aggregate demand has little or no effect on output and jobs, except perhaps in the short run, and will simply lead to higher inflation. Therefore, they argue that it is preferable to use fiscal policy as part of a supply side package to influence aggregate supply rather than aggregate demand (see Chapter 39).

However, there are a number of more general reasons why the effectiveness of fiscal policy in demand management has been questioned:

(a) *The inflexibility of government finance.* Adjusting the government's level of economic activity to suit changing circumstances is not as straightforward as it may seem. Much of the government's finance is inflexible. One of the reasons for this is that the major portion of almost any department's budget is wages and salaries, and it is not possible to play around with these to suit the short-run needs of the economy. In addition to this, it would be a strange way of ordering priorities if a government were to stop the construction of a half-built motorway, hospital or school because less expenditure was needed. Much of the government's expenditure involves long-run planning.

Another problem contributing to the inflexibility of government finance is the political problems associated with cuts in expenditure. It would not be easy, for example, to cut old age pensions, and cuts in health and education often bring unwelcome political criticism.

(b) *Information.* It is very difficult to assemble accurate information about the economy sufficiently quickly for it to be of use in the short-run management of the economy. There have been numerous occasions when, for example, the balance of payments has been declared to be in deficit in one quarter but a few months later, when more information is available, it has been discovered that the quarter was in fact in surplus. It is difficult, therefore, for a government to be sure about the accuracy of the information. Even if the figures are accurate, the government still has to decide what they mean. For example, if the balance of payments is still in deficit, is this the beginning of a long-run trend or just a freak result of that month or quarter? The same can be said for unemployment and inflation figures which sometimes suffer from temporary blips due to special circumstances.

(c) *Time lags*. One of the chief objectives of fiscal policy is stability, i.e. the government tries to avoid violent fluctuations in the level of economic activity. One way to do this is for the government to have a counter-cyclical policy so that if, for example, the level of economic activity were low, government activity would be high, i.e. it would have a budget deficit. Conversely, if there were a high level of activity then the government would budget for a surplus. This ideal policy approach is illustrated in Figure 36.1.

Unfortunately, it takes time for a government to appreciate the economic situation, to formulate a policy and then to implement it. This may mean that the government's policy works at the wrong time. For example, if the government decides to reflate the economy during a recession, it could be that by the time the policy works the economy would have recovered anyway. The government's actions therefore have the effect of boosting the economy beyond that which is desirable. When this happens the government decides to clamp down on the economy but, by the time the policy acts, the economy has naturally returned to recession. The government's action therefore makes the slump worse, and so on. This pattern will be familiar to anyone who lived through the stop–go policies of the 1950s and 1960s (see Chapter 43).

(d) *Crowding-out*. It is argued that government borrowing may starve industry of funds and force up interest rates. This argument is put forward by monetarists and neo-classicists. The argument runs something like this: an increase in government expenditure or a decrease in taxes means that the government must borrow more. It cannot borrow from the increased income generated by the multiplier, because that has not happened yet. It must therefore borrow from the existing pool of savings, thus pushing up interest rates. This increase in interest rates will reduce private sector expenditure on both investment and consumption. It may also push up the exchange rate, which will also have the effect of reducing expenditure on domestically produced goods. Any benefit from fiscal policy will be cancelled out by these ***crowding out effects***.

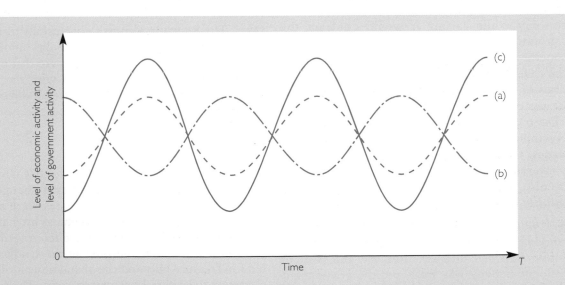

Figure 36.1 Counter-cyclical policy
(a) Fluctuations in the level of economic activity without government intervention. (b) Proposed pattern of government counter-cyclical activity. (c) Worsened fluctuations in the level of economic activity due to government policy acting at the wrong time.

The Keynesians reply that this increase in interest rates can be prevented by an increase in the money supply. The increase in the money supply will be needed anyway, because the economy is going to expand as a result of the multiplier effects of the fiscal policy. The monetarists cannot allow this escape from their argument, since they believe that an increase in the money supply will always be inflationary, while Keynesians argue that this will only be true for very sudden increases, or increases near to full employment levels.

The development of monetary policy

Monetary policy is the direction of the economy through the supply and price of money.

In most countries, as in the UK, the operation of monetary policy is undertaken by the central bank.

Early changes

It used to be believed that changes in the rate of interest (the price of money) determined the volume of investment in the economy. Thus, lowering the rate of interest would stimulate the economy while raising it would contract the economy. Up to the time of the First World War, monetary policy consisted of little more than minor changes in bank rate. The question of variations of the money supply hardly arose since the UK was on the gold standard.

During the 1930s the relationship between investment and interest was challenged by Keynes. Certainly, events seemed to support him as interest rates were very low but investment was also very low. This Keynes explained as the *liquidity trap*.

Thus, when Keynes's view became the economic orthodoxy after 1945 it was believed that the connection between interest rates and the level of economic activity was weak and the government relied upon fiscal policy as the principal method of directing the economy.

These points are explored further in the next chapter. Thus, in the immediate post-war years,

active monetary policy was severely curtailed and interest rates were held at a low level.

Monetary policy in the 1950s and 1960s

Monetary policy was revived in the 1950s, as evinced by the rise in bank rates over the decade. It came to be believed that raising interest rates would 'lock up' investment funds in financial institutions. This was because a large proportion of their assets were in government securities and a rise in interest rates would decrease their value, thus making institutions unwilling to sell them because they would make a loss. Thus the orthodox view at this time was that putting up rates would 'choke off' investment and was therefore useful in restricting the economy. However, lowering interest rates would not, of itself, be sufficient to stimulate the economy.

The Radcliffe Report (Committee on the Working of the Monetary System, 1959) endorsed the view that the control of overall liquidity was more important than control of the money supply. The Report was subsequently criticised for its lack of attention to control of the money supply. The Report argued that any contrived changes in the money supply (M) were as likely as not to be offset by changes in the velocity of circulation (V). The view was also challenged by monetarists in later years. The Radcliffe Report's conclusions formed the basis of government monetary policy until the early 1970s. In particular it was believed that monetary policy should be concerned with the fine tuning of the economy, while its overall direction was a matter for fiscal policy.

The rise of monetarist ideas

The Competition and Credit Control (CCC) regulations of 1971 were an important change in policy. From this date interest rates were supposed to be left free to be determined by market forces. Competition was to be encouraged by such measures as the abolition of the syndicated bid for Treasury bills and the abandonment of the clearing banks' cartel on interest rates. The CCC changes also abandoned the old 28 per cent liquid assets ratio in favour of a 12.5 per cent reserve assets ratio (itself abandoned in 1981). This resulted in an unprecedented rise in the money supply, which was one of the major causes of inflation in subsequent years.

Economists in the UK and the USA, especially the leader of the monetarist school, Milton Friedman, were convinced that the only way to control inflation was through control of the money supply (M).

The increasing severity of inflation and the apparent inability of traditional fiscal and incomes policy methods to deal with it won many people over to the monetarist school. In particular the IMF was convinced of the need to control M. Thus, when the UK was forced to apply for a major loan in 1976 it was granted if only on the condition that the money supply be controlled. The accession of monetarist ideas to dominance in monetary policy can be seen to date from 1976.

In 1979 a Conservative government was elected which placed control of the money supply at the centre of its policies. In 1980 the government adopted a *Medium Term Financial Strategy* (MTFS). This set down diminishing targets for the growth of the money supply so as to squeeze inflation out of the system. In most years the target rates were exceeded while, at the same time, measures of the money supply were changed and redefined. In October 1985 the MTFS was largely abandoned when the most favoured target, M_3, was suspended. By 1988 the only measure of money supply for which targets remained was M_0.

Despite these changes the Conservative government continued to see control of the money supply and of interest rates as central to its policies, although there was also an increased tendency to use interest rates to avoid fluctuations in exchange rates. In 1990 the UK joined the Exchange Rate Mechanism (ERM) and interest rates were primarily used to maintain the value of the pound within the requisite limits. However, the fact that the UK had entered the ERM at what many regarded as too high a level meant that interest rates were also kept high. In 1992 the UK left the ERM and interest rates fell. From 1993 the prime focus of government policy has been to use interest rates to keep inflation within certain 'target bands', the targeting of the money supply *per se* having been long since abandoned. This was also the policy adopted by the

Labour administration from 1997, the target rate for inflation being set at 2.5 per cent.

The predominance of the use of monetary policy as the key weapon in UK macroeconomic policy in the last twenty years has inevitably meant that fiscal policy is now no longer regarded as a prime demand management tool. Instead interest rates have come to be viewed as the principal fine tuners in the economy, particularly as regards the targetting of inflation. However, government spending still accounts for a significant share of national income and, as such, has an important influence on the economy. Government spending and taxation plans also continue to act as automatic stabilisers for the economy. In fact, some may view the announcement by the government in July 2000 to increase public spending in real terms by at least 3.3 per cent p.a. over the next three years as the return to a more active discretionary role for fiscal policy, although the effect of this spending surge will see public expenditure as a share of GDP simply rising to the levels of the mid-1990s (see Data response A at the end of this chapter).

STUDENT ACTIVITY 36.2

Why do you think that interest rates needed to be kept at a high level when the UK was in the ERM? What impact could such a policy have on the money supply and the level of spending in the economy?

● *Common misunderstanding*

It should be borne in mind that a government must have a fiscal policy. It is easy in the fiscal policy/monetary policy debate to assume that if the government adopts monetary policy as the chief weapon of policy it can abandon fiscal policy. This can never be so because in an economy where the government collects and spends over 40 per cent of the national income, how this is done must have profound effects upon the economy.

The stages of monetary policy

The five stages of policy

The Bank of England has a number of *weapons* or *instruments* of monetary policy at its disposal;

for example, it may lower interest rates in order to stimulate the economy.

● Common misunderstanding

It is sometimes thought that it is possible to use policy weapons to influence the economy and economic variables immediately. However, in most cases, policies do not take effect straight away. For example, there are several steps, or stages, along the monetary policy road.

These steps we may list as follows:

(a) *Instruments (or weapons) of policy*, which include, for example, open market operations, which are used to implement policy. It will take some time for these to act upon:

(b) *Operating policy targets* such as the liquidity of banks. These in turn will affect such things as the growth of money stock, which are termed:

(c) *Intermediate targets*. They are termed 'intermediate' because they are not the actual objective of policy but are important steps along the way. For example, restricting the money supply may be seen as essential in achieving the overall policy objective of controlling inflation. To do this the intermediate targets must affect:

(d) *Aggregate demand*. This is the actual level of national income as measured by GDP, NNP, etc., the control of which leads directly to:

(e) *Overall policy objectives*. This is the ultimate goal of policy such as the promotion of economic growth or the control of inflation.

Intermediate targets

The central link in the chain is intermediate targets. In choosing the best or most appropriate target, the monetary authorities are constrained by two major considerations: first, which target it is *possible* to control, i.e. it is no good selecting a target which is impossible to influence (perhaps we should say that some targets are more influenceable than others!); second, which intermediate target is thought to influence most the desired ultimate policy objective. Here there is considerable disagreement. Monetarists, for example, would argue that changes in interest rates have a significant influence on economic growth, while Keynesians would argue that the effect would be slight.

These are the main intermediate targets:

(a) the money stock;
(b) the volume of credit;
(c) interest rates;
(d) the exchange rate;
(e) the level of expenditure in the economy (or PSBR as a percentage of the level of expenditure, as was used in the early 1980s).

It is possible for expenditure to be considered an intermediate target as well as the fourth stage of monetary policy.

The weapons of monetary policy

Monetary policy is aimed at controlling the supply and price of money. However, elementary economics tells us that government cannot do both simultaneously, i.e. it can fix the interest rate but it will then be committed to creating a money supply which is appropriate to that rate, or it can control the money supply and leave market forces to determine the interest rate.

With the exception of M_0, whichever definition of the money supply we take (M_2, M_4, etc.), the major component of it is bank deposits. Thus monetary policy must be aimed at influencing the volume of bank deposits. The ability of banks to create deposits is determined by the ratio of liquid assets which they maintain. If, for example, banks keep to a 12.5 per cent liquid (or reserve) asset ratio, whether statutory or not, then because we have a bank multiplier of 8, each reduction of £1 in banks' liquid assets would cause a further reduction of £7 in their deposits. Much of monetary policy is therefore aimed at influencing the supply of liquid assets.

In order to effect its monetary policy the Bank of England uses a number of methods. These weapons of policy are considered below.

The issue of notes and coins

Theoretically the Bank could influence the volume of money by expanding or contracting the supply of cash. In practice it is very difficult for the Bank not to supply the cash which banks are demanding, so that it is not a viable method of restricting supply. The reverse may not be true, however, for expanding the issue of cash could conceivably expand the money supply. Indeed, many people would argue that the overprinting of banknotes, i.e. sale of government securities to the Bank's Issue Department, was one of the causes of inflation in the mid-1970s.

Table 36.2 traces the growth of the supply of notes and coins (this used to be called the fiduciary issue) over the last twenty years.

Table 36.2 **The growth of the value of notes and coins in the UK**

Year to end	Notes and coins at year end (£m)	Percentage increase over preceding year
1979	9225	–
1980	10075	9.2
1981	10600	5.2
1982	10775	1.7
1983	11300	4.9
1984	11900	5.3
1985	12190	2.4
1986	12370	1.5
1987	12970	4.9
1988	14020	8.1
1989	14750	5.2
1990	15680	6.3
1991	15910	1.5
1992	16770	5.4
1993	17795	6.1
1994	18752	5.3
1995	20007	6.6
1996	20843	4.2
1997	22447	7.7
1998	23318	3.9
1999	26008	11.5

Source: Bank of England and Financial Statistics, May 2000

The quantity of cash is now such a small proportion of the money supply that we might, in the words of the Radcliffe Report, regard it as the 'small change' of the monetary system. However, the fact that by 1988 M_0 (consisting of notes and coins in circulation plus banks' balances with the Bank of England) was the only money supply figure targeted suggests that the supply of cash had assumed some importance as a monetary

weapon. You can see from Table 36.2 that the growth of the supply of cash (and hence of M_0) has been relatively stable. This stability was one of the reasons which recommended it to the government as a target for control. However, credit booms, such as the one of the late 1980s, demonstrated that controlling the monetary base does not necessarily control spending in the economy. Besides, as noted above, money supply targeting had been effectively abandoned from about this time.

Liquidity ratios

In 1981 the Bank abandoned the reserve assets ratio. The only stated ratio now is the 0.13 per cent of eligible liabilities which the banks must keep with the Bank of England. However, as we saw in the previous chapter, although there is no overall liquid assets ratio, banks are still required to order their assets in particular ways. Since the Bank is able to influence the supply of liquid assets, it is therefore still able to influence bank lending. The Bank has stated that it regards these funds and, in addition, money which the banks voluntarily retain with it for clearing purposes as 'the fulcrum for money market management'.

Interest rates

Interest rate determination has dominated much of monetary policy since the Second World War; variations in interest rates were important means of helping to secure money supply targets when these were first introduced in the late 1970s. In this sense, a key technique for controlling monetary growth has been to influence money demand rather than money supply.

By lowering interest rates the Bank could hope to encourage economic activity by decreasing the cost of borrowing and hence increasing the demand for loans, while, conversely, raising interest rates should discourage borrowing. Most of the weapons of monetary policy will indirectly affect interest rates, but the Bank has a direct influence upon interest rates because, as lender of last resort, it guarantees the solvency of the financial system. Thus the rate at which the Bank is willing to lend is crucial. Great importance used to be attached to the bank rate but this was abandoned in 1972 in favour of the minimum lending rate (MLR) which was supposed to be determined by a formula geared to the Treasury bill rate, thus placing greater reliance on market forces. The announcement (or 'posting') of MLR was suspended in 1981. The Bank now works within an unpublished band of rates. Important money market rates such as the Treasury bill rate will stay close to the Bank's lending rate. This is because the Bank's rate is kept above Treasury bill rate, so that discount houses would lose money if they are forced to borrow. Thus all market rates tend to move in sympathy with the Bank's rates; the clearing banks' base rate, for example, is always at, or near, the Bank's rate.

Open-market operations

These are the sale or purchase of securities by the Bank of England on the open market with the intention of influencing the volume of money in circulation and the rate of interest. The selling of bills or bonds should reduce the volume of money and increase interest rates, while the repurchase of, or reduction in sales of, government securities should increase the volume of money and decrease interest rates.

In order to explain the effects of open-market operations it is necessary to explain their effect upon the balance sheets of commercial banks. Let us consider a bank whose assets and liabilities are arranged in the following manner:

Bank X before open-market sales

Liabilities (£)		Assets (£)	
Deposits	100 000	Liquid assets (10% ratio)	10 000
		Securities	40 000
		Advances	50 000
	100 000		100 000

You will note that bank X has a liquid asset ratio of 10 per cent. Let us now assume that the Bank of England *sells* securities, £1000 of which are bought by the depositors of bank X. The customers pay for these by cheques drawn on bank X and the Bank of England collects this money by deducting it from bank X's balance at the Bank. Thus after open-market sales, bank X's balance sheet will be as follows:

Bank X after open-market sales

Liabilities (£)		Assets (£)	
Deposits	99 000	Liquid assets (9.09% ratio)	9 000
		Securities	40 000
		Advances	50 000
	99 000		99 000

The Bank of England's actions will have immediate (or primary) effects by reducing the amount of money in circulation by the amount of open-market sales and may also increase the interest rate if increased sales depress the price of securities. However, the most important effects of open-market operations are the secondary effects which come about as a result of bank X's need to maintain its liquidity ratio. In order to restore its ratio the bank is forced to sell off securities, thus further reducing their price and thereby raising the rate of interest, and reduce its advances, which may involve both making advances harder to obtain and more expensive.

● *Common misunderstanding*

Students are often puzzled as to why selling securities does not increase the banks' reserves of cash. The supply of cash is effectively under the control of the monetary authorities so that as the banks sell securities these are paid for by customers running down their deposits. And after all, banks cannot deposit money in themselves!

Final position of bank X

Liabilities (£)		Assets (£)	
Deposits	90 000	Liquid assets (10% ratio)	9 000
		Securities	36 000
		Advances	45 000
	90 000		90 000

The final position of bank X's balance sheet shows that in order to restore its liquidity ratio it has been forced to reduce its balance sheet to £90 000. Thus £1000 of open-market operations have reduced the volume of money in circulation

STUDENT ACTIVITY 36.3

The magnitude of open-market operations is determined by the bank multiplier. If, in the above example, bank X worked to a 20 per cent ratio, what would be the effect on its balance sheet of the Bank of England selling £1000 of securities?

by £10 000. We have demonstrated here the effect of open-market sales. If the bank were to buy securities it would have exactly the opposite effect.

Funding

This is the conversion of short-term government debt into longer-term debt. Not only will this reduce liquidity but also, if the Bank of England is replacing securities which could be counted as liquid assets by securities which cannot, it could bring about the multiple contraction of deposits described above. In the mid-1980s the government was concerned to borrow money in a way which would not increase banks' supplies of liquid assets and therefore created more longer-term non-negotiable securities such as 'granny bonds'.

Special directives and special deposits

Since its nationalisation in 1946 the Bank of England has had the power to call for special deposits and to make special directives. However, these powers were not used until after the Radcliffe Report. If the Bank calls upon the members of the monetary sector to make a deposit of a certain percentage of their liabilities in cash at the Bank, and stipulates that these may not be counted as liquid assets, this brings about a multiple contraction of their lending in the same way as open-market operations, the difference being that it is more certain and less expensive. The power to call for special deposits was specifically retained in the Monetary Control Provisions of 1981, although they have not been used since then.

The Bank has issued special directives on both how much banks should lend (quantitative) and to whom they should lend (qualitative). However, since the competition and credit control changes of 1971 it ceased to make quantitative directives and has since only made qualitative ones (and these only rarely).

In 1973 a new scheme came into operation termed special supplementary deposits, which was nicknamed 'the corset'. By this scheme, if banks expanded their interest-bearing eligible liabilities (IBELs) too quickly they automatically had to make special deposits of cash with the Bank. This scheme was abandoned in 1980.

Problems of monetary policy

We have discussed the weapons of monetary policy but there are many doubts about their efficacy. These can be broadly classified into two groups. First, there are conceptual problems concerning the ability of monetary policy to influence the economy, as for instance the doubts about the ability of lower interest rates to stimulate investment (see also Chapter 37). Second, there are the more mechanistic problems which may prevent the weapons from being effective, as for example the existence of excess liquidity in the system preventing open-market operations from being effective. Some of these problems are discussed below.

Interest rate policy

It has already been suggested that decreasing the interest rate may not encourage investment but that raising the interest rate tends to lock up liquidity in the financial system. Businesses, however, might still be willing to borrow at a relatively high rate of interest if they are sufficiently confident: some investment decisions may be considered *non-marginal*, i.e. the entrepreneur will be anticipating a sufficiently large return on investment that small changes in the interest rate are unlikely to make a potentially profitable scheme unprofitable.

In considering the effect of interest rates we must also take account of the effect of time on investment decisions; the longer the term of an investment project the greater the proportion of total cost interest will represent.

STUDENT ACTIVITY 36.4

We can illustrate the latter point by an analogy with the individual consumer: which borrowing would be most influenced by a rise in the interest rate – borrowing to buy a car or borrowing over the longer term to buy a house?

Having mentioned house purchase above we have touched on another problem and that is that governments may be unwilling to put up interest rates because, as so many voters are home buyers, this is extremely unpopular.

There are other factors which make governments unwilling to face high interest rates. With a large National Debt to service, raising interest rates increases the government's own expenditure. Furthermore, higher interest rates may attract inflows of funds from overseas, thus making it more difficult to control the money supply. In addition, the inflow of funds from abroad increases the demand for the currency and pushes up its value; the rise in the exchange rate makes imports cheaper, but means that exports become more expensive, thus creating or enhancing a current account deficit on the balance of payments.

Governments from the 1980s onwards believed in using market forces as much as possible. Therefore, they came to view restriction of the money supply as unhelpful. The money supply is principally bank deposits, and in turning away from trying to control the size of banks' balance sheets, the Bank of England said that it was abandoning 'portfolio constraints'.

By the end of the 1980s the monetary authorities were relying almost entirely on interest rates to control the economy, a process which has continued ever since.

Liquidity and the multiple contraction of deposits

Many of the weapons of monetary policy depend upon limiting liquidity, which has a multiple effect upon banks' deposits through their liquidity ratios. If, however, banks keep surplus liquidity this will protect them against such measures as open-market operations and special deposits. Furthermore, if not all financial institutions were subject to some kind of restriction on their lending (through, say, the imposition of a statutory liquidity ratio for banks only), then lending activity would simply shift from the banks to these other institutions, a process known as *disintermediation.*

The efficacy of open-market sales is also affected by who purchases the securities. For open-market sales to be effective it is necessary that sales be to the general public. If the securities are bought by the banks they will have little effect upon their liquidity since most of the secu-

rities count as liquid assets. This problem was especially acute when governments were forced to borrow large amounts in the late 1970s and early 1980s. As banks acquired government securities they used them as a base to expand deposits. Thus, rather than controlling the money supply, sales of securities provided the springboard for its expansion. To counter this effect the monetary authorities adopted the practice of selling more government long-term debt to UK non-bank holders than was necessary to cover the PSBR. The object of doing so was to moderate the effects of rising bank lending on the M_3 definition of money supply, a practice known as *overfunding.* By creating more long-term debt than was actually needed the authorities hoped to reduce the rate of growth of 'broad' money.

Other problems

Funding may be effective in controlling liquidity and we have already mentioned the government's attempts to increase the sale of non-negotiable securities. However, it is expensive, since the rate of interest on long-term debt is usually much higher than on short-term debt. Considerable funding of the debt might therefore have the undesirable consequence of increasing long-term interest rates.

When we consider special deposits and special directives we discover that these can be simple, cheap, effective and quick acting. However, since the early 1980s governments have avoided using them because they tend to damage the relationship between the central bank and the commercial banks. They also have the effect of distorting market forces; government policy has tended to concentrate upon manipulating market forces rather than imposing its will directly on the system. The distorting effect of direct controls was well illustrated when the 'corset' was abolished in 1980. The immediate result was a surge in the money supply as banks, which had been keeping assets in eurocurrencies, switched them back to sterling.

The European dimension

As has been noted above, the UK belonged to the Exchange Rate Mechanism (ERM) of the

European Monetary System (EMS) from 1990 to 1992. Following the signing of the Maastricht treaty in 1992 the leaders of the 12 members of the EU established a programme for economic and monetary union (EMU). On 1 January 1999 11 member states (out of the 15 that now belonged to the expanded EU), but excluding the UK, commenced full EMU, comprising the operation of a single European currency (the 'euro') and the establishment of a European central bank with a common monetary policy for the EU. (These topics are discussed in Chapter 45.)

The independence of the Bank of England

Earlier in the chapter it was noted that the Labour administration elected in 1997 had granted the Bank of England 'operational independence' in the setting of interest rates; previously this function was the preserve of the government in the form of the Treasury. From May 1997 decisions on interest rates have been taken by a *monetary policy committee,* currently comprising the Governor of the Bank of England, four members of the staff of the Bank and four others, mainly professional economists. The MPC meets for two days every month to decide on whether to raise, lower or keep the base rate of interest unchanged. The decisions of the MPC on interest rates between June 1997 and June 2000 are shown in Table 36.3. The task of the MPC is to deliver price stability (defined by the government's inflation target of 2.5 per cent) and, through this, support the government's economic policy, including its objectives for growth and employment. Should the rate of inflation fall below 1.5 per cent or rise above 3.5 per cent the MPC would have to write to the Chancellor of the Exchequer explaining why the target had not been met and what the committee proposed to do about the situation.

In order to reach its decision each month, the MPC refers to a wide variety of data, such as the rate of increase in average earnings, the level of retail sales, changes in house values and stock market prices and the output gap or the differ-

Table 36.3 Monetary Policy Committee decisions, June 1997–June 2000

Date	Decision taken
2000	
7 June	Maintained at 6.0%
4 May	Maintained at 6.0%
6 April	Maintained at 6.0%
9 March	Maintained at 6.0%
10 February	**Raised** by 0.25% to 6.0%
13 January	**Raised** by 0.25% to 5.75%
1999	
9 December	Maintained at 5.5%
4 November	**Raised** by 0.25% to 5.5%
7 October	Maintained at 5.25%
8 September	**Raised** by 0.25% to 5.25%
5 August	Maintained at 5%
8 July	Maintained at 5%
10 June	*Reduced* by 0.25% to 5%
6 May	Maintained at 5.25%
8 April	*Reduced* by 0.25% to 5.25%
3 March	Maintained at 5.5%
4 February	*Reduced* by 0.5% to 5.5%
7 January	*Reduced* by 0.25% to 6%
1998	
10 December	*Reduced* by 0.5% to 6.25%
5 November	*Reduced* by 0.5% to 6.75%
8 October	*Reduced* by 0.25% to 7.25%
10 September	Maintained at 7.5%
6 August	Maintained at 7.5%
9 July	Maintained at 7.5%
4 June	**Raised** by 0.25% to 7.5%
7 May	Maintained at 7.25%
9 April	Maintained at 7.25%
5 March	Maintained at 7.25%
5 February	Maintained at 7.25%
8 January	Maintained at 7.25%
1997	
4 December	Maintained at 7.25%
6 November	**Raised** by 0.25% to 7.25%
9 October	Maintained at 7%
11 September	Maintained at 7%
7 August	**Raised** by 0.25% to 7%
10 July	**Raised** by 0.25% to 6.75%
6 June	**Raised** by 0.25% to 6.5%

Source: Teaching Business and Economics, Summer 2000

ence between the actual and potential levels of output in the economy. The problems that the MPC faces are that the data for a single month may not be wholly reliable and, even if it were, different interpretations may be placed on it by different members of the committee. Is a recent upturn in average earnings a temporary phenomenon or the start of a new trend, for example? So far, however, the MPC has not had to account for itself to the Chancellor of the Exchequer.

The main perceived advantage of central bank independence is that it is free from political control; it can thus concentrate on long-term economic objectives and targets rather than being under the influence of politicians who may have at least one eye on the potential short-term electoral impact of any policy change. Often interest rates have to be changed some months before they have an effect on inflation. Politicians may be reluctant to raise interest rates when there is no apparent short-term advantage of so doing, especially when close to an election. An independent central bank may be able to pre-empt higher inflation by raising interest rates immediately, thereby reducing the need for a higher interest rate rise later.

On the other hand, central bank independence means that democratic accountability for managing the economy is reduced. This can be particularly significant given the potential trade-off between inflation and unemployment. An independent central bank in charge of monetary policy is more likely to be committed to a regime of low and stable prices than to policies that result in creating more jobs; thus, it may increase interest rates in order to satisfy the former policy objective, even though such a strategy may adversely affect future employment prospects.

At both the national and international level the role of monetary policy has been the subject of much controversy in recent years. People have often expected monetary policy to accomplish tasks which it was never designed to do. In the best of all possible worlds the job of a central bank would be simply to maintain the system with small adjustments here and there. Monetary policy, however, has often been viewed as a way in which overall management of the economy could be achieved. For the UK there is also an extra dimension to the problem, for London is a world banking centre and the central bank must therefore contend not only with domestic economic problems but also with those of much of the world as well.

Summary

1 Fiscal policy is the regulation of the economy via government spending and taxation.
2 An increase in the budget deficit can have an expansionary effect on the economy, whereas an increase in the budget surplus can have a contractionary effect.
3 The fiscal stance describes how expansionary or contractionary a government's fiscal policy can be.
4 Discretionary fiscal changes are the result of conscious government decisions; automatic changes are the result of other changes in the economy.
5 The impact of fiscal policy on the economy depends on the assumed shape of the aggregate supply curve.
6 There are various practical problems of fiscal policy that limit its effectivenenss.
7 The weapons of monetary policy may be listed as the issue of notes, changing liquidity ratios, variations in interest rates, open-market operations, funding and special deposits and directives.
8 Interest rate variations have tended to dominate monetary policy since the Second World War; it continued to be an important weapon even when money supply targets were first introduced in the late 1970s.
9 There are many problems associated with the operating of monetary policy. In particular, interest rates do not appear to have a strong correlation with investment, and excess liquidity in the system may frustrate the Bank of England's ability to influence the money supply.
10 An independent central bank is free from political influence, although democratic accountability is reduced. Monetary policy is now at the centre of government policy and economic debate.

? QUESTIONS

1 Explain what is meant by the fiscal stance of the government. What factors should be considered when assessing the effectiveness of a government's fiscal policy?
2 Distinguish between discretionary and automatic fiscal changes and discuss their potential impact in a recession.

3 Discuss how the shape of the aggregate supply curve can influence the impact of an expansionary fiscal policy that shifts the aggregate demand curve to the right.

4 Discuss the relative merits of an independent central bank. Has the Monetary Policy Committee of the Bank of England been successful in achieving its objectives?

5 Examine the weapons of monetary policy. Comment on the view that the main thrust of monetary policy has been on controlling money demand rather than money supply.

6 What factors may limit the efficacy of variations in interest rates as a weapon of policy?

7 What conditions are necessary for open-market operations to be effective?

8 Explain how the monetary authorities might seek to influence the quantity of money in the economy. Describe how the monetary authorities have gone about this task since 1979.

Data response A
LOOSENING THE BELT

Read the article below (on pages 523–5) taken from *The Economist* of 15 July 2000 and answer the questions which follow.

1 What reasons can you suggest for the significant increase in public spending from 2001–2004?

2 Discuss whether this increase in public spending represents a return to a more discretionary role for fiscal policy.

3 Over the last twenty years or so public spending has hovered between 40 and 50 per cent of GDP. Should this share be reduced?

4 Discuss the problems of using fiscal policy to fine tune the economy.

Data response B
A GOOD START

Read the article on pages 525–6 taken from *The Economist* of 10 May 1997 and answer the questions which follow.

1 Why do you think the government granted the Bank of England 'operational independence' in monetary policy?

2 To what extent is this a 'historic' move?

3 To what extent do the arrangements in the UK counter the objections that an independent Bank of England reduces democratic accountability?

4 Discuss whether the arrangements for an independent Bank of England may increase the significance of some economic policy objectives at the expense of others. Comment on the potential drawbacks of such a situation.

Loosening the belt

After three years of tight control of public spending, the government is about to go on a splurge.

The unveiling of the Compre-hensive Spending Review (CSR) on July 18th will be a defining moment for an increasingly battered and fractious government. At stake is whether New Labour can retain its reputation for prudent fiscal management while convincing the electorate that real improvements in public services are on the way.

The CSR will set the course for public spending for three years, from 2001–02 to 2003–04. The new plans will set Departmental Expenditure limits (DELS) covering about half of public spending. These DELS are vital for the government since they set the spending limits for the politically sensitive public services like health. The other half of public spending remains subject to yearly control – hence another name and acronym, Annually Managed Expenditure (AME). The big-ticket items here are social security benefits and interest on the national debt.

Gordon Brown, the chancellor, revealed in his March budget the total amount of public spending in the three years ahead, and the share that the National Health Service (NHS) will get. Total expenditure will rise in real terms by 3.3% a year between 2000–01 and 2003–04 while resources for the NHS will rise at an annual rate of 5.6%. That left two principal uncertainties to be resolved next week. The first is the total amount other spending ministries will receive – the size of DELS, exclud-

Number crunching

	2000–01 £bn	2001–02 £bn	2003–04 £bn	Average annual % real increase 2000–01 to 2003–04
Budget announcements				
Total spending	371	392	440	3.3
NHS	54	59	69	5.6
Estimates				
Departmental expenditure limits	194	209	243	5.1
DELs (excluding NHS)	140	150	174	5.0
DELs (excluding NHS and education)	102	108	125	4.5
Annual managed expenditure	177	183	197	1.2

Sources: HM Treasury, IFS calculations based on press reports

ing health. The second is the carve-up between these ministries of the planned increase in spending.

Since the budget, government hints have indicated that DELS outside health will rise by £31 billion ($47 billion) by 2003–04, compared with the original plan for 2001–02 set in the government's 1998 three-year spending review. This would bring about an overall increase in departmental expenditure of around £43 billion. Piecing together these clues, a plausible scenario is that DELS outside the NHS will rise to £150 billion in 2001–02 and £174 billion in 2003–04. This is equivalent to an average real increase of 5% a year. If spending on education rises at the same rate as health, this will leave other departments with an annual real rise of around 4.5%.

Such increases sound impressive even before the spin. In a leaked memo, Alastair Campbell, the prime minister's press secretary, has ominously described the occasion as 'a very important moment'. But the spin-meisters will be bowling on a tricky wicket. They made such exaggerated claims at the time of the first spending review – double- and triple-counting the actual increases – that voters are now in a sceptical mood.

More important, the new splurge in public spending will simply compensate for Mr Brown's extraordinary success in reining in public expenditure. In real terms, total spending declined in Labour's first two years of

office and grew only modestly in its third year. Public expenditure is set to grow in 2000–01 by 5% after inflation. However, this will still leave the average rate of real increase over Labour's first four years at about half its long-run rate of growth from the early 1970s to the mid 1990s.

The intensity of Labour's squeeze is manifest in public spending's share of the economy. As a percentage of GDP, expenditure sank last year to its lowest since the first year of Harold Wilson's government in 1964–65 (see the chart below). Even with the big increases now under way, it will be under 40% of GDP next year, well below the share in the year before the last election.

Some of this decline in public spending is painless. Addressing the Royal Economic Society's conference in Scotland this week, Gordon Brown stressed that spending on debt interest would be lower because of the big receipts from the mobile phone licenses auction. This would provide scope for additional expenditure in the public services people care about The message was that the Chancellor's prudence will pay off before too long.

But the squeeze has also left its mark on the front-line services Labour has staked so much political capital on improving. When Tony Blair intoned the mantra of 'education, education, education' the public can hardly have expected this to mean a freeze in real spending in the first two years of office.

The increases now in the pipeline are undeniably substantial. This year, education spending will rise in real terms by 9% Expenditure on the NHS will rise by over 7% after inflation. While upward lurches in the health budget have been seen in the past, the next few years should deliver an unusually sustained increase in expenditure. By 2003–04, spending on the NHS will rise to 6.3% of GDP, up from 5.5% last year.

The question is whether the government will get the credit. It faces two difficulties, both largely of its own making. The first is that the full impact of the extra expenditure will now only come through in the next parliament. The second is that even this spending spree may fail to meet heightened public expectations. NHS spending also jumped sharply in the early 1990s but this did not change the public perception of an embattled service.

The ability to sustain this higher spending on public services also depends critically upon the Treasury's ability to constrain the real growth in annually-managed expenditure to 1.2% a year. Since AME has been shrinking in real terms in the past two years, this target looks attainable. However, the government is clearly under enormous pressure to provide a generous pensions settlement next year after the electoral backlash against the 75p increase in the basic pension. And an economic reverse could push up social-security outlays and cut tax revenues as well – repeating past bitter experience. The cost of the working families tax credit –

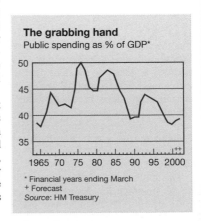

The grabbing hand
Public spending as % of GDP*

* Financial years ending March
+ Forecast
Source: HM Treasury

already approaching £5 billion – could also balloon.

The risk for the government is that it has left the spending too late. In their anxiety to avoid the mistakes of past Labour governments, Mr Blair and Mr Brown lashed themselves to the mast of austerity in the first two years of office. The chancellor prides himself on his achievement so far in preventing boom and bust in the economy. But in the public finances, he has presided over bust and boom. This has created a dangerous political gap for the government between the electoral and the expenditure timetables.

Source: The Economist Newspaper Limited, London, 15 July 2000. Reprinted with permission.

A good start

Gordon Brown's decision to grant the Bank of England 'operational independence' in monetary policy is an astonishingly bold start for the new chancellor. Henceforth the Bank, not the Treasury, will set British interest rates. After waiting 18 years for power, Labour's first step is to hand the larger part of its ability to steer the economy to somebody else. As a constitutional innovation it ranks alongside devolution, reform of the House of Lords, voting reform and the other measures on Labour's agenda for constitutional change.

The move is welcome and long overdue. Yet even enthusiasts cannot but be disconcerted by the manner of its coming. Unlike those other proposals, the idea was not in the party's manifesto. There are principled objections to it. One might have expected consultations, debate. But the City, which the chancellor was chiefly aiming to please, didn't mind: shares soared and long-term interest rates fell. Mr Brown has declared himself a bold reformer, dedicated to the long term and determined to get his way, all before his first budget.

The case for central-bank independence is much as Mr Brown described it. The essential difficulty of monetary policy is that interest rates need to be changed many months before they have any effect on inflation. Politics frowns on this. An independent central bank can anticipate higher inflation by raising interest rates promptly – and by less, therefore, than would be needed if the remedy were delayed. The result is smaller swings in inflation and interest rates, and a lower rate of inflation over the medium term. All this should foster investment and growth.

The main argument against is that democratic accountability is undermined. Britain's new arrangements, modelled on those of many other countries, meet this objection halfway. The chancellor will set the target for inflation (to begin with, 2½%), so the Bank will not have to decide for itself what 'stable prices' means. In addition, decisions on interest rates will be taken by a monetary-policy committee within the Bank, with members appointed by the government. Policy will be subject to review by both a committee of Parliament and the Bank's Court. In 'exceptional' circumstances the Treasury can take charge.

In all these ways, the Bank will be held accountable. But it is wrong to say that no 'democratic deficit' remains. The government may set the inflation target, but the Bank's committee will be left to decide how quickly the target should be pursued. It may be true that, in the long term, it is impossible to reduce unemployment by tolerating high inflation, that the power to make such a choice was always illusory, and that nothing is lost by giving it up. But such a trade-off undoubtedly exists in the short term. Much as the chancellor and Eddie George, the Bank's governor, might deny it, the Bank will be engaged in the highly political task of choosing how many jobs to sacrifice in order to hit the inflation target quickly rather than slowly. The true case for independence is not that there is no such democratic loss, but that the loss is more than matched by the economic gain.

In our view, it will be – provided the Bank is given space. It must be allowed to have its way even when, especially when, the Treasury sincerely believes it is wrong: otherwise, independence means nothing, and the benefits will not flow. Mr Brown cannot be so naïve as to suppose that such a time will never come, but when it does he may find it a sterner test than he suspects.

Whatever next?

Apart from its other virtues, the chancellor's first measure is a political masterstroke. It deflects blame for the coming increases in interest rates (this week's rise from 6% to 6¼% will not be enough). And it lends credibility to a promise Tony Blair made during his campaign, when he said that Labour would be more radical than many supposed – or, indeed, than his manifesto entitled anybody to think. What other startling initiatives, one cannot help but wonder, lie ahead?

It is easy to see where they are most needed. Success or failure for this administration is likely to turn on control of public spending. In some ways, the new approach to monetary policy already serves this cause. It frees the Treasury to concentrate its efforts on fiscal control. Also, the chancellor has armed himself with a potent new reason to resist demands from spending departments: if he gives way, the Bank will raise interest rates whether he likes it or not. So a kind of hell beckons for Labour's spending ministers, crushed on one side by expectations of more and better public services and on the other by a would-be iron chancellor and a newly independent Bank. Perhaps anticipating the protests that may ensue, the prime minister's first announcements have concentrated on strengthening the controls that his office and the Treasury will exert on the rest of the government.

But immovability will not suffice. The only hope of reconciling post-election expectations of better public services with low taxes and low interest rates is to embark on far-reaching reform of the biggest spending programmes: education, health and social security. There was no sign of such a reform in the manifesto – but, you may well ask, what does that prove? If four days is all it takes Gordon Brown to transform Britain's monetary-policy regime, think what Harriet Harman could do to pensions in, say, a week.

Source: The Economist Newspaper Limited, London, 10 May 1997. Reprinted with permission.

37 Monetary analysis and income analysis

Monetarists and Keynesians

In Section VII and at the beginning of the present section we have examined the determination of national income and monetary economics. We have treated them in a fairly neutral manner. However, we have been considering an area of economics over which there are fundamental theoretical disagreements. In this chapter we will review some of these disagreements. There are, of course, as many views on economics as there are economists. As **Bernard Shaw** said, 'If all the economists in the world were laid from end to end, they would not reach a conclusion!' It is therefore necessary for us to generalise. We will look on the one hand at those views which we may term *Keynesian* (and *neo-Keynesian*) and on the other at the views of monetarists and other neo-classicists.

What are monetarists?

One thing that *monetarists* are not is new; they are simply a modern variation of the neo-classical school which dominated economics from the 1870s to the Keynesian revolution of the late 1930s and 1940s. Monetarists share the same essential 'vision' as the *neo-classical school*, i.e. they reject theories of macro demand deficiencies and emphasise the efficiency of free markets; for instance, they believe that market forces act quickly to eliminate unemployment. Monetarists are new only in the sense that their theory is more sophisticated than that of their ancestors and that their doctrine has reasserted itself after a long period following 1945 in which Keynesians dominated both economics and economic policy. The modern term monetarist derives from the debate of the 1960s and 1970s concerning the role of money in determining aggregate demand.

Keynesian views of money

Keynes had argued that, in times of deep depression, monetary policy might be totally ineffective as a means of stimulating aggregate demand. By the time of the Radcliffe Report in 1959, most Keynesian economists held the view that there was no causal link between the quantity of money and aggregate demand. They argued, for example, that if an attempt was made to expand the money supply at a time when people in general did not want to spend, then either the money would be held in 'idle' money balances or banks would find it impossible to create new loans. Equally the Radcliffe Report had stated:

> We cannot find any reason for supposing or any experience in monetary history indicating that there is any limit to the velocity of circulation.

Hence, it seemed that a given quantity of money could support almost any level of aggregate demand.

Some Keynesians, such as **Kaldor**, accepted that there might be a correlation between nominal national income and the money supply but argued this merely reflected the fact that the money supply adjusted *passively* to people's desire to spend, i.e. that the money supply adjusted to national income and not vice versa. In short, Keynesian economists, for one reason or another, had come to the conclusion that manipulating the money supply was ineffective as a means of demand management and hence monetary policy should be set in relation to other objectives (see Chapter 47). Keynesian economists therefore emphasised *fiscal* policy rather than *monetary* policy as the means of implementing the demand management they believed necessary; for this reason they were known as 'Fiscalists' in the USA.

The rise of monetarism

The rise (or re-emergence) of monetarism within mainstream economics dates largely from **Milton Friedman's** 1956 restatement of the 'quantity theory of money'. Friedman argued that the demand for money depended in a stable and predictable manner on several major economic variables. Thus, if the money supply was expanded people would not simply wish to hold the extra money in 'idle' money balances. If they were in equilibrium before the increase they were already holding money balances to suit their requirements, and thus after the increase they would have money balances surplus to their requirements. These excess money balances would therefore be spent and hence aggregate demand would rise. Similarly, if the money supply were reduced people would want to replenish their holdings of money by reducing their spending. Thus Friedman challenged the Keynesian assertion that 'money does not matter'; he argued that the supply of money does affect the amount spent in an economy, and thus the word 'monetarist' was coined.

The rise of monetarism in political circles accelerated as Keynesian economics seemed unable to explain or cure the seemingly contra-dictory problems of simultaneously rising unemployment *and* inflation. On the one hand higher unemployment seemed to call for Keynesian reflation, but on the other hand rising inflation seemed to call for Keynesian deflation. The resulting disillusionment with Keynesian demand management was summed up in the now famous words of James Callaghan, the Labour party Prime Minister, in 1976:

> We used to think that you could just spend your way out of a recession and increase employment by cutting taxes and boosting government spending. I tell you, in all candour, that that option no longer exists; and insofar as it ever did exist, it only worked by injecting bigger doses of inflation into the economy followed by higher levels of unemployment as the next step. That is the history of the past twenty years.

Not only did monetarists seek to explain contemporary problems; they reinterpreted historical ones. **Milton Friedman** and **Anna Schwartz** in their book *A Monetary History of the United States, 1867–1960* argued that the depression of 1930 was caused by a massive contraction of the money supply and not by lack of investment as Keynes had argued. They also maintained that post-war inflation was caused by overexpansion of the money supply. They coined the famous assertion of monetarism that:

> inflation is always and everywhere a monetary phenomenon.

At first, to many economists whose perceptions had been set by Keynesian ideas, it seemed that the Keynesian–monetarist debate was merely about whether fiscal or monetary policy was the more effective tool of demand management. But by the mid-1970s the debate had moved on to more profound matters as monetarists presented a more fundamental challenge to Keynesian orthodoxy.

Keynesianism vs monetarism

Keynes had argued that the *volatility of expectations* meant that aggregate demand was subject to large fluctuations, and this in turn caused large fluctuations in the level of output and employment. The central political belief of Keynesians is therefore that it is necessary for governments to intervene and manage the level of demand in the economy in order to maintain full employment. As the Keynesian/monetarist debate progressed, monetarists sought to resurrect the pre-Keynesian orthodoxy that market economies are inherently stable (in the absence of major unexpected fluctuations in the money supply). Because of this belief in the stability of free market economies they asserted that active demand management is unnecessary and indeed likely to be harmful. The political right then adopted monetarism as an intellectual underpinning for its wish to return to a *laissez-faire* approach to economic policy in which economic outcomes are left to be determined by the free play of market forces. This was especially attractive to those on the right, such as Margaret Thatcher and Keith Joseph in the 1980s, who interpreted the expansion of the role of government as **back door socialism.**

There have been several developments in the debate since the 1970s, many of which (such as the *adaptive* versus *rational* expectations debate and the role of supply side economics) are examined in this book (see Chapter 38). But the central questions at the core of the debate, and which dominate the political discussion of economic policy, remain unchanged.

The first question is the extent to which market forces in a free market economy do, or do not, ensure desirable outcomes (see also Section II). The second question is the extent to which any government is able to correct for any failings of free market capitalism.

Money and national income

The Classical Dichotomy

The Classical Dichotomy provides a useful starting point for examining the technicalities of the Keynesian/monetarist debate. There is a problem, however, with the term classical. Keynes had lumped together all previous economists (with the exception of **Malthus**) under the title 'classical'. But many economists see the neo-classical or marginalist revolution of the 1870s as a watershed in the development of economic thought. Whether we wish to use the term classical or neoclassical the dichotomy referred to is central to the perspective of monetarists:

The Classical Dichotomy states that nominal prices are determined by the quantity of money but that the quantity of money has no effect on real things.

Nominal prices are prices in terms of the number of units of money that goods and services sell for, or factors of production are bought for. Hence we can speak of nominal (or money) prices, nominal wage rates and nominal income. Movements in the price 'level' record changes in these nominal prices. In contrast, *relative* prices are the price of one thing in terms of another. For example, if an egg costs 10p and a loaf 40p then the relative price of a loaf in terms of eggs is 4. If the price level were to rise by 100 per cent (i.e. if all nominal prices doubled) then relative prices would remain unchanged. The nominal price of an egg would now be 20p, and the nominal price of a loaf would be 80p, but the relative price of a loaf in terms of eggs would still be 4.

It should now be clear that if all prices were to increase by the same proportion then all relative prices would be unchanged. For example, suppose your money wage (the nominal price of your labour) has doubled, but at the same time the nominal price of everything that you buy has also doubled. You would soon realise that you are no better off than before. In this situation the money wage has doubled but the *real wage*, i.e. the price of labour relative to goods and services, has remained unchanged. Indeed, put like this, it is not apparent that anything real has changed. This is indeed the gist of the Classical Dichotomy: if an increase in the money supply merely increases all nominal prices proportionately, then all real variables such as relative prices, output, the goods and services earned in return for work, the level of employment/unemployment, the level of investment, etc., would be unaffected. It is in this sense that **Geoffrey Crowther** described money as a 'veil' thrown over the workings of the real economy.

To develop further our understanding of the debate we must now turn to the technicalities involved. First, we shall examine the debate concerning the link between the money supply and aggregate demand. Second, we shall examine the debate concerning what actually determines the level of real variables, such as output and employment, and how stable these variables are likely to be.

Money as a determinant of aggregate demand

The effectiveness of monetary policy as a determinant of the level of aggregate demand in the economy depends upon the nature of both the demand for and the supply of money. Most attention and research, however, has focused on the demand for money. Before we turn to this relatively modern concept, however, it is instructive to trace its development, starting with **Irving Fisher's** 'quantity equation' which was introduced in Chapter 35.

You will recall that Fisher's equation of exchange is:

$$M \times V \equiv P \times T$$

The symbol $\equiv$ denotes that this is an *identity,* i.e. something which is true by definition. For example, the statement 'All men who have never married are bachelors' is hardly the basis for further research! Similarly, Fisher's equation simply says that 'the amount spent is equal to the amount received'. The early quantity theorists, however, made three assumptions which turned the identity into a theory of the determination of the price level. They argued that the quantity of money (M) is 'exogenously' set (e.g. by the amount of gold mined or the quantity of notes printed) and that V and T are constant. If these assumptions are made it follows mechanically that, say, a doubling of the money supply must be associated with a doubling of the price level. Therefore we are back to the Classical Dichotomy and the assertion of the quantity theorists that the price level varies in direct proportion to changes in the quantity of money leaving real variables unchanged.

The velocity of circulation

Let us now concentrate on what determines V, i.e. the velocity of circulation of money. Later we shall return to the question of whether M is exogenously determined and also to the question of whether T is constant.

If M can be set by the monetary authorities and if we can predict V then it is easy to calculate the level of expenditure that would be 'caused' by any level of M. For example, if V is fixed at 3 a money stock of £50m would be associated with a total level of spending of £150m, whereas a money stock of £100m would give rise to expenditure of £300m, and so on. The early quantity theorists saw the determination of V in rather mechanical terms. They argued that any given level of spending in the economy would require a certain amount of money to finance it.

In much the same way as an engine running at a higher speed requires the oil within it to circulate at a faster rate to avoid friction reducing its speed, so a higher level of spending in the economy would require a given money stock to circulate faster so that money is always at hand for those desiring to make transactions. But the quantity theorists argued that the rate at which money can circulate around the economy is determined by the payment practices which prevail and the current structure of the economy. For example, if people are paid monthly rather than weekly they must keep more money 'idle', to be spent later in the month, and hence the rate at which the money stock can circulate is reduced. It was argued that factors such as payment practices changed only slowly. Hence, at any one time the *velocity of circulation* of money could be considered a **constant** and thus a higher level of spending would require a larger money stock to sustain it.

STUDENT ACTIVITY 37.1

1 If M is £10 billion, T is £50 billion and P is £5, what is the value of V?
2 Using the same figures, what would be the effect of increasing the money supply by a factor of two, assuming T and V are constant?
3 Using the same numbers as in 1, what would happen to V if aggregate demand (T) rose by 10 per cent, but the money stock and the price level remained the same? Why would monetarists find this unlikely?

The number of transactions

If V is a constant then the money value of transactions ($P \times T$) will vary in direct proportion to the quantity of money in the economy (M). We have explained earlier that T refers to all transactions in the economy and thus includes the purchases of **intermediate** goods and purely **financial** transactions. We are more interested, however, in the level of **output** of the economy. Hence it is more convenient to confine our definition of transactions only to those involving the sale of final goods and services. For direct proportionality of the money value of output to the quantity of money we thus require the further assumption that the number of transactions is directly related to the volume of output. We can thus write the quantity equation as:

$$M \times V = P \times Y$$

where Y is the level of output (real income) and P is the price level of final goods and services. In this equation V becomes the **income velocity of circulation**. If, therefore, V and Y are constants the nominal level of income ($P \times Y$; or money GDP) will vary in direct proportion to M.

The Cambridge approach and the demand for money

In the crude manner in which the quantity theory was formulated by Fisher, money appears as a technical input to spending, i.e. a certain quantity is required per unit of spending. There is no indication that the velocity of circulation might be affected by the decisions of people themselves to hold money. But the more people tend to want to keep their wealth in **liquid** form (e.g. cash and cheque/current/sight accounts) rather than time deposits or longer-term loans, the smaller the proportion of the existing stock of money that can be lent out by the financial institutions to be spent by borrowers.

Thus the more people wish to hold reserves of liquidity in money balances the lower will tend to be the velocity of circulation of money.

In the 1920s the notion of the demand for money was reintroduced as an explicit argument in the quantity theory. This approach was developed by the Cambridge economists, **Pigou** and **Marshall**; hence their formulation became known as the Cambridge equation. In their formulation the demand for money was written as:

$$M_d = k \times P \times Y$$

This states that the demand for money (M_d) is some proportion (k) of money income ($P \times Y$). Once we introduce the notion of a demand for money we can write the equilibrium condition for the economy as:

$$M = M_d$$

This states that for equilibrium the quantity of money demanded (M_d) must be equal to the quantity of money in the economy (M). For example, if M exceeded M_d there would be more money in existence than people wish to hold in their money balances. This would cause people with excess money balances to attempt to reduce them. For the economy as a whole, of course, the total level of money balances cannot be reduced. But the attempts to reduce excess money balances will lead to an increase in expenditure. This increase in expenditure will in turn increase the level of money income. Now, if the demand for money is some fraction of money income, the rise in money income will cause the increase in the demand for money that is required to restore equilibrium.

From the above we can now see that in equilibrium:

$$M = k \times P \times Y$$

By a simple rearrangement of this equilibrium result we have the Cambridge equation:

$$M \times 1/k = P \times Y$$

This looks very much like Fisher's crude representation of the quantity theory except that $1/k$ has taken the place of V. Indeed, if k is constant (i.e. the demand for money is a constant fraction of money income) it produces exactly the same proportionate relation between M and money income as Fisher's equation of exchange. That is, if k is constant and

$$V = 1/k$$

then V is also constant. For example, if $k = 1/5$ then $V = 5$; thus a money stock of £100m would imply an equilibrium level of money income of:

$$£100m \times 5 = £500m$$

If k were to change to, say, $k = 1/3$, then $V = 3$ and the same money stock would imply an equilibrium level of money income of only:

$$£100m \times 3 = £300m$$

This result also makes intuitive sense; it says that the velocity of circulation of money is inversely related to the demand for money. Hence if (*ceteris paribus*) the demand for money should rise, people will attempt to increase their holding of money balances. As more money is held rather than passed on, the rate at which money circulates in the economy falls. The fall in V in turn is seen in a fall in money income, until the fall in the level of money income reduces the demand for money back in line with the existing stock of money.

The Cambridge equation thus differs from the crude quantity theory in that it allows for the velocity of circulation to be affected by people's desire for money.

By introducing a role for human behaviour it is less mechanical than Fisher's version. Indeed, the early Cambridge school did explore the possibility that the demand for money (and hence the velocity of circulation) might be influenced by factors other than purely the level of money income. If this is the case, then a change in these other factors could 'disturb' the relationship between a given money stock and the level of money income making the level of money income for any quantity of money less predictable.

For example, perhaps a fall in interest rates reduces the opportunity cost of holding money *vis-à-vis* investing it in, say, a bank or building society to be lent out and spent on property. Such a change in interest rates might have explained the rise in the proportion of money income that people wanted to hold in 'idle' money balances in our example above when k rose from 1/5 to 1/3. If, then, an increase in the quantity of money is accompanied by a fall in interest rates the resulting rise in the demand for money as a proportion of money income might cause the velocity of circulation to fall. This could offset the rise in the quantity of money, thereby leaving money income unaltered. In short, *a rise in M might cause V to fall* such that there is no increase in aggregate demand and hence no increase in money income ($P \times Y$).

In fact the early Cambridge school, as with the earlier quantity theorists, placed most of the emphasis on money as a means of making transactions. Thus the role of other factors was usually ignored and k was treated as more or less constant. As we have seen, if k is constant the Cambridge equation simply reproduces the crude quantity theory assertion that the price level is directly proportionate to the stock of money. It was left for Keynes, the most famous of all Cambridge economists, to develop the notion of a demand for money other than as a means of making transactions.

Liquidity preference

Belief in the quantity theory of money and the Classical Dichotomy was challenged by the traumatic depression of the interwar years. As unemployment soared it no longer seemed possible to argue that free market capitalist economies are inherently stable; the failure of financial institutions cast doubt on the monetary authority's ability to control the money supply and large fluctuations in aggregate demand suggested that the velocity of circulation of money was highly volatile. We have yet to examine the exogeneity of the money supply (M) and the stability of output (Y), but here we are concerned with the possible *instability of V*. Keynes argued in *The General Theory of Employment, Interest and Money* (1936) that V can be unstable as money shifts in and out of 'idle' money balances reflecting changes in people's *liquidity preference*.

Unlike his predecessors, who focused upon money as a medium of exchange held only for transactions purposes, Keynes emphasised money as a store of wealth. Holding one's wealth in bonds, shares or real assets can be risky as the value of such assets can fluctuate widely, but this risk can be avoided by holding money instead. Thus in addition to money's usefulness for transactions purposes its quality of having relatively certain purchasing power means that money will also be held for its own sake. Thus, Keynes argued that a wave of pessimism concerning real-world prospects could precipitate a *retreat into liquidity* as people sought to increase their holdings of money. This increase in money holding would lower the velocity of circulation of money and thus aggregate demand would fall bringing about the recession which everyone had feared!

Portfolio balance

If we examine the wealth (or assets) of a person or society in general, we could arrange them in a spectrum of liquidity from most liquid to least liquid, the most liquid being cash and the least liquid being real physical assets such as buildings. People will attempt to find a balance in their holding of assets which they think most advantageous. The holding of money (cash and bank deposits) gives certainty and convenience. On the other hand, the person holding money is foregoing the earning or interest that could be gained by putting this money into bonds and equities. If money is put into earning assets then, although income is gained, certainty and convenience are sacrificed and risk is increased. This is illustrated in Figure 37.1.

Every individual will try to structure their assets to give maximum satisfaction. A selection of financial assets can be termed a *portfolio* and hence the distribution of assets within the portfolio is called a portfolio balance.

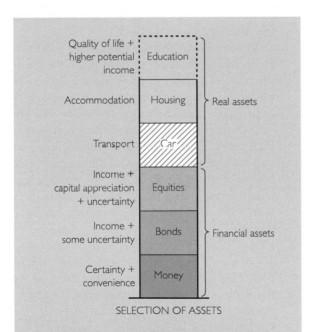

SELECTION OF ASSETS

Figure 37.1 Portfolio balance
People distribute their assets between money, financial assets such as bonds and real assets such as housing in a way which they consider maximises their utility.
Friedman included in the portfolio investment in human capital such as education.

Keynesian theory of the demand for money

Keynes argued that there are three motives for holding money: the transactions, precautionary and speculative motives.

(a) *The transactions motive.* This motive closely corresponds to the notion of money held by the quantity theorists. People hold cash and money in bank accounts simply to carry on the everyday business of life – to pay the gas bill, to buy petrol, to spend on groceries, and so on. Since people are usually paid weekly or monthly but spend money daily (i.e. their monetary receipts and expenditures are not perfectly synchronised) they therefore have to hold a proportion of their income as money rather than in more liquid assets. This gives a pattern as shown in Figure 37.2, where the peaks in the money balance are caused by monthly salary inputs and the downward slope of the curve shows money being spent over the month.

If the troughs are above zero there is an amount of idle money held in hand.

The lower jagged line shows what happens if a person is paid weekly. We can see there is a quicker turnover of money but the overall demand for money is smaller. There is thus a higher velocity of circulation. This type of regular pattern of income and payments is one of the reasons why the quantity theorists believed that the velocity of circulation of money is stable.

What determines the size of transactions demand for money? Keynes thought that it would be determined by the level of money income. Indeed, it is clear from our discussion of the transactions motive that this will tend to be the case. It has been demonstrated since (from stock control theory) that such transactions balances are also likely to be economised on when interest rates rise.

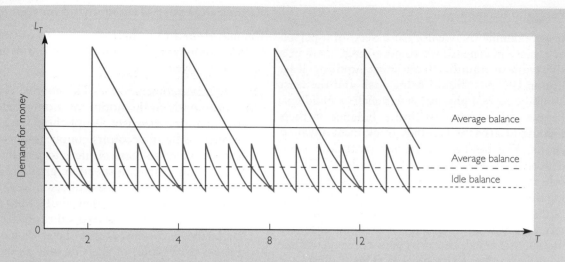

Figure 37.2 Transactions demand for money
Every fourth week there is an injection of salary. This runs out over the month as bills are paid. This gives an average balance (demand for money). If not all of the salary is spent, but is retained in the bank account, then this gives a level for the idle balance. The dotted line shows what would happen if a person was paid weekly instead of monthly. The demand for money is smaller but the velocity of circulation is greater.

(b) *The precautionary motive.* People hold money to guard against unexpected eventualities – the car breaking down, a period of illness, a large electricity bill, and so on. It seems reasonable to suppose that the higher the level of income the larger will be the size of precautionary balances. The reason for this is that the rich need higher precautionary balances; if, for example, you are running several cars and a large house, the unexpected bills are likely to be larger, thus demanding a larger precautionary stock of money. Again it is likely that a rise in interest rates might cause people to economise somewhat on precautionary balances. But because of the similarity with the transactions motive the two are often lumped together.

(c) *The speculative motive.* By emphasising this motive Keynes broke with the quantity theorists' view of money. The quantity theorists did not think that people will want to hold money for itself, but only for transactions purposes. Keynes, however, believed that people might speculate by holding money, just as they might speculate with other assets. The speculative demand for money is that money which is held in the hope of making a speculative gain, or to avoid a possible loss, as a result of the change in interest rates and the price of financial assets.

Keynes illustrated the speculative motive in terms of the decision to hold one's wealth in the form of cash or in fixed income bonds. To understand his argument it is necessary to appreciate that the price of bonds and the rate of interest are *inversely proportional* to each other. To make the argument simpler, we will assume that the bond is an eternal bond that will never be repaid by the government (such bonds are only usually issued in wartime). Consider, for example, a fixed income bond which yields an income of £5 per year. If the market rate of interest is 10 per cent the price of the bond will be £50. This is because the rate of interest on the bond must equal what savers could earn by investing their money elsewhere. If the market rate of interest were to fall to 2.5 per cent, the price of that same bond would rise to £200.

Keynes believed that investors had some notion of the normal rate of interest. If the current rate of interest was below this then people would

1 How will a fixed income bond which originally cost £100 and has a fixed return of 10 per cent (£10) be revalued under the following interest rates?

    (a) 10 per cent   (b) 5 per cent

    (c) 20 per cent   (d) $2\frac{1}{2}$ per cent

2 How would the value of the bond be affected in each case if you knew the bond was to be repaid next year?

3 How would the value of the bond be affected in each case if the investors believed that the next movement in interest rates would be upwards?

speculate by holding cash, anticipating that interest rates would rise and hence bond prices fall. Hence, the lower the interest rates the more people would expect the prices of bonds to fall and thus the more people would hold cash rather than bonds in their wealth portfolios. Thus, low interest rates are associated with a high speculative demand for money. Conversely, if the rate of interest was high, people would buy bonds because their price would be low and the chance of capital gains when interest rates came down would be high. Thus a high rate of interest is associated with a low speculative demand for money.

Later Keynesians, such as **J. Tobin,** tend to generalise risk to a wider range of assets than just bonds. Basically they argue that holding money is an insurance against the risk associated with other financial assets. If the interest rate increases then the cost of this insurance, i.e. the opportunity cost of holding money, is increased. Thus an increase in interest rates will cause a portfolio readjustment away from liquidity. Therefore they too arrive at the conclusion that the demand for money will be inversely related to the interest rate. Indeed, for the purpose of holding wealth, Keynesians regard money and many other financial assets as close substitutes. As with any commodity with *close substitutes*, the demand for money is expected to be sensitive to price changes, i.e. Keynesians hold that the demand for money is *elastic* with respect to changes in interest rates.

We can summarise the above discussion as follows:

The demand for money is positively related to income and negatively related to the interest rate.

Thus we have arrived at the result that the demand for money is rather like the demand for any normal good; if we put the price of holding money (i.e. the interest rate) on the vertical axis we have a demand curve that slopes downward and which shifts to the right as income increases. What we should emphasise, however, is that in Keynesian theory *expectations* play a large part. This means that the relationship between the demand for money and observable variables such as income and the interest rate is likely at any time to become unstable. For example, pessimistic views on the future prices of financial assets and the yield to investment in general could cause a large increase in the demand for money associated with previous levels of income and the interest rate.

Monetarist theory of the demand for money

In common with modern Keynesians, monetarists also take a portfolio adjustment approach to money. Again, individuals are seen to have a choice of different ways in which to hold their wealth. Again, these assets will have varying liquidity as well as other advantages and disadvantages. Thus individuals weigh up the various costs and benefits associated with each asset and arrange their portfolios such that their utility is maximised. But the monetarist concept of a wealth portfolio is much broader than that of Keynesians. Monetarists hold that the relevant portfolio includes not just financial assets but also physical goods. Thus an increase in the money supply which disturbs the equilibrium of wealth holders by making their portfolios 'too liquid' is just as likely to spill over into physical investment assets and *durable consumption goods* as into financial assets, as illustrated in Figure 37.3.

Monetarists, as did the earlier quantity theorists, concentrate on the convenience of money as a medium of exchange. Thus, unlike Keynesians,

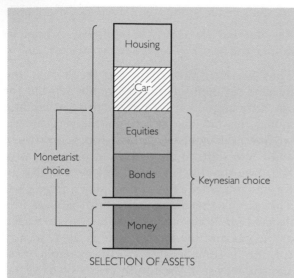

Figure 37.3 Different views of portfolio balance
Monetarists see portfolio balance as choice between
money and all other assets, but Keynesians see money
and financial assets as close substitutes.

they believe that there is a dividing line in the
portfolio between money and all other assets.
Therefore they do not regard money and other
financial assets as close substitutes. Monetarists
would state this condition in the following form:

Money is a substitute for all assets alike, real and
financial, rather than a close substitute for only a
small range of financial assets.

As money is not regarded as having close financial
substitutes, the demand for money is expected, in
contrast to the Keynesian view, to be inelastic with
respect to the rate of interest. In addition, monetarists do not include as a determinant of money
demand any variable which is likely to be volatile.
Thus, again in contrast to the Keynesian view, the
demand for money has a fairly stable and predictable relationship to its determinants.

Monetary transmission mechanisms

The transmission mechanisms in a car transmit
the power of the engine to the wheels. But how is
an increase in the money supply transmitted into
increased aggregate demand? We have already
touched upon this in our discussion of portfolio
adjustments. As would be expected from that
discussion monetarists and Keynesians differ as

to the mechanisms involved and the strength of
the links between variables.

What makes it more difficult for the author of
a textbook is that there is not complete unanim-
ity within each school of thought and that there
are many complex 'feedback' effects to consider.
The presentation here seeks to elucidate the differences which have generated most debate and
also serves as a useful introduction to more
'advanced' *IS/LM* presentations.

The Keynesian transmission mechanism

● *Common misunderstanding*

*Because of the way in which the difference between
Keynesians and monetarists is stressed in textbooks,
students often believe them to be complete opposites
and therefore conclude that Keynesians believe there is
no consequence of an increase in the money supply.
Except in the extreme case detailed below, this is not the
case, although it is true that Keynesians believe that the
responses will be much less dramatic.*

Figure 37.4 represents in diagrammatic form the
stages in the Keynesian view of the transmission
mechanism. In part (a) of Figure 37.4 we see that
there has been an increase in the supply of money
(M_{S1} to M_{S2}). At the previous equilibrium rate of
interest (r_1) there is now an excess supply of
money. Banks thus seek to expand their loans by
offering lower rates of interest, or people with
excess liquidity in their wealth portfolios will
seek to purchase other financial assets and in so
doing drive up the price of these assets thus
reducing interest rates. In short, interest rates will
fall to the new equilibrium indicated by r_2. In
part (b) we can see that the fall in the rate of
interest will cause an extension of the demand for
investment, i.e. the level of the investment will
increase by ΔI. Part (c) shows a shift in the aggregate demand curve to the right, i.e. the increase in
the money supply has finally led to an increase in
aggregate demand.

There are several important points to note
about this transmission mechanism:

(a) The link between changes in the money supply
    and aggregate demand is *indirect* as it operates
    only through the effect of money on the inter-
    est rates prevailing in financial markets.

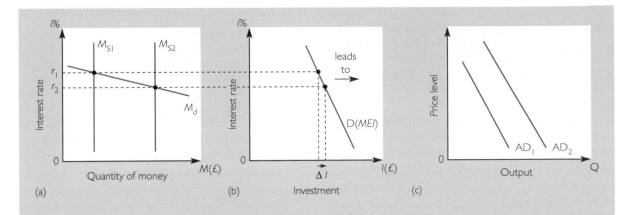

Figure 37.4 A Keynesian monetary transmission mechanism
An increase in the money supply in (a) causes a relatively small fall in the rate of interest. This causes a relatively small increase in investment (ΔI) in (b). This increase in investment leads to a small shift in the aggregate demand curve to the right in (c).

(b) Keynesians believe the demand for money to be interest elastic. Thus much of the impact of an increased money supply is absorbed because falls in the interest rate cause people readily to increase their holdings of 'idle' money balances.

(c) To the extent that interest rates do fall a little, the effect on investment and hence aggregate demand is slight. This is because Keynesians believe the interest elasticity of the demand for investment to be low.

(d) Both the demand for money and the demand for investment are likely to be highly *volatile* in the face of changes in expectations.

In short, Keynesians believe that the links between changes in the money supply and changes in aggregate demand are extremely tenuous; not only are the links weak, they are unstable. Therefore Keynesians prefer the more direct manipulation of spending and hence aggregate demand through fiscal measures.

An extreme Keynesian view

Some so-called 'extreme Keynesians', notably **Kaldor**, take a somewhat different tack. They deny money any causal role as a determinant of aggregate demand. Instead they argue that the money supply responds in an entirely *passive* manner to accommodate any increase in the desire to spend, i.e. the direction of causation flows from an autonomous increase in the desire to consume or invest to an increase in the money supply. Kaldor's famous example was the sharp increase in the money supply which occurs in the months of November and December. He teased those that ascribed a causal role to money by asking whether it was this increase in the money supply that caused increased consumer spending in the run-up to Christmas! Of course what actually happens is that the monetary authorities anticipate the increase in spending and therefore expand the money supply so that consumers and traders will have sufficient cash for their transactions.

Kaldor's point should not be dismissed lightly. We have seen that quasi- and near money can perform to some extent the functions of money. It is also the case that attempts since 1976 to control the money supply within pre-set target bands of growth were often unsuccessful and have now been largely abandoned (see the previous chapter). Part of the argument is that banks have access to reserve assets that cannot be directly controlled by central banks and that restrictions on such banks tend merely to cause *disintermediation* or the diversion of business to *fringe* banks or eurocurrency markets not covered by such regulations. Others stress that, historically, central banks have acted to accommodate the stock of money to changes in the needs for trade by giving their supportive responsibilities priority over their control duties. This latter argument explains why many Keynesians are not impressed by the historical evidence presented by Friedman and Schwartz of a correlation between nominal income and the money supply.

But the nature of money itself might make it difficult to control. Essentially, money is based on faith, e.g. we accept bank deposits as payment because it is believed that we could exchange them for cash. But equally any promissory note that one has faith in might be accepted as payment. The granting of credit is often extremely informal between regular trading partners. Credit arrangements can be extended by any large business that feels the advantages in attracting custom outweigh occasional defaults.

Whether they take the view that expansion of the money supply has a weak and unpredictable effect on aggregate demand, or that money is an entirely passive variable which is for practical purposes impossible to control, it is clear that such Keynesians would not emphasise monetary policy as a means of demand management.

The monetarist transmission mechanism

Figure 37.5 represents in diagrammatic form the monetarist view of the transmission mechanism. Again there are several important points to note:

(a) The links between the money supply and aggregate demand include not only indirect effects but also, through the cash balance effect of portfolio adjustment, direct effects. Moreover, not only does the fall in interest rates prevailing in financial markets cause an increase in business investment, it also causes consumers to increase their 'investment' in durable goods.

(b) The demand for money is interest inelastic. Thus large reductions in the interest rate can occur before excess money balances become absorbed by an extension of people's desire to hold money. (Indeed, most of the increase in the demand for money will come from the resulting increase in income. For simplicity such feedback effects are ignored.)

(c) Not only is the fall in interest rates from r_1 to r_2 likely to be substantial, it is also assumed that the interest elasticity of investment is high.

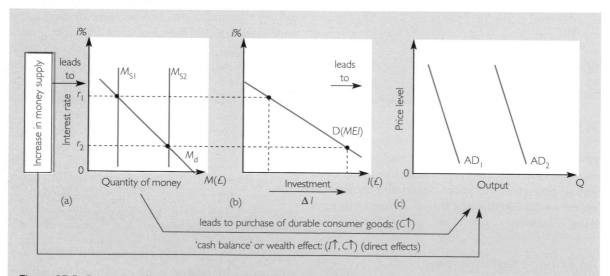

Figure 37.5 A monetarist monetary transmission mechanism
An increase in the money supply causes a large fall in interest rates in (a). This turn causes a large increase in investment (ΔI) in diagram (b). This increase in investment brings about a large increase in aggregate demand in diagram (c). Money national income is also boosted by the fall in interest rates causing people to buy more consumer durables. Aggregate demand is also boosted by the 'cash balance' effect. Notice the difference in slopes of demand for money and investment schedules compared with the Keynesian view in Figure 37.4.

(d) There will also be a relatively high and stable interest elasticity of consumption, particularly consumer durables.

In short, then, monetarists believe that the link between changes in the money supply and changes in aggregate demand is very strong and relatively stable.

Crowding out

Monetarists believe that Keynesians have overlooked the interest effects of fiscal policy. Expansionary fiscal policy involves an increase in the public sector net cash requirement (PSNCR). How will the government persuade people to buy this increased debt without an increase in interest rates? The increase in aggregate demand implied by fiscal policy will also create an upward pressure on the demand for money which will also increase interest rates. The only way to avoid interest rate rises is to increase the money supply, but monetarists believe that this would increase inflation and is therefore unwise.

Monetarists thus believe that an increase in government spending will raise interest rates which will in turn *crowd out* private spending on investment and consumption goods. This will render the fiscal policy ineffective.

Keynesians retort that a little increase in the money supply to finance the expansionary fiscal policy will just help to finance the increase in output, unless the whole economy is close to full employment.

Fine tuning

The crowding out effect is part of the argument against using fiscal policy to 'fine tune' the economy. Modern monetarists would also accept that fine tuning is not possible in monetary policy either. Instead, monetarists argue that the lags and the strength of links in the transmission mechanisms are uncertain in the short run.

However, monetarists argue that there is a fairly stable demand for money function which will be deviated from in the processes of adjustment but which will tend to re-establish itself as a new equilibrium is reached. Thus, despite significant short-term fluctuations, the velocity of circulation will tend to change only slowly over the long term. Hence monetarists argue that active or 'discretionary' stabilisation policies should not be attempted but, rather, a 'fixed throttle' non-discretionary monetary expansion regime should be adopted and then observed by all governments.

Ideally, the money supply should be set to grow roughly in line with the normal rate of growth of the economy, providing the extra money to absorb increases in output without causing inflation.

STUDENT ACTIVITY 37.4

Which of the following pieces of evidence (if they were correct) would tend to support a Keynesian viewpoint and which a monetarist viewpoint?

(a) Statistical evidence suggests the demand for money is inelastic.
(b) Statistical evidence suggests that investment is interest inelastic.
(c) The government increases public spending but unemployment remains stubbornly high.

The determination of aggregate real income

The debate concerning the monetary transmission mechanism has proceeded with each side conceding partial defeats. In terms of the view as to whether aggregate demand can be affected by fiscal or monetary policy it is now much more difficult to divide economists neatly into Keynesians and monetarists. Today the debate is between monetarists who hold that the level of output in the economy is self-adjusting to the level at which there is no involuntary unemployment, and Keynesians who believe that the level of aggregate demand must be managed by governments so as to produce full employment. It is to this more profound distinction that we now turn.

The nature of the debate

If the only difference between Keynesians and monetarists were that the former advocated fiscal policy to iron out fluctuations while the latter advocated monetary policy, then the debate would concern mere *technicalities* of policy rather than a fundamental difference of political vision. But it is this difference of vision concerning the nature of capitalist economies and the proper role of government that is at the heart of mainstream political debate today.

To use a medical analogy, Keynesians (except radical post-Keynesians; see Chapter 47) view the free market capitalist economy as an organism which works well when healthy but, from time to time, is prone to chronic illness. But it is believed that these illnesses can be cured if governments apply the correct treatments. Monetarists/neo-classicists especially admire the workings of free markets but they differ from Keynesians in that they believe the organism seldom suffers from malfunctions. From time to time capitalism might catch a chill but this will be cured by the system's own strong recuperative powers. Indeed, the only thing which is likely to turn a chill into serious ill health is the misguided prescription of Keynesian doctors! (For example, when attempts are made to preserve declining industries instead of allowing market forces to replace them in time with the growth industries of the future.)

As we have seen, Keynesians take the view that, when left unattended, fluctuations in aggregate demand are likely to destabilise the economy. Monetarists differ in that they believe that if the money supply is not allowed to fluctuate, fluctuations in aggregate demand will be slight.

Monetarists believe the economy is always, more or less, at an equilibrium at which there is no *involuntary unemployment*; the level of employment and hence the supply of output are determined more or less independently of aggregate demand. Hence, in the monetarist's view increases in aggregate demand are not met by an increased supply as all those who wish to work are already working as much as they wish to. It follows that increasing aggregate demand will result only in inflation:

Keynesians believe that aggregate output and thus employment are demand determined; monetarists believe that such 'real' aggregate variables are supply determined.

Aggregate supply

The notion that real variables are supply determined is easy to explain to anyone who has understood the microeconomic sections of this book. This is because monetarists believe that aggregate output and employment are determined by the same market forces that operate in individual competitive markets. Indeed, in such neo-classical analysis there is no clear distinction between micro- and macroeconomics. Whereas Keynes warned that those who extended micro analysis to analyse macro variables were guilty of a *fallacy of composition*, monetarists tend to view aggregate variables as only the sum of many millions of individually made 'micro' decisions. They make the assumption that the whole is the sum of the parts.

To understand how the level of employment, and hence output, is determined in the monetarist view we need only refer back to the neo-classical 'marginal distribution theory' of Chapter 25. In that chapter we saw how a firm in perfect competition in both its product and factor markets would be maximising its profits when:

Wage = Marginal revenue product

Before moving on we should remind ourselves that both sides of this equality are in money terms, i.e. 'wage' refers to money (nominal) wage and 'marginal revenue product' refers to marginal physical product multiplied by money (nominal) price:

$$W = MPP \times P$$

As we have seen, monetarists emphasise that real things are determined by real things. The above equality can be interpreted in real terms simply by dividing through by nominal price:

$$W/P = MPP$$

W/P can be thought of as the real wage, i.e. the actual purchasing power of the worker's money wage. There is an aggregation problem here in that *P* refers to a particular product's price whereas the wage of the worker will be spent on many products. Thus, to see how much the money wage could purchase in general terms we would have to divide it by some composite index of the price level (see for example the construction of the RPI in Chapter 32). It makes it easier to 'strip away the veil of money to reveal the real workings of the economy' if we assume that there is only one product which we will simply call 'output'. Thus, we assume that workers are paid in output and that firms employ workers to produce output. Therefore if the money wage is divided by the price of output we have the real wage in terms of units of output.

We can now interpret the equilibrium of the firm in real terms. In Figure 37.6 we represent the equilibrium of a perfectly competitive firm in monetary terms in part (a), and in real terms in part (b). In part (a) the employer will employ all workers up to L_E as each of these workers adds more money to revenue ($MPP \times P$) than they add to costs (W). In part (b) the same level of employment results as each worker up to L_E adds more to output (MPP) than the output they receive (W/P).

A numerical example will demonstrate the equivalence of part (a) and part (b) in Figure 37.6. Recall that in the short run the MPP depends only upon the number of workers employed by the firm and that, as employment increases, MPP falls owing to the law of dimin-

ishing marginal returns. Let us suppose that at L_E $MPP = 5$ units of output. If $W = £10$ and $P = £2$ then at L_E we have:

$$W = MPP \times P = 5 \times £2 = £10$$

or:

$$W/P = MPP = 5 \text{ units of output}$$

Hence the same profit-maximising equilibrium condition can be expressed in both real and monetary terms. Monetarists extend this micro analysis of equilibrium to the economy as a whole. In doing this they make use of the notion of an **aggregate production function**. Thus it is assumed that at any one time there is a fixed stock of capital in the economy as a whole. As total employment increases the MPP of labour therefore falls according to some aggregate version of the law of diminishing returns. It has to be said that the idea of a capital stock and aggregate production function raises logical problems that are complex but which cast doubt on the consistency of neo-classical theory. Nevertheless, as with other schools of thought, we brush aside these problems to present the monetarist/neo-classical view as simply as possible.

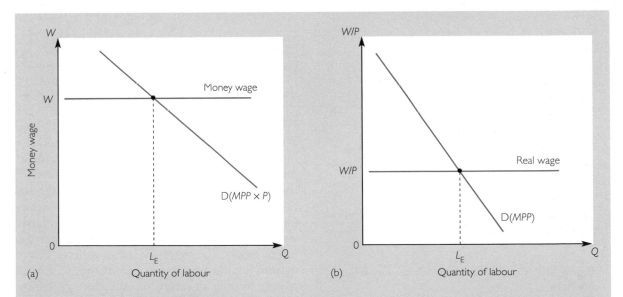

Figure 37.6 The same equilibrium (L_E) expressed in monetary and real terms
Diagram (a) shows the equilibrium of the perfectly competitive firm in money terms. This occurs where the MRP ($MPP \times P$) is equal to the wage rate. This equates with a quantity of labour employed of L_E. By dividing through by the price (P) we see the same equilibrium expressed in real terms.

In Figure 37.7 we have extended marginal distribution theory to the economy as a whole.

The demand curve for labour is the *MPP* of labour and slopes downward according to the law of diminishing returns. As we are now looking at the economy as a whole the supply of labour is upward sloping, indicating that higher wages will attract more people into the labour force (in fact the analysis is not significantly altered if the supply of labour is vertical or even slightly backward bending). We should note that everything in the diagram is in real terms, i.e. *MPP* is measured in units of output and the supply of labour is determined by the real wage. The equilibrium of the labour market occurs at the level of employment L_E where the real wage $(W/P)_E$ is equal to *MPP*.

It is instructive to examine the nature of the equilibrium in Figure 37.7. First, we can note that if the nominal prices W and P are increased by the same proportion, the real wage, and hence the equilibrium, is unchanged, i.e. $W/P = 2 \times W/2 \times P = 3 \times W/3 \times P = \ldots$. This assumes that workers are not fooled by increasing money wages into offering more labour than before even though the real wage has not changed; in short there is no ***money illusion***. Second, we should note that at L_E the demand for labour equals the supply of labour, i.e. anyone who wants to work at the equilibrium wage rate is able to find a job and thus there is no involuntary unemployment. Third, we should note that the economy is actually composed of many such labour markets each of which has its own clearing real wage. Thus if a worker's *MPP* is very low they will only find work if they are willing to accept a very low real wage; no employer will (or is obliged) to pay a worker more than that worker can actually contribute to output.

Recession or the natural rate of unemployment?

The neo-classical view: the natural rate of employment and output

We can now see more clearly what monetarists mean when they say that 'real things are determined by real things'. As we noted in Figure 37.7 the supply and demand functions that determine the level of employment are in real, not monetary, terms. The demand function reflects the productivity of labour when combined with the existing capital stock. The supply of labour reflects 'human nature', i.e. the amount of labour that people are willing to offer in return for any given real wage. Hence, far from the level of employment being the government's responsibility as is the implication of Keynesian theory, in monetarism the level of employment is not within the government's control to increase. The government cannot wave a magic

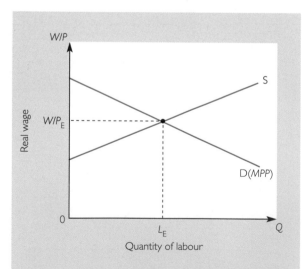

Figure 37.7 Equilibrium in the labour market as a whole
The demand curve for labour is the *MPP* curve. The supply curve represents the supply of labour for the whole economy. Equilibrium occurs where the real wage $(W/P)_E$ is equal to *MPP*.

wand to make people willing to work longer at the same real wage, nor would it be meaningful for the government to pass laws stating that the *MPP* of labour when combined with the actual capital stock is higher than it actually is. In short, within monetarist/neo-classical theory, insisting that the government should 'do something about unemployment' is rather like demanding that the government should increase the amount of rainfall in the UK.

Indeed, it is in their use of the term 'natural' that the political vision of the monetarists is most evident:

Monetarists use the term the natural rate of employment to summarise their belief that the operation of market forces, if not obstructed by government or powerful institutions, will quickly produce an equilibrium in which everybody is doing the best they can without infringing the rights of others.

This equilibrium is thus brought about by contracts between employers and employees which are voluntarily entered into because they confer mutual benefit. Monetarists believe that, in the short run, the equilibrium in the labour market also sets the level of output or aggregate supply.

Because the natural rate of employment is the result of mutually beneficial agreements, there will be a strong tendency for it to reassert itself if disturbed. For example, if (for some unspecified reason) the real wage is above $(W/P)_E$ in Figure 37.7, there will be an excess supply of labour. As long as the real wage is above $(W/P)_E$ there will be more people looking for work than employers wish to employ. But such involuntary unemployment will be only transitory. Monetarists argue that, as in any other market, an excess supply will cause a downward pressure on price. In this case it will be unemployed labour competing with the employed that will lower real wages. Hence involuntary unemployment is eradicated when the real wage falls to $(W/P)_E$ and the supply of labour once again matches the demand. Equally, a real wage below $(W/P)_E$ would cause an excess demand for labour and hence a rise in the real wage back to $(W/P)_E$.

The neutrality of money

We are now in a position to present the classical dichotomy in diagrammatic form. In Figure 37.8

the lower part of the diagram represents equilibrium in the labour market where L_N is the natural rate of employment. The initial money wage is W_1 and the initial price level is P_1. Thus the real wage which clears the labour market is W_1/P_1. The upper part of Figure 37.8 represents equilibrium in the goods or product market. Although the composition of aggregate output is determined by the interaction of demand and supply in individual markets, the arrow indicates that the level of aggregate output is set by the equilibrium of the labour market.

AD_1 represents the initial level of aggregate demand in the goods sector or product market(s). Note that, in accordance with monetarist views of the monetary transmission mechanism, AD_1 corresponds to a specific supply of money, i.e. M_1. According to monetarist theory the aggregate demand curve is downward sloping as lower levels of nominal prices mean a larger real money

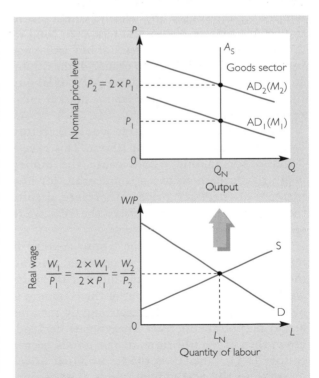

***Figure 37.8* The Classical Dichotomy and the neutrality of money**

A doubling of the money supply causes the money wage and the price level to double but leaves the equilibrium in the real economy unchanged.

supply. We can see that a nominal money supply of M_1 implies an equilibrium nominal price level in the product market of P_1. Hence, initially the real money supply is M_1/P_1. As the nominal money supply is exogenously set by the monetary authorities and the demand for money is stable there will be no change to the economy's equilibrium unless something real changes, e.g. if changes in the capital stock increase MPP or people's willingness to work somehow alters.

Now let us suppose that, perhaps in an attempt to increase employment and output, the government doubles the money supply. At the original price level of P_1 the real money supply will thus have also doubled. The effect, as shown in Figure 37.8, will be to shift aggregate demand from AD_1 to AD_2. This will cause excess demand which in turn will cause product prices to rise. If money wages were to remain at W_1 these increases in product prices would cause a decrease in the real wage. But this will not happen for the supply and demand conditions in the labour market are in real terms. As long as the people's willingness to work at any real wage is unchanged and there is no change in the capital stock or technology to change the MPP of labour, then the equilibrium in the labour market must remain at L_N.

A decrease in the real wage would therefore cause an excess demand for labour. This excess demand for labour would cause the money wage to increase so as to compensate for any increase in product prices. Therefore despite the increase in nominal prices the real wage would remain unchanged.

As the equilibrium in the labour market is undisturbed by the increase in aggregate demand in the product market(s) the number of hours worked and hence the output of the economy is also unaltered. Hence aggregate supply remains at Q_N despite the increase in aggregate demand. How then is equilibrium in the goods sector restored? The answer is that as nominal prices increase so the real money supply (i.e. its purchasing power) is reduced. This in turn, through the monetary transmission mechanism, causes the aggregate demand for products to contract until it is again equal to aggregate supply at Q_N.

It should be clear that once nominal prices have doubled the real money supply is the same as it was before; that is:

$$\frac{M_1}{P_1} = \frac{2 \times M_1}{2 \times P_1} = \frac{M_2}{P_2}$$

Equally, if product prices and money wages have doubled the real wage will be as it was before. Thus once nominal prices have doubled all things real are as they were before. The only difference is that the nominal price level has doubled. In short, attempts to increase employment and output through increasing aggregate demand will only result in inflation. Readers should now check their understanding by working back through the analysis on the assumption that the money supply is reduced once again to M_1.

The above analysis provides a theoretical underpinning for the Classical Dichotomy:

The Classical Dichotomy states that real and monetary things are separate; hence money plays a 'neutral' role in the economy in that an increase in the money supply merely causes an equiproportionate increase in the price level leaving real things unaltered.

A Keynesian recession or the natural rate of unemployment?

Monetarist theory implies that involuntary unemployment can exist only so long as it takes for the labour market to clear. As monetarism is based on the assumption of strong competitive forces this should not take too long. Indeed, for many Keynesians (often called 'neo-Keynesians') and monetarists the supposed speed of this adjustment is what distinguishes the two schools of thought.

Neo-Keynesians believe that persistent unemployment can be caused by the real wage being too high. If this were so there would be more people looking for jobs than there were jobs being offered. Thus some people would be voluntarily unemployed. Unlike monetarists these Keynesians believe that money wages are 'downwardly sticky' for institutional reasons. For example, workers are likely to resist a cut in money wages for fear of losing ground relative to other workers (erosion of 'relativities' or 'differentials' as union leaders often put it). Nevertheless, a decrease in the real wage brought about by product price inflation might be acceptable in that all workers are affected equally. Neo-Keynesians thus recommend that the necessary reduction in real wages can be speeded up by increasing aggregate demand in the economy until full employment is reached. Monetarists reject this account of things as it smacks of 'money illusion' and hence 'irrationality'.

Some 'extreme' Keynesians believe that the adjustment of prices plays a very minor role in the overall operation of the economy. They point out that the implicit assumption of perfect competition is hard to reconcile with the widespread existence of monopoly and oligopolistic power of both firms and organised labour. They argue that in such a world quantities rather than prices are likely to adjust to changes in aggregate demand. Thus, if there is a shortage of demand firms will cut back on output and labour without lowering prices or attempting to offer lower money wages. Thus although nominal prices and the real wage might be consistent with that needed for full employment the economy becomes 'stuck' in recession.

Figure 37.9 demonstrates a Keynesian recession brought about by lack of demand rather than incorrect prices. The top part of the diagram illustrates the equilibrium of aggregate demand in the economy. As can be seen from the lower part of the diagram this level of demand is insufficient to purchase the volume of output that would be produced at full employment. The arrow pointing downwards from Y_E indicates that this level of aggregate demand imposes a quantity constraint on the labour market. The nominal demand for labour as shown is again the *MPP* of labour. This shows how much labour it would be profitable to employ if it were possible to sell all the output so produced. It can be seen that at a real wage of $(W/P)_E$ the level of employment that would occur if the labour market cleared could be reached were there sufficient demand in the economy. But it would not be profitable to employ all this labour, at whatever real wage, if the output cannot be sold. Thus the *effective demand* for labour is constrained by the level of demand for products. Therefore *WX* amount of labour remains unemployed even though these people wish to work at the going wage rate and it would be profitable to employ them at this wage if their

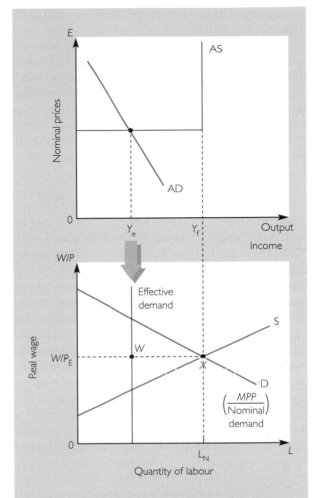

***Figure 37.9* Keynesian recession: demand deficiency**

In the upper part of the diagram a demand deficiency causes the equilibrium level of national income (Y_E) to be below the full employment equilibrium (Y_f). In the lower part of the diagram this imposes a quantity constraint on the labour market. At wage level $(W/P)_E$ *WX* amount of labour remains unemployed.

output could be sold. It should be clear that a cut in wages will not decrease unemployment in Figure 37.9. It will never be profitable for firms to employ more labour unless the level of demand for products is expanded. Indeed, if a reduction in wages acts to decrease the demand for products it will shift the quantity constraint in the labour market further away from L_N. Thus such a recession, if it existed, would not go away by itself. Keynesian theorists argue instead that government intervention to increase aggregate demand is essential.

Keynesian economists can thus account for persistent unemployment in terms of real wages being stuck too high or a general lack of demand in the economy. To this they can add frictional unemployment caused by people moving from one job to another and structural unemployment caused by a mismatch of labour and jobs in terms of either location or skills (see also Chapter 39).

Voluntary and involuntary unemployment

How then can monetarists account for the persistent high unemployment of the 1980s and early 1990s? As we have seen, in terms of involuntary unemployment this is difficult. Some monetarists do emphasise the role of unions in preventing real wage adjustment and lowering labour productivity. But more purist monetarists do not accept that unions can so bend market forces as to contribute significantly to unemployment. These monetarists make much of the distinction between involuntary and voluntary unemployment. In short they believe that persistent unemployment must be voluntary.

Monetarists thus argue that even at the natural rate of employment, where there is overall equilibrium in the labour market, there will be those that remain voluntarily unemployed. For example, at any one time there will be a flow of people through the unemployment register who are searching for better jobs. These people will search until the marginal cost of their search is equal to their expected marginal gain. They are voluntarily unemployed in that they are refusing the job offers already found in order to search for better jobs.

Monetarists point out that unemployed persons might not see themselves as voluntarily unemployed. For example, unskilled workers, or those whose skills are no longer in demand, can expect to be offered only jobs where low pay reflects their low market value. Such persons may well curse 'the system' or their own bad luck, but the monetarist argues that they are worth only a low wage and must thus accept the charity of the state or move house and/or retrain. Keynesians would argue that this is a harsh attitude but the monetarist would reply that attempting to eliminate such unemployment by demand measures will only result in inflation. For the monetarist

the only way to reduce the 'natural rate of unemployment' in an economy is through supply side measures such as skills training, reducing social security payments, lessening the disincentives present by taxation, facilitating the easier flow of finance to firms, removing restrictive practices, etc.

The natural rate of unemployment is defined by monetarists to be that level of unemployment which is consistent with overall equilibrium in the labour market. It cannot be reduced by increasing aggregate demand but only by making markets work better.

Conclusion

Monetarism appeared in the 1950s as a part of a technical debate concerning the importance of money in the functioning of the economy. It soon developed into a revival of the neo-classical school of 'macroeconomics' which Keynes had all but beaten into submission. By the 1980s it had gained (or regained) political ascendancy. This had led to a profound shift in economic policy from measures designed to influence demand to measures designed to improve the functioning of the supply side of the economy. These policies are examined at greater length in Chapter 39. The return of a Labour government in 1997 saw no headlong rush into fiscal expansion. Indeed the new Chancellor's first act was to give control of interest rates to a committee of the Bank of England. However, they may be thought of Keynesian in the sense that they do not believe that the market can be trusted to provide an adequate solution. Their policies are, however, as much supply side as demand side.

Summary

1 Keynesian and post-Keynesian economics had downgraded the importance of money in the determination of national income. Monetarism represents a return to the pre-Keynesian orthodoxy of the (neo-)classicists.

2 The Classical Dichotomy states that nominal prices are determined by the quantity of money but the quantity of money has no effect on real things.

3 In the quantity equation of money ($MV = PT$) monetarists argue for the stability of both V and T. This therefore establishes a firm link between the money supply (M) and the general price level (P).

4 In the Cambridge equation ($M \times 1/k = P \times Y$) the expression $1/k$ replaces the velocity of circulation. The symbol k is the proportion of nominal income which is demanded in money.

5 The theory of portfolio balance is concerned with the way in which people distribute their assets between money, financial assets and real assets.

6 The Keynesian view of the demand for money distinguishes three motives for demanding money:
(a) transactions;
(b) precautionary;
(c) speculative.
The first two are directly linked to income while the third is inversely proportional to the rate of interest.

7 Monetarists argue that there is a dividing line in the portfolio between money and other assets; thus there is only a weak line between the demand for money and the rate of interest.

8 The Keynesian view of the transmission mechanism is that increases in the money supply have weak indirect effects upon national income as falls in the interest rate lead to small increases in investment because the demand for money is interest elastic and the demand for investment is interest inelastic.

9 Monetarists argue for strong links between the money supply and national income through both direct and strong indirect effects. However, such effects act only upon nominal (or money) national income and not real national income.

10 Monetarists argue that the economy is essentially self-regulating while Keynesians maintain that periodic periods of imbalance are possible.

11 Keynesians have tended to focus on the demand side of the economy while monetarists and neo-classicists have stressed the importance of the supply side.

12 Neo-classicists have argued for the existence of a natural level of employment in the economy. It follows from this that such unemployment as exists is either temporary or voluntary.

13 Keynesian economists account for unemployment in terms of lack of demand or real wages being 'stuck' too high. To this can be added frictional and structural unemployment.

14 The political ascendancy of neo-classical views has led to profound shifts in policy designed to improve the functioning of the supply side of the economy.

QUESTIONS

1 What factors determine the demand for money in a modern society?

2 Contrast the effect of an increase in the money supply in both a Keynesian and a monetarist model of the economy:
(a) in the short run;
(b) in the long run.

3 What is meant by the theory of portfolio balance?

4 What effect upon the equilibrium level of national income would there be if the government were to lower interest rates?

5 Contrast Fisher's quantity equation of money with the Cambridge equation.

6 Describe the mechanism by which Keynes said increasing the money supply would lead to an increase in real GDP.

7 What is meant by 'money illusion'?

8 Evaluate the importance of the concept of the 'natural level of unemployment' in the neo-classical view of the economy.

9 Nobody doubts that monetarism will stop inflation if it is practised long enough and hard enough. At some point high interest rates stop all economic activity as well as inflation. But the price is very high, not equally distributed across the population and not endurable in a democracy.
Lester Thurow, *The Economist*, 23 January 1982

Critically evaluate Thurow's statement in the light of the Conservatives' performance while in government.

10 'Real things are determined by real things.' What is meant by this statement when monetarists use it to refer to the determination of the level of employment?

Figure 37.10 represents the equilibrium in the whole labour market of an economy. Answer the questions which follow.

1 Carefully explain what is being shown in Figure 37.10. Make sure that you make clear all the terms used in the construction of the graph.
2 Describe what assumptions are implicit in Figure 37.10.
3 What problems might a government have if it was faced with the situation shown in Figure 37.10? Suggest two measures that a government might take to deal with the situation.
4 Under what circumstances would the demand curve for labour shift to the right?
5 Suppose that there was a considerable increase in the money supply. How would the situation in the labour market be changed? In your answer make clear the difference in viewpoint between Keynesians and monetarists.

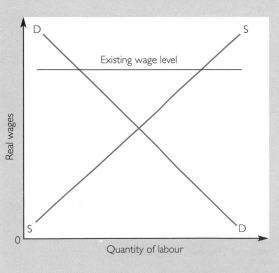

Figure 37.10 **Equilibrium in the labour market**

Study the following passage and then answer the questions below.

Monetarism came on to the political stage with great promise. It was to eliminate inflation and create the conditions for growth and reduced unemployment. Coming as it did after the decade of the seventies with unemployment rising above one million and inflation out of control, it seemed like a breath of fresh air. Looking back on the decade of the eighties, its fortunes seem a little more mixed. The massive recession of the early eighties must in part have been due to the excessively tight monetary policy that was introduced from 1979 onwards. There is no doubt, however, that inflation was squeezed out of the economy, so in that sense monetarism was a highly successful, if somewhat costly policy.

It is important to recognise the role which oil played in that period of economic history. We tend to forget in periods of relative calm in the oil markets what a pivotal role it played. The quadrupling of oil prices in 1973–4 undoubtedly had a major impact on the inflation of the seventies, and through its effect on plunging all but Japan and Germany into severe balance of payments deficit, created unemployment and generated worldwide deflationary policies. The impact of oil on Mrs Thatcher's first monetary experiment must also be remembered. As North Sea oil came on stream the oil prices doubled once again in 1979. The balance of payments in the UK moved into strong surplus, in contrast with most other industrial economies. It is not possible to blame all the strength of the pound, as it surged up from $1.50 to $2.40, on high interest rates. Oil seemed to be on our side in 1979. By 1982, we were not quite so sure as the strong pound decimated our manufacturing exports.

The mid-eighties were a period of relatively successful monetary policy with inflation falling and employment growing. Mrs Thatcher did not need a Falklands war to get re-elected in 1987 – the economy was doing well. For a brief period it seemed as though monetarism was going to deliver. Optimism on the stock exchange had never been so buoyant. Alas a contradiction of government policy was to undo this promising state of affairs. The control of the money supply and free competition in the financial markets both seemed to accord with conservative principles. Deregulation of the financial markets led to a massive expansion of credit which led to a consumer boom so large that consumer spending was actually growing faster than income.

The party had to end, and the recession of the early nineties was the price we paid. As inflation hit 10 per cent again in 1990, it was clear that interest rates had to rise. It was the early eighties all over again but without the benefit of a balance of payments surplus. Monetary targets for the control of the money supply were no longer the main government policy. A tendency for the financial markets to get around any monetary target by cleverly inventing new kinds of money meant there had been a subtle shift in monetary policy. It was now the demand for money that had to be controlled (via interest rates) rather than the supply.

A second major recession with unemployment over three million in just over 10 years dented faith in monetarism. In managing the recovery from 1992 onwards, the Conservatives allowed themselves a little passive Keynesianism. They allowed the PSBR to rise rather than trying to balance the government's finances as had been the case in the earlier recession.

The experience of these two major recessions has also dented belief in the market's ability to regulate itself. The Labour administration of 1997 was not ready to go back to the full blooded Keynesianism of its predecessors and promised to hold to the previous government's spending targets for the first two years. One suspects this has more to do with meeting the criteria for a single currency than dogmatic belief. They also had to convince the electorate that they were a prudent 'new' Labour party. The final convincing argument for fiscal restraint was the demutualisation of the building societies and some insurance companies. Consumers have received about £50 billion in new wealth which could have created a consumer boom every bit as damaging as that in 1987.

By giving control of interest rates to a committee of the Bank of England, the Labour party has more or less forced itself to take fiscal policy decisions that will convince the City that the economy is in good hands. The surge in public spending that has been announced for the three years from 2001 may simply be compensation for the strict clampdown on public expenditure during the previous three years. In addition, there has been a rise in the tax burden as a percentage of GDP of two points, due in good part to booming income tax revenues resulting from the healthy economic conditions. The alternative to taxes increases is high interest rates and a punishingly strong pound for our manufacturing exporters. Surely we have been down that road before. Perhaps it is time to try a little Keynesian policy for a change, or maybe it is happening already?

1 What were the problems of monetarist policies in the 1980s?
2 What kind of fiscal policy did the Conservative government use in the 1990s?
3 Why does giving interest rate control to the Bank of England mean that prudent fiscal policy is necessary?
4 What are the parallels between 1987 and 1997?
5 Does the record of monetarism under the Conservative government suggest that, left to themselves, markets will work? In which periods was this closest to being the case?
6 Does the recent increase in public spending by the Labour government represent a return to Keynesian values, or is it more the result of the operation of prudent fiscal policies in the past?

38 The control of inflation

Learning outcomes

At the end of this chapter you will be able to:

▶ Distinguish between those costs of inflation where inflation has been perfectly anticipated and the costs resulting from imperfectly anticipated inflation.

▶ Appreciate the relationship between inflation and unemployment as shown by the Phillips curve.

▶ Discuss the adaptive expectations school account of the relationship between inflation and unemployment.

▶ State the rational expectations (neo-classical) view of the relationship between inflation and unemployment.

▶ Outline the main causes of inflation.

▶ Explain the policies available to control inflation.

In Chapter 35 we defined inflation as a rise in the general level of prices and a fall in the value of money. We examined various measures of inflation such as the RPI. In this chapter we look at the control of inflation as an object of government policy. Since the mid-1970s control of inflation has become the chief objective of government policy. We will first examine the main costs of inflation for the economy.

The costs of inflation

There are various *costs of inflation* for the economy, although they are often difficult to quantify.

They can be divided into those costs where the rate of inflation has been perfectly anticipated and is fully taken into account in prices and incomes and the ostensibly much larger costs that result from imperfectly anticipated inflation which is not fully allowed for in economic transactions.

Anticipated inflation costs

If inflation is progressing at a steady and fully anticipated rate, then the main cost stems from the fact that interest is not paid on cash in circulation but is paid on bank and building society deposits. Hence, there is an opportunity cost of holding cash, which is the interest that could be gained from placing the money in an interest-bearing account; the higher the rate of anticipated inflation, generally the higher the likely rate of interest and the greater the prospective opportunity cost of holding cash. As a result, there are likely to be *'shoe-leather costs'* involved in placing cash in an interest-bearing account or in transferring funds from one account to another that pays a higher rate. Additional costs of anticipated inflation, known as **menu costs**, are incurred in the need to change prices: restaurants have to change their menus, firms have to issue new price lists and cash tills and vending machines have to be altered accordingly, all of which takes time and money.

Unanticipated inflation costs

A significant cost of unanticipated inflation is that it *redistributes income and wealth*. A fall in the value of money will remove purchasing power from those living on fixed incomes, such as pensioners, and redistribute it towards those who draw their living from prices. This is illustrated in Figure 38.1. Wages are seen as being in the middle of the spectrum, and the ability of wage earners to keep up with or ahead of inflation will depend upon the wage earners'

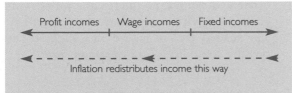

Figure 38.1 **Inflation and distribution of income in the UK**

bargaining power. This will mean that those whose skills are in demand or who have strong and well-organised trade unions, such as doctors and computer programmers, succeed in keeping ahead of inflation while those lacking the correct skills and/or who are poorly unionised, such as shopworkers, agricultural workers and bank workers, lag behind.

Furthermore, if inflation is not fully anticipated (i.e. if real interest rates should fall), there will be a redistribution of income from lenders to borrowers; borrowers will gain while savers will lose.

STUDENT ACTIVITY 38.1

If the rate of inflation is 8 per cent per annum and nominal interest rates currently lie at 5 per cent, who benefits – savers or borrowers?

It is argued by monetarists that inflation has a bad effect upon *economic growth*; this is because it *increases uncertainty* and *discourages investment*. If inflation is also accompanied by high nominal rates of interest, this will have a further detrimental effect on investment. A lower level of investment is usually associated with a reduced rate of economic growth.

While it is undoubtedly true that high rates of inflation are damaging to the economy, the evidence at lower rates of inflation is by no means convincing. Indeed it may be argued that some inflation is conducive to growth. This is because inflation may stimulate profits by reducing some costs of business but increasing their revenues. Certain business costs are usually incurred at a rate which is fixed for a period of time. For example, a business may lease premises at, say, £30 000 p.a. for 10 years. Inflation has the effect of reducing this rent in real terms while the price

of the business's product (and therefore its revenues) goes up with inflation. Inflation is generally supposed to have an adverse effect upon the *balance of payments*, especially if exchange rates do not fully adjust in purchasing power parity terms (see Chapter 42), because it makes imports cheaper and exports dearer. Theoretically this situation may be modified by a reversal of the Marshall–Lerner criterion (see page 629).

● *Common misunderstanding*

It should be remembered that, as far as the balance of payments is concerned, it is not the absolute but the relative rate of inflation which is important, i.e. the rate of inflation in the UK compared with that of its trading partners. If, for example, the domestic rate of inflation is 5 per cent but that of a trading partner is 10 per cent, then as far as foreign trade is concerned the price of exports will be falling and that of imports rising. Until fairly recently, however, the UK experienced consistently higher rates of inflation than those of its major trading partners.

Inflation and unemployment

A topic of great controversy is the relationship between the level of inflation and the *level of unemployment*. For many years it was claimed that there was a trade-off between the two, i.e. reducing inflation would cause more unemployment and vice versa. Monetarists and neo-classicists, however, claimed that such an inverse relationship between inflation and unemployment only held in the short run; eventually employment would return to its previous level, but at a higher rate of inflation. The controversy surrounds one of the best-known hypotheses of recent times – the *Phillips curve*. Since this is such an important topic we will now consider this controversy in more detail.

The Phillips curve

The original curve

Professor A.W.H. Phillips (1914–75) published research in 1962 which purported to show the relationship between unemployment, inflation and wage rises in the UK economy, 1861–1957.

The research appeared to show that the nearer the economy was to full employment the greater would be the rate of inflation. A diagram based upon the original Phillips curve is shown in Figure 38.2. It appeared that if unemployment were at 5.5 per cent then inflation would be zero.

The empirical evidence

Phillips's evidence seemed good for the period he investigated. However, since the mid-1960s the relationship seems to have broken down. Figure 38.6 (see page 554) shows the actual relationship between inflation and unemployment. You can see that on a scatter diagram it offers poor evidence for a Phillips curve. Three possible explanations therefore present themselves:

(a) No discernible relationship exists between prices and unemployment.
(b) A relationship exists, as described in the Phillips curve, but events have caused it to shift rightwards. This is illustrated in Figure 38.2. As you can see this could also be made to fit reasonably well with the evidence in Figure 38.6.
(c) **M. Sherman**, a radical American economist, has suggested that the relationship is the

other way round, i.e. increasing inflation is associated with increasing unemployment. The shaded area in Figure 38.6 suggests the possible trend line of the *Sherman curve*.

The adaptive expectations school

Milton Friedman put forward the view that there is a short-run trade-off between unemployment and inflation. That is to say, it is possible for the government, in the short run, to reduce unemployment by, for example, increasing the money supply. However, in the long run the jobs market will return to the previous level of employment but with a higher rate of inflation. This phenomenon is caused by the time it takes for people's *expectations* to adjust to the changes in prices and money wages.

The money illusion

This is the tendency of people to be fooled by changes in prices or wages when no real change has taken place.

● *Common misunderstanding*

If wages double but prices do as well, some people may still believe that they are better off because they are earning £25 000 a year instead of £12 500. In fact, of course, real wages have remained unchanged.

The effect of the money illusion

Suppose that the government, in an attempt to reduce unemployment, increases the money supply. This has the effect of increasing prices but has no immediate effect upon wages. This, therefore, means that prices have gone up but *real wages* have gone down.

We can illustrate the situation using the analysis which we developed in Chapter 37 (see pages 540–2). In Figure 38.3 real wages are on the vertical axis and the quantity of labour demanded and supplied is on the horizontal axis. The fall in real wages is shown as the shift of the supply curve from SS to S_1S_1. This is to say that people are offering their labour at a lower real wage because they do not appreciate that rising prices have devalued their wages.

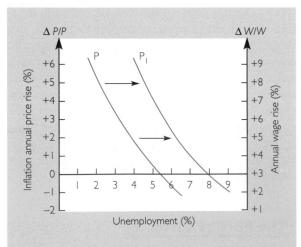

Figure 38.2 The Phillips curve
This shows the relationship between inflation and unemployment. A rate of wage increase of 3 per cent p.a. is consistent with zero inflation if 3 per cent represents the annual rate of increase of productivity.

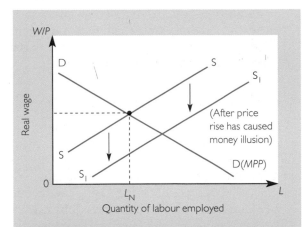

Figure 38.3 The effect of inflation with the money illusion
The real wage is W/P. If prices increase but wages do not, then the real wage declines. We can show this as a shift in the supply curve from SS to S_1S_1, because people are offering their labour at a lower real price not realising that inflation has devalued their wages.

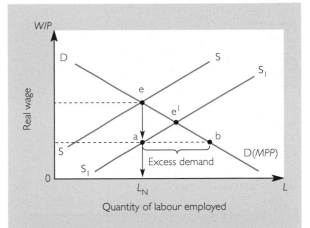

Figure 38.4 The money illusion disappears
Rise in prices shifts supply curve to S_1S_1. This creates an excess demand for labour because people are prepared to work for a lower real wage. Short-run equilibrium is e^1. As people demand higher real wages equilibrium returns to e with the original level of employment of L_N.

In Figure 38.4 we examine the effect which this has upon the employment situation. There is now a situation of excess demand for labour. This is because real wages are lower and businesses therefore find it profitable to employ more people. The excess demand for labour is shown as distance ab in Figure 38.4. This excess demand draws more people into the labour market and also begins to increase money wages. We reach a short-run equilibrium at e^1. Thus a rise in prices has caused the level of employment to rise. This is because the rise in money wages has fooled unemployed people into accepting jobs which they refused before.

You will note in Figure 38.4 that at the new equilibrium the real wage is still lower than the original one. The adaptive expectations school argues that this situation can persist only so long as the money illusion continues. In time expectations adapt and people realise that prices have risen; they therefore demand more wages and, thus, the supply curve of labour returns to its original position. When this happens money wages rise further to restore the level of real wages to what it was before the increase in the money supply.

Equilibrium in the whole economy

We can now have a look at how this affects the whole economy. Instead of equilibrium in the labour market(s) we look at aggregate demand and supply in the whole economy. In Figure 38.5 we see aggregate demand being increased from AD to AD_1. This is as a result of deliberate government policy to reduce the level of unemployment. In the short run the equilibrium changes to e^1 as people accept lower real wages. However, as they adapt to the inflationary situation and demand higher real wages we move to equilibrium at e^2. Thus, in the long run, we have higher prices but only the same amount of employment. It is argued that this is because there is a **natural level of unemployment** for the economy and any attempts to reduce unemployment below this level end in inflation rather than more employment.

STUDENT ACTIVITY 38.2

Adopting the same sort of reasoning as above, what would be the short-run and long-run effects of a fall in aggregate demand?

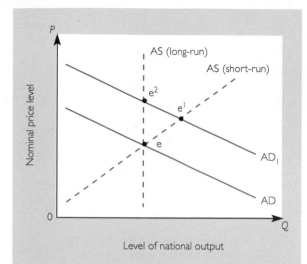

Figure 38.5 Equilibrium in the whole economy
Government policy increases aggregate demand from
AD to AD_1. This creates a short-run equilibrium of e^1 at
a high level of output and employment. As people adapt
to the new level or prices and demand higher wages,
the long-run equilibrium becomes e^2 – i.e. the same
level of output and employment but a higher level of
prices. Thus the short-run aggregate supply curve
appears to slope but in the long-run is vertical.

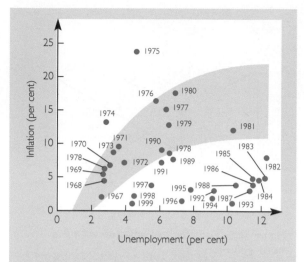

**Figure 38.6 Inflation and unemployment in
the UK**
This shows the relationship between inflation and
employment for the years 1967–99. This presents rather
poor evidence for the Phillips curve. The shaded area is
possible evidence that unemployment and inflation are
positively correlated, although various points on the
scattergraph are excluded from it

The expectations-augmented Phillips curve

Friedman has suggested that there is a vertical
long-run Phillips curve (you can see in
Figure 38.6 that the years 1967–75 give reasonable support to this view). The different results
are caused by short-run Phillips curves crossing
the long-run curve. This possibility is illustrated
in Figure 38.7. The solid vertical line is situated
at the 'natural level of unemployment'.

It is argued that at the natural rate inflation is
zero. This being the case, workers expect the
future inflation rate also to be zero. However, if
the government considers that OU unemployment is too much it may try to trade off
unemployment against inflation along the Phillips
curve P_0, to reach point V, where there is 4 per
cent inflation. Employers and unions are willing
to settle for this situation because they are under
the mistaken belief that their real incomes have
risen. But when 4 per cent inflation comes to be
anticipated we shift to a new Phillips curve P_4. To
maintain unemployment at a reduced level of OZ

and to meet expectations of higher real incomes it
is necessary to increase aggregate demand by
increasing the money supply. Thus the Phillips
curve is shifted outwards again to P_8 which is
consistent with the level of inflation of 8 per cent
at the natural level of unemployment.

This rightward shift of the Phillips curve due to
increased expectations produces the expectations-
augmented Phillips curve.

In order to get rid of this type of inflation
Friedman argued that a period of unemployment
above the natural rate is necessary.

The explanation is as follows. Suppose we are
at point V and the government refuses to expand
the money supply. Inflation has now been stabilised at 4 per cent. However, employers now
realise that they have ZU more workers than they
need; thus they move to point W, at the natural
rate of unemployment but at 4 per cent inflation.
In order to return to zero inflation it is necessary
to move to point X, which is a level of unemployment well above the natural rate. This will rid
people of their expectations of inflation and the
economy can gradually move back to point U.

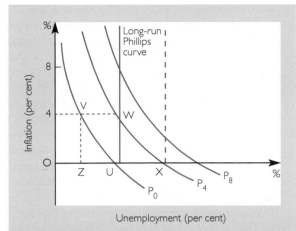

Figure 38.7 The effect of expectations upon the Phillips curve

The natural rate of unemployment is OU. P_0, P_4 and P_8 represents short-run Phillips curves based upon various expectations of inflation. If government decreases unemployment to OZ this causes 4 per cent inflation (point V). If inflation stabilises at 4 per cent employers reduce employment back to point W. However, getting rid of inflation altogether now involves increasing unemployment to OX because the economy has shifted to the expectations-augmented Phillips curve P_4. The blue dashed vertical line at OX represents an increase in the natural level of unemployment.

The rational expectations (neo-classical) school

According to this school of thought people are not fooled by changes in the price level. If there is an expansion of the money supply people correctly anticipate the effect on inflation and money wages adjust to keep the real wage the same, i.e. there is no money illusion.

In Figure 38.8(a) the labour market remains in equilibrium because wages adjust in line with inflation. Thus although prices and wages have risen the level of employment has remained at L_N. In Figure 38.8(b) we see the effect upon the whole economy. Here attempts to increase the level of employment lead the government to increase aggregate demand from AD to AD_1 but because there is no change in aggregate supply (because people are working the same amount that they did before) the aggregate supply curve AS is vertical and, therefore, the only result is

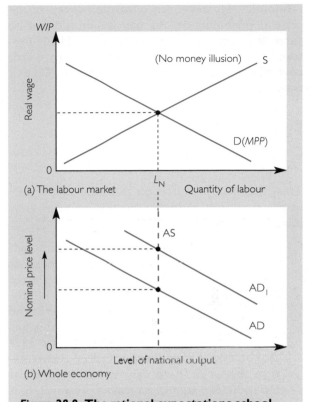

Figure 38.8 The rational expectations school

The labour market remains in equilibrium because wages adjust in line with inflation. In (b) we see that attempts to increase employment by increasing aggregate demand from AD to AD_1 only result in inflation. (See also page 543.)

inflation. Thus, both the adaptive expectations and the rational expectations schools agree that there is no long-run trade-off between inflation and unemployment.

For those who like logical puzzles the rational expectations school presents a nice example of circular logic. For the theory to work people must be able correctly to predict the effect of increases in the money stock upon inflation. This is possible only if the rational expectations model is correct. Thus the model can be correct only if it is correct and is believed to be correct!

The causes of inflation

With the causes of inflation we have reached one of the key areas of disagreement in modern economics. However, since inflation is one of the central problems of our day we should not be surprised that conflicting views are held. At present three explanations are put forward: *cost-push*; *demand-pull*; and *monetary*. We will now consider these.

Cost-push inflation

Cost-push inflation occurs when the increasing costs of production push up the general level of prices.

This, therefore, is inflation from the supply side of the economy. Evidence for this point of view includes the following.

(a) *Wage costs*. It is a widely held view (although perhaps rather less so than it used to be) that powerful trade unions have pushed up wage costs without corresponding increases in productivity. Since wages are usually one of the most important costs of production, this has an important effect upon prices. Figure 38.9 demonstrates that there is indeed a correlation between earnings and the level of inflation. We should remember, however, that correlation does not imply causation. The precise nature of the connection between wages and prices remains unclear.

(b) *Import prices*. Whatever one's view of inflation, it must be admitted that import costs play some part in it. The huge rise in commodity prices, especially oil, in the 1970s undoubtedly contributed to inflation. It should also be remembered that inflation is a worldwide phenomenon and it is not possible for a nation to cut itself off completely from rising prices in the rest of the world. A fall in the value of the pound relative to other currencies, such as occurred when the UK left the Exchange Rate Mechanism in 1992, makes imports more expensive and can fuel inflation.

(c) *Mark-up pricing and profits*. Many large firms fix their prices on a unit cost plus profit basis (see page 293). This makes prices more sensitive to supply than to demand influences and can mean that they tend to go up automatically with rising costs, whatever the state of the economy. In fact, some firms may use their monopoly power to raise prices independently of any other influences, simply to increase profits.

Demand-pull inflation

Demand-pull inflation is when aggregate demand exceeds the value of output (measured in constant prices) at full employment.

The excess demand for goods and services cannot be met in real terms and therefore it is met by rises in the price of goods. Figure 38.10 indicates the idea of the 'inflationary gap'. The aggregate demand line $C + I + G + (X - M)$ crosses the 45° line at point E, which is to the right of the full employment line. Thus at full employment there is excess demand of AB. It is this excess demand which *pulls up* prices.

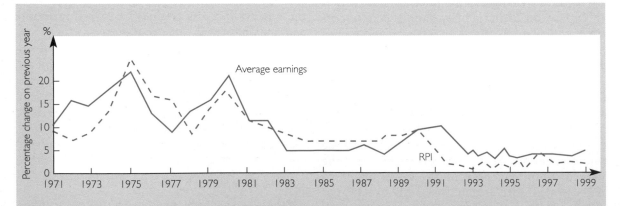

Figure 38.9 Earnings and inflation in the UK
The graph shows a reasonable correlation between the increase in weekly earnings (and therefore employers' costs) and prices.

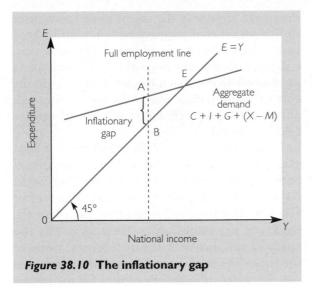

Figure 38.10 The inflationary gap

$$M \times V \equiv P \times T$$

and that this was turned into a theory by assuming that V and T are constant. Thus, we would obtain the formula:

$$M \times V = P \times T$$

We will briefly examine these two assumptions. Figure 38.11 shows the actual value of V for the UK M_0 and M_4 money stocks from 1970 to 1999. The velocity is worked out by dividing GDP by the money stock. Naturally, as M_0 is considerably smaller than M_4, the resultant value of V is much higher. This also emphasises another problem associated with monetarism: what is the correct measure of money stock? As you can see, the measures give quite different rates of change for V, sometimes even moving in opposite directions,

Those who support the demand-pull theory of inflation argue that it was the result of the pursuit of full employment policies after the Second World War. These policies meant that workers felt free to press for increases in wages in excess of productivity without fear of unemployment. In addition to this there was the political demand for high levels of public expenditure which were financed by budget deficits. Both these factors, therefore, put excess demand into the economy.

● *Common misunderstanding*

Ostensibly there would appear to be agreement between Keynesians and monetarists regarding the role of excess demand in inflation. However, in the demand-pull school it is the demand which brings about the expansion in the money supply and inflation, whereas monetarists see the causality reversed, with the release in the money stock occurring first.

Monetary inflation

'Inflation is always and anywhere a monetary phenomenon in the sense that it can *only* be produced by a more rapid increase in the quantity of money than in output' (our italics). Thus wrote Friedman in 1970. This note contains the core of monetary thinking, which is that inflation is *entirely* caused by a too-rapid increase in the money stock and by *nothing else*. We saw in Chapter 37 that the monetarist theory is based upon the identity:

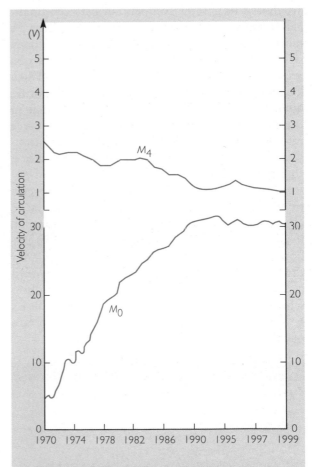

Figure 38.11 Velocity of money aggregates
Source: BEQB

although both measures have shown more stable values of V since the 1990s.

As regards M_4 the slowdown in velocity since 1980 is a feature common to all broad monetary aggregates and contrasts sharply with the behaviour of velocity through much of the 1970s and earlier. Apart from the sharp fall in 1971–3, which was soon reversed, the velocity of broad money had risen through most of the post-war period up to 1979. When, after this date, the velocity slowed down, it was important for the then authorities to establish why this was so. Did it mean that there was not a reliable connection between the growth of the money supply and inflation which the monetarists said there was?

The reasons for the fall of the velocity were varied, but in general terms they were due to a change in savings behaviour. This in turn may be attributed to greater competition between financial intermediaries for depositors, resulting in more attractive ways for investors to keep money with a bank or building society. It may also be attributed to high real interest rates in the 1980s. The stabilisation in velocity after 1990 can be associated with a decline in the pace of change in the financial markets, accompanied by lower rates of both inflation and nominal interest rates.

As you can see from Figure 38.11 there was a steady and continuous rise in the velocity of M_0 until the early 1990s. Bear in mind that a relatively small change in V could cause large changes in money national income; for example, if GDP were £525 billion and M were £150 billion this would give us the value $V = 3.5$. Under these circumstances a rise in V to 3.6 would cause an increase in money GDP by £15 billion whilst an increase to 4.0 would increase GDP by £75 billion. *Ceteris paribus*, this is equal to a rate of inflation of over 14 per cent.

STUDENT ACTIVITY 38.3

If GDP equals £400 billion and M is £100 billion, calculate V. What would be the effect on GDP if V then increased to 4.5?

The fall in velocity of M_0 after 1991 has been the result of a fall in the growth of credit and debit cards; the growth in the use of these cards prior to this meant that people had less need to hold cash, which thus circulated faster. The other contributory factor has been the fall in inflation mentioned above which has led to a drop in the cost of holding cash and increased its demand, allowing the relatively larger amount of cash to circulate slower.

Thus, as you can see, the idea that V is constant, or even stable, is dubious. Important criticisms of Friedman's views were raised in the *Bank of England Quarterly Bulletin* in December 1983 by **Hendry** and **Ericsson**. In the event the Bank did not publish the article as it was too much at variance with the authorities' views at the time. The most devastating claim made was that Friedman adjusted the figures for the money supply and the price levels to produce a constant V. Without a constant V there will be no predictable relationship between money, national income and prices.

The second assumption of monetarism is that T is constant. Put another way, it is the belief that the economy will tend towards a full employment equilibrium. This being the case, any increase in M can result only in price changes and not real changes in national income. Unemployment is caused by a temporary lack of adjustment in the economy when there is confusion between real national income and money national income – the *money illusion*. The unemployment experienced throughout the 1980s and 1990s is perhaps stretching the word 'temporary' to its limits.

Figure 38.12 shows the relationship between sterling M_3, M_2, M_0 and inflation. It is Friedman's contention that an increase in the money stock will cause a rise in inflation 18 months to two years later. As you can see the graph shows conflicting evidence. There does seem to be a close correlation between M_0 and the RPI during the 1980s. The period considered in the graph is probably too brief for a fair appraisal of Friedman's proposition. He obtained very good results for a whole century in the USA. However, even if there is a good fit it does not prove that one thing *causes* the other. Also, we have just seen above that the empirical basis of Friedman's research has been subject to criticism.

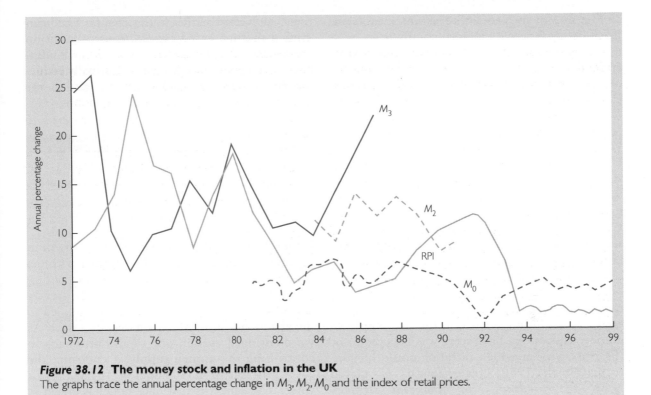

Figure 38.12 The money stock and inflation in the UK
The graphs trace the annual percentage change in M_3, M_2, M_0 and the index of retail prices.

Multicausal inflation

Having worked through the chapter the student might now legitimately ask, 'What does cause inflation then?' The answer is probably that inflation has a number of causes – increases in the money supply, excessive wage demands, excess demand and so on. It is also probably true that what may be the chief cause of inflation in one year may not be in the next. At this stage we need more research to separate out the different strands of inflation.

If inflation does have many causes, an important conclusion stems from this and that is that a variety of policy measures will be needed to deal with it. Thus a policy which places its trust entirely upon monetary control or entirely upon wage restraint is unlikely to be successful.

The control of inflation

As was noted in Chapter 18 governments have different areas of policy which they can use to regulate the economy. We will now look at these as they affect inflation.

Fiscal policy

Fiscal policy is based upon demand management, i.e. raising or lowering the level of aggregate demand. In Figure 38.10 you can see that the government could attempt to act upon any of the components in the $C + I + G + (X - M)$ line. The most obvious policy is that the government should reduce government expenditure and raise taxes. It should be stated here that this policy will be successful only against demand inflation. Fiscal policy was the chief counter-inflationary measure in the 1950s and 1960s. One of the reasons for its failure then was the clash of objectives. Governments were usually prone to put full employment higher on their list of priorities than control of inflation. Thus, after a short period of fiscal stringency, unemployment was likely to mount and this repeatedly caused governments to abandon tight fiscal policy and go over to expansion of the economy before inflation had been controlled.

The rise of monetarist ideas has meant that fiscal policy is seen as important only in so far as it affects the money supply. Thus in recent years emphasis has been placed upon reducing the size of the PSNCR (PSBR). This was discussed in Chapter 36.

Monetary policy

For many years monetary policy was seen as only supplementary to fiscal policy. The Radcliffe Report's conclusion, that 'money is not important', was widened into 'money does not matter'. Clearly this was an overstatement and we can see, for example, that the rapid expansion of the money supply in the 1970s was undoubtedly one of the causes of inflation.

If monetary policy had a role, Keynesians saw it as being through the rate of interest. The monetarist prescription is to control the supply of money. This, as we have seen, was believed to be the only way in which inflation could be controlled. In the 1980s great emphasis was placed upon the ***medium-term financial strategy*** (MTFS), i.e. setting targets for monetary growth for the next few years. Not only would reducing the supply of money in itself reduce inflation but the setting of *firm* targets would reduce expecta-

tions. As we saw earlier in this chapter Friedman argued that increased ***expectations*** of inflation are a reason for the rightward shift of the Phillips curve. The policy was aimed at gradually reducing the growth of the money supply until it was in line with the growth of the real economy.

Figure 38.13 shows the targets set for growth in the money supply in the 1980s, together with the actual growth of M_3. You can see from the diagram that MTFS targets were generally greatly exceeded and it was this which, in the end, led to the abandonment of M_3 as a monetary target. As we mentioned earlier, one of the problems in controlling the money supply is choosing the correct measure of it. Should it be M_1, M_2, M_3 or what? The danger is that once policy is aimed at controlling one of these variables it may tend to distort it. A Bank of England official, **Charles Goodhart**, formulated a principle based upon this difficulty.

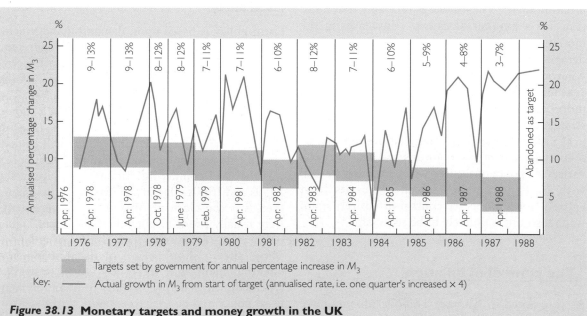

Figure 38.13 Monetary targets and money growth in the UK

Goodhart's law states that any statistical regularity will tend to collapse once pressure is placed upon it for control purposes.

In other words a measure such as M_3 is a good guide so long as we do not make its control the object of policy.

At the end of the 1980s the government had fixed on M_0 as the measure to control in its MTFS (see Figure 38.14). M_0 proved to be a stable and predictable measure of the money supply but, as you can see from Figure 38.11, the value of V for M_0 was increasing rapidly at this time. Thus, using the $MV = PT$ formula, it was still possible to have large increases in the nominal level of national income whilst keeping a strict control on M_0.

In the later years of the 1980s inflation dropped to below 5 per cent. However, following a drop in interest rates, inflation then escalated to over 10 per cent but then fell again in 1991 to around 5 per cent. Is it possible that we can attribute this to control of the money supply, whichever measure we take? The work of **Hendry** and **Ericsson** suggests that this is not so. They argue that the excessive growth of money supply such as that of the 1980s can even be restrictive! If this conclusion is correct it would make it virtually impossible for governments to formulate

money supply targets. Their findings also tend to repudiate the idea of the exogeneity of the money supply which is vital to Friedman's arguments (see page 535). Professor Hendry concluded: 'We have not been able to find any evidence that money supply creates either income growth or inflation.' If this were the case then the decrease in the rate of inflation must be due to some other factor, perhaps unemployment moderating wage demands. The government itself was disinclined to accept such a neo-Keynesian conclusion. Despite disillusionment with monetary targets it remained convinced of the primacy of monetary policy. Speaking in 1988 Nigel Lawson said:

> Experience in the '80s has demonstrated that . . . monetary policy is the only weapon for bearing down on inflation. The abolition of various controls within the financial system, which has brought enormous benefits, has made it difficult to rely solely on monetary targets.
>
> At the same time, the ending of controls inevitably places more weight on short-term interest rates as the essential weapon of monetary policy. Short-term interest rates are the market route to the defeat of inflation.

Thus we can conclude that a Conservative government committed to market forces had, by the end of the early 1990s, largely abandoned monetary targets in its fight against inflation and instead placed its faith in the ability of rising interest rates to control spending and hence inflation.

Following the decision by the government to leave the ERM in 1992, it was able to concentrate more on domestic issues rather than having to worry so much about the value of the pound. Since then, following the general dissatisfaction of employing monetary targets as a means for controlling inflation, the authorities have instead opted for explicit *inflation targets* in order to ensure price stability. Currently, the inflation target is that the RPI should, over the medium term, average 2.5 per cent or less. The advantage of such a policy is its apparent simplicity: a clear commitment is given by the monetary authorities, one that can be fairly easily understood by the public. Such a commitment is backed up by greater openness. The Bank of England now publishes monthly inflation forecasts and, should it miss its target, has to explain why it did so. An independent Bank of England has to account for

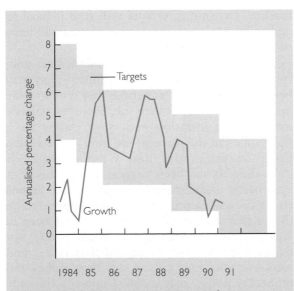

Figure 38.14 **Monetary targets and monetary growth of M_0 in the UK**

itself to the Chancellor of the Exchequer if inflation dips below 1.5 per cent or rises above 3.5 per cent.

On the other hand, such a monetary policy is based on inflation *forecasts* (of up to two years ahead given the time lags in the operation of monetary policy) rather than on inflation itself. If a target is set too tightly or if it is pursued too rigorously (i.e. by raising interest rates more than is necessary), then this could result in higher unemployment and lower growth.

So far the policy has been successful in keeping inflation inside its target range, although this was partly due to the existence of tight monetary conditions before targeting began. It remains to be seen whether the new system, in which the independent Bank of England has overall responsibility for setting interest rates, will continue to keep inflation within the target bands.

Direct intervention: prices and incomes policy

A prices and incomes policy is where the government takes measures to restrict the increase in wages (incomes) and prices.

Like other counter-inflationary measures, a prices and incomes policy tries to ensure that wages and other incomes do not rise faster than the improvement in productivity in the economy. If incomes can be kept below that level there is the added bonus of extra resources which are freed for investment. There are two main types of incomes policy.

(a) *Statutory*. This occurs when the government passes legislation to limit or to freeze wages and prices. Such policies were used in the UK at various times in the 1960s and 1970s, although they have not been formally employed since then.

(b) *Voluntary*. This is where the government tries through argument and persuasion to impose a wages and prices policy. Features of such a policy may include the setting up of a prices and incomes board to examine wage and price increases, exhortations to firms and unions to restrict increases and securing the cooperation of bodies such as the TUC and CBI.

● *Common misunderstanding*

A prices and incomes policy need not be legally enforced by the government; in fact it usually is not. Since 1979 a form of voluntary pay restraint has existed for much of the time in the form of cash limits for the public sector that restrict levels of pay increases.

An incomes policy is thought to be effective as a method of counteracting cost-push inflation caused by increasing wages. The rationale behind the Phillips curve is that it is wage costs which push up prices. Incomes policy could therefore be seen as a way to move the Phillips curve leftwards, achieving lower inflation without causing more unemployment. If inflation results from excess demand an incomes policy is only likely to lead to employers finding disguised ways of paying higher rewards to labour in order to attract people to jobs. Nowadays an incomes policy is more likely to be used in conjunction with other supply side measures, such as reducing the activities of trade unions, deregulation, monopoly legislation, tax incentives and training schemes, in order to attempt to lower the rate of increase in costs in general (see also Chapter 39).

Incomes policies often tend to be more effective in the public sector, thus restricting incomes there more than in the private sector. In addition, if all workers receive similar increases this will tend to distort market forces in the labour market. Expanding sectors will find it hard to attract labour while contracting sectors will hang on to labour for too long.

The UK experience of prices and incomes policies seems to have been that, although they may be successful for a short period, they tend to store up trouble for the future, i.e. incomes policies may restrain inflation and wage claims for a short time but the moment the policy is relaxed a flood of price rises and wage increases is unleashed. It has been suggested that this is at least partly caused because producers and unions see prices and incomes policies as temporary and that if they are permanent, as they have been in Austria and Sweden, this problem would not occur. It could also be argued that prices and incomes policy may fail, as may fiscal policy and monetary policy, if it is relied upon as the only method of controlling inflation, and that what is needed is a combination of policies.

STUDENT ACTIVITY 38.5

What effect do you think incomes polices may have on wage differentials?

Conclusion

We have demonstrated in this chapter that inflation can have a number of causes. The failure adequately to contain inflation except at the cost of other objectives of policy such as full employment may be at least partly attributable to treating inflation as if it were mono-causal, i.e. inflation is entirely caused by excess demand or entirely caused by expansion of the money supply. If inflation has a number of causes it seems likely that we need a 'package' of measures, namely fiscal, monetary and direct, to deal with it.

We must also consider the problem of inflation in the broader sphere. Inflation is a worldwide problem. Whatever measures have been taken domestically, it has been impossible to isolate the domestic economy. This points to the obvious conclusion, that inflation must also be cured on a worldwide basis. Furthermore, we may see the problem of inflation alongside our desire to achieve other objectives of policy such as full employment or economic growth. By the end of the 1980s the problem of inflation seemed to have been at least contained not only in the UK but also in other industrialised nations. However, there were at the same time levels of unemployment which a decade previously would have been considered unthinkable. Despite the current apparent success by the government and the Bank of England in keeping inflation within its target ranges, there still remain fundamental differences of opinion about the causes of inflation.

Summary

1 The costs of inflation are much greater when inflation is imperfectly anticipated than if it is perfectly anticipated.
2 The Phillips curve shows the relationship between inflation and unemployment. Monetarist theory suggests that expectations of inflation shift the Phillips curve rightwards.
3 The adaptive expectations school maintains that, because of the money illusion, there may be a short-term trade-off between inflation and unemployment. But in the long run attempts to reduce unemployment below the natural level result in inflation rather than jobs.
4 The rational expectations school argues that there is no money illusion and hence no trade-off between inflation and unemployment.
5 There are three concurrent explanations of inflation: demand-pull, cost-push and monetary inflation.
6 Fiscal policy has been used to control inflation by regulating aggregate demand. Policy in the 1980s came to regard fiscal policy as important only as a part of monetary policy.
7 The monetarist approach to monetary policy was based upon strict control of monetary aggregates. By the end of the 1980s monetary policy became almost entirely reliant upon control through interest rates. It has remained so despite a move towards inflation targeting.
8 Incomes policies can be either voluntary or statutory.
9 If inflation has a number of causes it is likely that a 'package deal' of various policy measures is necessary to deal with it.

? QUESTIONS

1 Distinguish between cost-push and demand-pull inflation and discuss the policies that may be used to counteract each.
2 Discuss the usefulness of the Phillips curve as a guide to economic policy.
3 To what extent are the consequences of inflation undesirable?
4 What part do expectations play in the determination of the rate of inflation?
5 Explain the monetarist theory of inflation and state its prescription for the cure.
6 Explain what is meant by prices and incomes policies and assess their effectiveness.
7 Distinguish between the adaptive expectations and the rational expectations views of inflation.
8 'Inflation is always and everywhere a monetary phenomenon.' Critically assess Milton Friedman's statement.
9 Examine the relationship between public borrowing and inflation.
10 In what ways may the control of interest rates be used to control inflation?

Study the following data and then answer the questions.

	Increase in M_4%	Inflation rate %	Increase in average earnings %	Growth rate %	Unemployment rate (%)
1988	17.2	4.9	8.8	5.0	8.3
1989	18.2	7.8	9.3	2.2	6.1
1990	17.6	9.5	9.9	0.4	5.4
1991	8.0	5.9	8.0	− 2.2	7.8
1992	4.4	3.7	6.6	− 0.6	9.4
1993	5.7	1.6	4.9	2.0	10.1
1994	4.1	2.5	4.5	4.5	9.2
1995	10.0	3.2	2.9	2.8	8.1
1996	9.5	2.4	3.9	2.6	7.3
1997	5.7	3.1	4.8	3.5	5.5
1998	8.4	3.4	4.5	2.2	4.7
1999	3.9	1.5	5.5	1.8	4.3

1 Outline the main theories of inflation.
2 To what extent, if any, do the above figures support any, or all, of the theories?

Read the following article taken from *The Guardian* of 18 August 1997 and then answer the questions which follow.

1 What does the Phillips curve purport to show?
2 Outline the 'expectations' view of inflation.
3 Explain the significance of the natural rate of unemployment for inflation.
4 Outline the reasons for the possible shifts in the Phillips curve according to the evidence of the last 30 years.

Dedicated followers of fashion

Ian Shepherdson offers an alternative with a notion that is very simple but heretical: exhume the Bill Phillips Curve. In fact, Mr Shepherdson argues, the Phillips Curve never really died – it simply moved position **Richard Thomas**

Economists are unlikely victims of fashion. The closest most get to the catwalk designs of Alexander McQueen is a subtle but daring contrast between the colour of their cords and elbow patches.

But intellectually, for all its seriousness, the profession has developed a butterfly tendency to flit between theoretical fads. Fundamental rules and equations are passé.

Ecomomists are being prodded further in this direction by their common room philosophy colleagues, who espouse postmodernism – a world in which everything is relative, nothing is sacred, and every idea can be dismissed as 'socially constructed' (whatever that means).

Politicians, too are enamoured of an accelerating, unpredictable world where trade is exploding, capital flows like water, workers jump between portfolio jobs and national governments are enfeebled by sweeping worldwide shifts.

Not that economists have given up on theories altogether – there is still too much of the scientist in their hearts – simply on the last one, whatever it happens to be. The half-life of theories is diminishing fast. Just look at monetarism. Economics, in short, has lost its confidence.

The process started in the 1970s when the old models appeared to have broken down and forecasting became a mug's game. The spectacular economic policy mistakes of that decade, and of the 1980s – most notably in the British boom and bust – finally snuffed out any remaining self-esteem.

This is a great shame. Partly because economics is more fun when it tries to provide answers as well as questions, but mostly because the profession may have given up its traditional tools of diligent analysis, correlation and prediction just when they are coming back into their own.

One of the quintessentially Old Economist approaches was the Phillips Curve, which shows a stable, inverse relationship between unemployment and wage inflation. It is learned religiously by every economics student and then put safely into the historical, do-not-touch file.

Bill Phillips himself personified the old approach, which assumed that economies could be tracked, graphed and controlled. His other contribution to intellectual progress was a machine which used water to represent money sluicing round the economy.

He was a practical man – his preparation for economic greatness included stints as a crocodile catcher, cinema manager and rebellious PoW in a Japanese camp. And his curve, unveiled in 1958, took a straightforward approach. Phillips used UK data on pay and unemployment between 1861–1957, and showed a robust predictable relationship between the two variables. Policy-makers had a choice between the two, and could decide where to strike the balance.

Unfortunately, most economies went pear-shaped about a decade after the curve was let loose on the world. Unemployment rose in parallel with inflation, in apparent contradiction of the Phillips hypothesis. A new, ugly word – stagflation – was born.

A new theory, needless to say, had popped up just in time. Milton Friedman, a decade after Phillips' breakthrough, delivered a powerful counter-blast which seemed to undercut fatally the elegant original theory. Friedman said that because workers *knew* that lower unemployment would cause higher inflation, they would build in the expected inflation to their current pay demands – and inflation would take off.

In the Friedman world, wages and prices could only be contained while unemployment remained above a 'natural' rate, later refined as the awkward Non-Accelerating Inflation Rate of Unemployment (Nairu).

The 1970s certainly looked a Nairuish sort of place, so Phillips and his near-century of data, were consigned to an early grave. (He died himself in the mid-1970s.) Now, of course, the Nairu thesis is in trouble, not least in the United States. Unemployment keeps falling: wages have not gone into orbit.

The hunt is now on for another model to explain the economy – is there a 'new economy' based on IT and invisible goods?

There are still some diehard economists trying, like truffle-hunters, to sniff out the 'true' Nairu so that it can be avoided. It isn't working. Every time they claim to have isolated it – say at a 5 per cent jobless rate – unemployment falls below it and still wages fail to lift off.

A paper to be published this week by Ian Shepherdson, chief US economist for HSBC[*] offers an alternative to sticking blindly to the Nairu or dashing off yet again to another theory. His notion is simple but heretical: exhume the Phillips Curve.

In fact, Mr Shepherdson argues, the Phillips Curve never really died – it simply moved position. At the end of the 1960s and early 1970s, the US Federal Reserve significantly loosened monetary policy, even though inflation was rising. From a peak of 9.25 per cent in 1969 the Federal funds rate was cut to 3.75 per cent by the spring of 1971. This took the real cost of borrowing (the Fed funds rate minus inflation) into negative territory for the first time in post-war history.

By cutting rates as prices rose, the Fed signalled to workers and firms that it was prepared to tolerate inflation. Workers therefore asked for more money (as Friedman predicted) while companies figured that they could accomodate the demands by passing the costs on to consumers through higher price tags.

The result was to significantly weaken, and worsen, the unemployment–price trade-off. And so it remained until Paul Volcker came along. The tough new Fed governor performed the opposite trick in 1979–1981, aggressively tightening monetary policy even as inflation eased.

Workers and bosses quickly got the new message, that inflation would not be tolerated, and curbed pay demands.

Mr Shepherdson argues that Mr Volcker – a 'visionary' – managed to re-establish a stable Phillips-style relationship to the economy, albeit at a high price. For the last decade, inflation has been a minor feature in US pay rounds.

So, Mr Shepherdson argues, it was the 1970s that were the abberation: 'the basic association – lower unemployment with greater pressure on earnings – did not disappear into a nightmare Nairu world of ever-accelerating inflation. Instead, the curve simply shifted once, upwards and to the right in the 1970s. It has since moved more or less back to where it was in the 1950s and 1960s.' The policy significance of this is profound. The Nairu school contends that once a certain point is reached inflation will suddenly become unstoppable. One more step and we might all be off the cliff into the inflationary abyss. By contrast, a Phillips world means we are on a clearly-marked slope, and that *we* control the descent.

This does not mean that unemployment can simply keep on falling. Indeed the curve gets steeper as the dole queue shrinks: HSBC estimates that while a 0.5 percentage point rise in the US unemployment rate would knock 0.5 percentage points off wage growth, a 0.5 percentage point *fall* in unemployment would add closer to 0.7 percentage points to wage growth.

But it does mean there is no need to panic. Policy-makers are in control, and have models to guide them. The US economy is not about to spiral out of control.

It is not clear whether the Phillips-curvy world extends beyond the US borders but, given the convergence of many labour and product markets towards American lines it seems likely that, if it doesn't yet, it will.

And on top of the greater leverage this implies for policy-makers, it should give economists pause for thought too. In their rush to be the next to produce a new theory, the boffins shouldn't forget there are some sharp tools available already, including Bill's curve. If economics is to thrive, it must tend to its roots.

[*]'Why wage inflation will stay low', HSBC Markets, 140 Broadway, New York, NY 10055.

Source: The Guardian, 18 August 1997

39 Unemployment and government policy

Learning outcomes

At the end of this chapter you will be able to:
- ▶ Understand the meanings of the terms employment and unemployment.
- ▶ Distinguish between the main methods of measuring unemployment.
- ▶ Appreciate the main costs of unemployment.
- ▶ Describe the relationship between job vacancies and unemployment.
- ▶ Distinguish between unemployment when the economy is in equilibrium and disequilibrium.
- ▶ Discuss the main reasons for regional policy and assess the efficacy of regional policy.
- ▶ Account for the rise of large-scale unemployment in the 1980s and 1990s.
- ▶ Explain the supply siders' view of the control of unemployment.
- ▶ Identify the key features of a flexible labour market.
- ▶ Explain the neo-Keynesian policy prescriptions for the control of unemployment.

Employment and unemployment

In many ways the control of unemployment is at the core of modern macroeconomics; it was the concern with unemployment which gave rise to the new economics of Keynes and his contemporaries during the 1930s. The pursuit of *full employment* (i.e. where all those who wish to work at the current wage are able to do so) as the prime objective of policy was specifically adopted by Western governments at the end of the Second World War and they adopted Keynesian demand management policies as the means of achieving it.

Compared with all previous eras this policy was successful, unemployment remaining at very low levels throughout the 1950s and 1960s, so much so that other objectives of policy such as the control of inflation came to be regarded as more important. Many people thought that mass unemployment was a problem which had been banished for ever. However, by the early 1980s the UK had a greater number of people unemployed than in the 1930s and the control of unemployment was once more at the centre of the stage.

Obviously not everyone in the economy works; the young, the old, some housewives, students, the sick and disabled, etc., may not be in employment.

Thus when we speak of employment we are speaking of those who are in some form of paid work and when we say the unemployed we are speaking of those who are actively seeking jobs.

As we saw in Chapter 26, the *working population* comprises all those who are working or who are seeking work. The *unemployment rate* is the number of unemployed expressed as a percentage of the working population. In early 2000 the working population in the UK was just over 29.5 million and of those 5.7 per cent (about 1 715 000 people according to the ILO definition, see below) were registered as unemployed and seeking work; the number of unemployed people has been falling quite sharply since late 1993, although a significant proportion of the growth of employment has been in part-time jobs, especially among women. The post-war high in unemployment was hit in December 1986, with a total of 3.4 million registered without a job.

● *Common misunderstanding*

The unemployed, although not actually officially working, are said to be economically active because they are actively seeking work. The employed and the unemployed are economically active, whereas other groups, such as the young, the old, housewives, students, the sick and disabled, etc., are defined as economically inactive.

STUDENT ACTIVITY 39.1

If the working population comprised 25 million people and of these 2.2 million were registered as unemployed, what is the unemployment rate?

There are two main methods of measuring unemployment: the first, which formed the basis of the UK's official statistics from 1982–1998, is based on the *claimant count*, i.e. those people receiving unemployment-related benefits. These figures were published monthly. However, they may have been slightly deceptive in that the figure for unemployment includes only those who have to register as available for work at employment offices. Many people such as married women lose their jobs but do not register as unemployed. In addition to this the government excluded certain categories of unemployed from the figures; for

example, those over 55 were not required to register as available for work, even though they were still able to draw unemployment benefit.

The history of unemployment since 1979 has become hard to follow because of the frequent changes in the way the statistics are compiled: there have been a total of 32 changes (see Table 39.1). Each change may have been defensible on the grounds of greater accuracy or practicality, yet all the changes until 1998, except one minor one, had the effect of reducing published unemployment totals! The inclusion of HM Forces and the self-employed in the size of the working population knocked 1.4 per cent off subsequent figures for unemployment.

The second method of measuring unemployment is by conducting *surveys* of the unemployed. In the UK the Labour Force Survey (LFS), based on the International Labour Office (ILO) definition of unemployment, is undertaken quarterly; people are defined as unemployed if they are without a job, available for work and have been actively seeking employment or are waiting to start a job. This definition of unemployment gives a higher figure than the claimant count by including people looking for work but not entitled to benefits (e.g. married women); on the other hand, it yields a lower figure by excluding those people claiming benefits but not

Table 39.1 **Major changes in the unemployment statistics**

Date	Change	Effect
October 79	Fortnightly payment of benefits	+20 000
November 81	Men over 60 offered higher supplementary benefit to leave working population	−37 000
October 82	Registration at Job Centres made voluntary. Computer count of benefit claimants substituted for clerical count of registrants	−190 000
March 83	Men aged 60 and over given national insurance credits or higher supplementary benefit without claiming unemployment benefit	−162 000
July 85	Correction of Northern Ireland discrepancies	−5 000
March 86	Two-week delay in compilation of figures to reduce overrecording	−50 000
July 86	Inclusion of self-employed and HM Forces in denominator of unemployed percentage	−1.4%
September 86	Nobody under 18 allowed to register as all 16 and 17 year olds guaranteed a Youth Training Scheme (YTS) place	−50 000
October 96	Introduction of Jobseeker's Allowance (JSA) replacing unemployment-related benefits; new allowance for six months only	−200 000
April 98	Move to ILO count of unemployment as main measure	+400 000
April 01	Revision of employment figures	−750 000

actively seeking work. It is usually reckoned that the 'tougher' the benefit regulations (i.e. the lower the *replacement ratio* or the rate of unemployment benefit relative to average earnings and/or the briefer the time period during which benefit can be claimed), then the lower the claimant count will be relative to the ILO measure. In April 1998 the Labour government in the UK switched from using the claimant count to the ILO definition as the main measure of unemployment. It was estimated that this move, at a stroke, added 400 000 to the unemployment figures.

Figure 39.1 compares the two measures over time for the UK. The broad trends in the two statistics are similar, although the ILO measure fluctuates less. Since the ILO is an international organisation it (and the Organisation for Economic Co-operation and Development, the OECD, which also uses survey data) is able to make international comparisons of unemployment rates using similar, or *standardised*, definitions. Some of these are shown in Table 39.2.

Unemployment rates were high in most countries in the 1980s, a legacy of the oil price hikes in the 1970s combined with the pursuit of deflationary policies to combat inflation. The rise in unemployment in the UK in the early 1980s was particularly steep. Unemployment rates rose again in the early 1990s owing to a worldwide and severe recession. Unemployment has traditionally tended to be much lower in Japan than elsewhere, the result of its policy of 'lifetime employment' in its largest companies, although the problems of the Japanese economy during the last decade has led to a rise in its level of unemployment. The success of the USA and to a lesser

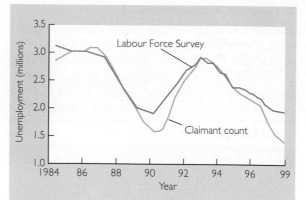

Figure 39.1 Claimant count and Labour Force Survey (ILO) measures of unemployment for the UK
The broad trends in the two measures are similar, although the Labour Force Survey shows less fluctuations.
Source: Adapted from *Labour Market Trends*, National Statistics.
© Crown Copyright 2001

extent the UK in reducing unemployment in recent years has been noticeable, yet controversial. Supporters of supply side economics claim that it is a result of tax cutting and other supply side measures, leading to a more 'flexible' labour market. Against this it is argued that many of the new jobs created have been either part time or temporary appointments, mainly among women; as a result, there is greater anxiety about job insecurity. However, there has also been a rise in male full-time employment in the UK since 1996.

A feature of the high levels of unemployment since the early 1980s in many countries has been the rise in the relative significance of *long-term unemployment*, although this has been more true

Table 39.2 Percentage rates of unemployment in the leading OECD countries

Country	1975	1985	1990	1992	1994	1996	1998
UK	4.3	11.2	6.9	10.1	9.5	7.9	6.3
USA	8.3	7.1	5.4	7.3	6.0	5.5	4.5
Japan	1.9	2.6	2.1	2.2	2.9	3.3	4.1
Germany*	3.6	7.1	4.8	4.6	8.4	10.3	9.4
France	4.0	10.2	8.9	10.4	12.3	12.1	11.7
Italy	5.8	9.6	10.3	10.5	11.1	11.4	12.2
Canada	6.9	10.5	8.1	11.3	10.3	9.2	8.3

*Until end 1990 West Germany, from then all Germany.
Source: OECD *Economic Outlook*, June 1999. Copyright © OECD

of events in the EU than in, say, the USA. It has been estimated that in the mid-1990s over 40 per cent of the unemployed within the EU had been jobless for more than a year, while the equivalent figure for the USA was only about 10 per cent. The reason for this may be the 'open-ended' nature of unemployment benefit payments in many European countries.

The costs of unemployment

There are many costs of unemployment and all sections of society are affected, but naturally the prime costs fall on the *unemployed themselves and their families*. These comprise not just the net drop in income (lost earnings minus unemployment benefit), but also the loss of self-esteem from not working and the resulting stresses that are placed upon family relationships. Many studies have reported a close association between unemployment and ill-health. The longer the extent of the unemployment, the greater the problems become; workers are increasingly distanced from the job market as skill-needs change and so they find it more and more difficult to find a job. Some short-term unemployment as people change jobs may be indicative of a dynamic economy and a flexible workforce. In general, however, unemployment can produce widespread costs for the *economy as a whole*. If some people are not working they are not producing anything (although some may be working in the 'hidden' economy'); hence, total output is less than it otherwise would be. In addition, there is the loss in tax revenue to the government to consider: the unemployed pay no income tax or national insurance contributions and also pay less in VAT and excise duties because they have less money to spend. Finally, there are the possible social costs of unemployment: there is some evidence that joblessness, particularly amongst the young, leads to increased crime, violence and alienation from society at large.

STUDENT ACTIVITY 39.2

Should unemployment benefits be considered a cost of unemployment for society at large?

Vacancies and unemployment

Figure 39.2 shows the trend in job vacancies in the UK from 1980 to 1999. It should come as no great surprise that, comparing this figure with Figure 39.1, some kind of inverse relationship can be seen, i.e. the level of vacancies tends to be higher when unemployment is lower and vice versa. When the economy emerges from recession and the demand for goods and services increases, then there is a tendency for the number of job vacancies to rise and the level of unemployment to fall; on the other hand, as demand falls vacancies decline and unemployment rises.

However, this relationship is not nearly as stable as it once was. In the last 30 years or so there has been a steady rise in the number of people unemployed at any particular level of vacancies; the unemployment rate today is three to four times higher than in 1971, but the number of vacancies is about the same. Furthermore, those people who are unemployed may not possess the right skills for the vacancies that are available; a newly redundant coal miner is not likely to be able to take a job as a computer programmer.

People often receive a financial payoff if made redundant and so can spend some time searching for a new job. Employers also engage in search

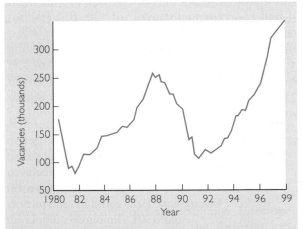

Figure 39.2 The level of vacancies in the UK
The graph shows the level of job vacancies in the UK for 1980 to 1999.
Source: Barclays Economic Review Third Quarter, 1997 and adapted from *Monthly Digest of Statistics,* Office for National Statistics

activities: looking for the right workers to fill vacant positions. Of course, information is not perfect about what jobs or workers are available; people may have to search for some time before finding the right job, just as employers may have to search for the right workers to take up vacancies. However, once people become unemployed for a long period they tend to lose not just the requisite skills for the workplace but also the heart to continue searching for a job. The main reason for the coexistence of both high unemployment and vacancies in the UK has been the growth in relative importance of long-term unemployment.

Types of unemployment

Unemployment is not a uniform phenomenon, it exists for a number of reasons. When we list those reasons we are therefore considering the *causes of unemployment*. A distinction can be made between unemployment when the economy is in *equilibrium* (i.e. when the aggregate or total demand for labour in the economy equals the aggregate or total supply of labour in the economy) and unemployment when the economy is in *disequilibrium* (i.e. when the wage rate is above the equilibrium level). Thus, in Figure 39.3, which shows the aggregate demand for and supply of labour curves, the equilibrium level of employment for the economy as a whole is OM at a wage rate of OW.

Disequilibrium unemployment

The main reasons for disequilibrium unemployment are as follows:

(a) *Classical or real wage unemployment* occurs when the real wage is above the equilibrium level and remains there. This may be because trade unions have secured wages above the market-clearing level or it could be due to minimum wage legislation. In Figure 39.4, for example, if wage levels are established at OW_1, then the demand for labour is OL while the supply of labour is ON; hence, unemployment is represented by the distance LN (see also page 360).

The so-called 'classical' economists pre-

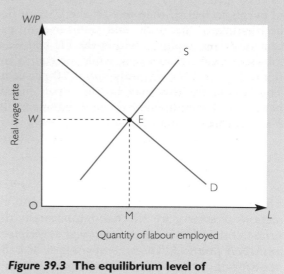

Figure 39.3 The equilibrium level of employment
Equilibrium occurs at point E, giving a level of employment of OM and a wage rate OW.

Keynes argued that the main reason for unemployment was that real wages were too high. In more recent times such arguments have been revived by supply side economists and have become popular within governments in both the UK and the USA.

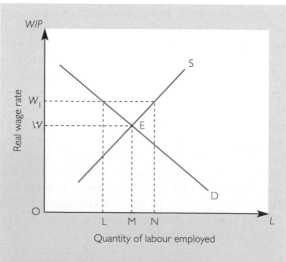

Figure 39.4 Classical or real wage unemployment
If the real wage settles at OW_1, unemployment of LN results.

(b) *Demand-deficient or cyclical unemployment* exists when an economy is in recession and there is a fall in the aggregate demand for goods and services. As a result, firms reduce their levels of output and eventually lay off workers. This is unemployment which we have traditionally associated with the **trade cycle** – hence the term cyclical unemployment (see also Chapter 16). This type of unemployment is also known as **Keynesian unemployment**, since Keynes was the first to postulate that the high unemployment of the 1930s was not associated with too high real wages but with a general decline in demand.

In Figure 39.5 the demand for labour falls from D to D_1 owing to a recession in the economy. Assuming that wages remain at O*W*, the level of employment declines from its original O*M* to O*N*. Demand-deficient unemployment equals N*M*. The downward 'stickiness' in wages may be due to trade unions wishing to protect the interests of their members or because firms are reluctant to lower wages and risk the wrath of their workers.

(c) *An increase in aggregate labour supply* due, say, to an increase in the numbers of women who wish to work. Should there be no corresponding increase in the demand for labour and assuming that wages are sticky downwards, then this can lead to unemployment.

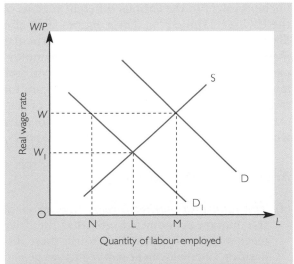

Figure 39.5 **Demand-deficient unemployment**
The demand for labour falls from D to D_1. As a result, demand-deficient unemployment equals N*M*.

Equilibrium unemployment

● *Common misunderstanding*

Unemployment may still occur even though there is equilibrium in the economy as a whole. This is because of a mismatch of labour supply and demand in particular markets or regions rather than at the aggregate level; there may be vacancies for hotel workers in London, while there are unemployed steelworkers in the north of England.

Such equilibrium unemployment is referred to by some economists as **natural unemployment** or **the natural rate of unemployment** because it is consistent with overall equilibrium in the labour market (see Chapter 37).

There are various types of equilibrium unemployment:

(a) *Frictional unemployment* refers to people displaced by the normal working of the economy. It is inevitable in a growing economy that people will, from time to time, change or lose their jobs and may perhaps be unemployed for some weeks as they wait to take up the next job or look for a new job. Since this procedure may take some time it is also referred to as **search unemployment**.

(b) *Seasonal unemployment* occurs because some jobs are dependent upon the weather and the season. Facetiously, we might say that this refers to deckchair attendants being unemployed in the winter or hot-chestnut sales people being unemployed in the summer. However, on a more serious level the construction industry is the most badly hit by seasonal unemployment, with tens or even hundreds of thousands of workers laid off in the winter when the bad weather makes work difficult.

(c) *Structural unemployment* results from a change in the structure of the economy; for example, it could be the result of the imbalance caused by the decline of one industry and (hopefully) the rise of another. Unemployment results when new industries do not create enough jobs to employ those made redundant, or because the new industry is in a different area or requires different skills.

Structural unemployment has plagued the UK economy for most of this century. For most of the period it has been caused by the decline of the *old staple industries* such as coal mining, iron and steel and textiles. These industries tended to be concentrated in the coalfields and thus, because of this heavy regional specialisation, structural unemployment manifested itself as *regional unemployment* (and see below).

In the 1970s and 1980s new forms of structural unemployment came about as previously prosperous industries such as motor vehicles were hit by foreign competition. This made the incidence of unemployment more widespread; the West Midlands, which beforehand was one of the most prosperous areas of the country, became one of the most profoundly depressed. In the early 1990s unemployment even hit the service industries in the previously prosperous south-east region.

(d) *Technological unemployment*, which occurs when improvements in technology reduce the demand for labour, is often regarded as a form of structural unemployment. There is nothing new about technological unemployment; the spinning jenny, for instance, allowed one person to do the work previously done by 100. What is new at the moment is the speed and breadth of technological change. Microchip technology has affected almost all industries and jobs. It affects unemployment in two ways, first by doing away with jobs and skills and, second, by creating new jobs which many of the unemployed are incapable of doing.

Let us consider the new technology as it affects one industry – banking. We have already seen computerised accounting, electronic transfer of funds, cash dispensers, speaking computers by which customers are able to telephone for statements of their accounts and so on. These changes are now supplemented by on-line banking. All these developments save on labour so that, although banking is one of the UK's fastest growing industries, its total workforce is not increasing; indeed there have been many redundancies. The new technology also produces a division in the workforce, creating a new managerial class of those able to comprehend and to control the technology on the one hand and, on the other, a class of semi-skilled people whose job

is to feed the machines. Whole areas of intermediate skills such as book-keeping are being swept away. This pattern is being repeated throughout whole sectors of UK industry and the potential for development seems to be showing no signs of slowing down.

Of course the new technology also creates jobs, both in terms of the manufacturing and the utilisation of computers and computer technology. However, some job prospects have been adversely affected in the UK by microtechnology because we have failed to keep pace with the manufacturing side of the industry (although we are better placed in the manufacture of software). The manufacture of microchips, for example, is effectively dominated by just two countries, the USA and Japan. Thus the UK and many other traditional manufacturing countries such as Germany and France are placed at a disadvantage.

STUDENT ACTIVITY 39.3

Consider the impact of microchip technology on unemployment – and employment – for the economy as a whole.

Regional unemployment

There are considerable differences in the rates of unemployment in the various different regions of the UK (see Table 39.3). These figures may also disguise much worse conditions in particular places. In Corby, for example, adult unemployment was greater than 50 per cent in the mid-1980s. This was not an untypical figure for the worst hit towns at the time. In a time of general unemployment, then, we must first consider whether there is a case for a special regional policy.

Arguments for regional policy

(a) *The failure of market forces*. Advocates of free market economics argue that the price mechanism will eventually abolish these disparities. Unemployment will reduce wage and other costs in the regions and this will eventually attract industry. However, it appears that, over any reasonable period of time,

Table 39.3 Percentage rates of unemployment in the UK

Region	1982	1996	1999
North East	16.5	10.8	9.6
Yorkshire and Humberside	13.4	8.0	6.3
East Midlands	11.0	7.0	5.4
East Anglia	9.9	6.2	4.2
South-east	8.7	5.5	3.9
South-west	10.8	6.3	4.5
West Midlands	14.9	7.5	6.8
North-west	14.7	6.9	6.3
Wales	15.6	8.3	7.3
Scotland	14.2	7.9	7.2
Northern Ireland	19.4	11.1	7.2
UK	12.2	7.6	6.0

Source: CSO *Annual Abstract of Statistics*, HMSO, and *Economic Trends* National Statistics. © Crown Copyright 2001

market forces are as likely to accentuate regional disparities as to remove them.

Neo-classical economists would also argue that the movement of workers should lessen regional differences, i.e. people will move out of the depressed regions thereby reducing the supply in that area and increasing it in other areas. Unfortunately, to the extent to which this is true, it tends to be the young and vigorous workers who move out of the depressed regions. This therefore leaves an older and less adaptable workforce. This may further add to the reluctance of firms to move to the region.

(b) *Cumulative decline.* The depressed areas have tended to have a legacy of labour troubles, a result of the decline of the old staple industries. This problem has diminished in recent years as the power of the unions has dwindled (see Chapter 26), but in the past the history of trade union disputes may have discouraged firms from moving to these areas. In addition to this the social capital of these areas, e.g. housing, transport and communications, tended to be run down. These factors may have further discouraged firms from moving to there. From this point of view there is therefore a need for positive government policy to encourage firms to move to these regions.

(c) *Inflationary pressures.* If national measures are taken to stimulate the economy in order to reduce unemployment it is quite likely that they will have an inflationary effect. Consider the following situation:

Area	Percentage employment of capacity in industry	
	X	Y
A	100	–
B	–	70

Industrial capacity in industry X is fully employed in area A but area B is dependent upon another industry (Y) and in this there is considerable unemployment. If the government tries to cure this by stimulating the general level of demand, it may well cause inflationary pressure in industry X before it cures the unemployment in industry Y.

(d) *Social costs.* A firm in choosing its location is likely to consider only its private costs. Socially, however, it must be considered that there is already enormous pressure upon resources in congested areas. Roads, schools, hospitals and housing are all much more expensive to provide in the prosperous areas, while in the depressed areas of the country there is often spare capacity. It may be worthwhile, therefore, encouraging firms to go to these regions in order that society may benefit from these lower social costs.

Government policy

The main choice which confronts the government is that of taking 'workers to the work' or 'work to the workers'. Methods of taking workers to the work include removal and relocation grants, retraining schemes and Job Centres. Since the Special Areas Act of 1935 the majority of government regional policy has been aimed at taking work to the workers by encouraging firms to locate in the less prosperous regions. Over the course of the 1980s and 1990s governments have reduced the scale of regional aid until it could be said that it was virtually relying on the market forces approach. The details of government regional policy are to be found on pages 146–50.

The efficacy of regional policy

There is little evidence to show that government policy had much success up until 1963. After that date there was a more aggressive regional policy. This policy succeeded for some time in reducing regional disparities but it was overtaken by the large-scale recession in the economy in the early 1980s and then by the government's effective abandonment of regional policy. (See also the comments on the north – south divide below.)

● *Common misunderstanding*

It may appear from Table 39.3 that, comparing unemployment in the regions in 1982 and 1999, the disparities between the regions have diminished. However, this has to be seen against the background of lower rates of unemployment nationally in 1999 than in 1982. While the figure for Wales was 27.8 per cent above the national average in 1982, it was 21.6 per cent above the average in 1999. On the other hand, despite a lower rate of unemployment in the North in 1999 (9.6 per cent) compared with 1982 (16.5 per cent), the 1999 figure was 60 per cent above the national average, while the 1982 figure was 35.2 per cent above the average for the country as a whole.

STUDENT ACTIVITY 39.4

Calculate the deviations from the national average level of unemployment for the other regions in the UK shown in Table 39.3 and comment on the implications for the efficacy of regional policy.

The north–south divide

The debate about whether the discrepancies between different regions have become more pronounced continues unabated (see also Chapter 10). The prosperous areas tend to be in the south of the country and the depressed ones in the north – hence the name. The existence of the north–south divide is vigorously denied by many politicians. However, we observed in Table 39.3 that there are considerable differences in rates of unemployment between the regions. You can also see from Table 39.4 that there are considerable differences in earnings and, if anything, that these have become more pronounced. We have already

Table 39.4 **Average gross weekly household incomes (£) in the UK**

Region	1980–81	1995–98 average
North	136.0	333
Yorkshire and Humberside	130.3	360
East Midlands	141.8	401
East Anglia	143.8	419
South-east	173.3	474
South-west	140.9	405
West Midlands	146.7	381
North-west	148.0	384
Wales	138.6	360
Scotland	144.2	371
Northern Ireland	119.2	336
UK	150.5	408

Source: Regional Trends 1996 and 1999, National Statistics.
© Crown Copyright 2001

mentioned that the decline of the northern regions began with the decline of the old staple industries. In some cases this situation was compounded by the decline of newer industries such as motor vehicles, although in more recent times multinational car firms, notably Japanese, have set up in these areas.

In the 1980s there were rapid improvements in productivity which also caused industries to shed labour. It is certainly true that the depressed areas are attracting new industry but they may not be doing it fast enough to offset the other trends. These trends tend to exacerbate, and be exacerbated by, other factors such as house prices which are much higher in the south than in the north. This in turn makes it more difficult for the people in the north to move south in search of work. This is not just a UK trend. Prosperity in the EU has tended to be concentrated in the 'golden triangle' which takes in northern Germany and France, the Benelux countries and the south-east of England.

The unemployment of the 1980s and 1990s

A study of Table 39.5 reveals that unemployment in the 1980s reached unprecedented levels. (Note that the unemployment percentages differ slightly from those for the UK shown in Table 39.2 because the figures in Table 39.5 are based on the claimant count.) Levels declined at the end of the

Table 39.5 **Unemployment and employment in the UK**

Year	Total unemployed (thousand)	Percentage unemployed (%)	Employed labour force (thousand)
1979	1234	5.3	25 393
1980	1513	6.8	25 327
1981	2394	10.5	24 344
1982	2770	11.6	23 908
1983	2984	11.7	23 610
1984	3030	11.7	24 060
1985	3179	11.9	24 445
1986	3229	11.9	24 542
1987	2953	10.6	25 142
1988	2370	8.4	26 413
1989	1798	6.3	26 725
1990	1664	5.9	26 800
1991	2241	7.8	26 305
1992	2678	9.4	25 775
1993	2865	10.1	25 391
1994	2586	9.2	25 400
1995	2255	8.1	25 741
1996	2104	7.5	25 865
1997	1602	5.5	27 305
1998	1362	4.7	27 625
1999	1263	4.3	27 899

Sources: CSO *Annual Abstract of Statistics* and *Economic Trends,* August 2000, National Statistics. © Crown Copyright 2001

1980s, only for them to rise again in the early 1990s, since when unemployment has fallen quite sharply once again.

The table also shows the figures for all those working. By comparing the unemployed and the employed figures between 1979 and 1988 you can see that although unemployment rose by 1 136 000, the employed total rose by 1 020 000. We were apparently faced with the curious paradox of employment and unemployment growing simultaneously.

● *Common misunderstanding*

It need not be the case that an increase in unemployment is always accompanied by a decrease in those employed. The growth in employment during the 1980s was caused by the growth of the relative size of the working population and was due to such factors as the changing age distribution of the population and the increased proportion of women working, often in part-time positions. Much of the increase in unemployment at the time comprised men in full-time jobs.

The rise of large-scale unemployment

We must now turn to consider the reasons for this rise in general unemployment that occurred in the 1980s and 1990s. No single explanation is satisfactory but the following factors are significant.

(a) *Deficiency of aggregate demand.* The Keynesian explanation of unemployment attributes it to lack of aggregate demand. While it must be true that unemployment is due to lack of demand, this begs the questions of what causes the depression of demand and also whether deficit financing to raise the level of aggregate demand would alleviate it.

(b) *Increase in structural and frictional unemployment.* Commentators have pointed to several factors in labour markets which have increased unemployment. In the early 1970s the rise in the **replacement ratio** (social security benefits relative to average wages) made unemployment more tolerable for some. The increase in unemployment has also made firms less willing to retrain employees or take on older ones, while employment protection legislation and redundancy payments may have made them more cautious about taking on labour.

We have already mentioned the decline in some UK industries which has increased unemployment. This was particularly noticeable in the manufacturing sector in the 1970s and early 1980s. The unemployment caused by these structural changes has been made worse by the difficulty that many people have when attempting to move to the south-east in search of jobs because of high housing prices.

(c) *International aspects.* Unemployment in the UK cannot be considered in isolation. Rates of unemployment have also been significantly higher in most of the UK's trading partners. This therefore contributed to the general depression of demand. Another international aspect is the import penetration of the UK's manufacturing industries such as iron and steel, motor vehicles and electronics. Exports on the other hand have often been hindered by a too-high exchange rate for the pound. This caused producers to cut prices, even though real wages were rising at the same time, so that profits were often squeezed to the point where firms closed down.

(d) *Oil prices.* The OPEC price rise in 1973 played a significant part in the rise in inflation and unemployment in the mid-1970s. The 1978 oil price rises had even more dramatic effects, increasing costs dramatically and thus squeezing profits still further. The 1978 oil price rise was a major factor in precipitating the worldwide recession of the early 1980s. The subsequent collapse in oil prices helped some of the UK's main trading rivals such as Japan and Germany who are major oil importers but further damaged the UK, which is an oil exporter.

(e) *Technology.* We have already seen that improvements in technology have reduced the demand for labour (see also the discussion on page 572). However, we may hope that in the long run improvements in technology and the resultant increases in productivity will create jobs by leading to an expansion of the economy.

(f) *Government policy.* Until the mid-1970s government policy was aimed at reducing unemployment by expansionary fiscal and monetary policies. However, at this time governments began to adopt contractionary policies, with the aim of squeezing inflation out of the economy. These policies therefore contributed to unemployment. Further, we saw in Chapter 38 that monetary thinking points to the necessity of raising unemployment as a method of eliminating inflation. The then Chancellor of the Exchequer, Norman Lamont, said in the Commons in 1991 that he was 'happy to pay the price of higher unemployment if it cures inflation'. Government policies must therefore be seen as a major factor in the rise of unemployment.

Changes in measurement and population

We discussed earlier in the chapter the many changes in measurement during the 1980s which made it difficult to say precisely what was happening to unemployment. Estimates by Christopher Johnson of Lloyds Bank suggest that unemployment was reduced by at least 400 000 by statistical redefinitions and that special employment measures such as YTS accounted for a further 400 000.

It is also the case that many of the new jobs created have been part-time jobs; this was especially so in the 1980s and early 1990s. Furthermore, some of these part-time jobs were in fact second jobs for those already employed. There was a growing tendency for newly created jobs to go to women. This could be, at least in part, because the jobs were part-time and/or low paid. In fact, while there were 2 548 000 less men employed in 1994 than in 1979 there were, in fact, 903 000 more women employed. Since the mid-1990s both male and female employment has risen as economic prospects have improved.

Because of demographic changes the population of working age was rising by about half a per cent a year, i.e. a figure of about 1.7 million, for the period 1979–91. It then declined slightly before increasing once again in the late 1990s. The unemployment figures have also been distorted by changes in the activity or participation rate, i.e. the percentage of those of working age who are working or seeking work. In the early 1980s the activity rate dropped to below 73 per cent but rose to reach nearly 77 per cent in 1990. It declined again in the early 1990s before rising to reach nearly 79 per cent in 2000. The falls in the activity rate made the unemployment figures worse. On the other hand, the official policy of discouraging benefit claims kept the activity rate below that which it would otherwise have been.

STUDENT ACTIVITY 39.5

During the 1980s the population of working age increased, as did the activity rate. What do you think were the implications of these trends for (a) unemployment, and (b) employment?

Hysteresis

This is a term for the tendency for equilibrium levels of a variable to gravitate towards actual values. For example, a prolonged increase in unemployment may actually cause an increase in the equilibrium level of unemployment. Economists have put forward several explanations for this phenomenon. These include:

(a) the likelihood of workers becoming discouraged in their search for a job and thus decreasing the intensity of their search;
(b) a rise in unemployment will decrease the numbers of insider employees (i.e. the tried and trusted employees) and thus the displaced workers find it difficult to obtain work when they attempt to return as outsiders;
(c) a prolonged recession is likely to decrease the capital stock and investment;
(d) a long period of unemployment will also decrease the skill that a worker possesses.

Hysteresis might be used to explain the change in the equilibrium of variables other than unemployment, such as inflation.

The control of unemployment: the supply side view

Introduction

For most of the period since the Second World War attempts to alleviate unemployment have centred on neo-Keynesian demand side management policies. For example, running a budget deficit was supposed to boost demand and reduce unemployment. During the late 1970s and 1980s various supply side schools of economics gained acceptance in government, not only in the UK but in the USA and most major Western economies. They argued that, not only were demand side policies ineffective but they made matters worse. Budget deficits created inflation and, in the end, created more unemployment, not less.

There are various supply side schools: monetarist, neo-classical, new classical and so on. While there are significant differences between them (see discussion on the *adaptive expectations* and the *rational expectations* schools on pages 552 and 555) there are common features and policy prescriptions and it is on these that we will concentrate in this section.

Supply side economics emphasises the 'natural' competitive forces in the economy. It is believed that the economy is essentially self-regulating (see pages 542–3). Problems arise because these 'natural' competitive forces are thwarted by government interference and by restrictive practices by firms and by unions. In short, we need to concentrate on the costs of production (hence supply side). This will reduce costs, control inflation and, in the long run, promote employment (see also Chapter 33).

One central idea of the supply side schools is that there is a natural level of unemployment and that it is the vain attempts to reduce this level that have been a key element in creating inflation. Only when the natural level has been achieved can we expect the economy to be operating efficiently and achieving the economic growth which will create more jobs (see discussion of this in Chapters 37 and 38). Common supply side policy prescriptions are:

(a) reduced welfare payments, such as unemployment benefits;
(b) lower levels of direct taxation;
(c) reduction of employee and trade union rights;
(d) abolition of wage floors;
(e) the promotion of training and retraining schemes.

We have already discussed the argument on lowering tax rates (see page 542). We will now consider the other points listed above.

Reducing welfare payments to the unemployed

It is argued that welfare benefits may be pitched at a level which is above the equilibrium wage rate in the lower-paid labour markets. This being the case, some people will not work since they would be worse off if they did so. Thus, welfare payments have artificially increased the level of unemployment.

In Figure 39.6 the 'benefits floor' is set at a level of OW_1 which is above the equilibrium wage in that labour market of OW. This being the case only OL will be employed instead of OM. Thus welfare benefits have created LN registered unemployed. The idea of making the level of welfare benefits less than the lowest standard of living achievable by those in work is not new, it is the principle of 'less eligibility' on which the Poor Law of 1834 was founded.

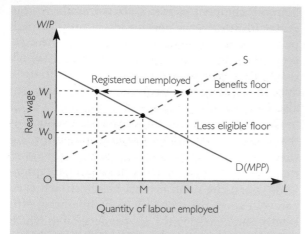

Figure 39.6 Effects of welfare benefits on unemployment
A benefits floor set at OW_1 which is above the equilibrium wage rate results in only OL being employed instead of OM. However, LN claim benefits thus there is less employment and a number of registered unemployed are created. Lowering the benefits floor to the 'less eligible' level eliminates the unemployment.

In order to eliminate the unemployment it is necessary to reduce the welfare benefits below the level of the lowest wage available in the labour market. In our example this could be OW_0. This argument contrasts with the Beveridge unemployment insurance argument that welfare insurance should sustain a person at or near their working standard of living while they are (temporarily) out of work (see also Chapter 28 for a discussion of the tax–benefit system).

● *Common misunderstanding*

The replacement ratio has fallen since the 1970s as unemployment regulations have hardened. It might be expected, therefore, that unemployment would also fall as people find it increasingly 'costly' to remain out of work. In fact, as has been seen, unemployment has increased sharply since this time, suggesting that other factors must also be responsible for the rise in the number of jobless people.

Reducing trade union rights

Many supply siders believe that overstrong trade unions through such things as closed-shop agreements hold the wage rate above the equilibrium.

In Figure 39.7 union power has lifted the wage rate to OW_1. This is above the equilibrium rate OW. As a result of this employers now only wish to employ OL workers rather than OM at the equilibrium (see discussion of this point on page 360).

Supply side policies also aim at increasing productivity by reducing union power. For example, the ending of demarcation agreements and overmanning is said to have a positive effect on both wages and employment. This is illustrated in Figure 39.8, where you can see that improvements in productivity have shifted the demand curve for labour to the right. Thus, before the ending of restrictive practices the equilibrium wage was OW and the quantity of labour employed was OM. After the resultant rises in productivity the wage rate has risen to OW_1 and the quantity of labour employed to ON.

There were substantial improvements in productivity during the 1980s; often, however, the highest rates of increase occurred in unionised firms compared with their non-unionised counterparts.

Training schemes

It is an obvious supply side point that improving the quality of factor inputs should improve productivity and output. Thus schemes to train and

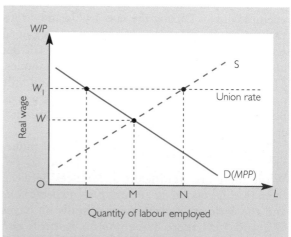

Figure 39.7 Wages and union power
Over-strong unions impose a wage rate at OW_1 which is above the equilibrium OW. Legislation to weaken unions allows the wage rate to return to the equilibrium and more employment to be created.

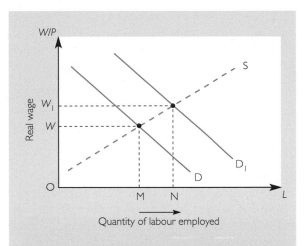

***Figure 39.8* The effect of increased productivity**
Productivity increases resulting from the reduction of restrictive practices such as demarcation, and/or improvement of the quality of the labour force through improved training shifts the demand curve for labour to the right. This results in both higher wages and increased employment.

retrain labour must have beneficial effects upon the economy. We can illustrate this point by reference to Figure 39.8. The result of better trained labour should be to shift the demand curve for labour to the right as it becomes more productive.

Governments during the 1980s introduced many training schemes such as TOPs (Training Opportunities Programme), YOPs (Youth Opportunities Programme) as well as YTS. These were politically controversial with many left-wingers claiming that real training was not being given and that the schemes were a method of keeping people off the unemployment register. In 1998 the Labour government introduced the New Deal scheme, whereby 18–24 year-olds unemployed for more than six months have the choice of working with an employer who receives a wage subsidy of £60 per week per person, pursuing full-time education or training, working with an environmental task force or taking a job with a voluntary organisation. The scheme also covers the over 25s unemployed for more than two years; here employers receive a wage subsidy of £75 per week. In April 2000 the scheme was extended to the over 50s and to those people with a long-term

disablity or illness. So far, however, evidence suggests that the New Deal has had only a small positive effect on employment, since, in a rapidly expanding economy, many who found work would have got jobs anyway.

It is worth noting that most of the measures described above are designed to improve ***labour market flexibility***, i.e. the ability for workers to move easily and speedily between different tasks and jobs (see also Data response B at the end of this chapter). Labour flexibility has a number of different facets:

(a) *Numerical flexibility* refers to the number of jobs; part-time and temporary or short-term appointments create a greater number of individual jobs. Such posts are both cheaper for firms to fill and easier for them to do without, should they need to reduce their number of staff. On the other hand, they may fit the employment needs of some workers, especially working mothers. Part-time workers comprised 16 per cent of the UK working population in 1973, but over 24 per cent in 2000.

(b) *Functional flexibility* denotes the extent to which workers possess a variety of skills or are able to undertake a range of tasks within a firm. This aspect of flexibility has, until recently, probably been the least developed within British firms, although the introduction of ***lean production techniques*** in the 1980s, traditionally associated with Japanese firms and that rely upon an increased level of automation and reduced levels of stockholding, hastened a greater flexibility in British industry.

(c) *Flexibility of time* can be viewed in terms of greater variability of working hours for staff; having employees adopt variable work patterns (i.e. starting or finishing at different times) is increasingly common among firms, although people are actually working longer hours on average than a decade ago. Flexibility of time can also be defined in terms of job tenure, i.e. how long people remain in their jobs. Average job tenure in the UK has fallen for men in the last 20 years, although not for women.

(d) *Wage flexibility* indicates the process by which pay is more closely related to the performance of a firm, e.g. through profit-sharing and productivity-bargaining schemes. Tax concessions have meant that these schemes have become more popular in a number of countries, although the 1996 budget in the UK began the process of phasing out tax relief on them.

STUDENT ACTIVITY 39.6

There are more people working part time in the UK than ever before. Is this a good thing?

It need hardly be said that the policy prescriptions proposed by the supply siders are hotly disputed by neo-Keynesians. They would see measures such as cutting wages as more likely to increase unemployment by creating a deficiency in demand. However, we may accept all the measures described above as effective and still be left with a problem. You will recall from our definition of labour as a factor of production that it has the unique characteristic of being 'the human factor'. Thus we may find that we have policy measures which are economically sound but which are politically or morally indefensible. This insight was one of the key starting points for Keynes. Below we will go on to look at the more traditional neo-Keynesian prescriptions for the control of unemployment.

The control of unemployment: neo-Keynesian views

Fiscal policy

Keynesian and neo-Keynesian policies emphasise the primacy of fiscal policy in the direction of the economy. The fiscal prescription for the cure of unemployment is to raise the level of aggregate demand and thus to close the deflationary gap. This is illustrated in Figure 39.9. Usually this would be done by running a budget deficit. However, two sets of problems are associated with this. First, there are the problems of forecasting and implementation which were discussed on pages 512–14. These problems raise the possi-

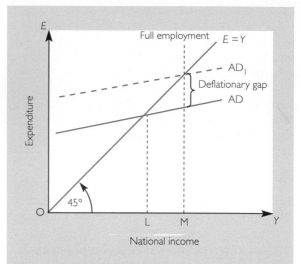

Figure 39.9 A deflationary gap
Unemployment occurs when the equilibrium level of national income (OL) is below the full employment level (OM). Unemployment could be eliminated by increasing the level of aggregate demand from AD to AD_1 $(AD = C + I + G + (X - M))$.

bility that fiscal policy may actually make the problem worse rather than better. Second, there is the problem that deficits in times of full or near-full employment tend to cause inflation. It is for these reasons that fiscal policy fell out of favour and monetary policy gained the ascendancy. We are here drawing together many threads of the argument. Assiduous readers should make sure that they are familiar with the contents of Chapter 37 and also with the discussion of the Phillips curve in Chapter 38. You will also find an aggregate supply and demand treatment of this argument in Chapter 33.

It should be remembered, however, that both problems considered above are most likely to occur at or near full employment. The problems associated with a finely balanced counter-cyclical fiscal policy can hardly be said to exist at a time of mass unemployment. It is also to be doubted whether expansionary policies would have the same inflationary effects when unemployment is at levels in the 2 to 3 million area. Many people have argued for an expansionary programme of public works. This would increase the level of aggregate demand and thus reduce unemployment. The cost of such schemes would be at least partly offset by the decrease in social security payments and the increase in tax revenues. It is also pointed out that public works programmes would not greatly stimulate the demand for imports since projects such as road building must mainly call upon domestic resources. Governments since 1979, both Conservative and Labour, have remained concerned about the inflationary aspects of such schemes.

Monetary policy

The conventional monetary policy response to unemployment is to lower interest rates and expand the money supply. As we have seen in previous chapters, the efficacy of monetary policy is a topic of fierce debate. Keynesians argue that reducing the rate of interest eventually causes some rise in national income by stimulating investment. You will recall from Chapters 37 and 38 that monetarists and neo-classicists reject the idea that employment can be created either by expanding the money supply or through budget deficits.

Incomes policy

The term neo-Keynesian embraces a wide spectrum of views and certainly not all would favour incomes policy. Incomes policy is usually regarded as an anti-inflationary device. We can see, however, from the arguments above concerning fiscal and monetary policies that the main reason for not stimulating the economy by such measures is fear of the inflationary consequences. If, therefore, inflation could be restrained by incomes policy while fiscal and monetary policies stimulated demand this could be a major contribution to the cure of unemployment. Incomes policies, however, have other drawbacks, as noted in Chapter 38.

Protection

In the 1970s and 1980s the Cambridge Economic Policy Group argued for protectionist measures to reduce unemployment in the UK, so that aggregate demand could be boosted without causing a severe current account deficit on the balance of payments. Conventionally, economists oppose calls for protection since these limit the benefits to be gained from comparative advantage. Some justification for the protectionist argument may be found in the fact that countries such as Japan have, for a long time, taken measures to prevent the UK's exports (and those of other countries) entering their country. Given that the UK is now part of the Single European Market, an independent protectionist stance is less likely as a policy weapon.

The political dimension

For 30 years after the Second World War positive economics was concerned with making statements which were scientifically verifiable. Increasingly it came to be recognised that major economic questions have a political dimension to them. If, for example, there is a trade-off between unemployment and inflation, as suggested by the Phillips curve, then whether it is more desirable to have 3 per cent inflation and 8 per cent unemployment or 3 per cent unemployment and 10 per cent inflation is a question which cannot be definitively answered by economics.

Conclusion

Having considered the problem of unemployment we may note that it has a national and international aspect. Whatever its causes, unemployment can be cured only if there is a significant increase in the growth of real national income (see Chapter 34).

Summary

1 There are different methods of measuring unemployment; the two most common ones are the claimant count and the survey technique.
2 The costs of unemployment fall mainly on the unemployed themselves and their families, but there are other costs for the economy as a whole.
3 There has been a steady increase in the number of unemployed at any level of vacancies, mainly because of the growth of the long-term unemployed.

4 There are many different types, or causes, of unemployment, which can be divided into those when the economy is in equilibrium or when it is in disequilibrium.

5 There are a number of valid reasons why governments should have a policy specifically designed to deal with regional unemployment. The efficacy of these policies, however, is open to debate.

6 There are many causes of the high level of unemployment in the 1980s and 1990s. The cure, however, is a matter of great controversy. The main concern has been that attempts to expand the economy might fuel inflation.

7 The supply side school places great emphasis on the promotion of competitive forces in the economy as the way to reduce unemployment, thereby aiming to make the labour market more flexible.

8 Neo-Keynesians favour demand management and other interventionist measures to reduce unemployment.

9 Unemployment is an international as well as a national problem. It is unlikely, therefore, that a purely national solution can be found to the problem.

? QUESTIONS

1 Comment on the different methods of measuring unemployment and describe the changes that have taken place in the UK's measurement techniques during the last 20 years.

2 Discuss the view that regional unemployment would be best solved through the operation of the price mechanism.

3 Explain why, at any time, job vacancies may co-exist alongside unemployment.

4 In the 1930s Keynes advocated that the government should 'spend its way' out of depression. Do you think that this view is still valid today, and if not, why not?

5 Study the figures in Tables 39.3 and 39.4 (pages 573 and 574) and then suggest reasons for the observed differences.

6 There was a considerable economic recovery in the UK in the late 1980s but the number of

unemployed remained high in historical terms. What are the implications of this for government policy?

7 In 1999 there were 1.7 million people unemployed in the UK according to the ILO definition. Attempt to assess the magnitude of the various types of unemployment involved, i.e. frictional, structural, etc.

8 Describe what measures supply side economists might favour to reduce unemployment. To what extent do they have empirical support?

9 During the 1980s employment was rising and so was unemployment. Explain how this was possible.

10 Examine the view that unemployment figures are not facts but, rather, they reflect economic theory.

Data response A
LABOUR STATS AREN'T WORKING

Read the following article which was taken from *The Economist* of 7 February 1998 and answer the questions which follow.

1 Distinguish between the claimant count and survey (ILO) methods of measuring unemployment.

2 Discuss the relative merits of each method.

3 Since the early 1980s the claimant count figure has often been below the ILO measure. Why do you think this is?

Data response B
STATISTICS BELIE BENEFITS OF FLEXIBLE LABOUR MARKET

The article was taken from *The Guardian* of 11 September 1997. Read it through and then answer the questions which follow.

1 Explain what is meant by the term 'the flexible labour market'.

2 Outline the supply side measures that can be taken to foster such a labour market.

3 There are various facets of a flexible labour market. What are they?

4 Supporters of the idea of a flexible labour market say that it reduces unemployment and can lead to faster growth. Discuss any potential disadvantages.

Labour stats aren't working

IN APRIL, according to official figures, unemployment in Britain will rise by more than 400 000 and the jobless rate will rise by about 1½% of the labour force. The reason is not that the economy is heading for a harder and earlier landing than anyone predicted, but a change (for the better) in the way the government presents unemployment statistics.

Officially, in December 1.4m Britons were unemployed – that is, they were claiming unemployment benefits. Compare that with the 3m-plus of the mid-1980s, or the near-3m of December 1992. Put another way, compare December's claimant count, at 5% of the British workforce, with 12.2% in France and 11.9% in Germany. Something for Britain to be proud of, no?

No. Or at least not without qualification. Unemployment has fallen, and the rate is far lower than either France's or Germany's, but the claimant count is misleading. It cannot be easily compared with past unemployment figures, because since 1979 umpteen changes to the definition of unemployment and to the rules for claiming benefit have taken hundreds of thousands off the jobless total. Nor can it be straightforwardly compared with other countries' figures, which are based on different definitions.

These failings of the claimant count are hardly news. Indeed, the Labour Party spent 18 years in opposition damning the Tories for fiddling the figures. Luckily, there is an international standard, supplied by the International Labour Organisation. Better still, Britain's Office for National Statistics already measures 'ILO unemployment', which counts people out of work and actively seeking it, whether or not they are entitled to benefits. The figure is compiled from the quarterly Labour Force Survey of 60 000 people, and is averaged over three months. According to the most recent survey, for autumn 1997, 1.8m people, or 6.6% of the workforce, are ILO unemployed.

From April, ILO unemployment will be given greater prominence, and the claimant count downgraded. The main advantage of this, apart from making year-by-year and international comparisons easier, is that it actually measures unemployment, rather than those eligible for benefit. More than this, the Labour Force Survey allows economists to look at the labour market in far more sophisticated ways than does the claimant count.

An article last October in the ONS's monthly Labour Market Trends, for instance, split the ILO unemployed into those looking for full-time and part-time work; and split those not looking for work, and so not classed as unemployed, into those who wanted to work and those who did not. By looking at how the numbers in these groups change over time, statisticians could get a much

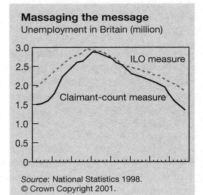

Massaging the message
Unemployment in Britain (million)

Source: National Statistics 1998.
© Crown Copyright 2001.

fuller picture of how labour-market participation varies over the economic cycle than they can from changes in the unemployment rate alone.

The new system has a snag, though. A figure for ILO unemployment will be released every month, but, as now, it will be a three-month average and will appear only after a long delay. Thus in April an average for December to February will be released; a claimant-count figure for mid-January, by contrast, will come out on February 11th. The ONS does not have the resources to carry out a full survey every month. Time to cut unemployment a bit more, and take on a few more statisticians?

Source: The Economist Newspaper Limited, London, 7 February 1998. Reprinted with permission.

Analysis

Larry Elliott studies the figures behind the latest buzz word, which too often means 'You're sacked'

JOHN Edmonds, leader of one of Britain's biggest unions said yesterday that flexibility in the labour market often meant 'You're sacked'.

But although the GMB general secretary said the use of the phrase made him shiver, flexibility was the new buzz word among policy makers. Germany, once admired for its economic strength, is pitied because its employees lack flexibility. The US, spiritual home of flexibility, is seen as a role model for the rest of the world.

On Monday the Prime Minister told the TUC he had no intention of abandoning the 'flexibility of the present labour market'. Mr Blair's theme was echoed at the same forum yesterday by Adair Turner, director general of the CBI.

Supporters of flexible labour markets believe they lead to more rapid growth, but there is no evidence of this. Growth in the UK and the US in the 1990s is slower than in the 1980s, which in turn was slower than in the 'inflexible' 1970s.

The Government's estimate of the average pace at which the economy can grow without running into difficulties with the balance of payments or inflation is the same now as 20 years ago – 2.25 per cent a year.

A second main argument is that flexible labour markets have delivered lower levels of unemployment. Employers in Britain and America have been more willing to hire workers than those in Germany and France because it is fairly easy to fire them if times get tough.

Recent figures seem to bear out this thesis. Unemployment in America is 4.8 per cent, only fractionally higher than in the last decade of the post-war boom which ended in 1973 while Britain's jobless rate is 5.5 per cent, less than half that in Germany and France.

But these figures rely on statistical sleight of hand. Two per cent of American men of working age are in prison, and the UK figure has been flattered by more than 30 changes since 1979 in the way unemployment is measured, all but one having had the effect of cutting the unemployment total.

Lord Eatwell, the economist who was once economic adviser to Neil Kinnock, also believes that the US and Britain suffer from heavy 'disguised unemployment', where a lack of demand for labour and ungenerous benefit regimes force people to take low-productivity jobs. Once these are included, jobless rates in the Anglo-Saxon economies look no better than those in continental Europe.

The Eatwell thesis is supported by a study of downsizing in the US showing that 29 per cent of those affected either left the workforce altogether or were jobless for two years or more, and that two-thirds of the remainder took a pay cut in their new job.

Ministers are keen to point out that the emphasis in flexible labour markets should be on training and education to make workers more employable. However, Alison Booth, of Essex University, will argue at the British Association for the Advancement of Science conference today that flexibility is incompatible with a 'learning society', because the low-paid jobs fostered by deregulation offer less training.

Further doubts about flexibility have been raised by the Organisation for Economic Co-operation and Development. Its research found that degregulated labour markets did not make workers more mobile, nor did they make it more likely that the low paid would move up the earnings ladder.

It said workers in the flexible labour markets of the US and the UK tended to be stuck in low pay jobs for much longer than employees in more regulated economies, tending to fluctuate between low pay and no pay.

Source: *The Guardian*, 11 September 1997. Reprinted with permission.

40 Advanced policy issues

Learning outcomes

At the end of this chapter you will be able to:
▶ Explain how utility theory underpins neoclassical economics.
▶ Identify points of conflict between optimal pollution and sustainability.
▶ Recognise the problems of indirect valuation.
▶ Understand the problems of using cost benefit analysis in practice.
▶ Identify situations in the real world where it is difficult to apply welfare economics.

About this chapter

The objective in this chapter is to use more complex analysis to analyse a range of problems. The topics chosen have some linkages in the area of sustainable development, but the objective is to introduce new techniques of public policy analysis. This is a case study chapter with student activities after each case. The chapter starts with a consideration of the philosophical underpinnings of modern neoclassical economics.

The philosophy behind neo-classical economics

In Chapters 9,10, 27 and 28, we have already examined the nature of government intervention in cases of market failure in terms of benefit to individuals. Up until now, when discussing the benefit of an activity, we have used the idea of willingness to pay as our measure of benefit. However, the history of economic thinking about how to measure benefit goes back to the philoso-

phy of utilitarianism. Before looking at some more advanced policy issues, this chapter explores how the idea of utility (or happiness) underpins much of what we have already studied, both in the area of the demand curve, and also government interventions in the economy.

Utility defined

Utility simply means the *satisfaction* which people derive from consuming goods or services. However, a good does not have to be 'useful' in the conventional sense; for example, cigarettes possess utility to the smoker even though they are harmful. As when we first discussed demand in Chapter 4, consumers are portrayed as rational and maximising individuals. In utility theory, it is of course utility that they are maximising.

Marginal utility

The law of diminishing marginal utility (LDMU) states that:

Other things being constant, as more and more units of a commodity are consumed the additional satisfaction, or utility, derived from the consumption of each successive unit will decrease.

For example, if you have nothing to drink all day, the utility of a glass of water would be very high indeed, and in consequence you would be willing to pay a high price for it. However, as you proceeded to drink a second, third and fourth glass of water the extra utility derived from each glass would become less. In this case you might have been willing to pay a great deal for the first glass of water but, as you continue to consume, the price you would be willing to pay would decrease because you would be deriving a smaller utility from each successive glass. This helps to clear up the puzzle of why we are willing to pay so little for bread, which is a necessity, and so much for diamonds, which have little practical value. The answer is that we have so much bread that the extra utility derived from another loaf is small, whereas we have so few diamonds that each one has a high marginal utility. Thus this principle helps to explain why more of a good is demanded at a lower price. The extra sales come from existing buyers, who buy more, and new buyers, who could not afford, or who did not think the good is worth buying, at the higher price.

When thinking about the LDMU, it is important to consider the *time period* over which decisions are made, since this may vary according to the nature of the commodity. For example, if we are considering food, a person who has not had a meal for several hours will place a high value on food. They will then not require another meal immediately, but after several hours will be equally willing to buy another meal. If, on the other hand, we consider a product such as a car, if a person has just bought a new car it will be a long time before they are willing to buy another one.

An important exception to LDMU occurs in the case of *addiction*. For example, smokers may find that the more they smoke, the more they want to smoke. The product need not necessarily be narcotic; for example, the avid philatelist may find a growing compulsion for stamp collecting. In the case of very rich individuals who still obsessively work to increase their wealth instead of taking leisure, the 'drug' may be power. This kind of behaviour is sometimes referred to as *monomania* since the individual pursues one activity to the detriment of all others.

STUDENT ACTIVITY 40.1

If the price of chocolate bars falls, persuading you to purchase more bars in any given week, which of the following would be true?

(a) Total utility from eating chocolate bars is falling as you eat more of them.
(b) Your marginal utility from the extra chocolate bars is less than from your first chocolate bar of the week.
(c) You are heartily sick of chocolate bars and never want to eat another in your life.

Demand and marginal utility

Cardinal utility

In the nineteenth century many economists, among them **Alfred Marshall**, believed that it was possible for utility to be measured in *cardinal numbers* as opposed to ordinal numbers. Hence these economists are termed cardinalists. A cardinal measure of utility implies that we can quantify how much more utility one unit of a good gives a person than the next. For example, we might say that a person derives 10 utils of utility from consuming the first unit of a commodity, 8 utils from the second, and so on. If we were taking an ordinal approach by contrast, all we could say is the first unit gives more utility than the second, but not by how much. The ordinal approach is discussed in the appendix to this chapter (see page 597), but we will proceed with the ordinal approach for now, partly because it is easier to explain.

No objective method of measuring the satisfaction that consumers enjoy from goods has ever been devised. It does, however, accord with subjective experience that different satisfaction is gained from consuming different goods. We can therefore learn something by following this approach a little further.

Equimarginal utility

Table 40.1 gives some hypothetical figures showing the total and marginal utility derived by a consumer from consumption of product X. Consuming 1 unit of X gives 15 utils of satisfaction, consuming 2 units gives 25 utils, and so on. The figures for marginal utility decline as each successive unit is consumed. If the consumer goes on consuming more and more units, eventually we see that the sixth unit yields no extra satisfaction at all, and, should a seventh unit be consumed, total utility actually decreases so that marginal utility becomes negative. Negative utility is referred to as disutility.

If we assume that consumers are utility maximisers, i.e. they wish to obtain as much utility as they can then, subject to no other constraints, the consumer in Table 40.1 would consume 5 units

Table 40.1 Diminishing marginal utility

Units of X consumed	Total utility (utils)	Marginal utility (utils)
0	0	
1	15	15
2	25	10
3	33	8
4	38	5
5	40	2
6	40	0
7	39	−1

of X, where total utility is greatest. However, we must now consider two complicating factors:

(a) The consumer's income is limited.
(b) The consumer must distribute expenditure between many different commodities.

Assume that the consumer has a choice between two products, X and Y. If X and Y both cost £1 each, and the consumer has £1 to spend, then, obviously, the commodity that yields the greater utility will be bought. If we were to apply this principle to each successive unit of the consumer's spending, we could conclude that utility will be maximised when income has been allocated in such a way that the utility derived from one extra pound's worth of X is equal to the utility derived from the consumption of one extra pound's worth of Y. If this condition is not fulfilled then the consumer could obviously increase the total utility derived by switching expenditure from X to Y or vice versa. For example, a consumer would not spend a pound more on vegetables if it was considered that the same pound spent on meat would give more satisfaction, or in the reverse situation would not spend a pound extra on meat (or nuts if you are a vegetarian) if the consumer considered that the same pound spent on vegetables would yield greater satisfaction. This fits in with the common phrase used when people are deciding whether to buy something: 'is it good value for money?'

The extra satisfaction derived from the consumption of one more unit of X is its marginal utility which we can write as MU_X and that of Y

as MU_Y, etc. We must also consider the relative price of X and Y which we can write as P_X and P_Y. We can then see that the **utility-maximising condition** is fulfilled when:

$$\frac{MU_X}{P_X} = \frac{MU_Y}{P_Y}$$

Any number of commodities may then be added to the equation. Table 40.2 gives hypothetical marginal utility figures for a consumer who wishes to distribute expenditure of £44 between three commodities, X, Y and Z.

Table 40.2 Equimarginal utility

Kg consumed	Kg marginal utility derived from each kg of: X (£8/kg)	Y (£4/kg)	Z (£2/kg)
1	72	60	64
2	48	44	56
3	40	32	40
4	36	24	28
5	32	20	16
6	20	8	12
7	12	4	8

In order to maximise utility, the consumer must distribute available income so that:

$$\frac{MU_X}{P_X} = \frac{MU_Y}{P_Y} = \frac{MU_Z}{P_Z}$$

By studying the table you can see that this yields a selection where the consumer buys 2 kg of X, 4 kg of Y and 6 kg of Z. Hence:

$$\frac{48}{8} = \frac{24}{4} = \frac{12}{2}$$

If the consumer wishes to spend all the £44 it is impossible to distribute it in any other way which would yield greater total utility. You can check this by totalling the marginal utilities for various other combinations.

This theorem, which we may term the concept of **equimarginal utilities**, should be carefully studied by the student, for it frequently forms the basis of data response or multiple choice questions.

STUDENT ACTIVITY 40.2

An individual derives the utility in Table 40.3 from consuming different quantities of three products: cheese, lamb and steak. The consumer lives in an ideal climate where it is only necessary to consume food in order to live. If this worries you, assume you make your own clothing.

Table 40.3 **Marginal utility**

Kilos	Cheese		Lamb		Steak	
	MU	MU/P	MU	MU/P	MU	MU/P
1	44		45		75	
2	30		36		60	
3	22		33		57	
4	20		31		55	
5	19		30		54	

(Hint: it is necessary to calculate values for the second column in each case in order to work out consumer equilibrium.)

What will the individual's consumption be if:

(a) The price in pounds per kilo is cheese 2; lamb 3; steak 5; and income is £35?

(b) All the conditions in (a) apply except the price of steak rises to £6 per kilo? Which is a better substitute for steak, lamb or cheese? Is steak consumption very sensitive to price for this income group?

(c) All the conditions in (a) apply except income falls to £12. Are all the products normal goods? Which products rise most strongly with income?

(d) Could you construct an individual demand curve using this information?

If you are vegetarian, substitute honey and nuts for lamb and steak. If you are a vegan, you could use soya, nuts and apples. Students are not recommended to follow the diet suggested by this exercise

The demand curve

The marginal utility approach gives us a rationalisation of the demand curve. Suppose that, starting from a condition of equilibrium, the price of X falls relative to Y. We now have a condition where the utility from the last penny spent on X will be greater than the utility from the last penny spent on Y. Mathematically this can be written as:

$$\frac{MU_X}{P_X} > \frac{MU_Y}{P_Y}$$

In order to restore the equilibrium the consumer will buy more of X (and less of Y), thus reducing the marginal utility of X. The consumer will continue substituting X for Y until equilibrium is achieved. Thus we have attained the normal demand relationship that, other things being equal, as the price of X falls, more of it is bought. We have therefore a normal downward-sloping demand curve. The demand curve we have derived is the individual's demand curve for a product. The market demand curve can then be obtained by aggregating all the individual demand curves.

Objections to utility theory

Theories based on utility place a great emphasis upon rationality and the search for utility maximisation. This is often hard to accord with observed behaviour. How many of your friends are completely rational? How many of your decisions to buy goods lack calm rational calculation?

Arguments that consumers are not in fact rational beings can in part be countered by the law of large numbers and 'as-if' methodology, first discussed in Chapter 3. If the purpose of demand theory is to *explain* consumers' behaviour, then the theory will not always succeed. If on the other hand the purpose of the theory is to *predict*, then the law of large numbers will result in the inconsistencies and irrationalities of individuals often cancelling out when aggregated at the level of the market. As long as people behave collectively 'as if' they were rational utility-maximising individuals, then demand theory will yield useful predictions.

The discipline of marketing is related to economics and comes up with different explanations of consumer behaviour, concentrating on what the firm can do to change demand for its product. Advertising can change people's tastes as well as give them more information. Distribution strategies can make the product more accessible to its target market. Product design and packaging can make the product more attractive to the consumer. Even the location on the supermarket shelves can affect sales. These ideas are not necessarily in conflict with traditional economic theory, since economics assumes that the consumer has full information about and access to the products. Many marketing strategies are just making sure this is the case. Informative advertising is also covered by this argument, but persuasive advertising is an attempt by the firm to manipulate the consumer rather than satisfy the consumer's preferences. Those who work in advertising are well aware that it is often the emotional content of a product that is more important than the rational. This does not necessarily contradict our analysis since the emotional satisfaction given by the consumption of a product is part of its utility.

Sustainability

The application of utility analysis to environmental policy raises important questions of sustainability. Should we only consider the utility of the current generation when deciding on policy, or should we take into account future generations? How can we know the preferences of future generations? People may have preferences in the current generation for environmental 'goods' but because of market failure it is difficult to value these goods and include them in policy decision making. Some of these issues have been raised in Chapters 13,14 and 27, but the following case studies look into these problems in more detail.

Case studies

The case studies in this chapter concern two areas covered in earlier chapters: the environment (Chapter 13) and transport (Chapter 14). The concepts developed in these two chapters will be used here.

Case study 40.1
ACID RAIN

Acid rain: the scientific background

A little science is needed to understand the nature of this problem. Burning coal and oil produces sulphur dioxide (SO_2) and nitrogen oxides. When mixed with water vapour in the atmosphere these gases turn into sulphuric acid and nitric acid. When rain falls, usually at some distance from the vehicle or power plant which caused the problem, the acidity of the rain corrodes buildings and makes the soil more acid. A more acid soil can reduce agricultural productivity and is thought to reduce growth in trees. Acid can build up in freshwater lakes eventually killing off fish. Once again, the culprits are the energy and transport industries.

Characteristics of the externality

Acid rain, like global warming, is a transfrontier pollution. Acid rain from the UK will often fall on Scandinavian countries because of prevailing southwesterly winds. It is also an operational pollutant because it is a side effect of normal production processes. Unlike global warming, it is not solely an intergenerational pollutant. Although the effects of acidification are passed on to later generations, it has an immediate impact on agricultural productivity, tree growth, and the erosion of buildings, although acidity does build up in the soil and in lakes. Although its effects are less serious than global warming, because they are more *immediate*, they have been taken more seriously.

Imports and exports

In the case of global warming, the externality is said to be a transfrontier pollutant because the whole planet could be affected by the actions of a single country. In the case of acid rain the effects are not global in this way, but rather the pollution is exported to a number of neighbouring countries. Which countries receive the pollution will depend on weather conditions at the time. Some of the acid rain which a country produces will, of course, fall locally in that country. Weather forecasters can keep track of the flow of air and rainfall and have produced information about which countries are polluting which. In Table 40.4 the imports and exports between some European countries, before major action was taken, are documented. The column under each country shows its 'exports' of acid rain to each of the countries on the left. The diagonal (top left to bottom right) shows how much acid rain is domestically produced for each country. Can you see why the Scandinavians have been so annoyed?

Table 40.4 Importers and exporters of acid rain, thousands of tonnes of sulphur p.a. (1989)

| Importers | Exporters | | | |
	UK	France	Scandinavia	West Germany
UK	571	14	0	15
France	43	332	0	40
Scandinavia	32	5	59	18
West Germany	45	69	0	330

Source: Adapted from EMEP data

Valuation

External costs are difficult to value because they do not pass through the market place, but are imposed on 'victims'. Where the costs are on other production processes, valuation is easier. It is possible to estimate the loss of timber or agricultural production as a result of acid rain. It is also possible to put a price on the damage caused to buildings and paintwork by the corrosive effects of acid rain. It is more difficult to put a value on consumption activities. If fishing is no longer possible because the fish have died as a result of rising acidity in Scandinavian lakes, how much is this worth? If landscapes are affected by dying trees, by how much is tourists' enjoyment reduced?

Stated preference

One way of obtaining values for external costs is to ask people directly how much they would be willing to pay for the pollution to be removed. There is a problem with this approach, because people are not actually asked to pay and the questions are hypothetical. People may be tempted to overstate their price because they think it may influence policy in their favour. This is known as **strategic bias**. There is a further

problem in that people are not used to buying and selling pollution. It is argued that consumers need the experience of real markets to practise on before finally deciding what price to pay. Values obtained from questionnaires are therefore subject to **hypothetical market bias**. Careful design of questionnaires is necessary to try and avoid these biased answers and to cross-check for consistency. Strand (1981) (in *Blueprint for a Green Economy*, D.W. Pearce *et al.*, Earthscan) found an average value of 800 Norwegian kroner per person to reduce acid rain in Norway to levels that would allow freshwater fish to survive. It is likely that this value is understated because some respondents would think it was more appropriate for the British or Germans to pay for the clean-up since they were causing about half of the pollution (see Table 40.4). There is a confusion here between **values** (how much is a clean-up worth) and **value judgements** (who should pay for it). This example underlines some of the difficulties of the technique.

The stated preference technique makes it possible to estimate different types of values, and not just the values of people who are users of an environmental resource, or its associated private goods. It is possible to ask people if they would be willing to pay for the **option** of using an environmental resource in the future, or simply for its **existence** to continue. it is possible to be willing to pay for the continued existence of the Brazilian rain forest without necessarily intending to visit it. A final kind of valuation concerns the wish to pass on environmental resource to the next generation, known as **bequest** valuations.

Revealed preference

An alternative approach is to infer from peoples' behaviour what value they place on an externality. In the case of acid rain a number of studies have been made on the relationship between air quality and house prices. The basis of these studies is that poor air quality will make a neighbourhood less desirable and this will be reflected in house prices. Differences in house prices for similar houses in different areas will reflect the value house-buyers put on the environment. In this way consumer preference is revealed. The main problem with studies of this sort is deciding what houses are similar. Consistent results from a number of studies suggest the values obtained are in fact fairly reliable. This method is also used to place a value on the noise around airports.

This helps planners to decide where to put airports: too close to the city and noise costs rise; too far away and passengers' time costs rise. It has also been used to study the effects of sulphur pollution in the USA, with the results of several studies suggesting house prices fall by about 0.1 per cent for each 1 per cent increase in sulphur levels.

Optimal pollution

Placing a value on an externality makes deciding policy towards it easier. An economic assessment of the problem would involve comparing the costs of the externality with the costs of reducing that externality. This is illustrated in Figure 40.1. The usual way of looking at an externality is as a social cost added to a private cost. Figure 40.1 takes a different approach. It looks at pollution as a good (or rather a bad) which is produced for which there is no market. Since no one wants pollution, benefits are achieved by moving from right to left on the diagram, by reducing pollution. The starting point is E_0, which is the **do nothing** situation. This is the outcome if there is no regulation or taxation of the polluter. As we move towards E_2, the optimal position, we start with the cheapest methods of reducing pollution, and as these are used up we gradually have to move on to more expensive methods. Where the marginal costs of reducing the externality (MRC) exceed the marginal costs of the pollution itself (MDC), there is a net loss to society as a whole if the pollution is further reduced. This would be the case if we reduced

pollution to level E_3. If on the other hand the marginal costs of pollution (MDC) are more than the costs of pollution reduction (MRC), then it makes sense to reduce the pollution further. This would be the case if we had only moved as far as E_1. The optimal level of pollution will be at point E_2 where the two costs are just equal at the margin.

Deep greens and light greens

Some people object that putting the two words 'optimal' and 'pollution' together in this way is a contradiction in terms. If all pollution is regarded as bad then should it not all be eliminated? The economist's answer to this viewpoint is that both the costs and benefits of pollution reduction should be considered. In the same way that economists are concerned with equilibrium and balance in the economic system, ecologists are also concerned with equilibrium and balance in ecological systems. If an economic activity is resulting in the breakdown of an ecological system, an ecologist is likely to object. Which of these two viewpoints is correct? The answer is that they both reflect different value judgements about what is important in the world. The economist's viewpoint only counts the costs and benefits which affect humankind. This approach is sometimes referred to as **anthropocentric** (centred on humankind) or **light green**. The ecological approach values all living systems and is sometimes referred to as **deep green** because it values the environment for itself, and not just for its value to humankind. You can hold either of these viewpoints, but if you are a deep green you must recognise that there are substantial economic costs of holding this position.

Policy

Since many of the costs of acid rain are easy to value, and the connection between the pollution and its effects are quite certain, policy has been quite direct. EU policy on power stations has directed member states to reduce output. The Large Combustion Plants Directive of 1988 required governments to reduce their countries emissions of sulphur dioxide by 60 per cent by 2003 and nitrous oxides by 30 per cent by 1998, starting with a 1980 baseline. More recently, the 1994 UNECE Second Sulphur Protocol, ratified by the UK in 1996 requires

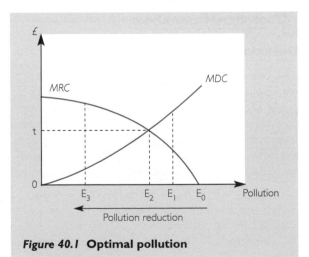

Figure 40.1 **Optimal pollution**

50 per cent reduction of sulphur dioxide emissions by 2000, rising to 70 per cent by 2005 and 80 per cent by 2010. This has been achieved partly by flue gas desulphurisation, but also by the 'dash for gas' which has no sulphur content, in the aftermath of electricity privatisation. In addition to this the government has recently reduced tax on low sulphur diesel for cars.

STUDENT ACTIVITY 40.3

Using Table 40.4 calculate which countries are the largest net exporters and which are the largest net importers. Could the problem be solved by the importers paying the exporters not to produce the acid rain? Alternatively, should the exporters have to pay the importers for the damage they cause them? What does your answer say about who 'owns' the environment?

STUDENT ACTIVITY 40.4

The costs of pollution reduction using alternative technologies are shown in Table 40.5. Using low-sulphur fuel oil results in less sulphur being burned with each tonne of oil in the power station. Flue gas desulphurisation involves putting an alkaline filter in the chimney of the power station which absorbs the sulphur, resulting in less of it reaching the atmosphere. Fluidised bed combustion is a technology which results in less of the sulphur being burned. You will notice that it is more expensive to put these technologies into old plant (retrofitting) rather than building them into new plant.

If the benefits of acid rain reduction are estimated to be $500 per tonne of SO_2, which acid rain reduction technologies would be worthwhile implementing? In what order should they be implemented? Does your answer depend on whether you hold a deep green or light green point of view?

Table 40.5 Estimates of reducing sulphur output (average of several studies)

	Cost ($) per tonne of SO_2 removed
Using low-sulphur fuel oil	600
Flue gas desulphurisation (FGD)	
New plant	300
Old plant	600
Fluidised bed combustion	
New plant	100
Old plant	2300

Case study 40.2
PROBLEMS OF DECISION MAKING IN THE PUBLIC SECTOR

The cases considered above indicate that the two criteria of equity and efficiency are sometimes in conflict with each other. The same thing has a tendency to happen in investment appraisal in the public sector. A *Pareto improvement* (see Chapter 27) implies no one has lost, even though someone has gained. Unfortunately, most economic changes in the real world do hurt someone. It is sometimes theoretically possible for the gainers to compensate the losers and still be better off themselves, but this is rarely done in practice. If we were willing to undertake projects only if an actual Pareto improvement were to result, most major changes would not be considered.

Cost–benefit analysis

Definition

This branch of economics is the result of the practical application of modern welfare economics to public sector decision making. Put simply, it attempts to evaluate the social costs and benefits of proposed investment projects as a guide when deciding upon the desirability of these projects. Cost–benefit analysis (CBA) differs from ordinary investment appraisal in that the latter considers only private costs and benefits. In short, it is intended to enable the decision maker to choose between alternative projects on the basis of their potential contribution to social welfare. **E.J. Mishan**, perhaps the leading authority on CBA, has summarised CBA concisely as follows:

> It transpires that the realisation of practically all proposed cost–benefit criteria . . . implies a concept of social betterment that amounts to a *potential* Pareto improvement. The project in question, to be considered as economically feasible, must, that is, be capable of producing an excess of benefits such that everyone in society could, by costless redistribution of the gains, be made better off.

The Hicks–Kaldor criterion

To get around the problem that in practice gainers rarely compensate losers, **Kaldor** and **Hicks** proposed that if the gainers could *in principle* compensate the losers and still enjoy a net increase in welfare then a project should still go ahead. This weaker test of the *potential* for a Pareto improvement is known as the Hicks–Kaldor criterion. This criterion has led to considerable controversy, particularly where the losers are the poorer people in society and there is a clear conflict with principles of equity. Suggestions have been made that the costs and benefits of poorer people should be given higher weights to reflect equity value judgements in society. No objective way has ever been found of arriving at such weights so these proposals have not usually been implemented. After a CBA has been undertaken, it must be remembered that there will still be gainers and losers, so a political dimension to the argument can be expected. Recent examples include the route of the high-speed channel tunnel link with London, the acceptability of a fifth terminal at Heathrow airport or an additional runway at Manchester airport. It should be noted that towns in northern France vied with each other to have the high-speed rail link with Paris pass their way because of the employment it would bring.

The imperfection of the world

The major difficulty in attempting a CBA stems from the fact that, in a world where imperfect competition, externalities and ignorance abound, market price will not reflect the true social costs and benefits.

The CBA thus estimates *shadow prices*. These are imputed prices that are intended to reflect more faithfully the true social costs and benefits of a project. For example, the value of the time saved by an individual following an improvement in transport facilities is often approximated using that person's average hourly wage for working drivers (leisure time is worth less). The Roskill Commission used the depreciation in house prices around Gatwick airport in estimating the negative value of noise around any proposed third London airport. The techniques for valuing costs and benefits which do not pass through the market place were discussed in Case study 40.1 above.

CBA in practice

CBA is quite expensive and is not used in many project appraisals because of difficulties in valuation. One area where it is still extensively used is in the assessment of road improvement schemes, using a Department of Transport computer program called **COBA**. The main costs and benefits that are assessed other than the building of the road itself are time, vehicle operating costs and death or injury. The change to the road system is simulated based on known experience elsewhere. Injury is costed in terms of treatment costs and lost income. Death is costed as the present value of a person's expected stream of income plus an amount for grief of those left behind. This is clearly less than adequate, but supporters of this approach argue that it is better than having no value at all. Working time is costed at the wage rate because it is assumed that the value of a person's output is equal to their wage rate (see Chapter 26). The gross wage rate (wages plus the costs of employing a person such as employer's national insurance contribution) is used because this is the cost to the employer. Leisure time is valued at about 40 per cent as a result of stated preference and revealed preference studies. The value that people place on time can be inferred by their choice between slow, cheap modes of transport and fast, more expensive modes of transport. For instance, if a person can get to work by bus for £1 in 30 minutes, or by train for £2 in 15 minutes, the person choosing the train is in effect buying 15 minutes for £1. The value for an hour of your time is thus £4 (see Figure 40.2). However, this choice is usually related to a person's income. Statistical techniques are used to relate the revealed preference of people for time to their income. The results show, unsurprisingly, that people on higher incomes value their time more. Time is therefore a normal good with a positive income elasticity of demand.

The Newbury bypass

COBA found that the Newbury bypass gave a positive return on the investment needed, but large numbers of environmental campaigners had a different point of view. The problem is that COBA does not value everything. In particular it does not have room for estimates of global warming, or the possible value of sites of special scientific interest (SSSIs). Where it is not possible to place values on such damage, a separate *environmental impact assessment* (EIA) can be undertaken. Where COBA and the EIA conflict there remains the political problem of how to resolve them. The idea of sustainable development discussed in Chapter 34 may be of use here.

Criticisms of CBA and welfare economics

There are many criticisms of this field of economics, some of which are extremely technical. It is important, though, that all students of economics appreciate the controversial nature of much of economics. Hence we will examine some of the simpler, but nevertheless important, objections. It should also be borne in mind, when reading these, that CBA utilises the concepts of modern welfare economics

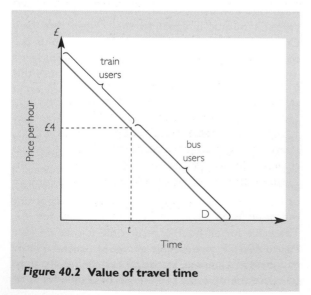

Figure 40.2 **Value of travel time**

and is thus subject to the same criticisms as that body of theory.

(a) CBA identifies only potential Pareto improvement using the Kaldor–Hicks criterion; it does not stipulate that the project should go ahead only if gainers actually compensate losers, i.e. that an actual Pareto improvement should take place. There are therefore potential problems of equity.

(b) The money values placed on intangibles such as the value of the environment are sometimes extremely speculative.

(c) CBA often involves estimates of consumer surplus, but it can be shown that, unless extremely unlikely assumptions are made, conventional measures of consumer surplus will be inaccurate. A simple example of this is the commonly used assumption that demand curves are linear, i.e. straight lines. Since this is extremely unlikely, considerable inaccuracy results when changes in consumer surplus are estimated following large price changes. Indeed, one authority on CBA, **I.M.D. Little**, has gone so far as to suggest that consumer surplus is 'a totally useless theoretical toy'.

(d) Welfare economics is ultimately normative, and this led early on to criticisms from positivists who felt that normative issues should not be the concern of the economists.

(e) Some economists feel that welfare economics concentrates on relatively insignificant welfare losses and ignores the far more important losses caused by cost inefficiency, e.g. in complacent monopolies (sometimes known as 'X-inefficiency' – see Chapter 23) and the loss of welfare caused by unemployment. This may be a valid criticism if the social returns to the development of welfare economics have been less than the social costs! However, it hardly seems fair to criticise a body of theory simply because it does not provide answers to all the questions one would like answered.

The response to criticisms of CBA in transport

The government has responded to criticisms of CBA by introducing a new framework for the assessment of new road developments. The new NATA framework sets the environmental assessments alongside the assessment of the road in terms of transport costs, time saving, and loss of life. Whereas the old framework gave pre-eminence to those costs that could be valued, and downplayed those which could not, the new framework attempts to place them on a more equal footing.

Critics of this new approach argue that, who ever makes the final decision on whether or not to go ahead with a new road, will make an implicit valuation of the environmental costs which are less easily valued. If the decision goes against the road, the implication will be that these environmental costs outweigh any net benefit in terms of lives saved, time saved, or reduction in transport costs. Supporters of this new innovation argue that the technocratic approach of the economist submerges the argument in jargon which is not intelligible to the intelligent layperson, and which therefore makes public sector decision making less democratic. They prefer a more discursive approach on the best lifestyle for the nation to adopt, which places more emphasis on value judgements than valuations.

STUDENT ACTIVITY 40.5

A bypass is about to be built around a local town, city or village. Make up a list of who the gainers and losers would be of such a project. How would you assess the environmental impacts of such a road improvement?

STUDENT ACTIVITY 40.6

What is the difference between a light green and a dark green approach to investment in roads? What changes in lifestyle would be necessary if roads are not expanded in line with expected demand growth ?

Case study 40.3
PRICING IN PRACTICE ON THE RAILWAYS

A related issue to the problem of investment in roads is the consequence of pricing on the privatised railway sytem. The free market may result in pricing which does not serve the public interest, but this case study also considers the problem of implement-

ing the recommendations of welfare economics in practice (see also Chapter 27).

Costs and indivisibilities

It is difficult to speak of the marginal cost of an extra rail user, because rail transport suffers from *indivisibilities*. An extra user of a rail service may impose virtually no additional costs on the railway if the train is not full. It is only if additional carriages or additional trains are required that substantial costs will result. It only makes sense to talk about reasonably large chunks of increased demand. There is a clear difference between the peak and off-peak, however. An additional chunk of demand in the peak period requires investment in new trains or carriages (rolling stock). In the off-peak period, however, it is a matter of making use of rolling stock already acquired for the peak. For this reason, revenue from off-peak demand only has to cover *variable* costs for there to be a *contribution* to profits. The capital costs should be attributed to the peak demand. This is one of the reasons for the difference in price between peak and off-peak journeys.

Load factor

Average costs will be affected by the proportion of seats which have been filled. It was noted in Case study 14.1 (page 196) that it is not possible to store transport from one period of time to another. The output of a train is the number of seats on the train times the number of kilometres it has travelled, the total being known as *seat kilometres*:

$$\text{Seat kilometres} = \text{Seats} \times \text{Kilometres}$$

Not all of this production will be consumed because some of the seats will be empty some of the time. The total transport consumed will be the total number of kilometres travelled by all the passengers, known as *passenger kilometres*. Any difference between the two will be wasted. This gives rise to a useful measure of transport efficiency – *load factor*:

$$\text{Load factor} = \frac{\text{Passenger kilometres}}{\text{Seat kilometres}} \times \frac{100}{1}$$

The higher the percentage figure, the more efficient the mode of transport. Intercity services usually manage the highest load factor, followed by commuter trains (which are often nearly empty on the return journey) and then provincial services last. Peak transport will normally achieve a higher load factor than the off-peak.

Joint costs

A final notable feature of railway costs is the existence of *joint costs*. Trains using the same track must pay for that track between them. There is no logical justification for any particular distribution of these jointly consumed *track costs* between two different services. An intercity train and a provincial service will frequently use the same track and the way in which the track costs are allocated between them will substantially affect the profitability of both. This was not very important before privatisation, but now has become a real issue.

Markets and market structure

Each railway service faces its own unique market structure, depending on the modes it is competing with. Commuter services into major cities enjoy a substantial degree of monopoly power as they are usually faster than the congested roads. Intercity services compete with both the car and the long-distance coach. On the longer haul services the speed of service provides an advantage over the coach, but air transport will be a serious competitor. Ferries and airlines will provide competition for the Channel tunnel route. Provincial services, particularly in less populated parts of the country, will face competition from bus and cars operating on much less congested roads and may have insufficient demand to break even at any price – see Figure 40.3.

For most services it will be possible to break the demand into different segments with different *elasticities*. Most estimates of commuter demand in the peak suggest a price elasticity between –0.2 and –0.4. The business traveller on intercity is also likely to have a more inelastic demand than the leisure traveller. Whole segments of the population can be identified who have lower elasticity of demand, such as young people and senior citizens. If methods can be found for the separation of these markets, then some degree of price discrimination can be practised.

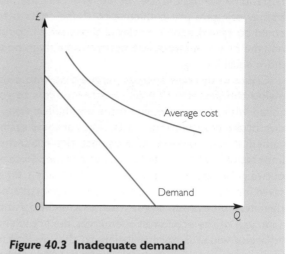

Figure 40.3 Inadequate demand

Pricing

Railway pricing is difficult to analyse because there are two distinct reasons why peak fares should be higher than off-peak fares. In the discussion on costs above it was pointed out that only variable costs should be considered in the off-peak, while the peak travellers should be charged the capital costs. This is usually referred to as *peak load pricing*. Higher prices in the peak will persuade some passengers to postpone their journey to later in the day. This will reduce the pressure in the peak and allow the railway to operate more cheaply with less capacity and therefore lower capital costs.

The second reason for higher prices in the peak has to do with inelastic demand which gives the opportunity for price discrimination. There are three conditions needed for this pricing strategy to work. Where there is some degree of monopoly power, where demand segments have different elasticity, and where markets can be separated, then price discrimination is possible. In the commuter market demand is more inelastic in the peak, the railways have some degree of monopoly power, and the markets can be separated by making off-peak tickets valid only after 9.30 a.m.

On the other hand, there are three reasons why this price difference should be minimised. First, higher load factors in the peak reduce average costs. Second, discounts are offered to season ticket holders as a reward for loyalty and to discourage occasional car use. Third, lower fares in the peak reduce congestion on the roads. This last point requires specific government intervention since it will not be in the interests of a profit-making railway.

STUDENT ACTIVITY 40.7

Each student should select different destinations and collect as much information as possible about different fares to that destination. You should try to work out how much market power the railways have in transporting people to each destination and identify the competitors. Try to work out which of the factors influencing pricing have been most important for each destination.

STUDENT ACTIVITY 40.8

Railtrack decided to charge the same amount for use of the track for an intercity express as a provincial train. Both trains use the same length of track at approximately the same time of day. Has Railtrack maximised its profit?

STUDENT ACTIVITY 40.9

If passenger kilometres are 20 million and seat kilometres are 50 million what is the load factor? What pricing techniques can be used to increase it and thus push down average costs?

Conclusions

The three cases introduced in this chapter have demonstrated the difficulties of making investment and pricing decisions in cases where there is market failure. These difficulties arise partly because of the problems of valuation, partly because of the need to make value judgements, and partly because of the problems of equity, between countries, between generations, or between different social groups. In practice the complex relationship between costs and prices can also create difficulties.

Summary

1 The marginal utility (or cardinalist) approach to demand maintains that the consumer maximises utility when the marginal utility of product A divided by its price is equated with the marginal utility of product B divided by its price, and so on.

2 The consumers' surplus is the extra utility enjoyed by consumers which they do not pay for.

3 The assumption of a rational utility-maximising consumer may not describe human beings exactly, but it can be used successfully to predict their behaviour.

4 The idea of optimal pollution requires us to place a value on environmental damage.

5 This may be easier for damage which can be costed in terms of resources than for costs which need to be assessed in terms of utility.

6 Revealed preference (or hedonic pricing), stated preference (or contingent valuation) and the travel cost method are all possible methods.

7 User, option, existence and bequest valuations are all possible.

8 Sustainable development means that we have to take into account future generations, but this may be difficult to do in an uncertain world.

9 Complex cost structures, external costs and price discrimination strategies all make it difficult to make judgements about the best price levels.

APPENDIX: Indifference curve analysis

The indifference curve approach to consumer theory is placed in an appendix, since it is not required by many syllabuses. The relationship between utility and demand has been adequately covered in the chapter so far, but indifference curve analysis provides a logically more precise analysis of the issues discussed above.

The ordinalist approach

The marginal utility approach is subject to the major criticism that we have never found a satisfactory way of quantifying utility. In the 1930s a group of economists, including **Sir John Hicks** and **Sir Roy Allen,** came to believe that cardinal measurement of utility was not necessary. They argued that consumer behaviour could be explained with *ordinal numbers* (i.e. is first, second, third and so on). This is because, it is argued, individuals are able to *rank their preferences,* saying that they would prefer this bundle of goods to that bundle of goods and so on. Finite measurement of utility therefore becomes unnecessary and it is sufficient simply to place in order consumers' preferences. To explain this we must investigate indifference curves.

Indifference curves

In order to explain indifference curves we will again make the simplifying assumption that the consumer buys only two goods, X and Y. Table 40.6 gives a number of combinations of X and Y which the consumer considers to give equal satisfaction; for example, combination C of 8X and 20Y is thought to yield the same satisfaction as D where 12X and 10Y are consumed. The consumer is thus said to be indifferent as to which combination the consumer has – hence the name given to this type of analysis. Figure 40.4 gives a graphical representation of the figures in

Table 40.6. Before proceeding any further with the analysis we must pause to consider several important features of indifference curves.

Table 40.6 An indifference schedule

Combination	Units of X	Units of Y
A	0	50
B	4	32
C	8	20
D	12	10
E	16	4
F	20	0

(a) *Indifference curves slope downwards from left to right.* Since we assume that consumers are rational then we must conclude that if consumers give up some of X they will want more of Y. This will therefore imply a negative, or inverse, slope for the indifference curve. This is illustrated in Figure 40.4. If the curve were to slope upwards from left to right, this would imply that as a consumer gave up some of X the consumer could only keep the level of utility constant by also giving up some of Y! This is clearly nonsense because it is illogical to assume that consumption of less of both goods can leave total utility undiminished.

(b) Indifference curves are *convex to the origin.* You will notice in Figure 40.4 that the indifference curve bends inwards towards the origin. This is because, as consumers give up more of X, they want relatively more and more of Y to compensate them.

(c) *The marginal rate of substitution.* As noted above the consumer requires more of X in return for Y (or vice versa) as the consumer moves along the indifference curve. In other words the rate of exchange of X for Y changes along the whole length of the curve.

The rate at which a consumer is willing to exchange one unit of one product for units of another is termed the marginal rate of substitution. It is given by the slope of the indifference curve.

As indifference curves are drawn convex to the origin the slope of the curve diminishes as

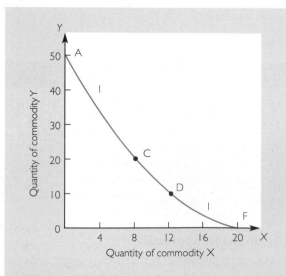

Figure 40.4 An indifference curve
At each point on the indifference curve the consumer believes that the same amount of utility is received.

we move up or down any curve (this was first illustrated in Figure 3.3, page 40), i.e. a diminishing marginal rate of substitution is assumed. Some textbooks incorrectly state that this is due to diminishing marginal utility. Such an error demonstrates a lack of knowledge of the development of economic thought and is clearly nonsense for, as we have seen, diminishing marginal utility assumes cardinal utility whereas indifference analysis assumes only ordinality.

(d) *An indifference map.* If we construct another indifference curve to the right of the original one (see Figure 40.5) this must show a situation where the consumer derives greater total utility, since for each point on the new curve the consumer is receiving more of both X and Y than the range NM on the old curve. We can say that:

Any movement of the indifference curve to the right is a movement to greater total utility.

Thus in Figure 40.5 point C_1 must yield more utility than point C, and so on. We are here at the heart of the ordinalist approach; we do not need to know how much utility the consumer obtains on indifference curve I to know that more is obtained on curve I_1 and more still on I_2. A series of indifference curves such as those in Figure 40.5 is known as an indifference map.

(e) *An infinite number of curves.* Given a consumer's scale of preferences, it is possible to construct any number of indifference curves on the indifference map. In each case a rightward shift gives more utility.

(f) *Indifference curves never cross.* It would be logically absurd for indifference curves to cross since this would imply that a consumer was equally happy with, for example, two combinations of X and Y, both of which have the same quantity of X but different quantities of Y.

The budget line

The indifference curve shows us consumers' preferences but it does not show us the situation in the market place. Here the consumer is constrained by income and by the prices of X and Y. They can both be shown by a budget line. Suppose that product X costs £5 per unit and product Y £2 per unit and that the consumer's income is £100.

A budget line shows all the combinations of two products which can be purchased with a given level of income. The slope of the line shows the relative prices of the two goods.

In Figure 40.6 you can see that the budget line AF stretches from 50 units of Y to 20 units of X. Thus X exchanges for Y at a rate of 2.5:1 which is their relative prices. The consumer is able to attain any point on the line, such as point C, or any point within the line, such as point U, where less than all of the budget is spent. However, given the constraint of an income of £100 it is not possible to obtain any combination of X and Y to the right of the budget line.

The line A_1F_1 shows the effect of an increase in income on the budget line. The whole line moves rightwards, showing that more of both X and Y may be consumed. Thus point C_1, which lies on the line A_1F_1, is unobtainable if the budget is limited to £100.

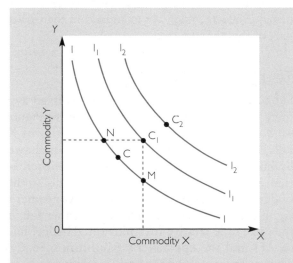

Figure 40.5 An indifference map
Each move to the right yields greater total unity. Thus C_1 gives more utility than C and so on. It is possible to construct an infinite number of curves.

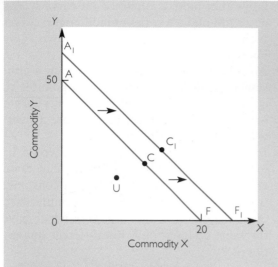

Figure 40.6 The budget line
A budget of £100 and prices for Y of £2/unit and for X of £5/unit gives a budget line AF, showing the ratio of prices of 1:2.5. The consumer can attain any position on the line, e.g. C, or within it, e.g. U. Line A_1F_1 shows an increase in the budget.

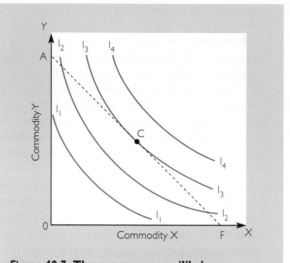

Figure 40.7 The consumer equilibrium
The consumer obtains maximum utility from a budget of AF by choosing the combination of X and Y represented by C, where the marginal rate of substitution is equal to the relative prices of X and Y.

Consumer equilibrium

To demonstrate the consumer's equilibrium, i.e. the point at which the consumer maximises utility with a given budget, we need to combine the indifference map and the budget line. In Figure 40.7 you can see that the consumer's equilibrium is at point C. This is because, with the budget line AF, it is the indifference curve the farthest to the right that can be reached. At this point the indifference curve I_3 is just tangential to the budget line.

Can we be sure that the indifference curve will be tangential to the budget line? Yes, because we have already shown that there can be an infinite number of indifference curves on an indifference map and therefore one of them must just touch the budget line without cutting it, i.e. be at a tangent to it.

Geometry tells us that when a tangent touches a straight line their slopes, at that point, are equal. Now in our model the budget line represents relative prices and the slope of the indifference curve the marginal rate of substitution. Thus we can conclude that:

The consumer's utility maximisation equilibrium occurs when relative prices are equal to the marginal rate of substitution.

Applications of indifference curve analysis

Having derived the consumer's equilibrium we can now use this to explain more fully the demand effects which we examined in the earlier part of this chapter.

The price–consumption line

Suppose that the consumer's budget is fixed and there are only two goods to choose from. Figure 40.8 shows us what happens as the price of X falls relative to Y. The original situation is shown by budget line AF where the consumer's equilibrium is at point C. As the price of X falls so the budget line pivots to AG and the consumer's equilibrium now changes to C_1. A further fall in the price of X relative to Y moves the budget line to AH and the consumer's equilibrium to C_2. Thus as the price of X has fallen relative to Y, so consumption of Y has fallen from OR to OS and then to OT, while consumption of X has grown from OC to OM and then to ON. These changes can be broken down into substitution and income effects.

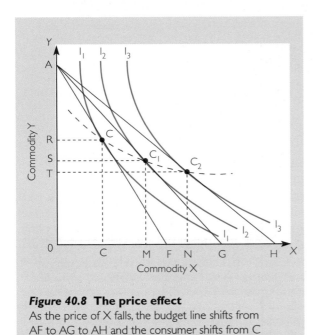

Figure 40.8 The price effect
As the price of X falls, the budget line shifts from AF to AG to AH and the consumer shifts from C to C_1 and C_2, substituting X and Y. CC_1C_2 is the price–consumption line.

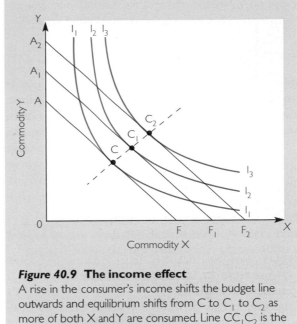

Figure 40.9 The income effect
A rise in the consumer's income shifts the budget line outwards and equilibrium shifts from C to C_1 to C_2 as more of both X and Y are consumed. Line CC_1C_2 is the income–consumption line.

The dashed line which joins points C, C_1 and C_2 shows how consumption alters in relation to price changes and is known as a price–consumption line.

Effect of a rise in income

We saw in Figure 40.6 that the effect of an increase in income is to shift the budget line outwards. This being the case, it can be seen in Figure 40.9 that as the budget line shifts outwards so the consumer moves to indifference curves further and further to the right. Thus as the budget line has shifted from AF to A_1F_1, and the equilibrium has changed from C to C_1, a further increase to A_2F_2 shifts the equilibrium C_2. Thus the effect of an increase in income is to increase the demand for both Y and X, provided that they are both normal goods.

Distinguishing between substitution and income effects

As the price of a product falls people may buy more of it for two reasons.

(a) It is cheaper (substitution effect).
(b) The fall in price in effect leaves them more income to spend (income effect).

By using indifference curve analysis it is possible to distinguish between the magnitude of these effects. In Figure 40.10 AF represents the original budget line and C the original equilibrium. The shift of the budget line to AG shows the effect of a fall in the price of X. As you can see this moves the consumer to a new equilibrium C_2 on indifference curve I_2; this means that the consumption of X increases from OM to OM_1. But how much of this increase is due to the fall in price and how much to the income effect of the fall in price making the consumer better off? In order to distinguish the two we project a new budget line A_1F_1 which is parallel to AG and tangential to the original indifference curve I_1. Remember, the fall in price increases the real income of consumers by leaving more money to spend. The line we have drawn, A_1F_1, shows the new relative prices of X and Y but at the original indifference curve or satisfaction level. This will tell us how much of X the consumer would have bought at that price if real income had not been increased.

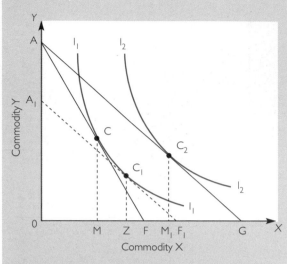

Figure 40.10 Separating income and substitution effects
Increase in demand, MZ, is due to substitution effect and ZM_1 to income effect. This is determined by projecting a hypothetical budget line A_1F_1 which is parallel to the new budget line AG and tangential to the original indifference line I_1.

It can be seen that at equilibrium C_1, OZ units of X would have been consumed. Thus the increase MZ is due to the substitution effect, while the rest of the increase in consumption at C_2, i.e. ZM_1, is due to the income effect alone.

Derivation of the demand curve

We can now use indifference curves to show how an individual's demand curve is derived. The upper portion of Figure 40.11 shows the effect of a price change similar to that in Figure 40.8. In this case we can see that the price–consumption line shows how demand for X grows as its price falls relative to Y. The lower portion of Figure 40.11 plots the price of X against the demand for it. If we correlate quantities of X demanded along the price–consumption line with the various prices on the demand curve we can see that we derive a normal downward-sloping demand curve. Thus as price has fallen from OA to OB to OC, so demand has expanded from OL to OM to ON.

As we concluded with marginal utility analysis, so we may also conclude here: if we can derive an

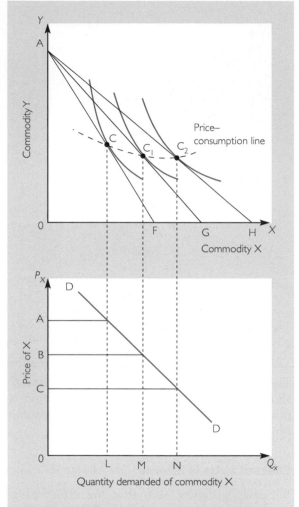

Figure 40.11 The derivation of the individual demand curve

individual's demand curve we can also derive a market demand curve by aggregating all the individual demand curves.

Inferior goods

We have demonstrated that a rise in a consumer's income will lead to an increase in demand. However, market observations tell us that this is not always so. In the case of inferior goods demand actually goes down as a result of an increase in income. The inferior goods phenomenon is due to the income effect and not to the substitution effect. In Figure 40.12 you can

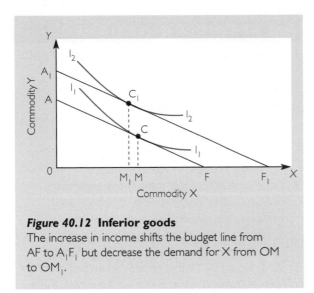

Figure 40.12 Inferior goods
The increase in income shifts the budget line from AF to A₁F₁ but decrease the demand for X from OM to OM₁.

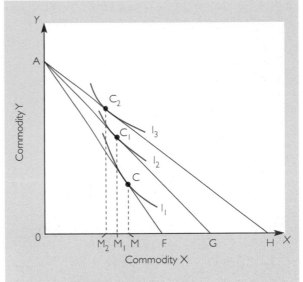

Figure 40.13 Giffen goods
The fall in the price of X is shown by the line pivoting outwards from AF to AG to AH, but instead of demand for X expanding it contracts from OM to OM₁ to OM₂.

observe that, as a result of the particular shape of the indifference curves, as the budget line has shifted outwards from AF to A_1F_1 the consumer's equilibrium has changed from C to C_1 involving a fall in the demand for X from OM to OM_1.

Giffen goods – again

It will be recalled that Giffen goods are those where a fall in the price of the good causes a fall in the demand. Figure 40.13 shows the fall in price of X by pivoting out the budget line from AF to AG and then to AH. As can be seen, owing to the peculiar shape of the indifference curves where Giffen goods are concerned, the demand for X does not expand but falls from OM to OM_1 and then to OM_2. This has come about because as Giffen goods are inferior there is a negative income effect as their price falls, and because they are such an important part of the household budget, the negative income effect has been sufficient to swamp the substitution effect.

Revealed preference theory

Professor Paul Samuelson developed a theory which was designed to do away with the subjective element which is implicit in the utility theories of both the marginal utility and the indifference curve approach. The only assumption necessary is that the consumer behaves rationally.

It is an analysis of consumer behaviour based only on the choices actually made by consumers in various price–income situations. Thus it is based on consumers' revealed preferences.

In Figure 40.14 AF represents the original budget line, with point E the consumer's revealed preference. A fall in the price of X pivots the budget line to AG. The consumer's revealed preference is now for the combination of X and Y represented by E_1. We can analyse this change by projecting a new budget line, parallel to AG and running through the original equilibrium E; that is, we have projected a set of circumstances where the individual is not able to consume more than was originally consumed but is on a budget line reflecting the new price. The consumer would then have to choose some combination along the line A_1F_1. It would be illogical to choose a combination to the left of E, i.e. along the part of the line A_1E, since this combination was available before the price fell. Logically, therefore, the consumer would choose some point to the right, e.g. Z. We are therefore able to attribute the increase in the demand for X of LM to the substitution effect alone, while the remaining increase in demand of MN to the new revealed preference of E_1 must be due to the

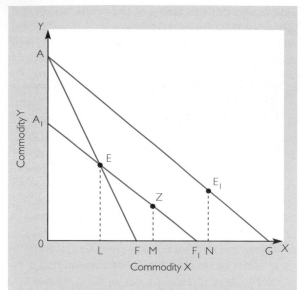

Figure 40.14 Revealed preference
A fall in the price of commodity X pivots the budget line from AF to AG. The consumer moves from E to E$_1$. Of the increase, LN, in demand, LM may be attributed to the price effect and MN to the income effect.

income effect. This analysis can then be extended to derive a demand curve for product X. We are thus able to analyse the effects of changes in price and incomes without reference to measures of utility or indifference curves.

Space precludes a fuller treatment of this theory; the interested reader should consult one of the more advanced texts on the subject.

Appendix summary

1 The indifference curve (or ordinalist) approach maintains that the consumer maximises utility when a person's marginal rate of substitution is equated with the relative price of products.
2 Indifference curve analysis can be used to explain price and income effects and to demonstrate the derivation of the demand curve.
3 Revealed preference theory is an attempt to explain consumers' behaviour without having to measure utility.

? APPENDIX QUESTIONS

1 Assume that a family has a weekly budget of £240 and a choice of only two goods that cost respectively £12 and £8.
   (a) Construct the family's budget line.
   (b) Show the effect of the price of the good which costs £12 increasing to £20.
   (c) In the original situation show the effect of the family's budget increasing to £360.
2 If one wished to avoid the subjective element involved in the marginal utility approach and indifference curve analysis, how could one justify the first law of demand, including the explanation of both the price effect and the income effect?
3 Study Figure 40.11 that shows the derivation of a normal demand curve and then show how the perverse demand curve for Giffen goods can be derived from Figure 40.13.
4 Describe and explain the equilibrium condition of a consumer when faced with a given income and relative prices. Starting from the equilibrium, how would the consumer respond to:
   (a) A rise in the price of one good?
   (b) A rise in the level of prices while the consumer's income remained constant?

Data response A
MAXIMISING UTILITY

Study the total utility figures given in Table 40.7 and then answer the following questions.

Table 40.7 Total utility schedules

Kg consumed	Cheese (£2/kg)	Fish (£4/kg)	Meat (£5/kg)
1	7	8	16
2	13	16	29
3	17	21	41
4	20.5	25	51
5	22	28.5	59
6	25	31.25	65
7	26	33.5	68

1 Assume that a poor family has a budget of £10, all of which it intends to spend, but only cheese is available. How many kilograms of cheese will be bought and why? Calculate the consumer's surplus under these conditions.
2 A richer family has a budget of £34 and a choice of all three commodities. Explain how the family will allocate its expenditure between the three commodities, assuming that it wishes to spend all of its budget. (Hint: remember the consumer equilibrium condition under the cardinalist approach.)
3 Do you notice anything unusual about the utility schedule for cheese? Explain your answer.

Data response B
CONSUMERS' EXPENDITURE

Study the information contained in Figure 40.15. This shows the indices of the sales of various categories of household goods and services. It also shows total consumers' expenditure. All figures are in real terms, but of course income was growing strongly over the period as a whole.

1 Describe the pattern of expenditure which the graph shows.
2 Which of the selected goods are normal goods?
3 Suppose that in 1978 the index for tobacco sales was 100 whereas in 1979 it was 97. Further suppose that the index for consumers' personal disposable income for those years rose from 108 to 110. Does this data suggest that tobacco is an inferior good or could the data be explained in some other way.
4 What would be the effect on the index for tobacco if the Chancellor were to increase significantly the tax on cigarettes?
5 What reasons account for the large increases in the index of sales of durable goods?

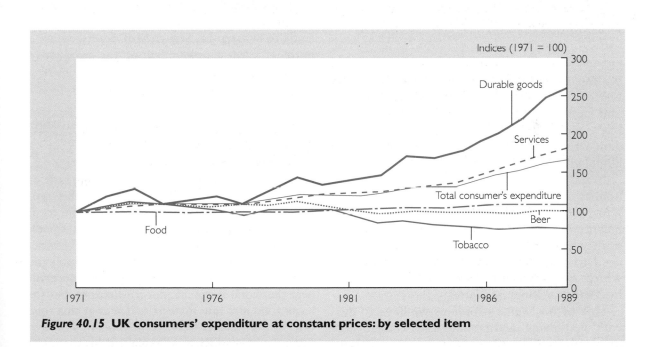

Figure 40.15 **UK consumers' expenditure at constant prices: by selected item**

41 The gains of international trade

Learning outcomes

At the end of this chapter you will be able to:
▶ Understand the theory of comparative advantage.
▶ Explain why countries may benefit from international trade.
▶ Appreciate the importance of economies of scale in determining the pattern of trade in differentiated products.
▶ Identify the major reasons why countries adopt protectionist measures.

We live in an increasingly international world. Nations trade more and more with one another and capital and finance is increasingly mobile. In the words of Marshall McLuhan, 'interdependence recreates the world in the image of a global village'.

In this section of the book we examine the economics of international trade, the accounting of international trade which is summarised in the balance of payments, and the monetary aspects of trade which determine exchange rates. Finally, we need to consider the major world institutions which are concerned with trade, such as the International Monetary Fund.

One of the major problems we have to deal with in studying international trade is the bias of nationalism. 'The notion dies hard', said **Lord Harlech**, 'that in some sort of way exports are patriotic but imports are immoral.' Many people believe it is best to buy the products of their own country; we are all familiar with slogans like 'buy British'. However, it makes no more sense to 'buy British' than it does to 'buy Lancastrian'. It does not occur to us in our private lives to feel threatened because we are dependent upon others for our food and clothing, but many people feel threatened by imports.

The bias of economic nationalism often obscures the benefits of specialisation which appear self-evident within the national economy. It is necessary, therefore, to examine the theory of the gains from trade – *the theory of comparative advantage* – and to see how international trade leads to what **John Stuart Mill** described as 'a more efficient employment of the productive forces of the world'.

The theory of comparative advantage

David Ricardo (1772–1823)

People and nations have traded since the time of the Phoenicians, but for most of this time they provided for most of their needs out of the local economy. Trade was for such things as spices, wines and precious metals. However, by the nineteenth century the UK had embarked upon the course which would see it export its products all over the world in return, not for luxuries, but for basic food and raw materials. It was at this time (1817) that, in his book, *Principles of Political Economy*, **David Ricardo** explained his theory of comparative advantage (sometimes called the theory of comparative costs). It is this theory, as subsequently modified by another great classical economist, **John Stuart Mill**, which is still the foundation of our theory of international trade today.

Absolute advantage and comparative advantage

One of the most fundamental reasons for trade is the diversity of conditions between different countries. For example, the UK can produce cars more cheaply than West African countries, but West African countries produce cocoa more cheaply than the UK. In these circumstances the UK is said to have an *absolute advantage* in cars and West African countries an absolute advantage in cocoa. If the West Africans want cars and the UK wants cocoa it is obviously to their mutual advantage to trade. However, trade depends not upon absolute advantage but upon *comparative advantage*; as **Professor Samuelson** says, 'it is not so immediately obvious, but it is no less true that international trade is mutually profitable even when one of the two can produce every commodity more cheaply'.

Consider the example of a town which has only one doctor but the doctor is also the best typist in town. Should this person be a doctor or a typist? Obviously the comparative advantage is in the medical field. If typing has to be done it would be better to employ a typist. The doctor will be better off because of concentrating on supplying a relatively rarer skill, the town will be better off because it gets more services of the doctor and a job will be created for the typist that is employed. The point is that although the doctor is better at both things than the typist, the doctor is much better as a doctor than the typist would be. So it is with international trade; a country should specialise not at what it is absolutely best at but at what it is relatively best at.

● *Common misunderstanding*

It is sometimes argued that some of the less developed countries are harmed by international trade because they do not have advantage in the production of any commodity. This argument is wrong because its advocates do not seem to understand that the basis for international trade is comparative and not absolute advantage. Thus while it may be possible to come up with a country that has no absolute advantage in the production of any one commodity it is bound to have comparative advantage in some commodities.

Comparative advantage: a model

Production possibilities

Ricardo illustrated his theory by considering trade between two countries, the UK and Portugal, and two products, wine and cloth. We will use two hypothetical countries, Richland and Poorland.

Richland has a population of 10 million and Poorland of 20 million. In Richland a day's labour will produce either 20 units of food or 18 units of clothing, whereas in Poorland a day's labour will only produce either 10 units of food or 4 units of clothing. It is apparent, therefore, that Richland has an absolute advantage in the production of both commodities.

If the two countries do not trade, they must produce both food and clothing for themselves, dividing their labour between the two commodities. Poorland's production possibilities are summarised in Table 41.1. Thus, if all resources were devoted to producing food, 200 million units could be produced, but no clothing. At the other extreme, 80 million units of clothing could be produced but no food. The Poorlanders must therefore choose some combination between those extremes. Say, for example, that the Poorlanders choose possibility D, producing 50 million units of food and 60 million units of clothing. These production possibilities can be represented graphically. Figure 41.1 shows that Poorland can obtain any combination of food or clothing along line AE, such as point D, or any combination within it such as U.

Table 41.1 **Poorland's production possibilities**

Possibility	Food (million units)	Clothing (million units)
A	200	0
B	150	20
C	100	40
D	50	60
E	0	80

The slope of the line shows the opportunity cost of food in terms of clothing; each 4 units of clothing given up will secure 10 units of food or

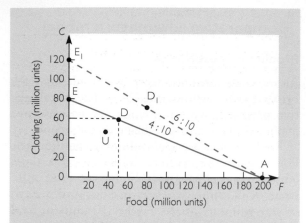

Figure 41.1 Poorland's production possibilities
The line AE shows Poorland's production possibilities before trade, i.e. any combination of food and clothing along line AE or within it. This represents a domestic ratio of 4:10. Line AE₁ shows possibilities not attainable at present.

vice versa. Thus we have a *domestic trading ratio* of 4:10. Position D_1 shows a better situation for Poorland, where it would be consuming both more food and clothing, but this is unattainable at the moment.

We can now construct a similar table and graph to show Richland's production possibilities. As you can see in Table 41.2, if Richland devoted all its resources to producing food 200 million units could be produced (possibility A) while, at the other extreme, if all resources were devoted to clothing production 180 million units could be produced (possibility K). If there is no

Table 41.2 **Richard's production possibilities**

Possibility	Food (million units)	Clothing (million units)
A	200	0
B	180	18
C	160	36
D	140	54
E	120	72
F	100	90
G	80	108
H	60	126
I	40	144
J	20	162
K	0	180

international trade, Richland must produce all its own food and clothing. One of the possible combinations must be chosen, e.g. possibility F which is 100 million units of food and 90 million units of clothing. This is illustrated in Figure 41.2. You can see from Table 41.2 and Figure 41.2 that the domestic trading ratio of food for clothing is 20 units of food given up gains 18 units of clothing. To make comparison with Poorland easier, instead of writing this as 20:18 we could express it as 10:9.

The opening up of trade

It might appear that there is little possibility of trade between the two nations.

In Richland
one day's labour will produce
either

20	or	18
units of food		units of clothing

In Poorland
one day's labour will produce
either

10	or	4
units of food		units of clothing

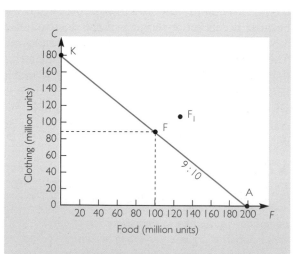

Figure 41.2 Richland's production possibilities
AK is the production possibility line. At point F Richland is producing and consuming 90 million units of clothing and 100 million units of food. Point F_1 shows a position where both more food and clothing would be consumed but which is at present unattainable.

Also, when we examine the production possibilities which each has chosen, i.e. possibility D for Poorland and F for Richland, and divide it by the respective populations we see that their per capita consumption of food and clothing is even more disproportionate.

| | Per capita consumption of: | |
	Food	Clothing
Richland	10.0	9.0
Poorland	2.5	3.0

If the possibility of trade between the two countries arises we can imagine the arguments which might be advanced against it in the two countries. In Richland it would be:

It is highly dangerous for us to trade with Poorland because the low wages of people there will enable producers to undercut our products by using cheap labour.

And in Poorland they would say:

If we trade with Richland we shall surely be swamped by the productive might of that country.

However, let us examine what is likely to happen if trade does begin between the two countries.

In Poorland 10 units of food can be exchanged for 4 units of clothing, but the same 10 units of food in Richland can be exchanged for 9 units of clothing. The Poorlanders therefore find that they can clothe themselves better by selling food to Richland rather than producing clothes themselves.

In Richland 10 units of food can be acquired at the cost of 9 units of clothing but in Poorland 10 units of food cost only 4 units of clothing. The Richlanders therefore find it more advantageous to produce clothing and export it to Poorland in exchange for food.

Thus it can be seen that although Richland has an absolute advantage in both commodities, it is to its advantage to specialise in the commodity in which it has the greater comparative advantage (clothing) and trade this for the other commodity. Similarly, Poorland has a comparative advantage in food and is better off specialising in producing this and trading it for clothing. We can draw from this the general principle that:

International trade is always potentially beneficial whenever the opportunity cost ratios of production within the countries differ from each other.

An international trading ratio

If trading is opened up between the two countries the two domestic trading ratios will be replaced by one international ratio. In our example, since the domestic ratios are 10:9 and 10:4, the international ratio must be somewhere between them. When Ricardo explained the theory he did not say how the ratio could be determined; he merely pointed out that any ratio which lay between the two domestic ratios could allow benefits from trade for both countries involved. It was John Stuart Mill who explained that the ratio would be determined by the forces of demand and supply in international markets. This is known as the *law of reciprocal demand*.

We cannot determine the ratio unless we have all the demand and supply information for both countries. Therefore, in order to proceed with an example we will simply assume an international ratio of 10:6. With the ratio of 10:6 we can demonstrate the advantage of trade to both countries. In Richland, 10 units of food previously cost 9 units of clothing but now they cost only 6 units, whereas in Poorland, 10 units of food bought only 4 units of clothing but with international trade they now buy 6. It is therefore to Richland's advantage to specialise in clothing and trade for food and for Poorland to specialise in food and trade for clothing.

The position after specialisation and trade

Let us assume that, once trade has begun, Richland specialises completely in the production of clothing and so produces 180 million units but no food at all. Similarly, Poorland specialises entirely in food production and therefore produces 200 million units. If you turn to Figure 41.3 you can see how Poorland's prospects have changed. It is now at A and if it were to trade all its food for clothing at the trade ratio of 10:6 it could obtain 120 million units instead of 80 million.

In order to complete the example we must make some assumption about the quantity of exports and imports. Let us suppose that Poorland exports 120 million units of food. If each 10 units of food buys 6 units of clothing then Poorland will be able to exchange its exports for 72 million units of clothing. Thus, before specialisation and trade

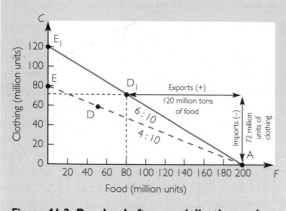

Figure 41.3 Poorland after specialisation and trade
By exporting food and importing clothing Poorland is able to attain position D_1 previously unattainable.

Poorland consumed 50 million units of food and 60 million units of clothing. After specialisation and trade it is now able to consume 80 million units of food and 72 million units of clothing. Thus its position has clearly improved. Figure 41.3 illustrates Poorland's position after trade.

Richland's position has similarly improved. It has specialised in clothing, producing 180 million units. Of these, 72 million have been exported, leaving it with 108 million units. The 72 million units of exports have earned it 120 million units of food, whereas before it consumed only 100 million units. Its position has therefore clearly improved. If you turn back to Figure 41.2 you will see that Richland is now at point F_1, a previously unattainable position.

Thus it can be seen that as a result of specialisation and trade both Richland and Poorland are better off. Not only that, but the total world production of both commodities has risen. These findings are summarised in Table 41.3.

Look again at the table on page 609 showing you the consumption per capita of both products in the two countries. You should now be able to determine that, after trade, the per capita consumption of both products in both countries has risen. For example, in Poorland consumption of food rises to 4 units per capita and clothing to 3.6. What are the figures for Richland?

Long-term versus short-term benefits

We have demonstrated that the levels of consumption and production increase as a result of international trade, so that we can argue that in the long run everyone benefits from trade. However, in the short and medium term we must consider the fortunes of those who work in industries without comparative advantage. In our example agriculture in Richland contracted as food was bought more cheaply in Poorland. This was to the advantage of the average Richland consumer, but the contraction of agriculture involved farmers going bankrupt and agricultural labourers losing their jobs.

This was indeed what happened in the UK in the late nineteenth century as the UK imported cheap food from the USA, Australia and Europe. As a result of this, agriculture in the UK experienced the 'Great Depression'. In the long term,

Table 41.3 Richland and Poorland before and after trade

Country	Trading ratio, food/ clothing	Clothing output	Clothing consumption	Clothing exports (+) or imports (−)	Food output	Food consumption	Food exports (+) or imports (−)
Situation before specialisation and trade:							
Richland	10 : 9	90	90	0	100	100	0
Poorland	10 : 4	60	60	0	50	50	0
Situation after specialisation and trade:							
Richland	10 : 6	180	108	+72	0	120	−120
Poorland	10 : 6	0	72	−72	200	80	+120
World gain from specialisation and trade:							
Total	−	30	30	−	50	50	−

however, it was also to the advantage of those in agriculture since it was better to enjoy high wages in a factory than low wages on a farm. At the present time the UK is going through great changes and many industries which traditionally had an advantage find that they have lost this advantage to new producers, for example in the Far East. Many arguments have been put forward in favour of protecting the UK's traditional industries against foreign competition. In the short term this may protect some jobs but in the long term protecting such industries will depress the living standard of everyone.

Comparative advantage and exchange rates

The overall theory of exchange rates is considered in Chapter 42, but we will here briefly consider the relationship between comparative advantage and exchange rates. Most international trade is not the swapping of one lot of goods for another but buying and selling through the medium of money and the exchange rate. Let us return to our Richland/Poorland example and assume that in Poorland food costs $2.00 a unit and clothing $5.00 a unit. These prices maintain the original domestic trading ratio of 10:4. Similarly we will assume that in Richland, food costs £1.00 a unit and clothing £1.11, thus retaining the ratio of 10:9.

If the exchange rate is such that in Richland imported goods are cheaper than domestically produced ones, then the Richlanders will buy them. Consider Figure 41.4. Here it can be seen that if the exchange rate is $1 = £1 no trade will take place because in Richland the price of imported goods is higher than that of domestically produced ones. Conversely, if the exchange rate were $5 = £1 then although imports would be cheap in Richland no trade would be possible because Richland's exports are too expensive for Poorlanders. However, if the exchange rate is $3 = £1 Richlanders will buy Poorland food, because it is cheaper than the domestic price, and, similarly, Poorlanders will buy Richland clothing because it is cheaper. Trade is therefore possible. In our example trade is possible so long as the exchange lies between the limits $2 = £1 and $4.50 = £1.

Domestic price of food and clothing (assuming the same domestic trading ratios as in the text)	Import prices at various exchange rates		
	Exchange rate 1 $1 = £1	Exchange rate 2 $3 = £1	Exchange rate 3 $5 = £1
Price of clothing in Richland = £1.11	£5.00	£1.67	£1.00
Price of food in Richland = £1.00	£2.00	£0.66	£0.40
Price of clothing in Poorland = $5.00	$1.11	$3.33	$5.55
Price of food in Poorland = $2.00	$1.00	$3.00	$5.00

☐ Import price higher than domestic price
No trade

▨ Import prices are lower than domestic prices in both countries
Trade will take place

▦ Import price lower than domestic but exports too expensive
No trade

Figure 41.4 Comparative advantage and exchange rates

It is disadvantageous to a country to have its exchange rate set incorrectly. An exchange rate set too high (overvalued) will cause a trade deficit, while if the rate is fixed too low (undervalued) consumers at home suffer although exporters may benefit. Governments are often tempted to manipulate exchange rates in the hope of benefiting trade. Although this may bring some short-term benefit it cannot alter the basic opportunity cost ratios on which international trade is based.

(a) In discussing our model of comparative advantage we have assumed constant opportunity costs. How realistic is this assumption?

(b) If the production possibilities in both Richland and Poorland were identical what would this imply for the opportunity cost ratios in both countries? Would international trade take place according to the principle of comparative advantage?

Extending the theory

In explaining the theory we have used a model with only two countries and two commodities. In practice the pattern of trade is much more complex than this. We must therefore consider a number of factors which bring about this complexity.

Many countries

The theory of comparative advantage will work better as more countries are brought into the example. This is because international trade not only requires a comparative advantage, but also depends upon countries wanting the goods which another country produces. In Figure 41.5 you can see that trade is possible between the four countries but would not be possible between two or even three. The UK wishes to import from Canada but Canada does not want the UK's exports, and so on. Multilateral trade allows for the international off-setting of debts from one country to another and so makes greater trade possible. In effect the UK pays for Canadian wheat with exports of machinery to Nigeria which in turn pays for these with exports of oil to the West Indies.

The greater the number of countries involved in trade the greater will be the opportunities for trade. It is for this reason that economists tend to favour multilateral trade agreements but oppose bilateral ones.

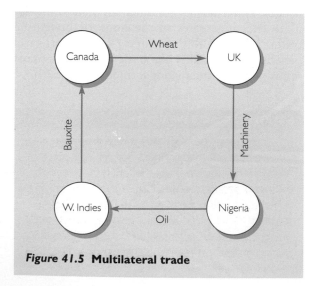

Figure 41.5 Multilateral trade

Many commodities

G. Harberler in his book, *Theory of International Trade*, demonstrated that when many commodities are introduced into the theory they can be arranged in order of comparative advantage. Figure 41.6 gives an illustration of this. The UK will tend to specialise in the commodities in the right-hand side of the diagram. As we move to the left so comparative advantage passes to the UK's trading partners. The extent to which a country is able to specialise in producing a commodity in which it has a comparative advantage will depend upon the strength of international demand for that commodity. For example, the greater the demand for, say, chemicals, the more the UK will be able to specialise in producing these and the less it will need to produce other products in which it lacks advantage, such as wheat.

It will be obvious to the reader that although the UK has no comparative advantage in wheat, it is still produced in the UK. This leads us to an important modification of the theory of comparative cost:

Specialisation is never complete.

Some wheat, and even some wine, can be produced in the UK because there are some domestic resources that are uniquely well suited to these products. Thus some of a product can be produced even though the country as a whole has no comparative advantage in it. Total specialisation may also be prevented by the **principle of increasing costs** (see page 616). For example, as more and more of a nation's available resources are devoted to a particular line of production the less suitable the available resources may be for this use.

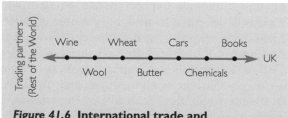

Figure 41.6 International trade and comparative advantage

Factor price equalisation

This idea was put forward by the economist, **Eli Hekscher**, later refined by **Bertil Ohlin**. Namely, that international trade would bring the prices of factors of production closer together. We might illustrate this Heckscher–Ohlin model of factor price equalisation hypothesis by considering the example of Europe and the USA in the nineteenth century. In the early nineteenth century rents were very high in Europe because land was scarce, and consequently food was also expensive. Wages on the other hand were low because people were plentiful. In the USA at the same time land was practically free. In the second half of the century improvements in transport allowed the USA to exploit its cheap land by exporting cheap food to Europe. This meant less land was needed for food in Europe which also utilised its labour by exporting manufactured goods to the USA. Consequently rents fell and wages rose in Europe and in the USA land became a valuable property as more and more of it was brought into food production. Thus the effect of international trade was to bring factor prices and commodity prices closer to each other. The effect of moving goods from country to country is a substitute for moving the factors of production themselves.

Again, we might note that international trade does not benefit every single person. Those that own the factors which are in very short supply have their incomes diminished as international trade lowers high factor prices and raises low ones. However, factor prices never completely equalise because factors of production are not homogeneous; national markets are protected by such things as transport costs and tariffs.

Economies of scale: decreasing costs

As a country specialises in the production of a particular commodity it could benefit from economies of scale. In our model so far we have assumed a constant cost case, i.e. the production possibility line is a straight line, indicating that the rate of exchange (food for clothing) is the same at all levels of output. Thus in Richland each time resources are switched from food to clothing production 9 units of clothing are gained for 10 of food. It could be, however, that, as

Richland specialises in clothing production, economies of scale reduce the cost of a unit of clothing. This is illustrated in Figure 41.7. Here the production possibility line is convex to the origin, illustrating decreasing costs. Originally Richland produced 90 million units of clothing at point F. It then specialises in clothing production and plans to move to position I (144 million units) but because of economies of scale it is able to produce more with the same amount of resources. Thus, it arrives at point I_1 (200 million units).

If an industry does experience decreasing costs as it specialises, this will increase the benefits of international trade. This was said to be one of the main reasons why the UK joined the European Community (now EU). The possibilities of achieving economies of scale could be a reason for specialisation and trade even when no comparative advantage exists.

To appreciate this consider the situation where Richland's and Poorland's production possibility frontiers are identical but both the food and clothing industries are characterised by economies of scale. Under the circumstances, at the pre-trade level, no country has comparative advantage, and thus there is no basis for mutually beneficial trade. However, even though neither

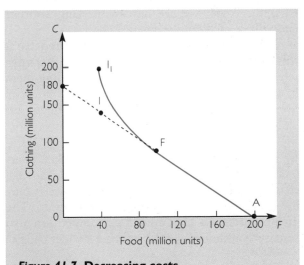

Figure 41.7 Decreasing costs
Richland starts from F and specialises in clothing, but experiences economies of scale so that instead of producing at point I (144 million units) it produces at point I_1 (200 million units).

country has comparative advantage, international trade will be beneficial for both countries if one country specialises in the production of food and the other in the production of clothing and trade with each other for the good they do not produce. Thus, economies of scale while increasing the benefits of trade when comparative advantage exists as illustrated in Figure 41.7 may also be a separate argument for international trade.

Differences in tastes: a reason for trade

Let us assume that Richland and Poorland can produce fish and meat equally successfully. Let us also assume that the Richlanders have no taste for fish but like meat, whereas the situation is the reverse in Poorland. The result will be that, if there is no trade, the fishing industry in Richland will languish, fish will be very cheap and meat expensive. The converse will be the case in Poorland. However, if trade takes place between them, Poorland will buy fish cheaply from Richland and Richland cheap meat from Poorland. This will reduce the cost of meat in Richland and of fish in Poorland, while the income of fishermen in Richland and of farmers in Poorland will go up. Thus trade will have proved beneficial to both countries even though no comparative advantage existed. (Note: we are here witnessing another example of factor price equalisation.)

The UK fishing industry has benefited from this principle for many years, catching herrings which are not popular in the UK and selling them at a good price in Scandinavia.

Increased competition

By bringing more producers into the market, international trade increases competition and, thereby, economic efficiency, and domestic monopolies may be broken down by foreign competition. The greater efficiency encouraged by competition also benefits consumers by offering them a wider choice.

Inter- versus intra-industry trade

The theory of comparative advantage is best at explaining international trade in goods that belong to different industries. For example, the UK exports cars to India and imports tea and

leather goods from India. Such trade is referred to as inter-industry trade. Yet, since the Second World War the dominant pattern of trade amongst the industrialised countries has been in the form of intra-industry trade – trade in goods that belong to the same/similar industry. For example, the EU exports cars and televisions to Japan and it also imports cars and televisions from Japan.

While it is true that differences in tastes amongst people living in different countries and within a single country explain why the overwhelming part of intra-industry trade is in differentiated products, economies of scale determine intra-industry specialisation. It would not be economically feasible for any one firm to specialise in the production of all possible types/brands of a particular product because of the enormous cost involved. For example, research and development costs in the pharmaceutical industry are huge. Thus, firms specialise in producing a small range of brands in order to benefit from economies of scale.

STUDENT ACTIVITY 41.2

(a) List the major trading partners of the UK and the major types of goods that are traded. Identify those countries where trade is overwhelmingly inter- or intra-industry.
(b) Outline the reasons why you believe consumers demand differentiated as opposed to homogeneous products.
(c) List the types of industries where economies of scale are of particular importance.
(d) Are the gains from trade likely to be greater when the production possibility frontiers for each country are characterised by increasing or decreasing opportunity costs?

Limitations of comparative advantage

There are a number of factors which prevent us from benefiting fully from comparative advantage. Some arise 'naturally' out of the economic situation, e.g. transport costs; others, however, are artificially imposed, e.g. customs duties. We will consider the more important of these limitations.

Obstacles to trade

There are a great many obstacles to trade which arise out of political considerations.

(a) *Tariffs and quotas.* Tariffs are taxes placed on imports. They may have the objective of either raising revenue or protecting industries. Which they accomplish will be determined by the elasticity of demand for imports. Quotas are a quantitative restriction on the amount of imports. Where restrictions successfully keep out imports they have the effect of protecting inefficient home producers. This means that although people employed in that industry may benefit, consumers generally are condemned to paying higher prices for goods.

(b) *Political frontiers.* Political frontiers can also be economic frontiers, as used to be the case between the Western world and the Communist bloc. Trade is further hindered by language differences and differing legal systems.

(c) *Currencies.* Foreign trade involves exchanging currency. This in itself is a barrier, but it is often added to by restrictions placed on currency exchange by governments.

(d) *Disguised barriers.* Governments may be able to discriminate in favour of home producers by such things as health and safety regulations. The Japanese safety requirements for cars are designed to favour Japanese methods of construction. In 1982 the UK imposed special health regulations on poultry, which had the effect of keeping out European imports. In the same year the French insisted that all video recorders entering France had to be processed by an obscure customs post in the centre of France, thus effectively limiting imports. Some observers have suggested that recent bans on UK beef in France and Germany had more to do with trade restriction than health risks from the outbreak of 'mad-cow' disease.

(e) *Trade diversion.* Before leaving obstacles to trade we must consider the phenomenon of trade diversion. This refers to the distortion of the pattern of world trade by tariffs and other artificial obstacles to trade. Suppose, for example, we consider three countries, Germany, France and Japan. The first two

have free trade because they are in the EU but have a common external tariff to keep out non-EU electrical goods. Both Germany and Japan produce video recorders but the German ones are more expensive. Without tariffs both Germany and France would import from Japan, but the effect of the tariff is that France now buys German video recorders even though they are more expensive to make. Thus the pattern of trade is distorted and French consumers suffer, as do Japanese exporters.

The creation of large trading blocks such as the EU introduces considerable trade diversion into the pattern of world trade. The effects of the abolition of tariff barriers between countries can be observed from the application of the Single European Act after 1992 that eliminated or greatly reduced barriers among EU countries.

Transport costs

Although a country may have a comparative advantage, this will be of little use if it is offset by high transport costs. Transport costs have a great influence upon the pattern of UK farming. UK farmers tend to produce products, such as milk or fresh vegetables, in which they are naturally protected by high transport costs.

Factor immobility

For a country to benefit from comparative advantage it is necessary for it to contract those industries in which it is at a disadvantage and expand those in which it has an advantage. This will involve wages, prices and employment falling in the declining industry. The fact that prices seem to go up easily but are very difficult to bring down is referred to as the downward inflexibility of prices or, more memorably, the 'sticky-upwardness' of prices. This will form part of a general resistance to change from those in the declining industry. We need only look at the recent problems in some UK industries such as coal to appreciate this. Such inflexibility may prevent an economy from benefiting fully from comparative advantage.

Increasing costs

Earlier in the chapter we considered the possibility that specialisation might produce decreasing costs. There is, on the other hand, the possibility that specialisation could lead to increasing costs. This could come about as the expansion of an industry drove up the price of labour and other factors, or it could occur as an industry expanded into less and less appropriate resources. This is illustrated in Figure 41.8. Here, starting from point F, forgoing the production of 60 million units of food at the constant cost ratio of 10:9 should have been expected to gain Richland a further 54 million units of clothing, thus moving it to point I. However, because of increasing costs, it has arrived at point I_1, a much lower level of production.

The principle of increasing costs also helps to explain why specialisation is not complete in international trade. If a country experiences increasing costs as it specialises then its domestic trading ratio is worsening. It would therefore stop specialising at the point where its domestic ratio became worse than the international ratio,

since at that point it would become more advantageous to import the product in which it was specialising. For example, in Figure 41.8, as Richland specialises in clothing production and moves from point F towards point I, it expects that each 10 units of food given up will gain it 9 units of clothing, but, because the production possibility line bends inwards, the rate deteriorates. Thus 10 units of food gain it only 8 of clothing and then 7 and so on. Once the rate has deteriorated to 10:6 (the international trading ratio) it would then be better to trade for clothing rather than produce more.

Other problems

Specialisation itself can create problems if there is a change in demand. For example, it could be argued that in the UK Lancashire overspecialised in cotton production so that when demand changed the whole area was plunged into depression. In recent years the dangers of overspecialisation were illustrated by the overdependence of the West Midlands in the UK on car production.

This problem also points to a shortcoming of the theory of comparative advantage, which is that it is static. The theory does not explain how comparative advantage arises in the first place, nor how it changes. The history of recent years illustrates only too well that comparative advantage can change; many Western nations which enjoyed an advantage in manufacturing have lost it to nations in the Far East.

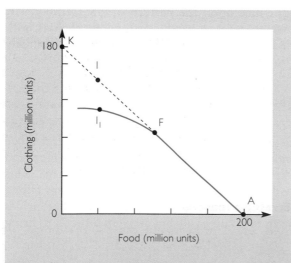

Figure 41.8 Increasing costs
As Richland moves from point F it arrives not at point I but at point I_1. If point I_1 is less than an output of 126 million units of clothing it would not be in Richland's interest to specialise this far because, at 126 million units of clothing 60 million units of food given up have gained only 36 million units of clothing, a rate equal to the international trading ratio of 10:6.

Protectionism considered

Adam Smith's *The Wealth of Nations* was designed to show the adverse effects of restrictions on trade. The majority of economists since his time have favoured free trade. However, the depression in the world economy in the late 1970s and early 1980s led to the revival of the protection lobby. Many prominent economists such as **Professor Wynne Godley** of Cambridge have argued for the need to protect the home market. The UK, however, has remained one of the most free markets in the world. Elsewhere protectionism is rife, not only through the use of tariffs but also through the subtler forms of economic nationalism. The UK has entered the EU which, while freeing trade between members, has erected tariff barriers to the rest of the world.

Many arguments are advanced in favour of protectionism. Some of the arguments are sounder than others, but all forms of protection suffer from the disadvantage that they may invite retaliation from trading partners. We will now consider the more significant arguments more fully.

Cheap labour

It is often argued that the economy must be protected from imports which are produced with cheap, or 'sweated', labour. Obviously there are important moral questions here, but unless there are international agreements about wages and working conditions there are dangers even for the exploited in pursuing this policy. It may be, for example, that banning exports from such countries simply depresses their labour markets further decreasing the demand for workers and further driving down wages and working conditions. In poor countries unemployment may literally mean death. If the poor wages and working conditions reflect market forces then preventing this trade is contrary to the whole principle of comparative advantage. For the poorer country it may deprive it of much needed exports that could eventually lead to increased wages in that country. Thus a ban could not only ensure that wages are kept low in the exporting country but also protect inefficient practices at home, in the long run depressing domestic living standards.

Dumping

If goods are sold on a foreign market below their cost of production this is referred to as dumping. This may be undertaken either by a foreign monopolist, using high profits at home to subsidise exports, or by foreign governments subsidising exports for political or strategic reasons. As dumping does not reflect comparative advantage and may damage home industries that would be important in the longer run, it is quite legitimate and necessary for a country to protect its industries from this type of unfair competition.

Infant industries

If a country is establishing an industry it may be necessary to protect it from competition temporarily until it reaches levels of production and costs which will allow it to compete with established industries elsewhere. This argument was advanced to support the protection of the European video cassette recorder industry. The problem is that protected industries tend to become dependent upon the protection. Nevertheless, Japan has used such policies in the past to protect industries in their early years that are now world leaders.

Unemployment and immobile factors

Imports may aggravate domestic unemployment and protection could be a way of alleviating this. As we have already noted, factors are immobile and protection could allow a country time to reallocate factors of production in a more efficient manner. However, in the long run such protection cannot be justified since it will protect inefficiency and ultimately depress the living standards of a nation.

Balance of payments

Perhaps the most immediate reason for bringing in protection is a balance of payments deficit. This has not been used much in the UK but an example is a package of measures brought in by the UK government in 1966 for this reason. They included exchange controls, an import surcharge and an import deposit scheme. Again this argument can be justified only in the short run, especially as it also invites retaliation from other countries.

Strategic reasons

Two world wars taught the UK the danger of being over-reliant on imports. For political or strategic reasons a country may not wish to be dependent upon imports and so may protect a home industry even if it is inefficient. Many countries maintain munitions industries for strategic reasons. In the UK, for example, the aerospace industry has received substantial 'protection' in the form of government money. Similarly, the EU is committed to protecting agriculture.

Bargaining

Even when a country can see no economic benefit in protection it may find it useful to have tariffs and restrictions as bargaining gambits in negotiating better terms with other nations.

Revenue

Customs duties are one of the oldest sources of government revenue. It should be remembered, however, that a tax on imports cannot both keep out imports and at the same time raise money. The effect of customs duties will depend upon the elasticity of demand for imports. If the demand is inelastic the tax will indeed make money for the government but will also add to domestic inflation. Where demand is elastic the government could increase its revenues by cutting the tax; this was confirmed as long ago as 1844 when **Sir Robert Peel** cut import duties. (The analysis of this is the same as that for any other indirect tax; see Chapter 6.)

The optimum tariff case

A country may be a 'large' country in the sense that it has purchasing power regarding a particular commodity (referred to in textbooks as monopsony power). A government by imposing a tariff on that commodity may succeed in forcing the foreign supplier to lower the price to such an extent that the country as a whole is better off than before the imposition of the tariff. The problem with this case is that in deciding on the optimum tariff very detailed information is needed about the supply and demand elasticities of the product.

Theory of second best

The neo-classical case for free trade is based on the assumption that the world is characterised by perfect competition. Needless to say this is not the case. For example, most governments in the world provide support for their agricultural industry. Let us take a situation where the government of a country is guaranteeing a price for wheat for its farmers at £2 a kilo whereas the world stands by to provide us with as much

wheat as we want for £1.50 a kilo. Under these circumstances if the government adopted a free trade policy it would be economic madness. Traders could simply import wheat and deliver it to the government at a profit. An example is the EU which often guarantees its farmers prices above the price of food on the world market. Thus, the EU has to set tariffs and impede imports. Such practices can take trading situations a long way from the assumption of international prices reflecting and allowing the working of comparative advantage.

Strategic trade policy argument

This is a 'new argument' for protectionism and is based on the observation that the most common form of market structure is oligopoly and not perfect competition. This argument is based on the premise that since abnormal profits are often being earned under oligopoly or monopoly, the government should intervene in order to obtain some or all of these abnormal profits from the foreign firm(s) either for itself by imposing a tariff or for the benefit of its domestic producers by providing them with subsidies. The problem with strategic trade policy is that a tremendous amount of information is needed in order to establish whether or not foreign forms are earning abnormal profits, never mind the magnitude. Furthermore, one needs to know how the rest of the economy will be affected by such a course of action.

Cultural reasons

A country may impose protectionist measures in order to safeguard the culture of its citizens. For example, the French government refused to remove the subsidies to its film industry on the ground that if it were to do so, it would have been destroyed and it feared the consequences for French culture.

Conclusion

We have endeavoured to show that the economic arguments are overwhelmingly in favour of a pattern of free world trade. However, in conclusion, we might note three qualifications upon this. First, the pattern of world trade which has grown up has not always reflected comparative advantage; it has all so often depended upon historical accident or upon the possession of surplus resources. Second, tariffs and other forms of protection have significantly modified the pattern of trade. Third, even where the country is committed to free trade and it has comparative advantage, it may be unwise to follow such a policy in a world of protectionism.

Summary

1 The bias of nationalism often prejudices our views on international trade.

2 The theory of comparative advantage explains that international trade is worthwhile and beneficial to both parties wherever there is any difference in their respective opportunity cost ratios.

3 The theory may be extended to include many countries and many commodities and comparative advantage may be improved by such things as decreasing costs.

4 There are many obstacles to free trade such as tariffs, quotas, exchange control and economic nationalism.

5 Comparative advantage is diminished by such things as transport costs, increasing costs and factor immobility.

6 Comparative cost ratios help to explain the determination of exchange rates.

7 Many arguments are advanced to support protectionism but few are valid in the long run.

8 Abraham Lincoln is supposed to have said 'I don't know much about the tariff. But I know this much, when we buy manufactured goods abroad, we get the goods and the foreigner gets the money. When we buy the manufactured goods at home we get both the goods and the money.' Identify the fallacy in Lincoln's statement.

? QUESTIONS

1 Explain the difference between absolute and comparative advantage.

2 Explain why every single country in the world is likely to have comparative advantage in the production of some commodity even though it may have no absolute advantage in the production of any one commodity.

3 Suppose that the production of olive oil and wine per unit of labour in Spain and the United States of America (USA) is as follows:

	Olive oil (litres)	Wine (litres)
Spain	50	30
USA	40	20

(a) Which country has absolute advantage in the production of both commodities?

(b) Which country has comparative advantage in the production of olive oil?

(c) Define the limits of possible international trading ratios within which the two countries may trade. (Hint: what are the domestic trading ratios in each country?)

(d) Explain how the international trading ratio will be determined.

(e) Wine costs 16.67 euros a litre and olive oil 6 euros in Spain whereas in the USA wine costs $4 and olive oil $2. Determine the limits of the exchange rate of the euro with the US dollars between which trade will be worthwhile for the two countries.

4 In your view, are there any valid arguments for protectionism?

5 Explain why business people often believe that protectionism will benefit the country whereas most economists believe the opposite?

6 With hindsight, can you think of any industries which should have been supported by the UK government owing to their beneficial externalities?

7 To what extent are exchange rates a result of the differing opportunity cost ratios between nations?

8 In an essay, evaluate the arguments for and against free trade.

Data response A
PUTTING TRADE IN ITS PLACE

Based on Larry Elliot's article which appeared in
The Guardian on 27 May 1996.

1 Outline the case for and against the proposal that
'trade should be linked to basic labour standards'.
2 Some commentators believe that globalisation
keeps workers in their place and wages down. Do
you agree with this view?

3 'Only around 5 per cent of exports to the west –
Europe, North America and Japan – come from
outside, and that percentage has actually fallen in
recent years.' Is this indicative of inter- or intra-
industry trade and what explanations can you offer
for this phenomenon?
4 Do you share the author's belief that growth and
rising incomes lead to trade rather than the
reverse?

Putting trade in its place

Globalisation is to the world economy what monetarism is to the
domestic economy. It represents the
final triumph of capital over labour,
since the corollary of the deregulation
of finance is the shackling of trade
unions. It means that national governments are left powerless in the face of
multinationals who will relocate at the
first whiff of interventionist policies.

Last week the OECD summed up
current thinking when it said globalisation 'gives all countries the possibility
of participating in world development
and all consumers the assurance of benefiting from increasingly vigorous
competition between producers'.

Yet these 'consumers' are also workers, and here the Panglossian view of
globalisation starts to break down. The
UK government strained every sinew to
prevent the OECD calling for the link
between trade and labour standards to be
discussed at the first ministerial meeting
of the World Trade Organisation in
Singapore later this year.

Britain argued that the International
Labour Organisation – a body anathema
to ministers these past 17 years – should
investigate. The intention, of course, is
to ensure that the issue is buried.

America thinks otherwise. It is insis-
tent that trade should be linked to basic
labour standards, and what the US
wants it usually gets. Nobody should
kid themselves that Washington's
actions are determined by altruism:

rather the US's approach is an amalgam
of Bill Clinton's political expediency in
the face of Pat Buchanan's blue-collar
protectionism and the naked self-interest of big business. The US likes global
rules and regulations in areas where it
perceives that it is at threat from international competition, but wants all
barriers removed where it is the dominant player.

For all that, the American stance is
welcome, because it offers some hope
that a human dimension can be added
to the trade debate. In an election year,
Clinton needs organised labour on his
side, and the unions are rightly out-
raged when they see US companies
being wooed to Bangladesh by adverts
boasting that unions are outlawed and
strikes illegal in special low-cost economic development zones.

Further, the debate over labour standards raises the question of whether the
cut-throat, lowest common denominator
approach has a long-run future. Trade
was certainly one of the three pillars of
the Golden Age of 1945–73 – along
with Keynesianism and postwar reconstruction – but it was ordered trade
developed within framework of rules
and capital controls.

The way in which US agribusiness
pushed through key parts of the
Uruguay Round is indicative of a brutal
new order in which powerful countries
decide what should be liberalised and
what shouldn't. This is the route to

anarchy and, ironically protectionism
as well.

Any challenge to globalisation
requires an understanding of what we
are dealing with. The theory is that liberalisation and deregulated capital
flows allow countries to specialise in
what they are good (or least bad) at,
and this international division of labour
raises global income. Free movement of
capital leads to higher foreign investment and the diffusion of best practice.
As a result, the developing countries
that do best are those with the least
state intervention and the freest trade
and these new 'tiger economies' pose a
massive competitive threat to living
standards in the developed world.

This last point is one of the keys to
the whole debate. Globalisation is an
important weapon for international capital because it keeps workers in their
place and wages down.

In fact, as the American economist
Paul Krugman has pointed out, the idea
of global competition bearing down on
Western living standards is a myth. Only
around 5 per cent of exports to the West
– Europe, North America and Japan –
come from outside, and that percentage
has actually fallen in recent years.

Professor Ajit Singh, of Cambridge
University, goes further. He finds no
evidence that globalisation has been
good for us and, to the extent that it is
symbiotically linked to deflationary
macro-economic policies, it is positively harmful.

Prof. Singh compares the past 15 years with the Golden Age of 1945–73 and concludes: 'Under the market supremacy model of the 1980s and 1990s, liberalisation and globalisation in industrial countries have not resulted in increased long-term economic growth, nor are these likely to do so in the foreseeable future under the present policy regime'.

This is a valid criticism. On almost any measure that real people could relate to – growth, unemployment, living standards, investment – the record of the past 20 years has been far poorer than in the Golden Age.

Prof. Singh does not advocate protectionism. Rather, he argues that the current euphoria for liberalism is potentially dangerous precisely because it could lead to a descent into the beggar-my-neighbour policies of the 1930s. On his reckoning, the Golden Age was not a fluke, but the consequence of the right policy choices and the creation of an appropriate institutional framework.

An Unctad paper by Paul Bairoch and Richard Kozul-Wright, argues that the pre-First World War era was not one of trade liberalisation, nor of diminished expectations for the role of the state. Rather, just as with Japan in the 1960s and Korea in the 1980s, countries grew more rapidly after they became more protectionist. Countries that experienced huge capital inflows – such as Argentina – were often destabilised.

The paper's thrust is that pre-1914 was not a golden age of economic growth and rapid convergence. Instead the internationalisation of finance capital was associated with uneven development, often reinforcing existing differences in the world economy rather than bringing about convergence.

This revisionism is long, long overdue. Internationalism and trade are grand ideals, much to be preferred to nationalism and protectionism, but history suggests that growth and rising incomes lead to trade rather than the reverse.

Source: The Guardian, 27 May 1996. Reprinted with permission.

42 The balance of payments and exchange rates

Learning outcomes

At the end of this chapter you will be able to:

▶ Describe the pattern of the UK's trade.
▶ List the main components of the balance of payments account.
▶ Relate the terms of trade to international competitiveness.
▶ Evaluate the methods of dealing with balance of payments problems.
▶ Explain the strengths and weaknesses of different exchange rate regimes.
▶ Appreciate the importance of non-trade factors in determining the exchange rate.
▶ Give a brief history of the UK's current exchange rate.

We have already briefly looked at the balance of payments in Chapter 16, here we give a more detailed account of movements in international trade and explore the determination of exchange rates in more depth.

The pattern of the UK's overseas trade

The importance of international trade

There are few nations in the world as dependent upon foreign trade as the UK. The UK depends upon imports for almost half its food requirements and for most of the raw materials needed by its industries. Equally, the continued well-being of the economy depends upon exporting a large proportion of the national product each year. Table 42.1 shows the importance for the UK of exports and imports.

Table 42.1 GDP and international trade in the UK

	Index of GDP (1995 = 100)	Exports as a percentage of GDP	Imports as a percentage of GDP
1985	78.5	28.7	27.8
1990	92.4	24.0	26.6
1995	100	28.3	28.7
1999	111.3	25.8	27.5

Source: Adapted from National Statistics. © Crown Copyright 2001

International trade is a vital component of national income, a major policy target and a source of fluctuations in aggregate demand.

The UK economy suffers from the structural problem that, as the economy expands, it tends to draw in raw materials which are necessary for its manufacturing industries. However, it often happens that, before these can be turned into exports, the flow of imports has caused a balance of payments crisis that necessitates contractionary policies to rectify the imbalance (see the stop–go cycle in Chapter 18).

In recent years a more disturbing trend has been the tendency for the expanding economy to draw in manufactured goods which the domestic economy is failing to produce. In 1983, for the first time since the industrial revolution, the UK imported more manufactured goods than it exported. The traditional situation is thus changed so that expansion of the domestic economy causes the balance of trade to deteriorate as consumers buy imported manufactured goods. By the late 1980s and early 1990s massive trade imbalances were recorded. Table 42.2 shows this has not reversed today with the surplus from North Sea oil now being more than off-set by deficits on manufactured goods and food.

Table 42.2 **UK Trade in goods (visibles) 1999**

	Goods exported		Goods imported	
	£m	%	£m	%
Food, beverages and tobacco	9929	6.0	16527	8.6
Basic materials	2280	1.4	5516	2.8
Oil	9050	5.5	4842	2.5
Other fuels	803	0.5	783	0.4
Semi-manufactured goods	43234	26.0	45437	23.6
Finished manufactured goods	98876	59.7	117540	61.0
Unspecified goods	1495	0.9	1789	0.9
Total	165667	100.0	192434	100.0

Source: National Statistics: *The Pink Book 2000.* © Crown Copyright 2001

In Table 42.2. you can see that there is often a sort of correspondence between the types of goods that are exported and imported, e.g. the UK both exports and imports large amounts of manufactured goods to and from Germany. On the surface this seems to fly in the face of the principle of comparative costs discussed in the previous chapter. But we saw then that the growing sophistication and fragmentation of consumer demand can explain this.

In addition to the trade in goods, which is termed 'visible' trade, there is trade in 'invisibles', i.e. services. For most of the last 100 years or so, the UK has had a deficit on visible trade that has been made up by a surplus on invisible earnings. However, while invisibles have become increasingly important, the UK has also enjoyed an improved position on visible trade due to North Sea oil, which has both added to exports and reduced the need for imports.

Figure 42.1 shows that the balance on current account has been largely determined by the balance of trade in goods and services. The years 1980–82 saw surpluses on visible trade which were due both to the impact of North Sea oil and the depressed state of the economy which restrained imports. However, after 1982 visible trade swung back into deficit. Thus from 1979 to 1986 the current account was in surplus but by 1987 the increasing deficit on visibles was pulling the current account back into deficit. This deficit in visibles grew rapidly to reach a record high in 1989 of £24.7bn but then improved in the 1990s to around £10bn. This allowed the growth in the surplus on invisibles, helped by higher surpluses on investment income, to pull the current account back to broad balance for the mid-1990s. Since 1997, however, there has been a rapid increase in the visibles deficit as imports have again been sucked in by a growing economy and exports have not kept pace. In 1999 there was a 6 per cent

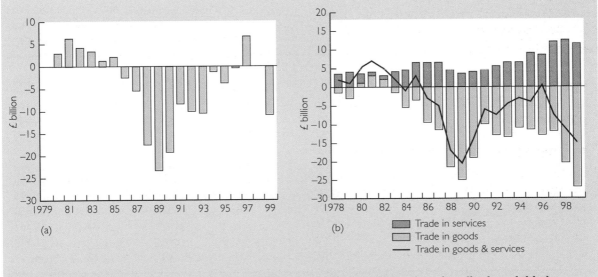

Figure 42.1 (a) Current account balance and (b) trade in goods and services (credits less debits)
Source: *United Kingdom Balance of Payments 2000.* National Statistics. © Crown Copyright 2001

rise in goods imports from non-EU countries with half of this £20.3bn deficit attributable to imports from SE Asia. Together with a £6.4bn goods deficit with EU, the result was a new record deficit for visibles of £26bn. Hence the current account has moved steeply back to overall deficit in 1999.

The direction of trade

In Table 42.3 you can see that over 70 per cent of the UK's overseas trade is with just a dozen countries. Despite this the UK continues to have a more worldwide pattern of trade than most other nations. Traditionally, the UK drew its imports of raw materials from the Commonwealth and former Empire to whom, in return, it exported its manufactures. Since 1945 there has been a growing dependence on North America and Europe. This trend was apparent before the UK joined the EU and was one of the main reasons for joining. Since joining the EU, the UK has become much more dependent upon EU trade. When the UK entered the EU around 27 per cent of visible trade was with the Community but by 1999 this was 59 per cent (see also Chapter 45). This is well illustrated by considering the position of one of the UK's traditional trading partners, Canada. In 1967 Canada was the second most important nation in the UK's overseas trade; by 1976 it was ninth, in 1999 it was thirteenth. Japan joined the list of the UK's top 10 trading partners only in 1985. This may seem a little surprising considering the vast quantities of cars and electronic equipment imported from there. However, the list measures both imports and exports and, as you can see from Table 42.3, there is a large deficit in the UK's balance of trade with Japan. This imbalance has been due, at least in part, to the protective measures the Japanese use to guard their home market and more recently the recession in Japan.

International competitiveness

The '*terms of trade*' is a measure of the relative prices of imports and exports. It is calculated by taking the *index of export prices* and dividing it by the *index of import prices*.

If the index increases this is said to be a favourable movement in the terms of trade; if it falls it is said to be unfavourable. A favourable movement in the terms of trade means that a given quantity of exports will buy more imports. The word favourable may, however, be mislead-

Table 42.3 **The UK's 12 leading trading partners (by value) 1999**

Country position (in order of importance in UK's trade)	International trade 1999				
	Imports		Exports		Total
	£m	%	£m	%	£m
1 USA	35 222	14.4	39 834	17.3	75 056
2 Germany	30 524	12.5	24 924	10.9	55 448
3 France	23 741	9.7	20 457	8.9	44 198
4 Netherlands	15 203	6.2	16 552	7.2	31 755
5 Irish Republic	10 220	4.2	13 319	5.8	23 539
6 Belgium/Luxembourg	11 039	4.5	11 136	4.8	22 175
7 Italy	11 384	4.6	9 812	4.3	21 196
8 Spain	11 255	4.6	9 240	4.0	20 495
9 Japan	10 115	4.1	5 798	4.4	15 913
10 Switzerland	6 299	2.6	4 631	2.0	10 930
11 Sweden	5 178	2.1	5 159	2.2	10 337
12 Hong Kong	5 526	2.3	3 233	1.4	8 759
World total	244 878	71.8	229 649	73.3	474 527

Source: National Statistics. © Crown Copyright 2001

Table 42.4 The UK's terms of trade (1995 = 100)

| | Price indices | | |
	Exports	Imports	Terms of trade
1975	28.5	30.9	92.2
1980	56.6	53.2	106.4
1985	80.1	78.2	102.4
1990	81.7	81.2	100.6
1995	100	100	100
1999	89.8	86.8	103.5

Source: National Statistics (*Economic Trends* and *Annual Supplement*).
© Crown Copyright 2001

ing: as a relative rise in the price of exports will be beneficial only if the demand for exports is inelastic (see below, page 629).

The relative price of exports and imports are affected by changes in the exchange rate but anything which reduces the relative price of UK exports will make the UK more competitive. Hence reductions in unit costs compared to other countries will allow relative reductions in export prices (and also reduce the competitiveness of imports on the home market). Reductions in input costs and relative increases in productivity will therefore tend to increase international competitiveness.

Table 42.4 reflects:

(a) Export and import prices rose for ten consecutive years from 1986 and 1996 but the largest rise was caused when the pound sterling depreciated rapidly after the UK left the ERM (see Chapter 18).

(b) From 1997 both exports and import prices have fallen, reflecting falls in input prices, including crude oil, and the weakening of the euro (see page 637).

STUDENT ACTIVITY 42.1

Define the expressions terms of trade and balance of trade. Discuss the possible relationship between the two.

The balance of payments

We have so far considered the export and import of goods and services. However, there are many other international transactions. These are brought together in the balance of payments account published in the *National Statistics 'Pink Book'*.

The balance of payments is an account of all the transactions of everyone living and working in the UK with the rest of the world.

You saw in Chapter 18 that if a person in the UK sells goods or services to someone abroad, this creates an inflow (+) of pounds, while anyone in the UK buying goods or services abroad creates an outflow (−), but if a foreigner invests in the UK, e.g. if a US company takes over a UK company, then an inflow (+) of currency is created. Not so obviously, if the UK reduces its reserves of foreign currency, this is recorded as a credit (+), as is the receipt of loans from abroad, while, conversely, increasing the reserves of foreign currency or making a loan is shown as a debit (−). When all these transactions are recorded we arrive at a balance of payments statement as in Table 42.5.

Table 42.5 Balance of payments of the UK, 1999

	£m (credits minus debits)
1. Current account	
A. Goods and services:	−15 229
1. Goods	−26 767
2. Services	+11 538
B. Income	
1. From employment	+191
2. From investments	+8 131
C. Transfers	
1. Central government	+2 186
2. Other sectors	−6 270
Total current account balance	**−10 981**
2. Capital and financial accounts	
Capital account	+776
Financial account	+5 853
Of which	
Direct investment	−72 962
Portfolio investment	+110 170
Other investment	−31 994
Reserve assets	−639
Total capital and financial account balance	**+6 629**
Total current, capital and financial accounts	**0***

* Net errors and omissions +4 352

Source: National Statistics *'The Pink Book'*, 2000 (published by The Stationery Office). © Crown Copyright 2001

Items in the account

Table 42.5 shows the various balances on the sections of the balance of payment accounts for 1999.

Current account

This has two main components: *visible trade*, which is the export and import of goods (which is sometimes called the balance of trade); and *invisible trade*, which is chiefly the sale and purchase of services. Major items in the trade in goods were shown in Table 42.2. The major components of services exports for the UK are transportation services; tourism; financial services; royalties and licence fees; communications, computer and information services; education.

● *Common misunderstanding*

The current account balance is often confused with the balance of payments. In Table 42.5 you can see that the balance of trade in goods and services is only a part of the balance of payments, albeit an important part. It is therefore possible to have a deficit in the trade on goods and services but a surplus on the balance of payments, or vice versa.

Capital and financial accounts

This involves the movement of capital (money) rather than goods and services, i.e. it is concerned with international loans and investment.

(a) The *capital account* records the transfer of ownership of fixed assets (e.g. land purchases and sales associated with embassies) or of non-produced, non-financial assets such as copyrights.

(b) *Direct investment* capital refers to finance provided to, or received from, an enterprise by an investor in another country who is also an owner of that enterprise. (The Nissan car plant in Sunderland is an example of Foreign Direct Investment (FDI) from Japan.)

(c) *Portfolio investment* refers to transactions in equity (shares) and financial instruments such as debt securities including bonds.

(d) *Other investment* records capital transactions not included in the other categories, e.g. trade credits and other loans; and also currency and deposits.

(e) *Reserve assets* refers chiefly to the increases or decreases in the reserves of gold and foreign currency held by the Bank of England. It is because of the 'reversed sign' on these flows that the overall account balances.

The transactions in external assets and liabilities from portfolio and other investments has been growing steadily in importance, as has its instability. This instability is caused by large movements of short-term capital. This so-called 'hot money' tends to move about in search of better interest rates or expectations of changes in the value of currencies. It should also be remembered that the UK is a major exporter of capital, as the figures for direct investment show. By this we mean that Britons invest in companies and property overseas to a greater extent than foreigners invest in the UK.

In the short term, therefore, this creates an outflow. However, we should recall that, in the longer term, money will flow back into the country by way of interest, profits and dividends on the current account. The UK is, in fact, one of the world's largest creditor nations.

● *Common misunderstanding*

'The balance of payments always balances, thus there is no need to worry about a country's external equilibrium position.' It is true that in an accounting sense the balance of payments always balances because for every debit there is a corresponding credit. However, from an economic policy view we need to look at the individual balances on the current and capital accounts.

The correct policy for a fundamental disequilibrium will depend upon its size, cause and upon the exchange rate policy which the government is pursuing. In this connection we must also consider the state of the domestic economy. Table 42.6 summarises some of the possible combinations of problems. A deficit on the balance of payments might be accompanied by either a high or a low level of domestic activity. The required solutions would obviously be very different; for example, if an external deficit was accompanied

Table 42.6 Problems and solutions with balance of payments

Causes of problem	Suggested remedies
Deficit problems **Problem 1:** (a) Inflationary pressures, exports low because prices too high, e.g. UK 1989. (b) Interest rates low and therefore 'hot' money flows out to earn high interest elsewhere.	(a) Increase productivity to lower prices and increase exports. (b) Tight fiscal policy and dear money policy to deflate economy; also higher interest rates attract 'hot money'.
Problem 2: (a) Currency overvalued, therefore exports low despite unemployment in the domestic economy, e.g. UK 1981 and 1992. (b) Capital outflow because of investment overseas or too much government expenditure overseas.	(a) Depreciate or devalue the currency if import/export elasticities are favourable. (b) Stop or reduce drain, e.g. by exchange control regulations on investment.
Surplus problems **Problem 3:** (a) Spare capacity in the economy, prices relatively low, exports high, e.g. West Germany 1982. (b) Interest rates high, 'hot' money flows in to earn high interest.	(a) Easy fiscal and cheap money policies, with low taxes and higher government expenditure, boost internal economy while lower interest rates reduce inflow of 'hot money'.
Problem 4: (a) Currency overvalued, embarrassment to trading partners, exports artificially cheap while imports dear, domestic living standards restricted, e.g. Japan 1983.	(a) Appreciate or revalue currency; this will reduce exports and increase imports if Marshall–Lerner conditions fulfilled. (b) Increase capital expenditure overseas or increase foreign aid.

by heavy unemployment domestically, a solution which aimed at further depressing the level of economic activity would hardly be ideal. Similarly, when we consider the possibility of a surplus on the balance of payments, this too could be accompanied by either a high or low level of domestic economic activity.

The type of exchange rate policy to which a country is committed will also influence the situation. When, as was the case with the UK up to 1972 and more recently when sterling was in the ERM (from October 1990 to September 1992), a country is committed to fixed exchange rates, this limits the options. Under these circumstances the UK was often obliged to subordinate internal policy, such as the pursuit of economic growth, to the external objective of maintaining the exchange rate. However, the adoption of a float-

ing exchange rate has still not entirely freed internal policy from external constraint.

The problems of a surplus

Why worry?

It might not be immediately obvious that a surplus presents problems. However, there are a number of reasons why it might.

(a) *De-industrialisation.* The UK's experience of surplus in the late 1970s and early 1980s has demonstrated that a surplus can lead to undesirable domestic consequences. The oil surpluses were used to finance industrial imports, thus leading to a rundown of the economy. The surpluses also attracted 'hot' money which led to an overvaluation of the currency, which in turn decreased the competitiveness of exports (see Chapter 18).

(b) *Feedback effects.* Since it is the case that overall the international payments of all nations must balance, a persistent surplus may, therefore, embarrass one's trading partners and force them to place restrictions on imports which are to the detriment of world trade. The activities of a country's trading partners in getting rid of their deficits may well decrease the demand for the surplus country's exports, thus 'feeding back' the effect of a deficit to the surplus country.

(c) *Inflationary consequences.* Both Keynesian and monetarist analysis of a balance of payments surplus points to possible inflationary consequences. In Keynesian analysis demand pull inflation will be caused if the economy is at, or near, full employment since a surplus is an injection into the economy. Monetarists argue that a surplus increases the money supply unless exchange rates are freely floating.

(d) *Depression of domestic living standards.* A country running a considerable balance of payments surplus is, in fact, keeping down the standard of living of its citizens. This is because the reserves of foreign currency built up by the surplus could be turned into goods and services for the population without any cost in resources to the economy. This was part of **Adam Smith's** objection to the mercantilists who had argued that a country got richer by hoarding gold earned from its exports.

Curing a surplus

A surplus might be reduced or eliminated by inflating the economy and/or revaluing the currency. Inflating the economy will tend to increase the demand for imports especially if the economy is at full employment. Revaluing the currency will reduce the price of imports and increase the price of exports, thus tending to eliminate the surplus.

Japan had huge current account surpluses during the 1980s. This was partly a result of productivity increases in Japanese industry but it was also due to protective measures. Under these circumstances getting rid of the protectionist measures could reduce the surplus. It would of

course also be possible for a nation to reduce its surplus by increasing overseas aid.

● *Common misunderstanding*

Although a surplus on the balance of payments is not as a pressing need for policy as a deficit, a persistent surplus indicates a country is not making the best use of its opportunities.

Deficit problems

Types of policy

The correct measures to remedy a deficit will depend upon its cause and also upon the exchange rate regime. A short-term deficit might be dealt with by running down reserves or by borrowing. Another short-term measure might be to raise interest rates to encourage the inflow of money. When there is a more fundamental payments deficit other measures will have to be taken.

We can divide measures to rectify a deficit into two main categories:

(a) *Expenditure reducing.* These are measures such as domestic deflation which aim to rectify the deficit by cutting expenditure.
(b) *Expenditure switching.* This refers to measures such as import controls, designed to switch expenditure from imports to domestically produced goods.

The two types of measures need not be regarded as alternatives but rather as complements; for example, a government might reduce expenditure to create spare capacity in the economy prior to creating extra demand through expenditure-switching policies.

Deflation

The demand for imports could be restrained (expenditure reducing) by restricting the total level of demand in the country through fiscal and monetary policies. It might appear that this is a very indirect method. However, there are three reasons it might be adopted. First, the country may wish to maintain a fixed exchange rate policy. Second, protective measures such as import controls may conflict with a nation's treaty obligations such as GATT/WTO and the Treaty of Rome (see Chapter 48). Third, protective measures also invite retaliation. These reasons explain why in the period 1947–72 deflation was the UK's chief method of rectifying a payment deficit. The recurring need to deflate the economy formed part of the so-called 'stop–go cycle'.

Using deflation to rectify a deficit is subordinating the needs of the domestic economy to the external need to maintain exchange rates. The cost of such a policy may be high in terms of unemployment. This is one of the most important disadvantages of fixed exchange rates. Deflation might have a secondary expenditure-switching effect if domestic rates of inflation are reduced below those of the nation's trading partners, thus giving it a price advantage.

Protection

It should also be remembered that protective measures do little or nothing about the underlying causes of the deficit but attempt to cure it by simply cutting off imports. Although recent years saw a rising tide of protectionism in world trade, the successful completion of the Uruguay round of GATT and the establishment of the World Trade Organisation should hopefully reverse this trend (see Chapter 44).

Devaluation or depreciation

If a nation operating a fixed exchange rate drops the external price of its currency, as the UK did in 1967 when the exchange rate changed from £1 = $2.80 to £1 = $2.40, this is referred to as devaluation. If a country has a 'floating' exchange rate and it allows the external value of its currency to decrease, this is referred to as depreciation.

STUDENT ACTIVITY 42.2

Suppose that a Prime Minister decides to devalue the pound and then tells the nation that it will not affect the value of the 'pound in your pocket'. Is this promise strictly true?

The UK allowed its currency to float when it left the ERM in September 1992 and sterling settled at a significantly lower level than its central par value under the ERM. Both of these actions have

the same effect, i.e. exports will now appear cheaper to foreigners while imports will appear more expensive to domestic consumers. These measures are thus expenditure switching. In order to assess devaluation or depreciation as a method, we need to consider the elasticities of demand for imports and exports.

The Marshall–Lerner criterion

A.P. Lerner in his book *Economics of Control* applied **Marshall's** elasticity concept to foreign trade. It should be clear that devaluation will increase total earnings from exports only if demand for exports and imports are sufficiently elastic. However, the question arises as to how the relative elasticities of demand affect the balance of payments position. The Marshall–Lerner criterion states that devaluation will improve the balance of trade only if the sum of the elasticities of demand for exports and imports is greater than unity. Conversely, a payment surplus would be reduced by revaluation if the same criterion was fulfilled.

We can demonstrate the Marshall–Lerner condition by taking the extreme position that the price elasticity of demand for a country's exports is perfectly inelastic (= 0). Given this assumption, devaluation will improve the balance of trade if, and only if, the price elasticity of demand for imports is elastic, i.e. greater than one.

Empirical studies strongly suggest that the Marshall–Lerner condition is satisfied.

The J-curve

It has frequently been observed that measures taken to rectify a balance of payments deficit have often led to an immediate deterioration in the payments position followed by a subsequent recovery. If we plot this on a graph we obtain the J-curve effect illustrated in Figure 42.2 A recent example of the J-curve effect was provided by the UK trade figures following sterling's exit from the ERM.

STUDENT ACTIVITY 42.3

Before reading the next section below, try to work out why would the sudden fall in the exchange rate upon leaving the ERM have a negative effect upon the balance of trade before it has a positive effect? Why should this occur?

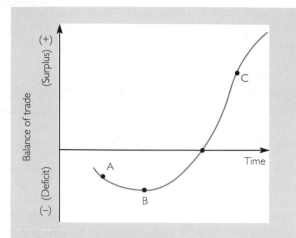

Figure 42.2 J-curve effect
In response to a trade deficit at point A the government depreciates the currency. Initially this causes a further deterioration to point B before moving the balance of trade into surplus (point C).

(a) *Crisis of confidence.* Measures taken to rectify a deficit may have the initial effect of creating anxiety, thus leading to an outflow of money which initially leads to a deterioration in the payments position before the (hoped for) recovery.

(b) *Insufficient capacity.* If the economy is at, or near, capacity then expenditure-switching policies are unlikely to be successful immediately until capacity can be increased.

(c) *Time lags.* Most of the beneficial effects of devaluation are quantitative effects. On the import side we are waiting for the domestic residents to reduce their demand for foreign commodities while on the export side we are waiting for foreigners to increase their demand for the devaluing country's commodities. Such quantity effects will take time to materialise.

(d) The disadvantages of devaluation are price effects. The price of imports in terms of the domestic currency will increase while the price of exports in terms of the domestic currency will either stay constant in the short run or rise in the long run. These inflationary effects will be immediate. Thus a country that has devalued is likely to see its total expenditure on imports increase at a faster rate than the increase in its total receipts from exports. Thus the balance of trade deteriorates in the short run.

The existence of the J-curve effect is an argument for taking expenditure-reducing measures preparatory to taking expenditure-switching measures.

STUDENT ACTIVITY 42.4

(a) What relationship would you expect to see between a country's exchange rate, unemployment rate and balance of payments?
(b) Does the recent history of the UK (post-September 1992) support your prediction?
(c) What explanations can you offer as to why the devaluation of sterling on leaving the ERM did not prove to be inflationary?

Exchange rates

The subject of international trade, and trade itself, is complicated by the existence of different currencies. Money is a complicating factor in studying national economies but in the international sphere we have to contend with different types of exchange rate, changes in the value of currencies, exchange control and different units of currency. In this chapter we will examine the different regimes that exist and the problems associated with them.

Exchange rates and nationalism

The problem of exchange rates is often complicated by national pride. Many countries have wasted vast sums of money supporting unrealistic rates.

● *Common misunderstanding*

Consider the vocabulary which is used if the exchange rate is high: we are said to have 'a strong pound'; conversely, a low rate is described as 'weak' and the newspapers often speak of 'defending the pound'. These can be very emotive words. However, what is important is not that the exchange rate is high or low but that it should be correct for the circumstances.

The theory of exchange rates

Although exchange rates are often complicated by government interference and hence different exchange rate 'regimes' are possible, we will first examine how exchange rates are set in a free market situation. This is normally termed a floating, or freely fluctuating, exchange rate.

An exchange rate is simply the price at which one currency can be traded for another. For example, if the exchange rate is £1 = 1.5 euros then one pound will exchange for 1.5 euros or one euro costs £0.6666 (i.e. 66.66 pence). We define the exchange rate as the amount of the foreign currency that may be bought for 1 unit of the domestic currency.

We saw in Chapter 18 that a floating exchange rate is determined like any other price. In Figure 42.3 we can see that the exchange rate is £1 = $1.60 or that $1 costs 62.5 pence. It is therefore possible for us to analyse changes in exchange rates in the same manner as other prices.

Exchange rate changes

Figure 42.4 shows the effect of an increase in demand for UK exports; foreigners are therefore offering more money so that demand for sterling increases. Thus the price of foreign currency has declined and the pound is said to have appreciated. If foreign currency becomes more expensive the pound is said to have depreciated.

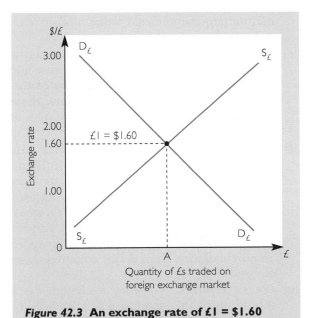

Figure 42.3 An exchange rate of £1 = $1.60
Behind the demand curve lies the USA's desire to buy UK exports, while behind the supply curve is the UK's desire to buy the USA's exports.

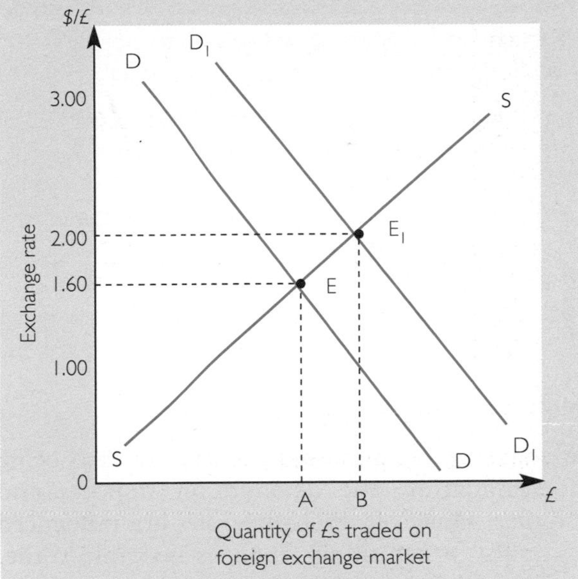

Figure 42.4 Effect of an increase in demand on the exchange rate
The effect of the shift of the demand curve from DD to D₁D₁ increases the exchange rate from £1 = $1.60 to £1 = $2. $1 now only costs 50p.

An appreciation in the rate of exchange could therefore be caused by either:

(a) an increased demand for UK exports; or
(b) a decreased UK demand for imports.

Alternatively a depreciation in the rate of exchange could be caused by:

(a) an increased UK demand for imports; or
(b) a reduced foreign demand for UK exports.

The effect of inflation

Let us assume the UK has inflation but Germany has not. This will mean that the sterling price of UK goods will rise. Thus, other things being equal, the demand for UK goods will decrease, while German goods will now appear cheaper to Britons who will, therefore, buy more. Thus the demand for sterling will decrease while the demand for Deutschmarks/euros will increase, and both the factors will cause a depreciation in the external value of sterling. If, on the other hand, the domestic rate of inflation is lower than that abroad, these factors may be expected to work in reverse.

STUDENT ACTIVITY 42.5

Explain what, if anything, will happen to sterling's exchange rate if the following events occur:

(a) The Bank of England raises interest rates.
(b) Foreign tastes change adversely against UK goods and services.
(c) The productivity of UK workers rises at a faster rate than our major competitors.
(d) The government announces its intention to join the Single European Currency.

Non-trade influences

We have, so far, discussed exchange rates as being determined by the demand for imports and exports. However, exchange rates are influenced by many other things such as invisible trade, interest rates, capital/financial movements, speculation and government activities. Confidence is also a vital factor in determining exchange rates. This is especially so because most large companies 'buy forward', i.e. they purchase foreign currency ahead of their needs. They are therefore very sensitive to factors which may influence future rates. Key indicators are such things as inflation and government policy. Thus the exchange rate at any particular moment may reflect the anticipated situation in a country rather than the present one.

The exchange rate debate

It is only since the early 1970s that floating exchange rates have become common. We will here consider the advantages and disadvantages of them.

Arguments in favour of floating exchange rates

(a) *Automatic stabilisation*. Any balance of payments disequilibrium should be rectified by a change in the exchange rate; for example, if a country has a balance of payments deficit then, other things being equal, the country's currency should depreciate. This would make the country's exports cheaper, thus increasing demand, while making imports dearer and decreasing demand. The balance of payments therefore will be brought back into equilibrium. Conversely, a balance of payments surplus should be eliminated by an appreciation of the currency.

(b) *Freeing internal policy*. Where a country has a floating exchange rate a balance of payments deficit can be rectified by a change in the external price of the currency. However, if a fixed exchange rate is adopted, then reducing a deficit could involve a general deflationary policy for the whole economy, resulting in unpleasant consequences such as increased unemployment. Thus a floating exchange rate allows a government to pursue internal policy objectives such as growth and full employment without external constraints.

(c) *Absence of crisis*. The periods of fixed exchange rates were frequently characterised by crisis as pressure was put on a currency to devalue or revalue. The fact that with floating exchange rates such changes occur automatically has removed the element of crisis from international relations.

(d) *Management*. Floating exchange rates have still left governments considerable freedom to manipulate the external value of their currency to their own advantage.

(e) *Flexibility*. Changes in world trade since the first oil crisis of 1973 have been immense and have caused great changes in the value of currencies. It is difficult to imagine how these could have been dealt with under a system of fixed exchange rates.

(f) *Avoiding inflation*. A floating exchange rate helps to insulate a country from inflation elsewhere. In the first place, if a country were on a fixed exchange rate it would 'import' inflation by way of higher import prices. Second, a country with a payments surplus and a fixed exchange rate would tend to 'import' inflation from deficit countries as its money supply grew.

(g) *Lower reserves*. Floating exchange rates should mean that there is a smaller need to maintain large reserves to defend the currency. These reserves can, therefore, be used more productively elsewhere.

Arguments against floating exchange rates

(a) *Uncertainty*. The fact that currencies change in value from day to day introduces a large element of uncertainty into trade. Sellers may be unsure of how much money they will receive when they sell goods abroad. Some of this uncertainty may be reduced by companies buying currency ahead in forward exchange contracts. However, the fact remains that this is costly and only short-term exchange rate risks can be hedged in this way.

(b) *Lack of investment*. The uncertainty induced by floating exchange rates may discourage foreign investment.

(c) *Speculation*. The day-to-day changes in exchange rates may encourage speculative movements of 'hot money' from country to country, thereby making changes in exchange rates greater.

(d) *Lack of discipline*. The need to maintain an exchange rate imposes a discipline upon an economy. It is possible that with a floating exchange rate such problems as inflation may be ignored until they have reached crisis proportions.

Fixed exchange rates

The gold standard

A gold standard occurs when a unit of a country's currency is valued in terms of a specific amount of gold. The Gold Standard Act of 1870 fixed the value of the pound sterling such that 1 ounce of gold cost £3.875. This remained constant until 1914. Between 1925 and 1931 the UK went back to the gold standard, during this period most Commonwealth and Empire countries also fixed their exchange rates by quoting their currency against sterling. After the Second World War the USA maintained the price of gold at $35 = 1 ounce of gold. However, in 1971 the USA was forced to abandon this and it is unlikely that a gold standard of any type will be readopted in the near future. This does not mean, however, that fixed exchange rates will not exist. Indeed, although not fixed to gold, the advent of a common currency for members of the European Union automatically fixes the exchange rate between them (see Chapter 45).

Pegged exchange rates

When a country is not on a gold standard but wishes to have a fixed exchange rate this can be done by the government 'pegging' the exchange rate, i.e. a rate is fixed and then guaranteed by the government. For example, after the UK left the gold standard in 1931 the government fixed the price of sterling against the dollar, in 1932, and made the rate of £1 = $4.03 effective by agreeing to buy or sell any amount of currency at this price.

Exchange control

One of the methods by which a government can attempt to make the stated exchange rate effective is through exchange control. Exchange control refers to restrictions placed upon the ability of citizens to exchange foreign currency freely; for example, in 1966 the UK government would allow Britons to convert only £50 into foreign currency for holidays abroad. The Mitterrand government in France imposed similar restrictions in 1983. A more serious restriction in the UK was the dollar premium. Under this arrangement any Briton wishing to change money into foreign currency for investment overseas had to pay a premium of 25 per cent. The Conservative government abolished all forms of exchange control in 1979. It was agreed in 1988 that, as part of the unification of EC markets, in 1992 there would be free movement of capital between EC nations. However, people may still find themselves subject to restrictions by other countries, e.g. as in some far eastern countries.

The adjustable peg

This was the system of fixed exchange rates operated by the members of the International Monetary Fund from 1947 to 1971. Members agreed not to let the value of their currencies vary by more than 1 per cent either side of a parity. Thus, for example, the UK's exchange rate in 1949 was £1 = $2.80 and sterling was allowed to appreciate to £1 = $2.82 or depreciate to £1 = $2.78. The system was termed 'adjustable' because it was possible for a country to devalue or revalue in the event of serious disequilibrium.

Some countries operated a so-called 'crawling peg'. Under this system a currency was allowed to depreciate (or appreciate) by a small percentage each year. Thus if, for example, a limit of 2 per cent was set and the currency devalued by this amount in year 1, it would be allowed to devalue by another 2 per cent in year 2, and so on.

Fixed rates evaluated

The chief advantage of fixed exchange rates is that they give certainty to international trade and investors. Price signals therefore become easier to interpret by all economic agents promoting greater economic efficiency both in consumption and production. It is also said that they reduce speculation. Fixed exchange rates also impose discipline on domestic economic policies because, in the event of an adverse balance of payments, deflationary measures will have to be taken to restore the situation.

On the other hand, if an exchange rate is fixed incorrectly then this will cause intense speculation against the currency. It can often be an expensive job defending a fixed exchange rate, requiring large reserves of foreign exchange. Defending a currency may also involve raising interest rates, and this can be both costly and damaging to the domestic economy. In September 1992 the Bank of England is reputed to have spent £20 billion in its futile attempts to stem the speculative flow against sterling and raised interest rates from 10 per cent to 15 per cent. It is possible, therefore, that a fixed exchange rate may result in domestic policy being subordinated to the external situation. Very sudden and destabilising change in exchange rates can occur when an economy is forced to abandon a fixed exchange rate as happened recently in south east Asia (see page 635).

The equilibrium exchange rate

We have considered some of the factors which can influence exchange rates. However, there is no completely satisfactory theory which explains

how the equilibrium rate of exchange is established. In Figure 42.3 we might make the assumption that the exchange rate is in equilibrium and that imbalances will cause shifts to new equilibriums. However, we would still like to explain why the exchange rate occurs at the level it does, i.e. why is it £1 = $2 and not £1 = $3 and so on? The Swedish economist **Gustav Cassell**, building on the idea of the classical economists and mercantilists, attempted to explain this in terms of purchasing power parity.

The theory of purchasing power parity

This theory suggests, for example, that the exchange rate would be in equilibrium if a situation existed where the same 'basket' of goods which costs £100 in the UK cost $140 in the USA and the exchange rate were £1 = $1.40. In order to do this we would have to discount transport costs and tariffs. Thus a measure we might use could appear as:

$$\text{Purchasing power parity} = \frac{\text{USA consumer price index}}{\text{UK consumer price index}}$$

From this we might deduce that a doubling of the general price level in the UK while prices in the USA remained constant would lead to the exchange rate being cut by one-half. However, no such strict proportionality exists. There are a number of reasons for this:

(a) The 'basket' of goods which determines domestic price levels is different from those which are traded internationally. Items which are important domestically, such as housing, bread, rail fares, etc., do not influence foreign trade significantly.
(b) Exchange rates are influenced by many other factors such as capital movements, speculation and interest rates.
(c) Confidence is also a very significant factor in determining exchange rates.

Thus, we may conclude that although domestic price levels do influence exchange rates, there is no strict proportionality.

Other exchange rate theories

We have discussed exchange rate stability in terms of the demand and supply of imports and exports. However, as we mentioned earlier, there are many other factors which influence the supply and demand for sterling. Other theories have, therefore, been put forward to explain the determination of exchange rates.

(a) *The portfolio balance theory*. This stresses the importance of international investment flows, including speculative movements, in determining exchange rates. It assumes that large investors are aware of investment opportunities worldwide. They therefore diversify their portfolios to gain higher yield in different countries until there is no further benefit from switching funds into pounds. The huge amount of highly liquid funds in international markets today makes interest rates a key factor in determining exchange rates. However, expectations of future interest rates and/or exchange rates may be more important than existing rates. This leads us to the theory of interest rate parity.

(b) *The theory of interest rate parity*. In the era of floating exchange rates much currency is bought 'forward'. For example, a company which may need large quantities of Deutschmarks in six months' time may place an order for them now and both buyer and seller agree to exchange the currency in six months' time at the rate agreed today. This rate may be higher or lower than today's 'spot' rate depending upon expectations of the future. Needless to say, there is a very large speculative market in currency futures.

The interest rate parity theory gets its name from the idea that differences in interest rates between countries will be reflected in the 'discount' or 'premium' at which currency futures are traded. The picture is complicated by the differences between real and nominal rates of interest, i.e. rates of inflation and expectations of rates of inflation.

Once we have progressed beyond the idea that exchange rates are determined by trade flows we can see the vital importance of other factors such as expectations, confidence, interest rates and speculation.

The amount of money changing hands on the world's foreign exchange markets is vast. It is estimated that well over 1 trillion dollars a day ($1 000 000 000 000) is exchanged by dealers, selling dollars for pounds, francs for Deutchmarks,

etc. Furthermore, only 5 per cent of the deals struck are for trade reasons. Another 15 per cent are due to foreign direct investment, and 80 per cent are purely speculative. People are simply gambling on whether currencies will go up or down. Thus we can see that the determination and explanation of the equilibrium exchange rate is a complex topic. It is very difficult to give a simple answer to the straightforward question, 'What is the correct exchange rate?'

STUDENT ACTIVITY 42.6

A UK exporter has won a major contract to supply a firm in the USA with equipment to the value of $3 million. When the equipment is dispatched and the invoice raised for $3 million, the sterling–dollar exchange rate is $1.60. By the time payment is made the sterling–dollar exchange rate is $1.70.

(a) How much has the UK firm lost as a result of the exchange rate movement?
(b) What, if anything, could the UK firm have done to avoid this exchange rate risk?
(c) What factors should a firm take into consideration in deciding whether or not to hedge a foreign exchange risk?

The Asian crisis

The 1990s provided several examples of severe currency instability. For example, in the late 1990s the south east Asia currency instability momentarily shook the strong faith in the market economics that had brought sustained and substantial growth for 'tiger economies' such as Korea, Malaysia and Singapore. The crisis began with Thailand in 1997 and rapidly spread to other countries in the region.

Before 1997 the Indonesian rupiah, Korean won and the Thai baht had been pegged to the US dollar and this, together with sustained economic growth had encouraged the flow of foreign finance to fund domestic investments. Doubtless some of these loans were overly risky and many economists point to inadequate financial reforms following the liberalisation of the Thai banking system, but things may not have reached crisis had the Thai economic growth rate not slowed and its balance of payments deficit worsened. This led to a belief that investments would not yield the returns needed to pay back investors leading to loan defaults. This fear and the growing deficit with the rest of the world led to speculation that there would have to be a devaluation of the baht.

To avoid this expected loss of value, holders of the baht began to sell. As speculative selling accelerated the Thai government was forced to unpeg the baht from the dollar. This speculative selling quickly spread to the currencies of other countries thought to have similar problems of risky investment and fragile financial sectors. The baht, and then, very quickly, the rupiah, began to tumble. Shortly after the won also fell very substantially as a contagion of speculative fear swept south east Asia. The fall in these currencies led to a substantial loss of wealth for many people in these countries and this in turn led to a fall in aggregate demand. This was an example of severe instability which caused hardship for many affected, however the depreciation of these currencies naturally increased still further the competitiveness of their exports, and long-term prospects continue to look good for South Korea and the four members of the Association of South-east Asian Nations (Asean).

Recent UK developments

The operation of the International Monetary Fund is discussed in detail in Chapter 44. We will here consider how developments since the early 1970s have influenced the UK economy.

Dirty floating

Following the USA's abandonment of the gold standard in 1971 and the failure of the Smithsonian Agreement, the UK floated the pound in 1972. The objective of the government was that the development of the economy should be free to continue without the constraint of having to maintain a fixed exchange rate. Although ostensibly the government allowed the exchange rate to find its own level, in fact it interfered to manipulate the exchange rate. This is termed managed flexibility, or, more memorably, a 'dirty float'.

Figure 42.5 illustrates government intervention in the foreign exchange market. Left to itself the exchange rate would be £1 = $1 but the government forces the rate up to £1 = $1.90 by buying sterling on the foreign exchange market, thus shifting the demand curve to the right.

Currency divergence

When countries were on a gold standard there was a simple way to show the value of their currencies. However, with floating exchange rates it becomes difficult. The most widely known measure of the UK exchange rate is that against the dollar, but the dollar itself is floating. Figure 42.6 shows that the pound sterling can move in different directions between currencies, in this case against the dollar and the euro. Trade-weighted indices are an attempt to overcome this problem by providing a measure of a currency in terms of a number of currencies

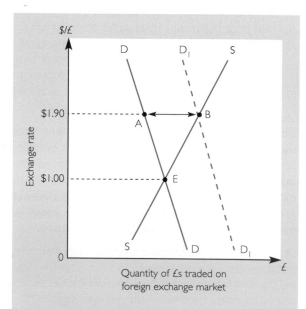

Figure 42.5 Dirty floating
The government forces up the exchange rate from £1 = $1 to £1 = $1.90 by purchasing AB £s on the foreign exchange market.

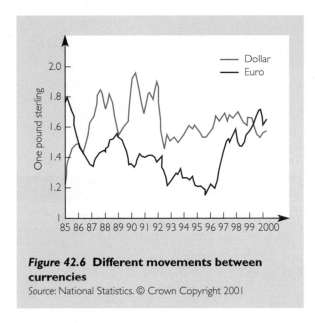

Figure 42.6 Different movements between currencies
Source: National Statistics. © Crown Copyright 2001

which are weighted in accordance with their importance in trade to the country whose currency is being measured.

Attempts at stabilisation

After the turbulence in currency markets during the 1970s various attempts were made in the 1980s to bring stability to exchange rates. These were mainly confined to the Western industrialised nations. The EU established the European Monetary System (EMS) which effectively fixed the rates of exchange between Common Market countries. The Plaza Agreement (1985) and the Louvre Accord (1987) attempted to limit the fluctuation in exchange rates between the G5 and G7 nations, respectively.

The cooperation between the leading industrial nations limited fluctuations. The growing importance of Germany and Japan meant that exchange rates of currencies against the yen and the Deutschmark became significant indicators as well as rates against the dollar. At the end of the 1980s the UK became a full member of the EMS, which limited the fluctuations of the pound against other EC currencies.

The UK: floating experience 1972–90 and 1992–97

How well has the floating rate worked for the UK? When the UK floated sterling in 1972 the exchange rate was £1 = $2.60; it reached a low of £1 = $1.55 in October 1976, an effective devaluation of 40.4 per cent. This massive drop was not altogether unwelcome to the UK government, who believed it would make exports more competitive. It should be remembered, however, that increasing the price of imports will also increase inflation. The UK government, however, seemed happy to settle for a rate of about £1 = $1.70, but no sooner had the rate stabilised around this level than the prospects of North Sea oil brought money flooding into London and the exchange rate soared, much to the displeasure of the government. It appeared that a pound that floated upwards was almost as difficult to live with as a sinking one.

The end of the 1970s saw the UK with a large balance of payments surplus and an exchange rate almost back to the 1971 level. The 'overvalued' pound had UK industry screaming for relief. The pound then collapsed, despite a sound balance of payments, and in 1983 dropped below £1 = $1.50 for the first time.

This fall continued until in February 1985 the pound dipped briefly below £1 = $1.10. It was during this crisis that the Bank of England reintroduced Minimum Lending Rate (MLR) (see Chapter 36) for one day in an attempt to stop the fall. This crisis for the pound was caused both by the weakness of the UK economy and by the strength of the dollar.

The recovery of the pound over the period 1985–88 was due both to increased confidence in the UK economy and to the weakness of the dollar. However, at the same time that the pound was rising in value against the dollar the balance of payments was moving into record deficits. The prospect for the pound was, therefore, uncertain. In addition, the UK inflation rate was increasing at a much faster rate than our major competitors. It had reached double figures by the time the UK joined the ERM in October 1990 (10.9 per cent). Sterling's membership of the ERM was short-lived and in September 1992 it was forced out of the ERM.

When the UK allowed sterling to float in September 1992, its value against the Deutschmark declined significantly. It stabilised at a rate of DM2.483 for 1993 and 1994 and then reached an all-time low in 1995 of DM2.261. It stayed at this level for 1996 but its fortunes reversed in 1997 when it rose to DM3.07 in July 1997. Sterling's dramatic rise against the other EU currencies has to a large extent been due to the fears on the foreign exchange markets that attempts to establish a European single currency could end in failure and thus sterling is seen as a 'safe haven'. Against the dollar sterling declined in 1993 from its 1992 average level of $1.7661 to $1.5. It remained relatively stable, standing in August 1997 at $1.58 but then towards the end of 1999 it fell to below $1.50.

We may conclude our discussion of floating exchange rates by saying that there have undoubtedly been unprecedented fluctuations in value, but there have also been unprecedented circumstances and it is doubtful if fixed exchange rates could have coped better with the situation. For the UK, as for the other members of the EU, the question of the single currency is now upmost on their minds (see Chapter 45).

Summary

1 The balance of payments is a summary of all a nation's dealings with the rest of the world.
2 Both deficits and surpluses on the balance of payments can lead to a loss of welfare but a deficit is a more pressing constraint.
3 The openness of the UK economy tends to cause imports to grow quicker than exports as the economy grows.
4 The terms of trade measures the relative prices of exports and imports.
5 Cures for a deficit can be categorised as expenditure reducing and expenditure switching.
6 The effect of a depreciation in the external value of a currency upon a country's balance

of payments depends upon the combined elasticities of demand for exports and imports.
7 In floating exchange rates the exchange rate is determined by expectations, confidence, investment flows as well as by trade.
8 There are advantages and disadvantages associated with fixed and floating exchange rates.

? QUESTIONS

1 The last Conservative government was very reluctant to devalue sterling in the summer of 1992, claiming that 'devaluation was fool's gold'. Explain why devaluation may be harmful to the balance of trade in the short run.
2 Explain why the conditions prevailing in the UK economy in September 1992 were favourable to devaluation.
3 What are the likely effects of the following on the balance of trade?
   (a) The country's propensity to save increases.
   (b) The government increases public expenditure on domestic goods and services.
   (c) Interest rates are lowered.
4 Assume that a country is in balance of payments equilibrium on current account such that total current debits are $40 000 million and total current credits are $40 000 million. Demonstrate that, as a result of the Marshall–Lerner criterion, a depreciation of 10 per cent in the country's exchange rate, *ceteris paribus*, will improve the balance of payments condition to a surplus of $4800 million if the combined elasticities of demand for exports and imports is $EX + EM = 12$.
5 In your view, which is worse: a balance of payments surplus or a deficit?

Data response A
ATLANTICA'S BALANCE OF PAYMENTS

The figures in Table 42.7 are taken from the annual balance of payments statement of Atlantica. Prepare Atlantica's balance of payments to show:

(a) the balance of visible trade;
(b) the invisible balance;
(c) the balance on current account;

Table 42.7

Items	$m
Capital transactions	+750
Banking earnings	+1 200
Insurance earnings	+500
Interest paid abroad	−300
Interest received from abroad	+900
Exports of manufactures	+18 000
Exports of raw materials and fuel	+8 000
Imports of manufactures	−15 000
Imports of raw materials and fuel	−14 000
Shipping earnings (net)	+250
Tourist earnings	+500
Change in reserves	−1 200

(d) transactions in the capital and financial accounts;
(e) net errors and omissions.

Data response B
CENTRAL BANKERS UPBEAT DESPITE EURO SLIDE

Read the following article from the *Financial Times* of 12 September 2000 and then answer the questions which follow.

1 Use a diagram to illustrate what might have happened to the euro exchange rate if the foreign exchange traders had been impressed by the meeting of euro-zone finance ministers.
2 Will the expected growth in the euro-zone definitely lead to an appreciation of the euro?
3 Why would the Bank of England governor be concerned about the euro's weakness?
4 Why would the support of the US Federal Reserve normally be considered important for successful intervention?

Central bankers upbeat despite euro slide

Hat trick of lows: foreign exchange markets unimpressed by results of euro-zone finance ministers' meeting. By **Tony Barber** in Frankfurt and **Christopher Swann** in London.

Central bankers continued to express confidence that the euro would recover yesterday as the currency hit a hat trick of lifetime lows against the dollar, yen and Swiss franc.

'I think the expectation generally is that the euro will at some point bottom and tend to strengthen because the expected growth in the euro-zone is really very encouraging,' Sir Eddie George, the Bank of England governor, said yesterday.

Speaking after a meeting of central bankers in Basle, Switzerland, Sir Eddie said he and his colleagues had also observed that high world oil prices had so far had a smaller impact on euro-zone economy than might have been expected.

'Even in the euro-zone, there has been less impact so far on demand and therefore output than one would have perhaps expected from the rise in the inflation rate,' he said.

But confidence in the foreign exchange markets continued to ebb. While the central bankers were meeting, the euro dived over a cent against the dollar to a low of $0.8570, representing a fall of 27 per cent since the currency was launched in January 1999. Economists and foreign exchange traders said financial markets had been left unimpressed by a weekend meeting in France at which euro-zone finance ministers reaffirmed their desire to see a strong euro.

Economists were alarmed by the breadth of the euro's loses yesterday.

'The dramatic fall against the Swiss franc demonstrates that euro's woes are not purely due to the strength of the US economy,' said Paul Meggyesi, senior economist at Deutsche Bank in London. 'There is a mounting problem of confidence in the currency among investors, many of whom are losing patience with the euro.'

But impressive economic figures from the US have continued to hurt the currency. 'The key aspect is that expectations of returns for dollar assets are still higher than for euro assets,' said Dieter Wermuth of Tokai Bank in Frankfurt.

Sir Eddie said the Basle meeting, attended by central bankers from Group of 10 countries including the US, Japan, Germany, France, the UK and other countries, had not dwelt on the possibility of market intervention in support of the euro.

Euro-zone finance ministers last weekend described intervention as an instrument available to them and to the European Central Bank. Economists believe the US Federal Reserve, whose support would normally be considered important for successful intervention, is unlikely to join action that could hurt the strong dollar before November's presidential election. 'Even though we are getting close to a point where intervention makes sense, I do not think the time has come already,' Mr Wermuth said.

Source: *Financial Times*, 12 September 2000. Reprinted with permission.

43 Conflicts between objectives

Learning outcomes

At the end of this chapter you will be able to:
▶ Recognise conflicts between objectives.
▶ Suggest policy combinations to deal with the conflict.
▶ Relate the discussion to current events.

The lessons of history

This is a case study chapter with student activities at the end of each section.

At different periods of history different objectives may be in conflict with each other. For instance, during the 1960s, the balance of payments was an obstacle to the achievement of full employment. The policy adopted in the 1960s and early 1970s was called the 'stop–go' policy, because governments repeatedly tried to expand the economy but were then forced back by the balance of payments constraint. Deficits on the current account created speculation against the pound, which had to be met by higher interest rates and fiscal restraint. Whether governments put the emphasis on tight monetary policy or deflationary fiscal policy, the consequence was a rise in unemployment and a slowing of growth – sometimes negative growth! Of course capitalist economies usually follow a growth path of expansion followed by contraction as a normal part of the business cycle. However, this expansion and contraction was a consequence of government intervention, not the normal operation of the market.

The balance of payments constraint lessened in the 1980s with the exploitation of North Sea oil. Unemployment and inflation then became the two conflicting objectives. To some extent this conflict existed during the earlier historical period, but in the 1980s the conflict became more apparent. New situations are confronting governments as history unfolds, but a return to consider historical examples is often instructive.

Unemployment and the balance of payments

The conflict between the balance of payments and reductions in unemployment discussed above resurfaced in the early 1990s. The advantage on the balance of payments current account that had been conferred by North Sea oil had finally been eroded by a combination of factors:

(a) High interest rates and exchange rates in the early 1980s had resulted in widespread loss of jobs and output in manufacturing industry, with a consequent loss of exports of manufactured goods.

(b) Deregulation of the financial sector in the 1980s resulted in an explosion of consumer credit. As house prices also shot up, people felt wealthier and therefore able to borrow against this wealth. This increased consumption sucked in imports.

(c) The economy was suddenly growing fast after the deep recession of the early 1980s. People believed that the Conservatives had finally solved the long-standing problems of the UK economy and that the expansion of the economy would last.

(d) The UK initially followed a policy of 'tracking the mark', which resulted in high exchange rates and then joined the ERM (see Chapter 42) at a high exchange rate in 1990. This made it difficult to export, but made importing very profitable.

(e) Partly as a result of the above factors, inflation took off again in the late 1980s and early 1990s, making British products less competitive.

It is widely recognised that the economy expanded too fast in the late 1980s, fuelled by a consumption boom rather than an investment boom. The Labour government faced similar problems with the expanding economy and high exchange rate that they inherited from the Conservative administration. Its response was to employ fairly restrictive fiscal and monetary policy to prevent a boom resulting in renewed inflation and balance of payments deficits. Nevertheless, house price inflation did take off, particularly from 1998 onwards. Higher interest rates, designed to contain this house price boom, contributed to the strong value of the pound. This has made exporting increasingly difficult, particularly in manufacturing jobs already under threat from low wage production from Eastern Europe and China.

The situation was resolved by:

(a) The recession of the early 1990s with 3 million unemployed reduced the demand for imports.
(b) High interest rates and high unemployment together reduced inflation rates.
(c) The collapse of the pound and the exit from the ERM meant that a cheap pound policy could be followed which discouraged imports and improved exports.

There is a view that in the age of a globalised economy a balance of payments has less significance. If there is a deficit on the current account, this can be offset by a surplus on the capital account. The problem with this approach is that high interest rates may be necessary to attract the capital in and will not work if confidence in the economy collapses.

STUDENT ACTIVITY 43.1

(a) Use economic statistics from 2000 onwards to see if the Labour government was successful in its objective of avoiding a repeat of 1990.
(b) If the pound is high in value, and the economy is overheating, which groups in society are most likely to lose and which will gain?

Unemployment and inflation

The trade-off between inflation and unemployment, and the arguments about the Phillips curve, were discussed in great detail in Chapter 38. After the expansion of the late 1980s resulted in a return of inflation, the *speed* of reduction in unemployment became an issue in the argument. It was argued that, if the economy was not given time to expand capacity and retrain workers in the expanding industries, it was argued that bottlenecks would develop in the fastest expanding industries, bidding up prices and wages and raising inflationary expectations in the economy as a whole. This process would also affect the balance of payments as in the case considered above, since consumer demand would suck in imports from abroad if there were insufficient capacity in the UK.

In the recovery from the recession of the early 1990s, inflation has been avoided, with the government meeting its objectives and largely keeping inflation in the 2 per cent to 2.5 per cent range. Whether there is a genuine trade-off between unemployment and inflation has been difficult to test in the UK in recent years because until recently unemployment has been so high. In the last three years of the century, unemployment was in the range of 1 million to 1.5 million (see Chapter 39). It will be interesting to see whether inflation starts to rise again if unemployment falls further. One indicator has been the sharp rise in house prices (see Chapter 11) which has necessitated an increase in interest rates.

STUDENT ACTIVITY 43.2

Trace the combinations of unemployment and inflation from 1990 to see whether there appears to be any relationship. Include data available after the publication date of this book, e.g. use www.statistics.gov.uk

Inflation and growth

There is no conflict between low inflation and growth; indeed it is often argued that low inflation is a prerequisite for sustained growth because of the stability it gives to the economy.

However, getting there is another matter. Most policies designed to reduce inflation are also damaging for growth. High interest rates have the effect of reducing investment. High interest rates often have the effect of increasing the value of the currency, thus reducing the demand for domestically produced output. Restrictive fiscal and monetary policy reduces aggregate demand, which in turn results in a reduction in investment in new capacity.

If this kind of anti-inflationary policy had the effect of permanently reducing inflation, then governments could use it, and then get on with the business of achieving economic growth. Unfortunately, when economies are reflated, eventually inflation tends to reappear. Some economies have been more successful in avoiding a return to inflation (e.g. Japan, Germany), but the UK has regularly been revisited with rising prices. After inflation was more or less squeezed out of the economy in the early 1980s, a period of growth in the mid- to late 1980s resulted in the return of inflation rates above 10 per cent in 1990. This was squeezed out of the economy during the early 1990s and then the economy began to expand again in the mid-1990s.

STUDENT ACTIVITY 43.3

Using recent data, assess whether the recovery of the economy in the mid-1990s led to substantial rises in inflation.

Income redistribution and growth

The effects of taxation on work effort and, by implication, on economic growth have been discussed in Chapter 28. If high rates of taxation are imposed on richer people in society, in order to finance those who are less well-off, we have to consider whether there is a cost in terms of reduced growth. Much of the tax policy of the Conservative government from 1979 onwards was based on the idea that there was such a trade-off, resulting in one of the lowest top rates of income tax in the developed world, at 40 per cent. It is fairly clear that the very high rates of tax that existed in 1979 were likely to create disincentives. Charging 98 per cent on marginal

income will not encourage people to work hard or to invest. Furthermore such people will normally be able to employ the best tax accountants to help them avoid paying such rates of tax. There is less evidence that reducing top tax rates to as low as 40 per cent creates substantial incentives. The process of globalisation and the greater mobility of both capital and labour means that countries are to some extent in competition with each other to provide the most attractive tax regime for the more affluent people who can move their resources around the world more easily.

STUDENT ACTIVITY 43.4

If there was a lower income tax rate in USA, would that persuade you to look for a job there? Would the same be true about Germany? Would you invest your savings in another country? What would be the risks of doing this? If income tax rates went down in the UK, would this give you the incentive to work harder, or would you be able to work shorter hours and earn the same money?

Economic freedom and other objectives

A balance of payments deficit can be resolved by import controls or tariff barriers (as all countries do to a greater or lesser extent). Inflation can be apparently cured by putting a freeze on wages or prices or both (as happened in the UK in the 1960s and 1970s). If growth is not occurring because of a lack of savings, then the government can require people to save (as has happened in Malaysia and Singapore). Unemployment can be 'solved' by requiring those without a job to undertake work in return for their benefit (the workfare system as used in the USA).

As can be seen, where the market has not succeeded in solving a problem, then compulsion can often do the job. There is a cost in terms of a loss of the economic freedom to choose. Sometimes this cost may be considered worthwhile because of the benefits it creates. Ideological arguments about the alleged superiority of the market will always arise when issues of this kind come up, and it will be difficult to separate value judgements from facts.

STUDENT ACTIVITY 43.5

Identify areas of current government policy that represent a restriction of economic freedom. Is it possible to justify these restrictions in each case?

Vicious circles and virtuous circles

The best hope for economic growth will occur when the conflicts discussed above are at a minimum. Some countries seem to have been more successful than others at achieving this state of affairs. When things go wrong, an economy is said to be in a vicious circle. A good example of an economy in a vicious circle would go something like this: a country suffering from a balance of payments deficit on current account and inflation above the average experiences speculation against its currency because of these problems. It deals with this situation by raising interest rates. This has the effect of supporting the currency and reducing domestic demand. Unemployment starts to rise and business confidence falls, resulting in a decline in investment. This policy eventually works, reducing both inflation and the balance of payments problem in the short term. Political pressure then turns the government's attention to unemployment. The government attempts to stimulate the economy using fiscal or monetary means, but the lack of investment means that there is little spare capacity in the economy, particularly in high-tech areas where demand is strong and new techniques have been introduced. Where there is sufficient capacity, new workers cannot be trained quickly enough to meet demand. The economy sucks in imports, the currency speculation returns, and as the currency falls in value, so higher import prices start to push up inflation.

A country in a vicious circle can solve one or more of its problems, but each solution brings a new problem into view. An economy with a virtuous circle can deal with one problem at a time and meet more of its objectives. An economy like this would develop something like this: starting from a position of unemployment, the government decides to expand the economy. This reduces the surplus on the balance of payments, but since this was large to begin with, this is not a problem. The increased demand for labour pushes up the wage rate, but prices do not have to rise as much because of the rising productivity of the workforce. The high cost of labour forces firms to continue to think of labour-saving inventions to raise productivity further. Inflation rates are modest and the currency is strong, so interest rates are low. This is a further incentive for businesses to invest, raising productivity and growth further. The low interest rates are a disincentive to savings, but firms are very profitable and able to generate funds internally for investment.

STUDENT ACTIVITY 43.6

Is the UK economy currently in a virtuous circle or a vicious circle?

Conclusion

We have ended this Section with a discussion of the dilemmas facing governments. Economics does not always provide straightforward answers, and economists do not always agree with each other. Whenever there are policies, there will also be politics about the correct priorities. Although history can provide us with precedents, each new situation facing policy makers will be in some way unique. Economics provides us with a way of thinking about the world, whether it is a government making decisions about the course of the economy, a business person making decisions about investment or pricing, or an individual making decisions about personal finance. There is, thank goodness, room for a wide range of opinions about the economy and politics.

Summary

1 Expanding employment may run into balance of payments constraints.
2 Inflation and unemployment may be conflicting goals.
3 Policies designed to reduce inflation may also reduce growth.
4 Although very high levels of taxation are likely to have effects on growth, current tax rates may not have significant effects.
5 Economies that can deal with one problem at a time are more likely to achieve a virtuous circle.

QUESTIONS

I   Explain why there has been a problem of stop–go policies in the past in the UK. Assess whether the UK has now solved this long-standing problem.

2   Is unemployment soluble without inflationary consequences?

3   Is it possible to have a fairer distribution of income without adversely affecting economic growth?

SECTION IX

The EU and wider perspectives

Economics is a subject that does not greatly respect one's wishes.

Nikita Khruschev

Learning outcomes

At the end this chapter you will be able to:
▶ Explain the role of international institutions such as the IMF in the international monetary system.
▶ Recognise the importance of eurocurrency markets in providing international liquidity.
▶ Understand the way in which the WTO has contributed to the reduction in trade barriers.

Introduction

Towards the end of the Second World War the Allied powers thoughts began to turn to peace and how to maintain it. Economic nationalism which had characterised the interwar years was seen to have been an important factor contributing to the depression and consequently to the rise of fascism and war. In particular protectionism and currency instability with competitive devaluations undermined trade, specialisation and economic efficiency. With the US in a hegemonic position in the world economy it was possible to develop institutions and rules for the international economy to achieve freer convertibility, improve international liquidity and to reduce and regulate protection.

This process commenced in July 1944 with a conference at Bretton Woods in New Hampshire, USA. **Keynes** and the American, **Harry Dexter-White,** dominated the conference. Keynes favoured strong international organisations but it was Dexter-White's American view with the nation states predominant that prevailed and compromise institutions were established. Thus in 1946 the'World Bank' International Bank for Reconstruction and Development (IBRD) was established, and in 1947 the International Monetary Fund (IMF) and the General Agreement on Tariffs and Trade.

STUDENT ACTIVITY 44.1

Consider the impact on world output and employment of the following general developments in the 1930s:
(a) Increasing protection.
(b) Competitive devaluations and currency instability.

The International Monetary Fund

It was the Bretton Woods System centred on the IMF, which dominated the pattern of international monetary payments from 1945 to 1972. The objectives of the IMF were to achieve free convertibility of all currencies for current account transactions and to promote stability in international money markets. Until 1972 the IMF system was stable underpinning for a period of unparalleled growth and prosperity for the world economy. Since 1972 most countries have adopted floating exchange rates, so the role of the IMF has changed to providing assistance to less developed and transition economies with payments difficulties. In 2000 the IMF had 182 members. Since 1985, 36 new members have joined. Many of these new members were former planned economies, including the countries, which emerged from the collapse of the Soviet Union and its satellite states.

Quotas

Each of the members of the IMF is required to contribute a quota to the fund. The size of the quota will depend upon the national income of the country concerned and upon its share in world trade. The quota used to be made up of 75 per cent in the country's own currency and 25 per cent in gold (now this is made up of other currencies from a country's foreign exchange reserves). In this way it was hoped that there would be enough of any currency in the pool for any members to draw on should they get into balance of payments difficulties. Members' quotas are now supplemented by an allocation of SDRs (see below). Table 44.1 shows the size of members' quotas in 2000.

Voting power in the IMF is related to the size of the quota. Each member is allocated 250 votes plus one vote for every 1 000 000 SDRs of its quota. In this way the USA and the other industrialised nations have managed to dominate the IMF for most of its life. It has been necessary to revise quotas to increase their overall size to take account of the growth of world trade and of inflation, and to revise the relative size of members' quotas. Thus the UK's quota was originally 14.9 per cent but in 2000 it was just 5.1 per cent reflecting the diminished importance of the UK in the world economy.

Table 44.1 IMF quotas, September 2000

Country	Amount (SDR million)	%
USA	37 149	17.5
Japan	13 313	6.3
Germany	13 008	6.1
UK	10 739	5.1
France	10 739	5.1
Italy	7 056	3.3
Canada	6 369	3.0
Netherlands	5 162	2.4
Belgium	4 605	2.2
Australia	3 236	1.5
Others	100 624	47.5
Total	212 000	100.0

Source: www.imf.org

Borrowing

Originally each member of the IMF could borrow in *tranches* (slices) equivalent to 25 per cent of their quota, taking up to five consecutive tranches, i.e. it was possible to borrow the equiv-

alent of 125 per cent of one's quota. Today a member country with serious balance of payments problems can obtain loans of more than six times the value of its quota over a three-year period. This is not, however, an unconditional right to borrow, for the IMF may, and usually does, impose conditions of increasing severity upon a member as it increases its borrowing.

There are several methods of borrowing from the IMF; the most important are standby arrangements and extended credit. *Standby arrangements* are the most usual form of assistance rendered by the IMF. Resources are made available to members, which they may draw on if they wish. Attaining a standby facility is often enough to stabilise a member's balance of payments without the member actually drawing it, in the same way that the guarantee of a bank overdraft will often stabilise a company's finances. It is still necessary for a member to agree to conditions for each tranche. Drawings are made over a three-year period after which they can be repaid over six years. The *extended fund facility* was introduced to give longer term assistance to members experiencing more protracted balance of payments difficulties.

It was not until the outbreak of the less developed countries' debt crisis in 1982 that the IMF really began to make loans on a large scale. In 1985, the outstanding loans reached a peak of almost SDR40 billion. They declined in subsequent years as repayments became due.

STUDENT ACTIVITY 44.2

1 Why might a country maintaining a fixed exchange rate with the dollar need to borrow from the IMF?
2 Why might a country with a floating exchange rate wish to borrow from the IMF. (Hint: consider the problems with a very large depreciation of a floating exchange rate.)

Special drawing rights (SDRs)

In 1967 it was decided to create international liquidity for the first time. This was done by giving members an allocation of *special drawing rights*. These do not exist as notes but merely as booking entries. When they were introduced in 1970 they were linked to the dollar and thus to gold (SDR1 = $1) and became known as 'paper gold'. However, since 1974 the value of a unit of SDR has been calculated by combining the value of leading currencies. Originally based on 16 currencies, this was reduced to five in 1981. Table 42.2 shows the weights within the basket in 2000.

Table 44.2 Weight and percentage weights in SDR currency 'basket', 2000

Currency	Currency amount	Weight %
US dollar	0.5821	44.3
Japanese yen	27.2000	18.9
Euro (Germany)	0.2280	16.0
Pound sterling	0.1050	12.0
Euro (France)	0.1239	8.7

Source: www.imf.org

The functions of SDRs can be summarised as follows:

(a) *A means of exchange.* SDRs can be used to settle indebtedness between nations, but only with the consent of the IMF. However, they cannot be used commercially.
(b) *A unit of account.* All IMF transactions are now denominated in SDRs. Several other institutions use the SDR as the unit of account, including the Asian Clearing Union, the Economic Community of West Africa and the Suez Canal Company.
(c) *A store of value.* In 1976 it was decided to reduce the role of gold and make the SDR the principal asset of the IMF.

It can therefore be seen that the SDR fulfils the most important functions of money but only to a limited extent. We could therefore best describe it as quasi-money (see Chapter 35). If world trade is not to be limited by lack of international liquidity, further development of SDRs is required.

The adjustable peg

At the heart of the Bretton Woods system was the regime of fixed exchange rates known as the *adjustable peg.* This was described in Chapter 42 (see pages 633–4). When the UK joined the IMF in 1947 its exchange rate was £1 = $4.03. In 1949 the UK, along with most other countries, devalued against the dollar so that the rate became £1 = $2.80. This rate lasted until 1967 when the UK devalued to £1 = $2.40. The Smithsonian Agreement of 1971 was an attempt to patch up the adjustable peg system and saw the pound revalued to £1 = $2.60. The 1970s, however, saw a collapse of the adjustable peg. We will now have a look at the break-up of this system.

The break-up of the Bretton Woods System

The 1967 crisis

Although it was not realised at the time, the UK's 1967 devaluation marked the beginning of the end for the adjustable peg system. It highlighted three fundamental problems of the system *adjustment*, *confidence* and *liquidity*. When the IMF was set up and the Bretton Woods System came into operation in 1947 the economies of West Germany and Japan lay in ruins and their new currencies were given undervalued exchange rates. Rapid productivity growth and low inflation led to very large balance of payments surpluses but West Germany and Japan refused to revalue their currencies. They were under little pressure to do so because their exchange rates could be maintained by buying foreign currency with their own currency. The current account surpluses also contributed positively to the growth of their economies. Thus the burden of adjustment fell on deficit countries such as the UK. If adjustment had been shared between deficit and surplus countries, for any country the adjustment would have been smaller and easier to make. In 1967 the UK could resist the pressure no longer and devalued.

This precipitated worldwide uncertainty and lack of confidence in the dollar the centre of the Bretton Woods System. Speculators realised that gold was undervalued at $35 an ounce and there was, therefore, great pressure on the USA to devalue. The final attempt to save the gold standard occurred in 1968 when a two-tier rate was established. This meant that the price of gold for monetary purposes was maintained at $35 while the price of gold for commercial purposes was allowed to float upwards.

The USA leaves the gold standard (1971)

The announcement by President Nixon in August 1971 that the USA would no longer exchange dollars for gold at the official price ended the gold standard. This was forced upon the USA by a massive balance of payments deficit. The reasons for this were:

(a) *Inflation.* This increasingly made the fixed price of gold ever more unrealistic.

(b) *Operation of the IMF system.* The dollar was the most important reserve asset under this system and an increase in dollar reserves undermined confidence in its value. This is because other countries could increase their dollar reserves in two ways. First by running a balance of payments current account surplus with the US, directly affecting confidence in the dollar. Second by having a balance of payments capital account surplus with the US, the resulting US ownership of foreign assets became increasingly resented. As more dollars were held as a reserve the extent of its gold backing was reduced.

(c) *Speculative pressure.* The vast US deficit meant that there was a large amount of dollars on the foreign exchange market which could be used to speculate upon a rise in the price of gold.

(d) *The Vietnam War.* One of the consequences of the unpopularity of this war was that the US government was not able to increase taxation to pay for it. The war was, therefore, partly financed by running up a deficit on the balance of payments.

(e) *The 'Watergate' election.* President Nixon desperately needed to reflate the economy to win the election of autumn 1971. This was fatal for the external position of the dollar.

STUDENT ACTIVITY 44.3

1 Explain what is meant by the following problems of the Bretton Woods System:
   (a) liquidity;
   (b) confidence;
   (c) adjustment.
2 Why did these problems become more acute the longer the system operated?

The Smithsonian Agreement 1971

The abandonment of the link to gold standard and decreased confidence in the dollar swept away the adjustable peg system since the world reference point for currencies had disappeared. The Smithsonian Agreement of December 1971 was an attempt to re-establish the adjustable peg. This agreement put the value of gold at $38 per ounce, an effective devaluation of the dollar of 8.9 per cent. The new rate for the pound was therefore £1 = $2.60.

The Smithsonian peg allowed a 2.25 per cent variation in the value of a currency (as opposed to the 1 per cent of the 1947 system). This meant that the maximum possible (Smithsonian) variation between three currencies (cross-parities) was 9 per cent. The variation was unacceptable to the EC countries and on 24 April 1972, they limited the variation between their own currencies of plus or minus 2.25 per cent. This arrangement was called the 'snake' because the narrower band of fluctuation among EC currencies looked like a snake when plotted on a graph. The UK joined the snake on 1 June 1972 but left 54 days later when Anthony Barber, the then Chancellor of the Exchequer, announced that the pound was to float.

The oil crises

The instability which started in 1971 was made much worse by the oil crises. As a result of the Yom Kippur War of 1973, oil supplies were cut off. When they were resumed the OPEC countries contrived a fourfold rise in price. It is possible to argue that the resulting transfer of money from the developed countries to OPEC nations brought about one of the most fundamental shifts in economic power of all time. It is estimated that this cost the oil-importing countries an extra $100 billion per year.

Then in 1978 oil prices were again raised dramatically, this time doubling, and causing a liquidity problem even greater than that of 1973. This price rise was a major factor in the subsequent world recession. This hit the industrialised countries hard but was disastrous for non-oil-exporting developing countries (NOEDCs). The subsequent slump in oil prices left some less developed oil exporters such as Mexico saddled with large debts which they found it impossible to service.

The Plaza Agreement 1985 and the Louvre Accord 1987

In the mid-1980s there was a consensus of opinion among the leading industrial nations that they would prefer to see a more stable system of exchange rates. The Plaza Agreement (named after the Plaza Hotel, New York) was an agreement by the monetary authorities of the G5 nations (see below) to bring about an orderly decline in the value of the dollar which was then considered overvalued.

The Louvre Accord (so called because it was arrived at in Paris) was an agreement among the G7 nations to stabilise variations in their exchange rates within certain limits. These limits were not published. However, they could be deduced, at least partly, from the actions of central banks. For example, in March 1988 it became obvious that the Bank of England was committed to holding the pound below the level of £1 = DM3. In the event this was not possible.

These agreements illustrate the urge to return to a more orderly pattern of exchange rates. The fact that they were not arrived at through the IMF also illustrates the decline in its importance. Intergovernmental groups such as the G5 and G7 have become increasingly important. The Group of Five leading industrialised nations – the USA, Japan, West Germany, France and the UK – became known as the G5 and, with the addition of Canada and Italy, G7, and with the addition of Russia in 1997, G8. This group meets yearly to discuss world economic and political issues.

The problem of international liquidity

Nations need to hold reserve assets such as gold and foreign currency to buy their currency, when a temporary balance of payments problem is threatening to undermine the exchange rate of their currency. The stock of official international liquidity is the gold and foreign currency reserves held by nations, plus their quotas at the IMF and their allocation of SDRs. As trade and capital flows have expanded, the required size of these reserves has increased enormously. Since the Second World War the dollar and, to a lesser extent, the deutschmark (now the euro) and the yen have been the major reserve currencies. The problem of international liquidity is how to achieve a sufficient growth in the volume of reserves without undermining confidence in the value of the reserve currency.

> ### STUDENT ACTIVITY 44.4
>
> 1 Why did West Germany and Japan refuse to revalue their currencies under the Bretton Woods System of exchange rates?
> 2 Consider why oil prices rose in the 1970s.
> 3 Are there any similarities with the rise of oil prices in 1999–2000?

The role of the IMF

At the 1976 annual conference of the IMF the Jamaica Agreement officially recognised the end of the system of fixed exchange rates and 'demonetised' gold, i.e. the official price of gold was abolished. Member countries were no longer allowed to use gold as part of their quota subscriptions to the IMF. The IMF was to reduce its stocks of gold by one third by sales and transfers to members.

The role of the IMF declined and changed significantly during the 1970s and 1980s. From 1947 to 1973 it was the organisation that oversaw and facilitated the operation of the fixed exchange rate IMF regime. Its lending was principally to industrial countries but the regime of floating exchange rates lessened the need to borrow foreign currency for official purposes. In addition to this the drop in oil prices got rid of the current deficits of many nations. Thus from the 1970s its role concentrated on providing loans to indebted less developing nations. The problem here was that the creditworthiness of these countries was in doubt. So the IMF combined loans with strict macroeconomic programmes containing austerity measures. The IMF was being drawn into a role overlapping with the World Bank. The problem was that the countries in most difficulties were considered uncreditworthy by the IMF. In addition, some nations were unwilling to borrow from the IMF because of the strict conditions the IMF imposed when giving loans. Debtor nations were attracted to seek concessions on their loans threatening default rather than turn to the IMF.

In 1995 the IMF made the biggest loan to a single nation ever when it bailed out Mexico. In August 1997, the IMF agreed a credit package to Thailand (see Data response A at the end of this chapter). The IMF, however, remains important because it is the main economic forum for discussions and agreements about currency and debt. It also is the organisation with the potential to provide a regulatory role in relation to international finance, if its members agreed to such a development. (The international debt crisis is also discussed in Chapter 46).

STUDENT ACTIVITY 44.5

1 Why has the significance of the IMF in the world economy diminished?
2 Assess the IMF's current role in the international economy.

● *Common misunderstanding*

With floating currencies it is often assumed that fluctuations against one currency such as the US dollar accurately measure the currency's value. With many floating currencies it is only possible to measure a currency's value by calculating its value as an index against the currencies of its major trading partners, with each currency weighted to its importance in a country's trade.

Eurocurrencies

There is no one institution which is concerned with eurocurrencies. However, it is convenient to consider them in this chapter since they loom so large in world trade and finance. For example, the amount of transactions in eurocurrencies is far greater than all IMF business.

Defining a eurocurrency

Eurocurrencies were referred to in Chapter 35 on page 503. We may formalise our definition thus:

A eurocurrency is any deposit in a financial institution which is not denominated in the national currency.

For example, deposits of sterling in a French bank which continue to be denominated as sterling and not as francs are eurocurrency deposits – in this case eurosterling. A glance at the balance sheet of any commercial bank will show just how much of this type of business they do. Most eurocurrency deposits are in dollars.

The origins and growth of the markets

The original market was the eurodollar market, which emerged in London in the 1950s to handle the supply of US dollars in Europe. The dollar, you will remember, was then (as now) the most important international unit of account. Therefore companies, not necessarily dealing with the USA, demanded dollars for the purposes of international trade.

(a) *Growth in the 1950s and 1960s.* Growth in the eurodollar market was further accelerated by the following factors:
  (i) US balance of payments deficits which created a supply of dollars outside the USA.
  (ii) COMECON countries preferring to hold their dollar reserves in London rather than the USA.
  (iii) Relaxation of exchange controls elsewhere in Europe allowing the holding of foreign currency reserves in London by individuals and institutions.
  (iv) Regulation Q, which restricted the interest rates which US banks could pay and therefore encouraged Americans to place deposits in London to gain higher rates.

The 1960s also saw the introduction of new financial instruments such as certificates of deposit which encouraged dealing. In this period we also saw the beginning of trade in other eurocurrencies, notably the eurodeutschmark. These forces combined to make London the world centre of eurocurrency dealing.

(b) *The 1970s.* There was a spectacular growth of the eurocurrency markets in the 1970s. Towards the end of the decade business was expanding at the rate of 30 per cent per year. There were two main reasons for the growth. First, the huge rise in oil prices in 1973 and again in 1978 left the oil exporting countries with huge dollar surpluses (all oil transactions are in dollars). A very large proportion of these surpluses were placed on short-term deposit in Europe. Second, the regime of floating exchange rates encouraged speculation and freed many currencies from exchange restrictions.

(c) *The 1980s.* This period saw a drastic slowing down in the expansion of the markets. This was partly a result of the worldwide recession but more especially of the world debt crisis. Many developing countries that had been borrowers in the 1970s found it impossible to service their debts in the 1980s when real interest rates were much higher. Despite this slowdown, by the end of the decade the total gross lending in eurocurrencies was over £3000 billion, an amount almost equal to the GDP of the USA and six times that of the UK.

What and where are the eurocurrency markets?

The leading eurocurrency is the dollar, accounting for something like 74 per cent of the market. The second most important is the Deutschmark; other eurocurrencies are the Swiss franc, the yen and sterling. There is nothing exclusively European about eurocurrencies. This is also reflected in the geographical location of the leading dealing centres. London is the pre-eminent centre. Other centres include Zurich, Hong Kong, Luxembourg, Paris, Tokyo, Singapore, Bahrain and Nassau. (Why isn't New York in the list?)

The importance of the eurocurrency markets

The sheer size of the markets makes them important but activities in the markets have important effects nationally and internationally. The markets are a source of finance for both companies and countries. In particular developing nations such as Brazil and Mexico have borrowed heavily on the eurocurrency markets. The level of interest rates in the markets influences interest rates worldwide. Many loans are at variable interest and are often tied to a key rate such as LIBOR (London InterBank Offered Rate).

The eurocurrency markets are largely beyond the effective control of government but they impinge upon the operation of domestic

monetary policy. The fact that banks can switch easily into and out of eurocurrencies makes it very difficult for direct controls (e.g. special deposits) on banks to be effective. This was well illustrated in 1980 when the government abolished the 'corset' (see Chapter 36). The immediate effect of this was a surge in $£M_3$ as banks switched liquidity they had been 'hiding' in eurocurrencies back into sterling. Because of these problems the monetary authorities have to rely to a much greater extent on the control of interest rates as a method of monetary policy.

The mobility of eurocurrency deposits is a source of instability bringing unwelcome changes in the exchange rate. For example, if interest rates were raised in the UK this could lead to a switch from eurodollars to sterling and hence to an appreciation of the pound and/or a growth in the money supply in the UK. Both of these consequences may be unwelcome. The existence of the eurocurrency markets reduces the effectiveness of national macroeconomic policy and may, therefore, provide an argument for global regulation of the international finance system.

STUDENT ACTIVITY 44.6

1　Why have eurocurrency markets developed?
2　What are the implications of eurocurrency markets for national governments' macroeconomic policy?
3　What are the problems for the world economy of the developments of such markets beyond national government control?

● *Common misunderstanding*

The eurocurrency markets are not to be confused with the new EU currency the euro.

The General Agreement on Tariffs and Trade (GATT) and its successor, the World Trade Organisation (WTO)

In 1944 when the Bretton Woods conference international payments was taking place at Bretton Woods, other negotiations were under way to establish an organisation to regulate protection to be named the International Trading

Organisation (ITO). However, the talks foundered and all that was achieved was the General Agreement on Tariffs and Trade (GATT). It is a chapter of 38 articles organised in four parts. None the less GATT has been the most important organisation for the promotion of freer trade.

Impediments to trade such as export subsidies and quotas were outlawed by the GATT and if a country wished to impose a new tariff it had to offset it by offering compensatory reductions in other tariffs. In reality, exemptions were granted. Thus, quantitative restrictions could be used to safeguard a balance of payments and to provide temporary relief for domestic industries. Developing countries can use quantitative restrictions to further development goals. Similarly, agriculture was not affected by the restriction on export subsidies.

The GATT attempted to achieve its objective of trade liberalisation by organising 'rounds of negotiations'. There have been eight such rounds. The most important rounds of negotiation were the last three, namely the Kennedy round, which took five years to complete (1962–67), the Tokyo round, which took seven years to complete (1973–79) and the Uruguay round, which took eight years to succeed (1986–93) and has been held by many to be the most important round ever completed.

The GATT is guided in its actions by two fundamental principles:

(a) *'Non-discrimination'*, also referred to as 'most favoured nation' (MFN) treatment. Every signatory was to be treated as 'a most favoured nation', i.e. trading privileges could not be extended to one member without extending them to all. Existing systems of preference were allowed to continue but could not be increased.
(b) *'Reciprocity'*. If a country granted a trade concession to another country then the latter must reciprocate by granting an equivalent trade concession.

Trading blocks such as the EU and NAFTA (North America Free Trade Area) were allowed even though they contravene the MFN principle, and developing countries were not bound by the 'reciprocity' principle.

Significant reductions in tariffs in industrial goods were achieved by the Kennedy and Tokyo rounds. By the end of the Tokyo round, average tariff levels on industrial goods were about 5 per cent in the main industrialised countries. This was a major achievement, given that at the start of the first round average tariffs exceeded 40 per cent.

This comparison however overstates GATT's successes, neither trade in agricultural goods nor trade in services was covered by these rounds. Non-tariff barriers to trade had been largely untouched. Some sectors such as the steel and textile industries had very high rates of protectionism and non-tariff barriers such as voluntary export restraints, dumping, government procurement policies, etc., were not addressed by these rounds. For example, the World Bank found that while 48 per cent of the imports of the industrialised countries were affected by non-tariff protection in 1986.

No wonder then that the Uruguay round took eight years to complete. The most 'conflict-ridden' areas were on the menu for discussion. Chief amongst them were agriculture, trade in services, trade in intellectual property rights (TRIPS), dumping, and non-tariff barriers. After a long and difficult round of negotiation, the round was finally concluded in 1993. The main results of the Uruguay round were as follows:

(a) Average reductions in tariff barriers by 50 per cent.
(b) Non-tariff barriers to be phased out.
(c) On agriculture, farm export subsidies to be reduced, the volume of subsidised exports reduced and there were minimum import volumes.
(d) Agreement to deregulate trade in services but the audio visual sector to be left out completely. No change in maritime transport. Financial services will not be subject to the MFN/non-discrimination principle.
(e) Provision to standardise patents.
(f) On textiles, the multifibre arrangements to be phased out and quotas to be replaced by tariffs.
(g) GATT to be replaced by the World Trade Organisation (WTO).

The World Trade Organisation

Established in January 1995, the WTO is responsible for administering multilateral trade agreements negotiated by its members such as the General Agreement on Tariffs and Trade (GATT), the General Agreement on Trade in Services (GATS) and the agreement on Trade in Intellectual Property Rights (TRIPS). Just like GATT, the WTO is to provide a forum for further negotiating rounds. It differs from GATT in that it has a much tighter dispute settlement procedure and a new trade policy review mechanism.

The dispute settlement procedure of the WTO

Under GATT it was possible for one of the parties to a dispute to block the establishment of a panel or the adoption of panel reports. Under the WTO, the adoption of panel reports can only be blocked by a consensus, which is extremely unlikely. The parties to a dispute must initially attempt to solve it themselves. If they fail to find a solution to their dispute within 60 days, the Dispute Settlement Body (DSB) will establish a panel to investigate and make a report to the parties involved and to the DSB. Creation of the panel is automatic. The report must be accepted by the DSB within 60 days. An appeal can be made on legal grounds only. Appeal proceedings should not exceed 60 days and must be completed within 90 days.

The offending party is expected to comply immediately. If this is not possible it will be given a reasonable time to do so. If the offending party fails to act within this period it must offer mutually acceptable compensation. Failure to do so may result in the complainant requesting authorisation from the DSB to retaliate against the offending party. Such authorisation is virtually automatic for a consensus is required to refuse it.

The trade policy review mechanism (TPRM) of the WTO

The TPRM is responsible for reporting on the trading policies of member countries and examining their impact on the trading system. Each member is requested to provide periodic reports

as to its trading policies. The frequency of review is dependent upon the member's share of world trade. The four largest players (the EU, the USA, Japan and Canada) are subject to a review every two years.

STUDENT ACTIVITY 44.7

(a) What, in your view, are the outstanding problems confronting the world trading system today? How successful do you think the WTO will be in resolving them?

(b) Was the French government right in refusing to give in to American pressures to liberate trade in the audio visual industry?

(c) Which countries (trading blocs) stand to gain the most from the implementation of the Uruguay round?

● *Common misunderstanding*

The WTO is seen by many people as a mechanism for rich industrial countries to impose restrictions on less developed countries. While the outcome of the Uruguay Round was shaped by the US and the EU it does have advantages for poorer countries. Access to developed country markets is made easier. In addition stricter dispute settlement procedures also make it harder for developed countries using their market power to impose restrictions on less developed countries.

Other international institutions

The World Bank (IBRD)

The International Bank for Reconstruction and Development, or World Bank, was set up in 1947 as the sister organisation to the IMF. Its original aim was to make loans to develop the war-shattered economies of Europe. Subsequently its activities shifted towards financing projects and programmes in developing countries on a long-term basis (ranging up to 35 years). The IMF's purpose is not to give loans to finance development projects; this is the job of the IBRD. Most World Bank loans are used to finance infrastructure investment in transportation, electric power, agriculture, water supply and education. One of the chief problems facing the IBRD is its lack of funds. Funds come from three sources:

(a) *Quotas.* The membership of the IBRD is the same as that of the IMF. Members make contributions in relation to their IMF quota. Of the quota, 10 per cent is subscribed while the other 90 per cent is promised as a guarantee for the World Bank's loans.

(b) *Bonds.* The World Bank sells bonds on the capital markets of the world.

(c) *Income.* A very small proportion of the World Bank's funds come from its earnings. As it developed the World Bank turned its attention from Europe to the poorer countries of the world. Today it is almost wholly concerned with helping LDCs. It is a source of advice and information, besides making loans.

As with the IMF, although there is a great need for the services of the IBRD its role is limited. The limitation comes both from lack of funds, from political disagreements and questions over the effectiveness of its operations in aiding development. Increasingly the work of the World Bank is overshadowed by that of commercial lending to developing nations.

OECD (the Organisation for Economic Co-operation and Development)

In 1947 the Organisation for European Economic Co-operation (OEEC) came into existence to administer the European recovery programme ('Marshall aid'). This was an important institution and, among other things, helped to establish the European Payments Union (EPU). By 1961 the OEEC became the OECD, a more widely based organisation. Its objectives are:

(a) to encourage growth, high employment and financial stability amongst members;

(b) to aid the economic development of less developed non-member countries.

The OECD now has 29 members, including most European countries, the USA, Canada, Australia, and Japan. Membership is limited only by the requirement that a country be committed to a market economy and a pluralistic democracy. The OECD enables member countries to:

(a) Discuss and develop economic and social policy.

(b) Compare experiences, seek answers to common problems and work to coordinate domestic and international policies that increasingly in today's globalised world must form a web of even practice across nations.

(c) Agree to legally-binding codes, e.g. on the free flow of capital and services, to crack down on bribery or to end subsidies for shipbuilding.

(d) Collect data, monitor trends, analyse and forecast economic developments.

(e) Carry out research, e.g. on social changes, evolving patterns in trade, environment, agriculture, technology, taxation, etc.

All the international organisations we have discussed in this chapter are important sources of information; their websites are invaluable information sources and their addresses are given at the end of this chapter.

The Bank for International Settlements (BIS)

This institution is based in Basle, Switzerland. It was set up after a proposal by the Young Committee in 1930. Its original purpose was to enable central banks to coordinate their international payments and receipts. Originally it arose out of the need to regulate German reparations. It is one of the oldest surviving and most successful of the international institutions.

Since the Second World War, the BIS has acted like a central bank for central banks. The board of the BIS is made up of representatives of the central banks of the UK, France, Germany, Belgium, Italy, Switzerland, The Netherlands and Sweden. Other countries such as the USA and Japan regularly attend meetings.

The chief functions of the BIS are as follows:

(a) the promotion of cooperation between central banks;

(b) organising finance for nations in payments difficulties;

(c) monitoring eurocurrency markets;

(d) provision of expert advice;

(e) administration of the EU's credit scheme.

Not only is the BIS one of the oldest and most successful of international institutions, but also it is a self-supporting and profit-making institution.

The European Bank for Reconstruction and Development (EBRD)

The aim of the EBRD is 'to foster the transition towards open market-orientated economies and to promote private and entrepreneurial initiative of Central and Eastern Europe'. The EBRD is the first international financial institution set up in the post Cold War era. The agreement establishing it is a response to the challenges of transition in Central and Eastern Europe (CEE), as the region moves from centrally planned command systems to market economies.

The structural transformation required in this process is enormous. It required the creation of an appropriate legal framework for property rights, contracts and financial transactions; the establishment of commercial codes and accounting systems; reform of the banking system; privatisation of most economic enterprises, liberalisation of prices; changes in managerial behaviour; and the fostering of competition throughout each economy. This radical set of reforms must be supported by sound advice, training and technical expertise and supplemented by major investments in the private and public sectors to ensure an effective supply response. Domestic capital will not be enough: external capital is therefore needed from both private and public sources.

The idea of the European Bank was put forward by President Mitterrand in 1989 and came to fruition in May 1990 with the signature of its agreement by 40 countries, the Commission of the EC and the European Investment Bank. The EBRD is a new institution where East and West can meet to build a future together. The Bank has its headquarters in London and began operations in April 1991. CEE countries such as the Czech Republic, Estonia, Hungary and Poland have made such progress with transition that they are currently in the final phase of negotiations for EU membership. But progress in many other countries such as Russia, the Ukraine, Romania, Bulgaria has been extremely limited. It seems that the heritage from the previous system and the policies adopted by individual countries are more important than external aid in the transition process.

Summary

1. The IMF and the IBRD were set up as a result of the Bretton Woods conference and were aimed at regulating international payments and helping economic development.
2. The IMF system is based on a system of quotas; members may borrow in relation to the size of their quotas.
3. The adjustable peg was central to the IMF system.
4. The 1970s saw a breakdown of the system of fixed exchange rates.
5. The SDR is a hypothetical unit of account, and is now the basis of all IMF transactions.
6. Both the IMF and the IBRD are hampered by lack of funds.
7. There has been a decline in the importance of the IMF and the IBRD.
8. The eurocurrency markets are an important source both of finance and of instability in the international system.
9. Negotiations under the GATT have succeeded in substantially reducing levels of protection in the world economy.
10. Gradually the emphasis has moved from tariff to non-tariff barriers and thus negotiations have become more difficult because they intrude more directly on national government policies.
11. The WTO which rules on disputes over government measures affecting trade is currently seen by many as simply facilitating globalisation and the exploitation of poorer countries.
12. The regulation of trade is, however, essential if large powerful economies are not to dictate to the rest of the world.

? QUESTIONS

1. Explain the reason for the abandonment of the adjustable peg system.
2. What is the problem of international liquidity and how does the IMF help to overcome it?
3. Describe the main functions of the IMF.
4. Trace the reasons for the variations in the level of economic cooperation in the 1970s and 1980s.
5. Outline the activities of the Bank for International Settlement (BIS).

6 Trace the origins and growth of the eurocurrency markets.

7 What is meant by the problem of international liquidity and how does the IMF help to overcome it?

8 Why have the reductions in trade barriers and regulation of trade under the GATT and the WTO been important in facilitating the growth of the world economy?

9 Explain why the WTO is thought to be an improvement on GATT?

Data response A
THE IMF AND THAILAND

The questions below should be answered after you have read the article by Ted Bardacke which appeared in the *Financial Times* on 7 August 1997. You should also refer to Chapter 42 'The balance of payments and exchange rates' and Chapter 47 'Schools of thought and future issues'.

1 Why did Thailand turn to the IMF for help?
2 What will the effect of the package be on the baht?
3 Will the IMF be successful in establishing control over Thailand's economy?
4 Was the IMF right to intervene in the internal economic affairs of Thailand?
5 Could and should the IMF have acted earlier to help Thailand?

A hole of its own making

FT

Holes are a common sight in Thailand.

Now, suddenly, comes the biggest hole yet – one in the public accounts. This has so far cost $20bn and shows signs of getting bigger.

On Tuesday, the Bank of Thailand detailed parts of an economic reform package designed to obtain between $12bn and $15bn in emergency credits from the International Monetary Fund. Simultaneously, it announced it had lent nearly $16bn to the finance companies it has now declared insolvent. Another $3bn in public money has been spent to bail out the fraud-ridden Bangkok Bank of Commerce over the past 18 months.

In addition to all that came yesterday's guarantee – worth at least $7bn and perhaps as much as $31bn – to protect all depositors and creditors at both the suspended and operating finance companies. In all, the size of Thailand's financial system bailout is comparable to the US Savings & Loan debacle.

It is little wonder then that the country was forced to turn to the

IMF. But after botching last month's flotation of the baht, the fact that the government had to be dragged to the negotiating table must cast doubts on its real commitment to reform.

'I have never seen Thailand in such a serious crisis,' Mr Anand Panyarachun told reporters this week. And he should know: twice this decade he was appointed prime minister after bloody military coups.

He added: 'There is nowhere else in this world where people have lost all faith in their own government and prefer their financial and monetary affairs to be managed by the IMF.'

The frustration of influential intellectuals and economists was, in large part, due to the belief that the Thai government could have forestalled the crisis on its own. The belief is that it should not have waited so long to float the baht and then to announce measures to deal with the aftermath of its 20 per cent fall.

By most economists' reckoning, at the start of the year the country faced no imminent balance of payments crisis. The currency was not seriously overvalued, the first budget deficit in a decade was going to be manageable and international financial markets were giving Thailand some breathing space. If at that point the government had taken some tough decisions – by introducing more flexibility to the baht, cutting government spending and being tough with insolvent financial institutions – it would have rescued the economy on its own with less pain.

Some in Thailand are worried that by, in effect, farming out the difficult economic decisions to the IMF, the government will never learn to tackle difficult issues on its own. There is a fear that, once the economy gets back on its feet, the government will fall into past patterns. This would risk turning Thailand into a boom-and-bust country more akin to Latin America in the 1970s than other south-east Asian tigers.

Most analysts agree that it will be at least two years before Thailand, one of the world's fastest growing economies between 1986 and 1996, can rejoin the ranks of the tiger cubs. Corporate Thailand has borrowed more money, both in absolute terms and as a percentage of gross domestic product, than its south-east Asian neighbours. Its domestic interest payments as a percentage of GDP are three times those of Mexico's at the time of the peso devaluation, according to Morgan Stanley and Goldman Sachs.

When Thailand's non-performing loans rise as a result of IMF-approved belt-tightening, the pressure on the government's balance sheet is going to grow further. This is not lost on other south-east Asian countries trying both to learn from Thailand and distance themselves from it at the same time.

'Long-term prospects for Thailand are good. But . . . we must never let this happen to us,' Mr Lee Hsien Loong, Singapore's deputy prime minister, told a gathering on Sunday to commemorate that country's National Day.

Yesterday, some commercial banks experienced a run on their deposits prompting a return of rumours, categorically denied by the central bank, that a number of small banks could also be shut.

But even if the Bank of Thailand's assurances are to be believed – difficult for some who have seen the institution reverse course with tidal regularity – brokerage W.I. Carr estimates that by closing down half of the financial institutions the central bank has locked up 10 per cent of the financial system's deposits and 15 per cent of its assets. This will deprive the already cash-strapped manufacturing companies of much needed liquidity.

'The impact on the real economy is going to be very, very large,' says Mr Warut Siwasariyanon, head of research at ING Barings in Bangkok.

'Companies and financial institutions are just hoarding cash right now. There isn't much scope for interest rates to come down for the next six to nine months,' he says.

Thai officials say this is now the IMF's problem. They have declared victory and retreated. Believing he has won the economic battle by calling up reinforcements, Mr Chavalit Yongchaiyudh, the prime minister, is now moving on to the even trickier problem of political reform.

Source: Financial Times, 7 August 1997. Reprinted with permission.

Websites

International Monetary Fund: www.imf.org
OECD: www.oecd.org
IBRD (World Bank): www.worldbank.org
Bank for International Settlement: www.bis.org
European Bank for Reconstruction and Development: www.ebrd.org

45 The European Union

Introduction

The origins of the EU

The origins of the EU lie in the desire for peace at the end of the Second World War. The integration of economies would, in the words of the founding father of European integration Jean Monnet, 'make war not only unthinkable but materially impossible'. Thus in 1952 to the European Coal and Steel Community (ECSC) was established with France, Italy, Belgium, West Germany, Holland and Luxembourg as members. The UK participated in the negotiations but declined to join. The ECSC was to abolish trade restrictions on coal and steel between member countries and to coordinate production and pricing policies. The idea was that integration in one sector would encourage the process of further political and economic integration and this has proved to be the case. The Treaties of Rome were signed in 1957 and on 1 January 1958 the European Economic Community (EEC) came into existence. Once again the UK participated in early negotiations but then withdrew.

After two abortive attempts to join the EC the UK finally became a member in 1973, together with Ireland and Denmark. Norway decided, by a referendum, not to become a member. Greece became a member in 1981 and Spain and Portugal in 1986. Sweden, Austria and Finland became members in January 1995.

Forms of economic integration

(a) *Free trade areas.* Countries agree to abolish internal tariff barriers usually on industrial goods, but retain their own national external tariffs and trade policy. The North American Free Trade Area (USA, Canada and Mexico) and the European Free Trade Area (Norway, Switzerland, Iceland, Liechtenstein) are examples of free trade areas but there are many others. Since a FTA does not have a Common External Tariff (CET) there have to be regulations called rules of origin to decide which goods are subject to free trade, otherwise extra-FTA imports would simply be channelled through the country with the lowest tariffs.

(b) *Customs union*. Central to the EEC Treaty was the establishment of a customs union abolishing tariffs between members and establishing a CET on imports from the rest of the world. The EEC's CET was to be set at the arithmetic mean of the previous four customs territories (Belgium, The Netherlands and Luxembourg, Benelux had common tariffs). Generally France and Italy had high tariffs and West Germany and the Benelux lower tariffs. So averaging would have led to tariffs on Germany and Benelux imports rising. This did not happen because GATT negotiations led to the first two rounds of internal tariff reductions being extended to all GATT members, so very few German and Benelux tariffs rose and Italian and French tariffs fell. The only exception was agriculture where levels of protection generally rose.

Special arrangements were made for imports for ex-colonies and these developed through a series of agreements into the Lomé Convention of 1975. Under this agreement, developing nations in Africa, the Caribbean and the Pacific (ACP states) were granted tariff concessions on their industrial exports and on some agricultural exports to the EU together with receiving aid.

(c) *Common market*. This colloquial term for the EU reflects the fact that the EEC Treaty provided not only for tariff-free trade in goods but also for the free movement of labour and capital. Restrictions on the movement of workers were removed in the 1960s but labour mobility within and between EU countries has remained low. Free movement of capital was not achieved until the run up to monetary union in the 1990s.

(d) *Single market*. Despite the fact that the EEC eliminated internal tariff barriers in 1968, non-tariff barriers (NTBs) remained to limit trade. These NTBs related to such factors as different product regulations (environmental regulations), border controls, government purchases and indirect tax differences. For example, France used to have higher duties on spirits distilled from grains, e.g. whisky and gin, as opposed to those distilled from grapes, e.g. brandy and armagnac, which were domestically produced. Although the EEC Treaty contained provisions to remove these barriers by the process of harmonisation of laws this proved extremely difficult because NTBs often involve sensitive issues. In the 1970s the use of NTBs in the EU actually increased. By signing the Single European Act in February 1986 the EU member states committed themselves to progressively completing the single 'common' market, envisaged in the EEC Treaty, by the end of 1992. The Act, which came into force in July 1987, defines the single market as 'an area without internal frontiers in which the free movement of goods, persons, services and capital is guaranteed'.

(e) *Economic and monetary union*. The use of different currencies restricts trade because of the cost of exchange and uncertainty over the exchange rate. Thus to have a truly single market the use of a single currency is necessary. Such a monetary union requires some coordination of other economic policies hence economic and monetary union (EMU).

STUDENT ACTIVITY 45.1

1 Why do free trade areas need rules of origin to decide which goods are to be sold without tariffs?
2 Why are there more free trade areas than customs union? (Hint: the major difference between the two is the CET and common external trade policy.)

The economics of integration

Most economists advocate the benefits of free world trade, it is argued that, in the long run societies' welfare will be improved as a result of specialisation on the basis of comparative advantage. But the single market is free trade in a limited geographical area; this is a 'second best', the 'first best' is World free trade. There can be no general rules in second best situations, thus the single market provides for benefits for freer trade between members but at the cost of discriminating against non-members. This is analysed by the theory of customs which distinguishes between short-run static effects and longer run dynamic effects of the formation, enlargement or intensification of customs unions.

The static effects of customs unions

The static effects of customs unions relate to the costs and benefits of the short-run reorganisation of production as a result of the change in trade patterns caused by the customs union. The benefits of freer internal trade are called *trade creation* and the cost of discrimination is called *trade diversion.*

Trade creation is additional trade caused by the internal tariff reductions in the customs union. This trade is beneficial because prices are reduced as imports from the partner are cheaper, leading to a reduction in higher cost domestic production and additional consumption. In Figure 45.1 S_{UK} is the UK supply of this good, D_{UK} is the UK demand for this good. For simplicity it is assumed that the EU supply of this good is infinitely elastic at the world price and the EU tariff is the same as the UK tariff. Thus before it was an EU member the UK market price would have been P_1 and at this price it would have imported Q_2Q_3 from the EU and received tariff revenue equal to $P_1P_2 \times Q_2Q_3$, the area 3. If the UK now joins the EU the price will fall to P_2, imports increase to Q_1Q_4. The trade creation is the additional imports $Q_1Q_2 + Q_3Q_4$, the net

benefit to the UK is equal to the areas 2 + 4. This is because consumers benefit by the price reduction on existing consumption, the areas 1 + 2 + 3, plus consumer surplus on additional consumption, the area 4. The area 1 represents a reduction in UK producers' surplus and area 3 lost tariff revenue, so the net benefit is the areas 2 + 4.

Trade diversion is an increase in trade with partner countries, which displaces lower cost imports from third countries. This is detrimental because the country is paying more for its imports as a result of switching from a lower to a higher cost partner supplier. In Figure 45.2 the pre-customs union price in the UK is P_1, at this price UK consumption is Q_3, UK production is Q_2 and imports from the world are Q_2Q_3 with tariff revenue of $P_1P_w \times Q_2Q_3$, the area 3 + 5. Joining the EU would lead to a fall in the price to consumers of P_1P_2, imports become Q_1Q_4, thus consumers gain 1 + 2 + 3 + 4. The pre-customs union imports Q_2Q_3 are now imported at higher cost from the EU, of the tariff revenue 3 + 5, the area 3 goes to the consumer as lower prices but the area 5 is a loss to the UK. There is also trade creation in this example $Q_1Q_2 + Q_3Q_4$ on which there is a net gain of consumer surplus of 2 + 4. So the net cost/benefit of EU membership in this case is (2 + 4)–5.

Whether joining the customs union is beneficial depends upon the relative extent of trade creation and trade diversion and thus depends upon the circumstances of the particular case.

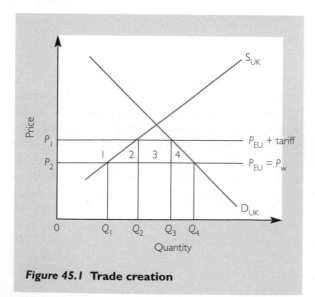

Figure 45.1 Trade creation

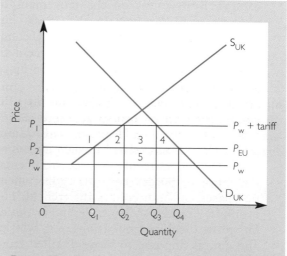

Figure 45.2 Trade creation and trade diversion

Trade creation is more likely:

- When the union's external tariff is low especially if it has been reduced as a result of the formation of the customs union.
- When the customs union is larger because it is likely to include efficient producers.
- When the countries that form the customs union are geographically close since this will reduce transport and communications costs encouraging trade.

The static benefits of customs unions are likely to be relatively small. For example suppose the formation of a customs union eliminates internal tariffs of 20 per cent of the price of imports, this leads to additional imports (trade creation) of 50 per cent of trade and that imports amount to 25 per cent of GNP. Thus the gain is as follows (the reason for the division by 2 is that the gain is the two triangles 2 and 4, the percentages are effectively measuring rectangles of similar dimensions).

$$\frac{\text{Tariff reduction} \quad \text{Additional trade} \quad \text{Trade/GNP}}{2} = \frac{20\% \quad \times \quad 50\% \quad \times \quad 25\%}{2} = 1.25\% \text{ of GDP}$$

Even with these relatively optimistic assumptions, the gain (the triangles 2 and 4) is only 1.25 per cent of GNP. The reasons for this are:

- Maximum gain is equal to the size of the original tariff.
- Gains only apply to additional trade.
- The gains are not cumulative they are just a percentage of trade created.
- There are potential losses from trade diversion as well as gains from trade creation.

This is a particular example of a more general rule in economics that the deadweight (static) costs of price distortions are relatively small. This is due to the fact that most of the loss to consumers goes to producers as higher surpluses. In the longer term price distortions are more significant because they can lead to cumulative distortions in the economy. Thus the dynamic effects of customs unions are likely to be much larger than the static effects.

The dynamic effects of customs unions

The dynamic effects of customs unions relate to the long-run changes in economic performance, which result from the formation of a customs union. These gains are cumulative and thus grow to be very significant with time.

- *Intensification of competition.* The reduction of trade barriers increases competition in domestic markets. Competition is essential to ensure that companies keep prices low, that quality is high and ensure that goods and services meet consumers' requirements. Additional competition is especially important for the oligopolistic markets that dominate modern economies, domestic firms may have slipped into tacitly collusive behaviour which opening up the market may undermine. A necessary adjunct to the customs union is an effective competition policy to ensure that cartels, dominant firms and mergers and takeovers do not prevent cross border competition from being effective.
- *Economies of scale.* The extent to which economies of scale can be exploited depends upon the size of the market, so a large market could potentially lead to significant cost savings. The problem here is that if economies of scale are really large international trade should exploit them. It may be that the market is closed as with government procurement.
- *Investment and the rate of economic growth.* Levels of investment depend upon the expectations of business, the creation of a customs union, its intensification or enlargement could be seen as a creating new opportunities which could encourage higher investment.
- *Foreign direct investment (FDI).* Impact of integration on FDI by multinationals. The major effect is likely to be an increase in FDI from outside the customs union. This effect is likely to be unevenly spread across the customs union thus the UK and Ireland have attracted a disproportionate share of inward investment to the EU.
- *Technology effects.* The effect of integration on technology and managerial efficiency. This could be the result of effects on profits, investment or competition.

STUDENT ACTIVITY 45.2

1 Explain why the formation of customs unions involves both freer trade and trade discrimination.

2 Why was the EEC a trade creating customs union?

● **Common misunderstanding**

A fortress Europe may be thought to be desirable with high levels of protection around a large single market. The theory of customs unions suggests that both the static and dynamic effects will be larger with lower external protection. This is because it will mean less trade diversion and greater competition.

The single market

The effect of the elimination of trade barriers in the single market is likely to be much greater than that suggested for customs unions. This is because it eliminates non-tariff barriers and it applies to sectors previously closed to competition:

(a) *The elimination of non-tariff barriers will yield greater benefits than the elimination of tariffs.* This is because NTBs are cost increasing rather than revenue generating this means the benefits of their elimination is much greater. In Figure 45.3 if P_1P_2 is a tariff on imports into the UK and the world (and EU) supply is represented by the line $P_{EU}P_W$ at price P_1. Under these circumstances the cost of the tariff to the consumers is shown by the area 1 + 2 + 3 + 4. Of this, area 1 is an increase in producer surplus and 3 is tariff revenue for the government. So the deadweight loss due to the tariff is the sum of the triangles 2 + 4, this will be net gain from trade creation if the UK joins the EU. If, however, P_1P_2 is a non-tariff barrier then there will be no tariff revenue. For many non-tariff barriers such as checks at borders the area 3 will be the additional cost of paying for customs officials, money lost to haulage companies as a result of delays, paperwork

and uncertainty. Thus the gain from eliminating such a non-tariff is larger by the area 1 + 3 than gain from eliminating tariffs.

(b) *Non-tariff barriers are likely to be higher than tariffs.* Since tariff levels have to be established by legislation tariff levels are known. This means that the government has to be prepared to justify very high levels of tariffs and negotiations to reduce tariff levels are relatively straightforward. Since NTBs are difficult to measure the level of such barriers can be very high and as they are related to other aspects of government policy negotiations to reduce non-tariff barriers have proved very problematic. For example when telecommunications switching equipment was purchased by national monopolies from national producers the average price in the EU was 60 per cent above the world price.

(c) *Protected sectors.* There were particular sectors of the economy where competition is extremely limited by non-tariff barriers. These included many financial services such as banking and insurance where the need to satisfy the financial regulations of each country in which operations took place severely limited competition. Thus in order to offer banking services in another EU country it was necessary to establish a subsidiary in that country and to satisfy the authorities that the

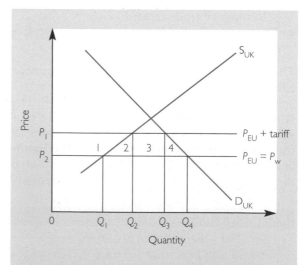

Figure 45.3 **The cost of tariff and non-tariff barriers to trade**

subsidiary had sufficient assets within the country. Defence equipment and government purchases more generally were overwhelmingly sought from the national suppliers. The public utilities gas, electricity, telecommunications and railways were usually national monopolies with little or no competition. These sectors represent very large parts of the economy, e.g. government purchases of goods and services are estimated to represent 16 per cent of the sales of private sector. With very little competition the scope for improvements in efficiency were very large. Substantial progress has been made in financial services, some progress has been made in opening up public utilities to competition.

STUDENT ACTIVITY 45.4

1 Why are the benefits from the elimination of non-tariff barriers likely to be much greater than the elimination of tariffs?

2 Consider why the following may act as non-tariff barriers to trade:

- an environmental regulation in Denmark that soft drinks be sold in returnable glass bottles could act as an NTB;
- border checks on lorries;
- government subsidies to the motor vehicle industry.

3 Explain why governments may be reluctant to abandon these measures.

Fiscal harmonisation

Fiscal harmonisation is the process of reducing differences in taxes between EU countries. The objective is to reduce tax differences to a level at which they do not distort economic decisions in the single market. The problems of differing tax levels vary between different taxes.

(a) *Indirect taxes.* Although tariffs and most NTBs have been eliminated in the EU the rates of indirect taxation vary substantially between countries. Now that customs checks have largely been eliminated in the EU differing rates of tax present two problems:

- *The collection and distribution of tax receipts on intra-EU trade.* Indirect taxes

are paid on consumption and should be revenue for the country where consumption takes place. Taxes such as VAT were repaid to exporters and were charged on imports, this is no longer possible without custom borders. So these taxes are charged on all intra-EU exports and an adjustment has to be made when the sale takes place. Thus if the local rate of tax is higher an additional tax has to be charged or if it is lower a deduction has to be made. There also has to be a clearing mechanism so that countries where the tax paid on imports exceeds the taxes paid on exports receive additional tax revenue and those where tax received from exports exceeds that levied on imports have to make an additional payment. Greater harmonisation of VAT and excise rates would avoid the need for elaborate calculations of tax payable on goods moving between countries.

There has been some progress towards narrowing the range of VAT rates. There is now a lower limit of 15 per cent on the standard rate of VAT, agreement to abolish higher rates of VAT on luxury items, and to no more than two lower rates on necessities.

- *Tax avoidance, evasion and smuggling.* There are very large differences in excise duties on tobacco and alcohol between EU states. This represents an enormous incentive to purchase the product in the cheaper countries. Individuals can, for example, go across the Channel from the UK and make enormous savings, often buying from outlets catering for such day shoppers. Then there are small scale operators bringing vans full of alcohol back across the Channel for illegal sale and finally there is large scale smuggling. An idea of the size of the problem can be gained from the estimate that one in five cigarettes smoked in the UK is smuggled. This represents a large loss of income to legitimate retailers, a significant loss of revenue for the UK Treasury and provides a lucrative source of criminal income. The large differences in excise duties make harmonisation extremely difficult with higher tax countries objecting on revenue and health grounds and lower tax countries claiming that, for example, cheap wine is part of their traditional way of life.

(b) *Income Taxes*. The situation with income taxes is less clear because although there are substantial differences in the level of income taxes between EU countries these to an extent are compensated for by differences in the level of public services. Scandinavian countries generally have the highest levels of income taxes but they also provide the most complete and generous welfare states. In addition, levels of labour mobility in the EU are very low because of problems of language and culture. Thus the only individuals likely to be sensitive to tax levels are high income earners whose occupation is relatively unaffected by their residence. Such individuals would be likely to reside in tax havens such as the Channel Islands, Monaco, etc. so the impact of differences in income taxes are likely to be limited. The other potential impact may be on those setting up new businesses and here there may be an effect but there is little evidence of relocation to avoid taxes.

(c) *Corporation taxes*. Capital unlike labour is very mobile and very different rates of tax between EU countries could encourage relocation in low tax states and the reorganisation of operations so that profits are recorded in low tax countries. Corporation tax payments are not just dependent upon the rates but also on the rules for assessing tax. So harmonisation of corporation tax has proved extremely difficult.

When considering the harmonisation of taxes it is important to remember that the US economy functions well with significant tax differences between states. Thus differences in taxes reflecting variations in national preferences are compatible with the single market provided that they are not so large that they significantly affect economic decisions.

STUDENT ACTIVITY 45.5

1 Why do differences in indirect taxes present problems for the single market?

2 Why are governments so reluctant to agree to harmonisation of direct taxes?

3 Why are differences in corporation taxes more likely to distort competition in the single market than differences in income tax?

● *Common misunderstanding*

Sometimes the single market is seen as purely being in the interests of business with a large market to achieve economies of scale. Consumers will, however, benefit from the reduction of non-tariff barriers and increased competition. Taxpayers will also benefit if governments get better value for money in their expenditure as a result of competitive tendering.

Economic and Monetary Union

With the inception of the euro on 1 January 1999 the EU took a fundamental step forward in the process of political and economic integration. The economic governance of eurozone members' economies became mainly the responsibility of EU institutions. A new supranational institution, the European Central Bank (ECB), has been established. This institution together with Ecofin (the Council of Finance Ministers) and the Euro 12 (the finance minsters of the 12 eurozone members) has responsibility for macroeconomic decisions in the eurozone.

The development of Economic and Monetary Union (EMU) has been slow: the EEC agreed in 1970 to achieve EMU by 1980. The first stage of moving to EMU, the 'Snake' system of tighter limits on exchange rate fluctuations between EEC members, was established, but this gradually broke down in the currency turmoil that followed the break-up of the Bretton Woods System and the first oil shock. In 1979 monetary integration was chosen to try to reinvigorate the integration process after the doldrums of the 1970s, thus the European Monetary System (EMS) was born. The exchange rate mechanism (ERM) of the EMS reintroduced fixed exchange rates among members' currencies (the UK was not a member of the ERM). The EMS was a success with ERM currencies achieving increasing stability of ERM exchange rates but countries had to modify their economic policies to maintain fixed exchange rates. In particular this meant maintaining the exchange rate with the strongest currency in the ERM the Deutschmark. This had the advantage that it was easier to control domestic inflation because a commitment to maintain a Deutschmark exchange rate carried more conviction than other commitments. Thus the effect on inflation expectations was greater. The disadvantage was that the Bundesbank effectively determined economic policy in the EMS and that policy was determined by German economic conditions. Since the Bundesbank was independent it was increasingly seen that the only effective way for other countries to have an influence on economic policy was to pool sovereignty in an economic and monetary union. This was what was agreed at Maastricht in 1991 when the Treaty on European Union was agreed. Subsequent instability in the EMS in 1992 and 1993 indicated that stability was only possible in a full EMU.

EMU fulfils the requirements for a complete monetary union:

- Permanently fixed exchange rates: with a single unit of account/currency, the euro.
- A single monetary authority, the European Central Bank, to control:
  - the money supply in the monetary union;
  - interest rates in the monetary union;
  - the exchange rate between the monetary union and the rest of the world.
- Some centralisation of fiscal policy, with the Growth and Stability Pact.

The costs of EMU

Having separate currencies is a trade-off, it:

- enables a country to pursue an independent economic policy;
- reduces economic efficiency as a result of transactions costs and uncertainty;
- the use of different currencies act as a non-tariff barrier to trade.

The Nobel prize winning economist **Robert Mundell** developed the theory of Optimum Currency Areas (OCA) in 1961. This suggested that there would be an optimum area over which a single currency should be used which would balance these factors. In practice the OCA theory has concentrated on the costs of losing the exchange rate instrument.

Whether losing the exchange rate as an instrument of economic policy is a problem depends upon:

(a) *The effectiveness of the exchange rate as an instrument of policy.* Changes in the exchange rate alter the relative price of domestic and foreign goods and services. Thus devaluation makes domestically produced goods and services relatively cheaper on home and foreign markets. Thus devaluation could be used to compensate for higher inflation in a country relative to its competitors. Devaluation will, however, increase the price of imported goods and this increases the costs of production directly. Wage costs will also tend to rise as workers try to maintain their real wages by increasing their nominal wages. The fact that past price increases have been accommodated also means that workers expectations are of further inflation. Thus the initial favourable effects of devaluation will be reduced and may completely disappear over time. The extent to which the effects disappear will depend upon: the openness of the economy; the extent to which workers can adjust their earnings to compensate for the loss of purchasing power; and the spare capacity in the economy to meet the extra domestic and foreign demand. Thus nominal devaluations tend to lead only to temporary *real* devaluations.

Even if devaluation is ineffective in the long run it may still be an effective short-term adjustment mechanism. In the absence of devaluation (an expenditure switching policy) a country in the short term may have to adjust for a balance of payments deficit by reducing demand and thereby imports. The cost of using such an expenditure reducing policy in terms of lost output may be high. The problem is that devaluation may also be used to avoid facing up to the economic problems that caused balance of payments difficulties. If this is the case further devaluations will occur with progressively diminishing effectiveness.

(b) *The extent to which economic performance differs between countries.* If the economic situation in similar in all countries within a monetary union then the same monetary policy will be suitable for them all. The performance of national economies does of course differ, part of this is due to the macroeconomic policies pursued by the government but there will be other characteristics of the economy that affect economic performance.

The UK for most of the last century grew more slowly than other developed economies, various explanations have been offered for this relatively poor performance such as a lower rate of investment, macroeconomic instability, inability to exploit innovation, limited entrepreneurial ability etc. If for whatever reason productivity in UK industry grows more slowly than in its competitors, then UK workers wages will have to rise more slowly than its competitors. If wages rose at the same rate UK industry would become uncompetitive, devaluation could provide a short-term adjustment for this situation but it does not resolve the fundamental problems. If the problem persists continued devaluations are unlikely to be effective. So the loss of exchange rate adjustment as an instrument of economic policy is not likely to adversely affect the long-term economic performance of an economy.

Economic performance will be determined not only by the nature of the economy and government policy but also by random shocks, e.g. oil price rises, the Russian crisis. For shocks to be a problem for EMU they must have a significant macroeconomic impact on one country. If the impact is sub-national adjusting the exchange rate would not help anyway. If the macroeconomic effect is felt across the union then a change in union policy will be the appropriate response.

A number of attempts have been made to ascertain the significance of asymmetric shocks but this has proved difficult because fluctuations in economic growth originate not just in external shocks but in national government policies. In addition, observed fluctuations are after government stabilisation and so differences reflect the success of these policies as well as differences in shocks. The research does seem to indicate the existence of a core where fluctuations from the normal growth path are correlated with Germany's; this predictably includes Austria, Switzerland, France, Denmark and the Benelux countries. More peripheral countries with much lower correlations are the UK, Italy, Spain, Portugal, Ireland, Greece and Finland. Economic cycles within Europe seem also to be becoming more synchronised as exchange rates have been stabilised.

(c) *The differences in economic preferences between countries.* The desired outcomes of macroeconomic policy may differ between countries. Thus post-1945 Germany seemed to have a preference for a lower rate of inflation than other developed economies. Such differences in economic preferences could cause two different types of problem for EMU. First, although monetary policy is the same across all eurozone countries, fiscal and other areas of economic policy remain the responsibility of national governments. If national governments pursued very different economic policies this could undermine the effectiveness of the common monetary policy. Second, public support for EMU could be undermined if economic performance differed substantially from national preferences. In reality this problem is not likely to be that serious. There has been substantial convergence of views on economic preferences between EU members, low inflation is seen as a high priority, as is the need to keep government expenditure and taxation and borrowing under control. Economic preferences are not likely to be very precisely defined, so as long as economic performance is reasonable preferences will be met. The extent to which it is possible to run the economy to achieve different preferences is questionable. Thus low unemployment may be unsustainable in the long term, i.e. it could lead to accelerating inflation.

STUDENT ACTIVITY 45.6

1 Why is the loss of the exchange rate as an instrument for economic adjustment more likely to be significant for the UK than it is for Ireland?
2 Consider whether the exchange rate is a useful economic instrument to compensate for differences in national economic performance.
3 Are there large differences in macroeconomic preferences between nations?

(d) *The availability and effectiveness of other adjustment mechanisms*. There are six other adjustment mechanisms that could be used in the absence of the exchange rate:

(i) *Price flexibility*. The most important means of achieving price flexibility is the maintenance of competitive markets. This is one of the major objectives of the single market and of EU competition policy.

(ii) *Wage flexibility*. If a country's goods are less competitive because of a negative demand or supply shock, a reduction in domestic prices would have the same effect as devaluation. A necessary condition for price flexibility is wage flexibility since prices are the major element of costs under the employers' control. Real wage flexibility seems to be achievable under two extreme wage bargaining systems: centralised national bargaining between employers organisations and trade unions; and decentralised company/plant level bargaining. In the first case the bargains have obvious macroeconomic effects so trade unions may be prepared to trade off lower wage increases for higher levels of employment. A significant part of German success in achieving low inflation was due to the centralisation of their wage bargaining system. The Netherlands and Ireland have been successful with agreements between the government and the social partners (trade unions, employers, etc.) to moderate wage demands in exchange for government commitments on employment, taxation, etc. With decentralised bargaining wage increases will have a direct impact on the performance of the company and on jobs so trade unions have to be realistic in their wage demands. This is the situation in the US and today in the UK. In between these two extremes the bargains may be too small for trade unions to appreciate their macroeconomic impact in total and too large to accept the effects on individual firms.

(iii) *Mobility of labour*. If the demand for goods and services produced by one nation diminishes relative to that of another nation then one way to prevent unemployment rising is for labour to move. Labour mobility is an important adjustment mechanism between states within the US monetary union. Europe is characterised by much more persistent regional unemployment than the US and low interregional and international migration. This low migration does not seem to be the result of low region specific shocks but an unwillingness to move. Therefore migration does not seem to be an adjustment mechanism available within EMU. European countries may also be less willing to accept the implications of migration of increased congestion in areas of inward migration and decline in areas of outward migration.

(iv) *Mobility of capital*. If workers will not move capital could move between areas. This could aid adjustment in two ways. First, low wages in areas of high unemployment could encourage an influx of investment, creating demand and employment. Second, if investment portfolios diversify away from a country as a result of EMU incomes will become less vulnerable to country specific shocks. In response to temporary shock private borrowing could increase moderating the impact. The cost and availability of borrowing is likely to be adversely affected by a downturn in the national economy. At the moment private capital mobility in the EU is too limited to achieve these effects.

(v) *Fiscal policy*. Governments could increase or decrease demand in their economy to offset the effects of a shock by altering the size of the public sector deficit. The ability to do this, however, is somewhat constrained by the Growth and Stability Pact (which is analysed in the section on EMU below, page 674).

(vi) *Interjurisdictional transfers*. National economies typically have large transfers between regions. These transfers have a countercyclical and a redistributional element. The countercyclical element is the one that permits adjustment in a monetary union. In a recession a region's payments of taxes to central government would fall as incomes and expenditure fall but central government expenditure in the area would rise with increased social security payments. In the USA empirical work suggests that fiscal stabilisation reduces falls in income in a recession by 20 per cent, in Europe the level of stabilisation seems higher. There is, however, no prospect of countries financing substantial international transfers on the US scale.

STUDENT ACTIVITY 45.7

1 Explain why centralised and decentralised systems of wage bargaining may lead to wage moderation.
2 Why is the mobility of labour low in the EU?
3 How can the mobility of capital provide a stabilising device in a monetary union?
4 Why are EU governments unwilling to finance large international fiscal transfers to facilitate adjustment in EMU?

The benefits of EMU

The gains from the use of a common currency in a monetary union are related to the lower transactions costs and reduced uncertainty:

(a) *Direct gains from elimination of transactions costs.* Resources are used in the billions of transactions every day when one currency is exchanged for another. The company or individual making the transaction has to pay for these resources. These costs for the EU are estimated to be around 0.5 per cent of GNP for intra-EU transactions, obviously transactions costs with non-EU currencies will remain. The small size of these gains may be a surprise compared with the high charges you incur when you buy foreign currency. This is because most international currency transactions take place in large amounts where costs are low and most transactions do not involve foreign exchange. Gains are much larger for consumers and small firms. There are also once and for all transition costs of adjusting records, computer systems and machines which use cash.

(b) *Welfare gains from reduced uncertainty.* Currencies such as sterling experience large fluctuations in their value against foreign currencies in general and even larger fluctuations against particular currencies. Individuals and companies are generally risk averse so by eliminating one source of uncertainty caused by fluctuating exchange rates monetary union should improve welfare.

(c) *Elimination of a non-tariff barrier to trade,* The use of different currencies acts as a very significant NTB because they deter trade by adding to costs and increasing uncertainty. Thus the use of different currencies was the largest remaining barrier to the completion of the single market. Using one currency will enable companies to buy their inputs where they are cheapest without worrying that exchange rate changes will eliminate the price advantage in the future. Thus the single currency will lead to gains from specialisation and economies of scale. It potentially could encourage greater regional specialisation within the EU.

(d) *Price transparency.* Similarly price differences across the EU should be reduced as direct price comparisons become possible and international payments become easy across frontiers. Both these effects are, of course, enormously enhanced by the potentialities of e-commerce.

(e) *Exchange rate uncertainty and economic growth.* There are two possible effects here. First, by eliminating fluctuations in your currency against other EU currencies economic stability is improved with lower uncertainty and potentially higher investment. Thus despite what is generally agreed to be successful macroeconomic policy in the UK, the rise in sterling against the euro over 1999–2000 period has caused significant problems for UK manufacturing industry. Second, since the use of a single currency reduces one source of uncertainty within EMU it could be argued that it leads to a lower level of interest rates. If this is correct the level of investment should be higher, increased investment could raise growth by raising productivity as a result of economies of scale or possibly technological improvements.

The problem with this argument is that fixing exchange rates has not eliminated risk it has merely shifted it. Thus the risk now is that the adjustment to shocks may be less efficient. So the question of the impact of EMU on risk, investment and growth is an empirical question. There is not an established empirical link between exchange rate stability and economic growth or between country size and economic growth.

(f) *Seigniorage.* If the ECU became accepted as stable rival to the $ countries, companies and individuals could be expected to hold significant reserves of the currency. So in exchange for paper money the monetary authorities of the EC would acquire the ability to buy overseas assets. The return on assets acquired as a result of the issue of paper money is called seigniorage.

(g) *Improved macroeconomic performance.* The EU as a whole potentially has a greater macroeconomic autonomy than individual countries. This ability could be used to create greater price stability and this will lead to higher growth. Both these assumptions are uncertain there is no guarantee that more independence in macroeconomic policy will lead to greater stability and that greater price stability will lead to increased economic growth.

(h) *Improved international economic coordination.* With the EC as a single economic bloc, the EC, the USA and Japan could exert enormous influence over the world economy situation coordinating their policies to achieve greater stability. This would depend upon agreement between the countries and although theoretically agreement would be easier with fewer players in reality this does not seem to be the case. The eurozone may use its greater autonomy to pursue its own economic objectives and a policy of benign neglect towards the exchange rate becomes possible. Thus the fall in the value of the euro against the US dollar has had a very limited impact on eurozone inflation and some governments have seen improved competitiveness as useful.

Institutions and decision making in EMU

The European Central Bank was created as an independent European institution because it is believed that there is an inflationary bias to discretionary policy making by political actors (see Chapter 36). The essential requirement of such an institution is that the markets should believe that it is credible, that it will achieve the objectives it sets itself. In EMU the approach to establishing the credibility of the ECB has been to make it exceptionally independent and to model it upon the Bundesbank, in the hope of inheriting its credibility and legitimacy. Independence is achieved by the appointment of members of the governing council of the ECB as individuals not representing or receiving instructions from other institutions. Since the governing council is composed of 6 ECB board members and 12 governors of national central banks no individual government has much leverage over the institution. The same applies to the EU which in the Council of Finance ministers again is composed of representatives of individual member states. So there is little possibility of the close relationship which may exist between a national government and its central bank. The ECB primary objective is clearly set in the Maastricht Treaty as being 'to maintain price stability'. It can aid the member states in achieving other objectives of economic policy such as economic growth or high employment only to the extent that this does not compromise its primary objective. Unlike the current system in the UK price stability is defined by the ECB not the government. Thus it enjoys considerable *goal independence* in deciding what the objective of policy should be as well as *instrument independence* in its ability to decide how to use policy instruments to achieve this objective. The ECB has defined its target of price stability, defined as a year-on-year increase in the Harmonised Index of Consumer Prices (HCIP) of below 2 per cent. This is to be achieved by using two pillars of policy. The first pillar is a target annual growth rate of the M_3 of 4.5 per cent. The second pillar is a broadly based assessment of the outlook for future price developments. This two-pillar approach especially when one of the pillars is so vague gives considerable discretion to the ECB in its monetary policy decisions. But this discretion makes it more difficult for the ECB to communicate the reasons for its decisions and to convince the markets that it is following its declared intentions. This creates special difficulties for a new institution such as the ECB, which has to establish its credibility.

Fiscal policy in the eurozone is controlled by the Stability and Growth Pact which limits public sector deficits to 3 per cent of GDP. When this limit is exceeded penalties can be imposed on the country concerned in the form of non-interest bearing deposits and ultimately fines. The purpose of this procedure is the achievement of medium-term budgetary positions close to balance or in surplus. When this is achieved changes in the deficit within the 3 per cent limit can act as an automatic stabiliser, the public sector deficit (PSD) expanding in a recession due to rising social security expenditure and falling tax revenue, this will tend to boost economic activity offsetting the effects of the recession. For this effect to operate there must be sufficient headroom with the 3 per cent deficit ceiling for the PSD to expand in a recession hence the aim for the medium term of balance or close to surplus.

STUDENT ACTIVITY 45.9

1 Why is it important that the European Central Bank is independent?
2 In what ways is the ECB exceptionally independent?
3 In what ways does the Growth and Stability Pact restrict the fiscal policy of national governments in EMU?

● *Common misunderstanding*

EMU is frequently described as a means of extending German influence over the rest of the EU. In fact the German's have less influence in EMU than they did in the EMS. In the EMS other members basically tied their currency to the Deutschmark and as a result had to follow German monetary policy. In EMU all members have a say in monetary policy via their national central bank, Germany has to accept a policy based on the situation as a whole. This is not to say that German ideas have not influenced the type of policies pursued in EMU, they have, because German macroeconomic management has been more successful than that of other countries.

The performance of the eurozone economy

The ultimate test of EMU is its impact on economic performance. Identifying an EMU effect separate from other influences on economic performance is difficult and it is too early to form a definitive judgement on EMU in operation. Accepting these qualifications how have the eurozone economies performed so far? Generally the economic performance has been good (see Table 45.1). Economic growth has accelerated with GDP growing considerably faster than the 1992–98 average. The improvement in employment creation has been dramatic. This improved real economic performance has been achieved with considerable economic stability; inflation has remained low and the balance of payments current account is in surplus. There has been a blip in inflation in 2000 caused by higher oil prices and the falling external value of the euro, but core inflation remains very low. Eurozone economic performance, however, suffers by comparison with the USA. In the USA the growth of GDP and of employment have been spectacular. The sustainability of this growth might be questioned given inflation pressures, which are being held in check by an overvalued exchange rate and a very large current account deficit.

This optimistic aggregate situation for the eurozone is marred by the falling exchange rate of the euro and the significant differences in economic performance which have arisen between eurozone countries. The euro has depreciated substantially in value relative to other currencies since its launch. The depreciation has been most spectacular against the Yen and the US$ but its trade weighted index fell over 15 per cent in nominal terms and just under 15 per cent in real terms. A trade-weighted index has to be used

Table 45.1 **Economic performance of the eurozone**

	1992–98	1999	2000 (estimate)	2001 (projection)
Growth of real GDP per capita %				
Advanced economies	2.0	2.7	3.6	2.7
USA	2.5	3.4	4.4	2.4
Euro area	1.5	2.3	3.3	3.3
Growth of employment %				
Advanced economies	0.8	1.3	1.3	0.9
USA	1.6	1.5	1.2	0.6
Euro area	0.1	1.9	1.9	1.4
Change in consumer prices %				
Advanced economies	2.5	1.4	2.3	2.1
USA	2.7	1.6	2.2	3.2
Euro area	2.7	1.2	2.1	1.7
Balance of payments current account % GDP				
USA	−1.6	−3.6	−4.2	−4.2
Euro area	0.7	0.5	0.7	1.0

Source: IMF (2000)

since most countries have floating exchange rates. Thus overall exchange rate movements can only be calculated as an index against other currencies whose weights depend upon their importance as trade partners. This fall in the value of the euro is particularly worrying at this early stage in its development because it is undermining public confidence in the currency.

Large fluctuations in currency values have been the norm since currencies floated in 1973. The fall in the value of the euro although unusual is not unprecedented. The euro was significantly above current levels for the whole of 1990s but its value was much lower against the US$ in the mid-1980s (see Figure 45.4). Any calculations of euro exchange rates before 1999 is artificial. In

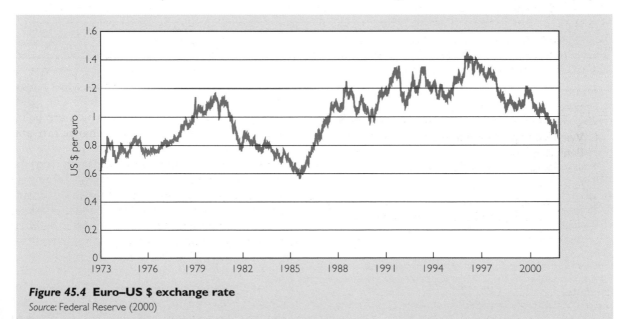

Figure 45.4 **Euro–US $ exchange rate**
Source: Federal Reserve (2000)

Figure 45.1 the Deutschmark has been used as a proxy for the euro for the pre-1999 period. The DM has the advantage that the Bundesbank was operating similar policies to the ECB. Most estimates suggest that the euro is now substantially undervalued but why did it fall to such low levels in the first place? The unexpected continuation of strong US growth and some revival in Japan encouraged purchases of these currencies. The growth potential of the US economy and of US companies was increasingly seen as having been enhanced by the 'new economy' effect of information technology. This together with higher interest rates in the US encouraged large outflows of direct and portfolio investment from the eurozone. These external factors were reinforced by a lack of market confidence engendered by apparent disagreements over economic policy, by the ECB and national governments. The fact that US Federal Reserve, the Bank of Japan and the Bank of England together with the ECB intervened to support the euro in October 2000 indicates that the currency is fundamentally undervalued and that there will be an upward correction in the future. An appreciating euro is also likely to

dispel many of the criticisms that have been levelled against the operation of the ECB and economic policy in the eurozone.

There remain substantial differences in economic performance within the eurozone (see Table 45.2). Variations in economic performance occur even within long established monetary unions so it is not surprising that there are quite large differences in the current period of adjustment to EMU. It is also to be expected that the poorer member states will register more rapid rates of GDP growth and of inflation. Higher growth is the result of improvements in productivity achieved by catching up with best practice. Higher inflation is due to the **Balassa–Samuelson** effect. Poorer countries have lower prices for non-traded goods and services but as productivity improves in the traded sectors wages generally will rise. Thus the price of non-traded goods and services will rise increasing inflation but not reducing competitiveness. It is also likely that the poorer member states will also run balance of payments deficits because they are likely to be importing capital. Differences in unemployment rates seem to stem from differences in medium-

Table 45.2 **National economic performance in the eurozone**

Eurozone states[1]	Growth of real GDP %			Unemployment %			Inflation[2] %			Balance of payments current account balance % GDP		
	1992–1998	1999	2000[3]	1992–1998	1999	2000[3]	1992–1998	1999	2000[3]	1992–1998	1999	2000[3]
Germany	1.3	1.6	2.9	8.2	8.3	7.9	2.3	0.9	0.4	4.1	−0.9	−0.2
Austria	1.7	2.2	3.5	4.1	4.4	3.5	2.2	0.6	1.5	2.5	−2.8	−2.0
Finland	2.4	4.0	5.0	14.1	10.3	9.0	2.0	0.7	1.6	4.7	5.2	5.6
Belgium	1.8	2.5	3.9	9.2	9.0	8.3	2.1	0.9	0.9	4.3	4.4	4.4
Netherlands	2.7	3.6	3.9	6.1	3.2	2.3	1.9	1.3	3.1	2.4	5.7	6.2
France	1.5	2.9	3.5	11.8	11.3	9.8	1.6	0.3	0.6	4.7	2.7	2.7
Ireland	6.9	9.9	8.7	12.2	5.6	4.5	3.4	6.2	5.5	4.8	0.3	−0.6
Italy	1.3	1.4	3.1	11.2	11.4	10.7	3.9	1.7	1.7	5.8	0.7	1.0
Spain	2.1	3.7	4.1	21.4	15.9	14.0	3.9	3.1	3.4	7.9	−2.2	−2.2
Greece	1.8	3.5	3.5	9.6	11.7	11.5	10.1	2.9	3.1	7.6	−4.1	−4.9
Portugal	2.4	3.0	3.4	6.1	4.4	4.1	6.0	3.2	2.2	3.8	−8.8	−10.4

Notes
[1] States listed in descending order of their GDP per head.
[2] Inflation measured by the GDP deflator rather than the consumer price index.
[3] Estimate.
Source: IMF (2000)

term growth and the success of structural reform. Whether these differences in national economic performance present problems for EMU is difficult to judge. The higher growth and inflation of the poorer member states is likely to persist and provided the divergences do not become too large they should not present significant difficulties. For other countries it is only persistent divergence of economic performance that will be problematic and it is still too early to judge whether this is the case.

STUDENT ACTIVITY 45.10

1 Assess the performance of the eurozone economy since the inception of the euro.
2 Why has the external value of the euro depreciated?
3 Is the depreciation of the exchange rate of the euro a cause for concern?
4 Why are there significant differences in inflation between individual eurozone countries?

● *Common misunderstanding*

The euro is often portrayed as a failure because of its falling external value, a 'toilet currency' according to one Sun *headline. This is not correct, with only one seventh of its output traded outside the eurozone changes in the external value of the euro only have a limited effect on its internal value, this is indeed a major advantage of the euro. So long as inflation remains low in the eurozone, the euro will retain its value. Experience suggests that large fluctuations in exchange rates unrelated to changes in relative price levels will subsequently be reversed.*

The UK and EMU

For the UK to join EMU it must meet convergence criteria and the UK government and Parliament must approve entry and the UK must vote for entry in a referendum. The convergence criteria are:

● *Price stability.* An average rate of inflation for one year that does not exceed by more than 1.5 per cent that of the three best performing member states in terms of price stability.
● *Government financial position.*
  – Government deficit: less than 3 per cent of GDP.
  – Government debt: less than 60 per cent of GDP.

● *ERM exchange rate.* The participation in the ERM and observance of its normal fluctuation margins for at least two years without devaluing.
● *Long-term interest rates.* For one year interest rates that do not exceed by more than 2 per cent the three best performing member states in terms of price stability.

There was some flexibility in the interpretation of these conditions in relation to the level of debt for Italy and Belgium and for ERM membership in the case of Finland. When Finland was accepted for membership it had not been in the ERM for two years, but it had completed its two years membership by 31 December 1998. The UK meets these requirements except for membership of the ERM, this is problematic. The consensus is that sterling is overvalued with an exchange rate of around 60 pence to 1 euro. A more appropriate exchange rate would have to be agreed with the EU and UK entry to the ERM engineered at this rate.

The real problem with EMU is political not economic. In 1997 the Labour government policy was that the UK would join when the time was right, defined by five tests:

1 Cyclical convergence: this partly dealt with by the convergence criteria but also requires similarity of growth both in terms of the rate and the direction of change.
2 Flexibility of products, wages and employment: two problems in particular are seen for UK in EMU skills shortages and the impact this could have on wage increases.
3 Investment: entry to EMU should not adversely affect investment, particularly FDI in the UK.
4 Financial services and the City of London: membership of EMU should not harm the UK financial services industry and the City of London as an international financial centre.
5 Growth, stability and jobs should not be adversely affected.

Arguably these tests are already meet but they are sufficiently vague to enable the government to postpone the decision until it feels it can win a referendum. But with a hostile press and an increasingly hardening public opinion and with the rejection of EMU membership in the Danish referendum of October 2000, early entry looks increasingly unlikely for the UK.

Regional problems and policy in the EU

A variety of indicators can be used to monitor the well-being of regions, although the most commonly used are GDP per head (a proxy for income) relative to the EU average, and the unemployment rate. Both have acknowledged shortcomings: GDP figures are a measure of production rather than income and thus ignore net transfers; Ireland exemplifies the problem as its GNP is some 10 per cent lower than its GDP because of interest, profit and dividends on foreign investment in Ireland. Unemployment rates are difficult to measure consistently across regions, especially where there is a substantial amount of undeclared employment, and do not always correlate closely with relative prosperity. Despite these caveats, the gaps revealed by both types of indicator are sufficiently large to be persuasive. Thus the ten most prosperous EU regions have a GDP per head three times as high as the ten least prosperous. These disparities in income are mirrored in other indicators of the standard of living, such as possession of consumer goods or access to care services. It is important to note, however, that the extent of regional disparities increased substantially as a result of the accession of the three Mediterranean member states (Greece, Spain, and Portugal) in the 1980s, all with levels of income per head substantially below the then Community average. Accession of much poorer countries from Eastern Europe will inevitably widen the disparities again. During the 1990s, the least favoured member states did well, with Portugal and Greece progressing from around half the EU average (expressed in Purchasing Power Standard, a measure that makes allowance for differences in price levels) to two-thirds, and Ireland having grown so rapidly that it now exceeds the EU average.

Unemployment disparities are also great, with particularly high rates of unemployment in the South and West of Spain, in Southern Italy, and in the eastern Länder of Germany. In Greece and Portugal, by contrast, unemployment is much less severe, although it is difficult to compare like with like. Comparing the US states with the EU regions at an equivalent level of territorial breakdown, there is a considerably greater spread of unemployment in the Community than in the US. Explanations for this include the much higher labour mobility in the US, which tends to equalise unemployment rates, the generally lower *level* of unemployment in the US, and the fact that there is greater social protection in much of the Community, which reduces pressure to migrate in search of work.

Types of regional disparity in the EU

Regional disparities in the EU stem from a variety of causes, an observation that is often overlooked in the search for an appropriate policy response.

(a) *Peripheral regions.* Most of the 'less-favoured' regions are on the periphery of the EU, suggesting that this, in itself, is part of the explanation. The notion of peripherality as a geographical one of distance from an economic 'core' implies that transport costs are the main obstacle, but it may be more accurate to analyse peripherality in terms of marginalisation in a wider sense. It is also important to note that there are many relatively prosperous regions (Grampian or North Yorkshire in the UK, Bavaria in Germany) in ostensibly remote locations, whereas some of the less-favoured regions, such as Hainaut in Belgium or the Saarland, could scarcely be more centrally located.

(b) *Underdeveloped agricultural regions.* An altogether different category of regional problem arises from lack of economic development. In much of Southern Europe, until very recently, agriculture remained the dominant industry and there was relatively little industrialisation. Advances in agricultural productivity have meant that fewer workers can be supported by farming, with the result that in such regions there has been a drift of population towards urban centres. This pattern of a shakeout in agriculture is likely to be repeated in many of the countries of Central and Eastern Europe, which are candidates for accession to the EU.

(c) *Declining industrial regions*. In Northern Europe, where the decline of agricultural employment occurred at an earlier stage, regional problems are associated mainly with the decline of staple industries, especially coal mining, steel making, textiles, and shipbuilding. More recently, some regions have been adversely affected by the relative decline of newer manufacturing industries, such as motor vehicles – the West Midlands of England being a prime example – and it is apparent that the 'sunrise' industries, such as computer software or biotechnology, are drawn to different sorts of locations. For most of the regions affected by industrial decline, adjustment has proved to be slow and painful, instead of happening quickly as might be predicted by the more sanguine economic theories. In addition, and in contrast to the experience in Southern Europe, there has been something of a drift away from large conurbations as both residents and businesses have found it more attractive to relocate to smaller cities and more rural areas.

In so far as they signal a lack of competitiveness, there is a common thread to these problems, but this does not mean that they are necessarily amenable to common solutions. In some regions, there are manifestly, still, shortcomings in much of the basic infrastructure of roads, telecommunications, and other services. In others, the problem may be more to do with training, while in others still, it is the promotion of small business and rates of innovation that are most urgent.

STUDENT ACTIVITY 45.12

1 Consider the relative merits of GDP per capita and the unemployment rate as measures of regional problems.
2 What are the characteristics of the EU's problem regions?

Reasons for regional policy

Regional policy is justified on the basis of economic efficiency and equity. Structural and cohesion policies raise overall economic efficiency by using unused or under-utilised resources more effectively and by improving the quality of resources available. Labour immobility means that labour may remain unemployed unless a region can be made more attractive to industry. Even if jobs are available the decline of some industries and the expansion of others in industrial restructuring may require retraining of the local workforce. In any case poorly skilled workers will need training to become employable. Congestion in prosperous regions like the South East England may mean it is desirable to encourage more widespread economic development.

Large differences in living standards between areas may be socially/politically unacceptable so there is a case in equity for regional policy. Government services such as health and education services should be reasonably similar in all regions. There is a minimum relative level of personal income, which is acceptable, a progressive tax and benefit systems, ensures that individuals reach this level. Since problem regions have lower income and higher unemployment such policies will redistribute income to these regions.

Why is an EU regional policy needed?

There are basically four sets of arguments for EU policies in relation to redistribution between regions:

(a) *Fair competition in the single market*. EU rules relating to national regional and social policy are necessary to ensure that competition is not distorted in the single market.
(b) *EU policies may increase inequality between regions*. This may vary with the degree of integration. In a customs union the elimination of internal trade barriers may lead to restructuring and unemployment in some regions/member states. A common market with the free movement of factors may exacerbate this uneven development with capital and the best qualified labour moving to the core developed areas. Economic and mone-

tary union with the loss of the exchange and monetary policy as instruments of economic adjustment may require the development of redistributive policies at the EU level. This is because specialisation and vulnerability to shocks may increase and national adjustment mechanisms are reduced in EMU. Redistributive policies could reduce the severity of shocks.

(c) *Side payments for political bargaining.* It may be necessary to 'bribe' countries to agree to policies which they argue may not be in their national interest, e.g. Spain extracted the Cohesion Fund as the price for agreeing EMU in the TEU.

(d) *Equality in the EU.* Some transfers from rich to poor nations may be necessary to ensure political cohesion in the EU.

STUDENT ACTIVITY 45.13

1 Explain why regional policy may enhance economic efficiency.

2 Why is there a case for an EU regional policy in addition to national regional policy.

The EU's regional policy

Although the regional impact is considered in relation to all its policies the EU has four specific policies or funds directed at regional policies:

(a) *European Regional Development Fund.* This fund finances policies to improve the infrastructure (roads, railways, telecommunications) of problem regions.

(b) *European Social Fund.* Training and education programmes for disadvantaged individuals and communities are financed by the ESF.

(c) *Agricultural Guidance Fund.* The expenditure under this fund is concentrated on improving the economic viability of farms and encouraging environmentally sensitive farming.

The expenditure under these policies is to be concentrated (70 per cent of the total) on poorer regions of the EU, defined as those with GDP per capita less than 75 per cent of the EU average.

(d) *Cohesion Fund.* This is to fund expenditure on transport and environmental projects in states with GNP per capita less than 90 per cent of the EU average, i.e. Greece, Ireland, Portugal and Spain.

The effects of EU regional policy

There has been a considerable reduction in regional inequality in the EU 15 (see Table 45.3) but this has largely been associated with reductions in disparities in income levels among countries. Since significant structural transfers between countries have only occurred since 1998 these changes are unlikely to be the result of structural policies. They may be related to other EU policies, particularly the single market.

Table 45.3 **Indices[a] of disparities of wealth in the EU 15**

	1950	1960	1970	1980	1990
1 Disparity among regions	0.124	0.100	0.079	0.058	0.057
2. Disparity among countries	0.096	0.080	0.063	0.043	0.040
3 2 : 1 (%)	77	80	80	75	70

[a] Thiel index of gross domestic product per capita at current exchange rates.
Source: Molle (1997), p. 437.

Evaluation of individual projects generally seems to show that they meet their objectives. The effect of the overall policy is more difficult to gauge. It is difficult to disentangle the independent effect of EU structural policy because we need to know what would have happened in its absence. The effect of structural policy is often in terms of the numbers employed on the projects, but it is extremely difficult to measure the independent effect of the project.

Most structural expenditure is on infrastructure and training and so it represents a supply side policy enhancing the potential growth rate of the regional economies. A number of studies suggest that these supply side improvements have been effective in improving the growth rate of regional economies. Thus the initial effect of the structural policies is to increase regional growth of GDP per head by 1 per cent but over time the effects are much greater because of time lags for the full effects to be felt.

There have been some problems with the operation of the structural funds. The present system puts considerable administrative burdens on the national and local governments within member states. This is the result of the multiplicity of programmes and the complexity of the regulations. The effectiveness of some of the expenditure has been questioned. There have also been some problems of fraud with countries such as Greece and Portugal having a problem of absorption, generating sufficient projects to use the available funds. The recent reform has addressed some of these problems so it is hoped the effectiveness of the fund will improve in the future.

STUDENT ACTIVITY 45.14

1 Why is it difficult to assess the effects of EU regional policy?
2 Has EU regional policy diminished regional differences in the EU?

Employment and social policy in the EU

Employment and social policy consists of government measures that seek to reduce inequalities in society by raising the standard of living or improving the quality of life of the poor. The policy takes two forms: work and welfare measures. Work measures seek to reduce unemployment and to improve the quality of and returns from work. Welfare measures are redistributive raising the living standards of the poor by transfers and by benefits in kind. This wide definition encompass an enormous range of polices from macroeconomic policy to social services. The EU has only a very limited role in this policy area because it accounts for a large share of government expenditure, different views about the appropriate policies and varying historical legacies mean that there are enormous differences in policy between countries.

Justifications of regulation of labour markets

(a) *Moral/ethical*. Workers should be treated humanely and fairly.
(b) *Asymmetric information*. The returns on employment are a complex mixture of wage/

salary, quality of work, stability and security of employment. The imposition of minimum standards might make the market work more efficiently by reducing the need for employees to gather information and preventing abuse by employers. Such regulation might also be justified on grounds of fairness.
(c) *Health and safety*. Where employers would not bear the cost of treatment of workers, health and safety standards of employment might be too low from society's point of view. So there is an efficiency reason for minimum standards as well as an ethical argument.
(d) *Human capital*. Providing employees with transferable skills is not profitable because such trained employees can be 'poached' by other companies that do not wish to bear the cost of training.

EU versus national employment and social policy

There are two basic requirements for a policy to be justified at the EU level. First, there must be advantages, which accrue to operating the policy at the EU, e.g. scale of the activity, cross border effects. Second, there must be sufficient commonality of interest among the member states to agree common objectives for the policy.

With regard to the areas of employment and social policy considered earlier most are ruled out by lack of commonality between countries:

- Macroeconomic policy (with EMU gradually becoming an EU responsibility).
- Manpower policy: some EU policy via ESF, free movement of labour.
- Regulation of employment standards and conditions (main thrust EU employment and social policy).
- Industrial relations (differences between member states too great).

Thus it is mainly in the employment sphere that EU action has been considered necessary. There are two main arguments for EU policy in this area:

(a) *Intra-EU mobility of labour*. This is an essential part of the single market. As the single market becomes more integrated and particularly with EMU variations in economic performance between countries must be reflected in flexible markets. Thus wages and prices must be flexible and labour must be mobile.

(b) *Social dumping*. This is the idea that higher labour standards in one EU country will be undermined by competition from other countries where labour regulations are weaker. This is not a persuasive argument. Labour regulations are just one (minor) factor influencing labour costs in different countries. Lower wages and poorer conditions in other countries will only undermine wages and social conditions in Germany if they are not offset by productivity differences. In this case the production should in any case move away from Germany. The movement of goods in the single market will effectively increase competition in the labour market and so the demand for protection from social dumping is really a plea for protection. German workers would be protected from additional competition by imposing higher social standards on other countries. But this is at the cost of German consumers and the wider German economy.

Social policy

In three areas of social policy the EU has a distinctive and important role:

(a) *Freedom of movement of workers*. This was an essential part of the Common Market provided for by the EEC Treaty. It is desirable that in a single market workers can move freely to respond to changes in the geographical demand for labour. Although legal impediments to the movement of workers have been eliminated such movement remains extremely limited because of language, social and cultural differences.

(b) *Equal treatment between men and women*. The Treaty of Rome recognised the principle that 'men and women should receive equal pay for equal work'. This was seen as quite radical for the period (1950s) and was introduced largely for competition reasons on the insistence of France which had quite advanced equal pay laws and therefore feared its industry would be undercut by low wages for female labour in other member states. More recently, the concept of equal opportunities has been expanded to include other social groups. The EU has been an important influence in developing non-discriminatory practices in employment.

(c) *The protection of workers' health and safety*. Common minimum standards were seen as essential for fair competition in a single market.

In other areas the EU's role is limited and unlikely to extend further:

- social security and social protection of workers;
- protection of workers where their employment contract is terminated;
- representation and collective defence of the interests of workers and employers including co-determination; this **does not apply to** pay, rights of association, the right to strike or to lock out;
- conditions of employment of third-country nationals legally residing in Community territory.

Developments in the social policy field have been limited by the very large and seemingly irreconcilable differences of philosophy and practice between member states. In the current climate of high unemployment, concerns over competitiveness and desire for more flexible labour markets there is little impetus for further legislation.

STUDENT ACTIVITY 45.15

1 Why have EU member states been reluctant to extend the EU's role in social policy?
2 Is social dumping a convincing argument for EU harmonisation of social policy?

● *Common misunderstanding*

Social policy it is suggested is being imposed on the UK by the Brussels bureaucracy; this is not correct. All policies have to be accepted by the governments of the member states to become part of EU law. In some areas such as health and safety (the work time directive was approved as a health and safety measure) an individual member state can be outvoted. But in contentious areas, e.g. social security, all member states must approve a measure before it becomes law.

Employment policy

Employment policy has come to the top of the political agenda. This is the result of the very high levels of unemployment in the EU (see Table 45.2, page 676) and the fact that with EMU macroeconomic policy is largely an EU responsibility. Thus, with the signing of the Treaty of Amsterdam (1997), the maintenance of a high level of employment became an EU responsibility: 'Member States . . . shall regard promoting employment as a matter of common concern and shall co-ordinate their action.' 'The objective of a high level of employment shall be taken into consideration in the formulation and implementation of Community Policies and activities.'

The EU has also tried to encourage member states to develop employment by peer pressure and learning from best practice. This has emphasised:

(a) *Employability*. Employability and developing skills especially of young people and the unemployed (particularly the long-term unemployed).

(b) *Entrepreneurship*. This is defined in a broad way, to cover the start-up and running of new enterprises, the development of existing enterprises, and the encouragement of initiative within large firms.

(c) *Adaptability*. The adaptability of enterprises and workers to changing technology and markets, industrial restructuring, and the development of new products and services.

(d) *Equal opportunities*. With the twin social and economic objective of modernising societies so that women and men can work on equal terms with equal responsibilities, to develop the full growth capacities of European economies.

(e) *Structural reform*. Making labour markets more flexible encouraging employers to increase employment and workers to accept jobs. By making social security less generous and conditions for receipt tougher and by reducing the regulation of employment contracts.

(f) *Technology*. Embracing new technology to make Europe competitive internationally.

The EU has developed only very limited responsibilities in employment and social policy. This is perhaps sensible given the limited justifications for EU as opposed to national employment and social policy, the substantial policy differences and the lack of consensus. There is no doubt that EMU and the employment situation in the EU is creating powerful pressures for further developments in this area. It is still too early to say what the effects of these pressures will be. Since the introduction of the euro economic growth in Europe has been much higher and unemployment levels have been falling. But unemployment remains too high and all EU member states recognise the need for increased flexibility to reduce unemployment to low levels.

STUDENT ACTIVITY 45.16

1 Why is the EU developing a role in employment policy?
2 Why may flexible labour markets enhance employment?

EU enlargement

By 2004 or 2005 the EU is likely to be enlarged to include additional countries from Central and Eastern Europe plus Cyprus and Malta. The front runners at the moment are the Czech Republic, Estonia, Hungary, Poland and Slovenia but these could well be joined by Latvia, Lithuania and the Slovak Republic. Enlargement, like the formation and intensification of the EU, will have effects on trade, competition, etc. as envisaged in the theory of customs unions. In addition, however, there will be changes related to the EU Budget, the application of EU legislation to Central and Eastern Europe (CEE) and the Common Agricultural Policy (CAP).

Impact of enlargement on trade

Central and Eastern European countries that are likely to join the EU already have a Free Trade Area with the EU. Membership will encourage further trade as a result of the elimination of NTBs. This is likely to be trade creation except perhaps in agriculture. Thus there will be increased EU exports to and increased EU imports from the CEE countries as a result of the elimination of the remaining barriers to trade. The effects are likely to be much more significant for the CEE countries than for the EU because the CEE countries' economies and markets are much smaller than the EU's (see Table 45.4). But over the medium to long term the potential is significant even for the EU. The population of the CEE 10 is much larger relative to the EU than its GDP. Population of the CEE 10 was 28.4 per cent of the EU 15 in 1999. The CEE 1 countries are also growing much more rapidly than the EU. Rapid growth of GNP, even in a comparatively difficult year like 1999 saw the CEE 5 grow by 3.5 per cent, compared to 2.4 per cent for the EU 15. This growing GDP is leading to a fast expansion of trade with consumers using their increasing incomes to buy imported durable goods and companies importing capital goods. As a result the EU is running an expanding current account surplus on its trade with the CEE countries. Enlargement is likely to intensify these effects by increasing the growth and trade between the CEE countries and the EU. So overall the trade effects of enlargement will add to GDP and employment in the EU and the CEE countries. In the EU the short-term effects will be minor but in the long term there is the potential for substantial trade.

Table 45.4 **Gross domestic product 1999 (current prices and exchange rates)**

	CEE 1	CEE 2	CEE 10	EU 15
Million ECU	264 700	77 700	342 400	7 469 700
% of EU15	3.4	1.0	4.5	100.0
Population	62.5	44.2	104.7	375.3
% of EU 15	16.7	11.8	28.4	100.0

CEE 1 = Czech Republic, Estonia, Hungary, Poland and Slovenia.
CEE 2 = Bulgaria, Latvia, Lithuania, Romania, Slovakia.
Source: Eurostat (1999a and 1999b), EP (2000)

Although the overall effects of enlargement will be positive this does not mean that all countries or all regions will benefit. The impact on the EU cannot be that large because of the small productive capacity of the CEE countries (see Table 45.4). It is the sectoral effects that are of particular concern, CEE exports may be concentrated on a narrow range of industries, with significant adjustment problems, which would be regionally (nationally) concentrated. These effects will depend upon the pattern of CEE specialisation and the size of the export flows.

Although most CEE countries are running large current account deficits this is to be expected during transition when capital inflows will be large. The fact that in 1997–98 the deficit was stable and in 1999 it fell is encouraging. These are short time periods and long-term trends are not apparent but it was only in 1999 that the EU economy was growing more quickly after a period of very slow growth, which limited imports. So the indications are that CEE industry will be able to compete in the single market. There may be problems for particular industries but some of these are associated with transition. So the ending of subsidies for steel production will lead to capacity reduction and unemployment. Mines producing brown coal will be closed because of the environmental effects of this fuel. These are however, changes associated with making production economically viable and environmentally responsible.

Table 45.5 **EU 15–CEE 10, trade in most important commodities (million ECU)**

	Machinery	Transport equipment	Textile and clothing	% of total
EU imports	20 698	10 459	9744	54.0
EU exports	30 509	11 708	8200	54.1

Source: EP (2000)

The industrial impact of enlargement is going to be muted because of:

(a) *Intra-industry trade.* It might be expected that since the CEE countries have very low labour costs compared with the EU they would specialise in particular labour cost sensitive sectors where the impact on EU industry would be very great. This does not seem to be the case, much trade with the CEE seems to be intra-industry with similar products being exported and imported. Thus even in textiles and clothing where low wage cost countries are at an advantage trade with the CEE is near to balance. It may of course be that within these broad categories there is specialisation. This is inevitable the high cost

EU cannot compete in labour intensive sectors, so European producers would have to move up market anyway.

(b) *Outward processing trade*. The EU exports semi-finished products for labour intensive processes to the CEE countries. The products are then reimported into the EU this seems to be the case with textile and clothing where EU–CEE trade is substantial in both directions. Such outward processing trade is a way of maintaining the competitiveness of EU industry.

Effect of enlargement on investment

Enlargement potentially can affect the size and location of investment. By providing new opportunities the overall level of investment in the EU could be raised. To the extent that overall investment increases the distribution of investment becomes less important.

New market opportunities in the CEE may encourage additional investment in the EU although this effect is likely to be limited because the elimination of tariffs on trade has meant that

many of these opportunities have already been exploited. The small size of the CEE economies also means the potential is limited but this will grow over time depending upon the performance of these economies.

Some diversion of investment particularly FDI is to be expected, as the CEE becomes a low cost production location within the EU. Thus EU firms may invest in the CEE rather than in the EU 15 but the CEE may also attract investment that would otherwise have gone to less developed economies. Non-EU firms may divert the investment to the CEE rather than the EU. Again these effects are likely to be minor because of the small size of the CEE economies. As these economies grow FDI might increase but growth will be associated with a reduction in their low wages as a comparative advantage. Foreign direct investment by multinationals is not very closely associated with wage levels, market size is more important.

It is likely that internal investment in the CEE countries will be encouraged. Greater economic and political stability that membership of the EU will bring will improve the climate for investment. Investment will be made in industries where opportunities to export to the EU have improved. As the CEE countries are likely to grow faster this will encourage increased investment. However the requirements to meet EU standards in health and safety and the environment will erode the cost advantages of CEE companies. There will need to be substantial investment in these areas which may divert investment resources from increasing productive capacity.

Table 45.6 **EU FDI in Central and Eastern Europe (ECU million)**

	1993	1994	1995	1996	1997	1998
Total (non EU)	24 157	24 129	45 580	48 750	93 260	192 937
CEE 10	3 196	2 757	5 303	5 327	6 736	8 864
(as a % of the total)	13.2	11.4	11.6	10.9	7.3	4.6
of which (ECU mill.)						
Poland	758	616	1 132	2 391	2 466	4 004
Hungary	1 217	839	2 102	1 066	1 351	1 671
Czech Republic	812	974	1 594	1 278	1 859	1 583

Source: EP (2000) www.europarl.eu.int/enlargement/briefings/pdf/22a1_en.pdf

There is no indication so far of a substantial diversion of EU investment to the CEE countries. EU FDI in the CEE countries has risen quickly in nominal terms by 177.3 per cent 1993–98. It has however, fallen as a proportion of total EU FDI beyond the EU because this has risen 698.7 per cent over the same period. Since most of this FDI is invested in developed countries especially the USA fears of enormous loss of jobs as FDI flows to CEE to take advantage of low labour costs seem misplaced. EU FDI is concentrated (over 80 per cent) in Poland, Hungary and the Czech Republic reflecting their economic size and the fact that they are at the forefront of the transition process.

Effect of EU regulations

Health and Safety requirements will impose some additional costs on the Central and Eastern Europe companies to the extent they are higher than existing regulations. There are also significant administrative requirements and costs. This can impose additional costs on potential entrants and can be a factor in competition. Thus the food industry in Central and Eastern Europe has found it difficult to compete because it finds it difficult to comply with these regulations. There are also problems with providing products of the requisite quality. Environmental regulations will impose significant extra costs ranging from water treatment to the closure and replacement of nuclear power stations. The additional resources the accessing countries will receive under the EU's structural funds will help to meet the costs of making these improvements.

● *Common misunderstanding*

With enlargement EU industry is frequently seen as being vulnerable from competition from low wage production in Central and Eastern Europe. The reverse is probably truer, CEE industry is vulnerable to competition from the EU. EU industry can compete with low wage industry because of its high productivity and good product quality is in many areas becoming more important than price. Thus the EU is running a very large trade surplus with CEE countries. CEE production is simply too small to have a significant effect on EU industry. The application of EU regulations will also increase the costs of CEE industry.

The Common Agricultural Policy and enlargement

Net food exporting CEE countries will benefit from the high internal prices, this effect is becoming less significant as CAP prices are reduced. There are very high informational and monitoring costs associated with operation of the CAP that will be incurred by new member states. At the moment the EU is running a surplus on food exports to the CEE countries this is associated with problems of transition in their agriculture and food industry. In particular the quality and volume requirements of food supermarkets are more easily satisfied by EU 15 producers. The major impact of enlargement on agriculture is that it is likely to encourage further reform of the CAP.

Enlargement overall

Enlargement is likely to provide net economic benefit for both the CEE countries and the EU. The effects to the CEE countries will be much more significant than those on the EU. Fears in the EU that particular industries, regions and countries will suffer significant economic losses from additional competition and diversion of investment seem misplaced. Estimates suggest that all EU 15 countries will benefit from enlargement.

Summary

1 The EU has developed from a customs union with no tariffs on internal trade, to a single market eliminating internal non-tariff barriers to an economic and monetary union.

2 In the short term customs unions can have benefits related to trade creation and costs related to trade diversion.

3 The dynamic effects of customs unions on competition, economies of scale, investment and FDI flows are likely to be much more important than the static effects of trade creation and diversion.

4 The single market has led to important gains in economic efficiency because it eliminates non-tariff barriers which are likely to be high and are increasing rather than revenue generating.

5 Economic and monetary union was agreed to complete the single market, to enable decision

on monetary policy to be based on the conditions of the eurozone as a whole and perhaps most importantly because of the political will to further develop integration.

6 The major cost of EMU is giving up an independent monetary policy and the exchange rates as mechanisms for adjustment.

7 The major benefit of EMU are increased stability and a substantial enhancement of the competitive effects of the single market.

8 The ECB which is responsible for monetary policy in EMU has a very high degree of independence.

9 Although it is early to judge, the economic performance of the eurozone has been very good.

10 The UK largely meets the convergence requirements for EMU membership the major problem with membership is political, for the government to commit the UK and the electorate to vote 'yes' in a referendum.

11 There are large disparities between EU regions in GDP per capita and unemployment.

12 Over time differences in GDP per capita are diminishing but whether this is the result of regional policy is unclear.

13 The EU has only developed a very limited role in relation to employment and social policy because of the political sensitivity of the area, differences in the policies of member states and divergences of opinion on the correct approach to such policy.

14 Enlargement will enhance the economic effects of the EU customs union but the relative size of the effects will be much greater for the CEE countries than for the EU 15.

15 Both the EU 15 and the CEE will benefit from enlargement, fears of significant impacts on employment in some EU 15 regions seems misplaced because the EU is running a surplus with the CEE and most trade is intra-industry.

? QUESTIONS

1 The EU has continually grown but EFTA has contracted, can the theory of customs union help explain why this has happened?

2 Why is the single market having a very large impact upon the economic performance of the EU?

3 Assess the extent to which further fiscal harmonisation is necessary in the EU?

4 Assess the economic costs and benefits of the UK joining EMU.

5 Does the fall in the value of the euro mean that EMU is a failure?

6 Evaluate the economic case for EU regional policy.

7 Consider the impact that EU structural (regional) policies have had on regional divergence in the EU.

8 Why is social policy such a contentious area for the EU?

9 Consider why the EU has began to develop an employment policy. Assess the likely effectiveness of the employment policy that the EU is developing.

10 Use the theory of customs unions to analyse the economic effects of further enlargement of the European Union.

11 'The economic impact of enlargement on the Central and East European countries is likely to be large, while the impact on the EU will be comparatively minor.' Explain.

12 Consider whether enlargement is going to have significant adverse economic impacts on particular regions and countries in the EU.

Data response A
EMPLOYMENT AND UNEMPLOYMENT IN THE EU

The questions below should be answered after referring to Tables 45.7–45.12 and Figure 45.5.

1 Compare the trends in employment and unemployment between the EU, USA and Japan (Table 45.7 and Figure 45.5).

2 What does the data in Table 45.8 indicate about the causes of unemployment in the EU?

3 It is often suggested that the USA employment is high because of the creation of low skilled jobs, does Table 45.9 support this conclusion?

4 How does employment vary with age (Table 45.12)?

5 Consider the reasons for the variation in employment by age and for the between countries EU member states, the USA and Japan. (Tables 45.10–45.12).

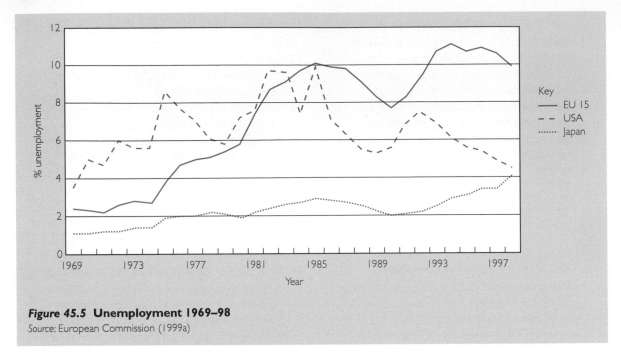

Figure 45.5 **Unemployment 1969–98**
Source: European Commission (1999a)

Table 45.7 **Participation and employment in the last three decades[1] (%)**

	1969–78		1979–88		1989–98	
	Participation rate	*Employment rate*	*Participation rate*	*Employment rate*	*Participation rate*	*Employment rate*
EU 15	66.3	64.1	66.2	60.5	67.2	60.6
USA	66.9	62.9	72.4	67.1	76.8	72.3
Japan	71.1	70.0	72.2	70.4	76.0	73.9

The participation rate is the proportion of the population aged 16–64 in employment or registered as unemployed.
The employment rate is the proportion of the population aged 16–64 in employment.
[1] Average of annual rates over the specified period.
Source: OECD (2000). Copyright © OECD

Table 45.8 **Sources of growth in real GDP per capita (average annual growth %)**

	1971–79	1980–89	1990–99	1971–99
Eurozone[1]				
Average growth rate of real GDP per capita	2.84	1.76	1.44	2.01
Working age population	0.20	0.51	0.00	0.25
Labour force participation rate	−0.02	−0.08	0.11	0.00
Unemployment rates	−0.36	−0.73	−0.22	−0.61
Hours worked[2]	−0.86	−0.73	−0.22	−0.61
Real GDP per man-hour	3.74	2.56	1.85	2.71
of which				
Labour efficiency	3.24	2.26	1.41	2.30
Capital deepening[3]	0.49	0.30	0.44	0.41
Terms of trade[4]	0.14	−0.08	−0.14	−0.03

Table 45.8 continued

	1971–79	1980–89	1990–99	1971–99
United States				
Average growth rate of real GDP per capita	2.54	1.56	1.89	1.98
Working age population	0.70	0.02	–0.01	0.22
Labour force participation rate	0.90	0.69	0.27	0.61
Unemployment rates	–0.10	0.06	0.11	0.03
Hours worked[2]	–0.05	0.24	0.03	0.08
Real GDP per man-hour	0.96	0.80	1.66	1.14
of which				
Labour efficiency	0.90	0.72	1.84	1.16
Capital deepening[3]	0.06	0.08	–0.18	–0.02
Terms of trade[4]	0.13	–0.25	–0.16	–0.10
Japan				
Average growth rate of real GDP per capita	2.53	2.82	0.96	2.09
Working age population	–0.26	0.33	–0.15	–0.02
Labour force participation rate	0.02	0.21	0.66	0.31
Unemployment rates	–0.10	–0.02	–0.26	–0.66
Hours worked[2]	–0.52	–0.27	–1.17	–0.66
Real GDP per man-hour	4.22	2.85	2.34	3.10
of which				
Labour efficiency	2.37	1.89	1.17	1.79
Capital deepening[3]	1.85	0.96	1.17	1.31
Terms of trade[4]	–0.82	0.29	0.46	–0.51

Notes

[1] Eurozone: Austria, Belgium, Finland, France, Germany, Ireland, Italy, Luxembourg, Netherlands, Portugal, Spain.

[2] Annual hours per employee.

[3] Capital deepening increase in output due to increased capital assuming constant returns to capital.

[4] Increase in output due to an increase in the price of exports relative to imports.

Source: OECD (2000) *EMU One Year On*. Copyright © OECD 2000

Table 45.9 Employment and growth of employment by occupation

	Employment % of working age population		Contribution to earnings growth %	
	US 1997	EU 15 1997	US 1990–97	Eurozone 1992–97
Managers, professionals, technicians	25.3	21.1	6.5	3.5
1 Managers, senior officials	10.5	4.9	3.1	0.6
2 Professionals	11.0	7.6	2.9	1.3
3 Technicians, associate professionals	3.8	8.6	0.6	1.5
Clerks and sales workers	26.3	16.3	1.9	0.4
4 Clerks	10.5	8.2	–0.3	–0.4
5 Sales and service workers	15.8	8.1	2.3	0.9
Manual workers	22.4	23.0	0.6	–4.3
6 Skilled agricultural and fisheries workers	2.0	2.4	0.0	–0.6
7 Craft and related trades workers	8.1	9.5	0.3	–1.0
8 Plant and machinery operators	7.6	5.3	0.2	–0.6
9 Elementary occupations	4.7	5.5	0.0	–1.9
Total	74.0	60.5	9.1	–0.4

Source: European Commission (1999)

Table 45.10 **Participation and employment in the last three decades (%)**

	1971–80		1981–90		1991–98	
	Participation rate	Employment rate	Participation rate	Employment rate	Participation rate	Employment rate
Sweden	76.7	75.1	81.2	79.1	78.4	74.0
Denmark	77.4	74.8	82.1	75.1	81.7	73.8
UK	73.2	70.7	74.4	67.4	75.7	69.7
Finland	71.9	69.5	76.2	72.3	74.0	65.8
Germany	68.6	67.2	67.9	63.5	71.0	65.5
Portugal	65.7	61.6	68.6	62.9	68.9	65.0
Austria	68.9	67.9	66.8	64.5	67.6	63.8
France	67.9	65.5	67.2	61.4	66.9	59.5
Netherlands	60.1	58.6	57.0	52.7	60.8	57.1
Belgium	61.5	59.1	61.8	54.9	63.0	55.8
Ireland	64.9	60.7	63.0	54.8	62.9	54.8
Greece	56.9	55.4	58.5	54.9	59.6	54.1
Italy	58.5	55.8	59.3	54.6	57.7	51.7
Spain	62.4	60.1	59.6	49.7	61.4	49.4
EU 15	66.3	64.1	66.2	60.5	67.2	60.6

Note: Countries are arranged in descending order of their employment rate in 1998.
Source: OECD (2000) *EMU One Year On.* Copyright © OECD 2000

Table 45.11 **Unemployment in the last three decades (%)**

	1971–80	1981–90	1991–98
Luxembourg	0.6	2.5	2.7
Austria	1.6	3.4	4.0
Portugal	2.5	7.0	5.9
Netherlands	4.4	8.5	5.9
Denmark	3.7	8.4	7.6
Sweden	2.1	2.6	8.0
Germany*	2.2	6.0	8.1
UK	3.8	8.8	8.6
Belgium	4.6	6.6	8.8
Greece	2.2	6.4	8.8
Italy	4.4	8.5	11.0
France	4.1	9.2	11.5
Ireland	7.7	14.7	12.7
Finland	2.1	2.6	13.3
Spain	5.4	18.5	20.8
EU 15	4.0	9.0	10.2
USA	6.4	7.1	6.0
Japan	1.8	2.1	3.0

* West Germany until 1990.
Source: European Commission (1999a)

Table 45.12 **Employment rates 1985 and 1997 (%)**

| | 1985 | | | 1997 | | |
Age	15–24	25–54	55–64	15–24	25–54	55–64
Denmark	68.4	84.7	51.2	69.4	84.4	52.2
UK	56.9	73.7	47.0	55.7	78.5	48.5
Austria	64.2	79.3	28.6	55.7	82.5	29.3
Sweden	58.6	90.6	66.8	32.1	80.6	61.8
Portugal	48.2	70.9	43.9	37.9	78.8	46.9
Netherlands	49.0	66.7	28.5	55.8	76.3	30.7
Finland	51.2	88.8	43.9	31.8	78.3	36.6
Germany	53.5	73.5	37.8	42.6	73.6	36.8
France	38.7	77.3	33.6	24.4	77.1	29.1
Luxembourg	55.1	68.4	25.6	31.3	74.3	21.4
Ireland	43.3	55.1	41.1	38.4	67.8	40.2
Belgium	32.4	68.6	25.9	25.2	74.8	22.0
Greece	30.8	66.4	45.1	24.5	69.8	40.7
Italy	31.8	65.7	32.7	25.2	65.5	27.4
Spain	24.7	54.3	36.6	24.9	61.8	33.7
EU 15	44.3	71.1	38.0	35.9	73.2	35.9
USA	53.4	77.5	58.0	52.0	80.9	57.2
Japan	40.8	76.9	60.4	45.1	79.6	63.6

Source: European Commission (1999b)

References

European Commission (1999a) 'Annual Economic Report for 1999' Statistical Annex, *European Economy*, No. 68.

European Commission (1999b) 'Employment Rates Report 1998', DG Employment and Social Affairs, Brussels.

European Commission (1999c) *Employment in Europe 1999*, OOPEC, Luxembourg.

Federal Reserve (2000) *www.federalreserve.gov*

Molle, W. (1997) *The Economics of European Integration: Theory, Practice and Policy*, 3rd Edition, Ashgate, Aldershot.

OECD (2000) *EMU One Year On*, OECD, Paris.

Websites

European Commission

General: www.europa.eu.int

Economic and financial affairs: www.europa.eu.int/comm/dgs/economy_finance/index_en.htm

Employment and social policy: www.europa.eu.int/comm/dgs/employment_social/index_en.htm

Structural policies: www.europa.eu.int/comm/dgs/regional_policy/index_en.htm

Taxation and the customs union: www.europa.eu.int/comm/dgs/taxation_customs/index_en.htm

Internal market: www.europa.eu.int/com/dgs/internal_market/index_en.htm

Statistics: www.europa.eu.int/comm/dgs/eurostat/index_en.htm

Enlargement: www.europa.eu.int/comm/dgs/enlargement/index_en.htm

Trade policy: www.europa.eu.int/comm/dgs/trade/index_en.htm

European Parliament Enlargement: www.europarl.eu.int/enlargement/default_en.htm

European Council EMU: http://ue.eu.int/emu/en/index.htm

European Central Bank EMU: www.ecb.int

House of Commons Library Research Papers: www.parliament.uk/commons/lib/research/rpintro.htm

House of Lords Select Committee on the European Union Reports:
www.parliament.the-stationery-office.co.uk/pa/ld/ldeucom.htm

The developing economies

Development economics

What's special about development economics?

This chapter is concerned with the problems of and economic policies towards relatively poor countries, in other words with *development economics*. In this book we have looked at many branches of economics such as monetary economics, foreign trade, and so on. It should come as no surprise, therefore, that there is a specialised branch of economics concerned with development. There is also here, as elsewhere, controversy. The argument is concerned with whether or not the principles and policies which apply to advanced economies also apply to relatively poor ones.

It is argued that the problems of developing economies are different from those of developed economies: first, because poor economies are starting out in a world in which there are already rich countries. Thus, for example, models based on the experience of the UK in the industrial revolution, when it was already the richest country in the world, are unlikely to be of use. Second, many people argue that there is a special case for state intervention and coordination in the economies of poor nations, the arguments for which are considered below.

On the other hand, there has, in recent years, been a tendency to absorb development economics back into mainstream economics and argue that the principles are no different. This, for example, has been the point of view of the World Bank. This accords with the neo-classical movement back towards market orientation seen elsewhere in the subject of economics.

A full treatment of development economics is beyond the scope of this book and the syllabus. We will, however, mention some of the main points. We will also consider why it is argued that development economics is a special discipline demanding different theory.

Categorising countries in terms of development

The World Bank classifies countries by their GDP per capita. In 1999 there were 50 countries classified as *low income*, with GDP per capita (based on purchasing power parity exchange rates) of less than $760. The poorest was Ethiopia with a per capita income of just $100. Countries with a per capita income of between $761 and $9 360 in 1999 are classified as *middle income* and those with a per capita income above $9 360 are *high income*.

In fact, there are a number of different ways in which the nations of the world are categorised. These categories sometimes cut across one another and categorisations are often rejected by nations. For example, many years ago economists spoke of *backward countries* or of *underdeveloped nations*. These terms were considered pejorative and are not now used.

One of the broadest classifications is that of the *three worlds*. The *First World* is the advanced industrial economies including most of those of Europe, Canada, the USA, Australia, New Zealand and Japan. The *Second World,* a term seldom used today, is the former communist countries of Eastern Europe and the old USSR, plus China. This leaves the *Third World* as all the remaining countries of Africa, Asia and Latin America. However, the collapse of communism in Eastern Europe has made this terminology somewhat obsolete.

Another expression which is used is that of the *north south divide*. This refers to the fact that the rich countries tend to be in the Northern Hemisphere while the poor are in the Southern. To be accurate the Southern Hemisphere would have to start well north of the equator in Africa and Asia to include some of the world's poorest nations. Australia and New Zealand, obviously, do not fit into this classification, since they are both relatively rich and yet are situated in the Southern Hemisphere.

An expression which is still in wide use is that of *less developed country* (LDC). This term is now also slipping from use and nowadays we tend to use the expression *developing countries* to describe the poorer nations.

A developing country is one where real per capita income is low when compared with that of industrialised nations.

Within this term there are distinctions. The very poorest such as Ethiopia and Burundi are, in fact, not developing at all and for them the term must be a bitter irony. To those which have experienced rapid economic development in more recent times, such as South Korea and Singapore, the name *newly industrialising countries* (NICs) has been applied.

Growth and the standard of living

It was noted in Chapter 34 that growth allows us all to enjoy an improved standard of living. However, there is not an exact correlation between the standard of living and the GDP per capita, although the fact that in 1999 it was only $100 in Ethiopia while in Switzerland it was $40 080 tells us something pretty fundamental about the two nations. The World Bank puts out a wealth of statistical information which is significant in assessing the present standard of living of a country and its potential for development. Thus, besides information on the growth of per capita GDP there is data on the debt owed by a country, the relative significance of agriculture in an economy, birth rates and death rates, life expectancy, infant mortality rates, literacy rates, the number of doctors per capita and the numbers enrolled in secondary education as a percentage of the relevant age group. (See also Data response A at the end of this chapter.)

Comparison of some of these other indicators confirms the huge discrepancy between the rich and the poor. In Malawi, for example, a newborn baby has a one in seven chance of dying before the age of 1 and just over a one in four chance of being dead before reaching the age of 5. This gives an overall infant mortality figure (for those aged under 5) for Malawi of 224 per thousand compared with a figure of 7 for the UK.

It should be noted that the economic and social organisation of the nation can significantly modify the picture presented by the GDP per capita figures. Thus, some countries classified as developing may, using the above indicators, achieve results similar to much richer nations. In terms of life expectancy, infant mortality, calorie intake and the number of doctors, communist countries such as China and Cuba have figures achieved only by nations with significantly higher GDPs per capita. This evidence conflicts with the World Bank's own conclusions (*World Development Report*, 1987) that development is linked to the degree of free enterprise in the organisation of the economy, although it should be remembered that free enterprise is now an important force in the Chinese economy.

We may, thus, conclude this section of the chapter by saying that economic development and improvements in the standard of living are influenced by social organisation, choices made and goals set as well as by growth in the real GDP per head. In 1990 the United Nations Development Programme (UNDP) introduced the Human Development Index (HDI), which incorporates data on life expectancy at birth, education (based on a measure of adult literacy plus average years of schooling) as well as real GDP per capita. Countries can then be classified as having low, medium or high levels of human development. India and Kenya are among those countries with a medium human development classification despite both having relatively low GDP per capita figures.

● *Common misunderstanding*

GDP per capita figures on their own may give a reasonable indication as to whether a country can be classified as developing, but they cannot give us the whole story. To get a better idea we need to refer to a range of data on factors such as life expectancy, infant mortality, the share of the economy devoted to agriculture, education, the numbers of doctors, the level of debt and so on.

STUDENT ACTIVITY 46.1

Which factors are able to provide some indication of a country's standard of living and potential for development? Make a list of countries that you would classify as developing economies.

Population and development

Population growth

The rate of change in the population for any country is affected by three main influences: the birth rate, the death rate and migration or the net figure from immigration and emigration.

The birth rate is usually expressed as a rate per thousand of the population. This is sometimes called a crude birth rate since it simply records the number of live births, no allowance being made for infant mortality or other circumstances.

The death rate is normally expressed as the number of people in a country that died in a year per thousand of the population. Again, this is sometimes called the crude death rate because it takes no account of the age of the person at death; they could be three months old or aged 90.

A way of presenting the change in population of a country can be arrived at by comparing the birth rate with the death rate; this gives a simple measure of the *rate of natural increase or decrease* of the population.

By taking into account migration figures the growth rate for the population of any country can be obtained. Table 46.1 shows the population growth rates for selected countries during the 1980s and 1990s. In general, average annual growth rates were much lower in the 1990s than in the 1980s.

Table 46.1 Growth of population, selected countries

Country	Average annual growth of population, percentage 1980–90	Average annual growth of population, percentage 1990–98
Bangladesh	3.7	1.9
Brazil	3.1	1.6
Burundi	4.7	2.7
Ethiopia	4.9	2.6
India	3.5	2.0
Japan	0.8	0.3
Kenya	5.7	3.1
Singapore	3.3	2.2
UK	0.5	0.4
USA	1.7	1.1

Source: World Development Report, 1999/2000, IBRD

As far as advanced economies are concerned it may be debated whether population growth is a spur to economic development or whether increased standards of living have increased population. It might be argued that the stagnation in population growth in Western Europe has had some connection with the lack of economic growth during the 1980s and early 1990s, but a similar stagnation in Japan did not seem to have had the same effect.

It would appear that, at least for the developed world, the predictions of British economist **Thomas Malthus** (1766–1834), concerning the rate of population growth and the growth of the available food supply, have not come to pass.

According to Malthus, since the amount of land on the planet is fixed, this would mean that there would be less and less food to feed each person. This would continue until population growth was halted by 'positive checks' of 'war, pestilence and famine'. This would give more food per person so that population would increase again, thus causing the positive checks to set in again, and so on. The gloomy forecast of Malthus was that world population would forever fluctuate around the point where most of it is on the point of starving to death. This is termed a *subsistence equilibrium* and featured in the work of classical economists such as **David Ricardo**.

Technological improvements (the debate over genetically modified crops being the latest in a long line) has meant that the growth in the supply of food has generally outstripped world population growth. This has not quelled the debate about the relevance of Malthusian economics for the developing world, however.

Population and developing countries

The developing nations account for over 80 per cent of the population of the world but only 54 per cent of the land area and under 20 per cent of total world output.

The poorer countries of the world are saddled with numerous problems. The huge discrepancy in levels of income per capita between the richest and the poorest countries in the world has been noted above. In many cases the poor are getting poorer, with average incomes actually falling. A number of countries have had their problems compounded by wars. Many of them are also burdened with large amounts of international debt. Other observers place the emphasis for their problems on the trade barriers facing the products of much of the developing world.

Despite all this, there can be little doubt that population growth is one of the main inhibiting factors in increasing GDP per capita. By far the greatest rates of population growth occur in the developing world; in fact, the developing nations account for over 95 per cent of world population growth. When one looks at the enormous spread of poverty, especially in Africa in recent years, one might be forgiven for thinking that Malthus was only too right. But estimates of a world

population consistent with sustainable economic development (see Chapter 13) vary enormously. Some neo-Malthusians place it 12 billion, others at far less than the current world population of a little over 6 billion! The 'technological optimists' argue that, just as Malthus underestimated the capacity of technology to provide, so the neo-Malthusians and pessimistic ecologists will be proved wrong.

Nevertheless, it would appear that any major advance in living standards will, for many countries, depend upon limiting the size of families. In recent years the country to take this most seriously has been China, the most populous nation on earth, where draconian measures have been taken to limit population growth. However, there are changes afoot in other parts of the developing world. The United Nation's Department for Social and Economic Affairs has recently lowered its most likely forecast for the world population for 2050 from 9.4 billion to 8.9 billion. About one-third of this drop is due to the ravages of AIDS in much of Africa and in parts of the Indian sub-continent. While advances in science have reduced infant mortality and increased lifespan, the fact that women are very slowly getting more say in the timing and size of their families has led to a fall in the average number of children and has contributed to a decline in the annual average growth rate of the population for a number of developing countries. Table 46.2 shows the fertility rates for women for various countries in 1980 and 1997. Of course, the enhanced role of women in society still clashes with cultural attitudes in some countries. There also remain substantial differences in the economic criteria for having children between much of the developed and developing worlds.

Children – investment goods or consumption goods?

It may seem bizarre to regard children as goods, but parents make decisions about whether or not to have children partly on economic criteria. If you live in a developing country without a welfare state, children can be regarded as an *investment* in your future. They will be cheap labour when they are young and they will look after you when you are no longer able to work.

Table 46.2 Total fertility rates, selected countries

Country	Total fertility rate* Births per woman	
	1980	1997
Bangladesh	6.1	3.2
Brazil	3.9	2.3
Burundi	6.8	6.3
Ethiopia	6.6	6.5
India	5.0	3.3
Japan	1.8	1.4
Kenya	7.8	4.7
Singapore	1.7	1.7
UK	1.9	1.7
USA	1.8	2.0

* Total fertility rate is the number of children who would be born to a woman if she were to live to the end of her child-bearing years and bear children in accordance with current fertility rates.

Source: World Development Report 1999/2000, IBRD

There is thus an inbuilt bias towards overpopulation which is no longer checked by such high levels of infant mortality. There is also a strong belief in many developing countries that you have to have a reasonably large number of children in order to ensure that at least some survive, although as medical standards rise, this belief is slowly disappearing.

Decision making about family size is quite different in developed countries where children are considered more as *consumption goods* to whom the law of diminishng marginal utility applies. The welfare state and private pensions provide for old age, and children, far from being a source of income, are considered to be a major expense. With the expansion of higher education, many do not join the workforce until they are in their twenties and must be supported through a lengthy period of education. It may be a case of one child, probably; two, perhaps; while three is often an accident!

Technological issues

Pioneers and latecomers

In order to advance the developing countries must adopt new technologies, especially in agriculture.

What they require, however, is technology which is *appropriate* to their situation. In many cases the adoption of modern techniques has been rejected by the population or else has created jobs for the few and unemployment for the many.

● *Common misunderstanding*

It can be argued that developing countries have the advantage of 'free' access to the ideas and inventions which the advanced nations pioneered. There is, as it were, a 'book of blueprints' which they can draw on. However, it may be doubted whether this access is free and whether the 'book of blueprints' is appropriate to developing nations. For example, the adoption of industrial techniques often throws thousands of skilled workers out of jobs.

Improvements in technology in the advanced nations also cause problems for the developing countries. New processes replace old products as, for example, when synthetic fibre replaced jute in carpets. Additionally, better technology facilitates economies in the use of materials as, for example, with the introduction of much thinner tin cans. Such developments have the effect of depressing the demand and therefore the price of primary products.

Rather than copy the technology of the developed world, it is argued that countries just starting out on the development road should use *intermediate technology*. This is capital equipment which is cheap to purchase and easy to use – which is appropriate in countries with low levels of savings and low educational levels.

Some nations, however, have made a spectacular success of borrowing the blueprints, e.g. Japan and, later, South Korea and the other Pacific rim countries known as the *Asian tigers* (although the major problems that many of these economies faced in the late 1990s may mean that such a term is rather less applicable than it once was).

STUDENT ACTIVITY 46.2

Choose an example of a newly industrialising country and discuss the reasons for its success and more recently for its failures.

The dual economy

Attention has been focused on the fact that development can create a *dual economy*. In one section there is the subsistence economy where wages are very low, and the other section is the newly industrialising one utilising capital. The existence of the first is important to the second in that it provides a pool of labour. In effect the industrialising sector can operate with a perfectly elastic supply of labour.

As the industrialising sector expands so it draws in a greater and greater percentage of the population. This process will be hindered if the expansion significantly increases wages. The successful expansion of the industrial sector increases the dualism. Dualism existed in economies such as the UK during the industrial revolution. (Some argue that it still exists now in some low-paid service sector jobs.) However, the relatively slow introduction of labour-saving technology kept the process in check. With a developing economy the ability to adopt the latest technology at once may dramatically increase dualism.

Sacred cows

It is a familiar theme in developed economies that advancement in the developing world is hindered by the people clinging to the practices of their forebears. A recent case cited is where resettled peasants in Ethiopia left their purpose-built houses and hundreds of new tractors to return to their traditional ways and practices.

● *Common misunderstanding*

Economic development is not just measured in terms of material success. It is about increasing the quality of life. This is made up not only of the consumption of material goods but also of social well-being, including a respect for traditional ways of life.

The problem of agriculture

We might expect in a simple economic model that developing countries would produce food to sell to the industrialised nations. This, however, is not the case: rather, it is the industrialised world which sells food to the developing world.

In the days of peasant agriculture people produced much of what they required themselves. In the push for development they were encouraged to produce cash crops. Their livelihood then becomes subject to the variations in market price of the crop. However, this market price is not freely determined. Massive intervention by governments in the developed world effectively precludes many producers in developing countries from the rich markets. Consider, for example, the variable import levy of the CAP which ensures that imported agricultural products are at least the same price as those produced domestically. Worse than this, the CAP produces food surpluses which further depress world prices if they are released.

Trade issues

Early thinking on development economics argued that the *terms of trade* (see Chapter 41) tended to move against latecomers especially where they are producers of primary products. This stems from a combination of low price and income elasticities of demand for primary products and a tendency towards the saving of raw material as technology improves in industrialised countries. To this we may add the 'learning by doing argument' which says that, whatever the level of technology a latecomer adopts, it becomes good at producing the goods only through the experience of doing so. By the time the latecomer has learnt the developed countries are likely to have moved on. For both these reasons, therefore, the latecomer (developing country) is likely to be at a disadvantage when trading.

The debate is thus whether, on the one hand, a developing country is at an advantage in the terms of trade by being able to adopt the latest technology and benefit from low wage costs or, on the other hand, the terms of trade are likely to move against it for the reasons stated above. If evidence did support the view that the terms of trade do move against the latecomer this could be an argument for (temporary) protection of *infant industries* in the 'learning by doing case'. On a non-theoretical basis it could be an argument for better organisation of primary procedures.

Many developing countries are 'one-horse' economies; that is to say, they are very dependent for their export earnings on one or two products. For example, virtually all of Uganda's export earnings comes from one crop, coffee, while Zambia is very heavily dependent on copper for its export earnings. This can be fortunate for the country if the price of the product goes up and very unfortunate if it comes down. Either way it makes life unstable and unpredictable.

STUDENT ACTIVITY 46.3

Can you think of any examples of a country (or countries) that is dependent on the revenue from a narrow range of primary good exports (or even from the exports of a single product) that have proved to be very lucrative?

After a dip in the early 1970s, the terms of trade of developing countries took a dramatic plunge following the OPEC oil price rise in 1973. A swift recovery followed after 1975 and then the second oil price rise in 1978 sent the terms of trade for non-oil exporters plunging. This drop was compounded by the world depression of the early 1980s, which depressed the demand for primary products. The collapse of oil prices was good news for the developed nations and brought some relief to developing nations, but the continued depression in commodity prices kept the terms of trade against them and this trend has continued ever since.

Protectionism

In those developing economies which have grown significantly since the Second World War we find that both the pace and the pattern of industrial growth have been influenced by a plethora of protective tariffs, subsidies, rebates, quotas and licences as well as direct investments by activist states. Many countries adopted a policy of *import substitution,* by which domestic industries were heavily protected in order to replace imports. These interventions attracted the attention of development economists from the 1960s onwards. Many focused on the effects of inter-vention on incentives and resource allocation. The pattern revealed was 'higgledy-piggledy'. The only discernible regularity was the taxation of agriculture and the subsidisation of some industries, especially those producing consumer goods. However, while a country is free to subsidise or protect an industry, it is still important for it to be able to assess its true opportunity cost. This is especially true for an economy attempting a balanced growth scenario, in which all real variables are assumed to grow at the same constant rate. Thus, it becomes necessary to undertake cost–benefit analyses based on world market prices. The difficulties of such an analysis (see pages 592–3) may be another reason for the reversion to the market forces viewpoint.

Import substitution policies can run counter to the principle of comparative advantage since a country is not likely to benefit from specialisation. The lack of competition from abroad can also breed inefficiency. Alternatively, a country might pursue a policy of *export-led growth* based on the gradual removal of trade barriers and the opening up of certain industries to the vagaries of world competition. These industries will obviously have to be efficient in order to survive and countries can benefit by specialising in those products in which they have a comparative advantage. The newly industrialised nations of Latin America and the Far East successfully exploited just this sort of strategy by temporarily subsidising selected manufacturing industries. The problem is that developed countries respond by erecting further trade barriers against the exported products from the developing world.

Cartelisation

The success of the OPEC oil price rise in 1973 dramatically demonstrated the effects of a successful cartel upon the price of a product. Never has there been a swifter redistribution of wealth from one group of countries to another. This lesson was well learned by the producers of other primary products but they have so far been unsuccessful in organising similar cartels.

A factor which works against the developing nations is that the buyers of primary products are frequently more organised than the sellers. The price of jute, for example, can effectively be set by a small group of people on the London Commodity Exchange. The position of the peasant producing the crop is often undermined by being heavily in debt and having sold the crop a year in advance.

When it comes to imports the developing nation is likely to find the situation reversed with the oligopolistic producers of manufactured goods much better organised. Consider the case of motor vehicles. It is the marketing requirements of the industrialised nations which determine the design and price of cars and these often bear little relation to the needs (or income) of developing nations.

The state and development

In many of the points made in this section, you can see that a key question for governments is whether or not they should intervene. Furthermore, if they intervene, does this mean wholesale direction of the economy or more discreet manipulation of markets?

Those arguing for some kind of *balanced growth* say that there is a need for central coordination and state control. The experience of the USSR before its break-up is often quoted. With all its disasters central coordination lifted this country from feudalism to superpower within a lifetime. Central control can direct scarce capital resources to where they are most needed, ensure that education is appropriate, restrict wasteful consumption and so on.

On the other hand those arguing for *unbalanced growth* urge the use of market forces in directing the economy. It is said that market forces will maximise the rate of growth. Some infrastructure projects may be neglected but in the long run the benefits created by a high, if unbalanced, rate of growth will 'trickle down' to the rest of the economy.

Until the late 1980s there were two competing models of development, capitalist and socialist. The collapse of the communist bloc in Eastern Europe and the adoption of market processes by the world's remaining communist countries, notably China, have resolved this dispute in favour of the market. Since its adoption of market mechanisms within a communist frame-

work, the Chinese economy has been growing strongly at about 10 per cent a year. It has started to develop some of the problems of capitalist economies as well with soaring unemployment and widening income distribution. Does this mean that the state has no role in development? The experience of developed countries suggests that its main role should be in *infrastructure* projects, such as transport and irrigation, and in improving *health* and *education*; these provide the basis for development of an industrialised market economy.

The debt problem of developing countries

In the 1970s many developing countries attempted to develop by borrowing heavily from abroad in order to industrialise. The argument in favour of such a policy was that a lack of internal savings meant that these countries were unable to build up the critical mass of capital needed to industrialise. The sudden massive surplus on the balance of payments of the oil-exporting countries in the middle of the 1970s meant that there was plenty of international capital looking for a home.

Unfortunately the two large oil price rises in 1973 and again in the late 1970s also depressed the economies of the developed economies. This meant that the promised export markets of many of the developing countries failed to live up to expectations and as a result these countries found themselves unable to repay the debt. Much of the money that was borrowed was not used for development purposes but simply to balance the books for the nations' overseas payments. Little found its way into the sort of projects which development economics would suggest.

This situation developed into a full-blown debt crisis in the 1980s with, in many developing countries, debt representing a high percentage of one year's national income.

By the mid-1990s the value of foreign debt was equivalent to over 60 per cent of the national income of the African countries and the total debt of developing countries reached almost $1800 billion. Banks that had previously been keen to lend were no longer willing to do so. International agencies either had insufficient funds substantially to affect the situation or imposed very stringent conditions on loans.

Solutions to the debt crisis

For some countries the burden of debt payments grew so great that it is difficult to see how they will ever get out of the situation. For instance, by 1997, following years of war and unrest, Angola's external debt was valued at more than 200 per cent of its current GDP!

It is said in banking that if you owe the bank £100, you have a problem, but if you owe the bank £1 million, the bank has a problem. This is the situation faced by the bankers who have lent to developing countries. Many imaginative solutions have been put forward ranging from the straightforward *write-off* or *write-down*, to *debt-for-equity* swaps, whereby the debt is sold at a discount and the purchaser buys shares in a country's companies, or *debt-for-nature* swaps. In the latter case debt is written off in return for a commitment for environmental policies such as preserving the rainforests. Some countries that have attempted to repay have had to introduce (often at the request of the IMF) such stringent budgetary and financial policies as to damage growth seriously. Developing countries are strongly discouraged from using protectionism to improve their balance of payments, so austerity measures are the only alternative. This often results in internal political problems and severe problems of poverty for the unemployed.

● *Common misunderstanding*

*The debt crisis is not as bad for some developing countries as it used to be. The debt problem has been relieved for many of the better-off developing countries through the **rescheduling** of the debt: both the governments of developed countries and banks have agreed to delay the repayment date for loans and/or to spread the repayments over a longer period. For the pooreset countries, however, despite recent initiatives, crippling levels of debt can still be the norm.*

However, for other developing countries, especially the poorest, the debt problem persists, despite recent intiatives. In 1996 the IMF announced a new plan to try to solve the debt crisis of the countries with the worst problems, or HIPCs (Heavily Indebted Poor Countries). As long as a country had conformed to the (often stringent) structural programme laid down for it by the IMF for a specified number of years, then that country would qualify for relief. However, by 2000 only four countries were actually receiving relief as part of the scheme.

The debt problems of developing countries were brought into sharp focus during 1997–98 when even the economies of the Asian tigers suffered from the effects of severe overborrowing (see also Chapter 42). The *Asian crisis* began in Thailand in 1997 when it was realised that it would not be able to repay its debts. As a result, governments and banks in Europe, Japan and the USA severely curtailed further lending to Thailand as well as to other countries in South-east Asia and Latin America. Businesses failed, demand slumped and growth forecasts were pegged back. However, by 1999 the crisis had ceased to have the severe implications for the newly industrialising nations as was initially feared. This was due to a combination of swift action by the countries themselves to rectify matters plus a package of loans from the IMF which helped to restore confidence in the regions.

Pressure from various organisations, and in particular from the All African Council of Churches, led to the birth of the Jubilee 2000 Coalition and the proposal that all unpayable debts of the HIPCs should be cancelled by 31 December 2000. In 1999 developed countries agreed a plan to write-off two-thirds of the official debts of the world's poorest nations. Despite other positive noises by banks, Western governments and multilateral agencies, however, the debt levels of many of the poorest developing countries are still equivalent to substantial shares of their respective GDPs.

STUDENT ACTIVITY 46.4

Explain why a solution to a country's debt crisis is beneficial to both parties in the arrangement.

What is necessary for development?

The four elements of development

Despite the disagreements on both theory and practice most people are agreed that there are four wheels to the development vehicle:

(a) *Human resources.* We must be concerned with the health, nutrition and education of the workforce. There is a growing recognition that investment in people is a key to development.

(b) *Natural resources.* The discovery of gold is doubtless a great boon but natural resources are not the key to development. Switzerland is an extremely rich nation which is almost devoid of mineral resources, has a terrible climate (unless you are a skier) and an impossible terrain. On the other hand there are oil-rich nations with money gushing out of the ground but which are still, to all intents and purposes, undeveloped with poor schools, health, roads and so on.

Perhaps for the developing country the key resource is agricultural land. Moreover, land ownership patterns are a key to providing farmers with strong incentives to invest in capital and technologies that will increase their land's yield.

(c) *Capital formation.* It is perhaps an obvious tautology that the rich are rich because they have wealth. Again we may turn to Switzerland as an example: it lacks almost everything except that it has enormous stocks of capital. The problem for a developing nation is how to accumulate capital. If possible the best way is the savings of its own people; Singapore and South Korea provide excellent examples of this. But for the poorest nations of the world this is impossible. If a nation is already reduced to the bare minimum of existence, depressing current consumption to accumulate capital is inviting mass starvation.

We can say that the poorest nations of the world are caught in a ***vicious circle of poverty.*** Low incomes lead to low saving; low saving retards the growth of capital; inadequate capital prevents rapid growth in productivity; low productivity leads to low

incomes, and so on. Other elements in poverty are self-reinforcing. Poverty is accompanied by low levels of skill, literacy and health; these in turn prevent the adoption of new processes and technologies (see Figure 46.1).

The alternative therefore is the importation of capital from abroad. This in turn is beset with problems as we saw above in the section on debt.

(d) *Technology.* The adoption of the appropriate technology is a difficult and controversial topic. (See the earlier discussion on pioneers and latecomers.)

World Bank policy

As we said in the section on the World Bank (see pages 657–8), it is not itself big enough to make a significant contribution to the problems of developing nations. However, we may take its attitude as being generally symptomatic of the approach of the developed nations towards the developing world.

In the early years of its development the World Bank concentrated on projects to improve the infrastructure of developing countries – irrigation projects, transport, power and similar projects. The emphasis has now changed. In the 1980s the World Bank became more concerned with the significance of improved health, nutrition and education in bringing about economic growth. It

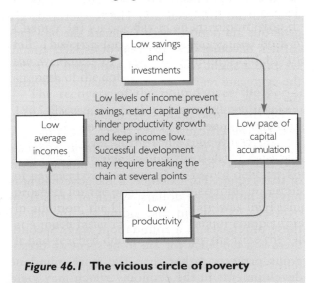

Figure 46.1 **The vicious circle of poverty**

regards them not only as important for economic development but also as desirable in themselves.

Whether the World Bank has achieved anything in this direction is another question. Despite its stated objectives the World Bank has been obsessed with the debt of developing countries and imposing sound financial packages on them in accordance with the policies of monetarist and neo-classical policies in the advanced world. Other international organisations such as the IMF have followed a similar line. The commercial banks which have lent billions to the developing world have also pressed financial stringency on developing nations. Thus, desperately poor nations have been constrained to deflate their economies, devalue their currencies, rein in government spending – in short, to apply classical supply side economics to their problems.

Does aid help?

There are two questions to be addressed when aid is considered: 'How much is given?' and 'Does it do any good?'

The targets are not ambitious. UNCTAD suggested that the developed nations should give 0.7 per cent of their GDP in aid, although even this modest target has long since been abandoned. Currently the West spends as little as 0.22 per cent of its wealth on aid, although there are significant exceptions to this fairly miserable figure. The Nordic countries and The Netherlands are generous aid donors, with Denmark the best performer, devoting 0.97 per cent of its GDP to aid. Despite a slight rise in 1998 and again in 1999, the aggregate real value of aid actually fell during the 1990s.

On the second point several doubts have been cast on the efficacy of aid. First, aid is usually given to governments or government agencies and thus may be perverted into the political aims of that regime. For example, if the government is buying millions of dollars' worth of arms from overseas, is not aid just aiding the finance of these purchases in a roundabout way? Second, there is a tendency for aid to be spent on prestigious projects rather than the more mundane developments in the economy which may yield better results. There is also concern as to whether aid really furthers development or whether it undermines the self-reliance of a nation. Finally, about half of the aid to the poorest countries is *tied* in some way, i.e. finance is only made available if the recipient country agrees to buy goods and services from the donor nation. Hence, a poor country may not be able to buy the cheapest products on the international market. Talks by rich countries to untie their aid, at least for the poorest nations, have yet to reach full agreement.

STUDENT ACTIVITY 46.5

Is there any type of aid that you think may do any good?

Conclusion

A developing country has low relative per capita income, although the term developing country covers a wide variety of situations, from very poor economies to those that are growing rapidly. Information on factors such as educational achievements, health matters and debt levels can provide further evidence of a country's standard of living.

Population growth is one of the main factors inhibiting an increase in per capita GDP. Despite a fall in the growth rate of the population of many developing countries, they are still responsible for most of the growth in world population.

The emphasis on the market process as the main means for development has had its successes, particularly among the Asian tiger economies. The debt cancellation programme is so far of limited scope and there are still many very poor countries which are caught in a vicious circle of debt repayment and financial stringency which prevents the growth needed to pay off the debt. Imaginative solutions to the problems of such countries are needed if they are to develop at all; more often than not the solutions that are put foward have a very restricted practical application.

Summary

1 Many different terms are used to describe the poorer nations of the world. Whatever terms are used the poor are those with a low GDP per capita.
2 The standard of living is not just the income per head but also all the other things which are important to the quality of life, such as health care and literacy.
3 Some of the major areas of controversy in development economics and those that need special review when considering developing economies are population growth, the appopriate level of technology, trade issues, environmental considerations, the position of agriculture and the role of the state.
4 The four elements of development are: human resources; natural resources; capital formation; and technology.
5 Despite recent improvements in the situation and moves towards debt cancellation, the world debt crisis still threatens to overwhelm some debtors and creditors.
6 The aggregate value of foreign aid fell in the 1990s. There are moves to reduce, or even eliminate, tied aid.

? QUESTIONS

1 What is meant by the term 'a developing nation'?
2 Discuss the view that economic growth is the sole indicator of a country's standard of living.
3 Explain the factors that determine country's rate of population growth. Comment on the trends in population growth in the developing world in the last twenty years.
4 Discuss whether developing countries can usefully apply Western technology.
5 Discuss those factors considered to be most important in aiding the development process.
6 'Trade not aid'. Evaluate this slogan as a prescription for development.
7 Discuss whether recent initiatives are likely to solve the debt crisis of developing nations.

Data response A
THE POTENTIAL FOR DEVELOPMENT

Study the information in Table 46.3 (based on 1998 data unless otherwise stated) and answer the questions that follow.

1 Developing economies can be classified as low income (≤ $760 GNP per capita), middle income ($761 to about $3030) and upper middle income ($3031 to about $9360). How else might they be characterised and categorised?
2 Do you think the information given here provides a sufficient overall indicator of the potential for development for each country? What other information may be useful?
3 How would you now classify Singapore?
4 Given this information, to what extent do you think a uniform programme of development for all developing countries would be a useful strategy?

Table 46.3 **The characteristics of development**

	Population (millions)	Population growth (% p.a.) (1990–98)	GNP per capita ($)	GNP per capita growth (% p.a.) (1997–98)	External debt as present value per cent of GNP 1997
Mozambique (Mo)	16.9	2.6	210	9.2	135
Ethiopia (E)	61.3	2.6	100	−3.2	131
Kenya (K)	29.3	3.1	330	−0.9	49
Mali (Ma)	10.6	3.2	250	2.2	73
India (I)	979.7	2.0	430	4.2	18
Nigeria (Ni)	121.3	3.3	–	–	72
Pakistan (Pa)	131.6	2.8	480	2.5	38
China (Ch)	1 238.6	1.2	750	6.5	15
Sri Lanka (SL)	18.8	1.4	810	–	35
Indonesia (Io)	203.7	1.9	680	−16.2	62
Senegal (Se)	9.0	3.0	530	3.1	56
Jamaica (J)	2.6	1.0	1 680	−1.9	90
Thailand (Th)	61.1	1.4	2 200	−8.5	61
Brazil (Br)	165.9	1.6	4 570	−1.4	23
Malaysia (My)	22.2	2.8	3 600	−8.4	48
Mexico (Me)	95.9	2.0	3 970	3.0	37
Korea, Rep. (Ko)	46.4	1.1	7 970	−7.1	33
UK	59.1	0.4	21 400	1.9	–
Singapore (Si)	3.2	2.2	30 060	−0.4	–
USA	270.0	1.1	29 340	2.8	–

	Life expectancy at birth 1997 (years)		Adult illiteracy 1997 (%)		Under 5 mortality rate 1997 (per 1000 live births)
	Males	Females	Males	Females	
Mo	44	47	43	75	201
E	42	44	59	71	175
K	51	53	13	28	112
Ma	49	52	57	72	235
I	62	64	33	61	88
Ni	52	55	31	49	122
Pa	61	63	45	75	136
Ch	68	71	9	25	39
SL	71	75	6	12	19
Io	63	67	9	20	60
Se	51	54	55	75	110
J	72	77	19	10	14
Th	66	72	3	7	38
Br	63	71	16	16	44
My	70	75	10	19	14
Me	69	75	8	12	38
Ko	69	76	1	4	11
UK	75	80	–	–	7
Si	73	79	4	13	6
USA	73	78	–	–	–

Source: *World Development Report* (WDR) *1999/2000*, IBRD

Schools of thought and future issues

Learning outcomes

At the end of this chapter you will be able to:
- Understand why some schools of thought reject key assumptions of neo-classical economics.
- Briefly describe the main alternatives to mainstream economics.
- Look at the economy from unfamiliar perspectives.
- List major unresolved problems for economics and economies.

Introduction

In this chapter we reflect on the overview of economics that this book has provided. It will assist if we briefly look at some alternative schools of thought that provide a contrast with the largely mainstream economics of this text. Examining these alternatives does not imply a belief in them, indeed it takes maturity to know that economics is to be used rather than believed, but even if alternatives are rejected it is often informative to consider the challenges posed and some new insights provided. Thinking about things from a different perspective is extremely useful for deepening our own understanding and making us aware of the weaknesses as well as strengths of our own views. We then conclude the book with a brief overview of some of the major economic issues for the future.

Political economy

Neo-classical economics, and the incorporation of Keynesian elements into essentially neo-classical aggregate demand and supply analysis (often called the *neo-classical synthesis*), have created the mainstream economics that dominates this and most other economics textbooks. Nevertheless, in the last twenty or so years, mainstream economists have moved away from asserting that economics is a completely value-free subject and that it is a purely 'scientific' body of knowledge. Nevertheless, there is still a strong belief among the majority of economists that the scientific method described in Chapter 1 is the best approach. Other economists, a minority, prefer the older term *political economy* to economics. The word 'political' emphasises that economic beliefs are intertwined with political beliefs and that evidence is usually interpreted and absorbed within a school of thought rather than providing an objective means of deciding between schools. Increasingly, however, economists are drawing eclectically on various schools in a *'heterodox'* way rather than conforming to narrower traditions.

Ben Fine, a left-wing radical political economist, goes as far as to say that the empirical part of a theory is precisely that, part of the theory! That would seem to make it difficult to evaluate schools against each other and mainstream economists reject this as an extreme position (although it is a more common position among other social sciences). But it does often seem to be the case that the 'big' changes in economics (e.g. Adam Smith's 'invisible hand', the neo-classical/marginalist revolution of the 1870s, the Keynesian 'revolution', Hayek and the Austrian School's dynamic view of capitalist processes, monetarism and the new-classical school) are born from fairly fundamental shifts in perception rather than more gradual scientific exploration.

You could probably spend a lifetime trying to identify the precise balance between fact and perception (in fact methodologists do!). We could do worse here than note the economic historian Deirdre McClosky's guidance that the rules of any serious investigation should be 'tolerance, honesty and clarity'. Indeed, you should not have confidence in your own views until you have made a reasonable effort to consider contrary arguments and evidence. Even then you should note John Beardshaw's warning 'avoid the OBE, the One Big Explanation for the economy!'

STUDENT ACTIVITY 47.1

Think back to when you did not know so much economics. Which of your previously held views have been challenged by reading this book? If you cannot think of any, ask friends who have not studied economics to comment on economic questions. To what extent do you think studying economics changes one's views of the world? Why do you think it is that economists from different schools of thought so often agree on what is not a valid economic argument?

Political economy

A critique of neo-classical economics

Neo-classical economics has been the subject matter of most of this book and is regarded as *mainstream* economics (this includes the incorporation of some Keynesian elements that are given a neo-classical treatment). In this section we consider more controversial viewpoints from both the right and left of the political spectrum. On the right are to be found the *Austrian* economists who believe in pure capitalism with as little government intervention as possible. On the left are the *post-Keynesians* who stress problems of income distribution and unemployment. Further to the left are *Marxists* who believe in the overthrow of capitalism by the working class. The newly developing *communitarian* school of thought is more difficult to classify since it emphasises the importance of the community as an important mediator between the individual and society. It can be thought of as left wing because it claims that the market often damages

communities, but it can also be thought of as right wing as it suggests a more authoritarian approach when the actions of individuals conflict with the interests of the community. Although these alternative *schools of thought* differ enormously in their views of the economy and economic policy, they share some common misgivings about neo-classical economics that are summarised below.

(a) *Microfoundations*. Neo-classical macroeconomics is based on the assumption of perfect competition. Although it is recognised that there are some market imperfections in the real world, neo-classical economists assume that the model of supply and demand is adequate to discuss problems of the whole economy. Post-Keynesians argue that this is no longer a realistic model of the economy in the late twentieth century because they believe the core of the economy is essentially *oligopolistic*. A more realistic pricing model to underpin macroeconomics would in their view be the mark-up model (see Chapter 33). Marxists also agree that the trend in capitalist economies is towards increasing monopoly power. Austrian economists also believe this to be the case, but they stress the benefit that monopoly power can bring in terms of the accumulation of capital, and innovation. Communitarians criticise the individualism of market processes and believe markets should be directed also towards social goals.

(b) *Equilibrium*. The emphasis in neo-classical economics is towards equilibrium, not just in individual markets but in the economy as a whole. This idea of general equilibrium is rejected by Austrian economists who argue that it is the dynamic creative powers of capitalism which make it the best system, and the price of this is some instability. Indeed they see a recession as an *opportunity* to reconstruct the economy in new creative ways and speak of 'gales of creative destruction'. Post-Keynesian economists regard equilibrium of the neo-classical kind in which markets clear as unlikely, but emphasise that equilibrium in which the economy gets stuck at low levels of output is more likely. Marxists also treat the economy as a dynamic rather than as a static system, but one which goes through periodic 'crises' which they believe will ultimately be fatal to the system.

(c) *Uncertainty*. Post-Keynesians emphasise the idea of uncertainty which was introduced in Keynes's *General Theory* (see Chapter 29). Sudden shifts in business confidence or expectations about interest rates will divert the economy from its predicted path. It is uncontrolled markets which are the uncertain element in the economy, so post-Keynesians generally favour an interventionist role for government. For Austrians it is this very uncertainty which leads them to argue against intervention since it may backfire on the government as intervention leads to unintended consequences.

(d) *Pareto optimality*. Austrians argue that choice is a subjective process which cannot be simulated by the state. Wherever there is market failure, the state can only guess at consumers' preferences. Instead of government intervention, it is better to create actual market processes, however imperfect, so that individuals can exercise their own choices directly. For post-Keynesians the manipulation of consumers by oligopolies, and the absence of full employment, mean that Pareto optimality is a pipe-dream. But also that, in any case, the larger part of welfare comes from membership and participation in the community rather than from the individualistic pleasures focused on in neo-classical welfare economics. Marxists also argue that the working class is deluded by capitalist ideology into believing that markets operate in their interests. The removal of this 'false consciousness' is seen as one of their most important tasks in the preparation for socialist revolution. Marx regarded the classical economics of Adam Smith as constructed to provide an ideological justification of capitalism. His followers today believe that neo-classical economics performs a similar function. Communitarians deny that the welfare of society can be thought of as merely the sum of the individuals that comprise it. Antisocial behaviour is likely to follow if the preferences of the individual are stressed to the exclusion of the interests of the community.

The Austrian school

It is easier to understand many aspects of Mrs Thatcher's Conservative government of the 1980s from the viewpoint of the Austrian school than by using neo-classical economic analysis. The term 'Austrian' refers to the school's beginnings in Vienna rather than the nationality of its modern followers. The Austrian school of thought differs in important respects from modern 'neo-classical' economics. We are using the term 'neo-classical' here as referring to that economic analysis which is based on utility- or profit-maximising equilibriums under perfectly competitive conditions. The two schools both stem from the 'marginalist' revolution in economic theory in the 1870s, and thus they also have much in common. An example of this is that both place an emphasis on explaining economic phenomena in terms of the choices made by utility-maximising individuals. However, the Austrian school has come to be distinguished by its insistence that markets can work effectively only in the complete absence of government 'interference' or of restrictions on the choices of buyers and sellers. Indeed, Friedrich Hayek, the twentieth century's leading champion of the Austrian school, believed that even the best intentioned intervention into the market is likely to have unforeseen side effects which result in a loss of overall welfare. For example, Austrian economists have argued that state intervention in education has caused a demand for educational certificates by employers which has adverse effects on the employment opportunities of young people.

Austrian economics is also distinguished from neo-classical economics in that it gives far less stress to the concept of equilibrium. The neo-classical welfare economics which we have looked at is based on the conditions which hold in equilibrium, whereas the Austrian school stresses the desirable welfare effects produced by the *dynamic* competitive processes which are generated by market forces within free market capitalism. For Austrian economists it is the process of learning and discovery which is made possible by free market systems that is the major source of economic welfare. This is in complete contrast to the certainty and perfect knowledge so often assumed in neo-classical economics.

Indeed, for many Austrian economists economic welfare is increased through time by allowing firms to compete for monopoly power. According to this perspective, rather than monopolies resulting in a welfare loss, prospective monopoly profit is the spur necessary to induce firms to undertake risky and expensive innovations designed to capture or maintain a monopoly position. The welfare gains to consumers from the 'gales of creative destruction' generated as firms compete for tenuous monopoly positions, are seen as far outweighing any static welfare losses arising from deviations of price from cost at the margin.

Austrian policy prescriptions

The role of government for Austrian economists is to reduce its activity to an absolute minimum (consistent with the maintenance of the rule of law, for Austrian economists are not anarchists!). Fiscal policy therefore consists of reducing government expenditure and taxation, privatising nationalised industries and balancing budgets. Monetary policy suggestions from Austrian economists have included the introduction of competitive currencies, with the most successful being the one which is used most. Austrian attitudes to market failure usually suggest ignoring it, since the imperfections of the market will be less than the imperfections of state intervention. Where intervention cannot be avoided, their preferred policy would be to create property rights over the environment as in the case of tradable permits (see Chapter 13) so that the market can be made to deliver on the policy.

Criticisms of the Austrian school

Market failure and income distribution are the Austrians' two weak points with committed environmentalists or socialists unlikely to find their approach attractive. Charitable giving is the basis for income redistribution and so if rich people don't feel like giving, too bad. Neo-classical economists' major complaint about the Austrians is their rejection of statistical testing of their hypotheses. Indeed, Austrian economists prize introspection over empiricism.

Post-Keynesian economics

This title is now used to refer to a broad group of economists who regard neo-classical economics as misleading and largely irrelevant to an analysis of actual economies. In particular they feel that the contributions of Keynes are misrepresented by their representation in the neo-classical synthesis. In the synthesis Keynes's arguments are reduced to the 'neo-Keynesian' arguments that there are price rigidities or restricted elasticities in an otherwise neo-classical (perfectly competitive) world. Thus, in the synthesis, unemployment is caused by wages being stuck above the labour market equilibrium, but real wages may be reduced by increasing aggregate demand, thereby restoring full employment. Post-Keynesians, in contrast, reject the notion that the economy would necessarily achieve full employment even in the absence of wage stickiness or other price rigidities.

Post-Keynesians emphasise quantity adjustments rather than the more familiar price adjustments of neo-classical analysis. In contrast to the notion of Pareto-efficient full employment equilibrium, post-Keynesians emphasise the *dynamic instability* of capitalism. There is no presumption that market forces create stability or that their outcome is necessarily desirable.

Many post-Keynesians follow Keynes's emphasis on *uncertainty*. They identify the assumption of perfect knowledge (or known probabilities) as an additional major flaw of mainstream (i.e. neo-classical and neo-classical synthesis) economics. In the timeless equilibriums of neo-classical economics the problem of uncertainty does not arise. But in the real world where fluctuations in economic activity are frequent and where fortunes ebb and flow, uncertainty is a ubiquitous problem. The same investment project can make or break an entrepreneur, depending on the future course of the economy. The stable relationship between economic variables assumed by neo-classical economists does not capture this uncertainty and instability.

To this is often added the assertion that smooth substitutions between goods and production techniques in response to changing relative prices are another fallacy of mainstream economics. Cambridge University in the UK has a tradition of great economists who dissent from the traditional textbook portrayal of the price mechanism as 'a marvelous computer' which efficiently balances the unlimited wants of consumers against the use of scarce resources. One such economist was Joan Robinson, who wrote in her book *A Guide to Post-Keynesian Economics*:

> The slogan that the free play of market forces allocates scarce resources between alternative uses is incomprehensible. At any moment the stocks of means of production in existence are more or less specific. The level of output may be higher or lower with the state of demand but there is very little play in the composition of output. Changes in the adaptation of resources to demand can come about only through the process of investment; but plans for investment are made in the light of expectations about the future which are rarely perfectly fulfilled, and therefore have to be drawn up with a wide margin of error.

For these writers economics cannot be separated from the wider analysis of society as a whole. The allocation of resources between competing uses is seen as interesting, but only a very small part of the wider economic and social dynamics that shape the evolution of societies and relations in the economy. In addition to competitive markets forces these political economists also analyse various forms of power and the interaction with political, social and economic life.

Criticisms of post-Keynesian economics

The main problem with post-Keynesian economists is that, because of their emphasis on uncertainty, they are less likely to make predictions that can be checked against historical events. This is not to say that they reject statistical evidence, but rather that they expect it to be inherently unstable. Critics argue that if the world is truly uncertain it is not clear what could be done about it! Post-Keynesians reply that the consequences of uncertainty, such as recession and currency instability, are obvious and require action to prevent serious loss of welfare and misery.

Marxist economics

● *Common misunderstanding*

The recent dramatic collapse of communist regimes in Eastern Europe has often been associated in the popular media with a failure of Marx's economics. Such an association is misleading because Marx offered a critique of capitalism rather than a detailed description of the system that would replace it. Moreover, given Marx's concern with human freedom, it seems unlikely that he would have approved of the oppressive totalitarian regimes that operated in his name.

Stages in the evolution of society

Karl Marx (1818–1883) identified four stages through which the relations of production and therefore society had passed – namely primitive communism, slavery, feudalism and capitalism. He argued that under feudalism the produce of labour was expropriated (by the lords from the serfs), through a complex social system based on hierarchies of land ownership. In Western Europe by the mid-nineteenth century this system of expropriation had been overthrown by the emerging capital-owning class and replaced by a social system which served its interests instead, i.e. capitalism. Just as feudalism had generated its own ideology, 'obligation' and 'divine right', so the ideology of the great liberal thinkers such as Adam Smith and John Stuart Mill was used to justify this new mode of production and social structure. Just as serfs had largely accepted their lot as inevitable and ordained by God so, Marx argued, workers typically are not aware of capitalist exploitation. They complain about their wages rather than the wage system.

Exploitation

The ideology of the liberal thinkers emphasised the right to equality under the law. Marx agreed that workers are indeed equal to capitalists in the sense that they can exchange their labour power in the market place in exchange for its market value. This equality allows them to withhold their services from an employer who does not pay this rate. Indeed, for Marx the distinguishing feature of capitalism is that labour power is sold in the market in exactly the same way as any other commodity, in contrast, say, to the ownership of a slave or the feudal obligation of a serf.

This equality in exchange, however, hides the inequality in production. If workers exercise their freedom to refuse to sell their labour power they have no other means of providing for their subsistence. This is because workers have no other access to the prevailing means of production, i.e. capital. In the extreme workers can exercise their freedom to refuse to work until starvation, but then in that sense slaves are equal to their masters! Thus, in Marx's economics, the capitalist's monopoly of the means of production enforces 'wage slavery' on the working class.

The idea of exploitation in Marx's economics is explained by the *labour theory of value*. Not only Marx, but also Smith, Ricardo and the other early classical economists argued that value of a commodity was based on the amount of labour that had gone into its production. Not until the marginalist revolution of the 1870s was utility used as the basis of value theory. Marx used the idea to emphasise the worker as the source of value. He pointed out that machinery used in production was itself a commodity that had been produced by labour. If the worker is the source of all value, it follows that profit (or *surplus value* as he called it) is value that has been taken from the worker. Class struggle would arise concerning the share of workers and capitalists in the value produced by labour, hence Marx argued that it was in the interests of the capitalists to have a *reserve army of the unemployed* in order to keep wages low and workers disciplined by the fear of unemployment.

Overproduction

Marx was very complimentary about the productive potential of the capitalist system. He accepted that capitalism is a very powerful engine for wealth creation, but argued that it had a tendency to *overproduce*. As capitalists increase their profits by reducing wages, making workers work harder so that some of the workforce can be made redundant etc., so the income in the economy to buy their products will be reduced. The capitalist system will produce more than it can consume. This is an example of what Marx calls an *internal contradiction* of the capitalist

system. The astute reader will recognise that overproduction is essentially the same as the Keynesian idea of underconsumption – when the level of aggregate demand is too low to keep people in employment. There is no multiplier or consumption function in Marx's theory, but the results are much the same. Unlike Keynes, Marx does not suggest fiscal policy to remedy the situation, but sees it as part of the logic of capitalist development and eventual self-destruction.

Concentration of capital

An important theme in Marx's work is his stress on 'competitive capital accumulation'. Capitalists compete with one another through time by accumulating capital and applying labour-saving technology. All capitalists seek to defend themselves against competitors or steal an advantage by reducing their costs of production. This capital accumulation reduces the costs of the capitalists by reducing the labour time necessary for the production of their commodities. As each capitalist adopts the more capital-intensive production technique the labour time for the production of commodities is reduced. Thus the value of the commodity falls and the profits of all capitalists producing that commodity fall with it. Those smaller capitalists left behind in the accumulation race are competed out of business by those who have accumulated more capital or adopted a more advanced labour-saving technology. The rule is 'accumulate or die', as the control of capital is concentrated more and more into the hands of fewer and larger centralisations of capital. Concentration of capital is increased during the periodic crises as certain companies become bankrupt and are taken over by the surviving companies.

STUDENT ACTIVITY 47.2

The firms that you are probably most familiar with are retail outlets. To what extent have trends in the retail trade reflected Marx's prediction of the concentration of capital. What other explanations for these retail trends are there?

Marx argued that the constant tendency of competition to expel labour from the production process would cause a continuous flow of workers into unemployment. As output expands the total level of employment might expand, but even while this is happening capitalist competition and accumulation will condemn workers in many regions and industries to unemployment. Workers in depressed regions or with redundant skills will become surplus to the requirements of capitalists. These are the reserve army of the unemployed referred to above. Within this army there will develop a core of the permanently unemployed who will be condemned to relative poverty and misery.

Revolution

Marx believed that as the extent of misery grew, and as capitalism appeared increasingly unable to provide for workers, the class consciousness of the working class (or 'proletariat') would develop, even among workers whose material conditions were being improved by the capitalists' development of the means of material production. When the proletariat finally recognised its class interest it would use the economic and political strength that capitalism had unwittingly bestowed upon it through the concentration of workers into places of mass production. The ensuing revolution would overthrow the capitalist order and replace it with a 'dictatorship of the proletariat' whereby the productive power developed through capitalist accumulation would be 'socialised' and coordinated to provide for the good of all.

Marx's 'law' or tendency for the rate of profit to fall

Although for Marx the 'anarchy' of capitalist production makes crisis likely, the inevitability of crises is predicted by his law of the tendency of the rate of profit to fall. This tendency rests upon Marx's assertion that capitalism has 'internal contradictions'. For example, only labour power creates value and that production will be by increasingly capital-intensive means. The concentration of capital means that more and more capital must be advanced by the capitalist in order just to compete with other capitalists. As the ratio of such capital to labour therefore rises, the surplus value generated by labour becomes

smaller and smaller as a percentage of the total capital. The process of capital concentration expels from production the living labour that is the very source of value! Hence profits eventually fall as a return on capital advanced falls.

Marx seemed to argue that the law of the falling rate of profit was a tendency rather than a once and for all event. It could be offset by such factors as cheaper raw materials, extending labour exploitation to the cheaper labour of Third World producers, and technology may alter the compositions of labour and capital. But there will be limits in the capitalist countries to how far the real or relative wage can fall without inducing widespread resistance and political dissent among workers. Marx pointed out that capitalists only advance their capital and produce in order to gain profit, if profits fall sufficiently the profit dynamic fails and capitalism falls into a recession that cannot be permanently delayed through demand management. In short, Marx argued that although most production problems will be overcome if profits are high, recurring crises caused by declining profits are inevitable. Marx predicted that it would be during one of these periodic crises that the proletariat will revolt and overthrow capitalism.

Criticisms of Marx's analysis

It should be remembered that Marx was writing at a time when democratic progress seemed unlikely and few, if any, of the benefits of the welfare state existed! He would have been surprised by the changes in capitalist countries since his day and this may have modified his predictions. He is criticised for not coming up with an internally consistent theory of how prices are formed in a capitalist economy. This is a more serious criticism which is too technical to discuss in this introductory text. However, criticisms have also been made of the neo-classical theory of pricing, partly because it depends on the assumption of perfect competition.

Perhaps the most effective criticism from a scientific point of view is the absence of testable hypotheses. The types of predictions made by Marx can always be put off into the future. The absence of a revolution in an advanced capitalist economy can be put down to its not having yet reached the right level of development. It should be noted that so-called communist revolutions have all taken place in countries which were not industrialised, such as China (feudal) and Russia (just out of feudalism). Those countries which had some degree of industrialisation, such as Czechoslovakia, had the communist system forced upon them by the advancing Red Army at the end of the Second World War.

Even economists to the left of the political spectrum have pointed out that Marx's predictions do not seem to describe modern capitalism and the mixed economy. For example, Joan Robinson used the famous battle cry of revolutionary Marxists 'Workers of the world unite you have nothing to lose but your chains!' to parody his prophecy of increasing proletarian misery. She pointed out that: '"You have nothing to lose but the prospect of a suburban home and a motor car" would not have been much of a slogan for a revolutionary movement.'

In support of Marx, capitalist 'crises' still seem to be occurring regularly, with unemployment going above 3 million in both the early 1980s and the early 1990s. Certainly it is possible to make a case for there being a world economic crisis and the idea of the reserve army of the unemployed forcing down wages has real meaning in the present world: as capitalism becomes more international, enormous reserves of very cheap labour are becoming available in the Indian subcontinent, China and elsewhere, which may create downward pressure on wages in the more industrialised nations.

More recently, and perhaps because the linking of Marx's name to totalitarian regimes has declined, Marx's economics is being re-assessed by some economists. For example, the role of profits in capitalist dynamics is being re-examined. In many ways Marx's picture of ever larger capitalist firms competing for ultimate survival is more realistic than the neo-classical model of perfect competition and hence some business schools are now teaching aspects of Marx's economics. In this, and other ways, elements of Marx's economics, as with Austrian and post-Keynesian economics, may help fill gaps and expose inadequacies in mainstream economics.

Where are we now?

Whatever its shortcomings may be, the discipline of Economics is the most powerful of the social sciences. In the two-and-a-quarter centuries since Adam Smith's *Wealth of Nations,* economists have developed rigorous and intellectually demanding analyses that provide understanding and deep insights into the economic consequences of human behaviour. For example, this book has shown that the theory of competitive markets has been developed to provide powerful tools of analysis such as supply and demand. But there are many other areas, such as oligopolistic competition and market dynamics, where our knowledge is certainly incomplete.

In macroeconomics, Keynes provided many new insights into why fluctuations in the overall level of economic activity occur. Since then, events, and the response from neo-classical economists, have greatly reduced the emphasis on discretionary macroeconomic policy. The instruments of policy have changed, but recent Chancellors of the Exchequers have emphasised 'stability' and creating a 'benign' environment for enterprise rather than the 'short-termism' of former active demand management. Nevertheless, it is still an open question as to when and why the economy may fall short of achieving acceptable performance so that governments feel compelled to take discretionary action. It is hoped that the current period of stability and growth will last, but if it does not economists may have at least provided a better understanding of what to do about it.

The emphasis today is less about radical change or even differences in political objectives.

The main political parties today are vying for the privilege of running mixed economies better than their opponents.

The extremes of socialism and *laissez-faire* are not the centre stage of debate; instead people are busy again trying to work out how better to run the mixed economy. For example, instead of welfare 'handouts', the 'smart state' is aimed at harnessing individual incentives towards social goals; governments in democracies must balance the desire for public spending with the unpopularity of taxation if they are to be re-elected. Economists who can assist in improving the performance of the private and/or public sectors, thereby improving this trade-off, are in demand.

STUDENT ACTIVITY 47.3

Use a production possibility frontier diagram to show how improving the efficiency of either the private or public sector can lead to an increase in the output of both sectors even though there as been no improvement in efficiency in the other sector. Explain why the growth of the private sector allows the expansion of the public sector without the need to raise the rate of taxation.

Future issues

There are very many issues for which there are currently less than satisfactory answers. On the domestic front, in addition to the issues listed above, we can point to:

(a) *Income distribution.* The development of the welfare state in the twentieth century involves the government in considerable expenditure on benefits for those who are less well-off, whether unemployed, sick or elderly. This will only increase as the population is an ageing one with an increasing number of retired persons dependent on the working population (see below). Certain services, such as education and health, also have the effect of redistributing income because they are provided free to everyone, but are paid for through the tax system. Although governments have introduced reforms to prevent welfare expenditure from growing, no serious political party is suggesting the abolition of the welfare state, and so expenditure in this area is a constraint on fiscal policy.

(b) *Correcting market failure.* Although the government may wish to control public expenditure, it is constrained in this objective by the existence of market failure. The 'correct' level of provision of public goods such as defence, quasi-public goods such as roads, and services with externalities and merit good

characteristics such as health and education (Chapter 28) is far from clear. Such questions are tackled by a branch of economics called 'social choice' theory.

(c) *The dependency ratio.* (See Chapter 34.) The effects of a falling birth rate and longer life have created an ageing population. This means that in the decades to come the number of people dependent on each member of the working population will increase. The bill for state pensions is not funded, and even if it were so, it would require redistribution of resources from providing for the working population to providing for the retired. It remains to be seen to what extent the working population of the future will be prepared to pay the burden of tax required to provide pensioners with an acceptable standard of living. This is one of the reasons that many have called for increased immigration to boost the numbers in the working population.

World issues

There are world issues of immense scale that remain unresolved and that will challenge more than just economists. Nevertheless, economists are also working here to provide better understanding. We end with a brief list of these, perhaps to put our day-to-day economic problems into better perspective:

(a) *Improvements to the environment.* (See Chapter 13.) This objective may partly be in conflict with the objective of economic growth because resources have to be diverted to minimise damage to the environment from industrial activity. The environmentalists would argue they are substituting the goal of 'sustainable development' for economic growth. The vast majority of observers now believe that global warming is a serious reality and point to the damage and loss of life from extreme weather. Questions here include: 'Is prosperity the enemy of the environment?' 'Which economic policies are best able to maintain output while providing incentives to reduce pollution?' 'Is it impossible to marry the aspirations of the developing world with a sustainable world environment and has anyone the right to object to such development?' 'Will market mechanisms provide an incentive to produce renewable energies or must this search be sponsored by governments?' 'Will there be technological solutions that protect the environment and allow high material consumption?'

(b) *Oil.* Despite advances in the efficient use of energy and development of alternative sources, economic production and consumption today is still heavily dependent on the fossil fuel of oil. Although we derive more units of GDP per barrel of oil, output growth means we use more oil in total than ever before. In 1970 North America consumed 16m barrels a day but by 2000 this had reached 22m a day. Over the same time period Western European use went from 12m barrels a day to 15m and Japan's from 4m to 6m. There have been many previous warnings that the oil is about to run out but this has not yet happened. It is the case that the supply of oil is dominated by the production of the middle-eastern Gulf states and unrest in the middle-east that affects this supply has, and could again, send shockwaves across the world economy.

(c) *The 'E-economy'.* In the 1990s and beginning of the new millennium, the USA has enjoyed a sustained period of increasing productivity and above-trend growth. Many commentators have linked this to the spread of the new 'Information and Communication Technologies' (ICT) such as the Internet and more powerful microprocessors. Other commentators have cast doubt on this and observe that the improvements do not seem to have spread beyond the booming new technology industries themselves. But the Internet is undoubtedly a powerful new form of communication and will supplement many older forms of doing business and may lead to new uses as yet unthought of. The question for economists is 'Will the new technologies lead to improvements in productivity and the expansion of markets that lift overall growth rates on a more permanent basis?'

(d) *Transition economies.* We saw in Chapter 1 that the introduction of market capitalism to former communist bloc countries has been successful for the Central European countries that already had significant private sectors and trading links with Western countries. For other former Soviet countries transition has been associated with massive falls in output that have taken millions of people from a basic living standard to third world levels of poverty. Time will tell if market forces can eventually raise output to alleviate this mass poverty and reduce the political tensions that are prone to arise with such desperation.

(e) *Globalisation.* To what extent have increased trade, financial movements and the growth of transnational/multinational companies rendered nations powerless to control their own economic destinies? Although the latter half of the twentieth century saw an increase in such international interdependence not all economists are convinced that the world economy is more globalised than it was one hundred years ago. Economic interdependence is easy to detect in the simultaneous movements of economies across the world, but differences do exist between countries. In any case, recognising such interdependence, is it impossible to organise international bodies to coordinate national policies and to control these forces?

(f) *World population.* The world's population has risen over twentyfold in the last 1000 years. The majority of this growth has been in the last 100 years. Some recent figures at last show some signs of slowing and a possible peaking of the world's population around the middle of this century, but trends are notoriously difficult to predict and there is still considerable potential for growth. The US Census Bureau has projected a world population of 9 400 million by 2050. Some believe that population growth can fuel its own production needs, others point to the poverty and starvation that can be seen already and the strains upon the environment. There can be no doubt, however, that sustaining the world's population is a daunting challenge.

(g) *World poverty.* (See Chapter 46.) In terms of human suffering this is the biggest issue on our planet. Perhaps it is because the richest one fifth of the world's population have over four fifths of the world's income whereas the poorest one fifth have less than one fiftieth of the world's income. Perhaps it is because of failures in the economic policies of poor countries. What is clear is that the scale of human suffering this represents dwarfs all other welfare issues. The number of chronically undernourished people in the world is over 800 million. To put this in perspective, almost 14 times the number of the UK population is currently on the verge of starvation.

It is certainly true that economic development has lifted many countries out of poverty but on a world scale there have never been so many people in poverty. All Western governments pay lip service to aiding the poorer countries of the world. The Brandt Report of 1981 suggested that each country should aim to contribute the equivalent of 0.7 per cent of its GDP to overseas aid, although in practice few countries attain this. Economists are addressing such questions in relation to development and world poverty as: How can self-generating economic development be initiated in poor countries? Are developed countries doing all they can to help or are restrictions on trade and crippling repayment of debt to rich countries keeping people in the Third World unnecessarily locked in poverty? Can poverty be solved through aid? Can aid sometimes worsen the situation? What are the most effective forms of aid? Are anti-capitalist demonstrators correct in asserting that globalisation is the enemy of the world's poor, or are unfettered world markets actually the best future hope for the poor?

Globalisation and the sheer scale of these issues will mean that they increasingly affect us all. We hope that this book has helped you to understand more about the power and weaknesses of economics as a means of understanding the process of wealth creation and for improving the welfare of humankind.

Summary

1 Mainstream economics provides very powerful tools of analysis, but powerful insights are also provided by other schools of thought.
2 The Austrian school rejects equilibrium approaches but claim that it is the dynamic properties of capitalism that make it so attractive.
3 Post-Keynesians do not feel that mainstream economics properly represents Keynes. They believe neo-classical models simply assume away much of reality such as the effects of uncertainty. They support intervention to control what they see as the inherent instability of capitalism.
4 Marx was complimentary about the productive performance of capitalism but believed that it would eventually be destroyed by its own internal contradictions and succeeded by socialist revolution. He was writing, however, before democratic reform and the advent of a mixed economy with a welfare state.
5 Despite much progress and reasons for optimism, the world's economic problems have never been bigger.

? QUESTIONS

1 In what ways might studying the alternative schools of thought in this chapter be more useful to a businessperson than studying neo-classical theory?
2 Why might some aspects of the changes brought by Mrs Thatcher's government be better understood from an Austrian rather than a neo-classical perspective?
3 What do you consider to be the main strengths and weaknesses of each of the neo-classical, Austrian, Marxist and post-Keynesian schools?
4 Contrast the view of Marx with that of Keynes concerning the stability of market capitalism.
5 Why have alternatives been put forward to the goal of continuing economic growth and what problems might arise if growth slowed?
6 The future is notoriously difficult to predict, but on the basis of what you know, argue the case for (a) an optimistic and (b) a pessimistic assessment of the world's economic future.

7 To what extent are the futures of rich and poor nations interdependent?

8 Return to the questions at the end of Chapter 1. How have your responses altered since you first did these?

Data response A
HOW DO DIFFERENT SCHOOLS OF THOUGHT INTERPRET DATA?

Refer again to Table 18.1 and Figure 16.5 and then give an account of the history of the UK economy according to the perspectives of the following schools of economics:

(a) Monetarist;   (d) Post-Keynesian;
(b) Marxist;   (e) Austrian.
(c) Keynesian;

Data response B
BUDGET INTERPRETATION

Using newspaper reports or official accounts of the latest budget:

1 Work out if the government is using fiscal policy to expand or contract the economy at present.

2 Try to work out which of the four macro objectives are most important at present.

3 What are currently the greatest problems facing the government in trying to manage the economy?

4 Are there any measures which could be described as direct intervention or supply side?

Index